Programming Python

Programming Python

Second Edition

Mark Lutz

O'REILLY®

Beijing · Cambridge · Farnham · Köln · Paris · Sebastopol · Taipei · Tokyo

Programming Python, Second Edition
by Mark Lutz

Copyright © 2001, 1996 O'Reilly Media, Inc. All rights reserved.
Printed in the United States of America.

Published by O'Reilly Media, Inc., 1005 Gravenstein Highway North, Sebastopol, CA 95472.

Editor: Laura Lewin and Frank Willison

Production Editor: Emily Quill

Cover Designer: Edie Freedman

Printing History:

October 1996:   First Edition.

March 2001:   Second Edition.

ISBN: 0-596-00085-5

[M]

Table of Contents

Foreword

Less than five years ago, I wrote the Foreword for the first edition of *Programming Python*. Since then, the book has changed about as much as the language and the Python community! I no longer feel the need to defend Python: the statistics and developments listed in Mark's Preface speak for themselves.

In the past year, Python has made great strides. We released Python 2.0, a big step forward, with new standard library features such as Unicode and XML support, and several new syntactic constructs, including augmented assignment: you can now write x += 1 instead of x = x+1. A few people wondered what the big deal was (answer: instead of x, imagine dict[key] or list[index]), but overall this was a big hit with those users who were already used to augmented assignment in other languages.

Less warm was the welcome for the extended print statement, print>>file, a shortcut for printing to a different file object than standard output. Personally, it's the Python 2.0 feature I use most frequently, but most people who opened their mouths about it found it an abomination. The discussion thread on the newsgroup berating this simple language extension was one of the longest ever—apart from the never-ending Python versus Perl thread.

Which brings me to the next topic. (No, not Python versus Perl. There are better places to pick a fight than a Foreword.) I mean the speed of Python's evolution, a topic dear to the heart of the author of this book. Every time I add a feature to Python, another patch of Mark's hair turns gray—there goes another chapter out of date! Especially the slew of new features added to Python 2.0, which appeared just as he was working on this second edition, made him worry: what if Python 2.1 added as many new things? The book would be out of date as soon as it was published!

Relax, Mark. Python will continue to evolve, but I promise that I won't remove things that are in active use! For example, there was a lot of worry about the string module. Now that string objects have methods, the string module is mostly redundant. I wish I could declare it obsolete (or deprecated) to encourage Python programmers to start using string methods instead. But given that a large majority of existing Python code—even many standard library modules—imports the string module, this change is obviously not going to happen overnight. The first likely opportunity to remove the string module will be when we introduce Python 3000; and even at that point, there will probably be a string module in the backwards compatibility library for use with old code.

Python 3000?! Yes, that's the nickname for the next generation of the Python interpreter. The name may be considered a pun on Windows 2000, or a reference to Mystery Science Theater 3000, a suitably Pythonesque TV show with a cult following. When will Python 3000 be released? Not for a loooooong time—although you won't quite have to wait until the year 3000.

Originally, Python 3000 was intended to be a complete rewrite and redesign of the language. It would allow me to make incompatible changes in order to fix problems with the language design that weren't solvable in a backwards compatible way. The current plan, however, is that the necessary changes will be introduced gradually into the current Python 2.x line of development, with a clear transition path that includes a period of backwards compatibility support.

Take, for example, integer division. In line with C, Python currently defines x/y with two integer arguments to have an integer result. In other words, 1/2 yields 0! While most dyed-in-the-wool programmers expect this, it's a continuing source of confusion for newbies, who make up an ever-larger fraction of the (exponentially growing) Python user population. From a numerical perspective, it really makes more sense for the / operator to yield the same value regardless of the type of the operands: after all, that's what all other numeric operators do. But we can't simply change Python so that 1/2 yields 0.5, because (like removing the string module) it would break too much existing code. What to do?

The solution, too complex to describe here in detail, will have to span several Python releases, and involves gradually increasing pressure on Python programmers (first through documentation, then through deprecation warnings, and eventually through errors) to change their code. By the way, a framework for issuing warnings will be introduced as part of Python 2.1. Sorry, Mark!

So don't expect the announcement of the release of Python 3000 any time soon. Instead, one day you may find that you are *already* using Python 3000—only it won't be called that, but rather something like Python 2.8.7. And most of what you've learned in this book will still apply! Still, in the meantime, references to

Python 3000 will abound; just know that this is intentionally vaporware in the purest sense of the word. Rather than worry about Python 3000, continue to use and learn more about the Python version that you do have.

I'd like to say a few words about Python's current development model. Until early 2000, there were hundreds of contributors to Python, but essentially all contributions had to go through my inbox. To propose a change to Python, you would mail me a context diff, which I would apply to my work version of Python, and if I liked it, I would check it into my CVS source tree. (CVS is a source code version management system, and the subject of several books.) Bug reports followed the same path, except I also ended up having to come up with the patch. Clearly, with the increasing number of contributions, my inbox became a bottleneck. What to do?

Fortunately, Python wasn't the only open source project with this problem, and a few smart people at VA Linux came up with a solution: SourceForge! This is a dynamic web site with a complete set of distributed project management tools available: a public CVS repository, mailing lists (using Mailman, a very popular Python application!), discussion forums, bug and patch managers, and a download area, all made available to any open source project for the asking.

We currently have a development group of 30 volunteers with SourceForge checkin privileges, and a development mailing list comprising twice as many folks. The privileged volunteers have all sworn their allegiance to the BDFL (Benevolent Dictator For Life—that's me :-). Introduction of major new features is regulated via a lightweight system of proposals and feedback called Python Enhancement Proposals (PEPs). Our PEP system proved so successful that it was copied almost verbatim by the Tcl community when they made a similar transition from Cathedral to Bazaar.

So, it is with confidence in Python's future that I give the floor to Mark Lutz. Excellent job, Mark. And to finish with my favorite Monty Python quote: Take it away, Eric, the orchestra leader!

Guido van Rossum
Reston, Virginia, January 2001

Preface for the Second Edition

"And Now for Something Completely Different . . . Again"

The first edition of this book was one of the first to present the Python language. This second edition is an almost completely new advanced Python topics book, designed to be a follow-up to the core language material in *Learning Python* and supplemented by the reference material in *Python Pocket Reference*.

That is, this edition is focused on ways to *use* Python, rather than on the language itself. Python development concepts are explored along the way—in fact, they really become meaningful only in the context of larger examples like those in this edition. But in general, this text now assumes that you already have at least a passing acquaintance with Python language fundamentals, and moves on to present the rest of the Python story.

In this preface, I'll explain some of the rationales for this major rewrite, describe the structure of this edition in more detail, and give a brief overview of how to use the Python programs shipped on the enclosed CD-ROM. First of all, though, a history lesson is in order.

Signs of the Python Times

It's been an exciting five years in the Python world. Since I wrote the first edition of this book between 1995 and 1996, Python has grown from a new kid on the scripting languages block to an established and widely used tool in companies around the world. Although measuring the popularity of an open source (*http://opensource.org*) and freely distributed tool such as Python is not always easy, most statistics available reveal exponential growth in Python's popularity over the last five years. Among the most recent signs of Python's explosive growth:

Books

As I write this in 2001, there are now over a dozen Python books on the market, with almost that many more on the way (in 1995 there were none). Some of these books are focused on a particular domain (e.g., Windows), and some are available in German, French, and Japanese language editions.

Users

In 1999, one leading industry observer suggested that there were as many as 300,000 Python users worldwide, based on various statistics. Other estimates are more optimistic still. In early 2000, for instance, the Python web site was already on track to service 500,000 new Python interpreter downloads by year end (in addition to other Python distribution mediums); this figure is likely closer to the true user-base size as I write this book.

Press

Python is now regularly featured in industry publications. In fact, since 1995, Python creator Guido van Rossum has appeared on the cover of prominent tech magazines such as *Linux Journal* and *Dr. Dobb's Journal*; the latter publication gave him a programming excellence award for Python.*

Applications

Real companies have adopted Python for real products. It has shown up animating the latest Star Wars movie (Industrial Light & Magic), serving up maps and directories on the Internet (Yahoo), guiding users through Linux operating system installation (Red Hat), testing chips and boards (Intel), managing Internet discussion forums (Egroups), scripting online games (Origin), talking to CORBA frameworks (TCSI), implementing web site tools (Digital Creations' Zope), scripting wireless products (Agilent), and much more.†

Newsgroup

User traffic on the main Python Internet newsgroup, *comp.lang.python*, has risen dramatically too. For instance, according to eGroups (see *http://www. egroups.com/group/python-list*), there were 76 articles posted on that list in

---

* As I was writing this book, *Linux Journal* also published a special Python supplement with their May 2000 edition—the cover of which, of course, featured a naked man seated outdoors in front of a computer desk instead of a piano. If you don't know why that is funny, you need to watch a few reruns from Python's namesake, the Monty Python television series (consider it a first suggested exercise). I'll say more about the implications of Python's name in the first chapter.

† See *http://www.python.org* for more details. Some companies don't disclose their Python use for competitive reasons, though many eventually become known when one of their web pages crashes and displays a Python error message in a browser. Hewlett Packard is generally counted among companies thus "outed."

January 1994, and 2678 in January 2000—a 35-fold increase. Recent months have been busier still (e.g., 4226 articles during June, 2000 alone—roughly 140 per day), and growth has been constant since the list's inception. This, and all other user-base figures cited in this preface, are likely to have increased by the time you read this text. But even at current traffic rates, Python forums are easily busy enough to consume the full-time attention of anyone with full-time attention to burn.

Conferences

There are now two annual Python conferences, one of which is hosted by O'Reilly & Associates. Attendance at Python conferences has roughly doubled in size every year. An annual Python Day is now also held in Europe.

Group therapy

Regional Python user groups have begun springing up in numerous sites in the U.S. and abroad, including Oregon, San Francisco, Washington D.C., Colorado, Italy, Korea, and England. Such groups work on Python-related enhancements, organize Python events, and more.

Domains

Python has grown to embrace both Microsoft Windows developers, with new support for COM and Active Scripting, as well as Java developers, with the new JPython (renamed "Jython") Java-based implementation of the language. As we'll see in this edition, the new COM support allows Python scripts to be both component server and client; Active Scripting allows Python code to be embedded in HTML web page code and run on either client or server; and JPython compiles Python scripts to Java Virtual Machine code so that they can be run in Java-aware systems and can seamlessly integrate Java class libraries for use by Python code. As an open source tool for simplifying web site construction, the Python-based Zope web application framework discussed in this edition has also begun capturing the attention of webmasters and CGI coders.

Services

On the pragmatics front, commercial support, consulting, prepackaged distributions, and professional training for Python are now readily available from a variety of sources. For instance, the Python interpreter can be obtained on CDs and packages sold by various companies (including Walnut Creek, *Dr. Dobb's Journal*, and ActiveState), and Python usually comes prebuilt and free with most Linux operating system distributions.

Jobs

It's now possible to make money as a Python programmer (without having to resort to writing large, seminal books). As I write this book, the Python job board at *http://www.python.org/Jobs.html* lists some 60 companies seeking

Python programmers in the U.S. and abroad. Searches for Python at popular employment sites yield even more hits—for instance, 285 Python-related jobs on Monster.com, and 369 on dice.com. Not that anyone should switch jobs, of course, but it's nice to know that you can now make a living by applying a language that also happens to be a pleasure to use.

Tools

Python has also played host to numerous tools development efforts. Among the most prominent as I write these words: the Software Carpentry project, which is developing new core software tools in Python; ActiveState, which is on the verge of releasing a set of Windows and Linux-focused Python development products; and PythonWare, which is about to release an integrated Python development environment and GUI builder.

Compilers

As I write this preface, ActiveState has also announced a new Python compiler for the Microsoft .NET framework and C# language environment—a true Python compiler and independent implementation of the Python language that generates DLL and EXE files, allows Python code to be developed under Visual Studio, and provides seamless .NET integration for Python scripts. It promises to be a third implementation of Python, along with the standard C-based Python, and the JPython Java-based system.

Education

Python has also begun attracting the attention of educators, many of whom see Python as a "Pascal of the 2000s"—an ideal language for teaching programming, due to its simplicity and structure. Part of this appeal was spawned by Guido van Rossum's proposed *Computer Programming for Everybody* (CP4E) project, aimed at making Python the language of choice for first-time programmers worldwide. At this writing the future of CP4E itself is uncertain, but a Python special interest group (SIG) has been formed to address education-related topics. Regardless of any particular initiative's outcome, Python promises to make programming more accessible to the masses of people who will surely soon grow tired of clicking preprogrammed links, as they evolve from computer users to computer scripters.

In other words, it's not 1995 anymore. Much of the preceding list was unimaginable when the first edition of this book was conceived. Naturally, this list is doomed to be out of date even before this book hits the shelves, but it is nonetheless representative of the sorts of milestones that have occurred over the last five years, and will continue to occur for years to come. As a language optimized to address the productivity demands of today's software world, Python's best is undoubtedly yet to come.

So What's Python?

If you are looking for a concise definition of this book's topic, try this:

Python is a general-purpose open source computer programming language, optimized for quality, productivity, portability, and integration. It is used by hundreds of thousands of developers around the world, in areas such as Internet scripting, systems programming, user interfaces, product customization, and more.

Among other things, Python sports object-oriented programming (OOP); a remarkably simple, readable, and maintainable syntax; integration with C components; and a vast collection of precoded interfaces and utilities. Although general-purpose, Python is often called a *scripting language* because it makes it easy to utilize and direct other software components. Perhaps Python's best asset is simply that it makes software development more rapid and enjoyable. To truly understand how, read on.

Why This Edition?

One consequence of the growing popularity of Python has been an influx of new users, programming styles, and applications, all of which have conspired to make parts of the first edition of this book prime for updates. Python itself has changed in smaller ways, but important extensions have simplified various aspects of Python development and merit new coverage.

Perhaps most relevant for this edition is that the Python "audience" has changed. Over the last five years, Python has transitioned from an emerging language of interest primarily to pioneers to a widely accepted tool used by programmers for day-to-day development tasks. This edition has been refocused for this new Python audience. You will find that it is now more of a nuts-and-bolts text, geared less toward introducing and popularizing the language than to showing how to apply it for realistically scaled programming tasks.

Because of the breadth of change, this edition is something of an entirely new book. To readers who enjoyed the first edition, I would like to express my gratitude, and I hope you will find the same spirit in this second edition. Although this is a major rewrite, I have tried to retain as much of the original book's material and flavor as possible (especially the jokes :-).

Since writing the first edition five years ago, I have also had the opportunity to teach Python classes in the U.S. and abroad, and some of the new examples reflect feedback garnered from these training sessions. The new application domain examples reflect common interests and queries of both myself and my students. Teaching Python to workers in the trenches, many of whom are now *compelled* to use Python on the job, also inspired a new level of practicality that you will notice in this edition's examples and topics.

Other new examples are simply the result of my having fun programming Python. Yes, fun; I firmly believe that one of Python's greatest intangible assets is its ability both to kindle the excitement of programming among newcomers, and to rekindle the excitement among those who have toiled for years with more demanding tools. As we will see in this edition, Python makes it incredibly easy to play with advanced but practical tools such as threads, sockets, GUIs, web sites, and OOP—areas that can be both tedious and daunting in traditional compiled languages like C and C++.

Frankly, even after eight years as a bona fide *Pythonista*,[*] I still find programming most enjoyable when it is done in Python. Python is a wildly productive language, and witnessing its application first-hand is an aesthetic delight. I hope this edition, as much as the first, will demonstrate how to reap Python's productivity benefits and communicate some of the satisfaction and excitement found in a rapid-development tool such as Python.

Major Changes in This Edition

The best way to get a feel for any book is to read it, of course. But especially for people who are familiar with the first edition, the next few sections go into more detail about what is new in this edition.

It's Been Updated for Python 2.0

This edition has been updated for Python 2.0, and the Graphical User Interface (GUI) material has been updated for Tk versions 8.0 or later. Technically, this update was begun under Python 1.5.2, but all examples were revisited for 2.0 before publication.

For the trivia buffs among you: release 2.0 was the first Python release following Guido's move to BeOpen, while 1.6 was the last release from Guido's prior employer, CNRI. Just before I finished this book's final draft and after the 2.0 release, Guido and the core Python development team moved from BeOpen to Digital Creations, home of the Zope web application construction kit, but this

---

[*] Since the first edition, Python zealots have struggled to come up with a label for themselves. *Pythonista* seems to be the most common, but an upstart handful still cling stubbornly to terms such as *Pythoneer*, among others. Pythonista comes with pseudo-militant overtones that may or may not reflect the nature of scripting-language politics.

move is independent of Python releases (see Chapter 1, *Introducing Python*, for more details).

Release 2.0 introduces a few language extensions, but 2.0 and 1.6 are similar in content, and the updates just add a handful of features. The examples in this book should generally work with later Python releases. Remarkably, almost all examples in the first edition still work five years later, with the latest Python releases; those that didn't work required only small fixes (e.g., GUI call formats and C API interfaces).

On the other hand, although the core language hasn't changed much since the first edition, a number of new constructs have been added, and we'll apply them all here. Among these new Python features: module packages, class exceptions, pseudo-private class attributes, unicode strings, the new regular expression module, new Tkinter features such as the grid manager, standard dialogs, and top-level menus, and so on. A new appendix summarizes all of the major changes in Python between the first and second editions of this book.

In addition to the language changes, this book presents new Python tools and applications that have emerged in recent years. Among them: the IDLE programming interface, the JPython (a.k.a. "Jython") compiler, Active Scripting and COM extensions, the Zope web framework, Python Server Pages (PSP), restricted execution mode, the HTMLgen and SWIG code generators, thread support, CGI and Internet protocol modules, and more (it's been a busy five years). Such applications are the heart and soul of this second edition.

It's Been Refocused for a More Advanced Audience

This edition presents Python programming by *advanced examples*. Becoming proficient in Python involves two distinct tasks: learning the core language itself, and then learning how to apply it in applications. This edition addresses the latter (and larger) of these tasks by presenting Python libraries, tools, and programming techniques. Since this is a very different focus, I should say a few words about its rationale here.

Because there were no other Python books on the horizon at the time, the first edition was written to appeal to many audiences at once—beginners and gurus alike. Since then, another O'Reilly book, *Learning Python*, has been developed to address the needs of beginners, and *Python Pocket Reference* was published for readers seeking a short Python reference. As a result, the core language introductory-level material and the original reference appendixes have been removed from this book.

Learning Python introduces the core language—its syntax, datatypes, and so on—using intentionally simplistic examples. Many have found it to be ideal for learning the language itself, but Python can become even more interesting once you master the basic syntax and can write simple examples at the interactive prompt. Very soon after you've learned how to slice a list, you find yourself wanting to do real things, like writing scripts to compare file directories, responding to user requests on the Internet, displaying images in a window, reading email, and so on. Most of the day-to-day action is in applying the language, not the language itself.

Programming Python focuses on the "everything else" of Python development. It covers libraries and tools beyond the core language, which become paramount when you begin writing real applications. It also addresses larger software design issues such as reusability and OOP, which can only be illustrated in the context of realistically scaled programs. In other words, *Programming Python*, especially in this new edition, is designed to pick up where *Learning Python* leaves off.

Therefore, if you find this book too advanced, I encourage you to read *Learning Python* as a prelude to this text, and return here for the rest of the story once you've mastered the basics. Unless you already have substantial programming experience, this edition might serve you best as a second Python text.

It Covers New Topics

Most of the changes in this edition were made to accommodate new topics. There are new chapters and sections on Internet scripting, CGI scripts, operating system interfaces, the SWIG integration code generator, advanced Tkinter topics, the HTMLgen web page generator, JPython, threads, restricted execution mode, and more. You should consult the Table of Contents for the full scoop, but here are some of the new topics and structural changes you'll find in this edition:

Topics

> The Internet, systems programming, Tkinter GUIs, and C integration domains get much more attention, and are arguably now the main focus of this text. For instance, you'll find six new chapters on Internet scripting, covering client-side tools, server-side scripts and web sites, and advanced Internet topics and systems. Four new chapters address systems topics: threads, directory processing, program launching, and so on. And the GUI material has also grown from one chapter to a much more complete four-chapter presentation, and now covers all widgets (including text and canvas), as well as new grid, menu, and dialog support.

C integration

> The C extending and embedding chapters have been expanded to cover new topics such as SWIG (*the* way to mix Python with C/C++ libraries today) and present new mixed-mode examples such as callback dispatch (extending plus embedding). C integration is at the heart of many Python systems, but the examples in this domain are inevitably complex, and involve large C programs

that are only useful to C users. In deference to readers who don't need to code C integrations, this material is now isolated at the end of the text. Some of the C code listings are gone as well—to reduce page count, I have opted instead to point readers to C source files on the enclosed CD-ROM where possible.

Although later chapters build upon material in earlier chapters, topics in this edition are covered fairly independently, and are associated by book parts. Because of that, it's not too much of a stretch to consider this edition to be akin to four or five books in one. Its top-level structure underscores its application topics focus:

Preface (you are here)
    Chapter 1, *Introducing Python*
Part I, *System Interfaces*
    Chapter 2, *System Tools*
    Chapter 3, *Parallel System Tools*
    Chapter 4, *Larger System Examples I*
    Chapter 5, *Larger System Examples II*
Part II, *GUI Programming*
    Chapter 6, *Graphical User Interfaces*
    Chapter 7, *A Tkinter Tour, Part 1*
    Chapter 8, *A Tkinter Tour, Part 2*
    Chapter 9, *Larger GUI Examples*
Part III, *Internet Scripting*
    Chapter 10, *Network Scripting*
    Chapter 11, *Client-Side Scripting*
    Chapter 12, *Server-Side Scripting*
    Chapter 13, *Larger Web Site Examples I*
    Chapter 14, *Larger Web Site Examples II*
    Chapter 15, *Advanced Internet Topics*
Part IV, *Assorted Topics*
    Chapter 16, *Databases and Persistence*
    Chapter 17, *Data Structures*
    Chapter 18, *Text and Language*
Part V, *Integration*
    Chapter 19, *Extending Python*
    Chapter 20, *Embedding Python*
Part VI, *The End*
    Chapter 21, *Conclusion: Python and the Development Cycle*
    Appendix A, *Recent Python Changes*
    Appendix B, *Pragmatics*
    Appendix C, *Python Versus C++*

Two notes here: First of all, don't let these titles fool you—although most have to do with application topics, Python language features and general design concepts are still explored along the way, in the context of real-world goals. Second, readers who use Python as a standalone tool can safely skip the integration chapters, though I still recommend a quick glance. C programming isn't nearly as fun or easy as Python programming. Yet because integration is central to Python's role as a scripting tool, a cursory understanding can be useful, regardless of whether you do integrating, scripting, or both.

First edition readers will notice that most of this material is new, and even chapters with old titles contain largely new material. Noticeably absent in this edition are the original Sneak Preview, Mini Reference, Tutorial Appendix, and all of the old Part II—a reflection of the new focus and intended readership.

It's More Example-Oriented

This book is largely about its examples. In this edition, old examples have been extended to become more realistic (e.g., PyForm and PyCalc), and new examples have been added throughout. Among the major examples, you'll find:

PyEdit
> A Python/Tk text file editor object and program

PyView
> A photo image and note-file slideshow

PyDraw
> A paint program for drawing and moving image objects

PyTree
> A tree data structure drawing program

PyClock
> A Python/Tk analog and digital clock widget

PyToe
> An AI-powered graphical tic-tac-toe program

PyForm
> A persistent object table browser

PyCalc
> A calculator widget in Python/Tk

PyMail
> A Python/Tk POP and SMTP email client

PyFtp

    A simple Python/Tk file-transfer GUI

PyErrata

    A web-based error report system

PyMailCgi

    A web-based email interface

There are also new mixed-mode C integration examples (e.g., callback registration and class object processing), SWIG examples (with and without "shadow" classes for C++), more Internet examples (FTP upload and download scripts, NNTP and HTTP examples, email tools, and new `socket` and `select` module examples), many new examples of Python threads, and new coverage of JPython, HTMLgen, Zope, Active Scripting, COM, and Python database interfaces. Many of the new examples are somewhat advanced, but of course this is now a somewhat advanced text.

In addition, the old Python/C embedding API (now called *ppembed*) has been extended to support precompiling strings to bytecode, and the original calculator example (now called *PyCalc*) has been beefed up to support keyboard entry, history lists, colors, and more.

In fact, the new book examples tree distributed on this edition's CD-ROM is *itself* a fairly sophisticated Python software system, and the examples within it have been upgraded structurally in a number of important ways:

Examples tree

    The entire examples distribution has been organized as one big Python *module package* to facilitate cross-directory imports and avoid name-clashes with other Python code installed on your computer. Using directory paths in import statements (instead of a complex PYTHONPATH) also tends to make it easier to tell where modules come from. Moreover, you now need to add only one directory to your PYTHONPATH search-path setting for the entire book examples tree: the directory containing the *PP2E* examples root directory. To reuse code in this book within your own applications, simply import through the *PP2E* package root (e.g., `from PP2E.Launcher import which`).

Example filenames

    Module names are generally much less cryptic now. I punted on 8.3 DOS compatibility long ago, and use more descriptive filenames. I've also fixed some old all-uppercase filenames, which were a last vestige of MS-DOS.

Example titles

    Labels of example listings now give the full directory pathname of the example's source file to help you locate it in the examples distribution. For instance, an example source-code file whose name is given as *Example N-M: PP2E\Internet\Ftp\sousa.py* refers to the file *sousa.py* in the *PP2E\Internet\ Ftp* subdirectory of the examples distribution directory.[*]

Example command lines

Similarly, when a command line is shown typed after a prompt such as C:\... \PP2E\System\Streams>, for example, it is really to be typed in the *PP2E\ System\Streams* subdirectory in your examples tree. Unix and Linux users: please think / when you see \ in filename paths (my official excuse for which is outlined in the next section).

Example launchers

Because it's just plain fun to click on things right away, there are new self-configuring demo launcher programs (described later in this preface in "The Short Story"), to give you a quick look at Python scripts in action with minimal configuration requirements. You can generally run them straight off the book's CD without setting any shell variables first.

It's More Platform-Neutral

Except for some C integration examples, the majority of the programs in this edition were developed on my Windows 98 laptop, with an eye toward portability to Linux and other platforms. In fact, some of the examples were born of my desire to provide portable Python equivalents of tools missing on Windows (e.g., file splitters). When programs are shown in action, it's usually on Windows; they are demonstrated on the Red Hat Linux 6.x platform only if they exercise Unix-specific interfaces.

This is not a political statement at all—I like Linux too. It's mostly a function of the fact that I wrote this book with MS Word; when time is tight, it's more convenient to run scripts on the same platform as your publishing tools than to frequently reboot into Linux. Luckily, because Python has now become so portable to both Windows and Linux, the underlying operating system is less of a concern to Python developers than it once was. Python, its libraries, and its Tkinter GUI framework all work extremely well on both platforms today.

---

[*] The "examples distribution directory" is the directory containing the top-level *PP2E* directory of the book examples tree. On the CD, it's the topmost *Examples* directory; if you've copied the examples to your machine, it's wherever you copied (or unpacked) the *PP2E* root directory. You can run most of the examples from the CD directly, but you'll want to copy them to your hard drive to make changes, and to allow Python to save *.pyc* compiled bytecode files for quicker startups.

Because I'm not a politician, though, I've tried to make the examples as platform-neutral as possible, and point out platform-specific issues along the way. Generally speaking, most of the scripts should work on common Python platforms unchanged. For instance, all the GUI examples were tested on both Windows (98, 95) and Linux (KDE, Gnome), and most of the command-line and thread examples were developed on Windows but work on Linux too. Because Python's system interfaces are generally built to be portable, this is easier than it may sound.

On the other hand, this book does delve into platform-specific topics where appropriate. There is new coverage of many Windows-specific topics—Active Scripting, COM, program launch options, and so on. Linux and Unix readers will also find material geared towards their platforms—forks, pipes, and the like. There is also new discussion of ways to edit and run Python programs on most major platforms.

The one place where readers may still catch a glimpse of platform biases is in the Python/C integration examples. For simplicity, the C compilation details covered in this text are still somewhat Unix/Linux-biased. One can at least make a reasonable case for such a focus—not only does Linux come with C compilers for free, but its development environment grew up around that language. On Windows, the C extension code shown in this book will work, but you may need to use different build procedures that vary per Windows compiler. O'Reilly has published an outstanding text, *Python Programming on Win32*, that covers Windows-specific Python topics like this, and should help address some of the disparity here. If you do Windows-specific programming, please see that book for all Windows details skipped here.

But It's Still Not a Reference Manual

Please note that this edition, like the first, is still more of a *tutorial* than a reference manual (despite sharing a title pattern with a popular Perl reference text). This book aims to teach, not document. You can use its table of contents and index to track down specifics, and the new structure helps make this easy to do. But this edition is still designed to be used in conjunction with, rather than to replace, Python reference manuals. Because Python's manuals are free, well-written, available online, and change frequently, it would be folly to devote space to parroting their contents. For an exhaustive list of all tools available in the Python system, consult other books (e.g., O'Reilly's *Python Pocket Reference*) or the standard manuals at Python's web site and on this book's CD-ROM.

Using the Examples and Demos

I want to briefly describe how to use the book's examples here. In general, though, please see the following text files in the examples distribution directory for more details:

- *README-root.txt:* package structure notes
- *PP2E\README-PP2E.txt:* general usage notes
- *PP2E\Config\setup-pp.bat:* Windows configuration
- *PP2E\Config\setup-pp.csh:* Unix and Linux configuration

Of these, the *README-PP2E.txt* file is the most informative, and the *PP2E\Config* directory contains all configuration file examples. I give an overview here, but the files listed give a complete description.

The Short Story

If you want to see some Python examples right away, do this:

1. Install Python from the book's CD-ROM, unless it is already installed on your computer. On Windows, click on the name of the self-installer program on the CD and do a default install (say "yes" or "next" to every prompt). On other systems, see the README file (the gzipped source distribution on the CD can be used to build Python locally).

2. Start one of the following *self-configuring scripts* located in the top-level *Examples\PP2E* directory on the CD. Either click on their icons in your file explorer, or run them from your system prompt (e.g., DOS console box, Linux Xterm) using command lines of the form `python script-name` (you may need to use the full path to `python` if it's not on your system):

   — *Launch_PyDemos.pyw:* the main Python/Tk demo launcher toolbar

   — *Launch_PyGadgets_bar.pyw:* a Python/Tk utilities launcher bar

   — *Launch_PyGadgets.py:* starts standard Python/Tk utilities

   — *LaunchBrowser.py:* opens web examples index in web browser

The `Launch_*` scripts start Python programs portably[*] and require only that Python be installed—you don't need to set environment variables first or tweak the included *PP2E\Config* setup files to run them. `LaunchBrowser` will work if it can

---

[*] All the demo and launcher scripts are written portably but are known to work only on Windows 95/98 and Linux at the time of this writing; they may require minor changes on other platforms. Apologies if you're using a platform that I could not test: Tk runs on Windows, X11, and Macs; Python itself runs on everything from handheld PDAs to mainframes; and my advance for writing this book wasn't as big as you may think.

find a web browser on your machine, even if you don't have an Internet link (though some Internet examples won't work completely without a live link).

If installing Python isn't an option, you can still run a few Python web demos by visiting *http://starship.python.net/~lutz/PyInternetDemos.html* with your browser. Because these examples execute scripts on a server, they tend to work best when run live from this site, rather than from the book's CD.

The Details

To help organize the new examples, I've provided a demo launcher program, *PyDemos.pyw*, in the top-level *PP2E* directory of the examples distribution. Figure P-1 shows PyDemos in action on Windows after pressing a few buttons. The launcher bar appears on the left of the screen; with it, you can run most of the major graphical examples in the book with a mouse click. The demo launcher bar can also be used to start major Internet book examples if a browser can be located on your machine (see the following launcher description).

Besides launching demos, the PyDemos source code provides pointers to major examples in the distribution; see its source code for details. You'll also find Linux automated build scripts for the Python/C integration examples in the top-level examples directory, which serve as indexes to major C examples.

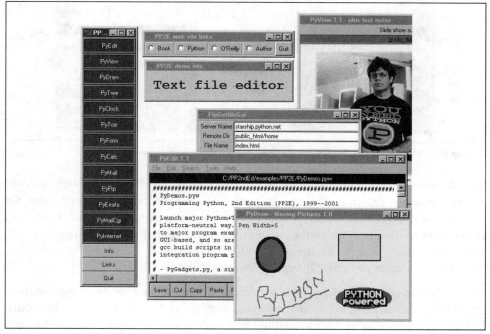

Figure P-1. The PyDemos launcher with pop-ups and demos (Guido's photo reprinted with permission from Dr. Dobb's Journal)

I've also included a top-level program called *PyGadgets.py*, and its relative *PyGadgets_bar.pyw*, to launch some of the more useful GUI book examples for real use instead of demonstration (mostly, the programs I use often; configure as desired). Figure P-2 shows what `PyGadgets_bar` looks like on Windows, along with a few of the utilities that its buttons can launch. All of the programs are presented in this book and included in the examples distribution. Most gadgets require a Python with Tkinter support, but that is the default configuration for the standard Windows port on the book's CD.

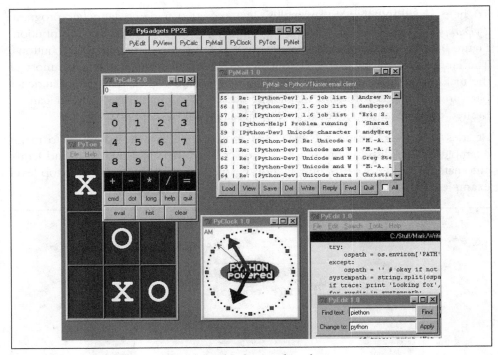

Figure P-2. The PyGadgets utilities launcher bar, with gadgets

To run the files listed in the prior paragraph directly, you'll need to set up your Python module search path (see the top-level `PP2E/Config/setup*` files for hints). But if you want to run a collection of Python demos from the book and don't want to bother with setting up your environment first, simply run the self-launching utility scripts in the *PP2E* directory instead: *Launch_PyDemos.pyw*, *Launch_PyGadgets.py*, and *Launch_PyGadgets_bar.pyw*.

These Python-coded launcher scripts assume Python has already been installed, but will automatically find your Python executable and the book examples distribution, and set up your Python module and system search paths as needed to run the demos. You can probably run these launch scripts by simply clicking on their names in a file explorer, and you should also be able to run them directly from the book's CD-ROM. See the comments at the top of *Launcher.py* for more details (or read about these scripts in Chapter 4, *Larger System Examples I*).

Many of the browser-based Internet examples from the book can also be found online at *http://starship.python.net/~lutz/PyInternetDemos.html*, where you can test-drive a few Python Internet scripting examples. Because these examples run in your web browser, they can be tested even if you haven't installed Python (or Python's Tk support) on your machine.

The PyDemos program also attempts to launch a web browser on the major example web pages by starting the *LaunchBrowser.py* script in the examples root directory. That script tries to find a usable browser on your machine, with generally good results; see the script for more details if it fails. Provided `LaunchBrowser` can find a browser on your machine, some demo buttons will pop up web pages automatically, whether you have a live Internet connection or not (if not, you'll see local files in your browser). Figure P-3 shows what the PyInternetDemos page looks like under Internet Explorer on Windows.

Of special interest, the *getfile.html* link on this page allows you to view the source code of any other file on the book's site—HTML code, Python CGI scripts, and so on; see Chapter 12 for details. To summarize, here is what you'll find in the top-level *PP2E* directory of the book's examples distribution:

PyDemos.pyw
> Button bar for starting major GUI and Internet examples

PyGadgets.py
> Starts programs in non-demo mode for regular use

PyGadgets_bar.pyw
> Button bar for starting PyGadgets on demand

Launch_*.py*
> Starts PyDemos and PyGadgets programs using *Launcher.py* to autoconfigure search paths (run these for a quick look)

Launcher.py
> Used to start programs without environment settings—finds Python, sets PYTHONPATH, spawns Python programs

LaunchBrowser.py
> Opens example web pages with an automatically located web browser, either live off the Net or by opening local web page files; if started directly, opens the PyInternetDemos index page

There are also subdirectories for examples from each major topic area of the book.

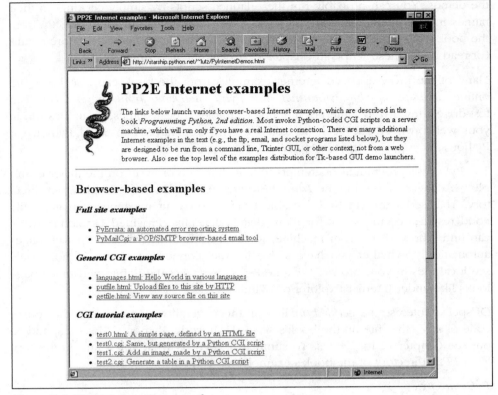

Figure P-3. The PyInternetDemos web page

In addition, the top-level *PP2E\PyTools* directory contains Python-coded command-line utilities for converting line-feeds in all example text files to DOS or Unix format (useful if they look odd in your text editor), making all example files writable (useful if you drag-and-drop off the book's CD), deleting old *.pyc* bytecode files in the tree, and more. Again, see the distribution's *README-PP2E.txt* file for more details on all example issues.

Where It's At

The book examples distribution can be found on the CD-ROM that accompanies this book. See the CD's top-level README file for usage details, or browse the CD's example root directory in your favorite file explorer for a quick tour.

In addition to the book examples, the CD also contains various Python-related packages, including a full Windows *self-installer* program with Python and Tk support (double-click and say "yes" at all prompts to install), the full Python *source code distribution* (unpack and compile on your machine), and Python's *standard documentation* set in HTML form (click to view in your web browser).

Extra open source packages such as the latest releases (at the time of publication) of the SWIG code generator and JPython are also included, but you can always find up-to-date releases of Python and other packages at Python's web site, *http://www.python.org*.

Conventions Used in This Book

The following font conventions are used in this book:

Italic
> Used for file and directory names, URLs, commands, to emphasize new terms when first introduced, and for some comments within code sections

`Constant width`
> Used for code listings and to designate modules, methods, options, classes, functions, statements, programs, objects, and HTML tags

`Constant width bold`
> Used in code sections to show user input

`Constant width italic`
> Used to mark replaceables

 The owl icon designates a note related to the nearby text.

 The turkey icon designates a warning related to the nearby text.

Where to Look for Updates

As before, updates, corrections, and supplements for this book will be maintained at the author's web site, *http://www.rmi.net/~lutz*. Look for the second edition's link on that page for all supplemental information related to this version of the book. As for the first edition, I will also be maintaining a log on this web site of Python changes over time, which you should consider a supplement to this text.

Beginning with this edition, I am making available a user-driven book errata reporting system on the World Wide Web, at this site:

>   *http://starship.python.net/~lutz/PyErrata/pyerrata.html*

There, you'll find forms for submitting book problem reports and comments, as well as viewing the report database by various sort keys. Reports are stored in a publicly browsable database by default, but an option lets you email them privately instead. The PyErrata system also happens to be written in Python, and is an example presented and shipped with this book; see Chapter 14. Figure P-4 shows what the root page of PyErrata looks like.

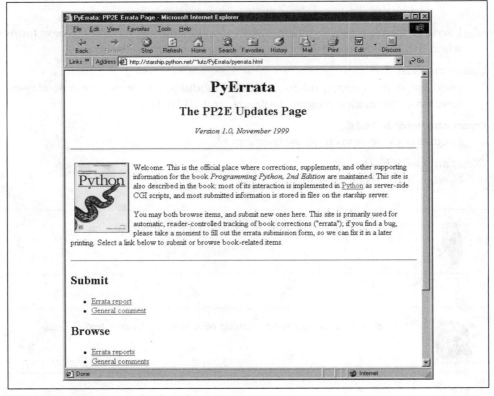

Figure P-4. The PyErrata book updates site

If any of these addresses stop working over time, these pages might also be accessible from O'Reilly's web site, *http://www.oreilly.com.** I'm still happy to receive

---

* O'Reilly has an errata report system at their site too, and you should consider the union of these two lists to be the official word on book bugs and updates.

direct emails from readers, of course, but the PyErrata site will hopefully stream-line the report-posting process.

Contacting O'Reilly

You can also address comments and questions about this book to the publisher:

O'Reilly & Associates, Inc.
1005 Gravenstein Highway North
Sebastopol, CA 95472
(800) 998-9938 (in the United States or Canada)
(707) 829-0515 (international/local)
(707) 829-0104 (fax)

O'Reilly has a web page for this book, which lists errata, examples, and any addi-tional information. You can access this page at:

http://www.oreilly.com/catalog/python2/

To comment or ask technical questions about this book, send email to:

bookquestions@oreilly.com

For more information about books, conferences, software, Resource Centers, and the O'Reilly Network, see the O'Reilly web site at:

http://www.oreilly.com

Acknowledgments

In addition to the people I mentioned in the first edition's preface, I'd like to extend appreciation to a few of the people who helped in some way during this second edition project:

- To this book's first editor, Frank Willison, for overseeing this update, as well as championing the Python cause at O'Reilly and beyond. To this book's later editor, Laura Lewin, for picking up the ball and lighting necessary fires.

- To Python creator Guido van Rossum for making this stuff fun again.

- To the people who took part in a review of an early draft of this edition: Eric Raymond, Mark Hammond, David Ascher, Tim Peters, and Dave Beazley.

- To Tim O'Reilly and the staff of O'Reilly & Associates, both for producing this book, and supporting open source software in general.

- To the Python community at large, for diligence, hard work, and humor—both in the early years and today. We've come far, but to steal a line from the 1970s: You aint' seen nothin' yet.

- And to the students of the many Python classes I have taught, as well as the scores of readers who took the time to send me comments about the first edition; your opinions helped shape this update.

Finally, a few personal notes of thanks. To my children, Michael, Samantha, and Roxanne, for purpose. If they are at all representative of their generation, the future of our species seems in very good hands. You'll have to pardon me if that sounds proud; with kids like mine, it's impossible to feel otherwise.

And most of all to Lisa, the mother of those amazing kids. I owe her my largest debt of gratitude, for everything from enduring my flights from reality while writing books like this, to keeping me out of jail in our youth. No matter what the future may hold, I'll always be glad that something threw us together two decades ago.

Mark Lutz
November 2000
Somewhere in Colorado

"When Billy Goes Down, He's Going Down Fast"

The last five years have also been host to the rise of the open source movement. Open source refers to software that is distributed free of charge with full source code, and is usually the product of many developers working in a loosely knit collaborative fashion. Python, the Linux operating system, and many other tools such as Perl and the Apache web server fall into this category. Partly because of its challenge to the dominance of mega-companies, the open source movement has quickly spread through society in profound ways.

Let me tell you about an event that recently underscored the scope of this movement's impact on me. To understand this story, you first need to know that as I was writing this book, I lived in a small town in Colorado not generally known for being on the cutting edge of technological innovation. To put that more colorfully, it's the sort of place that is sometimes called a "cowboy town."

I was at a small local bookstore hunting for the latest *Linux Journal.* After browsing for a while, I found a copy and walked it to the checkout. Behind the counter were two clerks who looked as if they might be more at home at a rodeo than behind the counter of this establishment. The older of the two sported gray hair, a moustache, and the well-worn skin of a person accustomed to life on a ranch. Both wore obligatory baseball caps. Cowboys, to be sure.

As I put the magazine down, the elder clerk looked up for a moment, and said, in classic cowboy drawl, "Linux, huh? I tell you what, when Billy goes down, he's goin' down fast!" Of course, this was in reference to the widely publicized competition between Linux and Bill Gates' Microsoft Windows, spurred by the open source movement.

Now, in another time and place, these two might have instead been discussing livestock and firearms over strong cups of coffee. Yet somehow, somewhere, they had become passionate advocates of the Linux open source operating system. After collecting my chin from the floor, we wound up having a lively discussion about Linux, Microsoft, Python, and all things open. You might even say we had a good-old time.

I'm not trying to express a preference for one operating system over another here; both have merits, and Python runs equally well on either platform (indeed, this book's examples were developed on both systems). But I am amazed that an idea that software developers often take for granted has had such a deep, mainstream impact. That seems a very hopeful thing to me; if technology is to truly improve the quality of life in the next millennium, we need all the cowboys we can get.

1

Introducing Python

"And Now for Something Completely Different"

This book is about using Python, a very high-level, object-oriented, open source[*] programming language, designed to optimize development speed. Although it is completely general-purpose, Python is often called an object-oriented *scripting language*, partly because of its sheer ease of use, and partly because it is commonly used to orchestrate or "glue" other software components in an application.

If you are new to Python, chances are you've heard about the language somewhere, but are not quite sure what it is about. To help you get started, this chapter provides a nontechnical introduction to Python's features and roles. Most of it will make more sense once you have seen real Python programs, but let's first take a quick pass over the forest before wandering among the trees.

In the preface, I mentioned that Python emphasizes concepts such as quality, productivity, portability, and integration. Since these four terms summarize most of the reasons for using Python, I'd like to define them in a bit more detail:

Quality

> Python makes it easy to write software that can be reused and maintained. It was deliberately designed to raise development quality expectations in the scripting world. Python's clear syntax and coherent design almost forces programmers to write readable code—a critical feature for software that may be

---

[*] Open source systems are sometimes called *freeware*, in that their source code is freely distributed and community-controlled. Don't let that concept fool you, though; with roughly half a million users in that community today, Python is very well supported.

1

changed by others. The Python language really does look like it was designed, not accumulated. Python is also well tooled for modern software reuse methodologies. In fact, writing high-quality Python components that may be applied in multiple contexts is almost automatic.

Productivity

Python is optimized for speed of development. It's easy to write programs fast in Python, because the interpreter handles details you must code explicitly in lower-level languages. Things like type declarations, memory management, and build procedures are nowhere to be found in Python scripts. But fast initial development is only one component of productivity. In the real world, programmers must write code both for a computer to execute and for other programmers to read and maintain. Because Python's syntax resembles *executable pseudocode*, it yields programs that are easy to understand long after they have been written. In addition, Python supports (but does not impose) advanced paradigms such as object-oriented programming, which further boost developer productivity and shrink development schedules.

Portability

Most Python programs run without change on almost every computer system in use today. In fact, Python programs run today on everything from IBM mainframes and Cray Supercomputers to notebook PCs and handheld PDAs. Although some platforms offer nonportable extensions, the core Python language and libraries are platform-neutral. For instance, most Python scripts developed on Linux will generally run on Windows immediately, and vice versa—simply copy the script over. Moreover, a graphical user interface (GUI) program written with Python's standard Tkinter library will run on the X Windows system, Microsoft Windows, and the Macintosh, with native look-and-feel on each, and without modifying the program's source code at all.

Integration

Python is designed to be integrated with other tools. Programs written in Python can be easily mixed with and *script* (i.e., direct) other components of a system. Today, for example, Python scripts can call out to existing C and C++ libraries, talk to Java classes, integrate with COM and CORBA components, and more. In addition, programs written in other languages can just as easily run Python scripts by calling C and Java API functions, accessing Python-coded COM servers, and so on. Python is not a closed box.

In an era of increasingly short development schedules, faster machines, and heterogeneous applications, these strengths have proven to be powerful allies in both small and large development projects. Naturally, there are other aspects of Python that attract developers, such as its simple learning curve for developers and users alike, libraries of precoded tools to minimize up-front development, and completely free nature that cuts product development and deployment costs.

But Python's productivity focus is perhaps its most attractive and defining quality. As I write this, the main problem facing the software development world is not just writing programs quickly, but finding developers with time to write programs at all. Developers' time has become paramount—much more critical than execution speed. There are simply more projects than programmers to staff them.

As a language optimized for developer productivity, Python seems to be the right answer to the questions being asked by the development world. Not only can Python developers implement systems quickly, but the resulting systems will be maintainable, portable, and easily integrated with other application components.

The Life of Python

Python was invented around 1990 by Guido van Rossum, when he was at CWI in Amsterdam. Despite the reptiles, it is named after the BBC comedy series *Monty Python's Flying Circus*, of which Guido is a fan (see the following silly sidebar). Guido was also involved with the Amoeba distributed operating system and the ABC language. In fact, the original motivation for Python was to create an advanced scripting language for the Amoeba system.

But Python's design turned out to be general enough to address a wide variety of domains. It's now used by hundreds of thousands of engineers around the world, in increasingly diverse roles. Companies use Python today in commercial products, for tasks such as testing chips and boards, developing GUIs, searching the Web, animating movies, scripting games, serving up maps and email on the Internet, customizing C++ class libraries, and much more.* In fact, because Python is a completely general-purpose language, its target domains are only limited by the scope of computers in general.

Since it first appeared on the public domain scene in 1991, Python has continued to attract a loyal following, and spawned a dedicated Internet newsgroup, *comp. lang.python*, in 1994. And as the first edition of this book was being written in 1995, Python's home page debuted on the WWW at *http://www.python.org*—still the official place to find all things Python.

To help manage Python's growth, organizations aimed at supporting Python developers have taken shape over the years: among them, Python Software Activity (PSA) was formed to help facilitate Python conferences and web sites, and the

---

* See the preface for more examples of companies using Python in these ways, and see *http://www. python.org* for a more comprehensive list of commercial applications.

What's in a Name?

Python gets its name from the 1970s British TV comedy series, *Monty Python's Flying Circus*. According to Python folklore, Guido van Rossum, Python's creator, was watching reruns of the show at about the same time he needed a name for a new language he was developing. And, as they say in show business, "the rest is history."

Because of this heritage, references to the comedy group's work often show up in examples and discussion. For instance, the name "Spam" has a special connotation to Python users, and confrontations are sometimes referred to as "The Spanish Inquisition." As a rule, if a Python user starts using phrases that have no relation to reality, they're probably borrowed from the Monty Python series or movies. Some of these phrases might even pop up in this book. You don't have to run out and rent *The Meaning of Life* or *The Holy Grail* to do useful work in Python, of course, but it can't hurt.

While "Python" turned out to be a distinctive name, it's also had some interesting side effects. For instance, when the Python newsgroup, *comp.lang.python*, came online in 1994, its first few weeks of activity were almost entirely taken up by people wanting to discuss topics from the TV show. More recently, a special Python supplement in the *Linux Journal* magazine featured photos of Guido garbed in an obligatory "nice red uniform."

There's still an occasional post from fans of the show on Python's news list. For instance, one poster innocently offered to swap Monty Python scripts with other fans. Had he known the nature of the forum, he might have at least mentioned whether they ran under DOS or Unix.

Python Consortium was formed by organizations interested in helping to foster Python's growth. Although the future of the PSA is unclear as I write these words, it has helped to support Python through the early years.

Today, Guido and a handful of other key Python developers, are employed by a company named Digital Creations to do Python development on a full-time basis. Digital Creations, based in Virginia, is also home to the Python-based Zope web application toolkit (see *http://www.zope.org*). However, the Python language is owned and managed by an independent body, and remains a true open source, community-driven system.

Other companies have Python efforts underway as well. For instance, ActiveState and PythonWare develop Python tools, O'Reilly (the publisher of this book) and a company named Foretech both organize annual Python conferences, and O'Reilly manages a supplemental Python web site (see the O'Reilly Network's Python Dev-Center at *http://www.oreillynet.com/python*). The O'Reilly Python Conference is held as part of the annual Open Source Software Convention. Although the world of professional organizations and companies changes more frequently than do published books, it seems certain that the Python language will continue to meet the needs of its user community.

The Compulsory Features List

One way to describe a language is by listing its features. Of course, this will be more meaningful after you've seen Python in action; the best I can do now is speak in the abstract. And it's really how Python's features work together, that make it what it is. But looking at some of Python's attributes may help define it; Table 1-1 lists some of the common reasons cited for Python's appeal.

Table 1-1. Python Language Features

Features	Benefits
No compile or link steps	Rapid development cycle turnaround
No type declarations	Simpler, shorter, and more flexible programs
Automatic memory management	Garbage collection avoids bookkeeping code
High-level datatypes and operations	Fast development using built-in object types
Object-oriented programming	Code reuse, C++, Java, and COM integration
Embedding and extending in C	Optimization, customization, system "glue"
Classes, modules, exceptions	Modular "programming-in-the-large" support
A simple, clear syntax and design	Readability, maintainability, ease of learning
Dynamic loading of C modules	Simplified extensions, smaller binary files
Dynamic reloading of Python modules	Programs can be modified without stopping
Universal "first-class" object model	Fewer restrictions and special-case rules
Runtime program construction	Handles unforeseen needs, end-user coding
Interactive, dynamic nature	Incremental development and testing
Access to interpreter information	Metaprogramming, introspective objects
Wide interpreter portability	Cross-platform programming without ports
Compilation to portable bytecode	Execution speed, protecting source code
Standard portable GUI framework	Tkinter scripts run on X, Windows, and Macs
Standard Internet protocol support	Easy access to email, FTP, HTTP, CGI, etc.
Standard portable system calls	Platform-neutral system scripting
Built-in and third-party libraries	Vast collection of precoded software components
True open source software	May be freely embedded and shipped

To be fair, Python is really a conglomeration of features borrowed from other languages. It includes elements taken from C, C++, Modula-3, ABC, Icon, and others. For instance, Python's modules came from Modula, and its slicing operation from Icon (as far as anyone can seem to remember, at least). And because of Guido's background, Python borrows many of ABC's ideas, but adds practical features of its own, such as support for C-coded extensions.

What's Python Good For?

Because Python is used in a wide variety of ways, it's almost impossible to give an authoritative answer to this question. In general, any application that can benefit from the inclusion of a language optimized for speed of development is a good target Python application domain. Given the ever-shrinking schedules in software development, this a very broad category.

A more specific answer is less easy to formulate. For instance, some use Python as an embedded extension language, while others use it exclusively as a standalone programming tool. And to some extent, this entire book will answer this very question—it explores some of Python's most common roles. For now, here's a summary of some of the more common ways Python is being applied today:

System utilities
> Portable command-line tools, testing systems

Internet scripting
> CGI web sites, Java applets, XML, ASP, email tools

Graphical user interfaces
> With APIs such as Tk, MFC, Gnome, KDE

Component integration
> C/C++ library front-ends, product customization

Database access
> Persistent object stores, SQL database system interfaces

Distributed programming
> With client/server APIs like CORBA, COM

Rapid-prototyping/development
> Throwaway or deliverable prototypes

Language-based modules
> Replacing special-purpose parsers with Python

And more
> Image processing, numeric programming, AI, etc.

"Buses Considered Harmful"

The PSA organization described earlier was originally formed in response to an early thread on the Python newsgroup, which posed the semiserious question: "What would happen if Guido was hit by a bus?"

These days, Guido van Rossum is still the ultimate arbiter of proposed Python changes, but Python's user base helps support the language, work on extensions, fix bugs, and so on. In fact, Python development is now a completely open process—anyone can inspect the latest source-code files or submit patches by visiting a web site (see *http://www.python.org* for details).

As an open source package, Python development is really in the hands of a very large cast of developers working in concert around the world. Given Python's popularity, bus attacks seem less threatening now than they once did; of course, I can't speak for Guido.

On the other hand, Python is not really tied to any particular application area at all. For example, Python's integration support makes it useful for almost any system that can benefit from a frontend, programmable interface. In abstract terms, Python provides services that span domains. It is:

- A dynamic programming language, for situations in which a compile/link step is either impossible (on-site customization), or inconvenient (prototyping, rapid development, system utilities)

- A powerful but simple programming language designed for development speed, for situations in which the complexity of larger languages can be a liability (prototyping, end-user coding)

- A generalized language tool, for situations where we might otherwise need to invent and implement yet another "little language" (programmable system interfaces, configuration tools)

Given these general properties, Python can be applied to any area we're interested in by extending it with domain libraries, embedding it in an application, or using it all by itself. For instance, Python's role as a system tools language is due as much to its built-in interfaces to operating system services as to the language itself. In fact, because Python was built with integration in mind, it has naturally given rise to a growing library of extensions and tools, available as off-the-shelf components to Python developers. Table 1-2 names just a few; you can find more about most of these components in this book or on Python's web site.

Table 1-2. A Few Popular Python Tools and Extensions

Domain	Extensions
Systems programming	Sockets, threads, signals, pipes, RPC calls, POSIX bindings
Graphical user interfaces	Tk, PMW, MFC, X11, wxPython, KDE, Gnome
Database interfaces	Oracle, Sybase, PostGres, mSQL, persistence, dbm
Microsoft Windows tools	MFC, COM, ActiveX, ASP, ODBC, .NET
Internet tools	JPython, CGI tools, HTML/XML parsers, email tools, Zope
Distributed objects	DCOM, CORBA, ILU, Fnorb
Other popular tools	SWIG, PIL, regular expressions, NumPy, cryptography

What's Python Not Good For?

To be fair again, some tasks are outside of Python's scope. Like all dynamic languages, Python (as currently implemented) isn't as fast or efficient as static, compiled languages like C. In many domains, the difference doesn't matter; for programs that spend most of their time interacting with users or transferring data over networks, Python is usually more than adequate to meet the performance needs of the entire application. But efficiency is still a priority in some domains.

Because it is interpreted today,* Python alone usually isn't the best tool for delivery of performance-critical components. Instead, computationally intensive operations can be implemented as compiled *extensions* to Python, and coded in a low-level language like C. Python can't be used as the sole implementation language for such components, but it works well as a frontend scripting interface to them.

For example, numerical programming and image processing support has been added to Python by combining optimized extensions with a Python language interface. In such a system, once the optimized extensions have been developed, most of the programming occurs at the higher-level Python scripting level. The net result is a numerical programming tool that's both efficient and easy to use.

Moreover, Python can still serve as a prototyping tool in such domains. Systems may be implemented in Python first, and later moved in whole or piecemeal to a language like C for delivery. C and Python have distinct strengths and roles; a

---

* Python is "interpreted" in the same way that Java is: Python source code is automatically compiled (translated) to an intermediate form called "bytecode," which is then executed by the Python virtual machine (that is, the Python runtime system). This makes Python scripts more portable and faster than a pure interpreter that runs raw source code or trees. But it also makes Python slower than true compilers that translate source code to binary machine code for the local CPU. Keep in mind, though, that some of these details are specific to the standard Python implementation; the JPython (a.k.a. "Jython") port compiles Python scripts to Java bytecode, and the new C#/.NET port compiles Python scripts to binary *.exe* files. An optimizing Python compiler might make most of the performance cautions in this chapter invalid (we can hope).

hybrid approach, using C for compute-intensive modules, and Python for proto-typing and frontend interfaces, can leverage the benefits of both.

In some sense, Python solves the efficiency/flexibility tradeoff by not solving it at all. It provides a language optimized for ease of use, along with tools needed to integrate with other languages. By combining components written in Python and compiled languages like C and C++, developers may select an appropriate mix of usability and performance for each particular application. While it's unlikely that it will ever be as fast as C, Python's speed of development is at least as important as C's speed of execution in most modern software projects.

On Truth in Advertising

In this book's conclusion we will return to some of the bigger ideas introduced in this chapter, after we've had a chance to study Python in action. I want to point out up front, though, that my background is in Computer Science, not marketing. I plan to be brutally honest in this book, both about Python's features and its downsides. Despite the fact that Python is one of the most easy-to-use programming languages ever created, there are indeed some pitfalls, which we will examine in this book.

Let's start now. Perhaps the biggest pitfall you should know about is this one: *Python makes it incredibly easy to throw together a bad design quickly.* It's a genuine problem. Because developing programs in Python is so simple and fast compared to traditional languages, it's easy to get wrapped up in the act of programming itself, and pay less attention to the problem you are really try-ing to solve.

In fact, Python can be downright seductive—so much so that you may need to consciously resist the temptation to quickly implement a program in Python that works, and is arguably "cool," but leaves you as far from a maintainable imple-mentation of your original conception as you were when you started. The nat-ural delays built in to compiled language development—fixing compiler error messages, linking libraries, and the like—aren't there to apply the brakes in Python work.

This isn't necessarily all bad. In most cases, the early designs that you throw together fast are stepping stones to better designs that you later keep. But be warned: even with a rapid development language like Python, *there is no sub-stitute for brains*—it's always best to think before you start typing code. To date, at least, no computer programing language has managed to make intelli-gence obsolete.

I

System Interfaces

This first technical part of the book presents Python's system programming tools—interfaces to services in the underlying operating system, as well as the context of an executing program. It consists of the following chapters:

- Chapter 2, *System Tools*. This chapter is a comprehensive look at commonly used system interface tools, and will teach you how to process streams, files, directories, command-line arguments, shell variables, and more. This chapter starts slowly, and is partially meant as a reference.

- Chapter 3, *Parallel System Tools*. This chapter is an introduction to Python's library support for running programs in parallel. Here, you'll find coverage of threads, process forks, pipes, signals, and the like.

- Chapter 4, *Larger System Examples I*, and Chapter 5, *Larger System Examples II*. This is a two-chapter collection of typical system programming examples that draw upon the material of the first two chapters. Among other things, Python scripts here demonstrate how to do things like split and join files, compare and copy directories, generate web pages from templates, and launch programs and web browsers portably. The second of these chapters focuses on advanced file and directory examples; the first presents assorted system tools case studies.

Although this part of the book emphasizes systems programming tasks, the tools introduced are general-purpose, and are used often in later chapters.

2

System Tools

"The os.path to Knowledge"

This chapter begins our look at ways to apply Python to real programming tasks. In this and the following chapters, we'll see how to use Python to write system tools, graphical user interfaces, database applications, Internet scripts, web sites, and more. Along the way we'll also study larger Python programming concepts in action: code reuse, maintainability, object-oriented programming, and so on.

In this first part of the book, we begin our Python programming tour by exploring the *systems application domain*—scripts that deal with files, programs, and the environment surrounding a program in general. Although the examples in this domain focus on particular kinds of tasks, the techniques they employ will prove to be useful in later parts of the book as well. In other words, you should begin your journey here, unless you already are a Python systems programming wizard.

Why Python Here?

Python's system interfaces span application domains, but for the next four chapters, most of our examples fall into the category of *system tools*—programs sometimes called command-line utilities, shell scripts, or some permutation of such words. Regardless of their title, you are probably familiar with this sort of script already; they accomplish tasks like processing files in a directory, launching test scripts, and so on. Such programs historically have been written in nonportable and syntactically obscure shell languages such as DOS batch files, csh, and awk.

Even in this relatively simple domain, though, some of Python's better attributes shine brightly. For instance, Python's ease of use and extensive built-in library make it simple (and even fun) to use advanced system tools such as threads, signals, forks, sockets, and their kin; such tools are much less accessible under the obscure syntax of shell languages and the slow development cycles of compiled languages. Python's support for concepts like code clarity and object-oriented programming also help us write shell tools that can be read, maintained, and reused. When using Python, there is no need to start every new script from scratch.

Moreover, we'll find that Python not only includes all the interfaces we need to write system tools, it also fosters script *portability*. By employing Python's standard library, most system scripts written in Python are automatically portable to all major platforms. A Python directory-processing script written in Windows, for instance, can usually also be run in Linux without changing its source code at all—simply copy over the source code. If used well, Python is the only system scripting tool you need to know.

"Batteries Included"

This chapter and those that follow deal with both the Python language and its standard library. Although Python itself provides an easy-to-use scripting language, much of the action in real Python development involves the vast library of programming tools (some 200 modules at last count) that ship with the Python package. In fact, the standard libraries are so powerful that it is not uncommon to hear Python described by the term "batteries included"—a phrase generally credited to Frank Stajano, meaning that most of what you need for real day-to-day work is already there for the importing.

As we'll see, the standard libraries form much of the challenge in Python programming. Once you've mastered the core language, you'll find that most of your time is spent applying the built-in functions and modules that come with the system. On the other hand, libraries are where most of the fun happens. In practice, programs become most interesting when they start using services external to the language interpreter: networks, files, GUIs, databases, and so on. All of these are supported in the Python standard library, a collection of precoded modules written in Python and C that are installed with the Python interpreter.

Beyond the Python standard library, there is an additional collection of third-party packages for Python that must be fetched and installed separately. At this writing, most of these third-party extensions can be found via searches and links at *http://www.python.org*, and at the "Starship" and "Vaults of Parnassus" Python sites (also reachable from links at *http://www.python.org*). If you have to do something special with Python, chances are good that you can find a free and open source module that will help. Most of the tools we'll employ in this text are a standard part of Python, but I'll be careful to point out things that must be installed separately.

System Scripting Overview

The next two sections will take a quick tour through `sys` and `os`, before this chapter moves on to larger system programming concepts. As I'm not going to demonstrate every item in every built-in module, the first thing I want to do is show you how to get more details on your own. Officially, this task also serves as an excuse for introducing a few core system scripting concepts—along the way, we'll code a first script to format documentation.

Python System Modules

Most system-level interfaces in Python are shipped in just two modules: `sys` and `os`. That's somewhat oversimplified; other standard modules belong to this domain too (e.g., `glob`, `socket`, `thread`, `time`, `fcntl`), and some built-in functions are really system interfaces as well (e.g., `open`). But `sys` and `os` together form the core of Python's system tools arsenal.

In principle at least, `sys` exports components related to the Python *interpreter* itself (e.g., the module search path), and `os` contains variables and functions that map to the operating system on which Python is run. In practice, this distinction may not always seem clear-cut (e.g., the standard input and output streams show up in `sys`, but they are at least arguably tied to operating system paradigms). The good news is that you'll soon use the tools in these modules so often that their locations will be permanently stamped on your memory.*

The `os` module also attempts to provide a *portable* programming interface to the underlying operating system—its functions may be implemented differently on different platforms, but they look the same everywhere to Python scripts. In addition, the `os` module exports a nested submodule, `os.path`, that provides a portable interface to file and directory processing tools.

Module Documentation Sources

As you can probably deduce from the preceding paragraphs, learning to write system scripts in Python is mostly a matter of learning about Python's system modules. Luckily, there are a variety of information sources to make this task easier—from module attributes to published references and books.

For instance, if you want to know everything that a built-in module exports, you can either read its library manual entry, study its source code (Python is open

---

* They may also work their way into your subconscious. Python newcomers sometimes appear on Internet discussion forums to express joy after "dreaming in Python" for the first time. All possible Freudian interpretations aside, it's not bad as dream motifs go; after all, there are worse languages to dream in.

source software, after all), or fetch its attribute list and documentation string inter-actively. Let's import `sys` and see what it's got:

```
C:\...\PP2E\System> python
>>> import sys
>>> dir(sys)
['__doc__', '__name__', '__stderr__', '__stdin__', '__stdout__', 'argv',
'builtin_module_names', 'copyright', 'dllhandle', 'exc_info', 'exc_type',
'exec_prefix', 'executable', 'exit', 'getrefcount', 'hexversion', 'maxint',
'modules', 'path', 'platform', 'prefix', 'ps1', 'ps2', 'setcheckinterval',
'setprofile', 'settrace', 'stderr', 'stdin', 'stdout', 'version', 'winver']
```

The `dir` function simply returns a list containing the string names of all the attributes in any object with attributes; it's a handy memory-jogger for modules at the interactive prompt. For example, we know there is something called `sys.version`, because the name `version` came back in the `dir` result. If that's not enough, we can always consult the `__doc__` string of built-in modules:

```
>>> sys.__doc__
...
...lots of text deleted here...
...
count for an object (plus one :-)\012setcheckinterval() -- control how often
the interpreter checks for events\012setprofile() -- set the global profiling
function\012settrace() -- set the global debug tracing function\012"
```

Paging Documentation Strings

The `__doc__` built-in attribute usually contains a string of documentation, but may look a bit weird when printed—it's one long string with embedded line-feed char-acters that print as \012, not a nice list of lines. To format these strings for more humane display, I usually use a utility script like the one in Example 2-1.

Example 2-1. PP2E\System\more.py

```
#########################################################
# split and interactively page a string or file of text;
#########################################################

import string

def more(text, numlines=15):
    lines = string.split(text, '\n')
    while lines:
        chunk = lines[:numlines]
        lines = lines[numlines:]
        for line in chunk: print line
        if lines and raw_input('More?') not in ['y', 'Y']: break

if __name__ == '__main__':
```

Example 2-1. PP2E\System\more.py (continued)

```
import sys                              # when run, not imported
more(open(sys.argv[1]).read(), 10)     # page contents of file on cmdline
```

The meat of this file is its **more** function, and if you know any Python at all, it should be fairly straightforward—it simply splits up a string around end-of-line characters, and then slices off and displays a few lines at a time (15 by default) to avoid scrolling off the screen. A slice expression `lines[:15]` gets the first 15 items in a list, and `lines[15:]` gets the rest; to show a different number of lines each time, pass a number to the **numlines** argument (e.g., the last line in Example 2-1 passes 10 to the **numlines** argument of the **more** function).

The `string.split` built-in call this script employs returns a list of sub-strings (e.g., `["line", "line",...]`). As we'll see later in this chapter, the end-of-line character is always \n (which is \012 in octal escape form) within a Python script, no matter what platform it is run upon. (If you don't already know why this matters, DOS \r characters are dropped when read.)

Introducing the string Module

Now, this is a simple Python program, but it already brings up three important topics that merit quick detours here: it uses the **string** module, reads from a file, and is set up to be run or imported. The Python **string** module isn't a system-related tool per se, but it sees action in most Python programs. In fact, it is going to show up throughout this chapter and those that follow, so here is a quick review of some of its more useful exports. The **string** module includes calls for searching and replacing:

```
>>> import string
>>> string.find('xxxSPAMxxx', 'SPAM')        # return first offset
3
>>> string.replace('xxaaxxaa', 'aa', 'SPAM') # global replacement
'xxSPAMxxSPAM'

>>> string.strip('\t  Ni\n')                 # remove whitespace
'Ni'
```

The `string.find` call returns the offset of the first occurrence of a substring, and `string.replace` does global search and replacement. With this module, substrings are just strings; in Chapter 18, *Text and Language*, we'll also see modules that allow regular expression *patterns* to show up in searches and replacements. The **string** module also provides constants and functions useful for things like case conversions:

```
>>> string.lowercase                         # case constants, converters
'abcdefghijklmnopqrstuvwxyz'
```

```
>>> string.lower('SHRUBBERRY')
'shrubberry'
```

There are also tools for splitting up strings around a substring delimiter and putting them back together with a substring between. We'll explore these tools later in this book, but as an introduction, here they are at work:

```
>>> string.split('aaa+bbb+ccc', '+')          # split into substrings list
['aaa', 'bbb', 'ccc']
>>> string.split('a b\nc\nd')                   # default delimiter: whitespace
['a', 'b', 'c', 'd']

>>> string.join(['aaa', 'bbb', 'ccc'], 'NI')   # join substrings list
'aaaNIbbbNIccc'
>>> string.join(['A', 'dead', 'parrot'])       # default delimiter: space
'A dead parrot'
```

These calls turn out to be surprisingly powerful. For example, a line of data columns separated by tabs can be parsed into its columns with a single `split` call; the *more.py* script uses it to split a string into a list of line strings. In fact, we can emulate the `string.replace` call with a split/join combination:

```
>>> string.join(string.split('xxaaxxaa', 'aa'), 'SPAM')   # replace the hard way
'xxSPAMxxSPAM'
```

For future reference, also keep in mind that Python doesn't automatically convert strings to numbers, or vice versa; if you want to use one like the other, you must say so, with manual conversions:

```
>>> string.atoi("42"), int("42"), eval("42")   # string to int conversions
(42, 42, 42)

>>> str(42), `42`, ("%d" % 42)                  # int to string conversions
('42', '42', '42')

>>> "42" + str(1), int("42") + 1                # concatenation, addition
('421', 43)
```

In the last command here, the first expression triggers string concatenation (since both sides are strings) and the second invokes integer addition (because both objects are numbers). Python doesn't assume you meant one or the other and convert automatically; as a rule of thumb, Python tries to avoid magic when possible. String tools will be covered in more detail later in this book (in fact, they get a full chapter in Part IV, *Assorted Topics*), but be sure to also see the library manual for additional `string` module tools.

As of Python 1.6, `string` *objects* have grown *methods* corresponding to functions in the `string` *module*. For instance, given a name `X` assigned to a `string` object, `X.split()` now does the same work as `string.split(X)`. In Example 2-1, that means that these two lines would be equivalent:

```
lines = string.split(text, '\n')
lines = text.split('\n')
```

but the latter form doesn't require an import statement. The `string` module will still be around for the foreseeable future and beyond, but `string` methods are likely to be the next wave in the Python text-processing world.

File Operation Basics

The *more.py* script also opens the external file whose name is listed on the command line with the built-in **open** function, and reads its text into memory all at once with the file object **read** method. Since file objects returned by **open** are part of the core Python language itself, I assume that you have at least a passing familiarity with them at this point in the text. But just in case you've flipped into this chapter early on in your Pythonhood, the calls:

```
open('file').read()        # read entire file into string
open('file').read(N)       # read next N bytes into string
open('file').readlines()   # read entire file into line strings list
open('file').readline()    # read next line, through '\n'
```

load a file's contents into a string, load a fixed size set of bytes into a string, load a file's contents into a list of line strings, and load the next line in the file into a string, respectively. As we'll see in a moment, these calls can also be applied to shell commands in Python. File objects also have **write** methods for sending strings to the associated file. File-related topics are covered in depth later in this chapter.

Using Programs Two Ways

The last few lines in the *more.py* file also introduce one of the first big concepts in shell tool programming. They instrument the file to be used two ways: as *script* or *library*. Every Python module has a built-in **__name__** variable that is set by Python to the string **__main__** only when the file is run as a program, not when imported as a library. Because of that, the **more** function in this file is executed automatically by the last line in the file when this script is run as a top-level program, not when it is imported elsewhere. This simple trick turns out to be one key to writing reusable script code: by coding program logic as *functions* instead of top-level code, it can also be imported and reused in other scripts.

The upshot is that we can either run *more.py* by itself, or import and call its more function elsewhere. When running the file as a top-level program, we list the name of a file to be read and paged on the command line: as we'll describe fully later in this chapter, words typed in the command used to start a program show up in the built-in sys.argv list in Python. For example, here is the script file in action paging itself (be sure to type this command line in your *PP2E\System* directory, or it won't find the input file; I'll explain why later):

```
C:\...\PP2E\System>python more.py more.py
#########################################################
# split and interactively page a string or file of text;
#########################################################

import string

def more(text, numlines=15):
    lines = string.split(text, '\n')
    while lines:
        chunk = lines[:numlines]
More?y
        lines = lines[numlines:]
        for line in chunk: print line
        if lines and raw_input('More?') not in ['y', 'Y']: break

if __name__ == '__main__':
    import sys                              # when run, not imported
    more(open(sys.argv[1]).read(), 10)      # page contents of file on cmdline
```

When the *more.py* file is imported, we pass an explicit string to its more function, and this is exactly the sort of utility we need for documentation text. Running this utility on the sys module's documentation string gives us a bit more information about what's available to scripts, in human-readable form:

```
>>> from more import more
>>> more(sys.__doc__)
This module provides access to some objects used or maintained by the
interpreter and to functions that interact strongly with the interpreter.

Dynamic objects:

argv -- command line arguments; argv[0] is the script pathname if known
path -- module search path; path[0] is the script directory, else ''
modules -- dictionary of loaded modules
exitfunc -- you may set this to a function to be called when Python exits
```

```
stdin -- standard input file object; used by raw_input() and input()
stdout -- standard output file object; used by the print statement
stderr -- standard error object; used for error messages
  By assigning another file object (or an object that behaves like a file)
  to one of these, it is possible to redirect all of the interpreter's I/O.
More?
```

Pressing "y" (and the Enter key) here makes the function display the next few lines of documentation, and then prompt again unless you've run past the end of the lines list. Try this on your own machine to see what the rest of the module's documentation string looks like.

Python Library Manuals

If that still isn't enough detail, your next step is to read the Python library manual's entry for **sys** to get the full story. All of Python's standard manuals ship as HTML pages, so you should be able to read them in any web browser you have on your computer. They are available on this book's CD, and are installed with Python on Windows, but here are a few simple pointers:

- On Windows, click the Start button, pick Programs, select the Python entry there, and then choose the manuals item. The manuals should magically appear on your display within a browser like Internet Explorer.

- On Linux, you may be able to click on the manuals' entries in a file explorer, or start your browser from a shell command line and navigate to the library manual's HTML files on your machine.

- If you can't find the manuals on your computer, you can always read them online. Go to Python's web site, *http://www.python.org*, and follow the documentation links.

However you get started, be sure to pick the "Library" manual for things like **sys**; Python's standard manual set also includes a short tutorial, language reference, extending references, and more.

Commercially Published References

At the risk of sounding like a marketing droid, I should mention that you can also purchase the Python manual set, printed and bound; see the book information page at *http://www.python.org* for details and links. Commercially published Python reference books are also available today, including *Python Essential Reference* (New Riders Publishing) and *Python Pocket Reference* (O'Reilly). The former is more complete and comes with examples, but the latter serves as a convenient memory-jogger once you've taken a library tour or two.* Also watch for O'Reilly's upcoming book *Python Standard Library*.

The sys Module

On to module details. As mentioned earlier, the `sys` and `os` modules form the core of much of Python's system-related toolset. Let's now take a quick, interactive tour through some of the tools in these two modules, before applying them in bigger examples.

Platforms and Versions

Like most modules, `sys` includes both informational names and functions that take action. For instance, its attributes give us the name of the underlying operating system the platform code is running on, the largest possible integer on this machine, and the version number of the Python interpreter running our code:

```
C:\...\PP2E\System>python
>>> import sys
>>> sys.platform, sys.maxint, sys.version
('win32', 2147483647, '1.5.2 (#0, Apr 13 1999, 10:51:12) [MSC 32 bit (Intel)]')
>>>
>>> if sys.platform[:3] == 'win': print 'hello windows'
...
hello windows
```

If you have code that must act differently on different machines, simply test the `sys.platform` string as done here; although most of Python is cross-platform, nonportable tools are usually wrapped in `if` tests like the one here. For instance, we'll see later that program launch and low-level console interaction tools vary per platform today—simply test `sys.platform` to pick the right tool for the machine your script is running on.

The Module Search Path

The `sys` module also lets us inspect the module search path both interactively and within a Python program. `sys.path` is a list of strings representing the true search path in a running Python interpreter. When a module is imported, Python scans this list from left to right, searching for the module's file on each directory named

---

* I also wrote the latter as a replacement for the reference appendix that appeared in the first edition of this book; it's meant to be a supplement to the text you're reading. Since I'm its author, though, I won't say more here . . . except that you should be sure to pick up a copy for friends, coworkers, old college roommates, and every member of your extended family the next time you're at the bookstore (yes, I'm kidding).

in the list. Because of that, this is the place to look to verify that your search path
is really set as intended.*

The `sys.path` list is simply initialized from your PYTHONPATH setting plus system defaults, when the interpreter is first started up. In fact, you'll notice quite a
few directories that are not on your PYTHONPATH if you inspect `sys.path` interactively—it also includes an indicator for the script's home directory (an empty
string—something I'll explain in more detail after we meet `os.getcwd`), and a set
of standard library directories that may vary per installation:

```
>>> sys.path
['', 'C:\\PP2ndEd\\examples', ...plus standard paths deleted... ]
```

Surprisingly, `sys.path` can actually be *changed* by a program too—a script can
use list operations like `append`, `del`, and the like to configure the search path at
runtime. Python always uses the current `sys.path` setting to import, no matter
what you've changed it to be:

```
>>> sys.path.append(r'C:\mydir')
>>> sys.path
['', 'C:\\PP2ndEd\\examples', ...more deleted... , 'C:\\mydir']
```

Changing `sys.path` directly like this is an alternative to setting your PYTHON-
PATH shell variable, but not a very good one—changes to `sys.path` are retained
only until the Python process ends, and must be remade every time you start a
new Python program or session.

The Loaded Modules Table

The `sys` module also contains hooks into the interpreter; `sys.modules`, for example, is a dictionary containing one `name:module` entry for every module imported
in your Python session or program (really, in the calling Python process):

```
>>> sys.modules
{'os.path': <module 'ntpath' from 'C:\Program Files\Python\Lib\ntpath.pyc'>,...

>>> sys.modules.keys()
['os.path', 'os', 'exceptions', '__main__', 'ntpath', 'strop', 'nt', 'sys',
'__builtin__', 'site', 'signal', 'UserDict', 'string', 'stat']
>>>
>>> sys
<module 'sys' (built-in)>
>>> sys.modules['sys']
<module 'sys' (built-in)>
```

---

* It's not impossible that Python sees PYTHONPATH differently than you do. A syntax error in your system shell configuration files may botch the setting of PYTHONPATH, even if it looks fine to you. On
  Windows, for example, if a space appears around the = of a DOS *set* command in your *autoexec.bat*
  file (e.g., set NAME = VALUE), you will actually set NAME to an empty string, not VALUE!

Windows Directory Paths

Because *backslashes* normally introduce escape code sequences in Python strings, Windows users should be sure to either double up on backslashes when using them in DOS directory path strings (e.g., in `"C:\\dir"`, `\\` is an escape sequence that really means `\`), or use *raw string* constants to retain backslashes literally (e.g., `r"C:\dir"`).

If you inspect directory paths on Windows (as in the `sys.path` interaction listing), Python prints double `\\` to mean a single `\`. Technically, you can get away with a single `\` in a string if it is followed by a character Python does not recognize as the rest of an escape sequence, but doubles and raw strings are usually easier than memorizing escape code tables.

Also note that most Python library calls accept either forward (`/`) or backward (`\`) slashes as directory path separators, regardless of the underlying platform. That is, `/` usually works on Windows too, and aids in making scripts portable to Unix. Tools in the `os` and `os.path` modules, described later in this chapter, further aid in script path portability.

We might use such a hook to write programs that display or otherwise process all the modules loaded by a program (just iterate over the keys list of `sys.modules`). `sys` also exports tools for getting an object's reference count used by Python's garbage collector (`getrefcount`), checking which modules are built in to this Python (`builtin_module_names`), and more.

Exception Details

Some of the `sys` module's attributes allow us to fetch all the information related to the most recently raised Python exception. This is handy if we want to process exceptions in a more generic fashion. For instance, the `sys.exc_info` function returns the latest exception's type, value, and traceback object:

```
>>> try:
...     raise IndexError
... except:
...     print sys.exc_info()
...
(<class exceptions.IndexError at 7698d0>, <exceptions.IndexError instance at
797140>, <traceback object at 7971a0>)
```

We might use such information to format our own error message to display in a GUI pop-up window or HTML web page (recall that by default, uncaught exceptions terminate programs with a Python error display). Portability note—the most recent exception type, value, and traceback objects are also available via other names:

```
>>> try:
...     raise TypeError, "Bad Thing"
... except:
...     print sys.exc_type, sys.exc_value
...
exceptions.TypeError Bad Thing
```

But these names represent a single, global exception, and are not specific to a particular *thread* (threads are covered in the next chapter). If you mean to raise and catch exceptions in multiple threads, `exc_info()` provides thread-specific exception details.

Other sys Module Exports

The `sys` module exports additional tools we will meet in the context of larger topics and examples later in this chapter and book. For instance:

- *Command-line arguments* show up as a list of strings called `sys.argv`
- *Standard streams* are available as `stdin`, `stdout`, and `stderr`
- *Program exit* can be forced with `sys.exit` calls

Since these all lead us to bigger topics, though, we cover them in sections of their own later in this and the next chapters.

The os Module

As mentioned, `os` contains all the usual operating-system calls you may have used in your C programs and shell scripts. Its calls deal with directories, processes, shell variables, and the like. Technically, this module provides *POSIX* tools—a portable standard for operating-system calls—along with platform-independent directory processing tools as nested module `os.path`. Operationally, `os` serves as a largely portable interface to your computer's system calls: scripts written with `os` and `os.path` can usually be run on any platform unchanged.

In fact, if you read the `os` module's source code, you'll notice that it really just imports whatever platform-specific system module you have on your computer (e.g., `nt`, `mac`, `posix`). See the file *os.py* in the Python source library directory—it simply runs a `from*` statement to copy all names out of a platform-specific module. By always importing `os` instead of platform-specific modules, though, your scripts are mostly immune to platform implementation differences.

The Big os Lists

Let's take a quick look at the basic interfaces in os. If you inspect this module's attributes interactively, you get a huge list of names that will vary per Python release, will likely vary per platform, and isn't incredibly useful until you've learned what each name means:

```
>>> import os
>>> dir(os)
['F_OK', 'O_APPEND', 'O_BINARY', 'O_CREAT', 'O_EXCL', 'O_RDONLY', 'O_RDWR',
'O_TEXT', 'O_TRUNC', 'O_WRONLY', 'P_DETACH', 'P_NOWAIT', 'P_NOWAITO',
'P_OVERLAY', 'P_WAIT', 'R_OK', 'UserDict', 'W_OK', 'X_OK', '_Environ',
'__builtins__', '__doc__', '__file__', '__name__', '_execvpe', '_exit',
'_notfound', 'access', 'altsep', 'chdir', 'chmod', 'close', 'curdir',
'defpath', 'dup', 'dup2', 'environ', 'error', 'execl', 'execle', 'execlp',
'execlpe', 'execv', 'execve', 'execvp', 'execvpe', 'fdopen', 'fstat', 'getcwd',
'getpid', 'i', 'linesep', 'listdir', 'lseek', 'lstat', 'makedirs', 'mkdir',
'name', 'open', 'pardir', 'path', 'pathsep', 'pipe', 'popen', 'putenv', 'read',
'remove', 'removedirs', 'rename', 'renames', 'rmdir', 'sep', 'spawnv',
'spawnve', 'stat', 'strerror', 'string', 'sys', 'system', 'times', 'umask',
'unlink', 'utime', 'write']
```

Besides all of these, the nested os.path module exports even more tools, most of which are related to processing file and directory names portably:

```
>>> dir(os.path)
['__builtins__', '__doc__', '__file__', '__name__', 'abspath', 'basename',
'commonprefix', 'dirname', 'exists', 'expanduser', 'expandvars', 'getatime',
'getmtime', 'getsize', 'isabs', 'isdir', 'isfile', 'islink', 'ismount', 'join',
'normcase', 'normpath', 'os', 'split', 'splitdrive', 'splitext', 'splitunc',
'stat', 'string', 'varchars', 'walk']
```

Administrative Tools

Just in case those massive listings aren't quite enough to go on, let's experiment with some of the simpler os tools interactively. Like sys, the os module comes with a collection of informational and administrative tools:

```
>>> os.getpid()
-510737
>>> os.getcwd()
'C:\\PP2ndEd\\examples\\PP2E\\System'

>>> os.chdir(r'c:\temp')
>>> os.getcwd()
'c:\\temp'
```

As shown here, the os.getpid function gives the calling process's *process ID* (a unique system-defined identifier for a running program), and os.getcwd returns the *current working directory*. The current working directory is where files opened by your script are assumed to live, unless their names include explicit directory paths. That's why I told you earlier to run the following command in the directory where *more.py* lives:

```
C:\...\PP2E\System>python more.py more.py
```

The input filename argument here is given without an explicit directory path (though you could add one to page files in another directory). If you need to run in a different working directory, call the os.chdir function to change to a new directory; your code will run relative to the new directory for the rest of the program (or until the next os.chdir call). This chapter has more to say about the notion of a current working directory, and its relation to module imports, when it explores *script execution context* later.

Portability Constants

The os module also exports a set of names designed to make *cross-platform* programming simpler. The set includes platform-specific settings for path and directory separator characters, parent and current directory indicators, and the characters used to terminate lines on the underlying computer:[*]

```
>>> os.pathsep, os.sep, os.pardir, os.curdir, os.linesep
(';', '\\', '..', '.', '\015\012')
```

Name os.sep whatever character is used to separate directory components on the platform Python is running on; it is automatically preset to "\" on Windows, "/" for POSIX machines, and ":" on the Mac. Similarly, os.pathsep provides the character that separates directories on directory lists—":" for POSIX and ";" for DOS and Windows. By using such attributes when composing and decomposing system-related strings in our scripts, they become fully portable. For instance, a call of the form string.split(dirpath,os.sep) will correctly split platform-specific directory names into components, even though dirpath may look like "dir\dir" on Windows, "dir/dir" on Linux, and "dir:dir" on Macintosh.

Basic os.path Tools

The nested module os.path provides a large set of directory-related tools of its own. For example, it includes portable functions for tasks such as checking a file's type (isdir, isfile, and others), testing file existence (exists), and fetching the size of a file by name (getsize):

```
>>> os.path.isdir(r'C:\temp'),        os.path.isfile(r'C:\temp')
(1, 0)
```

---

[*] os.linesep comes back as \015\012 here—the octal escape code equivalent of \r\n, reflecting the carriage-return+line-feed line terminator convention on Windows. See the discussion of end-of-line translations in the "File Tools" section later in this chapter.

```
>>> os.path.isdir(r'C:\config.sys'),  os.path.isfile(r'C:\config.sys')
(0, 1)
>>> os.path.isdir('nonesuch'),        os.path.isfile('nonesuch')
(0, 0)

>>> os.path.exists(r'c:\temp\data.txt')
0
>>> os.path.getsize(r'C:\autoexec.bat')
260
```

The os.path.isdir and os.path.isfile calls tell us whether a filename is a directory or a simple file; both return 0 (false) if the named file does not exist. We also get calls for splitting and joining directory path strings, which automatically use the directory name conventions on the platform on which Python is running:

```
>>> os.path.split(r'C:\temp\data.txt')
('C:\\temp', 'data.txt')
>>> os.path.join(r'C:\temp', 'output.txt')
'C:\\temp\\output.txt'

>>> name = r'C:\temp\data.txt'                          # Windows paths
>>> os.path.basename(name), os.path.dirname(name)
('data.txt', 'C:\\temp')

>>> name = '/home/lutz/temp/data.txt'                   # Unix-style paths
>>> os.path.basename(name), os.path.dirname(name)
('data.txt', '/home/lutz/temp')

>>> os.path.splitext(r'C:\PP2ndEd\examples\PP2E\PyDemos.pyw')
('C:\\PP2ndEd\\examples\\PP2E\\PyDemos', '.pyw')
```

Call os.path.split separates a filename from its directory path, and os.path.join puts them back together—all in entirely portable fashion, using the path conventions of the machine on which they are called. The basename and dirname calls here simply return the second and first items returned by a split as a convenience, and splitext strips the file extension (after the last "."). This module also has an abspath call that portably returns the absolute full directory pathname of a file; it accounts for adding the current directory, ".." parents, and more:

```
>>> os.getcwd()
'C:\\PP2ndEd\\cdrom\\WindowsExt'
>>> os.path.abspath('temp')                    # expand to full path name
'C:\\PP2ndEd\\cdrom\\WindowsExt\\temp'
>>> os.path.abspath(r'..\examples')            # relative paths expanded
'C:\\PP2ndEd\\examples'
>>> os.path.abspath(r'C:\PP2ndEd\chapters')    # absolute paths unchanged
'C:\\PP2ndEd\\chapters'
>>> os.path.abspath(r'C:\temp\spam.txt')       # ditto for file names
'C:\\temp\\spam.txt'
>>> os.path.abspath('')                        # empty string means the cwd
'C:\\PP2ndEd\\cdrom\\WindowsExt'
```

Because filenames are relative to the current working directory when they aren't fully specified paths, the `os.path.abspath` function helps if you want to show users what directory is truly being used to store a file. On Windows, for example, when GUI-based programs are launched by clicking on file explorer icons and desktop shortcuts, the execution directory of the program is the clicked file's home directory, but that is not always obvious to the person doing the clicking; printing a file's `abspath` can help.

Running Shell Commands from Scripts

The `os` module is also the place where we run shell commands from within Python scripts. This concept is intertwined with others we won't cover until later in this chapter, but since this a key concept employed throughout this part of the book, let's take a quick first look at the basics here. Two `os` functions allow scripts to run any command line that you can type in a console window:

`os.system`
> Run a shell command from a Python script

`os.popen`
> Run a shell command and connect to its input or output streams

What's a shell command?

To understand the scope of these calls, we need to first define a few terms. In this text the term *shell* means the system that reads and runs command-line strings on your computer, and *shell command* means a command-line string that you would normally enter at your computer's shell prompt.

For example, on Windows, you can start an MS-DOS console window and type DOS commands there—things like *dir* to get a directory listing, *type* to view a file, names of programs you wish to start, and so on. DOS is the system shell, and commands like *dir* and *type* are shell commands. On Linux, you can start a new shell session by opening an xterm window and typing shell commands there too—*ls* to list directories, *cat* to view files, and so on. There are a variety of shells available on Unix (e.g., `csh`, `ksh`), but they all read and run command lines. Here are two shell commands typed and run in an MS-DOS console box on Windows:

```
C:\temp>dir /B                    ...type a shell command-line
about-pp.html                     ...its output shows up here
python1.5.tar.gz                  ...DOS is the shell on Windows
about-pp2e.html
about-ppr2e.html
newdir

C:\temp>type helloshell.py
# a Python program
print 'The Meaning of Life'
```

Running shell commands

None of this is directly related to Python, of course (despite the fact that Python command-line scripts are sometimes confusingly called "shell tools"). But because the os module's system and popen calls let Python scripts run any sort of command that the underlying system shell understands, our scripts can make use of every command-line tool available on the computer, whether it's coded in Python or not. For example, here is some Python code that runs the two DOS shell commands typed at the shell prompt shown previously:

```
C:\temp>python
>>> import os
>>> os.system('dir /B')
about-pp.html
python1.5.tar.gz
about-pp2e.html
about-ppr2e.html
newdir
0

>>> os.system('type helloshell.py')
# a Python program
print 'The Meaning of Life'
0
```

The "0"s at the end here are just the return values of the system call itself. The system call can be used to run any command line that we could type at the shell's prompt (here, C:\temp>). The command's output normally shows up in the Python session's or program's standard output stream.

Communicating with shell commands

But what if we want to grab a command's output within a script? The os.system call simply runs a shell command line, but os.popen also connects to the standard input or output streams of the command—we get back a *file-like object* connected to the command's output by default (if we pass a "w" mode flag to popen, we connect to the command's input stream instead). By using this object to read the output of a command spawned with popen, we can intercept the text that would normally appear in the console window where a command line is typed:

```
>>> open('helloshell.py').read()
"# a Python program\012print 'The Meaning of Life'\012"

>>> text = os.popen('type helloshell.py').read()
>>> text
"# a Python program\012print 'The Meaning of Life'\012"

>>> listing = os.popen('dir /B').readlines()
```

```
>>> listing
['about-pp.html\012', 'python1.5.tar.gz\012', 'helloshell.py\012',
 'about-pp2e.html\012', 'about-ppr2e.html\012', 'newdir\012']
```

Here, we first fetch a file's content the usual way (using Python files), then as the output of a shell *type* command. Reading the output of a *dir* command lets us get a listing of files in a directory which we can then process in a loop (we'll meet other ways to obtain such a list later in this chapter). So far, we've run basic DOS commands; because these calls can run *any* command line that we can type at a shell prompt, they can also be used to launch other Python scripts:

```
>>> os.system('python helloshell.py')        # run a Python program
The Meaning of Life
0
>>> output = os.popen('python helloshell.py').read()
>>> output
'The Meaning of Life\012'
```

In all of these examples, the command-line strings sent to `system` and `popen` are hardcoded, but there's no reason Python programs could not *construct* such strings at runtime using normal string operations (+, %, etc.). Given that commands can be dynamically built and run this way, `system` and `popen` turn Python scripts into flexible and portable tools for launching and orchestrating other programs. For example, a Python test "driver" script can be used to run programs coded in any language (e.g., C++, Java, Python) and analyze their outputs. We'll explore such a script in "A Regression Test Script" in Chapter 4, *Larger System Examples I.*

Shell command limitations

You should keep in mind two limitations of `system` and `popen`. First, although these two functions themselves are fairly portable, their use is really only as portable as the commands that they run. The preceding examples that run DOS *dir* and *type* shell commands, for instance, work only on Windows, and would have to be changed to run *ls* and *cat* commands on Unix-like platforms. As I wrote this, the `popen` call on Windows worked for command-line programs only; it failed when called from a program running on Windows with any sort of user interface (e.g., under the IDLE Python development GUI). This has been improved in the Python 2.0 release—`popen` now works much better on Windows—but this fix naturally works only on machines with the latest version of Python installed.

Second, it is important to remember that running Python files as programs this way is very different, and generally much slower, than importing program files and calling functions they define. When `os.system` and `os.popen` are called, they must start a brand-new independent program running on your operating system (on Unix-like platforms, they run the command in a newly forked process). When *importing* a program file as a module, the Python interpreter simply loads and runs the file's code in the same process, to generate a module object. No other program is spawned along the way.[*]

There are good reasons to build systems as separate programs too, and we'll later explore things like command-line arguments and streams that allow programs to pass information back and forth. But for most purposes, imported modules are a faster and more direct way to compose systems.

If you plan to use these calls in earnest, you should also know that the `os.system` call normally *blocks* (that is, pauses) its caller until the spawned command line exits. On Linux and Unix-like platforms, the spawned command can generally be made to run independently and in parallel with the caller, by adding an `&` shell background operator at the end of the command line:

```
os.system("python program.py arg arg &")
```

On Windows, spawning with a DOS *start* command will usually launch the command in parallel too:

```
os.system("start program.py arg arg")
```

The `os.popen` call generally does not block its caller—by definition, the caller must be able to read or write the file object returned—but callers may still occasionally become blocked under both Windows and Linux if the pipe object is closed (e.g., when garbage is collected) before the spawned program exits, or the pipe is read exhaustively (e.g., with its `read()` method). As we will see in the next chapter, the Unix `os.fork/exec` and Windows `os.spawnv` calls can also be used to run parallel programs without blocking.

Because the `os system` and `popen` calls also fall under the category of program launchers, stream redirectors, and cross-process communication devices, they will show up again in later parts of this and the following chapters, so we'll defer further details for the time being.

Other os Module Exports

Since most other `os` module tools are even more difficult to appreciate outside the context of larger application topics, we'll postpone a deeper look until later

---

[*] The Python `execfile` built-in function also runs a program file's code, but within the same process that called it. It's similar to an import in that regard, but works more as if the file's text had been *pasted* into the calling program at the place where the `execfile` call appears (unless explicit global or local namespace dictionaries are passed). Unlike imports, `execfile` unconditionally reads and executes a file's code (it may be run more than once per process), and no module object is generated by the file's execution.

sections. But to let you sample the flavor of this module, here is a quick preview for reference. Among the os module's other weapons are these:

os.environ
> Fetch and set shell environment variables

os.fork
> Spawn a new child process on Unix

os.pipe
> Communicate between programs

os.execlp
> Start new programs

os.spawnv
> Start new programs on Windows

os.open
> Open a low-level descriptor-based file

os.mkdir
> Create a new directory

os.mkfifo
> Create a new named pipe

os.stat
> Fetch low-level file information

os.remove
> Delete a file by its pathname

os.path.walk
> Apply a function to files in an entire directory tree

And so on. One caution up front: the os module provides a set of file open, read, and write calls, but these all deal with low-level file access and are entirely distinct from Python's built-in stdio file objects that we create with the built-in **open** function. You should normally use the built-in **open** function (not the os module) for all but very special file-processing needs.

Throughout this chapter, we will apply sys and os tools such as these to implement common system-level tasks, but this book doesn't have space to provide an exhaustive list of the contents of the modules we meet along the way. If you have not already done so, you should become acquainted with the contents of modules like os and sys by consulting the Python library manual. For now, let's move on to explore additional system tools, in the context of broader system programming concepts.

Script Execution Context

Python scripts don't run in a vacuum. Depending on platforms and startup procedures, Python programs may have all sorts of enclosing *context*—information automatically passed-in to the program by the operating system when the program
starts up. For instance, scripts have access to the following sorts of system-level
inputs and interfaces:

Current working directory
> os.getcwd gives access to the directory from which a script is started, and
> many file tools use its value implicitly.

Command-line arguments
> sys.argv gives access to words typed on the command line used to start the
> program that serve as script inputs.

Shell variables
> os.environ provides an interface to names assigned in the enclosing shell
> (or a parent program) and passed in to the script.

Standard streams
> sys.stdin, stdout, and stderr export the three input/output streams that
> are at the heart of command-line shell tools.

Such tools can serve as inputs to scripts, configuration parameters, and so on. In
the next few sections, we will explore these context tools—both their Python
interfaces and their typical roles.

Current Working Directory

The notion of the current working directory (CWD) turns out to be a key concept
in some scripts' execution: it's always the implicit place where files processed by
the script are assumed to reside, unless their names have absolute directory paths.
As we saw earlier, os.getcwd lets a script fetch the CWD name explicitly, and
os.chdir allows a script to move to a new CWD.

Keep in mind, though, that filenames without full pathnames map to the CWD,
and have nothing to do with your PYTHONPATH setting. Technically, the CWD is
always where a script is launched from, not the directory containing the script file.
Conversely, *imports* always first search the directory containing the script, not the
CWD (unless the script happens to also be located in the CWD). Since this distinction is subtle and tends to trip up beginners, let's explore it in more detail.

CWD, Files, and Import Paths

When you run a Python script by typing a shell command line like `python dir1\`
`dir2\file.py`, the CWD is the directory you were in when you typed this command, not *dir1\dir2*. On the other hand, Python automatically adds the identity of
the script's home directory to the front of the module search path, such that *file.py*
can always import other files in *dir1\dir2*, no matter where it is run from. To illustrate, let's write a simple script to echo both its CWD and module search path:

```
C:\PP2ndEd\examples\PP2E\System>type whereami.py
import os, sys
print 'my os.getcwd =>', os.getcwd()          # show my cwd execution dir
print 'my sys.path  =>', sys.path[:6]         # show first 6 import paths
raw_input()                                    # wait for keypress if clicked
```

Now, running this script in the directory in which it resides sets the CWD as
expected, and adds an empty string (`' '`) to the front of the module search path, to
designate the CWD (we met the `sys.path` module search path earlier):

```
C:\PP2ndEd\examples\PP2E\System>set PYTHONPATH=C:\PP2ndEd\examples
C:\PP2ndEd\examples\PP2E\System>python whereami.py
my os.getcwd => C:\PP2ndEd\examples\PP2E\System
my sys.path  => ['', 'C:\\PP2ndEd\\examples', 'C:\\Program Files\\Python
\\Lib\\plat-win', 'C:\\Program Files\\Python\\Lib', 'C:\\Program Files\\
Python\\DLLs', 'C:\\Program Files\\Python\\Lib\\lib-tk']
```

But if we run this script from other places, the CWD moves with us (it's the directory where we type commands), and Python adds a directory to the front of the
module search path that allows the script to still see files in its own home directory. For instance, when running from one level up (`".."`), the "System" name
added to the front of `sys.path` will be the first directory Python searches for
imports within *whereami.py*; it points imports back to the directory containing the
script run. Filenames without complete paths, though, will be mapped to the CWD
(*C:\PP2ndEd\examples\PP2E*), not the *System* subdirectory nested there:

```
C:\PP2ndEd\examples\PP2E\System>cd ..
C:\PP2ndEd\examples\PP2E>python System\whereami.py
my os.getcwd => C:\PP2ndEd\examples\PP2E
my sys.path  => ['System', 'C:\\PP2ndEd\\examples', ...rest same... ]

C:\PP2ndEd\examples\PP2E>cd ..
C:\PP2ndEd\examples>python PP2E\System\whereami.py
my os.getcwd => C:\PP2ndEd\examples
my sys.path  => ['PP2E\\System', 'C:\\PP2ndEd\\examples', ...rest same... ]

C:\PP2ndEd\examples\PP2E\System>cd PP2E\System\App
C:\PP2ndEd\examples\PP2E\System\App>python ..\whereami.py
my os.getcwd => C:\PP2ndEd\examples\PP2E\System\App
my sys.path  => ['..', 'C:\\PP2ndEd\\examples', ...rest same... ]
```

The net effect is that *filenames* without directory paths in a script will be mapped to the place where the command was typed (os.getcwd), but *imports* still have access to the directory of the script being run (via the front of sys.path). Finally, when a file is launched by clicking its icon, the CWD is just the directory that contains the clicked file. The following output, for example, appears in a new DOS console box, when *whereami.py* is double-clicked in Windows explorer:

```
my os.getcwd => C:\PP2ndEd\examples\PP2E\System
my sys.path  => ['C:\\PP2NDED\\EXAMPLES\\PP2E\\SYSTEM', 'C:\\PP2ndEd\\examples',
 'C:\\Program Files\\Python\\Lib\\plat-win', 'C:\\Program Files\\Python\\Lib',
 'C:\\Program Files\\Python\\DLLs']
```

In this case, both the CWD used for filenames and the first import search directory are the directory containing the script file. This all usually works out just as you expect, but there are two pitfalls to avoid:

- Filenames might need to include complete directory paths if scripts cannot be sure from where they will be run.

- Command-line scripts cannot use the CWD to gain import visibility to files not in their own directories; instead, use PYTHONPATH settings and package import paths to access modules in other directories.

For example, files in this book can always import other files in their own *home directories* without package path imports, regardless of how they are run (import filehere) but must go through the *PP2E* package root to find files anywhere else in the examples tree (from PP2E.dir1.dir2 import filethere) even if they are run from the directory containing the desired external module. As usual for modules, the *PP2E\dir1\dir2* directory name could also be added to PYTHON-PATH to make filethere visible everywhere without package path imports (though adding more directories to PYTHONPATH increases the likelihood of name clashes). In either case, though, imports are always resolved to the script's home directory or other Python search path settings, not the CWD.

CWD and Command Lines

This distinction between the CWD and import search paths explains why many scripts in this book designed to operate in the current working directory (instead of one whose name is passed in) are run with command lines like this:

```
C:\temp>python %X%\PyTools\cleanpyc-py.py                        process cwd
```

In this example, the Python script file itself lives in the directory *C:\PP2ndEd\ examples\PP2E\PyTools*, but because it is run from *C:\temp*, it processes the files located in *C:\temp* (i.e., in the CWD, not in the script's home directory). To process files elsewhere with such a script, simply *cd* to the directory to be processed to change the CWD:

```
C:\temp>cd C:\PP2nEd\examples
C:\PP2ndEd\examples>python %X%\PyTools\cleanpyc-py.py      process cwd
```

Because the CWD is always implied, a *cd* tells the script which directory to process in no less certain terms that passing a directory name to the script explicitly like this:

```
C:\...\PP2E\PyTools>python find.py *.py C:\temp      process named dir
```

In this command line, the CWD is the directory containing the script to be run (notice that the script filename has no directory path prefix); but since this script processes a directory named explicitly on the command line (*C:\temp*), the CWD is irrelevant. Finally, if we want to run such a script located in some other directory to process files located in some other directory, we can simply give directory paths to both:

```
C:\temp>python %X%\PyTools\find.py *.cxx C:\PP2ndEd\examples\PP2E
```

Here, the script has import visibility to files in its *PP2E\PyTools* home directory and processes files in the *PP2E* root, but the CWD is something else entirely (*C:\temp*). This last form is more to type, of course, but watch for a variety of CWD and explicit script-path command lines like these in this book.

Whenever you see a %X% in command lines like those in the preceding examples, it refers to the value of the shell environment variable named X. It's just a shorthand for the full directory pathname of the *PP2E* book examples package root directory, which I use to point to scripts' files. On my machines, it is preset in my PP2E\Config setup-pp* files like this:

```
set X=C:\PP2ndEd\examples\PP2E            --DOS
setenv X /home/mark/PP2ndEd/examples/PP2E --Unix/csh
```

That is, it is assigned and expanded to the directory where *PP2E* lives on the system. See the Config\setup-pp* files for more details, and see later in this chapter for more on shell variables. You can instead type full paths everywhere you see %X% in this book, but your fingers and your keyboard are probably both better off if you set X to your examples root.

Command-Line Arguments

The sys module is also where Python makes available the words typed on the command used to start a Python script. These words are usually referred to as *command-line arguments*, and show up in sys.argv, a built-in list of strings. C programmers may notice its similarity to the C "argv" array (an array of C strings). It's not much to look at interactively, because no command-line arguments are passed to start up Python in this mode:

```
>>> sys.argv
['']
```

To really see what arguments are about, we need to run a script from the shell command line. Example 2-2 shows an unreasonably simple one that just prints the `argv` list for inspection.

Example 2-2. PP2E\System\testargv.py

```
import sys
print sys.argv
```

Running this script prints the command-line arguments list; note that the first item is always the name of the executed Python script file itself, no matter how the script was started (see the sidebar "Executable Scripts on Unix" later in this chapter):

```
C:\...\PP2E\System>python testargv.py
['testargv.py']

C:\...\PP2E\System>python testargv.py spam eggs cheese
['testargv.py', 'spam', 'eggs', 'cheese']

C:\...\PP2E\System>python testargv.py -i data.txt -o results.txt
['testargv.py', '-i', 'data.txt', '-o', 'results.txt']
```

The last command here illustrates a common convention. Much like function arguments, command-line options are sometimes passed by position, and sometimes by name using a "–name value" word pair. For instance, the pair `-i data.txt` means the `-i` option's value is `data.txt` (e.g., an input filename). Any words can be listed, but programs usually impose some sort of structure on them.

Command-line arguments play the same role in programs that function arguments do in functions: they are simply a way to pass information to a program that can vary per program run. Because they don't have to be hardcoded, they allow scripts to be more generally useful. For example, a file-processing script can use a command-line argument as the name of the file it should process; see the *more.py* script we met in Example 2-1 for a prime example. Other scripts might accept processing mode flags, Internet addresses, and so on.

Once you start using command-line arguments regularly, though, you'll probably find it inconvenient to keep writing code that fishes through the list looking for words. More typically, programs translate the arguments list on startup into structures more conveniently processed. Here's one way to do it: the script in Example 2-3 scans the `argv` list looking for `-optionname optionvalue` word pairs, and stuffs them into a dictionary by option name for easy retrieval.

Example 2-3. PP2E\System\testargv2.py

```
# collect command-line options in a dictionary

def getopts(argv):
    opts = {}
    while argv:
        if argv[0][0] == '-':            # find "-name value" pairs
            opts[argv[0]] = argv[1]      # dict key is "-name" arg
            argv = argv[2:]
        else:
            argv = argv[1:]
    return opts

if __name__ == '__main__':
    from sys import argv                 # example client code
    myargs = getopts(argv)
    if myargs.has_key('-i'):
        print myargs['-i']
    print myargs
```

You might import and use such a function in all your command-line tools. When run by itself, this file just prints the formatted argument dictionary:

```
C:\...\PP2E\System>python testargv2.py
{}

C:\...\PP2E\System>python testargv2.py -i data.txt -o results.txt
data.txt
{'-o': 'results.txt', '-i': 'data.txt'}
```

Naturally, we could get much more sophisticated here in terms of argument patterns, error checking, and the like. We could also use standard and more advanced command-line processing tools in the Python library to parse arguments; see module `getopt` in the library manual for another option. In general, the more configurable your scripts, the more you must invest on command-line processing logic complexity.

Shell Environment Variables

Shell variables, sometimes known as environment variables, are made available to Python scripts as `os.environ`, a Python dictionary-like object with one entry per variable setting in the shell. Shell variables live outside the Python system; they are often set at your system prompt or within startup files, and typically serve as systemwide configuration inputs to programs.

In fact, by now you should be familiar with a prime example: the PYTHONPATH module search path setting is a shell variable used by Python to import modules. By setting it once in your system startup files, its value is available every time a

Executable Scripts on Unix

Unix and Linux users: you can also make text files of Python source code directly executable by adding a special line at the top with the path to the Python interpreter and giving the file executable permission. For instance, type this code into a text file called "myscript":

```
#!/usr/bin/python
print 'And nice red uniforms'
```

The first line is normally taken as a comment by Python (it starts with a #); but when this file is run, the operating system sends lines in this file to the interpreter listed after #! on line 1. If this file is made directly executable with a shell command of the form chmod +x myscript, it can be run directly, without typing python in the command, as though it were a binary executable program:

```
% myscript a b c
And nice red uniforms
```

When run this way, sys.argv will still have the script's name as the first word in the list: ["myscript", "a", "b", "c"], exactly as if the script had been run with the more explicit and portable command form python myscript a b c. Making scripts directly executable is really a Unix trick, not a Python feature, but it's worth pointing out that it can be made a bit less machine-dependent by listing the Unix *env* command at the top instead of a hardcoded path to the Python executable:

```
#!/usr/bin/env python
print 'Wait for it...'
```

When coded this way, the operating system will employ your environment variable settings to locate your Python interpreter (your PATH variable, on most platforms). If you run the same script on many machines, you need only change your environment settings on each machine, not edit Python script code. Of course, you can always run Python files with a more explicit command line:

```
% python myscript a b c
```

This assumes that the python interpreter program is on your system's search path setting (else you need to type its full path), but works on any Python platform with a command line. Since this is more portable, I generally use this convention in the book's examples, but consult your Unix man pages for more details on any of the topics mentioned here. Even so, these special #! lines will show up in many examples in this book just in case readers want to run them as executables on Unix or Linux; on other platforms, they are simply ignored as Python comments. Note that on Windows NT/2000, you can usually type a script's filename directly (without the "python" word) to make it go too, and you don't have to add a #! line at the top.

Python program is run. Shell variables can also be set by programs to serve as inputs to other programs in an application; because their values are normally inherited by spawned programs, they can be used as a simple form of interprocess communication.

Fetching Shell Variables

In Python, the surrounding shell environment becomes a simple preset object, not special syntax. Indexing `os.environ` by the desired shell variable's name string (e.g., `os.environ['USER']`) is the moral equivalent of adding a dollar sign before a variable name in most Unix shells (e.g., $USER), using surrounding percent signs on DOS (%USER%), and calling `getenv("USER")` in a C program. Let's start up an interactive session to experiment:

```
>>> import os
>>> os.environ.keys()
['WINBOOTDIR', 'PATH', 'USER', 'PP2HOME', 'CMDLINE', 'PYTHONPATH', 'BLASTER',
'X', 'TEMP', 'COMSPEC', 'PROMPT', 'WINDIR', 'TMP']
>>> os.environ['TEMP']
'C:\\windows\\TEMP'
```

Here, the `keys` method returns a list of variables set, and indexing fetches the value of shell variable TEMP on Windows. This works the same on Linux, but other variables are generally preset when Python starts up. Since we know about PYTHONPATH, let's peek at its setting within Python to verify its content:[*]

```
>>> os.environ['PYTHONPATH']
'C:\\PP2ndEd\\examples\\Part3;C:\\PP2ndEd\\examples\\Part2;C:\\PP2ndEd\\
examples\\Part2\\Gui;C:\\PP2ndEd\\examples'
>>>
>>> import string
>>> for dir in string.split(os.environ['PYTHONPATH'], os.pathsep):
...     print dir
...
C:\PP2ndEd\examples\Part3
C:\PP2ndEd\examples\Part2
C:\PP2ndEd\examples\Part2\Gui
C:\PP2ndEd\examples
```

PYTHONPATH is a string of directory paths separated by whatever character is used to separate items in such paths on your platform (e.g., ";" on DOS/Window, ":" on Unix and Linux). To split it into its components, we pass `string.split` a delimiter `os.pathsep`, a portable setting that gives the proper separator for the underlying machine.

---

[*] For color, these results reflect an old path setting used during development; this variable now contains just the single directory containing the *PP2E* root.

Changing Shell Variables

Like normal dictionaries, the os.environ object supports both key indexing and *assignment.* As usual, assignments change the value of the key:

```
>>> os.environ['TEMP'] = r'c:\temp'
>>> os.environ['TEMP']
'c:\\temp'
```

But something extra happens here. In recent Python releases, values assigned to os.environ keys in this fashion are automatically *exported* to other parts of the application. That is, key assignments change both the os.environ object in the Python program as well as the associated variable in the enclosing *shell* environment of the running program's process. Its new value becomes visible to the Python program, all linked-in C modules, and any programs spawned by the Python process. Internally, key assignments to os.environ call os.putenv—a function that changes the shell variable outside the boundaries of the Python interpreter. To demonstrate this how this works, we need a couple scripts that set and fetch shell variables; the first is shown in Example 2-4.

Example 2-4. PP2E\System\Environment\setenv.py

```
import os
print 'setenv...',
print os.environ['USER']                 # show current shell variable value

os.environ['USER'] = 'Brian'             # runs os.putenv behind the scenes
os.system('python echoenv.py')

os.environ['USER'] = 'Arthur'            # changes passed to spawned programs
os.system('python echoenv.py')           # and linked-in C library modules

os.environ['USER'] = raw_input('?')
print os.popen('python echoenv.py').read()
```

This *setenv.py* script simply changes a shell variable, USER, and spawns another script that echoes this variable's value, shown in Example 2-5.

Example 2-5. PP2E\System\Environment\echoenv.py

```
import os
print 'echoenv...',
print 'Hello,', os.environ['USER']
```

No matter how we run *echoenv.py*, it displays the value of USER in the enclosing shell; when run from the command line, this value comes from whatever we've set the variable to in the shell itself:

```
C:\...\PP2E\System\Environment>set USER=Bob
```

```
C:\...\PP2E\System\Environment>python echoenv.py
echoenv... Hello, Bob
```

When spawned by another script like *setenv.py*, though, *echoenv.py* gets whatever USER settings its parent program has made:

```
C:\...\PP2E\System\Environment>python setenv.py
setenv... Bob
echoenv... Hello, Brian
echoenv... Hello, Arthur
?Gumby
echoenv... Hello, Gumby

C:\...\PP2E\System\Environment>echo %USER%
Bob
```

This works the same way on Linux. In general terms, a spawned program always *inherits* environment settings from its parents. "Spawned" programs are programs started with Python tools such as `os.spawnv` on Windows, the `os.fork/exec` combination on Unix and Linux, and `os.popen` and `os.system` on a variety of platforms—all programs thus launched get the environment variable settings that exist in the parent at launch time.*

Setting shell variables like this before starting a new program is one way to pass information into the new program. For instance, a Python configuration script might tailor the PYTHONPATH variable to include custom directories, just before launching another Python script; the launched script will have the custom search path because shell variables are passed down to children (in fact, watch for such a launcher script to appear at the end of Chapter 4).

 Notice the last command in the preceding example, though—the USER variable is back to its original value after the top-level Python program exits. Assignments to `os.environ` keys are passed outside the interpreter and *down* the spawned programs chain, but never back *up* to parent program processes (including the system shell). This is also true in C programs that use the `putenv` library call, and isn't a Python limitation per se. It's also likely to be a nonissue if a Python script is at the top of your application. But keep in mind that shell settings made within a program only endure for that program's run, and that of its spawned children.

---

* This is by default. Some program-launching tools also let scripts pass environment settings different from their own to child programs. For instance, the `os.spawnve` call is like `os.spawnv`, but accepts a dictionary argument representing the shell environment to be passed to the started program. Some `os.exec*` variants (ones with an "e" at the end of their names) similarly accept explicit environments; see the `os.exec` call formats in Chapter 3, *Parallel System Tools*, for more details.

Standard Streams

Module `sys` is also the place where the standard input, output, and error streams of your Python programs live:

```
>>> for f in (sys.stdin, sys.stdout, sys.stderr): print f
...
<open file '<stdin>', mode 'r' at 762210>
<open file '<stdout>', mode 'w' at 762270>
<open file '<stderr>', mode 'w' at 7622d0>
```

The standard streams are simply pre-opened Python file objects that are automatically connected to your program's standard streams when Python starts up. By default, they are all tied to the console window where Python (or a Python program) was started. Because the `print` statement and `raw_input` functions are really nothing more than user-friendly interfaces to the standard output and input streams, they are similar to using `stdout` and `stdin` in `sys` directly:

```
>>> print 'hello stdout world'
hello stdout world

>>> sys.stdout.write('hello stdout world' + '\n')
hello stdout world

>>> raw_input('hello stdin world>')
hello stdin world>spam
'spam'

>>> print 'hello stdin world>',; sys.stdin.readline()[:-1]
hello stdin world>eggs

'eggs'
```

Redirecting Streams to Files and Programs

Technically, standard output (and `print`) text appears in the console window where a program was started, standard input (and `raw_input`) text comes from the keyboard, and standard error is used to print Python error messages to the console window. At least that's the default. It's also possible to *redirect* these streams both to files and other programs at the system shell, and to arbitrary objects within a Python script. On most systems, such redirections make it easy to reuse and combine general-purpose command-line utilities.

Redirecting streams to files

Redirection is useful for things like canned (precoded) test inputs: we can apply a single test script to any set of inputs by simply redirecting the standard input stream to a different file each time the script is run. Similarly, redirecting the standard output stream lets us save and later analyze a program's output; for example,

Standard Streams on Windows

Windows users: if you click a *.py* Python program's filename in a Windows file explorer to start it (or launch it with **os.system**), a DOS console box automatically pops up to serve as the program's standard stream. If your program makes windows of its own, you can avoid this console pop-up window by naming your program's source-code file with a *.pyw* extension, not *.py*. The *.pyw* extension simply means a *.py* source file without a DOS pop-up on Windows.

One caveat: in the Python 1.5.2 release, *.pyw* files can only be run, not imported—the *.pyw* is not recognized as a module name. If you want a program to *both* be run without a DOS console pop-up and be importable elsewhere, you need both *.py* and *.pyw* files; the *.pyw* may simply serve as top-level script logic that imports and calls the core logic in the *.py*. See "PyEdit: A Text Editor Program/Object" in Chapter 9, *Larger GUI Examples*, for an example.

Also note that because printed output goes to this DOS pop-up when a program is clicked, scripts that simply print text and exit will generate an odd "flash"—the DOS console box pops up, output is printed into it, and the pop-up goes immediately away (not the most user-friendly of features!). To keep the DOS pop-up box around so you can read printed output, simply add a **raw_input()** call at the bottom of your script to pause for an Enter key press before exiting.

testing systems might compare the saved standard output of a script with a file of expected output, to detect failures.

Although it's a powerful paradigm, redirection turns out to be straightforward to use. For instance, consider the simple read-evaluate-print loop program in Example 2-6.

Example 2-6. PP2E\System\Streams\teststreams.py

```
# read numbers till eof and show squares

def interact():
    print 'Hello stream world'                    # print sends to sys.stdout
    while 1:
        try:
            reply = raw_input('Enter a number>')   # raw_input reads sys.stdin
        except EOFError:
            break                                  # raises an except on eof
        else:                                      # input given as a string
            num = int(reply)
            print "%d squared is %d" % (num, num ** 2)
    print 'Bye'

if __name__ == '__main__':
    interact()                                     # when run, not imported
```

As usual, the `interact` function here is automatically executed when this file is run, not when it is imported. By default, running this file from a system command line makes that standard stream appear where you typed the Python command. The script simply reads numbers until it reaches end-of-file in the standard input stream (on Windows, end-of-file is usually the two-key combination Ctrl+Z; on Unix, type Ctrl+D instead[*]):

```
C:\...\PP2E\System\Streams>python teststreams.py
Hello stream world
Enter a number>12
12 squared is 144
Enter a number>10
10 squared is 100
Enter a number>
```

But on both Windows and Unix-like platforms, we can redirect the standard input stream to come from a file with the `< filename` shell syntax. Here is a command session in a DOS console box on Windows that forces the script to read its input from a text file, *input.txt*. It's the same on Linux, but replace the DOS *type* command with a Unix *cat* command:

```
C:\...\PP2E\System\Streams>type input.txt
8
6

C:\...\PP2E\System\Streams>python teststreams.py < input.txt
Hello stream world
Enter a number>8 squared is 64
Enter a number>6 squared is 36
Enter a number>Bye
```

Here, the *input.txt* file automates the input we would normally type interactively—the script reads from this file instead of the keyboard. Standard output can be similarly redirected to go to a file, with the `> filename` shell syntax. In fact, we can combine input and output redirection in a single command:

```
C:\...\PP2E\System\Streams>python teststreams.py < input.txt > output.txt

C:\...\PP2E\System\Streams>type output.txt
Hello stream world
Enter a number>8 squared is 64
Enter a number>6 squared is 36
Enter a number>Bye
```

---

[*] Notice that `raw_input` raises an exception to signal end-of-file, but file read methods simply return an empty string for this condition. Because `raw_input` also strips the end-of-line character at the end of lines, an empty string result means an empty line, so an exception is necessary to specify the end-of-file condition. File read methods retain the end-of-line character, and denote an empty line as `\n` instead of `""`. This is one way in which reading `sys.stdin` directly differs from `raw_input`. The latter also accepts a prompt string that is automatically printed before input is accepted.

This time, the Python script's input and output are both mapped to text files, not the interactive console session.

Chaining programs with pipes

On Windows and Unix-like platforms, it's also possible to send the standard output of one program to the standard input of another, using the | shell character between two commands. This is usually called a "pipe" operation—the shell creates a pipeline that connects the output and input of two commands. Let's send the output of the Python script to the standard "more" command-line program's input to see how this works:

```
C:\...\PP2E\System\Streams>python teststreams.py < input.txt | more

Hello stream world
Enter a number>8 squared is 64
Enter a number>6 squared is 36
Enter a number>Bye
```

Here, `teststreams`'s standard input comes from a file again, but its output (written by `print` statements) is sent to another program, not a file or window. The receiving program is `more`—a standard command-line paging program available on Windows and Unix-like platforms. Because Python ties scripts into the standard stream model, though, Python scripts can be used on both ends—one Python script's output can always be piped into another Python script's input:

```
C:\...\PP2E\System\Streams>type writer.py
print "Help! Help! I'm being repressed!"
print 42

C:\...\PP2E\System\Streams>type reader.py
print 'Got this" "%s"' % raw_input()
import sys
data = sys.stdin.readline()[:-1]
print 'The meaning of life is', data, int(data) * 2

C:\...\PP2E\System\Streams>python writer.py | python reader.py
Got this" "Help! Help! I'm being repressed!"
The meaning of life is 42 84
```

This time, two Python programs are connected. Script `reader` gets input from script `writer`; both scripts simply read and write, oblivious to stream mechanics. In practice, such chaining of programs is a simple form of cross-program communications. It makes it easy to *reuse* utilities written to communicate via `stdin` and `stdout` in ways we never anticipated. For instance, a Python program that sorts `stdin` text could be applied to any data source we like, including the output of other scripts. Consider the Python command-line utility scripts in Examples 2-7 and 2-8 that sort and sum lines in the standard input stream.

Example 2-7. PP2E\System\Streams\sorter.py

```
import sys
lines = sys.stdin.readlines()        # sort stdin input lines,
lines.sort()                         # send result to stdout
for line in lines: print line,       # for further processing
```

Example 2-8. PP2E\System\Streams\adder.py

```
import sys, string
sum = 0
while 1:
    try:
        line = raw_input()           # or call sys.stdin.readlines():
    except EOFError:                 # or sys.stdin.readline() loop
        break
    else:
        sum = sum + string.atoi(line)    # int(line[:-1]) treats 042 as octal
print sum
```

We can apply such general-purpose tools in a variety of ways at the shell command line, to sort and sum arbitrary files and program outputs:

```
C:\...\PP2E\System\Streams>type data.txt
123
000
999
042

C:\...\PP2E\System\Streams>python sorter.py < data.txt          sort a file
000
042
123
999

C:\...\PP2E\System\Streams>type data.txt | python adder.py      sum program output
1164

C:\...\PP2E\System\Streams>type writer2.py
for data in (123, 0, 999, 42):
    print '%03d' % data

C:\...\PP2E\System\Streams>python writer2.py | python sorter.py   sort py output
000
042
123
999

C:\...\PP2E\System\Streams>python writer2.py | python sorter.py | python adder.py
1164
```

The last command here connects three Python scripts by standard streams—the output of each prior script is fed to the input of the next via pipeline shell syntax.

If you look closely, you'll notice that `sorter` reads all of `stdin` at once with the `readlines` method, but `adder` reads one line at a time. If the input source is another program, some platforms run programs connected by pipes in *parallel*. On such systems, reading line-by-line works better if the data streams being passed about are large—readers need not wait until writers are completely finished to get busy processing data. Because `raw_input` just reads `stdin`, the line-by-line scheme used by `adder` can always be coded with `sys.stdin` too:

```
C:\...\PP2E\System\Streams>type adder2.py
import sys, string
sum = 0
while 1:
    line = sys.stdin.readline()
    if not line: break
    sum = sum + string.atoi(line[:-1])
print sum
```

Changing `sorter` to read line-by-line may not be a big performance boost, though, because the list `sort` method requires the list to already be complete. As we'll see in Chapter 17, *Data Structures*, manually coded sort algorithms are likely to be much slower than the Python list sorting method.

Redirected streams and user interaction

At the start of the last section, we piped *teststreams.py* output into the standard `more` command-line program with a command like this:

```
C:\...\PP2E\System\Streams>python teststreams.py < input.txt | more
```

But since we already wrote our own "more" paging utility in Python near the start of this chapter, why not set it up to accept input from `stdin` too? For example, if we change the last three lines of file *more.py* listed earlier in this chapter to this:

```
if __name__ == '__main__':              # when run, not when imported
    if len(sys.argv) == 1:              # page stdin if no cmd args
        more(sys.stdin.read())
    else:
        more(open(sys.argv[1]).read())
```

Then it almost seems as if we should be able to redirect the standard output of *teststreams.py* into the standard input of *more.py*:

```
C:\...\PP2E\System\Streams>python teststreams.py < input.txt | python ..\more.py
Hello stream world
Enter a number>8 squared is 64
Enter a number>6 squared is 36
Enter a number>Bye
```

This technique works in general for Python scripts. Here, *teststreams.py* takes input from a file again. And, as in the last section, one Python program's output is piped to another's input—the *more.py* script in the parent ("..") directory.

Reading keyboard input. But there's a subtle problem lurking in the preceding *more.py* command. Really, chaining only worked there by sheer luck: if the first script's output is long enough for **more** to have to ask the user if it should continue, the script will utterly fail. The problem is that the augmented *more.py* uses **stdin** for two disjoint purposes. It reads a reply from an interactive user on **stdin** by calling **raw_input**, but now *also* accepts the main input text on **stdin**. When the **stdin** stream is really redirected to an input file or pipe, we can't use it to input a reply from an interactive user; it contains only the text of the input source. Moreover, because **stdin** is redirected before the program even starts up, there is no way to know what it meant prior to being redirected in the command line.

If we intend to accept input on **stdin** *and* use the console for user interaction, we have to do a bit more. Example 2-9 shows a modified version of the **more** script that pages the standard input stream if called with no arguments, but also makes use of lower-level and platform-specific tools to converse with a user at a keyboard if needed.

Example 2-9. PP2E\System\moreplus.py

```
###############################################################
# split and interactively page a string, file, or stream of
# text to stdout; when run as a script, page stdin or file
# whose name is passed on cmdline; if input is stdin, can't
# use it for user reply--use platform-specific tools or gui;
###############################################################

import sys, string

def getreply():
    """
    read a reply key from an interactive user
    even if stdin redirected to a file or pipe
    """
    if sys.stdin.isatty():                   # if stdin is console
        return raw_input('?')                # read reply line from stdin
    else:
        if sys.platform[:3] == 'win':        # if stdin was redirected
            import msvcrt                     # can't use to ask a user
            msvcrt.putch('?')
            key = msvcrt.getche()             # use windows console tools
            msvcrt.putch('\n')                # getch() does not echo key
            return key
        elif sys.platform[:5] == 'linux':    # use linux console device
            print '?',                        # strip eoln at line end
            console = open('/dev/tty')
            line = console.readline()[:-1]
            return line
        else:
            print '[pause]'                   # else just pause--improve me
            import time                       # see also modules curses, tty
            time.sleep(5)                     # or copy to temp file, rerun
            return 'y'                        # or gui popup, tk key bind
```

Example 2-9. PP2E\System\moreplus.py (continued)

```
def more(text, numlines=10):
    """
    split multi-line string to stdout
    """
    lines = string.split(text, '\n')
    while lines:
        chunk = lines[:numlines]
        lines = lines[numlines:]
        for line in chunk: print line
        if lines and getreply() not in ['y', 'Y']: break

if __name__ == '__main__':                      # when run, not when imported
    if len(sys.argv) == 1:                      # if no command-line arguments
        more(sys.stdin.read())                  # page stdin, no raw_inputs
    else:
        more(open(sys.argv[1]).read())          # else page filename argument
```

Most of the new code in this version shows up in its `getreply` function. The file
`isatty` method tells us if `stdin` is connected to the console; if it is, we simply
read replies on `stdin` as before. Unfortunately, there is no portable way to input a
string from a console user independent of `stdin`, so we must wrap the non-`stdin`
input logic of this script in a `sys.platform` test:

- On Windows, the built-in `msvcrt` module supplies low-level console input
  and output calls (e.g., `msvcrt.getch()` reads a single key press).

- On Linux, the system device file named */dev/tty* gives access to keyboard input
  (we can read it as though it were a simple file).

- On other platforms, we simply run a built-in `time.sleep` call to pause for
  five seconds between displays (this is not at all ideal, but is better than not
  stopping at all, and serves until a better nonportable solution can be found).

Of course, we only have to add such extra logic to scripts that intend to interact
with console users *and* take input on `stdin`. In a GUI application, for example,
we could instead pop up dialogs, bind keyboard-press event to run callbacks, and
so on (we'll meet GUIs in Chapter 6, *Graphical User Interfaces*).

Armed with the reusable `getreply` function, though, we can safely run our
`moreplus` utility in a variety of ways. As before, we can import and call this module's function directly, passing in whatever string we wish to page:

```
>>> from moreplus import more
>>> more(open('System.txt').read())
This directory contains operating system interface examples.

Many of the examples in this unit appear elsewhere in the examples
distribution tree, because they are actually used to manage other
programs.  See the README.txt files in the subdirectories here
for pointers.
```

Also as before, when run with a command-line *argument*, this script interactively pages through the named file's text:

```
C:\...\PP2E\System>python moreplus.py System.txt
This directory contains operating system interface examples.

Many of the examples in this unit appear elsewhere in the examples
distribution tree, because they are actually used to manage other
programs.  See the README.txt files in the subdirectories here
for pointers.

C:\...\PP2E\System>python moreplus.py moreplus.py
############################################################
# split and interactively page a string, file, or stream of
# text to stdout; when run as a script, page stdin or file
# whose name is passed on cmdline; if input is stdin, can't
# use it for user reply--use platform-specific tools or gui;
############################################################

import sys, string

def getreply():
?n
```

But now the script also correctly pages text redirected in to `stdin` from either a *file* or command *pipe*, even if that text is too long to fit in a single display chunk. On most shells, we send such input via redirection or pipe operators like these:

```
C:\...\PP2E\System>python moreplus.py < moreplus.py
############################################################
# split and interactively page a string, file, or stream of
# text to stdout; when run as a script, page stdin or file
# whose name is passed on cmdline; if input is stdin, can't
# use it for user reply--use platform-specific tools or gui;
############################################################

import sys, string

def getreply():
?n

C:\...\PP2E\System>type moreplus.py | python moreplus.py
############################################################
# split and interactively page a string, file, or stream of
# text to stdout; when run as a script, page stdin or file
# whose name is passed on cmdline; if input is stdin, can't
# use it for user reply--use platform-specific tools or gui;
############################################################

import sys, string

def getreply():
?n
```

This works the same on Linux, but again use the *cat* command instead of *type*. Finally, piping one Python script's output into this script's input now works as expected, without botching user interaction (and not just because we got lucky):

```
C:\......\System\Streams>python teststreams.py < input.txt | python ..\moreplus.py
Hello stream world
Enter a number>8 squared is 64
Enter a number>6 squared is 36
Enter a number>Bye
```

Here, the standard *output* of one Python script is fed to the standard *input* of another Python script located in the parent directory: *moreplus.py* reads the output of *teststreams.py*.

All of the redirections in such command lines work only because scripts don't care what standard input and output really are—interactive users, files, or pipes between programs. For example, when run as a script, *moreplus.py* simply reads stream `sys.stdin`; the command-line shell (e.g., DOS on Windows, `csh` on Linux) attaches such streams to the source implied by the command line before the script is started. Scripts use the preopened `stdin` and `stdout` file objects to access those sources, regardless of their true nature.

And for readers keeping count, we have run this single `more` pager script in four different ways: by importing and calling its function, by passing a filename command-line argument, by redirecting `stdin` to a file, and by piping a command's output to `stdin`. By supporting importable functions, command-line arguments, and standard streams, Python system tools code can be reused in a wide variety of modes.

Redirecting Streams to Python Objects

All of the above standard stream redirections work for programs written in any language that hooks into the standard streams, and rely more on the shell's command-line processor than on Python itself. Command-line redirection syntax like `< filename` and `| program` is evaluated by the shell, not Python. A more Pythonesque form of redirection can be done within scripts themselves, by resetting `sys.stdin` and `sys.stdout` to file-like objects.

The main trick behind this mode is that anything that looks like a file in terms of methods will work as a standard stream in Python. The object's protocol, not the object's specific datatype, is all that matters. That is:

- Any object that provides file-like *read* methods can be assigned to `sys.stdin` to make input come from that object's read methods.

- Any object that defines file-like *write* methods can be assigned to `sys.stdout`; all standard output will be sent to that object's methods.

Because `print` and `raw_input` simply call the **write** and **readline** methods of whatever objects `sys.stdout` and `sys.stdin` happen to reference, we can use this trick to both provide and intercept standard stream text with objects implemented as classes. Example 2-10 shows a utility module that demonstrates this concept.

Example 2-10. PP2E\System\Streams\redirect.py

```python
###########################################################
# file-like objects that save all standard output text in
# a string, and provide standard input text from a string;
# redirect runs a passed-in function with its output and
# input streams reset to these file-like class objects;
###########################################################

import sys, string                             # get built-in modules

class Output:                                   # simulated output file
    def __init__(self):
        self.text = ''                          # empty string when created
    def write(self, string):                    # add a string of bytes
        self.text = self.text + string
    def writelines(self, lines):                # add each line in a list
        for line in lines: self.write(line)

class Input:                                     # simulated input file
    def __init__(self, input=''):               # default argument
        self.text = input                       # save string when created
    def read(self, *size):                      # optional argument
        if not size:                            # read N bytes, or all
            res, self.text = self.text, ''
        else:
            res, self.text = self.text[:size[0]], self.text[size[0]:]
        return res
    def readline(self):
        eoln = string.find(self.text, '\n')     # find offset of next eoln
        if eoln == -1:                          # slice off through eoln
            res, self.text = self.text, ''
        else:
            res, self.text = self.text[:eoln+1], self.text[eoln+1:]
        return res

def redirect(function, args, input):            # redirect stdin/out
    savestreams = sys.stdin, sys.stdout         # run a function object
    sys.stdin   = Input(input)                  # return stdout text
    sys.stdout  = Output()
    try:
        apply(function, args)
    except:
        sys.stderr.write('error in function! ')
        sys.stderr.write("%s, %s\n" % (sys.exc_type, sys.exc_value))
    result = sys.stdout.text
    sys.stdin, sys.stdout = savestreams
    return result
```

This module defines two classes that masquerade as real files:

- **Output** provides the write method protocol expected of output files, but saves all output as it is written, in an in-memory string.

- **Input** provides the protocol expected of input files, but provides input on demand from an in-memory string, passed in at object construction time.

The **redirect** function at the bottom of this file combines these two objects to run a single function with input and output redirected entirely to Python class objects. The passed-in function so run need not know or care that its **print** statements, **raw_input** calls, and **stdin** and **stdout** method calls are talking to a class instead of a real file, pipe, or user.

To demonstrate, import and run the **interact** function at the heart of the **teststreams** script we've been running from the shell (to use the redirection utility function, we need to deal in terms of functions, not files). When run directly, the function reads from the keyboard and writes to the screen, just as if it were run as a program without redirection:

```
C:\...\PP2E\System\Streams>python
>>> from teststreams import interact
>>> interact()
Hello stream world
Enter a number>2
2 squared is 4
Enter a number>3
3 squared is 9
Enter a number
>>>
```

Now, let's run this function under the control of the redirection function in *redirect.py*, and pass in some canned input text. In this mode, the **interact** function takes its input from the string we pass in (`'4\n5\n6\n'`—three lines with explicit end-of-line characters), and the result of running the function is a string containing all the text written to the standard output stream:

```
>>> from redirect import redirect
>>> output = redirect(interact, (), '4\n5\n6\n')
>>> output
'Hello stream world\012Enter a number>4 squared is 16\012Enter a number>
5 squared is 25\012Enter a number>6 squared is 36\012Enter a number>Bye\012'
```

The result is a single, long string, containing the concatenation of all text written to standard output. To make this look better, we can split it up with the standard **string** module:

```
>>> from string import split
>>> for line in split(output, '\n'): print line
...
Hello stream world
```

```
Enter a number>4 squared is 16
Enter a number>5 squared is 25
Enter a number>6 squared is 36
Enter a number>Bye
```

Better still, we can reuse the *more.py* module we saw earlier in this chapter; it's less to type and remember, and is already known to work well:

```
>>> from PP2E.System.more import more
>>> more(output)
Hello stream world
Enter a number>4 squared is 16
Enter a number>5 squared is 25
Enter a number>6 squared is 36
Enter a number>Bye
```

This is an artificial example, of course, but the techniques illustrated are widely applicable. For example, it's straightforward to add a GUI interface to a program written to interact with a command-line user. Simply intercept standard output with an object like the Output class shown earlier, and throw the text string up in a window. Similarly, standard input can be reset to an object that fetches text from a graphical interface (e.g., a popped-up dialog box). Because classes are plug-and-play compatible with real files, we can use them in any tool that expects a file. Watch for a GUI stream-redirection module named guiStreams in Chapter 9.

Other Redirection Options

Earlier in this chapter, we also studied the built-in os.popen function, which provides a way to redirect another command's streams from within a Python program. As we saw, this function runs a shell command line (e.g., a string we would normally type at a DOS or csh prompt), but returns a Python file-like object connected to the command's input or output stream. Because of that, the os.popen tool can be considered another way to redirect streams of spawned programs, and a cousin to the techniques we just met: Its effect is much like the shell | command-line pipe syntax for redirecting streams to programs (in fact its name means "pipe open"), but it is run within a script and provides a file-like interface to piped streams. It's similar in spirit to the redirect function, but is based on running programs (not calling functions), and the command's streams are processed in the spawning script as files (not tied to class objects).

By passing in the desired mode flag, we redirect a spawned program's input or output streams to a file in the calling scripts:

```
C:\...\PP2E\System\Streams>type hello-out.py
print 'Hello shell world'

C:\...\PP2E\System\Streams>type hello-in.py
input = raw_input()
open('hello-in.txt', 'w').write('Hello ' + input + '\n')
```

```
C:\...\PP2E\System\Streams>python
>>> import os
>>> pipe = os.popen('python hello-out.py')          # 'r' is default--read stdout
>>> pipe.read()
'Hello shell world\012'

>>> pipe = os.popen('python hello-in.py', 'w')
>>> pipe.write('Gumby\n')                            # 'w'--write to program stdin
>>> pipe.close()                                     # \n at end is optional
>>> open('hello-in.txt').read()
'Hello Gumby\012'
```

The popen call is also smart enough to run the command string as an independent process on Unix and Linux. There are additional popen-like tools in the Python library that allow scripts to connect to more than one of the commands' streams. For instance, the popen2 module includes functions for hooking into *both* a command's input and output streams (popen2.popen2), and another for connecting to standard error as well (popen2.popen3):

```
import popen2
childStdout, childStdin = popen2.popen2('python hello-in-out.py')
childStdin.write(input)
output = childStdout.read()

childStdout, childStdin, childStderr = popen2.popen3('python hello-in-out.py')
```

These two calls work much like os.popen, but connect additional streams. When I originally wrote this, these calls only worked on Unix-like platforms, not on Windows, because they relied on a fork call in Python 1.5.2. As of the Python 2.0 release, they now work well on Windows too.

Speaking of which: on Unix-like platforms, the combination of the calls os.fork, os.pipe, os.dup, and some os.exec variants can be used to start a new independent program with streams connected to the parent program's streams (that's how popen2 works its magic). As such, it's another way to redirect streams, and a low-level equivalent to tools like os.popen. See Chapter 3 for more on all these calls, especially its section on pipes.

Python 2.0 now also makes the popen2 and popen3 calls available in the os module. (For example, os.popen2 is the same as popen2. popen2, except that the order of stdin and stdout in the call's result tuple is swapped.) In addition, the 2.0 release extends the print statement to include an explicit file to which output is to be sent. A statement of the form print >>file stuff prints stuff to file, instead of stdout. The net effect is similar to simply assigning sys.stdout to an object.

Also note that when opening in "w" mode, Python either creates the external file if it does not yet exist, or erases the file's current contents if it is already present on your machine (so be careful out there).

Writing. Notice that we added an explicit \n end-of-line character to lines written to the file; unlike the print statement, file write methods write exactly what they are passed, without any extra formatting. The string passed to write shows up byte-for-byte on the external file.

Output files also sport a writelines method, which simply writes all the strings in a list one at a time, without any extra formatting added. For example, here is a writelines equivalent to the two write calls shown earlier:

```
file.writelines(['Hello file world!\n', 'Bye   file world.\n'])
```

This call isn't as commonly used (and can be emulated with a simple for loop), but is convenient in scripts that save output in a list to be written later.

Closing. The file close method used earlier finalizes file contents and frees up system resources. For instance, closing forces buffered output data to be flushed out to disk. Normally, files are automatically closed when the file object is garbage collected by the interpreter (i.e., when it is no longer referenced), and when the Python session or program exits. Because of that, close calls are often optional. In fact, it's common to see file-processing code in Python like this:

```
open('somefile.txt').write("G'day Bruce\n")
```

Since this expression makes a temporary file object, writes to it immediately, and does not save a reference to it, the file object is reclaimed and closed right away without ever having called the close method explicitly.

But note that it's not impossible that this *auto-close on reclaim* file feature may change in future Python releases. Moreover, the JPython Java-based Python implementation discussed later does not reclaim files as immediately as the standard Python system (it uses Java's garbage collector). If your script makes many files and your platform limits the number of open files per program, explicit close calls are a robust habit to form.

Input files

Reading data from external files is just as easy as writing, but there are more methods that let us load data in a variety of modes. Input text files are opened with either a mode flag of "r" (for "read") or no mode flag at all (it defaults to "r" if omitted). Once opened, we can read the lines of a text file with the `readlines` method:

```
>>> file = open('data.txt', 'r')          # open input file object
>>> for line in file.readlines():         # read into line string list
...     print line,                       # lines have '\n' at end
...
Hello file world!
Bye    file world.
```

The `readlines` method loads the entire contents of the file into memory, and gives it to our scripts as a list of line strings that we can step through in a loop. In fact, there are many ways to read an input file:

- `file.read()` returns a string containing all the bytes stored in the file.

- `file.read(N)` returns a string containing the next N bytes from the file.

- `file.readline()` reads through the next \n and returns a line string.

- `file.readlines()` reads the entire file and returns a list of line strings.

Let's run these method calls to read files, lines, and bytes:

```
>>> file.seek(0)                          # go back to the front of file
>>> file.read()                           # read entire file into string
'Hello file world!\012Bye    file world.\012'

>>> file.seek(0)
>>> file.readlines()
['Hello file world!\012', 'Bye    file world.\012']

>>> file.seek(0)
>>> file.readline()
'Hello file world!\012'
>>> file.readline()
'Bye    file world.\012'

>>> file.seek(0)
>>> file.read(1), file.read(8)
('H', 'ello fil')
```

All these input methods let us be specific about how much to fetch. Here are a few rules of thumb about which to choose:

- `read()` and `readlines()` load the *entire file* into memory all at once. That makes them handy for grabbing a file's contents with as little code as possible. It also makes them very fast, but costly for huge files—loading a multi-gigabyte file into memory is not generally a good thing to do.

- On the other hand, because the `readline()` and `read(N)` calls fetch just *part of the file* (the next line, or N-byte block), they are safer for potentially big files, but a bit less convenient, and usually much slower. If speed matters and your files aren't huge, `read` or `readlines` may be better choices.

By the way, the `seek(0)` call used repeatedly here means "go back to the start of the file." In files, all read and write operations take place at the current position; files normally start at offset 0 when opened and advance as data is transferred. The `seek` call simply lets us move to a new position for the next transfer operation. Python's `seek` method also accepts an optional second argument having one of three values—0 for absolute file positioning (the default), 1 to seek relative to the the current position, and 2 to seek relative to the file's end. When `seek` is passed only an offset argument 0 as above, it's roughly a file *rewind* operation.

Other file object modes

Besides "w" and "r", most platforms support an "a" open mode string, meaning "append." In this output mode, `write` methods add data to the end of the file, and the `open` call will not erase the current contents of the file:

```
>>> file = open('data.txt', 'a')          # open in append mode: doesn't erase
>>> file.write('The Life of Brian')       # added at end of existing data
>>> file.close()
>>>
>>> open('data.txt').read()               # open and read entire file
'Hello file world!\012Bye   file world.\012The Life of Brian'
```

Most files are opened using the sorts of calls we just ran, but `open` actually allows up to three arguments for more specific processing needs—the filename, the open mode, and a buffer size. All but the first of these are optional: if omitted, the open mode argument defaults to "r" (input), and the buffer size policy is to enable buffering on most platforms. Here are a few things you should know about all three `open` arguments:

Filename

As mentioned, filenames can include an explicit directory path to refer to files in arbitrary places on your computer; if they do not, they are taken to be names relative to the current working directory (described earlier). In general, any filename form you can type in your system shell will work in an `open` call. For instance, a filename argument `r'..\temp\spam.txt'` on Windows means *spam.txt* in the *temp* subdirectory of the current working directory's parent—up one, and down to directory *temp*.

Open mode

The `open` function accepts other modes too, some of which are not demonstrated in this book (e.g., `r+`, `w+`, and `a+` to open for updating, and any mode string with a "b" to designate binary mode). For instance, mode `r+` means both reads and writes are allowed on the file, and `wb` writes data in binary mode (more on this in the next section). Generally, whatever you could use as a mode string in the C language's `fopen` call on your platform will work in the Python `open` function, since it really just calls `fopen` internally. (If you don't know C, don't sweat this point.) Notice that the contents of files are always strings in Python programs regardless of mode: read methods return a string, and we pass a string to write methods.

Buffer size

The `open` call also takes an optional third *buffer size* argument, which lets you control `stdio` buffering for the file—the way that data is queued up before being transferred to boost performance. If passed, 0 means file operations are unbuffered (data is transferred immediately), 1 means they are line buffered, any other positive value means use a buffer of approximately that size, and a negative value means to use the system default (which you get if no third argument is passed, and generally means buffering is enabled). The buffer size argument works on most platforms, but is currently ignored on platforms that don't provide the `sevbuf` system call.

Binary data files

The preceding examples all process simple text files. On most platforms, Python scripts can also open and process files containing *binary* data—JPEG images, audio clips, and anything else that can be stored in files. The primary difference in terms of code is the *mode* argument passed to the built-in open function:

```
>>> file = open('data.txt', 'wb')      # open binary output file
>>> file = open('data.txt', 'rb')      # open binary input file
```

Once you've opened binary files in this way, you may read and write their contents using the same methods just illustrated: `read`, `write`, and so on. (`readline` and `readlines` don't make sense here, though: binary data isn't line-oriented.)

In all cases, data transferred between files and your programs is represented as Python *strings* within scripts, even if it is binary data. This works because Python string objects can always contain character bytes of any value (though some may look odd if printed). Interestingly, even a byte of value zero can be embedded in a Python string; it's called \0 in escape-code notation, and does not terminate strings in Python as it does in C. For instance:

```
>>> data = "a\0b\0c"
>>> data
'a\000b\000c'
>>> len(data)
5
```

Instead of relying on a terminator character, Python keeps track of a string's length explicitly. Here, `data` references a string of length 5, that happens to contain two zero-value bytes; they print in octal escape form as \000. Because no character codes are reserved, it's okay to read binary data with zero bytes (and other values) into a string in Python.

End-of-line translations on Windows

Strictly speaking, on some platforms you may not need the "b" at the end of the open mode argument to process binary files; the "b" is simply ignored, so modes "r" and "w" work just as well. In fact, the "b" in mode flag strings is usually only required for binary files on Windows. To understand why, though, you need to know how lines are terminated in text files.

For historical reasons, the end of a line of text in a file is represented by different characters on different platforms: it's a single \n character on Unix and Linux, but the two-character sequence \r\n on Windows.* That's why files moved between Linux and Windows may look odd in your text editor after transfer—they may still be stored using the original platform's end-of-line convention. For example, most Windows editors handle text in Unix format, but Notepad is a notable exception—text files copied from Unix or Linux usually look like one long line when viewed in Notepad, with strange characters inside (\n).

Python scripts don't normally need to care, because the Windows port (really, the underlying C compiler on Windows) automatically maps the DOS \r\n sequence to a single \n. It works like this—when scripts are run on Windows:

- For files opened in text mode, \r\n is translated to \n when input.
- For files opened in text mode, \n is translated to \r\n when output.
- For files opened in binary mode, no translation occurs on input or output.
- On Unix-like platforms, no translations occur, regardless of open modes.

There are two important consequences of all these rules to keep in mind. First, the end of line character is almost always represented as a single \n in all Python scripts, regardless of how it is stored in external files on the underlying platform. By mapping to and from \n on input and output, the Windows port hides the platform-specific difference.

The second consequence of the mapping is more subtle: if you mean to process *binary data files* on Windows, you generally must be careful to open those files in binary mode ("rb", "wb"), not text mode ("r", "w"). Otherwise, the translations listed previously could very well corrupt data as it is input or output. It's not impossible that binary data would by chance contain bytes with values the same

---

* Actually, it gets worse: on the Mac, lines in text files are terminated with a single \r (not \n or \r\n). Whoever said proprietary software was good for the consumer probably wasn't speaking about users of multiple platforms, and certainly wasn't talking about programmers.

as the DOS end-line characters, \r and \n. If you process such binary files in *text* mode on Windows, \r bytes may be incorrectly discarded when read, and \n bytes may be erroneously expanded to \r\n when written. The net effect is that your binary data will be trashed when read and written—probably not quite what you want! For example, on Windows:

```
>>> len('a\0b\rc\r\nd')                          # 4 escape code bytes
8
>>> open('temp.bin', 'wb').write('a\0b\rc\r\nd')  # write binary data to file

>>> open('temp.bin', 'rb').read()                # intact if read as binary
'a\000b\015c\015\012d'

>>> open('temp.bin', 'r').read()                 # loses a \r in text mode!
'a\000b\015c\012d'

>>> open('temp.bin', 'w').write('a\0b\rc\r\nd')   # adds a \r in text mode!
>>> open('temp.bin', 'rb').read()
'a\000b\015c\015\015\012d'
```

This is only an issue when running on Windows, but using binary open modes "rb" and "wb" for binary files everywhere won't hurt on other platforms, and will help make your scripts more portable (you never know when a Unix utility may wind up seeing action on your PC).

There are other times you may want to use binary file open modes too. For instance, in Chapter 5, *Larger System Examples II*, we'll meet a script called `fixeoln_one` that translates between DOS and Unix end-of-line character conventions in text files. Such a script also has to open *text* files in *binary* mode to see what end-of-line characters are truly present on the file; in text mode, they would already be translated to \n by the time they reached the script.

File Tools in the os Module

The `os` module contains an additional set of file-processing functions that are distinct from the built-in file *object* tools demonstrated in previous examples. For instance, here is a very partial list of `os` file-related calls:

`os.open(`*path, flags, mode*`)`
  Opens a file, returns its descriptor

`os.read(`*descriptor, N*`)`
  Reads at most *N* bytes, returns a string

`os.write(`*descriptor, string*`)`
  Writes bytes in *string* to the file

`os.lseek(`*descriptor, position*`)`
  Moves to *position* in the file

Technically, os calls process files by their *descriptors*—integer codes or "handles" that identify files in the operating system. Because the descriptor-based file tools in os are lower-level and more complex than the built-in file objects created with the built-in open function, you should generally use the latter for all but very special file-processing needs.[*]

To give you the general flavor of this tool-set, though, let's run a few interactive experiments. Although built-in file objects and os module descriptor files are processed with distinct toolsets, they are in fact related—the stdio filesystem used by file objects simply adds a layer of logic on top of descriptor-based files.

In fact, the fileno file object method returns the integer descriptor associated with a built-in file object. For instance, the standard stream file objects have descriptors 0, 1, and 2; calling the os.write function to send data to stdout by descriptor has the same effect as calling the sys.stdout.write method:

```
>>> import sys
>>> for stream in (sys.stdin, sys.stdout, sys.stderr):
...     print stream.fileno(),
...
0 1 2

>>> sys.stdout.write('Hello stdio world\n')        # write via file method
Hello stdio world

>>> import os
>>> os.write(1, 'Hello descriptor world\n')        # write via os module
Hello descriptor world
23
```

Because file objects we open explicitly behave the same way, it's also possible to process a given real external file on the underlying computer, through the built-in open function, tools in module os, or both:

```
>>> file = open(r'C:\temp\spam.txt', 'w')          # create external file
>>> file.write('Hello stdio file\n')               # write via file method
>>>
>>> fd = file.fileno()
>>> print fd
3
>>> os.write(fd, 'Hello descriptor file\n')        # write via os module
22
>>> file.close()
>>>
C:\WINDOWS>type c:\temp\spam.txt                   # both writes show up
Hello descriptor file
Hello stdio file
```

---

[*] For instance, to process *pipes*, described in Chapter 3. The Python pipe call returns two file descriptors, which can be processed with os module tools or wrapped in a file object with os.fdopen.

Open mode flags

So why the extra file tools in os? In short, they give more low-level control over file processing. The built-in open function is easy to use, but is limited by the underlying stdio filesystem that it wraps—buffering, open modes, and so on, are all per stdio defaults.* Module os lets scripts be more specific; for example, the following opens a descriptor-based file in read-write and binary modes, by performing a binary "or" on two mode flags exported by os:

```
>>> fdfile = os.open(r'C:\temp\spam.txt', (os.O_RDWR | os.O_BINARY))
>>> os.read(fdfile, 20)
'Hello descriptor fil'
>>> os.lseek(fdfile, 0, 0)                    # go back to start of file
0
>>> os.read(fdfile, 100)                      # binary mode retains "\r\n"
'Hello descriptor file\015\012Hello stdio file\015\012'

>>> os.lseek(fdfile, 0, 0)
0
>>> os.write(fdfile, 'HELLO')                 # overwrite first 5 bytes
5
```

On some systems, such open flags let us specify more advanced things like *exclusive access* (O_EXCL) and *nonblocking* modes (O_NONBLOCK) when a file is opened. Some of these flags are not portable across platforms (another reason to use built-in file objects most of the time); see the library manual or run a dir(os) call on your machine for an exhaustive list of other open flags available.

We saw earlier how to go from file object to field descriptor with the fileno file method; we can also go the other way—the os.fdopen call wraps a file descriptor in a file object. Because conversions work both ways, we can generally use either tool set—file object, or os module:

```
>>> objfile = os.fdopen(fdfile)
>>> objfile.seek(0)
>>> objfile.read()
'HELLO descriptor file\015\012Hello stdio file\015\012'
```

Other os file tools

The os module also includes an assortment of file tools that accept a file pathname string, and accomplish file-related tasks such as renaming (os.rename), deleting (os.remove), and changing the file's owner and permission settings (os.chown, os.chmod). Let's step through a few examples of these tools in action:

```
>>> os.chmod('spam.txt', 0777)               # enabled all accesses
```

---

* To be fair to the built-in file object, the open function accepts a mode "rb+", which is equivalent to the combined mode flags used here, and can also be made nonbuffered with a 0 buffer size argument. Whenever possible, use open, not os.open.

This `os.chmod` file permissions call passes a nine-bit bitstring, composed of three sets of three bits each. From left to right, the three sets represent the file's owning user, the file's group, and all others. Within each set, the three bits reflect read, write, and execute access permissions. When a bit is "1" in this string, it means that the corresponding operation is allowed for the assessor. For instance, octal 0777 is a string of nine "1" bits in binary, so it enables all three kinds of accesses, for all three user groups; octal 0600 means that the file can be only read and written by the user that owns it (when written in binary, 0600 octal is really bits 110 000 000).

This scheme stems from Unix file permission settings, but works on Windows as well. If it's puzzling, either check a Unix manpage for *chmod*, or see the `fixreadonly` example in Chapter 5, *Larger System Examples II*, for a practical application (it makes read-only files copied off a CD-ROM writable).

```
>>> os.rename(r'C:\temp\spam.txt', r'C:\temp\eggs.txt')       # (from, to)
>>>
>>> os.remove(r'C:\temp\spam.txt')                            # delete file
Traceback (innermost last):
  File "<stdin>", line 1, in ?
OSError: [Errno 2] No such file or directory: 'C:\\temp\\spam.txt'
>>>
>>> os.remove(r'C:\temp\eggs.txt')
```

The `os.rename` call used here changes a file's name; the `os.remove` file deletion call deletes a file from your system, and is synonymous with `os.unlink`; the latter reflects the call's name on Unix, but was obscure to users of other platforms. The `os` module also exports the `stat` system call:

```
>>> import os
>>> info = os.stat(r'C:\temp\spam.txt')
>>> info
(33206, 0, 2, 1, 0, 0, 41, 968133600, 968176258, 968176193)

>>> import stat
>>> info[stat.ST_MODE], info[stat.ST_SIZE]
(33206, 41)

>>> mode = info[stat.ST_MODE]
>>> stat.S_ISDIR(mode), stat.S_ISREG(mode)
(0, 1)
```

The `os.stat` call returns a tuple of values giving low-level information about the named file, and the `stat` module exports constants and functions for querying this information in a portable way. For instance, indexing an `os.stat` result on offset `stat.ST_SIZE` returns the file's size, and calling `stat.S_ISDIR` with the mode item from an `os.stat` result checks whether the file is a directory. As shown earlier, though, both of these operations are available in the `os.path` module too, so it's rarely necessary to use `os.stat` except for low-level file queries:

```
>>> path = r'C:\temp\spam.txt'
>>> os.path.isdir(path), os.path.isfile(path), os.path.getsize(path)
(0, 1, 41)
```

File Scanners

Unlike some shell-tool languages, Python doesn't have an implicit file-scanning loop procedure, but it's simple to write a general one that we can reuse for all time. The module in Example 2-11 defines a general file-scanning routine, which simply applies a passed-in Python function to each line in an external file.

Example 2-11. PP2E\System\Filetools\scanfile.py

```
def scanner(name, function):
    file = open(name, 'r')              # create a file object
    while 1:
        line = file.readline()          # call file methods
        if not line: break              # until end-of-file
        function(line)                  # call a function object
    file.close()
```

The **scanner** function doesn't care what line-processing function is passed in, and that accounts for most of its generality—it is happy to apply *any* single-argument function that exists now or in the future to all the lines in a text file. If we code this module and put it in a directory on PYTHONPATH, we can use it any time we need to step through a file line-by-line. Example 2-12 is a client script that does simple line translations.

Example 2-12. PP2E\System\Filetools\commands.py

```
#!/usr/local/bin/python
from sys import argv
from scanfile import scanner

def processLine(line):                  # define a function
    if line[0] == '*':                  # applied to each line
        print "Ms.", line[1:-1]
    elif line[0] == '+':
        print "Mr.", line[1:-1]         # strip 1st and last char
    else:
        raise 'unknown command', line   # raise an exception

filename = 'data.txt'
if len(argv) == 2: filename = argv[1]   # allow file name cmd arg
scanner(filename, processLine)          # start the scanner
```

If, for no readily obvious reason, the text file *hillbillies.txt* contains the following lines:

```
*Granny
+Jethro
```

```
*Elly-Mae
+"Uncle Jed"
```

then our commands script could be run as follows:

```
C:\...\PP2E\System\Filetools>python commands.py hillbillies.txt
Ms. Granny
Mr. Jethro
Ms. Elly-Mae
Mr. "Uncle Jed"
```

As a rule of thumb, though, we can usually speed things up by shifting process-ing from Python code to built-in tools. For instance, if we're concerned with speed (and memory space isn't tight), we can make our file scanner faster by using the `readlines` method to load the file into a list all at once, instead of the manual `readline` loop in Example 2-11:

```
def scanner(name, function):
    file = open(name, 'r')            # create a file object
    for line in file.readlines():     # get all lines at once
        function(line)                # call a function object
    file.close()
```

And if we have a list of lines, we can work more magic with the `map` built-in func-tion. Here's a minimalist's version; the `for` loop is replaced by `map`, and we let Python close the file for us when it is garbage-collected (or the script exits):

```
def scanner(name, function):
    map(function, open(name, 'r').readlines())
```

But what if we also want to *change* a file while scanning it? Example 2-13 shows two approaches: one uses explicit files, and the other uses the standard input/out-put streams to allow for redirection on the command line.

Example 2-13. PP2E\System\Filetools\filters.py

```
def filter_files(name, function):       # filter file through function
    input  = open(name, 'r')            # create file objects
    output = open(name + '.out', 'w')   # explicit output file too
    for line in input.readlines():
        output.write(function(line))    # write the modified line
    input.close()
    output.close()                      # output has a '.out' suffix

def filter_stream(function):
    import sys                          # no explicit files
    while 1:                            # use standard streams
        line = sys.stdin.readline()     # or: raw_input()
        if not line: break
        print function(line),           # or: sys.stdout.write()

if __name__ == '__main__':
    filter_stream(lambda line: line)    # copy stdin to stdout if run
```

Since the standard streams are preopened for us, they're often easier to use. This module is more useful when imported as a library (clients provide the line-processing function); when run standalone it simply parrots `stdin` to `stdout`:

```
C:\...\PP2E\System\Filetools>python filters.py < ..\System.txt
This directory contains operating system interface examples.

Many of the examples in this unit appear elsewhere in the examples
distribution tree, because they are actually used to manage other
programs.  See the README.txt files in the subdirectories here
for pointers.
```

> Brutally observant readers may notice that this last file is named *filters.py* (with an "s"), not *filter.py*. I originally named it the latter, but changed its name when I realized that a simple import of the filename (e.g., "import filter") assigns the module to a local name "filter," thereby hiding the built-in `filter` function. This is a built-in functional programming tool, not used very often in typical scripts; but be careful to avoid picking built-in names for module files. I will if you will.

Making Files Look Like Lists

One last file-related trick has proven popular enough to merit an introduction here. Although file objects only export method calls (e.g., `file.read()`), it is easy to use classes to make them look more like data structures, and hide some of the underlying file call details. The module in Example 2-14 defines a `FileList` object that "wraps" a real file to add sequential indexing support.

Example 2-14. PP2E\System\Filetools\filelist.py

```
class FileList:
    def __init__(self, filename):
        self.file = open(filename, 'r')        # open and save file
    def __getitem__(self, i):                  # overload indexing
        line = self.file.readline()
        if line:
            return line                        # return the next line
        else:
            raise IndexError                   # end 'for' loops, 'in'
    def __getattr__(self, name):
        return getattr(self.file, name)        # other attrs from real file
```

This class defines three specially named methods:

- The `__init__` method is called whenever a new object is created.

- The `__getitem__` method intercepts indexing operations.

- The `__getattr__` method handles undefined attribute references.

This class mostly just extends the built-in file object to add indexing. Most standard file method calls are simply delegated (passed off) to the wrapped file by __getattr__. Each time a FileList object is indexed, though, its __getitem__ method returns the next line in the actual file. Since for loops work by repeatedly indexing objects, this class lets us iterate over a wrapped file as though it were an in-memory list:

```
>>> from filelist import FileList
>>> for line in FileList('hillbillies.txt'):
...     print '>', line,
...
> *Granny
> +Jethro
> *Elly-Mae
> +"Uncle Jed"
```

This class could be made much more sophisticated and list-like too. For instance, we might overload the + operation to concatenate a file onto the end of an output file, allow random indexing operations that seek among the file's lines to resolve the specified offset, and so on. But since coding all such extensions takes more space than I have available here, I'll leave them as suggested exercises.

Directory Tools

One of the more common tasks in the shell utilities domain is applying an operation to a set of files in a *directory*—a "folder" in Windows-speak. By running a script on a batch of files, we can automate (that is, *script*) tasks we might have to otherwise run repeatedly by hand.

For instance, suppose you need to search all of your Python files in a development directory for a global variable name (perhaps you've forgotten where it is used). There are many platform-specific ways to do this (e.g., the *grep* command in Unix), but Python scripts that accomplish such tasks will work on every platform where Python works—Windows, Unix, Linux, Macintosh, and just about any other in common use today. Simply copy your script to any machine you wish to use it on, and it will work, regardless of which other tools are available there.

Walking One Directory

The most common way to go about writing such tools is to first grab hold of a list of the names of the files you wish to process, and then step through that list with a Python for loop, processing each file in turn. The trick we need to learn here, then, is how to get such a directory list within our scripts. There are at least three options: running shell listing commands with os.popen, matching filename patterns with glob.glob, and getting directory listings with os.listdir. They vary in interface, result format, and portability.

Running shell listing commands with os.popen

Quick: How did you go about getting directory file listings before you heard of Python? If you're new to shell tools programming, the answer may be: "Well, I started a Windows file explorer and clicked on stuff," but I'm thinking in terms of less GUI-oriented command-line mechanisms here (and answers submitted in Perl and Tcl only get partial credit).

On Unix, directory listings are usually obtained by typing *ls* in a shell; on Windows, they can be generated with a *dir* command typed in an MS-DOS console box. Because Python scripts may use `os.popen` to run any command line we can type in a shell, they also are the most general way to grab a directory listing inside a Python program. We met `os.popen` earlier in this chapter; it runs a shell command string and gives us a file object from which we can read the command's output. To illustrate, let's first assume the following directory structures (yes, I have both *dir* and *ls* commands on my Windows laptop; old habits die hard):

```
C:\temp>dir /B
about-pp.html
python1.5.tar.gz
about-pp2e.html
about-ppr2e.html
newdir

C:\temp>ls
about-pp.html      about-ppr2e.html  python1.5.tar.gz
about-pp2e.html    newdir

C:\temp>ls newdir
more    temp1  temp2  temp3
```

The *newdir* name is a nested subdirectory in *C:\temp* here. Now, scripts can grab a listing of file and directory names at this level by simply spawning the appropriate platform-specific command line, and reading its output (the text normally thrown up on the console window):

```
C:\temp>python
>>> import os
>>> os.popen('dir /B').readlines()
['about-pp.html\012', 'python1.5.tar.gz\012', 'about-pp2e.html\012',
'about-ppr2e.html\012', 'newdir\012']
```

Lines read from a shell command come back with a trailing end-line character, but it's easy enough to slice off:

```
>>> for line in os.popen('dir /B').readlines():
...       print line[:-1]
...
about-pp.html
python1.5.tar.gz
about-pp2e.html
about-ppr2e.html
newdir
```

Both *dir* and *ls* commands let us be specific about filename patterns to be matched and directory names to be listed; again, we're just running shell commands here, so anything you can type at a shell prompt goes:

```
>>> os.popen('dir *.html /B').readlines()
['about-pp.html\012', 'about-pp2e.html\012', 'about-ppr2e.html\012']

>>> os.popen('ls *.html').readlines()
['about-pp.html\012', 'about-pp2e.html\012', 'about-ppr2e.html\012']

>>> os.popen('dir newdir /B').readlines()
['temp1\012', 'temp2\012', 'temp3\012', 'more\012']

>>> os.popen('ls newdir').readlines()
['more\012', 'temp1\012', 'temp2\012', 'temp3\012']
```

These calls use general tools and all work as advertised. As we noted earlier, though, the downsides of os.popen are that it is nonportable (it doesn't work well in a Windows GUI application in Python 1.5.2 and earlier, and requires using a platform-specific shell command), and it incurs a performance hit to start up an independent program. The following two alternative techniques do better on both counts.

The glob module

The term "globbing" comes from the * wildcard character in filename patterns—per computing folklore, a * matches a "glob" of characters. In less poetic terms, globbing simply means collecting the names of all entries in a directory—files and subdirectories—whose names match a given filename pattern. In Unix shells, globbing expands filename patterns within a command line into all matching filenames before the command is ever run. In Python, we can do something similar by calling the glob.glob built-in with a pattern to expand:

```
>>> import glob
>>> glob.glob('*')
['about-pp.html', 'python1.5.tar.gz', 'about-pp2e.html', 'about-ppr2e.html',
'newdir']

>>> glob.glob('*.html')
['about-pp.html', 'about-pp2e.html', 'about-ppr2e.html']

>>> glob.glob('newdir/*')
['newdir\\temp1', 'newdir\\temp2', 'newdir\\temp3', 'newdir\\more']
```

The glob call accepts the usual filename pattern syntax used in shells (e.g., ? means any one character, * means any number of characters, and [] is a character selection set).* The pattern should include a directory path if you wish to glob in

---

* In fact, glob just uses the standard fnmatch module to match name patterns; see the fnmatch description later in this chapter in the section titled "Rolling Your Own find Module" for more details.

something other than the current working directory, and the module accepts either Unix or DOS-style directory separators (/ or \). This call also is implemented without spawning a shell command, and so is likely to be faster and more portable across all Python platforms than the os.popen schemes shown earlier.

Technically speaking, glob is a bit more powerful than described so far. In fact, using it to list files in one directory is just one use of its pattern-matching skills. For instance, it can also be used to collect matching names across multiple directories, simply because each level in a passed-in directory path can be a pattern too:

```
C:\temp>python
>>> import glob
>>> for name in glob.glob('*examples/L*.py'): print name
...
cpexamples\Launcher.py
cpexamples\Launch_PyGadgets.py
cpexamples\LaunchBrowser.py
cpexamples\launchmodes.py
examples\Launcher.py
examples\Launch_PyGadgets.py
examples\LaunchBrowser.py
examples\launchmodes.py

>>> for name in glob.glob(r'*\*\visitor_find*.py'): print name
...
cpexamples\PyTools\visitor_find.py
cpexamples\PyTools\visitor_find_quiet2.py
cpexamples\PyTools\visitor_find_quiet1.py
examples\PyTools\visitor_find.py
examples\PyTools\visitor_find_quiet2.py
examples\PyTools\visitor_find_quiet1.py
```

In the first call here, we get back filenames from two different directories that matched the *examples pattern; in the second, both of the first directory levels are wildcards, so Python collects all possible ways to reach the base filenames. Using os.popen to spawn shell commands only achieves the same effect if the underlying shell or listing command does too.

The os.listdir call

The os module's listdir call provides yet another way to collect filenames in a Python list. It takes a simple directory name string, not a filename pattern, and returns a list containing the names of all entries in that directory—both simple files and nested directories—for use in the calling script:

```
>>> os.listdir('.')
['about-pp.html', 'python1.5.tar.gz', 'about-pp2e.html', 'about-ppr2e.html',
'newdir']

>>> os.listdir(os.curdir)
['about-pp.html', 'python1.5.tar.gz', 'about-pp2e.html', 'about-ppr2e.html',
```

```
'newdir']

>>> os.listdir('newdir')
['temp1', 'temp2', 'temp3', 'more']
```

This too is done without resorting to shell commands, and so is portable to all major Python platforms. The result is not in any particular order (but can be sorted with the list sort method), returns base filenames without their directory path prefixes, and includes names of both files and directories at the listed level.

To compare all three listing techniques, let's run them side by side on an explicit directory here. They differ in some ways but are mostly just variations on a theme—os.popen sorts names and returns end-of-lines, glob.glob accepts a pattern and returns filenames with directory prefixes, and os.listdir takes a simple directory name and returns names without directory prefixes:

```
>>> os.popen('ls C:\PP2ndEd').readlines()
['README.txt\012', 'cdrom\012', 'chapters\012', 'etc\012', 'examples\012',
'examples.tar.gz\012', 'figures\012', 'shots\012']

>>> glob.glob('C:\PP2ndEd\*')
['C:\\PP2ndEd\\examples.tar.gz', 'C:\\PP2ndEd\\README.txt',
'C:\\PP2ndEd\\shots', 'C:\\PP2ndEd\\figures', 'C:\\PP2ndEd\\examples',
'C:\\PP2ndEd\\etc', 'C:\\PP2ndEd\\chapters', 'C:\\PP2ndEd\\cdrom']

>>> os.listdir('C:\PP2ndEd')
['examples.tar.gz', 'README.txt', 'shots', 'figures', 'examples', 'etc',
'chapters', 'cdrom']
```

Of these three, glob and listdir are generally better options if you care about script portability, and listdir seems fastest in recent Python releases (but gauge its performance yourself—implementations may change over time).

Splitting and joining listing results

In the last example, I pointed out that glob returns names with directory paths, but listdir gives raw base filenames. For convenient processing, scripts often need to split glob results into base files, or expand listdir results into full paths. Such translations are easy if we let the os.path module do all the work for us. For example, a script that intends to copy all files elsewhere will typically need to first split off the base filenames from glob results so it can add different directory names on the front:

```
>>> dirname = r'C:\PP2ndEd'
>>> for file in glob.glob(dirname + '/*'):
...       head, tail = os.path.split(file)
...       print head, tail, '=>', ('C:\\Other\\' + tail)
...
C:\PP2ndEd examples.tar.gz => C:\Other\examples.tar.gz
```

```
C:\PP2ndEd README.txt => C:\Other\README.txt
C:\PP2ndEd shots => C:\Other\shots
C:\PP2ndEd figures => C:\Other\figures
C:\PP2ndEd examples => C:\Other\examples
C:\PP2ndEd etc => C:\Other\etc
C:\PP2ndEd chapters => C:\Other\chapters
C:\PP2ndEd cdrom => C:\Other\cdrom
```

Here, the names after the `=>` represent names that files might be moved to. Conversely, a script that means to process all files in a different directory than the one it runs in will probably need to prepend `listdir` results with the target directory name, before passing filenames on to other tools:

```
>>> for file in os.listdir(dirname):
...     print os.path.join(dirname, file)
...
C:\PP2ndEd\examples.tar.gz
C:\PP2ndEd\README.txt
C:\PP2ndEd\shots
C:\PP2ndEd\figures
C:\PP2ndEd\examples
C:\PP2ndEd\etc
C:\PP2ndEd\chapters
C:\PP2ndEd\cdrom
```

Walking Directory Trees

Notice, though, that all of the preceding techniques only return the names of files in a *single* directory. What if you want to apply an operation to every file in every directory and subdirectory in a directory tree?

For instance, suppose again that we need to find every occurrence of a global name in our Python scripts. This time, though, our scripts are arranged into a module *package*: a directory with nested subdirectories, which may have subdirectories of their own. We could rerun our hypothetical single-directory searcher in every directory in the tree manually, but that's tedious, error-prone, and just plain no fun.

Luckily, in Python it's almost as easy to process a directory tree as it is to inspect a single directory. We can either collect names ahead of time with the `find` module, write a recursive routine to traverse the tree, or use a tree-walker utility built-in to the `os` module. Such tools can be used to search, copy, compare, and otherwise process arbitrary directory trees on any platform that Python runs on (and that's just about everywhere).

The find module

The first way to go hierarchical is to collect a list of all names in a directory tree ahead of time, and step through that list in a loop. Like the single-directory tools

we just met, a call to the `find.find` built-in returns a list of both file and directory names. Unlike the tools described earlier, `find.find` also returns pathnames
of matching files nested in subdirectories, all the way to the bottom of a tree:

```
C:\temp>python
>>> import find
>>> find.find('*')
['.\\about-pp.html', '.\\about-pp2e.html', '.\\about-ppr2e.html',
'.\\newdir', '.\\newdir\\more', '.\\newdir\\more\\xxx.txt',
'.\\newdir\\more\\yyy.txt', '.\\newdir\\temp1', '.\\newdir\\temp2',
'.\\newdir\\temp3', '.\\python1.5.tar.gz']

>>> for line in find.find('*'): print line
...
.\about-pp.html
.\about-pp2e.html
.\about-ppr2e.html
.\newdir
.\newdir\more
.\newdir\more\xxx.txt
.\newdir\more\yyy.txt
.\newdir\temp1
.\newdir\temp2
.\newdir\temp3
.\python1.5.tar.gz
```

We get back a list of full pathnames, that each include the top-level directory's
path. By default, find collects names matching the passed-in pattern in the tree
rooted at the current working directory, known as ".". If we want a more specific
list, we can pass in both a filename pattern and a directory tree root to start at;
here's how to collect HTML filenames at "." and below:

```
>>> find.find('*.html', '.')
['.\\about-pp.html', '.\\about-pp2e.html', '.\\about-ppr2e.html']
```

Incidentally, `find.find` is also the Python library's equivalent to platform-specific
shell commands such as a *find –print* on Unix and Linux, and *dir /B /S* on DOS
and Windows. Since we can usually run such shell commands in a Python script
with `os.popen`, the following does the same work as `find.find`, but is inherently nonportable, and must start up a separate program along the way:

```
>>> import os
>>> for line in os.popen('dir /B /S').readlines(): print line,
...
C:\temp\about-pp.html
C:\temp\python1.5.tar.gz
C:\temp\about-pp2e.html
C:\temp\about-ppr2e.html
C:\temp\newdir
C:\temp\newdir\temp1
C:\temp\newdir\temp2
C:\temp\newdir\temp3
C:\temp\newdir\more
```

```
C:\temp\newdir\more\xxx.txt
C:\temp\newdir\more\yyy.txt
```

 If the `find` calls don't seem to work in your Python, try changing the import statement used to load the module from `import find` to `from PP2E.PyTools import find`. Alas, the Python standard library's `find` module has been marked as "deprecated" as of Python 1.6. That means it may be deleted from the standard Python distribution in the future, so pay attention to the next section; we'll use its topic later to write our own `find` module—one that is also shipped on this book's CD.

The os.path.walk visitor

To make it easy to apply an operation to all files in a tree, Python also comes with a utility that scans trees for us, and runs a provided function at every directory along the way. The `os.path.walk` function is called with a directory root, function object, and optional data item, and walks the tree at the directory root and below. At each directory, the function object passed in is called with the optional data item, the name of the current directory, and a list of filenames in that directory (obtained from `os.listdir`). Typically, the function we provide scans the filenames list to process files at each directory level in the tree.

That description might sound horribly complex the first time you hear it, but `os.path.walk` is fairly straightforward once you get the hang of it. In the following code, for example, the `lister` function is called from `os.path.walk` at each directory in the tree rooted at ".". Along the way, `lister` simply prints the directory name, and all the files at the current level (after prepending the directory name). It's simpler in Python than in English:

```
>>> import os
>>> def lister(dummy, dirname, filesindir):
...     print '[' + dirname + ']'
...     for fname in filesindir:
...         print os.path.join(dirname, fname)        # handle one file
...
>>> os.path.walk('.', lister, None)
[.]
.\about-pp.html
.\python1.5.tar.gz
.\about-pp2e.html
.\about-ppr2e.html
.\newdir
[.\newdir]
.\newdir\temp1
.\newdir\temp2
.\newdir\temp3
.\newdir\more
```

```
[.\newdir\more]
.\newdir\more\xxx.txt
.\newdir\more\yyy.txt
```

In other words, we've coded our own custom and easily changed recursive directory listing tool in Python. Because this may be something we would like to tweak and reuse elsewhere, let's make it permanently available in a module file, shown in Example 2-15, now that we've worked out the details interactively.

Example 2-15. PP2E\System\Filetools\lister_walk.py

```
# list file tree with os.path.walk
import sys, os

def lister(dummy, dirName, filesInDir):        # called at each dir
    print '[' + dirName + ']'
    for fname in filesInDir:                   # includes subdir names
        path = os.path.join(dirName, fname)    # add dir name prefix
        if not os.path.isdir(path):            # print simple files only
            print path

if __name__ == '__main__':
    os.path.walk(sys.argv[1], lister, None)    # dir name in cmdline
```

This is the same code, except that directory names are filtered out of the filenames list by consulting the `os.path.isdir` test, to avoid listing them twice (see—it's been tweaked already). When packaged this way, the code can also be run from a shell command line. Here it is being launched from a different directory, with the directory to be listed passed in as a command-line argument:

```
C:\...\PP2E\System\Filetools>python lister_walk.py C:\Temp
[C:\Temp]
C:\Temp\about-pp.html
C:\Temp\python1.5.tar.gz
C:\Temp\about-pp2e.html
C:\Temp\about-ppr2e.html
[C:\Temp\newdir]
C:\Temp\newdir\temp1
C:\Temp\newdir\temp2
C:\Temp\newdir\temp3
[C:\Temp\newdir\more]
C:\Temp\newdir\more\xxx.txt
C:\Temp\newdir\more\yyy.txt
```

The `walk` paradigm also allows functions to tailor the set of directories visited by changing the file list argument in place. The library manual documents this further, but it's probably more instructive to simply know what `walk` truly looks like. Here is its actual Python-coded implementation for Windows platforms, with comments added to help demystify its operation:

```
def walk(top, func, arg):                   # top is the current dirname
    try:
        names = os.listdir(top)             # get all file/dir names here
```

```
        except os.error:                    # they have no path prefix
            return
        func(arg, top, names)               # run func with names list here
        exceptions = ('.', '..')
        for name in names:                   # step over the very same list
            if name not in exceptions:       # but skip self/parent names
                name = join(top, name)        # add path prefix to name
                if isdir(name):
                    walk(name, func, arg)     # descend into subdirs here
```

Notice that **walk** generates filename lists at each level with **os.listdir**, a call
that collects both file and directory names in no particular order, and returns them
without their directory paths. Also note that **walk** uses the very same list returned
by **os.listdir** and passed to the function you provide, to later descend into subdirectories (variable **names**). Because lists are mutable objects that can be changed
in place, if your function modifies the passed-in filenames list, it will impact what
walk does next. For example, deleting directory names will prune traversal
branches, and sorting the list will order the walk.

Recursive os.listdir traversals

The **os.path.walk** tool does tree traversals for us, but it's sometimes more flexible, and hardly any more work, to do it ourself. The following script recodes the
directory listing script with a manual recursive traversal function. The **mylister**
function in Example 2-16 is almost the same as **lister** in the prior script, but calls
os.listdir to generate file paths manually, and calls itself recursively to descend
into subdirectories.

Example 2-16. PP2E\System\Filetools\lister_recur.py

```
# list files in dir tree by recursion
import sys, os

def mylister(currdir):
    print '[' + currdir + ']'
    for file in os.listdir(currdir):            # list files here
        path = os.path.join(currdir, file)       # add dir path back
        if not os.path.isdir(path):
            print path
        else:
            mylister(path)                       # recur into subdirs

if __name__ == '__main__':
    mylister(sys.argv[1])                        # dir name in cmdline
```

This version is packaged as a script too (this is definitely too much code to type at
the interactive prompt); its output is identical when run as a script:

```
C:\...\PP2E\System\Filetools>python lister_recur.py C:\Temp
[C:\Temp]
C:\Temp\about-pp.html
```

```
C:\Temp\python1.5.tar.gz
C:\Temp\about-pp2e.html
C:\Temp\about-ppr2e.html
[C:\Temp\newdir]
C:\Temp\newdir\temp1
C:\Temp\newdir\temp2
C:\Temp\newdir\temp3
[C:\Temp\newdir\more]
C:\Temp\newdir\more\xxx.txt
C:\Temp\newdir\more\yyy.txt
```

But this file is just as useful when imported and called elsewhere:

```
C:\temp>python
>>> from PP2E.System.Filetools.lister_recur import mylister
>>> mylister('.')
[.]
.\about-pp.html
.\python1.5.tar.gz
.\about-pp2e.html
.\about-ppr2e.html
[.\newdir]
.\newdir\temp1
.\newdir\temp2
.\newdir\temp3
[.\newdir\more]
.\newdir\more\xxx.txt
.\newdir\more\yyy.txt
```

We will make better use of most of this section's techniques in later examples in Chapter 5, and this book at large. For example, scripts for copying and comparing directory trees use the tree-walker techniques listed previously. Watch for these tools in action along the way. If you are interested in directory processing, also see the coverage of Python's old `grep` module in Chapter 5; it searches files, and can be applied to all files in a directory when combined with the `glob` module, but simply prints results and does not traverse directory trees by itself.

Rolling Your Own find Module

Over the last eight years, I've learned to trust Python's Benevolent Dictator. Guido generally does the right thing, and if you don't think so, it's usually only because you haven't yet realized how your own position is flawed. Trust me on this. On the other hand, it's not completely clear why the standard `find` module I showed you seems to have fallen into deprecation; it's a useful tool. In fact, I use it a lot— it is often nice to be able to grab a list of files to process in a single function call, and step through it in a `for` loop. The alternatives—`os.path.walk`, and recursive functions—are more code-y, and tougher for beginners to digest.

I suppose the `find` module's followers (if there be any) could have defended it in long, drawn-out debates on the Internet, that would have spanned days or weeks, been joined by a large cast of heroic combatants, and gone just about nowhere. I decided to spend ten minutes whipping up a custom alternative instead. The module in Example 2-17 uses the standard `os.path.walk` call described earlier to reimplement a find operation for Python.

Example 2-17. PP2E\PyTools\find.py

```
#!/usr/bin/python
#####################################################
# custom version of the now deprecated find module
# in the standard library--import as "PyTools.find";
# equivalent to the original, but uses os.path.walk,
# has no support for pruning subdirs in the tree, and
# is instrumented to be runnable as a top-level script;
# results list sort differs slightly for some trees;
# exploits tuple unpacking in function argument lists;
#####################################################

import fnmatch, os

def find(pattern, startdir=os.curdir):
    matches = []
    os.path.walk(startdir, findvisitor, (matches, pattern))
    matches.sort()
    return matches

def findvisitor((matches, pattern), thisdir, nameshere):
    for name in nameshere:
        if fnmatch.fnmatch(name, pattern):
            fullpath = os.path.join(thisdir, name)
            matches.append(fullpath)

if __name__ == '__main__':
    import sys
    namepattern, startdir = sys.argv[1], sys.argv[2]
    for name in find(namepattern, startdir): print name
```

There's not much to this file; but calling its **find** function provides the same utility as the deprecated **find** standard module, and is noticeably easier than rewriting all of this file's code every time you need to perform a find-type search. To process every Python file in a tree, for instance, I simply type:

```
from PP2E.PyTools import find
for name in find.find('*.py'):
    ...do something with name...
```

As a more concrete example, I use the following simple script to clean out any old output text files located anywhere in the book examples tree:

```
C:\...\PP2E>type PyTools\cleanoutput.py
import os                                    # delete old output files in tree
```

```
from PP2E.PyTools.find import find          # only need full path if I'm moved
for filename in find('*.out.txt'):          # use cat instead of type in Linux
    print filename
    if raw_input('View?') == 'y':
        os.system('type ' + filename)
    if raw_input('Delete?') == 'y':
        os.remove(filename)
```

```
C:\temp\examples>python %X%\PyTools\cleanoutput.py
.\Internet\Cgi-Web\Basics\languages.out.txt
View?
Delete?
.\Internet\Cgi-Web\PyErrata\AdminTools\dbaseindexed.out.txt
View?
Delete?y
```

To achieve such code economy, the custom `find` module calls `os.path.walk` to register a function to be called per directory in the tree, and simply adds matching filenames to the result list along the way.

New here, though, is the `fnmatch` module—a standard Python module that performs Unix-like pattern matching against filenames, and was also used by the original `find`. This module supports common operators in name pattern strings: `*` (to match any number of characters), `?` (to match any single character), and `[...]` and `[!...]` (to match any character inside the bracket pairs, or not); other characters match themselves.* To make sure that this alternative's results are similar, I also wrote the test module shown in Example 2-18.

Example 2-18. PP2E\PyTools\find-test.py

```
##########################################################
# test custom find; the builtin find module is deprecated:
# if it ever goes away completely, replace all "import find"
# with "from PP2E.PyTools import find" (or add PP2E\PyTools
# to your path setting and just "import find"); this script
# takes 4 seconds total time on my 650mhz Win98 notebook to
# run 10 finds over a directory tree of roughly 1500 names;
##########################################################

import sys, os, string
for dir in sys.path:
    if string.find(os.path.abspath(dir), 'PyTools') != -1:
        print 'removing', repr(dir)
        sys.path.remove(dir)    # else may import both finds from PyTools, '.'!

import find                 # get deprecated builtin (for now)
import PP2E.PyTools.find    # later use: from PP2E.PyTools import find
```

---

* Unlike the `re` module, fnmatch supports only common Unix shell matching operators, not full-blown regular expression patterns; to understand why this matters, see Chapter 18 for more details.

Example 2-18. PP2E\PyTools\find-test.py (continued)

```
print  find
print  PP2E.PyTools.find

assert find.find != PP2E.PyTools.find.find          # really different?
assert string.find(str(find), 'Lib') != -1          # should be after path remove
assert string.find(str(PP2E.PyTools.find), 'PyTools') != -1

startdir = r'C:\PP2ndEd\examples\PP2E'
for pattern in ('*.py', '*.html', '*.c', '*.cgi', '*'):
    print pattern, '=>'
    list1 = find.find(pattern, startdir)
    list2 = PP2E.PyTools.find.find(pattern, startdir)
    print len(list1), list1[-1]
    print len(list2), list2[-1]
    print list1 == list2,; list1.sort(); print list1 == list2
```

There is some magic at the top of this script that I need to explain. To make sure that it can load both the standard library's find module *and* the custom one in *PP2E\PyTools*, it must delete the entry (or entries) on the module search path that point to the *PP2E\PyTools* directory, and import the custom version with a full package directory—PP2E.PyTools.find. If not, we'd always get the same find module, the one in *PyTools*, no matter where this script is run from.

Here's why. Recall that Python always adds the directory containing a script being run to the *front* of sys.path. If we didn't delete that entry here, the **import find** statement would always load the custom find in **PyTools**, because the custom *find.py* module is in the same directory as the *find-test.py* script. The script's home directory would effectively hide the standard library's find. If that doesn't make sense, go back and reread the "Current Working Directory" section earlier in this chapter.

Below is the output of this tester, along with a few command-line invocations; unlike the original find, the custom version in Example 2-18 can be run as a command-line tool too. If you study the test output closely, you'll notice that the custom find differs only in an occasional sort order that I won't go into further here (the original find module used a recursive function, not os.path.walk); the "0 1" lines mean that results differ in order, but not content. Since find callers don't generally depend on precise filename result ordering, this is trivial:

```
C:\temp>python %X%\PyTools\find-test.py
removing 'C:\\PP2ndEd\\examples\\PP2E\\PyTools'
<module 'find' from 'C:\Program Files\Python\Lib\find.pyc'>
<module 'PP2E.PyTools.find' from 'C:\PP2ndEd\examples\PP2E\PyTools\find.pyc'>
*.py =>
657 C:\PP2ndEd\examples\PP2E\tounix.py
657 C:\PP2ndEd\examples\PP2E\tounix.py
```

```
0 1
*.html =>
37 C:\PP2ndEd\examples\PP2E\System\Filetools\template.html
37 C:\PP2ndEd\examples\PP2E\System\Filetools\template.html
1 1
*.c =>
46 C:\PP2ndEd\examples\PP2E\Other\old-Integ\embed.c
46 C:\PP2ndEd\examples\PP2E\Other\old-Integ\embed.c
0 1
*.cgi =>
24 C:\PP2ndEd\examples\PP2E\Internet\Cgi-Web\PyMailCgi\onViewSubmit.cgi
24 C:\PP2ndEd\examples\PP2E\Internet\Cgi-Web\PyMailCgi\onViewSubmit.cgi
1 1
* =>
1519 C:\PP2ndEd\examples\PP2E\xferall.linux.csh
1519 C:\PP2ndEd\examples\PP2E\xferall.linux.csh
0 1


C:\temp>python %X%\PyTools\find.py *.cxx C:\PP2ndEd\examples\PP2E
C:\PP2ndEd\examples\PP2E\Extend\Swig\Shadow\main.cxx
C:\PP2ndEd\examples\PP2E\Extend\Swig\Shadow\number.cxx


C:\temp>python %X%\PyTools\find.py *.asp C:\PP2ndEd\examples\PP2E
C:\PP2ndEd\examples\PP2E\Internet\Other\asp-py.asp


C:\temp>python %X%\PyTools\find.py *.i C:\PP2ndEd\examples\PP2E
C:\PP2ndEd\examples\PP2E\Extend\Swig\Environ\environ.i
C:\PP2ndEd\examples\PP2E\Extend\Swig\Shadow\number.i
C:\PP2ndEd\examples\PP2E\Extend\Swig\hellolib.i


C:\temp>python %X%\PyTools\find.py setup*.csh C:\PP2ndEd\examples\PP2E
C:\PP2ndEd\examples\PP2E\Config\setup-pp-embed.csh
C:\PP2ndEd\examples\PP2E\Config\setup-pp.csh
C:\PP2ndEd\examples\PP2E\EmbExt\Exports\ClassAndMod\setup-class.csh
C:\PP2ndEd\examples\PP2E\Extend\Swig\setup-swig.csh


[filename sort scheme]
C:\temp> python
>>> l = ['ccc', 'bbb', 'aaa', 'aaa.xxx', 'aaa.yyy', 'aaa.xxx.nnn']
>>> l.sort()
>>> l
['aaa', 'aaa.xxx', 'aaa.xxx.nnn', 'aaa.yyy', 'bbb', 'ccc']
```

Finally, if an example in this book fails in a future Python release because there is no `find` to be found, simply change find-module imports in the source code to say `from PP2E.PyTools import find` instead of `import find`. The former form will find the custom `find` module in the book's example package directory tree; the old module in the standard Python library is ignored (if it is still there at all). And if you are brave enough to add the *PP2E\PyTools* directory itself to your PYTHONPATH setting, all original `import find` statements will continue to work unchanged.

Better still, do nothing at all—most find-based examples in this book automatically pick the alternative by catching import exceptions, just in case they aren't located in the *PyTools* directory:

```
try:
    import find
except ImportError:
    from PP2E.PyTools import find
```

The **find** module may be gone, but it need not be forgotten.

Python Versus csh

If you are familiar with other common shell script languages, it might be useful to see how Python compares. Here is a simple script in a Unix shell language called **csh** that mails all the files in the current working directory having a suffix of *.py* (i.e., all Python source files) to a hopefully fictitious address:

```
#!/bin/csh
foreach x (*.py)
    echo $x
    mail eric@halfabee.com -s $x < $x
end
```

The equivalent Python script looks similar:

```
#!/usr/bin/python
import os, glob
for x in glob.glob('*.py'):
    print x
    os.system('mail eric@halfabee.com -s %s < %s' % (x, x))
```

but is slightly more verbose. Since Python, unlike **csh**, isn't meant just for shell scripts, system interfaces must be imported, and called explicitly. And since Python isn't just a string-processing language, character strings must be enclosed in quotes as in C.

Although this can add a few extra keystrokes in simple scripts like this, being a general-purpose language makes Python a better tool, once we leave the realm of trivial programs. We could, for example, extend the preceding script to do things like transfer files by FTP, pop up a GUI message selector and status bar, fetch messages from an SQL database, and employ COM objects on Windows—all using standard Python tools.

Python scripts also tend to be more portable to other platforms than **csh**. For instance, if we used the Python SMTP interface to send mail rather than relying on a Unix command-line mail tool, the script would run on any machine with Python and an Internet link (as we'll see in Chapter 11, *Client-Side Scripting*, SMTP only requires sockets). And like C, we don't need $ to evaluate variables; what else would you expect in a free language?

3

Parallel System Tools

"Telling the Monkeys What to Do"

Most computers spend a lot of time doing nothing. If you start a system monitor tool and watch the CPU utilization, you'll see what I mean—it's rare to see one hit 100%, even when you are running multiple programs.* There are just too many delays built in to software: disk accesses, network traffic, database queries, waiting for users to click a button, and so on. In fact, the majority of a modern CPU's capacity is often spent in an idle state; faster chips help speed up performance demand peaks, but much of their power can go largely unused.

Early on in computing, programmers realized that they could tap into such unused processing power, by running more than one program at the same time. By dividing up the CPU's attention among a set of tasks, its capacity need not go to waste while any given task is waiting for an external event to occur. The technique is usually called *parallel processing*, because tasks seem to be performed at once, overlapping and parallel in time. It's at the heart of modern operating systems, and gave rise to the notion of multiple active-window computer interfaces we've all grown to take for granted. Even within a single program, dividing processing up into tasks that run in parallel can make the overall system faster, at least as measured by the clock on your wall.

Just as importantly, modern software systems are expected to be responsive to users, regardless of the amount of work they must perform behind the scenes. It's

---

* To watch on Windows, click the Start button, select Programs/Accessories/System Tools/System Monitor, and monitor Processor Usage. The graph rarely climbed above 50% on my laptop machine while writing this (at least until I typed `while 1: pass` in a Python interactive session console window).

usually unacceptable for a program to stall while busy carrying out a request. Consider an email-browser user interface, for example; when asked to fetch email from a server, the program must download text from a server over a network. If you have enough email and a slow enough Internet link, that step alone can take minutes to finish. But while the download task proceeds, the program as a whole shouldn't stall—it still must respond to screen redraws, mouse clicks, etc.

Parallel processing comes to the rescue here too. By performing such long-running tasks in parallel with the rest of the program, the system at large can remain responsive no matter how busy some of its parts may be.

There are two built-in ways to get tasks running at the same time in Python—process *forks*, and spawned *threads*. Functionally, both rely on underlying operating system services to run bits of Python code in parallel. Procedurally, they are very different in terms of interface, portability, and communication. At this writing, process forks don't work on Windows (more on this in a later note), but Python's thread support works on all major platforms. Moreover, there are additional Windows-specific ways to launch programs that are similar to forks.

In this chapter, which is a continuation of our look at system interfaces available to Python programmers, we explore Python's built-in tools for starting programs in parallel, as well as communicating with those programs. In some sense, we've already starting doing so—the os.system and os.popen calls introduced and applied in the prior chapter are a fairly portable way to spawn and speak with command-line programs too. Here, our emphasis is on introducing more direct techniques—forks, threads, pipes, signals, and Windows-specific launcher tools. In the next chapter (and the remainder of this book), we use these techniques in more realistic programs, so be sure you understand the basics here before flipping ahead.

Forking Processes

Forked processes are the traditional way to structure parallel tasks, and are a fundamental part of the Unix tool set. Forking is based on the notion of *copying* programs: when a program calls the fork routine, the operating system makes a new copy of that program in memory, and starts running that copy in parallel with the original. Some systems don't really copy the original program (it's an expensive operation), but the new copy works as if it was a literal copy.

After a fork operation, the original copy of the program is called the *parent* process, and the copy created by os.fork is called the *child* process. In general, parents can make any number of children, and children can create child processes of their own—all forked processes run independently and in parallel under the operating system's control. It is probably simpler in practice than theory, though; the Python script in Example 3-1 forks new child processes until you type a "q" at the console.

Example 3-1. PP2E\System\Processes\fork1.py

```
# forks child processes until you type 'q'

import os

def child():
    print 'Hello from child', os.getpid()
    os._exit(0)   # else goes back to parent loop

def parent():
    while 1:
        newpid = os.fork()
        if newpid == 0:
            child()
        else:
            print 'Hello from parent', os.getpid(), newpid
        if raw_input() == 'q': break

parent()
```

Python's process forking tools, available in the os module, are simply thin wrappers over standard forking calls in the C library. To start a new, parallel process, call the os.fork built-in function. Because this function generates a copy of the calling program, it returns a different value in each copy: zero in the child process, and the process ID of the new child in the parent. Programs generally test this result to begin different processing in the child only; this script, for instance, runs the child function in child processes only.*

Unfortunately, this won't work on Windows today; fork is at odds with the Windows model, and a port of this call is still in the works. But because forking is ingrained into the Unix programming model, this script works well on Unix and Linux:

```
[mark@toy]$ python fork1.py
Hello from parent 671 672
Hello from child 672

Hello from parent 671 673
Hello from child 673
```

---

* At least in the current Python implementation, calling os.fork in a Python script actually copies the Python interpreter process (if you look at your process list, you'll see two Python entries after a fork). But since the Python interpreter records everything about your running script, it's okay to think of fork as copying your program directly. It really will, if Python scripts are ever compiled to binary machine code.

```
Hello from parent 671 674
Hello from child 674
q
```

These messages represent three forked child processes; the unique identifiers of all the processes involved are fetched and displayed with the `os.getpid` call. A subtle point: The `child` process function is also careful to exit explicitly with an `os._exit` call. We'll discuss this call in more detail later in this chapter, but if it's not made, the child process would live on after the `child` function returns (remember, it's just a copy of the original process). The net effect is that the child would go back to the loop in `parent` and start forking children of its own (i.e., the parent would have grandchildren). If you delete the exit call and rerun, you'll likely have to type more than one "q" to stop, because multiple processes are running in the `parent` function.

In Example 3-1, each process exits very soon after it starts, so there's little overlap in time. Let's do something slightly more sophisticated to better illustrate multiple forked processes running in parallel. Example 3-2 starts up 10 copies of itself, each copy counting up to 10 with a one-second delay between iterations. The `time.sleep` built-in call simply pauses the calling process for a number of seconds (pass a floating-point value to pause for fractions of seconds).

Example 3-2. PP2E\System\Processes\fork-count.py

```
############################################################
# fork basics: start 10 copies of this program running in
# parallel with the original; each copy counts up to 10
# on the same stdout stream--forks copy process memory,
# including file descriptors; fork doesn't currently work
# on Windows: use os.spawnv to start programs on Windows
# instead; spawnv is roughly like a fork+exec combination;
############################################################

import os, time

def counter(count):
    for i in range(count):
        time.sleep(1)
        print '[%s] => %s' % (os.getpid(), i)

for i in range(10):
    pid = os.fork()
    if pid != 0:
        print 'Process %d spawned' % pid
    else:
        counter(10)
        os._exit(0)

print 'Main process exiting.'
```

When run, this script starts 10 processes immediately and exits. All 10 forked processes check in with their first count display one second later, and every second thereafter. Child processes continue to run, even if the parent process that created them terminates:

```
mark@toy]$ python fork-count.py
Process 846 spawned
Process 847 spawned
Process 848 spawned
Process 849 spawned
Process 850 spawned
Process 851 spawned
Process 852 spawned
Process 853 spawned
Process 854 spawned
Process 855 spawned
Main process exiting.
[mark@toy]$
[846] => 0
[847] => 0
[848] => 0
[849] => 0
[850] => 0
[851] => 0
[852] => 0
[853] => 0
[854] => 0
[855] => 0
[847] => 1
[846] => 1
...more output deleted...
```

The output of all these processes shows up on the same screen, because they all share the standard output stream. Technically, a forked process gets a copy of the original process's global memory, including open file descriptors. Because of that, global objects like files start out with the same values in a child process. But it's important to remember that global memory is copied, not shared—if a child process changes a global object, it changes its own copy only. (As we'll see, this works differently in threads, the topic of the next section.)

The fork/exec Combination

Examples 3-1 and 3-2 child processes simply ran a function within the Python program and exited. On Unix-like platforms, forks are often the basis of starting independently running programs that are completely different from the program that performed the `fork` call. For instance, Example 3-3 forks new processes until we type "q" again, but child processes run a brand new program instead of calling a function in the same file.

Example 3-3. PP2E\System\Processes\fork-exec.py

```
# starts programs until you type 'q'

import os

parm = 0
while 1:
    parm = parm+1
    pid = os.fork()
    if pid == 0:                                         # copy process
        os.execlp('python', 'python', 'child.py', str(parm)) # overlay program
        assert 0, 'error starting program'              # shouldn't return
    else:
        print 'Child is', pid
        if raw_input() == 'q': break
```

If you've done much Unix development, the fork/exec combination will probably look familiar. The main thing to notice is the os.execlp call in this code. In a nutshell, this call *overlays* (i.e., replaces) the program running in the current process with another program. Because of that, the *combination* of os.fork and os.execlp means start a new process, and run a new program in that process—in other words, launch a new program in parallel with the original program.

os.exec call formats

The arguments to os.execlp specify the program to be run by giving command-line arguments used to start the program (i.e., what Python scripts know as sys.argv). If successful, the new program begins running and the call to os.execlp itself never returns (since the original program has been replaced, there's really nothing to return to). If the call does return, an error has occurred, so we code an assert after it that will always raise an exception if reached.

There are a handful of os.exec variants in the Python standard library; some allow us to configure environment variables for the new program, pass command-line arguments in different forms, and so on. All are available on both Unix and Windows, and replace the calling program (i.e., the Python interpreter). exec comes in eight flavors, which can be a bit confusing unless you generalize:

os.execv(*program, commandlinesequence*)
> The basic "v" exec form is passed an executable program's name, along with a list or tuple of command-line argument strings used to run the executable (that is, the words you would normally type in a shell to start a program).

os.execl(*program, cmdarg1, cmdarg2, ... cmdargN*)
> The basic "l" exec form is passed an executable's name, followed by one or more command-line arguments passed as individual function arguments. This is the same as os.execv(*program, (cmdarg1, cmdarg2, ...)*).

os.execlp, os.execvp

> Adding a "p" to the execv and execl names means that Python will locate the executable's directory using your system search-path setting (i.e., PATH).

os.execle, os.execve

> Adding an "e" to the execv and execl names means an extra, *last* argument is a dictionary containing shell environment variables to send to the program.

os.execvpe, os.execlpe

> Adding both "p" and "e" to the basic exec names means to use the search-path, *and* accept a shell environment settings dictionary.

So, when the script in Example 3-3 calls os.execlp, individually passed parameters specify a command line for the program to be run on, and the word "python" maps to an executable file according to the underlying system search-path setting ($PATH). It's as if we were running a command of the form python child.py 1 in a shell, but with a different command-line argument on the end each time.

Spawned child program

Just as when typed at a shell, the string of arguments passed to os.execlp by the fork-exec script in Example 3-3 starts another Python program file, shown in Example 3-4.

Example 3-4. PP2E\System\Processes\child.py

```
import os, sys
print 'Hello from child', os.getpid(), sys.argv[1]
```

Here is this code in action on Linux. It doesn't look much different from the original *fork1.py*, but it's really running a new *program* in each forked process. The more observant readers may notice that the child process ID displayed is the same in the parent program and the launched *child.py* program—os.execlp simply overlays a program in the same process:

```
[mark@toy]$ python fork-exec.py
Child is 1094
Hello from child 1094 1

Child is 1095
Hello from child 1095 2

Child is 1096
Hello from child 1096 3
q
```

There are other ways to start up programs in Python, including the os.system and os.popen we met in Chapter 2, *System Tools* (to start shell command lines), and the os.spawnv call we'll meet later in this chapter (to start independent programs on Windows); we further explore such process-related topics in more detail later in this chapter. We'll also discuss additional process topics in later chapters of this book. For instance, forks are revisited in Chapter 10, *Network Scripting*, to deal with "zombies"—dead processes lurking in system tables after their demise.

Threads

Threads are another way to start activities running at the same time. They sometimes are called "lightweight processes," and they are run in parallel like forked processes, but all run within the same single process. For applications that can benefit from parallel processing, threads offer big advantages for programmers:

Performance
> Because all threads run within the same process, they don't generally incur a big startup cost to copy the process itself. The costs of both copying forked processes and running threads can vary per platform, but threads are usually considered less expensive in terms of performance overhead.

Simplicity
> Threads can be noticeably simpler to program too, especially when some of the more complex aspects of processes enter the picture (e.g., process exits, communication schemes, and "zombie" processes covered in Chapter 10).

Shared global memory
> Also because threads run in a single process, every thread shares the same global memory space of the process. This provides a natural and easy way for threads to communicate—by fetching and setting data in global memory. To the Python programmer, this means that global (module-level) variables and interpreter components are shared among all threads in a program: if one thread assigns a global variable, its new value will be seen by other threads. Some care must be taken to control access to shared global objects, but they are still generally simpler to use than the sorts of process communication tools necessary for forked processes we'll meet later in this chapter (e.g., pipes, streams, signals, etc.).

Portability
> Perhaps most importantly, threads are more portable than forked processes. At this writing, the `os.fork` is not supported on Windows at all, but threads are. If you want to run parallel tasks portably in a Python script today, threads are likely your best bet. Python's thread tools automatically account for any platform-specific thread differences, and provide a consistent interface across all operating systems.

Using threads is surprisingly easy in Python. In fact, when a program is started it is already running a thread—usually called the "main thread" of the process. To start new, independent threads of execution within a process, we either use the Python `thread` module to run a function call in a spawned thread, or the Python `threading` module to manage threads with high-level objects. Both modules also provide tools for synchronizing access to shared objects with locks.

The thread Module

Since the basic `thread` module is a bit simpler than the more advanced threading module covered later in this section, let's look at some of its interfaces first. This module provides a *portable* interface to whatever threading system is available in your platform: its interfaces work the same on Windows, Solaris, SGI, and any system with an installed "pthreads" POSIX threads implementation (including Linux). Python scripts that use the Python thread module work on all of these platforms without changing their source code.

Let's start off by experimenting with a script that demonstrates the main thread interfaces. The script in Example 3-5 spawns threads until you reply with a "q" at the console; it's similar in spirit to (and a bit simpler than) the script in Example 3-1, but goes parallel with threads, not forks.

Example 3-5. PP2E\System\Threads\thread1.py

```
# spawn threads until you type 'q'

import thread

def child(tid):
    print 'Hello from thread', tid

def parent():
    i = 0
    while 1:
        i = i+1
        thread.start_new(child, (i,))
        if raw_input() == 'q': break

parent()
```

There are really only two thread-specific lines in this script: the import of the `thread` module, and the thread creation call. To start a thread, we simply call the `thread.start_new` function, no matter what platform we're programming on.[*] This call takes a function object and an arguments tuple, and starts a new thread to execute a call to the passed function with the passed arguments. It's almost like the built-in `apply` function (and like `apply`, also accepts an optional keyword

---

[*] This call is also available as `thread.start_new_thread`, for historical reasons. It's possible that one of the two names for the same function may become deprecated in future Python releases, but both appear in this text's examples.

arguments dictionary), but in this case, the function call begins running in parallel with the rest of the program.

Operationally speaking, the `thread.start_new` call itself returns immediately with no useful value, and the thread it spawns silently exits when the function being run returns (the return value of the threaded function call is simply ignored). Moreover, if a function run in a thread raises an uncaught exception, a stack trace is printed and the thread exits, but the rest of the program continues.

In practice, though, it's almost trivial to use threads in a Python script. Let's run this program to launch a few threads; it can be run on both Linux and Windows this time, because threads are more portable than process forks:

```
C:\...\PP2E\System\Threads>python thread1.py
Hello from thread 1

Hello from thread 2

Hello from thread 3

Hello from thread 4
q
```

Each message here is printed from a new thread, which exits almost as soon as it is started. To really understand the power of threads running in parallel, we have to do something more long-lived in our threads. The good news is that threads are both easy and fun to play with in Python. Let's mutate the **fork-count** program of the prior section to use threads. The script in Example 3-6 starts 10 copies of its **counter** running in parallel threads.

Example 3-6. PP2E\System\Threads\thread-count.py

```python
##################################################
# thread basics: start 10 copies of a function
# running in parallel; uses time.sleep so that
# main thread doesn't die too early--this kills
# all other threads on both Windows and Linux;
# stdout shared: thread outputs may be intermixed
##################################################

import thread, time

def counter(myId, count):                 # this function runs in threads
    for i in range(count):
        #time.sleep(1)
        print '[%s] => %s' % (myId, i)

for i in range(10):                        # spawn 10 threads
    thread.start_new(counter, (i, 3))      # each thread loops 3 times

time.sleep(4)
print 'Main thread exiting.'               # don't exit too early
```

Each parallel copy of the `counter` function simply counts from zero up to two here. When run on Windows, all 10 threads run at the same time, so their output is intermixed on the standard output stream:

```
C:\...\PP2E\System\Threads>python thread-count.py
...some lines deleted...
  [5] => 0
  [6] => 0
  [7] => 0
  [8] => 0
  [9] => 0
  [3] => 1
  [4] => 1
  [1] => 0
  [5] => 1
  [6] => 1
  [7] => 1
  [8] => 1
  [9] => 1
  [3] => 2
  [4] => 2
  [1] => 1
  [5] => 2
  [6] => 2
  [7] => 2
  [8] => 2
  [9] => 2
  [1] => 2
Main thread exiting.
```

In fact, these threads' output is mixed arbitrarily, at least on Windows—it may even be in a *different* order each time you run this script. Because all 10 threads run as independent entities, the exact ordering of their overlap in time depends on nearly random system state at large at the time they are run.

If you care to make this output a bit more coherent, uncomment (that is, remove the `#` before) the `time.sleep(1)` call in the `counter` function and rerun the script. If you do, each of the 10 threads now pauses for one second before printing its current count value. Because of the pause, all threads check in at the same time with the same count; you'll actually have a one-second delay before each batch of 10 output lines appears:

```
C:\...\PP2E\System\Threads>python thread-count.py
...some lines deleted...
  [7] => 0
  [6] => 0                                 pause...
  [0] => 1
  [1] => 1
  [2] => 1
  [3] => 1
```

```
 [5] => 1
 [7] => 1
 [8] => 1
 [9] => 1
 [4] => 1
 [6] => 1                              pause...
 [0] => 2
 [1] => 2
 [2] => 2
 [3] => 2
 [5] => 2
 [9] => 2
 [7] => 2
 [6] => 2
 [8] => 2
 [4] => 2
Main thread exiting.
```

Even with the sleep synchronization active, though, there's no telling in what order the threads will print their current count. It's random on purpose—the whole point of starting threads is to get work done independently, in parallel.

Notice that this script sleeps for four seconds at the end. It turns out that, at least on my Windows and Linux installs, the main thread cannot exit while any spawned threads are running; if it does, all spawned threads are immediately terminated. Without the sleep here, the spawned threads would die almost immediately after they are started. This may seem ad hoc, but isn't required on all platforms, and programs are usually structured such that the main thread naturally lives as long as the threads it starts. For instance, a user interface may start an FTP download running in a thread, but the download lives a much shorter life than the user interface itself. Later in this section, we'll see different ways to avoid this sleep with global flags, and will also meet a "join" utility in a different module that lets us wait for spawned threads to finish explicitly.

Synchronizing access to global objects

One of the nice things about threads is that they automatically come with a cross-task communications mechanism: *shared global memory*. For instance, because every thread runs in the same process, if one Python thread changes a global variable, the change can be seen by every other thread in the process, main or child. This serves as a simple way for a program's threads to pass information back and forth to each other—exit flags, result objects, event indicators, and so on.

The downside to this scheme is that our threads must sometimes be careful to avoid changing global objects at the same time—if two threads change an object at once, it's not impossible that one of the two changes will be lost (or worse, will corrupt the state of the shared object completely). The extent to which this becomes an issue varies per application, and is sometimes a nonissue altogether.

But even things that aren't obviously at risk may be at risk. Files and streams, for example, are shared by all threads in a program; if multiple threads write to one stream at the same time, the stream might wind up with interleaved, garbled data. Here's an example: if you edit Example 3-6, comment-out the sleep call in `counter`, and increase the per-thread `count` parameter from 3 to 100, you might occasionally see the same strange results on Windows that I did:

```
C:\...\PP2E\System\Threads\>python thread-count.py | more
...more deleted...
[5] => 14
[7] => 14
[9] => 14
[3] => 15
[5] => 15
[7] => 15
[9] => 15
[3] => 16 [5] => 16 [7] => 16 [9] => 16


[3] => 17
[5] => 17
[7] => 17
[9] => 17
...more deleted...
```

Because all 10 threads are trying to write to `stdout` at the same time, once in a while the output of more than one thread winds up on the same line. Such an oddity in this script isn't exactly going to crash the Mars Lander, but it's indicative of the sorts of clashes in time that can occur when our programs go parallel. To be robust, thread programs need to control access to shared global items like this such that only one thread uses it at once.[*]

Luckily, Python's `thread` module comes with its own easy-to-use tools for synchronizing access to shared objects among threads. These tools are based on the concept of a *lock*—to change a shared object, threads *acquire* a lock, make their changes, and then *release* the lock for other threads to grab. Lock objects are allocated and processed with simple and portable calls in the `thread` module, and are automatically mapped to thread locking mechanisms on the underlying platform.

---

[*] For a more detailed explanation of this phenomenon, see upcoming sidebar "The Global Interpreter Lock and Threads."

For instance, in Example 3-7, a lock object created by `thread.allocate_lock` is acquired and released by each thread around the `print` statement that writes to the shared standard output stream.

Example 3-7. PP2E\System\Threads\thread-count-mutex.py

```
#################################################
# synchronize access to stdout: because it is
# shared global, thread outputs may be intermixed
#################################################

import thread, time

def counter(myId, count):
    for i in range(count):
        mutex.acquire()
        #time.sleep(1)
        print '[%s] => %s' % (myId, i)
        mutex.release()

mutex = thread.allocate_lock()
for i in range(10):
    thread.start_new_thread(counter, (i, 3))

time.sleep(6)
print 'Main thread exiting.'
```

Python guarantees that only one thread can acquire a lock at any given time; all other threads that request the lock are blocked until a release call makes it available for acquisition. The net effect of the additional lock calls in this script is that no two threads will ever execute a `print` statement at the same point in time—the lock ensures *mutually exclusive* access to the `stdout` stream. Hence, the output of this script is the same as the original *thread_count.py*, except that standard output text is never munged by overlapping prints.

Incidentally, uncommenting the `time.sleep` call in this version's `counter` function makes each output line show up one second apart. Because the sleep occurs while a thread holds the lock, all other threads are blocked while the lock holder sleeps. One thread grabs the lock, sleeps one second and prints; another thread grabs, sleeps, and prints, and so on. Given 10 threads counting up to 3, the program as a whole takes 30 seconds (10 × 3) to finish, with one line appearing per second. Of course, that assumes that the main thread sleeps at least that long too; to see how to remove this assumption, we need to move on to the next section.

The Global Interpreter Lock and Threads

Strictly speaking, Python currently uses a *global interpreter lock* mechanism, which guarantees that at most one thread is running code within the Python interpreter at any given point in time. In addition, to make sure that each thread gets a chance to run, the interpreter automatically switches its attention between threads at regular intervals (by releasing and acquiring the lock after a number of bytecode instructions), as well as at the start of long-running operations (e.g., on file input/output requests).

This scheme avoids problems that could arise if multiple threads were to update Python system data at the same time. For instance, if two threads were allowed to simultaneously change an object's reference count, the result may be unpredictable. This scheme can also have subtle consequences. In this chapter's threading examples, for instance, the `stdout` stream is likely corrupted only because each thread's call to write text is a long-running operation that triggers a thread switch within the interpreter. Other threads are then allowed to run and make write requests while a prior write is in progress.

Moreover, even though the global interpreter lock prevents more than one Python thread from running at the same time, it is not enough to ensure thread safety in general, and does not address higher-level synchronization issues at all. For example, if more than one thread might attempt to *update* the same variable at the same time, they should generally be given exclusive access to the object with locks. Otherwise, it's not impossible that thread switches will occur in the middle of an update statement's bytecode. Consider this code:

```
import thread, time
count = 0

def adder():
    global count
    count = count + 1      # concurrently update a shared global
    count = count + 1      # thread swapped out in the middle of this

for i in range(100):
    thread.start_new(adder, ())   # start 100 update threads
time.sleep(5)
print count
```

As is, this code fails on Windows due to the way its threads are interleaved (you get a different result each time, not 200), but works if lock acquire/release calls are inserted around the addition statements. Locks are not strictly required for all shared object access, especially if a single thread updates an object inspected by other threads. As a rule of thumb, though, you should generally use locks to synchronize threads whenever update rendezvous are possible, rather than relying on the current thread implementation.

—Continued—

Interestingly, the above code also works if the thread-switch check interval is made high enough to allow each thread to finish without being swapped out. The `sys.setcheckinterval(N)` call sets the frequency with which the interpreter checks for things like thread switches and signal handlers. This interval defaults to 10, the number of bytecode instructions before a switch; it does not need to be reset for most programs, but can be used to tune thread performance. Setting higher values means that switches happen less often: threads incur less overhead, but are less responsive to events.

If you plan on mixing Python with C, also see the thread interfaces described in the Python/C API standard manual. In threaded programs, C extensions must release and reacquire the global interpreter lock around long-running operations, to let other Python threads run.

Waiting for spawned thread exits

Thread module locks are surprisingly useful. They can form the basis of higher-level synchronization paradigms (e.g., semaphores), and can be used as general thread communication devices.* For example, Example 3-8 uses a global list of locks to know when all child threads have finished.

Example 3-8. PP2E\System\Threads\thread-count-wait1.py

```
###################################################
# uses mutexes to know when threads are done
# in parent/main thread, instead of time.sleep;
# lock stdout to avoid multiple prints on 1 line;
###################################################

import thread

def counter(myId, count):
    for i in range(count):
        stdoutmutex.acquire()
        print '[%s] => %s' % (myId, i)
        stdoutmutex.release()
    exitmutexes[myId].acquire()  # signal main thread

stdoutmutex = thread.allocate_lock()
exitmutexes = []
for i in range(10):
    exitmutexes.append(thread.allocate_lock())
    thread.start_new(counter, (i, 100))
```

---

* They cannot, however, be used to directly synchronize processes. Since processes are more independent, they usually require locking mechanisms that are more long-lived and external to programs. In Chapter 14, *Larger Web Site Examples II*, we'll meet a `fcntl.flock` library call that allows scripts to lock and unlock files, and so is ideal as a cross-process locking tool.

Example 3-8. PP2E\System\Threads\thread-count-wait1.py (continued)

```
for mutex in exitmutexes:
    while not mutex.locked(): pass
print 'Main thread exiting.'
```

A lock's `locked` method can be used to check its state. To make this work, the main thread makes one lock per child, and tacks them onto a global `exitmutexes` list (remember, the threaded function shares global scope with the main thread). On exit, each thread acquires its lock on the list, and the main thread simply watches for all locks to be acquired. This is much more accurate than naively sleeping while child threads run, in hopes that all will have exited after the sleep.

But wait—it gets even simpler: since threads share global memory anyhow, we can achieve the same effect with a simple global list of *integers*, not locks. In Example 3-9, the module's namespace (scope) is shared by top-level code and the threaded function as before—name `exitmutexes` refers to the same list object in the main thread and all threads it spawns. Because of that, changes made in a thread are still noticed in the main thread without resorting to extra locks.

Example 3-9. PP2E\System\Threads\thread-count-wait2.py

```
##################################################
# uses simple shared global data (not mutexes) to
# know when threads are done in parent/main thread;
##################################################

import thread
stdoutmutex = thread.allocate_lock()
exitmutexes = [0] * 10

def counter(myId, count):
    for i in range(count):
        stdoutmutex.acquire()
        print '[%s] => %s' % (myId, i)
        stdoutmutex.release()
    exitmutexes[myId] = 1  # signal main thread

for i in range(10):
    thread.start_new(counter, (i, 100))

while 0 in exitmutexes: pass
print 'Main thread exiting.'
```

The main threads of both of the last two scripts fall into busy-wait loops at the end, which might become significant performance drains in tight applications. If so, simply add a `time.sleep` call in the wait loops to insert a pause between end tests and free up the CPU for other tasks. Even threads must be good citizens.

Both of the last two counting thread scripts produce roughly the same output as the original *thread_count.py*—albeit, without **stdout** corruption, and with different random ordering of output lines. The main difference is that the main thread exits immediately after (and no sooner than!) the spawned child threads:

```
C:\...\PP2E\System\Threads>python thread-count-wait2.py
...more deleted...
[2] => 98
[6] => 97
[0] => 99
[7] => 97
[3] => 98
[8] => 97
[9] => 97
[1] => 99
[4] => 98
[5] => 98
[2] => 99
[6] => 98
[7] => 98
[3] => 99
[8] => 98
[9] => 98
[4] => 99
[5] => 99
[6] => 99
[7] => 99
[8] => 99
[9] => 99
Main thread exiting.
```

Of course, threads are for much more than counting. We'll put shared global data like this to more practical use in a later chapter, to serve as *completion signals* from child processing threads transferring data over a network, to a main thread controlling a Tkinter GUI user interface display (see "The PyMailGui Email Client" in Chapter 11, *Client-Side Scripting*).

The threading Module

The standard Python library comes with two thread modules—thread, the basic lower-level interface illustrated thus far, and threading, a higher-level interface based on objects. The threading module internally uses the thread module to implement objects that represent threads and common synchronization tools. It is loosely based on a subset of the Java language's threading model, but differs in ways that only Java programmers would notice.* Example 3-10 morphs our counting threads example one last time to demonstrate this new module's interfaces.

---

* But in case this means you: Python's lock and condition variables are distinct objects, not something inherent in all objects, and Python's Thread class doesn't have all the features of Java's. See Python's library manual for further details.

Example 3-10. PP2E\System\Threads\thread-classes.py

```
#####################################################
# uses higher-level java like threading module object
# join method (not mutexes or shared global vars) to
# know when threads are done in parent/main thread;
# see library manual for more details on threading;
#####################################################

import threading

class mythread(threading.Thread):        # subclass Thread object
    def __init__(self, myId, count):
        self.myId = myId
        self.count = count
        threading.Thread.__init__(self)
    def run(self):                       # run provides thread logic
        for i in range(self.count):      # still synch stdout access
            stdoutmutex.acquire()
            print '[%s] => %s' % (self.myId, i)
            stdoutmutex.release()

stdoutmutex = threading.Lock()           # same as thread.allocate_lock()
threads = []
for i in range(10):
    thread = mythread(i, 100)            # make/start 10 threads
    thread.start()                       # start run method in a thread
    threads.append(thread)

for thread in threads:
    thread.join()                        # wait for thread exits
print 'Main thread exiting.'
```

The output of this script is the same as that shown for its ancestors earlier (again, randomly distributed). Using the **threading** module is largely a matter of special-izing classes. Threads in this module are implemented with a **Thread** object—a Python class which we customize per application by providing a **run** method that defines the thread's action. For example, this script subclasses **Thread** with its own **mythread** class; **mythread**'s **run** method is what will be executed by the **Thread** framework when we make a **mythread** and call its **start** method.

In other words, this script simply provides methods expected by the **Thread** frame-work. The advantage of going this more coding-intensive route is that we get a set of additional thread-related tools from the framework "for free." The **Thread.join** method used near the end of this script, for instance, waits until the thread exits (by default); we can use this method to prevent the main thread from exiting too early, rather than the **time.sleep** calls and global locks and variables we relied on in earlier threading examples.

The example script also uses **threading.Lock** to synchronize stream access (though this name is just a synonym for **thread.allocate_lock** in the current implementation). Besides **Thread** and **Lock**, the **threading** module also includes higher-level objects for synchronizing access to shared items (e.g., `Semaphore`, `Condition`, `Event`), and more; see the library manual for details. For more examples of threads and forks in general, see the following section and the examples in Part III, *Internet Scripting*.

Program Exits

As we've seen, unlike C there is no "main" function in Python—when we run a program, we simply execute all the code in the top-level file, from top to bottom (i.e., in the filename we listed in the command line, clicked in a file explorer, and so on). Scripts normally exit when Python falls off the end of the file, but we may also call for program exit explicitly with the built-in `sys.exit` function:

```
>>> sys.exit()          # else exits on end of script
```

Interestingly, this call really just raises the built-in `SystemExit` exception. Because of this, we can catch it as usual to intercept early exits and perform cleanup activities; if uncaught, the interpreter exits as usual. For instance:

```
C:\...\PP2E\System>python
>>> import sys
>>> try:
...     sys.exit()              # see also: os._exit, Tk().quit()
... except SystemExit:
...     print 'ignoring exit'
...
ignoring exit
>>>
```

In fact, explicitly raising the built-in `SystemExit` exception with a Python `raise` statement is equivalent to calling `sys.exit`. More realistically, a `try` block would catch the exit exception raised elsewhere in a program; the script in Example 3-11 exits from within a processing function.

Example 3-11. PP2E\System\Exits\testexit_sys.py

```
def later():
    import sys
    print 'Bye sys world'
    sys.exit(42)
    print 'Never reached'

if __name__ == '__main__': later()
```

Running this program as a script causes it to exit before the interpreter falls off the end of the file. But because `sys.exit` raises a Python exception, importers of its function can trap and override its exit exception, or specify a `finally` cleanup block to be run during program exit processing:

```
C:\...\PP2E\System\Exits>python testexit_sys.py
Bye sys world
```

```
C:\...\PP2E\System\Exits>python
>>> from testexit_sys import later
>>> try:
...     later()
... except SystemExit:
...     print 'Ignored...'
...
Bye sys world
Ignored...
>>> try:
...     later()
... finally:
...     print 'Cleanup'
...
Bye sys world
Cleanup

C:\...\PP2E\System\Exits>
```

os Module Exits

It's possible to exit Python in other ways too. For instance, within a forked child process on Unix we typically call the os._exit function instead of sys.exit, threads may exit with a thread.exit call, and Tkinter GUI applications often end by calling something named Tk().quit(). We'll meet the Tkinter module later in this book, but os and thread exits merit a look here. When os._exit is called, the calling process exits immediately rather than raising an exception that could be trapped and ignored, as shown in Example 3-12.

Example 3-12. PP2E\System\Exits\testexit_os.py

```
def outahere():
    import os
    print 'Bye os world'
    os._exit(99)
    print 'Never reached'

if __name__ == '__main__': outahere()
```

Unlike sys.exit, os._exit is immune to both try/except and try/finally interception:

```
C:\...\PP2E\System\Exits>python testexit_os.py
Bye os world

C:\...\PP2E\System\Exits>python
>>> from testexit_os import outahere
>>> try:
...     outahere()
... except:
...     print 'Ignored'
...
Bye os world
```

```
C:\...\PP2E\System\Exits>python
>>> from testexit_os import outahere
>>> try:
...        outahere()
... finally:
...        print 'Cleanup'
...
Bye os world
```

Exit Status Codes

Both the sys and os exit calls we just met accept an argument that denotes the exit status code of the process (it's optional in the sys call, but required by os). After exit, this code may be interrogated in shells, and by programs that ran the script as a child process. On Linux, we ask for the "status" shell variable's value to fetch the last program's exit status; by convention a nonzero status generally indicates some sort of problem occurred:

```
[mark@toy]$ python testexit_sys.py
Bye sys world
[mark@toy]$ echo $status
42
[mark@toy]$ python testexit_os.py
Bye os world
[mark@toy]$ echo $status
99
```

In a chain of command-line programs, exit statuses could be checked along the way as a simple form of cross-program communication. We can also grab hold of the exit status of a program run by another script. When launching shell commands, it's provided as the return value of an os.system call, and the return value of the close method of an os.popen object; when forking programs, the exit status is available through the os.wait and os.waitpid calls in a parent process. Let's look at the shell commands case first:

```
[mark@toy]$ python
>>> import os
>>> pipe = os.popen('python testexit_sys.py')
>>> pipe.read()
'Bye sys world\012'
>>> stat = pipe.close()              # returns exit code
>>> stat
10752
>>> hex(stat)
'0x2a00'
>>> stat >> 8
42

>>> pipe = os.popen('python testexit_os.py')
>>> stat = pipe.close()
>>> stat, stat >> 8
(25344, 99)
```

When using `os.popen`, the exit status is actually packed into specific bit positions of the return value, for reasons we won't go into here; it's really there, but we need to shift the result right by eight bits to see it. Commands run with `os.system` send their statuses back through the Python library call:

```
>>> import os
>>> for prog in ('testexit_sys.py', 'testexit_os.py'):
...     stat = os.system('python ' + prog)
...     print prog, stat, stat >> 8
...
Bye sys world
testexit_sys.py 10752 42
Bye os world
testexit_os.py 25344 99
```

Unfortunately, neither the `popen` nor `system` interfaces for fetching exit statuses worked reliably on Windows as I wrote this. Moreover, `fork` isn't supported at all, and `popen` in Python 1.5.2 and earlier fails in applications that create windows (though it works in code run from DOS console command lines, and works better in general in 2.0). On Windows:

```
>>> import os
>>> stat = os.system('python testexit_sys.py')
Bye sys world
>>> print stat
0
>>> pipe = os.popen('python testexit_sys.py')
>>> print pipe.read(),
Bye sys world
>>> print pipe.close()
None
>>> os.fork
Traceback (innermost last):
  File "<stdin>", line 1, in ?
AttributeError: fork
```

For now, you may need to utilize Windows-specific tools to accomplish such goals (e.g., `os.spawnv`, and running a DOS *start* command with `os.system`; see later in this chapter). Be sure to watch for changes on this front, though; Python 2.0 fixes Windows `popen` problems, and ActiveState, a company that created a `fork` call for Perl on Windows, has begun focusing on Python tools development.

To learn how to get the exit status from forked processes, let's write a simple forking program: the script in Example 3-13 forks child processes and prints child process exit statuses returned by `os.wait` calls in the parent, until a "q" is typed at the console.

Example 3-13. PP2E\System\Exits\testexit_fork.py

```
############################################################
# fork child processes to watch exit status with os.wait;
# fork works on Linux but not Windows as of Python 1.5.2;
# note: spawned threads share globals, but each forked
# process has its own copy of them--exitstat always the
# same here but will vary if we start threads instead;
############################################################

import os
exitstat = 0

def child():                           # could os.exit a script here
    global exitstat                    # change this process's global
    exitstat = exitstat + 1            # exit status to parent's wait
    print 'Hello from child', os.getpid(), exitstat
    os._exit(exitstat)
    print 'never reached'

def parent():
    while 1:
        newpid = os.fork()             # start a new copy of process
        if newpid == 0:                # if in copy, run child logic
            child()                    # loop until 'q' console input
        else:
            pid, status = os.wait()
            print 'Parent got', pid, status, (status >> 8)
            if raw_input() == 'q': break

parent()
```

Running this program on Linux (remember, `fork` also didn't work on Windows as I wrote the second edition of this book) produces the following results:

```
[mark@toy]$ python testexit_fork.py
Hello from child 723 1
Parent got 723 256 1

Hello from child 724 1
Parent got 724 256 1

Hello from child 725 1
Parent got 725 256 1
q
```

If you study this output closely, you'll notice that the exit status (the last number printed) is always the same—the number 1. Because forked processes begin life as *copies* of the process that created them, they also have copies of global memory. Because of that, each forked child gets and changes its own `exitstat` global variable, without changing any other process's copy of this variable.

Thread Exits

In contrast, threads run in parallel within the *same* process and share global memory. Each thread in Example 3-14 changes the single shared global variable `exitstat`.

Example 3-14. PP2E\System\Exits\testexit_thread.py

```
###########################################################
# spawn threads to watch shared global memory change;
# threads normally exit when the function they run returns,
# but thread.exit() can be called to exit calling thread;
# thread.exit is the same as sys.exit and raising SystemExit;
# threads communicate with possibly locked global vars;
###########################################################

import thread
exitstat = 0

def child():
    global exitstat
    exitstat = exitstat + 1                  # process global names
    threadid = thread.get_ident()            # shared by all threads
    print 'Hello from child', threadid, exitstat
    thread.exit()
    print 'never reached'

def parent():
    while 1:
        thread.start_new_thread(child, ())
        if raw_input() == 'q': break

parent()
```

Here is this script in action on Linux; the global `exitstat` is changed by each thread, because threads share global memory within the process. In fact, this is often how threads communicate in general—rather than exit status codes, threads assign module-level globals to signal conditions (and use `thread` module locks to synchronize access to shared globals if needed):

```
[mark@toy]$ /usr/bin/python testexit_thread.py
Hello from child 1026 1

Hello from child 2050 2

Hello from child 3074 3
q
```

Unlike forks, threads run on Windows today too; this program works the same there, but thread identifiers differ—they are arbitrary but unique among active threads, and so may be used as dictionary keys to keep per-thread information:

```
C:\...\PP2E\System\Exits>python testexit_thread.py
Hello from child -587879 1
```

```
Hello from child -587879 2

Hello from child -587879 3
q
```

Speaking of exits, a thread normally exits silently when the function it runs returns, and the function return value is ignored. Optionally, the `thread.exit` function can be called to terminate the calling thread explicitly. This call works almost exactly like `sys.exit` (but takes no return status argument), and works by raising a `SystemExit` exception in the calling thread. Because of that, a thread can also prematurely end by calling `sys.exit`, or directly raising `SystemExit`. Be sure to not call `os._exit` within a thread function, though—doing so hangs the entire process on my Linux system, and kills every thread in the process on Windows!

When used well, exit status can be used to implement error-detection and simple communication protocols in systems composed of command-line scripts. But having said that, I should underscore that most scripts do simply fall off the end of the source to exit, and most thread functions simply return; explicit exit calls are generally employed for exceptional conditions only.

Interprocess Communication

As we saw earlier, when scripts spawn *threads*—tasks that run in parallel within the program—they can naturally communicate by changing and inspecting shared global memory. As we also saw, some care must be taken to use locks to synchronize access to shared objects that can't be updated concurrently, but it's a fairly straightforward communication model.

Things aren't quite as simple when scripts start processes and programs. If we limit the kinds of communications that can happen between programs, there are many options available, most of which we've already seen in this and the prior chapters. For example, the following can all be interpreted as cross-program communication devices:

- Command-line arguments
- Standard stream redirections
- Pipes generated by `os.popen` calls
- Program exit status codes
- Shell environment variables
- Even simple files

For instance, sending command-line options and writing to input streams lets us pass in program execution parameters; reading program output streams and exit codes gives us a way to grab a result. Because shell variable settings are inherited by spawned programs, they provide another way to pass context in. Pipes made by os.popen and simple files allow even more dynamic communication—data can be sent between programs at arbitrary times, not only at program start and exit.

Beyond this set, there are other tools in the Python library for doing IPC—Inter-Process Communication. Some vary in portability, and all vary in complexity. For instance, in Chapter 10 of this text we will meet the Python socket module, which lets us transfer data between programs running on the same computer, as well as programs located on remote networked machines.

In this section, we introduce *pipes*—both anonymous and named—as well as *signals*—cross-program event triggers. Other IPC tools are available to Python programmers (e.g., shared memory; see module mmap), but not covered here for lack of space; search the Python manuals and web site for more details on other IPC schemes if you're looking for something more specific.

Pipes

Pipes, another cross-program communication device, are made available in Python with the built-in os.pipe call. Pipes are unidirectional channels that work something like a shared memory buffer, but with an interface resembling a simple file on each of two ends. In typical use, one program writes data on one end of the pipe, and another reads that data on the other end. Each program only sees its end of the pipes, and processes it using normal Python file calls.

Pipes are much more within the operating system, though. For instance, calls to read a pipe will normally block the caller until data becomes available (i.e., is sent by the program on the other end), rather than returning an end-of-file indicator. Because of such properties, pipes are also a way to synchronize the execution of independent programs.

Anonymous Pipe Basics

Pipes come in two flavors—*anonymous* and *named*. Named pipes (sometimes called "fifos") are represented by a file on your computer. Anonymous pipes only exist within processes, though, and are typically used in conjunction with process *forks* as a way to link parent and spawned child processes within an application—parent and child converse over shared pipe file descriptors. Because named pipes are really external files, the communicating processes need not be related at all (in fact, they can be independently started programs).

Since they are more traditional, let's start with a look at anonymous pipes. To illustrate, the script in Example 3-15 uses the os.fork call to make a copy of the calling process as usual (we met forks earlier in this chapter). After forking, the original parent process and its child copy speak through the two ends of a pipe created with os.pipe prior to the fork. The os.pipe call returns a tuple of two *file descriptors*—the low-level file identifiers we met earlier—representing the input and output sides of the pipe. Because forked child processes get *copies* of their parents' file descriptors, writing to the pipe's output descriptor in the child sends data back to the parent on the pipe created before the child was spawned.

Example 3-15. PP2E\System\Processes\pipe1.py

```
import os, time

def child(pipeout):
    zzz = 0
    while 1:
        time.sleep(zzz)                            # make parent wait
        os.write(pipeout, 'Spam %03d' % zzz)       # send to parent
        zzz = (zzz+1) % 5                           # goto 0 after 4

def parent():
    pipein, pipeout = os.pipe()                    # make 2-ended pipe
    if os.fork() == 0:                             # copy this process
        child(pipeout)                             # in copy, run child
    else:                                          # in parent, listen to pipe
        while 1:
            line = os.read(pipein, 32)             # blocks until data sent
            print 'Parent %d got "%s" at %s' % (os.getpid(), line, time.time())

parent()
```

If you run this program on Linux (`pipe` is available on Windows today, but `fork` is not), the parent process waits for the child to send data on the pipe each time it calls `os.read`. It's almost as if the child and parent act as client and server here— the parent starts the child and waits for it to initiate communication.[*] Just to tease, the child keeps the parent waiting one second longer between messages with `time.sleep` calls, until the delay has reached four seconds. When the `zzz` delay counter hits 005, it rolls back down to 000 and starts again:

```
[mark@toy]$ python pipe1.py
Parent 1292 got "Spam 000" at 968370008.322
Parent 1292 got "Spam 001" at 968370009.319
Parent 1292 got "Spam 002" at 968370011.319
Parent 1292 got "Spam 003" at 968370014.319
Parent 1292 got "Spam 004Spam 000" at 968370018.319
Parent 1292 got "Spam 001" at 968370019.319
Parent 1292 got "Spam 002" at 968370021.319
Parent 1292 got "Spam 003" at 968370024.319
Parent 1292 got "Spam 004Spam 000" at 968370028.319
```

---

[*] We will clarify the notions of "client" and "server" in Chapter 10. There, we'll communicate with *sockets* (which are very roughly like bidirectional pipes for networks), but the overall conversation model is similar. Named pipes (fifos), described later, are a better match to the client/server model, because they can be accessed by arbitrary, unrelated processes (no forks are required). But as we'll see, the socket port model is generally used by most Internet scripting protocols.

```
Parent 1292 got "Spam 001" at 968370029.319
Parent 1292 got "Spam 002" at 968370031.319
Parent 1292 got "Spam 003" at 968370034.319
```

If you look closely, you'll see that when the child's delay counter hits 004, the parent ends up reading two messages from the pipe *at once*—the child wrote two distinct messages, but they were close enough in time to be fetched as a single unit by the parent. Really, the parent blindly asks to read at most 32 bytes each time, but gets back whatever text is available in the pipe (when it becomes available at all). To distinguish messages better, we can mandate a separator character in the pipe. An end-of-line makes this easy, because we can wrap the pipe descriptor in a *file object* with os.fdopen, and rely on the file object's readline method to scan up through the next \n separator in the pipe. Example 3-16 implements this scheme.

Example 3-16. PP2E\System\Processes\pipe2.py

```
# same as pipe1.py, but wrap pipe input in stdio file object
# to read by line, and close unused pipe fds in both processes

import os, time

def child(pipeout):
    zzz = 0
    while 1:
        time.sleep(zzz)                          # make parent wait
        os.write(pipeout, 'Spam %03d\n' % zzz)   # send to parent
        zzz = (zzz+1) % 5                         # roll to 0 at 5

def parent():
    pipein, pipeout = os.pipe()                  # make 2-ended pipe
    if os.fork() == 0:                           # in child, write to pipe
        os.close(pipein)                         # close input side here
        child(pipeout)
    else:                                        # in parent, listen to pipe
        os.close(pipeout)                        # close output side here
        pipein = os.fdopen(pipein)               # make stdio input object
        while 1:
            line = pipein.readline()[:-1]        # blocks until data sent
            print 'Parent %d got "%s" at %s' % (os.getpid(), line, time.time())

parent()
```

This version has also been augmented to *close* the unused end of the pipe in each process (e.g., after the fork, the parent process closes its copy of the output side of the pipe written by the child); programs should close unused pipe ends in general. Running with this new version returns a single child message to the parent each time it reads from the pipe, because they are separated with markers when written:

```
[mark@toy]$ python pipe2.py
Parent 1296 got "Spam 000" at 968370066.162
Parent 1296 got "Spam 001" at 968370067.159
Parent 1296 got "Spam 002" at 968370069.159
```

```
Parent 1296 got "Spam 003" at 968370072.159
Parent 1296 got "Spam 004" at 968370076.159
Parent 1296 got "Spam 000" at 968370076.161
Parent 1296 got "Spam 001" at 968370077.159
Parent 1296 got "Spam 002" at 968370079.159
Parent 1296 got "Spam 003" at 968370082.159
Parent 1296 got "Spam 004" at 968370086.159
Parent 1296 got "Spam 000" at 968370086.161
Parent 1296 got "Spam 001" at 968370087.159
Parent 1296 got "Spam 002" at 968370089.159
```

Bidirectional IPC with Pipes

Pipes normally only let data flow in *one direction*—one side is input, one is output. What if you need your programs to talk back and forth, though? For example, one program might send another a request for information, and then wait for that information to be sent back. A single pipe can't generally handle such bidirectional conversations, but two pipes can—one pipe can be used to pass requests to a program, and another can be used to ship replies back to the requestor.[*]

The module in Example 3-17 demonstrates one way to apply this idea to link the input and output streams of two programs. Its **spawn** function forks a new child program, and connects the input and output streams of the parent to the output and input streams of the child. That is:

- When the parent reads from its standard input, it is reading text sent to the child's standard output.

- When the parent writes to its standard output, it is sending data to the child's standard input.

The net effect is that the two independent programs communicate by speaking over their standard streams.

Example 3-17. PP2E\System\Processes\pipes.py

```
#########################################################
# spawn a child process/program, connect my stdin/stdout
# to child process's stdout/stdin -- my reads and writes
# map to output and input streams of the spawned program;
# much like popen2.popen2 plus parent stream redirection;
#########################################################

import os, sys
```

---

[*] This really does have real-world applications. For instance, I once added a GUI interface to a command-line debugger for a C-like programming language by connecting two processes with pipes. The GUI ran as a separate process that constructed and sent commands to the existing debugger's input stream pipe and parsed the results that showed up in the debugger's output stream pipe. In effect, the GUI acted like a programmer typing commands at a keyboard. By spawning command-line programs with streams attached by pipes, systems can add new interfaces to legacy programs.

Example 3-17. PP2E\System\Processes\pipes.py (continued)

```
def spawn(prog, *args):                  # pass progname, cmdline args
    stdinFd  = sys.stdin.fileno()        # get descriptors for streams
    stdoutFd = sys.stdout.fileno()       # normally stdin=0, stdout=1

    parentStdin, childStdout  = os.pipe()   # make two ipc pipe channels
    childStdin,  parentStdout = os.pipe()   # pipe returns (inputfd, outoutfd)
    pid = os.fork()                         # make a copy of this process
    if pid:
        os.close(childStdout)            # in parent process after fork:
        os.close(childStdin)             # close child ends in parent
        os.dup2(parentStdin,  stdinFd)   # my sys.stdin copy  = pipe1[0]
        os.dup2(parentStdout, stdoutFd)  # my sys.stdout copy = pipe2[1]
    else:
        os.close(parentStdin)            # in child process after fork:
        os.close(parentStdout)           # close parent ends in child
        os.dup2(childStdin,  stdinFd)    # my sys.stdin copy  = pipe2[0]
        os.dup2(childStdout, stdoutFd)   # my sys.stdout copy = pipe1[1]
        args = (prog,) + args
        os.execvp(prog, args)            # new program in this process
        assert 0, 'execvp failed!'       # os.exec call never returns here

if __name__ == '__main__':
    mypid = os.getpid()
    spawn('python', 'pipes-testchild.py', 'spam')   # fork child program

    print 'Hello 1 from parent', mypid          # to child's stdin
    sys.stdout.flush()                           # subvert stdio buffering
    reply = raw_input()                          # from child's stdout
    sys.stderr.write('Parent got: "%s"\n' % reply)   # stderr not tied to pipe!

    print 'Hello 2 from parent', mypid
    sys.stdout.flush()
    reply = sys.stdin.readline()
    sys.stderr.write('Parent got: "%s"\n' % reply[:-1])
```

This **spawn** function in this module does not work on Windows—remember, **fork** isn't yet available there today. In fact, most of the calls in this module map straight to Unix system calls (and may be arbitrarily terrifying on first glance to non-Unix developers). We've already met some of these (e.g., **os.fork**), but much of this code depends on Unix concepts we don't have time to address well in this text. But in simple terms, here is a brief summary of the system calls demonstrated in this code:

- **os.fork** copies the calling process as usual, and returns the child's process ID in the parent process only.

- **os.execvp** overlays a new program in the calling process; it's just like the **os.execlp** used earlier but takes a *tuple* or *list* of command-line argument strings (collected with the ***args** form in the function header).

- `os.pipe` returns a tuple of file descriptors representing the input and output ends of a pipe, as in earlier examples.

- `os.close(fd)` closes descriptor-based file `fd`.

- `os.dup2(fd1,fd2)` copies all system information associated with the file named by file descriptor `fd1` to the file named by `fd2`.

In terms of connecting standard streams, `os.dup2` is the real nitty-gritty here. For example, the call `os.dup2(parentStdin,stdinFd)` essentially assigns the parent process's `stdin` file to the input end of one of the two pipes created; all `stdin` reads will henceforth come from the pipe. By connecting the other end of this pipe to the child process's copy of the `stdout` stream file with `os.dup2(childStdout,stdoutFd)`, text written by the child to its `sdtdout` winds up being routed through the pipe to the parent's `stdin` stream.

To test this utility, the self-test code at the end of the file spawns the program shown in Example 3-18 in a child process, and reads and writes standard streams to converse with it over two pipes.

Example 3-18. PP2E\System\Processes\pipes-testchild.py

```
import os, time, sys
mypid     = os.getpid()
parentpid = os.getppid()
sys.stderr.write('Child %d of %d got arg: %s\n' %
                                (mypid, parentpid, sys.argv[1]))
for i in range(2):
    time.sleep(3)             # make parent process wait by sleeping here
    input = raw_input()       # stdin tied to pipe: comes from parent's stdout
    time.sleep(3)
    reply = 'Child %d got: [%s]' % (mypid, input)
    print reply               # stdout tied to pipe: goes to parent's stdin
    sys.stdout.flush()        # make sure it's sent now else blocks
```

Here is our test in action on Linux; its output is not incredibly impressive to read, but represents two programs running independently and shipping data back and forth through a pipe device managed by the operating system. This is even more like a client/server model (if you imagine the child as the server). The text in square brackets in this output went from the parent process, to the child, and back to the parent again—all through pipes connected to standard streams:

```
[mark@toy]$ python pipes.py
Child 797 of 796 got arg: spam
Parent got: "Child 797 got: [Hello 1 from parent 796]"
Parent got: "Child 797 got: [Hello 2 from parent 796]"
```

Deadlocks, flushes, and unbuffered streams

These two processes engage in a simple dialog, but it's already enough to illustrate some of the dangers lurking in cross-program communications. First of all, notice that both programs need to write to `stderr` to display a message—their `stdout` streams are tied to the other program's input stream. Because processes share file descriptors, `stderr` is the same in both parent and child, so status messages show up in the same place.

More subtly, note that both parent and child call `sys.stdout.flush` after they print text to the `stdout` stream. Input requests on pipes normally block the caller if there is no data available, but it seems that shouldn't be a problem in our example—there are as many writes as there are reads on the other side of the pipe. By default, though, `sys.stdout` is *buffered*, so the printed text may not actually be transmitted until some time in the future (when the `stdio` output buffers fill up). In fact, if the flush calls are not made, both processes will get stuck waiting for input from the other—input that is sitting in a buffer and is never flushed out over the pipe. They wind up in a *deadlock* state, both blocked on `raw_input` calls waiting for events that never occur.

Keep in mind that output buffering is really a function of the filesystem used to access pipes, not pipes themselves (pipes do queue up output data, but never hide it from readers!). In fact it only occurs in this example because we copy the pipe's information over to `sys.stdout`—a built-in file object that uses `stdio` buffering by default. However, such anomalies can also occur when using other cross-process tools, such as the `popen2` and `popen3` calls introduced in Chapter 2.

In general terms, if your programs engage in a two-way dialogs like this, there are at least three ways to avoid buffer-related deadlock problems:

* As demonstrated in this example, manually *flushing* output pipe streams by calling file `flush` method is an easy way to force buffers to be cleared.

* It's possible to use pipes in *unbuffered mode*—either use low-level `os` module calls to read and write pipe descriptors directly, or (on most systems) pass a buffer size argument of 0 to `os.fdopen` to disable `stdio` buffering in the file object used to wrap the descriptor. For fifos, described in the next section, do the same for `open`.

* Simply use the `-u` Python command-line flag to turn off buffering for the `sys.stdout` stream.

The last technique merits a few more words. Try this: delete all the `sys.stdout.flush` calls in both Examples 3-17 and 3-18 (files *pipes.py* and *pipes-testchild.py*) and change the parent's spawn call in *pipes.py* to this (i.e., add a −u command-line argument):

```
spawn('python', '-u', 'pipes-testchild.py', 'spam')
```

Then start the program with a command line like this: python −u pipes.py. It will work as it did with manual stdout flush calls, because stdout will be operating in *unbuffered* mode. Deadlock in general, though, is a bigger problem than we have space to address here; on the other hand, if you know enough to want to do IPC in Python, you're probably already a veteran of the deadlock wars.

Named Pipes (Fifos)

On some platforms, it is also possible to create a pipe that exists as a file. Such files are called "named pipes" (or sometimes, "fifos"), because they behave just like the pipes created within the previous programs, but are associated with a real file somewhere on your computer, external to any particular program. Once a named pipe file is created, processes read and write it using normal file operations. Fifos are unidirectional streams, but a set of two fifos can be used to implement bidirectional communication just as we did for anonymous pipes in the prior section.

Because fifos are files, they are longer-lived than in-process pipes and can be accessed by programs started independently. The unnamed, in-process pipe examples thus far depend on the fact that file descriptors (including pipes) are copied to child processes. With fifos, pipes are accessed instead by a filename visible to all programs regardless of any parent/child process relationships. Because of that, they are better suited as IPC mechanisms for independent client and server programs; for instance, a perpetually running server program may create and listen for requests on a fifo, that can be accessed later by arbitrary clients not forked by the server.

In Python, named pipe files are created with the os.mkfifo call, available today on Unix-like platforms and Windows NT (but not on Windows 95/98). This only creates the external file, though; to send and receive data through a fifo, it must be opened and processed as if it were a standard file. Example 3-19 is a derivation of the *pipe2.py* script listed earlier, written to use fifos instead of anonymous pipes.

Example 3-19. PP2E\System\Processes\pipefifo.py

```
#########################################################
# named pipes; os.mkfifo not avaiable on Windows 95/98;
# no reason to fork here, since fifo file pipes are
# external to processes--shared fds are irrelevent;
#########################################################

import os, time, sys
fifoname = '/tmp/pipefifo'                    # must open same name
```

Here is what this script looks like running on Linux: a signal number to watch for (12) is passed in on the command line, and the program is made to run in the background with a & shell operator (available in most Unix-like shells):

```
[mark@toy]$ python signal1.py 12 &
[1] 809
[mark@toy]$ ps
  PID TTY          TIME CMD
  578 ttyp1    00:00:00 tcsh
  809 ttyp1    00:00:00 python
  810 ttyp1    00:00:00 ps
[mark@toy]$ kill -12 809
[mark@toy]$ Got signal 12 at Fri Sep  8 00:27:01 2000
kill -12 809
[mark@toy]$ Got signal 12 at Fri Sep  8 00:27:03 2000
kill -12 809
[mark@toy]$ Got signal 12 at Fri Sep  8 00:27:04 2000

[mark@toy]$ kill -9 809           # signal 9 always kills the process
```

Inputs and outputs are a bit jumbled here, because the process prints to the same screen used to type new shell commands. To send the program a signal, the *kill* shell command takes a signal number and a process ID to be signalled (809); every time a new *kill* command sends a signal, the process replies with a message generated by a Python signal handler function.

The `signal` module also exports a `signal.alarm` function for scheduling a SIGALRM signal to occur at some number of seconds in the future. To trigger and catch timeouts, set the alarm and install a SIGALRM handler as in Example 3-21.

Example 3-21. PP2E\System\Processes\signal2.py

```
#########################################################
# set and catch alarm timeout signals in Python;
# time.sleep doesn't play well with alarm (or signal
# in general in my Linux PC), so call signal.pause
# here to do nothing until a signal is received;
#########################################################

import sys, signal, time
def now(): return time.ctime(time.time())

def onSignal(signum, stackframe):                   # python signal handler
    print 'Got alarm', signum, 'at', now()          # most handlers stay in effect

while 1:
    print 'Setting at', now()
    signal.signal(signal.SIGALRM, onSignal)         # install signal handler
    signal.alarm(5)                                 # do signal in 5 seconds
    signal.pause()                                  # wait for signals
```

Running this script on Linux causes its `onSignal` handler function to be invoked every five seconds:

```
[mark@toy]$ python signal2.py
Setting at Fri Sep  8 00:27:53 2000
Got alarm 14 at Fri Sep  8 00:27:58 2000
Setting at Fri Sep  8 00:27:58 2000
Got alarm 14 at Fri Sep  8 00:28:03 2000
Setting at Fri Sep  8 00:28:03 2000
Got alarm 14 at Fri Sep  8 00:28:08 2000
Setting at Fri Sep  8 00:28:08 2000
```

Generally speaking, signals must be used with cautions not made obvious by the examples we've just seen. For instance, some system calls don't react well to being interrupted by signals, and only the main thread can install signal handlers and respond to signals in a multithreaded program.

When used well, though, signals provide an event-based communication mechanism. They are less powerful than data streams like pipes, but are sufficient in situations where you just need to tell a program that something important has occurred at all, and not pass along any details about the event itself. Signals are sometimes also combined with other IPC tools. For example, an initial signal may inform a program that a client wishes to communicate over a named pipe—the equivalent of tapping someone's shoulder to get their attention before speaking. Most platforms reserve one or more `SIGUSR` signal numbers for user-defined events of this sort.

Launching Programs on Windows

Suppose just for a moment, that you've been asked to write a big Python book, and want to provide a way for readers to easily start the book's examples on just about any platform that Python runs on. Books are nice, but it's awfully fun to be able to click on demos right away. That is, you want to write a general and portable launcher program in Python, for starting other Python programs. What to do?

In this chapter, we've seen how to portably spawn threads, but these are simply parallel functions, not external programs. We've also learned how to go about starting new, independently running programs, with both the `fork`/`exec` combination, and tools for launching shell commands such as `os.popen`. Along the way, though, I've also been careful to point out numerous times that the `os.fork` call doesn't work on Windows today, and `os.popen` fails in Python release 1.5.2 and earlier when called from a GUI program on Windows; either of these constraints may be improved by the time you read this book (e.g., 2.0 improves `os.popen` on Windows), but they weren't quite there yet as I wrote this chapter. Moreover, for reasons we'll explore later, the `os.popen` call is prone to blocking (pausing) its caller in some scenarios.

Luckily, there are other ways to start programs in the Python standard library, albeit in platform-specific fashion:

- The `os.spawnv` and `os.spawnve` calls launch programs on Windows, much like a `fork`/`exec` call combination on Unix-like platforms.

- The `os.system` call can be used on Windows to launch a DOS *start* command, which opens (i.e., runs) a file independently based on its Windows filename associations, as though it were clicked.

- Tools in the Python `win32all` extensions package provide other, less standardized ways to start programs (e.g., the `WinExec` call).

The os.spawnv Call

Of these, the `spawnv` call is the most complex, but also the most like forking programs in Unix. It doesn't actually copy the calling process (so shared descriptor operations won't work), but can be used to start a Windows program running completely independent of the calling program. The script in Example 3-22 makes the similarity more obvious—it launches a program with a `fork`/`exec` combination in Linux, or an `os.spawnv` call on Windows.

Example 3-22. PP2E\System\Processes\spawnv.py

```
############################################################
# start up 10 copies of child.py running in parallel;
# use spawnv to launch a program on Windows (like fork+exec)
# P_OVERLAY replaces, P_DETACH makes child stdout go nowhere
############################################################

import os, sys

for i in range(10):
    if sys.platform[:3] == 'win':
        pypath  = r'C:\program files\python\python.exe'
        os.spawnv(os.P_NOWAIT, pypath, ('python', 'child.py', str(i)))
    else:
        pid = os.fork()
        if pid != 0:
            print 'Process %d spawned' % pid
        else:
            os.execlp('python', 'python', 'child.py', str(i))
print 'Main process exiting.'
```

Call `os.spawnv` with a process mode flag, the full directory path to the Python interpreter, and a tuple of strings representing the DOS command line with which to start a new program. The *process mode* flag is defined by Visual C++ (whose library provides the underlying spawnv call); commonly used values include:

*   P_OVERLAY: spawned program replaces calling program, like os.exec
*   P_DETACH: starts a program with full independence, without waiting
*   P_NOWAIT: runs the program without waiting for it to exit; returns its handle
*   P_WAIT: runs the program and pauses until it finishes; returns its exit code

Run a dir(os) call to see other process flags available, and either run a few tests or see VC++ documentation for more details; things like standard stream connection policies vary between the P_DETACH and P_NOWAIT modes in subtle ways. Here is this script at work on Windows, spawning 10 independent copies of the *child.py* Python program we met earlier in this chapter:

```
C:\...\PP2E\System\Processes>type child.py
import os, sys
print 'Hello from child', os.getpid(), sys.argv[1]

C:\...\PP2E\System\Processes>python spawnv.py
Hello from child -583587 0
Hello from child -558199 2
Hello from child -586755 1
Hello from child -562171 3
Main process exiting.
Hello from child -581867 6
Hello from child -588651 5
Hello from child -568247 4
Hello from child -563527 7
Hello from child -543163 9
Hello from child -587083 8
```

Notice that the copies print their output in random order, and the parent program exits before all children do; all these programs are really running in parallel on Windows. Also observe that the child program's output shows up in the console box where *spawnv.py* was run; when using P_NOWAIT standard output comes to the parent's console, but seems to go nowhere when using P_DETACH instead (most likely a feature, when spawning GUI programs).

The os.spawnve call works the same as os.spawnv, but accepts an extra fourth dictionary argument to specify a different shell environment for the spawned program (which, by default, inherits all the parent's settings).

Running DOS Command Lines

The os.system and os.popen calls can be used to start command lines on Windows just as on Unix-like platforms (but with the portability caveats about popen mentioned earlier). On Windows, though, the DOS *start* command combined with `os.system` provides an easy way for scripts to launch any file on the system, using Windows filename associations. Starting a program file this way makes it run as independently as its starter. Example 3-23 demonstrates these launch techniques.

Example 3-23. PP2E\System\Processes\dosstart.py

```
#############################################################
# start up 5 copies of child.py running in parallel;
# - on Windows, os.system always blocks its caller,
#   and os.popen currently fails in a GUI programs
# - using DOS start command pops up a DOS box (which goes
#   away immediately when the child.py program exits)
# - running child-wait.py with DOS start, 5 independent
#   DOS console windows popup and stay up (1 per program)
# DOS start command uses file name associations to know
# to run Python on the file, as though double-clicked in
# Windows explorer (any filename can be started this way);
#############################################################

import os, sys

for i in range(5):
    #print os.popen('python child.py ' + str(i)).read()[:-1]
    #os.system('python child.py ' + str(i))
    #os.system('start child.py ' + str(i))
     os.system('start child-wait.py ' + str(i))
print 'Main process exiting.'
```

Uncomment one of the lines in this script's `for` loop to experiment with these schemes on your computer. On mine, when run with either of the first two calls in the loop uncommented, I get the following sort of output—the text printed by five spawned Python programs:

```
C:\...\PP2E\System\Processes>python dosstart.py
Hello from child -582331 0
Hello from child -547703 1
Hello from child -547703 2
Hello from child -547651 3
Hello from child -547651 4
Main process exiting.
```

The `os.system` call usually blocks its caller until the spawned program exits; reading the output of a `os.popen` call has the same blocking effect (the reader waits for the spawned program's output to be complete). But with either of the last two statements in the loop uncommented, I get output that simply looks like this:

```
C:\...\PP2E\System\Processes>python dosstart.py
Main process exiting.
```

In both cases, I also see five new and completely independent DOS console windows appear on my display; when the third line in the loop is uncommented, all the DOS boxes go away right after they appear; when the last line in the loop is active, they remain on the screen after the `dosstart` program exits because the `child-wait` script pauses for input before exit.

Using the DOS start command

To understand why, you first need to know how the DOS *start* command works in general. Roughly, a DOS command line of the form `start command` works as if `command` were typed in the Windows "Run" dialog box available in the Start button menu. If `command` is a filename, it is opened exactly as if its name had been double-clicked in the Windows Explorer file selector GUI.

For instance, the following three DOS commands automatically start Internet Explorer on a file *index.html*, my registered image viewer program on a *uk-1.jpg*, and my sound media player program on file *sousa.au*. Windows simply opens the file with whatever program is associated to handle filenames of that form. Moreover, all three of these programs run independently of the DOS console box where the command is typed:

```
C:\temp>start c:\stuff\website\public_html\index.html
C:\temp>start c:\stuff\website\public_html\uk-1.jpg
C:\...\PP2E\System\Processes>start ..\..\Internet\Ftp\sousa.au
```

Now, because the *start* command can run any file and command line, there is no reason it cannot also be used to start an independently running Python program:

```
C:\...\PP2E\System\Processes>start child.py 1
```

Because Python is registered to open names ending in *.py* when it is installed, this really does work—script *child.py* is launched independently of the DOS console window, even though we didn't provide the name or path of the Python interpreter program. Because *child.py* simply prints a message and exits, though, the result isn't exactly satisfying: a new DOS window pops up to serve as the script's standard output, and immediately goes away when the child exits (it's that Windows "flash feature" described earlier!). To do better, add a `raw_input` call at the bottom of the program file to wait for a key press before exiting:

```
C:\...\PP2E\System\Processes>type child-wait.py
import os, sys
print 'Hello from child', os.getpid(), sys.argv[1]
raw_input("Press <Enter>")    # don't flash on Windows

C:\...\PP2E\System\Processes>start child-wait.py 2
```

Now the child's DOS window pops up and stays up after the *start* command has returned. Pressing the Enter key in the pop-up DOS window makes it go away.

Using start in Python scripts

Since we know that Python's `os.system` and `os.popen` can be called by a script to run *any* command line that can be typed at a DOS shell prompt, we can also start independently running programs from a Python script by simply running a DOS *start* command line. For instance:

```
C:\...\PP2E>python
>>> import os
>>>
>>> cmd = r'start c:\stuff\website\public_html\index.html'   # start IE browser
>>> os.system(cmd)                                           # runs independent
0
>>> file = r'gui\gifs\pythonPowered.gif'                     # start image viewer
>>> os.system('start ' + file)                               # IE opens .gif for me
0
>>> os.system('start ' + 'Gui/gifs/PythonPowered.gif')       # fwd slashes work too
0
>>> os.system(r'start Internet\Ftp\sousa.au')                # start media bar
0
```

The four Python `os.system` calls here start whatever web-page browser, image viewer, and sound player are registered on your machine to open *.html*, *.gif*, and *.au* files (unless these programs are already running). The launched programs run completely independent of the Python session—when running a DOS start command, `os.system` does not wait for the spawned program to exit. For instance, Figure 3-1 shows the *.gif* file handler in action on my machine, generated by both the second and third `os.system` calls in the preceding code.

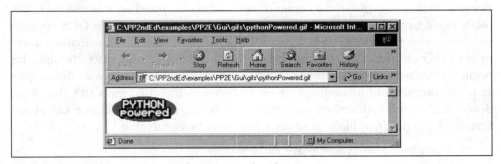

Figure 3-1. Started image viewer (Internet Explorer)

Now, since we also know that a Python program be can started from a command line, this yields two ways to launch Python programs:

```
C:\...\PP2E>python
>>> os.system(r'python Gui\TextEditor\textEditor.pyw')    # start and wait
0
>>> os.system(r'start  Gui\TextEditor\textEditor.pyw')    # start, go on
0
```

When running a `python` command, the `os.system` call waits (blocks) for the command to finish. When running a *start* command it does not—the launched Python program (here, PyEdit, a text editor GUI we'll meet in Chapter 9, *Larger GUI Examples*) runs independent of the `os.system` caller. And finally, that's why the following call in *dosstart.py* generates a new, independent instance of *child-wait.py*:

```
C:\...\PP2E\System\Processes>python
>>> os.system('start child-wait.py 1')
0
```

When run, this call pops up a new, independent DOS console window to serve as the standard input and output streams of the child-wait program. It truly is independent—in fact, it keeps running if we exit both this Python interpreter session and the DOS console box where the command was typed.* An `os.popen` call can launch a *start* command too; but since it normally starts commands independently anyhow, the only obvious advantages of *start* here are the pop-up DOS box, and the fact that Python need not be in the system search path setting:

```
>>> file = os.popen('start child-wait.py 1')      # versus: python child-wait...
>>> file.read()
'Hello from child -413849 1\012Press <Enter>'
```

Which scheme to use, then? Using `os.system` or `os.popen` to run a `python` command works fine, but only if your users have added the *python.exe* directory to their system search path setting. Running a DOS *start* command is often a simpler alternative to both running `python` commands and calling the `os.spawnv` function, since filename associations are automatically installed along with Python, and `os.spawnv` requires a full directory path to the Python interpreter program (*python.exe*). On the other hand, running *start* commands with `os.system` calls can fail on Windows for very long command-line strings:

```
>>> os.system('start child-wait.py ' + 'Z'*425)   # okay- 425 Zs in dos popup
0
>>> os.system('start child-wait.py ' + 'Z'*450)   # fails- msg, not exception
Access is denied.
0
>>> os.popen('python child-wait.py ' + 'Z'*500).read()   # works if PATH set
>>> os.system('python child-wait.py ' + 'Z'*500)         # works if PATH set

>>> pypath = r'C:\program files\python\python.exe'        # this works too
>>> os.spawnv(os.P_NOWAIT, pypath, ('python', 'child-wait.py', 'Z'*500))
```

---

* And remember, if you want to start a Python GUI program this way and not see the new DOS standard stream console box at all, simply name the script *child-wait.pyw*; the "w" on the end tells the Windows Python port to avoid the DOS box. For DOS jockeys: the *start* command also allows a few interesting options: /m (run minimized), /max (run maximized), /r (run restored—the default), and /w (don't return until the other program exits—this adds caller blocking if you need it). Type start /? for help. And for any Unix developers peeking over the fence: you can also launch independent programs with `os.system`—append the & background operator to the command line.

As a rule of thumb, use `os.spawnv` if your commands are (or may be) long. For instance, we'll meet a script in Chapter 4, *Larger System Examples I*, that launches web browsers to view HTML files; even though a *start* command applied to an HTML file will automatically start a browser program, this script instead must use `os.spawnv` to accommodate potentially long directory paths in HTML filenames.

For more information on other Windows-specific program launcher tools, see O'Reilly's *Python Programming on Win32*. Other schemes are even less standard than those shown here, but are given excellent coverage in that text.

A Portable Program-Launch Framework

With all these different ways to start programs on different platforms, it can be difficult to remember what tools to use in a given situation. Moreover, some of these tools are called in ways that are complicated enough to easily forget (for me, at least). I write scripts that need to launch Python programs often enough that I eventually wrote a module to try and hide most of the underlying details. While I was at it, I made this module smart enough to automatically pick a launch scheme based on the underlying platform. Laziness is the mother of many a useful module.

Example 3-24 collects many of the techniques we've met in this chapter in a single module. It implements an abstract superclass, `LaunchMode`, which defines what it means to start a Python program, but doesn't define how. Instead, its subclasses provide a `run` method that actually starts a Python program according to a given scheme, and (optionally) define an `announce` method to display a program's name at startup time.

Example 3-24. PP2E\launchmodes.py

```
#############################################################
# launch Python programs with reusable launcher scheme classes;
# assumes 'python' is on your system path (but see Launcher.py)
#############################################################

import sys, os, string
pycmd = 'python'    # assume it is on your system path

class LaunchMode:
    def __init__(self, label, command):
        self.what  = label
        self.where = command
    def __call__(self):                     # on call, ex: button press callback
        self.announce(self.what)
        self.run(self.where)                # subclasses must define run()
    def announce(self, text):               # subclasses may redefine announce()
        print text                          # methods instead of if/elif logic
    def run(self, cmdline):
        assert 0, 'run must be defined'
```

Example 3-24. PP2E\launchmodes.py (continued)

```
class System(LaunchMode):                   # run shell commands
    def run(self, cmdline):                 # caveat: blocks caller
        os.system('%s %s' % (pycmd, cmdline))   # unless '&' added on Linux

class Popen(LaunchMode):                     # caveat: blocks caller
    def run(self, cmdline):                  # since pipe closed too soon
        os.popen(pycmd + ' ' + cmdline)      # 1.5.2 fails in Windows GUI

class Fork(LaunchMode):
    def run(self, cmdline):
        assert hasattr(os, 'fork')           # for linux/unix today
        cmdline = string.split(cmdline)      # convert string to list
        if os.fork() == 0:                   # start new child process
            os.execvp(pycmd, [pycmd] + cmdline)  # run new program in child

class Start(LaunchMode):
    def run(self, cmdline):                  # for windows only
        assert sys.platform[:3] == 'win'     # runs independent of caller
        os.system('start ' + cmdline)        # uses Windows associations

class Spawn(LaunchMode):                      # for windows only
    def run(self, cmdline):                   # run python in new process
        assert sys.platform[:3] == 'win'      # runs independent of caller
        #pypath = r'C:\program files\python\python.exe'
        try:                                              # get path to python
            pypath = os.environ['PP2E_PYTHON_FILE']       # run by launcher?
        except KeyError:                                  # if so configs env
            from Launcher import which, guessLocation
            pypath = which('python.exe', 0) or guessLocation('python.exe', 1,0)
        os.spawnv(os.P_DETACH, pypath, ('python', cmdline)) # P_NOWAIT: dos box

class Top_level(LaunchMode):
    def run(self, cmdline):                              # new window, same process
        assert 0, 'Sorry - mode not yet implemented'     # tbd: need GUI class info

if sys.platform[:3] == 'win':
    PortableLauncher = Spawn            # pick best launcher for platform
else:                                   # need to tweak this code elsewhere
    PortableLauncher = Fork

class QuietPortableLauncher(PortableLauncher):
    def announce(self, text):
        pass

def selftest():
    myfile = 'launchmodes.py'
    program = 'Gui/TextEditor/textEditor.pyw ' + myfile     # assume in cwd
    raw_input('default mode...')
    launcher = PortableLauncher('PyEdit', program)
    launcher()                                             # no block

    raw_input('system mode...')
```

Example 3-24. PP2E\launchmodes.py (continued)

```
    System('PyEdit', program)()                                    # blocks

    raw_input('popen mode...')
    Popen('PyEdit', program)()                                     # blocks

    if sys.platform[:3] == 'win':
        raw_input('DOS start mode...')
        Start('PyEdit', program)()                                 # no block

if __name__ == '__main__': selftest()
```

Near the end of the file, the module picks a default class based on the `sys.platform` attribute: `PortableLauncher` is set to a class that uses `spawnv` on Windows and one that uses the `fork/exec` combination elsewhere. If you import this module and always use its `PortableLauncher` attribute, you can forget many of the platform-specific details enumerated in this chapter.

To run a Python program, simply import the `PortableLauncher` class, make an instance by passing a label and command line (without a leading "python" word), and then call the instance object as though it were a function. The program is started by a *call* operation instead of a method, so that the classes in this module can be used to generate *callback handlers* in Tkinter-based GUIs. As we'll see in the upcoming chapters, button-presses in Tkinter invoke a callable-object with no arguments; by registering a `PortableLauncher` instance to handle the press event, we can automatically start a new program from another program's GUI.

When run standalone, this module's `selftest` function is invoked as usual. On both Windows and Linux, all classes tested start a new Python text editor program (the upcoming PyEdit GUI program again) running independently with its own window. Figure 3-2 shows one in action on Windows; all spawned editors open the *launchmodes.py* source file automatically, because its name is passed to PyEdit as a command-line argument. As coded, both `System` and `Popen` block the caller until the editor exits, but `PortableLauncher` (really, `Spawn` or `Fork`) and `Start` do not:*

```
    C:\...\PP2E>python launchmodes.py
    default mode...
```

---

* This is fairly subtle. Technically, `Popen` only blocks its caller because the input pipe to the spawned program is closed too early, when the `os.popen` call's result is garbage-collected in `Popen.run`; `os.popen` normally does not block (in fact, assigning its result here to a global variable postpones blocking, but only until the next `Popen` object run frees the prior result). On Linux, adding a `&` to the end of the constructed command line in the `System` and `Popen.run` methods makes these objects no longer block their callers when run. Since the `fork/exec`, `spawnv`, and `system/start` schemes seem at least as good in practice, these `Popen` block states have not been addressed. Note too that the `Start` scheme does not generate a DOS console pop-up window in the self-test, only because the text editor program file's name ends in a *.pyw* extension; starting *.py* program files with `os.system` normally creates the console pop-up box.

```
PyEdit
system mode...
PyEdit
popen mode...
PyEdit
DOS start mode...
PyEdit
```

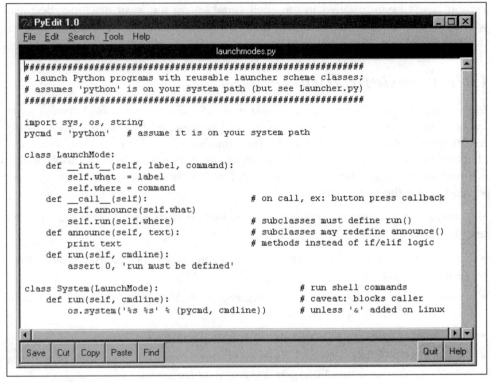

Figure 3-2. PyEdit program spawned from launchmodes

As a more practical application, this file is also used by launcher scripts designed to run examples in this book in a portable fashion. The PyDemos and PyGadgets scripts at the top of this book's examples directory tree (see the enclosed CD) simply import `PortableLauncher`, and register instances to respond to GUI events. Because of that, these two launcher GUIs run on both Windows and Linux unchanged (Tkinter's portability helps too, of course). The PyGadgets script even customizes `PortableLauncher` to update a label in a GUI at start time:

```
class Launcher(launchmodes.PortableLauncher):    # use wrapped launcher class
    def announce(self, text):                    # customize to set GUI label
        Info.config(text=text)
```

We'll explore these scripts in Part II, *GUI Programming* (but feel free to peek at the end of Chapter 8, *A Tkinter Tour, Part 2*, now). Because of this role, the `Spawn` class in this file uses additional tools to search for the Python executable's path—required by `os.spawnv`. It calls two functions exported by a file *Launcher.py* to find a suitable *python.exe*, whether or not the user has added its directory to their system PATH variable's setting. The idea is to start Python programs, even if Python hasn't been installed in the shell variables on the local machine. Because we're going to meet *Launcher.py* in Chapter 4, though, I'm going to postpone further details for now.

Other System Tools

In this and the prior chapters, we've met most of the commonly used system tools in the Python library. Along the way, we've also learned how to use them to do useful things like start programs, process directories, and so on. The next two chapters are something of a continuation of this topic—they use the tools we've just met to implement scripts that do useful and more realistic system-level work, so read on for the rest of this story.

Still, there are other system-related tools in Python that appear even later in this text. For instance:

- *Sockets* (used to communicate with other programs and networks) are introduced in Chapter 10.

- *Select* calls (used to multiplex among tasks) are also introduced in Chapter 10 as a way to implement servers.

- *File locking* calls in the `fcntl` module appear in Chapter 14.

- *Regular expressions* (string pattern matching used by many text processing tools) don't appear until Chapter 18, *Text and Language*.

Moreover, things like *forks* and *threads* are used extensively in the Internet scripting chapters: see the server implementations in Chapter 10 and the FTP and email GUIs in Chapter 11. In fact, most of this chapter's tools will pop up constantly in later examples in this book—about what one would expect of general-purpose, portable libraries.

Last but not necessarily least, I'd like to point out one more time that there are many additional tools in the Python library that don't appear in this book at all—with some 200 library modules, Python book authors have to pick and choose their topics frugally! As always, be sure to browse the Python library manuals early and often in your Python career.

4

Larger System Examples I

"Splits and Joins and Alien Invasions"

This chapter and the next continue our look at the *system utilities* domain in Python. They present a collection of larger Python scripts that do real systems work—comparing and copying directory trees, splitting files, searching files and directories, testing other programs, configuring program shell environments, launching web browsers, and so on. To make this collection easier to absorb, it's been split into a two-chapter set. This chapter presents assorted Python system utility programs that illustrate typical tasks and techniques in this domain. The next chapter presents larger Python programs that focus on more advanced file and directory tree processing.

Although the main point of these two case-study chapters is to give you a feel for realistic scripts in action, the size of these examples also gives us an opportunity to see Python's support for development paradigms like OOP and reuse at work. It's really only in the context of nontrivial programs like the ones we'll meet here that such tools begin to bear tangible fruit. These chapters also emphasize the "why" of systems tools, not just the "how"—along the way, I'll point out real-world needs met by the examples we'll study, to help you put the details in context.

One note up front: these chapters move quickly, and a few of their examples are largely just listed for independent study. Because all the scripts here are all heavily documented and use Python system tools described in the prior two chapters, I won't go through all code in detail. You should read the source code listings and experiment with these programs on your own computer, to get a better feel for how to combine system interfaces to accomplish realistic tasks. They are all available in source code form on the book's CD-ROM, and most work on all major platforms.

I should also mention that these are programs I really *use*—not examples written just for this book. In fact, they were coded over years and perform widely differing tasks, so there is no obvious common thread to connect the dots here. On the other hand, they help explain why system tools are useful in the first place, demonstrate larger development concepts that simpler examples cannot, and bear collective witness to the simplicity and portability of automating system tasks with Python. Once you've mastered the basics, you'll probably wish you had done so sooner.

Splitting and Joining Files

Like most kids, mine spend a lot of time on the Internet. As far as I can tell, it's the thing to do these days. Among this latest generation, computer geeks and gurus seem to be held with the same sort of esteem that rock stars once were by mine. When kids disappear into their rooms, chances are good that they are hacking on computers, not mastering guitar riffs. It's probably healthier than some of the diversions of my own misspent youth, but that's a topic for another kind of book.

But if you have teenage kids and computers, or know someone who does, you probably know that it's not a bad idea to keep tabs on what those kids do on the Web. Type your favorite four-letter word in almost any web search engine and you'll understand the concern—it's much better stuff than I could get during my teenage career. To sidestep the issue, only a few of the machines in my house have Internet feeds.

Now, while they're on one of these machines, my kids download lots of games. To avoid infecting our Very Important Computers with viruses from public-domain games, though, my kids usually have to download games on a computer with an Internet feed, and transfer them to their own computers to install. The problem is that game files are not small; they are usually much too big to fit on a floppy (and burning a CD takes away valuable game playing time).

If all the machines in my house ran Linux, this would be a nonissue. There are standard command-line programs on Unix for chopping a file into pieces small enough to fit on a floppy (*split*), and others for putting the pieces back together to recreate the original file (*cat*). Because we have all sorts of different machines in the house, though, we needed a more portable solution.

Splitting Files Portably

Since all the computers in my house run Python, a simple portable Python script came to the rescue. The Python program in Example 4-1 distributes a single file's contents among a set of part files, and stores those part files in a directory.

Example 4-1. PP2E\System\Filetools\split.py

```
#!/usr/bin/python
###########################################################
# split a file into a set of portions; join.py puts them
# back together; this is a customizable version of the
# standard unix split command-line utility; because it
# is written in Python, it also works on Windows and can
# be easily tweaked; because it exports a function, it
# can also be imported and reused in other applications;
###########################################################

import sys, os
kilobytes = 1024
megabytes = kilobytes * 1000
chunksize = int(1.4 * megabytes)               # default: roughly a floppy

def split(fromfile, todir, chunksize=chunksize):
    if not os.path.exists(todir):              # caller handles errors
        os.mkdir(todir)                        # make dir, read/write parts
    else:
        for fname in os.listdir(todir):        # delete any existing files
            os.remove(os.path.join(todir, fname))
    partnum = 0
    input = open(fromfile, 'rb')               # use binary mode on Windows
    while 1:                                   # eof=empty string from read
        chunk = input.read(chunksize)          # get next part <= chunksize
        if not chunk: break
        partnum  = partnum+1
        filename = os.path.join(todir, ('part%04d' % partnum))
        fileobj  = open(filename, 'wb')
        fileobj.write(chunk)
        fileobj.close()                        # or simply open().write()
    input.close()
    assert partnum <= 9999                     # join sort fails if 5 digits
    return partnum

if __name__ == '__main__':
    if len(sys.argv) == 2 and sys.argv[1] == '-help':
        print 'Use: split.py [file-to-split target-dir [chunksize]]'
    else:
        if len(sys.argv) < 3:
            interactive = 1
            fromfile = raw_input('File to be split? ')        # input if clicked
            todir    = raw_input('Directory to store part files? ')
        else:
            interactive = 0
            fromfile, todir = sys.argv[1:3]                   # args in cmdline
            if len(sys.argv) == 4: chunksize = int(sys.argv[3])
        absfrom, absto = map(os.path.abspath, [fromfile, todir])
        print 'Splitting', absfrom, 'to', absto, 'by', chunksize

        try:
            parts = split(fromfile, todir, chunksize)
```

Example 4-1. PP2E\System\Filetools\split.py (continued)

```
    except:
        print 'Error during split:'
        print sys.exc_type, sys.exc_value
    else:
        print 'Split finished:', parts, 'parts are in', absto
    if interactive: raw_input('Press Enter key') # pause if clicked
```

By default, this script splits the input file into chunks that are roughly the size of a floppy disk—perfect for moving big files between electronically isolated machines. Most important, because this is all portable Python code, this script will run on just about any machine, even ones without a file splitter of their own. All it requires is an installed Python. Here it is at work splitting the Python 1.5.2 self-installer executable on Windows:

```
C:\temp>echo %X%          shorthand shell variable
C:\PP2ndEd\examples\PP2E

C:\temp>ls -l py152.exe
-rwxrwxrwa   1 0          0          5028339 Apr 16  1999 py152.exe

C:\temp>python %X%\System\Filetools\split.py -help
Use: split.py [file-to-split target-dir [chunksize]]

C:\temp>python %X%\System\Filetools\split.py py152.exe pysplit
Splitting C:\temp\py152.exe to C:\temp\pysplit by 1433600
Split finished: 4 parts are in C:\temp\pysplit

C:\temp>ls -l pysplit
total 9821
-rwxrwxrwa   1 0          0          1433600 Sep 12 06:03 part0001
-rwxrwxrwa   1 0          0          1433600 Sep 12 06:03 part0002
-rwxrwxrwa   1 0          0          1433600 Sep 12 06:03 part0003
-rwxrwxrwa   1 0          0           727539 Sep 12 06:03 part0004
```

Each of these four generated part files represent one binary chunk of file *py152.exe*, small enough to fit comfortably on a floppy disk. In fact, if you add the sizes of the generated part files given by the *ls* command, you'll come up with 5,028,339 bytes—exactly the same as the original file's size. Before we see how to put these files back together again, let's explore a few of the splitter script's finer points.

Operation modes

This script is designed to input its parameters in either *interactive* or *command-line* modes; it checks the number of command-line arguments to know in which mode it is being used. In command-line mode, you list the file to be split and the output directory on the command line, and can optionally override the default part file size with a third command-line argument.

In interactive mode, the script asks for a filename and output directory at the console window with `raw_input`, and pauses for a keypress at the end before exiting. This mode is nice when the program file is started by clicking on its icon—on Windows, parameters are typed into a pop-up DOS box that doesn't automatically disappear. The script also shows the absolute paths of its parameters (by running them through `os.path.abspath`) because they may not be obvious in interactive mode. We'll see examples of other split modes at work in a moment.

Binary file access

This code is careful to open both input and output files in binary mode (`rb`, `wb`), because it needs to portably handle things like executables and audio files, not just text. In Chapter 2, *System Tools*, we learned that on Windows, text-mode files automatically map \r\n end-of-line sequences to \n on input, and map \n to \r\n on output. For true binary data, we really don't want any \r characters in the data to go away when read, and we don't want any superfluous \r characters to be added on output. Binary-mode files suppress this \r mapping when the script is run on Windows, and so avoid data corruption.

Manually closing files

This script also goes out of its way to manually close its files. For instance:

```
fileobj  = open(partname, 'wb')
fileobj.write(chunk)
fileobj.close()
```

As we also saw in Chapter 2, these three lines can usually be replaced with this single line:

```
open(partname, 'wb').write(chunk)
```

This shorter form relies on the fact that the current Python implementation automatically closes files for you when file objects are reclaimed (i.e., when they are garbage collected, because there are no more references to the file object). In this line, the file object would be reclaimed immediately, because the `open` result is temporary in an expression, and is never referenced by a longer-lived name. The `input` file similarly is reclaimed when the `split` function exits.

As I was writing this chapter, though, there was some possibility that this automatic-close behavior may go away in the future.* Moreover, the JPython Java-based Python implementation does not reclaim unreferenced objects as immediately as

---

* I hope this doesn't happen—such a change would be a major break from backward compatibility, and could impact Python systems all over the world. On the other hand, it's just a possibility for a future mutation of Python. I'm told that publishers of technical books love language changes, and this isn't a text on politics.

the standard Python. If you care about the Java port (or one possible future), your script may potentially create many files in a short amount of time, and your script may run on a machine that has a limit on the number of open files per program, then close manually. The close calls in this script have never been necessary for my purposes, but because the split function in this module is intended to be a general-purpose tool, it accommodates such worst-case scenarios.

Joining Files Portably

Back to moving big files around the house. After downloading a big game program file, my kids generally run the previous splitter script by clicking on its name in Windows Explorer and typing filenames. After a split, they simply copy each part file onto its own floppy, walk the floppies upstairs, and recreate the split output directory on their target computer by copying files off the floppies. Finally, the script in Example 4-2 is clicked or otherwise run to put the parts back together.

Example 4-2. PP2E\System\Filetools\join.py

```python
#!/usr/bin/python
##########################################################
# join all part files in a dir created by split.py.
# This is roughly like a 'cat fromdir/* > tofile' command
# on unix, but is a bit more portable and configurable,
# and exports the join operation as a reusable function.
# Relies on sort order of file names: must be same length.
# Could extend split/join to popup Tkinter file selectors.
##########################################################

import os, sys
readsize = 1024

def join(fromdir, tofile):
    output = open(tofile, 'wb')
    parts  = os.listdir(fromdir)
    parts.sort()
    for filename in parts:
        filepath = os.path.join(fromdir, filename)
        fileobj  = open(filepath, 'rb')
        while 1:
            filebytes = fileobj.read(readsize)
            if not filebytes: break
            output.write(filebytes)
        fileobj.close()
    output.close()

if __name__ == '__main__':
    if len(sys.argv) == 2 and sys.argv[1] == '-help':
        print 'Use: join.py [from-dir-name to-file-name]'
    else:
        if len(sys.argv) != 3:
```

Example 4-2. PP2E\System\Filetools\join.py (continued)

```
        interactive = 1
        fromdir = raw_input('Directory containing part files? ')
        tofile  = raw_input('Name of file to be recreated? ')
    else:
        interactive = 0
        fromdir, tofile = sys.argv[1:]
    absfrom, absto = map(os.path.abspath, [fromdir, tofile])
    print 'Joining', absfrom, 'to make', absto

    try:
        join(fromdir, tofile)
    except:
        print 'Error joining files:'
        print sys.exc_type, sys.exc_value
    else:
        print 'Join complete: see', absto
    if interactive: raw_input('Press Enter key') # pause if clicked
```

After running the join script, they still may need to run something like zip, gzip, or tar to unpack an archive file, unless it's shipped as an executable;* but at least they're much closer to seeing the Starship Enterprise spring into action. Here is a join in progress on Windows, combining the split files we made a moment ago:

```
C:\temp>python %X%\System\Filetools\join.py -help
Use: join.py [from-dir-name to-file-name]

C:\temp>python %X%\System\Filetools\join.py pysplit mypy152.exe
Joining C:\temp\pysplit to make C:\temp\mypy152.exe
Join complete: see C:\temp\mypy152.exe

C:\temp>ls -l mypy152.exe py152.exe
-rwxrwxrwa   1 0        0         5028339 Sep 12 06:05 mypy152.exe
-rwxrwxrwa   1 0        0         5028339 Apr 16  1999 py152.exe

C:\temp>fc /b mypy152.exe py152.exe
Comparing files mypy152.exe and py152.exe
FC: no differences encountered
```

The join script simply uses os.listdir to collect all the part files in a directory created by split, and sorts the filename list to put the parts back together in the correct order. We get back an exact byte-for-byte copy of the original file (proved by the DOS *fc* command above; use *cmp* on Unix).

Some of this process is still manual, of course (I haven't quite figured out how to script the "walk the floppies upstairs" bit yet), but the split and join scripts

---

* See also the built-in module *gzip.py* in the Python standard library; it provides tools for reading and writing gzip files, usually named with a *.gz* filename extension. It can be used to unpack gzipped files, and serves as an all-Python equivalent of the standard gzip and gunzip command-line utility programs. This built-in module uses another called zlib that implements gzip-compatible data compressions. In Python 2.0, see also the new zipfile module for handling ZIP format archives (different from gzip).

make it both quick and simple to move big files around. Because this script is also portable Python code, it runs on any platform we care to move split files to. For instance, it's typical for my kids to download both Windows and Linux games; since this script runs on either platform, they're covered.

Reading by blocks or files

Before we move on, there are a couple of details worth underscoring in the join script's code. First of all, notice that this script deals with files in binary mode, but also reads each part file in blocks of 1K bytes each. In fact, the `readsize` setting here (the size of each block read from an input part file) has no relation to `chunksize` in *split.py* (the total size of each output part file). As we learned in Chapter 2, this script could instead read each part file all at once:

```
filebytes = open(filepath, 'rb').read()
output.write(filebytes)
```

The downside to this scheme is that it really does load all of a file into memory at once. For example, reading a 1.4M part file into memory all at once with the file object `read` method generates a 1.4M string in memory to hold the file's bytes. Since `split` allows users to specify even larger chunk sizes, the `join` script plans for the worst and reads in terms of limited-size blocks. To be completely robust, the `split` script could read its input data in smaller chunks too, but this hasn't become a concern in practice.

Sorting filenames

If you study this script's code closely, you may also notice that the join scheme it uses relies completely on the sort order of filenames in the parts directory. Because it simply calls the list `sort` method on the filenames list returned by `os.listdir`, it implicitly requires that filenames have the same length and format when created by split. The splitter uses zero-padding notation in a string formatting expression (`'part%04d'`) to make sure that filenames all have the same number of digits at the end (four), much like this list:

```
>>> list = ['xx008', 'xx010', 'xx006', 'xx009', 'xx011', 'xx111']
>>> list.sort()
>>> list
['xx006', 'xx008', 'xx009', 'xx010', 'xx011', 'xx111']
```

When sorted, the leading zero characters in small numbers guarantee that part files are ordered for joining correctly. Without the leading zeroes, `join` would fail whenever there were more than nine part files, because the first digit would dominate:

```
>>> list = ['xx8', 'xx10', 'xx6', 'xx9', 'xx11', 'xx111']
>>> list.sort()
>>> list
['xx10', 'xx11', 'xx111', 'xx6', 'xx8', 'xx9']
```

Because the list `sort` method accepts a comparison function as an argument, we could in principle strip off digits in filenames and sort numerically:

```
>>> list = ['xx8', 'xx10', 'xx6', 'xx9', 'xx11', 'xx111']
>>> list.sort(lambda x, y: cmp(int(x[2:]), int(y[2:])))
>>> list
['xx6', 'xx8', 'xx9', 'xx10', 'xx11', 'xx111']
```

But that still implies that filenames all must start with the same length substring, so this doesn't quite remove the file naming dependency between the `split` and `join` scripts. Because these scripts are designed to be two steps of the same process, though, some dependencies between them seem reasonable.

Usage Variations

Let's run a few more experiments with these Python system utilities to demonstrate other usage modes. When run without full command-line arguments, both `split` and `join` are smart enough to input their parameters *interactively*. Here they are chopping and gluing the Python self-installer file on Windows again, with parameters typed in the DOS console window:

```
C:\temp>python %X%\System\Filetools\split.py
File to be split? py152.exe
Directory to store part files? splitout
Splitting C:\temp\py152.exe to C:\temp\splitout by 1433600
Split finished: 4 parts are in C:\temp\splitout
Press Enter key

C:\temp>python %X%\System\Filetools\join.py
Directory containing part files? splitout
Name of file to be recreated? newpy152.exe
Joining C:\temp\splitout to make C:\temp\newpy152.exe
Join complete: see C:\temp\newpy152.exe
Press Enter key

C:\temp>fc /B py152.exe newpy152.exe
Comparing files py152.exe and newpy152.exe
FC: no differences encountered
```

When these program files are double-clicked in a file explorer GUI, they work the same way (there usually are no command-line arguments when launched this way). In this mode, absolute path displays help clarify where files are really at. Remember, the current working directory is the script's home directory when clicked like this, so the name *tempsplit* actually maps to a source code directory; type a full path to make the split files show up somewhere else:

```
[in a popup DOS console box when split is clicked]
File to be split? c:\temp\py152.exe
Directory to store part files? tempsplit
Splitting c:\temp\py152.exe to C:\PP2ndEd\examples\PP2E\System\Filetools\
tempsplit by 1433600
Split finished: 4 parts are in C:\PP2ndEd\examples\PP2E\System\Filetools\
```

```
tempsplit
Press Enter key
```

[in a popup DOS console box when join is clicked]
```
Directory containing part files? tempsplit
Name of file to be recreated? c:\temp\morepy152.exe
Joining C:\PP2ndEd\examples\PP2E\System\Filetools\tempsplit to make
c:\temp\morepy152.exe
Join complete: see c:\temp\morepy152.exe
Press Enter key
```

Because these scripts package their core logic up in functions, though, it's just as easy to reuse their code by importing and calling from another Python component:

```
C:\temp>python
>>> from PP2E.System.Filetools.split import split
>>> from PP2E.System.Filetools.join  import join
>>>
>>> numparts = split('py152.exe', 'calldir')
>>> numparts
4
>>> join('calldir', 'callpy152.exe')
>>>
>>> import os
>>> os.system(r'fc /B py152.exe callpy152.exe')
Comparing files py152.exe and callpy152.exe
FC: no differences encountered
0
```

A word about performance: All the `split` and `join` tests shown so far process a 5M file, but take at most one second of real wall-clock time to finish on my Windows 98 300 and 650 MHz laptop computers—plenty fast for just about any use I could imagine. (They run even faster after Windows has cached information about the files involved.) Both scripts run just as fast for other reasonable part file sizes too; here is the splitter chopping up the file into 500,000- and 50,000-byte parts:

```
C:\temp>python %X%\System\Filetools\split.py py152.exe tempsplit 500000
Splitting C:\temp\py152.exe to C:\temp\tempsplit by 500000
Split finished: 11 parts are in C:\temp\tempsplit

C:\temp>ls -l tempsplit
total 9826
-rwxrwxrwa   1 0        0            500000 Sep 12 06:29 part0001
-rwxrwxrwa   1 0        0            500000 Sep 12 06:29 part0002
-rwxrwxrwa   1 0        0            500000 Sep 12 06:29 part0003
-rwxrwxrwa   1 0        0            500000 Sep 12 06:29 part0004
-rwxrwxrwa   1 0        0            500000 Sep 12 06:29 part0005
-rwxrwxrwa   1 0        0            500000 Sep 12 06:29 part0006
-rwxrwxrwa   1 0        0            500000 Sep 12 06:29 part0007
-rwxrwxrwa   1 0        0            500000 Sep 12 06:29 part0008
-rwxrwxrwa   1 0        0            500000 Sep 12 06:29 part0009
-rwxrwxrwa   1 0        0            500000 Sep 12 06:29 part0010
-rwxrwxrwa   1 0        0             28339 Sep 12 06:29 part0011
```

```
C:\temp>python %X%\System\Filetools\split.py py152.exe tempsplit 50000
Splitting C:\temp\py152.exe to C:\temp\tempsplit by 50000
Split finished: 101 parts are in C:\temp\tempsplit

C:\temp>ls tempsplit
part0001   part0014   part0027   part0040   part0053   part0066   part0079   part0092
part0002   part0015   part0028   part0041   part0054   part0067   part0080   part0093
part0003   part0016   part0029   part0042   part0055   part0068   part0081   part0094
part0004   part0017   part0030   part0043   part0056   part0069   part0082   part0095
part0005   part0018   part0031   part0044   part0057   part0070   part0083   part0096
part0006   part0019   part0032   part0045   part0058   part0071   part0084   part0097
part0007   part0020   part0033   part0046   part0059   part0072   part0085   part0098
part0008   part0021   part0034   part0047   part0060   part0073   part0086   part0099
part0009   part0022   part0035   part0048   part0061   part0074   part0087   part0100
part0010   part0023   part0036   part0049   part0062   part0075   part0088   part0101
part0011   part0024   part0037   part0050   part0063   part0076   part0089
part0012   part0025   part0038   part0051   part0064   part0077   part0090
part0013   part0026   part0039   part0052   part0065   part0078   part0091
```

Split can take longer to finish, but only if the part file's size is set small enough to generate thousands of part files—splitting into 1006 parts works, but runs slower (on my computer this split and join take about five and two seconds, respectively, depending on what other programs are open):

```
C:\temp>python %X%\System\Filetools\split.py py152.exe tempsplit 5000
Splitting C:\temp\py152.exe to C:\temp\tempsplit by 5000
Split finished: 1006 parts are in C:\temp\tempsplit

C:\temp>python %X%\System\Filetools\join.py tempsplit mypy152.exe
Joining C:\temp\tempsplit to make C:\temp\py152.exe
Join complete: see C:\temp\py152.exe

C:\temp>fc /B py152.exe mypy152.exe
Comparing files py152.exe and mypy152.exe
FC: no differences encountered

C:\temp>ls -l tempsplit
...1000 lines deleted...
-rwxrwxrwa   1 0         0         5000 Sep 12 06:30 part1001
-rwxrwxrwa   1 0         0         5000 Sep 12 06:30 part1002
-rwxrwxrwa   1 0         0         5000 Sep 12 06:30 part1003
-rwxrwxrwa   1 0         0         5000 Sep 12 06:30 part1004
-rwxrwxrwa   1 0         0         5000 Sep 12 06:30 part1005
-rwxrwxrwa   1 0         0         3339 Sep 12 06:30 part1006
```

Finally, the splitter is also smart enough to create the output directory if it doesn't yet exist, or clear out any old files there if it does exist. Because the joiner combines whatever files exist in the output directory, this is a nice ergonomic touch—if the output directory was not cleared before each split, it would be too easy to forget that a prior run's files are still there. Given that my kids are running these scripts, they need to be as forgiving as possible; your user base may vary, but probably not by much.

```
C:\temp>python %X%\System\Filetools\split.py py152.exe tempsplit 700000
Splitting C:\temp\py152.exe to C:\temp\tempsplit by 700000
Split finished: 8 parts are in C:\temp\tempsplit

C:\temp>ls -l tempsplit
total 9827
-rwxrwxrwa   1 0        0           700000 Sep 12 06:32 part0001
-rwxrwxrwa   1 0        0           700000 Sep 12 06:32 part0002
-rwxrwxrwa   1 0        0           700000 Sep 12 06:32 part0003
...
...only new files here...
...
-rwxrwxrwa   1 0        0           700000 Sep 12 06:32 part0006
-rwxrwxrwa   1 0        0           700000 Sep 12 06:32 part0007
-rwxrwxrwa   1 0        0           128339 Sep 12 06:32 part0008
```

Generating Forward-Link Web Pages

Moving is rarely painless, even in the brave new world of cyberspace. Changing your web site's Internet address can lead to all sorts of confusion—you need to ask known contacts to use the new address, and hope that others will eventually stumble onto it themselves. But if you rely on the Internet, moves are bound to generate at least as much confusion as an address change in the real world.

Unfortunately, such site relocations are often unavoidable. Both ISPs (Internet Service Providers) and server machines come and go over the years. Moreover, some ISPs let their service fall to intolerable levels; if you are unlucky enough to have signed up with such an ISP, there is not much recourse but to change providers, and that often implies a change of web addresses.[*]

Imagine, though, that you are an O'Reilly author, and have published your web site's address in multiple books sold widely all over the world. What to do, when your ISP's service level requires a site change? Notifying the tens or hundreds of thousands of readers out there isn't exactly a practical solution.

Probably the best you can do is to leave forwarding instructions at the old site, for some reasonably long period of time—the virtual equivalent of a "We've Moved" sign in a storefront window. On the Web, such a sign can also send visitors to the new site automatically: simply leave a page at the old site containing a hyperlink to the page's address at the new site. With such *forward-link files* in place, visitors to the old addresses will be only one click away from reaching the new ones.

---

[*] It happens. In fact, most people who spend any substantial amount of time in cyberspace probably could tell a horror story or two. Mine goes like this: I had an account with an ISP that went completely offline for a few weeks in response to a security breach by an ex-employee. Worse, personal email was not only disabled, but queued up messages were permanently lost. If your livelihood depends on email and the Web as much as mine does, you'll appreciate the havoc such an outage can wreak.

That sounds simple enough. But because visitors might try to directly access the address of *any* file at your old site, you generally need to leave one forward-link file for every old file—HTML pages, images, and so on. If you happen to enjoy doing lots of mindless typing, you could create each forward-link file by hand. But given that my home site contains 140 files today, the prospect of running one editor session per file was more than enough motivation for an automated solution.

Page Template File

Here's what I came up with. First of all, I create a general *page template* text file, shown in Example 4-3, to describe how all the forward-link files should look, with parts to be filled in later.

Example 4-3. PP2E\System\Filetools\template.html

```
<HTML><BODY>
<H1>This page has moved</H1>

<P>This page now lives at this address:

<P><A HREF="http://$server$/$home$/$file$">
http://$server$/$home$/$file$</A>

<P>Please click on the new address to jump to this page, and
update any links accordingly.
</P>

<HR>
<H3><A HREF="ispmove.html">Why the move? - The ISP story</A></H3>

</BODY></HTML>
```

To fully understand this template, you have to know something about HTML—a web page description language that we'll explore in Chapter 12, *Server-Side Scripting*. But for the purposes of this example, you can ignore most of this file and focus on just the parts surrounded by dollar signs: the strings `$server$`, `$home$`, and `$file$` are targets to be replaced with real values by global text substitutions. They represent items that vary per site relocation and file.

Page Generator Script

Now, given a page template file, the Python script in Example 4-4 generates all the required forward-link files automatically.

Example 4-4. PP2E\System\Filetools\site-forward.py

```
#####################################################
# Create forward link pages for relocating a web site.
# Generates one page for every existing site file;
```

Example 4-4. PP2E\System\Filetools\site-forward.py (continued)

```
# upload the generated files to your old web site.
# Performance note: the first 2 string.replace calls
# could be moved out of the for loop, but this runs
# in < 1 second on my Win98 machine for 150 site files.
# Lib note: the os.listdir call can be replaced with:
# sitefiles = glob.glob(sitefilesdir + os.sep + '*')
# but then the file/directory names must be split
# with: dirname, filename = os.path.split(sitefile);
#####################################################

import os, string
servername   = 'starship.python.net'    # where site is relocating to
homedir      = '~lutz/home'             # where site will be rooted
sitefilesdir = 'public_html'           # where site files live locally
uploaddir    = 'isp-forward'           # where to store forward files
templatename = 'template.html'         # template for generated pages

try:
    os.mkdir(uploaddir)                # make upload dir if needed
except OSError: pass

template  = open(templatename).read()   # load or import template text
sitefiles = os.listdir(sitefilesdir)    # filenames, no directory prefix

count = 0
for filename in sitefiles:
    fwdname = os.path.join(uploaddir, filename)         # or + os.sep + filename
    print 'creating', filename, 'as', fwdname

    filetext = string.replace(template, '$server$', servername)  # insert text
    filetext = string.replace(filetext, '$home$',   homedir)     # and write
    filetext = string.replace(filetext, '$file$',    filename)   # file varies
    open(fwdname, 'w').write(filetext)
    count = count + 1

print 'Last file =>\n', filetext
print 'Done:', count, 'forward files created.'
```

Notice that the template's text is loaded by reading a *file*; it would work just as well to code it as an imported Python string variable (e.g., a triple-quoted string in a module file). Also observe that all configuration options are assignments at the top of the *script*, not command-line arguments; since they change so seldom, it's convenient to type them just once in the script itself.

But the main thing worth noticing here is that this script doesn't care what the template file looks like at all; it simply performs global substitutions blindly in its text, with a different filename value for each generated file. In fact, we can change the template file any way we like, without having to touch the script. Such a division of labor can be used in all sorts of contexts—generating "makefiles," form-letters, and so on. In terms of library tools, the generator script simply:

- Uses os.listdir to step through all the filenames in the site's directory

- Uses string.replace to perform global search-and-replace operations that fill in the $-delimited targets in the template file's text

- Uses os.path.join and built-in file objects to write the resulting text out to a forward-link file of the same name, in an output directory

The end result is a mirror-image of the original web site directory, containing only forward-link files generated from the page template. As an added bonus, the generator script can be run on just about any Python platform—I can run it on both my Windows laptop (where my web site files are maintained), as well as a Unix server where I keep a copy of my site. Here it is in action on Windows:

```
C:\Stuff\Website>python %X%\System\Filetools\site-forward.py
creating about-hop1.html as isp-forward\about-hop1.html
creating about-lp-toc.html as isp-forward\about-lp-toc.html
creating about-lp.html as isp-forward\about-lp.html
creating about-pp-japan.html as isp-forward\about-pp-japan.html
...
...more lines deleted...
...
creating whatsold.html as isp-forward\whatsold.html
creating xlate-lp.html as isp-forward\xlate-lp.html
creating about-pp2e.html as isp-forward\about-pp2e.html
creating about-ppr2e.html as isp-forward\about-ppr2e.html
Last file =>
<HTML><BODY>
<H1>This page has moved</H1>

<P>This page now lives at this address:

<P><A HREF="http://starship.python.net/~lutz/home/about-ppr2e.html">
http://starship.python.net/~lutz/home/about-ppr2e.html</A>

<P>Please click on the new address to jump to this page, and
update any links accordingly.
</P>

<HR>
<H3><A HREF="ispmove.html">Why the move? - The ISP story</A></H3>

</BODY></HTML>

Done: 137 forward files created.
```

To verify this script's output, double-click on any of the output files to see what they look like in a web browser (or run a *start* command in a DOS console on

Windows, e.g., `start isp-forward\about-ppr2e.html`). Figure 4-1 shows what one generated page looks like on my machine.

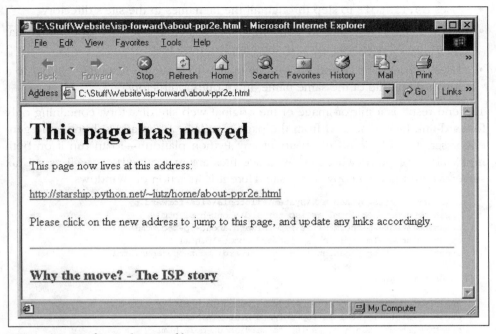

Figure 4-1. Site-forward output file page

To complete the process, you still need to install the forward links: upload all the generated files in the output directory to your old site's web directory. If that's too much to do by hand too, be sure to also see the FTP site upload scripts in Chapter 11, *Client-Side Scripting*, for an automatic way to do it with Python (*PP2E\Internet\Ftp\uploadflat.py* will do the job). Once you've caught the scripting bug, you'll be amazed at how much manual labor Python can automate.

A Regression Test Script

As we've seen, Python provides interfaces to a variety of system services, along with tools for adding others. Example 4-5 shows some commonly used services in action. It implements a simple *regression-test* system, by running a command-line program with a set of given input files and comparing the output of each run to the prior run's results. This script was adapted from an automated testing system I wrote to catch errors introduced by changes in program source files; in a big system, you might not know when a fix is really a bug in disguise.

Example 4-5. PP2E\System\Filetools\regtest.py

```
#!/usr/local/bin/python
import os, sys                          # get unix, python services
from stat import ST_SIZE                # or use os.path.getsize
from glob import glob                   # file name expansion
from os.path import exists             # file exists test
from time import time, ctime           # time functions

print 'RegTest start.'
print 'user:', os.environ['USER']      # environment variables
print 'path:', os.getcwd()             # current directory
print 'time:', ctime(time()), '\n'
program = sys.argv[1]                   # two command-line args
testdir = sys.argv[2]

for test in glob(testdir + '/*.in'):    # for all matching input files
    if not exists('%s.out' % test):
        # no prior results
        os.system('%s < %s > %s.out 2>&1' % (program, test, test))
        print 'GENERATED:', test
    else:
        # backup, run, compare
        os.rename(test + '.out', test + '.out.bkp')
        os.system('%s < %s > %s.out 2>&1' % (program, test, test))
        os.system('diff %s.out %s.out.bkp > %s.diffs' % ((test,)*3) )
        if os.stat(test + '.diffs')[ST_SIZE] == 0:
            print 'PASSED:', test
            os.remove(test + '.diffs')
        else:
            print 'FAILED:', test, '(see %s.diffs)' % test

print 'RegTest done:', ctime(time())
```

Some of this script is Unix-biased. For instance, the 2>&1 syntax to redirect **stderr** works on Unix and Windows NT/2000, but not on Windows 9x, and the *diff* command line spawned is a Unix utility. You'll need to tweak such code a bit to run this script on some platforms. Also, given the improvements to the **os** module's **popen** calls in Python 2.0, they have now become a more portable way to redirect streams in such a script, and an alternative to shell command redirection syntax.

But this script's basic operation is straightforward: for each filename with an *.in* suffix in the test directory, this script runs the program named on the command line and looks for deviations in its results. This is an easy way to spot changes (called "regressions") in the behavior of programs spawned from the shell. The real secret of this script's success is in the filenames used to record test information: within a given test directory *testdir*:

- `testdir/`*test*`.in` files represent standard input sources for program runs.
- `testdir/`*test*`.in.out` files represent the output generated for each input file.

- `testdir/`*`test`*`.in.out.bkp` files are backups of prior *.in.out* result files.

- `testdir/`*`test`*`.in.diffs` files represent regressions; output file differences.

Output and difference files are generated in the test directory, with distinct suffixes. For example, if we have an executable program or script called **shrubbery**, and a test directory called *test1* containing a set of *.in* input files, a typical run of the tester might look something like this:

```
% regtest.py shrubbery test1
RegTest start.
user: mark
path: /home/mark/stuff/python/testing
time: Mon Feb 26 21:13:20 1996

FAILED: test1/t1.in (see test1/t1.in.diffs)
PASSED: test1/t2.in
FAILED: test1/t3.in (see test1/t3.in.diffs)
RegTest done: Mon Feb 26 21:13:27 1996
```

Here, **shrubbery** is run three times, for the three *.in* canned input files, and the results of each run are compared to output generated for these three inputs the last time testing was conducted. Such a Python script might be launched once a day, to automatically spot deviations caused by recent source code changes (e.g., from a **cron** job on Unix).

We've already met system interfaces used by this script; most are fairly standard Unix calls, and not very Python-specific to speak of. In fact, much of what happens when we run this script occurs in programs spawned by **os.system** calls. This script is really just a *driver*; because it is completely independent of both the program to be tested and the inputs it will read, we can add new test cases on the fly by dropping a new input file in a test directory.

So given that this script just drives other programs with standard Unix-like calls, why use Python here instead of something like C? First of all, the equivalent program in C would be much longer: it would need to declare variables, handle data structures, and more. In C, all external services exist in a single global scope (the linker's scope); in Python, they are partitioned into module namespaces (**os**, **sys**, etc.) to avoid name clashes. And unlike C, the Python code can be run immediately, without compiling and linking; changes can be tested much quicker in Python. Moreover, with just a little extra work we could make this script run on Windows 9x too. As you can probably tell by now, Python excels when it comes to portability and productivity.

Because of such benefits, automated testing is a very common role for Python scripts. If you are interested in using Python for testing, be sure to see Python's web site (*http://www.python.org*) for other available tools (e.g., the PyUnit system).

Testing Gone Bad?

Once we learn about sending email from Python scripts in Chapter 11, you might also want to augment this script to automatically send out email when regularly run tests fail. That way, you don't even need to remember to check results. Of course, you could go further still.

One company I worked at added sound effects to compiler test scripts; you got an audible round of applause if no regressions were found, and an entirely different noise otherwise. (See the end of this chapter and *playfile.py* in Chapter 11 for audio hints.)

Another company in my development past ran a nightly test script that automatically isolated the source code file check-in that triggered a test regression, and sent a nasty email to the guilty party (and their supervisor). Nobody expects the Spanish Inquisition!

Packing and Unpacking Files

Many moons ago (about five years), I used machines that had no tools for bundling files into a single package for easy transport. The situation is this: you have a large set of text files lying around that you need to transfer to another computer. These days, tools like `tar` are widely available for packaging many files into a single file that can be copied, uploaded, mailed, or otherwise transferred in a single step. Even Python itself has grown to support zip archives in the 2.0 standard library (see module `zipfile`).

Before I managed to install such tools on my PC, though, portable Python scripts served just as well. Example 4-6 copies all the files listed on the command line to the standard output stream, separated by marker lines.

Example 4-6. PP2E\System\App\Clients\textpack.py

```
#!/usr/local/bin/python
import sys                         # load the system module
marker = ':'*10 + 'textpak=>'     # hopefully unique separator

def pack():
    for name in sys.argv[1:]:      # for all command-line arguments
        input = open(name, 'r')    # open the next input file
        print marker + name        # write a separator line
        print input.read(),        # and write the file's contents

if __name__ == '__main__': pack()  # pack files listed on cmdline
```

The first line in this file is a Python comment (#...), but it also gives the path to the Python interpreter using the Unix executable-script trick discussed in Chapter 2. If we give *textpack.py* executable permission with a Unix *chmod* command, we can pack files by running this program file directly from a Unix shell, and redirect its standard output stream to the file we want the packed archive to show up in. It works the same on Windows, but we just type the interpreter name "python" instead:

```
C:\...\PP2E\System\App\Clients\test>type spam.txt
SPAM
spam

C:\......\test>python ..\textpack.py spam.txt eggs.txt ham.txt > packed.all

C:\......\test>type packed.all
:::::::::textpak=>spam.txt
SPAM
spam
::::::::::textpak=>eggs.txt
EGGS
:::::::::::textpak=>ham.txt
ham
```

Running the program this way creates a single output file called *packed.all*, which contains all three input files, with a header line giving the original file's name before each file's contents. Combining many files into one like this makes it easy to transfer in a single step—only one file need be copied to floppy, emailed, and so on. If you have hundreds of files to move, this can be a big win.

After such a file is transferred, though, it must somehow be unpacked on the receiving end, to recreate the original files. To do so, we need to scan the combined file line by line, watching for header lines left by the packer to know when a new file's contents begins. Another simple Python script, shown in Example 4-7, does the trick.

Example 4-7. PP2E\System\App\Clients\textunpack.py

```
#!/usr/local/bin/python
import sys
from textpack import marker                  # use common seperator key
mlen = len(marker)                           # file names after markers

for line in sys.stdin.readlines():           # for all input lines
    if line[:mlen] != marker:                # write real lines
        print line,
    else:
        sys.stdout = open(line[mlen:-1], 'w') # or make new output file
```

We could code this in a function like we did in **textpack**, but there is little point here—as written, the script relies on standard streams, not function parameters.

Run this in the directory where you want unpacked files to appear, with the
packed archive file piped in on the command line as the script's standard input
stream:

```
C:\......\test\unpack>python ..\..\textunpack.py < ..\packed.all

C:\......\test\unpack>ls
eggs.txt   ham.txt    spam.txt

C:\......\test\unpack>type spam.txt
SPAM
Spam
```

Packing Files "++"

So far so good; the `textpack` and `textunpack` scripts made it easy to move lots
of files around, without lots of manual intervention. But after playing with these
and similar scripts for a while, I began to see *commonalities* that almost cried out
for reuse. For instance, almost every shell tool I wrote had to scan command-line
arguments, redirect streams to a variety of sources, and so on. Further, almost
every command-line utility wound up with a different command-line option pattern, because each was written from scratch.

The following few classes are one solution to such problems. They define a *class
hierarchy* that is designed for reuse of common shell tool code. Moreover,
because of the reuse going on, every program that ties into its hierarchy sports a
common look-and-feel in terms of command-line options, environment variable
use, and more. As usual with object-oriented systems, once you learn which methods to overload, such a class framework provides a lot of work and consistency
for free. The module in Example 4-8 adapts the `textpack` script's logic for integration into this hierarchy.

Example 4-8. PP2E\System\App\Clients\packapp.py

```
#!/usr/local/bin/python
###################################################
# pack text files into one, separated by marker line;
# % packapp.py -v -o target src src...
# % packapp.py *.txt -o packed1
# >>> apptools.appRun('packapp.py', args...)
# >>> apptools.appCall(PackApp, args...)
###################################################

from textpack import marker
from PP2E.System.App.Kinds.redirect import StreamApp

class PackApp(StreamApp):
    def start(self):
        StreamApp.start(self)
```

Example 4-8. PP2E\System\App\Clients\packapp.py (continued)

```
            if not self.args:
                self.exit('packapp.py [-o target]? src src...')
    def run(self):
        for name in self.restargs():
            try:
                self.message('packing: ' + name)
                self.pack_file(name)
            except:
                self.exit('error processing: ' + name)
    def pack_file(self, name):
        self.setInput(name)
        self.write(marker + name + '\n')
        while 1:
            line = self.readline()
            if not line: break
            self.write(line)

if __name__ == '__main__':  PackApp().main()
```

Here, `PackApp` inherits members and methods that handle:

* Operating system services

* Command-line processing

* Input/output stream redirection

from the `StreamApp` class, imported from another Python module file (listed in Example 4-10). `StreamApp` provides a "read/write" interface to redirected streams, and provides a standard "start/run/stop" script execution protocol. `PackApp` simply redefines the `start` and `run` methods for its own purposes, and reads and writes *itself* to access its standard streams. Most low-level system interfaces are hidden by the `StreamApp` class; in OOP terms, we say they are *encapsulated*.

This module can both be run as a program, and imported by a client (remember, Python sets a module's name to `__main__` when it's run directly, so it can tell the difference). When run as a program, the last line creates an instance of the `PackApp` class, and starts it by calling its `main` method—a method call exported by `StreamApp` to kick off a program run:

```
C:\......\test>python ..\packapp.py -v -o packedapp.all spam.txt eggs.txt ham.txt
PackApp start.
packing: spam.txt
packing: eggs.txt
packing: ham.txt
PackApp done.

C:\......\test>type packedapp.all
::::::::::textpak=>spam.txt
SPAM
spam
```

```
:::::::::::textpak=>eggs.txt
EGGS
:::::::::::::textpak=>ham.txt
ham
```

This has the same effect as the *textpack.py* script, but command-line options (-v for verbose mode, -o to name an output file) are inherited from the StreamApp superclass. The unpacker in Example 4-9 looks similar when migrated to the OO framework, because the very notion of running a program has been given a standard structure.

Example 4-9. PP2E\System\App\Clients\unpackapp.py

```
#!/usr/bin/python
##########################################
# unpack a packapp.py output file;
# % unpackapp.py -i packed1 -v
# apptools.appRun('unpackapp.py', args...)
# apptools.appCall(UnpackApp, args...)
##########################################

import string
from textpack import marker
from PP2E.System.App.Kinds.redirect import StreamApp

class UnpackApp(StreamApp):
    def start(self):
        StreamApp.start(self)
        self.endargs()                  # ignore more -o's, etc.
    def run(self):
        mlen = len(marker)
        while 1:
            line = self.readline()
            if not line:
                break
            elif line[:mlen] != marker:
                self.write(line)
            else:
                name = string.strip(line[mlen:])
                self.message('creating: ' + name)
                self.setOutput(name)

if __name__ == '__main__':  UnpackApp().main()
```

This subclass redefines start and run methods to do the right thing for this script—prepare for and execute a file unpacking operation. All the details of parsing command-line arguments and redirecting standard streams are handled in superclasses:

```
C:\......\test\unpackapp>python ..\..\unpackapp.py -v -i ..\packedapp.all
UnpackApp start.
creating: spam.txt
creating: eggs.txt
```

```
        creating: ham.txt
        UnpackApp done.

        C:\......\test\unpackapp>ls
        eggs.txt    ham.txt     spam.txt

        C:\......\test\unpackapp>type spam.txt
        SPAM
        spam
```

Running this script does the same job as the original *textunpack.py*, but we get command-line flags for free (`-i` specifies the input files). In fact, there are more ways to launch classes in this hierarchy than I have space to show here. A command line pair, `-i -`, for instance, makes the script read its input from `stdin`, as though it were simply piped or redirected in the shell:

```
        C:\......\test\unpackapp>type ..\packedapp.all | python ..\..\unpackapp.py -i -
        creating: spam.txt
        creating: eggs.txt
        creating: ham.txt
```

Application Hierarchy Superclasses

This section lists the source code of `StreamApp` and `App`—the classes that do all this extra work on behalf of `PackApp` and `UnpackApp`. We don't have space to go through all this code in detail, so be sure to study these listings on your own for more information. It's all straight Python code.

I should also point out that the classes listed in this section are just the ones used by the object-oriented mutations of the `textpack` and `textunpack` scripts. They represent just one branch of an overall application framework class tree, that you can study on this book's CD (browse directory *PP2E\System\App*). Other classes in the tree provide command menus, internal string-based file streams, and so on. You'll also find additional clients of the hierarchy that do things like launch other shell tools, and scan Unix-style email mailbox files.

StreamApp: Adding stream redirection

`StreamApp` adds a few command-line arguments (`-i`, `-o`) and input/output stream redirection to the more general `App` root class listed later; `App` in turn defines the most general kinds of program behavior, to be inherited in Examples 4-8, 4-9, and 4-10, i.e., in all classes derived from `App`.

Example 4-10. PP2E\System\App\Kinds\redirect.py

```
###########################################################################
# App subclasses for redirecting standard streams to files
###########################################################################
```

Example 4-10. PP2E\System\App\Kinds\redirect.py (continued)

```python
import sys
from PP2E.System.App.Bases.app import App

##############################################################################
# an app with input/output stream redirection
##############################################################################

class StreamApp(App):
    def __init__(self, ifile='-', ofile='-'):
        App.__init__(self)                          # call superclass init
        self.setInput( ifile or self.name + '.in')  # default i/o file names
        self.setOutput(ofile or self.name + '.out') # unless '-i', '-o' args

    def closeApp(self):                             # not __del__
        try:
            if self.input != sys.stdin:             # may be redirected
                self.input.close()                  # if still open
        except: pass
        try:
            if self.output != sys.stdout:           # don't close stdout!
                self.output.close()                 # input/output exist?
        except: pass

    def help(self):
        App.help(self)
        print '-i <input-file |"-">   (default: stdin  or per app)'
        print '-o <output-file|"-">   (default: stdout or per app)'

    def setInput(self, default=None):
        file = self.getarg('-i') or default or '-'
        if file == '-':
            self.input = sys.stdin
            self.input_name = '<stdin>'
        else:
            self.input = open(file, 'r')            # cmdarg | funcarg | stdin
            self.input_name = file                  # cmdarg '-i -' works too

    def setOutput(self, default=None):
        file = self.getarg('-o') or default or '-'
        if file == '-':
            self.output = sys.stdout
            self.output_name = '<stdout>'
        else:
            self.output = open(file, 'w')           # error caught in main()
            self.output_name = file                 # make backups too?

class RedirectApp(StreamApp):
    def __init__(self, ifile=None, ofile=None):
        StreamApp.__init__(self, ifile, ofile)
        self.streams = sys.stdin, sys.stdout
        sys.stdin    = self.input                   # for raw_input, stdin
        sys.stdout   = self.output                  # for print, stdout
```

Example 4-10. PP2E\System\App\Kinds\redirect.py (continued)

```
    def closeApp(self):                         # not __del__
        StreamApp.closeApp(self)                # close files?
        sys.stdin, sys.stdout = self.streams    # reset sys files


#########################################################
# to add as a mix-in (or use multiple-inheritance...)
#########################################################

class RedirectAnyApp:
    def __init__(self, superclass, *args):
        apply(superclass.__init__, (self,) + args)
        self.super   = superclass
        self.streams = sys.stdin, sys.stdout
        sys.stdin    = self.input               # for raw_input, stdin
        sys.stdout   = self.output              # for print, stdout

    def closeApp(self):
        self.super.closeApp(self)               # do the right thing
        sys.stdin, sys.stdout = self.streams    # reset sys files
```

App: The root class

The top of the hierarchy knows what it means to be a shell application, but not
how to accomplish a particular utility task (those parts are filled in by subclasses).
App, listed in Example 4-11, exports commonly used tools in a standard and simplified interface, and a customizable **start/run/stop** method protocol that
abstracts script execution. It also turns application objects into file-like objects:
when an application reads itself, for instance, it really reads whatever source its
standard input stream has been assigned to by other superclasses in the tree (like
StreamApp).

Example 4-11. PP2E\System\App\Bases\app.py

```
#############################################################################
# an application class hierarchy, for handling top-level components;
# App is the root class of the App hierarchy, extended in other files;
#############################################################################

import sys, os, traceback
AppError = 'App class error'                            # errors raised here

class App:                                              # the root class
    def __init__(self, name=None):
        self.name    = name or self.__class__.__name__  # the lowest class
        self.args    = sys.argv[1:]
        self.env     = os.environ
        self.verbose = self.getopt('-v') or self.getenv('VERBOSE')
        self.input   = sys.stdin
        self.output  = sys.stdout
```

Example 4-11. PP2E\System\App\Bases\app.py (continued)

```python
        self.error   = sys.stderr                       # stdout may be piped
    def closeApp(self):                                 # not __del__: ref's?
        pass                                            # nothing at this level
    def help(self):
        print self.name, 'command-line arguments:'      # extend in subclass
        print '-v (verbose)'


    ##############################
    # script environment services
    ##############################

    def getopt(self, tag):
        try:                                            # test "-x" command arg
            self.args.remove(tag)                       # not real argv: > 1 App?
            return 1
        except:
            return 0
    def getarg(self, tag, default=None):
        try:                                            # get "-x val" command arg
            pos = self.args.index(tag)
            val = self.args[pos+1]
            self.args[pos:pos+2] = []
            return val
        except:
            return default                              # None: missing, no default
    def getenv(self, name, default=''):
        try:                                            # get "$x" environment var
            return self.env[name]
        except KeyError:
            return default
    def endargs(self):
        if self.args:
            self.message('extra arguments ignored: ' + `self.args`)
            self.args = []
    def restargs(self):
        res, self.args = self.args, []                  # no more args/options
        return res
    def message(self, text):
        self.error.write(text + '\n')                   # stdout may be redirected
    def exception(self):
        return (sys.exc_type, sys.exc_value)            # the last exception
    def exit(self, message='', status=1):
        if message:
            self.message(message)
        sys.exit(status)
    def shell(self, command, fork=0, inp=''):
        if self.verbose:
            self.message(command)                              # how about ipc?
        if not fork:
            os.system(command)                                 # run a shell cmd
        elif fork == 1:
```

Example 4-11. PP2E\System\App\Bases\app.py (continued)

```
        return os.popen(command, 'r').read()      # get its output
    else:                                          # readlines too?
        pipe = os.popen(command, 'w')
        pipe.write(inp)                            # send it input
        pipe.close()


################################################
# input/output-stream methods for the app itself;
# redefine in subclasses if not using files, or
# set self.input/output to file-like objects;
################################################

def read(self, *size):
    return apply(self.input.read, size)
def readline(self):
    return self.input.readline()
def readlines(self):
    return self.input.readlines()
def write(self, text):
    self.output.write(text)
def writelines(self, text):
    self.output.writelines(text)


################################################
# to run the app
# main() is the start/run/stop execution protocol;
################################################

def main(self):
    res = None
    try:
        self.start()
        self.run()
        res = self.stop()                          # optional return val
    except SystemExit:                             # ignore if from exit()
        pass
    except:
        self.message('uncaught: ' + `self.exception()`)
        traceback.print_exc()
    self.closeApp()
    return res

def start(self):
    if self.verbose: self.message(self.name + ' start.')
def stop(self):
    if self.verbose: self.message(self.name + ' done.')
def run(self):
    raise AppError, 'run must be redefined!'
```

Why use classes here?

Now that I've listed all this code, some readers might naturally want to ask, "So why go to all this trouble?" Given the amount of *extra* code in the OO version of these scripts, it's a perfectly valid question. Most of the code listed in Example 4-11 is general-purpose logic, designed to be used by many applications. Still, that doesn't explain why the `packapp` and `unpackapp` OO scripts are larger than the original equivalent `textpack` and `textunpack` non-OO scripts.

The answers will become more apparent after the first few times you *don't* have to write code to achieve a goal, but there are some concrete benefits worth summarizing here:

Encapsulation

> `StreamApp` clients need not remember all the system interfaces in Python, because `StreamApp` exports its own unified view. For instance, arguments, streams, and shell variables are split across Python modules (e.g., `sys.argv`, `sys.stdout`, `os.environ`); in these classes, they are all collected in the same single place.

Standardization

> From the shell user's perspective, `StreamApp` clients all have a common look-and-feel, because they inherit the same interfaces to the outside world from their superclasses (e.g., -i and -v flags).

Maintenance

> All the common code in the `App` and `StreamApp` superclasses must be debugged only once. Moreover, localizing code in superclasses makes it easier to understand and change in the future.

Reuse

> Such a framework can provide an extra precoded utility we would otherwise have to recode in every script we write (command-line argument extraction, for instance). That holds true both now and in the future—services added to the `App` root class become immediately usable and customizable among all applications derived from this hierarchy.

Utility

> Because file access isn't hardcoded in `PackApp` and `UnpackApp`, they can easily take on new behavior, just by changing the class they inherit from. Given the right superclass, `PackApp` and `UnpackApp` could just as easily read and write to strings or sockets, as to text files and standard streams.

Although it's not obvious until you start writing larger class-based systems, code reuse is perhaps the biggest win for class-based programs. For instance, in

Chapter 9, *Larger GUI Examples*, we will reuse the OO-based packer and unpacker scripts by invoking them from a menu GUI like this:

```
from PP2E.System.App.Clients.packapp import PackApp
...get dialog inputs, glob filename patterns
app = PackApp(ofile=output)              # run with redirected output
app.args = filenames                     # reset cmdline args list
app.main()


from PP2E.System.App.Clients.unpackapp import UnpackApp
...get dialog input
app = UnpackApp(ifile=input)             # run with input from file
app.main()                               # execute app class
```

Because these classes encapsulate the notion of streams, they can be imported and called, not just run as top-level scripts. Further, their code is reusable two ways: not only do they export common system interfaces for reuse in subclasses, but they can also be used as software *components* as in the previous code listing. See the *PP2E\Gui\Shellgui* directory for the full source code of these clients.

Python doesn't impose OO programming, of course, and you can get a lot of work done with simpler functions and scripts. But once you learn how to structure class trees for reuse, going the extra OO mile usually pays off in the long run.

User-Friendly Program Launchers

Suppose, for just a moment, that you wish to ship Python programs to an audience that may be in the very early stages of evolving from computer user to computer programmer. Maybe you are shipping a Python application to nontechnical users; or perhaps you're interested in shipping a set of cool Python demo programs on a Python book's CD-ROM. Whatever the reason, some of the people who will use your software can't be expected to do any more than click a mouse—much less edit their system configuration files to set things like PATH and PYTHONPATH per your programs' assumptions. Your software will have to configure itself.

Luckily, Python scripts can do that too. In the next two sections, we're going to see two modules that aim to automatically launch programs with minimal assumptions about the environment on the host machine:

- *Launcher.py* is a library of tools for automatically configuring the shell environment in preparation for launching a Python script. It can be used to set required shell variables—both the PATH system program search path (used to find the "python" executable), and the PYTHONPATH module search path (used to resolve imports within scripts). Because such variable settings made in a parent program are *inherited* by spawned child programs, this interface lets scripts preconfigure search paths for other scripts.

• *LaunchBrowser.py* aims to portably locate and start an Internet browser program on the host machine to view a local file or remote web page. It uses tools in *Launcher.py* to search for a reasonable browser to run.

Both of these modules are designed to be reusable in any context where you want your software to be user-friendly. By searching for files and configuring environments automatically, your users can avoid (or at least postpone) having to learn the intricacies of environment configuration.

Launcher Module Clients

The two modules in this section see action in many of this book's examples. In fact, we've already used some of these tools. The `launchmodes` script we met at the end of the prior chapter imported `Launcher` functions to hunt for the local *python.exe* interpreter's path, needed by `os.spawnv` calls. That script could have assumed that everyone who installs it on their machine will edit its source code to add their own Python location; but the technical know-how required for even that task is already light-years beyond many potential users.* It's much nicer to invest a negligible amount of startup time to locate Python automatically.

The two modules listed in Examples 4-14 and 4-15, together with `launchmodes`, also form the core of the *demo-launcher programs* at the top of the examples distribution on this book's CD. There's nothing quite like being able to witness programs in action first-hand, so I wanted to make it as easy as possible to launch Python examples in the book. Ideally, they should run straight off the CD when clicked, and not require readers to wade through a complex environment installation procedure.

However, many demos perform cross-directory imports, and so require the book's module package directories to be installed in PYTHONPATH; it is not enough just to click on some programs' icons at random. Moreover, when first starting out, users can't be assumed to have added the Python executable to their system search path either; the name "python" might not mean anything in the shell.

At least on platforms tested thus far, the following modules solve such configuration problems. For example, script *Launch_PyDemos.pyw* in the root directory automatically configures the system and Python execution environments using

---

* You gurus and wizards out there will just have to take my word for it. One of the very first things you learn from flying around the world teaching Python to beginners is just how much knowledge developers take for granted. In the book *Learning Python*, for example, my co-author and I directed readers to do things like "open a file in your favorite text editor" and "start up a DOS command console." We had no shortage of email from beginners wondering what in the world we meant.

Launcher.py tools, and then spawns *PyDemos.py*, a Tkinter GUI Demo interface we'll meet later in this book. PyDemos in turn uses `launchmodes` to spawn other programs, that also inherit the environment settings made at the top. The net effect is that clicking any of the `Launch_*` scripts starts Python programs even if you haven't touched your environment settings at all.

You still need to install Python if it's not present, of course, but the Python Windows self-installer is a simple point-and-click affair too. Because searches and configuration take extra time, it's still to your advantage to *eventually* configure your environment settings and run programs like PyDemos directly, instead of through the launcher scripts. But there's much to be said for instant gratification when it comes to software.

These tools will show up in other contexts later in this text, too. For instance, the PyMail email interface we'll meet in Chapter 11 uses `Launcher` to locate its own source code file; since it's impossible to know what directory it will be run from, the best it can do is search. Another GUI example, `big_gui`, will use a similar `Launcher` tool to locate canned Python source-distribution demo programs in arbitrary and unpredictable places on the underlying computer.

The `LaunchBrowser` script in Example 4-15 also uses `Launcher` to locate suitable web browsers, and is itself used to start Internet demos in the PyDemos and PyGadgets launcher GUIs—that is, `Launcher` starts PyDemos, which starts `LaunchBrowser`, which uses `Launcher`. By optimizing generality, these modules also optimize reusability.

Launching Programs Without Environment Settings

Because the *Launcher.py* file is heavily documented, I won't go over its fine points in narrative here. Instead, I'll just point out that all of its functions are useful by themselves, but the main entry point is the `launchBookExamples` function near the end; you need to work your way from the bottom of this file up to glimpse its larger picture.

The `launchBookExamples` function uses all the others, to configure the environment and then spawn one or more programs to run in that environment. In fact, the top-level demo launcher scripts shown in Examples 4-12 and 4-13 do nothing more than ask this function to spawn GUI demo interface programs we'll meet later (e.g., *PyDemos.pyw*, *PyGadgets_bar.pyw*). Because the GUIs are spawned indirectly through this interface, all programs they spawn inherit the environment configurations too.

Example 4-12. PP2E\Launch_PyDemos.pyw

```
#!/bin/env python
###############################################
# PyDemos + environment search/config first
# run this if you haven't setup your paths yet
# you still must install Python first, though
###############################################

import Launcher
Launcher.launchBookExamples(['PyDemos.pyw'], 0)
```

Example 4-13. PP2E\Launch_PyGadgets_bar.pyw

```
#!/bin/env python
#################################################
# PyGadgets_bar + environment search/config first
# run this if you haven't setup your paths yet
# you still must install Python first, though
#################################################

import Launcher
Launcher.launchBookExamples(['PyGadgets_bar.pyw'], 0)
```

When run directly, *PyDemos.pyw* and *PyGadgets_bar.pyw* instead rely on the configuration settings on the underlying machine. In other words, `Launcher` effectively *hides* configuration details from the GUI interfaces, by enclosing them in a
configuration program layer. To understand how, study Example 4-14.

Example 4-14. PP2E\Launcher.py

```
#!/usr/bin/env python
"""
-----------------------------------------------------------------------------
Tools to find files, and run Python demos even if your environment has
not been manually configured yet.  For instance, provided you have already
installed Python, you can launch Tk demos directly off the book's CD by
double-clicking this file's icon, without first changing your environment
config files.  Assumes Python has been installed first (double-click on the
python self-install exe on the CD), and tries to guess where Python and the
examples distribution live on your machine.  Sets Python module and system
search paths before running scripts: this only works because env settings
are inherited by spawned programs on both windows and linux.  You may want
to tweak the list of directories searched for speed, and probably want to
run one of the Config/setup-pp files at startup time to avoid this search.
This script is friendly to already-configured path settings, and serves to
demo platform-independent directory path processing.  Python programs can
always be started under the Windows port by clicking (or spawning a 'start'
DOS command), but many book examples require the module search path too.
-----------------------------------------------------------------------------
"""

import sys, os, string
```

Example 4-14. PP2E\Launcher.py (continued)

```
def which(program, trace=1):
    """
    Look for program in all dirs in the system's search
    path var, PATH; return full path to program if found,
    else None. Doesn't handle aliases on Unix (where we
    could also just run a 'which' shell cmd with os.popen),
    and it might help to also check if the file is really
    an executable with os.stat and the stat module, using
    code like this: os.stat(filename)[stat.ST_MODE] & 0111
    """
    try:
        ospath = os.environ['PATH']
    except:
        ospath = ''  # okay if not set
    systempath = string.split(ospath, os.pathsep)
    if trace: print 'Looking for', program, 'on', systempath
    for sysdir in systempath:
        filename = os.path.join(sysdir, program)      # adds os.sep between
        if os.path.isfile(filename):                  # exists and is a file?
            if trace: print 'Found', filename
            return filename
        else:
            if trace: print 'Not at', filename
    if trace: print program, 'not on system path'
    return None


def findFirst(thisDir, targetFile, trace=0):
    """
    Search directories at and below thisDir for a file
    or dir named targetFile.  Like find.find in standard
    lib, but no name patterns, follows unix links, and
    stops at the first file found with a matching name.
    targetFile must be a simple base name, not dir path.
    """
    if trace: print 'Scanning', thisDir
    for filename in os.listdir(thisDir):              # skip . and ..
        if filename in [os.curdir, os.pardir]:        # just in case
            continue
        elif filename == targetFile:                  # check name match
            return os.path.join(thisDir, targetFile)  # stop at this one
        else:
            pathname = os.path.join(thisDir, filename)  # recur in subdirs
            if os.path.isdir(pathname):                 # stop at 1st match
                below = findFirst(pathname, targetFile, trace)
                if below: return below


def guessLocation(file, isOnWindows=(sys.platform[:3]=='win'), trace=1):
    """
    Try to find directory where file is installed
    by looking in standard places for the platform.
```

Example 4-14. PP2E\Launcher.py (continued)

```
    Change tries lists as needed for your machine.
    """
    cwd = os.getcwd()                                # directory where py started
    tryhere = cwd + os.sep + file                    # or os.path.join(cwd, file)
    if os.path.exists(tryhere):                      # don't search if it is here
        return tryhere                               # findFirst(cwd,file) descends
    if isOnWindows:
        tries = []
        for pydir in [r'C:\Python20', r'C:\Program Files\Python']:
            if os.path.exists(pydir):
                tries.append(pydir)
        tries = tries + [cwd, r'C:\Program Files']
        for drive in 'CGDEF':
            tries.append(drive + ':\\')
    else:
        tries = [cwd, os.environ['HOME'], '/usr/bin', '/usr/local/bin']
    for dir in tries:
        if trace: print 'Searching for %s in %s' % (file, dir)
        try:
            match = findFirst(dir, file)
        except OSError:
            if trace: print 'Error while searching', dir    # skip bad drives
        else:
            if match: return match
    if trace: print file, 'not found! - configure your environment manually'
    return None


PP2EpackageRoots = [                                 # python module search path
  #'%sPP2E' % os.sep,                                # pass in your own elsewhere
  '']                                                # '' adds examplesDir root


def configPythonPath(examplesDir, packageRoots=PP2EpackageRoots, trace=1):
    """
    Setup the Python module import search-path directory
    list as necessary to run programs in the book examples
    distribution, in case it hasn't been configured already.
    Add examples package root, plus nested package roots.
    This corresponds to the setup-pp* config file settings.
    os.environ assignments call os.putenv internally in 1.5,
    so these settings will be inherited by spawned programs.
    Python source lib dir and '.' are automatically searched;
    unix|win os.sep is '/' | '\\', os.pathsep is ':' | ';'.
    sys.path is for this process only--must set os.environ.
    adds new dirs to front, in case there are two installs.
    could also try to run platform's setup-pp* file in this
    process, but that's non-portable, slow, and error-prone.
    """
    try:
        ospythonpath = os.environ['PYTHONPATH']
    except:
```

Example 4-14. PP2E\Launcher.py (continued)

```
            ospythonpath = '' # okay if not set
        if trace: print 'PYTHONPATH start:\n', ospythonpath
        addList = []
        for root in packageRoots:
            importDir = examplesDir + root
            if importDir in sys.path:
                if trace: print 'Exists', importDir
            else:
                if trace: print 'Adding', importDir
                sys.path.append(importDir)
                addList.append(importDir)
        if addList:
            addString = string.join(addList, os.pathsep) + os.pathsep
            os.environ['PYTHONPATH'] = addString + ospythonpath
            if trace: print 'PYTHONPATH updated:\n', os.environ['PYTHONPATH']
        else:
            if trace: print 'PYTHONPATH unchanged'


def configSystemPath(pythonDir, trace=1):
    """
    Add python executable dir to system search path if needed
    """
    try:
        ospath = os.environ['PATH']
    except:
        ospath = '' # okay if not set
    if trace: print 'PATH start', ospath
    if (string.find(ospath, pythonDir) == -1 and           # not found?
        string.find(ospath, string.upper(pythonDir)) == -1):   # case diff?
            os.environ['PATH'] = ospath + os.pathsep + pythonDir
            if trace: print 'PATH updated:', os.environ['PATH']
    else:
        if trace: print 'PATH unchanged'


def runCommandLine(pypath, exdir, command, isOnWindows=0, trace=1):
    """
    Run python command as an independent program/process on
    this platform, using pypath as the Python executable,
    and exdir as the installed examples root directory.
    Need full path to python on windows, but not on unix.
    On windows, a os.system('start ' + command) is similar,
    except that .py files pop up a dos console box for i/o.
    Could use launchmodes.py too but pypath is already known.
    """
    command = exdir + os.sep + command           # rooted in examples tree
    os.environ['PP2E_PYTHON_FILE'] = pypath       # export directories for
    os.environ['PP2E_EXAMPLE_DIR'] = exdir        # use in spawned programs

    if trace: print 'Spawning:', command
    if isOnWindows:
```

Example 4-14. PP2E\Launcher.py (continued)

```
        os.spawnv(os.P_DETACH, pypath, ('python', command))
    else:
        cmdargs = [pypath] + string.split(command)
        if os.fork() == 0:
            os.execv(pypath, cmdargs)              # run prog in child process


def launchBookExamples(commandsToStart, trace=1):
    """
    Toplevel entry point: find python exe and
    examples dir, config env, spawn programs
    """
    isOnWindows  = (sys.platform[:3] == 'win')
    pythonFile   = (isOnWindows and 'python.exe') or 'python'
    examplesFile = 'README-PP2E.txt'
    if trace:
        print os.getcwd(), os.curdir, os.sep, os.pathsep
        print 'starting on %s...' % sys.platform

    # find python executable: check system path, then guess
    pypath = which(pythonFile) or guessLocation(pythonFile, isOnWindows)
    assert pypath
    pydir, pyfile = os.path.split(pypath)          # up 1 from file
    if trace:
        print 'Using this Python executable:', pypath
        raw_input('Press <enter> key')

    # find examples root dir: check cwd and others
    expath = guessLocation(examplesFile, isOnWindows)
    assert expath
    updir = string.split(expath, os.sep)[:-2]      # up 2 from file
    exdir = string.join(updir,   os.sep)           # to PP2E pkg parent
    if trace:
        print 'Using this examples root directory:', exdir
        raw_input('Press <enter> key')

    # export python and system paths if needed
    configSystemPath(pydir)
    configPythonPath(exdir)
    if trace:
        print 'Environment configured'
        raw_input('Press <enter> key')

    # spawn programs
    for command in commandsToStart:
        runCommandLine(pypath, os.path.dirname(expath), command, isOnWindows)


if __name__ == '__main__':
    #
    # if no args, spawn all in the list of programs below
    # else rest of cmd line args give single cmd to be spawned
```

Example 4-14. PP2E\Launcher.py (continued)

```
#
if len(sys.argv) == 1:
    commandsToStart = [
        'Gui/TextEditor/textEditor.pyw',        # either slash works
        'Lang/Calculator/calculator.py',        # os normalizes path
        'PyDemos.pyw',
       #'PyGadgets.py',
        'echoEnvironment.pyw'
    ]
else:
    commandsToStart = [ string.join(sys.argv[1:], ' ') ]
launchBookExamples(commandsToStart)
import time
if sys.platform[:3] == 'win': time.sleep(10)    # to read msgs if clicked
```

One way to understand the Launcher script is to trace the messages it prints along the way. When run by itself without a PYTHONPATH setting, the script finds a suitable Python and the examples root directory (by hunting for its README file), uses those results to configure PATH and PYTHONPATH settings if needed, and spawns a precoded list of program examples. To illustrate, here is a launch on Windows with an empty PYTHONPATH:

```
C:\temp\examples>set PYTHONPATH=

C:\temp\examples>python Launcher.py
C:\temp\examples . \ ;
starting on win32...
Looking for python.exe on ['C:\\WINDOWS', 'C:\\WINDOWS',
'C:\\WINDOWS\\COMMAND', 'C:\\STUFF\\BIN.MKS', 'C:\\PROGRAM FILES\\PYTHON']
Not at C:\WINDOWS\python.exe
Not at C:\WINDOWS\python.exe
Not at C:\WINDOWS\COMMAND\python.exe
Not at C:\STUFF\BIN.MKS\python.exe
Found C:\PROGRAM FILES\PYTHON\python.exe
Using this Python executable: C:\PROGRAM FILES\PYTHON\python.exe
Press <enter> key
Using this examples root directory: C:\temp\examples
Press <enter> key
PATH start C:\WINDOWS;C:\WINDOWS;C:\WINDOWS\COMMAND;C:\STUFF\BIN.MKS;
C:\PROGRAM FILES\PYTHON
PATH unchanged
PYTHONPATH start:

Adding C:\temp\examples\Part3
Adding C:\temp\examples\Part2
Adding C:\temp\examples\Part2\Gui
Adding C:\temp\examples
PYTHONPATH updated:
C:\temp\examples\Part3;C:\temp\examples\Part2;C:\temp\examples\Part2\Gui;
C:\temp\examples;
Environment configured
```

```
Press <enter> key
Spawning: C:\temp\examples\Part2/Gui/TextEditor/textEditor.pyw
Spawning: C:\temp\examples\Part2/Lang/Calculator/calculator.py
Spawning: C:\temp\examples\PyDemos.pyw
Spawning: C:\temp\examples\echoEnvironment.pyw
```

Four programs are spawned with PATH and PYTHONPATH preconfigured according to the location of your Python interpreter program, the location of your examples distribution tree, and the list of required PYTHONPATH entries in script variable `PP2EpackageRoots`.

The PYTHONPATH directories that are added by preconfiguration steps may be different when you run this script, because the `PP2EpackageRoots` variable may have an arbitrarily different setting by the time this book's CD is burned. In fact, to make this example more interesting, the outputs listed were generated at a time when the book's PYTHONPATH requirements were much more complex than they are now:

```
PP2EpackageRoots = [
    '%sPart3' % os.sep,   # python module search path
    '%sPart2' % os.sep,   # required by book demos
    '%sPart2%sGui' % ((os.sep,)*2),
    '']                   # '' adds examplesDir root
```

Since then, the tree has been reorganized so that only one directory needs to be added to the module search path—the one containing the *PP2E* root directory. That makes it easier to configure (only one entry is added to PYTHONPATH now), but the code still supports a list of entries for generality. Like most developers, I can't resist playing with the directories.

When used by the PyDemos launcher script, `Launcher` does not pause for key presses along the way (the `trace` argument is passed in false). Here is the output generated when using the module to launch PyDemos with PYTHONPATH already set to include all the required directories; the script both avoids adding settings redundantly, and retains any exiting settings already in your environment:

```
C:\PP2ndEd\examples>python Launch_PyDemos.pyw
Looking for python.exe on ['C:\\WINDOWS', 'C:\\WINDOWS',
'C:\\WINDOWS\\COMMAND', 'C:\\STUFF\\BIN.MKS', 'C:\\PROGRAM FILES\\PYTHON']
Not at C:\WINDOWS\python.exe
Not at C:\WINDOWS\python.exe
Not at C:\WINDOWS\COMMAND\python.exe
Not at C:\STUFF\BIN.MKS\python.exe
Found C:\PROGRAM FILES\PYTHON\python.exe
PATH start C:\WINDOWS;C:\WINDOWS;C:\WINDOWS\COMMAND;C:\STUFF\BIN.MKS;
C:\PROGRAM FILES\PYTHON
PATH unchanged
PYTHONPATH start:
```

```
C:\PP2ndEd\examples\Part3;C:\PP2ndEd\examples\Part2;C:\PP2ndEd\examples\
Part2\Gui;C:\PP2ndEd\examples
Exists C:\PP2ndEd\examples\Part3
Exists C:\PP2ndEd\examples\Part2
Exists C:\PP2ndEd\examples\Part2\Gui
Exists C:\PP2ndEd\examples
PYTHONPATH unchanged
Spawning: C:\PP2ndEd\examples\PyDemos.pyw
```

And finally, here is the trace output of a launch on my Linux system; because Launcher is written with portable Python code and library calls, environment configuration and directory searches work just as well there:

```
[mark@toy ~/PP2ndEd/examples]$ unsetenv PYTHONPATH
[mark@toy ~/PP2ndEd/examples]$ python Launcher.py
/home/mark/PP2ndEd/examples . / :
starting on linux2...
Looking for python on ['/home/mark/bin', '.', '/usr/bin', '/usr/bin', '/usr/local/
bin', '/usr/X11R6/bin', '/bin', '/usr/X11R6/bin', '/home/mark/
bin', '/usr/X11R6/bin', '/home/mark/bin', '/usr/X11R6/bin']
Not at /home/mark/bin/python
Not at ./python
Found /usr/bin/python
Using this Python executable: /usr/bin/python
Press <enter> key
Using this examples root directory: /home/mark/PP2ndEd/examples
Press <enter> key
PATH start /home/mark/bin:.:/usr/bin:/usr/bin:/usr/local/bin:/usr/X11R6/bin:/bin:/
usr
/X11R6/bin:/home/mark/bin:/usr/X11R6/bin:/home/mark/bin:/usr/X11R6/bin
PATH unchanged
PYTHONPATH start:

Adding /home/mark/PP2ndEd/examples/Part3
Adding /home/mark/PP2ndEd/examples/Part2
Adding /home/mark/PP2ndEd/examples/Part2/Gui
Adding /home/mark/PP2ndEd/examples
PYTHONPATH updated:
/home/mark/PP2ndEd/examples/Part3:/home/mark/PP2ndEd/examples/Part2:/home/
mark/PP2ndEd/examples/Part2/Gui:/home/mark/PP2ndEd/examples:
Environment configured
Press <enter> key
Spawning: /home/mark/PP2ndEd/examples/Part2/Gui/TextEditor/textEditor.py
Spawning: /home/mark/PP2ndEd/examples/Part2/Lang/Calculator/calculator.py
Spawning: /home/mark/PP2ndEd/examples/PyDemos.pyw
Spawning: /home/mark/PP2ndEd/examples/echoEnvironment.pyw
```

In all of these launches, the Python interpreter was found on the system search-path, so no real searches were performed (the "Not at" lines near the top represent the module's which function). In a moment, we'll also use the Launcher's which and guessLocation functions to look for web browsers in a way that kicks off searches in standard install directory trees. Later in the book, we'll use this module in other ways—for instance, to search for demo programs and source code files somewhere on the machine, with calls of this form:

```
C:\temp>python
>>> from PP2E.Launcher import guessLocation
>>> guessLocation('hanoi.py')
Searching for hanoi.py in C:\Program Files\Python
Searching for hanoi.py in C:\temp\examples
Searching for hanoi.py in C:\Program Files
Searching for hanoi.py in C:\
'C:\\PP2ndEd\\cdrom\\Python1.5.2\\SourceDistribution\\Unpacked\\Python-1.5.2
\\Demo\\tkinter\\guido\\hanoi.py'

>>> from PP2E.Launcher import findFirst
>>> findFirst('.', 'PyMailGui.py')
'.\\examples\\Internet\\Email\\PyMailGui.py'
```

Such searches aren't necessary if you can rely on an environment variable to give at least part of the path to a file; for instance, paths scripts within the *PP2E* examples tree can be named by joining the PP2EHOME shell variable, with the rest of the script's path (assuming the rest of the script's path won't change, and we can rely on that shell variable being set everywhere).

Some scripts may also be able to compose relative paths to other scripts using the sys.path[0] home-directory indicator added for imports (see the section "Current Working Directory" in Chapter 2). But in cases where a file can appear at arbitrary places, searches like those shown previously are sometimes the best scripts can do. The earlier *hanoi.py* program file, for example, can be anywhere on the underlying machine (if present at all); searching is a more user-friendly final alternative than simply giving up.

Launching Web Browsers Portably

Web browsers can do amazing things these days. They can serve as document viewers, remote program launchers, database interfaces, media players, and more. Being able to open a browser on a local or remote page file *from within a script* opens up all kinds of interesting user-interface possibilities. For instance, a Python system might automatically display its HTML-coded documentation when needed, by launching the local web browser on the appropriate page file.[*] Because most browsers know how to present pictures, audio files, and movie clips, opening a browser on such a file is also a simple way for scripts to deal with multimedia.

The last script listed in this chapter is less ambitious than *Launcher.py*, but equally reusable: *LaunchBrowser.py* attempts to provide a *portable* interface for starting a

---

[*] For example, the PyDemos demo bar GUI we'll meet in Chapter 8, *A Tkinter Tour, Part 2*, has buttons that automatically open a browser on web pages related to this book when pressed—the publisher's site, the Python home page, my update files, and so on.

Finding Programs on Windows

Per a tip from a Python Windows guru, it may also be possible to determine the location of the installed Python interpreter on Windows with platform-specific code like this:

```
import _winreg
try:
    keyname = "SOFTWARE\\Microsoft\\Windows\\" +
              "CurrentVersion\\AppPaths\\python.exe"
    pyexe   =_winreg.QueryValue(
              _winreg.HKEY_LOCAL_MACHINE, keyname)
except _winreg.error:
    # not found
```

This code uses the **_winreg** module (new as of Python 1.6) to find Python if it has been installed correctly. The same sort of code will work for most other well-installed applications (e.g., web browsers), but not for some other kinds of files (e.g., Python scripts). It's also too Windows-specific to cover better in this text; see Windows resources for more details.

---

web browser. Because techniques for launching browsers vary per platform, this script provides an interface that aims to hide the differences from callers. Once launched, the browser runs as an independent program, and may be opened to view either a local file or a remote page on the Web.

Here's how it works. Because most web browsers can be started with shell command lines, this script simply builds and launches one as appropriate. For instance, to run a Netscape browser on Linux, a shell command of the form **netscape** *url* is run, where *url* begins with "file://" for local files, and "http://" for live remote-page accesses (this is per URL conventions we'll meet in more detail later, in Chapter 12). On Windows, a shell command like **start** *url* achieves the same goal. Here are some platform-specific highlights:

Windows platforms

On Windows, the script either opens browsers with DOS *start* commands, or searches for and runs browsers with the **os.spawnv** call. On this platform, browsers can usually be opened with simple *start* commands (e.g., **os. system("start xxx.html")**). Unfortunately, *start* relies on the underlying filename associations for web page files on your machine, picks a browser for you per those associations, and has a command-line length limit that this script might exceed for long local file paths or remote page addresses.

Because of that, this script falls back on running an explicitly named browser with **os.spawnv**, if requested or required. To do so, though, it must find the full path to a browser executable. Since it can't assume that users will add it to the PATH system search path (or this script's source code), the script searches for a suitable browser with `Launcher` module tools in both directories on PATH and in common places where executables are installed on Windows.

Unix-like platforms

On other platforms, the script relies on `os.system` and the system PATH setting on the underlying machine. It simply runs a command line naming the first browser on a candidates list that it can find on your PATH setting. Because it's much more likely that browsers are in standard search directories on platforms like Unix and Linux (e.g., */usr/bin*), the script doesn't look for a browser elsewhere on the machine. Notice the `&` at the end of the browser command-line run; without it, `os.system` calls block on Unix-like platforms.

All of this is easily customized (this is Python code, after all), and you may need to add additional logic for other platforms. But on all of my machines, the script makes reasonable assumptions that allow me to largely forget most of the platform-specific bits previously discussed; I just call the same `launchBrowser` function everywhere. For more details, let's look at Example 4-15.

Example 4-15. PP2E\LaunchBrowser.py

```
#!/bin/env python
################################################################
# Launch a web browser to view a web page, portably.  If run
# in '-live' mode, assumes you have a Internet feed and opens
# a page at a remote site.  Otherwise, assumes the page is a
# full file path name on your machine, and opens the page file
# locally.  On Unix/Linux, finds first browser on your $PATH.
# On Windows, tries DOS "start" command first, or searches for
# the location of a browser on your machine for os.spawnv by
# checking PATH and common Windows executable directories. You
# may need to tweak browser executable name/dirs if this fails.
# This has only been tested in Win98 and Linux, so you may need
# to add more code for other machines (mac: ic.launcurl(url)?).
################################################################

import os, sys
from Launcher import which, guessLocation      # file search utilities
useWinStart = 1                                 # 0=ignore name associations
onWindows   = sys.platform[:3] == 'win'
helptext    = "Usage: LaunchBrowser.py [ -file path | -live path site ]"
#browser    = r'c:\"Program Files"\Netscape\Communicator\Program\netscape.exe'

# defaults
Mode = '-file'
Page = os.getcwd() + '/Internet/Cgi-Web/PyInternetDemos.html'
Site = 'starship.python.net/~lutz'

def launchUnixBrowser(url, verbose=1):          # add your platform if unique
    tries = ['netscape', 'mosaic', 'lynx']      # order your preferences here
    for program in tries:
```

Example 4-15. PP2E\LaunchBrowser.py (continued)

```
        if which(program): break          # find one that is on $path
    else:
        assert 0, 'Sorry - no browser found'
    if verbose: print 'Running', program
    os.system('%s %s &' % (program, url))    # or fork+exec; assumes $path

def launchWindowsBrowser(url, verbose=1):
    if useWinStart and len(url) <= 400:      # on windows: start or spawnv
        try:                                 # spawnv works if cmd too long
            if verbose: print 'Starting'
            os.system('start ' + url)        # try name associations first
            return                           # fails if cmdline too long
        except: pass
    browser = None                           # search for a browser exe
    tries   = ['IEXPLORE.EXE', 'netscape.exe']  # try explorer, then netscape
    for program in tries:
        browser = which(program) or guessLocation(program, 1)
        if browser: break
    assert browser != None, 'Sorry - no browser found'
    if verbose: print 'Spawning', browser
    os.spawnv(os.P_DETACH, browser, (browser, url))

def launchBrowser(Mode='-file', Page=Page, Site=None, verbose=1):
    if Mode == '-live':
        url = 'http://%s/%s' % (Site, Page)    # open page at remote site
    else:
        url = 'file://%s' % Page               # open page on this machine
    if verbose: print 'Opening', url
    if onWindows:
        launchWindowsBrowser(url, verbose)     # use windows start, spawnv
    else:
        launchUnixBrowser(url, verbose)        # assume $path on unix, linux

if __name__ == '__main__':
    # get command-line args
    argc = len(sys.argv)
    if argc > 1:  Mode = sys.argv[1]
    if argc > 2:  Page = sys.argv[2]
    if argc > 3:  Site = sys.argv[3]
    if Mode not in ['-live', '-file']:
        print helptext
        sys.exit(1)
    else:
        launchBrowser(Mode, Page, Site)
```

Launching browsers with command lines

This module is designed to be both run and imported. When run by itself on my
Windows machine, Internet Explorer starts up. The requested page file is always
displayed in a new browser window when os.spawnv is applied, but in the currently open browser window (if any) when running a *start* command:

```
C:\...\PP2E>python LaunchBrowser.py
Opening file://C:\PP2ndEd\examples\PP2E/Internet/Cgi-Web/PyInternetDemos.html
Starting
```

The seemingly odd mix of forward and backward slashes in the URL here works fine within the browser; it pops up the window shown in Figure 4-2.

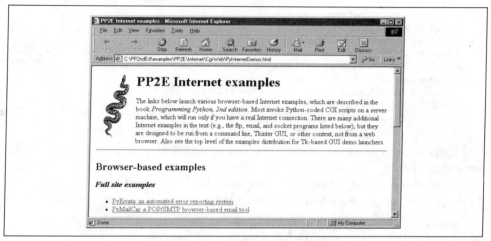

Figure 4-2. Launching a Windows browser on a local file

By default, a *start* command is spawned; to see the browser search procedure in action on Windows, set the script's useWinStart variable to 0. The script will search for a browser on your PATH settings, and then in common Windows install directories hardcoded in *Launcher.py*:

```
C:\...\PP2E>python LaunchBrowser.py
                   -file C:\Stuff\Website\public_html\about-pp.html
Opening file://C:\Stuff\Website\public_html\about-pp.html
Looking for IEXPLORE.EXE on ['C:\\WINDOWS', 'C:\\WINDOWS',
'C:\\WINDOWS\\COMMAND', 'C:\\STUFF\\BIN.MKS', 'C:\\PROGRAM FILES\\PYTHON']
Not at C:\WINDOWS\IEXPLORE.EXE
Not at C:\WINDOWS\IEXPLORE.EXE
Not at C:\WINDOWS\COMMAND\IEXPLORE.EXE
Not at C:\STUFF\BIN.MKS\IEXPLORE.EXE
Not at C:\PROGRAM FILES\PYTHON\IEXPLORE.EXE
IEXPLORE.EXE not on system path
Searching for IEXPLORE.EXE in C:\Program Files\Python
Searching for IEXPLORE.EXE in C:\PP2ndEd\examples\PP2E
Searching for IEXPLORE.EXE in C:\Program Files
Spawning C:\Program Files\Internet Explorer\IEXPLORE.EXE
```

If you study these trace message you'll notice that the browser wasn't on the system search path, but was eventually located in a local *C:\Program Files* subdirectory—this is just the Launcher module's which and guessLocation functions at work. As coded, the script searches for Internet Explorer first; if that's not to your liking, try changing the script's `tries` list to make Netscape first:

```
C:\...\PP2E>python LaunchBrowser.py
Opening file://C:\PP2ndEd\examples\PP2E/Internet/Cgi-Web/PyInternetDemos.html
Looking for netscape.exe on ['C:\\WINDOWS', 'C:\\WINDOWS',
'C:\\WINDOWS\\COMMAND', 'C:\\STUFF\\BIN.MKS', 'C:\\PROGRAM FILES\\PYTHON']
Not at C:\WINDOWS\netscape.exe
Not at C:\WINDOWS\netscape.exe
Not at C:\WINDOWS\COMMAND\netscape.exe
Not at C:\STUFF\BIN.MKS\netscape.exe
Not at C:\PROGRAM FILES\PYTHON\netscape.exe
netscape.exe not on system path
Searching for netscape.exe in C:\Program Files\Python
Searching for netscape.exe in C:\PP2ndEd\examples\PP2E
Searching for netscape.exe in C:\Program Files
Spawning C:\Program Files\Netscape\Communicator\Program\netscape.exe
```

Here, the script eventually found Netscape in a different install directory on the local machine. Besides automatically finding a user's browser for them, this script also aims to be portable. When running this file unchanged on Linux, the local Netscape browser starts, if it lives on your PATH; otherwise, others are tried:

```
[mark@toy ~/PP2ndEd/examples/PP2E]$ python LaunchBrowser.py
Opening file:///home/mark/PP2ndEd/examples/PP2E/Internet/Cgi-
Web/PyInternetDemos.html
Looking for netscape on ['/home/mark/bin', '.', '/usr/bin', '/usr/bin',
'/usr/local/bin', '/usr/X11R6/bin', '/bin', '/usr/X11R6/bin', '/home/mark/
bin', '/usr/X11R6/bin', '/home/mark/bin', '/usr/X11R6/bin']
Not at /home/mark/bin/netscape
Not at ./netscape
Found /usr/bin/netscape
Running netscape
[mark@toy ~/PP2ndEd/examples/PP2E]$
```

I have Netscape installed, so running the script this way on my machine generates the window shown in Figure 4-3, seen under the KDE window manager.

If you have an Internet connection, you can open pages at *remote* servers too— the next command opens the root page at my site on the *starship.python.net* server, located somewhere on the East Coast the last time I checked:

```
C:\...\PP2E>python LaunchBrowser.py -live ~lutz starship.python.net
Opening http://starship.python.net/~lutz
Starting
```

In Chapter 8, we'll see that this script is also run to start Internet examples in the top-level demo launcher system: the PyDemos script presented in that chapter portably opens local or remote web page files with this button-press callback:

```
[File mode]
    pagepath = os.getcwd() + '/Internet/Cgi-Web'
    demoButton('PyErrata',
               'Internet-based errata report system',
```

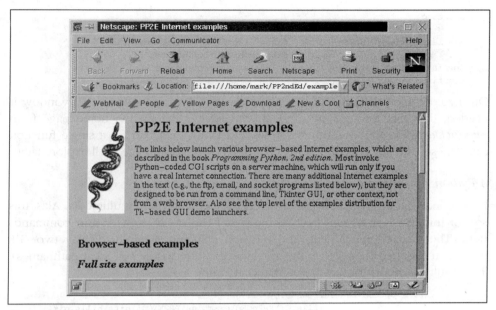

Figure 4-3. Launching a browser on Linux

```
        'LaunchBrowser.py -file %s/PyErrata/pyerrata.html' % pagepath)

[Live mode]
    site = 'starship.python.net/~lutz'
    demoButton('PyErrata',
               'Internet-based errata report system',
               'LaunchBrowser.py -live PyErrata/pyerrata.html ' + site)
```

Launching browsers with function calls

Other programs can spawn *LaunchBrowser.py* command lines like those shown previously with tools like `os.system`, as usual; but since the script's core logic is coded in a function, it can just as easily be imported and called:

```
>>> from PP2E.LaunchBrowser import launchBrowser
>>> launchBrowser(Page=r'C:\Stuff\Website\Public_html\about-pp.html')
Opening file://C:\Stuff\Website\Public_html\about-pp.html
Starting
>>>
```

When called like this, `launchBrowser` isn't much different from spawning a *start* command on DOS or a *netscape* command on Linux, but the Python `launchBrowser` function is designed to be a portable interface for browser startup across platforms. Python scripts can use this interface to pop up local HTML documents in web browsers; on machines with live Internet links, this call even lets scripts open browsers on remote pages on the Web:

```
>>> launchBrowser(Mode='-live', Page='index.html', Site='www.python.org')
Opening http://www.python.org/index.html
```

```
Starting

>>> launchBrowser(Mode='-live', Page='~lutz/PyInternetDemos.html',
...                           Site='starship.python.net')
Opening http://starship.python.net/~lutz/PyInternetDemos.html
Starting
```

On my computer, the first call here opens a new Internet Explorer GUI window if needed, dials out through my modem, and fetches the Python home page from *http://www.python.org* on both Windows and Linux—not bad for a single function call. The second call does the same, but with a web demos page we'll explore later.

A Python "multimedia extravaganza"

I mentioned earlier that browsers are a cheap way to present multimedia. Alas, this sort of thing is best viewed live, so the best I can do is show startup commands here. The next command line and function call, for example, display two GIF images in Internet Explorer on my machine (be sure to use full local pathnames). The result of the first of these is captured in Figure 4-4.

```
C:\...\PP2E>python LaunchBrowser.py
                       -file C:\PP2ndEd\examples\PP2E\Gui\gifs\hills.gif
Opening file://C:\PP2ndEd\examples\PP2E\Gui\gifs\hills.gif
Starting

C:\temp>python
>>> from LaunchBrowser import launchBrowser
>>> launchBrowser(Page=r'C:\PP2ndEd\examples\PP2E\Gui\gifs\mp_lumberjack.gif')
Opening file://C:\PP2ndEd\examples\PP2E\Gui\gifs\mp_lumberjack.gif
Starting
```

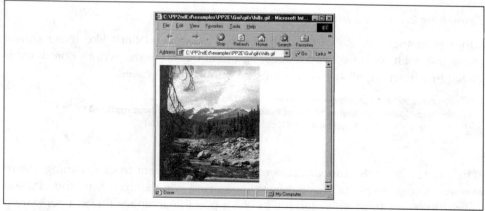

Figure 4-4. Launching a browser on an image file

The next command line and call open the *sousa.au* audio file on my machine too; the second of these downloads the file from *http://www.python.org* first. If all goes as planned, they'll make the Monty Python theme song play on your computer too:

```
C:\PP2ndEd\examples>python LaunchBrowser.py
                   -file C:\PP2ndEd\examples\PP2E\Internet\Ftp\sousa.au
Opening file://C:\PP2ndEd\examples\PP2E\Internet\Ftp\sousa.au
Starting

>>> launchBrowser(Mode='-live',
...               Site='www.python.org',
...               Page='ftp/python/misc/sousa.au',
...               verbose=0)
>>>
```

Of course, you could just pass these filenames to a spawned *start* command on Windows, or run the appropriate handler program directly with something like `os.system`. But opening these files in a browser is a more portable approach—you don't need to keep track of a set of file-handler programs per platform. Provided your scripts use a portable browser launcher like `LaunchBrowser`, you don't even need to keep track of a browser per platform.

In closing, I want to point out that `LaunchBrowser` reflects browsers that I tend to use. For instance, it tries to find Internet Explorer before Netscape on Windows, and prefers Netscape over Mosaic and Lynx on Linux, but you should feel free to change these choices in your copy of the script. In fact, both `LaunchBrowser` and `Launcher` make a few heuristic guesses when searching for files that may not make sense on every computer. As always, hack on; this is Python, after all.

Reptilian Minds Think Alike

A postscript: roughly one year after I wrote the `LaunchBrowser` script, Python release 2.0 sprouted a new standard library module that serves a similar purpose: `webbrowser.open(url)` also attempts to provide a portable interface for launching browsers from scripts. This module is more complex, but likely to support more options than the `LaunchBrowser` script presented here (e.g., Macintosh browsers are directly supported with the Mac `ic.launcurl(url)` call—a call I'd add to `LaunchBrowser` too, if I had a Mac lying around the office). See the library manual in releases 2.0 and later for details.

Just before publication, I stumbled onto another script called *FixTk.py* in the *lib-tk* subdirectory of the Python source library; at least in Python 1.5.2, this script tries to locate the Tcl/Tk 8.0 DLLs on Windows by checking common install directories, in order to allow Python/Tkinter programs to work without Tcl/Tk PATH settings. It doesn't recursively search directory trees like the `Launcher` module presented in this chapter, and may be defunct by the time you read this (Tk is copied into Python's own install directory as of Python 2.0), but it is similar in spirit to some of the tools in this chapter's last section.

5

Larger System Examples II

"The Greps of Wrath"

This chapter continues our exploration of systems programming case studies. Here, the focus is on Python scripts that perform more advanced kinds of file and directory processing. The examples in this chapter do system-level tasks such as converting files, comparing and copying directories, and searching files and directories for strings—a task idiomatically known as "grepping."

Most of the tools these scripts employ were introduced in Chapter 2, *System Tools*. Here, the goal is to show these tools in action, in the context of more useful and realistic programs. As in the prior chapter, learning about Python programming techniques such as OOP and encapsulation is also a hidden subgoal of most of the examples presented here.

Fixing DOS Line Ends

When I wrote the first edition of this book, I shipped two copies of every example file on the CD-ROM—one with Unix line-end markers, and one with DOS markers. The idea was that this would make it easy to view and edit the files on either platform. Readers would simply copy the examples directory tree designed for their platform onto their hard drive, and ignore the other one.

If you read Chapter 2, you know the issue here: DOS (and by proxy, Windows) marks line ends in text files with the two characters \r\n (carriage-return, line-feed), but Unix uses just a single \n. Most modern text editors don't care—they happily display text files encoded in either format. Some tools are less forgiving, though. I still occasionally see odd \r characters when viewing DOS files on Unix, or an entire file in a single line when looking at Unix files on DOS (the Notepad accessory does this on Windows, for example).

Because this is only an occasional annoyance, and because it's easy to forget to keep two distinct example trees in sync, I adopted a different policy for this second edition: we're shipping a single copy of the examples (in DOS format), along with a portable converter tool for changing to and from other line-end formats.

The main obstacle, of course, is how to go about providing a portable and easy to use converter—one that runs "out of the box" on almost every computer, without changes or recompiles. Some Unix platforms have commands like *fromdos* and *dos2unix*, but they are not universally available even on Unix. DOS batch files and csh scripts could do the job on Windows and Unix, respectively, but neither solution works on both platforms.

Fortunately, Python does. The scripts presented in Examples 5-1, 5-3, and 5-4 convert end-of-line markers between DOS and Unix formats; they convert a single file, a directory of files, and a directory tree of files. In this section, we briefly look at each of the three scripts, and contrast some of the system tools they apply. Each reuses the prior's code, and becomes progressively more powerful in the process.

The last of these three scripts, Example 5-4, is the portable converter tool I was looking for; it converts line ends in the entire examples tree, in a single step. Because it is pure Python, it also works on *both* DOS and Unix unchanged; as long as Python is installed, it is the only line converter you may ever need to remember.

Converting Line Ends in One File

These three scripts were developed in stages on purpose, so I could first focus on getting line-feed conversions right, before worrying about directories and tree walking logic. With that scheme in mind, Example 5-1 addresses just the task of converting lines in a single text file.

Example 5-1. PP2E\PyTools\fixeoln_one.py

```
#####################################################################
# Use: "python fixeoln_one.py [tounix|todos] filename".
# Convert end-of-lines in the single text file whose name is passed
# in on the command line, to the target format (tounix or todos).
# The _one, _dir, and _all converters reuse the convert function
# here.  convertEndlines changes end-lines only if necessary:
# lines that are already in the target format are left unchanged,
# so it's okay to convert a file > once with any of the 3 fixeoln
# scripts.  Notes: must use binary file open modes for this to
# work on Windows, else default text mode automatically deletes
# the \r on reads, and adds an extra \r for each \n on writes;
# Mac format not supported; PyTools\dumpfile.py shows raw bytes;
#####################################################################

import os
listonly = 0    # 1=show file to be changed, don't rewrite
```

Example 5-1. PP2E\PyTools\fixeoln_one.py (continued)

```
def convertEndlines(format, fname):              # convert one file
    if not os.path.isfile(fname):                # todos:  \n   => \r\n
        print 'Not a text file', fname           # tounix: \r\n => \n
        return                                   # skip directory names

    newlines = []
    changed  = 0
    for line in open(fname, 'rb').readlines():   # use binary i/o modes
        if format == 'todos':                    # else \r lost on Win
            if line[-1:] == '\n' and line[-2:-1] != '\r':
                line = line[:-1] + '\r\n'
                changed = 1
        elif format == 'tounix':                 # avoids IndexError
            if line[-2:] == '\r\n':              # slices are scaled
                line = line[:-2] + '\n'
                changed = 1
        newlines.append(line)

    if changed:
        try:                                     # might be read-only
            print 'Changing', fname
            if not listonly: open(fname, 'wb').writelines(newlines)
        except IOError, why:
            print 'Error writing to file %s: skipped (%s)' % (fname, why)

if __name__ == '__main__':
    import sys
    errmsg = 'Required arguments missing: ["todos"|"tounix"] filename'
    assert (len(sys.argv) == 3 and sys.argv[1] in ['todos', 'tounix']), errmsg
    convertEndlines(sys.argv[1], sys.argv[2])
    print 'Converted', sys.argv[2]
```

This script is fairly straightforward as system utilities go; it relies primarily on the built-in file object's methods. Given a target format flag and filename, it loads the file into a lines list using the `readlines` method, converts input lines to the target format if needed, and writes the result back to the file with the `writelines` method if any lines were changed:

```
C:\temp\examples>python %X%\PyTools\fixeoln_one.py tounix PyDemos.pyw
Changing PyDemos.pyw
Converted PyDemos.pyw


C:\temp\examples>python %X%\PyTools\fixeoln_one.py todos PyDemos.pyw
Changing PyDemos.pyw
Converted PyDemos.pyw


C:\temp\examples>fc PyDemos.pyw %X%\PyDemos.pyw
Comparing files PyDemos.pyw and C:\PP2ndEd\examples\PP2E\PyDemos.pyw
FC: no differences encountered


C:\temp\examples>python %X%\PyTools\fixeoln_one.py todos PyDemos.pyw
Converted PyDemos.pyw
```

```
C:\temp\examples>python %X%\PyTools\fixeoln_one.py toother nonesuch.txt
Traceback (innermost last):
  File "C:\PP2ndEd\examples\PP2E\PyTools\fixeoln_one.py", line 45, in ?
    assert (len(sys.argv) == 3 and sys.argv[1] in ['todos', 'tounix']), errmsg
AssertionError: Required arguments missing: ["todos"|"tounix"] filename
```

Here, the first command converts the file to Unix line-end format (*tounix*), and the second and fourth convert to the DOS convention—all regardless of the platform on which this script is run. To make typical usage easier, converted text is written back to the file *in place*, instead of to a newly created output file. Notice that this script's filename has a "_" in it, not a "-"; because it is meant to be both run as a script and imported as a library, its filename must translate to a legal Python *variable* name in importers (*fixeoln-one.py* won't work for both roles).

 In all the examples in this chapter that change files in directory trees, the *C:\temp\examples* and *C:\temp\cpexamples* directories used in testing are full copies of the real *PP2E* examples root directory. I don't always show the copy commands used to create these test directories along the way (at least not until we've written our own in Python).

Slinging bytes and verifying results

The *fc* DOS file-compare command in the preceding interaction confirms the conversions, but to better verify the results of this Python script, I wrote another, shown in Example 5-2.

Example 5-2. PP2E\PyTools\dumpfile.py

```
import sys
bytes = open(sys.argv[1], 'rb').read()
print '-'*40
print repr(bytes)

print '-'*40
while bytes:
    bytes, chunk = bytes[4:], bytes[:4]           # show 4-bytes per line
    for c in chunk: print oct(ord(c)), '\t',      # show octal of binary value
    print

print '-'*40
for line in open(sys.argv[1], 'rb').readlines():
    print repr(line)
```

To give a clear picture of a file's contents, this script opens a file in binary mode (to suppress automatic line-feed conversions), prints its raw contents (**bytes**) all at once, displays the octal numeric ASCII codes of it contents four bytes per line, and shows its raw lines. Let's use this to trace conversions. First of all, use a simple text file to make wading through bytes a bit more humane:

```
C:\temp>type test.txt
a
b
c

C:\temp>python %X%\PyTools\dumpfile.py test.txt
-----------------------------------------
'a\015\012b\015\012c\015\012'
-----------------------------------------
0141    015     012     0142
015     012     0143    015
012

-----------------------------------------
'a\015\012'
'b\015\012'
'c\015\012'
```

The *test.txt* file here is in DOS line-end format—the escape sequence \015\012 displayed by the dumpfile script is simply the DOS \r\n line-end marker in octal character-code escapes format. Now, converting to Unix format changes all the DOS \r\n markers to a single \n (\012) as advertised:

```
C:\temp>python %X%\PyTools\fixeoln_one.py tounix test.txt
Changing test.txt
Converted test.txt

C:\temp>python %X%\PyTools\dumpfile.py test.txt
-----------------------------------------
'a\012b\012c\012'
-----------------------------------------
0141    012     0142    012
0143    012

-----------------------------------------
'a\012'
'b\012'
'c\012'
```

And converting back to DOS restores the original file format:

```
C:\temp>python %X%\PyTools\fixeoln_one.py todos test.txt
Changing test.txt
Converted test.txt

C:\temp>python %X%\PyTools\dumpfile.py test.txt
-----------------------------------------
'a\015\012b\015\012c\015\012'
-----------------------------------------
0141    015     012     0142
015     012     0143    015
012

-----------------------------------------
```

```
'a\015\012'
'b\015\012'
'c\015\012'
```

```
C:\temp>python %X%\PyTools\fixeoln_one.py todos test.txt      # makes no changes
Converted test.txt
```

Nonintrusive conversions

Notice that no "Changing" message is emitted for the last command just run, because no changes were actually made to the file (it was already in DOS format). Because this program is smart enough to avoid converting a line that is already in the target format, it is safe to rerun on a file even if you can't recall what format the file already uses. More naive conversion logic might be simpler, but may not be repeatable. For instance, a **string.replace** call can be used to expand a Unix \n to a DOS \r\n (\015\012), but only once:

```
>>> import string
>>> lines = 'aaa\nbbb\nccc\n'
>>> lines = string.replace(lines, '\n', '\r\n')          # okay: \r added
>>> lines
'aaa\015\012bbb\015\012ccc\015\012'
>>> lines = string.replace(lines, '\n', '\r\n')          # bad: double \r
>>> lines
'aaa\015\015\012bbb\015\015\012ccc\015\015\012'
```

Such logic could easily trash a file if applied to it twice.* To really understand how the script gets around this problem, though, we need to take a closer look at its use of slices and binary file modes.

Slicing strings out-of-bounds

This script relies on subtle aspects of string slicing behavior to inspect parts of each line without size checks. For instance:

- The expression **line[-2:]** returns the last two characters at the end of the line (or one or zero characters, if the line isn't at least two characters long).

- A slice like **line[-2:-1]** returns the second to last character (or an empty string, if the line is too small to have a second to last character).

- The operation **line[:-2]** returns all characters except the last two at the end (or an empty string, if there are fewer than three characters).

---

* In fact, see the files *old_todos.py*, *old_tounix.py*, and *old_toboth.py* in the *PyTools* directory on the examples CD for a complete earlier implementation built around **string.replace**. It was repeatable for to-Unix changes, but not for to-DOS conversion (only the latter may add characters). The **fixeoln** scripts here were developed as a replacement, after I got burned by running to-DOS conversions twice.

Because out-of-bounds slices scale slice limits to be in-bounds, the script doesn't need to add explicit tests to guarantee that the line is big enough to have end-line characters at the end. For example:

```
>>> 'aaaXY'[-2:], 'XY'[-2:], 'Y'[-2:], ''[-2:]
('XY', 'XY', 'Y', '')

>>> 'aaaXY'[-2:-1], 'XY'[-2:-1], 'Y'[-2:-1], ''[-2:-1]
('X', 'X', '', '')

>>> 'aaaXY'[:-2], 'aaaY'[:-1], 'XY'[:-2], 'Y'[:-1]
('aaa', 'aaa', '', '')
```

If you imagine characters like \r and \n instead of the X and Y here, you'll understand how the script exploits slice scaling to good effect.

Binary file mode revisited

Because this script aims to be portable to Windows, it also takes care to open files in binary mode, even though they contain text data. As we've seen, when files are opened in text mode on Windows, \r is stripped from \r\n markers on input, and \r is added before \n markers on output. This automatic conversion allows scripts to represent the end-of-line marker as \n on all platforms. Here, though, it would also mean that the script would never see the \r it's looking for to detect a DOS-encoded line—the \r would be dropped before it ever reached the script:

```
>>> open('temp.txt', 'w').writelines(['aaa\n', 'bbb\n'])
>>> open('temp.txt', 'rb').read()
'aaa\015\012bbb\015\012'
>>> open('temp.txt', 'r').read()
'aaa\012bbb\012'
```

Without binary open mode, this can lead to fairly subtle and incorrect behavior on Windows. For example, if files are opened in text mode, converting in "todos" mode on Windows would actually produce double \r characters: the script might convert the stripped \n to \r\n, which is then expanded on output to \r\r\n!

```
>>> open('temp.txt', 'w').writelines(['aaa\r\n', 'bbb\r\n'])
>>> open('temp.txt', 'rb').read()
'aaa\015\015\012bbb\015\015\012'
```

With binary mode, the script inputs a full \r\n, so no conversion is performed. Binary mode is also required for output on Windows, to suppress the insertion of \r characters; without it, the "tounix" conversion would fail on that platform.*

---

* But wait—it gets worse. Because of the auto-deletion and insertion of \r characters in Windows text mode, we might simply read and write files in text mode to perform the "todos" line conversion when run on Windows; the file interface will automatically add the \r on output if it's missing. However, this fails for other usage modes—"tounix" conversions on Windows (only binary writes can omit the \r), and "todos" when running on Unix (no \r is inserted). Magic is not always our friend.

If all that is too subtle to bear, just remember to use the "b" in file open mode strings if your scripts might be run on Windows, and you mean to process either true binary data or text data as it is actually stored in the file.

Macintosh Line Conversions

As coded, the `convertEndlines` function does not support Macintosh single \r line terminators at all. It neither converts *to* Macintosh terminators from DOS and Unix format (\r\n and \n to \r), nor converts *from* Macintosh terminators to DOS or Unix format (\r to \r\n or \n). Files in Mac format pass untouched through both the "todos" and "tounix" conversions in this script (study the code to see why). I don't use a Mac, but some readers may.

Since adding Mac support would make this code more complex, and since I don't like publishing code in books unless it's been well tested, I'll leave such an extension as an exercise for the Mac Python users in the audience. But for implementation hints, see file *PP2E\PyTools\fixeoln_one_mac.py* on the CD. When run on Windows, it does to-Mac conversions:

```
C:\temp>python %X%\PyTools\fixeoln_one_mac.py tomac test.txt
Changing test.txt
Converted test.txt

C:\temp>python %X%\PyTools\dumpfile.py test.txt
----------------------------------------
'a\015b\015c\015'
----------------------------------------
0141     015     0142     015
0143     015
----------------------------------------
'a\015b\015c\015'
```

but fails to convert files already in Mac format to Unix or DOS, because the file `readlines` method does not treat a bare \r as a line break on that platform. The last output line is a single file line, as far as Windows is concerned; converting back to DOS just adds a single \n at its end.

Converting Line Ends in One Directory

Armed with a fully debugged single file converter, it's an easy step to add support for converting all files in a single directory. Simply call the single file converter on every filename returned by a directory listing tool. The script in Example 5-3 uses the `glob` module we met in Chapter 2 to grab a list of files to convert.

Example 5-3. PP2E\PyTools\fixeoln_dir.py

```
#########################################################
# Use: "python fixeoln_dir.py [tounix|todos] patterns?".
# convert end-lines in all the text files in the current
# directory (only: does not recurse to subdirectories).
# Reuses converter in the single-file _one version.
#########################################################

import sys, glob
from fixeoln_one import convertEndlines
listonly = 0
patts = ['*.py', '*.pyw', '*.txt', '*.cgi', '*.html',      # text file names
         '*.c',  '*.cxx', '*.h',   '*.i',   '*.out',       # in this package
         'README*', 'makefile*', 'output*', '*.note']

if __name__ == '__main__':
    errmsg = 'Required first argument missing: "todos" or "tounix"'
    assert (len(sys.argv) >= 2 and sys.argv[1] in ['todos', 'tounix']), errmsg

    if len(sys.argv) > 2:                    # glob anyhow: '*' not applied on dos
        patts = sys.argv[2:]                 # though not really needed on linux
    filelists = map(glob.glob, patts)        # name matches in this dir only

    count = 0
    for list in filelists:
        for fname in list:
            if listonly:
                print count+1, '=>', fname
            else:
                convertEndlines(sys.argv[1], fname)
            count = count + 1

    print 'Visited %d files' % count
```

This module defines a list, `patts`, containing filename patterns that match all the kinds of text files that appear in the book examples tree; each pattern is passed to the built-in `glob.glob` call by `map`, to be separately expanded into a list of matching files. That's why there are nested `for` loops near the end—the outer loop steps through each `glob` result list, and the inner steps through each name within each list. Try the `map` call interactively if this doesn't make sense:

```
>>> import glob
>>> map(glob.glob, ['*.py', '*.html'])
[['helloshell.py'], ['about-pp.html', 'about-pp2e.html', 'about-ppr2e.html']]
```

This script requires a convert mode flag on the command line, and assumes that it is run in the directory where files to be converted live; *cd* to the directory to be converted before running this script (or change it to accept a directory name argument too):

```
C:\temp\examples>python %X%\PyTools\fixeoln_dir.py tounix
Changing Launcher.py
```

```
Changing Launch_PyGadgets.py
Changing LaunchBrowser.py
...lines deleted...
Changing PyDemos.pyw
Changing PyGadgets_bar.pyw
Changing README-PP2E.txt
Visited 21 files

C:\temp\examples>python %X%\PyTools\fixeoln_dir.py todos
Changing Launcher.py
Changing Launch_PyGadgets.py
Changing LaunchBrowser.py
...lines deleted...
Changing PyDemos.pyw
Changing PyGadgets_bar.pyw
Changing README-PP2E.txt
Visited 21 files

C:\temp\examples>python %X%\PyTools\fixeoln_dir.py todos      # makes no changes
Visited 21 files

C:\temp\examples>fc PyDemos.pyw %X%\PyDemos.pyw
Comparing files PyDemos.pyw and C:\PP2ndEd\examples\PP2E\PyDemos.pyw
FC: no differences encountered
```

Notice that the third command generated no "Changing" messages again. Because
the `convertEndlines` function of the single-file module is reused here to perform the actual updates, this script inherits that function's *repeatability*: it's okay to
rerun this script on the same directory any number of times. Only lines that
require conversion will be converted. This script also accepts an optional list of
filename patterns on the command line, to override the default `patts` list of files
to be changed:

```
C:\temp\examples>python %X%\PyTools\fixeoln_dir.py tounix *.pyw *.csh
Changing echoEnvironment.pyw
Changing Launch_PyDemos.pyw
Changing Launch_PyGadgets_bar.pyw
Changing PyDemos.pyw
Changing PyGadgets_bar.pyw
Changing cleanall.csh
Changing makeall.csh
Changing package.csh
Changing setup-pp.csh
Changing setup-pp-embed.csh
Changing xferall.linux.csh
Visited 11 files

C:\temp\examples>python %X%\PyTools\fixeoln_dir.py tounix *.pyw *.csh
Visited 11 files
```

Also notice that the single-file script's `convertEndlines` function performs an initial `os.path.isfile` test to make sure the passed-in filename represents a *file*,
not a directory; when we start globbing with patterns to collect files to convert, it's

not impossible that a pattern's expansion might include the name of a directory along with the desired files.

Unix and Linux users: Unix-like shells automatically glob (i.e., expand) filename pattern operators like * in command lines before they ever reach your script. You generally need to *quote* such patterns to pass them in to scripts verbatim (e.g., `"*.py"`).

The `fixeoln_dir` script will still work if you don't—its `glob.glob` calls will simply find a single matching filename for each already-globbed name, and so have no effect:

```
>>> glob.glob('PyDemos.pyw')
['PyDemos.pyw']
```

Patterns are not pre-globbed in the DOS shell, though, so the `glob.glob` calls here are still a good idea in scripts that aspire to be as portable as this one.

Converting Line Ends in an Entire Tree

Finally, Example 5-4 applies what we've already learned to an entire directory tree. It simply runs the file-converter function to every filename produced by tree-walking logic. In fact, this script really just orchestrates calls to the original and already debugged `convertEndlines` function.

Example 5-4. PP2E\PyTools\fixeoln_all.py

```
#########################################################
# Use: "python fixeoln_all.py [tounix|todos] patterns?".
# find and convert end-of-lines in all text files at and
# below the directory where this script is run (the dir
# you are in when you type 'python'). If needed, tries to
# use the Python find.py library module, else reads the
# output of a unix-style find command; uses a default
# filename patterns list if patterns argument is absent.
# This script only changes files that need to be changed,
# so it's safe to run brute-force from a root-level dir.
#########################################################

import os, sys, string
debug   = 0
pyfind  = 0        # force py find
listonly = 0       # 1=show find results only

def findFiles(patts, debug=debug, pyfind=pyfind):
    try:
        if sys.platform[:3] == 'win' or pyfind:
            print 'Using Python find'
            try:
                import find                  # use python-code find.py
```

Example 5-4. PP2E\PyTools\fixeoln_all.py (continued)

```
            except ImportError:                 # use mine if deprecated!
                from PP2E.PyTools import find   # may get from my dir anyhow
            matches = map(find.find, patts)     # startdir default = '.'
        else:
            print 'Using find executable'
            matches = []
            for patt in patts:
                findcmd = 'find . -name "%s" -print' % patt   # run find command
                lines = os.popen(findcmd).readlines()         # remove endlines
                matches.append(map(string.strip, lines))      # lambda x: x[:-1]
    except:
        assert 0, 'Sorry - cannot find files'
    if debug: print matches
    return matches


if __name__ == '__main__':
    from fixeoln_dir import patts
    from fixeoln_one import convertEndlines

    errmsg = 'Required first argument missing: "todos" or "tounix"'
    assert (len(sys.argv) >= 2 and sys.argv[1] in ['todos', 'tounix']), errmsg

    if len(sys.argv) > 2:                  # quote in unix shell
        patts = sys.argv[2:]              # else tries to expand
    matches = findFiles(patts)

    count = 0
    for matchlist in matches:              # a list of lists
        for fname in matchlist:            # one per pattern
            if listonly:
                print count+1, '=>', fname
            else:
                convertEndlines(sys.argv[1], fname)
            count = count + 1
    print 'Visited %d files' % count
```

On Windows, the script uses the portable `find.find` built-in tool we met in Chapter 2 (either Python's or the hand-rolled equivalent)[*] to generate a list of all matching file and directory names in the tree; on other platforms, it resorts to spawning a less portable and probably slower *find* shell command just for illustration purposes.

Once the file pathname lists are compiled, this script simply converts each found file in turn using the single-file converter module's tools. Here is the collection of

---

[*] Recall that the home directory of a running script is always added to the front of `sys.path` to give the script import visibility to other files in the script's directory. Because of that, this script would normally load the *PP2E\PyTools\find.py* module anyhow (not the one in the Python library), by just saying `import find`; it need not specify the full package path in the import. The `try` handler and full path import are useful here only if this script is moved to a different source directory. Since I move files a lot, I tend to code with self-inflicted worst-case scenarios in mind.

scripts at work converting the book examples tree on Windows; notice that this script also processes the current working directory (CWD; *cd* to the directory to be converted before typing the command line), and that Python treats forward and backward slashes the same in the program filename:

```
C:\temp\examples>python %X%/PyTools/fixeoln_all.py tounix
Using Python find
Changing .\LaunchBrowser.py
Changing .\Launch_PyGadgets.py
Changing .\Launcher.py
Changing .\Other\cgimail.py
...lots of lines deleted...
Changing .\EmbExt\Exports\ClassAndMod\output.prog1
Changing .\EmbExt\Exports\output.prog1
Changing .\EmbExt\Regist\output
Visited 1051 files

C:\temp\examples>python %X%/PyTools/fixeoln_all.py todos
Using Python find
Changing .\LaunchBrowser.py
Changing .\Launch_PyGadgets.py
Changing .\Launcher.py
Changing .\Other\cgimail.py
...lots of lines deleted...
Changing .\EmbExt\Exports\ClassAndMod\output.prog1
Changing .\EmbExt\Exports\output.prog1
Changing .\EmbExt\Regist\output
Visited 1051 files

C:\temp\examples>python %X%/PyTools/fixeoln_all.py todos
Using Python find
Not a text file .\Embed\Inventory\Output
Not a text file .\Embed\Inventory\WithDbase\Output
Visited 1051 files
```

The first two commands convert over 1000 files, and usually take some eight seconds of real-world time to finish on my 650 MHz Windows 98 machine; the third takes only six seconds, because no files have to be updated (and fewer messages have to be scrolled on the screen). Don't take these figures too seriously, though; they can vary by system load, and much of this time is probably spent scrolling the script's output to the screen.

The view from the top

This script and its ancestors are shipped on the book's CD, as that portable converter tool I was looking for. To convert all examples files in the tree to Unix line-terminator format, simply copy the entire *PP2E* examples tree to some "examples" directory on your hard drive, and type these two commands in a shell:

```
cd examples/PP2E
python PyTools/fixeoln_all.py tounix
```

Of course, this assumes Python is already installed (see the CD's README file for details), but will work on almost every platform in use today.* To convert back to DOS, just replace "tounix" with "todos" and rerun. I ship this tool with a training CD for Python classes I teach too; to convert those files, we simply type:

```
cd Html\Examples
python ..\..\Tools\fixeoln_all.py tounix
```

Once you get accustomed to the command lines, you can use this in all sorts of contexts. Finally, to make the conversion easier for beginners to run, the top-level examples directory includes *tounix.py* and *todos.py* scripts that can be simply double-clicked in a file explorer GUI; Example 5-5 shows the "tounix" converter.

Example 5-5. PP2E\tounix.py

```
#!/usr/local/bin/python
####################################################################
# Run me to convert all text files to UNIX/Linux line-feed format.
# You only need to do this if you see odd '\r' characters at the end
# of lines in text files in this distribution, when they are viewed
# with your text editor (e.g., vi).  This script converts all files
# at and below the examples root, and only converts files that have
# not already been converted (it's okay to run this multiple times).
#
# Since this is a Python script which runs another Python script,
# you must install Python first to run this program; then from your
# system command-line (e.g., a xterm window), cd to the directory
# where this script lives, and then type "python tounix.py".  You
# may also be able to simply click on this file's icon in your file
# system explorer, if it knows what '.py' file are.
####################################################################

import os
prompt = """
This program converts all text files in the book
examples distribution to UNIX line-feed format.
Are you sure you want to do this (y=yes)? """

answer = raw_input(prompt)
if answer not in ['y', 'Y', 'yes']:
    print 'Cancelled'
else:
    os.system('python PyTools/fixeoln_all.py tounix')
```

This script addresses the *end user's* perception of usability, but other factors impact *programmer* usability—just as important to systems that will be read or changed by others. For example, the file, directory, and tree converters are coded in separate script files, but there is no law against combining them into a single program that

---

* Except Macs, perhaps—see the "Macintosh Line Conversions" sidebar earlier in this chapter. To convert to Mac format, try replacing the script's import of `fixeoln_one` to load `fixeoln_one_mac`.

relies on a command-line arguments pattern to know which of the three modes to run. The first argument could be a mode flag, tested by such a program:

```
if    mode == '-one':
    ...
elif mode == '-dir':
    ...
elif mode == '-all':
    ...
```

That seems more confusing than separate files per mode, though; it's usually much easier to botch a complex command line than to type a specific program file's name. It will also make for a confusing mix of global names, and one very big piece of code at the bottom of the file. As always, simpler is usually better.

Fixing DOS Filenames

The heart of the prior script was `findFiles`, a function than knows how to portably collect matching file and directory names in an entire tree, given a list of filename patterns. It doesn't do much more than the built-in `find.find` call, but can be augmented for our own purposes. Because this logic was bundled up in a function, though, it automatically becomes a *reusable* tool.

For example, the next script imports and applies `findFiles`, to collect *all* file names in a directory tree, by using the filename pattern * (it matches everything). I use this script to fix a legacy problem in the book's examples tree. The names of some files created under MS-DOS were made all uppercase; for example, *spam.py* became *SPAM.PY* somewhere along the way. Because case is significant both in Python and on some platforms, an import statement like "import spam" will sometimes fail for uppercase filenames.

To repair the damage everywhere in the thousand-file examples tree, I wrote and ran Example 5-6. It works like this: For every filename in the tree, it checks to see if the name is all uppercase, and asks the console user whether the file should be renamed with the `os.rename` call. To make this easy, it also comes up with a reasonable default for most new names—the old one in all-lowercase form.

Example 5-6. PP2E\PyTools\fixnames_all.py

```
#########################################################
# Use: "python ..\..\PyTools\fixnames_all.py".
# find all files with all upper-case names at and below
# the current directory ('.'); for each, ask the user for
# a new name to rename the file to; used to catch old
# uppercase file names created on MS-DOS (case matters on
# some platforms, when importing Python module files);
# caveats: this may fail on case-sensitive machines if
# directory names are converted before their contents--the
# original dir name in the paths returned by find may no
```

Example 5-6. PP2E\PyTools\fixnames_all.py (continued)

```
# longer exist; the allUpper heuristic also fails for
# odd filenames that are all non-alphabetic (ex: '.');
########################################################

import os, string
listonly = 0

def allUpper(name):
    for char in name:
        if char in string.lowercase:     # any lowercase letter disqualifies
            return 0                      # else all upper, digit, or special
    return 1

def convertOne(fname):
    fpath, oldfname = os.path.split(fname)
    if allUpper(oldfname):
        prompt = 'Convert dir=%s file=%s? (y|Y)' % (fpath, oldfname)
        if raw_input(prompt) in ['Y', 'y']:
            default  = string.lower(oldfname)
            newfname = raw_input('Type new file name (enter=%s): ' % default)
            newfname = newfname or default
            newfpath = os.path.join(fpath, newfname)
            os.rename(fname, newfpath)
            print 'Renamed: ', fname
            print 'to:      ', str(newfpath)
            raw_input('Press enter to continue')
            return 1
    return 0

if __name__ == '__main__':
    patts = "*"                          # inspect all file names
    from fixeoln_all import findFiles    # reuse finder function
    matches = findFiles(patts)

    ccount = vcount = 0
    for matchlist in matches:            # list of lists, one per pattern
        for fname in matchlist:          # fnames are full directory paths
            print vcount+1, '=>', fname  # includes names of directories
            if not listonly:
                ccount = ccount + convertOne(fname)
            vcount = vcount + 1
    print 'Converted %d files, visited %d' % (ccount, vcount)
```

As before, the `findFiles` function returns a list of simple filename lists, representing the expansion of all patterns passed in (here, just one result list, for the wildcard pattern `*`).[*] For each file and directory name in the result, this script's `convertOne` function prompts for name changes; an `os.path.split` and an `os.`

---

[*] Interestingly, using string `'*'` for the patterns list works the same as using list `['*']` here, only because a single-character string is a sequence that contains itself; compare the results of `map(find.find, '*')` with `map(find.find, ['*'])` interactively to verify.

`path.join` call combination portably tacks the new filename onto the old directory name. Here is a renaming session in progress on Windows:

```
C:\temp\examples>python %X%\PyTools\fixnames_all.py
Using Python find
1 => .\.cshrc
2 => .\LaunchBrowser.out.txt
3 => .\LaunchBrowser.py
...
...more deleted...
...
218 => .\Ai
219 => .\Ai\ExpertSystem
220 => .\Ai\ExpertSystem\TODO
Convert dir=.\Ai\ExpertSystem file=TODO? (y|Y)n
221 => .\Ai\ExpertSystem\__init__.py
222 => .\Ai\ExpertSystem\holmes
223 => .\Ai\ExpertSystem\holmes\README.1ST
Convert dir=.\Ai\ExpertSystem\holmes file=README.1ST? (y|Y)y
Type new file name (enter=readme.1st):
Renamed:   .\Ai\ExpertSystem\holmes\README.1st
to:        .\Ai\ExpertSystem\holmes\readme.1st
Press enter to continue
224 => .\Ai\ExpertSystem\holmes\README.2ND
Convert dir=.\Ai\ExpertSystem\holmes file=README.2ND? (y|Y)y
Type new file name (enter=readme.2nd): readme-more
Renamed:   .\Ai\ExpertSystem\holmes\README.2nd
to:        .\Ai\ExpertSystem\holmes\readme-more
Press enter to continue
...
...more deleted...
...
1471 => .\todos.py
1472 => .\tounix.py
1473 => .\xferall.linux.csh
Converted 2 files, visited 1473
```

This script could simply convert every all-uppercase name to an all-lowercase equivalent automatically, but that's potentially dangerous (some names might require mixed-case). Instead, it asks for input during the traversal, and shows the results of each renaming operation along the way.

Rewriting with os.path.walk

Notice, though, that the pattern-matching power of the `find.find` call goes completely unused in this script. Because it always must visit *every* file in the tree, the `os.path.walk` interface we studied in Chapter 2 would work just as well, and avoids any initial pause while a filename list is being collected (that pause is negligible here, but may be significant for larger trees). Example 5-7 is an equivalent version of this script that does its tree traversal with the `walk` callbacks-based model.

Example 5-7. PP2E\PyTools\fixnames_all2.py

```
############################################################
# Use: "python ..\..\PyTools\fixnames_all2.py".
# same, but use the os.path.walk interface, not find.find;
# to make this work like the simple find version, puts of
# visiting directories until just before visiting their
# contents (find.find lists dir names before their contents);
# renaming dirs here can fail on case-sensitive platforms
# too--walk keeps extending paths containing old dir names;
############################################################

import os
listonly = 0
from fixnames_all import convertOne

def visitname(fname):
    global ccount, vcount
    print vcount+1, '=>', fname
    if not listonly:
        ccount = ccount + convertOne(fname)
    vcount = vcount + 1

def visitor(myData, directoryName, filesInDirectory):   # called for each dir
    visitname(directoryName)                             # do dir we're in now,
    for fname in filesInDirectory:                       # and non-dir files here
        fpath = os.path.join(directoryName, fname)       # fnames have no dirpath
        if not os.path.isdir(fpath):
            visitname(fpath)

ccount = vcount = 0
os.path.walk('.', visitor, None)
print 'Converted %d files, visited %d' % (ccount, vcount)
```

This version does the same job, but visits one extra file (the topmost root directory), and may visit directories in a different order (`os.listdir` results are unordered). Both versions run in under a dozen seconds for the example directory tree on my computer.* We'll revisit this script, as well as the `fixeoln` line-end fixer, in the context of a general tree-walker class hierarchy later in this chapter.

---

* Very subtle thing: both versions of this script might fail on platforms where case matters, if they rename directories along the way. If a directory is renamed *before* the contents of that directory have been visited (e.g., a directory *SPAM* renamed to *spam*), then later reference to the directory's contents using the old name (e.g., *SPAM/filename*) will no longer be valid on case-sensitive platforms. This can happen in the `find.find` version, because directories can and do show up in the result list *before* their contents. It's also a potential with the `os.path.walk` version, because the prior directory path (with original directory names) keeps being extended at each level of the tree. I only use this script on Windows (DOS), so I haven't been bitten by this in practice. Workarounds—ordering find result lists, walking trees in a bottom-up fashion, making two distinct passes for files and directories, queuing up directory names on a list to be renamed later, or simply not renaming directories at all—are all complex enough to be delegated to the realm of reader experiments. As a rule of thumb, changing a tree's names or structure while it is being walked is a risky venture.

Searching Directory Trees

Engineers love to change things. As I was writing this book, I found it almost *irresistible* to move and rename directories, variables, and shared modules in the book examples tree, whenever I thought I'd stumbled on to a more coherent structure. That was fine early on, but as the tree became more intertwined, this became a maintenance nightmare. Things like program directory paths and module names were hardcoded all over the place—in package import statements, program startup calls, text notes, configuration files, and more.

One way to repair these references, of course, is to edit every file in the directory by hand, searching each for information that has changed. That's so tedious as to be utterly impossible in this book's examples tree, though; as I wrote these words, the example tree contained 118 directories and 1342 files! (To count for yourself, run a command-line `python PyTools/visitor.py 1` in the *PP2E* examples root directory.) Clearly, I needed a way to automate updates after changes.

Greps and Globs in Shells and Python

There is a standard way to search files for strings on Unix and Linux systems: the command-line program *grep* and its relatives list all lines in one or more files containing a string or string pattern.* Given that Unix shells expand (i.e., "glob") filename patterns automatically, a command such as `grep popen *.py` will search a single directory's Python files for string "popen". Here's such a command in action on Windows (I installed a commercial Unix-like *fgrep* program on my Windows 98 laptop because I missed it too much there):

```
C:\...\PP2E\System\Filetools>fgrep popen *.py
diffall.py:# - we could also os.popen a diff (unix) or fc (dos)
dirdiff.py:# - use os.popen('ls...') or glob.glob + os.path.split
dirdiff6.py:    files1 = os.popen('ls %s' % dir1).readlines()
dirdiff6.py:    files2 = os.popen('ls %s' % dir2).readlines()
testdirdiff.py:   expected = expected + os.popen(test % 'dirdiff').read()
testdirdiff.py:       output = output + os.popen(test % script).read()
```

DOS has a command for searching files too—*find*, not to be confused with the Unix *find* directory walker command:

```
C:\...\PP2E\System\Filetools>find /N "popen" testdirdiff.py

---------- testdirdiff.py
[8]     expected = expected + os.popen(test % 'dirdiff').read()
[15]        output = output + os.popen(test % script).read()
```

You can do the same within a Python script, by either running the previously mentioned shell command with `os.system` or `os.popen`, or combining the `grep`

---

* In fact, the act of searching files often goes by the colloquial name "grepping" among developers who have spent any substantial time in the Unix ghetto.

and `glob` built-in modules. We met the `glob` module in Chapter 2; it expands a filename pattern into a list of matching filename strings (much like a Unix shell). The standard library also includes a `grep` module, which acts like a Unix *grep* command: `grep.grep` prints lines containing a pattern string among a set of files. When used with `glob`, the effect is much like the *fgrep* command:

```
>>> from grep import grep
>>> from glob import glob
>>> grep('popen', glob('*.py'))
diffall.py:  16: # - we could also os.popen a diff (unix) or fc (dos)
dirdiff.py:  12: # - use os.popen('ls...') or glob.glob + os.path.split
dirdiff6.py: 19:     files1 = os.popen('ls %s' % dir1).readlines()
dirdiff6.py: 20:     files2 = os.popen('ls %s' % dir2).readlines()
testdirdiff.py:  8:    expected = expected + os.popen(test % 'dirdiff')...
testdirdiff.py: 15:        output = output + os.popen(test % script).read()

>>> import glob, grep
>>> grep.grep('system', glob.glob('*.py'))
dirdiff.py:  16: # - on unix systems we could do something similar by
regtest.py:  18:       os.system('%s < %s > %s.out 2>&1' % (program, ...
regtest.py:  23:       os.system('%s < %s > %s.out 2>&1' % (program, ...
regtest.py:  24:       os.system('diff %s.out %s.out.bkp > %s.diffs' ...
```

The `grep` module is written in pure Python code (no shell commands are run), is completely portable, and accepts both simple strings and general regular expression patterns as the search key (regular expressions appear later in this text). Unfortunately, it is also limited in two major ways:

- It simply *prints* matching lines instead of returning them in a list for later processing. We could intercept and split its output by redirecting `sys.stdin` to an object temporarily (Chapter 2 showed how), but that's fairly inconvenient.[*]

- More crucial here, the `grep`/`glob` combination still inspects only a *single directory*; as we also saw in Chapter 2, we need to do more to search all files in an entire directory tree.

On Unix systems, we can work around the second of these limitations by running a *grep* shell command from within a *find* shell command. For instance, the following Unix command line:

```
find . -name "*.py" -print -exec fgrep popen {} \;
```

would pinpoint lines and files at and below the current directory that mention "popen". If you happen to have a Unix-like *find* command on every machine you will ever use, this is one way to process directories.

---

[*] Due to its limitations, the `grep` module has been tagged as "deprecated" as of Python 1.6, and may disappear completely in future releases. It was never intended to become a widely reusable tool. Use other tree-walking techniques in this book to search for strings in files, directories, and trees. Of the original Unix-like `grep`, `glob`, and `find` modules in Python's library, only `glob` remains nondeprecated today (but see also the custom `find` implementation presented in Chapter 4, *Larger System Examples I*).

Cleaning up bytecode files

I used to run the script in Example 5-8 on some of my machines to remove all *.pyc* bytecode files in the examples tree before packaging or upgrading Pythons (it's not impossible that old binary bytecode files are not forward-compatible with newer Python releases).

Example 5-8. PP2E\PyTools\cleanpyc.py

```
############################################################
# find and delete all "*.pyc" bytecode files at and below
# the directory where this script is run; this assumes a
# Unix-like find command, and so is very non-portable; we
# could instead use the Python find module, or just walk
# the directry trees with portable Python code; the find
# -exec option can apply a Python script to each file too;
############################################################

import os, sys

if sys.platform[:3] == 'win':
    findcmd = r'c:\stuff\bin.mks\find . -name "*.pyc" -print'
else:
    findcmd = 'find . -name "*.pyc" -print'
print findcmd

count = 0
for file in os.popen(findcmd).readlines():      # for all file names
    count = count + 1                           # have \n at the end
    print str(file[:-1])
    os.remove(file[:-1])

print 'Removed %d .pyc files' % count
```

This script uses `os.popen` to collect the output of a commercial package's `find` program installed on one of my Windows computers, or else the standard `find` tool on the Linux side. It's also *completely nonportable* to Windows machines that don't have the commercial `find` program installed, and that includes other computers in my house, and most of the world at large.

Python scripts can reuse underlying shell tools with `os.popen`, but by so doing they lose much of the portability advantage of the Python language. The Unix *find* command is both not universally available, and is a complex tool by itself (in fact, too complex to cover in this book; see a Unix manpage for more details). As we saw in Chapter 2, spawning a shell command also incurs a performance hit, because it must start a new independent program on your computer.

To avoid some of the portability and performance costs of spawning an underlying *find* command, I eventually recoded this script to use the `find` utilities we met and wrote Chapter 2. The new script is shown in Example 5-9.

Example 5-9. PP2E\PyTools\cleanpyc-py.py

```
##########################################################
# find and delete all "*.pyc" bytecode files at and below
# the directory where this script is run; this uses a
# Python find call, and so is portable to most machines;
# run this to delete .pyc's from an old Python release;
# cd to the directory you want to clean before running;
##########################################################

import os, sys, find               # here, gets PyTools find

count = 0
for file in find.find("*.pyc"):    # for all file names
    count = count + 1
    print file
    os.remove(file)

print 'Removed %d .pyc files' % count
```

This works portably, and avoids external program startup costs. But `find` is really just a tree-searcher that doesn't let you hook into the tree search—if you need to do something unique while traversing a directory tree, you may be better off using a more manual approach. Moreover, `find` must collect all names before it returns; in very large directory trees, this may introduce significant performance and memory penalties. It's not an issue for my trees, but your trees may vary.

A Python Tree Searcher

To help ease the task of performing global searches on all platforms I might ever use, I coded a Python script to do most of the work for me. Example 5-10 employs standard Python tools we met in the preceding chapters:

*   `os.path.walk` to visit files in a directory
*   `string.find` to search for a string in a text read from a file
*   `os.path.splitext` to skip over files with binary-type extensions
*   `os.path.join` to portably combine a directory path and filename
*   `os.path.isdir` to skip paths that refer to directories, not files

Because it's pure Python code, though, it can be run the same way on both Linux and Windows. In fact, it should work on any computer where Python has been installed. Moreover, because it uses direct system calls, it will likely be faster than using `op.popen` to spawn a *find* command that spawns many *grep* commands.

Example 5-10. PP2E\PyTools\search_all.py

```
##########################################################
# Use: "python ..\..\PyTools\search_all.py string".
# search all files at and below current directory
# for a string; uses the os.path.walk interface,
# rather than doing a find to collect names first;
##########################################################

import os, sys, string
listonly = 0
skipexts = ['.gif', '.exe', '.pyc', '.o', '.a']         # ignore binary files

def visitfile(fname, searchKey):                        # for each non-dir file
    global fcount, vcount                               # search for string
    print vcount+1, '=>', fname                         # skip protected files
    try:
        if not listonly:
            if os.path.splitext(fname)[1] in skipexts:
                print 'Skipping', fname
            elif string.find(open(fname).read(), searchKey) != -1:
                raw_input('%s has %s' % (fname, searchKey))
                fcount = fcount + 1
    except: pass
    vcount = vcount + 1

def visitor(myData, directoryName, filesInDirectory):   # called for each dir
    for fname in filesInDirectory:                      # do non-dir files here
        fpath = os.path.join(directoryName, fname)      # fnames have no dirpath
        if not os.path.isdir(fpath):                    # myData is searchKey
            visitfile(fpath, myData)

def searcher(startdir, searchkey):
    global fcount, vcount
    fcount = vcount = 0
    os.path.walk(startdir, visitor, searchkey)

if __name__ == '__main__':
    searcher('.', sys.argv[1])
    print 'Found in %d files, visited %d' % (fcount, vcount)
```

This file also uses the **sys.argv** command-line list and the **__name__** trick for running in two modes. When run standalone, the search key is passed on the command line; when imported, clients call this module's **searcher** function directly. For example, to search (grep) for all appearances of directory name "Part2" in the examples tree (an old directory that really did go away!), run a command line like this in a DOS or Unix shell:

```
C:\...\PP2E>python PyTools\search_all.py Part2
1 => .\autoexec.bat
2 => .\cleanall.csh
3 => .\echoEnvironment.pyw
4 => .\Launcher.py
.\Launcher.py has Part2
```

```
5 => .\Launcher.pyc
Skipping .\Launcher.pyc
6 => .\Launch_PyGadgets.py
7 => .\Launch_PyDemos.pyw
8 => .\LaunchBrowser.out.txt
.\LaunchBrowser.out.txt has Part2
9 => .\LaunchBrowser.py
.\LaunchBrowser.py has Part2
...
```
...more lines deleted
```
...
1339 => .\old_Part2\Basics\unpack2b.py
1340 => .\old_Part2\Basics\unpack3.py
1341 => .\old_Part2\Basics\__init__.py
Found in 74 files, visited 1341
```

The script lists each file it checks as it goes, tells you which files it is skipping (names that end in extensions listed in variable skipexts that imply binary data), and pauses for an Enter key press each time it announces a file containing the search string (bold lines). A solution based on find could not pause this way; although trivial in this example, find doesn't return until the entire tree traversal is finished. The search_all script works the same when *imported* instead of run, but there is no final statistics output line (fcount and vcount live in the module, and so would have to be imported to be inspected here):

```
>>> from PP2E.PyTools.search_all import searcher
>>> searcher('.', '-exec')              # find files with string '-exec'
1 => .\autoexec.bat
2 => .\cleanall.csh
3 => .\echoEnvironment.pyw
4 => .\Launcher.py
5 => .\Launcher.pyc
Skipping .\Launcher.pyc
6 => .\Launch_PyGadgets.py
7 => .\Launch_PyDemos.pyw
8 => .\LaunchBrowser.out.txt
9 => .\LaunchBrowser.py
10 => .\Launch_PyGadgets_bar.pyw
11 => .\makeall.csh
12 => .\package.csh
.\package.csh has -exec
```
...more lines deleted...

However launched, this script tracks down all references to a string in an entire directory tree—a name of a changed book examples file, object, or directory, for instance.[*]

---

[*] See the coverage of regular expressions in Chapter 18, *Text and Language*. The search_all script here searches for a simple string in each file with string.find, but it would be trivial to extend it to search for a regular expression pattern match instead (roughly, just replace string.find with a call to a regular expression object's search method). Of course, such a mutation will be much more trivial after we've learned how to do it.

Visitor: Walking Trees Generically

Armed with the portable `search_all` script from Example 5-10, I was able to better pinpoint files to be edited, every time I changed the book examples tree structure. At least initially, I ran `search_all` to pick out suspicious files in one window, and edited each along the way by hand in another window.

Pretty soon, though, this became tedious too. Manually typing filenames into editor commands is no fun, especially when the number of files to edit is large. The search for "Part2" shown earlier returned 74 files, for instance. Since there are at least occasionally better things to do than manually start 74 editor sessions, I looked for a way to *automatically* run an editor on each suspicious file.

Unfortunately, `search_all` simply prints results to the screen. Although that text could be intercepted and parsed, a more direct approach that spawns edit sessions during the search may be easier, but may require major changes to the tree search script as currently coded. At this point, two thoughts came to mind.

First, I knew it would be easier in the long-run to be able to add features to a general directory searcher as *external components*, not by changing the original script. Because editing files was just one possible extension (what about automating text replacements too?), a more generic, customizable, and reusable search component seemed the way to go.

Second, after writing a few directory walking utilities, it became clear that I was rewriting the same sort of code over and over again. Traversals could be even further simplified by wrapping common details for easier reuse. The `os.path.walk` tool helps, but its use tends to foster redundant operations (e.g., directory name joins), and its function-object-based interface doesn't quite lend itself to customization the way a class can.

Of course, both goals point to using an OO framework for traversals and searching. Example 5-11 is one concrete realization of these goals. It exports a general `FileVisitor` class that mostly just wraps `os.path.walk` for easier use and extension, as well as a generic `SearchVisitor` class that generalizes the notion of directory searches. By itself, `SearchVisitor` simply does what `search_all` did, but it also opens up the search process to customization—bits of its behavior can be modified by overloading its methods in subclasses. Moreover, its core search logic can be reused everywhere we need to search; simply define a subclass that adds search-specific extensions.

Example 5-11. PP2E\PyTools\visitor.py

```
##############################################################
# Test: "python ..\..\PyTools\visitor.py testmask [string]".
# Uses OOP, classes, and subclasses to wrap some of the
```

Example 5-11. PP2E\PyTools\visitor.py (continued)

```
# details of using os.path.walk to walk and search; testmask
# is an integer bitmask with 1 bit per available selftest;
# see also: visitor_edit/replace/find/fix*/.py subclasses,
# and the fixsitename.py client script in Internet\Cgi-Web;
#############################################################

import os, sys, string
listonly = 0

class FileVisitor:
    """
    visits all non-directory files below startDir;
    override visitfile to provide a file handler
    """
    def __init__(self, data=None, listonly=0):
        self.context  = data
        self.fcount   = 0
        self.dcount   = 0
        self.listonly = listonly
    def run(self, startDir=os.curdir):                    # default start='.'
        os.path.walk(startDir, self.visitor, None)
    def visitor(self, data, dirName, filesInDir):         # called for each dir
        self.visitdir(dirName)                            # do this dir first
        for fname in filesInDir:                          # do non-dir files
            fpath = os.path.join(dirName, fname)          # fnames have no path
            if not os.path.isdir(fpath):
                self.visitfile(fpath)
    def visitdir(self, dirpath):                          # called for each dir
        self.dcount = self.dcount + 1                     # override or extend me
        print dirpath, '...'
    def visitfile(self, filepath):                        # called for each file
        self.fcount = self.fcount + 1                     # override or extend me
        print self.fcount, '=>', filepath                # default: print name

class SearchVisitor(FileVisitor):
    """
    search files at and below startDir for a string
    """
    skipexts = ['.gif', '.exe', '.pyc', '.o', '.a']       # skip binary files
    def __init__(self, key, listonly=0):
        FileVisitor.__init__(self, key, listonly)
        self.scount = 0
    def visitfile(self, fname):                           # test for a match
        FileVisitor.visitfile(self, fname)
        if not self.listonly:
            if os.path.splitext(fname)[1] in self.skipexts:
                print 'Skipping', fname
            else:
                text = open(fname).read()
                if string.find(text, self.context) != -1:
                    self.visitmatch(fname, text)
                    self.scount = self.scount + 1
```

Example 5-11. PP2E\PyTools\visitor.py (continued)

```
    def visitmatch(self, fname, text):            # process a match
        raw_input('%s has %s' % (fname, self.context))   # override me lower


# self-test logic
dolist   = 1
dosearch = 2     # 3=do list and search
donext   = 4     # when next test added

def selftest(testmask):
    if testmask & dolist:
        visitor = FileVisitor()
        visitor.run('.')
        print 'Visited %d files and %d dirs' % (visitor.fcount, visitor.dcount)

    if testmask & dosearch:
        visitor = SearchVisitor(sys.argv[2], listonly)
        visitor.run('.')
        print 'Found in %d files, visited %d' % (visitor.scount, visitor.fcount)

if __name__ == '__main__':
    selftest(int(sys.argv[1]))     # e.g., 5 = dolist | dorename
```

This module primarily serves to export classes for external use, but it does something useful when run standalone too. If you invoke it as a script with a single argument "1", it makes and runs a `FileVisitor` object, and prints an exhaustive listing of every file and directory at and below the place you are at when the script is invoked (i.e., ".", the current working directory):

```
C:\temp>python %X%\PyTools\visitor.py 1
. ...
1 => .\autoexec.bat
2 => .\cleanall.csh
3 => .\echoEnvironment.pyw
4 => .\Launcher.py
5 => .\Launcher.pyc
6 => .\Launch_PyGadgets.py
7 => .\Launch_PyDemos.pyw
...more deleted...
479 => .\Gui\Clock\plotterGui.py
480 => .\Gui\Clock\plotterText.py
481 => .\Gui\Clock\plotterText1.py
482 => .\Gui\Clock\__init__.py
.\Gui\gifs ...
483 => .\Gui\gifs\frank.gif
484 => .\Gui\gifs\frank.note
485 => .\Gui\gifs\gilligan.gif
486 => .\Gui\gifs\gilligan.note
...more deleted...
1352 => .\PyTools\visitor_fixnames.py
1353 => .\PyTools\visitor_find_quiet2.py
```

```
1354 => .\PyTools\visitor_find.pyc
1355 => .\PyTools\visitor_find_quiet1.py
1356 => .\PyTools\fixeoln_one.doc.txt
Visited 1356 files and 119 dirs
```

If you instead invoke this script with a "2" as its first argument, it makes and runs
a `SearchVisitor` object, using the second argument as the search key. This form
is equivalent to running the *search_all.py* script we met earlier; it pauses for an
Enter key press after each matching file is reported (lines in bold font here):

```
C:\temp\examples>python %X%\PyTools\visitor.py 2 Part3
. ...
1 => .\autoexec.bat
2 => .\cleanall.csh
.\cleanall.csh has Part3
3 => .\echoEnvironment.pyw
4 => .\Launcher.py
.\Launcher.py has Part3
5 => .\Launcher.pyc
Skipping .\Launcher.pyc
6 => .\Launch_PyGadgets.py
7 => .\Launch_PyDemos.pyw
8 => .\LaunchBrowser.out.txt
9 => .\LaunchBrowser.py
10 => .\Launch_PyGadgets_bar.pyw
11 => .\makeall.csh
.\makeall.csh has Part3
...
...more deleted
...
1353 => .\PyTools\visitor_find_quiet2.py
1354 => .\PyTools\visitor_find.pyc
Skipping .\PyTools\visitor_find.pyc
1355 => .\PyTools\visitor_find_quiet1.py
1356 => .\PyTools\fixeoln_one.doc.txt
Found in 49 files, visited 1356
```

Technically, passing this script a first argument "3" runs *both* a `FileVisitor` and
a `SearchVisitor` (two separate traversals are performed). The first argument is
really used as a bitmask to select one or more supported self-tests—if a test's bit is
on in the binary value of the argument, the test will be run. Because 3 is 011 in
binary, it selects both a search (010) and a listing (001). In a more user-friendly
system we might want to be more symbolic about that (e.g., check for "–search"
and "–list" arguments), but bitmasks work just as well for this script's scope.

Editing Files in Directory Trees

Now, after genericizing tree traversals and searches, it's an easy step to add automatic file editing in a brand-new, separate component. Example 5-12 defines a
new `EditVisitor` class that simply customizes the `visitmatch` method of the

Text Editor War and Peace

In case you don't know, the vi setting used in the *visitor_edit.py* script is a Unix text editor; it's available for Windows too, but is not standard there. If you run this script, you'll probably want to change its `editor` setting on your machine. For instance, "emacs" should work on Linux, and "edit" or "notepad" should work on all Windows boxes.

These days, I tend to use an editor I coded in Python (PyEdit), so I'll leave the editor wars to more politically-minded readers. In fact, changing the script to assign `editor` either of these ways:

```
editor = r'python Gui\TextEditor\textEditor.pyw'
editor = r'start  Gui\TextEditor\textEditor.pyw'
```

will open the matched file in a pure and portable Python text editor GUI—one coded in Python with the Tkinter interface, which runs on all major GUI plat-forms, and which we'll meet in Chapter 9, *Larger GUI Examples*. If you read about the *start* command in Chapter 3, *Parallel System Tools*, you know that the first editor setting pauses the traversal while the editor runs, but the second does not (you'll get as many PyEdit windows as there are matched files).

This may fail, however, for very long file directory names (remember, `os.system` has a length limit unlike `os.spawnv`). Moreover, the path to the *textEditor.pyw* program may vary depending on where you are when you run *visitor_edit.py* (i.e., the CWD). There are ways around this latter problem:

- Prefixing the script's path string with the value of the `PP2EHOME` shell variable, fetched with `os.environ`; with the standard book setup scripts, `PP2EHOME` gives the absolute root directory, from which the editor script's path can be found.

- Prefixing the path with `sys.path[0]` and a `'../'` to exploit the fact that the first import directory is always the script's home directory (see the "Current Working Directory" section in Chapter 2).

- Windows shortcuts or Unix links to the editor script from the CWD.

- Searching for the script naively with `Launcher.findFirst` or `guessLocation`, described near the end of Chapter 4.

But these are all beyond the scope of a sidebar on text editor politics.

SearchVisitor class, to open a text editor on the matched file. Yes, this is the complete program—it needs to do something special only when visiting matched files, and so need provide only that behavior; the rest of the traversal and search logic is unchanged and inherited.

Example 5-12. PP2E\PyTools\visitor_edit.py

```
###########################################################
# Use: "python PyTools\visitor_edit.py string".
# add auto-editor start up to SearchVisitor in an external
# component (subclass), not in-place changes; this version
# automatically pops up an editor on each file containing the
# string as it traverses; you can also use editor='edit' or
# 'notepad' on windows; 'vi' and 'edit' run in console window;
# editor=r'python Gui\TextEditor\textEditor.pyw' may work too;
# caveat: we might be able to make this smarter by sending
# a search command to go to the first match in some editors;
###########################################################

import os, sys, string
from visitor import SearchVisitor
listonly = 0

class EditVisitor(SearchVisitor):
    """
    edit files at and below startDir having string
    """
    editor = 'vi'   # ymmv
    def visitmatch(self, fname, text):
        os.system('%s %s' % (self.editor, fname))

if __name__ == '__main__':
    visitor = EditVisitor(sys.argv[1], listonly)
    visitor.run('.')
    print 'Edited %d files, visited %d' % (visitor.scount, visitor.fcount)
```

When we make and run an `EditVisitor`, a text editor is started with the `os.system` command-line spawn call, which usually blocks its caller until the spawned program finishes. On my machines, each time this script finds a matched file during the traversal, it starts up the vi text editor within the console window where the script was started; exiting the editor resumes the tree walk.

Let's find and edit some files. When run as a script, we pass this program the search string as a command argument (here, the string "–exec" is the search key, not an option flag). The root directory is always passed to the `run` method as ".", the current run directory. Traversal status messages show up in the console as before, but each matched file now automatically pops up in a text editor along the way. Here, the editor is started eight times:

```
C:\...\PP2E>python PyTools\visitor_edit.py -exec
1 => .\autoexec.bat
2 => .\cleanall.csh
3 => .\echoEnvironment.pyw
4 => .\Launcher.py
5 => .\Launcher.pyc
Skipping .\Launcher.pyc
...more deleted...
```

```
1340 => .\old_Part2\Basics\unpack2.py
1341 => .\old_Part2\Basics\unpack2b.py
1342 => .\old_Part2\Basics\unpack3.py
1343 => .\old_Part2\Basics\__init__.py
Edited 8 files, visited 1343
```

This, finally, is the exact tool I was looking for to simplify global book examples tree maintenance. After major changes to things like shared modules and file and directory names, I run this script on the examples root directory with an appropriate search string, and edit any files it pops up as needed. I still need to change files by hand in the editor, but that's often safer than blind global replacements.

Global Replacements in Directory Trees

But since I brought it up: given a general tree traversal class, it's easy to code a global search-and-replace subclass too. The `FileVisitor` subclass in Example 5-13, `ReplaceVisitor`, customizes the `visitfile` method to globally replace any appearances of one string with another, in all text files at and below a root directory. It also collects the names of all files that were changed in a list, just in case you wish to go through and verify the automatic edits applied (a text editor could be automatically popped up on each changed file, for instance).

Example 5-13. PP2E\PyTools\visitor_replace.py

```
#############################################################
# Use: "python PyTools\visitor_replace.py fromStr toStr".
# does global search-and-replace in all files in a directory
# tree--replaces fromStr with toStr in all text files; this
# is powerful but dangerous!! visitor_edit.py runs an editor
# for you to verify and make changes, and so is much safer;
# use CollectVisitor to simply collect a list of matched files;
#############################################################

import os, sys, string
from visitor import SearchVisitor
listonly = 0

class ReplaceVisitor(SearchVisitor):
    """
    change fromStr to toStr in files at and below startDir;
    files changed available in obj.changed list after a run
    """
    def __init__(self, fromStr, toStr, listonly=0):
        self.changed = []
        self.toStr   = toStr
        SearchVisitor.__init__(self, fromStr, listonly)
    def visitmatch(self, fname, text):
        fromStr, toStr = self.context, self.toStr
        text = string.replace(text, fromStr, toStr)
        open(fname, 'w').write(text)
        self.changed.append(fname)
```

Example 5-13. PP2E\PyTools\visitor_replace.py (continued)

```
if __name__ == '__main__':
    if raw_input('Are you sure?') == 'y':
        visitor = ReplaceVisitor(sys.argv[1], sys.argv[2], listonly)
        visitor.run(startDir='.')
        print 'Visited %d files' % visitor.fcount
        print 'Changed %d files:' % len(visitor.changed)
        for fname in visitor.changed: print fname
```

To run this script over a directory tree, go to the directory to be changed and run
the following sort of command line, with "from" and "to" strings. On my current
machine, doing this on a 1354-file tree and changing 75 files along the way takes
roughly six seconds of real clock time when the system isn't particularly busy:

```
C:\temp\examples>python %X%/PyTools/visitor_replace.py Part2 SPAM2
Are you sure?y
. ...
1 => .\autoexec.bat
2 => .\cleanall.csh
3 => .\echoEnvironment.pyw
4 => .\Launcher.py
5 => .\Launcher.pyc
Skipping .\Launcher.pyc
6 => .\Launch_PyGadgets.py
...more deleted...
1351 => .\PyTools\visitor_find_quiet2.py
1352 => .\PyTools\visitor_find.pyc
Skipping .\PyTools\visitor_find.pyc
1353 => .\PyTools\visitor_find_quiet1.py
1354 => .\PyTools\fixeoln_one.doc.txt
Visited 1354 files
Changed 75 files:
.\Launcher.py
.\LaunchBrowser.out.txt
.\LaunchBrowser.py
.\PyDemos.pyw
.\PyGadgets.py
.\README-PP2E.txt
...more deleted...
.\PyTools\search_all.out.txt
.\PyTools\visitor.out.txt
.\PyTools\visitor_edit.py

[to delete, use an empty toStr]
C:\temp\examples>python %X%/PyTools/visitor_replace.py SPAM ""
```

This is both wildly powerful and dangerous. If the string to be replaced is something that can show up in places you didn't anticipate, you might just ruin an
entire tree of files by running the ReplaceVisitor object defined here. On the
other hand, if the string is something very specific, this object can obviate the
need to automatically edit suspicious files. For instance, we will use this approach

to automatically change web site addresses in HTML files in Chapter 12, *Server-Side Scripting*; the addresses are likely too specific to show up in other places by chance.

Collecting Matched Files in Trees

The scripts so far search and replace in directory trees, using the same traversal code base (module `visitor`). Suppose, though, that you just want to get a Python *list* of files in a directory containing a string. You could run a search and parse the output messages for "found." Much simpler, simply knock off another `SearchVisitor` subclass to collect the list along the way, as in Example 5-14.

Example 5-14. PP2E\PyTools\visitor_collect.py

```
#############################################################
# Use: "python PyTools\visitor_collect.py searchstring".
# CollectVisitor simply collects a list of matched files, for
# display or later processing (e.g., replacement, auto-editing);
#############################################################

import os, sys, string
from visitor import SearchVisitor

class CollectVisitor(SearchVisitor):
    """
    collect names of files containing a string;
    run this and then fetch its obj.matches list
    """
    def __init__(self, searchstr, listonly=0):
        self.matches = []
        SearchVisitor.__init__(self, searchstr, listonly)
    def visitmatch(self, fname, text):
        self.matches.append(fname)

if __name__ == '__main__':
    visitor = CollectVisitor(sys.argv[1])
    visitor.run(startDir='.')
    print 'Found these files:'
    for fname in visitor.matches: print fname
```

`CollectVisitor` is just tree search again, with a new kind of specialization—collecting files, instead of printing messages. This class is useful from other scripts that mean to collect a matched files list for later processing; it can be run by itself as a script too:

```
C:\...\PP2E>python PyTools\visitor_collect.py -exec
...
...more deleted...
...
1342 => .\old_Part2\Basics\unpack2b.py
1343 => .\old_Part2\Basics\unpack3.py
```

```
1344 => .\old_Part2\Basics\__init__.py
Found these files:
.\package.csh
.\README-PP2E.txt
.\readme-old-pp1E.txt
.\PyTools\cleanpyc.py
.\PyTools\fixeoln_all.py
.\System\Processes\output.txt
.\Internet\Cgi-Web\fixcgi.py
```

Suppressing status messages

Here, the items in the collected list are displayed at the end—all the files containing the string "–exec". Notice, though, that traversal status messages are still printed along the way (in fact, I deleted about 1600 lines of such messages here!). In a tool meant to be called from another script, that may be an undesirable side effect; the calling script's output may be more important than the traversal's.

We could add mode flags to `SearchVisitor` to turn off status messages, but that makes it more complex. Instead, the following two files show how we might go about collecting matched filenames without letting any traversal messages show up in the console, all without changing the original code base. The first, shown in Example 5-15, simply takes over and copies the search logic, without print statements. It's a bit redundant with `SearchVisitor`, but only in a few lines of mimicked code.

Example 5-15. PP2E\PyTools\visitor_collect_quiet1.py

```
##############################################################
# Like visitor_collect, but avoid traversal status messages
##############################################################

import os, sys, string
from visitor import FileVisitor, SearchVisitor

class CollectVisitor(FileVisitor):
    """
    collect names of files containing a string, silently;
    """
    skipexts = SearchVisitor.skipexts
    def __init__(self, searchStr):
        self.matches = []
        self.context = searchStr
    def visitdir(self, dname): pass
    def visitfile(self, fname):
        if (os.path.splitext(fname)[1] not in self.skipexts and
            string.find(open(fname).read(), self.context) != -1):
            self.matches.append(fname)

if __name__ == '__main__':
    visitor = CollectVisitor(sys.argv[1])
```

Example 5-15. PP2E\PyTools\visitor_collect_quiet1.py (continued)

```
visitor.run(startDir='.')
print 'Found these files:'
for fname in visitor.matches: print fname
```

When this class is run, only the contents of the matched filenames list show up at
the end; no status messages appear during the traversal. Because of that, this form
may be more useful as a general-purpose tool used by other scripts:

```
C:\...\PP2E>python PyTools\visitor_collect_quiet1.py -exec
Found these files:
.\package.csh
.\README-PP2E.txt
.\readme-old-pp1E.txt
.\PyTools\cleanpyc.py
.\PyTools\fixeoln_all.py
.\System\Processes\output.txt
.\Internet\Cgi-Web\fixcgi.py
```

A more interesting and less redundant way to suppress printed text during a traversal is to apply the stream redirection tricks we met in Chapter 2. Example 5-16
sets `sys.stdin` to a `NullOut` object that throws away all printed text for the duration of the traversal (its `write` method does nothing).

The only real complication with this scheme is that there is no good place to insert
a restoration of `sys.stdout` at the end of the traversal; instead, we code the
restore in the `__del__` destructor method, and require clients to delete the visitor
to resume printing as usual. An explicitly called method would work just as well, if
you prefer less magical interfaces.

Example 5-16. PP2E\PyTools\visitor_collect_quiet2.py

```
#############################################################
# Like visitor_collect, but avoid traversal status messages
#############################################################

import os, sys, string
from visitor import SearchVisitor

class NullOut:
    def write(self, line): pass

class CollectVisitor(SearchVisitor):
    """
    collect names of files containing a string, silently
    """
    def __init__(self, searchstr, listonly=0):
        self.matches = []
        self.saveout, sys.stdout = sys.stdout, NullOut()
        SearchVisitor.__init__(self, searchstr, listonly)
    def __del__(self):
```

Example 5-16. PP2E\PyTools\visitor_collect_quiet2.py (continued)

```
            sys.stdout = self.saveout
    def visitmatch(self, fname, text):
        self.matches.append(fname)

if __name__ == '__main__':
    visitor = CollectVisitor(sys.argv[1])
    visitor.run(startDir='.')
    matches = visitor.matches
    del visitor
    print 'Found these files:'
    for fname in matches: print fname
```

When this script is run, output is identical to the prior run—just the matched file-names at the end. Perhaps better still, why not code and debug just one verbose CollectVisitor utility class, and require *clients* to wrap calls to its run method in the redirect.redirect function we wrote back in Example 2-10?

```
>>> from PP2E.PyTools.visitor_collect import CollectVisitor
>>> from PP2E.System.Streams.redirect import redirect
>>> walker = CollectVisitor('-exec')              # object to find '-exec'
>>> output = redirect(walker.run, ('.',), '')     # function, args, input
>>> for line in walker.matches: print line         # print items in list
...
.\package.csh
.\README-PP2E.txt
.\readme-old-pp1E.txt
.\PyTools\cleanpyc.py
.\PyTools\fixeoln_all.py
.\System\Processes\output.txt
.\Internet\Cgi-Web\fixcgi.py
```

The redirect call employed here resets standard input and output streams to file-like objects for the duration of *any* function call; because of that, it's a more general way to suppress output than recoding every outputter. Here, it has the effect of intercepting (and hence suppressing) printed messages during a walker. run('.') traversal. They really *are* printed, but show up in the string result of the redirect call, not on the screen:

```
>>> output[:60]
'. ...\0121 => .\\autoexec.bat\0122 => .\\cleanall.csh\0123 => .\\echoEnv'

>>> import string
>>> len(output), len(string.split(output, '\n'))   # bytes, lines
(67609, 1592)

>>> walker.matches
['.\\package.csh', '.\\README-PP2E.txt', '.\\readme-old-pp1E.txt',
'.\\PyTools\\cleanpyc.py', '.\\PyTools\\fixeoln_all.py',
'.\\System\\Processes\\output.txt',
'.\\Internet\\Cgi-Web\\fixcgi.py']
```

Because `redirect` saves printed text in a string, it may be less appropriate than the two quiet `CollectVisitor` variants for functions that generate much output. Here, for example, 67,609 bytes of output was queued up in an in-memory string (see the `len` call results); such a buffer may or may not be significant in some applications.

In more general terms, redirecting `sys.stdout` to dummy objects as done here is a simple way to turn off outputs (and is the equivalent to the Unix notion of redirecting output to file */dev/null*—a file that discards everything sent to it). For instance, we'll pull this trick out of the bag again in the context of server-side Internet scripting, to prevent utility status messages from showing up in generated web page output streams.[*]

Recoding Fixers with Visitors

Be warned: once you've written and debugged a class that knows how to do something useful like walking directory trees, it's easy for it to spread throughout your system utility libraries. Of course, that's the whole point of code reuse. For instance, very soon after writing the visitor classes presented in the prior sections, I recoded both the *fixnames_all.py* and *fixeoln_all.py* directory walker scripts listed earlier in Examples 5-6 and 5-4, respectively, to use visitor instead of proprietary tree-walk logic (they both originally used `find.find`). Example 5-17 combines the original `convertLines` function (to fix end-of-lines in a single file) with visitor's tree walker class, to yield an alternative implementation of the line-end converter for directory trees.

Example 5-17. PP2E\PyTools\visitor_fixeoln.py

```
#############################################################
# Use: "python visitor_fixeoln.py todos|tounix".
# recode fixeoln_all.py as a visitor subclass: this version
# uses os.path.walk, not find.find to collext all names first;
# limited but fast: if os.path.splitext(fname)[1] in patts:
#############################################################

import visitor, sys, fnmatch, os
from fixeoln_dir import patts
from fixeoln_one import convertEndlines

class EolnFixer(visitor.FileVisitor):
    def visitfile(self, fullname):                          # match on basename
```

---

[*] For the impatient: see `commonhtml.runsilent` in the PyMailCgi system presented in Chapter 13, *Larger Web Site Examples I*. It's a variation on `redirect.redirect` that discards output as it is printed (instead of retaining it in a string), returns the return value of the function called (not the output string), and lets exceptions pass via a `try`/`finally` statement (instead of catching and reporting them with a `try`/`except`). It's still redirection at work, though.

Example 5-17. PP2E\PyTools\visitor_fixeoln.py (continued)

```
                basename = os.path.basename(fullname)       # to make result same
                for patt in patts:                          # else visits fewer
                    if fnmatch.fnmatch(basename, patt):
                        convertEndlines(self.context, fullname)
                        self.fcount = self.fcount + 1        # could break here
                                                            # but results differ
if __name__ == '__main__':
    walker = EolnFixer(sys.argv[1])
    walker.run()
    print 'Files matched (converted or not):', walker.fcount
```

As we saw in Chapter 2, the built-in `fnmatch` module performs Unix shell-like file-name matching; this script uses it to match names to the previous version's file-name patterns (simply looking for filename extensions after a "." is simpler, but not as general):

```
C:\temp\examples>python %X%/PyTools/visitor_fixeoln.py tounix
. ...
Changing .\echoEnvironment.pyw
Changing .\Launcher.py
Changing .\Launch_PyGadgets.py
Changing .\Launch_PyDemos.pyw
...more deleted...
Changing .\PyTools\visitor_find.py
Changing .\PyTools\visitor_fixnames.py
Changing .\PyTools\visitor_find_quiet2.py
Changing .\PyTools\visitor_find_quiet1.py
Changing .\PyTools\fixeoln_one.doc.txt
Files matched (converted or not): 1065

C:\temp\examples>python %X%/PyTools/visitor_fixeoln.py tounix
...more deleted...
.\Extend\Swig\Shadow ...
.\ ...
.\EmbExt\Exports ...
.\EmbExt\Exports\ClassAndMod ...
.\EmbExt\Regist ...
.\PyTools ...
Files matched (converted or not): 1065
```

If you run this script and the original *fixeoln_all.py* on the book examples tree, you'll notice that this version visits two fewer matched files. This simply reflects the fact that `fixeoln_all` also collects and skips over two directory names for its patterns in the `find.find` result (both called "Output"). In all other ways, this version works the same way even when it could do better—adding a break statement after the `convertEndlines` call here avoids visiting files that appear redundantly in the original's find results lists.

The first command here takes roughly six seconds on my computer, and the second takes about four (there are no files to be converted). That's faster than the

eight- and six-second figures for the original find.find-based version of this
script, but they differ in amount of output, and benchmarks are usually much more
subtle than you imagine. Most of the real clock time is likely spent scrolling text in
the console, not doing any real directory processing. Since both are plenty fast for
their intended purposes, finer-grained performance figures are left as exercises.

The script in Example 5-18 combines the original **convertOne** function (to rename
a single file or directory) with the visitor's tree walker class, to create a directory
tree-wide fix for uppercase filenames. Notice that we redefine both file and directory visitation methods here, as we need to rename both.

Example 5-18. PP2E\PyTools\visitor_fixnames.py

```
#############################################################
# recode fixnames_all.py name case fixer with the Visitor class
# note: "from fixnames_all import convertOne" doesn't help at
# top-level of the fixnames class, since it is assumed to be a
# method and called with extra self argument (an exception);
#############################################################

from visitor import FileVisitor

class FixnamesVisitor(FileVisitor):
    """
    check filenames at and below startDir for uppercase
    """
    import fixnames_all
    def __init__(self, listonly=0):
        FileVisitor.__init__(self, listonly=listonly)
        self.ccount = 0
    def rename(self, pathname):
        if not self.listonly:
            convertflag = self.fixnames_all.convertOne(pathname)
            self.ccount = self.ccount + convertflag
    def visitdir(self, dirname):
        FileVisitor.visitdir(self, dirname)
        self.rename(dirname)
    def visitfile(self, filename):
        FileVisitor.visitfile(self, filename)
        self.rename(filename)

if __name__ == '__main__':
    walker = FixnamesVisitor()
    walker.run()
    allnames = walker.fcount + walker.dcount
    print 'Converted %d files, visited %d' % (walker.ccount, allnames)
```

This version is run like the original find.find based version, **fixnames_all**, but
visits one more name (the top-level root directory), and there is no initial delay
while filenames are collected on a list—we're using **os.path.walk** again, not

`find.find`. It's also close to the original `os.path.walk` version of this script, but is based on a class hierarchy, not direct function callbacks:

```
C:\temp\examples>python %X%/PyTools/visitor_fixnames.py
...more deleted...
303 => .\__init__.py
304 => .\__init__.pyc
305 => .\Ai\ExpertSystem\holmes.tar
306 => .\Ai\ExpertSystem\TODO
Convert dir=.\Ai\ExpertSystem file=TODO? (y|Y)
307 => .\Ai\ExpertSystem\__init__.py
308 => .\Ai\ExpertSystem\holmes\cnv
309 => .\Ai\ExpertSystem\holmes\README.1ST
Convert dir=.\Ai\ExpertSystem\holmes file=README.1ST? (y|Y)
...more deleted...
1353 => .\PyTools\visitor_find.pyc
1354 => .\PyTools\visitor_find_quiet1.py
1355 => .\PyTools\fixeoln_one.doc.txt
Converted 1 files, visited 1474
```

Both of these fixer scripts work roughly the same as the originals, but because the directory walking logic lives in just one file (*visitor.py*), it only needs to be debugged once. Moreover, improvements in that file will automatically be inherited by every directory-processing tool derived from its classes. Even when coding system-level scripts, reuse and reduced redundancy pay off in the end.

Fixing File Permissions in Trees

Just in case the preceding visitor-client sections weren't quite enough to convince you of the power of code reuse, another piece of evidence surfaced very late in this book project. It turns out that copying files off a CD using Windows drag-and-drop makes them *read-only* in the copy. That's less than ideal for the book examples directory on the enclosed CD—you must copy the directory tree onto your hard drive to be able to experiment with program changes (naturally, files on CD can't be changed in place). But if you copy with drag-and-drop, you may wind up with a tree of over 1000 read-only files.

Since drag-and-drop is perhaps the most common way to copy off a CD on Windows, I needed a portable and easy-to-use way to undo the read-only setting. Asking readers to make these all writable by hand would be impolite to say the least. Writing a full-blown install system seemed like overkill. Providing different fixes for different platforms doubles or triples the complexity of the task.

Much better, the Python script in Example 5-19 can be run in the root of the copied examples directory to repair the damage of a read-only drag-and-drop operation. It specializes the traversal implemented by the `FileVisitor` class again—this time to run an `os.chmod` call on every file and directory visited along the way.

Example 5-19. PP2E\PyTools\fixreadonly-all.py

```
#!/usr/bin/env python
##############################################################
# Use: python PyTools\fixreadonly-all.py
# run this script in the top-level examples directory after
# copying all examples off the book's CD-ROM, to make all
# files writeable again--by default, copying files off the
# CD with Windows drag-and-drop (at least) creates them as
# read-only on your hard drive; this script traverses entire
# dir tree at and below the dir it is run in (all subdirs);
##############################################################

import os, string
from PP2E.PyTools.visitor import FileVisitor       # os.path.walk wrapper
listonly = 0

class FixReadOnly(FileVisitor):
    def __init__(self, listonly=0):
        FileVisitor.__init__(self, listonly=listonly)
    def visitDir(self, dname):
        FileVisitor.visitfile(self, fname)
        if self.listonly:
            return
        os.chmod(dname, 0777)
    def visitfile(self, fname):
        FileVisitor.visitfile(self, fname)
        if self.listonly:
            return
        os.chmod(fname, 0777)

if __name__ == '__main__':
    # don't run auto if clicked
    go = raw_input('This script makes all files writeable; continue?')
    if go != 'y':
        raw_input('Canceled - hit enter key')
    else:
        walker = FixReadOnly(listonly)
        walker.run()
        print 'Visited %d files and %d dirs' % (walker.fcount, walker.dcount)
```

As we saw in Chapter 2, the built-in os.chmod call changes the permission settings on an external file (here, to 0777—global read, write, and execute permissions). Because os.chmod and the FileVisitor's operations are portable, this same script will work to set permissions in an entire tree on both Windows and Unix-like platforms. Notice that it asks whether you really want to proceed when it first starts up, just in case someone accidentally clicks the file's name in an explorer GUI. Also note that Python must be installed before this script can be run to make files writable; that seems a fair assumption to make of users about to change Python scripts.

```
C:\temp\examples>python PyTools\fixreadonly-all.py
This script makes all files writeable; continue?y
. ...
1 => .\autoexec.bat
2 => .\cleanall.csh
3 => .\echoEnvironment.pyw
```
...more deleted...
```
1352 => .\PyTools\visitor_find.pyc
1353 => .\PyTools\visitor_find_quiet1.py
1354 => .\PyTools\fixeoln_one.doc.txt
Visited 1354 files and 119 dirs
```

Copying Directory Trees

The next three sections conclude this chapter by exploring a handful of additional utilities for processing directories (a.k.a. "folders") on your computer with Python. They present directory *copy*, *deletion*, and *comparison* scripts that demonstrate system tools at work. All of these were born of necessity, are generally portable among all Python platforms, and illustrate Python development concepts along the way.

Some of these scripts do something too unique for the `visitor` module's classes we've been applying in early sections of this chapter, and so require more custom solutions (e.g., we can't remove directories we intend to walk through). Most have platform-specific equivalents too (e.g., drag-and-drop copies), but the Python utilities shown here are portable, easily customized, callable from other scripts, and surprisingly fast.

A Python Tree Copy Script

My CD writer sometimes does weird things. In fact, copies of files with odd names can be totally botched on the CD, even though other files show up in one piece. That's not necessarily a show-stopper—if just a few files are trashed in a big CD backup copy, I can always copy the offending files to floppies one at a time. Unfortunately, Windows drag-and-drop copies don't play nicely with such a CD: the copy operation stops and exits the moment the first bad file is encountered. You only get as many files as were copied up to the error, but no more.

There may be some magical Windows setting to work around this feature, but I gave up hunting for one as soon as I realized that it would be easier to code a copier in Python. The *cpall.py* script in Example 5-20 is one way to do it. With this script, I control what happens when bad files are found—skipping over them with Python exception handlers, for instance. Moreover, this tool works with the same interface and effect on other platforms. It seems to me, at least, that a few minutes spent writing a portable and reusable Python script to meet a need is a better investment than looking for solutions that work on only one platform (if at all).

Example 5-20. PP2E\System\Filetools\cpall.py

```
#######################################################
# Usage: "python cpall.py dir1 dir2".
# Recursive copy of a directory tree. Works like a
# unix "cp -r dirFrom/* dirTo" command, and assumes
# that dirFrom and dirTo are both directories.  Was
# written to get around fatal error messages under
# Windows drag-and-drop copies (the first bad file
# ends the entire copy operation immediately), but
# also allows you to customize copy operations.
# May need more on Unix--skip links, fifos, etc.
#######################################################

import os, sys
verbose = 0
dcount = fcount = 0
maxfileload = 100000
blksize = 1024 * 8

def cpfile(pathFrom, pathTo, maxfileload=maxfileload):
    """
    copy file pathFrom to pathTo, byte for byte
    """
    if os.path.getsize(pathFrom) <= maxfileload:
        bytesFrom = open(pathFrom, 'rb').read()       # read small file all at once
        open(pathTo, 'wb').write(bytesFrom)           # need b mode on Windows
    else:
        fileFrom = open(pathFrom, 'rb')               # read big files in chunks
        fileTo   = open(pathTo,   'wb')               # need b mode here too
        while 1:
            bytesFrom = fileFrom.read(blksize)        # get one block, less at end
            if not bytesFrom: break                   # empty after last chunk
            fileTo.write(bytesFrom)

def cpall(dirFrom, dirTo):
    """
    copy contents of dirFrom and below to dirTo
    """
    global dcount, fcount
    for file in os.listdir(dirFrom):                  # for files/dirs here
        pathFrom = os.path.join(dirFrom, file)
        pathTo   = os.path.join(dirTo,   file)        # extend both paths
        if not os.path.isdir(pathFrom):               # copy simple files
            try:
                if verbose > 1: print 'copying', pathFrom, 'to', pathTo
                cpfile(pathFrom, pathTo)
                fcount = fcount+1
            except:
                print 'Error copying', pathFrom, to, pathTo, '--skipped'
                print sys.exc_type, sys.exc_value
        else:
            if verbose: print 'copying dir', pathFrom, 'to', pathTo
            try:
```

Example 5-20. PP2E\System\Filetools\cpall.py (continued)

```
                os.mkdir(pathTo)                           # make new subdir
                cpall(pathFrom, pathTo)                     # recur into subdirs
                dcount = dcount+1
        except:
            print 'Error creating', pathTo, '--skipped'
            print sys.exc_type, sys.exc_value

def getargs():
    try:
        dirFrom, dirTo = sys.argv[1:]
    except:
        print 'Use: cpall.py dirFrom dirTo'
    else:
        if not os.path.isdir(dirFrom):
            print 'Error: dirFrom is not a directory'
        elif not os.path.exists(dirTo):
            os.mkdir(dirTo)
            print 'Note: dirTo was created'
            return (dirFrom, dirTo)
        else:
            print 'Warning: dirTo already exists'
            if dirFrom == dirTo or (hasattr(os.path, 'samefile') and
                                os.path.samefile(dirFrom, dirTo)):
                print 'Error: dirFrom same as dirTo'
            else:
                return (dirFrom, dirTo)

if __name__ == '__main__':
    import time
    dirstuple = getargs()
    if dirstuple:
        print 'Copying...'
        start = time.time()
        apply(cpall, dirstuple)
        print 'Copied', fcount, 'files,', dcount, 'directories',
        print 'in', time.time() - start, 'seconds'
```

This script implements its own recursive tree traversal logic, and keeps track of both the "from" and "to" directory paths as it goes. At every level, it copies over simple files, creates directories in the "to" path, and recurs into subdirectories with "from" and "to" paths extended by one level. There are other ways to code this task (e.g., other cpall variants on the book's CD change the working directory along the way with os.chdir calls), but extending paths on descent works well in practice.

Notice this script's reusable cpfile function—just in case there are multigigabyte files in the tree to be copied, it uses a file's size to decide whether it should be read all at once or in chunks (remember, the file read method without arguments really loads the while file into an in-memory string). Also note that this script creates the "to" directory if needed, but assumes it is empty when a copy starts up; be sure to remove the target directory before copying a new tree to its name (more on this in the next section).

Here is a big book examples tree copy in action on Windows; pass in the name of the "from" and "to" directories to kick off the process, and run a *rm* shell command (or similar platform-specific tool) to delete the target directory first:

```
C:\temp>rm -rf cpexamples

C:\temp>python %X%\system\filetools\cpall.py examples cpexamples
Note: dirTo was created
Copying...
Copied 1356 files, 118 directories in 2.41999995708 seconds

C:\temp>fc /B examples\System\Filetools\cpall.py
          cpexamples\System\Filetools\cpall.py
Comparing files examples\System\Filetools\cpall.py and
cpexamples\System\Filetools\cpall.py
FC: no differences encountered
```

This run copied a tree of 1356 files and 118 directories in 2.4 seconds on my 650 MHz Windows 98 laptop (the built-in `time.time` call can be used to query the system time in seconds). It runs a bit slower if programs like MS Word are open on the machine, and may run arbitrarily faster or slower for you. Still, this is at least as fast as the best drag-and-drop I've timed on Windows.

So how does this script work around bad files on a CD backup? The secret is that it catches and ignores file *exceptions*, and keeps walking. To copy all the files that are good on a CD, I simply run a command line like this:

```
C:\temp>python %X%\system\filetools\cpall_visitor.py
                    g:\PP2ndEd\examples\PP2E cpexamples
```

Because the CD is addressed as "G:" on my Windows machine, this is the command-line equivalent of drag-and-drop copying from an item in the CD's top-level folder, except that the Python script will recover from errors on the CD and get the rest. In general, `cpall` can be passed any absolute directory path on your machine—even ones that mean devices like CDs. To make this go on Linux, try a root directory like */dev/cdrom* to address your CD drive.

Recoding Copies with a Visitor-Based Class

When I first wrote the `cpall` script just discussed, I couldn't see a way that the `visitor` class hierarchy we met earlier would help—*two* directories needed to be traversed in parallel (the original and the copy), and `visitor` is based on climbing one tree with `os.path.walk`. There seemed no easy way to keep track of where the script is at in the copy directory.

The trick I eventually stumbled onto is to not keep track at all. Instead, the script in Example 5-21 simply replaces the "from" directory path string with the "to" directory path string, at the front of all directory and pathnames passed-in from `os.path.walk`. The results of the string replacements are the paths that the original files and directories are to be copied to.

Example 5-21. PP2E\System\Filetools\cpall_visitor.py

```
###########################################################
# Use: "python cpall_visitor.py fromDir toDir"
# cpall, but with the visitor classes and os.path.walk;
# the trick is to do string replacement of fromDir with
# toDir at the front of all the names walk passes in;
# assumes that the toDir does not exist initially;
###########################################################

import os
from PP2E.PyTools.visitor import FileVisitor
from cpall import cpfile, getargs
verbose = 1

class CpallVisitor(FileVisitor):
    def __init__(self, fromDir, toDir):
        self.fromDirLen = len(fromDir) + 1
        self.toDir      = toDir
        FileVisitor.__init__(self)
    def visitdir(self, dirpath):
        toPath = os.path.join(self.toDir, dirpath[self.fromDirLen:])
        if verbose: print 'd', dirpath, '=>', toPath
        os.mkdir(toPath)
        self.dcount = self.dcount + 1
    def visitfile(self, filepath):
        toPath = os.path.join(self.toDir, filepath[self.fromDirLen:])
        if verbose: print 'f', filepath, '=>', toPath
        cpfile(filepath, toPath)
        self.fcount = self.fcount + 1

if __name__ == '__main__':
    import sys, time
    fromDir, toDir = sys.argv[1:3]
    if len(sys.argv) > 3: verbose = 0
    print 'Copying...'
    start = time.time()
    walker = CpallVisitor(fromDir, toDir)
    walker.run(startDir=fromDir)
    print 'Copied', walker.fcount, 'files,', walker.dcount, 'directories',
    print 'in', time.time() - start, 'seconds'
```

This version accomplishes roughly the same goal as the original, but has made a few assumptions to keep code simple—the "to" directory is assumed to not exist initially, and exceptions are not ignored along the way. Here it is copying the book examples tree again on Windows:

```
C:\temp>rm -rf cpexamples

C:\temp>python %X%\system\filetools\cpall_visitor.py
                                examples cpexamples -quiet
Copying...
Copied 1356 files, 119 directories in 2.09000003338 seconds

C:\temp>fc /B examples\System\Filetools\cpall.py
           cpexamples\System\Filetools\cpall.py
Comparing files examples\System\Filetools\cpall.py and
cpexamples\System\Filetools\cpall.py
FC: no differences encountered
```

Despite the extra string slicing going on, this version runs just as fast as the original. For tracing purposes, this version also prints all the "from" and "to" copy paths during the traversal, unless you pass in a third argument on the command line, or set the script's **verbose** variable to 0:

```
C:\temp>python %X%\system\filetools\cpall_visitor.py examples cpexamples
Copying...
d examples => cpexamples\
f examples\autoexec.bat => cpexamples\autoexec.bat
f examples\cleanall.csh => cpexamples\cleanall.csh
...more deleted...
d examples\System => cpexamples\System
f examples\System\System.txt => cpexamples\System\System.txt
f examples\System\more.py => cpexamples\System\more.py
f examples\System\reader.py => cpexamples\System\reader.py
...more deleted...
Copied 1356 files, 119 directories in 2.31000006199 seconds
```

Deleting Directory Trees

Both of the copy scripts in the last section work as planned, but they aren't very forgiving of existing directory trees. That is, they implicitly assume that the "to" target directory is either empty or doesn't exist at all, and fail badly if that isn't the case. Presumably, you will first somehow delete the target directory on your machine. For my purposes, that was a reasonable assumption to make.

The copiers could be changed to work with existing "to" directories too (e.g., ignore os.mkdir exceptions), but I prefer to start from scratch when copying trees; you never know what old garbage might be laying around in the "to" directory. So when testing the copies above, I was careful to run a rm -rf cpexamples command line to recursively delete the entire *cpexamples* directory tree before copying another tree to that name.

Unfortunately, the *rm* command used to clear the target directory is really a Unix utility that I installed on my PC from a commercial package; it probably won't work on your computer. There are other platform-specific ways to delete directory trees (e.g., deleting a folder's icon in a Windows explorer GUI), but why not do it once in Python for every platform? Example 5-22 deletes every file and directory at and below a passed-in directory's name. Because its logic is packaged as a function, it is also an *importable* utility that can be run from other scripts. Because it is pure Python code, it is a *cross-platform* solution for tree removal.

Example 5-22. PP2E\System\Filetools\rmall.py

```
#!/usr/bin/python
##############################################################
# Use: "python rmall.py directoryPath directoryPath..."
# recursive directory tree deletion: removes all files and
# directories at and below directoryPaths; recurs into subdirs
# and removes parent dir last, because os.rmdir requires that
# directory is empty; like a Unix "rm -rf directoryPath"
##############################################################

import sys, os
fcount = dcount = 0

def rmall(dirPath):                              # delete dirPath and below
    global fcount, dcount
    namesHere = os.listdir(dirPath)
    for name in namesHere:                       # remove all contents first
        path = os.path.join(dirPath, name)
        if not os.path.isdir(path):              # remove simple files
            os.remove(path)
            fcount = fcount + 1
        else:                                    # recur to remove subdirs
            rmall(path)
    os.rmdir(dirPath)                            # remove now-empty dirPath
    dcount = dcount + 1

if __name__ == '__main__':
    import time
    start = time.time()
    for dname in sys.argv[1:]: rmall(dname)
    tottime = time.time() - start
    print 'Removed %d files and %d dirs in %s secs' % (fcount, dcount, tottime)
```

The great thing about coding this sort of tool in Python is that it can be run with the same command-line interface on any machine where Python is installed. If you don't have a `rm -rf` type command available on your Windows, Unix, or Macintosh computer, simply run the Python `rmall` script instead:

```
C:\temp>python %X%\System\Filetools\cpall.py examples cpexamples
Note: dirTo was created
Copying...
Copied 1379 files, 121 directories in 2.68999993801 seconds
```

```
C:\temp>python %X%\System\Filetools\rmall.py cpexamples
Removed 1379 files and 122 dirs in 0.549999952316 secs

C:\temp>ls cpexamples
ls: File or directory "cpexamples" is not found
```

Here, the script traverses and deletes a tree of 1379 files and 122 directories in about half a second—substantially impressive for a noncompiled programming language, and roughly equivalent to the commercial **rm −rf** program I purchased and installed on my PC.

One subtlety here: this script must be careful to delete the contents of a directory *before* deleting the directory itself—the os.rmdir call mandates that directories must be empty when deleted (and throws an exception if they are not). Because of that, the recursive calls on subdirectories need to happen before the os.mkdir call. Computer scientists would recognize this as a *postorder*, depth-first tree traversal, since we process parent directories after their children. This also makes any traversals based on os.path.walk out of the question: we need to *return* to a parent directory to delete it after visiting its descendents.

To illustrate, let's run interactive os.remove and os.rmdir calls on a *cpexample* directory containing files or nested directories:

```
>>> os.path.isdir('cpexamples')
1
>>> os.remove('cpexamples')
Traceback (innermost last):
  File "<stdin>", line 1, in ?
OSError: [Errno 2] No such file or directory: 'cpexamples'
>>> os.rmdir('cpexamples')
Traceback (innermost last):
  File "<stdin>", line 1, in ?
OSError: [Errno 13] Permission denied: 'cpexamples'
```

Both calls always fail if the directory is not empty. But now, delete the contents of *cpexamples* in another window and try again:

```
>>> os.path.isdir('cpexamples')
1
>>> os.remove('cpexamples')
Traceback (innermost last):
  File "<stdin>", line 1, in ?
OSError: [Errno 2] No such file or directory: 'cpexamples'
>>> os.rmdir('cpexamples')
>>> os.path.exists('cpexamples')
0
```

The os.remove still fails—it's only meant for deleting nondirectory items—but os.rmdir now works because the directory is empty. The upshot of this is that a tree deletion traversal must generally remove directories "on the way out."

Recoding Deletions for Generality

As coded, the `rmall` script only processes directory names and fails if given names of simple files, but it's trivial to generalize the script to eliminate that restriction. The recoding in Example 5-23 accepts an arbitrary command-line list of file and directory names, deletes simple files, and recursively deletes directories.

Example 5-23. PP2E\System\Filetools\rmall2.py

```
#!/usr/bin/python
##############################################################
# Use: "python rmall2.py fileOrDirPath fileOrDirPath..."
# like rmall.py, alternative coding, files okay on cmd line
##############################################################

import sys, os
fcount = dcount = 0

def rmone(pathName):
    global fcount, dcount
    if not os.path.isdir(pathName):              # remove simple files
        os.remove(pathName)
        fcount = fcount + 1
    else:                                        # recur to remove contents
        for name in os.listdir(pathName):
            rmone(os.path.join(pathName, name))
        os.rmdir(pathName)                       # remove now-empty dirPath
        dcount = dcount + 1

if __name__ == '__main__':
    import time
    start = time.time()
    for name in sys.argv[1:]: rmone(name)
    tottime = time.time() - start
    print 'Removed %d files and %d dirs in %s secs' % (fcount, dcount, tottime)
```

This shorter version runs the same, and just as fast, as the original:

```
C:\temp>python %X%\System\Filetools\cpall.py examples cpexamples
Note: dirTo was created
Copying...
Copied 1379 files, 121 directories in 2.52999997139 seconds

C:\temp>python %X%\System\Filetools\rmall2.py cpexamples
Removed 1379 files and 122 dirs in 0.550000071526 secs

C:\temp>ls cpexamples
ls: File or directory "cpexamples" is not found
```

but can also be used to delete simple files:

```
C:\temp>python %X%\System\Filetools\rmall2.py spam.txt eggs.txt
Removed 2 files and 0 dirs in 0.0600000619888 secs
```

```
C:\temp>python %X%\System\Filetools\rmall2.py spam.txt eggs.txt cpexamples
Removed 1381 files and 122 dirs in 0.630000042915 secs
```

As usual, there is more than one way to do it in Python (though you'll have to try harder to find many spurious ways). Notice that these scripts trap no exceptions; in programs designed to blindly delete an entire directory tree, exceptions are all likely to denote truly bad things. We could get more fancy, and support filename patterns by using the built-in fnmatch module along the way too, but this was beyond the scope of these script's goals (for pointers on matching, see Example 5-17, and also *find.py* in Chapter 2).

Comparing Directory Trees

Engineers can be a paranoid sort (but you didn't hear that from me). At least I am. It comes from decades of seeing things go terribly wrong, I suppose. When I create a CD backup of my hard drive, for instance, there's still something a bit too magical about the process to trust the CD writer program to do the right thing. Maybe I should, but it's tough to have a lot of faith in tools that occasionally trash files, and seem to crash my Windows 98 machine every third Tuesday of the month. When push comes to shove, it's nice to be able to verify that data copied to a backup CD is the same as the original—or at least spot deviations from the original—as soon as possible. If a backup is ever needed, it will be *really* needed.

Because data CDs are accessible as simple directory trees, we are once again in the realm of tree walkers—to verify a backup CD, we simply need to walk its top-level directory. We've already written a generic walker class (the visitor module), but it won't help us here directly: we need to walk *two* directories in parallel and inspect common files along the way. Moreover, walking either one of the two directories won't allow us to spot files and directories that only exist in the other. Something more custom seems in order here.

Finding Directory Differences

Before we start coding, the first thing we need to clarify is what it means to compare two directory trees. If both trees have exactly the same branch structure and depth, this problem reduces to comparing corresponding files in each tree. In general, though, the trees can have arbitrarily different shapes, depth, and so on.

More generally, the contents of a directory in one tree may have more or fewer entries than the corresponding directory in the other tree. If those differing contents are filenames, there is no corresponding file to compare; if they are directory names, there is no corresponding branch to descend through. In fact, the only way to detect files and directories that appear in one tree but not the other is to detect differences in each level's directory.

In other words, a tree comparison algorithm will also have to perform *directory* comparisons along the way. Because this is a nested, and simpler operation, let's start by coding a single-directory comparison of filenames in Example 5-24.

Example 5-24. PP2E\System\Filetools\dirdiff.py

```python
#!/bin/env python
#########################################################
# use: python dirdiff.py dir1-path dir2-path
# compare two directories to find files that exist
# in one but not the other;  this version uses the
# os.listdir function and list difference;  note
# that this script only checks filename, not file
# contents--see diffall.py for an extension that
# does the latter by comparing .read() results;
#########################################################

import os, sys

def reportdiffs(unique1, unique2, dir1, dir2):
    if not (unique1 or unique2):
        print 'Directory lists are identical'
    else:
        if unique1:
            print 'Files unique to', dir1
            for file in unique1:
                print '...', file
        if unique2:
            print 'Files unique to', dir2
            for file in unique2:
                print '...', file

def unique(seq1, seq2):
    uniques = []                        # return items in seq1 only
    for item in seq1:
        if item not in seq2:
            uniques.append(item)
    return uniques

def comparedirs(dir1, dir2):
    print 'Comparing', dir1, 'to', dir2
    files1  = os.listdir(dir1)
    files2  = os.listdir(dir2)
    unique1 = unique(files1, files2)
    unique2 = unique(files2, files1)
    reportdiffs(unique1, unique2, dir1, dir2)
    return not (unique1 or unique2)          # true if no diffs

def getargs():
    try:
        dir1, dir2 = sys.argv[1:]            # 2 command-line args
    except:
        print 'Usage: dirdiff.py dir1 dir2'
        sys.exit(1)
```

Example 5-24. PP2E\System\Filetools\dirdiff.py (continued)

```
    else:
        return (dir1, dir2)

if __name__ == '__main__':
    dir1, dir2 = getargs()
    comparedirs(dir1, dir2)
```

Given listings of names in two directories, this script simply picks out unique names in the first, unique names in the second, and reports any unique names found as differences (that is, files in one directory but not the other). Its comparedirs function returns a true result if no differences were found—useful for detecting differences in callers.

Let's run this script on a few directories; differences are detected and reported as names unique in either passed-in directory pathname. Notice that this is only a *structural* comparison that just checks names in listings, not file contents (we'll add the latter in a moment):

```
C:\temp>python %X%\system\filetools\dirdiff.py examples cpexamples
Comparing examples to cpexamples
Directory lists are identical

C:\temp>python %X%\system\filetools\dirdiff.py
                                examples\PyTools cpexamples\PyTools
Comparing examples\PyTools to cpexamples\PyTools
Files unique to examples\PyTools
... visitor.py

C:\temp>python %X%\system\filetools\dirdiff.py
                                examples\System\Filetools
                                cpexamples\System\Filetools
Comparing examples\System\Filetools to cpexamples\System\Filetools
Files unique to examples\System\Filetools
... dirdiff2.py
Files unique to cpexamples\System\Filetools
... cpall.py
```

The unique function is the heart of this script: it performs a simple list difference operation. Here's how it works apart from the rest of this script's code:

```
>>> L1 = [1, 3, 5, 7, 9]
>>> L2 = [2, 3, 6, 8, 9]
>>> from dirdiff import unique
>>> unique(L1, L2)              # items in L1 but not in L2
[1, 5, 7]
>>> unique(L2, L1)              # items in L2 but not in L1
[2, 6, 8]
```

These two lists have objects 3 and 9 in common; the rest appear only in one of the two. When applied to directories, *unique* items represent tree differences, and *common* items are names of files or subdirectories that merit further comparisons or traversal. There are other ways to check this code; see the `dirdiff` variants in the book's CD for a few.

Finding Tree Differences

Now all we need is a tree walker that applies `dirdiff` at each level to pick out unique files and directories, explicitly compares the contents of files in common, and descends through directories in common. Example 5-25 fits the bill.

Example 5-25. PP2E\System\Filetools\diffall.py

```
#########################################################
# Usage: "python diffall.py dir1 dir2".
# recursive tree comparison--report files that exist
# in only dir1 or dir2, report files of same name in
# dir1 and dir2 with differing contents, and do the
# same for all subdirectories of the same names in
# and below dir1 and dir2; summary of diffs appears
# at end of output (but search redirected output for
# "DIFF" and "unique" strings for further details);
#########################################################

import os, dirdiff

def intersect(seq1, seq2):
    commons = []                    # items in seq1 and seq2
    for item in seq1:
        if item in seq2:
            commons.append(item)
    return commons

def comparedirs(dir1, dir2, diffs, verbose=0):
    # compare filename lists
    print '-'*20
    if not dirdiff.comparedirs(dir1, dir2):
        diffs.append('unique files at %s - %s' % (dir1, dir2))

    print 'Comparing contents'
    files1 = os.listdir(dir1)
    files2 = os.listdir(dir2)
    common = intersect(files1, files2)

    # compare contents of files in common
    for file in common:
        path1 = os.path.join(dir1, file)
        path2 = os.path.join(dir2, file)
        if os.path.isfile(path1) and os.path.isfile(path2):
            bytes1 = open(path1, 'rb').read()
            bytes2 = open(path2, 'rb').read()
```

Example 5-25. PP2E\System\Filetools\diffall.py (continued)

```
            if bytes1 == bytes2:
                if verbose: print file, 'matches'
            else:
                diffs.append('files differ at %s - %s' % (path1, path2))
                print file, 'DIFFERS'

    # recur to compare directories in common
    for file in common:
        path1 = os.path.join(dir1, file)
        path2 = os.path.join(dir2, file)
        if os.path.isdir(path1) and os.path.isdir(path2):
            comparedirs(path1, path2, diffs, verbose)

if __name__ == '__main__':
    dir1, dir2 = dirdiff.getargs()
    mydiffs = []
    comparedirs(dir1, dir2, mydiffs)          # changes mydiffs in-place
    print '='*40                              # walk, report diffs list
    if not mydiffs:
        print 'No diffs found.'
    else:
        print 'Diffs found:', len(mydiffs)
        for diff in mydiffs: print '-', diff
```

At each directory in the tree, this script simply runs the `dirdiff` tool to detect unique names, and then compares names in common by intersecting directory lists. Since we've already studied the tree-walking tools this script employs, let's jump right into a few example runs. When run on identical trees, status messages scroll during the traversal, and a "No diffs found" message appears at the end:

```
C:\temp>python %X%\system\filetools\diffall.py examples cpexamples
--------------------
Comparing examples to cpexamples
Directory lists are identical
Comparing contents
--------------------
Comparing examples\old_Part2 to cpexamples\old_Part2
Directory lists are identical
Comparing contents
--------------------
...more lines deleted...
--------------------
Comparing examples\EmbExt\Regist to cpexamples\EmbExt\Regist
Directory lists are identical
Comparing contents
--------------------
Comparing examples\PyTools to cpexamples\PyTools
Directory lists are identical
Comparing contents
========================================
No diffs found.
```

To show how differences are reported, we need to generate a few. Let's run the global search-and-replace script we met earlier, to change a few files scattered about one of the trees (see—I told you global replacement could trash your files!):

```
C:\temp\examples>python %X%\PyTools\visitor_replace.py -exec SPAM
Are you sure?y
...
1355 => .\PyTools\visitor_find_quiet1.py
1356 => .\PyTools\fixeoln_one.doc.txt
Visited 1356 files
Changed 8 files:
.\package.csh
.\README-PP2E.txt
.\readme-old-pp1E.txt
.\temp
.\remp
.\Internet\Cgi-Web\fixcgi.py
.\System\Processes\output.txt
.\PyTools\cleanpyc.py
```

While we're at it, let's remove a few common files so directory uniqueness differences show up on the scope too; the following three removal commands will make two directories differ (the last two commands impact the same directory in different trees):

```
C:\temp>rm cpexamples\PyTools\visitor.py
C:\temp>rm cpexamples\System\Filetools\dirdiff2.py
C:\temp>rm examples\System\Filetools\cpall.py
```

Now, rerun the comparison walker to pick out differences, and pipe its output report to a file for easy inspection. The following lists just the parts of the output report that identify differences. In typical use, I inspect the summary at the bottom of the report first, and then search for strings "DIFF" and "unique" in the report's text if I need more information about the differences summarized:

```
C:\temp>python %X%\system\filetools\diffall.py examples cpexamples > diffs
C:\temp>type diffs
--------------------
Comparing examples to cpexamples
Directory lists are identical
Comparing contents
package.csh DIFFERS
README-PP2E.txt DIFFERS
readme-old-pp1E.txt DIFFERS
temp DIFFERS
remp DIFFERS
--------------------
Comparing examples\old_Part2 to cpexamples\old_Part2
Directory lists are identical
Comparing contents
--------------------
...
--------------------
```

```
Comparing examples\Internet\Cgi-Web to cpexamples\Internet\Cgi-Web
Directory lists are identical
Comparing contents
fixcgi.py DIFFERS
--------------------
...
--------------------
Comparing examples\System\Filetools to cpexamples\System\Filetools
Files unique to examples\System\Filetools
... dirdiff2.py
Files unique to cpexamples\System\Filetools
... cpall.py
Comparing contents
--------------------
...
--------------------
Comparing examples\System\Processes to cpexamples\System\Processes
Directory lists are identical
Comparing contents
output.txt DIFFERS
--------------------
...
--------------------
Comparing examples\PyTools to cpexamples\PyTools
Files unique to examples\PyTools
... visitor.py
Comparing contents
cleanpyc.py DIFFERS
==========================================
Diffs found: 10
- files differ at examples\package.csh - cpexamples\package.csh
- files differ at examples\README-PP2E.txt - cpexamples\README-PP2E.txt
- files differ at examples\readme-old-pp1E.txt - cpexamples\readme-old-pp1E.txt
- files differ at examples\temp - cpexamples\temp
- files differ at examples\remp - cpexamples\remp
- files differ at examples\Internet\Cgi-Web\fixcgi.py -
        cpexamples\Internet\Cgi-Web\fixcgi.py
- unique files at examples\System\Filetools -
        cpexamples\System\Filetools
- files differ at examples\System\Processes\output.txt -
        cpexamples\System\Processes\output.txt
- unique files at examples\PyTools - cpexamples\PyTools
- files differ at examples\PyTools\cleanpyc.py - cpexamples\PyTools\cleanpyc.py
```

I added line breaks and tabs in a few of these output lines to make them fit on this page, but the report is simple to understand. Ten differences were found—the eight files we changed (trashed) with the replacement script, and the two directories we threw out of sync with the three *rm* remove commands.

Verifying CD backups

So how does this script placate CD backup paranoia? To double-check my CD writer's work, I run a command like the following. I can also use a command like this to find out what has been changed since the last backup. Again, since the CD is "G:" on my machine when plugged in, I provide a path rooted there; use a root such as */dev/cdrom* on Linux:

```
C:\temp>python %X%\system\filetools\diffall.py
               examples g:\PP2ndEd\examples\PP2E > exdiffs091500

C:\temp>more exdiffs091500
--------------------
Comparing examples to g:\PP2ndEd\examples\PP2E
Files unique to examples
... .cshrc
Comparing contents
tounix.py DIFFERS
--------------------
Comparing examples\old_Part2 to g:\PP2ndEd\examples\PP2E\old_Part2
Directory lists are identical
Comparing contents
--------------------
...more
visitor_fixeoln.py DIFFERS
visitor_fixnames.py DIFFERS
=====================================
Diffs found: 41
- unique files at examples - g:\PP2ndEd\examples\PP2E
- files differ at examples\tounix.py - g:\PP2ndEd\examples\PP2E\tounix.py
...more
```

The CD spins, the script compares, and a summary of 41 differences appears at the end of the report (in this case, representing changes to the examples tree since the latest backup CD was burned). For an example of a full difference report, see file *exdiffs091500* on the book's CD. More typically, this is what turns up for most of my example backups—files with a leading "." are not copied to the CD:

```
C:\temp>python %X%\System\Filetools\diffall.py
               examples g:\PP2ndEd\examples\PP2E
...
--------------------
Comparing examples\Config to g:\PP2ndEd\examples\PP2E\Config
Files unique to examples\Config
... .cshrc
Comparing contents
=====================================
Diffs found: 1
- unique files at examples\Config - g:\PP2ndEd\examples\PP2E\Config
```

And to *really* be sure, I run the following global comparison command against the true book directory, to verify the entire book tree backup on CD:

```
C:\>python %X%\System\Filetools\diffall.py PP2ndEd G:\PP2ndEd
--------------------
Comparing PP2ndEd to G:\PP2ndEd
```

```
Files unique to G:\PP2ndEd
... examples.tar.gz
Comparing contents
README.txt DIFFERS
--------------------
```
...more
```
--------------------
Comparing PP2ndEd\examples\PP2E\Config to G:\PP2ndEd\examples\PP2E\Config
Files unique to PP2ndEd\examples\PP2E\Config
... .cshrc
Comparing contents
--------------------
```
...more
```
--------------------
Comparing PP2ndEd\chapters to G:\PP2ndEd\chapters
Directory lists are identical
Comparing contents
ch01-intro.doc DIFFERS
ch04-os3.doc DIFFERS
ch05-gui1.doc DIFFERS
ch06-gui2.doc DIFFERS
--------------------
```
...more
```
========================================
Diffs found: 11
- unique files at PP2ndEd - G:\PP2ndEd
- files differ at PP2ndEd\README.txt - G:\PP2ndEd\README.txt
```
...more

This particular run indicates that I've changed a "readme" file, four chapter files, and a bunch more since the last backup; if run immediately after making a backup, only the *.cshrc* unique file shows up on `diffall` radar. This global comparison can take a few minutes—it performs byte-for-byte comparisons of all chapter files and screen shots, the examples tree, an image of the book's CD, and more, but it's an accurate and complete verification. Given that this book tree contained roughly 119M of data in 7300 files and 570 directories the last time I checked, a more manual verification procedure without Python's help would be utterly impossible.

Finally, it's worth noting that this script still only *detects* differences in the tree, but does not give any further details about individual file differences. In fact, it simply loads and compares the binary contents of corresponding files with a single string comparison—it's a simple yes/no result.[*] If and when I need more details about

---

[*] We might try to do a bit better here, by opening text files in text mode to ignore line-terminator differences, but it's not clear that such differences should be blindly ignored (what if the caller wants to know if line-end markers have been changed?). We could also be smarter by avoiding the load and compare steps for files that differ in size, and read files in small chunks, instead of all at once, to minimize memory requirements for huge files (see earlier examples such as the `cpall` script for hints). For my comparisons, such optimizations are unnecessary.

how two reported files actually differ, I either edit the files, or run the file-comparison command on the host platform (e.g., *fc* on Windows/DOS, *diff* or *cmp* on Unix and Linux). That's not a portable solution for this last step; but for my purposes, just finding the differences in a 1300-file tree was much more critical than reporting which lines differ in files flagged in the report.

Of course, since we can always run shell commands in Python, this last step could be automated by spawning a *diff* or *fc* command with `os.popen` as differences are encountered (or after the traversal, by scanning the report summary). Because Python excels at processing files and strings, though, it's possible to go one step further and code a Python equivalent of the *fc* and *diff* commands. Since this is beyond both this script's scope and this chapter's size limits, that will have to await the attention of a curious reader.

II

GUI Programming

This part of the book shows you how to apply Python to build portable graphical user interfaces, primarily with Python's standard Tkinter library. The following chapters cover this topic in depth:

- Chapter 6, *Graphical User Interfaces*. This chapter outlines GUI options available to Python developers, and then presents a tutorial that illustrates core Tkinter coding concepts in the context of simple user interfaces.

- Chapter 7, *A Tkinter Tour, Part 1*. This chapter begins a tour of the Tkinter library—its widget set and related tools. This first tour chapter covers simpler library tools and widgets: pop-up windows, various types of buttons, and so on.

- Chapter 8, *A Tkinter Tour, Part 2*. This chapter continues the library tour begun in the prior chapter. It presents the rest of the Tkinter widget library—menus, images, text, canvases, grids, and time-based events and animation.

- Chapter 9, *Larger GUI Examples*. This chapter pulls the earlier chapters' ideas together to implement a collection of user interfaces. It begins with a look at GUI automation techniques, and concludes by presenting larger GUIs—clocks, text editors, drawing programs, image viewers, and more.

As in the first part of this book, the material presented here is applicable to a wide variety of domains and will be utilized again to build domain-specific user interfaces in later chapters of this book.

II

GUI Programming

6

Graphical User Interfaces

"Here's Looking at You, Kid"

For most software systems, a graphical user interface (GUI) has become an expected part of the package. Even if the GUI acronym is new to you, chances are that you are already familiar with such interfaces—the windows, buttons, and menus that we use to interact with software programs. In fact, most of what we do on computers today is done with some sort of point-and-click graphical interface. From web browsers to system tools, programs are routinely dressed-up with a GUI component to make them more flexible and easy to use.

In this part of the book, we will learn how to make Python scripts sprout such graphical interfaces too, by studying examples of programming with the Tkinter module—a portable GUI library that is a standard part of the Python system. As we'll see, it's easy to program user interfaces in Python scripts, thanks both to the simplicity of the language and the power of its GUI libraries. As an added bonus, GUIs programmed in Python with Tkinter are automatically portable to all major computer systems.

GUI Programming Topics

Because GUIs are a major area, I want to say a few more words about this part of the book. To make them easier to absorb, GUI programming topics are split over the next four chapters of this book:

- This chapter begins with a quick Tkinter tutorial to teach coding basics. Interfaces are kept simple here on purpose, so you can master the fundamentals before moving on to the following chapter's interfaces. On the other hand, this chapter covers all the basics: event processing, the `pack` geometry manager, using inheritance and composition in GUIs, and more. As we'll see, OOP (object-oriented programming) isn't required for Tkinter, but it makes GUIs structured and reusable.

- Chapters 7 and 8 take you on a tour of the Tkinter widget set.* Roughly, Chapter 7, *A Tkinter Tour, Part 1*, presents simple widgets, and Chapter 8, *A Tkinter Tour, Part 2*, covers more advanced widgets and related tools. Most of the interfaces devices you're accustomed to seeing show up here: sliders, menus, dialogs, images, and their kin. These two chapters are not a fully complete Tkinter reference (which could easily fill a large book by itself), but should be enough to help you get started coding substantial Python GUIs. The examples in these chapters are focused on widgets and Tkinter tools, but Python's support for code reuse is also explored along the way.

- Chapter 9, *Larger GUI Examples,* presents more complex examples that use coding and widget techniques presented in the three preceding chapters. It begins with an exploration of techniques for automating common GUI tasks with Python. Although Tkinter is a full-featured library, a small amount of reusable Python code can make its interfaces even more powerful and easy to use. This chapter wraps up by presenting a handful of complete GUI programs that implement text editors, image viewers, clocks, and more.

Because GUIs are really cross-domain tools, other GUI examples will also show up throughout the remainder of this book. For example, we'll later see email GUIs, calculators, tree viewers, table browsers, and so on. See the fourth GUI chapter for a list of forward pointers to other Tkinter examples in this text.

One point I'd like to make right away: most GUIs are dynamic and interactive interfaces, and the best I can do here is show static screen shots representing selected states in the interactions such programs implement. This really won't do justice to most examples. If you are not working along with the examples already, I encourage you to run the GUI examples in this and later chapters on your own.

On Windows, the standard Python install comes with Tkinter support built-in, so all these examples should work immediately. For other systems, Pythons with Tkinter support are readily available as well (see Appendix B, *Pragmatics*, and the top-level *README-PP2E.txt* file for more details). It's worth whatever extra install details you may need to absorb, though; experimenting with these programs is a great way to learn about both GUI programming, and Python itself.

---

* The term "widget set" refers to the objects used to build familiar point-and-click user interface devices— push-buttons, sliders, input fields, and so on. Tkinter comes with Python classes that correspond to all the widgets you're accustomed to seeing in graphical displays. Besides widgets, Tkinter also comes with tools for other activities, such as scheduling events to occur, waiting for socket data to arrive, and so on.

Has Anyone Noticed That "GUI" Are
the First Three Letters of "GUIDO"?

Python's creator didn't originally set out to build a GUI development tool, but Python's ease of use and rapid turnaround have made this one of its primary roles. From an implementation perspective, GUIs in Python are really just instances of C extensions, and extendability was one of the main ideas behind Python. When a script builds push-buttons and menus, it ultimately talks to a C library; and when a script responds to a user event, a C library ultimately talks back to Python.

But from a practical point of view, GUIs are a critical part of modern systems, and an ideal domain for a tool like Python. As we'll see, Python's simple syntax and object-oriented flavor blend well with the GUI model—it's natural to represent each device drawn on a screen as a Python class. Moreover, Python's quick turnaround lets programmers experiment with alternative layouts and behavior rapidly, in ways not possible with traditional development techniques. In fact, you can usually make a change to a Python-based GUI, and observe its effects in a matter of seconds. Don't try this with C or C++.

Python GUI Development Options

Before we start wading into the Tkinter pond, let's begin with some perspective on Python GUI options in general. Because Python has proven to be such a good match for GUI work, this domain has seen much activity in recent years. In fact, although Tkinter is the most widely used GUI toolkit in Python, there is a variety of ways to program user interfaces in Python today. Some are specific to Windows or X Windows,* some are cross-platform solutions, and all have followings and strong points all their own. To be fair to all the alternatives, here is a brief inventory of GUI toolkits available to Python programmers as I write these words:

Tkinter (shipped with Python)
  An open-source, portable GUI library, used as the de facto standard for GUI development in Python. Tkinter makes it easy to build simple GUIs quickly, and can be straightforwardly augmented with larger component frameworks in Python. Python scripts that use Tkinter to build GUIs run portably on Windows, X Windows (Unix), and Macintosh, and display a native look-and-feel

---

* In this book, "Windows" refers to the Microsoft Windows interface common on PCs, and "X Windows" refers to the X11 interface most commonly found on Unix and Linux platforms. These two interfaces are generally tied to the Microsoft and Unix platforms, respectively. It's possible to run X Windows on top of a Microsoft operating system and Windows emulators on Unix and Linux, but not common.

on each of these. The underlying Tk library used by Tkinter is a standard in the open source world at large, and is also used by the Perl and Tcl scripting languages.

wxPython (http://wxpython.org)

An open-source Python interface for wxWindows—a portable GUI class framework originally written to be used from the C++ programming language. The wxPython system is an extension module that wraps wxWindows classes. This library is generally considered to excel at building sophisticated interfaces, and is probably the second most popular Python GUI toolkit today, behind Tkinter. At this writing, wxPython code is portable to Windows and Unix-like platforms, but not the Macintosh. The underlying wxWindows library best supports Windows and GTK (on Unix), but it is generally portable to Windows, Unix-like platforms, and the Macintosh.

JPython (http://www.jpython.org)

As we will see in Chapter 15, *Advanced Internet Topics*, JPython (a.k.a. "Jython") is a Python port for Java, which gives Python scripts seamless access to Java class libraries on the local machine. Because of that, Java GUI libraries such as `swing` and `awt` become another way to construct GUIs in Python code run by the JPython system. Such solutions are obviously Java-specific, and limited in portability to the portability of Java and its libraries. A new package named `jTkinter` also provides a Tkinter port to JPython using Java's JNI; if installed, Python scripts may also use Tkinter to build GUIs under JPython.

KDE and Qt (http://www.thekompany.com/projects/pykde)
Gnome and GTK (ftp://ftp.daa.com.au/pub/james/python)

On Linux, developers can find Python interfaces to the underlying GUI libraries at the core of the KDE and Gnome window systems. The PyKDE and PyQt extension packages provide access to KDE development libraries (PyKDE requires PyQt). The gnome-python and PyGTK extension packages export Gnome and GTK toolkit calls for use in Python scripts (gnome-python requires PyGTK). Both of these sets of extensions are as portable as the underlying libraries they use. Today, the Qt class library runs on Unix and Windows, KDE runs on Linux and Unix platforms, and GTK and Gnome run on Linux and Unix platforms (though a Windows port of GTK is in the works). See relevant web sites for more recent details.

MFC (http://www.python.org/windows)

The Windows *win32all.exe* extensions package for Python, available at Python's web site and on this book's CD-ROM, includes wrappers for the Microsoft Foundation Classes (MFC) framework—a development library that includes user interface components. With the Windows extensions, Python programs can construct Windows GUIs using the same MFC calls applied in languages such as Visual C++. Pythonwin, an MFC sample program that implements a Python development GUI, is included with the extensions package. This is a Windows-only solution, but may be an appealing option for developers with a prior intellectual investment in using the MFC framework from Visual C++.

WPY (http://www.python.org/ftp/python/wpy)

An MFC-like GUI library for Python, ported to run on both X Windows for Unix (where it uses Tk) and Windows for PCs (where it uses MFC). WPY scripts run unchanged on each platform, but use MFC coding styles.

X11 (http://www.cwi.nl/ftp/sjoerd/index.html)

Interfaces to the raw X Windows and Motif libraries also exist for Python. They provide maximum control over the X11 development environment, but are an X-only solution.

There are other lesser-known GUI toolkits for Python, and new ones are likely to emerge by the time you read this book (e.g., the newly announced Python port to the .NET framework on Windows may offer user interface options as well).[*] Moreover, package and web site names like those in this list mutate over time. For an up-to-date list of available tools, see *http://www.python.org* and the new "Vaults of Parnassus" third-party packages site currently at *http://www.vex.net/parnassus*.

Tkinter Overview

Of all these GUI options, though, Tkinter is by far the de facto standard way to implement portable user interfaces in Python today, and the focus of this part of the book. Tkinter's portability, availability, accessibility, documentation, and extensions have made it the most widely used Python GUI solution for many years running. Here are some of the reasons why:

Accessibility

Tkinter is generally regarded as a lightweight toolkit, and one of the simplest GUI solutions for Python available today. Unlike larger frameworks, it is easy to get started in Tkinter right away, without first having to grasp a much larger class interaction model. As we'll see, programmers can create simple Tkinter GUIs in a few lines of Python code, and scale up to writing industrial-strength GUIs gradually.

Portability

A Python script that builds a GUI with Tkinter will run without source code changes on all major window platforms today: Microsoft Windows, X Windows

---

[*] In Part III, *Internet Scripting*, we'll learn how to build user interfaces within a web browser. For now, we'll focus on more traditional GUIs that may or may not be connected to a network.

(on Unix and Linux), and the Macintosh. Further, that same script will provide a native look-and-feel to its users on each of these platforms. A Python/Tkinter script looks like a Windows program on Windows; on Unix and Linux, it provides the same interaction but sports an appearance familiar to X Windows users; and on the Mac, it looks like a Mac program should.

Availability

Tkinter is a standard module in the Python library, shipped with the interpreter. If you have Python, you have Tkinter. Moreover, most Python installation packages (including the standard Python self-installer for Windows) come with Tkinter support bundled. Because of that, scripts written to use the Tkinter module work immediately on most Python interpreters, without any extra installation steps.* Tkinter is also generally better supported than its alternatives today. Because the underlying Tk library is also used by the Tcl and Perl programming languages, it tends to receive more development time and effort than other toolkits available.

Naturally, other factors such as documentation and extensions are important when using a GUI toolkit too; let's take a quick look at the story Tkinter has to tell on these fronts as well.

Tkinter Documentation

This book explores Tkinter fundamentals and most widgets tools, and should be enough to get started with substantial GUI development in Python. On the other hand, it is not an exhaustive reference to the Tkinter library. Happily, at least one book dedicated to using Tkinter in Python is now commercially available as I write this paragraph, and others are on the way (see the Python books list at *http://www.python.org* for details). Besides books, you can also now find Tkinter documentation online; a complete set of Tkinter manuals is currently maintained on the web at *http://www.pythonware.com/library*.

In addition, because the underlying Tk toolkit used by Tkinter is also a de facto standard in the open source scripting community at large, other documentation sources apply. For instance, because Tk has also been adopted by the Tcl and Perl programming languages, Tk-oriented books and documentation written for both of these are directly applicable to Python/Tkinter as well (albeit, with some syntactic mapping).

---

* Some Python distributions on Unix-like platforms still come without Tk support bundled, so you may need to add it on your machine. On some Unix and Linux platforms, you may also need to set your Tcl/Tk library shell variables to use Tkinter. See Appendix B for install details; you can usually sidestep Tk build details by finding an alternative Python distribution with Tk bundled (e.g., Linux RPMs).

Frankly, I learned Tkinter by studying Tcl/Tk texts and references—just replace Tcl strings with Python objects and you have additional reference libraries at your disposal (see Table 6-2, the Tk to Tkinter conversion guide, at the end of this chapter for help reading Tk documentation). For instance, the *Tcl/Tk Pocket Reference* (O'Reilly) can serve as a nice supplement to the Tkinter tutorial material in this part of the book. Moreover, since Tk concepts are familiar to a large body of programmers, Tk support is also readily available on the Net.

Tkinter Extensions

Because Tkinter is so widely used, programmers also have access to precoded Python extensions designed to work with or augment it. For instance:

PIL (http://www.pythonware.com/products/pil/)
> The Python Imaging Library is an open source extension package that adds image-processing tools to Python. Among other things, it extends the basic Tkinter image object set, to add support for displaying many image file types (see the section "Images" at the end of Chapter 7 for details). Besides developing PIL, PythonWare is also building GUI development tools for Python and Tkinter programming, known as PythonWorks; visit their web site for more details.

PMW (http://www.dscpl.com.au/pmw)
> Python Mega Widgets is an extension toolkit for building high-level compound widgets in Python using the Tkinter module. It extends the Tkinter API with a collection of more sophisticated widgets for advanced GUI development, and a framework for implementing some of your own. Among the precoded and extensible megawidgets shipped with the package are notebooks, comboboxes, selection widgets, paned widgets, scrolled widgets, dialog windows, button boxes, and an interface to the Blt graph widget. The interface to PMW megawidgets is similar to that of basic Tkinter widgets, so Python scripts can freely mix PMW megawidgets with standard Tkinter widgets.

IDLE (shipped with Python)
> The IDLE integrated Python development environment is both written in Python with Tkinter and shipped and installed with the Python package (if you have a recent Python interpreter, you should have IDLE too—on Windows, click the Start button, select the Programs menu, and click the Python entry to find it). As described in Appendix B, IDLE provides syntax-coloring text editors for Python code, point-and-click debugging, and more, and is an example of Tkinter's utility.

If you plan on doing any commercial-grade GUI development with Tkinter, you'll probably want to explore extensions such as PMW and PIL after learning Tkinter basics in this text. They can save development time and add pizzazz to your GUIs. See the Python-related web sites mentioned earlier for up-to-date details and links.

Tkinter Structure

From a more nuts-and-bolts perspective, Tkinter is an integration system that implies a somewhat unique program structure. We'll see what this means in terms of code in a moment, but here is a brief introduction to some of the terms and concepts at the core of Python GUI programming.

Strictly speaking, Tkinter is simply the name of Python's interface to Tk—a GUI library originally written for use with the Tcl programming language, and developed by Tcl's creator, John Ousterhout. Python's Tkinter module talks to Tk, and the Tk API in turn interfaces with the underlying window system: Microsoft Windows, X Windows on Unix, or Macintosh.

Python's Tkinter adds a software layer on top of Tk that allows Python scripts to call out to Tk to build and configure interfaces, and routes control back to Python scripts that handle user-generated events (e.g., mouseclicks). That is, GUI *calls* are internally routed from Python script, to Tkinter, to Tk; GUI *events* are routed from Tk, to Tkinter, and back to a Python script. In Part V, *Integration*, we'll know these transfers by their C integration terms, *extending* and *embedding*.[*]

Luckily, Python programmers don't normally need to care about all this call routing going on internally; they simply make widgets and register Python functions to handle widget events. Because of the overall structure, though, event handlers are usually known as *callback handlers*, because the GUI library "calls back" to Python code when events occur.

In fact, we'll find that Python/Tkinter programs are entirely *event-driven*: they build displays and register handlers for events, and then do nothing but wait for events to occur. During the wait, the Tk GUI library runs an *event loop* that watches for mouseclicks, keyboard presses, and so on. All application program processing happens in the registered callback handlers, in response to events. Further, any information needed across events must be stored in long-lived references like global variables and class instance attributes. The notion of a traditional linear program control-flow doesn't really apply in the GUI domain; you need to think in terms of smaller chunks.

---

[*] Since I brought it up: Tkinter is structured as a combination of the Python-coded `Tkinter` module file, and an extension module called `_tkinter` that is written in C. `_tkinter` interfaces with the Tk library and dispatches callbacks back to Python objects using embedding tools; `Tkinter` adds a class-based interface on top of `_tkinter`. You should always import `Tkinter` (not `_tkinter`) in your scripts, though; the latter is an implementation module for internal use only (it was oddly named for a reason).

In Python, Tk also becomes *object-oriented* just because Python is object-oriented: the Tkinter layer exports Tk's API as Python classes. With Tkinter, we can either use a simple function-call approach to create widgets and interfaces, or apply OO techniques such as inheritance and composition to customize and extend the base set of Tkinter classes. Larger Tkinter GUIs generally are constructed as trees of linked Tkinter widget objects, and are often implemented as Python classes to provide structure and retain state information between events. As we'll see in this part of the book, a Tkinter GUI coded with classes almost by default becomes a reusable software component.

Climbing the GUI Learning Curve

On to the details. Let's start out by quickly stepping through a few small examples that illustrate basic concepts, and show the windows they create on the screen. The examples will become more sophisticated as we move along.

"Hello World" in Four Lines (or Less)

The usual first example for GUI systems is to show how to display a "Hello World" message in a window. As coded in Example 6-1, it's just four lines in Python.

Example 6-1. PP2E\Gui\Intro\gui1.py

```
from Tkinter import Label                          # get a widget object
widget = Label(None, text='Hello GUI world!')      # make one
widget.pack()                                      # arrange it
widget.mainloop()                                  # start event loop
```

This is a complete Python Tkinter GUI program. When this script is run, we get a simple window with a label in the middle; it looks like Figure 6-1 on Windows.

Figure 6-1. "Hello World" (gui1) on Windows

This isn't much to write home about yet; but notice that this is a completely functional, independent window on the computer's display. It can be maximized to take up the entire screen, minimized to hide it in the system bar, and resized. Click on the window's "X" box in the top right to kill the window and exit the program.

The script that builds this window is also fully portable—when this same file is run on Linux it produces a similar window, but it behaves according to the underlying

Linux window manager. For instance, Figures 6-2 and 6-3 show this simple script in action on the Linux X Windows system, under the KDE and Gnome window managers, respectively. Even on the same operating system, the same Python code yields a different look and feel for different window systems.

Figure 6-2. "Hello World" on Linux with KDE

Figure 6-3. "Hello World" on Linux with Gnome

The same script file would look different still when run on Macintosh and other Unix-like window managers. On all platforms, though, its basic functional behavior will be the same.

Tkinter Coding Basics

The `gui1` script is a trivial example, but it illustrates steps common to most Tkinter programs. This Python code:

1. Loads a widget class from the `Tkinter` module

2. Makes an instance of the imported `Label` class

3. Packs (arranges) the new `Label` in its parent widget

4. Calls `mainloop` to bring up the window and start the Tkinter event loop

The `mainloop` method called last puts the label on the screen and enters a Tkinter *wait state*, which watches for user-generated GUI events. Within the `mainloop` function, Tkinter internally monitors things like the keyboard and mouse, to detect user-generated events. Because of this model, the `mainloop` call here never returns to our script while the GUI is displayed on-screen.[*] As we'll see when we reach larger scripts, the only way we can get anything done after calling `mainloop` is to register callback handlers to respond to events.

---

[*] Technically, the `mainloop` call returns to your script only after the Tkinter event loop exits. This normally happens when the GUI's main window is closed, but may also occur in response to explicit `quit` method calls that terminate nested event loops but leave the GUI at large open. You'll see why this matters in Chapter 7.

Note that you really need *both* steps 3 and 4 to open this script's GUI. To display a GUI's window at all, you need to call `mainloop`; to display widgets within the window they must be packed (or otherwise arranged) so that the Tkinter geometry manager knows about them. In fact, if you call either `mainloop` or `pack` without calling the other, your window won't show up as expected: a `mainloop` without a `pack` shows an empty window, and a `pack` without a `mainloop` in a script shows nothing since the script never enters an event wait state (try it). Since the concepts illustrated by this simple script are at the core of most Tkinter programs, let's take a deeper look a some of them before moving on.

Making widgets

When widgets are constructed in Tkinter, we can specify how they should be configured. The `gui1` script passes two arguments to the `Label` class constructor:

- The first is a *parent-widget* object, which we want the new label to be attached to. Here, `None` means: "attach the new `Label` to the default top-level window of this program." Later, we'll pass real widgets in this position, to attach our labels to other container objects.

- The second is a *configuration option* for the `Label`, passed as a keyword argument: the `text` option specifies a text string to appear as the label's message. Most widget constructors accept multiple keyword arguments for specifying a variety of options (color, size, callback handlers, and so on). Most widget configuration options have reasonable defaults per platform, though, and this accounts for much of Tkinter's simplicity—you only need to set most options if you wish to do something custom.

As we'll see, the parent-widget argument is the hook we use to build-up complex GUIs as widget trees. Tkinter works on a "what-you-build-is-what-you-get" principle: we construct widget object trees as models of what we want to see on the screen, and then ask the tree to display itself by calling `mainloop`.

Geometry managers

The `pack` widget method called by the `gui1` script invokes the *packer geometry manager*—one of three ways to control how widgets are arranged in a window. Tkinter geometry managers simply arrange one or more widgets within a container (sometimes called a parent, or master). Both top-level windows and frames (a special kind of widget we'll meet later) can serve as containers, and containers may be nested inside other containers to build hierarchical displays.

The packer geometry manager uses *constraint* option settings to automatically position widgets in a window. Scripts supply higher-level instructions (e.g., "attach this widget to the top of its container, and stretch it to fill its space vertically"), not absolute pixel coordinates. Because such constraints are so abstract, the packer provides a powerful and easy-to-use layout system. In fact, you don't even have to specify constraints—if you don't pass any arguments to `pack`, you get default packing, which attaches the widget to side *top*.

We'll visit the packer repeatedly in this chapter, and use it in many of the examples in this book. In Chapter 8 we will also meet an alternative `grid` geometry manager and layout system that arranges widgets within a container in tabular form (i.e., by rows and columns). A third alternative, the *placer* geometry manager system, is described in Tk documentation, but not in this book; it's less popular than the `pack` and `grid` managers, and can be difficult to use for larger GUIs.

Running GUI programs

Like all Python code, the module in Example 6-1 can be started in a number of ways: by running it as a top-level program file:

```
C:\...\PP2E\Gui\Intro>python gui1.py
```

by importing it from a Python session or another module file:

```
>>> import gui1
```

by running it as a Unix executable, if we add the special `#!` line at the top:

```
% gui1.py &
```

and in any other way that Python programs can be launched on your platform. For instance, the script can also be run by clicking on the file's name in a Windows file explorer, and its code can be typed interactively at the `>>>` prompt. It can even be run from a C program, by calling the appropriate embedding API function (see Chapter 20, *Embedding Python*, for details).

In other words, there really are no special rules to follow when running GUI Python code. The Tkinter interface (and Tk itself) are linked into the Python interpreter. When a Python program calls GUI functions, they're simply passed to the embedded GUI system behind the scenes. That makes it easy to write command-line tools that pop up windows; they are run the same way as the purely text-based scripts we studied in the prior part of this book.

Avoiding DOS consoles on Windows

Earlier in this book we learned that if a program's name ends in a *.pyw* extension instead of *.py*, the Windows Python port does not pop up a DOS console box to serve as its standard streams when the file is launched by clicking its filename icon. Now that we've finally started making windows of our own, that filename trick will start to become even more useful.

If you just want to see the windows that your script makes no matter how it is launched, be sure to name your GUI scripts with a *.pyw* if they might be run on Windows. For instance, clicking on the file in Example 6-2 in a Windows explorer creates *just* the window in Figure 6-1.

Example 6-2. PP2E\Gui\Intro\gui1.pyw

...same as gui1.py...

You can also avoid the DOS popup on Windows by running the program with the *pythonw.exe* executable, not *python.exe* (in fact, *.pyw* files are simply registered to be opened by *pythonw*). On Linux, the *.pyw* doesn't hurt, but isn't necessary— there is no notion of a streams popup on Unix-like machines. On the other hand, if your GUI scripts might run on Windows in the future, adding an extra "w" at the end of their names now might save porting effort later. In this book, *.py* filenames are still sometimes used to pop up console windows for viewing printed messages on Windows.

Tkinter Coding Alternatives

As you might expect, there are a variety of ways to code the `gui1` example. For instance, if you want to make all your Tkinter imports more explicit in your script, grab the whole module and prefix all its names with the module's name, as in Example 6-3.

Example 6-3. PP2E\Gui\Intro\gui1b.py – import versus from

```
import Tkinter
widget = Tkinter.Label(None, text='Hello GUI world!')
widget.pack()
widget.mainloop()
```

That will probably get tedious in realistic examples, though—Tkinter exports dozens of widget classes and constants that show up all over Python GUI scripts. In fact, it is usually easier to use a * to import *everything* from the Tkinter module by name in one shot. This is demonstrated in Example 6-4.

Example 6-4. PP2E\Gui\Intro\gui1c.py – roots, sides, pack in-place

```
from Tkinter import *
root = Tk()
Label(root, text='Hello GUI world!').pack(side=TOP)
root.mainloop()
```

The Tkinter module goes out of its way to only export things that we really need, so it's one of the few for which the * import form is relatively safe to apply.* The TOP constant in the pack call here, for instance, is one of those many names exported by the Tkinter module. It's simply a variable name (TOP="top") preassigned in Tkconstants, a module automatically loaded by Tkinter.

When widgets are packed, we can specify which side of their parent they should be attached to—TOP, BOTTOM, LEFT, or RIGHT. If no side option is sent to pack (as in prior examples), a widget is attached to its parent's TOP by default. In general, larger Tkinter GUIs can be constructed as sets of rectangles, attached to the appropriate sides of other, enclosing rectangles. As we'll see later, Tkinter arranges widgets in a rectangle according to both their packing order and their side attachment options. When widgets are gridded, they are assigned row and column numbers instead. None of this will become very meaningful, though, until we have more than one widget in a window, so let's move on.

Notice that this version calls the pack method right away after creating the label, without assigning it a variable. If we don't need to save a widget, we can pack it *in place* like this to eliminate a statement. We'll use this form when a widget is attached to a larger structure and never again referenced. This can be tricky if you assign the pack result, though, but I'll postpone an explanation of why until we've covered a few more basics.

We also use a Tk widget class instance as the *parent* here, instead of None. Tk represents the main ("root") window of the program—the one that starts when the program does. Tk is also used as the default parent widget, both when we don't pass *any* parent to other widget calls, and when we pass the parent as None. In other words, widgets are simply attached to the main program window by default. This script just makes this default behavior explicit, by making and passing the Tk object itself. In Chapter 7, we'll see that Toplevel widgets are typically used to generate new pop-up windows that operate independently of the program's main window.

In Tkinter, some widget methods are exported as functions too, and this lets us shave Example 6-5 to just three lines of code.

Example 6-5. PP2E\Gui\Intro\gui1d.py – a minimal version

```
from Tkinter import *
Label(text='Hello GUI world!').pack()
mainloop()
```

---

* If you study file *Tkinter.py* in the Python source library, you'll notice that top-level module names not meant for export start with a single underscore. Python never copies over such names when a module is accessed with the * form of the from statement.

The Tkinter `mainloop` can be called with or without a widget (i.e., as a function or method). We didn't pass `Label` a parent argument in this version either: it simply defaults to `None` when omitted (which in turn defaults to `Tk`). But relying on that default is less useful once we start building larger displays—things like labels are more typically attached to other widget containers.

Widget resizing basics

Top-level windows, like the one all of the coding variants seen thus far build, can normally be *resized* by the user—simply drag out the window with your mouse. Figure 6-4 shows how our window looks when it is expanded.

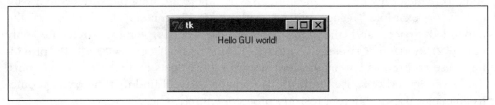

Figure 6-4. Expanding gui1

This isn't very good—the label stays attached to the top of the parent window instead of staying in the middle on expansion—but it's easy to improve on this with a pair of `pack` options, demonstrated in Example 6-6.

Example 6-6. PP2E\Gui\Intro\gui1e.py – expansion

```
from Tkinter import *
Label(text='Hello GUI world!').pack(expand=YES, fill=BOTH)
mainloop()
```

When widgets are packed, we can specify whether a widget should expand to take up all available space, and if so, how it should stretch to fill that space. By default, widget are not expanded when their parent is. But in this script, names `YES` and `BOTH` (imported from the Tkinter module) specify that the label should grow along with its parent, the main window. It does, in Figure 6-5.

Figure 6-5. gui1e with widget resizing

Technically, the packer geometry manager assigns a size to each widget in a display, based on what it contains (text string lengths, etc.). By default, a widget only can occupy its allocated space, and is no bigger than its assigned size. The **expand** and **fill** options let us be more specific about such things:

- The **expand=YES** option asks the packer to expand the allocated space for the widget in general, into any unclaimed space in the widget's parent.

- The **fill** option can be used to stretch the widget to occupy all of its allocated space.

Combinations of these two options produce different layout and resizing effects, some of which only become meaningful when there are multiple widgets in a window. For example, using **expand** without **fill** centers the widget in the expanded space, and the **fill** option can specify vertical stretching only (**fill=Y**), horizontal stretching only (**fill=X**), or both (**fill=BOTH**). By providing these constraints and attachment sides for all widgets in a GUI, we can control the layout in fairly precise terms. In later chapters, we'll find that the **grid** geometry manager uses a different resizing protocol entirely.

This all can be confusing the first time you hear it, and we'll return to this later. But if you're not sure what an **expand** and **fill** combination will do, simply try it out—this is Python after all. For now, remember that the combination of **expand=YES** and **fill=BOTH** is perhaps the most common setting; it means "expand my space allocation to occupy all available space, and stretch me to fill the expanded space in both directions." For our "Hello World" example, the net result is that label grows as the window is expanded, and so is always centered.

Configuring widget options and window titles

So far, we've been telling Tkinter what to display on our label by passing its text as a keyword argument in label *constructor* calls. It turns out that there are two other ways to specify widget configuration options. In Example 6-7, the **text** option of the label is set after it is constructed, by assigning to the widget's **text** key—widget objects overload index operations such that options are also available as mapping keys, much like a dictionary.

Example 6-7. PP2E\Gui\Intro\guif.py – option keys

```
from Tkinter import *
widget = Label()
widget['text'] = 'Hello GUI world!'
widget.pack(side=TOP)
mainloop()
```

More commonly, widget options can be set after construction by calling the widget **config** method, as in Example 6-8.

Example 6-8. PP2E\Gui\Intro\gui1g.py – config and titles

```
from Tkinter import *
root = Tk()
widget = Label(root)
widget.config(text='Hello GUI world!')
widget.pack(side=TOP, expand=YES, fill=BOTH)
root.title('gui1g.py')
root.mainloop()
```

The **config** method (which can also be called by its synonym, **configure**) can be called at any time after construction to change the appearance of a widget on the fly. For instance, we could call this label's **config** method again later in the script to change the text that it displays; watch for such dynamic reconfigurations in later examples in this part of the book.

Notice that this version also calls a **root.title** method—this call sets the label that appears at the top of the window, as pictured in Figure 6-6. In general terms, top-level windows like the **Tk root** here export window-manager interfaces: things that have to do with the border around the window, not its contents.

Figure 6-6. gui1g with expansion and a window title

Just for fun, this version also centers the label on resizes by setting the **expand** and **fill** pack options too. In fact, this version makes just about *everything* explicit, and is more representative of how labels are often coded in full-blown interfaces—their parents, expansion policies, and attachments are usually all spelled out, rather than defaulted.

One more for old times' sake

Finally, if you are both a minimalist and nostalgic for old Python code, you can also program this "Hello World" example as in Example 6-9.

Example 6-9. PP2E\Gui\Intro\gui1-old.py – dictionary calls

```
from Tkinter import *
Label(None, {'text': 'Hello GUI world!', Pack: {'side': 'top'}}).mainloop()
```

This makes the window in just two lines—albeit gruesome ones! This scheme relies on an old coding style that was widely used until Python 1.3 that passed configuration options in a dictionary instead of keyword arguments.* In this scheme, packer options can be sent as values of the key `Pack` (a class in the Tkinter module).

The dictionary call scheme still works, and you may see it in old Python code, but please don't do this—use keywords to pass options, and explicit `pack` method calls in your Tkinter scripts instead. In fact, the only reason I didn't cut this example completely is that dictionaries can still be useful if you want to compute and pass a set of options dynamically. On the other hand, the built-in `apply` function now also allows you to pass an explicit dictionary of keyword arguments in its third argument slot, so there's no compelling reason to ever use the pre–1.3 Tkinter dictionary call form at all.

Packing widgets without saving them

In *gui1c.py* (shown in Example 6-4), I started packing labels without assigning them to names. This works, and is an entirely valid coding style; but because it tends to confuse beginners at first glance, I need to explain *why* it works in more detail here.

In Tkinter, Python class objects correspond to real objects displayed on a screen; we make the Python object to make a screen object, and call the Python object's methods to configure that screen object. Because of this correspondence, the *lifetime* of the Python object must generally correspond to the lifetime of the corresponding object on the screen.

Luckily, Python scripts don't usually need to care about managing object lifetimes. In fact, they do not normally need to maintain a reference to widget objects created along the way at all, unless they plan to reconfigure those objects later. For instance, it's common in Tkinter programming to pack a widget immediately after creating it, if no further reference to the widget is required:

```
Label(text='hi').pack()                        # okay
```

This expression is evaluated left to right as usual—it creates a new label, and then immediately calls the new object's `pack` method, to arrange it in the display. Notice, though, that the Python `Label` object is temporary in this expression; because it is not assigned to a name, it would normally be garbage collected (destroyed and reclaimed) by Python immediately after running its `pack` method.

---

* In fact, Python's pass-by-name keyword arguments were first introduced to help clean up Tkinter calls like this. Internally, keyword arguments really are passed as a dictionary (which can be collected with the `**name` argument form in a `def` header), so the two schemes are similar in implementation. But they vary widely in the amount of characters you need to type and debug.

However, because Tkinter emits Tk calls when objects are constructed, the label will be drawn on the display as expected, even though we haven't held on to the corresponding Python object in our script. In fact, Tkinter internally cross-links widget objects into a long-lived tree used to represent the display, so the `Label` object made during this statement really is retained, even if not by our code.*

In other words, your scripts don't generally need to care about widget object lifetimes, and it's okay to make widgets and pack them right away in the same statement. But that does not mean that it's okay to say something like this:

```
widget = Label(text='hi').pack()             # wrong!
...use widget...
```

This statement almost seems like it should assign a newly packed label to name **widget**, but it does not. In fact, it's really a notorious Tkinter beginner's mistake. The widget **pack** method packs the widget but does not return the widget thus packed. Really, **pack** returns the Python object **None**; after such a statement, **widget** will be a reference to **None**, and any further widget operations through that name will fail. For instance, the following fails too, for the same reason:

```
Label(text='hi').pack().mainloop()           # wrong!
```

Since **pack** returns **None**, asking for its **mainloop** attribute generates an exception (as it should). If you really want to both pack a widget and retain a reference to it, say this instead:

```
widget = Label(text='hi')                    # okay too
widget.pack()
...use widget...
```

This form is a bit more verbose, but is less tricky than packing a widget in the same statement that creates it, and allows you to hold onto the widget for later processing. On the other hand, scripts that compose layouts often add widgets once and for all when they are created, and never need to reconfigure them later; assigning to long-lived names in such program is pointless and unnecessary.†

---

* Ex-Tcl programmers in the audience may be interested to know that Python not only builds the widget tree internally, but uses it to automatically generate widget pathname strings coded manually in Tcl/Tk (e.g., `.panel.row.cmd`). Python uses the addresses of widget class objects to fill in the path components, and records path names in the widget tree. A label attached to a container, for instance, might have an assigned name like `.8220096.8219408` inside Tkinter. You don't need to care, though—simply make and link widget objects by passing parents, and let Python manage pathname details based on the object tree. See the end of this chapter for more on Tk/Tkinter mappings.

† In Chapter 7, we'll meet two exceptions to this rule. Scripts must manually retain a reference to *image* objects because the underlying image data is discarded if the Python image object is garbage-collected. Tkinter *variable* class objects temporarily unset an associated Tk variable if reclaimed, but this is uncommon and less harmful.

Adding Buttons and Callbacks

So far, we've learned how to display messages in labels, and met Tkinter core concepts along the way. Labels are nice for teaching the basics, but user interfaces usually need to do a bit more—like actually responding to users. The program in Example 6-10 creates the window in Figure 6-7.

Example 6-10. PP2E\Gui\Intro\gui2.py

```
import sys
from Tkinter import *
widget = Button(None, text='Hello widget world', command=sys.exit)
widget.pack()
widget.mainloop()
```

Figure 6-7. A button on the top

Here, instead of making a label, we create an instance of the Tkinter `Button` class. It's attached to the default top-level as before, on the default `TOP` packing side. But the main thing to notice here is the button's configuration arguments: we set an option called `command` to the `sys.exit` function.

For buttons, the `command` option is the place where we specify a callback handler function to be run when the button is later pressed. In effect, we use `command` to *register* an action for Tkinter to call when a widget's event occurs. The callback handler used here isn't very interesting: as we learned in an earlier chapter, the built-in `sys.exit` function simply shuts down the calling program. Here, that means pressing this button makes the window go away.

Just as for labels, there are other ways to code buttons. Example 6-11 is a version that packs the button in place without assigning it to a name, attaches it to the `LEFT` side of its parent window explicitly, and specifies `root.quit` as the callback handler—a standard `Tk` object method that shuts down the GUI, and so ends the program (really, it ends the current `mainloop` event loop call).

Example 6-11. PP2E\Gui\Intro\gui2b.py

```
from Tkinter import *
root = Tk()
Button(root, text='press', command=root.quit).pack(side=LEFT)
root.mainloop()
```

This version produces the window in Figure 6-8. Because we didn't tell the button to expand into all available space, it does not.

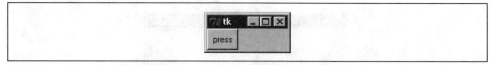

Figure 6-8. A button on the left

In both of the last two examples, pressing the button makes the GUI program exit. In older Tkinter code, you may sometimes see the string "exit" assigned to the command option to make the GUI go away when pressed. This exploits a tool in the underlying Tk library, and is less Pythonic than sys.exit or root.quit.

Widget resizing revisited: expansion

Even with a GUI this simple, there are many ways to lay out its appearance with Tkinter's constraint-based pack geometry manager. For example, to center the button in its window, add an expand=YES option to the button's pack method call, and generate a window like Figure 6-9. This makes the packer allocate all available space to the button, but does not stretch the button to fill that space.

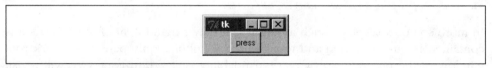

Figure 6-9. side=LEFT, expand=YES

If you want the button to be given all available space, and to stretch to fill all of its assigned space horizontally, add expand=YES and fill=X keyword arguments to the pack call, and create the scene in Figure 6-10.

Figure 6-10. side=LEFT, expand=YES, fill=X

This makes the button fill the whole window initially (its allocation is expanded, and it is stretched to fill that allocation). It also makes the button grow as the parent window is resized. As shown in Figure 6-11, the button in this window does expand when its parent expands, but only along the X horizontal axis.

To make the button grow in both directions, specify both expand=YES and fill=BOTH in the pack call; now, resizing the window makes the button grow in general, as shown in Figure 6-12. In fact, for a good time, maximize this window to fill the entire screen; you'll get one very big Tkinter button indeed.

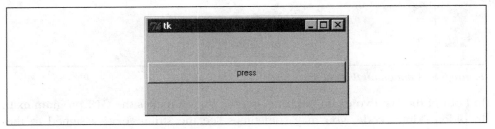

Figure 6-11. Resizing with expand=YES, fill=X

Figure 6-12. Resizing with expand=YES, fill=BOTH

In more complex displays, such a button will only expand if all of the widgets it is contained by are set to expand too. Here, the button's only parent is the Tk root window of the program, so parent expandability isn't yet an issue. We will revisit the packer geometry manager when we meet multiple-widget displays later in this tutorial, and again when we study the alternative `grid` call in Chapter 8.

Adding User-Defined Callback Handlers

In the simple button examples in the previous section, the callback handler was simply an existing function that killed the GUI program. It's not much more work to register callback handlers that do something a bit more useful. Example 6-12 defines a callback handler of its own in Python.

Example 6-12. PP2E\Gui\Intro\gui3.py

```
from Tkinter import *

def quit():                                 # a custom callback handler
    print 'Hello, I must be going...'       # kill windows and process
    import sys; sys.exit()

widget = Button(None, text='Hello event world', command=quit)
widget.pack()
widget.mainloop()
```

The window created by this script is shown in Figure 6-13. This script and its GUI are almost identical to the last example. But here, the `command` option specifies a *function* we've defined locally. When the button is pressed, Tkinter calls the `quit` function in this file to handle the event. Inside `quit`, the `print` statement types a message on the program's `stdout` stream, and the GUI process exits as before.

Figure 6-13. A button that runs a Python function

As usual, `stdout` is normally the window that the program was started from, unless it's been redirected to a file. It's a pop-up DOS console if you run this program by clicking it on Windows—add a `raw_input` call before `sys.exit` if you have trouble seeing the message before the pop-up disappears. Here's what the printed output looks like back in standard stream world when the button is pressed; it is generated by a Python function called automatically by Tkinter:

```
C:\...\PP2E\Gui\Intro>python gui3.py
Hello, I must be going...

C:\...\PP2E\Gui\Intro>
```

Normally, such messages would be displayed in another window, but we haven't gotten far enough to know how just yet. Callback functions usually do more, of course (and may even pop up new windows altogether), but this example illustrates the basics.

In general, *callback handlers* can be any callable object: functions, anonymous functions generated with lambda expressions, bound methods of class or type instances, or class instances that inherit a `__call__` operator overload method. For `Button` press callbacks, callback handlers always receive no arguments (other than a `self`, for bound-methods).

Lambda callback handlers

To make the last paragraph a bit more concrete, let's take a quick look at some other ways to code the callback handler in this example. Recall that the Python lambda expression generates a new, unnamed function object when run. If we need extra data passed in to the handler function, we can register lambda expressions with default argument values to specify the extra data needed. We'll see how this can be useful later in this part of the book, but to illustrate the basic idea, Example 6-13 shows what this example looks like when recoded to use a lambda instead of a `def`.

Example 6-13. PP2E\Gui\Intro\gui3b.py

```
from Tkinter import *
from sys import stdout, exit                # lambda generates a function
widget = Button(None,                       # but contains just an expression
                text='Hello event world',
                command=(lambda: stdout.write('Hello lambda world\n') or exit()) )
widget.pack()
widget.mainloop()
```

This code is a bit tricky because lambdas can only contain an expression; to emulate the original script, this version uses an or operator to force two expressions to be run, and writes to stdout to mimic a print. More typically, lambdas are used to pass along extra data to a callback handler using defaults:

```
def handler(X, Y):                 # would normallly be called with no args
    use original X and Y here...

X = something here...
Y = something else here...
Button(text='ni', command=(lambda save1=X, save2=Y: handler(save1, save2)))
```

Although Tkinter invokes command callbacks with no arguments, such a lambda can be used to provide an indirect anonymous function that wraps the real handler call, and passes along information that existed when the GUI was first constructed. Since default arguments are evaluated and saved when the lambda runs (not when its result is later called), they are a way to remember objects that must be accessed again later, during event processing. We'll see this put to more concrete use later. If its syntax confuses you, remember that a lambda expression like the one in the preceding code can usually be coded as a simple nested def statement instead:

```
X = something here...
Y = something else here...
def func(save1=X, save2=Y): handler(save1, save2)
Button(text='ni', command=func)
```

Bound method callback handlers

Class *bound methods* work particularly well as callback handlers too: they record both an instance to send the event to, and an associated method to call. As a preview, Example 6-14 shows Example 6-12 rewritten to register a bound class method, instead of a function or lambda result.

Example 6-14. PP2E\Gui\Intro\gui3c.py

```
from Tkinter import *

class HelloClass:
    def __init__(self):
        widget = Button(None, text='Hello event world', command=self.quit)
        widget.pack()
```

Example 6-14. PP2E\Gui\Intro\gui3c.py (continued)

```
    def quit(self):
        print 'Hello class method world'      # self.quit is a bound method
        import sys; sys.exit()                 # retains the self+quit pair

HelloClass()
mainloop()
```

On a button press, Tkinter calls this class's `quit` method with no arguments as usual. But really, is does receive one argument—the original `self` object—even though Tkinter doesn't pass it explicitly. Because the `self.quit` bound method retains both `self` and `quit`, it's compatible with a simple function call; Python automatically passes the `self` argument along to the method function. Conversely, registering an *unbound* method like `HelloClass.quit` won't work, because there is no `self` object to pass along when the event later occurs.

Later, we'll see that class callback handler coding schemes provide a natural place to remember information for use on events too: simply assign it to `self` instance attributes:

```
    class someGuiClass:
        def __init__(self):
            self.X = something here...
            self.Y = something else here...
            Button(text='Hi', command=self.handler)
        def handler(self):
            use self.X, self.Y here...
```

Because the event will be dispatched to this class's method with a reference to the original instance object, `self` gives access to attributes that retain original data.

Callable class object callback handlers

Because Python class instance objects can also be *called* if they inherit a `__call__` method to intercept the operation, we can pass one of these to serve as a callback handler too, as in Example 6-15.

Example 6-15. PP2E\Gui\Intro\gui3d.py

```
from Tkinter import *

class HelloCallable:
    def __init__(self):                        # __init__ run on object creation
        self.msg = 'Hello __call__ world'
    def __call__(self):                        # __call__ run later when called
        print self.msg                         # class object looks like a function
        import sys; sys.exit()

widget = Button(None, text='Hello event world', command=HelloCallable())
widget.pack()
widget.mainloop()
```

Here, the `HelloCallable` instance registered with `command` can be called like a normal function too—Python invokes its `__call__` method to handle the call operation made in Tkinter on the button press. Notice that `self.msg` is used to retain information for use on events here; `self` is the original instance when the special `__call__` method is automatically invoked.

All four `gui3` variants create the same GUI window, but print different messages to `stdout` when their button is pressed:

```
C:\...\PP2E\Gui\Intro>python gui3.py
Hello, I must be going...

C:\...\PP2E\Gui\Intro>python gui3b.py
Hello lambda world

C:\...\PP2E\Gui\Intro>python gui3c.py
Hello class method world

C:\...\PP2E\Gui\Intro>python gui3d.py
Hello __call__ world
```

There are good reasons for each callback coding scheme (function, lambda, class method, callable class), but we need to move on to larger examples to uncover them in less theoretical terms.

Other Tkinter callback protocols

For future reference, also keep in mind that using `command` options to intercept user-generated button press events is just one way to register callbacks in Tkinter. In fact, there are a variety of ways for Tkinter scripts to catch events:

Button command options

As we've just seen, button press events are intercepted by providing a callable object in widget `command` options. This is true of other kinds of button-like widgets we'll meet in Chapter 7 (e.g., radio and check buttons, scales).

Menu command options

In the upcoming Tkinter tour chapters, we'll also find that a `command` option is used to specify callback handlers for menu selections.

Scrollbar protocols

Scrollbar widgets register handlers with `command` options too, but they have a unique event protocol that allows them to be cross-linked with the widget they are meant to scroll (e.g., listboxes, text displays, and canvases): moving the scrollbar automatically moves the widget, and vice versa.

General widget bind methods

A more general Tkinter event `bind` method mechanism can be used to register callback handlers for lower-level interface events—key presses, mouse movement and clicks, and so on. Unlike `command` callbacks, `bind` callbacks receive an event object argument (an instance of the Tkinter `Event` class), that gives context about the event—subject widget, screen coordinates, etc.

Window manager protocols

In addition, scripts can also intercept window manager events (e.g., window close requests) by tapping into the window manager `protocol` method mechanism available on top-level window objects: setting a handler for `WM_DELETE_WINDOW`, for instance, takes over window close buttons.

Scheduled event callbacks

Finally, Tkinter scripts can also register callback handlers to be called in special contexts, such as timer expirations, input data arrival, and event-loop idle states. Scripts can also pause for state-change events related to windows and special variables. We'll meet these event interfaces in more detail near the end of Chapter 8.

Binding events

Of all these, `bind` is the most general, but also perhaps the most complex. We'll study it in more detail later, but to let you sample its flavor now, Example 6-16 uses `bind`, not `command`, to catch button presses.

Example 6-16. PP2E\Gui\Intro\gui3e.py

```
from Tkinter import *

def hello(event):
    print 'Press twice to exit'          # on single-left click

def quit(event):                          # on double-left click
    print 'Hello, I must be going...'     # event gives widget, x/y, etc.
    import sys; sys.exit()

widget = Button(None, text='Hello event world')
widget.pack()
widget.bind('<Button-1>', hello)          # bind left mouse clicks
widget.bind('<Double-1>', quit)           # bind double-left clicks
widget.mainloop()
```

In fact, this version doesn't specify a `command` option for the button at all. Instead, it binds lower-level callback handlers for both left mouseclicks (`<Button-1>`) and double-left mouseclicks (`<Double-1>`) within the button's display area. The `bind` method accepts a large set of such event identifiers in a variety of formats, which we'll meet in Chapter 7.

When run, this script makes the same window again (see Figure 6-13). Clicking on the button once prints a message but doesn't exit; you need to double-click on the button now to exit as before. Here is the output after clicking twice and double-clicking once (a double-click fires the single-click callback first):

```
C:\...\PP2E\Gui\Intro>python gui3e.py
Press twice to exit
Press twice to exit
Press twice to exit
Hello, I must be going...
```

Although this script intercepts button clicks manually, the end result is roughly the same; widget-specific protocols like button `command` options are really just higher-level interfaces to events you can also catch with `bind`.

We'll meet `bind` and all of the other Tkinter event callback handler hooks again in more detail later in this book. First, though, let's focus on building GUIs larger than a single button, and other ways to use classes in GUI work.

Adding Multiple Widgets

It's time to start building user interfaces with more than one widget. Example 6-17 makes the window shown in Figure 6-14.

Example 6-17. PP2E\Gui\Intro\gui4.py

```
from Tkinter import *

def greeting():
    print 'Hello stdout world!...'

win = Frame()
win.pack()
Label(win,  text='Hello container world').pack(side=TOP)
Button(win, text='Hello', command=greeting) .pack(side=LEFT)
Button(win, text='Quit',  command=win.quit).pack(side=RIGHT)

win.mainloop()
```

Figure 6-14. A multiple-widget window

This example makes a `Frame` widget (another Tkinter class), and attaches three other widget objects to it, a `Label` and two `Buttons`, by passing the `Frame` as their first argument. In Tkinter terms, we say that the `Frame` becomes a *parent* to the other three widgets. Both buttons on this display trigger callbacks:

- Pressing the Hello button triggers the `greeting` function defined within this file, which prints to `stdout` again.

- Pressing the Quit button calls the standard Tkinter `quit` method, inherited by `win` from the `Frame` class (`Frame.quit` has the same effect as the `Tk.quit` we used earlier).

Here is the `stdout` text that shows up on Hello button presses, wherever this script's standard streams may be:

```
C:\...\PP2E\Gui\Intro>python gui4.py
Hello stdout world!...
Hello stdout world!...
Hello stdout world!...
Hello stdout world!...
```

The notion of attaching widgets to containers turns out to be at the core of layouts in Tkinter. Before we go into more detail on that topic, though, let's get small.

Widget resizing revisited: clipping

Earlier, we saw how to make widgets expand along with their parent window, by passing `expand` and `fill` options to the `pack` geometry manager. Now that we have a window with more than one widget, I can let you in on one of the more useful secrets in the packer. As a rule, widgets packed first are clipped last, when a window is shrunk. That is, the order in which you pack items determines which will be cut out of the display if it is made too small—widgets packed later are cut out first. For example, Figure 6-15 shows what happens when the `gui4` window is shrunk interactively.

Figure 6-15. gui4 gets small

Try reordering the label and button lines in the script and see what happens when the window shrinks; the first packed is always the last to go away. For instance, if the label is packed last, Figure 6-16 shows that it is clipped first even though it is attached to the top: `side` attachments and packing order both impact the overall layout, but only packing order matters when windows shrink.

Figure 6-16. Label packed last, clipped first

Tkinter keeps track of the packing order internally to make this work. Scripts can plan ahead for shrinkage by calling `pack` methods of more important widgets first. For instance, on the upcoming Tkinter tour we'll meet code that builds menus and toolbars at the top and bottom of the window; to make sure these are lost last as a window is shrunk, they are packed first, before the application components in the middle. Similarly, displays that include scrollbars normally pack them before the items they scroll (e.g., text, lists), so that the scrollbars remain as the window shrinks.

Attaching widgets to frames

In larger terms, the critical innovation in this example is its use of frames: `Frame` widgets are just *containers* for other widgets, and so give rise to the notion of GUIs as widget hierarchies, or *trees*. Here, `win` serves as an enclosing window for the other three widgets. In general, though, by attaching widgets to frames, and frames to other frames, we can build up arbitrary GUI layouts. Simply divide the user interface into a set of increasingly smaller rectangles, implement each as a Tkinter `Frame`, and attach basic widgets to the frame in the desired screen position.

In this script, by specifying `win` in the first argument to the `Label` and `Button` constructors, they are attached to the `Frame` by Tkinter (they become children of the `win` parent). `win` itself is attached to the default top-level window, since we didn't pass a parent to the Frame constructor. When we ask `win` to run itself (by calling `mainloop`), Tkinter draws all the widgets in the tree we've built.

The three child widgets also provide `pack` options now: the `side` arguments tell which part of the containing frame (i.e., `win`) to attach the new widget to. The label hooks onto the top, and the buttons attach to the sides. `TOP`, `LEFT`, and `RIGHT` are all preassigned string variables imported from Tkinter. Arranging widgets is a bit more subtle than simply giving a side, though, but we need to take a quick detour into packer geometry management details to see why.

Packing order and side attachments

When a widget tree is displayed, child widgets appear inside their parents, and are arranged according to their order of packing and their packing options. Because of this, the order in which widgets are packed not only gives their clipping order, it also determines how their `side` settings play out in the generated display.

Here's how the packer's layout system works:

1. The packer starts out with an available space *cavity* that includes the entire parent container (e.g., the whole `Frame` or top-level window).

2. As each widget is packed on a side, that widget is given the *entire* requested side in the remaining space cavity, and the space cavity is shrunk.

3. Later pack requests are given an entire side of what is left, after earlier pack requests have shrunk the cavity.

4. After widgets are given cavity space, **expand** divides up any space left, and **fill** and **anchor** stretch and position widgets within their assigned space.

For instance, if you recode the **gui4** child widget creation logic like this:

```
Button(win, text='Hello', command=greeting).pack(side=LEFT)
Label(win,  text='Hello container world').pack(side=TOP)
Button(win, text='Quit',  command=win.quit).pack(side=RIGHT)
```

You will wind up with the very different display in Figure 6-17, even though you've only moved the label code one line down in the source file (contrast with Figure 6-14).

Figure 6-17. Packing the label second

Despite its **side** setting, the label does not get the entire top of the window now, and you have to think in terms of shrinking cavities to understand why. Because the Hello button is packed first, it is given the entire **LEFT** side of the **Frame**. Next, the label is given the entire **TOP** side of what is left. Finally, the Quit button gets the **RIGHT** side of the remainder—a rectangle to the right of the Hello button and under the label. When this window shrinks, widgets are clipped in reverse order of their packing: the Quit button disappears first, followed by the label.* In the original version of this example, the label spans the entire top side just because it is the first packed, not because of its **side** option.

The packer's expand and fill revisited

Beyond all this, the **fill** option we met earlier can be used to stretch the widget to occupy all the space in the cavity side it has been given, and any cavity space left after all packing is evenly allocated among widgets with the **expand=YES** we saw before. For example, coding this way makes the window in Figure 6-18:

```
Button(win, text='Hello', command=greeting).pack(side=LEFT, fill=Y)
Label(win,  text='Hello container world').pack(side=TOP)
Button(win, text='Quit', command=win.quit).pack(side=RIGHT, expand=YES, fill=X)
```

---

* Technically, the packing steps are just rerun again after a window resize. But since this means that there won't be enough space left for widgets packed last when the window shrinks, it works the same as saying that widgets packed first are clipped last.

Figure 6-18. Packing with expand and fill options

To make these all grow along with their window, though, we also need to make the container frame expandable—widgets only expand beyond their initial packer arrangement if all of their parents expand too:

```
win = Frame()
win.pack(side=TOP, expand=YES, fill=BOTH)
Button(win, text='Hello', command=greeting).pack(side=LEFT, fill=Y)
Label(win,  text='Hello container world').pack(side=TOP)
Button(win, text='Quit', command=win.quit).pack(side=RIGHT, expand=YES,fill=X)
```

When this code runs, the Frame is assigned the entire top side of its parent as before (that is, the top parcel of the root window); but because it is now marked to expand into unused space in its parent and fill that space both ways, it and all its attached children expand along with the window. Figure 6-19 shows how.

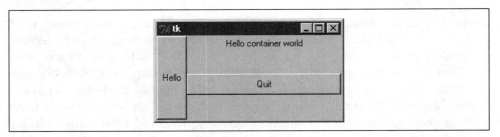

Figure 6-19. gui4 gets big with an expandable frame

Using anchor to position instead of stretch

And as if that isn't flexible enough, packer also allows widgets to be positioned within their allocated space with an anchor option, instead of filling that space with a fill. The anchor option accepts Tkinter constants identifying all eight points of the compass (N, NE, NW, S, etc.) and CENTER as its value (e.g., anchor=NW). It instructs the packer to position the widget at the desired position within its allocated space, if the space allocated for the widget is larger than the space needed to display the widget.

The default anchor is CENTER, so widgets show up in the middle of their space (the cavity side they were given) unless they are positioned with anchor, or stretched with fill. To demonstrate, change gui4 to use this sort of code:

```
Button(win, text='Hello', command=greeting).pack(side=LEFT, anchor=N)
Label(win,  text='Hello container world').pack(side=TOP)
Button(win, text='Quit',  command=win.quit).pack(side=RIGHT)
```

The only thing new here is that the Hello button is anchored to the north side of its space allocation. Because this button was packed first, it got the entire left side of the parent frame—more space than needed to show the button, so it shows up in the middle of that side by default as in Figure 6-17 (i.e., anchored to the center). Setting the anchor to N moves it to the top of its side, as shown in Figure 6-20.

Figure 6-20. Anchoring a button to the north

Keep in mind that fill and **anchor** are applied *after* a widget has been allocated cavity side space by its **side**, packing order, and **expand** extra space request. By playing with packing orders, sides, fills, and anchors, you can generate lots of layout and clipping effects, and you should take a few moments to experiment with alternatives if you haven't already. In the original version of this example, for instance, the label spans the entire top side just because it is the first packed.

As we'll see later, frames can be *nested* in other frames too, to make more complex layouts. In fact, because each parent container is a distinct space cavity, this provides a sort of escape mechanism for the packer cavity algorithm: to better control where a set of widgets show up, simply pack them within a nested subframe, and attach the frame as a package to a larger container. A row of pushbuttons, for example, might be easier laid out in a frame of its own than mixed with other widgets in the display directly.

Finally, also keep in mind that the widget tree created by these examples is really an implicit one; Tkinter internally records the relationships implied by passed parent widget arguments. In OOP terms, this is a *composition* relationship—the Frame contains a Label and Buttons; let's look at *inheritance* relationships next.

Customizing Widgets with Classes

You don't have to use OOP in Tkinter scripts, but it can definitely help. As we just saw, Tkinter GUIs are built up as class-instance object trees. Here's another way Python's OOP features can be applied to GUI models: specializing widgets by inheritance. Example 6-18 builds the window in Figure 6-21.

Example 6-18. PP2E\Gui\Intro\gui5.py

```
from Tkinter import *

class HelloButton(Button):
```

Example 6-18. PP2E\Gui\Intro\gui5.py (continued)

```
    def __init__(self, parent=None, **config):      # add callback method
        Button.__init__(self, parent, config)       # and pack myself
        self.pack()
        self.config(command=self.callback)
    def callback(self):                             # default press action
        print 'Goodbye world...'                    # replace in subclasses
        self.quit()

if __name__ == '__main__':
    HelloButton(text='Hello subclass world').mainloop()
```

Figure 6-21. A button subclass in action

This example isn't anything special to look at: it just displays a single button that prints a message and exits when pressed. But this time, it is a button widget we created on our own. The HelloButton class inherits everything from the Tkinter Button class, but adds a callback method and constructor logic to set the command option to self.callback, a bound method of the instance. When the button is pressed this time, the new widget class's callback *method* is invoked, not a simple function.

The **config argument here is assigned unmatched keyword arguments; they're passed along to the Button constructor. We met the config widget method called in HelloButton's constructor earlier; it is just an alternative way to pass configuration options after the fact (instead of passing constructor arguments).

So what's the point of subclassing widgets like this? It allows widgets to be configured by *subclassing*, instead of passing in options. HelloButton is a true button; we pass in configuration options as usual when one is made. But we can also specify callback handlers by overriding the callback method in subclasses, as shown in Example 6-19.

Example 6-19. PP2E\Gui\Intro\gui5b.py

```
from gui5 import HelloButton

class MyButton(HelloButton):      # subclass HelloButton
    def callback(self):           # redefine press-handler method
        print "Ignoring press!..."

if __name__ == '__main__':
    MyButton(None, text='Hello subclass world').mainloop()
```

Instead of exiting, this MyButton button prints to stdout and stays up when pressed. Here is its standard output after being pressed a few times:

```
C:\PP2ndEd\examples\PP2E\Gui\Intro>python gui5b.py
Ignoring press!...
Ignoring press!...
Ignoring press!...
Ignoring press!...
```

Whether it's simpler to customize widgets by subclassing or passing in options is probably a matter of taste. But the point to notice is that Tk becomes truly object-oriented in Python, just because Python is object-oriented: we can specialize widget classes using normal class-based OO techniques. The next example provides yet another way to arrange for specialization.

Reusable GUI Components with Classes

Larger GUI interfaces are often built up as subclasses of Frame, with callback handlers implemented as methods. This structure gives us a natural place to store information between events: instance attributes record *state*. It also allows us to both specialize GUIs by overriding their methods in new subclasses, and attach them to larger GUI structures to reuse them as general components. For instance, a GUI text editor implemented as a Frame subclass can be attached to and configured by any number of other GUIs; if done well, we can plug such a text editor into any user interface that needs text editing tools.

We'll meet such a text editor component in Chapter 9. For now, Example 6-20 is a simple example to illustrate the concept. Script *gui6.py* produces the window in Figure 6-22.

Example 6-20. PP2E\Gui\Intro\gui6.py

```
from Tkinter import *

class Hello(Frame):                              # an extended Frame
    def __init__(self, parent=None):
        Frame.__init__(self, parent)             # do superclass init
        self.pack()
        self.data = 42
        self.make_widgets()                      # attach widgets to self
    def make_widgets(self):
        widget = Button(self, text='Hello frame world!', command=self.message)
        widget.pack(side=LEFT)
    def message(self):
        self.data = self.data + 1
        print 'Hello frame world %s!' % self.data

if __name__ == '__main__': Hello().mainloop()
```

Figure 6-22. A custom Frame in action

This example pops up a single button window. When pressed, the button triggers the `self.message` bound method to print to `stdout` again. Here is the output after pressing this button four times; notice how `self.data` (a simple counter here) retains its state between presses:

```
C:\...\PP2E\Gui\Intro>python gui6.py
Hello frame world 43!
Hello frame world 44!
Hello frame world 45!
Hello frame world 46!
```

This may seem like a roundabout way to show a `Button` (we did it in fewer lines in Examples 6-10, 6-11, and 6-12). But the `Hello` class provides an enclosing organizational structure for building GUIs. In the examples prior to the last section, we made GUIs using a function-like approach: we called widget constructors as though they were functions and hooked widgets together manually by passing in parents to widget construction calls. There was no notion of an enclosing context, apart from the global scope of the module file containing the widget calls. This works for simple GUIs, but can make for brittle code when building up larger GUI structures.

But by subclassing `Frame` as we've done here, the class becomes an enclosing context for the GUI:

- Widgets are added by attaching objects to `self`, an instance of a `Frame` container subclass (e.g., `Button`).

- Callback handlers are registered as bound methods of `self`, and so are routed back to code in the class (e.g., `self.message`).

- State information is retained between events by assigning to attributes of `self`, visible to all callback methods in the class (e.g., `self.data`).

- It's easy to make multiple copies of such a GUI component, because each class instance is a distinct namespace.

In a sense, entire GUIs become specialized `Frame` objects, with extensions for an application. Classes can also provide protocols for building widgets (e.g., the `make_widgets` method here), handle standard configuration chores (like setting window manager options), and so on. In short, `Frame` subclasses provide a simple way to organize collections of other widget-class objects.

Attaching class components

Perhaps more important, subclasses of **Frame** are true widgets: they can be further extended and customized by subclassing, and can be attached to enclosing widgets. For instance, to attach the entire package of widgets that a class builds to something else, simply create an instance of the class with a real parent widget passed in. To illustrate, running the script in Example 6-21 creates the window shown in Figure 6-23.

Example 6-21. PP2E\Gui\Intro\gui6b.py

```
from sys import exit
from Tkinter import *                   # get Tk widget classes
from gui6 import Hello                  # get the subframe class

parent = Frame(None)                    # make a container widget
parent.pack()
Hello(parent).pack(side=RIGHT)          # attach Hello instead of running it

Button(parent, text='Attach', command=exit).pack(side=LEFT)
parent.mainloop()
```

Figure 6-23. An attached class component on the right

This script just adds **Hello**'s button to the right side of **parent**—a container **Frame**. In fact, the button on the right in this window represents an embedded component: its button really represents an attached Python class object. Pressing the embedded class's button on the right prints a message as before; pressing the new button exits the GUI by a **sys.exit** call:

```
C:\...\PP2E\Gui\Intro>python gui6b.py
Hello frame world 43!
Hello frame world 44!
Hello frame world 45!
Hello frame world 46!
```

In more complex GUIs, we might instead attach large **Frame** subclasses to other container components and develop each independently. For instance, Example 6-22 is yet another specialized **Frame** itself, but attaches an instance of the original **Hello** class in a more OO fashion. When run as a top-level program, it creates a window identical to the one shown in Figure 6-23.

Example 6-22. PP2E\Gui\Intro\gui6c.py

```
from Tkinter import *                    # get Tk widget classes
from gui6 import Hello                   # get the subframe class

class HelloContainer(Frame):
    def __init__(self, parent=None):
        Frame.__init__(self, parent)
        self.pack()
        self.makeWidgets()
    def makeWidgets(self):
        Hello(self).pack(side=RIGHT)        # attach a Hello to me
        Button(self, text='Attach', command=self.quit).pack(side=LEFT)

if __name__ == '__main__': HelloContainer().mainloop()
```

This looks and works exactly like gui6b, but registers the added button's callback handler as self.quit, which is just the standard quit widget method this class inherits from Frame. The window this time represents two Python classes at work—the embedded component's widgets on the right (the original Hello button), and the container's widgets on the left.

Naturally, this is a simple example (we only attached a single button here, after all). But in more practical user interfaces, the set of widget class objects attached in this way can be much larger. Imagine replacing the Hello call in this script with a call to attach an already-coded and fully debugged calculator object, and you'll begin to better understand the power of this paradigm. If we code all of our GUI components as classes, they automatically become a library of reusable widgets, which we can combine in other applications as often as we like.

Extending class components

When GUIs are built with classes, there are a variety of ways to reuse their code in other displays. To extend Hello instead of attaching it, we just override some of its methods in a new subclass (which itself becomes a specialized Frame widget). This technique is shown in Example 6-23.

Example 6-23. PP2E\Gui\Intro\gui6d.py

```
from Tkinter import *
from gui6 import Hello

class HelloExtender(Hello):
    def make_widgets(self):                       # extend method here
        Hello.make_widgets(self)
        Button(self, text='Extend', command=self.quit).pack(side=RIGHT)
    def message(self):
        print 'hello', self.data                  # redefine method here

if __name__ == '__main__': HelloExtender().mainloop()
```

This subclass's `make_widgets` method here first builds the superclass's widgets, then adds a second Extend button on the right, as shown in Figure 6-24.

Figure 6-24. A customized class's widgets, on the left

Because it redefines the `message` method, pressing the original superclass's button on the left now prints a different string to `stdout` (when searching up from `self`, the `message` attribute is found first in this subclass, not the superclass):

```
C:\...\PP2E\Gui\Intro>python gui6d.py
hello 42
hello 42
hello 42
hello 42
```

But pressing the new Extend button on the right, added by this subclass, exits immediately, since the `quit` method (inherited from `Hello`, which inherits it from `Frame`) is the added button's callback handler. The net effect is that this class customizes the original, to add a new button and change `message`'s behavior.

Although this example is simple, it demonstrates a technique that can be powerful in practice—to change a GUI's behavior, we can write a new class that customizes its parts, rather than changing the existing GUI code in place. The main code need be debugged only once, and customized with subclasses as unique needs arise.

The moral of this story is that Tkinter GUIs can be coded without ever writing a single new class, but using classes to structure your GUI code makes it much more reusable in the long run. If done well, you can both attach already-debugged components to new interfaces, and specialize their behavior in new external subclasses as needed for custom requirements. Either way, the initial up-front investment to use classes is bound to save coding time in the end.

Standalone container classes

Before we move on, I want to point out that it's possible to reap most of the benefits previously mentioned by creating standalone classes not derived from Tkinter `Frames` or other widgets. For instance, the class in Example 6-24 generates the window shown in Figure 6-25.

Example 6-24. PP2E\Gui\Intro\gui7.py

```
from Tkinter import *

class HelloPackage:                         # not a widget subbclass
    def __init__(self, parent=None):
        self.top = Frame(parent)            # embed a Frame
        self.top.pack()
        self.data = 0
        self.make_widgets()                 # attach widgets to self.top
    def make_widgets(self):
        Button(self.top, text='Bye', command=self.top.quit).pack(side=LEFT)
        Button(self.top, text='Hye', command=self.message).pack(side=RIGHT)
    def message(self)):
        self.data = self.data + 1
        print 'Hello number', self.data

if __name__ == '__main__': HelloPackage().top.mainloop()
```

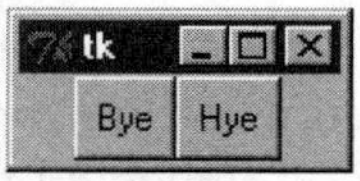

Figure 6-25. A standalone class package in action

When run, the Hye button here prints to `stdout`, and Bye closes and exits the GUI, much as before:

```
C:\...\PP2E\Gui\Intro>python gui7.py
Hello number 1
Hello number 2
Hello number 3
Hello number 4
```

Also as before, `self.data` retains state between events, and callbacks are routed to the `self.message` method within this class. Unlike before, the `HelloPackage` class is not itself a kind of `Frame` widget. In fact, it's not a kind of anything—it only serves as a generator of namespaces for storing away real widget objects and state. Because of that, widgets are attached to a `self.top` (an embedded `Frame`), not `self`. Moreover, all references to the object as widget must descend to the embedded frame—as in the `top.mainloop` call to start the GUI.

This makes for a bit more coding within the class, but avoids potential name clashes with both attributes added to `self` by the Tkinter framework, and existing Tkinter widget methods. For instance, if you define a `config` method in your class, it will hide the `config` call exported by Tkinter. With the standalone class package in this example, you only get the methods and instance attributes that your class defines.

In practice, Tkinter doesn't use very many names, so this is not generally a big concern.* It can happen, of course; but frankly, I've never seen a real Tkinter name clash in widget subclasses in some eight years of Python coding. Moreover, using standalone classes is not without other downsides. Although they can generally be attached and subclassed as before, they are not quite plug-and-play compatible with real widget objects. For instance, the configuration calls made in Example 6-21 for the `Frame` subclass fail in Example 6-25.

Example 6-25. PP2E\Gui\Intro\gui7b.py

```
from Tkinter import *
from gui7 import HelloPackage       # or get from gui7c--__getattr__ added

frm = Frame()
frm.pack()
Label(frm, text='hello').pack()

part = HelloPackage(frm)
part.pack(side=RIGHT)              # fails!--need part.top.pack(side=RIGHT)
frm.mainloop()
```

This won't quite work, because `part` isn't really a widget. To treat it as such, you must descend to `part.top` before making GUI configurations, and hope that the name `top` never changes. The class could make this better by defining a method that always routes unknown attribute fetches to the embedded `Frame`, as in Example 6-26.

Example 6-26. PP2E\Gui\Intro\gui7c.py

```
import gui7
from Tkinter import *

class HelloPackage(gui7.HelloPackage):
    def __getattr__(self, name):
        return getattr(self.top, name)      # pass off to a real widget

if __name__ == '__main__': HelloPackage().top.mainloop()
```

But that then requires even more extra coding in standalone package classes. As usual, though, the significance of all these trade-offs varies per application.

---

* If you study the *Tkinter.py* module's source code, you'll notice that many of the attribute names it creates start with a single underscore to make them unique; others do not because they are potentially useful outside of the Tkinter implementation (e.g., `self.master`, `self.children`). Oddly, most of Tkinter still does not use the new Python "pseudo-private attributes" trick of prefixing attribute names with two leading underscores to automatically add the enclosing class's name, and thus localize them to the creating class. If Tkinter is ever rewritten to employ this feature, name clashes will be much less common in widget subclasses.

The End of the Tutorial

In this chapter, we have learned the core concepts of Python/Tkinter programming, and met a handful of simple widget objects along the way—labels, buttons, frames, and the packer geometry manager. We've seen enough to construct simple interfaces, but have really only scratched the surface of the Tkinter widget set.

In the next two chapters, we will apply what we've learned here to study the rest of the Tkinter library, and learn how to use it to generate the kinds of interfaces you expect to see in realistic GUI programs. As a preview and roadmap, Table 6-1 lists the kinds of widgets we'll meet there, in roughly their order of appearance. Note that this table lists only widget classes; along the way, we will also meet a few additional widget-related topics that don't appear in this table.

Table 6-1. Tkinter Widget Classes

Widget Class	Description
Label	A simple message area
Button	A simple labeled pushbutton widget
Frame	A container for attaching and arranging other widget objects
Toplevel, Tk	A new window managed by the window manager
Message	A multiline label
Entry	A simple single-line text-entry field
Checkbutton	A two-state button widget, typically used for multiple-choice selections
Radiobutton	A two-state button widget, typically used for single-choice selections
Scale	A slider widget with scalable positions
PhotoImage	An image object used for displaying full-color images on other widgets
BitmapImage	An image object used for displaying bitmap images on other widgets
Menu	A set of options associated with a Menubutton or top-level window
Menubutton	A button that opens a Menu of selectable options and submenus
Scrollbar	A control for scrolling other widgets (e.g., listbox, canvas, text)
Listbox	A list of selection names
Text	A multiline text browse/edit widget, with support for fonts, etc.
Canvas	A graphic drawing area, which supports lines, circles, photos, text, etc.

We've already met the Label, Button, and Frame in this chapter's tutorial. To make the remaining topics easier to absorb, they are split over the next two chapters: Chapter 7 covers the first widgets in this table up to but not including Menu, and Chapter 8 presents widgets lower in this table.

Besides the widget classes in this table, there are additional classes and tools in the Tkinter library, many of which we'll explore in the following two chapters as well:

Geometry management
   pack, grid, place

Tkinter linked variables
   StringVar, IntVar, DoubleVar, BooleanVar

Composite widgets
   Dialog, ScrolledText, OptionMenu

Scheduled callbacks
   Widget after, wait, and update methods

Other tools
   Standard dialogs, clipboard, bind and Event, widget configuration options, custom and modal dialogs, animation techniques

Most Tkinter widgets are familiar user interface devices. Some are remarkably rich in functionality. For instance, the Text class implements a sophisticated multiline text widget that supports fonts, colors, and special effects, and is powerful enough to implement a web browser, and the Canvas class provides extensive drawing tools powerful enough for image-processing applications. Beyond this, Tkinter extensions such as PMW add even richer widgets to a GUI programmer's toolbox.

Python/Tkinter for Tcl/Tk Converts

At the start of this chapter, I mentioned that Tkinter is Python's interface to the Tk GUI library, originally written for the Tcl language. To help readers migrating from Tcl to Python, and to summarize some of the main topics we met in this chapter, this section contrasts Python's Tk interface with Tcl's. This mapping also helps make Tk references written for other languages more useful to Python developers.

In general terms, Tcl's command-string view of the world differs widely from Python's object-based approach to programming. In terms of Tk programming, though, the syntactic differences are fairly small. Here are some of the main distinctions in Python's Tkinter interface:

Creation
   Widgets are created as class instance objects by calling a widget class.

Masters (parents)
   Parents are previously created objects, passed to widget-class constructors.

Widget options
   Options are constructor or config keyword arguments, or indexed keys.

Operations

Widget operations (actions) become Tkinter widget class object methods.

Callbacks

Callback handlers are any callable objects: function, method, lambda, etc.

Extension

Widgets are extended using Python class inheritance mechanisms.

Composition

Interfaces are constructed by attaching objects, not concatenating names.

Linked variables (next chapter)

Variables associated with widgets are Tkinter class objects with methods.

In Python, widget creation commands (e.g., `button`) are Python class names that start with an uppercase letter (e.g., `Button`), two-word widget operations (e.g., `add command`) become a single method name with an underscore (e.g., `add_command`), and the "configure" method can be abbreviated as "config" as in Tcl. In Chapter 7, we will also see that Tkinter "variables" associated with widgets take the form of class instance objects (e.g., `StringVar`, `IntVar`) with `get` and `set` methods, not simple Python or Tcl variable names. Table 6-2 shows some of the primary language mappings in more concrete terms.

Table 6-2. Tk to Tkinter Mappings

Operation	Tcl/Tk	Python/Tkinter
Creation	`frame .panel`	`panel = Frame()`
Masters	`button .panel.quit`	`quit = Button(panel)`
Options	`button .panel.go -fg black`	`go = Button(panel, fg='black')`
Configure	`.panel.go config -bg red`	`go.config(bg='red')` `go['bg'] = 'red'`
Actions	`.popup invoke`	`popup.invoke()`
Packing	`pack .panel -side left -fill x`	`panel.pack(side=LEFT, fill=X)`

Some of these differences are more than just syntactic, of course. For instance, Python builds an internal widget object tree based on parent arguments passed to widget constructors, without ever requiring concatenated widget pathname strings. Once you've made a widget object, you can use it directly by reference. Tcl coders can hide some dotted pathnames by manually storing them in variables, but that's not quite the same as Python's purely object-based model.

Once you've written a few Python/Tkinter scripts, though, the coding distinctions in the Python object world will probably seem trivial. At the same time, Python's support for OO techniques adds an entirely new component to Tk development; you get the same widgets, plus Python's support for code structure and reuse.

A Tkinter Tour, Part 1

"Widgets and Gadgets and GUIs, Oh My!"

This chapter is a continuation of our look at GUI programming in Python. The previous chapter used simple widgets to demonstrate the fundamentals of Tkinter coding in Python—buttons, labels, and the like. That was simple by design: it's easier to grasp the big GUI picture if widget interface details don't get in the way. But now that we've seen the basics, this chapter and the next move on to present a tour of more advanced widget objects and tools available in the Tkinter library.

As we'll find, this is where GUI scripting starts getting both practical and fun. In these two chapters we'll meet classes that build the interface devices you expect to see in real programs—sliders, checkboxes, menus, scrolled lists, dialogs, graphics, and so on. After these chapters, the last GUI chapter moves on to present larger GUIs that utilize the coding techniques and the interfaces shown in all prior GUI chapters. In these two chapters, though, examples are small and self-contained so that we can focus on widget details.

This Chapter's Topics

Technically, we've already used a handful of simple widgets in Chapter 6, *Graphical User Interfaces*. So far we've met `Label`, `Button`, `Frame`, and `Tk`, and studied `pack` geometry management concepts along the way. Although these are all basic, they are representative of Tkinter interfaces in general, and can be workhorses in typical GUIs. `Frame` containers, for instance, are the basis of hierarchical display layout.

In this and the following chapter, we'll explore additional options for widgets we've already seen, and move beyond the basics to cover the rest of the Tkinter widget set. Here are some of the widgets and topics we'll explore in this chapter:

- `Toplevel` and `Tk` widgets

- `Message` and `Entry` widgets

- `Checkbutton`, `Radiobutton`, and `Scale` widgets

- Images: `PhotoImage` and `BitmapImage` objects

- Dialogs: both standard and custom

- Widget configuration options

- Low-level event binding

- Tkinter variable objects

Chapter 8, *A Tkinter Tour, Part 2*, concludes the tour by presenting the remainder of the Tkinter library's tool set: menus, text, canvases, animation, and more.

To make this tour interesting, I'll also introduce a few notions of *component reuse* along the way. For instance, some later examples will be built using components written for prior examples. Although these two tour chapters introduce widget interfaces, this book is really about Python programming in general; as we'll see, Tkinter programming in Python can be much more than simply drawing circles and arrows.

Configuring Widget Appearance

So far, all the buttons and labels in examples have been rendered with a default look-and-feel that is standard for the underlying platform. That usually means gray on Windows, with my machine's color scheme. Tkinter widgets can be made to look arbitrarily different, though, using a handful of widget and packer options.

Because I generally can't resist the temptation to customize widgets in examples, I want to cover this topic early on the tour. Example 7-1 introduces some of the configuration options available in Tkinter.

Example 7-1. PP2E\Gui\Tour\config-label.py

```
from Tkinter import *
root = Tk()
labelfont = ('times', 20, 'bold')              # family, size, style
widget = Label(root, text='Hello config world')
widget.config(bg='black', fg='yellow')         # yellow text on black label
widget.config(font=labelfont)                  # use a larger font
widget.config(height=3, width=20)              # initial size: lines,chars
widget.pack(expand=YES, fill=BOTH)
root.mainloop()
```

Remember, we can call a widget's `config` method to reset its options at any time, instead of passing them all to the object's constructor. Here, we use it to set options that produce the window in Figure 7-1.

Figure 7-1. A custom label appearance

This may not be completely obvious unless you run this script on a real computer (alas, I can't show it in color here), but the label's text here shows up in yellow on a black background, and with a font that's very different from what we've seen so far. In fact, this script customizes the label in number of ways:

Color

By setting the `bg` option of the label widget here, its background is displayed in black; the `fg` option similarly changes the foreground (text) color of the widget to yellow. These color options work on most Tkinter widgets, and accept either a simple color name (e.g., `'blue'`) or a hexadecimal string. Most of the color names you are familiar with are supported (unless you happen to work for Crayola). You can also pass a hexadecimal color identifier string to these options to be more specific; they start with a `#` and name a color by its red, green, and blue saturations, with an equal number of bits in the string for each. For instance, `'#ff0000'` specifies eight bits per color, and defines pure red—"f" means four "1" bits in hexadecimal. We'll come back to this hex form when we meet the color selection dialog later in this chapter.

Size

The label is given a preset size in lines high and characters wide by setting its `height` and `width` attributes. You can use this setting to make the widget larger than the Tkinter geometry manager would by default.

Font

This script specifies a custom font for the label's text by setting the label's `font` attribute to a three-item tuple giving the font family, size, and style (here: Times, 20-point, and bold). Font style can be `normal`, `bold`, `roman`, `italic`, `underline`, `overstrike`, and combinations of these (e.g., "bold italic"). Tkinter guarantees that `Times`, `Courier`, and `Helvetica` font family names exist on all platforms, but others may work too (e.g., `system` gives the system font on Windows). Font settings like this work on all widgets with text, such as labels, buttons, entry fields, listboxes, and `Text` (the latter of which can display more than one font at once with "tags"). The `font` option still accepts older X-style font indicators—long strings with dashes and stars—but the new tuple font indicator form is more platform independent.

Layout and expansion

Finally, the label is made generally expandable and stretched by setting the **pack expand** and **fill** options we met in the last chapter; the label grows as the window does. If you maximize this window, its black background fills the whole screen and the yellow message is centered in the middle—try it.

In this script, the net effect of all these settings is that this label looks radically different then the ones we've been making so far. It no longer follows the Windows standard look-and-feel, but such conformance isn't always important. Tkinter provides additional ways to customize appearance, not used by this script:

Border and relief

A **bd=N** widget option can be used to set border width, and a **relief=S** option can specify a border style; S can be FLAT, SUNKEN, RAISED, GROOVE, SOLID, or RIDGE—all constants exported by the Tkinter module.

Cursor

A **cursor** option can be given to change the appearance of the mouse pointer when it moves over the widget. For instance, **cursor='gumby'** changes the pointer to a Gumby figure (the green kind). Other common cursor names used in this book include **watch**, **pencil**, **cross**, and **hand2**.

State

Some widgets also support the notion of a state, which impacts their appearance. For example, a **state=DISABLED** option will generally stipple (gray out) a widget on screen, and make it unresponsive; **NORMAL** does not.

Padding

Extra space can be added around many widgets (e.g., buttons, labels, and text) with the **padx=N** and **pady=N** options. Interestingly, you can set these options both in **pack** calls (where it adds empty space around the widget in general), and in a widget object itself (where it makes the widget larger).

To illustrate some of these extra settings, Example 7-2 configures the custom button captured in Figure 7-2 and changes the mouse pointer when above it.

Example 7-2. PP2E\Gui\Tour\config-button.py

```
from Tkinter import *
widget = Button(text='Spam', padx=10, pady=10)
widget.pack(padx=20, pady=20)
widget.config(cursor='gumby')
widget.config(bd=8, relief=RAISED)
widget.config(bg='dark green', fg='white')
widget.config(font=('helvetica', 20, 'underline italic'))
mainloop()
```

Figure 7-2. Config button at work

To see the effects generated by these two script's settings, try out a few changes on your computer. Most widgets can be given a custom appearance in the same way, and we'll see such options used repeatedly in this text. We'll also meet *operational* configurations, such as `focus` (for focusing input), and more. In fact, widgets can have dozens of options; most have reasonable defaults that produce a native look-and-feel on each windowing platform, and this is one reason for Tkinter's simplicity. But Tkinter lets you build more custom displays when you want to.

Toplevel Windows

Tkinter GUIs always have a *root* window, whether you get it by default or create it explicitly by calling the `Tk` object constructor. This main root window is the one that opens when your program runs, and is where you generally pack your most important widgets. In addition, Tkinter scripts can create any number of independent windows, generated and popped up on demand, by creating `Toplevel` widget objects.

Each `Toplevel` object created produces a new window on the display, and automatically adds it to the program's GUI event-loop processing stream (you don't need to call the `mainloop` method of new windows to activate them). Example 7-3 builds a root and two pop-up windows.

Example 7-3. PP2E\Gui\Tour\toplevel0.py

```python
import sys
from Tkinter import Toplevel, Button, Label

win1 = Toplevel()                  # two independent windows
win2 = Toplevel()                  # but part of same process

Button(win1, text='Spam', command=sys.exit).pack()
Button(win2, text='SPAM', command=sys.exit).pack()

Label(text='Popups').pack()        # on default Tk() root window
win1.mainloop()
```

The `toplevel0` script gets a root window by default (that's what the `Label` is attached to, since it doesn't specify a real parent), but also creates two standalone `Toplevel` windows that appear and function independently of the root window, as seen in Figure 7-3.

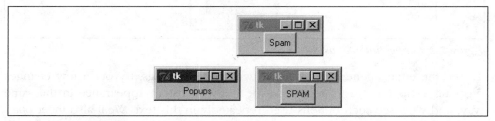

Figure 7-3. Two Toplevel windows and a root window

The two `Toplevel` windows on the right are full-fledged windows; they can be independently iconified, maximized, and so on. `Toplevel`s are typically used to implement multiple-window displays, and pop-up modal and nonmodal *dialogs* (more on dialogs in the next section). They stay up until explicitly destroyed, or the application that created them exits.

But it's important to know that although `Toplevel`s are independently active windows, they are not separate processes—if your program exits, all its windows are erased, including all `Toplevel` windows it may have created. We'll learn how to work around this rule later by launching independent GUI programs.

Toplevel and Tk Widgets

A `Toplevel` is roughly like a `Frame` that is split off into its own window, and has additional methods that allow you to deal with top-level window properties. The `Tk` widget is roughly like a `Toplevel`, but is used to represent the application root window. We got one for free in Example 7-3 because the `Label` had a default parent; in other scripts, we've made the `Tk` root more explicit by creating it directly like this:

```
root = Tk()
Label(root, text='Popups').pack()        # on explicit Tk() root window
root.mainloop()
```

In fact, because Tkinter GUIs are built as a hierarchy, you always get a root window by default, whether it is named explicitly like this or not. You should generally use the root to display top-level information of some sort—if you don't attach widgets to the root, it shows up as an odd empty window when you run your script. Technically, you can suppress the default root creation logic and make multiple root windows with the `Tk` widget, as in Example 7-4.

Example 7-4. PP2E\Gui\Tour\toplevel1.py

```
import Tkinter
from Tkinter import Tk, Button
Tkinter.NoDefaultRoot()

win1 = Tk()            # two independent root windows
win2 = Tk()

Button(win1, text='Spam', command=win1.destroy).pack()
Button(win2, text='SPAM', command=win2.destroy).pack()
win1.mainloop()
```

When run, this script displays the two pop-up windows of the screen shot in Figure 7-3 only (there is no third root window). But it's more common to use the Tk root as a main window, and create Toplevel widgets for an application's pop-up windows.

Top-Level Window Protocols

Both Tk and Toplevel widgets export extra methods and features tailored for their top-level role, as illustrated by Example 7-5.

Example 7-5. PP2E\Gui\Tour\toplevel2.py

```
###############################################################
# popup three new window, with style
# destroy() kills one window, quit() kills all windows and app;
# top-level windows have title, icon (on Unix), iconify/deiconify
# and protocol for wm events; there always is an app root window,
# whether by default or created as an explicit Tk() object; all
# top-level windows are containers, but never packed or gridded;
# Toplevel is like frame, but is a new window, and can have menu;
###############################################################

from Tkinter import *
root = Tk()                                         # explicit root

trees = [('The Larch!',            'light blue'),
         ('The Pine!',             'light green'),
         ('The Giant Redwood!',    'red')]

for (tree, color) in trees:
    win = Toplevel(root)                            # new window
    win.title('Sing...')                           # set border
    win.protocol('WM_DELETE_WINDOW', lambda:0)     # ignore close

    msg = Button(win, text=tree, command=win.destroy)   # kills one win
    msg.pack(expand=YES, fill=BOTH)
    msg.config(padx=10, pady=10, bd=10, relief=RAISED)
    msg.config(bg='black', fg=color, font=('times', 30, 'bold italic'))
```

Example 7-5. PP2E\Gui\Tour\toplevel2.py (continued)

```
root.title('Lumberjack demo')
Label(root, text='Main window', width=30).pack()
Button(root, text='Quit All', command=root.quit).pack()              # kills all app
root.mainloop()
```

This program adds widgets to the `Tk` root window, immediately pops up three `Toplevel` windows with attached buttons, and uses special top-level protocols. When run, it generates the scene captured in living black-and-white by Figure 7-4 (the buttons' text shows up blue, green, and red on a color display).

Figure 7-4. Three Toplevel windows with configurations

There are a few operational details worth noticing here, all of which are more obvious if you run this script on your machine:

Intercepting closes: protocol

> Because the window manager close event has been intercepted by this script using the top-level widget `protocol` method, pressing the X in the top-right corner doesn't do anything in the three `Toplevel` pop-ups. The name string `WM_DELETE_WINDOW` identifies the close operation. You can use this interface to disallow closes apart from the widgets your script creates—the function created by this script's `lambda:0` does nothing but return zero.

Killing one window: destroy

> Pressing the big black buttons in any one of the three pop-ups only kills that pop-up, because the pop-up runs the widget `destroy` method. The other windows live on, much as you would expect of a pop-up dialog window.

Killing all windows: quit

To kill all the windows at once and end the GUI application (really, its active `mainloop` call), the root window's button runs the `quit` method instead. Pressing the root window's button ends the application.

Window titles: title

As introduced in Chapter 6, top-level window widgets (`Tk` and `Toplevel`) have a `title` method that lets you change the text displayed on the top border. Here, the window title text is set to the string "Sing…" to override the default "tk".

Geometry management

Top-level windows are containers for other widgets, much like a standalone `Frame`. Unlike frames, though, top-level window widgets are never themselves packed (or gridded, or placed). To embed widgets, this script passes its windows as parent arguments to label and button constructors.

In addition, top-level window widgets support other kinds of protocols that we will utilize later on this tour:

State

The `iconify` and `withdraw` top-level widget methods allow scripts to hide and erase a window on the fly; `deiconify` redraws a hidden or erased window. The `state` method queries a window's state (it returns "iconic", "withdrawn", or "normal"), and `lift` and `lower` raise and lower a window with respect to others. See the alarm scripts near the end of Chapter 8 for usage.

Menus

Each top-level window can have its own window menus too; both the `Tk` and `Toplevel` widgets have a `menu` option used to associate a horizontal menu bar of pull-down option lists. This menu bar looks as it should on each platform on which your scripts are run. We'll explore menus early in Chapter 8.

Notice that this script passes its `Toplevel` constructor calls an explicit parent widget—the `Tk` root window (that is, `Toplevel(root)`). `Toplevel`s can be associated with a parent like other widgets, even though they are not visually embedded in their parents. I coded the script this way to avoid what seems like an odd feature; if coded instead like this:

```
win = Toplevel()                          # new window
```

If no `Tk` root yet exists, this call actually generates a *default* `Tk` root window to serve as the `Toplevel`'s parent, just like any other widget call without a parent argument. The problem is that this makes the position of the following line crucial:

```
root = Tk()                               # explicit root
```

If this line shows up *above* the `Toplevel` calls, it creates the single root window as expected. But if you move this line *below* the `Toplevel` calls, Tkinter creates a default `Tk` root window that is different than the one created by the script's explicit `Tk` call. You wind up with two `Tk` roots just as in Example 7-5. Move the `Tk` call below the `Toplevel` calls and rerun it to see what I mean—you'll get a fourth window that is completely empty! As a rule of thumb, to avoid such oddities, make your `Tk` root windows early and explicit.

All of the top-level protocol interfaces are only available on top-level window widgets, but you can often access them by going through other widgets' `master` attributes—links to the widget parents. For example, to set the title of a window in which a frame is contained, say something like this:

```
theframe.master.title('Spam demo')    # master is the container window
```

Naturally, you should only do so if you're sure that the frame will only be used in one kind of window. General-purpose attachable components coded as classes, for instance, should leave window property settings to their client applications.

Top-level widgets have additional tools, some of which we may not meet in this book. For instance, under Unix window managers, you can also call icon-related methods to change the bitmap used for top-level windows (`iconbitmask`), and set the name used on the window's icon (`iconname`). Because such icon options are only useful when scripts run on Unix, see other Tk and Tkinter resources for more details on this topic. For now, the next scheduled stop on this tour explores one of the more common uses of top-level windows.

Dialogs

Dialogs are windows popped up by a script to provide or request additional information. They come in two flavors, modal and nonmodal:

- *Modal* dialogs block the rest of the interface until the dialog window is dismissed; users must reply to the dialog before the program continues.

- *Nonmodal* dialogs can remain on screen indefinitely without interfering with other windows in the interface; they can usually accept inputs at any time.

Regardless of their modality, dialogs are generally implemented with the `Toplevel` window object we met in the prior section, whether you make the `Toplevel` or not. There are essentially three ways to present pop-up dialogs to users with Tkinter: by using common dialog calls, by using the now-dated `Dialog` object, and by creating custom dialog windows with `Toplevel`s and other kinds of widgets. Let's explore the basics of all three schemes.

Standard (Common) Dialogs

Because standard dialog calls are simpler, let's start here first. Tkinter comes with a collection of precoded dialog windows that implement many of the most common pop-ups programs generate—file selection dialogs, error and warning pop-ups, and question and answer prompts. They are called standard dialogs (and sometimes "common" dialogs), because they are part of the Tkinter library, and use platform-specific library calls to look like they should on each platform. A Tkinter file open dialog, for instance, looks like any other on Windows.

All standard dialog calls are modal (they don't return until the dialog box is dismissed by the user), and block the program's main window while displayed. Scripts can customize these dialogs' windows by passing message text, titles, and the like. Since they are so simple to use, let's jump right into Example 7-6.

Example 7-6. PP2E\Gui\Tour\dlg1.pyw

```
from Tkinter import *
from tkMessageBox import *

def callback():
    if askyesno('Verify', 'Do you really want to quit?'):
        showwarning('Yes', 'Quit not yet implemented')
    else:
        showinfo('No', 'Quit has been cancelled')

errmsg = 'Sorry, no Spam allowed!'
Button(text='Quit', command=callback).pack(fill=X)
Button(text='Spam', command=(lambda: showerror('Spam', errmsg))).pack(fill=X)
mainloop()
```

A lambda anonymous function is used here to wrap the call to **showerror**, so that it is passed two hardcoded arguments (remember, button press callbacks get no arguments from Tkinter itself). When run, this script creates the main window in Figure 7-5.

Figure 7-5. dlg1 main window: buttons to trigger pop-ups

Pressing this window's Quit button pops up the dialog in Figure 7-6, by calling the standard **askyesno** function in the **tkmessagebox** module. This looks different on Unix and Macintosh, but looks like you'd expect when run on Windows. This dialog blocks the program until the user clicks one of its buttons; if the dialog's Yes button is clicked (or the Enter key is pressed), the dialog call returns with a true value and the script pops up the standard dialog in Figure 7-7 by calling `showwarning`.

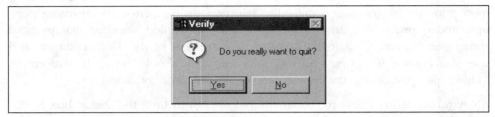

Figure 7-6. dlg1 askyesno dialog (Windows)

Figure 7-7. dlg1 showwarning dialog

There is nothing the user can do with Figure 7-7's dialog but press OK. If No is clicked in Figure 7-6's quit verification dialog, a `showinfo` call makes the pop-up in Figure 7-8 instead. Finally, if the Spam button is clicked in the main window, the standard dialog captured in Figure 7-9 is generated with the standard `showerror` call.

Figure 7-8. dlg1 showinfo dialog

Figure 7-9. dlg1 showerror dialog

This all makes for a lot of window pop-ups, of course, and you need to be careful not to rely on these dialogs too much (it's generally better to use input fields in long-lived windows, than to distract the user with pop-ups). But where appropriate, such pop-ups save coding time and provide a nice native look-and-feel.

A "smart" and reusable quit button

Let's put some of these canned dialogs to better use. Example 7-7 implements an attachable Quit button that uses standard dialogs to verify the quit request. Because it's a class, it can be attached and reused in any application that needs a verifying Quit button. Because it uses standard dialogs, it looks as it should on each GUI platform.

Example 7-7. PP2E\Gui\Tour\quitter.py

```
#############################################
# a quit button that verifies exit requests;
# to reuse, attach an instance to other guis
#############################################

from Tkinter import *                        # get widget classes
from tkMessageBox import askokcancel         # get canned std dialog

class Quitter(Frame):                        # subclass our GUI
    def __init__(self, parent=None):         # constructor method
        Frame.__init__(self, parent)
        self.pack()
        widget = Button(self, text='Quit', command=self.quit)
        widget.pack(side=LEFT)
    def quit(self):
        ans = askokcancel('Verify exit', "Really quit?")
        if ans: Frame.quit(self)

if __name__ == '__main__':  Quitter().mainloop()
```

This module is mostly meant to be used elsewhere, but puts up the button it implements when run standalone. Figure 7-10 shows the Quit button itself in the upper left, and the askokcancel verification dialog popped up when Quit is pressed.

If you press OK here, Quitter runs the Frame quit method to end the GUI to which this button is attached (really, the mainloop call). But to really understand how such a spring-loaded button can be useful, we need to move on to study a client GUI in the next section.

A dialog demo launcher bar

So far, we've seen a handful of standard dialogs, but there quite a few more. But rather than just throwing these up in dull screen shots, let's write a Python demo

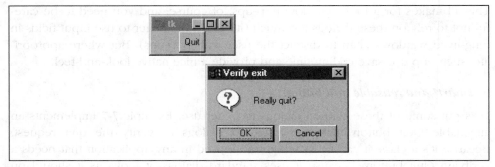

Figure 7-10. Quitter, with askokcancel dialog

script to generate them on demand. Here's one way to do it. First of all, in
Example 7-8 we write a module to define a table that maps a demo name to a
standard dialog call (and use lambda to wrap the call if we need to pass extra
arguments to the dialog function).

Example 7-8. PP2E\Gui\Tour\dialogTable.py

```
# define a name:callback demos table

from tkFileDialog    import askopenfilename        # get standard dialogs
from tkColorChooser import askcolor                # they live in Lib/lib-tk
from tkMessageBox    import askquestion, showerror
from tkSimpleDialog import askfloat

demos = {
    'Open':  askopenfilename,
    'Color': askcolor,
    'Query': lambda: askquestion('Warning', 'You typed "rm *"\nConfirm?'),
    'Error': lambda: showerror('Error!', "He's dead, Jim"),
    'Input': lambda: askfloat('Entry', 'Enter credit card number')
}
```

I put this table in a module so that it might be reused as the basis of other demo
scripts later (dialogs are more fun than printing to stdout). Next, we'll write a
Python script, Example 7-9, that simply generates buttons for all of this table's
entries—use its keys as button labels, and its values as button callback handlers.

Example 7-9. PP2E\Gui\Tour\demoDlg.py

```
from Tkinter import *            # get base widget set
from dialogTable import demos    # button callback handlers
from quitter import Quitter      # attach a quit object to me

class Demo(Frame):
    def __init__(self, parent=None):
        Frame.__init__(self, parent)
        self.pack()
        Label(self, text="Basic demos").pack()
```

Example 7-9. PP2E\Gui\Tour\demoDlg.py (continued)

```
    for (key, value) in demos.items():
        Button(self, text=key, command=value).pack(side=TOP, fill=BOTH)
    Quitter(self).pack(side=TOP, fill=BOTH)

if __name__ == '__main__': Demo().mainloop()
```

This script creates the window shown in Figure 7-11 when run as a standalone program; it's a bar of demo buttons, that simply route control back to the values of the table in module `dialogTable` when pressed.

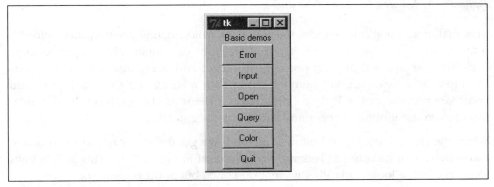

Figure 7-11. demoDlg main window

Notice that because this script is driven by the contents of the `dialogTable` module's dictionary, we can change the set of demo buttons displayed by changing just `dialogTable` (we don't need to change any executable code in `demoDlg`). Also note that the Quit button here is an attached instance of the `Quitter` class of the prior section—it's at least one bit of code that you never have to write again.

We've already seen some of the dialogs triggered by this demo bar window's other buttons, so I'll just step through the new ones here. Pressing the main window's Query button, for example, generates the standard pop-up in Figure 7-12.

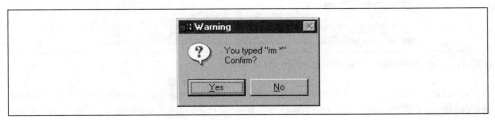

Figure 7-12. demoDlg query, askquestion dialog

This `askquestion` dialog looks like the `askyesno` we saw earlier, but actually returns either string "yes" or "no" (`askyesno` and `askokcancel` return 1 or 0, true or false). Pressing the demo bar's Input button generates the standard `askfloat` dialog box shown in Figure 7-13.

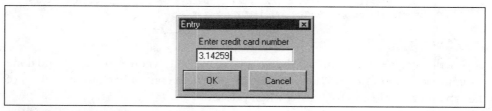

Figure 7-13. demoDlg input, askfloat dialog

This dialog automatically checks the input for valid floating-point syntax before it returns, and is representative of a collection of single-value input dialogs (`askinteger` and `askstring` prompt for integer and string inputs too). It returns the input as a floating-point number object (not a string) on the OK button and enter key presses, or the Python **None** object if the user clicks Cancel. Its two relatives return the input as integer and string objects instead.

When the demo bar's Open button is pressed, we get the standard file open dialog made by calling `askopenfilename`, and captured in Figure 7-14. This is Windows look-and-feel; it looks radically different on Linux, but appropriately so.

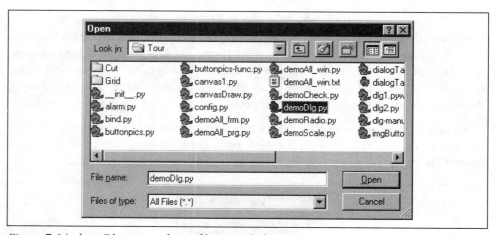

Figure 7-14. demoDlg open, askopenfilename dialog

A similar dialog for selecting a save-as filename is produced by calling `asksaveasfilename` (see the **Text** widget section under "Text" in Chapter 8 for an example). Both file dialogs let the user navigate through the filesystem to select a subject filename, returned with its full directory pathname when Open is pressed; an empty string comes back if Cancel is pressed instead. Both also have additional protocols not demonstrated by this example:

- They can be passed a `filetypes` keyword argument—a set of name patterns used to select files, that appear in the "Files of type" pulldown at the bottom of the dialog.

- They can be passed an `initialdir` (start directory), `initialfile` (for "File name"), `title` (for the dialog window), `defaultextension` (appended if the selection has none), and `parent` (to appear as an embedded child, instead of a pop-up dialog).

- They can be made to remember the last directory selected, by using exported objects instead of these function calls.

We'll use most of these interfaces later in the book, especially for the file dialogs in the PyEdit example in Chapter 9, *Larger GUI Examples* (but feel free to flip ahead for more details now). Finally, the demo bar's Color button triggers a standard `askcolor` call, which generates the standard color selection dialog shown in Figure 7-15.

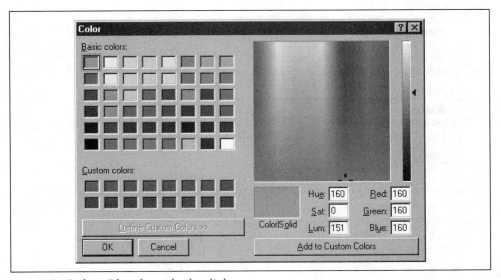

Figure 7-15. demoDlg color, askcolor dialog

If you press its OK button it returns a data structure the identifies the selected color, which can be used in all color contexts in Tkinter. It includes RGB values and a hexadecimal color string (e.g., `((160, 160, 160), '#a0a0a0')`). More on how this tuple can be useful in a moment. If you press Cancel, the script gets back a tuple containing two nones (Nones of the Python variety, that is).

Printing dialog results (and passing callback data with lambdas)

The dialog demo launcher bar displays standard dialogs, and can be made to display others by simply changing the `dialogTable` module it imports. As coded, though, it really only *shows* dialogs; it would also be nice to see their return values so we know how to use them in scripts. Example 7-10 adds printing of standard dialog results to the `stdout` standard output stream.

Example 7-10. PP2E\Gui\Tour\demoDlg-print.py

```
###################################################
# same, but show returns values of dialog calls;
# the lambda saves data from the local scope to be
# passed to the handler (button handlers normally
# get no args) and works like this def statement:
# def func(self=self, name=key): self.printit(name)
###################################################

from Tkinter import *              # get base widget set
from dialogTable import demos      # button callback handlers
from quitter import Quitter        # attach a quit object to me

class Demo(Frame):
    def __init__(self, parent=None):
        Frame.__init__(self, parent)
        self.pack()
        Label(self, text="Basic demos").pack()
        for (key, value) in demos.items():
            func = (lambda self=self, name=key: self.printit(name))
            Button(self, text=key, command=func).pack(side=TOP, fill=BOTH)
        Quitter(self).pack(side=TOP, fill=BOTH)
    def printit(self, name):
        print name, 'returns =>', demos[name]()        # fetch, call, print

if __name__ == '__main__': Demo().mainloop()
```

This script builds the same main button-bar window, but notice that the callback handler is an anonymous function made with a lambda now, not a direct reference to dialog calls in the imported `dialogTable` dictionary:

```
func = (lambda self=self, name=key: self.printit(name))
```

This is the first time we've actually used lambda like this, so let's get the facts straight. Because button press callbacks are run with no arguments, if we need to pass extra data to the handler it must be wrapped in an object that remembers that extra data and passes it along. Here, a button press runs the function generated by the lambda—an indirect call layer that retains information from the enclosing scope by assigning it to default arguments. The net effect is that the real handler, `printit`, receives an extra `name` argument giving the demo associated with the button pressed, even though this argument wasn't passed back from Tkinter itself.

Notice, though, that this lambda assigns both `self` and `key` to defaults, to retain them for use on callbacks. Like all functions, lambda results only have access to their local scope, the enclosing global module scope, and the built-in names scope—not the local scope of the method function that created them, and that is where name `self` really lives. Because *bound methods* remember both a `self` object and a method function, this lambda could also be written like this:

```
func = (lambda handler=self.printit, name=key: handler(name))
```

You can also use a callable class object here that retains state as instance attributes (see the tutorial's `__call__` example in Chapter 6 for hints). But as a rule of thumb, if you want a lambda's result to use any names from the enclosing scope when later called, simply pass them in as defaults.

When run, this script prints dialog return values; here is the output after clicking all the demos buttons in the main window, and picking both Cancel/No and OK/Yes buttons in each dialog:

```
C:\...\PP2E\Gui\Tour>python demoDlg-print.py
Error returns => ok
Input returns => None
Input returns => 3.14159
Open returns =>
Open returns => C:/PP2ndEd/examples/PP2E/Gui/Tour/demoDlg-print.py
Query returns => no
Query returns => yes
Color returns => (None, None)
Color returns => ((160, 160, 160), '#a0a0a0')
```

Now that I've shown you these dialog results, I want to next show you how one of them can actually be useful.

Letting users select colors on the fly

The standard color selection dialog isn't just another pretty face—scripts can pass the hexadecimal color string it returns to the `bg` and `fg` widget color configuration options we met earlier. That is, `bg` and `fg` accept both a color name (e.g., "blue") and an `askcolor` result strings that starts with a # (e.g., the #a0a0a0 in the last output line of the prior section).

This adds another dimension of customization to Tkinter GUIs: Rather than hard-coding colors in your GUI products, you can provide a button that pops up color selectors that let users choose color preferences on the fly. Simply pass the color string to widget `config` methods in callback handlers, as in Example 7-11.

Example 7-11. PP2E\Gui\Tour\setcolor.py

```
from Tkinter import *
from tkColorChooser import askcolor

def setBgColor():
```

Example 7-11. PP2E\Gui\Tour\setcolor.py (continued)

```
    (triple, hexstr) = askcolor()
    if hexstr:
        print hexstr
        push.config(bg=hexstr)

root = Tk()
push = Button(root, text='Set Background Color', command=setBgColor)
push.config(height=3, font=('times', 20, 'bold'))
push.pack(expand=YES, fill=BOTH)
root.mainloop()
```

This script makes the window in Figure 7-16 when launched (its button's background is a sort of green, but you'll have to trust me on this). Pressing the button pops up the color selection dialog shown earlier; the color you pick in that dialog becomes the background color of this button after you press OK.

Figure 7-16. setcolor main window

Color strings are also printed to the stdout stream (the console window); run this on your computer to experiment with available color settings:

```
C:\...\PP2E\Gui\Tour>python setcolor.py
#c27cc5
#5fe28c
#69d8cd
```

Other standard dialog calls

We've seen most of the standard dialogs and will use these pop-ups in examples throughout the rest of this book. But for more details on other calls and options available, either consult other Tkinter documentation, or browse the source code of the modules used at the top of the dialogTable module; all are simple Python files installed in the *lib-tk* subdirectory of the Python source library on your machine. And keep this demo bar example filed away for future reference; we'll reuse it later in the tour when we meet other button-like widgets.

The Old-Style Dialog Module

In older Python code, you may see dialogs occasionally coded with the standard Dialog module. This is a bit dated now, and uses an X Windows look-and-feel; but just in case you run across such code in your Python maintenance excursions, Example 7-12 gives you a feel for the interface.

Example 7-12. PP2E\Gui\Tour\dlg-old.py

```
from Tkinter import *
from Dialog import Dialog

class OldDialogDemo(Frame):
    def __init__(self, master=None):
        Frame.__init__(self, master)
        Pack.config(self)  # same as self.pack()
        Button(self, text='Pop1', command=self.dialog1).pack()
        Button(self, text='Pop2', command=self.dialog2).pack()
    def dialog1(self):
        ans = Dialog(self,
                     title  = 'Popup Fun!',
                     text   = 'An example of a popup-dialog '
                              'box, using older "Dialog.py".',
                     bitmap = 'questhead',
                     default = 0, strings = ('Yes', 'No', 'Cancel'))
        if ans.num == 0: self.dialog2()
    def dialog2(self):
        Dialog(self, title  = 'HAL-9000',
                     text   = "I'm afraid I can't let you do that, Dave...",
                     bitmap = 'hourglass',
                     default = 0, strings = ('spam', 'SPAM'))

if __name__ == '__main__': OldDialogDemo().mainloop()
```

You supply `Dialog` a tuple of button labels and a message, and get back the index of the button pressed (the leftmost is index zero). `Dialog` windows are modal: the rest of the application's windows are disabled until the `Dialog` receives a response from the user. When you press the Pop2 button in the main window created by this script, the second dialog pops up, as shown in Figure 7-17.

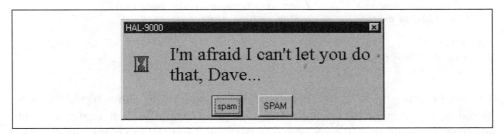

Figure 7-17. Old-style dialog

This is running on Windows, and as you can see, is nothing like what you would expect on that platform for a question dialog. In fact, this dialog generates an X Windows look-and-feel, regardless of the underlying platform. Because of both `Dialog`'s appearance and the extra complexity required to program it, you are probably better off using the standard dialog calls of the prior section instead.

Custom Dialogs

The dialogs we've seen so far all have a standard appearance and interaction. They are fine for many purposes, but often we need something a bit more custom. For example, *forms* that request multiple field inputs (e.g., name, age, shoe size) aren't directly addressed by the common dialog library. We could pop-up one single-input dialog in turn for each requested field, but that isn't exactly user-friendly.

Custom dialogs support arbitrary interfaces, but they are also the most complicated to program. Even so, there's not much to it—simply create a pop-up window as a `Toplevel` with attached widgets, and arrange a callback handler to fetch user inputs entered in the dialog (if any) and destroy the window. To make such a custom dialog modal, we also need to wait for a reply, by giving the window input focus, making other windows inactive, and waiting for an event. Example 7-13 illustrates the basics.

Example 7-13. PP2E\Gui\Tour\dlg-custom.py

```python
import sys
from Tkinter import *
makemodal = (len(sys.argv) > 1)

def dialog():
    win = Toplevel()                                        # make a new window
    Label(win,  text='Hard drive reformatted!').pack()      # add a few widgets
    Button(win, text='OK', command=win.destroy).pack()      # set destroy callback
    if makemodal:
        win.focus_set()             # take over input focus,
        win.grab_set()              # disable other windows while I'm open,
        win.wait_window()           # and wait here until win destroyed
    print 'dialog exit'             # else returns right away

root = Tk()
Button(root, text='popup', command=dialog).pack()
root.mainloop()
```

This script is set up to create a pop-up dialog window in either modal or non-modal mode, depending on its `makemodal` global variable. If it is run with no command-line arguments, it picks nonmodal style, captured in Figure 7-18.

The window in the upper right is the root window here; pressing its "popup" button creates a new pop-up dialog window. Because dialogs are nonmodal in this mode, the root window remains active after a dialog is popped up. In fact, non-modal dialogs never block other windows, so you can keep pressing the root's button to generate as many copies of the pop-up window as will fit on your screen. Any or all of the pop-ups can be killed by pressing their OK buttons, without killing other windows in this display.

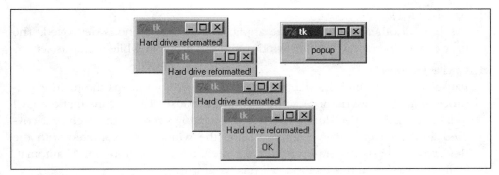

Figure 7-18. Nonmodal custom dialogs at work

Making custom dialogs modal

Now, when the script is run with a command-line argument (e.g., `python dlg-custom.py 1`), it makes its pop-ups modal instead. Because modal dialogs grab all of the interface's attention, the main window becomes inactive in this mode until the pop-up is killed; you can't even click on it to reactivate it while the dialog is open. Because of that, you can never make more than one copy of the pop-up on screen at once, as shown in Figure 7-19.

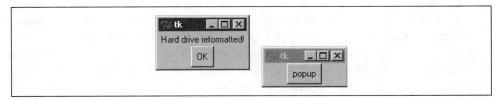

Figure 7-19. A modal custom dialog at work

In fact, the call to the `dialog` function in this script doesn't return until the dialog window on the left is dismissed by pressing its OK button. The net effect is that modal dialogs impose a function call–like model on an otherwise event-driven programming model—user inputs can be processed right away, not in a callback handler triggered at some arbitrary point in the future.

Forcing such a linear control flow on a GUI takes a bit of extra work, though. The secret to locking other windows and waiting for a reply boils down to three lines of code, which are a general pattern repeated in most custom modal dialogs:

`win.focus_set()`
> Makes the window take over the application's input focus, as if it had been clicked with the mouse to make it the active window. This method is also known by synonym `focus`, and it's also common to set the focus on an input widget within the dialog (e.g., an `Entry`) rather than the entire window.

`win.grab_set()`

> Disables all other windows in the application until this one is destroyed. The
> user cannot interact with other windows in the program while a grab is set.

`win.wait_window()`

> Pauses the caller until the `win` widget is destroyed, but keeps the main event-
> processing loop (`mainloop`) active during the pause. That means that the GUI
> at large remains active during the wait; its windows redraw themselves if cov-
> ered and uncovered, for example. When the window is destroyed with the
> `destroy` method, it is erased from the screen, the application grab is automat-
> ically released, and this method call finally returns.

Because the script waits for a window destroy event, it must also arrange for a callback handler to destroy the window in response to interaction with widgets in the
dialog window (the only window active). This example's dialog is simply informational, so its OK button calls the window's `destroy` method. In user-input dialogs,
we might instead install an Enter key-press callback handler that fetches data typed
into an `Entry` widget, and then calls `destroy` (see later in this chapter).

Other ways to be modal

Modal dialogs are typically implemented by waiting for a newly created pop-up
window's `destroy` event, as in this example. But other schemes are viable too.
For example, it's possible to create dialog windows ahead of time, and show and
hide them as needed with the top-level window's `deiconify` and `withdraw`
methods (see the alarm scripts in Chapter 8 under "Time Tools, Threads, and Animation" for details). Given that window creation speed is generally fast enough as
to appear instantaneous today, this is much less common than making and
destroying a window from scratch on each interaction.

It's also possible to implement a modal state by waiting for a Tkinter *variable* to
change its value, instead of waiting for a window to be destroyed. See this chapter's discussion of Tkinter variables (which are class objects, not normal Python
variables) and the `wait_variable` method discussed near the end of Chapter 8
for more details. This scheme allows a long-lived dialog box's callback handler to
signal a state change to a waiting main program, without having to destroy the
dialog box.

Finally, if you call the `mainloop` method recursively, the call won't return until the
widget `quit` method has been invoked. The `quit` method terminates a `mainloop`
call, and so normally ends a GUI program. But it will simply exit a recursive
`mainloop` level if one is active. Because of this, modal dialogs can also be written
without wait method calls if you are careful. For instance, Example 7-14 works the
same as `dlg-custom`.

Example 7-14. PP2E\Gui\Tour\dlg-recursive.py

```
from Tkinter import *

def dialog():
    win = Toplevel()                                # make a new window
    Label(win,  text='Hard drive reformatted!').pack()  # add a few widgets
    Button(win, text='OK', command=win.quit).pack()     # set quit callback
    win.protocol('WM_DELETE_WINDOW', win.quit)          # quit on wm close too!

    win.focus_set()          # take over input focus,
    win.grab_set()           # disable other windows while I'm open,
    win.mainloop()           # and start a nested event loop to wait
    win.destroy()
    print 'dialog exit'

root = Tk()
Button(root, text='popup', command=dialog).pack()
root.mainloop()
```

If you go this route, be sure to call `quit` instead of `destroy` in dialog callback handlers (`destroy` doesn't terminate the `mainloop` level), and be sure to use `protocol` to make the window border close button call `quit` too (or else it doesn't end the recursive `mainloop` level call, and will generate odd error messages when your program finally exits). Because of this extra complexity, you're probably better off using `wait_window` or `wait_variable`, not recursive `mainloop` calls.

We'll see how to build form-like dialogs with labels and input fields later in this chapter when we meet `Entry`, and again when we study the `grid` manager in Chapter 8. For more custom dialog examples, see ShellGui (Chapter 9), PyMailGui (Chapter 11), PyCalc (Chapter 18), and the nonmodal *form.py* (Chapter 10). Here, we're moving on to learn more about events that will prove to be useful currency at later tour destinations.

Binding Events

We met the `bind` widget method in the last chapter, when we used it to catch button presses in the tutorial. Because bind is commonly used in conjunction with other widgets (e.g., to catch return key presses for input boxes), we're going to make a stop early on the tour here as well. Example 7-15 illustrates more `bind` event protocols.

Example 7-15. PP2E\Gui\Tour\bind.py

```
from Tkinter import *

def showPosEvent(event):
    print 'Widget=%s X=%s Y=%s' % (event.widget, event.x, event.y)
```

Example 7-15. PP2E\Gui\Tour\bind.py (continued)

```python
def showAllEvent(event):
    print event
    for attr in dir(event):
        print attr, '=>', getattr(event, attr)

def onKeyPress(event):
    print 'Got key press:', event.char

def onArrowKey(event):
    print 'Got up arrow key press'

def onReturnKey(event):
    print 'Got return key press'

def onLeftClick(event):
    print 'Got left mouse button click:',
    showPosEvent(event)

def onRightClick(event):
    print 'Got right mouse button click:',
    showPosEvent(event)

def onMiddleClick(event):
    print 'Got middle mouse button click:',
    showPosEvent(event)
    showAllEvent(event)

def onLeftDrag(event):
    print 'Got left mouse button drag:',
    showPosEvent(event)

def onDoubleLeftClick(event):
    print 'Got double left mouse click',
    showPosEvent(event)
    tkroot.quit()

tkroot = Tk()
labelfont = ('courier', 20, 'bold')               # family, size, style
widget = Label(tkroot, text='Hello bind world')
widget.config(bg='red', font=labelfont)           # red background, large font
widget.config(height=5, width=20)                 # initial size: lines,chars
widget.pack(expand=YES, fill=BOTH)

widget.bind('<Button-1>',   onLeftClick)          # mouse button clicks
widget.bind('<Button-3>',   onRightClick)
widget.bind('<Button-2>',   onMiddleClick)        # middle=both on some mice
widget.bind('<Double-1>',   onDoubleLeftClick)    # click left twice
widget.bind('<B1-Motion>',  onLeftDrag)           # click left and move

widget.bind('<KeyPress>',   onKeyPress)           # all keyboard presses
widget.bind('<Up>',         onArrowKey)           # arrow button pressed
widget.bind('<Return>',     onReturnKey)          # return/enter key pressed
widget.focus()                                    # or bind keypress to tkroot
tkroot.title('Click Me')
tkroot.mainloop()
```

Most of this file consists of callback handler functions triggered when bound events occur. As we learned in Chapter 6, these callbacks all receive an event object argument that gives details about the event that fired. Technically, this argument is an instance of the Tkinter **Event** class, and its details are attributes; most of the callbacks simply trace events by displaying relevant event attributes.

When run, this script makes the window shown in Figure 7-20; it's mostly intended just as a surface for clicking and pressing event triggers.

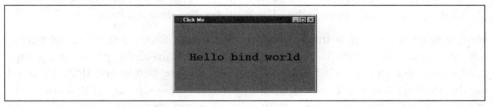

Figure 7-20. A bind window for the clicking

The black-and-white medium of the book you're holding won't really do justice to this script—when run live, it uses the configuration options shown earlier to make the window show up as black on red, with a large Courier font. You'll have to take my word for it (or run this on your own).

But the main point of this example is to demonstrate other kinds of event binding protocols at work. We saw a script that intercepted left and double-left mouse-clicks with the widget **bind** method earlier; the script here demonstrates other kinds of events that are commonly caught with **bind**:

<KeyPress>

To catch the press of a single key on the keyboard, register a handler for the **<KeyPress>** event identifier; this is a low-level way to input data in GUI programs than the **Entry** widget covered in the next section. The key pressed is returned in ASCII form in the event object passed to the callback handler (**event.char**). Other attributes in the event structure identify the key pressed in lower-level detail. Key presses can be intercepted by the top-level root window widget or a widget that has been assigned keyboard focus with the **focus** method used by this script.

<B1-Motion>

This script also catches mouse motion while a button is held down: the registered **<B1-Motion>** event handler is called every time the mouse is moved while the left button is pressed, and receives the current X/Y coordinates of the mouse pointer in its event argument (**event.x**, **event.y**). Such information can be used to implement object moves, drag-and-drop, pixel-level painting, and so on (e.g., see the PyDraw examples in Chapter 9).

<Button-3>, <Button-2>

This script also catches right and middle mouse button clicks (known as buttons 3 and 2). To make the middle button 2 click work on a two-button mouse, try clicking both buttons at the same time; if that doesn't work, check your mouse setting in your properties interface (Control Panel on Windows).

<Return>, <Up>

To catch more specific kinds of key presses, this script registers for the Return/ Enter and up-arrow key press events; these events would otherwise be routed to the general <KeyPress> handler, and require event analysis.

Here is what shows up in the stdout output stream, after a left click, right click, left click and drag, a few key presses, a Return and up-arrow press, and a final double-left click to exit. When you press the left mouse button and drag it around on the display, you'll get lots of drag event messages—one is printed for every move during the drag (and one Python callback is run for each):

```
C:\...\PP2E\Gui\Tour>python bind.py
Got left mouse button click: Widget=.7871632 X=209 Y=79
Got right mouse button click: Widget=.7871632 X=209 Y=79
Got left mouse button click: Widget=.7871632 X=83 Y=63
Got left mouse button drag: Widget=.7871632 X=83 Y=65
Got left mouse button drag: Widget=.7871632 X=84 Y=66
Got left mouse button drag: Widget=.7871632 X=85 Y=66
Got left mouse button drag: Widget=.7871632 X=85 Y=67
Got left mouse button drag: Widget=.7871632 X=85 Y=68
Got key press: s
Got key press: p
Got key press: a
Got key press: m
Got key press: 1
Got key press: -
Got key press: 2
Got key press: .
Got return key press
Got up arrow key press
Got left mouse button click: Widget=.7871632 X=85 Y=68
Got double left mouse click Widget=.7871632 X=85 Y=68
```

For mouse-related events, callbacks print the X and Y coordinates of the mouse pointer, in the event object passed in. Coordinates are usually measured in pixels from the upper-left corner (0,0), but are relative to the widget being clicked. Here's what is printed for a left, middle, and double-left click. Notice that the middle-click callback dumps the entire argument—all of the Event object's attributes. Different event types set different event attributes; most key presses put something in char, for instance:

```
C:\...\PP2E\Gui\Tour>python bind.py
Got left mouse button click: Widget=.7871632 X=163 Y=18
```

```
Got middle mouse button click: Widget=.7871632 X=152 Y=110
<Tkinter.Event instance at 7b3640>
char => ??
height => 0
keycode => 2
keysym => ??
keysym_num => 2
num => 2
send_event => 0
serial => 14
state => 0
time => 5726238
type => 4
widget => .7871632
width => 0
x => 152
x_root => 156
y => 110
y_root => 133
Got left mouse button click: Widget=.7871632 X=152 Y=110
Got double left mouse click Widget=.7871632 X=152 Y=110
```

Besides the ones illustrated in this example, there are additional kinds of bindable events that a Tkinter script can register to catch. For example:

- `<ButtonRelease>` fires when a button is released (`<ButtonPress>` is run when the button first goes down).

- `<Motion>` is triggered when a mouse pointer is moved.

- `<Enter>` and `<Leave>` handlers intercept mouse entry and exit in a window's display area (useful for automatically highlighting a widget).

- `<Configure>` is invoked when the window is resized, repositioned, and so on (e.g., the event object's `width` and `height` give the new window size).

- `<Destroy>` is invoked when the window widget is destroyed (and differs from the `protocol` mechanism for window manager close button presses).

- `<FocusIn>` and `<FocusOut>` are run as the widget gains and loses focus.

- `<Map>` and `<Unmap>` are run when a window is opened and iconified.

- `<Escape>`, `<BackSpace>`, and `<Tab>` catch other special key presses.

- `<Down>`, `<Left>`, and `<Right>` catch other arrow key presses.

This is not a complete list, and event names can be written with a somewhat sophisticated syntax all their own. For example:

- *Modifiers* can be added to event identifiers to make them even more specific; for instance, `<B1-Motion>` means moving the mouse with the left button pressed, and `<KeyPress-a>` refers to pressing the "a" key only.

- *Synonyms* can be used for some common event names; for instance, <ButtonPress-1>, <Button-1>, and <1> all mean a left mouse button press, and <KeyPress-a> and <Key-a> both mean the "a" key. All forms are case-sensitive: use <Key-Escape>, not <KEY-ESCAPE>.

- *Virtual* event identifiers can be defined within double bracket pairs (e.g., <<PasteText>>) to refer to a selection of one or more event sequences.

In the interest of space, though, we'll defer to other Tk and Tkinter reference sources for an exhaustive list of details on this front. Alternatively, changing some of the settings in the example script and rerunning can help clarify some event behavior too; this is Python, after all.

Message and Entry

The Message and Entry widgets allow for display and input of simple text. Both are essentially functional subsets of the Text widget we'll meet later—Text can do everything Message and Entry can, but not vice versa.

Message

The Message widget is simply a place to display text. Although the standard showinfo dialog we met earlier is perhaps a better way to display pop-up messages, Message splits up long strings automatically and flexibly, and can be embedded inside container widgets anytime you need to add some read-only text to a display. Moreover, this widget sports over a dozen configuration options that let you customize its appearance. Example 7-16 and Figure 7-21 illustrate Message basics; see a Tk or Tkinter reference for other options it supports.

Example 7-16. PP2E\Gui\tour\message.py

```
from Tkinter import *
msg = Message(text="Oh by the way, which one's Pink?")
msg.config(bg='pink', font=('times', 16, 'italic'))
msg.pack()
mainloop()
```

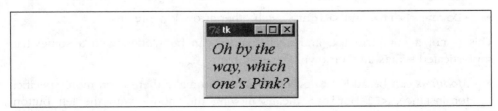

Figure 7-21. A Message widget at work

Entry

The Entry widget is a simple, single-line text input field. It is typically used for
input fields in form-like dialogs, and anywhere else you need the user to type a
value into a field of a larger display. Entry also supports advanced concepts such
as scrolling, key bindings for editing, and text selections, but it's simple to use in
practice. Example 7-17 builds the input window shown in Figure 7-22.

Example 7-17. PP2E\Gui\tour\entry1.py

```
from Tkinter import *
from quitter import Quitter

def fetch():
    print 'Input => "%s"' % ent.get()              # get text

root = Tk()
ent = Entry(root)
ent.insert(0, 'Type words here')                    # set text
ent.pack(side=TOP, fill=X)                           # grow horiz

ent.focus()                                          # save a click
ent.bind('<Return>', (lambda event: fetch()))       # on enter key
btn = Button(root, text='Fetch', command=fetch)     # and on button
btn.pack(side=LEFT)
Quitter(root).pack(side=RIGHT)
root.mainloop()
```

Figure 7-22. entry1 caught in the act

On startup, the entry1 script fills the input field in this GUI with the text "Type
words here" by calling the widget's insert method. Because both the Fetch button and the Enter key are set to trigger the script's fetch callback function, either
user event gets and displays the current text in the input field, using the widget's
get method:

```
C:\...\PP2E\Gui\Tour>python entry1.py
Input => "Type words here"
Input => "Have a cigar"
```

We met the <Return> event earlier when we studied bind; unlike button presses,
these lower-level callbacks get an event argument, so the script uses a lambda
wrapper to ignore it. This script also packs the entry field with fill=X to make it

expand horizontally with the window (try it out), and calls the widget `focus` method to give the entry field input focus when the window first appears. Manually setting the focus like this saves the user from having to click the input field before typing.

Programming Entry widgets

Generally speaking, the values typed into and displayed by `Entry` widgets are set and fetched with either tied "variable" objects (described later in this chapter), or with `Entry` widget method calls like this:

```
ent.insert(0, 'some text')         # set value
value = ent.get()                  # fetch value (a string)
```

The first parameter to the `insert` method gives the position where the text is to be inserted. Here, "0" means the front because offsets start at zero, and integer `0` and string `'0'` mean the same thing (Tkinter method arguments are always converted to strings if needed). If the `Entry` widget might already contain text, you also generally need to delete its contents before setting it to a new value, or else new text will be simply added to the text already present:

```
ent.delete(0, END)                 # first, delete from start to end
ent.insert(0, 'some text')         # then set value
```

The name `END` here is a preassigned Tkinter constant denoting the end of the widget; we'll revisit it in Chapter 8 when we meet the full-blown and multiple-line `Text` widget (`Entry`'s more powerful cousin). Since the widget is empty after the deletion, this statement sequence is equivalent to the prior:

```
ent.delete('0', END)               # delete from start to end
ent.insert(END, 'some text')       # add at end of empty text
```

Either way, if you don't delete the text first, new text inserted is simply added. If you want to see how, try changing the `fetch` function to look like this—an "x" is added at the front and end of the input field on each button or key press:

```
def fetch():
    print 'Input => "%s"' % ent.get()     # get text
    ent.insert(END, 'x')                   # to clear: ent.delete('0', END)
    ent.insert(0, 'x')                     # new text simply added
```

In later examples, we'll also see the `Entry` widget's `state='disabled'` option, which makes it read-only, as well as its `show='*'` option, which makes it display each character as a `*` (useful for password-type inputs). Try this out on your own by changing and running this script, for a quick look. `Entry` supports other options we'll skip here too; see later examples and other resources for additional details.

Laying out input forms

As mentioned, `Entry` widgets are often used to get field values in form-like displays. We're going to create such displays often in this book, but to show you how this works in simpler terms, Example 7-18 combines labels and entries to achieve the multiple-input display captured in Figure 7-23.

Example 7-18. PP2E\Gui\Tour\entry2.py

```
# use Entry widgets directly and layout by rows

from Tkinter import *
from quitter import Quitter
fields = 'Name', 'Job', 'Pay'

def fetch(entries):
    for entry in entries:
        print 'Input => "%s"' % entry.get()         # get text

def makeform(root, fields):
    entries = []
    for field in fields:
        row = Frame(root)                            # make a new row
        lab = Label(row, width=5, text=field)        # add label, entry
        ent = Entry(row)
        row.pack(side=TOP, fill=X)                   # pack row on top
        lab.pack(side=LEFT)
        ent.pack(side=RIGHT, expand=YES, fill=X)     # grow horizontal
        entries.append(ent)
    return entries

if __name__ == '__main__':
    root = Tk()
    ents = makeform(root, fields)
    root.bind('<Return>', (lambda event, e=ents: fetch(e)))
    Button(root, text='Fetch',
                command=(lambda e=ents: fetch(e))).pack(side=LEFT)
    Quitter(root).pack(side=RIGHT)
    root.mainloop()
```

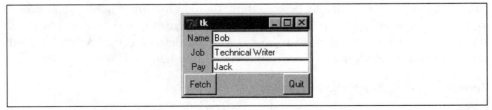

Figure 7-23. entry2 (and entry3) form displays

The input fields here are just simple `Entry` widgets. The script builds an explicit list of these widgets to be used to fetch their values later. Every time you press this window's Fetch button, it grabs the current values in all the input fields and prints them to the standard output stream:

```
C:\...\PP2E\Gui\Tour>python entry2.py
Input => "Bob"
Input => "Technical Writer"
Input => "Jack"
```

You get the same field dump if you press the Enter key any time this window has the focus on your screen—this event has been bound to the whole root window this time, not to a single input field.

Most of the art in form layout has to do with arranging widgets in a hierarchy. This script builds each label/entry row as a new `Frame` attached to the window's current `TOP`; labels are attached to the `LEFT` of their row, and entries to its `RIGHT`. Because each row is a distinct `Frame`, its contents are insulated from other packing going on in this window. The script also arranges for *just* the entry fields to grow vertically on a resize, as in Figure 7-24.

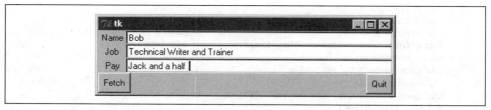

Figure 7-24. entry2 (and entry3) expansion at work

Going modal again

Later on this tour, we'll see how to make similar form layouts with the `grid` geometry manager too. But now that we have a handle on form layout, let's see how to apply the *modal dialog* techniques we met earlier to a more complex input display like this.

Example 7-19 uses the prior's `makeform` and `fetch` functions to generate a form and prints its contents much as before. Here, though, the input fields are attached to a new `Toplevel` pop-up window created on demand, and an OK button is added to the pop-up window to trigger a window destroy event. As we learned earlier, the `wait_window` call pauses until the destroy happens.

Example 7-19. PP2E\Gui\Tour\entry2-modal.py

```
# must fetch before destroy with entries

from Tkinter import *
from entry2 import makeform, fetch, fields

def show(entries):
    fetch(entries)                    # must fetch before window destroyed!
```

Example 7-19. PP2E\Gui\Tour\entry2-modal.py (continued)

```
    popup.destroy()                   # fails with msgs if stmt order is reversed

def ask():
    global popup
    popup = Toplevel()                # show form in modal dialog window
    ents = makeform(popup, fields)
    Button(popup, text='OK', command=(lambda e=ents: show(e)) ).pack()
    popup.grab_set()
    popup.focus_set()
    popup.wait_window()               # wait for destroy here

root = Tk()
Button(root, text='Dialog', command=ask).pack()
root.mainloop()
```

When run, pressing the button in this program's main window creates the blocking form input dialog in Figure 7-25, as expected.

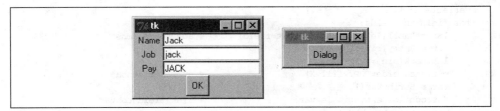

Figure 7-25. entry2-modal (and entry3-modal) displays

But there is a subtle danger lurking in this modal dialog code: because it fetches user inputs from **Entry** widgets embedded in the popped-up display, it must fetch those inputs *before* destroying the pop-up window in the OK press callback handler. It turns out that a **destroy** call really does destroy all the child widgets of the window destroyed; trying to fetch values from a destroyed **Entry** not only doesn't work, but generates a host of error messages in the console window—try reversing the statement order in the **show** function to see for yourself.

To avoid this problem, we can either be careful to fetch before destroying, or we can use Tkinter variables, the subject of the next section.

Tkinter "variables"

Entry widgets (among others) support the notion of an associated variable; changing the associated variable changes the text displayed in the **Entry**, and changing the text in the **Entry** changes the value of the variable. These aren't normal Python variable names, though—variables tied to widgets are instances of variable *classes* in the Tkinter module library. These classes are named **StringVar**, **IntVar**, **DoubleVar**, and **BooleanVar**; you pick one based on the context in which it is to be used. For example, a **StringVar** class instance can be associated with an **Entry** field, as demonstrated by Example 7-20.

Example 7-20. PP2E\Gui\Tour\entry3.py

```
# use StringVar variables and layout by columns

from Tkinter import *
from quitter import Quitter
fields = 'Name', 'Job', 'Pay'

def fetch(variables):
    for variable in variables:
        print 'Input => "%s"' % variable.get()      # get from var

def makeform(root, fields):
    form = Frame(root)                               # make outer frame
    left = Frame(form)                               # make two columns
    rite = Frame(form)
    form.pack(fill=X)
    left.pack(side=LEFT)
    rite.pack(side=RIGHT, expand=YES, fill=X)        # grow horizontal

    variables = []
    for field in fields:
        lab = Label(left, width=5, text=field)       # add to columns
        ent = Entry(rite)
        lab.pack(side=TOP)
        ent.pack(side=TOP, fill=X)                   # grow horizontal
        var = StringVar()
        ent.config(textvariable=var)                 # link field to var
        var.set('enter here')
        variables.append(var)
    return variables

if __name__ == '__main__':
    root = Tk()
    vars = makeform(root, fields)
    Button(root, text='Fetch',
                 command=(lambda v=vars: fetch(v))).pack(side=LEFT)
    Quitter(root).pack(side=RIGHT)
    root.bind('<Return>', (lambda event, v=vars: fetch(v)))
    root.mainloop()
```

Except for the fact that this script initializes input fields with the string "enter here", it makes a window identical in appearance and function to that created by script entry2 (see Figure 7-23). For illustration purposes, the window is laid out differently—as a Frame containing two nested subframes used to build the left and right columns of the form area—but the end result is the same when displayed on screen.

The main thing to notice here, though, is the use of StringVar variables. Rather than use a list of Entry widgets to fetch input values, this version keeps a list of StringVar objects that have been associated with the Entry widgets like this:

```
ent = Entry(rite)
var = StringVar()
ent.config(textvariable=var)                 # link field to var
```

Once you've tied variables like this, changing and fetching the variable's value:

```
var.set('text here')
value = var.get()
```

will really change and fetch the corresponding display's input field value.* The variable object `get` method returns as a string for `StringVar`, an integer for `IntVar`, and a floating-point number for `DoubleVar`.

Of course, we've already seen that it's easy to set and fetch text in `Entry` fields directly, without adding extra code to use variables. So why the bother about variable objects? For one thing, it clears up that nasty fetch-after-destroy peril we met in the prior section. Because `StringVars` live on after the `Entry` widgets they are tied to have been destroyed, it's okay to fetch input values from them long after a modal dialog has been dismissed, as shown in Example 7-21.

Example 7-21. PP2E\Gui\Tour\entry3-modal.py

```
# can fetch values after destroy with stringvars

from Tkinter import *
from entry3 import makeform, fetch, fields

def show(variables):
    popup.destroy()                    # order doesn't matter here
    fetch(variables)                   # variables live on after window destroyed

def ask():
    global popup
    popup = Toplevel()                 # show form in modal dialog window
    vars = makeform(popup, fields)
    Button(popup, text='OK', command=(lambda v=vars: show(v)) ).pack()
    popup.grab_set()
    popup.focus_set()
    popup.wait_window()                # wait for destroy here

root = Tk()
Button(root, text='Dialog', command=ask).pack()
root.mainloop()
```

This version is the same as the original (shown in Example 7-19 and Figure 7-25), but `show` now destroys the pop-up *before* inputs are fetched through `StringVars` in the list created by `makeform`. In other words, variables are a bit more robust in some contexts because they are not part of a real display tree. For example, they are also associated with checkboxes, radioboxes, and scales, to provide access to

---

* In a now-defunct Tkinter release shipped with Python 1.3, you could also set and fetch variable values by calling them like functions, with and without an argument (e.g., `var(value)` and `var()`). Today, you should call variable `set` and `get` methods instead. For unknown reasons, the function call form stopped working years ago, but you may still see it in older Python code (and first editions of at least one O'Reilly Python book).

current settings and link multiple widgets together. Almost coincidentally, that's the topic of the next section.

Checkbutton, Radiobutton, and Scale

This section introduces three widget types—the Checkbutton (a multiple-choice input widget), the Radionbutton (a single-choice device), and the Scale (sometimes known as a "slider"). All are variations on a theme, and somewhat related to simple buttons, so we'll explore them as a group here. To make these widgets more fun to play with, we'll reuse the dialogTable module shown in Example 7-8 to provide callbacks for widget selections (callbacks pop up dialog boxes). Along the way, we'll also use the Tkinter variables we just met to communicate with these widgets' state settings.

Checkbuttons

The Checkbutton and Radiobutton widgets are designed to be associated with Tkinter variables: pushing the button changes the value of the variable, and setting the variable changes the state of the button it is linked to. In fact, Tkinter variables are central to the operation of these widgets:

- A collection of *checkbuttons* implements a multiple-choice interface, by assigning each button a variable of its own.

- A collection of *radiobuttons* imposes a mutually exclusive single-choice model, by giving each button a unique value and the same Tkinter variable.

Both kinds of buttons provide both command and variable options. The command option lets you register a callback to be run immediately on button-press events, much like normal Button widgets. But by associating a Tkinter variable with the variable option, you can also fetch or change widget state at any time, by fetching or changing the value of the widget's associated variable.

Since it's a bit simpler, let's start with the Tkinter checkbutton. Example 7-22 creates the set of five, captured in Figure 7-26. To make this more useful, it also adds a button that dumps the current state of all checkbuttons, and attaches an instance of the Quitter button we built earlier in the tour.

Example 7-22. PP2E\Gui\Tour\demoCheck.py

```
from Tkinter import *            # get base widget set
from dialogTable import demos    # get canned dialogs
from quitter import Quitter      # attach a quitter object to "me"

class Demo(Frame):
    def __init__(self, parent=None, **args):
        Frame.__init__(self, parent, args)
```

Example 7-22. PP2E\Gui\Tour\demoCheck.py (continued)

```
        self.pack()
        self.tools()
        Label(self, text="Check demos").pack()
        self.vars = []
        for key in demos.keys():
            var = IntVar()
            Checkbutton(self,
                            text=key,
                            variable=var,
                            command=demos[key]).pack(side=LEFT)
            self.vars.append(var)
    def report(self):
        for var in self.vars:
            print var.get(),    # current toggle settings: 1 or 0
        print
    def tools(self):
        frm = Frame(self)
        frm.pack(side=RIGHT)
        Button(frm, text='State', command=self.report).pack(fill=X)
        Quitter(frm).pack(fill=X)

if __name__ == '__main__': Demo().mainloop()
```

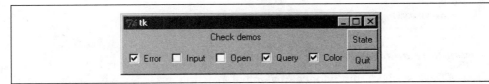

Figure 7-26. demoCheck in action

In terms of program code, checkbuttons resemble normal buttons; they are even packed within a container widget. Operationally, though, they are a bit different. As you can probably tell from this figure (and can better tell by running this live), a checkbutton works as a *toggle*—pressing one changes its state from off to on (deselected to selected); or from on to off again. When a checkbox is selected, it has a checked display, and its associated `IntVar` variable has a value of 1; when deselected, its display is empty, and its `IntVar` has value 0.

To simulate an enclosing application, the State button in this display triggers the script's `report` method to display the current values of all five toggles on the `stdout` stream. Here is the output after a few pushes:

```
C:\...\PP2E\Gui\Tour>python demoCheck.py
0 0 0 0 0
1 0 0 0 0
1 0 1 0 0
1 0 1 1 0
1 0 0 1 0
1 0 0 1 1
```

Really, these are the values of the five Tkinter variables associated with the check-buttons with `variable` options, but they give the buttons' values when queried. This script associates `Intvar` variables with each of checkbuttons in this display, since they are 0 or 1 binary indicators. `StringVars` will work here too, although their `get` methods would return strings "0" or "1" (not integers), and their initial state is an empty string (not the integer 0).

This widget's `command` option lets you register a callback to be run each time the button is pressed. To illustrate, this script registers a *standard dialog* demo call as a handler for each of the checkbuttons: pressing a button changes the toggle's state, but also pops up one of the dialog windows we visited earlier on this tour.

Interestingly, you can run the `report` method interactively too. When working this way, widgets pop up as lines are typed and are fully active even without call-ing `mainloop`:

```
C:\...\PP2E\Gui\Tour>python
>>> from demoCheck import Demo
>>> d = Demo()
>>> d.report()
0 0 0 0 0
>>> d.report()
1 0 0 0 0
>>> d.report()
1 0 0 1 1
```

Checkbuttons and variables

When I first studied this widget, my initial reaction was: So why do we need Tkinter variables here at all when we can register button-press callbacks? Linked variables may seem superfluous at first glance, but they simplify some GUI chores. Rather than asking you to accept this blindly, though, let me explain why.

Keep in mind that a checkbuttons's `command` callback will be run on *every* press—whether the press toggles the checkbutton to a selected or deselected state. Because of that, if you want to run an action immediately when a checkbutton is pressed, you will generally want to check the button's current *value* in the callback handler. Because there is no checkbutton "get" method for fetching values, you usually need to interrogate an associated variable to see if the button is on or off.

Moreover, some GUIs simply let users set checkbuttons without running `command` callbacks at all, and fetch button settings at some later point in the program. In such a scenario, variables serve to automatically keep track of button settings. The `demoCheck` script's `report` method is representative of this latter approach.

Of course, you could manually keep track of each button's state in press callback handlers too. Example 7-23 keeps its own list of state toggles, and updates it man-ually on `command` press callbacks.

Example 7-23. PP2E\Gui\Tour\demo-check-manual.py

```
# check buttons, the hard way (without variables)

from Tkinter import *
states = []
def onPress(i):                         # keep track of states
    states[i] = not states[i]           # changes 0->1, 1->0

root = Tk()
for i in range(10):
    chk = Checkbutton(root, text=str(i), command=(lambda i=i: onPress(i)) )
    chk.pack(side=LEFT)
    states.append(0)
root.mainloop()
print states                            # show all states on exit
```

The lambda here passes along the pressed button's index in the **states** list (or else we would need a separate callback function for each button). When run, this script makes the 10-checkbutton display in Figure 7-27.

Figure 7-27. Manual checkbutton state window

Manually maintained state toggles are updated on every button press, and are printed when the GUI exits (technically, when the **mainloop** call returns):

```
C:\...\PP2E\Gui\Tour>python demo-check-manual.py
[0, 0, 1, 0, 1, 0, 0, 0, 1, 0]
```

This works, and isn't too horribly difficult to manage manually. But linked Tkinter variables make this task noticeably easier, especially if you don't need to process checkbutton states until some time in the future. This is illustrated in Example 7-24.

Example 7-24. PP2E\Gui\Tour\demo-check-auto.py

```
# check buttons, the easy way

from Tkinter import *
root = Tk()
states = []
for i in range(10):
    var = IntVar()
    chk = Checkbutton(root, text=str(i), variable=var)
    chk.pack(side=LEFT)
    states.append(var)
root.mainloop()                                    # let Tkinter keep track
print map((lambda var: var.get()), states)         # show all states on exit
```

This looks and works the same, but there is no **command** button-press callback handler at all, because toggle state is tracked by Tkinter automatically:

```
C:\...\PP2E\Gui\Tour>python demo-check-auto.py
[0, 0, 1, 0, 0, 0, 1, 0, 0, 0]
```

The point here is that you don't necessarily have to link variables with checkbuttons, but your GUI life will be simpler if you do.

Radiobuttons

Radiobuttons are toggles too, but they are generally used in groups: just like the mechanical station selector pushbuttons on radios of times gone by, pressing one **Radiobutton** widget in a group automatically deselects the one pressed last. In other words, at most one can be selected at once. In Tkinter, associating all radiobuttons in a group with unique values and the same variable guarantees that at most one can ever be selected at a given time.

Like checkbuttons and normal buttons, radiobuttons support a **command** option for registering a callback to handle presses immediately. Like checkbuttons, radiobuttons also have a **variable** attribute for associating single-selection buttons in a group and fetching the current selection at arbitrary times.

In addition, radiobuttons have a **value** attribute that lets you tell Tkinter what value the button's associated variable should have when the button is selected. Because more than one radiobutton is associated with the same variable, you need to be explicit about each button's value (it's not just a 1 or 0 toggle scenario). Example 7-25 demonstrates radiobutton basics.

Example 7-25. PP2E\Gui\Tour\demoRadio.py

```
from Tkinter import *                 # get base widget set
from dialogTable import demos         # button callback handlers
from quitter import Quitter           # attach a quit object to "me"

class Demo(Frame):
    def __init__(self, parent=None):
        Frame.__init__(self, parent)
        self.pack()
        Label(self, text="Radio demos").pack(side=TOP)
        self.var = StringVar()
        for (key, value) in demos.items():
            Radiobutton(self, text=key,
                              command=self.onPress,
                              variable=self.var,
                              value=key).pack(anchor=NW)
        Button(self, text='State', command=self.report).pack(fill=X)
        Quitter(self).pack(fill=X)
    def onPress(self):
```

Example 7-25. PP2E\Gui\Tour\demoRadio.py (continued)

```
        pick = self.var.get()
        print 'you pressed', pick
        print 'result:', demos[pick]()
    def report(self):
        print self.var.get()

if __name__ == '__main__': Demo().mainloop()
```

Figure 7-28 shows what this script generates when run. Pressing any of this window's radiobuttons triggers its `command` handler, pops up one of the standard dialog boxes we met earlier, and automatically deselects the button previously pressed. Like checkbuttons, radiobuttons are packed; this script packs them to the the top to arrange vertically, and then anchors each on the northwest corner of its allocated space so that they align well.

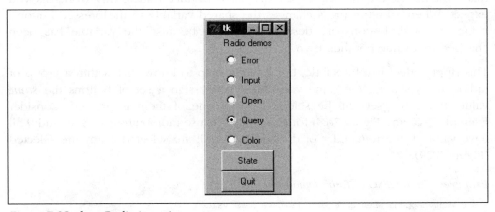

Figure 7-28. demoRadio in action

Like the checkbutton demo script, this one also puts up a State button to run the class's `report` method, and show the current radio state (the button selected). Unlike the checkbutton demo, this script also prints the return values of dialog demo calls run as its buttons are pressed. Here is what the `stdout` stream looks like after a few presses and state dumps; states are shown in bold:

```
C:\...\PP2E\Gui\Tour>python demoRadio.py
you pressed Input
result: 3.14
Input
you pressed Open
result: C:/PP2ndEd/examples/PP2E/Gui/Tour/demoRadio.py
Open
you pressed Query
result: yes
Query
```

Radiobuttons and variables

So why variables here? For one thing, radiobuttons also have no "get" widget method to fetch the selection in the future. More importantly, in radiobutton groups, the `value` and `variable` settings turn out to be the whole basis of single-choice behavior. In fact, to make radiobuttons work normally at all, it's crucial that they all are associated with the *same* Tkinter variable, and all have *distinct* value settings. To truly understand why, though, you need to know a bit more about how radiobuttons and variables do their stuff.

We've already seen that changing a widget changes its associated Tkinter variable, and vice versa. But it's also true that changing a variable in any way automatically changes *every* widget it is associated with. In the world of radiobuttons, pressing a button sets a shared variable, which in turn impacts other buttons associated with that variable. Assuming that all buttons have distinct values, this works as you expect: When a button press changes the shared variable to the pressed button's value, all other buttons are deselected, simply because the variable has been changed to a value not their own.

This ripple effect is a bit subtle, but it might help to know that within a group of radiobuttons sharing the same variable, if you assign a set of buttons the *same* value, the entire set will be selected if any one of them is pressed. Consider Example 7-26 and Figure 7-29, for example; because radiobuttons 0, 3, 6, and 9 all have value 0 (the remainder of division by 3), all are selected if any are selected (Figure 7-29).

Example 7-26. PP2E\Gui\Tour\demo-radio-multi.py

```
# see what happens when some buttons have same value

from Tkinter import *
root = Tk()
var = StringVar()
for i in range(10):
    rad = Radiobutton(root, text=str(i), variable=var, value=str(i % 3))
    rad.pack(side=LEFT)
root.mainloop()
```

Figure 7-29. Radiobuttons gone bad?

If you press 1, 4, or 7 now, all three of these are selected, and any existing selections are cleared (they don't have value "1"). That's not normally what you want, so be sure to give each button the same variable but a unique value if you want radiobuttons to work as expected. In the `demoRadio` script, for instance, the name of the demo provides a naturally unique value for each button.

Radiobuttons without variables

In Example 7-27, too, you could implement a single-selection model *without* variables, by manually selecting and deselecting widgets in the group, in a callback handler of your own. On each press event, for example, you could issue `deselect` calls for every widget object in the group and `select` the one pressed.

Example 7-27. PP2E\Gui\Tour\demo-radio-manual.py

```
# radio buttons, the hard way (without variables)
# note that deselect for radio buttons simply sets the button's
# associated value to a null string, so we either need to still
# give buttons unique values, or use checkbuttons here instead;

from Tkinter import *
state = ''
buttons = []

def onPress(i):
    global state
    state = i
    for btn in buttons:
        btn.deselect()
    buttons[i].select()

root = Tk()
for i in range(10):
    rad = Radiobutton(root, text=str(i),
                         value=str(i), command=(lambda i=i: onPress(i)) )
    rad.pack(side=LEFT)
    buttons.append(rad)
root.mainloop()
print state                 # show state on exit
```

This works—it creates a 10-radiobutton window that looks just like the one in Figure 7-29, but implements a single-choice radio style interface, with current state available in a global Python variable printed on script exit. By associating Tkinter variables and unique values, though, you can let Tkinter do all this work for you, as shown in Example 7-28.

Example 7-28. PP2E\Gui\Tour\demo-radio-auto.py

```
# radio buttons, the easy way

from Tkinter import *
root = Tk()                       # IntVars work too
var  = IntVar()                   # state = var.get()
for i in range(10):
    rad = Radiobutton(root, text=str(i), value=i, variable=var)
```

Example 7-28. PP2E\Gui\Tour\demo-radio-auto.py (continued)

```
    rad.pack(side=LEFT)
root.mainloop()
print var.get()                        # show state on exit
```

This works the same, but is a lot less to type and debug. Notice that this script associates the buttons with an `IntVar`, the integer type sibling of `StringVar`; as long as button values are unique, integers work fine for radiobuttons too.

Hold on to your variables

One minor word of caution: you should generally hold on to the Tkinter variable object used to link radiobuttons for as long as the radiobuttons are displayed. Assign it to a module global variable, store it in a long-lived data structure, or save it as an attribute of a long-lived class object as done by `demoRadio`—just as long as you retain a reference to it somehow. You normally will fetch state anyhow, so it's unlikely that you'll ever care about what I'm about to tell you.

But in the current Tkinter, variable classes have a `__del__` destructor that automatically *unsets* a generated `Tk` variable when the Python object is reclaimed (i.e., garbage-collected). The upshot is that your radiobuttons may all be deselected if the variable object is collected, at least until the next press resets the `Tk` variable to a new value. Example 7-29 shows one way to trigger this.

Example 7-29. PP2E\Gui\Tour\demo-radio-clear.py

```
# hold on to your radio variables (an obscure thing, indeed)

from Tkinter import *
root = Tk()

def radio1():                  # local vars are temporary
    #global tmp                 # making it global fixes the problem
    tmp = IntVar()
    for i in range(10):
        rad = Radiobutton(root, text=str(i), value=i, variable=tmp)
        rad.pack(side=LEFT)
    tmp.set(5)

radio1()
root.mainloop()
```

This should come up with button 5 selected initially, but doesn't. The variable referenced by local `tmp` is reclaimed on function exit, the `Tk` variable is unset, and the 5 setting is lost (all buttons come up unselected). These radiobuttons work fine, though, one you start pressing them, because that resets the `Tk` variable. Uncommenting the `global` statement here makes 5 start out set, as expected.

Of course, this is an atypical example—as coded, there is no way to know which button is pressed, because the variable isn't saved (and **command** isn't set). In fact, this is so obscure that I'll just refer you to *demo-radio-clear2.py* on the CD for an example that works hard to trigger this oddity in other ways. You probably won't care, but you can't say that I didn't warn you if you ever do.

Scales (Sliders)

Scales (sometimes called "sliders") are used to select among a *range* of numeric values. Moving the scale's position with mouse drags or clicks moves the widget's value among a range of integers, and triggers Python callbacks if registered.

Like checkbuttons and radiobuttons, scales have both a **command** option for registering an event-driven callback handler to be run right away when the scale is moved, as well as a **variable** option for associating a Tkinter variable that allows the scale's position to be fetched and set at arbitrary times. You can process scale settings when they are made, or let the user pick a setting for later use.

In addition, scales have a third processing option—**get** and **set** methods that scripts may call to access scale values directly without associating variables. Because scale **command** movement callbacks also get the current scale setting value as an *argument*, it's often enough just to provide a callback for this widget, without resorting to either linked variables or get/set method calls.

To illustrate the basics, Example 7-30 makes two scales—one horizontal and one vertical—and links them with an associated variable to keep them in sync.

Example 7-30. PP2E\Gui\Tour\demoScale.py

```
from Tkinter import *              # get base widget set
from dialogTable import demos      # button callback handlers
from quitter import Quitter        # attach a quit frame to me

class Demo(Frame):
    def __init__(self, parent=None):
        Frame.__init__(self, parent)
        self.pack()
        Label(self, text="Scale demos").pack()
        self.var = IntVar()
        Scale(self, label='Pick demo number',
                command=self.onMove,                    # catch moves
                variable=self.var,                      # reflects position
                from_=0, to=len(demos)-1).pack()
        Scale(self, label='Pick demo number',
                command=self.onMove,                    # catch moves
                variable=self.var,                      # reflects position
                from_=0, to=len(demos)-1,
                length=200, tickinterval=1,
                showvalue=YES, orient='horizontal').pack()
```

Example 7-30. PP2E\Gui\Tour\demoScale.py (continued)

```
        Quitter(self).pack(side=RIGHT)
        Button(self, text="Run demo",  command=self.onRun).pack(side=LEFT)
        Button(self, text="State",     command=self.report).pack(side=RIGHT)
    def onMove(self, value):
        print 'in onMove', value
    def onRun(self):
        pos = self.var.get()
        print 'You picked', pos
        pick = demos.keys()[pos]      # map from position to key
        print demos[pick]()
    def report(self):
        print self.var.get()

if __name__ == '__main__':
    print demos.keys()
    Demo().mainloop()
```

Besides value access and callback registration, scales have options tailored to the notion of a range of selectable values, most of which are demonstrated in this example's code:

- The `label` option provides text that appears along with the scale, `length` specifies an initial size in pixels, and `orient` specifies an axis.

- The `from_` and `to` options set the scale range's minimum and maximum values (note that "from" is a Python reserved word, but "from_" is not).

- The `tickinterval` option sets the number of units between marks drawn at regular intervals next to the scale (the default 0 means no marks are drawn).

- The `resolution` option provides the number of units that the scale's value jumps on each drag or left mouseclick event (defaults to 1).

- The `showvalue` option can be used to show or hide the scale's current value next to its slider bar (the default `showvalue=YES` means it is drawn).

Note that scales are also *packed* in their container, just like other Tkinter widgets. Let's see how these ideas translate in practice; Figure 7-30 shows the window you get if you run this script live on Windows (you get a similar one on Unix and Macs).

For illustration purposes, this window's State button shows the scales' current values, and "Run demo" runs a standard dialog call as before using the integer value of the scales to index the demos table. The script also registers a `command` handler that fires every time either of the scales is moved, and prints their new positions. Here is a set of messages sent to `stdout` after a few moves, demo runs (italic), and state requests (bold):

```
C:\...\PP2E\Gui\Tour>python demoScale.py
['Error', 'Input', 'Open', 'Query', 'Color']
```

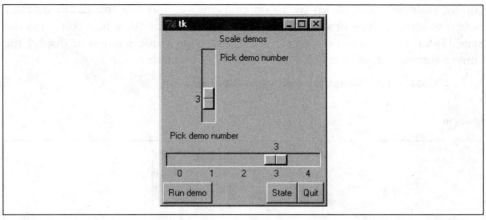

Figure 7-30. demoScale in action

```
in onMove 0
in onMove 0
in onMove 1
1
in onMove 2
You picked 2
C:/PP2ndEd/examples/PP2E/Gui/Tour/demoScale.py
in onMove 3
3
You picked 3
yes
```

Scales and variables

As you can probably tell, scales offer a variety of ways to process their selections: immediately in move callbacks, or later by fetching current position with variables or scale method calls. In fact, Tkinter variables aren't needed to program scales at all—simply register movement callbacks, or call the scale **get** method to fetch scale values on demand as in the simpler scale example in Example 7-31.

Example 7-31. PP2E\Gui\Tour\demo-scale-simple.py

```python
from Tkinter import *
root = Tk()
scl = Scale(root, from_=-100, to=100, tickinterval=50, resolution=10)
scl.pack(expand=YES, fill=Y)
def report(): print scl.get()
Button(root, text='state', command=report).pack(side=RIGHT)
root.mainloop()
```

Figure 7-31 shows two instances of this program running on Windows—one stretched and one not (the scales are packed to grow vertically on resizes). Its scale displays a range from −100 to 100, uses the **resolution** option to adjust the current position up or down by 10 on every move, and sets the `tickinterval` option to show values next to the scale in increments of 50. When you press the State button in this script's window, it calls the scale's `get` method to display the current setting, without variables or callbacks of any kind:

```
C:\...\PP2E\Gui\Tour>python demo-scale-simple.py
0
60
-70
```

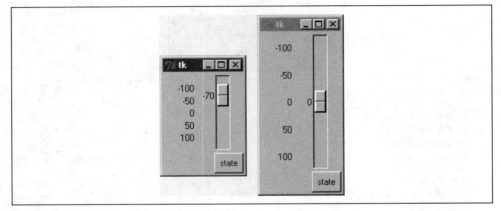

Figure 7-31. A simple scale without variables

Frankly, the only reason Tkinter variables are used in the `demoScale` script at all is to synchronize scales. To make the demo interesting, this script associates the *same* Tkinter variable object with both scales. As we learned in the last section, changing a widget changes its variable, but changing a variable also changes *all* the widgets it is associated with. In the world of sliders, moving the slide updates that variable, which in turn might update other widgets associated with the same variable. Because this script links one variable with two scales, it keeps them automatically in sync: moving one scale moves the other too, because the shared variable is changed in the process and so updates the other scale as a side effect.

Linking scales like this may or may not be typical of your applications (and borders on deep magic), but it's a powerful tool once you get your mind around it. By linking multiple widgets on a display with Tkinter variables, you can keep them automatically in sync, without making manual adjustments in callback handlers. On the other hand, the synchronization could be implemented without a shared variable at all by calling one scale's `set` method from a move callback handler of the other. I'll leave such a manual mutation as a suggested exercise, though. One person's deep magic might be another's evil hack.

Running GUI Code Three Ways

Now that we've built a handful of similar demo launcher programs, let's write a few top-level scripts to combine them. Because the demos were coded as both reusable classes and scripts, they can be deployed as attached frame components, run in their own top-level windows, and launched as standalone programs. All three options illustrate *code reuse* in action.

Attaching Frames

To illustrate hierarchical GUI composition on a grander scale than we've seen so far, Example 7-32 arranges to show all four of the dialog launcher bar scripts of this chapter in a single frame. It reuses Examples 7-9, 7-22, 7-25, and 7-30.

Example 7-32. PP2E\Gui\Tour\demoAll-frm.py

```
######################################################
# 4 demo class components (subframes) on one window;
# there are 5 Quitter buttons on this one window too;
# guis can be reused as frames, windows, processes;
######################################################

from Tkinter import *
from quitter import Quitter
demoModules = ['demoDlg', 'demoCheck', 'demoRadio', 'demoScale']
parts = []

def addComponents(root):
    for demo in demoModules:
        module = __import__(demo)             # import by name string
        part = module.Demo(root)              # attach an instance
        part.config(bd=2, relief=GROOVE)
        part.pack(side=LEFT, fill=BOTH)
        parts.append(part)                    # change list in-place

def dumpState():
    for part in parts:                        # run demo report if any
        print part.__module__ + ':',
        if hasattr(part, 'report'):
            part.report()
        else:
            print 'none'

root = Tk()                                    # default toplevel window
Label(root, text='Multiple Frame demo', bg='white').pack()
Button(root, text='States', command=dumpState).pack(fill=X)
Quitter(root).pack(expand=YES, fill=X)
addComponents(root)
mainloop()
```

Because all four demo launcher bars are coded to attach themselves to parent container widgets, this is easier than you might think: simply pass the same parent widget (here, the `root` window) to all four demo constructor calls, and pack and configure the demo objects as desired. Figure 7-32 shows this script's graphical result—a single window embedding instances of all four of the dialog demo launcher demos we saw earlier.

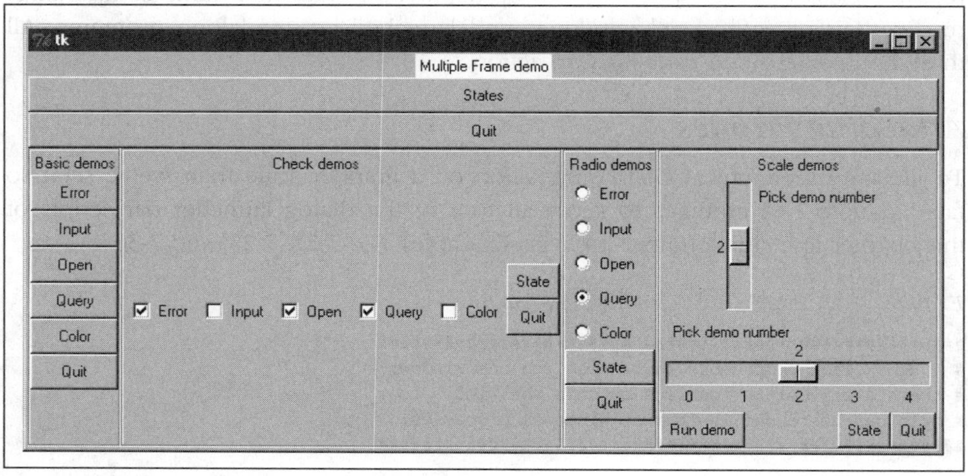

Figure 7-32. demoAll_frm: nested subframes

Naturally, this example is artificial, but it illustrates the power of composition when applied to building larger GUI displays. If you pretend that each of the four attached demo objects was something more useful, like a text editor, calculator, or clock, you'll better appreciate the point of this example.

Besides demo object frames, this composite window also contains no less than five instances of the Quitter button we wrote earlier (any one of which can end the GUI), and a States button to dump the current values of all the embedded demo objects at once (it calls each object's `report` method, if it has one). Here is a sample of the sort of output that shows up in the `stdout` stream after interacting with widgets on this display; States output is in bold:

```
C:\...\PP2E\Gui\Tour>python demoAll_frm.py
in onMove 0
in onMove 0
demoDlg: none
demoCheck: 0 0 0 0 0
demoRadio:
demoScale: 0
you pressed Input
result: 1.234
demoDlg: none
demoCheck: 1 0 1 1 0
demoRadio: Input
demoScale: 0
you pressed Query
```

```
result: yes
in onMove 1
in onMove 2
You picked 2
C:/PP2ndEd/examples/PP2E/Gui/Tour/demoAll_frm.py
demoDlg: none
demoCheck: 1 0 1 1 0
demoRadio: Query
demoScale: 2
```

The only substantially tricky part of this script is its use of Python's built-in __import__ function to import a module by a name string. Look at the following two lines from the script's addComponents function:

```
module = __import__(demo)          # import module by name string
part = module.Demo(root)           # attach an instance of its Demo
```

This is equivalent to saying something like this:

```
import 'demoDlg'
part = 'demoDlg'.Demo(root)
```

except that this is not legal Python syntax—the module name in import statements must be a Python variable, not a string. To be generic, addComponents steps through a list of name strings, and relies on __import__ to import and return the module identified by each string. It's as though all of these statements were run:

```
import demoDlg, demoRadio, demoCheck, demoScale
part = demoDlg.Demo(root)
part = demoRadio.Demo(root)
part = demoCheck.Demo(root)
part = demoScale.Demo(root)
```

But because the script uses a list of name strings, it's easier to change the set of demos embedded—simply change the list, not lines of executable code. Moreover, such *data-driven* code tends to be more compact, less redundant, and easier to debug and maintain. Incidentally, modules can also be imported from name strings by dynamically constructing and running import statements like this:

```
for demo in demoModules:
    exec 'from %s import Demo' % demo      # make and run a from
    part = Demo(root)                      # or eval('Demo')(window)
```

The exec statement compiles and runs a Python statement string (here, a from to load a module's Demo class); it works here as if the statement string were pasted into the source code where the exec statement appears. Because it supports any sort of Python statement, this technique is more general than the __import__ call, but, it can also be slower, since it must parse code strings before running them.[*] But that slowness may not matter in a GUI; users tend to be slower than parsers.

---

[*] As we'll see later, exec can also be dangerous if running code strings fetched from users or network connections. That's not an issue for the hardcoded strings in this example.

As we saw in Chapter 6, attaching nested frames like this is really just one way to reuse GUI code structured as classes. It's just as easy to customize such interfaces by subclassing, rather than embedding. Here, though, we're more interested in deploying an existing widget package, rather than changing it; the next two sections show two other ways to present such packages to users.

Independent Windows

Once you have a set of component classes, any parent will work—both frames, and brand new top-level windows. Example 7-33 attaches instances of all four demo bar objects to their own `Toplevel` windows, not the same `Frame`.

Example 7-33. PP2E\Gui\Tour\demoAll-win.py

```
###################################################
# 4 demo classes in independent top-level windows;
# not processes: when one is quit all others go away
# because all windows run in the same process here
###################################################

from Tkinter import *
demoModules = ['demoDlg', 'demoRadio', 'demoCheck', 'demoScale']

demoObjects = []
for demo in demoModules:
    module = __import__(demo)        # import by name string
    window = Toplevel()              # make a new window
    demo   = module.Demo(window)     # parent is the new window
    demoObjects.append(demo)

def allstates():
    for obj in demoObjects:
        if hasattr(obj, 'report'):
            print obj.__module__,
            obj.report()

Label(text='Multiple Toplevel window demo', bg='white').pack()
Button(text='States', command=allstates).pack(fill=X)
mainloop()
```

We met the `Toplevel` class earlier; every instance generates a new window on your screen. The net result is captured in Figure 7-33—each demo runs in an independent window of its own, instead of being packed together in a single display.

The main root window of this program appears in the lower left of this screen shot; it provides a States button that runs the `report` method of each of the demo objects, producing this sort of `stdout` text:

```
C:\...\PP2E\Gui\Tour>python demoAll_win.py
in onMove 0
in onMove 0
in onMove 1
```

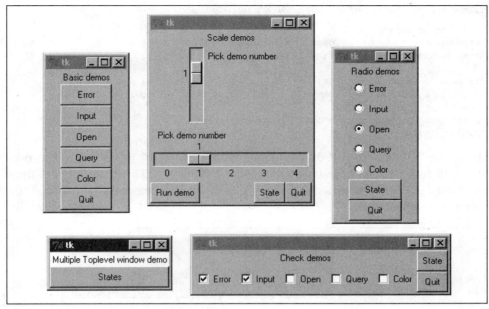

Figure 7-33. demoAll_win: new Toplevel windows

```
you pressed Open
result: C:/PP2ndEd/examples/PP2E/Gui/Tour/demoAll_win.txt
demoRadio Open
demoCheck 1 1 0 0 0
demoScale 1
```

Running Programs

Finally, as we learned earlier in this chapter, `Toplevel` windows function independently, but they are not really independent programs. Quitting any of the windows created by Example 7-33 quits them all, because all run in the same program process. That's okay in some applications, but not all.

To go truly independent, Example 7-34 spawns each of the four demo launchers as independent programs, using the `launchmodes` module we wrote at the end of Chapter 3, *Parallel System Tools.* This only works because the demos were written as both importable classes and runnable scripts—launching them here makes all their names `__main__` when run.

Example 7-34. PP2E\Gui\Tour\demoAll-prg.py

```
#######################################################
# 4 demo classes run as independent program processes;
# if one window is quit now, the others will live on;
# there is no simple way to run all report calls here,
# and some launch schemes drop child program stdout;
#######################################################
```

Example 7-34. PP2E\Gui\Tour\demoAll-prg.py (continued)

```
from Tkinter import *
demoModules = ['demoDlg', 'demoRadio', 'demoCheck', 'demoScale']
from PP2E.launchmodes import PortableLauncher

for demo in demoModules:                        # see Parallel System Tools
    PortableLauncher(demo, demo+'.py')()        # start as top-level programs

Label(text='Multiple program demo', bg='white').pack()
mainloop()
```

As Figure 7-34 shows, the display generated by this script is similar to the prior
one—all four demos come up in windows of their own. This time, though, these
are really independent programs: if any one of the five windows here is quit, the
others live on.

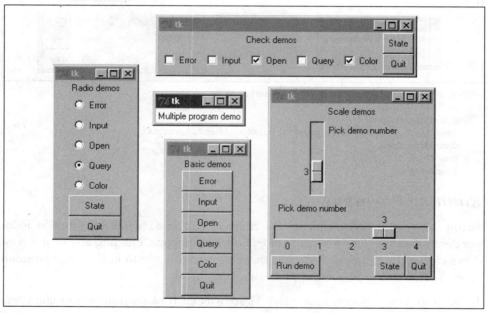

Figure 7-34. demoAll_prg: independent programs

Cross-program communication

Spawning GUIs as programs is the ultimate in code independence, but makes the
lines of communication between components more complex. For instance,
because the demos run as programs here, there is no easy way to run all their
`report` methods from the launching script's window pictured in the middle of
Figure 7-34. In fact, the States button is gone this time, and we only get
`PortableLauncher` messages in `stdout` as the demos start up:

```
C:\...\PP2E\Gui\Tour>python demoAll_prg.py
demoDlg
```

```
demoRadio
demoCheck
demoScale
```

On some platforms, messages printed by the demo programs (including their own State buttons) may show up the original console window where this script is launched; on Windows, the `os.spawnv` call used to start programs in `launchmodes` completely disconnects the child program's `stdout` stream from its parent. Regardless, there is no way to call all demos' `report` methods at once— they are spawned programs in distinct address spaces, not imported modules.

Of course, we could trigger report methods in the spawned programs with some of the IPC mechanisms we met in Chapter 3. For instance:

- The demos could be instrumented to catch a user signal, and run their `report` in response.

- They could also watch for request strings sent by the launching program to show up in pipes or fifos—the `demoAll` launching program would essentially act as a client, and the demo GUIs as servers.

- Independent programs can also converse this way over sockets—a tool we'll meet in Part III, *Internet Scripting.*

Given their event-driven nature, GUI-based programs may need to be augmented with threads or timer-event callbacks to periodically check for such incoming messages on pipes, fifos, or sockets (e.g., see the `after` method call described near the end of the next chapter). But since this is all well beyond the scope of these simple demo programs, I'll leave such cross-program extensions up to more parallel-minded readers.

Coding for reusability

A postscript: I coded all the demo launcher bars deployed by the last three examples to demonstrate all the different ways that their widgets can be used. They were not developed with general-purpose reusability in mind; in fact, they're not really useful outside the context of introducing widgets in this book.

That was by design; most Tkinter widgets are easy to use once you learn their interfaces, and Tkinter already provides lots of configuration flexibility by itself. But if I had in mind to code checkboxes and radiobutton classes to be reused as general library components, they would have to be structured differently:

Extra widgets
They would not display anything but radio- and checkbuttons. As is, the demos each embed State and Quit buttons for illustration, but there really should be just one Quit per top-level window.

Geometry management

They would allow for different button arrangements, and not pack (or grid) themselves at all. In a true general-purpose reuse scenario, it's often better to leave a component's geometry management up to its caller.

Usage mode limitations

They would either have to export complex interfaces to support all possible Tkinter configuration options and modes, or make some limiting decisions that support one common use only. For instance, these buttons can either run callbacks at press time or provide their state later in the application.

Example 7-35 shows one way to code check and radiobutton bars as library components. It encapsulates the notion of associating Tkinter variables, and imposes a common usage mode on callers to keep the interface simple—state fetches, instead of press callbacks.

Example 7-35. PP2E\Gui\Tour\buttonbars.py

```
# check and radio button bar classes for apps that fetch state later;
# pass a list of options, call state(), variable details automated

from Tkinter import *

class Checkbar(Frame):
    def __init__(self, parent=None, picks=[], side=LEFT, anchor=W):
        Frame.__init__(self, parent)
        self.vars = []
        for pick in picks:
            var = IntVar()
            chk = Checkbutton(self, text=pick, variable=var)
            chk.pack(side=side, anchor=anchor, expand=YES)
            self.vars.append(var)
    def state(self):
        return map((lambda var: var.get()), self.vars)

class Radiobar(Frame):
    def __init__(self, parent=None, picks=[], side=LEFT, anchor=W):
        Frame.__init__(self, parent)
        self.var = StringVar()
        for pick in picks:
            rad = Radiobutton(self, text=pick, value=pick, variable=self.var)
            rad.pack(side=side, anchor=anchor, expand=YES)
    def state(self):
        return self.var.get()

if __name__ == '__main__':
    root = Tk()
    lng = Checkbar(root, ['Python', 'C#', 'Java', 'C++'])
    gui = Radiobar(root, ['win', 'x11', 'mac'], side=TOP, anchor=NW)
    tgl = Checkbar(root, ['All'])
    gui.pack(side=LEFT, fill=Y)
```

Example 7-35. PP2E\Gui\Tour\buttonbars.py (continued)

```
    lng.pack(side=TOP,  fill=X)
    tgl.pack(side=LEFT)
    lng.config(relief=GROOVE, bd=2)
    gui.config(relief=RIDGE,  bd=2)
    from quitter import Quitter
    def allstates(): print gui.state(), lng.state(), tgl.state()
    Quitter(root).pack(side=RIGHT)
    Button(root, text='Peek', command=allstates).pack(side=RIGHT)
    root.mainloop()
```

To reuse these classes in your scripts, import and call with a list of the options you want to appear in a bar of checkboxes or radiobuttons. This module's self-test code at the bottom of the file gives further usage details. It generates Figure 7-35 when this file is run as a program instead of imported—a top-level window that embeds two Checkbars, one Radiobar, a Quitter button to exit, and a Peek button to show bar states.

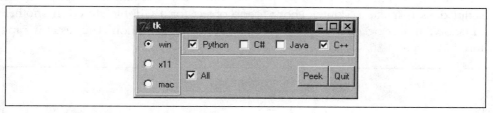

Figure 7-35. buttonbars self-test window

Here's the stdout text you get after pressing Peek—the results of these classes' state methods:

```
    x11 [1, 0, 1, 1] [0]
    win [1, 0, 0, 1] [1]
```

The two classes in this module demonstrate how easy it is to wrap Tkinter interfaces to make them easier to use—they completely abstract away many of the tricky parts of radiobutton and checkbox bars. For instance, you can forget about linked variable details completely if you use such higher-level classes instead; simply make objects with option lists and call their state methods later. If you follow this path to its conclusion, you might just wind up with a higher-level widget library on the order of the PMW package mentioned in Chapter 6.

On the other hand, these classes are still not universally applicable; if you need to run actions when these buttons are pressed, for instance, you'll need to use other high-level interfaces. Luckily, Python/Tkinter already provides plenty. Later in this book, we'll again use the widget combination and reuse techniques introduced in this section to construct larger GUIs. For now, this first widget tour chapter is about to make one last stop—the photo shop.

Images

In Tkinter, graphical images are displayed by creating independent `PhotoImage` or `BitmapImage` objects, and then attaching those image objects to other widgets via `image` attribute settings. Buttons, labels, canvases, text, and menus can all display images by associating prebuilt image objects this way. To illustrate, Example 7-36 throws a picture up on a button.

Example 7-36. PP2E\Gui\Tour\imgButton.py

```
gifdir = "../gifs/"
from Tkinter import *
win = Tk()
igm = PhotoImage(file=gifdir+"ora-pp.gif")
Button(win, image=igm).pack()
win.mainloop()
```

I could try to come up with a simpler example, but it would be tough—all this script does is make a Tkinter `PhotoImage` object for a GIF file stored in another directory, and associate it with a `Button` widget's `image` option. The result is captured in Figure 7-36.

Figure 7-36. imgButton in action

`PhotoImage` and its cousin, `BitmapImage`, essentially load graphics files, and allow those graphics to be attached to other kinds of widgets. To open a picture file, pass its name to the `file` attribute of these image objects. `Canvas` widgets—general drawing surfaces discussed in more detail later on this tour—can display pictures too; Example 7-37 renders Figure 7-37.

Example 7-37. PP2E\Gui\Tour\imgCanvas.py

```
gifdir = "../gifs/"
from Tkinter import *
win = Tk()
img = PhotoImage(file=gifdir+"ora-lp.gif")
can = Canvas(win)
can.pack(fill=BOTH)
can.create_image(2, 2, image=img, anchor=NW)          # x, y coordinates
win.mainloop()
```

Figure 7-37. An image on canvas

Buttons are automatically sized to fit an associated photo, but canvases are not (because you can add objects to a canvas, as we'll see in Chapter 8). To make a canvas fit the picture, size it according to the **width** and **height** methods of image objects as in Example 7-38. This version will make the canvas smaller or larger than its default size as needed, lets you pass in a photo file's name on the command line, and can be used as a simple image viewer utility. The visual effect of this script is captured in Figure 7-38.

Example 7-38. PP2E\Gui\Tour\imgCanvas2.py

```
gifdir = "../gifs/"
from sys import argv
from Tkinter import *
filename = (len(argv) > 1 and argv[1]) or 'ora-lp.gif'    # name on cmdline?
win = Tk()
img = PhotoImage(file=gifdir+filename)
can = Canvas(win)
can.pack(fill=BOTH)
can.config(width=img.width(), height=img.height())        # size to img size
can.create_image(2, 2, image=img, anchor=NW)
win.mainloop()
```

Figure 7-38. Sizing the canvas to match the photo

And that's all there is to it. In Chapter 8, well see images show up in a `Menu`, other `Canvas` examples, and the image-friendly `Text` widget. In later chapters, we'll find them in an image slideshow (PyView), in a paint program (PyDraw), on clocks (PyClock), and so on. It's easy to add graphics to GUIs in Python/Tkinter.

Once you start using photos in earnest, though, you're likely to run into two tricky bits which I want to warn you about here:

Supported file types

   At present, the `PhotoImage` widget only supports GIF, PPM, and PGM graphic file formats, and `BitmapImage` supports X Windows–style *.xbm* bitmap files. This may be expanded in future releases, and you can convert photos in other formats to these supported formats, of course; but I'll wait to address this issue in more detail in the sidebar titled "Other Image File Formats: PIL" later in this section.

Hold on to your photos

   Unlike all other Tkinter widgets, an image is utterly lost if the corresponding Python image object is garbage-collected. That means that you must retain an explicit reference to image objects for as long as your program needs them (e.g., assign them to a long-lived variable name or data structure component). Python does not automatically keep a reference to the image, even if it is linked to other GUI components for display; moreover, image destructor methods erase the image from memory. We saw earlier that Tkinter variables can behave oddly when reclaimed too, but the effect is much worse and more likely to happen with images. This may change in future Python releases (though there are good reasons for not retaining big image files in memory indefinitely); for now, though, images are a "use it or lose it" widget.

Fun with Buttons and Pictures

I tried to come up with an image demo for this section that was both fun and useful. I settled for the fun part. Example 7-39 displays a button that changes its image at random each time it is pressed.

Example 7-39. PP2E\Gui\Tour\buttonpics-func.py

```
from Tkinter import *                  # get base widget set
from glob import glob                  # file name expansion list
import demoCheck                       # attach checkbutton demo to me
import random                          # pick a picture at random
gifdir = '../gifs/'                    # where to look for gif files

def draw():
    name, photo = random.choice(images)
    lbl.config(text=name)
    pix.config(image=photo)

root=Tk()
lbl = Label(root,  text="none", bg='blue', fg='red')
pix = Button(root, text="Press me", command=draw, bg='white')
lbl.pack(fill=BOTH)
pix.pack(pady=10)
demoCheck.Demo(root, relief=SUNKEN, bd=2).pack(fill=BOTH)

files = glob(gifdir + "*.gif")                       # gifs for now
images = map(lambda x: (x, PhotoImage(file=x)), files)  # load and hold
print files
root.mainloop()
```

This code uses a handful of built-in tools from the Python library:

- The Python `glob` module we met earlier in the book gives a list of all files ending in *.gif* in a directory; in other words, all GIF files stored there.

- The Python `random` module is used to select a random GIF from files in the directory: `random.choice` picks and returns an item from a list at random.

- To change the image displayed (and the GIF file's name in a label at the top of the window), the script simply calls the widget `config` method with new option settings; changing on the fly like this changes the widget's display.

Just for fun, this script also attaches an instance of the `demoCheck` checkbox demo bar, which in turn attaches an instance of the `Quitter` button we wrote earlier. This is an artificial example, of course, but again demonstrates the power of component class attachment at work.

Notice how this script builds and holds onto all images in its `images` list. The `map` here applies a `PhotoImage` constructor call to every *.gif* file in the photo directory, producing a list of (`file,image`) tuples that is saved in a global variable.

Remember, this guarantees that image objects won't be garbage-collected as long as the program is running. Figure 7-39 shows this script in action on Windows.

Figure 7-39. buttonpics in action

Although it may not be obvious in this grayscale book, the name of the GIF file being displayed is shown in red text in the blue label at the top of this window. This program's window grows and shrinks automatically when larger and smaller GIF files are displayed; Figure 7-40 shows it randomly picking a taller photo globbed from the image directory.

Figure 7-40. buttonpics showing a taller photo

And finally, Figure 7-41 captures this script's GUI displaying one of the wider GIFs, selected completely at random from the photo file directory.*

---

* This particular image appeared as a banner ad on developer-related web sites like *slashdot.com* when the book *Learning Python* was first published. It generated enough of a backlash from Perl zealots that O'Reilly eventually pulled the ad altogether. Which is why, of course, it appears in this book.

Figure 7-41. buttonpics gets political

While we're playing, let's recode this script as a class in case we ever want to attach or customize it later (it could happen). It's mostly a matter of indenting and adding `self` before global variable names, as shown in Example 7-40.

Example 7-40. PP2E\Gui\Tour\buttonpics.py

```python
from Tkinter import *              # get base widget set
from glob import glob             # file name expansion list
import demoCheck                  # attach checkbox example to me
import random                     # pick a picture at random
gifdir = '../gifs/'              # default dir to load gif files

class ButtonPicsDemo(Frame):
    def __init__(self, gifdir=gifdir, parent=None):
        Frame.__init__(self, parent)
        self.pack()
        self.lbl = Label(self,  text="none", bg='blue', fg='red')
        self.pix = Button(self, text="Press me", command=self.draw, bg='white')
        self.lbl.pack(fill=BOTH)
        self.pix.pack(pady=10)
        demoCheck.Demo(self, relief=SUNKEN, bd=2).pack(fill=BOTH)
        files = glob(gifdir + "*.gif")
        self.images = map(lambda x: (x, PhotoImage(file=x)), files)
        print files

    def draw(self):
        name, photo = random.choice(self.images)
        self.lbl.config(text=name)
        self.pix.config(image=photo)

if __name__ == '__main__': ButtonPicsDemo().mainloop()
```

This version works the same as the original, but can now be attached to any other GUI where you would like to include such an unreasonably silly button.

Other Image File Formats: PIL

As mentioned, Python Tkinter scripts show images by associating independently created image objects with real widget objects. At this writing, Tkinter GUIs can display photo image files in GIF, PPM, and PGM formats by creating a `PhotoImage` object, as well as X11-style bitmap files (usually suffixed with a *.xbm* extension) by creating a `BitmapImage` object.

This set of supported file formats is limited by the underlying Tk library, not Tkinter itself, and may expand in the future. But if you want to display files in other formats today (e.g., JPEG and BMP), you can either convert your files to one of the supported formats with an image-processing program, or install the PIL Python extension package mentioned at the start of Chapter 6.

PIL currently supports nearly 30 graphic file formats (including JPEG and BMP). To make use of its tools, you must first fetch and install the PIL package (see *http://www.pythonware.com*). Then, simply use special `PhotoImage` and `BitmapImage` objects imported from the PIL `ImageTk` module to open files in other graphic formats. These are compatible replacements for the standard Tkinter classes of the same name, and may be used anywhere Tkinter expects a `PhotoImage` or `BitmapImage` object (i.e., in label, button, canvas, text, and menu object configurations). That is, replace standard Tkinter code like this:

```
from Tkinter import *
imgobj = PhotoImage(file=imgdir+"spam.gif")
Button(image=imgobj).pack()
```

With code of this form:

```
from Tkinter import *
import ImageTk
imgobj = ImageTk.PhotoImage(file=imgdir+"spam.jpg")
Button(image=imgobj).pack()
```

Or the more verbose equivalent:

```
from Tkinter import *
import Image, ImageTk
imagefile = Image.open(imgdir+"spam.jpeg")
imageobj  = ImageTk.PhotoImage(imagefile)
Label(image=imageobj).pack()
```

PIL installation details vary per platform; on my Windows laptop, it was just a matter of downloading, unzipping, and adding PIL directories to the front of PYTHONPATH. There is much more to PIL than we have time to cover here; for instance, it also provides image conversion, resizing, and transformation tools, some of which can be run as command-line programs that have nothing to do with GUIs directly. See *http://www.pythonware.com* for more information, as well as online PIL and Tkinter documentation sets.

8

A Tkinter Tour, Part 2

"On Today's Menu: Spam, Spam, and Spam"

This chapter is the second in a two-part tour of the Tkinter library. It picks up where Chapter 7, *A Tkinter Tour, Part 1*, left off, and covers some of the more advanced widgets and tools in the Tkinter arsenal. Among the topics presented in this chapter:

- `Menu`, `Menubutton`, and `OptionMenu` widgets

- The `Scrollbar` widget: for scrolling text, lists, and canvases

- The `Listbox` widget: a list of multiple selections

- The `Text` widget: a general text display and editing tool

- The `Canvas` widget: a general graphical drawing tool

- The `grid` table-based geometry manager

- Time-based tools: `after`, `update`, `wait`, and threads

- Basic Tkinter animation techniques

- Clipboards, erasing widgets and windows, etc.

By the time you've finished this chapter, you will have seen the bulk of the Tkinter library, and have all the information you need to compose larger portable user interfaces of your own. You'll also be ready to tackle the larger GUI examples presented in Chapter 9, *Larger GUI Examples*. As a segue to the next chapter, this one also closes with a look at the PyDemos and PyGadgets launcher toolbars—GUIs used to start larger GUI examples.

Menus

Menus are the pull-down lists you're accustomed to seeing at the top of a window (or the entire display, if you're accustomed to seeing them on a Macintosh). Move the mouse cursor to the menu bar at the top, click on a name (e.g., File), and a list of selectable options pops up under the name you clicked (e.g., Open, Save). The options within a menu might trigger actions, much like clicking on a button; they may also open other "cascading" submenus that list more options, pop-up dialog windows, and so on. In Tkinter, there are two kinds of menus you can add to your scripts: top-level window menus and frame-based menus. The former option is better suited to whole windows, but the latter also works as a nested component.

Top-Level Window Menus

In more recent Python releases (using Tk 8.0 and beyond), you can associate a horizontal menu bar with a top-level window object (e.g., a `Tk` or `Toplevel`). On Windows and Unix (X Windows), this menu bar is displayed along the top of the window; on Macintosh, this menu replaces the one shown at the top of the screen when the window is selected. In other words, window menus look like you would expect on whatever underlying platform your script runs upon.

This scheme is based on building trees of `Menu` widget objects. Simply associate one top-level `Menu` with the window, add other pull-down `Menu` objects as cascades of the top-level `Menu`, and add entries to each of the pull-downs. `Menus` are cross-linked with the next higher level, by using parent widget arguments and the `Menu` widget's `add_cascade` method. It works like this:

1. Create a topmost `Menu` as the child of the window widget, and configure the window's `menu` attribute to be the new `Menu`.

2. For each pull-down, make a new `Menu` as the child of the topmost `Menu`, and add the child as a cascade of the topmost `Menu` using `add_cascade`.

3. Add menu selections to each pull-down `Menu` from Step 2, using the `command` options of `add_command` to register selection callback handlers.

4. Add a cascading submenu by making a new `Menu` as the child of the `Menu` the cascade extends, and using `add_cascade` to link parent to child.

The end result is a tree of `Menu` widgets with associated `command` callback handlers. This is all probably simpler in code than in words, though. Example 8-1 makes a main menu with two pull-downs, File and Edit; the Edit pull-down in turn has a nested submenu of its own.

Example 8-1. PP2E\Gui\Tour\menu_win.py

```
# Tk8.0 style top-level window menus

from Tkinter import *                                  # get widget classes
from tkMessageBox import *                             # get standard dialogs

def notdone():
    showerror('Not implemented', 'Not yet available')

def makemenu(win):
    top = Menu(win)                                    # win=top-level window
    win.config(menu=top)                               # set its menu option

    file = Menu(top)
    file.add_command(label='New...',   command=notdone,   underline=0)
    file.add_command(label='Open...',  command=notdone,   underline=0)
    file.add_command(label='Quit',     command=win.quit,  underline=0)
    top.add_cascade(label='File',      menu=file,         underline=0)

    edit = Menu(top, tearoff=0)
    edit.add_command(label='Cut',      command=notdone,   underline=0)
    edit.add_command(label='Paste',    command=notdone,   underline=0)
    edit.add_separator()
    top.add_cascade(label='Edit',      menu=edit,         underline=0)

    submenu = Menu(edit, tearoff=0)
    submenu.add_command(label='Spam',  command=win.quit,  underline=0)
    submenu.add_command(label='Eggs',  command=notdone,   underline=0)
    edit.add_cascade(label='Stuff',    menu=submenu,      underline=0)

if __name__ == '__main__':
    root = Tk()                                        # or Toplevel()
    root.title('menu_win')                             # set window-mgr info
    makemenu(root)                                     # associate a menu bar
    msg = Label(root, text='Window menu basics')       # add something below
    msg.pack(expand=YES, fill=BOTH)
    msg.config(relief=SUNKEN, width=40, height=7, bg='beige')
    root.mainloop()
```

There is a lot of code in this file devoted to setting callbacks and such, so it might help to isolate the bits involved with the menu tree building process. For the File menu, it's done like this:

```
    top = Menu(win)                        # attach Menu to window
    win.config(menu=top)                   # cross-link window to menu
    file = Menu(top)                       # attach a Menu to top Menu
    top.add_cascade(label='File', menu=file) # cross-link parent to child
```

Apart from building up the menu object tree, this script also demonstrates some of the most common menu configuration options:

Separator lines

The script makes a separator in the Edit menu with `add_separator`; it's just a line used to set off groups of related entries.

Tear-offs

The script also disables menu tear-offs in the Edit pull-down by passing a `tearoff=0` widget option to `Menu`. Tear-offs are dashed lines that appear by default at the top of Tkinter menus, and create a new window containing the menu's contents when clicked. They can be a convenient shortcut device (you can click items in the tear-off window right away, without having to navigate through menu trees), but are not widely used on all platforms.

Keyboard shortcuts

The script uses the `underline` option to make a unique letter in a menu entry a keyboard shortcut. It gives the offset of the shortcut letter in the entry's label string. On Windows, for example, the Quit option in this script's File menu can be selected with the mouse as usual, but also by pressing the Alt key, then "f", then "q", You don't strictly have to use `underline`—on Windows, the first letter of a pull-down name is a shortcut automatically, and arrow and Enter keys can be used to move through and select pull-down items. But explicit keys can enhance usability in large menus; for instance, the key sequence Alt+E+S+S runs the quit action in this script's nested submenu, without any mouse or arrow key movement.

Let's see what all this translates to in the realm of the pixel. Figure 8-1 shows the window that first appears when this script is run live on Windows; it looks different, but similar, on Unix and Macintosh.

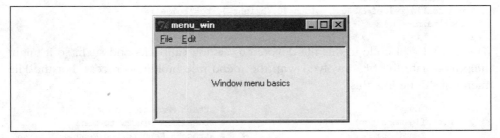

Figure 8-1. menu_win: a top-level window menu bar

Figure 8-2 shows the scene when the File pull-down is selected. Notice that `Menu` widgets are linked, not packed (or gridded)—the geometry manager doesn't really come into play here. If you run this script, you'll also notice that all of its menu entries either quit the program immediately or pop up a "Not Implemented" standard error dialog. This example is about menus, after all, but menu selection callback handlers generally do more useful work in practice.

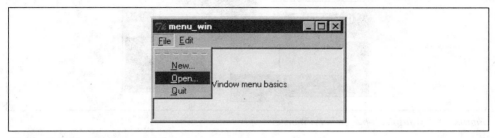

Figure 8-2. The File menu pull-down

And finally, Figure 8-3 shows what happens after clicking the File menu's tear-off line and selecting the cascading submenu in the Edit pull-down. Cascades can be nested as deep as you like, but your users probably won't be happy if this gets silly.

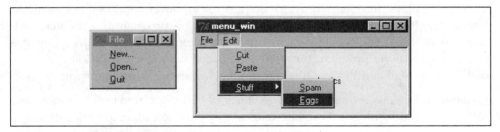

Figure 8-3. A File tear-off and Edit cascade

In Tkinter, every top-level window can have a menu bar, including pop-ups that you create with the `Toplevel` widget. Example 8-2 makes three pop-up windows with the same menu bar as the one we just met; when run, it constructs the scene captured in Figure 8-4.

Example 8-2. PP2E\Gui\Tour\menu_win-multi.py

```
from menu_win import makemenu
from Tkinter import *

root = Tk()
for i in range(3):                      # 3 popup windows with menus
    win = Toplevel(root)
    makemenu(win)
    Label(win, bg='black', height=5, width=15).pack(expand=YES, fill=BOTH)
Button(root, text="Bye", command=root.quit).pack()
root.mainloop()
```

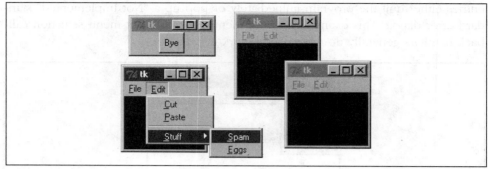

Figure 8-4. Multiple Toplevels with menus

Frame- and Menubutton-Based Menus

Although less commonly used for top-level windows, it's also possible to create a menu bar as a horizontal `Frame`. Before I show you how, though, let me explain why you should care. Because this frame-based scheme doesn't depend on top-level window protocols, it can also be used to add menus as *nested* components of larger displays. In other words, it's not just for top-level windows. For example, Chapter 9's PyEdit text editor can be used both as a program and an attachable component. We'll use window menus to implement PyEdit selections when it is run as a standalone program, but use frame-based menus when PyEdit is embedded in the PyMail and PyView displays. Both schemes are worth knowing.

Frame-based menus require a few more lines of code, but aren't much more complex than window menus. To make one, simply pack `Menubutton` widgets within a `Frame` container, associate `Menu` widgets with the `Menubuttons`, and associate the `Frame` with the top of a container window. Example 8-3 creates the same menu as Example 8-1, but using the frame-based approach.

Example 8-3. PP2E\Gui\Tour\menu_frm.py

```
# Frame-based menus: for top-levels and components

from Tkinter import *                          # get widget classes
from tkMessageBox import *                     # get standard dialogs

def notdone():
    showerror('Not implemented', 'Not yet available')

def makemenu(parent):
    menubar = Frame(parent)                    # relief=RAISED, bd=2...
    menubar.pack(side=TOP, fill=X)

    fbutton = Menubutton(menubar, text='File', underline=0)
    fbutton.pack(side=LEFT)
    file = Menu(fbutton)
```

Example 8-3. PP2E\Gui\Tour\menu_frm.py (continued)

```
    file.add_command(label='New...',  command=notdone,     underline=0)
    file.add_command(label='Open...', command=notdone,     underline=0)
    file.add_command(label='Quit',    command=parent.quit, underline=0)
    fbutton.config(menu=file)

    ebutton = Menubutton(menubar, text='Edit', underline=0)
    ebutton.pack(side=LEFT)
    edit = Menu(ebutton, tearoff=0)
    edit.add_command(label='Cut',    command=notdone,     underline=0)
    edit.add_command(label='Paste',  command=notdone,     underline=0)
    edit.add_separator()
    ebutton.config(menu=edit)

    submenu = Menu(edit, tearoff=0)
    submenu.add_command(label='Spam', command=parent.quit, underline=0)
    submenu.add_command(label='Eggs', command=notdone,     underline=0)
    edit.add_cascade(label='Stuff',   menu=submenu,        underline=0)
    return menubar

if __name__ == '__main__':
    root = Tk()                                     # or TopLevel or Frame
    root.title('menu_frm')                          # set window-mgr info
    makemenu(root)                                  # associate a menu bar
    msg = Label(root, text='Frame menu basics')     # add something below
    msg.pack(expand=YES, fill=BOTH)
    msg.config(relief=SUNKEN, width=40, height=7, bg='beige')
    root.mainloop()
```

Again, let's isolate the linkage logic here to avoid getting distracted by other details. For the File menu case, here is what this boils down to:

```
    menubar = Frame(parent)                     # make a Frame for the menubar
    fbutton = Menubutton(menubar, text='File')  # attach a MenuButton to Frame
    file    = Menu(fbutton)                      # attach a Menu to MenuButton
    fbutton.config(menu=file)                    # crosslink button to menu
```

There is an extra `Menubutton` widget in this scheme, but it's not much more complex than making top-level window menus. Figures 8-5 and 8-6 show this script in action on Windows.

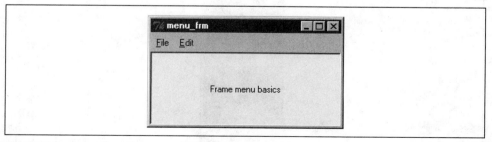

Figure 8-5. menu_frm: Frame and Menubutton menu bar

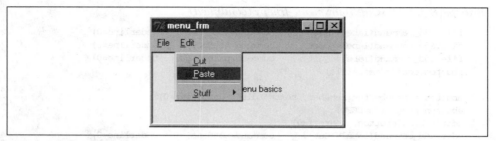

Figure 8-6. With the Edit menu selected

The menu widgets in this script provide a default set of event bindings that automatically pop up menus when selected with a mouse. This doesn't look or behave
exactly like the top-level window menu scheme shown earlier, but it is close, can
be configured in any way that frames can (i.e., with colors and borders), and will
look similar on every platform (though this is probably not a feature).

The biggest advantage of frame-based menu bars, though, is that they can also be
attached as nested components in larger displays. Example 8-4 and its resulting
interface (Figure 8-7) show how.

Example 8-4. PP2E\Gui\Tour\menu_frm-multi.py

```
from menu_frm import makemenu         # can't use menu_win here--one window
from Tkinter import *                 # but can attach from menus to windows

root = Tk()
for i in range(2):                    # 2 menus nested in one window
    mnu = makemenu(root)
    mnu.config(bd=2, relief=RAISED)
    Label(root, bg='black', height=5, width=15).pack(expand=YES, fill=BOTH)
Button(root, text="Bye", command=root.quit).pack()
root.mainloop()
```

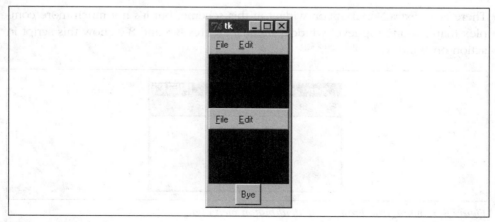

Figure 8-7. Multiple Frame menus on one window

Because they are not tied to the enclosing window, frame-based menus can also be used as part of another attachable component's widget package. For example, the menu embedding behavior in Example 8-5 even works if the menu's parent is another `Frame` container, not the top-level window.

Example 8-5. PP2E\Gui\Tour\menu_frm-multi2.py

```
from menu_frm import makemenu          # can't use menu_win here--root=Frame
from Tkinter import *

root = Tk()
for i in range(3):                     # 3 menus nested in the containers
    frm = Frame()
    mnu = makemenu(frm)
    mnu.config(bd=2, relief=RAISED)
    frm.pack(expand=YES, fill=BOTH)
    Label(frm, bg='black', height=5, width=15).pack(expand=YES, fill=BOTH)
Button(root, text="Bye", command=root.quit).pack()
root.mainloop()
```

Using Menubuttons and Optionmenus

In fact, menus based on `Menubutton` are even more general than Example 8-3 implies—they can actually show up anywhere on a display that normal buttons can, not just within a menubar `Frame`. Example 8-6 makes a `Menubutton` pull-down list that simply shows up by itself, attached to the root window; Figure 8-8 shows the GUI it produces.

Example 8-6. PP2E\Gui\Tour\mbutton.py

```
from Tkinter import *
root    = Tk()
mbutton = Menubutton(root, text='Food')        # the pull-down stands alone
picks   = Menu(mbutton)
mbutton.config(menu=picks)
picks.add_command(label='spam',  command=root.quit)
picks.add_command(label='eggs',  command=root.quit)
picks.add_command(label='bacon', command=root.quit)
mbutton.pack()
mbutton.config(bg='white', bd=4, relief=RAISED)
root.mainloop()
```

Figure 8-8. A Menubutton all by itself

The related Tkinter `Optionmenu` widget displays an item selected from a pull-down menu. It's roughly like a `Menubutton` plus a display label, and displays a menu of choices when clicked; but you must link Tkinter variables (described in Chapter 7) to fetch the choice after the fact instead of registering callbacks, and menu entries are passed as arguments in the widget constructor call after the variable.

Example 8-7 illustrates typical `Optionmenu` usage, and builds the interface captured in Figure 8-9. Clicking on either of the first two buttons opens a pull-down menu of options; clicking on the third "state" button fetches and prints the current values displayed in the first two.

Example 8-7. PP2E\Gui\Tour\optionmenu.py

```
from Tkinter import *
root = Tk()
var1 = StringVar()
var2 = StringVar()
opt1 = OptionMenu(root, var1, 'spam', 'eggs',  'toast')      # like Menubutton
opt2 = OptionMenu(root, var2, 'ham',  'bacon', 'sausage')    # but shows choice
opt1.pack(fill=X)
opt2.pack(fill=X)
var1.set('spam')
var2.set('ham')
def state(): print var1.get(), var2.get()                    # linked variables
Button(root, command=state, text='state').pack()
root.mainloop()
```

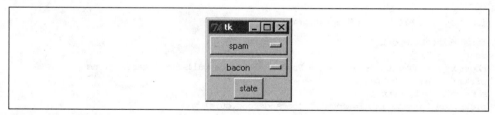

Figure 8-9. An Optionmenu at work

There are other menu-related topics that we'll skip here in the interest of space. For instance, scripts can add entries to *system menus*, and generate *pop-up menus* (posted in response to events, without an associated button). Refer to Tk and Tkinter resources for more details on this front.

In addition to simple selections and cascades, menus can also contain disabled entries, checkbutton and radiobutton selections, and bitmap and photo images. The next section demonstrates how some of these special menu entries are programmed.

Windows with Both Menus and Toolbars

Besides showing a menu at the top, it is common for windows to display a row of buttons at the bottom. This bottom button row is usually called a *toolbar*, and often contains shortcuts to items also available in the menus at the top. It's easy to add a toolbar to windows in Tkinter—simply pack buttons (and other kinds of widgets) into a frame, pack the frame on the bottom of the window, and set it to expand horizontally only. This is really just hierarchical GUI layout at work again, but make sure to pack toolbars (and frame-based menu bars) early, so that other widgets in the middle of the display are clipped first when the window shrinks.

Example 8-8 shows one way to go about adding a toolbar to a window. It also demonstrates how to add photo images in menu entries (set the **image** attribute to **PhotoImage** object), and how to disable entries and give them a grayed-out appearance (call the menu **entryconfig** method with the index of the item to disable, starting from 1). Notice that **PhotoImage** objects are saved as a list; remember, unlike other widgets, these go away if you don't hold onto them.

Example 8-8. PP2E\Gui\Tour\menuDemo.py

```python
#!/usr/local/bin/python
###########################################################################
# Tk8.0 style main window menus
# menu/tool bars packed before middle, fill=X (pack first=clip last);
# adds photos menu entries; see also: add_checkbutton, add_radiobutton
###########################################################################

from Tkinter import *                         # get widget classes
from tkMessageBox import *                     # get standard dialogs

class NewMenuDemo(Frame):                       # an extended frame
    def __init__(self, parent=None):            # attach to top-level?
        Frame.__init__(self, parent)            # do superclass init
        self.pack(expand=YES, fill=BOTH)
        self.createWidgets()                    # attach frames/widgets
        self.master.title("Toolbars and Menus") # set window-manager info
        self.master.iconname("tkpython")        # label when iconified

    def createWidgets(self):
        self.makeMenuBar()
        self.makeToolBar()
        L = Label(self, text='Menu and Toolbar Demo')
        L.config(relief=SUNKEN, width=40, height=10, bg='white')
        L.pack(expand=YES, fill=BOTH)

    def makeToolBar(self):
        toolbar = Frame(self, cursor='hand2', relief=SUNKEN, bd=2)
        toolbar.pack(side=BOTTOM, fill=X)
        Button(toolbar, text='Quit',  command=self.quit    ).pack(side=RIGHT)
        Button(toolbar, text='Hello', command=self.greeting).pack(side=LEFT)
```

Example 8-8. PP2E\Gui\Tour\menuDemo.py (continued)

```
    def makeMenuBar(self):
        self.menubar = Menu(self.master)
        self.master.config(menu=self.menubar)     # master=top-level window
        self.fileMenu()
        self.editMenu()
        self.imageMenu()

    def fileMenu(self):
        pulldown = Menu(self.menubar)
        pulldown.add_command(label='Open...', command=self.notdone)
        pulldown.add_command(label='Quit',    command=self.quit)
        self.menubar.add_cascade(label='File', underline=0, menu=pulldown)

    def editMenu(self):
        pulldown = Menu(self.menubar)
        pulldown.add_command(label='Paste',   command=self.notdone)
        pulldown.add_command(label='Spam',    command=self.greeting)
        pulldown.add_separator()
        pulldown.add_command(label='Delete',  command=self.greeting)
        pulldown.entryconfig(4, state=DISABLED)
        self.menubar.add_cascade(label='Edit', underline=0, menu=pulldown)

    def imageMenu(self):
        photoFiles = ('guido.gif', 'pythonPowered.gif', 'ppython_sm_ad.gif')
        pulldown = Menu(self.menubar)
        self.photoObjs = []
        for file in photoFiles:
            img = PhotoImage(file='../gifs/' + file)
            pulldown.add_command(image=img, command=self.notdone)
            self.photoObjs.append(img)    # keep a reference
        self.menubar.add_cascade(label='Image', underline=0, menu=pulldown)

    def greeting(self):
        showinfo('greeting', 'Greetings')
    def notdone(self):
        showerror('Not implemented', 'Not yet available')
    def quit(self):
        if askyesno('Verify quit', 'Are you sure you want to quit?'):
            Frame.quit(self)

if __name__ == '__main__': NewMenuDemo().mainloop()  # if I'm run as a script
```

When run, this script generates the scene in Figure 8-10 at first. Figure 8-11 shows this window after being stretched a bit, with its File and Edit menus torn off, and its Image menu selected. That's Python creator Guido van Rossum in this script's third menu (wearing his now-deprecated eyeglasses). Run this on your own computer to get a better feel for its behavior.[*]

---

[*] Also note that toolbar items can be pictures too—simply associate small images with toolbar buttons, as shown at the end of Chapter 7.

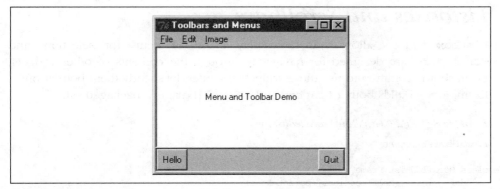

Figure 8-10. menuDemo: menus and toolbars

Figure 8-11. Images and tear-offs on the job

Automating menu construction

Menus are a powerful Tkinter interface device. If you're like me, though, the examples in this section probably seem like a lot of work. Menu construction can be both code-intensive and error-prone if done by calling Tkinter methods directly. A better approach might automatically build and link up menus from a higher-level description of their contents. In fact, we will—in Chapter 9, we'll meet a tool called *GuiMixin* that automates the menu construction process, given a data structure that contains all menus desired. As an added bonus, it supports both window and frame-style menus, so it can be used by both standalone programs and nested components. Although it's important to know the underlying calls used to make menus, you don't necessarily have to remember them for long.

Listboxes and Scrollbars

Listbox widgets allow you to display a list of items for selection, and Scrollbars are designed for navigating through the contents of other widgets. Because it is common to use these widgets together, let's study them both at once. Example 8-9 builds both a Listbox and a Scrollbar, as a packaged set.

Example 8-9. PP2E\Gui\Tour\scrolledlist.py

```
from Tkinter import *

class ScrolledList(Frame):
    def __init__(self, options, parent=None):
        Frame.__init__(self, parent)
        self.pack(expand=YES, fill=BOTH)                # make me expandable
        self.makeWidgets(options)
    def handleList(self, event):
        index = self.listbox.curselection()            # on list double-click
        label = self.listbox.get(index)                # fetch selection text
        self.runCommand(label)                         # and call action here
    def makeWidgets(self, options):                    # or get(ACTIVE)
        sbar = Scrollbar(self)
        list = Listbox(self, relief=SUNKEN)
        sbar.config(command=list.yview)                # xlink sbar and list
        list.config(yscrollcommand=sbar.set)           # move one moves other
        sbar.pack(side=RIGHT, fill=Y)                  # pack first=clip last
        list.pack(side=LEFT, expand=YES, fill=BOTH)    # list clipped first
        pos = 0
        for label in options:                          # add to list-box
            list.insert(pos, label)                    # or insert(END,label)
            pos = pos + 1
       #list.config(selectmode=SINGLE, setgrid=1)      # select,resize modes
        list.bind('<Double-1>', self.handleList)       # set event handler
        self.listbox = list
    def runCommand(self, selection):                   # redefine me lower
        print 'You selected:', selection

if __name__ == '__main__':
    options = map((lambda x: 'Lumberjack-' + str(x)), range(20))
    ScrolledList(options).mainloop()
```

This module can be run standalone to experiment with these widgets, but is also designed to be useful as a library object. By passing in different selection lists to the options argument and redefining the runCommand method in a subclass, the ScrolledList component class defined here can be reused any time you need to display a scrollable list. With just a little forethought, it's easy to extend the Tkinter library with Python classes.

When run standalone, this script generates the window shown in Figure 8-12. It's a Frame, with a Listbox on its left containing 20 generated entries (the fifth has been clicked), along with an associated `Scrollbar` on its right for moving through the list. If you move the scroll, the list moves, and vice versa.

Figure 8-12. scrolledlist at the top

Programming Listboxes

Listboxes are straightforward to use, but they are populated and processed in somewhat unique ways compared to the widgets we've seen so far. Many listbox calls accept a passed-in *index* to refer to an entry in the list. Indexes start at integer 0 and grow higher, but Tkinter also accepts special name strings in place of integer offsets—"end" to refer to the end of the list, "active" to denote the line selected, and more. This generally yields more than one way to code listbox calls.

For instance, this script adds items to the listbox in this window by calling its `insert` method, with successive offsets (starting at zero):

```
list.insert(pos, label)
pos = pos + 1
```

But you can also fill a list by simply adding items at the *end* without keeping a position counter at all, with either of these statements:

```
list.insert('end', label)      # add at end: no need to count positions
list.insert(END, label)        # END is preset to 'end' inside Tkinter
```

The listbox widget doesn't have anything like the `command` option we use to register callback handlers for button presses, so you either need to fetch listbox selections while processing other widgets' events (e.g., a button press elsewhere in the GUI), or tap into other event protocols to process user selections. To fetch a selected value, this script binds the `<Double-1>` left mouse button double-click event to a callback handler method with `bind` (seen earlier on this tour).

In the double-click handler, this script grabs the selected item out of the listbox with this pair of listbox method calls:

```
index = self.listbox.curselection()    # get selection index
label = self.listbox.get(index)        # fetch text by its index
```

Here, too, you can code this differently. Either of the following lines have the same effect; they get the contents of the line at index "active"—the one selected:

```
label = self.listbox.get('active')     # fetch from active index
label = self.listbox.get(ACTIVE)        # ACTIVE='active' in Tkinter
```

For illustration purposes, the class's default runCommand method prints the value selected each time you double-click an entry in the list—as fetched by this script, it comes back as a string reflecting the text in the selected entry:

```
C:\...\PP2E\Gui\Tour>python scrolledlist.py
You selected: Lumberjack-2
You selected: Lumberjack-19
You selected: Lumberjack-4
You selected: Lumberjack-12
```

Programming Scrollbars

The deepest magic in this script, though, boils down to two lines of code:

```
sbar.config(command=list.yview)            # call list.yview when I move
list.config(yscrollcommand=sbar.set)       # call sbar.set when I move
```

The scrollbar and listbox are effectively cross-linked to each other through these configuration options; their values simply refer to bound widget methods of the other. By linking like this, Tkinter automatically keeps the two widgets in sync with each other as they move. Here's how this works:

- Moving a *scrollbar* invokes the callback handler registered with its command option. Here, list.yview refers to a built-in listbox method that adjusts the listbox display proportionally, based on arguments passed to the handler.

- Moving a *listbox* vertically invokes the callback handler registered with its yscrollcommand option. In this script, the sbar.set built-in method adjusts a scrollbar proportionally.

In other words, moving one automatically moves the other. It turns out that every scrollable object in Tkinter—Listbox, Entry, Text, and Canvas—has built-in yview and xview methods to process incoming *vertical* and *horizontal* scroll callbacks, as well as yscrollcommand and xscrollcommand options for specifying an associated scrollbar's callback handler. Scrollbars all have a command option, to name a handler to call on moves. Internally, Tkinter passes information to all these methods that specifies their new position (e.g., "go 10% down from the top"), but your scripts need never deal with that level of detail.

Because the scrollbar and listbox have been cross-linked in their option settings, moving the scrollbar automatically moves the list, and moving the list automatically moves the scrollbar. To move the scrollbar, either drag the solid part or click on its arrows or empty areas. To move the list, click on the list and move the mouse pointer above or below the listbox without releasing the mouse button. In both cases, the list and scrollbar move in unison. Figure 8-13 is the scene after moving down a few entries in the list, one way or another.

Figure 8-13. scrolledlist in the middle

Packing Scrollbars

Finally, remember that widgets packed last are always clipped first when a window is shrunk. Because of that, it's important to pack scrollbars in a display as soon as possible, so that they are the last to go when the window becomes too small for everything. You can generally make due with less than complete listbox text, but the scrollbar is crucial for navigating through the list. As Figure 8-14 shows, shrinking this script's window cuts out part of the list, but retains the scrollbar.

Figure 8-14. scrolledlist gets small

At the same time, you don't generally want a scrollbar to expand with a window, so be sure to pack it with just a `fill=Y` (or `fill=X` for a horizontal scroll), and *not* an `expand=YES`. Expanding this example's window, for instance, makes the listbox grow along with the window, but keeps the scrollbar attached to the right, and of the same size.

We'll see both scrollbars and listboxes repeatedly in later examples in this and later chapters (flip ahead to PyEdit, PyForm, PyTree, and ShellGui for more examples). And although the example script in this section captures the fundamentals, I should point out that there is more to both scrollbars and listboxes than meets the eye here.

For example, it's just as easy to add *horizontal* scrollbars to scrollable widgets; they are programmed almost exactly like the vertical one implemented here, but callback handler names start with "x", not "y", and an `orient='horizontal'` configuration option is set for the scrollbar object (see the later PyEdit and PyTree programs for examples). Listboxes can also be useful input devices even without attached scrollbars; they also accept color, font, and relief configuration options, and support multiple selections (the default is `selectmode=SINGLE`).

Scrollbars see more kinds of GUI action too—they can be associated with other kinds of widgets in the Tkinter library. For instance, it is common to attach one to the `Text` widget; which brings us to the next point of interest on this tour.

Text

It's been said that Tkinter's strongest points may be its text and canvas widgets. Both provide a remarkable amount of functionality. For instance, the Tkinter `Text` widget was powerful enough to implement the Grail web browser, discussed in Chapter 15, *Advanced Internet Topics*; it supports complex font style settings, embedded images, and much more. The Tkinter `Canvas` widget, a general-purpose drawing device, has also been the basis of sophisticated image processing and visualization applications.

In Chapter 9, we'll put these two widgets to use to implement text editors (PyEdit), paint programs (PyDraw), clock GUIs (PyClock), and photo slideshows (PyView). For the purposes of this tour chapter, though, let's start out using these widgets in simpler ways. Example 8-10 implements a simple scrolled-text display, which knows how to fill its display with a text string or file.

Example 8-10. PP2E\Gui\Tour\scrolledtext.py

```
# a simple text or file viewer component

print 'PP2E scrolledtext'
from Tkinter import *

class ScrolledText(Frame):
    def __init__(self, parent=None, text='', file=None):
        Frame.__init__(self, parent)
        self.pack(expand=YES, fill=BOTH)                # make me expandable
        self.makewidgets()
        self.settext(text, file)
    def makewidgets(self):
        sbar = Scrollbar(self)
        text = Text(self, relief=SUNKEN)
        sbar.config(command=text.yview)                 # xlink sbar and text
        text.config(yscrollcommand=sbar.set)            # move one moves other
        sbar.pack(side=RIGHT, fill=Y)                   # pack first=clip last
        text.pack(side=LEFT, expand=YES, fill=BOTH)     # text clipped first
```

Example 8-10. PP2E\Gui\Tour\scrolledtext.py (continued)

```
        self.text = text
    def settext(self, text='', file=None):
        if file:
            text = open(file, 'r').read()
        self.text.delete('1.0', END)             # delete current text
        self.text.insert('1.0', text)            # add at line 1, col 0
        self.text.mark_set(INSERT, '1.0')        # set insert cursor
        self.text.focus()                        # save user a click
    def gettext(self):                           # returns a string
        return self.text.get('1.0', END+'-1c')   # first through last

if __name__ == '__main__':
    root = Tk()
    try:
        st = ScrolledText(file=sys.argv[1])      # filename on cmdline
    except IndexError:
        st = ScrolledText(text='Words\ngo here')  # or not: 2 lines
    def show(event): print repr(st.gettext())    # show as raw string
    root.bind('<Key-Escape>', show)              # esc = dump text
    root.mainloop()
```

Like the `ScrolledList` of Example 8-9, the `ScrolledText` object in this file is designed to be a reusable component, but can also be run standalone to display text file contents. Also like the last section, this script is careful to pack the scrollbar first so that it is cut out of the display last as the window shrinks, and arranges for the embedded `Text` object to expand in both directions as the window grows. When run with a filename argument, this script makes the window shown in Figure 8-15; it embeds a `Text` widget on the left, and a cross-linked `Scrollbar` on the right.

Just for fun, I populated the text file displayed in the window with the following code and command lines (and not just because I happen to live near an infamous hotel in Colorado):

```
C:\...\PP2E\Gui\Tour>type temp.py
f = open('temp.txt', 'w')
for i in range(250):
    f.write('%03d  All work and no play makes Jack a dull boy.\n' % i)
f.close()

C:\...\PP2E\Gui\Tour>python temp.py

C:\...\PP2E\Gui\Tour>python scrolledtext.py temp.txt
PP2E scrolledtext
```

To view a file, pass its name on the command line—its text is automatically displayed in the new window. By default, it is shown in a non-fixed-width font, but we'll pass a `font` option to the text widget in the next example to change that.

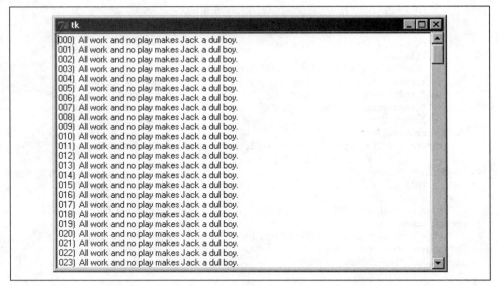

Figure 8-15. scrolledtext in action

Notice the "PP2E scrolledtext" message printed when this script runs. Because there is also a *ScrolledText.py* file in the standard Python distribution with a very different interface, the one here identifies itself when run or imported so you can tell which one you've got. If the standard one ever goes away, import the one listed here for a simple text browser, and adjust configuration calls to include a ".text" qualifier level (the library version subclasses `Text`, not `Frame`).

Programming the Text Widget

To understand how this script works at all, though, we have to detour into a few `Text` widget details here. Earlier we met the `Entry` and `Message` widgets, which address a subset of the `Text` widget's uses. The `Text` widget is much richer in both features and interfaces—it supports both input and display of multiple lines of text, editing operations for both programs and interactive users, multiple fonts and colors, and much more. `Text` objects are created, configured, and packed just like any other widget, but they have properties all their own.

Text is a Python string

Although the `Text` widget is a powerful tool, its interface seems to boil down to two core concepts. First of all, the content of a `Text` widget is represented as a string in Python scripts, and multiple lines are separated with the normal \n line terminator. The string `'Words\ngo here'`, for instance, represents two lines when stored in or fetched from a `Text` widget; it would normally have a trailing \n too, but doesn't have to.

To help illustrate this point, this script binds the Escape key press to fetch and print the entire contents of the `Text` widget it embeds:

```
C:\...\PP2E\Gui\Tour>python scrolledtext.py
PP2E scrolledtext
'Words\012go here'
'Always look\012on the bright\012side of life\012'
```

When run with arguments, the script stores a file's contents in the text widget. When run without arguments, the script stuffs a simple literal string into the widget, displayed by the first Escape press output here (recall that \012 is the octal escape form of the \n line terminator). The second output here happens when pressing Escape in the shrunken window captured in Figure 8-16.

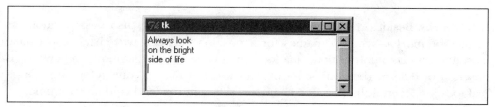

Figure 8-16. scrolledtext gets a positive outlook

String positions

The second key to understanding `Text` code has to do with the ways you specify a *position* in the text string. Like the listbox, text widgets allow you to specify such a position in a variety of ways. In `Text`, methods that expect a position to be passed in will accept an *index*, a *mark*, or a *tag* reference. Moreover, some special operations are invoked with predefined marks and tags—the insert cursor is mark `INSERT`, and the current selection is tag `SEL`.

Text indexes. Because it is a multiple-line widget, `Text` indexes identify both a line and a column. For instance, consider the interfaces of the basic insert, delete, and fetch text operations used by this script:

```
self.text.insert('1.0', text)           # insert text at the start
self.text.delete('1.0', END)            # delete all current text
return self.text.get('1.0', END+'-1c')  # fetch first through last
```

In all of these, the first argument is an absolute *index* that refers to the start of the text string: string "1.0" means row 1, column 0 (rows are numbered from 1 and columns from 0). An index "2.1" refers to the second character in the second row.

Like the listbox, text indexes can also be symbolic names: the `END` in the preceding `delete` call refers to the position just past the last character in the text string (it's a Tkinter variable preset to string "end"). Similarly, the symbolic index `INSERT` (really, string "insert") refers to the position immediately after the insert cursor—the place where characters would appear if typed at the keyboard. Symbolic names like `INSERT` can also be called marks, described in a moment.

For added precision, you can add simple arithmetic extensions to index strings. The index expression `END+'-1c'` in the `get` call in the previous example, for instance, is really the string "end-1c", and refers to one character back from `END`. Because `END` points to just beyond the last character in the text string, this expression refers to the last character itself. The `-1c` extension effectively strips the trailing `\n` that this widget adds to its contents (and may add a blank line if saved in a file).

Similar index string extensions let you name characters ahead (`+1c`), lines ahead and behind (`+2l`, `-2l`), and specify things like word and line starts around an index (`lineend`, `wordstart`). Indexes show up in most `Text` widget calls.

Text marks. Besides row/column identifier strings, you can also pass positions as names of *marks*—symbolic names for a position between two characters. Unlike absolute row/column positions, marks are virtual locations that move as new text is inserted or deleted (by your script or your user). A mark always refers to its original location, even if that location shifts to a different row and column over time.

To create a mark, call the `text mark_set` method with a string name and an index to give its logical location. For instance, this script sets the insert cursor at the start of the text initially, with a call like the first one here:

```
self.text.mark_set(INSERT, '1.0')         # set insert cursor to start
self.text.mark_set('linetwo', '2.0')      # mark current line 2
```

The name `INSERT` is a predefined special mark that identifies the insert cursor position; setting it changes the insert cursor's location. To make a mark of your own, simply provide a unique name as in the second call here, and use it anywhere you need to specify a text position. The `mark_unset` call deletes marks by name.

Text tags. In addition to absolute indexes and symbolic mark names, the `Text` widget supports the notion of *tags*—symbolic names associated with one or more substrings within the `Text` widget's string. Tags can be used for many things, but they also serve to represent a position anywhere you need one: tagged items are named by their beginning and ending indexes, which can be later passed to position-based calls.

For example, Tkinter provides a built-in tag name `SEL`—a Tkinter name preassigned to string "sel"—which automatically refers to currently selected text. To fetch the text selected (highlighted) with a mouse, run either of these calls:

```
text = self.text.get(SEL_FIRST, SEL_LAST)     # use tags for from/to indexes
text = self.text.get('sel.first', 'sel.last') # strings and constants work
```

The names SEL_FIRST and SEL_LAST are just preassigned variables in the Tkinter module that refer to the strings used in the second line here. The text get method expects two indexes; to fetch text names by a tag, add .first and .last to the tag's name to get its start and end indexes.

To tag a substring, call the text widget's tag_add method with a tag name string and start and stop positions (text can also be tagged as added in insert calls). To remove a tag from all characters in a range of text, call tag_remove:

```
self.text.tag_add('alltext', '1.0', END)    # tag all text in the widget
self.text.tag_add(SEL, index1, index2)      # select from index1 up to index2
self.text.tag_remove(SEL, '1.0', END)       # remove selection from all text
```

The first line here creates a new tag that names all text in the widget—from start through end positions. The second line adds a range of characters to the built-in SEL selection tag—they are automatically highlighted, because this tag is pre-defined to configure its members that way. The third line removes all characters in the text string from the SEL tag (all selections are unselected). Note that the tag_remove call just untags text within the named range; to really delete a tag completely, call tag_delete instead.

You can map indexes to tags dynamically too. For example, the text search method returns the row.column index of the first occurrence of a string between start and stop positions. To automatically select the text thus found, simply add its index to the built-in SEL tag:

```
where = self.text.search(target, INSERT, END)   # search from insert cursor
pastit = where + ('+%dc' % len(target))         # index beyond string found
self.text.tag_add(SEL, where, pastit)           # tag and select found string
self.text.focus()                               # select text widget itself
```

If you only want one string to be selected, be sure to first run the tag_remove call listed earlier—this code adds a selection *in addition* to any selections that already exist (it may generate multiple selections in the display). In general, you can add any number of substrings to a tag to process them as a group.

To summarize: indexes, marks, and tag locations can be used anytime you need a text position. For instance, the text see method scrolls the display to make a position visible; it accepts all three kinds of position specifiers:

```
self.text.see('1.0')            # scroll display to top
self.text.see(INSERT)           # scroll display to insert cursor mark
self.text.see(SEL_FIRST)        # scroll display to selection tag
```

Text tags can also be used in broader ways for formatting and event bindings, but I'll defer those details until the end of this section.

Adding Text-Editing Operations

Example 8-11 puts some of these concepts to work. It adds support for four common text-editing operations—file *save*, text *cut* and *paste*, and string *find* searching—by subclassing `ScolledText` to provide additional buttons and methods. The `Text` widget comes with a set of default keyboard bindings that perform some common editing operations too, but they roughly mimic the Unix Emacs editor, and are somewhat obscure; it's more common and user-friendly to provide GUI interfaces to editing operations in a GUI text editor.

Example 8-11. PP2E\Gui\Tour\simpleedit.py

```
#########################################################
# add common edit tools to scrolled text by inheritance;
# composition (embedding) would work just as well here;
# this is not robust! see PyEdit for a feature superset;
#########################################################

from Tkinter import *
from tkSimpleDialog import askstring
from tkFileDialog   import asksaveasfilename
from quitter        import Quitter
from scrolledtext   import ScrolledText               # here, not Python's

class SimpleEditor(ScrolledText):                     # see PyEdit for more
    def __init__(self, parent=None, file=None):
        frm = Frame(parent)
        frm.pack(fill=X)
        Button(frm, text='Save',  command=self.onSave).pack(side=LEFT)
        Button(frm, text='Cut',   command=self.onCut).pack(side=LEFT)
        Button(frm, text='Paste', command=self.onPaste).pack(side=LEFT)
        Button(frm, text='Find',  command=self.onFind).pack(side=LEFT)
        Quitter(frm).pack(side=LEFT)
        ScrolledText.__init__(self, parent, file=file)
        self.text.config(font=('courier', 9, 'normal'))
    def onSave(self):
        filename = asksaveasfilename()
        if filename:
            alltext = self.gettext()                  # first through last
            open(filename, 'w').write(alltext)        # store text in file
    def onCut(self):
        text = self.text.get(SEL_FIRST, SEL_LAST)     # error if no select
        self.text.delete(SEL_FIRST, SEL_LAST)         # should wrap in try
        self.clipboard_clear()
        self.clipboard_append(text)
    def onPaste(self):                                # add clipboard text
        try:
            text = self.selection_get(selection='CLIPBOARD')
            self.text.insert(INSERT, text)
        except TclError:
            pass                                      # not to be pasted
    def onFind(self):
```

Example 8-11. PP2E\Gui\Tour\simpleedit.py (continued)

```
        target = askstring('SimpleEditor', 'Search String?')
        if target:
            where = self.text.search(target, INSERT, END)   # from insert cursor
            if where:                                        # returns an index
                print where
                pastit = where + ('+%dc' % len(target))      # index past target
                #self.text.tag_remove(SEL, '1.0', END)       # remove selection
                self.text.tag_add(SEL, where, pastit)        # select found target
                self.text.mark_set(INSERT, pastit)           # set insert mark
                self.text.see(INSERT)                        # scroll display
                self.text.focus()                            # select text widget

if __name__ == '__main__':
    try:
        SimpleEditor(file=sys.argv[1]).mainloop()   # filename on command line
    except IndexError:
        SimpleEditor().mainloop()                   # or not
```

This, too, was written with one eye toward reuse—the SimpleEditor class it defines could be attached or subclassed by other GUI code. As I'll explain at the end of this section, though, it's not yet as robust as a general-purpose library tool should be. Still, it implements a functional text editor in a small amount of portable code. When run standalone, it brings up the window in Figure 8-17 (shown running in Windows); index positions are printed on stdout after each successful find operation:

```
C:\...\PP2E\Gui\Tour>python simpleedit.py simpleedit.py
PP2E scrolledtext
14.4
24.4
```

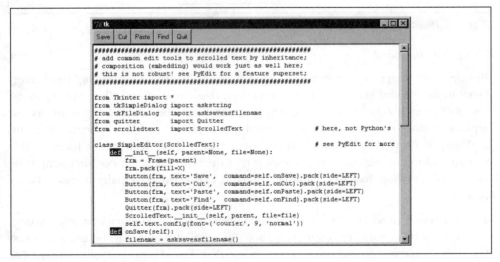

Figure 8-17. simpleedit in action

The save operation pops up the common save dialog available in Tkinter, and tailored to look native on each platform. Figure 8-18 shows this dialog in action on Windows. Find operations also pop up a standard dialog box to input a search string (Figure 8-19); in a full-blown editor, you might want to save this string away to repeat the find again (we will, in the next chapter's PyEdit).

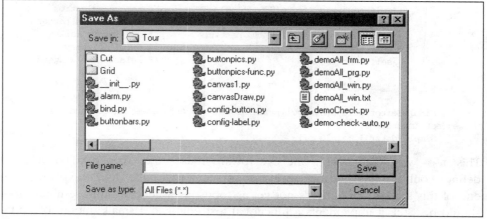

Figure 8-18. Save pop-up dialog on Windows

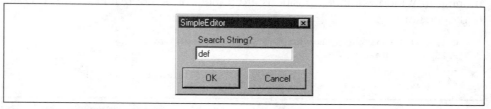

Figure 8-19. Find pop-up dialog

Using the clipboard

Besides text widget operations, Example 8-11 applies the Tkinter clipboard interfaces in its cut and paste functions. Together, these operations allow you to move text within a file (cut in one place, paste in another). The clipboard they use is just a place to store data temporarily—deleted text is placed on the clipboard on a cut, and text is inserted from the clipboard on a paste. If we restrict our focus to this program alone, there really is no reason that the text string cut couldn't simply be stored in a Python instance variable. But the clipboard is actually a much larger concept.

The clipboard used by this script is an interface to a *systemwide* storage space, shared by all programs on your computer. Because of that, it can be used to transfer data between applications, even ones that know nothing of Tkinter. For instance, text cut or copied in a Microsoft Word session can be pasted in a `SimpleEditor` window, and text cut in `SimpleEditor` can be pasted in a Microsoft Notepad window (try it). By using the clipboard for cut and paste, `SimpleEditor` automatically integrates with the window system at large. Moreover, the clipboard is not just for the text widget—it can also be used to cut and paste graphical objects in the `Canvas` widget (discussed next).

As used in this script, the basic Tkinter clipboard interface looks like this:

```
self.clipboard_clear()                          # clear the clipboard
self.clipboard_append(text)                     # store a text string on it
text = self.selection_get(selection='CLIPBOARD')  # fetch contents, if any
```

All of these calls are available as methods inherited by all Tkinter widget objects because they are global in nature. The `CLIPBOARD` selection used by this script is available on all platforms (a `PRIMARY` selection is also available, but is only generally useful on X Windows, so we'll ignore it here). Notice that the clipboard `selection_get` call throws a `TclError` exception if it fails; this script simply ignores it and abandons a paste request, but we'll do better later.

Composition versus inheritance

As coded, `SimpleEditor` uses *inheritance* to extend `ScrolledText` with extra buttons and callback methods. As we've seen, it's also reasonable to attach (embed) GUI objects coded as components, like `ScrolledText`. The attachment model is usually called *composition*; some people find it simpler to understand, and less prone to name clashes than extension by inheritance.

To give you an idea of the differences between these two approaches, the following sketches the sort of code you would write to attach a `ScrolledText` to `SimpleEditor` with changed lines in bold font (see file *simpleedit-2.py* on the CD for a complete composition implementation). It's mostly a matter of passing in the right parents, and adding an extra "st" attribute name to get to the `Text` widget's methods:

```
class SimpleEditor(Frame):
    def __init__(self, parent=None, file=None):
        Frame.__init__(self, parent)
        self.pack()
        frm = Frame(self)
        frm.pack(fill=X)
        Button(frm, text='Save',  command=self.onSave).pack(side=LEFT)
        ...more...
        Quitter(frm).pack(side=LEFT)
        self.st = ScrolledText(self, file=file)           # attach, not subclass
        self.st.text.config(font=('courier', 9, 'normal'))
    def onSave(self):
        filename = asksaveasfilename()
        if filename:
```

```
        alltext = self.st.gettext()                    # go through attribute
        open(filename, 'w').write(alltext)
    def onCut(self):
        text = self.st.text.get(SEL_FIRST, SEL_LAST)
        self.st.text.delete(SEL_FIRST, SEL_LAST)
        ...more...
```

The window looks identical when such code is run. I'll let you be the judge of whether composition or inheritance is better here. If you code your Python GUI classes right, they will work under either regime.

It's called "Simple" for a reason

Finally, before you change your system registry to make `SimpleEditor` your default text file viewer, I should mention that although it shows the basics, it's something of a stripped-down version of the PyEdit example we'll meet in Chapter 9. In fact, you should study that example now if you're looking for more complete Tkinter text processing code in general. Because the text widget is so powerful, it's difficult to demonstrate more of its features without the volume of code that is already listed in the PyEdit program.

I should also point out that `SimpleEditor` is not only limited in function, it's just plain careless—many boundary cases go unchecked and trigger uncaught exceptions that don't kill the GUI, but are not handled or reported. Even errors that are caught are not reported to the user (e.g., a paste, with nothing to be pasted). Be sure to see the PyEdit example for a more robust and complete implementation of the operations introduced in `SimpleEditor`.

Advanced Text and Tag Operations

Besides position specifiers, text tags can also be used to apply formatting and behavior to both all characters in a substring, and all substrings added to a tag. In fact, this is where much of the power of the text widget lies:

• Tags have *formatting* attributes for setting color, font, tabs, and line spacing and justification; to apply these to many parts of the text at once, associate them with a tag and apply formatting to the tag with the `tag_config` method, much like the general widget `config` we've been using.

• Tags can also have associated *event bindings*, which lets you implement things like hyperlinks in a `Text` widget: clicking the text triggers its tag's event handler. Tag bindings are set with a `tag_bind` method, much like the general widget `bind` method we've already met.

With tags, it's possible to display multiple configurations within the same text widget; for instance, you can apply one font to the text widget at large, and other fonts to tagged text. In addition, the text widget allows you to embed other widgets at an index (they are treated like a single character), as well as images.

Example 8-12 illustrates the basics of all these advanced tools at once, and draws the interface captured in Figure 8-20. This script applies formatting and event bindings to three tagged substrings, displays text in two different font and color schemes, and embeds an image and a button. Double-clicking any of the tagged substrings (or the embedded button) with a mouse triggers an event that prints a "Got tag event" message to `stdout`.

Example 8-12. PP2E\Gui\Tour\texttags.py

```
# demo advanced tag and text interfaces

from Tkinter import *
root = Tk()
def hello(event): print 'Got tag event'

# make and config a Text
text = Text()
text.config(font=('courier', 15, 'normal'))              # set font for all
text.config(width=20, height=12)
text.pack(expand=YES, fill=BOTH)
text.insert(END, 'This is\n\nthe meaning\n\nof life.\n\n')   # insert 6 lines

# embed windows and photos
btn = Button(text, text='Spam', command=lambda: hello(0))   # embed a button
btn.pack()
text.window_create(END, window=btn)                     # embed a photo
text.insert(END, '\n\n')
img = PhotoImage(file='../gifs/PythonPowered.gif')
text.image_create(END, image=img)

# apply tags to substrings
text.tag_add('demo', '1.5', '1.7')                      # tag 'is'
text.tag_add('demo', '3.0', '3.3')                      # tag 'the'
text.tag_add('demo', '5.3', '5.7')                      # tag 'life'
text.tag_config('demo', background='purple')            # change colors in tag
text.tag_config('demo', foreground='white')             # not called bg/fg here
text.tag_config('demo', font=('times', 16, 'underline')) # change font in tag
text.tag_bind('demo', '<Double-1>', hello)              # bind events in tag
root.mainloop()
```

Such embedding and tag tools could ultimately be used to render a web page. In fact, Python's standard `htmllib` HTML parser module can help automate web page GUI construction. As you can probably tell, though, the text widget offers more GUI programming options than we have space to list here. For more details on tag and text options, consult other Tk and Tkinter references. Right now, art class is about to begin.

Figure 8-20. Text tags in action

Canvas

When it comes to graphics, the Tkinter `Canvas` widget is the most free-form device in the library. It's a place to draw shapes, move objects dynamically, and place other kinds of widgets. The canvas is based on a structured graphic object model: everything drawn on a canvas can be processed as an object. You can get down to the pixel-by-pixel level in a canvas, but you can also deal in terms of larger objects like shapes, photos, and embedded widgets.

Basic Canvas Operations

Canvases are ubiquitous in much nontrivial GUI work, and we'll see larger canvas examples show up later in this book under the names PyDraw, PyView, PyClock, and PyTree. For now, let's jump right into an example that illustrates the basics. Example 8-13 runs most of the major canvas drawing methods.

Example 8-13. PP2E\Gui\Tour\canvas1.py

```
# demo all basic canvas interfaces
from Tkinter import *

canvas = Canvas(width=300, height=300, bg='white')    # 0,0 is top left corner
canvas.pack(expand=YES, fill=BOTH)                     # increases down, right

canvas.create_line(100, 100, 200, 200)                 # fromX, fromY, toX, toY
canvas.create_line(100, 200, 200, 300)                 # draw shapes
for i in range(1, 20, 2):
    canvas.create_line(0, i, 50, i)
```

Example 8-13. PP2E\Gui\Tour\canvas1.py (continued)

```
canvas.create_oval(10, 10, 200, 200, width=2, fill='blue')
canvas.create_arc(200, 200, 300, 100)
canvas.create_rectangle(200, 200, 300, 300, width=5, fill='red')
canvas.create_line(0, 300, 150, 150, width=10, fill='green')

photo=PhotoImage(file='../gifs/guido.gif')
canvas.create_image(250, 0, image=photo, anchor=NW)   # embed a photo

widget = Label(canvas, text='Spam', fg='white', bg='black')
widget.pack()
canvas.create_window(100, 100, window=widget)        # embed a widget
canvas.create_text(100, 280, text='Ham')             # draw some text
mainloop()
```

When run, this script draws the window captured in Figure 8-21. We saw how to place a photo on canvas and size a canvas for a photo earlier on this tour (see the section "Images" near the end of Chapter 7). This script also draws shapes, text, and even an embedded `Label` widget. Its window gets by on looks alone; in a moment we'll learn how to add event callbacks that let users interact with drawn items.

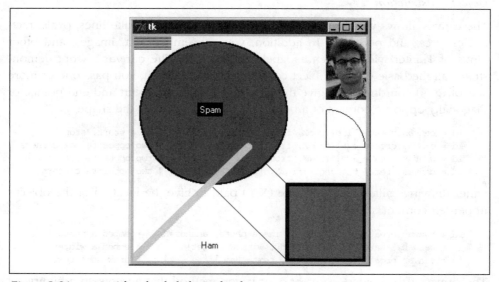

Figure 8-21. canvas1 hardcoded object sketches

Programming the Canvas Widget

Canvases are easy to use, but rely on a coordinate system, define unique drawing methods, and name objects by identifier or tag. This section introduces these core canvas concepts.

Coordinates

All items drawn on a canvas are distinct objects, but they are not really widgets. If you study the `canvas1` script closely, you'll notice that canvases are created and *packed* (or gridded or placed) within their parent container just like any other widget in Tkinter. But the items drawn on a canvas are not—shapes, images, and so on are positioned and moved on the canvas by coordinates, identifiers, and tags. Of these, coordinates are the most fundamental part of the canvas model.

Canvases define an (X,Y) coordinate system for their drawing area; X means the horizontal scale, Y means vertical. By default, coordinates are measured in screen pixels (dots), the upper-left corner of the canvas has coordinates (0,0), and X and Y coordinates increase to the right and down, respectively. To draw and embed objects within a canvas, you supply one or more (X,Y) coordinate pairs to give absolute canvas locations. This is different than the constraints we've used to pack widgets thus far, but allows very fine-grained control over graphical layouts, and supports more freeform interface techniques such as animation.[*]

Object construction

The canvas allows you to draw and display common *shapes* like lines, ovals, rectangles, arcs, and polygons. In addition, you can embed text, images, and other kinds of Tkinter widgets such as labels and buttons. The `canvas1` script demonstrates all the basic graphic object constructor calls; to each, you pass one or more sets of (X,Y) coordinates to give the new object's location, start and end points, or diagonally opposite corners of a bounding box that encloses the shape:

```
id = canvas.create_line(fromX, fromY, toX, toY)       # line start, stop
id = canvas.create_oval(fromX, fromY, toX, toY)       # two opposite box corners
id = canvas.create_arc( fromX, fromY, toX, toY)       # two opposite oval corners
id = canvas.create_rectangle(fromX, fromY, toX, toY)  # two opposite corners
```

Other drawing calls specify just one (X,Y) pair, to give the location of the object's upper-left corner:

```
id = canvas.create_image(250, 0, image=photo, anchor=NW)  # embed a photo
id = canvas.create_window(100, 100, window=widget)        # embed a widget
id = canvas.create_text(100, 280, text='Ham')             # draw some text
```

The canvas also provides a `create_polygon` method that accepts an arbitrary set of coordinate arguments defining the end-points of connected lines; it's useful for drawing more arbitrary kinds of shapes composed of straight lines.

---

[*] Animation techniques are covered at the end of this tour. Because you can embed other widgets in a canvas's drawing area, their coordinate system also makes them ideal for implementing GUIs that let users design other GUIs by dragging embedded widgets around on the canvas—a useful canvas application we would explore in this book if I had a few hundred pages to spare.

In addition to coordinates, most of these drawing calls let you specify common configuration options, such as outline `width`, `fill` color, `outline` color, and so on. Individual object types have unique configuration options all their own too; for instance, lines may specify the shape of an optional arrow, and text, widgets, and images may all be anchored to a point of the compass (this looks like the packer's `anchor`, but really gives a point on the object that is positioned at the (X,Y) coordinates given in the create call; `NW` puts the upper-left corner at (X,Y)).

Perhaps the most important thing to notice here, though, is that Tkinter does most of the "grunt" work for you—when drawing graphics, you provide coordinates, and shapes are automatically plotted and rendered in the pixel world. If you've ever done any lower-level graphics work, you'll appreciate the difference.

Object identifiers and operations

Although not used by the `canvas1` script, every object you put on a canvas has an identifier, returned by the `create_` method that draws or embeds the object (what was coded as "id" in the last section's examples). This identifier can later be passed to other methods that move the object to new coordinates, set its configuration options, delete it from the canvas, raise or lower it among other overlapping objects, and so on.

For instance, the canvas `move` method accepts both an object identifier and X and Y *offsets* (not coordinates), and moves the named object by the offsets given:

```
canvas.move(objectIdOrTag, offsetX, offsetY)   # move object(s) by offset
```

If this happens to move the object offscreen, it is simply clipped (not shown). Other common canvas operations process objects too:

```
canvas.delete(objectIdOrTag)                # delete object(s) from canvas
canvas.tkraise(objectIdOrTag)               # raise object(s) to front
canvas.lower(objectIdOrTag)                 # lower object(s) below others
canvas.itemconfig(objectIdOrTag, fill='red') # fill object(s) with red color
```

Notice the `tkraise` name—`raise` by itself is a reserved word in Python. Also note that the `itemconfig` method is used to configure objects drawn on a canvas after they have been created; use `config` to set configuration options for the canvas itself. The best thing to notice here, though, is that because Tkinter is based on structured objects, you can process a graphic object all at once; there is no need to erase and redraw each pixel manually to implement a move or raise.

Canvas object tags

But it gets even better: In addition to object identifiers, you can also perform canvas operations on entire sets of objects at once, by associating them all with a *tag*, a name that you make up and apply to objects on the display. Tagging objects in a `Canvas` is at least similar in spirit to tagging substrings in the `Text` widget we studied in the prior section. In general terms, canvas operation methods accept either a single object's identifier or a tag name.

For example, you can move an entire set of drawn objects by associating all with the same tag, and passing the tag name to the canvas move method. In fact, this is why move takes offsets, not coordinates—when given a tag, each object associated with the tag is moved by the same (X,Y) offsets; absolute coordinates would make all the tagged objects appear on top of each other.instead.

To associate an object with a tag, either specify the tag name in the object drawing call's tag option, or call the addtag_withtag(tag, objectIdOrTag) canvas method (or its relatives). For instance:

```
canvas.create_oval(x1, y1, x2, y2, fill='red', tag='bubbles')
canvas.create_oval(x3, y3, x4, y4, fill='red', tag='bubbles')
objectId = canvas.create_oval(x5, y5, x6, y6, fill='red')
canvas.addtag_withtag('bubbles', objectId)
canvas.move('bubbles', diffx, diffy)
```

This makes three ovals and moves them at the same time by associating them all with the same tag name. Many objects can have the same tag, many tags can refer to the same object, and each tag can be individually configured and processed.

As in Text, Canvas widgets have predefined tag names too: tag "all" refers to all objects on the canvas, and "current" refers to whatever object is under the mouse cursor. Besides asking for an object under the mouse, you can also *search* for objects with the find_ canvas methods: canvas.find_closest(X,Y), for instance, returns a tuple whose first item is the identifier of the closest object to the supplied coordinates—handy after you've received coordinates in a general mouseclick event callback.

We'll revisit the notion of canvas tags by example later in this chapter (see the animation scripts near the end if you can't wait). Canvases support additional operations and options that we don't have space to cover here (e.g., the canvas postscript method lets you save the canvas in a postscript file). See later examples in this book such as PyDraw for more details, and consult other Tk or Tkinter references for an exhaustive list of canvas object options.

Scrolling Canvases

As demonstrated by Example 8-14, scrollbars can be cross-linked with a canvas using the same protocols we used to add them to listboxes and text earlier, but with a few unique requirements.

Example 8-14. PP2E\Gui\Tour\scrolledcanvas.py

```
from Tkinter import *

class ScrolledCanvas(Frame):
```

Example 8-14. PP2E\Gui\Tour\scrolledcanvas.py (continued)

```
    def __init__(self, parent=None, color='brown'):
        Frame.__init__(self, parent)
        self.pack(expand=YES, fill=BOTH)                  # make me expandable
        canv = Canvas(self, bg=color, relief=SUNKEN)
        canv.config(width=300, height=200)               # display area size
        canv.config(scrollregion=(0,0,300, 1000))        # canvas size corners
        canv.config(highlightthickness=0)                # no pixels to border

        sbar = Scrollbar(self)
        sbar.config(command=canv.yview)                  # xlink sbar and canv
        canv.config(yscrollcommand=sbar.set)             # move one moves other
        sbar.pack(side=RIGHT, fill=Y)                    # pack first=clip last
        canv.pack(side=LEFT, expand=YES, fill=BOTH)      # canv clipped first

        for i in range(10):
            canv.create_text(150, 50+(i*100), text='spam'+str(i), fill='beige')
        canv.bind('<Double-1>', self.onDoubleClick)      # set event handler
        self.canvas = canv
    def onDoubleClick(self, event):
        print event.x, event.y
        print self.canvas.canvasx(event.x), self.canvas.canvasy(event.y)

if __name__ == '__main__': ScrolledCanvas().mainloop()
```

This script makes the window in Figure 8-22. It is similar to prior scroll examples, but scrolled canvases introduce two kinks:

- You can specify the size of the displayed view window, but must specify the size of the scrollable canvas at large.

- In addition, you must map between event *view area* coordinates and overall *canvas* coordinates if the canvas is larger than its view area. In a scrolling scenario, the canvas will almost always be larger than the part displayed, so mapping is often needed when canvases are scrolled.

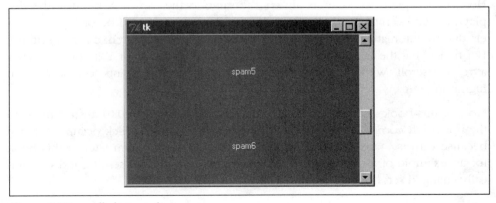

Figure 8-22. scrolledcanvas live

Sizes are given as configuration options. To specify a *view area* size, use canvas
`width` and `height` options. To specify an overall *canvas* size, give the (X,Y) coordinates of the upper-left and lower-right corners of the canvas in a four-item tuple
passed to the `scrollregion` option. If no view area size is given, a default size is
used. If no `scrollregion` is given, it defaults to the view area size; this makes
the scrollbar useless, since the view is assumed to hold the entire canvas.

Mapping coordinates is a bit more subtle. If the scrollable view area associated
with a canvas is smaller than the canvas at large, then the (X,Y) coordinates
returned in event objects are view area coordinates, not overall canvas coordinates. You'll generally want to scale the event coordinates to canvas coordinates,
by passing them to the `canvasx` and `canvasy` canvas methods before using them
to process objects.

For example, if you run the scrolled canvas script and watch the messages printed
on mouse double-clicks, you'll notice that the event coordinates are always relative to the displayed view window, not the overall canvas:

```
C:\...\PP2E\Gui\Tour>python scrolledcanvas.py
2  0                        event x,y when scrolled to top of canvas
2.0 0.0                     canvas x,y –same, as long as no border pixels
150 106
150.0 106.0
299 197
299.0 197.0
3  2                        event x,y when scrolled to bottom of canvas
3.0 802.0                   canvas x,y –y differs radically
296 192
296.0 992.0
152 97                      when scrolled to a mid point in the canvas
152.0 599.0
16 187
16.0 689.0
```

Here, the mapped canvas X is always the same as the canvas X because the display area and canvas are both set at 300 pixels wide (it would be off by two pixels due to automatic borders if not for the script's `highlightthickness` setting).
But notice that the mapped Y is wildly different from the event Y if you click after
a vertical scroll. Without scaling, the event's Y incorrectly points to a spot much
higher in the canvas.

Most of this book's canvas examples need no such scaling—(0,0) always maps to
the upper-left corner of the canvas display in which a mouseclick occurs—but just
because canvases are not scrolled. But see the PyTree program later in this book
for an example of a canvas with both horizontal and vertical scrolls, and dynamically changed scroll region sizes.

As a rule of thumb, if your canvases scroll, be sure to scale event coordinates to true canvas coordinates in callback handlers that care about positions. Some handlers might not care if events are bound to individual drawn objects instead of the canvas at large; but we need to talk more about events to see why.

Using Canvas Events

Like `Text` and `Listbox`, there is no notion of a single `command` callback for `Canvas`. Instead, canvas programs generally use other widgets, or the lower-level `bind` call to set up handlers for mouse-clicks, key-presses, and the like, as in Example 8-14. Example 8-15 shows how to bind events for the canvas itself, in order to implement a few of the more common canvas drawing operations.

Example 8-15. PP2E\Gui\Tour\canvasDraw.py

```
###############################################################
# draw elastic shapes on a canvas on drag, move on right click;
# see canvasDraw_tags*.py for extensions with tags and animation
###############################################################

from Tkinter import *
trace = 0

class CanvasEventsDemo:
    def __init__(self, parent=None):
        canvas = Canvas(width=300, height=300, bg='beige')
        canvas.pack()
        canvas.bind('<ButtonPress-1>', self.onStart)       # click
        canvas.bind('<B1-Motion>',     self.onGrow)        # and drag
        canvas.bind('<Double-1>',      self.onClear)       # delete all
        canvas.bind('<ButtonPress-3>', self.onMove)        # move latest
        self.canvas = canvas
        self.drawn  = None
        self.kinds = [canvas.create_oval, canvas.create_rectangle]
    def onStart(self, event):
        self.shape = self.kinds[0]
        self.kinds = self.kinds[1:] + self.kinds[:1]       # start dragout
        self.start = event
        self.drawn = None
    def onGrow(self, event):                               # delete and redraw
        canvas = event.widget
        if self.drawn: canvas.delete(self.drawn)
        objectId = self.shape(self.start.x, self.start.y, event.x, event.y)
        if trace: print objectId
        self.drawn = objectId
    def onClear(self, event):
        event.widget.delete('all')                         # use tag all
    def onMove(self, event):
        if self.drawn:                                     # move to click spot
            if trace: print self.drawn
            canvas = event.widget
```

Example 8-15. PP2E\Gui\Tour\canvasDraw.py (continued)

```
        diffX, diffY = (event.x - self.start.x), (event.y - self.start.y)
        canvas.move(self.drawn, diffX, diffY)
        self.start = event

if __name__ == '__main__':
    CanvasEventsDemo()
    mainloop()
```

This script intercepts and processes three mouse-controlled actions:

Clearing the canvas

To erase everything on the canvas, the script binds the double left-click event to run the canvas's `delete` method with tag "all"—again, a built-in tag that associates every object on the screen. Notice that the canvas widget clicked is available in the event object passed in to the callback handler (it's also available as `self.canvas`).

Dragging out object shapes

Pressing the left mouse button and dragging (moving it while the button is still pressed) creates a rectangle or oval shape as you drag. This is often called dragging out an object—the shape grows and shrinks in an elastic, rubberband fashion as you drag the mouse, and winds up with a final size and location given by the point where you release the mouse button.

To make this work in Tkinter, all you need to do is delete the old shape and draw another as each drag event fires; both delete and draw operations are fast enough to achieve the elastic drag-out effect. Of course, to draw a shape to the current mouse location you need a starting point; and to delete before a redraw you also must remember the last drawn object's identifier. Two events come into play: the initial *button press* event saves the start coordinates (really, the initial press event object, which contains the start coordinates), and *mouse movement* events erase and redraw from the start coordinates to the new mouse coordinates, and save the new object ID for the next event's erase.

Object moves

When you click the right mouse button (button 3), the script moves the most recently drawn object to the spot you clicked in a single step. The event argument gives the (X,Y) coordinates of the spot clicked, and we subtract the saved starting coordinates of the last drawn object to get the (X,Y) *offsets* to pass to the canvas move method (again, move does not take positions). Remember to scale event coordinates first if your canvas is scrolled.

The net result creates a window like that shown in Figure 8-23 after user interaction. As you drag out objects, the script alternates between ovals and rectangles; set the script's `trace` global to watch object identifiers scroll on `stdout` as new objects are drawn during a drag. This screen shot was taken after a few object drag-outs and moves, but you'd never tell from looking at it; run this example on your own computer to get a better feel for the operations it supports.

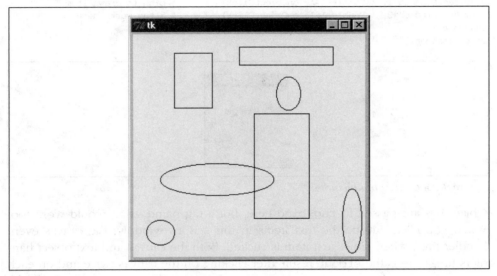

Figure 8-23. canvasDraw after a few drags and moves

Binding events on specific items

Much like we did for the `Text` widget, it is also possible to bind events for one or more specific objects drawn on a `Canvas` with its `tag_bind` method. This call accepts either a tag name string or object ID in its first argument. For instance, you can register a different callback handler for mouseclicks on every drawn item, or on any in a group of drawn and tagged items, rather than for the entire canvas at large. Example 8-16 binds a double-click handler in both the canvas itself and on two specific text items within it, to illustrate the interfaces; it generates Figure 8-24 when run.

Example 8-16. PP2E\Gui\Tour\canvas-bind.py

```
from Tkinter import *

def onCanvasClick(event):
    print 'Got canvas click', event.x, event.y, event.widget
def onObjectClick(event):
    print 'Got object click', event.x, event.y, event.widget,
    print event.widget.find_closest(event.x, event.y)   # find text object's id

root = Tk()
canv = Canvas(root, width=100, height=100)
obj1 = canv.create_text(50, 30, text='Click me one')
obj2 = canv.create_text(50, 70, text='Click me two')
```

Example 8-16. PP2E\Gui\Tour\canvas-bind.py (continued)

```
canv.bind('<Double-1>', onCanvasClick)          # bind to whole canvas
canv.tag_bind(obj1, '<Double-1>', onObjectClick)   # bind to drawn item
canv.tag_bind(obj2, '<Double-1>', onObjectClick)   # a tag works here too
canv.pack()
root.mainloop()
```

Figure 8-24. Canvas-bind window

Object IDs are passed to `tag_bind` here, but a tag name string would work too. When you click outside the text items in this script's window, the canvas event handler fires; when either text item is clicked, both the canvas and text object handlers fire. Here is the `stdout` result after clicking on the canvas twice and on each text item once; the script uses the canvas `find_closest` method to fetch the object ID of the particular text item clicked (the one closest to the click spot):

```
C:\...\PP2E\Gui\Tour>python canvas-bind.py
Got canvas click 3 6 .8217952              canvas clicks
Got canvas click 46 52 .8217952
Got object click 51 33 .8217952 (1,)       first text click
Got canvas click 51 33 .8217952
Got object click 55 69 .8217952 (2,)       second text click
Got canvas click 55 69 .8217952
```

We'll revisit the notion of events bound to canvases in the PyDraw example in Chapter 9, where we'll use them to implement a feature-rich paint and motion program. We'll also return to the `canvasDraw` script later in this chapter, to add tag-based moves and simple animation with time-based tools, so keep this page bookmarked for reference. First, though, let's follow a promising side road to explore another way to lay out widgets within windows.

Grids

So far, we've been arranging widgets in displays by calling their `pack` methods—an interface to the packer geometry manager in Tkinter. This section introduces `grid`, the most commonly used alternative to the packer.

As we learned earlier, Tkinter geometry managers work by arranging child widgets within a parent container widget (parents are typically `Frames` or top-level windows). When we ask a widget to pack or grid itself, we're really asking its parent to place it among its siblings. With pack, we provide constraints and let the geometry manager lay out widgets appropriately. With grid, we arrange widgets in rows and columns in their parent, as though the parent container widget was a table.

Gridding is an entirely distinct geometry management system in Tkinter. In fact, at this writing pack and grid are mutually exclusive for widgets that have the same parent—within a given parent container, we can either pack widgets or grid them, but not both. That makes sense, if you realize that geometry managers do their jobs at parents, and a widget can only be arranged by one geometry manager.

At least within one container, though, that means that you must pick either grid or pack and stick with it. So why grid, then? In general, grid is handy for laying out *form-like* displays; arranging input fields in row/column fashion can be at least as easy as laying out the display with nested frames. As we'll see, though, grid doesn't offer substantial code or complexity savings compared to equivalent packer solutions in practice, especially when things like resizability are added to the GUI picture. In other words, the choice between the two layout schemes is largely one of style, not technology.

Grid Basics

Let's start off with the basics; Example 8-17 lays out a table of Labels and Entry fields—widgets we've already met. Here, though, they are arrayed on a grid.

Example 8-17. PP2E\Gui\Tour\Grid\grid1.py

```
from Tkinter import *
colors = ['red', 'green', 'orange', 'white', 'yellow', 'blue']

r = 0
for c in colors:
    Label(text=c, relief=RIDGE,  width=25).grid(row=r, column=0)
    Entry(bg=c,   relief=SUNKEN, width=50).grid(row=r, column=1)
    r = r+1

mainloop()
```

When run, this script creates the window shown in Figure 8-25, pictured with data typed into a few of the input fields. Once again, this book won't do justice to the colors displayed on the right, so you'll have to stretch your imagination a little (or run this script on a computer of your own).

This is a classic input form layout: labels on the left describe data to type into entry fields on the right. Just for fun, this script displays color names on the left

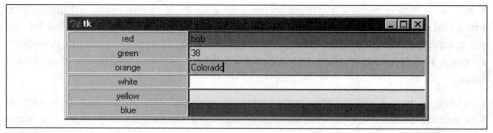

Figure 8-25. The grid geometry manager in pseudo–living color

and the entry field of the corresponding color on the right. It achieves its nice table-like layout with the following two lines:

```
Label(...).grid(row=r, column=0)
Entry(...).grid(row=r, column=1)
```

From the perspective of the container window, the *label* is gridded to column 0 in the current row number (a counter that starts at 0), and the *entry* is placed in column 1. The upshot is that the grid system lays out all the labels and entries in a two-dimensional table automatically, with evenly sized columns large enough to hold the largest item in each column.

grid Versus pack

Time for some compare-and-contrast: Example 8-18 implements the same sort of colorized input form with both `grid` and `pack`, to make it easy to see the differences between the two approaches.

Example 8-18. PP2E\Gui\Tour\Grid\grid2.py

```
# add equivalent pack window

from Tkinter import *
colors = ['red', 'green', 'yellow', 'orange', 'blue', 'navy']

def gridbox(parent):
    r = 0
    for c in colors:
        l = Label(parent, text=c, relief=RIDGE,  width=25)
        e = Entry(parent, bg=c,   relief=SUNKEN, width=50)
        l.grid(row=r, column=0)
        e.grid(row=r, column=1)
        r = r+1

def packbox(parent):
    for c in colors:
        f = Frame(parent)
        l = Label(f, text=c, relief=RIDGE,  width=25)
        e = Entry(f, bg=c,   relief=SUNKEN, width=50)
        f.pack(side=TOP)
```

Example 8-18. PP2E\Gui\Tour\Grid\grid2.py (continued)

```
        l.pack(side=LEFT)
        e.pack(side=RIGHT)

if __name__ == '__main__':
    root = Tk()
    gridbox(Toplevel())
    packbox(Toplevel())
    Button(root, text='Quit', command=root.quit).pack()
    mainloop()
```

The basic label and entry widgets are created the same way by these two functions, but they are arranged in very different ways:

- With `pack`, we use `side` options to attach labels and rows on the left and right, and create a `Frame` for each row (itself attached to the parent's top).

- With `grid`, we instead assign each widget a `row` and `column` position in the implied tabular grid of the parent, using options of the same name.

The difference in the amount code required for each scheme is roughly a wash: the `pack` scheme must create a `Frame` per row, but the `grid` scheme must keep track of the current row number. Running the script makes the windows in Figure 8-26.

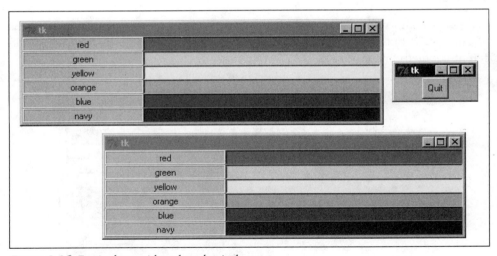

Figure 8-26. Equivalent grid and pack windows

Combining grid and pack

Notice that the prior script passes a brand new `Toplevel` to each form constructor function, so that the `grid` and `pack` versions wind up in distinct top-level windows. Because the two geometry managers are mutually exclusive within a given parent, we have to be careful not to mix them carelessly. For instance,

Example 8-19 is able to put both the packed and gridded widgets on the same window, but only by isolating each in its own `Frame` container widget.

Example 8-19. PP2E\Gui\Tour\Grid\grid2-same.py

```
####################################################################
# can't grid and pack in same parent container (e.g., root window)
# but can mix in same window if done in different parent frames;
####################################################################

from Tkinter import *
from grid2 import gridbox, packbox

root = Tk()

Label(root, text='Grid:').pack()
frm = Frame(root, bd=5, relief=RAISED); frm.pack(padx=5, pady=5)
gridbox(frm)

Label(root, text='Pack:').pack()
frm = Frame(root, bd=5, relief=RAISED); frm.pack(padx=5, pady=5)
packbox(frm)

Button(root, text='Quit', command=root.quit).pack()
mainloop()
```

We get a composite window when this runs with two forms that look identical (Figure 8-27), but the two nested frames are actually controlled by completely different geometry managers.

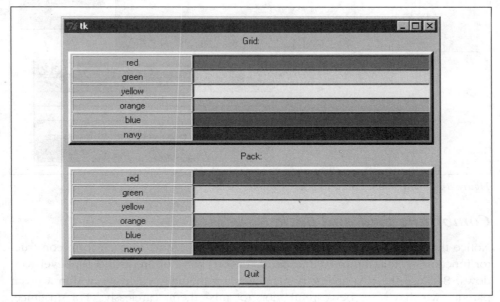

Figure 8-27. grid and pack in the same window

On the other hand, the sort of code in Example 8-20 fails badly, because it attempts to use `pack` and `grid` at the same parent—only one geometry manager can be used on any one parent.

Example 8-20. PP2E\Gui\Tour\Grid\grid2-fails.py

```
#################################################################
# FAILS-- can't grid and pack in same parent (root window)
#################################################################

from Tkinter import *
from grid2 import gridbox, packbox

root = Tk()
gridbox(root)
packbox(root)
Button(root, text='Quit', command=root.quit).pack()
mainloop()
```

This script passes the *same* parent (the top-level window) to each function in an effort to make both forms appear in one window. It also utterly hangs the Python process on my machine, without ever showing any windows at all (on Windows 98, I had to resort to Ctrl-Alt-Delete to kill it). Geometry manager combinations can be subtle until you get the hang of this; to make this example work, for instance, we simply need to isolate the grid box in a parent container all its own to keep it away from the packing going on in the root window:

```
root = Tk()
frm = Frame(root)
frm.pack()              # this works
gridbox(frm)            # gridbox must have its own parent in which to grid
packbox(root)
Button(root, text='Quit', command=root.quit).pack()
mainloop()
```

Again, today you must either `pack` or `grid` within one parent, but not both. It's possible that this restriction may be lifted in the future, but seems unlikely given the disparity in the two window manager schemes; try your Python to be sure.

Making Gridded Widgets Expandable

And now, some practical bits. The grids we've seen so far are fixed in size; they do not grow when the enclosing window is resized by a user. Example 8-21 implements an unreasonably patriotic input form with both `grid` and `pack` again, but adds the configuration steps needed to make all widgets in both windows expand along with their window on a resize.

Example 8-21. PP2E\Gui\Tour\Grid\grid3.py

```
# add label and resizing

from Tkinter import *
colors = ['red',   'white',   'blue']

def gridbox(root):
    Label(root, text='Grid').grid(columnspan=2)
    r = 1
    for c in colors:
        l = Label(root, text=c, relief=RIDGE,  width=25)
        e = Entry(root, bg=c,    relief=SUNKEN, width=50)
        l.grid(row=r, column=0, sticky=NSEW)
        e.grid(row=r, column=1, sticky=NSEW)
        root.rowconfigure(r, weight=1)
        r = r+1
    root.columnconfigure(0, weight=1)
    root.columnconfigure(1, weight=1)

def packbox(root):
    Label(root, text='Pack').pack()
    for c in colors:
        f = Frame(root)
        l = Label(f, text=c, relief=RIDGE,  width=25)
        e = Entry(f, bg=c,    relief=SUNKEN, width=50)
        f.pack(side=TOP,    expand=YES, fill=BOTH)
        l.pack(side=LEFT,   expand=YES, fill=BOTH)
        e.pack(side=RIGHT, expand=YES, fill=BOTH)

root = Tk()
gridbox(Toplevel(root))
packbox(Toplevel(root))
Button(root, text='Quit', command=root.quit).pack()
mainloop()
```

When run, this script makes the scene in Figure 8-28. It builds distinct pack and
grid windows again, with entry fields on the right colored red, white, and blue (or
for readers not working along on a computer: gray, white, and an arguably darker
gray).

This time, though, resizing both windows with mouse drags makes all their
embedded labels and entry fields expand along with the parent window, as we
see in Figure 8-29.

Resizing in grids

Now that I've shown you what these windows do, I need to explain how they do
it. We learned earlier how to make widgets expand with **pack**: we use **expand** and
fill options to increase space allocations and stretch into them. To make expansion work for widgets arranged by **grid**, we need to use different protocols: rows

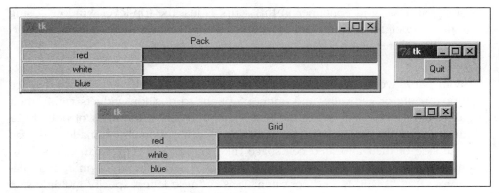

Figure 8-28. grid and pack windows before resizing

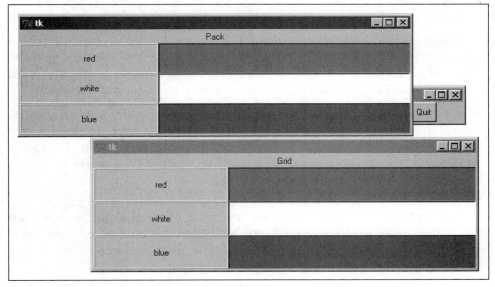

Figure 8-29. grid and pack windows resized

and columns must be marked with a *weight* to make them expandable, and widgets must also be made *sticky* so that they are stretched within their allocated grid cell:

Heavy rows and columns

With `pack`, we make each row expandable by making the corresponding `Frame` expandable, with `expand=YES` and `fill=BOTH`. Gridders must be a bit more specific: to get full expandability, call the grid container's `rowconfigure` method for each row, and its `columnconfigure` for each column. To both methods, pass a weight option with a value greater than zero to enable rows and columns to expand. Weight defaults to zero (which means no expansion), and the grid container in this script is just the top-level window. Using different weights for different rows and columns makes them grow at proportionally different rates.

Sticky widgets

With `pack`, we use `fill` options to stretch widgets to fill their allocated space horizontally or vertically, and `anchor` options to position widgets within their allocated space. With `grid`, the `sticky` option serves the roles of both `fill` and `anchor` in the packer. Gridded widgets can optionally be made sticky on one side of their allocated cell space (like `anchor`) or more than one side to make them stretch (like `fill`). Widgets can be made sticky in four directions—`N`, `S`, `E`, and `W`, and concatenations of these letters specify multiple-side stickiness. For instance, a sticky setting of `W` left-justifies the widget in its allocated space (like a packer `anchor=W`), and `NS` stretches the widget vertically within its allocated space (like a packer `fill=Y`).

Widget stickiness hasn't been useful in examples thus far because the layouts were regularly sized (widgets were no smaller than their allocated grid cell space), and resizes weren't supported at all. Here, this script specifies `NSEW` stickiness to make widgets stretch in all directions with their allocated cells.

Different combinations of row and column weights and sticky settings generate different resize effects. For instance, deleting the `columnconfig` lines in the `grid3` script makes the display expand vertically but not horizontally. Try changing some of these settings yourself to see the sorts of effects they produce.

Spanning columns and rows

There is one other big difference in how the `grid3` script configures its windows. Both the `grid` and `pack` windows display a label on the top that spans the entire window. For the packer scheme, we simply make a label attached to the top of the window at large (remember, `side` defaults to `TOP`):

```
Label(root, text='Pack').pack()
```

Because this label is attached to the window's top before any row frames are, it appears across the entire window top as expected. But laying out such a label takes a bit more work in the rigid world of grids; the first line of the grid implementation function does it like this:

```
Label(root, text='Grid').grid(columnspan=2)
```

To make a widget span across multiple columns, we pass grid a `columnspan` option with spanned-column count. Here, it just specifies that the label at the top of the window should stretch over the entire window—across both the label and entry columns. To make a widget span across multiple rows, pass a `rowspan` option instead. The regular layouts of grids can be either an asset or a liability, depending on how regular your user interface will be; these two span settings let you specify exceptions to the rule when needed.

So which geometry manager comes out on top here? When resizing is factored in, as in this script, gridding actually becomes slightly *more* complex (in fact, gridding requires three extra lines of code here). On the other hand, `grid` is nice for simple forms, and your grids and packs may vary.

Laying Out Larger Tables with grid

So far, we've been building two-column arrays of labels and input fields. That's typical of input forms, but the Tkinter grid manager is capable of configuring much grander matrixes. For instance, Example 8-22 builds a five-row by four-column array of labels, where each label simply displays its row and column number (`row.col`). When run, the window in Figure 8-30 appears on screen.

Example 8-22. PP2E\Gui\Tour\Grid\grid4.py

```
# simple 2d table

from Tkinter import *

for i in range(5):
    for j in range(4):
        l = Label(text='%d.%d' % (i, j), relief=RIDGE)
        l.grid(row=i, column=j, sticky=NSEW)

mainloop()
```

Figure 8-30. A 5x4 array of coordinates labels

If you think this is starting to look like it might be a way to program spreadsheets, you may be on to something. Example 8-23 takes this idea a bit further, and adds a button that prints the table's current input field values to the `stdout` stream (usually, to the console window).

Example 8-23. PP2E\Gui\Tour\Grid\grid5.py

```
# 2d table of input fields

from Tkinter import *
```

Example 8-23. PP2E\Gui\Tour\Grid\grid5.py (continued)

```
rows = []
for i in range(5):
    cols = []
    for j in range(4):
        e = Entry(relief=RIDGE)
        e.grid(row=i, column=j, sticky=NSEW)
        e.insert(END, '%d.%d' % (i, j))
        cols.append(e)
    rows.append(cols)

def onPress():
    for row in rows:
        for col in row:
            print col.get(),
        print

Button(text='Fetch', command=onPress).grid()
mainloop()
```

When run, this script creates the window in Figure 8-31, and saves away all the grid's entry field widgets in a two-dimensional list of lists. When its Fetch button is pressed, the script steps through the saved list of lists of entry widgets, to fetch and display all the current values in the grid. Here is the output of two Fetch presses—one before I made input field changes, and one after:

```
C:\...\PP2E\Gui\Tour\Grid>python grid5.py
0.0 0.1 0.2 0.3
1.0 1.1 1.2 1.3
2.0 2.1 2.2 2.3
3.0 3.1 3.2 3.3
4.0 4.1 4.2 4.3
0.0 0.1 0.2 42
1.0 1.1 1.2 43
2.0 2.1 2.2 44
3.0 3.1 3.2 45
4.0 4.1 4.2 46
```

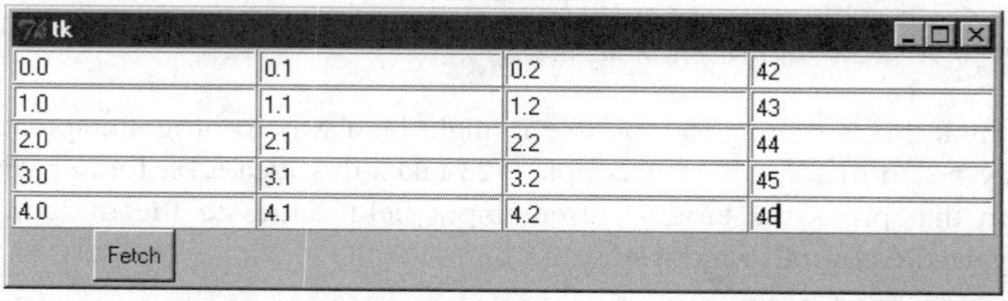

Figure 8-31. A larger grid of input fields

Now that we know how to build and step through arrays of input fields, let's add a few more useful buttons. Example 8-24 adds another row to display column sums, and buttons to clear all fields to zero and calculate column sums.

Example 8-24. PP2E\Gui\Tour\Grid\grid5b.py

```python
# add column sums, clearing

from Tkinter import *
numrow, numcol = 5, 4

rows = []
for i in range(numrow):
    cols = []
    for j in range(numcol):
        e = Entry(relief=RIDGE)
        e.grid(row=i, column=j, sticky=NSEW)
        e.insert(END, '%d.%d' % (i, j))
        cols.append(e)
    rows.append(cols)

sums = []
for i in range(numcol):
    l = Label(text='?', relief=SUNKEN)
    l.grid(row=numrow, column=i, sticky=NSEW)
    sums.append(l)

def onPrint():
    for row in rows:
        for col in row:
            print col.get(),
        print
    print

def onSum():
    t = [0] * numcol
    for i in range(numcol):
        for j in range(numrow):
            t[i]= t[i] + eval(rows[j][i].get())
    for i in range(numcol):
        sums[i].config(text=str(t[i]))

def onClear():
    for row in rows:
        for col in row:
            col.delete('0', END)
            col.insert(END, '0.0')
    for sum in sums:
        sum.config(text='?')

import sys
```

Example 8-24. PP2E\Gui\Tour\Grid\grid5b.py (continued)

```
Button(text='Sum',   command=onSum).grid(row=numrow+1, column=0)
Button(text='Print', command=onPrint).grid(row=numrow+1, column=1)
Button(text='Clear', command=onClear).grid(row=numrow+1, column=2)
Button(text='Quit',  command=sys.exit).grid(row=numrow+1, column=3)
mainloop()
```

Figure 8-32 shows this script at work summing up four columns of numbers; to get a different size table, change the `numrow` and `numcol` variables at the top of the script.

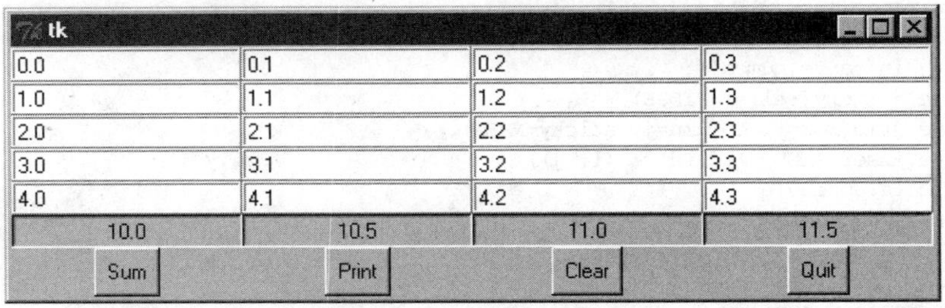

Figure 8-32. Adding column sums

And finally, Example 8-25 is one last extension that is coded as a class for reusability, and adds a button to load the table from a data file. Data files are assumed to be coded as one line per row, with whitespace (spaces or tabs) between each column within a row line. Loading a file of data automatically resizes the table GUI to accommodate the number of columns in the table.

Example 8-25. PP2E\Gui\Tour\Grid\grid5c.py

```
# recode as an embeddable class

from Tkinter import *
from PP2E.Gui.Tour.quitter import Quitter         # reuse, pack, and grid

class SumGrid(Frame):
    def __init__(self, parent=None, numrow=5, numcol=5):
        Frame.__init__(self, parent)
        self.numrow = numrow                        # I am a frame container
        self.numcol = numcol                        # caller packs or grids me
        self.makeWidgets(numrow, numcol)            # else only usable one way

    def makeWidgets(self, numrow, numcol):
        self.rows = []
        for i in range(numrow):
            cols = []
            for j in range(numcol):
                e = Entry(self, relief=RIDGE)
                e.grid(row=i+1, column=j, sticky=NSEW)
```

Example 8-25. PP2E\Gui\Tour\Grid\grid5c.py (continued)

```
                e.insert(END, '%d.%d' % (i, j))
                cols.append(e)
            self.rows.append(cols)

        self.sums = []
        for i in range(numcol):
            l = Label(self, text='?', relief=SUNKEN)
            l.grid(row=numrow+1, column=i, sticky=NSEW)
            self.sums.append(l)

        Button(self, text='Sum',   command=self.onSum).grid(row=0, column=0)
        Button(self, text='Print', command=self.onPrint).grid(row=0, column=1)
        Button(self, text='Clear', command=self.onClear).grid(row=0, column=2)
        Button(self, text='Load',  command=self.onLoad).grid(row=0, column=3)
        Quitter(self).grid(row=0, column=4)     # fails: Quitter(self).pack()

    def onPrint(self):
        for row in self.rows:
            for col in row:
                print col.get(),
            print
        print

    def onSum(self):
        t = [0] * self.numcol
        for i in range(self.numcol):
            for j in range(self.numrow):
                t[i]= t[i] + eval(self.rows[j][i].get())
        for i in range(self.numcol):
            self.sums[i].config(text=str(t[i]))

    def onClear(self):
        for row in self.rows:
            for col in row:
                col.delete('0', END)
                col.insert(END, '0.0')
        for sum in self.sums:
            sum.config(text='?')

    def onLoad(self):
        import string
        from tkFileDialog import *
        file = askopenfilename()
        if file:
            for r in self.rows:
                for c in r: c.grid_forget()
            for s in self.sums:
                s.grid_forget()
            filelines   = open(file, 'r').readlines()
            self.numrow = len(filelines)
            self.numcol = len(string.split(filelines[0]))
            self.makeWidgets(self.numrow, self.numcol)
```

Example 8-25. PP2E\Gui\Tour\Grid\grid5c.py (continued)

```
                row = 0
                for line in filelines:
                        fields = string.split(line)
                        for col in range(self.numcol):
                                self.rows[row][col].delete('0', END)
                                self.rows[row][col].insert(END, fields[col])
                        row = row+1

if __name__ == '__main__':
    import sys
    root = Tk()
    root.title('Summer Grid')
    if len(sys.argv) != 3:
        SumGrid(root).pack()        # .grid() works here too
    else:
        rows, cols = eval(sys.argv[1]), eval(sys.argv[2])
        SumGrid(root, rows, cols).pack()
    mainloop()
```

Notice that this module's `SumGrid` class is careful not to either grid or pack *itself*. In order to be attachable to containers where other widgets are being gridded or packed, it leaves its own geometry management ambiguous, and requires callers to pack or grid its instances. It's okay for containers to pick either scheme for their own children, because they effectively seal off the pack-or-grid choice. But attachable component classes that aim to be reused under *both* geometry managers cannot manage themselves, because they cannot predict their parent's policy.

This is a fairly long example that doesn't say much else about gridding or widgets in general, so I'll leave most of it as suggested reading and just show what it does. Figure 8-33 shows the initial window created by this script after changing the last column and requesting a sum.

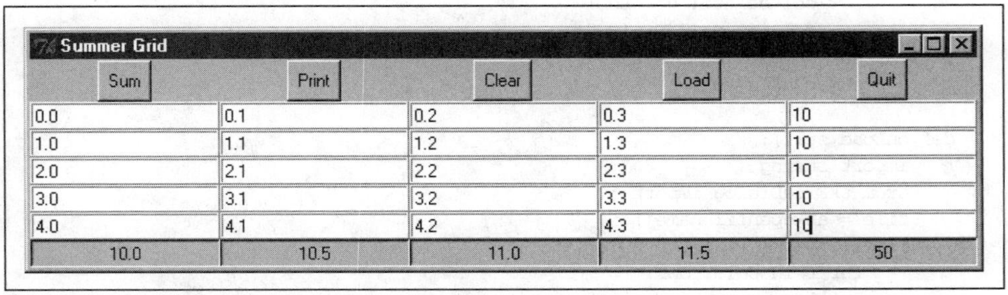

Figure 8-33. Adding data file loads

By default, the class makes the 5-by-5 grid here, but we can pass in other dimensions to both the class constructor and the script's command line. When you press the Load button, you get the standard file selection dialog we met earlier on this tour (Figure 8-34).

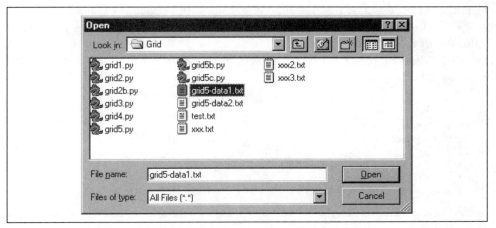

Figure 8-34. Opening a data file for SumGrid

Data file *grid-data1.txt* contains seven rows and six columns of data:

```
C:\...\PP2E\Gui\Tour\Grid>type grid5-data1.txt
1 2 3 4 5 6
1 2 3 4 5 6
1 2 3 4 5 6
1 2 3 4 5 6
1 2 3 4 5 6
1 2 3 4 5 6
1 2 3 4 5 6
```

Loading this into our GUI makes the dimensions of the grid change accordingly—the class simply reruns its widget construction logic after erasing all the old entry widgets with the `grid_forget` method.* Figure 8-35 captures the scene after a file load.

Summer Grid					
Sum	Print	Clear	Load	Quit	
1	2	3	4	5	6
1	2	3	4	5	6
1	2	3	4	5	6
1	2	3	4	5	6
1	2	3	4	5	6
1	2	3	4	5	6
1	2	3	4	5	6
7	14	21	28	35	42

Figure 8-35. Data file loaded, displayed, and summed

---

* `grid_forget` unmaps gridded widgets, and so effectively erases them from the display. Also see the widget `pack_forget` and window `withdraw` methods used in the `after` event "alarm" examples of the next section, for other ways to erase and redraw GUI components.

Data file *grid5-data2.txt* has the same dimensions, but contains expressions in two of its columns, not just simple numbers. Because this script converts input field values with the Python `eval` built-in function, any Python syntax will work in this table's fields, as long as it can be parsed and evaluated within the scope of the `onSum` method:

```
C:\...\PP2E\Gui\Tour\Grid>type grid5-data2.txt
1 2 3 2*2 5 6
1 3-1 3 2<<1 5 6
1 5%3 3 pow(2,2) 5 6
1 2 3 2**2 5 6
1 2 3 [4,3][0] 5 6
1 {'a':2}['a'] 3 len('abcd') 5 6
1 abs(-2) 3 eval('2+2') 5 6
```

Summing these fields runs the Python code they contain, as seen in Figure 8-36. This can be a powerful feature; imagine a full-blown spreadsheet grid, for instance—field values could be Python code "snippets" that compute values on the fly, call functions in modules, even download current stock quotes over the Internet with tools we'll meet in the next part of this book.

It's also a potential dangerous tool—a field might just contain an expression that erases your hard drive! If you're not sure what expressions may do, either don't use `eval` (convert with more limited built-in functions like `int` and `float` instead), or see Chapter 15 for details on the Python `rexec` restricted-execution mode module.

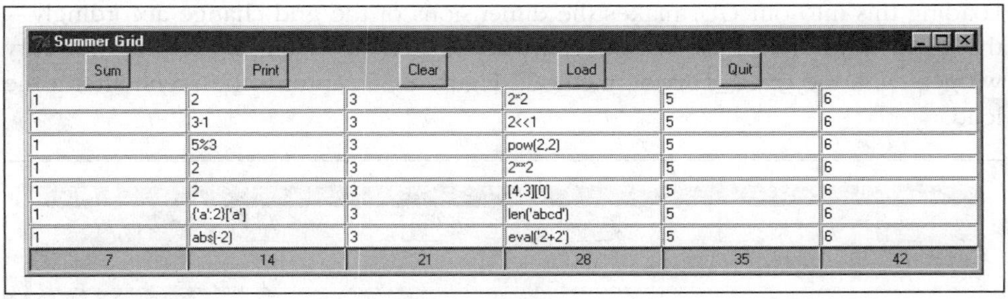

Figure 8-36. Python expressions in the data and table

Of course, this still is nowhere near a true spreadsheet program; further mutations towards that goal are left as exercises. I should also point out that there is more to gridding than we have time to present fully here. For instance, by creating sub-frames that have grids of their own, we can build up more sophisticated layouts in much the same way as nested frames arranged with the packer. For now, let's move on to one last widget survey topic.

Time Tools, Threads, and Animation

The last stop on our widget tour is the most unique. Tkinter also comes with a handful of tools that have to do with the event-driven programming model, not graphics displayed on a computer screen.

Some GUI applications need to perform background activities periodically. For example, to "blink" a widget's appearance, we'd like to register a callback handler to be invoked at regular time intervals. Similarly, it's not a good idea to let a long-running file operation block other activity in a GUI; if the event loop could be forced to update periodically, the GUI could remain responsive. Tkinter comes with tools for both scheduling such delayed actions and forcing screen updates:

`widget.after(`*milliseconds, function, *args*`)`

> This tool schedules the function to be called after a number of milliseconds. `function` can be any callable Python object: a function, bound method, etc. This form of the call does not pause the program—the callback function is run later from the normal Tkinter event loop. The milliseconds value can be a floating point number, to specify fractions of a second. This returns an ID which can be passed to `after_cancel` to cancel the callback. Since this method is so commonly used, I'll say more about it by example in a moment.

`widget.after(`*milliseconds*`)`

> This tool pauses the program for a number of milliseconds. For example, an argument of 5000 pauses for 5 seconds. This is essentially the same as Python's library function `time.sleep`, and both calls can be used to add a delay in time-sensitive displays (e.g., animation programs like PyDraw and the simpler examples ahead).

`widget.after_idle(`*function, *args*`)`

> This tool schedules the function to be called when there are no more pending events to process. That is, `function` becomes an idle handler, which is invoked when the GUI isn't busy doing anything else.

`widget.after_cancel(`*id*`)`

> This tool cancels a pending `after` callback event before it occurs.

`widget.update()`

> This tool forces Tkinter to process all pending events in the event queue, including geometry resizing, and widget updates and redraws. You can call this periodically from a long-running callback handler to refresh the screen and perform any updates to it that your handler has already requested. If you don't, your updates may not appear on screen until your callback handler exits. In fact, your display may hang completely during long-running handlers if not manually updated (and handlers are not run in threads, as described in the next section); the window won't even redraw itself until the handler

returns if covered and uncovered by another. For instance, programs that animate by repeatedly moving an object and pausing must call for an update before the end of the animation, or only the final object position will appear on screen; worse, the GUI will be completely inactive until the animation callback returns (see the simple animation examples later in this chapter, and PyDraw in the next chapter).

`widget.update_idletasks()`

This tool processes any pending idle events. This may sometimes be safer than `after` which has the potential to set up race (looping) conditions in some scenarios. Tk widgets use idle events to display themselves.

`_tkinter.createfilehandler(`*file, mask, function*`)`

This tool schedules the function to be called when a file's status changes. The function may be invoked when the file has data for reading, is available for writing, or triggers an exception. File handlers are often used to process pipes or sockets, since normal input/output requests can block the caller. This is not available on Windows under Tk 8.0, and so won't be used in this book.

`widget.wait_variable(var)`
`widget.wait_window(win)`
`widget.wait_visibility(win)`

These tools pause the caller until a Tkinter variable changes its value, a window is destroyed, or a window becomes visible. All of these enter a local event loop, such that the application's `mainloop` continues to handle events. Note that `var` is a Tkinter variable object (discussed earlier), not a simple Python variable. To use for modal dialogs, first call `widget.focus()` (to set input focus) and `widget.grab()` (to make a window be the only one active).

We won't go into further details on all of these tools here; see other Tk and Tkinter documentation for more information.

Using Threads with GUIs

Keep in mind that for many programs, Python's thread support that we met in Chapter 3, *Parallel System Tools*, can serve some of the same roles as the Tkinter tools listed in the previous section. For instance, to avoid blocking a GUI during a long-running file or socket transfer, the transfer can simply be run in a spawned thread, while the rest of the program continues to run normally. We'll meet such threaded GUI programs in Part III, *Internet Scripting* (e.g., PyMailGui in Chapter 11, *Client-Side Scripting*). Similarly, GUIs that must watch for inputs on pipes or sockets can do so in spawned threads (or `after` callbacks), without blocking the GUI itself.

If you do use threads in Tkinter programs, however, only the *main* thread (the one that built the GUI and started the `mainloop`) can make GUI calls. Even things like the `update` method described in the previous section cannot be called from spawned threads in a GUI program—they'll likely trigger very strange program crashes. This GUI thread story may be improved in future Python and Tkinter releases, but imposes a few structural and platform-specific constraints today.

For example, because spawned threads cannot perform GUI processing, they must generally communicate with the main thread using global variables, as required by the application. A thread that watches a socket, for instance, might simply set global variables that trigger GUI changes in `after` event callbacks. Note that this is not a Python or Tkinter limitation (it's much lower in the software hierarchy that runs your GUI), and may go away in the future. In addition, some Tkinter canvas calls may actually be thread-safe (see the animation script in Example 8-31). We'll revisit this limitation later in this book, when we meet larger threaded GUI programs.

Using the after Method

The `after` method allows scripts to schedule a callback handler to be run at some time in the future, and we'll use this often in later examples in this book. For instance, in Chapter 9 we'll meet a *clock* program that uses `after` to wake up 10 times per second and check for a new time, and an image *slideshow* program that uses `after` to schedule the next photo display (see PyClock and PyView). To illustrate the basics of scheduled callbacks, Example 8-26 does something a bit different.

Example 8-26. PP2E\Gui\Tour\alarm.py

```
#!/usr/local/bin/python
from Tkinter import *

class Alarm(Frame):
    def repeater(self):                      # on every N millisecs
        self.bell()                          # beep now
        self.stopper.flash()                 # flash button now
        self.after(self.msecs, self.repeater) # reschedule handler
    def __init__(self, msecs=1000):          # default = 1 second
        Frame.__init__(self)
        self.msecs = msecs
        self.pack()
        stopper = Button(self, text='Stop the beeps!', command=self.quit)
        stopper.pack()
        stopper.config(bg='navy', fg='white', bd=8)
        self.stopper = stopper
        self.repeater()

if __name__ == '__main__': Alarm(msecs=1000).mainloop()
```

This script builds the window in Figure 8-37 and periodically calls both the button widget's `flash` method to make the button flash momentarily (it alternates colors quickly), and the Tkinter `bell` method to call your system's sound interface. The `repeater` method beeps and flashes once, and schedules a callback to be invoked after a specific amount of time with the `after` method.

Figure 8-37. Stop the beeps!

But `after` doesn't pause the caller: callbacks are scheduled to occur in the background, while the program performs other processing—technically, as soon as the Tk event loop is able to notice the time rollover. To make this work, `repeater` calls `after` each time through, to reschedule the callback. Delayed events are *one-shot* callbacks; to repeat the event, we need to reschedule.

The net effect is that when this script runs, it starts beeping and flashing once its one-button window pops up. And it keeps beeping and flashing. And beeping. And flashing. Other activities and GUI operations don't affect it. Even if the window is iconified, the beeping continues because Tkinter timer events fire in the background. You need to kill the window or press the button to stop the alarm. By changing the `msecs` delay, you can make this beep as fast or slow as your system allows (some platforms can't beep as fast as others). And this may or may not be the best demo to launch in a crowded office, but at least you've been warned.

Hiding and redrawing widgets and windows

The button `flash` method flashes the widget, but it's easy to dynamically change other appearance options of widgets like buttons, labels, and text, with the widget `config` method. For instance, you can also achieve a flash-like effect by manually reversing foreground and background colors with the widget `config` method, in scheduled `after` callbacks. Just for fun, Example 8-27 specializes the alarm to go a step further.

Example 8-27. PP2E\Gui\Tour\alarm-hide.py

```
from Tkinter import *
import alarm

class Alarm(alarm.Alarm):                     # change alarm callback
    def repeater(self):                       # on every N millisecs
        self.bell()                           # beep now
        if self.shown:
            self.stopper.pack_forget()        # hide or erase button now
        else:                                 # or reverse colors, flash...
            self.stopper.pack()
        self.shown = not self.shown           # toggle state for next time
```

Example 8-27. PP2E\Gui\Tour\alarm-hide.py (continued)

```
        self.after(self.msecs, self.repeater)    # reschedule handler
    def __init__(self, msecs=1000):              # default = 1 second
        self.shown = 0
        alarm.Alarm.__init__(self, msecs)

if __name__ == '__main__': Alarm(msecs=500).mainloop()
```

When this script is run, the same window appears, but the button is erased or redrawn on alternating timer events. The widget `pack_forget` method erases (unmaps) a drawn widget, and `pack` makes it show up again; `grid_forget` and `grid` similarly hide and show widgets in a grid. The `pack_forget` method is useful for dynamically drawing and changing a running GUI. For instance, you can be selective about which components are displayed, and build widgets ahead of time and show them only as needed. Here, it just means that users must press the button while it's displayed, or else the noise keeps going.

To hide and unhide the *entire window* instead of just one widget within it, use the top-level window widget `withdraw` and `deiconify` methods. The `withdraw` method, demonstrated in Example 8-28, completely erases the window and its icon (use `iconify` if you want the window's icon to appear during a hide), and the `state` method returns the window's current state ("normal", "iconic", or "withdrawn"). These are also useful to pop up prebuilt dialog windows dynamically, but are perhaps less practical here.

Example 8-28. PP2E\Gui\Tour\alarm-withdraw.py

```
from Tkinter import *
import alarm

class Alarm(alarm.Alarm):
    def repeater(self):                          # on every N millisecs
        self.bell()                              # beep now
        if self.master.state() == 'normal':      # is window displayed?
            self.master.withdraw()               # hide entire window, no icon
        else:                                    # iconify shrinks to an icon
            self.master.deiconify()              # else redraw entire window
            self.master.lift()                   # and raise above others
        self.after(self.msecs, self.repeater)    # reschedule handler

if __name__ == '__main__': Alarm().mainloop()    # master = default Tk root
```

This works the same, but the entire window appears or disappears on beeps—you have to press it when it's shown. There are lots of other effects you could add to the alarm. Whether your buttons and windows should flash and disappear or not, though, probably depends less on Tkinter technology than on your users' patience.

Simple Animation Techniques

Apart from the direct shape moves in the `canvasDraw` example, all of the GUIs presented so far in this part of the book have been fairly static. This last section shows you how to change that, by adding simple shape movement *animations* to the canvas drawing example listed in Example 8-15. It also demonstrates the notion of *canvas tags*—the move operations performed here move all canvas objects associated with a tag at once. All oval shapes move if you press "o", and all rectangles move if you press "r"; as mentioned earlier, canvas operation methods accept both object IDs and tag names.

But the main goal here is to illustrate simple animation techniques using the time-based tools described earlier in this section. There are three basic ways to move objects around a canvas:

- By loops that use `time.sleep` to pause for fractions of a second between multiple move operations, along with manual `update` calls. The script moves, sleeps, moves a bit more, and so on. A `time.sleep` call pauses the caller, and so fails to return control to the GUI event loop—any new requests that arrive during a move are deferred. Because of that, `canvas.update` must be called to redraw the screen after each move, or else updates don't appear until the entire movement loop callback finishes and returns. This is a classic long-running callback scenario; without manual update calls, *no* new GUI events are handled until the callback returns in this scheme (even window redraws).

- By using the `widget.after` method to schedule multiple move operations to occur every few milliseconds. Because this approach is based upon scheduled events dispatched by Tkinter to your handlers, it allows multiple moves to occur in parallel, and doesn't require `canvas.update` calls. You rely on the event loop to run moves, so there's no reason for sleep pauses, and the GUI is not blocked while moves are in progress.

- By using threads to run multiple copies of the `time.sleep` pausing loops of the first approach. Because threads run in parallel, a sleep in any thread blocks neither the GUI nor other motion threads. GUIs should not be updated from spawned threads in general (in fact, calling `canvas.update` from a spawned thread will likely crash the GUI today), but some canvas calls such as movement seem to be thread safe in the current implementation.

Of these three schemes, the first yields the smoothest animations but makes other operations sluggish during movement, the second seems to yield slower motion than the others but is safer than using threads in general, and the last two both allow multiple objects to be in motion at the same time.

Using time.sleep loops

The next three sections demonstrate the code structure of all three approaches in turn, with new subclasses of the **canvasDraw** example we met in Example 8-15. Example 8-29 illustrates the first approach.

Example 8-29. PP2E\Gui\Tour\canvasDraw_tags.py

```
###################################################################
# add tagged moves with time.sleep (not widget.after or threads);
# time.sleep does not block the gui event loop while pausing, but
# screen not redrawn until callback returns or widget.update call;
# the currently running onMove callback gets exclusive attention
# until it returns: others pause if press 'r' or 'o' during move;
###################################################################

from Tkinter import *
import canvasDraw, time

class CanvasEventsDemo(canvasDraw.CanvasEventsDemo):
    def __init__(self, parent=None):
        canvasDraw.CanvasEventsDemo.__init__(self, parent)
        self.canvas.create_text(75, 8, text='Press o and r to move shapes')
        self.canvas.master.bind('<KeyPress-o>', self.onMoveOvals)
        self.canvas.master.bind('<KeyPress-r>', self.onMoveRectangles)
        self.kinds = self.create_oval_tagged, self.create_rectangle_tagged
    def create_oval_tagged(self, x1, y1, x2, y2):
        objectId = self.canvas.create_oval(x1, y1, x2, y2)
        self.canvas.itemconfig(objectId, tag='ovals', fill='blue')
        return objectId
    def create_rectangle_tagged(self, x1, y1, x2, y2):
        objectId = self.canvas.create_rectangle(x1, y1, x2, y2)
        self.canvas.itemconfig(objectId, tag='rectangles', fill='red')
        return objectId
    def onMoveOvals(self, event):
        print 'moving ovals'
        self.moveInSquares(tag='ovals')            # move all tagged ovals
    def onMoveRectangles(self, event):
        print 'moving rectangles'
        self.moveInSquares(tag='rectangles')
    def moveInSquares(self, tag):                  # 5 reps of 4 times per sec
        for i in range(5):
            for (diffx, diffy) in [(+20, 0), (0, +20), (-20, 0), (0, -20)]:
                self.canvas.move(tag, diffx, diffy)
                self.canvas.update()               # force screen redraw/update
                time.sleep(0.25)                   # pause, but don't block gui

if __name__ == '__main__':
    CanvasEventsDemo()
    mainloop()
```

All three of the scripts in this section create a window of blue ovals and red rectangles as you drag new shapes out with the left mouse button. The drag-out implementation itself is inherited from the superclass. A right mouse button click still moves a single shape immediately, and a double-left click still clears the canvas too—other operations inherited from the original superclass. In fact, all this new script really does is change the object creation calls to add tags and colors here, add a text field, and add bindings and callbacks for motion. Figure 8-38 shows what this subclass's window looks like after dragging out a few shapes to be animated.

Figure 8-38. Drag-out objects ready to be animated

The "o" and "r" keys are set up to start animation of all the ovals and rectangles you've drawn, respectively. Pressing "o", for example, makes all the blue ovals start moving synchronously. Objects are animated to mark out five squares around their location, and move four times per second. New objects drawn while others are in motion start to move too, because they are tagged. You need to run these live to get a feel for the simple animations they implement, of course (you could try moving this book back and forth and up and down, but it's not quite the same, and might look silly in public places).

Using widget.after events

The main drawback of this first approach is that only one animation can be going at once: if you press "r" or "o" while a move is in progress, the new request puts the prior movement on hold until it finishes because each move callback handler assumes the only thread of control while it runs. Screen updates are a bit sluggish while moves are in progress too, because they only happen as often as manual update calls are made (try a drag-out or a cover/uncover of the window during a move to see for yourself). Example 8-30 specializes just the `moveInSquares` method to remove such limitations.

Example 8-30. PP2E\Gui\Tour\canvasDraw_tags_after.py

```
###########################################################################
# similar, but with .after scheduled events, not time.sleep loops;
# because these are scheduled events, this allows both ovals and
# rectangles to be moving at the _same_ time and does not require
# update calls to refresh the gui (only one time.sleep loop callback
# can be running at once, and blocks others started until it returns);
# the motion gets wild if you press 'o' or 'r' while move in progress,
# though--multiple move updates start firing around the same time;
###########################################################################

from Tkinter import *
import canvasDraw_tags

class CanvasEventsDemo(canvasDraw_tags.CanvasEventsDemo):
    def moveEm(self, tag, moremoves):
        (diffx, diffy), moremoves = moremoves[0], moremoves[1:]
        self.canvas.move(tag, diffx, diffy)
        if moremoves:
            self.canvas.after(250, self.moveEm, tag, moremoves)
    def moveInSquares(self, tag):
        allmoves = [(+20, 0), (0, +20), (-20, 0), (0, -20)] * 5
        self.moveEm(tag, allmoves)

if __name__ == '__main__':
    CanvasEventsDemo()
    mainloop()
```

This version lets you make both ovals and rectangles move at the same time—drag out a few ovals and rectangles, and then press "o" and then "r" right away to make this go. In fact, try pressing both keys a few times; the more you press, the more the objects move, because multiple scheduled events are firing and moving objects from wherever they happen to be positioned. If you drag out a new shape during a move, it starts moving immediately as before.

Using multiple time.sleep loop threads

Running animations in threads can sometimes achieve the same effect; it can be dangerous to update the screen from a spawned thread in general, but works in this example, at least on Windows. Example 8-31 runs each animation task as an independent and parallel thread. That is, each time you press the "o" or "r" keys to start an animation, a new thread is spawned to do the work. This works on Windows, but failed on Linux at the time I was writing this book—the screen is not updated as threads change it, so you won't see any changes until later GUI events.

Example 8-31. PP2E\Gui\Tour\canvasDraw_tags_thread.py

```
#####################################################################
# similar, but run time.sleep loops in parallel with threads, not
# .after events or single active time.sleep loop; because threads run
# in parallel, this also allows ovals and rectangles to be moving at
# the _same_ time and does not require update calls to refresh the gui:
# in fact, calling .update() can make this _crash_ today, though some
# canvas calls seem to be thread safe or else this wouldn't work at all;
#####################################################################

from Tkinter import *
import canvasDraw_tags
import thread, time

class CanvasEventsDemo(canvasDraw_tags.CanvasEventsDemo):
    def moveEm(self, tag):
        for i in range(5):
            for (diffx, diffy) in [(+20, 0), (0, +20), (-20, 0), (0, -20)]:
                self.canvas.move(tag, diffx, diffy)
                time.sleep(0.25)                        # pause this thread only
    def moveInSquares(self, tag):
        thread.start_new_thread(self.moveEm, (tag,))

if __name__ == '__main__':
    CanvasEventsDemo()
    mainloop()
```

This version lets you move shapes at the same time just like Example 8-30, but this time it's a reflection of threads running in parallel. In fact, this uses the same scheme as the first `time.sleep` version. Here, though, there is more than one active thread of control, so move handlers can overlap in time—`time.sleep` only blocks the calling thread, not the program at large. This seems to work (at least on Windows), but it is usually safer to have your threads do number crunching only, and let the main thread (the one that built the GUI) handle any screen updates. It's not impossible that GUI threads may be better supported in later Tkinter releases, so see more recent releases for more details.

Other animation options

We'll revisit animation in Chapter 9's PyDraw example; there, all three techniques will be resurrected to move shapes, text, and photos to arbitrary spots on a canvas marked with a mouseclick. And although the canvas widget's absolute coordinate system make it the workhorse of most nontrivial animations, Tkinter animation in general is limited mostly by your imagination. As we saw in the flashing and hiding `alarm` examples earlier, it's easy to change the appearance of other kinds of widgets dynamically too; you can even erase and redraw widgets and windows on the fly.

I should also note that the sorts of movement and animation techniques shown in this chapter and the next are suitable for many game-like programs, but not all.

For more advanced 3D animation needs, be sure to also see the support in the PIL extension package for common animation and movie file formats such as FLI and MPEG. As currently implemented, Python is not widely used as the sole implementation language of graphic-intensive game programs, but it can still be used as both a prototyping and scripting language for such products.* And when integrated with 3D graphics libraries, it can serve even broader roles. See *http://www. python.org* for links to other available extensions in this domain.

The End of the Tour

And that's a wrap for our tour around the Tkinter library. You have now seen all the widgets and tools previewed at the end of Chapter 6, *Graphical User Interfaces* (flip back for a summary of territory covered on this tour). For more details, watch for all of the tools introduced here to appear again in larger GUI examples in Chapter 9, and the remainder of the book at large. And consult Tk and Tkinter resources for options not listed explicitly here; although other Tkinter options are analogous to those presented on this tour, the space I have for illustrating such options in this book is limited by both my publisher and my fingers.

The PyDemos and PyGadgets Launchers

To close out this chapter, I want to show the implementations of the two GUIs used to run major book examples. The following GUIs, PyDemos and PyGadgets, are simply GUIs for launching other GUI programs. In fact, we've now come to the end of the demo launcher story: both of the programs here interact with modules that we met earlier in Chapters 3 and 3:

- *launchmodes.py* starts independent Python programs portably.
- *Launcher.py* finds programs, and ultimately runs both PyDemos and PyGadgets when used by the self-configuring top-level launcher scripts.
- *LaunchBrowser.py* spawns web browsers.

See Examples 3-24, 4-14, and 4-15 for the code for these modules. The programs listed here add the GUI components to the program launching system—they simply provide easy-to-use pushbuttons that spawn most of the larger examples in this text when pressed.

Both these scripts also assume that they will be run with the current working directory set to their directory (they hardcode paths to other programs relative to that). Either click on their names in a file explorer, or run them from a command-line

---

* Origin Systems, a major game software development company, uses Python in this role to script the animation in some of their games. At last report, their online game product Ultima Online II was to be scripted with Python.

shell after a *cd* to the top-level *PP2E* examples root directory. These scripts could allow invocations from other directories by prepending the `PP2EHOME` environment variable's value to program script paths, but they were really only designed to be run out of the *PP2E* root.

PyDemos Launcher Bar

The PyDemos script constructs a bar of buttons that run programs in demonstration mode, not for day-to-day use. I use PyDemos to show off Python programs whenever I can—it's much easier to press its buttons than to run command lines or fish through a file explorer GUI to find scripts. You should use PyDemos to start and interact with examples presented in this book—all of the buttons on this GUI represent examples we will meet in later chapters.

To make this launcher bar even easier to run, drag it out to your desktop to generate a clickable Windows shortcut (do something similar on other systems). Since this script hardcodes command lines for running programs elsewhere in the examples tree, it is also useful as an index to major book examples. Figure 8-39 shows what PyDemos looks like when run on Windows; it looks slightly different but works the same on Linux.

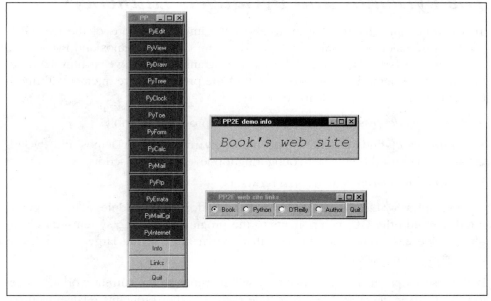

Figure 8-39. PyDemos with its pop-ups

The source code that constructs this scene is listed in Example 8-32. PyDemos doesn't present much new in terms of GUI interface programming; its `demoButton` function simply attaches a new button to the main window, spring-loaded to spawn a Python program when pressed. To start programs, PyDemos calls an instance of the `launchmodes.PortableLauncher` object we met at the end of Chapter 3—its role as a Tkinter callback handler here is why a *call* operation is used to kick off the launched program.

As pictured in Figure 8-39, PyDemos also constructs two pop-up windows when buttons at the bottom of the main window are pressed—an Info pop-up giving a short description of the last demo spawned, and a Links pop-up containing radiobuttons that open a local web browser on book-related sites when pressed:

- The Info pop-up displays a simple message line, and changes its font every second to draw attention to itself; since this can be a bit distracting, the pop-up starts out iconified (click the Info button to see or hide it).

- The Links pop-up's radiobuttons are much like hyperlinks in a web page, but this GUI isn't a browser: when pressed, the portable `LaunchBrowser` script we met in a prior chapter is used to find and start a web browser used to connect to the relevant site, assuming you have an Internet connection.

PyDemos runs on Windows and Linux, but that's largely due to the inherent portability of both Python and Tkinter. For more details, consult the source, which is shown in Example 8-32.

Example 8-32. PP2E\PyDemos.pyw

```
##############################################################################
# PyDemos.pyw
# Programming Python, 2nd Edition (PP2E), 1999--2001
#
# Launch major Python+Tk GUI examples from the book, in a
# platform-neutral way.  This file also serves as an index
# to major program examples, though many book examples aren't
# GUI-based, and so aren't listed here (e.g., see the Linux
# gcc build scripts in the examples root directory for C
# integration program pointers).  Also see:
#
# - PyGadgets.py, a simpler script for starting programs in
#   non-demo mode that you wish to use on a regular basis
# - PyGadgets_bar.pyw, which creates a button bar for starting
#   all PyGadgets programs on demand, not all at once
# - Launcher.py for starting programs without environment
#   settings--finds Python, sets PYTHONPATH, etc.
# - Launch_*.py for starting PyDemos and PyGadgets with
#   Launcher.py--run these for a quick look
# - LaunchBrowser.py for running example web pages with an
#   automatically-located web browser
# - README-PP2E.txt, for general examples information
#
# Internet-based demos live here:
#      http://starship.python.net/~lutz/PyInternetDemos.html
# but this program tries to start a browser on the main web pages
# automatically, either on the site above or on local page files.
```

Example 8-32. PP2E\PyDemos.pyw (continued)

```
# Additional program comments were moved to file PyDemos.doc.txt
###############################################################################

import sys, time, os, launchmodes
from Tkinter import *

# -live loads root pages off net, -file loads local files
InternetMode = '-file'

################################
# start building main gui windows
################################

Root = Tk()
Root.title('PP2E Demos')

# build message window
Stat = Toplevel()
Stat.protocol('WM_DELETE_WINDOW', lambda:0)     # ignore wm delete
Stat.title('PP2E demo info')

Info = Label(Stat, text = 'Select demo',
                font=('courier', 20, 'italic'), padx=12, pady=12, bg='lightblue')
Info.pack(expand=YES, fill=BOTH)

############################################
# add launcher buttons with callback objects
############################################

# demo launcher class
class Launcher(launchmodes.PortableLauncher):     # use wrapped launcher class
    def announce(self, text):                     # customize to set GUI label
        Info.config(text=text)

def demoButton(name, what, where):
    b = Button(Root, bg='navy', fg='white', relief=RIDGE, border=4)
    b.config(text=name, command=Launcher(what, where))
    b.pack(side=TOP, expand=YES, fill=BOTH)

demoButton('PyEdit',
           'Text file editor',                                # edit myself
           'Gui/TextEditor/textEditor.pyw PyDemos.pyw')       # assume in cwd
demoButton('PyView',
           'Image slideshow, plus note editor',
           'Gui/SlideShow/slideShowPlus.py Gui/gifs')
demoButton('PyDraw',
           'Draw and move graphics objects',
           'Gui/MovingPics/movingpics.py Gui/gifs')
demoButton('PyTree',
           'Tree data structure viewer',
           'Dstruct/TreeView/treeview.py')
demoButton('PyClock',
           'Analog/digital clocks',
```

Example 8-32. PP2E\PyDemos.pyw (continued)

```
              'Gui/Clock/clockStyles.py Gui/gifs')
demoButton('PyToe',
              'Tic-tac-toe game (AI)',
              'Ai/TicTacToe/tictactoe.py')
demoButton('PyForm',                                    # view in-memory dict
              'Persistent table viewer/editor',         # or cwd shelve of class
           #'Dbase/TableBrowser/formgui.py')            # 0=do not reinit shelve
           #'Dbase/TableBrowser/formtable.py  shelve 0 pyformData-1.5.2')
              'Dbase/TableBrowser/formtable.py  shelve 1 pyformData')
demoButton('PyCalc',
              'Calculator, plus extensions',
              'Lang/Calculator/calculator_plusplus.py')
demoButton('PyMail',
              'Python+Tk pop/smtp email client',
              'Internet/Email/PyMailGui.py')
demoButton('PyFtp',
              'Python+Tk ftp clients',
              'Internet/Ftp/PyFtpGui.pyw')

if InternetMode == '-file':
    pagepath = os.getcwd() + '/Internet/Cgi-Web'
    demoButton('PyErrata',
                'Internet-based errata report system',
                'LaunchBrowser.py -file %s/PyErrata/pyerrata.html' % pagepath)
    demoButton('PyMailCgi',
                'Browser-based pop/smtp email interface',
                'LaunchBrowser.py -file %s/PyMailCgi/pymailcgi.html' % pagepath)
    demoButton('PyInternet',
                'Internet-based demo launcher page',
                'LaunchBrowser.py -file %s/PyInternetDemos.html' % pagepath)
else:
    site = 'starship.python.net/~lutz'
    demoButton('PyErrata',
                'Internet-based errata report system',
                'LaunchBrowser.py -live PyErrata/pyerrata.html ' + site)
    demoButton('PyMailCgi',
                'Browser-based pop/smtp email interface',
                'LaunchBrowser.py -live PyMailCgi/pymailcgi.html ' + site)
    demoButton('PyInternet',
                'Main Internet demos launcher page',
                'LaunchBrowser.py -live PyInternetDemos.html ' + site)

#To try: bind mouse entry events to change info text when over a button
#See also: site http://starship.python.net/~lutz/PyInternetDemos.html


############################################
# toggle info message box font once a second
############################################

def refreshMe(info, ncall):
    slant = ['normal', 'italic', 'bold', 'bold italic'][ncall % 4]
    info.config(font=('courier', 20, slant))
    Root.after(1000, (lambda info=info, ncall=ncall: refreshMe(info, ncall+1)) )
```

Example 8-32. PP2E\PyDemos.pyw (continued)

```
#######################################
# unhide/hide status box on info clicks
#######################################

Stat.iconify()
def onInfo():
    if Stat.state() == 'iconic':
        Stat.deiconify()
    else:
        Stat.iconify()  # was 'normal'


###########################################
# popup a few web link buttons if connected
###########################################

radiovar = StringVar() # use a global

def onLinks():
    popup = Toplevel()
    popup.title('PP2E web site links')
    links = [("Book",     'LaunchBrowser.py -live about-pp.html rmi.net/~lutz'),
             ("Python",   'LaunchBrowser.py -live index.html www.python.org'),
             ("O'Reilly", 'LaunchBrowser.py -live index.html www.oreilly.com'),
             ("Author",   'LaunchBrowser.py -live index.html rmi.net/~lutz')]

    for (name, command) in links:
        callback = Launcher((name + "'s web site"), command)
        link = Radiobutton(popup, text=name, command=callback)
        link.config(relief=GROOVE, variable=radiovar, value=name)
        link.pack(side=LEFT, expand=YES, fill=BOTH)
    Button(popup, text='Quit', command=popup.destroy).pack(expand=YES,fill=BOTH)

    if InternetMode != '-live':
        from tkMessageBox import showwarning
        showwarning('PP2E Demos', 'Web links require an Internet connection')


###########################################
# finish building main gui, start event loop
###########################################

Button(Root, text='Info',  command=onInfo).pack(side=TOP, fill=X)
Button(Root, text='Links', command=onLinks).pack(side=TOP, fill=X)
Button(Root, text='Quit',  command=Root.quit).pack(side=BOTTOM, fill=X)
refreshMe(Info, 0)  # start toggling
Root.mainloop()
```

PyGadgets Launcher Bar

The PyGadgets script runs some of the same programs as PyDemos, but for real, practical use, not as flashy demonstrations. Both scripts use `launchmodes` to spawn other programs and display bars of launcher buttons, but this one is a bit simpler because its task is more focused. PyGadgets also supports two spawning modes: it can either start a canned list of programs immediately and all at once, or display a GUI for running each program on demand (Figure 8-40 shows the launch bar GUI made in on-demand mode).

Because of such differences, PyGadgets takes a more data-driven approach to building the GUI: it stores program names in a list and steps through it as needed, rather than using a sequence of precoded `demoButton` calls. The set of buttons on the launcher bar GUI in Figure 8-40, for example, depends entirely upon the contents of the programs list.

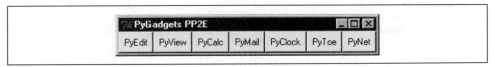

Figure 8-40. PyGadgets launcher bar

The source code behind this GUI is listed in Example 8-33; it's not much, because it relies on other modules (`launchmodes`, `LaunchBrowser`) to work most of its magic. PyGadgets is always open on my machines (I have a clickable shortcut to this script on my Windows desktop too). I use it to gain easy access to Python tools that I use on a daily basis—text editors, calculators, and so on—all of which we'll meet in upcoming chapters.

To customize PyGadgets for your own use, simply import and call its functions with program command-line lists of your own, or change the `mytools` list of spawnable programs near the end of this file. This is Python, after all.

Example 8-33. PP2E\PyGadgets.py

```python
#!/bin/env python
###################################################################
# Start various examples; run me at system boot time to make them
# always available.  This file is meant for starting programs you
# actually wish to use; see PyDemos for starting Python/Tk demos
# and more details on program start options.  Windows usage note:
# this is a '.py' file, so you get a dos box console window when it
# is clicked; the dos box is used to show a startup message (and we
# sleep 5 seconds to make sure it's visible while gadgets start up).
# If you don't want the dos popup, run with the 'pythonw' program
# (not 'python'), use a '.pyw' suffix, mark with a 'run minimized'
# Windows property, or spawn the file from elsewhere; see PyDemos.
###################################################################

import sys, time, os, time
from Tkinter import *
from launchmodes import PortableLauncher      # reuse program start class

def runImmediate(mytools):
```

Example 8-33. PP2E\PyGadgets.py (continued)

```
        # launch gadget programs immediately
        print 'Starting Python/Tk gadgets...'        # msgs to temp stdout screen
        for (name, commandLine) in mytools:
            PortableLauncher(name, commandLine)()     # call now to start now
        print 'One moment please...'                  # \b means a backspace
        if sys.platform[:3] == 'win':
            # on Windows keep stdio console window up for 5 seconds
            for i in range(5): time.sleep(1); print ('\b' + '.'*10),

def runLauncher(mytools):
    # put up a simple launcher bar for later use
    root = Tk()
    root.title('PyGadgets PP2E')
    for (name, commandLine) in mytools:
        b = Button(root, text=name, fg='black', bg='beige', border=2,
                   command=PortableLauncher(name, commandLine))
        b.pack(side=LEFT, expand=YES, fill=BOTH)
    root.mainloop()

mytools = [
    ('PyEdit',   'Gui/TextEditor/textEditor.pyw'),
    ('PyView',   'Gui/SlideShow/slideShowPlus.py Gui/gifs'),
    ('PyCalc',   'Lang/Calculator/calculator.py'),
    ('PyMail',   'Internet/Email/PyMailGui.py'),
    ('PyClock',  'Gui/Clock/clock.py -size 175 -bg white'
                 '          -picture Gui/gifs/pythonPowered.gif'),
    ('PyToe',    'Ai/TicTacToe/tictactoe.py'
                 '          -mode Minimax -fg white -bg navy'),
    ('PyNet',    'LaunchBrowser.py -file ' + os.getcwd() +
                 '/Internet/Cgi-Web/PyInternetDemos.html')
]

if __name__ == '__main__':
    prestart, toolbar = 1, 0
    if prestart:
        runImmediate(mytools)
    if toolbar:
        runLauncher(mytools)
```

By default, PyGadgets starts programs immediately when it is run. To run PyGadgets in launcher-bar mode instead, Example 8-34 simply imports and calls the appropriate function with an imported program list. Because it is a *.pyw* file, you only see the launcher bar GUI it constructs initially, not a DOS console streams window.

Example 8-34. PP2E\PyGadgets_bar.pyw

```
# run PyGadgets tool bar only, instead of starting all the
# gadgets immediately; filename avoids dos popup on windows

import PyGadgets
PyGadgets.runLauncher(PyGadgets.mytools)
```

This script is the file my desktop shortcut invokes; I prefer to run gadget GUIs on demand. You can also run a script like this at your system's startup to make it always available (and save a mouseclick). For instance:

- On Windows, such a script can be automatically started by adding it to your StartUp folder—click on your system's Start button, select Settings, go to the Taskbar & Start Menu dialog, and click your way through remaining steps.

- On Linux and Unix, you can automatically start this script by spawning it with a command line in your startup scripts (e.g., your home directory's *.cshrc, .profile,* or *.login*) after X Windows has been started.

Whether run via a shortcut, file explorer click, typed command line, or other means, the PyGadgets launcher bar at the top of Figure 8-41 appears.

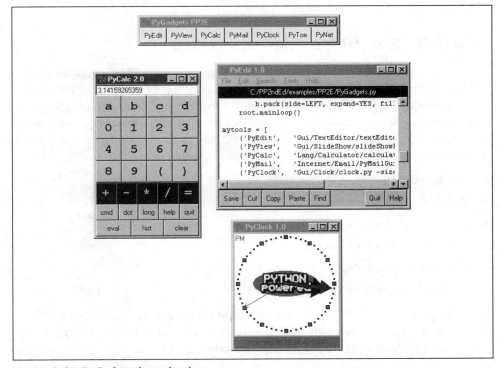

Figure 8-41. PyGadgets launcher bar

Of course, the whole point of PyGadgets is to spawn other programs. Pressing on its launcher bar's buttons starts programs like those shown in the rest of Figure 8-41, but if you want to know more about those, you'll have to turn the page and move on to the next chapter.

9

Larger GUI Examples

"Building a Better Mouse Trap"

This chapter continues our look at building graphical user interfaces with Python and its standard Tkinter library by presenting a collection of realistic GUI programs. In the previous three chapters, we met all the basics of Tkinter programming and toured the core set of *widgets*—Python classes that generate devices on a computer screen and may reply to user-generated events like mouseclicks. Here, our focus is on putting those widgets together to create more useful GUIs. We'll study:

- Advanced GUI coding techniques

- *PyEdit*—a text editor program

- *PyView*—an image slideshow

- *PyDraw*—a painting program

- *PyClock*—a graphical clock

- *PyToe*—and even a simple game just for fun[*]

As in Chapter 4, *Larger System Examples I*, and Chapter 5, *Larger System Examples II*, I've pulled the examples in this chapter from my own library of Python programs that I really use. For instance, the text editor and clock GUIs that we'll meet here are day-to-day workhorses on my machines. Because they are written in

---

[*] All of the larger examples in this book have a "Py" at the start of their names. This is by convention in the Python world. If you shop around at *http://www.python.org*, you'll find other free software that follows this pattern too: PyApache (a Python interface to the Apache web server), PySol (a Python/Tkinter solitaire game system), and many more. I'm not sure who started this pattern, but it has turned out to be a more or less subtle way to advertise programming language preferences to the rest of the open source world. Pythonistas are nothing if not subtle.

Python and Tkinter, they work unchanged on both my Windows and Linux machines, and they should work on Macs, too.

And since these are pure Python scripts, their future evolution is entirely up to their users—once you get a handle on Tkinter interfaces, changing or augmenting the behavior of such programs by editing their Python code is a snap. Although some of these examples are similar to commercially available programs (e.g., PyEdit is reminiscent of the Windows Notepad accessory), the portability and almost infinite configurability of Python scripts can be a decided advantage.

Examples in Other Chapters

Later in the book, we'll meet other Tkinter GUI programs that put a good face on specific application domains. For instance, the following larger GUI examples show up in later chapters, too:

- *PyMail*—an email client in Chapter 11, *Client-Side Scripting*

- *PyForm*—a persistent object table viewer in Chapter 16, *Databases and Persistence*

- *PyTree*—a tree data structure viewer in Chapter 17, *Data Structures*

- *PyCalc*—a calculator widget in Chapter 18, *Text and Language*

Most of these programs see regular action on my desktop, too. Because GUI libraries are general-purpose tools, there are few domains that cannot benefit from an easy-to-use, easy-to-program, and widely portable user interface coded in Python and Tkinter.

Beyond the examples in this book, you can also find higher-level GUI toolkits for Python, such as the PMW system mentioned in Chapter 6, *Graphical User Interfaces*. Such systems build upon Tkinter to provide compound components such as notebook and tabbed widgets. We'll also later meet programs that build user interfaces in web browsers, not Tkinter. But apart from simple web-based interfaces, Tkinter GUIs can be an indispensable feature of almost any Python program you write.

This Chapter's Strategy

As for all case-study chapters in this text, this one is largely a "learn by example" exercise; most of the programs here are listed with minimal details. Along the way I'll point out new Tkinter features that each example introduces, but I'll also assume that you will study the listed source code and its comments for more details. Python's readability becomes a substantial advantage for programmers (and writers), especially once we reach the level of complexity demonstrated by programs here.

Finally, I want to remind you that all of the larger programs listed in the previous sections can be run from the PyDemos and PyGadgets launcher-bar GUIs that we met at the end of the previous chapter. Although I will try hard to capture some of their behavior in screen shots here, GUIs are event-driven systems by nature, and there is nothing quite like running one live to sample the flavor of its user interactions. Because of that, the launcher bars are really a supplement to the material in this chapter. They should run on most platforms and are designed to be easy to start (see the top-level *README-PP2E.txt* file for hints). You should go there and start clicking things immediately, if you haven't done so already.

Advanced GUI Coding Techniques

If you read Chapter 8, *A Tkinter Tour, Part 2*, you know that the code used to construct non-trivial GUIs can become large if we make each widget by hand. Not only do we have to manually link up all the widgets, but there are dozens of options to be set and remember. If we stick to this strategy, GUI programming often becomes an exercise in typing, or at least in cut-and-paste text editor operations.

GuiMixin: Shared Behavior in "Mixin" Classes

Rather than doing each step by hand, a better idea is to wrap or automate as much of the GUI construction process as possible. One approach is to code functions that provide typical widget configurations; for instance, we could define a button function to handle configuration details and support most of the buttons we draw.

Alternatively, we can implement common methods in a class and inherit them everywhere they are needed. Such classes are commonly called *mixin* classes, because their methods are "mixed in" with other classes. Mixins serve to package generally useful tools as methods. The concept is almost like importing a module, but mixin classes can access the subject instance, *self*, to utilize per-instance state and inherited methods. The script in Example 9-1 shows how.

Example 9-1. PP2E\Gui\Tools\guimixin.py

```
#########################################################
# a "mixin" class for other frames: common methods for
# canned-dialogs, spawning programs, etc; must be mixed
# with a class derived from Frame for its quit method
#########################################################

from Tkinter import *
from tkMessageBox import *
from tkFileDialog import *
```

Example 9-1. PP2E\Gui\Tools\guimixin.py (continued)

```python
from ScrolledText import ScrolledText
from PP2E.launchmodes import PortableLauncher, System

class GuiMixin:
    def infobox(self, title, text, *args):            # use standard dialogs
        return showinfo(title, text)                  # *args for bkwd compat
    def errorbox(self, text):
        showerror('Error!', text)
    def question(self, title, text, *args):
        return askyesno(title, text)

    def notdone(self):
        showerror('Not implemented', 'Option not available')
    def quit(self):
        ans = self.question('Verify quit', 'Are you sure you want to quit?')
        if ans == 1:
            Frame.quit(self)                          # quit not recursive!
    def help(self):
        self.infobox('RTFM', 'See figure 1...')       # override this better

    def selectOpenFile(self, file="", dir="."):       # use standard dialogs
        return askopenfilename(initialdir=dir, initialfile=file)
    def selectSaveFile(self, file="", dir="."):
        return asksaveasfilename(initialfile=file, initialdir=dir)

    def clone(self):
        new = Toplevel()                   # make a new version of me
        myclass = self.__class__           # instance's (lowest) class object
        myclass(new)                       # attach/run instance to new window

    def spawn(self, pycmdline, wait=0):
        if not wait:
            PortableLauncher(pycmdline, pycmdline)()   # run Python progam
        else:
            System(pycmdline, pycmdline)()             # wait for it to exit

    def browser(self, filename):
        new  = Toplevel()                              # make new window
        text = ScrolledText(new, height=30, width=90)  # Text with scrollbar
        text.config(font=('courier', 10, 'normal'))    # use fixed-width font
        text.pack()
        new.title("Text Viewer")                       # set window mgr attrs
        new.iconname("browser")
        text.insert('0.0', open(filename, 'r').read() ) # insert file's text

if __name__ == '__main__':
    class TestMixin(GuiMixin, Frame):      # stand-alone test
        def __init__(self, parent=None):
            Frame.__init__(self, parent)
            self.pack()
            Button(self, text='quit',  command=self.quit).pack(fill=X)
            Button(self, text='help',  command=self.help).pack(fill=X)
```

Example 9-1. PP2E\Gui\Tools\guimixin.py (continued)

```
        Button(self, text='clone', command=self.clone).pack(fill=X)
    TestMixin().mainloop()
```

Although Example 9-1 is geared towards GUIs, it's really about design concepts. The `GuiMixin` class implements common operations with standard interfaces that are immune to changes in implementation. In fact, the implementations of some of this class's method did change—between the first and second editions of this book, old-style `Dialog` calls were replaced with the new Tk standard dialog calls. Because this class's interface hides such details, its clients did not have to be changed to use the new dialog techniques.

As is, `GuiMixin` provides methods for common dialogs, window cloning, program spawning, text file browsing, and so on. We can add more methods to such a mixin later if we find ourselves coding the same methods repeatedly; they will all become available immediately everywhere this class is imported and mixed. Moreover, `GuiMixin`'s methods can be inherited and used as is, or they can be redefined in subclasses.

There are a few things to notice here:

- The `quit` method serves some of the same purpose as the reusable `Quitter` button we used in earlier chapters. Because mixin classes can define a large library of reusable methods, they can be a more powerful way to package reusable components than individual classes. If the mixin is packaged well, we can get a lot more from it than a single button's callback.

- The `clone` method makes a new copy of the most specific class that mixes in a `GuiMixin`, in a new top-level window (`self.__class__` is the class object that the instance was created from). This opens a new independent copy of the window.

- The `browser` method opens the standard library's `ScrolledText` object in a new window and fills it with the text of a file to be viewed. We wrote our own `ScrolledText` in the last chapter; you might need to use it here instead, if the standard library's class ever becomes deprecated (please, no wagering).

- The `spawn` method launches a Python program command line as a new process, and waits for it to end or not (depending on the `wait` argument). This method is simple, though, because we wrapped launching details in the `launchmodes` module presented at the end of Chapter 3, *Parallel System Tools*. `GuiMixin` both fosters and practices good code reuse habits.

The `GuiMixin` class is meant to be a library of reusable tool methods and is essentially useless by itself. In fact, it must generally be mixed with a `Frame`-based class to be used: `quit` assumes it's mixed with a `Frame`, and `clone` assumes it's mixed with a widget class. To satisfy such constraints this module's self-test code at the bottom combines `GuiMixin` with a `Frame` widget. Figure 9-1 shows the scene created by the self-test after pressing "clone" twice, and then "help" in one of the three copies.

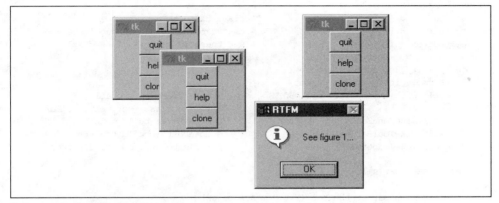

Figure 9-1. GuiMixin self-test code in action

We'll see this class show up again as a mixin in later examples, too—that's the whole point of code reuse, after all.

GuiMaker: Automating Menus and Toolbars

The last section's mixin class makes common tasks simpler, but it still doesn't address the complexity of linking up widgets like menus and toolbars. Of course, if we had access to a GUI layout tool that generated Python code, this would not be an issue. We'd design our widgets interactively, press a button, and fill in the callback handler blanks.

For now, a programming-based approach can work just as well. What we'd like is to be able to inherit something that does all the grunt work of construction for us, given a template for the menus and toolbars in a window. Here's one way it can be done—using trees of simple objects. The class in Example 9-2 interprets data structure representations of menus and toolbars, and builds all the widgets automatically.

Example 9-2. PP2E\Gui\Tools\guimaker.py

```
###########################################################################
# An extended Frame that makes window menus and tool-bars automatically.
# Use GuiMakerFrameMenu for embedded components (makes frame-based menus).
# Use GuiMakerWindowMenu for top-level windows (makes Tk8.0 window menus).
# See the self-test code (and PyEdit) for an example layout tree format.
###########################################################################
```

Example 9-2. PP2E\Gui\Tools\guimaker.py (continued)

```
import sys
from Tkinter import *                  # widget classes
from types   import *                  # type constants

class GuiMaker(Frame):
    menuBar    = []                    # class defaults
    toolBar    = []                    # change per instance in subclasses
    helpButton = 1                     # set these in start() if need self

    def __init__(self, parent=None):
        Frame.__init__(self, parent)
        self.pack(expand=YES, fill=BOTH)           # make frame stretchable
        self.start()                               # for subclass: set menu/toolBar
        self.makeMenuBar()                         # done here: build menu-bar
        self.makeToolBar()                         # done here: build tool-bar
        self.makeWidgets()                         # for subclass: add middle part

    def makeMenuBar(self):
        """
        make menu bar at the top (Tk8.0 menus below)
        expand=no, fill=x so same width on resize
        """
        menubar = Frame(self, relief=RAISED, bd=2)
        menubar.pack(side=TOP, fill=X)

        for (name, key, items) in self.menuBar:
            mbutton  = Menubutton(menubar, text=name, underline=key)
            mbutton.pack(side=LEFT)
            pulldown = Menu(mbutton)
            self.addMenuItems(pulldown, items)
            mbutton.config(menu=pulldown)

        if self.helpButton:
            Button(menubar, text    = 'Help',
                            cursor  = 'gumby',
                            relief  = FLAT,
                            command = self.help).pack(side=RIGHT)

    def addMenuItems(self, menu, items):
        for item in items:                        # scan nested items list
            if item == 'separator':               # string: add separator
                menu.add_separator({})
            elif type(item) == ListType:          # list: disabled item list
                for num in item:
                    menu.entryconfig(num, state=DISABLED)
            elif type(item[2]) != ListType:
                menu.add_command(label     = item[0],   # command:
                                 underline = item[1],    # add command
                                 command   = item[2])    # cmd=callable
            else:
                pullover = Menu(menu)
```

Example 9-2. PP2E\Gui\Tools\guimaker.py (continued)

```
                self.addMenuItems(pullover, item[2])          # sublist:
                menu.add_cascade(label     = item[0],         # make submenu
                                 underline = item[1],         # add cascade
                                 menu      = pullover)

    def makeToolBar(self):
        """
        make button bar at bottom, if any
        expand=no, fill=x so same width on resize
        """
        if self.toolBar:
            toolbar = Frame(self, cursor='hand2', relief=SUNKEN, bd=2)
            toolbar.pack(side=BOTTOM, fill=X)
            for (name, action, where) in self.toolBar:
                Button(toolbar, text=name, command=action).pack(where)

    def makeWidgets(self):
        """
        make 'middle' part last, so menu/toolbar
        is always on top/bottom and clipped last;
        override this default, pack middle any side;
        for grid: grid middle part in a packed frame
        """
        name = Label(self,
                     width=40, height=10,
                     relief=SUNKEN, bg='white',
                     text    = self.__class__.__name__,
                     cursor  = 'crosshair')
        name.pack(expand=YES, fill=BOTH, side=TOP)

    def help(self):
        """
        override me in subclass
        """
        from tkMessageBox import showinfo
        showinfo('Help', 'Sorry, no help for ' + self.__class__.__name__)

    def start(self): pass   # override me in subclass


##############################################################################
# For Tk 8.0 main window menubar, instead of a frame
##############################################################################

GuiMakerFrameMenu = GuiMaker            # use this for embedded component menus

class GuiMakerWindowMenu(GuiMaker):     # use this for top-level window menus
    def makeMenuBar(self):
        menubar = Menu(self.master)
        self.master.config(menu=menubar)
```

Example 9-2. PP2E\Gui\Tools\guimaker.py (continued)

```
        for (name, key, items) in self.menuBar:
            pulldown = Menu(menubar)
            self.addMenuItems(pulldown, items)
            menubar.add_cascade(label=name, underline=key, menu=pulldown)

        if self.helpButton:
            if sys.platform[:3] == 'win':
                menubar.add_command(label='Help', command=self.help)
            else:
                pulldown = Menu(menubar)   # linux needs real pulldown
                pulldown.add_command(label='About', command=self.help)
                menubar.add_cascade(label='Help', menu=pulldown)


###########################################################################
# Self test when file run stand-alone: 'python guimaker.py'
###########################################################################

if __name__ == '__main__':
    from guimixin import GuiMixin             # mixin a help method

    menuBar = [
        ('File', 0,
            [('Open',  0, lambda:0),          # lambda:0 is a no-op
             ('Quit',  0, sys.exit)]),        # use sys, no self here
        ('Edit', 0,
            [('Cut',   0, lambda:0),
             ('Paste', 0, lambda:0)]) ]
    toolBar = [('Quit', sys.exit, {'side': LEFT})]

    class TestAppFrameMenu(GuiMixin, GuiMakerFrameMenu):
        def start(self):
            self.menuBar = menuBar
            self.toolBar = toolBar
    class TestAppWindowMenu(GuiMixin, GuiMakerWindowMenu):
        def start(self):
            self.menuBar = menuBar
            self.toolBar = toolBar
    class TestAppWindowMenuBasic(GuiMakerWindowMenu):
        def start(self):
            self.menuBar = menuBar
            self.toolBar = toolBar     # guimaker help, not guimixin

    root = Tk()
    TestAppFrameMenu(Toplevel())
    TestAppWindowMenu(Toplevel())
    TestAppWindowMenuBasic(root)
    root.mainloop()
```

To make sense of this module, you have to be familiar with the menu fundamentals introduced in the last chapter. If you are, though, it's straightforward—the GuiMaker class simply traverses the menu and toolbar structures and builds menu and toolbar widgets along the way. This module's self-test code includes a simple example of the data structures used to lay out menus and toolbars:

Menubar templates

Lists and nested sublists of (`label, underline, handler`) triples. If a `handler` is a sublist instead of a function or method, it is assumed to be a cascading submenu.

Toolbar templates

List of (`label, handler, pack-options`) triples. `pack-options` is coded as a dictionary of options passed on to the widget `pack` method (it accepts dictionaries, but we could also transform the dictionary into keyword arguments by passing it as a third argument to `apply`).

Subclass protocols

In addition to menu and toolbar layouts, clients of this class can also tap into and customize the method and geometry protocols it implements:

Template attributes

Clients of this class are expected to set `menuBar` and `toolBar` attributes somewhere in the inheritance chain by the time the `start` method has finished.

Initialization

The `start` method can be overridden to construct menu and toolbar templates dynamically (since `self` is then available); `start` is also where general initializations should be performed—GuiMixin's `__init__` constructor must be run, not overridden.

Adding widgets

The `makeWidgets` method can be redefined to construct the middle part of the window—the application portion between the menubar and toolbar. By default, `makeWidgets` adds a label in the middle with the name of the most specific class, but this method is expected to be specialized.

Packing protocol

In a specialized `makeWidgets` method, clients may attach their middle portion's widgets to any side of "self" (a `Frame`), since the menu and toolbars have already claimed the container's top and bottom by the time `makeWidgets` is run. The middle part does not need to be a nested frame if its parts are packed. The menu and toolbars are also automatically packed first so that they are clipped last if the window shrinks.

Gridding protocol

The middle part can contain a grid layout, as long as it is gridded in a nested `Frame` that is itself packed within the `self` parent. (Remember, that each container level may use `grid` or `pack`, not both, and `self` is a `Frame` with

already-packed bars by the time `makeWidgets` is called.) Because the
`GuiMaker` `Frame` packs itself within its parent, it is not directly embeddable in
a container with widgets arranged in a grid for similar reasons—add an intermediate gridded `Frame` to use it in this context.

GuiMaker classes

In return for conforming to `GuiMaker` protocols and templates, client subclasses
get a `Frame` that knows how to automatically build up its own menus and toolbars from template data structures. If you read the last chapter's menu examples,
you probably know that this is a big win in terms of reduced coding requirements. `GuiMaker` is also clever enough to export interfaces for both menu styles
that we met in the last chapter:

- `GuiMakerWindowMenu` implements Tk 8.0–style top-level window menus, useful for menus associated with standalone programs and pop-ups.

- `GuiMakerFrameMenu` implements alternative `Frame/Menubutton`-based menus,
  useful for menus on objects embedded as components of a larger GUI.

Both classes build toolbars, export the same protocols, and expect to find the
same template structures; they differ only in the way they process menu templates. In fact, one is simply a subclass of the other with a specialized menu maker
method—only top-level menu processing differs between the two styles (a `Menu`
with `Menu` cascades, instead of a `Frame` with `Menubuttons`).

GuiMaker self-test

Like `GuiMixin`, when we run Example 9-2 as a top-level program, we trigger the
self-test logic at the bottom; Figure 9-2 shows the windows we get. Three windows come up, representing each of the self-test code's `TestApp` classes. All three
have a menu and toolbar with the options specified in the template data structures created in the self-test code: File and Edit menu pull-downs, plus a Quit toolbar button, and a standard Help menu button. In the screen shot, one window's
File menu has been torn off, and the Edit menu of another is being pulled down.

Because of the superclass relationships coded, two of the three windows get their
`help` callback handler from `GuiMixin`; `TestAppWindowMenuBasic` gets
`GuiMaker`'s instead. Notice that the order in which these two classes are mixed
can be important: because both `GuiMixin` and `Frame` define a `quit` method, we
need to list the class we want to get it from first in the mixed class's header line
due to the left-to-right search rule of multiple inheritance. To select `GuiMixin`'s
methods, it should usually be listed before a superclass derived from real widgets.

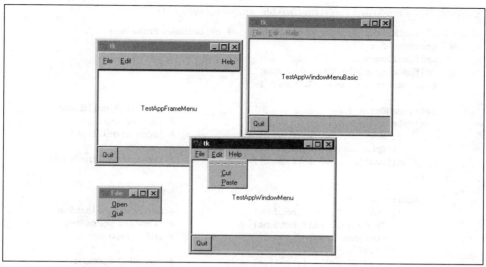

Figure 9-2. GuiMaker self-test at work

We'll put `GuiMaker` to more practical use in examples such as PyEdit later in this chapter. The next module shows another way to use `GuiMaker`'s templates to build up a sophisticated interface.

BigGui: A Client Demo Program

Let's look at a program that makes better use of the two automation classes we just wrote. In the module in Example 9-3, the `Hello` class inherits from both `GuiMixin` and `GuiMaker`. `GuiMaker` provides the link to the `Frame` widget, plus the menu/toolbar construction logic. `GuiMixin` provides extra common-behavior methods. Really, `Hello` is another kind of extended `Frame` widget because it is derived from `GuiMaker`. To get a menu and toolbar for free, it simply follows the protocols defined by `GuiMaker`—it sets the `menuBar` and `toolBar` attributes in its `start` method, and overrides `makeWidgets` to put a label in the middle.

Example 9-3. PP2E\Gui\Tools\BigGui\big_gui.py

```
#!/usr/bin/python
#######################################################
# gui implementation - combines maker, mixin, and this
#######################################################

import sys, os, string
from Tkinter import *                        # widget classes
from PP2E.Gui.Tools.guimixin import *        # mix-in methods
from PP2E.Gui.Tools.guimaker import *        # frame, plus menu/toolbar builder
from find_demo_dir import findDemoDir        # Python demos search
```

Example 9-3. PP2E\Gui\Tools\BigGui\big_gui.py (continued)

```
class Hello(GuiMixin, GuiMakerWindowMenu):    # or GuiMakerFrameMenu
    def start(self):
        self.hellos = 0
        self.master.title("GuiMaker Demo")
        self.master.iconname("GuiMaker")

        self.menuBar = [                                 # a tree: 3 pulldowns
          ('File', 0,                                    # (pull-down)
             [('New...',  0, self.notdone),              # [menu items list]
              ('Open...', 0, self.fileOpen),
              ('Quit',    0, self.quit)]                 # label,underline,action
          ),

          ('Edit', 0,
             [('Cut',   -1, self.notdone),               # no underline|action
              ('Paste',-1, self.notdone),               # lambda:0 works too
              'separator',                               # add a separator
              ('Stuff', -1,
                  [('Clone', -1, self.clone),            # cascaded submenu
                   ('More',  -1, self.more)]
              ),
              ('Delete', -1, lambda:0),
              [5]]                                       # disable 'delete'
          ),

          ('Play', 0,
             [('Hello',     0, self.greeting),
              ('Popup...',  0, self.dialog),
              ('Demos', 0,
                  [('Hanoi', 0,
                      lambda x=self:
                        x.spawn(findDemoDir() + '\guido\hanoi.py', wait=0)),
                   ('Pong',  0,
                      lambda x=self:
                        x.spawn(findDemoDir() + '\matt\pong-demo-1.py', wait=0)),
                   ('Other...', -1, self.pickDemo)]
              )]
          )]

        self.toolBar = [
          ('Quit',  self.quit,     {'side': RIGHT}),     # add 3 buttons
          ('Hello', self.greeting, {'side': LEFT}),
          ('Popup', self.dialog,   {'side': LEFT, 'expand':YES}) ]

    def makeWidgets(self):                               # override default
        middle = Label(self, text='Hello maker world!', width=40, height=10,
                       cursor='pencil', bg='white', relief=SUNKEN)
        middle.pack(expand=YES, fill=BOTH)

    def greeting(self):
        self.hellos = self.hellos + 1
```

Example 9-3. PP2E\Gui\Tools\BigGui\big_gui.py (continued)

```
        if self.hellos % 3:
            print "hi"
        else:
            self.infobox("Three", 'HELLO!')     # on every third press

    def dialog(self):
        button = self.question('OOPS!',
                                   'You typed "rm*" ... continue?',
                                   'questhead', ('yes', 'no', 'help'))
        [lambda:0, self.quit, self.help][button]()

    def fileOpen(self):
        pick = self.selectOpenFile(file='big_gui.py')
        if pick:
            self.browser(pick)        # browse my source file, or other

    def more(self):
        new = Toplevel()
        Label(new,  text='A new non-modal window').pack()
        Button(new, text='Quit', command=self.quit).pack(side=LEFT)
        Button(new, text='More', command=self.more).pack(side=RIGHT)

    def pickDemo(self):
        pick = self.selectOpenFile(dir=findDemoDir()+'\guido')
        if pick:
            self.spawn(pick, wait=0)     # spawn any python program

if __name__ == '__main__': Hello().mainloop()    # make one, run one
```

This script lays out a fairly large menu and toolbar structure that we'll see in moment. It also adds callback methods of its own that print `stdout` messages, pop up text file browsers and new windows, and run other programs. Many of the callbacks don't do much more than run the `notDone` method inherited from `GuiMixin`, though; this code is intended mostly as a `GuiMaker` and `GuiMixin` demo.

The `big_gui` script is almost a complete program, but not quite: it relies on a utility module to search for canned demo programs that come packaged with the Python full source distribution. (These demos are not part of this book's example collection.) The Python source distribution might be unpacked anywhere on the host machine.

Because of that, it's impossible to know where the demo directory is located (if it is present at all). But rather than expecting beginners to change the source code of this script to hardcode a path, the `guessLocation` tool in the `Launcher` module we met at the end of Chapter 4 is used to hunt for the demo directory (see Example 9-4). Flip back if you've forgotten how this works (though the beauty of code reuse is that it's often okay to forget).

Example 9-4. PP2E\Gui\Tools\BigGui\find_demo_dir.py

```
######################################################
# search for demos shipped in Python source distribution;
# PATH and PP2EHOME won't help here, because these demos
# are not part of the standard install or the book's tree
######################################################

import os, string, PP2E.Launcher
demoDir  = None
myTryDir = ''

#sourceDir = r'C:\Stuff\Etc\Python-ddj-cd\distributions'
#myTryDir  = sourceDir + r'\Python-1.5.2\Demo\tkinter'

def findDemoDir():
    global demoDir
    if not demoDir:                             # only searches on first call
        if os.path.exists(myTryDir):            # use hard-coded dir, or search
            demoDir = myTryDir                  # save in global for next call
        else:
            print 'Searching for standard demos on your machine...'
            path = PP2E.Launcher.guessLocation('hanoi.py')
            if path:
                demoDir = string.join(string.split(path, os.sep)[:-2], os.sep)
                print 'Using demo dir:', demoDir
    assert demoDir, 'Where is your demo directory?'
    return demoDir
```

When `big_gui` is run as a top-level program, it creates a window with four menu pull-downs on top, and a three-button toolbar on the bottom, shown in Figure 9-3 along with some of the pop-up windows its callbacks create. The menus have separators, disabled entries, and cascading submenus, all as defined by the `menuBar` template.

Figure 9-4 shows this script's window again, after its Play pull-down has been used to launch two independently running instances of the *hanoi.py* demo script that is shipped in the Python source distribution and coded by Python creator Guido van Rossum. This demo shows a simple animation of solutions to the "Towers of Hanoi" puzzle—a classic recursive problem popular on computer science quizzes (if you never heard of it, I'll spare you the gory details here).

To find this demo, the script searches directory trees on your machine rooted at common places; it was found on mine only by a last-resort traversal of my entire *C:* hard drive:

```
C:\...\PP2E\Gui\Tools\BigGui>python big_gui.py
Searching for standard demos on your machine...
Searching for hanoi.py in C:\Program Files\Python
Searching for hanoi.py in C:\PP2ndEd\examples\PP2E\Gui\Tools\BigGui
Searching for hanoi.py in C:\Program Files
Searching for hanoi.py in C:\
```

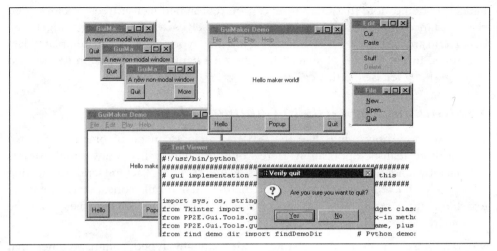

Figure 9-3. big_gui with various pop-ups

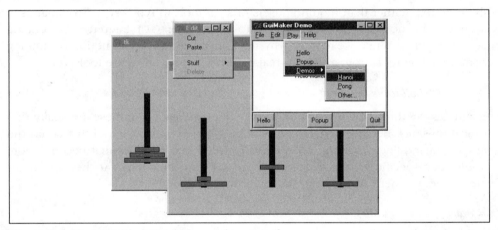

Figure 9-4. big_gui with spawned hanoi demos on the move

```
Using demo dir: C:\PP2ndEd\cdrom\Python1.5.2\SourceDistribution\Unpacked\Python-
1.5.2\Demo\tkinter
C:\PP2ndEd\cdrom\Python1.5.2\SourceDistribution\Unpacked\Python-1.5.2\Demo\tkint
er\guido\hanoi.py
```

This search takes about 20 seconds on my 650 MHz Windows laptop, but is done only the first time you select one of these demos—after a successful search, the `find_demo_dir` module caches away the directory name in a global variable for immediate retrieval the next time you start a demo. If you want to run demos from other directories (e.g., one of the book demos in the *PP2E* tree), select the Play menu's Other option to pop up a standard file selection dialog instead and navigate to the desired program's file.

Finally, I should note that `GuiMaker` can be redesigned to use trees of embedded class instances that know how to apply themselves to the Tkinter widget tree being constructed, instead of branching on the types of items in template data structures. In the interest of space, though, we'll banish that extension to the land of suggested exercises in this edition.

ShellGui: Adding GUIs to Command-Line Tools

To better show how things like the `GuiMixin` class can be of practical use, we need a more realistic application. Here's one: in Chapter 4, we saw simple scripts for packing and unpacking text files (see the section "Packing and Unpacking Files"). The *packapp.py* script we met there, you'll recall, concatenates multiple text files into a single file, and *unpackapp.py* extracts the original files from the combined file.

We ran these scripts in that chapter with manually typed command lines that weren't the most complex ever devised, but were complicated enough to be easily forgotten. Rather than requiring users of such tools to type cryptic commands at a shell, why not also provide an easy-to-use Tkinter GUI interface for running such programs? While we're at it, why not generalize the whole notion of running command-line tools from a GUI, to make it easy to support future tools, too?

A generic shell-tools display

Examples 9-5 through 9-8 are one concrete implementation of these artificially rhetorical musings. Because I wanted this to be a general-purpose tool that could run any command-line program, its design is factored into modules that become more application-specific as we go lower in the software hierarchy. At the top, things are about as generic as they can be, as shown in Example 9-5.

Example 9-5. PP2E\Gui\ShellGui\shellgui.py.py

```
#!/usr/local/bin/python
#####################################################################
# tools launcher; uses guimaker templates, guimixin std quit dialog;
# I am just a class library: run mytools script to display the gui;
#####################################################################

from Tkinter import *                          # get widgets
from PP2E.Gui.Tools.guimixin import GuiMixin   # get quit, not done
from PP2E.Gui.Tools.guimaker import *          # menu/toolbar builder

class ShellGui(GuiMixin, GuiMakerWindowMenu):  # a frame + maker + mixins
    def start(self):                           # use GuiMaker if component
        self.setMenuBar()
        self.setToolBar()
        self.master.title("Shell Tools Listbox")
```

Example 9-5. PP2E\Gui\ShellGui\shellgui.py.py (continued)

```
        self.master.iconname("Shell Tools")

    def handleList(self, event):              # on listbox double-click
        label = self.listbox.get(ACTIVE)      # fetch selection text
        self.runCommand(label)                # and call action here

    def makeWidgets(self):                    # add listbox in middle
        sbar = Scrollbar(self)                # cross link sbar, list
        list = Listbox(self, bg='white')      # or use Tour.ScrolledList
        sbar.config(command=list.yview)
        list.config(yscrollcommand=sbar.set)
        sbar.pack(side=RIGHT, fill=Y)         # pack 1st=clip last
        list.pack(side=LEFT, expand=YES, fill=BOTH)   # list clipped first
        for (label, action) in self.fetchCommands():  # add to list-box
            list.insert(END, label)           # and menu/toolbars
        list.bind('<Double-1>', self.handleList)  # set event handler
        self.listbox = list

    def forToolBar(self, label):              # put on toolbar?
        return 1                              # default = all

    def setToolBar(self):
        self.toolBar = []
        for (label, action) in self.fetchCommands():
            if self.forToolBar(label):
                self.toolBar.append((label, action, {'side': LEFT}))
        self.toolBar.append(('Quit', self.quit, {'side': RIGHT}))

    def setMenuBar(self):
        toolEntries  = []
        self.menuBar = [
            ('File',  0, [('Quit', -1, self.quit)]),  # pull-down name
            ('Tools', 0, toolEntries)             # menu items list
            ]                                     # label,underline,action
        for (label, action) in self.fetchCommands():
            toolEntries.append((label, -1, action))  # add app items to menu


###################################################
# delegate to template type-specific subclasses
# which delegate to app toolset-specific subclasses
###################################################

class ListMenuGui(ShellGui):
    def fetchCommands(self):            # subclass: set 'myMenu'
        return self.myMenu              # list of (label, callback)
    def runCommand(self, cmd):
        for (label, action) in self.myMenu:
            if label == cmd: action()

class DictMenuGui(ShellGui):
    def fetchCommands(self):    return self.myMenu.items()
    def runCommand(self, cmd): self.myMenu[cmd]()
```

The `ShellGui` class in this module knows how to use the `GuiMaker` and `GuiMix` interfaces to construct a selection window that displays tool names in menus, a scrolled list, and a toolbar. It also provides an overridable `forToolBar` method that allows subclasses to specify which tools should and should not be added to the window's toolbar (the toolbar can get crowded in a hurry). However, it is deliberately ignorant about both the names of tools that should be displayed in those places, and the actions to be run when tool names are selected.

Instead, `ShellGui` relies on the `ListMenuGui` and `DictMenuGui` subclasses in this file to provide a list of tool names from a `fetchCommands` method and dispatch actions by name in a `runCommand` method. These two subclasses really just serve to interface to application-specific tool sets laid out as lists or dictionaries, though; they are still naive about what tool names really go up on the GUI. That's by design, too—because the tool sets displayed are defined by lower subclasses, we can use `ShellGui` to display a variety of different tool sets.

Application-specific tool set classes

To get to the actual tool sets, we need to go one level down. The module in Example 9-6 defines subclasses of the two type-specific `ShellGui` classes, to provide sets of available tools in both list and dictionary format (you would normally need only one, but this module is meant for illustration). This is also the module that is actually *run* to kick off the GUI—the `shellgui` module is a class library only.

Example 9-6. PP2E\Gui\ShellGui\mytools.py

```
#!/usr/local/bin/python
from shellgui import *                 # type-specific shell interfaces
from packdlg  import runPackDialog     # dialogs for data entry
from unpkdlg  import runUnpackDialog    # they both run app classes


class TextPak1(ListMenuGui):
    def __init__(self):
        self.myMenu = [('Pack',    runPackDialog),
                       ('Unpack',  runUnpackDialog),    # simple functions
                       ('Mtool',   self.notdone)]        # method from guimixin
        ListMenuGui.__init__(self)

    def forToolBar(self, label):
        return label in ['Pack', 'Unpack']


class TextPak2(DictMenuGui):
    def __init__(self):
        self.myMenu = {'Pack':    runPackDialog,         # or use input here...
                       'Unpack':  runUnpackDialog,       # instead of in dialogs
                       'Mtool':   self.notdone}
```

Example 9-6. PP2E\Gui\ShellGui\mytools.py (continued)

```
        DictMenuGui.__init__(self)


if __name__ == '__main__':                          # self-test code...
    from sys import argv                            # 'menugui.py list|^'
    if len(argv) > 1 and argv[1] == 'list':
        print 'list test'
        TextPak1().mainloop()
    else:
        print 'dict test'
        TextPak2().mainloop()
```

The classes in this module are specific to a particular tools set; to display a different set of tool names, simply code and run a new subclass. By separating out application logic into distinct subclasses and modules like this, software can become widely reusable.

Figure 9-5 shows the main `ShellGui` window created when the `mytools` script is run with its dictionary-based menu layout class on Windows, along with menu tear-offs so you can see what they contain. This window's menu and toolbar are built by `GuiMaker`, and its Quit and Help buttons and menu selections trigger quit and help methods inherited from `GuiMixin` through the `ShellGui` module's superclasses. Are you starting to see why this book preaches code reuse so often?

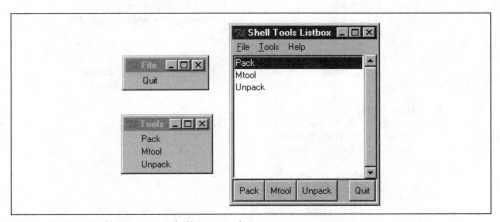

Figure 9-5. mytools items in a ShellGui window

Adding GUI frontends to command lines

The callback actions named within the prior module's classes, though, should normally do something GUI-oriented. Because the original file packing and unpacking scripts live in the world of text-based streams, we need to code wrappers around them that accept input parameters from more GUI-minded users.

The module in Example 9-7 uses the custom modal dialog techniques we studied in Chapter 7, *A Tkinter Tour, Part 1*, to pop up an input display to collect pack script parameters. Its `runPackDialog` function is the actual callback handler invoked when tool names are selected in the main `ShellGui` window.

Example 9-7. PP2E\Gui\ShellGui\packdlg.py.

```
# added file select dialogs, empties test; could use grids

import string
from glob import glob                                      # filename expansion
from Tkinter import *                                       # gui widget stuff
from tkFileDialog import *                                  # file selector dialog
from PP2E.System.App.Clients.packapp import PackApp         # use pack class

def runPackDialog():
    s1, s2 = StringVar(), StringVar()                      # run class like a function
    PackDialog(s1, s2)                                     # pop-up dialog: sets s1/s2
    output, patterns = s1.get(), s2.get()                  # whether 'ok' or wm-destroy
    if output != "" and patterns != "":
        patterns = string.split(patterns)
        filenames = []
        for sublist in map(glob, patterns):                # do expansion manually
            filenames = filenames + sublist                # Unix does auto on command-line
        print 'PackApp:', output, filenames
        app = PackApp(ofile=output)                        # run with redirected output
        app.args = filenames                               # reset cmdline args list
        app.main()                                         # should show msgs in gui too

class PackDialog(Toplevel):
    def __init__(self, target1, target2):
        Toplevel.__init__(self)                            # a new top-level window
        self.title('Enter Pack Parameters')               # 2 frames plus a button

        f1 = Frame(self)
        l1 = Label(f1,  text='Output file?', relief=RIDGE, width=15)
        e1 = Entry(f1,  relief=SUNKEN)
        b1 = Button(f1, text='browse...')
        f1.pack(fill=X)
        l1.pack(side=LEFT)
        e1.pack(side=LEFT, expand=YES, fill=X)
        b1.pack(side=RIGHT)
        b1.config(command= (lambda x=target1: x.set(askopenfilename())) )

        f2 = Frame(self)
        l2 = Label(f2,  text='Files to pack?', relief=RIDGE, width=15)
        e2 = Entry(f2,  relief=SUNKEN)
        b2 = Button(f2, text='browse...')
        f2.pack(fill=X)
        l2.pack(side=LEFT)
        e2.pack(side=LEFT, expand=YES, fill=X)
        b2.pack(side=RIGHT)
        b2.config(command=
```

Example 9-7. PP2E\Gui\ShellGui\packdlg.py. (continued)

```
                (lambda x=target2: x.set(x.get() +' '+ askopenfilename())) )

        Button(self, text='OK', command=self.destroy).pack()
        e1.config(textvariable=target1)
        e2.config(textvariable=target2)

        self.grab_set()        # make myself modal:
        self.focus_set()       # mouse grab, keyboard focus, wait...
        self.wait_window()     # till destroy; else returns to caller now
if __name__ == '__main__':
    root = Tk()
    Button(root, text='pop', command=runPackDialog).pack(fill=X)
    Button(root, text='bye', command=root.quit).pack(fill=X)
    root.mainloop()
```

When run, this script makes the input form shown in Figure 9-6. Users may either type input and output filenames into the entry fields, or press the "browse…" buttons to pop up standard file selection dialogs. They can also enter filename patterns—the manual `glob.glob` call in this script expands filename patterns to match names and filters out nonexistent input filenames. The Unix command line does this pattern expansion automatically when running `PackApp` from a shell, but Windows does not (see Chapter 2, *System Tools*, for more details).

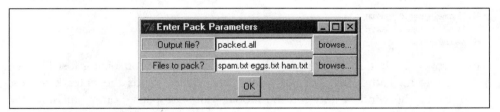

Figure 9-6. The packdlg input form

When the form is filled in and submitted with its OK button, parameters are finally passed to an instance of the `PackApp` class we wrote in Chapter 4 to do file concatenations. The GUI interface to the unpacking script is simpler, because there is only one input field—the name of the packed file to scan. The script in Example 9-8 generated the input form window shown in Figure 9-7.

Example 9-8. PP2E\Gui\ShellGui\unpkdlg.py

```
# added file select dialog, handles cancel better

from Tkinter import *                                # widget classes
from tkFileDialog import *                           # file open dialog
from PP2E.System.App.Clients.unpackapp import UnpackApp  # use unpack class

def runUnpackDialog():
```

Example 9-8. PP2E\Gui\ShellGui\unpkdlg.py (continued)

```
        input = UnpackDialog().input          # get input from GUI
        if input != '':                        # do non-gui file stuff
            print 'UnpackApp:', input
            app = UnpackApp(ifile=input)        # run with input from file
            app.main()                          # execute app class

class UnpackDialog(Toplevel):
    def __init__(self):                        # a function would work too
        Toplevel.__init__(self)                # resizable root box
        self.input = ''                        # a label and an entry
        self.title('Enter Unpack Parameters')
        Label(self, text='input file?', relief=RIDGE, width=11).pack(side=LEFT)
        e = Entry(self, relief=SUNKEN)
        b = Button(self, text='browse...')
        e.bind('<Key-Return>', self.gotit)
        b.config(command=(lambda x=e: x.insert(0, askopenfilename())))
        b.pack(side=RIGHT)
        e.pack(side=LEFT, expand=YES, fill=X)
        self.entry = e
        self.grab_set()                        # make myself modal
        self.focus_set()
        self.wait_window()                     # till I'm destroyed on return->gotit
    def gotit(self, event):                    # on return key: event.widget==Entry
        self.input = self.entry.get()          # fetch text, save in self
        self.destroy()                         # kill window, but instance lives on

if __name__ == "__main__":
    Button(None, text='pop', command=runUnpackDialog).pack()
    mainloop()
```

The "browse..." button in Figure 9-7 pops up a file selection dialog just like the packdlg form. Rather than an OK button, this dialog binds the enter key-press event to kill the window and end the modal wait state pause; on submission, the name of the file is passed to an instance of the UnpackApp class shown in Chapter 4 to perform the actual file scan process.

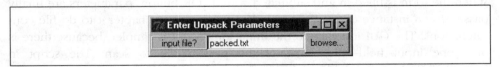

Figure 9-7. The unpkdlg input form

This all works as advertised—by making command-line tools available in graphical form like this, they become much more attractive to users accustomed to the GUI way of life. Still, there are two aspects of this design that seem prime for improvement.

First of all, both of the input dialogs use custom code to render a unique appearance, but we could probably simplify them substantially by importing a common form-builder module instead. We met generalized form builder code in Chapters 7 and 8, and we'll meet more later; see the *form.py* module in Chapter 10, *Network Scripting*, for pointers on genericizing form construction, too.

Secondly, at the point where the user submits input data in either form dialog, we've lost the GUI trail—`PackApp` and `UnpackApp` messages still show up in the `stdout` console window:

```
C:\...\PP2E\Gui\ShellGui\test>python ..\mytools.py
dict test
PackApp: packed.all ['spam.txt', 'eggs.txt', 'ham.txt']
packing: spam.txt
packing: eggs.txt
packing: ham.txt
UnpackApp: packed.all
creating: spam.txt
creating: eggs.txt
creating: ham.txt
```

We can do better here, by *redirecting* `stdout` to an object that throws text up in a GUI window as it is received. You'll have to read the next section to see how.

GuiStreams: Redirecting Streams to GUI Widgets

The script in Example 9-9 arranges to map input and output sources to pop-up windows in a GUI application, much as we did with strings in the stream redirection topics in Chapter 2. Although this module is really just a first-cut prototype and needs improvement itself (e.g., each input line request pops up a new input dialog), it demonstrates the concepts in general.

Its `GuiOutput` and `GuiInput` objects define methods that allow them to masquerade as files in any interface that expects a file. As we learned earlier in Chapter 2, this includes standard stream processing tools like `print`, `raw_input`, and explicit `read` and `write` calls. The `redirectedGuiFunc` function in this module uses this plug-and-play compatibility to run a function with its standard input and output streams mapped completely to pop-up windows instead of the console window (or wherever streams would otherwise be mapped).

Example 9-9. PP2E\Gui\Tools\guiStreams.py

```
#############################################################################
# first-cut implementation of file-like classes that can be used to redirect
# input and output streams to GUI displays; as is, input comes from a common
# dialog popup (a single output+input interface or a persistent Entry field
# for input would be better); this also does not properly span lines for read
# requests with a byte count > len(line); see guiStreamsTools.py for more;
#############################################################################

from Tkinter import *
from ScrolledText import ScrolledText
```

Example 9-9. PP2E\Gui\Tools\guiStreams.py (continued)

```python
from tkSimpleDialog import askstring

class GuiOutput:
    def __init__(self, parent=None):
        self.text = None
        if parent: self.popupnow(parent)          # popup now or on first write
    def popupnow(self, parent=None):               # in parent now, Toplevel later
        if self.text: return
        self.text = ScrolledText(parent or Toplevel())
        self.text.config(font=('courier', 9, 'normal'))
        self.text.pack()
    def write(self, text):
        self.popupnow()
        self.text.insert(END, str(text))
        self.text.see(END)
        self.text.update()
    def writelines(self, lines):                   # lines already have '\n'
        for line in lines: self.write(line)        # or map(self.write, lines)

class GuiInput:
    def __init__(self):
        self.buff = ''
    def inputLine(self):
        line = askstring('GuiInput', 'Enter input line + <crlf> (cancel=eof)')
        if line == None:
            return ''                               # popup dialog for each line
        else:                                       # cancel button means eof
            return line + '\n'                      # else add end-line marker
    def read(self, bytes=None):
        if not self.buff:
            self.buff = self.inputLine()
        if bytes:                                   # read by byte count
            text = self.buff[:bytes]                # doesn't span lines
            self.buff = self.buff[bytes:]
        else:
            text = ''                               # read all till eof
            line = self.buff
            while line:
                text = text + line
                line = self.inputLine()             # until cancel=eof=''
        return text
    def readline(self):
        text = self.buff or self.inputLine()        # emulate file read methods
        self.buff = ''
        return text
    def readlines(self):
        lines = []                                  # read all lines
        while 1:
            next = self.readline()
            if not next: break
            lines.append(next)
        return lines
```

Example 9-9. PP2E\Gui\Tools\guiStreams.py (continued)

```python
def redirectedGuiFunc(func, *pargs, **kargs):
    import sys
    saveStreams = sys.stdin, sys.stdout          # map func streams to popups
    sys.stdin   = GuiInput()                      # pops up dialog as needed
    sys.stdout  = GuiOutput()                     # new output window per call
    sys.stderr  = sys.stdout
    result = apply(func, pargs, kargs)            # this is a blocking func call
    sys.stdin, sys.stdout = saveStreams
    return result

def redirectedGuiShellCmd(command):
    import os
    input  = os.popen(command, 'r')
    output = GuiOutput()
    def reader(input, output):                    # show a shell command's
        while 1:                                  # standard output in a new
            line = input.readline()               # popup text box widget
            if not line: break
            output.write(line)
    reader(input, output)

if __name__ == '__main__':
    import string
    def makeUpper():                              # use standard streams
        while 1:
            try:
                line = raw_input('Line? ')
            except:
                break
            print string.upper(line)
        print 'end of file'

    def makeLower(input, output):                 # use explicit files
        while 1:
            line = input.readline()
            if not line: break
            output.write(string.lower(line))
        print 'end of file'

    root = Tk()
    Button(root, text='test streams',
           command=lambda: redirectedGuiFunc(makeUpper)).pack(fill=X)
    Button(root, text='test files  ',
           command=lambda: makeLower(GuiInput(), GuiOutput()) ).pack(fill=X)
    Button(root, text='test popen  ',
           command=lambda: redirectedGuiShellCmd('dir *')).pack(fill=X)
    root.mainloop()
```

As coded here, `GuiOutput` either attaches a `ScrolledText` to a parent container, or pops up a new top-level window to serve as the container on the first write call. `GuiInput` pops up a new standard input dialog every time a read request requires a new line of input. Neither one of these policies is ideal for all scenarios (input would be better mapped to a more long-lived widget), but they prove the general point. Figure 9-8 shows the scene generated by this script's self-test code, after capturing the output of a shell *dir* listing command (on the left), and two interactive loop tests (the one with "Line?" prompts and uppercase letters represents the `makeUpper` streams test). An input dialog has just popped up for a new `makeLower` files test.

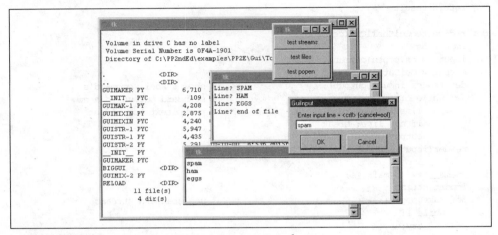

Figure 9-8. guiStreams routing streams to pop-up windows

Using redirection for the packing scripts

Now, to use such redirection tools to map command-line script output back to a GUI, simply run calls and command lines with the two redirected functions in this module. Example 9-10 shows one way to wrap the packing operation to force its printed output to appear in a pop-up window when generated, instead of the console.

Example 9-10. PP2E\Gui\ShellGui\packdlg-redirect.py

```
# wrap command-line script in GUI redirection tool to popup its output

from Tkinter import *
from packdlg import runPackDialog
from PP2E.Gui.Tools.guiStreams import redirectedGuiFunc

def runPackDialog_Wrapped():
    redirectedGuiFunc(runPackDialog)      # wrap entire callback handler

if __name__ == '__main__':
    root = Tk()
    Button(root, text='pop', command=runPackDialog_Wrapped).pack(fill=X)
    root.mainloop()
```

You can run this script directly to test its effect, without bringing up the ShellGui window. Figure 9-9 shows the resulting stdout window after the pack input dialog is dismissed. This window pops up as soon as script output is generated, and is a bit more GUI user-friendly than hunting for messages in a console. You can similarly code the unpack parameters dialog to route its output to a pop-up too.[*] In fact, you can use this technique to route the output of any function call or command line to a pop-up window; as usual, the notion of compatible object interfaces are at the heart of much of Python's flexibility.

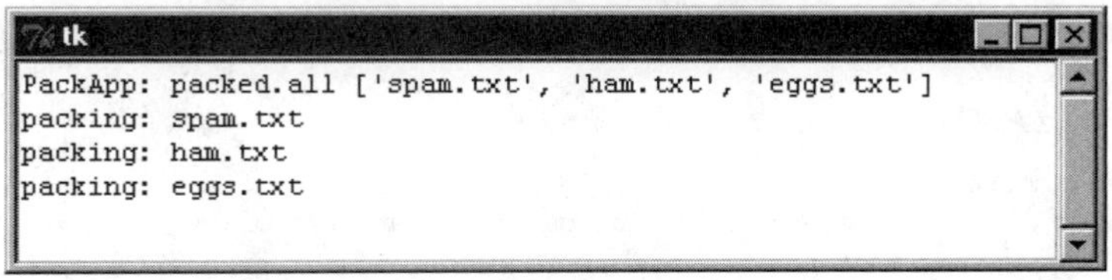

```
PackApp: packed.all ['spam.txt', 'ham.txt', 'eggs.txt']
packing: spam.txt
packing: ham.txt
packing: eggs.txt
```

Figure 9-9. Routing script outputs to GUI pop-ups

Reloading GUI Callback Handlers Dynamically

One last GUI programming technique merits a quick look here. The Python reload function lets you dynamically change and reload a program's modules without stopping the program. For instance, you can bring up a text editor window to change the source code of selected parts of a system while it is running and see those changes show up immediately after reloading the changed module.

This is a powerful feature, especially for developing programs that take a long time to restart. Programs that connect to databases or network servers, initialize large objects, or travel through a long series of steps to retrigger a callback are prime candidates for reload. It can shave substantial time from the development cycle.

The catch for GUIs, though, is that because callback handlers are registered as *object references* instead of module and object names, reloads of callback handler functions are ineffective after the callback has been registered. The Python reload operation works by changing a module object's contents in place. Because Tkinter stores a pointer to the registered handler object directly, though, it is oblivious to any reloads of the module that the handler came from. That is, Tkinter will still reference a module's old objects even after the module is reloaded and changed.

---

[*] These two scripts are something of a unique case; because the App superclass they employ saves away standard streams in its own attributes at object creation time, you must kick off the GUI redirection wrapper calls as soon as possible so that App finds the redirected GUI streams in sys when saving them locally. Most other scripts aren't quite as tricky when it comes to internal stream redirections.

This is a subtle thing, but you really only need to remember that you must do something special to reload callback handler functions dynamically. Not only do you need to explicitly request reloading of the modules that you change, but you must also generally provide an indirection layer that routes callbacks from registered objects to modules, so that reloads have impact.

For example, the script in Example 9-11 goes the extra mile to indirectly dispatch callbacks to functions in an explicitly reloaded module. The callback handlers registered with Tkinter are method objects that do nothing but reload and dispatch again. Because the true callback handler functions are fetched through a module object, reloading that module makes the latest versions of the functions accessible.

Example 9-11. PP2E\Gui\Tools\Reload\rad.py

```
from Tkinter import *
import actions                   # get initial callback handlers

class Hello(Frame):
    def __init__(self, master=None):
        Frame.__init__(self, master)
        self.pack()
        self.make_widgets()

    def make_widgets(self):
        Button(self, text='message1', command=self.message1).pack(side=LEFT)
        Button(self, text='message2', command=self.message2).pack(side=RIGHT)

    def message1(self):
        reload(actions)            # need to reload actions module before calling
        actions.message1()         # now new version triggered by pressing button

    def message2(self):
        reload(actions)            # changes to actions.py picked up by reload
        actions.message2(self)     # call the most recent version; pass self

    def method1(self):
        print 'exposed method...'    # called from actions function

Hello().mainloop()
```

When run, this script makes a two-button window that triggers the `message1` and `message2` methods. Example 9-12 contains the actual callback handlers' code. Its functions receive a `self` argument that gives access back to the `Hello` class object, as though these were real methods. You can change this file any number of times while the `rad` script's GUI is active; each time you do so, you'll change the behavior of the GUI when a button press occurs.

Example 9-12. PP2E\Gui\Tools\Reload\actions.py

```
# callback handlers: reloaded each time triggered

def message1():
    print 'spamSpamSPAM'          # change me
                                  # could build a dialog...

def message2(self):
    print 'Ni! Ni!'               # change me
    self.method1()                # access the 'Hello' instance...
```

Try running `rad` and editing the messages printed by `actions` in another window; you should see your new messages printed in the `stdout` console window each time the GUI's buttons are pressed. This example is deliberately simple to illustrate the concept, but the actions reloaded like this in practice might build pop-up dialogs, new top-level windows, and so on. Reloading the code that creates such windows would also let us dynamically change their appearances.

There are other ways to change a GUI while it's running. For instance, we saw in Chapter 8 that appearances can be altered at any time by calling the widget `config` method, and widgets can be added and deleted from a display dynamically with methods like `pack_forget` and `pack` (and their `grid` manager relatives). Furthermore, passing a new `command=action` option setting to a widget's `config` method might reset a callback handler to a new action object on the fly; with enough support code, this may be a viable alternative to the indirection scheme used above to make reloads more effective in GUIs.

Complete Program Examples

The rest of this chapter presents a handful of complete GUI programs, as examples of how far Python and Tkinter can take you. Because I've already shown the interfaces these scripts employ, this section is mostly screen shots, program listings, and a few bullets describing some of the most important aspects of these programs. In other words, this is a self-study section: read the source, run the examples on your own computer, and refer to the previous chapters for further details on the code listed here. Many of these scripts also are accompanied on the book CD by alternative or experimental implementations not listed here; see the CD for extra code examples.

PyEdit: A Text Editor Program/Object

In the last few decades, I've typed text into a lot of programs. Most were closed systems (I had to live with whatever decisions their designers made), and many ran on only one platform. The PyEdit program presented in this section does better on both counts: it implements a full-featured, graphical text editor program in roughly 470 lines of portable Python code (including whitespace and comments). Despite its size, PyEdit was sufficiently powerful and robust to serve as the primary tool used to code most examples in this book.

PyEdit supports all the usual mouse and keyboard text-editing operations: cut and paste, search and replace, open and save, and so on. But really, PyEdit is a bit more than just another text editor—it is designed to be used as both a program and a library component, and can be run in a variety of roles:

Standalone mode

> As a *standalone* text editor program, with or without the name of a file to be edited passed in on the command line. In this mode, PyEdit is roughly like other text-editing utility programs (e.g., Notepad on Windows), but also provides advanced functions such as running Python program code being edited, changing fonts and colors, and so on. More importantly, because it is coded in Python, PyEdit is easy to customize, and runs portably on Windows, X Windows, and Macintosh.

Pop-up mode

> Within a new pop-up window, allowing an arbitrary number of copies to appear as pop-ups at once in a program. Because state information is stored in class instance attributes, each PyEdit object created operates independently. In this mode and the next, PyEdit serves as a library object for use in other scripts, not a canned application.

Embedded mode

> As an *attached* component, to provide a text- editing widget for other GUIs. When attached, PyEdit uses a frame-based menu, and can optionally disable some of its menu options for an embedded role. For instance, PyView (later in this chapter) uses PyEdit in embedded mode this way to serve as a note editor for photos, and PyMail (in Chapter 11) attaches it to get an email text editor for free.

While such mixed-mode behavior may sound complicated to implement, most of PyEdit's modes are a natural by-product of coding GUIs with the class-based techniques we've seen in the last three chapters.

Running PyEdit

PyEdit sports lots of features, and the best way to learn how it works is to test drive it for yourself—it can be run by starting the file *textEditor.pyw*, or from the PyDemo and PyGadget launcher bars described in the previous chapter (the launchers themselves live in the top level of the book examples directory tree). To give you a sampling of its interfaces, Figure 9-10 shows the main window's default appearance, after opening PyEdit's source code file.

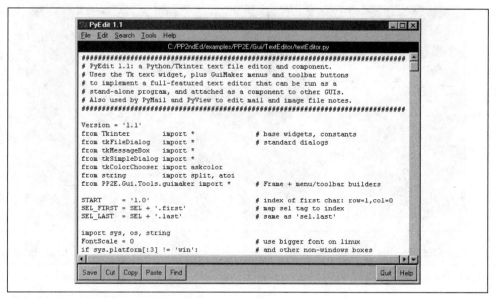

```
PyEdit 1.1                                                      _ □ ×
File  Edit  Search  Tools  Help
             C:/PP2ndEd/examples/PP2E/Gui/TextEditor/textEditor.py
####################################################################
# PyEdit 1.1: a Python/Tkinter text file editor and component.
# Uses the Tk text widget, plus GuiMaker menus and toolbar buttons
# to implement a full-featured text editor that can be run as a
# stand-alone program, and attached as a component to other GUIs.
# Also used by PyMail and PyView to edit mail and image file notes.
####################################################################

Version = '1.1'
from Tkinter         import *          # base widgets, constants
from tkFileDialog    import *          # standard dialogs
from tkMessageBox    import *
from tkSimpleDialog  import *
from tkColorChooser  import askcolor
from string          import split, atoi
from PP2E.Gui.Tools.guimaker import *  # Frame + menu/toolbar builders

START    = '1.0'                       # index of first char: row=1,col=0
SEL_FIRST = SEL + '.first'             # map sel tag to index
SEL_LAST  = SEL + '.last'              # same as 'sel.last'

import sys, os, string
FontScale = 0                          # use bigger font on linux
if sys.platform[:3] != 'win':          # and other non-windows boxes

Save   Cut   Copy   Paste   Find                          Quit   Help
```

Figure 9-10. PyEdit main window, editing itself

The main part of this window is a **Text** widget object, and if you read the last chapter's coverage of this widget, PyEdit text-editing operations will be familiar. It uses text marks, tags, and indexes, and implements cut-and-paste operations with the system clipboard so that PyEdit can paste data to and from other applications. Both vertical and horizontal scrollbars are cross-linked to the **Text** widget, to support movement through arbitrary files.

If PyEdit's menu and toolbars look familiar, they should—it builds the main window with minimal code and appropriate clipping and expansion policies, by mixing in the **GuiMaker** class we met earlier in this chapter. The toolbar at the bottom contains shortcut buttons for operations I tend to use most often; if my preferences don't match yours, simply change the toolbar list in the source code to show the buttons you want (this is Python, after all). As usual for Tkinter menus, shortcut key combinations can be used to invoke menu options quickly, too—press Alt plus all the underlined keys of entries along the path to the desired action.

PyEdit pops up a variety of modal and nonmodal dialogs, both standard and custom. Figure 9-11 shows the custom and nonmodal change dialog, along with a standard dialog used to display file statistics.

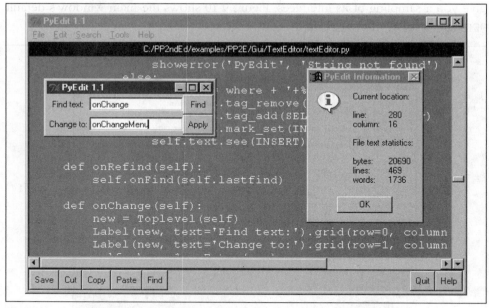

Figure 9-11. PyEdit with colors, font, and a few pop-ups

The main window here has been given new foreground and background colors (with the standard color selection dialog), and a new text font has been selected from a canned list in the script that users can change to suit their preferences (this is Python, after all). The standard file open and save selection dialogs in PyEdit use object-based interfaces to remember the last directory visited, so you don't have to renavigate there every time.

One of the more unique features of PyEdit is that it can actually run Python program code that you are editing. This isn't as hard as it may sound either—because Python provides built-ins for both compiling and running code strings and launching programs, PyEdit simply has to make the right calls for this to work. For example, it's easy to code a simple-minded Python interpreter in Python (though you need a bit more to handle multiple-line statements), as shown in Example 9-13.

Example 9-13. PP2E\Gui\TextEditor\simpleshell.py

```python
namespace= {}
while 1:
    try:
        line = raw_input('>>> ')          # single line statements only
    except EOFError:
        break
    else:
        exec line in namespace            # or eval() and print result
```

Depending on the user's preference, PyEdit either does something similar to this to run code fetched from the text widget, or uses the `launchmodes` module we wrote at the end of Chapter 3 to run the code's file as an independent program. There are a variety of options in both schemes that you can customize as you like (this is Python, after all). See the `onRunCode` method for details, or simply edit and run some Python code on your own.

Figure 9-12 shows four independently started instances of PyEdit running with a variety of color schemes, sizes, and fonts. This figure also captures two PyEdit torn-off menus (lower right) and the PyEdit help pop-up (upper right). The edit windows' backgrounds are shades of yellow, blue, purple, and orange; use the Tools menu's Pick options to set colors as you like.

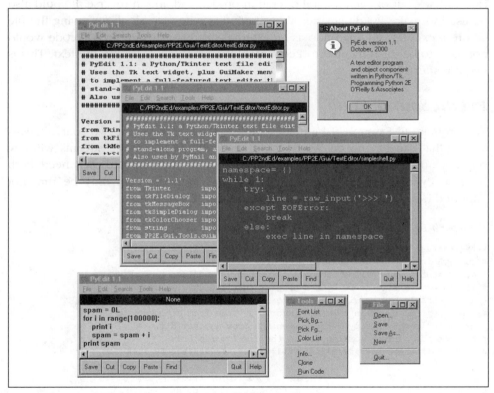

Figure 9-12. Multiple PyEdit sessions at work

Since these four PyEdit sessions are all editing Python source-coded text, you can run their contents with the Run Code option in the Tools pull-down menu. Code run from files is spawned independently; the standard streams of code run not from a file (i.e., fetched from the text widget itself) are mapped to the PyEdit session's console window. This isn't an IDE by any means; it's just something I added because I found it to be useful. It's nice to run code you're editing without fishing through directories.

One caveat before I turn you loose on the source code: PyEdit does not yet have an Undo button in this release. I don't use such a mode myself, and it's easy to undo cuts and pastes right after you've done them (simply paste back from the clipboard, or cut the pasted and selected text). Adding a general undo option would make for a fun exercise if you are so motivated. An interesting approach may be to subclass either the `TextEditor` class here or the Tkinter `Text` class itself. Such a subclass would record text operations on a limited-length list and run calls to back out of each logged operation on demand and in reverse. It could also be used to make PyEdit smarter about knowing when to ask about saving the file before it exits. By adding undo as an external subclass, existing PyEdit code would not have to be instrumented to keep track of everything it does to the text. This is Python, after all.

PyEdit Source Code

The program in Example 9-14 and Example 9-15 consists of just two source files— a *.pyw* that can be run on Windows to avoid the DOS console streams window pop-up, and a main *.py* that can be either run or imported. We need both because PyEdit is both script and library, and *.pyw* files can only be run, not imported (see Chapter 2 if you've forgotten what that implies).

Example 9-14. PP2E\Gui\TextEditor\textEditor.pyw

```
###################################################################
# run PyEdit without DOS console popup for os.system on Windows;
# at present, ".pyw" files cannot be imported as modules;
# if you want a file to be both a program that launches without
# a dos console box on windows, and be imported from elsewhere,
# use ".py" for the main file and import .py code from a ".pyw";
# execfile('textEditor.py') fails when run from another dir,
# because the current working dir is the dir I'm run from;
###################################################################

import textEditor          # grab .py (or .pyc) file
textEditor.main()          # run top-level entry point
```

The module in Example 9-15 is PyEdit's implementation; the main classes used to start and embed a PyEdit object appear at the end of this file. Study this listing while you experiment with PyEdit, to learn about its features and techniques.

Example 9-15. PP2E\Gui\TextEditor\textEditor.py

```
###############################################################################
# PyEdit 1.1: a Python/Tkinter text file editor and component.
# Uses the Tk text widget, plus GuiMaker menus and toolbar buttons
# to implement a full-featured text editor that can be run as a
# stand-alone program, and attached as a component to other GUIs.
# Also used by PyMail and PyView to edit mail and image file notes.
###############################################################################

Version = '1.1'
from Tkinter          import *            # base widgets, constants
from tkFileDialog     import *            # standard dialogs
from tkMessageBox     import *
from tkSimpleDialog   import *
from tkColorChooser import askcolor
from string           import split, atoi
from PP2E.Gui.Tools.guimaker import *     # Frame + menu/toolbar builders

START    = '1.0'                          # index of first char: row=1,col=0
SEL_FIRST = SEL + '.first'                # map sel tag to index
SEL_LAST  = SEL + '.last'                 # same as 'sel.last'

import sys, os, string
FontScale = 0                             # use bigger font on linux
if sys.platform[:3] != 'win':            # and other non-windows boxes
    FontScale = 3

class TextEditor:                         # mix with menu/toolbar Frame class
    startfiledir = '.'
    ftypes = [('All files',     '*'),            # for file open dialog
              ('Text files',   '.txt'),          # customize in subclass
              ('Python files', '.py')]           # or set in each instance

    colors = [{'fg':'black',      'bg':'white'},    # color pick list
              {'fg':'yellow',     'bg':'black'},    # first item is default
              {'fg':'white',      'bg':'blue'},     # tailor me as desired
              {'fg':'black',      'bg':'beige'},    # or do PickBg/Fg chooser
              {'fg':'yellow',     'bg':'purple'},
              {'fg':'black',      'bg':'brown'},
              {'fg':'lightgreen', 'bg':'darkgreen'},
              {'fg':'darkblue',   'bg':'orange'},
              {'fg':'orange',     'bg':'darkblue'}]

    fonts  = [('courier',    9+FontScale, 'normal'),  # platform-neutral fonts
              ('courier',   12+FontScale, 'normal'),  # (family, size, style)
              ('courier',   10+FontScale, 'bold'),    # or popup a listbox
              ('courier',   10+FontScale, 'italic'),  # make bigger on linux
              ('times',     10+FontScale, 'normal'),
              ('helvetica', 10+FontScale, 'normal'),
              ('ariel',     10+FontScale, 'normal'),
              ('system',    10+FontScale, 'normal'),
              ('courier',   20+FontScale, 'normal')]
```

Example 9-15. PP2E\Gui\TextEditor\textEditor.py (continued)

```python
    def __init__(self, loadFirst=''):
        if not isinstance(self, GuiMaker):
            raise TypeError, 'TextEditor needs a GuiMaker mixin'
        self.setFileName(None)
        self.lastfind   = None
        self.openDialog = None
        self.saveDialog = None
        self.text.focus()                              # else must click in text
        if loadFirst:
            self.onOpen(loadFirst)

    def start(self):                                   # run by GuiMaker.__init__
        self.menuBar = [                               # configure menu/toolbar
            ('File', 0,
                [('Open...',     0, self.onOpen),
                 ('Save',        0, self.onSave),
                 ('Save As...',  5, self.onSaveAs),
                 ('New',         0, self.onNew),
                 'separator',
                 ('Quit...',     0, self.onQuit)]
            ),
            ('Edit', 0,
                [('Cut',         0, self.onCut),
                 ('Copy',        1, self.onCopy),
                 ('Paste',       0, self.onPaste),
                 'separator',
                 ('Delete',      0, self.onDelete),
                 ('Select All', 0, self.onSelectAll)]
            ),
            ('Search', 0,
                [('Goto...',     0, self.onGoto),
                 ('Find...',     0, self.onFind),
                 ('Refind',      0, self.onRefind),
                 ('Change...',   0, self.onChange)]
            ),
            ('Tools', 0,
                [('Font List',    0, self.onFontList),
                 ('Pick Bg...',   4, self.onPickBg),
                 ('Pick Fg...',   0, self.onPickFg),
                 ('Color List',   0, self.onColorList),
                 'separator',
                 ('Info...',      0, self.onInfo),
                 ('Clone',        1, self.onClone),
                 ('Run Code',     0, self.onRunCode)]
            )]
        self.toolBar = [
            ('Save',  self.onSave,   {'side': LEFT}),
            ('Cut',   self.onCut,    {'side': LEFT}),
            ('Copy',  self.onCopy,   {'side': LEFT}),
            ('Paste', self.onPaste,  {'side': LEFT}),
            ('Find',  self.onRefind, {'side': LEFT}),
            ('Help',  self.help,     {'side': RIGHT}),
```

Example 9-15. PP2E\Gui\TextEditor\textEditor.py (continued)

```
            ('Quit',  self.onQuit,   {'side': RIGHT})]

    def makeWidgets(self):                        # run by GuiMaker.__init__
        name = Label(self, bg='black', fg='white')  # add below menu, above tool
        name.pack(side=TOP, fill=X)               # menu/toolbars are packed

        vbar  = Scrollbar(self)
        hbar  = Scrollbar(self, orient='horizontal')
        text  = Text(self, padx=5, wrap='none')

        vbar.pack(side=RIGHT,  fill=Y)
        hbar.pack(side=BOTTOM, fill=X)                  # pack text last
        text.pack(side=TOP,    fill=BOTH, expand=YES)  # else sbars clipped

        text.config(yscrollcommand=vbar.set)     # call vbar.set on text move
        text.config(xscrollcommand=hbar.set)
        vbar.config(command=text.yview)          # call text.yview on scroll move
        hbar.config(command=text.xview)          # or hbar['command']=text.xview

        text.config(font=self.fonts[0],
                    bg=self.colors[0]['bg'], fg=self.colors[0]['fg'])
        self.text = text
        self.filelabel = name

    #####################
    # Edit menu commands
    #####################

    def onCopy(self):                             # get text selected by mouse,etc
        if not self.text.tag_ranges(SEL):         # save in cross-app clipboard
            showerror('PyEdit', 'No text selected')
        else:
            text = self.text.get(SEL_FIRST, SEL_LAST)
            self.clipboard_clear()
            self.clipboard_append(text)

    def onDelete(self):                           # delete selected text, no save
        if not self.text.tag_ranges(SEL):
            showerror('PyEdit', 'No text selected')
        else:
            self.text.delete(SEL_FIRST, SEL_LAST)

    def onCut(self):
        if not self.text.tag_ranges(SEL):
            showerror('PyEdit', 'No text selected')
        else:
            self.onCopy()                         # save and delete selected text
            self.onDelete()

    def onPaste(self):
        try:
            text = self.selection_get(selection='CLIPBOARD')
```

Example 9-15. PP2E\Gui\TextEditor\textEditor.py (continued)

```
        except TclError:
            showerror('PyEdit', 'Nothing to paste')
            return
        self.text.insert(INSERT, text)              # add at current insert cursor
        self.text.tag_remove(SEL, '1.0', END)
        self.text.tag_add(SEL, INSERT+'-%dc' % len(text), INSERT)
        self.text.see(INSERT)                       # select it, so it can be cut

    def onSelectAll(self):
        self.text.tag_add(SEL, '1.0', END+'-1c')    # select entire text
        self.text.mark_set(INSERT, '1.0')           # move insert point to top
        self.text.see(INSERT)                       # scroll to top

    #####################
    # Tools menu commands
    #####################

    def onFontList(self):
        self.fonts.append(self.fonts[0])            # pick next font in list
        del self.fonts[0]                           # resizes the text area
        self.text.config(font=self.fonts[0])

    def onColorList(self):
        self.colors.append(self.colors[0])          # pick next color in list
        del self.colors[0]                          # move current to end
        self.text.config(fg=self.colors[0]['fg'], bg=self.colors[0]['bg'])

    def onPickFg(self):
        self.pickColor('fg')                        # added on 10/02/00
    def onPickBg(self):                             # select arbitrary color
        self.pickColor('bg')                        # in standard color dialog
    def pickColor(self, part):                      # this is way too easy
        (triple, hexstr) = askcolor()
        if hexstr:
            apply(self.text.config, (), {part: hexstr})

    def onInfo(self):
        text  = self.getAllText()                   # added on 5/3/00 in 15 mins
        bytes = len(text)                           # words uses a simple guess:
        lines = len(string.split(text, '\n'))       # any separated by whitespace
        words = len(string.split(text))
        index = self.text.index(INSERT)
        where = tuple(string.split(index, '.'))
        showinfo('PyEdit Information',
                 'Current location:\n\n' +
                 'line:\t%s\ncolumn:\t%s\n\n' % where +
                 'File text statistics:\n\n' +
                 'bytes:\t%d\nlines:\t%d\nwords:\t%d\n' % (bytes, lines, words))

    def onClone(self):
        new = Toplevel()                # a new edit window in same process
        myclass = self.__class__        # instance's (lowest) class object
```

Example 9-15. PP2E\Gui\TextEditor\textEditor.py (continued)

```
        myclass(new)                            # attach/run instance of my class

    def onRunCode(self, parallelmode=1):
        """
        run Python code being edited--not an ide, but handy;
        tries to run in file's dir, not cwd (may be pp2e root);
        inputs and adds command-line arguments for script files;
        code's stdin/out/err = editor's start window, if any;
        but parallelmode uses start to open a dos box for i/o;
        """
        from PP2E.launchmodes import System, Start, Fork
        filemode = 0
        thefile  = str(self.getFileName())
        cmdargs  = askstring('PyEdit', 'Commandline arguments?') or ''
        if os.path.exists(thefile):
            filemode = askyesno('PyEdit', 'Run from file?')
        if not filemode:                                      # run text string
            namespace = {'__name__': '__main__'}             # run as top-level
            sys.argv = [thefile] + string.split(cmdargs)     # could use threads
            exec self.getAllText() + '\n' in namespace       # exceptions ignored
        elif askyesno('PyEdit', 'Text saved in file?'):
            mycwd = os.getcwd()                              # cwd may be root
            os.chdir(os.path.dirname(thefile) or mycwd)      # cd for filenames
            thecmd  = thefile + ' ' + cmdargs
            if not parallelmode:                             # run as file
                System(thecmd, thecmd)()                     # block editor
            else:
                if sys.platform[:3] == 'win':                # spawn in parallel
                    Start(thecmd, thecmd)()                  # or use os.spawnv
                else:
                    Fork(thecmd, thecmd)()                   # spawn in parallel
            os.chdir(mycwd)


    #####################
    # Search menu commands
    #####################

    def onGoto(self):
        line = askinteger('PyEdit', 'Enter line number')
        self.text.update()
        self.text.focus()
        if line is not None:
            maxindex = self.text.index(END+'-1c')
            maxline  = atoi(split(maxindex, '.')[0])
            if line > 0 and line <= maxline:
                self.text.mark_set(INSERT, '%d.0' % line)    # goto line
                self.text.tag_remove(SEL, '1.0', END)        # delete selects
                self.text.tag_add(SEL, INSERT, 'insert + 1l') # select line
                self.text.see(INSERT)                        # scroll to line
            else:
                showerror('PyEdit', 'Bad line number')
```

Example 9-15. PP2E\Gui\TextEditor\textEditor.py (continued)

```
    def onFind(self, lastkey=None):
        key = lastkey or askstring('PyEdit', 'Enter search string')
        self.text.update()
        self.text.focus()
        self.lastfind = key
        if key:
            where = self.text.search(key, INSERT, END)       # don't wrap
            if not where:
                showerror('PyEdit', 'String not found')
            else:
                pastkey = where + '+%dc' % len(key)           # index past key
                self.text.tag_remove(SEL, '1.0', END)         # remove any sel
                self.text.tag_add(SEL, where, pastkey)        # select key
                self.text.mark_set(INSERT, pastkey)           # for next find
                self.text.see(where)                          # scroll display

    def onRefind(self):
        self.onFind(self.lastfind)

    def onChange(self):
        new = Toplevel(self)
        Label(new, text='Find text:').grid(row=0, column=0)
        Label(new, text='Change to:').grid(row=1, column=0)
        self.change1 = Entry(new)
        self.change2 = Entry(new)
        self.change1.grid(row=0, column=1, sticky=EW)
        self.change2.grid(row=1, column=1, sticky=EW)
        Button(new, text='Find',
                command=self.onDoFind).grid(row=0, column=2, sticky=EW)
        Button(new, text='Apply',
                command=self.onDoChange).grid(row=1, column=2, sticky=EW)
        new.columnconfigure(1, weight=1)    # expandable entrys

    def onDoFind(self):
        self.onFind(self.change1.get())                      # Find in change box

    def onDoChange(self):
        if self.text.tag_ranges(SEL):                        # must find first
            self.text.delete(SEL_FIRST, SEL_LAST)            # Apply in change
            self.text.insert(INSERT, self.change2.get())     # deletes if empty
            self.text.see(INSERT)
            self.onFind(self.change1.get())                  # goto next appear
            self.text.update()                               # force refresh

####################
# File menu commands
####################

    def my_askopenfilename(self):        # objects remember last result dir/file
        if not self.openDialog:
            self.openDialog = Open(initialdir=self.startfiledir,
                                   filetypes=self.ftypes)
        return self.openDialog.show()
```

Example 9-15. PP2E\Gui\TextEditor\textEditor.py (continued)

```python
    def my_asksaveasfilename(self):        # objects remember last result dir/file
        if not self.saveDialog:
            self.saveDialog = SaveAs(initialdir=self.startfiledir,
                                     filetypes=self.ftypes)
        return self.saveDialog.show()

    def onOpen(self, loadFirst=''):
        doit = self.isEmpty() or askyesno('PyEdit', 'Disgard text?')
        if doit:
            file = loadFirst or self.my_askopenfilename()
            if file:
                try:
                    text = open(file, 'r').read()
                except:
                    showerror('PyEdit', 'Could not open file ' + file)
                else:
                    self.setAllText(text)
                    self.setFileName(file)

    def onSave(self):
        self.onSaveAs(self.currfile)  # may be None

    def onSaveAs(self, forcefile=None):
        file = forcefile or self.my_asksaveasfilename()
        if file:
            text = self.getAllText()
            try:
                open(file, 'w').write(text)
            except:
                showerror('PyEdit', 'Could not write file ' + file)
            else:
                self.setFileName(file)           # may be newly created

    def onNew(self):
        doit = self.isEmpty() or askyesno('PyEdit', 'Disgard text?')
        if doit:
            self.setFileName(None)
            self.clearAllText()

    def onQuit(self):
        if askyesno('PyEdit', 'Really quit PyEdit?'):
            self.quit()                          # Frame.quit via GuiMaker

####################################
# Others, useful outside this class
####################################

    def isEmpty(self):
        return not self.getAllText()

    def getAllText(self):
        return self.text.get('1.0', END+'-1c')  # extract text as a string
```

Example 9-15. PP2E\Gui\TextEditor\textEditor.py (continued)

```
    def setAllText(self, text):
        self.text.delete('1.0', END)              # store text string in widget
        self.text.insert(END, text)               # or '1.0'
        self.text.mark_set(INSERT, '1.0')         # move insert point to top
        self.text.see(INSERT)                     # scroll to top, insert set

    def clearAllText(self):
        self.text.delete('1.0', END)              # clear text in widget

    def getFileName(self):
        return self.currfile

    def setFileName(self, name):
        self.currfile = name   # for save
        self.filelabel.config(text=str(name))

    def help(self):
        showinfo('About PyEdit',
                 'PyEdit version %s\nOctober, 2000\n\n'
                 'A text editor program\nand object component\n'
                 'written in Python/Tk.\nProgramming Python 2E\n'
                 "O'Reilly & Associates" % Version)


#############################################################
# ready-to-use editor classes
# mix in a Frame subclass that builds menu/toolbars
#############################################################


# when editor owns the window

class TextEditorMain(TextEditor, GuiMakerWindowMenu):  # add menu/toolbar maker
    def __init__(self, parent=None, loadFirst=''):     # when fills whole window
        GuiMaker.__init__(self, parent)                # use main window menus
        TextEditor.__init__(self, loadFirst)           # self has GuiMaker frame
        self.master.title('PyEdit ' + Version)         # title if stand-alone
        self.master.iconname('PyEdit')                 # catch wm delete button
        self.master.protocol('WM_DELETE_WINDOW', self.onQuit)

class TextEditorMainPopup(TextEditor, GuiMakerWindowMenu):
    def __init__(self, parent=None, loadFirst=''):
        self.popup = Toplevel(parent)                  # create own window
        GuiMaker.__init__(self, self.popup)            # use main window menus
        TextEditor.__init__(self, loadFirst)
        assert self.master == self.popup
        self.popup.title('PyEdit ' + Version)
        self.popup.iconname('PyEdit')
    def quit(self):
        self.popup.destroy()                           # kill this window only
```

Example 9-15. PP2E\Gui\TextEditor\textEditor.py (continued)

```
# when embedded in another window

class TextEditorComponent(TextEditor, GuiMakerFrameMenu):
    def __init__(self, parent=None, loadFirst=''):      # use Frame-based menus
        GuiMaker.__init__(self, parent)                 # all menus, buttons on
        TextEditor.__init__(self, loadFirst)            # GuiMaker must init 1st

class TextEditorComponentMinimal(TextEditor, GuiMakerFrameMenu):
    def __init__(self, parent=None, loadFirst='', deleteFile=1):
        self.deleteFile = deleteFile
        GuiMaker.__init__(self, parent)
        TextEditor.__init__(self, loadFirst)
    def start(self):
        TextEditor.start(self)                          # GuiMaker start call
        for i in range(len(self.toolBar)):              # delete quit in toolbar
            if self.toolBar[i][0] == 'Quit':            # delete file menu items
                del self.toolBar[i]; break              # or just disable file
        if self.deleteFile:
            for i in range(len(self.menuBar)):
                if self.menuBar[i][0] == 'File':
                    del self.menuBar[i]; break
        else:
            for (name, key, items) in self.menuBar:
                if name == 'File':
                    items.append([1,2,3,4,6])


# stand-alone program run

def testPopup():
    # see PyView and PyMail for component tests
    root = Tk()
    TextEditorMainPopup(root)
    TextEditorMainPopup(root)
    Button(root, text='More', command=TextEditorMainPopup).pack(fill=X)
    Button(root, text='Quit', command=root.quit).pack(fill=X)
    root.mainloop()

def main():                                             # may be typed or clicked
    try:                                                # or associated on Windows
        fname = sys.argv[1]                             # arg = optional filename
    except IndexError:
        fname = None
    TextEditorMain(loadFirst=fname).pack(expand=YES, fill=BOTH)
    mainloop()

if __name__ == '__main__':                              # when run as a script
    #testPopup()
    main()                                              # run .pyw for no dos box
```

PyView: An Image and Notes Slideshow

A picture may be worth a thousand words, but it takes considerably fewer to display one with Python. The next program, PyView, implements a simple photo slideshow program in portable Python/Tkinter code.

Running PyView

PyView pulls together many of the topics we studied in the last chapter: it uses `after` events to sequence a slideshow, displays image objects in an automatically sized canvas, and so on. Its main window displays a photo on a canvas; users can either open and view a photo directly or start a slideshow mode that picks and displays a random photo from a directory, at regular intervals specified with a scale widget.

By default, PyView slideshows show images in the book's image file directory (though the Open button allows you to load images in arbitrary directories). To view other sets of photos, either pass a directory name in as a first command-line argument or change the default directory name in the script itself. I can't show you a slideshow in action here, but I can show you the main window in general. Figure 9-13 shows the main PyView window's default display.

Figure 9-13. PyView without notes

Though it's not obvious as rendered in this book, the black-on-red label at the top gives the pathname of the photo file displayed. For a good time, move the slider at the bottom all the way over to "0" to specify no delay between photo changes, and click Start to begin a very fast slideshow. If your computer is at least as fast as mine, photos flip by much too fast to be useful for anything but subliminal advertising. Slideshow photos are loaded on startup to retain references to them (remember, you must hold on to image objects). But the speed with which large GIFs can be thrown up in a window in Python is impressive, if not downright exhilarating.

The GUI's Start button changes to a Stop button during a slideshow (its text attribute is reset with the widget `config` method). Figure 9-14 shows the scene after pressing Stop at an opportune moment.

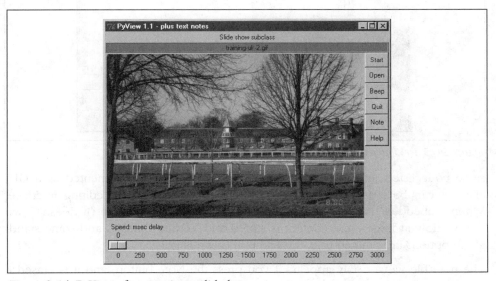

Figure 9-14. PyView after stopping a slideshow

In addition, each photo can have an associated "notes" text file which is automatically opened along with the image. You can use this feature to record basic information about the photo. Press the Note button to open an additional set of widgets that let you view and change the note file associated with the currently displayed photo. This additional set of widgets should look familiar—the PyEdit text editor of the previous section is attached to PyView to serve as a display and editing widget for photo notes. Figure 9-15 shows PyView with the attached PyEdit note-editing component opened.

This makes for a very big window, usually best view maximized (taking up the entire screen). The main thing to notice, though, is the lower right corner of this display above the scale—it's simply an attached PyEdit object, running the very

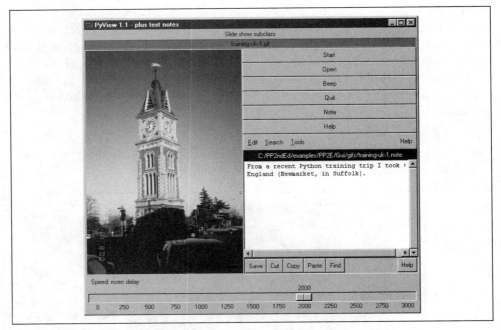

Figure 9-15. PyView with notes

same code listed in the prior section. Because PyEdit is implemented as a GUI class, it can be reused like this in any GUI that needs a text editing interface. When embedded like this, PyEdit's menus are based on a frame (it doesn't own the window at large), text content is stored and fetched directly, and some stand-alone options are omitted (e.g, the File pull-down is gone).

The note file viewer only appears if you press the Note button, and it is erased if you press it again; PyView uses widget `pack` and `pack_forget` methods introduced at the end of the last chapter to show and hide the note viewer frame. The window automatically expands to accommodate the note viewer when it is packed and displayed. It is also possible to open the note file in a PyEdit pop-up window, but PyView embeds the editor to retain a direct visual association. Watch for PyEdit to show up embedded within another GUI like this when we meet PyMail in Chapter 11.

A caveat here: out of the box, PyView supports as many photo formats as Tkinter's `PhotoImage` object does; that's why it looks for GIF files by default. You can improve this by installing the PIL extension to view JPEGs (and many others). But because PIL is an optional extension today, it's not incorporated into this PyView release. See the end of Chapter 7 for more on PIL and image formats.

PyView Source Code

Because the PyView program was implemented in stages, you need to study the union of two files and classes to understand how it truly works. One file implements a class that provides core slideshow functionality; the other implements a class the extends the original class, to add additional features on top of the core behavior. Let's start with the extension class: Example 9-16 adds a set of features to an imported slideshow base class—note editing, a delay scale and file label, etc. This is the file that is actually run to start PyView.

Example 9-16. PP2E\Gui\SlideShow\slideShowPlus.py

```
###################################################################
# SlideShowPlus: add note files with an attached PyEdit object,
# a scale for setting the slideshow delay interval, and a label
# that gives the name of the image file currently being displayed;
###################################################################

import os, string
from Tkinter import *
from PP2E.Gui.TextEditor.textEditor import *
from slideShow import SlideShow
#from slideShow_threads import SlideShow

class SlideShowPlus(SlideShow):
    def __init__(self, parent, picdir, editclass, msecs=2000):
        self.msecs = msecs
        self.editclass = editclass
        SlideShow.__init__(self, parent=parent, picdir=picdir, msecs=msecs)
    def makeWidgets(self):
        self.name = Label(self, text='None', bg='red', relief=RIDGE)
        self.name.pack(fill=X)
        SlideShow.makeWidgets(self)
        Button(self, text='Note', command=self.onNote).pack(fill=X)
        Button(self, text='Help', command=self.onHelp).pack(fill=X)
        s = Scale(label='Speed: msec delay', command=self.onScale,
                    from_=0, to=3000, resolution=50, showvalue=YES,
                    length=400, tickinterval=250, orient='horizontal')
        s.pack(side=BOTTOM, fill=X)
        s.set(self.msecs)
        if self.editclass == TextEditorMain:          # make editor now
            self.editor = self.editclass(self.master) # need root for menu
        else:
            self.editor = self.editclass(self)        # embedded or popup
        self.editor.pack_forget()                     # hide editor initially
        self.editorUp = self.image = None
    def onStart(self):
        SlideShow.onStart(self)
        self.config(cursor='watch')
    def onStop(self):
        SlideShow.onStop(self)
        self.config(cursor='hand2')
```

Example 9-16. PP2E\Gui\SlideShow\slideShowPlus.py (continued)

```
def onOpen(self):
    SlideShow.onOpen(self)
    if self.image:
        self.name.config(text=os.path.split(self.image[0])[1])
    self.config(cursor='crosshair')
    self.switchNote()
def quit(self):
    self.saveNote()
    SlideShow.quit(self)
def drawNext(self):
    SlideShow.drawNext(self)
    if self.image:
        self.name.config(text=os.path.split(self.image[0])[1])
    self.loadNote()
def onScale(self, value):
    self.msecs = string.atoi(value)
def onNote(self):
    if self.editorUp:                          # if editor already open
        #self.saveNote()                        # save text, hide editor
        self.editor.pack_forget()
        self.editorUp = 0
    else:
        self.editor.pack(side=TOP)             # else unhide/pack editor
        self.editorUp = 1                      # and load image note text
        self.loadNote()
def switchNote(self):
    if self.editorUp:
        self.saveNote()                        # save current image's note
        self.loadNote()                        # load note for new image
def saveNote(self):
    if self.editorUp:
        currfile = self.editor.getFileName()       # or self.editor.onSave()
        currtext = self.editor.getAllText()        # but text may be empty
        if currfile and currtext:
            try:
                open(currfile, 'w').write(currtext)
            except:
                pass # this may be normal if run off cd
def loadNote(self):
    if self.image and self.editorUp:
        root, ext = os.path.splitext(self.image[0])
        notefile  = root + '.note'
        self.editor.setFileName(notefile)
        try:
            self.editor.setAllText(open(notefile).read())
        except:
            self.editor.clearAllText()
def onHelp(self):
    showinfo('About PyView',
             'PyView version 1.1\nJuly, 1999\n'
             'An image slide show\nProgramming Python 2E')
```

Example 9-16. PP2E\Gui\SlideShow\slideShowPlus.py (continued)

```
if __name__ == '__main__':
    import sys
    picdir = '../gifs'
    if len(sys.argv) >= 2:
        picdir = sys.argv[1]

    editstyle = TextEditorComponentMinimal
    if len(sys.argv) == 3:
        try:
            editstyle = [TextEditorMain,
                         TextEditorMainPopup,
                         TextEditorComponent,
                         TextEditorComponentMinimal][string.atoi(sys.argv[2])]
        except: pass

    root = Tk()
    root.title('PyView 1.1 - plus text notes')
    Label(root, text="Slide show subclass").pack()
    SlideShowPlus(parent=root, picdir=picdir, editclass=editstyle)
    root.mainloop()
```

The core functionality extended by `SlideShowPlus` lives in Example 9-17. This was the initial slideshow implementation; it opens images, displays photos, and cycles through a slideshow. You can run it by itself, but you won't get advanced features like notes and sliders added by the `SlideShowPlus` subclass.

Example 9-17. PP2E\Gui\SlideShow\slideShow.py

```
#########################################################################
# SlideShow: a simple photo image slideshow in Python/Tkinter;
# the base feature set coded here can be extended in subclasses;
#########################################################################

from Tkinter import *
from glob import glob
from tkMessageBox import askyesno
from tkFileDialog import askopenfilename
import random
Width, Height = 450, 450

imageTypes = [('Gif files', '.gif'),      # for file open dialog
              ('Ppm files', '.ppm'),      # plus jpg with a Tk patch,
              ('Pgm files', '.pgm'),      # plus bitmaps with BitmapImage
              ('All files', '*')]

class SlideShow(Frame):
    def __init__(self, parent=None, picdir='.', msecs=3000, **args):
        Frame.__init__(self, parent, args)
        self.makeWidgets()
        self.pack(expand=YES, fill=BOTH)
        self.opens = picdir
        files = []
```

Example 9-17. PP2E\Gui\SlideShow\slideShow.py (continued)

```python
        for label, ext in imageTypes[:-1]:
            files = files + glob('%s/*%s' % (picdir, ext))
        self.images = map(lambda x: (x, PhotoImage(file=x)), files)
        self.msecs  = msecs
        self.beep   = 1
        self.drawn  = None
    def makeWidgets(self):
        self.canvas = Canvas(self, bg='white', height=Height, width=Width)
        self.canvas.pack(side=LEFT, fill=BOTH, expand=YES)
        self.onoff = Button(self, text='Start', command=self.onStart)
        self.onoff.pack(fill=X)
        Button(self, text='Open',  command=self.onOpen).pack(fill=X)
        Button(self, text='Beep',  command=self.onBeep).pack(fill=X)
        Button(self, text='Quit',  command=self.onQuit).pack(fill=X)
    def onStart(self):
        self.loop = 1
        self.onoff.config(text='Stop', command=self.onStop)
        self.canvas.config(height=Height, width=Width)
        self.onTimer()
    def onStop(self):
        self.loop = 0
        self.onoff.config(text='Start', command=self.onStart)
    def onOpen(self):
        self.onStop()
        name = askopenfilename(initialdir=self.opens, filetypes=imageTypes)
        if name:
            if self.drawn: self.canvas.delete(self.drawn)
            img = PhotoImage(file=name)
            self.canvas.config(height=img.height(), width=img.width())
            self.drawn = self.canvas.create_image(2, 2, image=img, anchor=NW)
            self.image = name, img
    def onQuit(self):
        self.onStop()
        self.update()
        if askyesno('PyView', 'Really quit now?'):
            self.quit()
    def onBeep(self):
        self.beep = self.beep ^ 1
    def onTimer(self):
        if self.loop:
            self.drawNext()
            self.after(self.msecs, self.onTimer)
    def drawNext(self):
        if self.drawn: self.canvas.delete(self.drawn)
        name, img = random.choice(self.images)
        self.drawn = self.canvas.create_image(2, 2, image=img, anchor=NW)
        self.image = name, img
        if self.beep: self.bell()
        self.canvas.update()

if __name__ == '__main__':
    import sys
```

Example 9-17. PP2E\Gui\SlideShow\slideShow.py (continued)

```
if len(sys.argv) == 2:
    picdir = sys.argv[1]
else:
    picdir = '../gifs'
root = Tk()
root.title('PyView 1.0')
root.iconname('PyView')
Label(root, text="Python Slide Show Viewer").pack()
SlideShow(root, picdir=picdir, bd=3, relief=SUNKEN)
root.mainloop()
```

To give you a better idea of what this core base class implements, Figure 9-16 shows what it looks like if run by itself (actually, two copies run by themselves) by a script called `slideShow_frames`, which is on this book's CD.

Figure 9-16. Two attached SlideShow objects

The simple `slideShow_frames` scripts attach two instances of `SlideShow` to a single window—a feat possible only because state information is recorded in class instance variables, not globals. The `slideShow_toplevels` script also on the CD attaches two `SlideShow`s to two top-level pop-up windows instead. In both cases, the slideshows run independently, but are based on `after` events fired from the same single event loop in a single process.

PyDraw: Painting and Moving Graphics

The previous chapter introduced simple Tkinter animation techniques (see the tour's `canvasDraw` variants). The PyDraw program listed here builds upon those ideas to implement a more feature-rich painting program in Python. It adds new trails and scribble drawing modes, object and background color fills, embedded photos, and more. In addition, it implements object movement and animation techniques—drawn objects may be moved around the canvas by clicking and dragging, and any drawn object can be gradually moved across the screen to a target location clicked with the mouse.

Running PyDraw

PyDraw is essentially a Tkinter canvas with lots of keyboard and mouse event bindings to allow users to perform common drawing operations. This isn't a professional-grade paint program by any definition, but it's fun to play with. In fact, you really should—it is impossible to capture things like object motion in the medium afforded by this book. Start PyDraw from the launcher bars (or run the file *movingpics.py* from Example 9-18 directly). Press the ? key to view a help message giving available commands (or read the help string in the code listings).

Figure 9-17 shows PyDraw after a few objects have been drawn on the canvas. To move any object shown here, either click it with the middle mouse button and drag to move it with the mouse cursor, or middle-click the object and then right-click in the spot you want it to move towards. In the latter case, PyDraw performs an animated (gradual) movement of the object to the target spot. Try this on the picture of Python creator Guido van Rossum near the top to start the famous "Moving Guido Demo" (yes, he has a sense of humor, too).

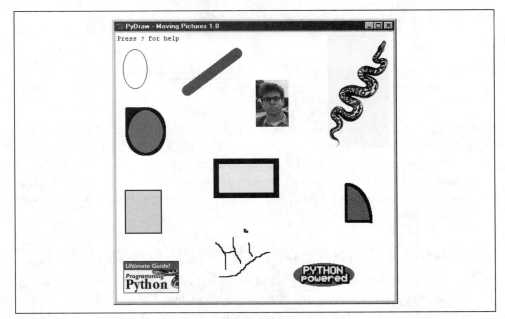

Figure 9-17. PyDraw with draw objects ready to be moved

Press "p" to insert photos, and use left-button drags to draw shapes. Windows users—middle-click is usually both mouse buttons at once, but you may need to configure this in your control panel. In addition to mouse events, there are 17 key-press commands for tailoring sketches that I won't cover here. It takes a while to get the hang of what all the keyboard and mouse commands do; but once you've mastered the bindings, you too can begin generating senseless electronic artwork like that in Figure 9-18.

Figure 9-18. PyDraw after substantial play

PyDraw Source Code

Like PyEdit, PyDraw lives in a single file. Two extensions that customize motion implementations are listed following the main module shown in Example 9-18.

Example 9-18. PP2E\Gui\MovingPics\movingpics.py

```
#############################################################################
# PyDraw: simple canvas paint program and object mover/animator
# uses time.sleep loops to implement object move loops, such that only
# one move can be in progress at once; this is smooth and fast, but see
# the widget.after and thread-based subclasses here for other techniques;
#############################################################################

helpstr = """--PyDraw version 1.0--
Mouse commands:
  Left        = Set target spot
  Left+Move   = Draw new object
  Double Left = Clear all objects
  Right       = Move current object
  Middle      = Select closest object
  Middle+Move = Drag current object
```

Example 9-18. PP2E\Gui\MovingPics\movingpics.py (continued)

```
Keyboard commands:
  w=Pick border width  c=Pick color
  u=Pick move unit     s=Pick move delay
  o=Draw ovals         r=Draw rectangles
  l=Draw lines         a=Draw arcs
  d=Delete object      1=Raise object
  2=Lower object       f=Fill object
  b=Fill background    p=Add photo
  z=Save postscript    x=Pick pen modes
  ?=Help               other=clear text
"""

import time, sys
from Tkinter import *
from tkFileDialog import *
from tkMessageBox import *
PicDir = '../gifs'

if sys.platform[:3] == 'win':
    HelpFont = ('courier', 9, 'normal')
else:
    HelpFont = ('courier', 12, 'normal')

pickDelays = [0.01, 0.025, 0.05, 0.10, 0.25, 0.0, 0.001, 0.005]
pickUnits  = [1, 2, 4, 6, 8, 10, 12]
pickWidths = [1, 2, 5, 10, 20]
pickFills  = [None,'white','blue','red','black','yellow','green','purple']
pickPens   = ['elastic', 'scribble', 'trails']

class MovingPics:
    def __init__(self, parent=None):
        canvas = Canvas(parent, width=500, height=500, bg= 'white')
        canvas.pack(expand=YES, fill=BOTH)
        canvas.bind('<ButtonPress-1>',   self.onStart)
        canvas.bind('<B1-Motion>',       self.onGrow)
        canvas.bind('<Double-1>',        self.onClear)
        canvas.bind('<ButtonPress-3>',   self.onMove)
        canvas.bind('<Button-2>',        self.onSelect)
        canvas.bind('<B2-Motion>',       self.onDrag)
        parent.bind('<KeyPress>',        self.onOptions)
        self.createMethod = Canvas.create_oval
        self.canvas = canvas
        self.moving = []
        self.images = []
        self.object = None
        self.where  = None
        self.scribbleMode = 0
        parent.title('PyDraw - Moving Pictures 1.0')
        parent.protocol('WM_DELETE_WINDOW', self.onQuit)
        self.realquit = parent.quit
        self.textInfo = self.canvas.create_text(
                                5, 5, anchor=NW,
```

Example 9-18. PP2E\Gui\MovingPics\movingpics.py (continued)

```python
                                font=HelpFont,
                                text='Press ? for help')
    def onStart(self, event):
        self.where  = event
        self.object = None
    def onGrow(self, event):
        canvas = event.widget
        if self.object and pickPens[0] == 'elastic':
            canvas.delete(self.object)
        self.object = self.createMethod(canvas,
                        self.where.x, self.where.y,     # start
                        event.x,  event.y,              # stop
                        fill=pickFills[0], width=pickWidths[0])
        if pickPens[0] == 'scribble':
            self.where = event  # from here next time
    def onClear(self, event):
        if self.moving: return          # ok if moving but confusing
        event.widget.delete('all')      # use all tag
        self.images = []
        self.textInfo = self.canvas.create_text(
                        5, 5, anchor=NW,
                        font=HelpFont,
                        text='Press ? for help')
    def plotMoves(self, event):
        diffX = event.x - self.where.x            # plan animated moves
        diffY = event.y - self.where.y            # horizontal then vertical
        reptX = abs(diffX) / pickUnits[0]         # incr per move, number moves
        reptY = abs(diffY) / pickUnits[0]         # from last to event click
        incrX = pickUnits[0] * ((diffX > 0) or -1)
        incrY = pickUnits[0] * ((diffY > 0) or -1)
        return incrX, reptX, incrY, reptY
    def onMove(self, event):
        traceEvent('onMove', event, 0)            # move current object to click
        object = self.object                      # ignore some ops during mv
        if object and object not in self.moving:
            msecs = int(pickDelays[0] * 1000)
            parms = 'Delay=%d msec, Units=%d' % (msecs, pickUnits[0])
            self.setTextInfo(parms)
            self.moving.append(object)
            canvas = event.widget
            incrX, reptX, incrY, reptY = self.plotMoves(event)
            for i in range(reptX):
                canvas.move(object, incrX, 0)
                canvas.update()
                time.sleep(pickDelays[0])
            for i in range(reptY):
                canvas.move(object, 0, incrY)
                canvas.update()                   # update runs other ops
                time.sleep(pickDelays[0])         # sleep until next move
            self.moving.remove(object)
            if self.object == object: self.where  = event
    def onSelect(self, event):
        self.where  = event
        self.object = self.canvas.find_closest(event.x, event.y)[0]    # tuple
```

Example 9-18. PP2E\Gui\MovingPics\movingpics.py (continued)

```
    def onDrag(self, event):
        diffX = event.x - self.where.x          # ok if object in moving
        diffY = event.y - self.where.y          # throws it off course
        self.canvas.move(self.object, diffX, diffY)
        self.where = event
    def onOptions(self, event):
        keymap = {
            'w': lambda self: self.changeOption(pickWidths, 'Pen Width'),
            'c': lambda self: self.changeOption(pickFills,  'Color'),
            'u': lambda self: self.changeOption(pickUnits,  'Move Unit'),
            's': lambda self: self.changeOption(pickDelays, 'Move Delay'),
            'x': lambda self: self.changeOption(pickPens,   'Pen Mode'),
            'o': lambda self: self.changeDraw(Canvas.create_oval,      'Oval'),
            'r': lambda self: self.changeDraw(Canvas.create_rectangle, 'Rect'),
            'l': lambda self: self.changeDraw(Canvas.create_line,      'Line'),
            'a': lambda self: self.changeDraw(Canvas.create_arc,       'Arc'),
            'd': MovingPics.deleteObject,
            '1': MovingPics.raiseObject,
            '2': MovingPics.lowerObject,        # if only 1 call pattern
            'f': MovingPics.fillObject,         # use unbound method objects
            'b': MovingPics.fillBackground,     # else lambda passed self
            'p': MovingPics.addPhotoItem,
            'z': MovingPics.savePostscript,
            '?': MovingPics.help}
        try:
            keymap[event.char](self)
        except KeyError:
            self.setTextInfo('Press ? for help')
    def changeDraw(self, method, name):
        self.createMethod = method             # unbound Canvas method
        self.setTextInfo('Draw Object=' + name)
    def changeOption(self, list, name):
        list.append(list[0])
        del list[0]
        self.setTextInfo('%s=%s' % (name, list[0]))
    def deleteObject(self):
        if self.object != self.textInfo:       # ok if object in moving
            self.canvas.delete(self.object)    # erases but move goes on
            self.object = None
    def raiseObject(self):
        if self.object:                        # ok if moving
            self.canvas.tkraise(self.object)   # raises while moving
    def lowerObject(self):
        if self.object:
            self.canvas.lower(self.object)
    def fillObject(self):
        if self.object:
            type = self.canvas.type(self.object)
            if type == 'image':
                pass
            elif type == 'text':
                self.canvas.itemconfig(self.object, fill=pickFills[0])
```

Example 9-18. PP2E\Gui\MovingPics\movingpics.py (continued)

```
            else:
                self.canvas.itemconfig(self.object,
                                  fill=pickFills[0], width=pickWidths[0])
        def fillBackground(self):
            self.canvas.config(bg=pickFills[0])
        def addPhotoItem(self):
            if not self.where: return
            filetypes=[('Gif files', '.gif'), ('All files', '*')]
            file = askopenfilename(initialdir=PicDir, filetypes=filetypes)
            if file:
                image = PhotoImage(file=file)                # load image
                self.images.append(image)                    # keep reference
                self.object = self.canvas.create_image(      # add to canvas
                               self.where.x, self.where.y,    # at last spot
                               image=image, anchor=NW)
        def savePostscript(self):
            file = asksaveasfilename()
            if file:
                self.canvas.postscript(file=file)  # save canvas to file
        def help(self):
            self.setTextInfo(helpstr)
            #showinfo('PyDraw', helpstr)
        def setTextInfo(self, text):
            self.canvas.dchars(self.textInfo, 0, END)
            self.canvas.insert(self.textInfo, 0, text)
            self.canvas.tkraise(self.textInfo)
        def onQuit(self):
            if self.moving:
                self.setTextInfo("Can't quit while move in progress")
            else:
                self.realquit()  # std wm delete: err msg if move in progress

def traceEvent(label, event, fullTrace=1):
    print label
    if fullTrace:
        for key in dir(event): print key, '=>', getattr(event, key)


if __name__ == '__main__':
    from sys import argv                        # when this file is executed
    if len(argv) == 2: PicDir = argv[1]         # '..' fails if run elsewhere
    root = Tk()                                 # make, run a MovingPics object
    MovingPics(root)
    root.mainloop()
```

Just as in the last chapter's `canvasDraw` examples, we can add support for moving more than one object at the same time with either **after** scheduled-callback events, or threads. Example 9-19 shows a `MovingPics` subclass that codes the necessary customizations to do parallel moves with **after** events. Run this file directly to see the difference; I could try to capture the notion of multiple objects in motion with a screen shot, but would almost certainly fail.

Example 9-19. PP2E\Gui\MovingPics\movingpics_after.py

```
###########################################################################
# PyDraw-after: simple canvas paint program and object mover/animator
# use widget.after scheduled events to implement object move loops, such
# that more than one can be in motion at once without having to use threads;
# this does moves in parallel, but seems to be slower than time.sleep version;
# see also canvasDraw in Tour: builds and passes the incX/incY list at once:
# here, would be allmoves = ([(incrX, 0)] * reptX) + ([(0, incrY)] * reptY)
###########################################################################

from movingpics import *

class MovingPicsAfter(MovingPics):
    def doMoves(self, delay, objectId, incrX, reptX, incrY, reptY):
        if reptX:
            self.canvas.move(objectId, incrX, 0)
            reptX = reptX - 1
        else:
            self.canvas.move(objectId, 0, incrY)
            reptY = reptY - 1
        if not (reptX or reptY):
            self.moving.remove(objectId)
        else:
            self.canvas.after(delay,
                self.doMoves, delay, objectId, incrX, reptX, incrY, reptY)
    def onMove(self, event):
        traceEvent('onMove', event, 0)
        object = self.object                        # move cur obj to click spot
        if object:
            msecs  = int(pickDelays[0] * 1000)
            parms  = 'Delay=%d msec, Units=%d' % (msecs, pickUnits[0])
            self.setTextInfo(parms)
            self.moving.append(object)
            incrX, reptX, incrY, reptY = self.plotMoves(event)
            self.doMoves(msecs, object, incrX, reptX, incrY, reptY)
            self.where = event

if __name__ == '__main__':
    from sys import argv                            # when this file is executed
    if len(argv) == 2:
        import movingpics                           # not this module's global
        movingpics.PicDir = argv[1]                 # and from* doesn't link names
    root = Tk()
    MovingPicsAfter(root)
    root.mainloop()
```

Now, while one or more moves are in progress, you can start another by middle-clicking on another object and right-clicking on the spot you want it to move to. It starts its journey immediately, even if other objects are in motion. Each object's scheduled **after** events are added to the same event loop queue and dispatched by Tkinter as soon as possible after a timer expiration. If you run this subclass module directly, you'll probably notice that movement isn't quite as fast or as smooth as in the original, but multiple moves can overlap in time.

Example 9-20 shows how to achieve such parallelism with threads. This process works, but as we learned in the last chapter, updating GUIs in spawned threads is generally a dangerous affair. On my machine, the movement that this script implements with threads is a bit more jerky than the original version—a reflection of the overhead incurred for switching the interpreter (and CPU) between multiple threads.

Example 9-20. PP2E\Gui\MovingPics\movingpics_threads.py

```
#################################################################
# use threads to move objects; seems to work on Windows provided
# that canvas.update() not called by threads(else exits with fatal
# errors, some objs start moving immediately after drawn, etc.);
# at least some canvas method calls must be thread safe in Tkinter;
# this is less smooth than time.sleep, and is dangerous in general:
# threads are best coded to update global vars, not change GUI;
#################################################################

import thread, time, sys, random
from Tkinter import Tk, mainloop
from movingpics import MovingPics, pickUnits, pickDelays

class MovingPicsThreaded(MovingPics):
    def __init__(self, parent=None):
        MovingPics.__init__(self, parent)
        self.mutex = thread.allocate_lock()
        import sys
        #sys.setcheckinterval(0) # switch after each vm op- doesn't help
    def onMove(self, event):
        object = self.object
        if object and object not in self.moving:
            msecs  = int(pickDelays[0] * 1000)
            parms  = 'Delay=%d msec, Units=%d' % (msecs, pickUnits[0])
            self.setTextInfo(parms)
            #self.mutex.acquire()
            self.moving.append(object)
            #self.mutex.release()
            thread.start_new_thread(self.doMove, (object, event))
    def doMove(self, object, event):
        canvas = event.widget
        incrX, reptX, incrY, reptY = self.plotMoves(event)
        for i in range(reptX):
            canvas.move(object, incrX, 0)
            # canvas.update()
            time.sleep(pickDelays[0])           # this can change
        for i in range(reptY):
            canvas.move(object, 0, incrY)
            # canvas.update()                   # update runs other ops
            time.sleep(pickDelays[0])           # sleep until next move
```

Example 9-20. PP2E\Gui\MovingPics\movingpics_threads.py (continued)

```
        #self.mutex.acquire()
        self.moving.remove(object)
        if self.object == object: self.where  = event
        #self.mutex.release()

if __name__ == '__main__':
    root = Tk()
    MovingPicsThreaded(root)
    mainloop()
```

PyClock: An Analog/Digital Clock Widget

One of the first things I always look for when exploring a new computer interface is a clock. Because I spend so much time glued to computers, it's essentially impossible for me to keep track of the time unless it is right there on the screen in front of me (and even then, it's iffy). The next program, *PyClock*, implements such a clock widget in Python. It's not substantially different than clock programs you may be used to seeing on the X Windows system. Because it is coded in Python, though, this one is both easily customized, and fully portable among Windows, the X Windows system, and Macs, like all the code in this chapter. In addition to advanced GUI techniques, this example demonstrates Python `math` and `time` module tools.

A Quick Geometry Lesson

Before I show you PyClock, though, a little background and a confession. Quick—how do you plot points on a circle? This, along with time formats and events, turns out to be a core concept in clock widget programs. To draw an analog clock face on a canvas widget, you essentially need to be able to sketch a circle—the clock face itself is composed of points on a circle, and the second, minute, and hour hands of the clock are really just lines from a circle's center out to a point on the circle. Digital clocks are simpler to draw, but not much to look at.

Now the confession: when I started writing PyClock, I couldn't answer the last paragraph's opening question. I had utterly forgotten the math needed to sketch out points on a circle (as had most of the professional software developers I queried about this magic formula). It happens. After going unused for a few decades, such knowledge tends to be garbage-collected. I finally was able to dust off a few neurons long enough to code the plotting math needed, but it wasn't my finest intellectual hour.

If you are in the same boat, I don't have space to teach geometry in depth here, but I can show you one way to code the point-plotting formulas in Python in simple terms. Before tackling the more complex task of implementing a clock, I wrote the `plotterGui` script shown in Example 9-21 to focus on just the circle-plotting logic.

Its `point` function is where the circle logic lives—it plots the (X,Y) coordinates of a point on the circle, given the relative point number, the total number of points to be placed on the circle, and the circle's radius (the distance from the circle's center to the points drawn upon it). It first calculates the point's angle from the top by dividing 360 by the number of points to be plotted, and then multiplying by the point number; in case you've forgotten, too, it's 360 degrees around the whole circle (e.g., if you plot 4 points on a circle, each is 90 degrees from the last, or 360/ 4). Python's standard `math` module gives all the required constants and functions from that point forward—*pi*, *sine*, and *cosine*. The math is really not too obscure if you study this long enough (in conjunction with your old geometry text if necessary). See the book's CD for alternative ways to code the number crunching.[*]

Even if you don't care about the math, though, check out this script's `circle` function. Given the (X,Y) coordinates of a point on the circle returned by `point`, it draws a line from the circle's center out to the point and a small rectangle around the point itself—not unlike the hands and points of an analog clock. Canvas tags are used to associate drawn objects for deletion before each plot.

Example 9-21. PP2E\Gui\Clock\plotterGui.py

```
# plot circles (like I did in high school)

import math, sys
from Tkinter import *

def point(tick, range, radius):
    angle = tick * (360.0 / range)
    radiansPerDegree = math.pi / 180
    pointX = int( round( radius * math.sin(angle * radiansPerDegree) ))
    pointY = int( round( radius * math.cos(angle * radiansPerDegree) ))
    return (pointX, pointY)

def circle(points, radius, centerX, centerY, slow=0):
    canvas.delete('lines')
    canvas.delete('points')
    for i in range(points):
        x, y = point(i+1, points, radius-4)
        scaledX, scaledY = (x + centerX), (centerY - y)
        canvas.create_line(centerX, centerY, scaledX, scaledY, tag='lines')
        canvas.create_rectangle(scaledX-2, scaledY-2,
                                scaledX+2, scaledY+2,
                                       fill='red', tag='points')
        if slow: canvas.update()
```

---

[*] And if you do enough number crunching to have followed this paragraph, you will probably also be interested in exploring the NumPy numeric programming extension for Python. It adds things like vector objects and advanced mathematical operations, and effectively turns Python into a scientific programming tool. It's been used effectively by many organizations, including Lawrence Livermore National Labs. NumPy must be fetched and installed separately; see Python's web site for links. Python also has a built-in complex number type for engineering work; see the library manual for details.

Example 9-21. PP2E\Gui\Clock\plotterGui.py (continued)

```
def plotter():
    circle(scaleVar.get(), (Width / 2), originX, originY, checkVar.get())

def makewidgets():
    global canvas, scaleVar, checkVar
    canvas = Canvas(width=Width, height=Width)
    canvas.pack(side=TOP)
    scaleVar = IntVar()
    checkVar = IntVar()
    scale = Scale(label='Points on circle', variable=scaleVar, from_=1, to=360)
    scale.pack(side=LEFT)
    Checkbutton(text='Slow mode', variable=checkVar).pack(side=LEFT)
    Button(text='Plot', command=plotter).pack(side=LEFT, padx=50)

if __name__ == '__main__':
    Width = 500                                       # default width, height
    if len(sys.argv) == 2: Width = int(sys.argv[1])   # width cmdline arg?
    originX = originY = Width / 2                      # same as circle radius
    makewidgets()                                     # on default Tk root
    mainloop()
```

The circle defaults to 500 pixels wide unless you pass a width on the command line. Given a number of points on a circle, this script marks out the circle in clockwise order every time you press Plot, by drawing lines out from the center to small rectangles at points on the circle's shape. Move the slider to plot a different number of points, and click the checkbutton to make the drawing happen slow enough to notice the clockwise order in which lines and points are drawn (this forces the script to update the display after each line is drawn). Figure 9-19 shows the result for plotting 120 points with the circle width set to 400 on the command line; if you ask for 60 and 12 points on the circle, the relationship to clock faces and hands starts becoming more clear.

For more help, the book CD also includes text-based versions of this plotting script that print circle point coordinates to the stdout stream for review, rather than rendering them in a GUI. See the plotterText scripts in the clock's directory. Here is the sort of output they produce when plotting 4 and 12 points on a circle that is 400 points wide and high; the output format is simply:

```
    pointnumber : angle = (Xcoordinate, Ycoordinate)
```

and assumes that the circle is centered at coordinate (0,0):

```
    ----------
    1 : 90.0 = (200, 0)
    2 : 180.0 = (0, -200)
    3 : 270.0 = (-200, 0)
    4 : 360.0 = (0, 200)
    ----------
    1 : 30.0 = (100, 173)
    2 : 60.0 = (173, 100)
```

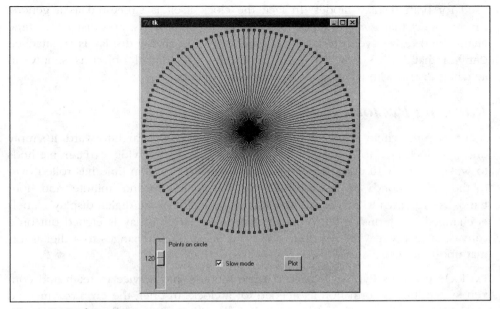

Figure 9-19. plotterGui in action

```
 3 : 90.0 = (200, 0)
 4 : 120.0 = (173, -100)
 5 : 150.0 = (100, -173)
 6 : 180.0 = (0, -200)
 7 : 210.0 = (-100, -173)
 8 : 240.0 = (-173, -100)
 9 : 270.0 = (-200, 0)
10 : 300.0 = (-173, 100)
11 : 330.0 = (-100, 173)
12 : 360.0 = (0, 200)
----------
```

To understand how these points are mapped to a canvas, you first need to know that the width and height of a circle are always the same—the radius × 2. Because Tkinter canvas (X,Y) coordinates start at (0,0) in the upper left corner, the plotter GUI must offset the circle's center point to coordinates (width/2, width/2)—the origin point from which lines are drawn. For instance, in a 400-by-400 circle, the canvas center is (200,200). A line to the 90-degree angle point on the right side of the circle runs from (200,200) to (400,200)—the result of adding the (200,0) point coordinates plotted for the radius and angle. A line to the bottom at 180 degrees runs from (200,200) to (200,400) after factoring in the (0,–200) point plotted.

This point-plotting algorithm used by `plotterGui`, along with a few scaling constants, is at the heart of the PyClock analog display. If this still seems a bit much, I suggest you focus on the PyClock script's *digital* display implementation first; the analog geometry plots are really just extensions of underlying timing mechanisms used for both display modes. In fact, the clock itself is structured as a generic Frame object that *embeds* digital and analog display objects, and dispatches time change and resize events to both the same way. The analog display is an attached Canvas that knows how to draw circles, but the digital object is simply an attached Frame with labels to show time components.

Running PyClock

Apart from the circle geometry bit, the rest of PyClock is straightforward. It simply draws a clock face to represent the current time and uses widget after methods to wake itself up 10 times per second to check if the system time has rolled over to the next second. On second rollovers, the analog second, minute, and hour hands are redrawn to reflect the new time (or the text of the digital display's labels is changed). In terms of GUI construction, the analog display is etched out on a canvas, is redrawn whenever the window is resized, and changes to a digital format upon request.

PyClock also puts Python's standard time module into service to fetch and convert system time information as needed for a clock. In brief, the onTimer method gets system time with time.time, a built-in tool that returns a floating-point number giving seconds since the "epoch"—the point from which your computer counts time. The time.localtime call is then used to convert epoch time into a tuple that contains hour, minute, and second values; see the script and Python library manual for additional time-related call details.

Checking the system time 10 times per second may seem intense, but it guarantees that the second hand ticks when it should without jerks or skips (after events aren't precisely timed), and is not a significant CPU drain on systems I use.[*] On Linux and Windows, PyClock uses negligible processor resources, and what it does use is spent largely on screen updates in analog display mode, not after events. To minimize screen updates, PyClock redraws only clock hands on second rollovers; points on the clock's circle are redrawn at startup and on window resizes only. Figure 9-20 shows the default initial PyClock display format you get when file *clock.py* is run directly.

The clock hand lines are given arrows at their endpoints with the canvas line object's arrow and arrowshape options. The arrow option can be "first", "last", "none", or "both"; the arrowshape option takes a tuple giving the length of the arrow touching the line, its overall length, and its width.

---

[*] Speaking of performance, I've run multiple clocks on all test machines—from a 650 MHz Pentium III to an "old" 200 MHz Pentium I—without seeing any degraded performance in any running clocks. The PyDemos script, for instance, launches six clocks running in the same process, and all update smoothly. They probably do on older machines, too, but mine have collected too much dust to yield useful metrics.

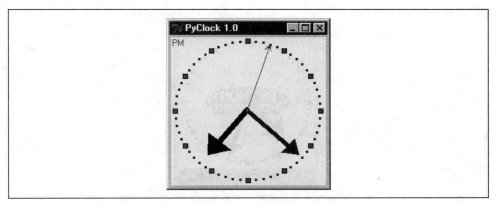

Figure 9-20. PyClock default analog display

Like PyView, PyClock also uses the widget `pack_forget` and `pack` methods to dynamically erase and redraw portions of the display on demand (i.e., in response to bound events). Clicking on the clock with a left mouse button changes its display to digital by erasing the analog widgets and drawing the digital interface; you get the simpler display captured in Figure 9-21.

Figure 9-21. PyClock goes digital

This digital display form is useful if you want to conserve real estate on your computer screen and minimize PyClock CPU utilization (it incurs very little screen update overhead). Left-clicking on the clock again changes back to the analog display. The analog and digital displays are both constructed when the script starts, but only one is ever packed at any given time.

A right mouseclick on the clock in either display mode shows or hides an attached label that gives the current date in simple text form. Figure 9-22 shows a PyClock running with a digital display, a clicked-on date label, and a centered photo image object.

The image in the middle of Figure 9-22 is added by passing in a configuration object with appropriate settings to the PyClock object constructor. In fact, almost everything about this display can be customized with attributes in PyClock configuration objects—hand colors, clock tick colors, center photos, and initial size.

Because PyClock's analog display is based upon a manually sketched figure on a canvas, it has to process window *resize* events itself: whenever the window shrinks or expands, the clock face has to be redrawn and scaled for the new window size.

Figure 9-22. PyClock extended display with an image

To catch screen resizes, the script registers for the <Configure> event with bind;
surprisingly, this isn't a top-level window manager event like the close button. As
you expand a PyClock, the clock face gets bigger with the window—try expanding, shrinking, and maximizing the clock window on your computer. Because the
clock face is plotted in a square coordinate system, PyClock always expands in
equal horizontal and vertical proportions, though; if you simply make the window
only wider or taller, the clock is unchanged.

Finally, like PyEdit, PyClock can be run either standalone or attached to and
embedded in other GUIs that need to display the current time. To make it easy to
start preconfigured clocks, a utility module called clockStyles provides a set of
clock configuration objects you can import, subclass to extend, and pass to the
clock constructor; Figure 9-23 shows a few of the preconfigured clock styles and
sizes in action, ticking away in sync.

Each of these clocks uses after events to check for system-time rollover 10 times
per second. When run as top-level windows in the same process, all receive a
timer event from the same event loop. When started as independent programs,
each has an event loop of its own. Either way, their second hands sweep in unison each second.

PyClock Source Code

PyClock source code all lives in one file, except for the precoded configuration
style objects. If you study the code at the bottom of the file shown in
Example 9-22, you'll notice that you can either make a clock object with a configuration object passed in, or specify configuration options by command line arguments (in which case, the script simply builds a configuration object for you).
More generally, you can run this file directly to start a clock, import and make its
objects with configuration objects to get a more custom display, or import and

Figure 9-23. A few canned clock styles (Guido's photo reprinted with permission from Dr. Dobb's Journal)

attach its objects to other GUIs. For instance, PyGadgets runs this file with command line options to tailor the display.

Example 9-22. PP2E\Gui\Clock\clock.py

```
#############################################################################
# PyClock: a clock GUI, with both analog and digital display modes, a
# popup date label, clock face images, resizing, etc.  May be run both
# stand-alone, or embedded (attached) in other GUIs that need a clock.
#############################################################################

from Tkinter import *
import math, time, string


#############################################################################
# Option configuration classes
#############################################################################


class ClockConfig:
    # defaults--override in instance or subclass
    size = 200                                      # width=height
```

Example 9-22. PP2E\Gui\Clock\clock.py (continued)

```
    bg, fg = 'beige', 'brown'                # face, tick colors
    hh, mh, sh, cog = 'black', 'navy', 'blue', 'red'  # clock hands, center
    picture = None                           # face photo file

class PhotoClockConfig(ClockConfig):
    # sample configuration
    size    = 320
    picture = '../gifs/ora-pp.gif'
    bg, hh, mh = 'white', 'blue', 'orange'


###########################################################################
# Digital display object
###########################################################################

class DigitalDisplay(Frame):
    def __init__(self, parent, cfg):
        Frame.__init__(self, parent)
        self.hour = Label(self)
        self.mins = Label(self)
        self.secs = Label(self)
        self.ampm = Label(self)
        for label in self.hour, self.mins, self.secs, self.ampm:
            label.config(bd=4, relief=SUNKEN, bg=cfg.bg, fg=cfg.fg)
            label.pack(side=LEFT)

    def onUpdate(self, hour, mins, secs, ampm, cfg):
        mins = string.zfill(str(mins), 2)
        self.hour.config(text=str(hour), width=4)
        self.mins.config(text=str(mins), width=4)
        self.secs.config(text=str(secs), width=4)
        self.ampm.config(text=str(ampm), width=4)

    def onResize(self, newWidth, newHeight, cfg):
        pass  # nothing to redraw here


###########################################################################
# Analog display object
###########################################################################

class AnalogDisplay(Canvas):
    def __init__(self, parent, cfg):
        Canvas.__init__(self, parent,
                        width=cfg.size, height=cfg.size, bg=cfg.bg)
        self.drawClockface(cfg)
        self.hourHand = self.minsHand = self.secsHand = self.cog = None

    def drawClockface(self, cfg):                        # on start and resize
        if cfg.picture:                                  # draw ovals, picture
            try:
                self.image = PhotoImage(file=cfg.picture)        # bkground
            except:
                self.image = BitmapImage(file=cfg.picture)      # save ref
```

Example 9-22. PP2E\Gui\Clock\clock.py (continued)

```
        imgx = (cfg.size - self.image.width())  / 2           # center it
        imgy = (cfg.size - self.image.height()) / 2
        self.create_image(imgx+1, imgy+1,  anchor=NW, image=self.image)
    originX =  originY = radius = cfg.size/2
    for i in range(60):
        x, y = self.point(i, 60, radius-6, originX, originY)
        self.create_rectangle(x-1, y-1, x+1, y+1, fill=cfg.fg)  # mins
    for i in range(12):
        x, y = self.point(i, 12, radius-6, originX, originY)
        self.create_rectangle(x-3, y-3, x+3, y+3, fill=cfg.fg)  # hours
    self.ampm = self.create_text(3, 3, anchor=NW, fill=cfg.fg)

def point(self, tick, units, radius, originX, originY):
    angle = tick * (360.0 / units)
    radiansPerDegree = math.pi / 180
    pointX = int( round( radius * math.sin(angle * radiansPerDegree) ))
    pointY = int( round( radius * math.cos(angle * radiansPerDegree) ))
    return (pointX + originX+1), (originY+1 - pointY)

def onUpdate(self, hour, mins, secs, ampm, cfg):        # on timer callback
    if self.cog:                                        # redraw hands, cog
        self.delete(self.cog)
        self.delete(self.hourHand)
        self.delete(self.minsHand)
        self.delete(self.secsHand)
    originX = originY = radius = cfg.size/2
    hour = hour + (mins / 60.0)
    hx, hy = self.point(hour, 12, (radius * .80), originX, originY)
    mx, my = self.point(mins, 60, (radius * .90), originX, originY)
    sx, sy = self.point(secs, 60, (radius * .95), originX, originY)
    self.hourHand = self.create_line(originX, originY, hx, hy,
                        width=(cfg.size * .04),
                        arrow='last', arrowshape=(25,25,15), fill=cfg.hh)
    self.minsHand = self.create_line(originX, originY, mx, my,
                        width=(cfg.size * .03),
                        arrow='last', arrowshape=(20,20,10), fill=cfg.mh)
    self.secsHand = self.create_line(originX, originY, sx, sy,
                        width=1,
                        arrow='last', arrowshape=(5,10,5), fill=cfg.sh)
    cogsz = cfg.size * .01
    self.cog = self.create_oval(originX-cogsz, originY+cogsz,
                            originX+cogsz, originY-cogsz, fill=cfg.cog)
    self.dchars(self.ampm, 0, END)
    self.insert(self.ampm, END, ampm)

def onResize(self, newWidth, newHeight, cfg):
    newSize = min(newWidth, newHeight)
    #print 'analog onResize', cfg.size+4, newSize
    if newSize != cfg.size+4:
        cfg.size = newSize-4
        self.delete('all')
        self.drawClockface(cfg)  # onUpdate called next
```

Example 9-22. PP2E\Gui\Clock\clock.py (continued)

```python
#############################################################################
# Clock composite object
#############################################################################

ChecksPerSec = 10   # second change timer

class Clock(Frame):
    def __init__(self, config=ClockConfig, parent=None):
        Frame.__init__(self, parent)
        self.cfg = config
        self.makeWidgets(parent)                    # children are packed but
        self.labelOn = 0                            # clients pack or grid me
        self.display = self.digitalDisplay
        self.lastSec = -1
        self.onSwitchMode(None)
        self.onTimer()

    def makeWidgets(self, parent):
        self.digitalDisplay = DigitalDisplay(self, self.cfg)
        self.analogDisplay  = AnalogDisplay(self,  self.cfg)
        self.dateLabel      = Label(self, bd=3, bg='red', fg='blue')
        parent.bind('<ButtonPress-1>', self.onSwitchMode)
        parent.bind('<ButtonPress-3>', self.onToggleLabel)
        parent.bind('<Configure>',     self.onResize)

    def onSwitchMode(self, event):
        self.display.pack_forget()
        if self.display == self.analogDisplay:
            self.display = self.digitalDisplay
        else:
            self.display = self.analogDisplay
        self.display.pack(side=TOP, expand=YES, fill=BOTH)

    def onToggleLabel(self, event):
        self.labelOn = self.labelOn + 1
        if self.labelOn % 2:
            self.dateLabel.pack(side=BOTTOM, fill=X)
        else:
            self.dateLabel.pack_forget()
        self.update()

    def onResize(self, event):
        if event.widget == self.display:
            self.display.onResize(event.width, event.height, self.cfg)

    def onTimer(self):
        secsSinceEpoch = time.time()
        timeTuple      = time.localtime(secsSinceEpoch)
        hour, min, sec = timeTuple[3:6]
        if sec != self.lastSec:
            self.lastSec = sec
            ampm = ((hour >= 12) and 'PM') or 'AM'          # 0...23
            hour = (hour % 12) or 12                        # 12..11
```

Example 9-22. PP2E\Gui\Clock\clock.py (continued)

```
            self.display.onUpdate(hour, min, sec, ampm, self.cfg)
            self.dateLabel.config(text=time.ctime(secsSinceEpoch))
        self.after(1000 / ChecksPerSec, self.onTimer)   # run N times per second


##############################################################################
# Stand-alone clocks
##############################################################################

class ClockWindow(Clock):
    def __init__(self, config=ClockConfig, parent=None, name=''):
        Clock.__init__(self, config, parent)
        self.pack(expand=YES, fill=BOTH)
        title = 'PyClock 1.0'
        if name: title = title + ' - ' + name
        self.master.title(title)                # master=parent or default
        self.master.protocol('WM_DELETE_WINDOW', self.quit)


##############################################################################
# Program run
##############################################################################

if __name__ == '__main__':
    def getOptions(config, argv):
        for attr in dir(ClockConfig):           # fill default config obj,
            try:                                 # from "-attr val" cmd args
                ix = argv.index('-' + attr)
            except:
                continue
            else:
                if ix in range(1, len(argv)-1):
                    if type(getattr(ClockConfig, attr)) == type(0):
                        setattr(config, attr, int(argv[ix+1]))
                    else:
                        setattr(config, attr, argv[ix+1])
    import sys
    config = ClockConfig()
    #config = PhotoClockConfig()
    if len(sys.argv) >= 2:
        getOptions(config, sys.argv)            # clock.py -size n -bg 'blue'...
    myclock = ClockWindow(config, Tk())         # parent is Tk root if standalone
    myclock.mainloop()
```

And finally, Example 9-23 shows the module that is actually run from the PyDemos launcher script—it predefines a handful of clock styles, and runs six of them at once attached to new top-level windows for demo effect (though one clock per screen is usually enough in practice, even for me).*

---

* Note that images named in this script may be missing on your CD due to copyright concerns. Insert lawyer joke here.

Example 9-23. PP2E\Gui\Clock\clockStyles.py

```
from clock import *
from Tkinter import mainloop

gifdir = '../gifs/'
if __name__ == '__main__':
    from sys import argv
    if len(argv) > 1:
        gifdir = argv[1] + '/'

class PPClockBig(PhotoClockConfig):
    picture, bg, fg = gifdir + 'ora-pp.gif', 'navy', 'green'

class PPClockSmall(ClockConfig):
    size    = 175
    picture = gifdir + 'ora-pp.gif'
    bg, fg, hh, mh = 'white', 'red', 'blue', 'orange'

class GilliganClock(ClockConfig):
    size    = 550
    picture = gifdir + 'gilligan.gif'
    bg, fg, hh, mh = 'black', 'white', 'green', 'yellow'

class GuidoClock(GilliganClock):
    size = 400
    picture = gifdir + 'guido_ddj.gif'
    bg = 'navy'

class GuidoClockSmall(GuidoClock):
    size, fg = 278, 'black'

class OusterhoutClock(ClockConfig):
    size, picture = 200, gifdir + 'ousterhout-new.gif'
    bg, fg, hh    = 'black', 'gold', 'brown'

class GreyClock(ClockConfig):
    bg, fg, hh, mh, sh = 'grey', 'black', 'black', 'black', 'white'

class PinkClock(ClockConfig):
    bg, fg, hh, mh, sh = 'pink', 'yellow', 'purple', 'orange', 'yellow'

class PythonPoweredClock(ClockConfig):
    bg, size, picture = 'white', 175, gifdir + 'pythonPowered.gif'

if __name__ == '__main__':
    for configClass in [
        ClockConfig,
        PPClockBig,
        #PPClockSmall,
        GuidoClockSmall,
        #GilliganClock,
        OusterhoutClock,
        #GreyClock,
```

Example 9-23. PP2E\Gui\Clock\clockStyles.py (continued)

```
        PinkClock,
        PythonPoweredClock
    ]:
        ClockWindow(configClass, Toplevel(), configClass.__name__)
    Button(text='Quit Clocks', command='exit').pack()
    mainloop()
```

PyToe: A Tic-Tac-Toe Game Widget

Finally, a bit of fun to close out this chapter. Our last example, *PyToe*, implements an artificially intelligent tic-tac-toe (sometimes called "naughts and crosses") game-playing program in Python. Most readers are probably familiar with this simple game, so I won't dwell on its details. In short, players take turns marking board positions, in an attempt to occupy an entire row, column, or diagonal. The first player to fill such a pattern wins.

In PyToe, board positions are marked with mouseclicks, and one of the players is a Python program. The gameboard itself is displayed with a simple Tkinter GUI; by default, PyToe builds a 3-by-3 game board (the standard tic-tac-toe setup), but can be configured to build and play an arbitrary N-by-N game.

When it comes time for the computer to select a move, artificial intelligence (AI) algorithms are used to score potential moves and search a tree of candidate moves and countermoves. This is a fairly simple problem as gaming programs go, and the heuristics used to pick moves are not perfect. Still, PyToe is usually smart enough to spot wins a few moves in advance of the user.

Running PyToe

PyToe's GUI is implemented as a frame of packed labels, with mouse-click bindings on the labels to catch user moves. The label's text is configured with the player's mark after each move, computer or user. The `GuiMaker` class we coded earlier in this chapter is also reused here to add a simple menu bar at the top (but no toolbar is drawn at the button, because PyToe leaves its descriptor empty). By default, the user's mark is "X", and PyToe's is "O". Figure 9-24 shows PyToe on the verge of beating me one of two ways.

Figure 9-25 shows PyToe's help pop-up dialog, which lists its command-line configuration options. You can specify colors and font sizes for board labels, the player who moves first, the mark of the user ("X" or "O"), the board size (to override the 3-by-3 default), and the move selection strategy for the computer (e.g., "Minimax" performs a move tree search to spot wins and losses, and "Expert1" and "Expert2" use static scoring heuristics functions).

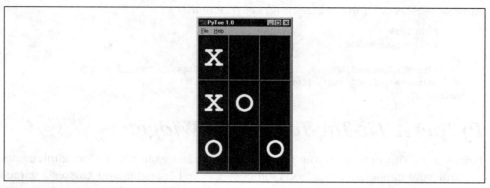

Figure 9-24. PyToe thinks its way to a win

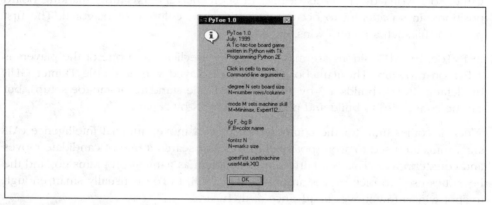

Figure 9-25. PyToe help pop-up with options info

The AI gaming techniques used in PyToe are CPU-intensive, and some computer move selection schemes take longer than others, but their speed varies mostly with the speed of your computer. Move selection delays are fractions of a second long on my 650 MHz machine for a 3-by-3 game board, for all "-mode" move-selection strategy options.

Figure 9-26 shows an alternative PyToe configuration just after it beat me. Despite the scenes captured for this book, under some move selection options, I do still win once in awhile. In larger boards and more complex games, PyToe's move selection algorithms become even more useful.

PyToe Source Code (on CD)

PyToe is a big system that assumes some AI background knowledge and doesn't really demonstrate anything new in terms of GUIs. Partly because of that, but mostly because I've already exceeded my page limit for this chapter, I'm going to

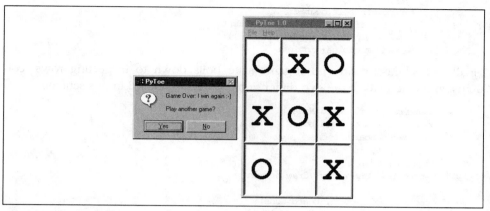

Figure 9-26. an alternative layout

refer you to the book's CD for its source code rather than listing it all here. Please see these two files in the examples distribution for PyToe implementation details:

- *PP2E\Ai\TicTacToe\tictactoe.py*, a top-level wrapper script
- *PP2E\Ai\TicTacToe\tictactoe_lists.py*, the meat of the implementation

If you do look, though, probably the best hint I can give you is that the data structure used to represent board state is the crux of the matter. That is, if you understand the way that boards are modeled, the rest of the code comes naturally.

For instance, the lists-based variant uses a list-of-lists to representation the board's state, along with a simple dictionary of entry widgets for the GUI indexed by board coordinates. Clearing the board after a game is simply a matter of clearing the underlying data structures, as shown in this code excerpt from the examples named above:

```
def clearBoard(self):
    for row, col in self.label.keys():
        self.board[row][col] = Empty
        self.label[(row, col)].config(text=' ')
```

Similarly, picking a move, at least in random mode, is simply a matter of picking a nonempty slot in the board array and storing the machine's mark there and in the GUI (degree is the board's size):

```
def machineMove(self):
    row, col = self.pickMove()
    self.board[row][col] = self.machineMark
    self.label[(row, col)].config(text=self.machineMark)

def pickMove(self):
    empties = []
    for row in self.degree:
```

```
            for col in self.degree:
                if self.board[row][col] == Empty:
                    empties.append((row, col))
        return random.choice(empties)
```

Finally, checking for an end-of-game state boils down to inspecting rows, columns, and diagonals in the two-dimensional list-of-lists board in this scheme:

```
    def checkDraw(self, board=None):
        board = board or self.board
        for row in board:
            if Empty in row:
                return 0
        return 1 # none empty: draw or win


    def checkWin(self, mark, board=None):
        board = board or self.board
        for row in board:
            if row.count(mark) == self.degree:     # check across
                return 1
        for col in range(self.degree):
            for row in board:                      # check down
                if row[col] != mark:
                    break
            else:
                return 1
        for row in range(self.degree):             # check diag1
            col = row                              # row == col
            if board[row][col] != mark: break
        else:
            return 1
        for row in range(self.degree):             # check diag2
            col = (self.degree-1) - row            # row+col = degree-1
            if board[row][col] != mark: break
        else:
            return 1


    def checkFinish(self):
        if self.checkWin(self.userMark):
            outcome = "You've won!"
        elif self.checkWin(self.machineMark):
            outcome = 'I win again :-)'
        elif self.checkDraw():
            outcome = 'Looks like a draw'
```

Other move-selection code mostly just performs other kinds of analysis on the board data structure or generates new board states to search a tree of moves and countermoves.

You'll also find relatives of these files in the same directory that implement alternative search and move-scoring schemes, different board representations, and so on. For additional background on game scoring and searches in general, consult an AI text. It's fun stuff, but too advanced to cover well in this book.

Where to Go from Here

This concludes the GUI section of this book, but is not an end to its GUI coverage. If you want to learn more about GUIs, be sure to see the Tkinter examples that appear later in this book and are described at the start of this chapter. PyMail, PyCalc, PyForm, and PyTree all provide additional GUI case studies. In the next section of this book, we'll also learn how to build user interfaces that run in web browsers—a very different concept, but another option for simple interface design.

Keep in mind, too, that even if you don't see a GUI example in this book that looks very close to one you need to program, you've already met all the building blocks. Constructing larger GUIs for your application is really just a matter of laying out hierarchical composites of the widgets presented in this part of the text.

For instance, a complex display might be composed as a collection of radio-buttons, listboxes, scales, text fields, menus, and so on—all arranged in frames or grids to achieve the desired appearance. Pop-up top-level windows, as well as independently run GUI programs linked with IPC mechanisms like pipes, signals, and sockets, can further supplement a complex graphical interface.

Moreover, you can implement larger GUI components as Python classes and attach or extend them anywhere you need a similar interface device (see PyEdit for a prime example). With a little creativity, Tkinter's widget set and Python support a virtually unlimited number of layouts.

Beyond this book, see the documentation and books departments at Python's web site, *http://www.python.org*. I would plug Tkinter-related texts here, but I suspect that the offerings in this department will expand during the shelf-life of this book. Finally, if you catch the Tkinter bug, I want to again recommend downloading and experimenting with packages introduced in Chapter 6—especially PMW and PIL. Both add additional tools to the Tkinter arsenal that can make your GUIs more sophisticated with minimal coding.

III

Internet Scripting

This part of the book explores Python's role as a language for programming Internet-based applications, and its library tools that support this role. Along the way, system and GUI tools presented earlier in the book are put to use as well. Because this is a popular Python domain, chapters here cover all fronts:

- Chapter 10, *Network Scripting*. This chapter introduces Internet concepts, presents Python low-level network communication tools such as sockets and select calls, and illustrates common client/server programming techniques in Python.

- Chapter 11, *Client-Side Scripting*. This chapter shows you how your scripts can use Python to access common client-side network protocols such as FTP, email, HTTP, and more.

- Chapter 12, *Server-Side Scripting*. This chapter covers the basics of Python server-side CGI scripts—a kind of program used to implement interactive web sites.

- Chapter 13, *Larger Web Site Examples I*. This chapter demonstrates Python web site implementation techniques such as security, by presenting a web-based email system.

- Chapter 14, *Larger Web Site Examples II*. This chapter presents additional web site techniques including persistent data on the server, by presenting a bug report system.

- Chapter 15, *Advanced Internet Topics*. This chapter gives an overview of Python Internet systems and tools, such as JPython, Active Scripting, Zope, and HTMLgen.

III

Internet Scripting

10

Network Scripting

"Tune in, Log on, and Drop out"

In the last few years, the Internet has virtually exploded onto the mainstream stage. It has rapidly grown from a simple communication device used primarily by academics and researchers into a medium that is now nearly as pervasive as the television and telephone. Social observers have likened the Internet's cultural impact to that of the printing press, and technical observers have suggested that all new software development of interest occurs only on the Internet. Naturally, time will be the final arbiter for such claims, but there is little doubt that the Internet is a major force in society, and one of the main application contexts for modern software systems.

The Internet also happens to be one of the primary application domains for the Python programming language. Given Python and a computer with a socket-based Internet connection, we can write Python scripts to read and send email around the world, fetch web pages from remote sites, transfer files by FTP, program interactive web sites, parse HTML and XML files, and much more, simply by using the Internet modules that ship with Python as standard tools.

In fact, companies all over the world do: Yahoo, Infoseek, Hewlett-Packard, and many others rely on Python's standard tools to power their commercial web sites. Many also build and manage their sites with the *Zope* web application server, which is itself written and customizable in Python. Others use Python to script Java web applications with *JPython* (a.k.a. "Jython")—a system that compiles Python programs to Java bytecode, and exports Java libraries for use in Python scripts.

As the Internet has grown, so too has Python's role as an Internet tool. Python has proven to be well-suited to Internet scripting for some of the very same reasons that make it ideal in other domains. Its modular design and rapid turnaround mix well with the intense demands of Internet development. In this part of the book, we'll find that Python does more than simply support Internet scripts; it also fosters qualities such as productivity and maintainability that are essential to Internet projects of all shapes and sizes.

Internet Scripting Topics

Internet programming entails many topics, so to make the presentation easier to digest, I've split this subject over the next six chapters of this book. This chapter introduces Internet fundamentals and explores sockets, the underlying communications mechanism of the Internet. From there, later chapters move on to discuss the client, the server, web site construction, and more advanced topics.

Each chapter assumes you've read the previous one, but you can generally skip around, especially if you have any experience in the Internet domain. Since these chapters represent a big portion (about a third) of this book at large, the following sections go into a few more details about what we'll be studying.

What we will cover

In conceptual terms, the Internet can roughly be thought of as being composed of multiple functional layers:

Low-level networking layers
> Mechanisms such as the TCP/IP transport mechanism, which deal with transferring bytes between machines, but don't care what they mean

Sockets
> The programmer's interface to the network, which runs on top of physical networking layers like TCP/IP

Higher-level protocols
> Structured communication schemes such as FTP and email, which run on top of sockets and define message formats and standard addresses

Server-side web scripting (CGI)
> Higher-level client/server communication protocols between web browsers and web servers, which also run on top of sockets

Higher-level frameworks and tools
> Third-party systems such as Zope and JPython, which address much larger problem domains

In this chapter and Chapter 11, *Client-Side Scripting*, our main focus is on programming the second and third layers: sockets and higher-level protocols. We'll start this chapter at the bottom, learning about the socket model of network programming. Sockets aren't strictly tied to Internet scripting, but they are presented here because this is their primary role. As we'll see, most of what happens on the Internet happens through sockets, whether you notice or not.

After introducing sockets, the next chapter makes its way up to Python's client-side interfaces to higher-level protocols—things like email and FTP transfers, which run on top of sockets. It turns out that a lot can be done with Python on the client alone, and Chapter 11 will sample the flavor of Python client-side scripting. The next three chapters then go on to present server-side scripting (programs that run on a server computer and are usually invoked by a web browser). Finally, the last chapter in this part, Chapter 15, *Advanced Internet Topics*, briefly introduces even higher-level tools such as JPython and Zope.

Along the way, we will also put to work some of the operating-system and GUI interfaces we've studied earlier (e.g., processes, threads, signals, and Tkinter), and investigate some of the design choices and challenges that the Internet presents.

That last statement merits a few more words. Internet scripting, like GUIs, is one of the sexier application domains for Python. As in GUI work, there is an intangible but instant gratification in seeing a Python Internet program ship information all over the world. On the other hand, by its very nature, network programming imposes speed overheads and user interface limitations. Though it may not be a fashionable stance these days, some applications are still better off not being deployed on the Net. In this part of the book, we will take an honest look at the Net's trade-offs as they arise.

The Internet is also considered by many to be something of an ultimate proof of concept for open source tools. Indeed, much of the Net runs on top of a large number of tools, such as Python, Perl, the Apache web server, the sendmail program, and Linux. Moreover, new tools and technologies for programming the Web sometimes seem to appear faster than developers can absorb.

The good news is that Python's integration focus makes it a natural in such a heterogeneous world. Today, Python programs can be installed as client-side and server-side tools, embedded within HTML code, used as applets and servlets in Java applications, mixed into distributed object systems like CORBA and DCOM, integrated with XML-coded objects, and more. In more general terms, the rationale for using Python in the Internet domain is exactly the same as in any other: Python's emphasis on productivity, portability, and integration make it ideal for writing Internet programs that are open, maintainable, and delivered according to the ever-shrinking schedules in this field.

What we won't cover

Now that I've told you what we will cover in this book, I should also mention what we won't cover. Like Tkinter, the Internet is a large domain, and this part of the book is mostly an introduction to core concepts and representative tasks, not an exhaustive reference. There are simply too many Python Internet modules to include each in this text, but the examples here should help you understand the library manual entries for modules we don't have time to cover.

I also want to point out that higher-level tools like JPython and Zope are large systems in their own right, and they are best dealt with in more dedicated documents. Because books on both topics are likely to appear soon, we'll merely scratch their surfaces here. Moreover, this book says almost nothing about lower-level networking layers such as TCP/IP. If you're curious about what happens on the Internet at the bit-and-wire level, consult a good networking text for more details.

Running examples in this part of the book

Internet scripts generally imply execution contexts that earlier examples in this book have not. That is, it usually takes a bit more to run programs that talk over networks. Here are a few pragmatic notes about this part's examples up front:

- You don't need to download extra packages to run examples in this part of the book. Except in Chapter 15, all of the examples we'll see are based on the standard set of Internet-related modules that come with Python (they are installed in Python's library directory).

- You don't need a state-of-the-art network link or an account on a web server to run most of the examples in this and the following chapters; a PC and dial-up Internet account will usually suffice. We'll study configuration details along the way, but client-side programs are fairly simple to run.

- You don't need an account on a web server machine to *run* the server-side scripts in later chapters (they can be run by any web browser connected to the Net), but you will need such an account to *change* these scripts.

When a Python script opens an Internet connection (with the `socket` or protocol modules), Python will happily use whatever Internet link exists on your machine, be that a dedicated T1 line, a DSL line, or a simple modem. For instance, opening a socket on a Windows PC automatically initiates processing to create a dial-up connection to your Internet Service Provider if needed (on my laptop, a Windows modem connection dialog automatically pops up). In other words, if you have a way to connect to the Net, you likely can run programs in this chapter.

Moreover, as long as your machine supports sockets, you probably can run many of the examples here even if you have no Internet connection at all. As we'll see, a machine name "localhost" or "" usually means the local computer itself. This allows you to test both the client and server sides of a dialog on the same computer without connecting to the Net. For example, you can run both socket-based clients and servers locally on a Windows PC without ever going out to the Net.

Some later examples assume that a particular kind of server is running on a server machine (e.g., FTP, POP, SMTP), but client-side scripts work on any Internet-aware machine with Python installed. Server-side examples in Chapters 12, 13, and 14 require more: you'll need a web server account to code CGI scripts, and you must download advanced third-party systems like JPython and Zope separately (or find them on this book's CD).

In the Beginning There Was Grail

Besides creating the Python language, Guido van Rossum also wrote a World Wide Web browser in Python, named (appropriately enough) Grail. Grail was partly developed as a demonstration of Python's capabilities. It allows users to browse the Web much like Netscape or Internet Explorer, but can also be programmed with Grail applets—Python/Tkinter programs downloaded from a server when accessed and run on the client by the browser. Grail applets work much like Java applets in more widespread browsers (more on applets in Chapter 15).

Grail is no longer under development and is mostly used for research purposes today. But Python still reaps the benefits of the Grail project, in the form of a rich set of Internet tools. To write a full-featured web browser, you need to support a wide variety of Internet protocols, and Guido packaged support for all of these as standard library modules that are now shipped with the Python language.

Because of this legacy, Python now includes standard support for Usenet news (NNTP), email processing (POP, SMTP, IMAP), file transfers (FTP), web pages and interactions (HTTP, URLs, HTML, CGI), and other commonly used protocols (Telnet, Gopher, etc.). Python scripts can connect to all of these Internet components by simply importing the associated library module.

Since Grail, additional tools have been added to Python's library for parsing XML files, OpenSSL secure sockets, and more. But much of Python's Internet support can be traced back to the Grail browser—another example of Python's support for code reuse at work. At this writing, you can still find the Grail at *http://www.python.org*.

Plumbing the Internet

Unless you've been living in a cave for the last decade, you are probably already familiar with what the Internet is about, at least from a user's perspective. Functionally, we use it as a communication and information medium, by exchanging email, browsing web pages, transferring files, and so on. Technically, the Internet consists of many layers of abstraction and device—from the actual wires used to send bits across the world to the web browser that grabs and renders those bits into text, graphics, and audio on your computer.

In this book, we are primarily concerned with the programmer's interface to the Internet. This too consists of multiple layers: *sockets*, which are programmable interfaces to the low-level connections between machines, and standard *protocols*, which add structure to discussions carried out over sockets. Let's briefly look at each of these layers in the abstract before jumping into programming details.

The Socket Layer

In simple terms, sockets are a programmable interface to network connections between computers. They also form the basis, and low-level "plumbing," of the Internet itself: all of the familiar higher-level Net protocols like FTP, web pages, and email, ultimately occur over sockets. Sockets are also sometimes called *communications endpoints* because they are the portals through which programs send and receive bytes during a conversation.

To programmers, sockets take the form of a handful of calls available in a library. These socket calls know how to send bytes between machines, using lower-level operations such as the TCP network transmission control protocol. At the bottom, TCP knows how to transfer bytes, but doesn't care what those bytes mean. For the purposes of this text, we will generally ignore how bytes sent to sockets are physically transferred. To understand sockets fully, though, we need to know a bit about how computers are named.

Machine identifiers

Suppose for just a moment that you wish to have a telephone conversation with someone halfway across the world. In the real world, you would probably either need that person's telephone number, or a directory that can be used to look up the number from his or her name (e.g., a telephone book). The same is true on the Internet: before a script can have a conversation with another computer somewhere in cyberspace, it must first know that other computer's number or name.

Luckily, the Internet defines standard ways to name both a remote machine, and a service provided by that machine. Within a script, the computer program to be contacted through a socket is identified by supplying a pair of values—the machine name, and a specific port number on that machine:

Machine names

A machine name may take the form of either a string of numbers separated by dots called an *IP address* (e.g., 166.93.218.100), or a more legible form known as a *domain name* (e.g., *starship.python.net*). Domain names are automatically mapped into their dotted numeric address equivalent when used, by something called a domain name server—a program on the Net that serves the same purpose as your local telephone directory assistance service.

Port numbers

A port number is simply an agreed-upon numeric identifier for a given conversation. Because computers on the Net can support a variety of services, port numbers are used to name a particular conversation on a given machine. For two machines to talk over the Net, both must associate sockets with the same machine name and port number when initiating network connections.

The combination of a machine name and a port number uniquely identifies every dialog on the Net. For instance, an Internet Service Provider's computer may provide many kinds of services for customers—web pages, Telnet, FTP transfers, email, and so on. Each service on the machine is assigned a unique port number to which requests may be sent. To get web pages from a web server, programs need to specify both the web server's IP or domain name, and the port number on which the server listens for web page requests.

If this all sounds a bit strange, it may help to think of it in old-fashioned terms. In order to have a telephone conversation with someone within a company, for example, you usually need to dial both the company's phone number, as well as the extension of the person you want to reach. Moreover, if you don't know the company's number, you can probably find it by looking up the company's name in a phone book. It's almost the same on the Net—machine names identify a collection of services (like a company), port numbers identify an individual service within a particular machine (like an extension), and domain names are mapped to IP numbers by domain name servers (like a phone book).

When programs use sockets to communicate in specialized ways with another machine (or with other processes on the same machine), they need to avoid using a port number reserved by a standard protocol—numbers in the range of 0–1023—but we first need to discuss protocols to understand why.

The Protocol Layer

Although sockets form the backbone of the Internet, much of the activity that happens on the Net is programmed with *protocols*,* which are higher-level message models that run on top of sockets. In short, Internet protocols define a structured way to talk over sockets. They generally standardize both message formats and socket port numbers:

- *Message formats* provide structure for the bytes exchanged over sockets during conversations.

- *Port numbers* are reserved numeric identifiers for the underlying sockets over which messages are exchanged.

Raw sockets are still commonly used in many systems, but it is perhaps more common (and generally easier) to communicate with one of the standard higher-level Internet protocols.

Port number rules

Technically speaking, socket port numbers can be any 16-bit integer value between 0 and 65,535. However, to make it easier for programs to locate the standard protocols, port numbers in the range of 0–1023 are reserved and preassigned to the standard higher-level protocols. Table 10-1 lists the ports reserved for many of the standard protocols; each gets one or more preassigned numbers from the reserved range.

Table 10-1. Port Numbers Reserved for Common Protocols

Protocol	Common Function	Port Number	Python Module
HTTP	Web pages	80	`httplib`
NNTP	Usenet news	119	`nntplib`
FTP data default	File transfers	20	`ftplib`
FTP control	File transfers	21	`ftplib`
SMTP	Sending email	25	`smtplib`
POP3	Fetching email	110	`poplib`
IMAP4	Fetching email	143	`imaplib`
Finger	Informational	79	n/a
Telnet	Command lines	23	`telnetlib`
Gopher	Document transfers	70	`gopherlib`

---

* Some books also use the term *protocol* to refer to lower-level transport schemes such as TCP. In this book, we use protocol to refer to higher-level structures built on top of sockets; see a networking text if you are curious about what happens at lower levels.

Clients and servers

To socket programmers, the standard protocols mean that port numbers 0–1023 are off-limits to scripts, unless they really mean to use one of the higher-level protocols. This is both by standard and by common sense. A Telnet program, for instance, can start a dialog with any Telnet-capable machine by connecting to its port 23; without preassigned port numbers, each server might install Telnet on a different port. Similarly, web sites listen for page requests from browsers on port 80 by standard; if they did not, you might have to know and type the HTTP port number of every site you visit while surfing the Net.

By defining standard port numbers for services, the Net naturally gives rise to a *client/server architecture*. On one side of a conversation, machines that support standard protocols run a set of perpetually running programs that listen for connection requests on the reserved ports. On the other end of a dialog, other machines contact those programs to use the services they export.

We usually call the perpetually running listener program a *server* and the connecting program a *client*. Let's use the familiar web browsing model as an example. As shown in Table 10-1, the HTTP protocol used by the Web allows clients and servers to talk over sockets on port 80:

Server

A machine that hosts web sites usually runs a web server program that constantly listens for incoming connection requests, on a socket bound to port 80. Often, the server itself does nothing but watch for requests on its port perpetually; handling requests is delegated to spawned processes or threads.

Clients

Programs that wish to talk to this server specify the server machine's name and port 80 to initiate a connection. For web servers, typical clients are web browsers like Internet Explorer or Netscape, but any script can open a client-side connection on port 80 to fetch web pages from the server.

In general, many clients may connect to a server over sockets, whether it implements a standard protocol or something more specific to a given application. And in some applications, the notion of client and server is blurred—programs can also pass bytes between each other more as *peers* than as master and subordinate. For the purpose of this book, though, we usually call programs that listen on sockets servers, and those that connect, clients. We also sometimes call the machines that these programs run on server and client (e.g., a computer on which a web server program runs may be called a web server machine, too), but this has more to do with the physical than the functional.

Protocol structures

Functionally, protocols may accomplish a familiar task like reading email or post-ing a Usenet newsgroup message, but they ultimately consist of message bytes sent over sockets. The structure of those message bytes varies from protocol to protocol, is hidden by the Python library, and is mostly beyond the scope of this book, but a few general words may help demystify the protocol layer.

Some protocols may define the contents of messages sent over sockets; others may specify the sequence of control messages exchanged during conversations. By defining regular patterns of communication, protocols make communication more robust. They can also minimize deadlock conditions—machines waiting for mes-sages that never arrive.

For example, the FTP protocol prevents deadlock by conversing over *two* sockets: one for control messages only, and one to transfer file data. An FTP server listens for control messages (e.g., "send me a file") on one port, and transfers file data over another. FTP clients open socket connections to the server machine's control port, send requests, and send or receive file data over a socket connected to a data port on the server machine. FTP also defines standard message structures passed between client and server. The control message used to request a file, for instance, must follow a standard format.

Python's Internet Library Modules

If all of this sounds horribly complex, cheer up: Python's standard protocol mod-ules handle all the details. For example, the Python library's `ftplib` module man-ages all the socket and message-level handshaking implied by the FTP protocol. Scripts that import `ftplib` have access to a much higher-level interface for FTPing files and can be largely ignorant of both the underlying FTP protocol, and the sockets over which it runs.*

In fact, each supported protocol is represented by a standard Python module file with a name of the form *xxxlib.py*, where *xxx* is replaced by the protocol's name, in lowercase. The last column in Table 10-1 gives the module name for protocol standard modules. For instance, FTP is supported by module file *ftplib.py*. More-over, within the protocol modules, the top-level interface object is usually the name of the protocol. So, for instance, to start an FTP session in a Python script,

---

* Since Python is an open source system, you can read the source code of the `ftplib` module if you are curious about how the underlying protocol actually works. See file *ftplib.py* in the standard source library directory in your machine. Its code is complex (since it must format messages and manage two sockets), but with the other standard Internet protocol modules, it is a good example of low-level socket programming.

you run `import ftplib` and pass appropriate parameters in a call to `ftplib.FTP()`; for Telnet, create a `telnetlib.Telnet()`.

In addition to the protocol implementation modules in Table 10-1, Python's standard library also contains modules for parsing and handling data once it has been transferred over sockets or protocols. Table 10-2 lists some of the more commonly used modules in this category.

Table 10-2. Common Internet-Related Standard Modules

Python Modules	Utility
`socket`	Low-level network communications support (TCP/IP, UDP, etc.).
`cgi`	Server-side CGI script support: parse input stream, escape HTML text, etc.
`urllib`	Fetch web pages from their addresses (URLs), escape URL text
`httplib, ftplib, nntplib`	HTTP (web), FTP (file transfer), and NNTP (news) protocol modules
`poplib, imaplib, smtplib`	POP, IMAP (mail fetch), and SMTP (mail send) protocol modules
`telnetlib, gopherlib`	Telnet and Gopher protocol modules
`htmllib, sgmllib, xmllib`	Parse web page contents (HTML, SGML, and XML documents)
`xdrlib`	Encode binary data portably (also see the `struct` and `socket` modules)
`rfc822`	Parse email-style header lines
`mhlib, mailbox`	Process complex mail messages and mailboxes
`mimetools, mimify`	Handle MIME-style message bodies
`multifile`	Read messages with multiple parts
`uu, binhex, base64, binascii, quopri`	Encode and decode binary (or other) data transmitted as text
`urlparse`	Parse URL string into components
`SocketServer`	Framework for general net servers
`BaseHTTPServer`	Basic HTTP server implementation
`SimpleHTTPServer, CGIHTTPServer`	Specific HTTP web server request handler modules
`rexec, bastion`	Restricted code execution modes

We will meet many of this table's modules in the next few chapters of this book, but not all. The modules demonstrated are representative, but as always, be sure to see Python's standard Library Reference Manual for more complete and up-to-date lists and details.

More on Protocol Standards

If you want the full story on protocols and ports, at this writing you can find a comprehensive list of all ports reserved for protocols, or registered as used by various common systems, by searching the web pages maintained by the Internet Engineering Task Force (IETF) and the Internet Assigned Numbers Authority (IANA). The IETF is the organization responsible for maintaining web protocols and standards. The IANA is the central coordinator for the assignment of unique parameter values for Internet protocols. Another standards body, the W3 (for WWW), also maintains relevant documents. See these web pages for more details:

> *http://www.ietf.org*
> *http://www.iana.org/numbers.html*
> *http://www.isi.edu/in-notes/iana/assignments/port-numbers*
> *http://www.w3.org*

It's not impossible that more recent repositories for standard protocol specifications will arise during this book's shelf-life, but the IETF web site will likely be the main authority for some time to come. If you do look, though, be warned that the details are, well, detailed. Because Python's protocol modules hide most of the socket and messaging complexity documented in the protocol standards, you usually don't need to memorize these documents to get web work done in Python.

Socket Programming

Now that we've seen how sockets figure into the Internet picture, let's move on to explore the tools that Python provides for programming sockets with Python scripts. This section shows you how to use the Python socket interface to perform low-level network communications; in later chapters, we will instead use one of the higher-level protocol modules that hide underlying sockets.

The basic socket interface in Python is the standard library's socket module. Like the os POSIX module, Python's socket module is just a thin wrapper (interface layer) over the underlying C library's socket calls. Like Python files, it's also *object-based*: methods of a socket object implemented by this module call out to the corresponding C library's operations after data conversions. The socket module also includes tools for converting bytes to a standard network ordering, wrapping socket objects in simple file objects, and more. It supports socket programming on any machine that supports BSD-style sockets—MS Windows, Linux, Unix, etc.— and so provides a portable socket interface.

Socket Basics

To create a connection between machines, Python programs import the `socket` module, create a socket object, and call the object's methods to establish connections and send and receive data. Socket object methods map directly to socket calls in the C library. For example, the script in Example 10-1 implements a program that simply listens for a connection on a socket, and echoes back over a socket whatever it receives through that socket, adding `'Echo=>'` string prefixes.

Example 10-1. PP2E\Internet\Sockets\echo-server.py

```
#########################################################
# Server side: open a socket on a port, listen for
# a message from a client, and send an echo reply;
# this is a simple one-shot listen/reply per client,
# but it goes into an infinite loop to listen for
# more clients as long as this server script runs;
#########################################################

from socket import *                 # get socket constructor and constants
myHost = ''                          # server machine, '' means local host
myPort = 50007                       # listen on a non-reserved port number

sockobj = socket(AF_INET, SOCK_STREAM)       # make a TCP socket object
sockobj.bind((myHost, myPort))               # bind it to server port number
sockobj.listen(5)                            # listen, allow 5 pending connects

while 1:                                     # listen until process killed
    connection, address = sockobj.accept()   # wait for next client connect
    print 'Server connected by', address     # connection is a new socket
    while 1:
        data = connection.recv(1024)         # read next line on client socket
        if not data: break                   # send a reply line to the client
        connection.send('Echo=>' + data)     # until eof when socket closed
    connection.close()
```

As mentioned earlier, we usually call programs like this that listen for incoming connections *servers* because they provide a service that can be accessed at a given machine and port on the Internet. Programs that connect to such a server to access its service are generally called *clients*. Example 10-2 shows a simple client implemented in Python.

Example 10-2. PP2E\Internet\Sockets\echo-client.py

```
#########################################################
# Client side: use sockets to send data to the server, and
# print server's reply to each message line; 'localhost'
# means that the server is running on the same machine as
# the client, which lets us test client and server on one
# machine;  to test over the Internet, run a server on a remote
# machine, and set serverHost or argv[1] to machine's domain
```

Example 10-2. PP2E\Internet\Sockets\echo-client.py (continued)

```
# name or IP addr;  Python sockets are a portable BSD socket
# interface, with object methods for standard socket calls;
############################################################

import sys
from socket import *              # portable socket interface plus constants
serverHost = 'localhost'          # server name, or: 'starship.python.net'
serverPort = 50007                # non-reserved port used by the server

message = ['Hello network world']            # default text to send to server
if len(sys.argv) > 1:
    serverHost = sys.argv[1]                 # or server from cmd line arg 1
    if len(sys.argv) > 2:                    # or text from cmd line args 2..n
        message = sys.argv[2:]               # one message for each arg listed

sockobj = socket(AF_INET, SOCK_STREAM)       # make a TCP/IP socket object
sockobj.connect((serverHost, serverPort))    # connect to server machine and port

for line in message:
    sockobj.send(line)                       # send line to server over socket
    data = sockobj.recv(1024)                # receive line from server: up to 1k
    print 'Client received:', `data`

sockobj.close()                              # close socket to send eof to server
```

Server socket calls

Before we see these programs in action, let's take a minute to explain how this client and server do their stuff. Both are fairly simple examples of socket scripts, but they illustrate common call patterns of most socket-based programs. In fact, this is boilerplate code: most socket programs generally make the same socket calls that our two scripts do, so let's step through the important points of these scripts line by line.

Programs such as Example 10-1 that provide services for other programs with sockets generally start out by following this sequence of calls:

sockobj = socket(AF_INET, SOCK_STREAM)

Uses the Python socket module to create a TCP socket object. The names AF_INET and SOCK_STREAM are preassigned variables defined by and imported form the socket module; using them in combination means "create a TCP/IP socket," the standard communication device for the Internet. More specifically, AF_INET means the IP address protocol, and SOCK_STREAM means the TCP transfer protocol.

If you use other names in this call, you can instead create things like UDP connectionless sockets (use SOCK_DGRAM second) and Unix domain sockets on the local machine (use AF_UNIX first), but we won't do so in this book. See the Python library manual for details on these and other socket module options.

```
sockobj.bind((myHost, myPort))
```
Associates the socket object to an address—for IP addresses, we pass a server machine name and port number on that machine. This is where the server identifies the machine and port associated with the socket. In server programs, the hostname is typically an empty string (""), which means the machine that the script runs on and the port is a number outside the range 0–1023 (which is reserved for standard protocols, described earlier). Note that each unique socket dialog you support must have its own port number; if you try to open a socket on a port already in use, Python will raise an exception. Also notice the nested parenthesis in this call—for the `AF_INET` address protocol socket here, we pass the host/port socket address to `bind` as a two-item tuple object (pass a string for `AF_UNIX`). Technically, `bind` takes a tuple of values appropriate for the type of socket created (but see the next Note box about the older and deprecated convention of passing values to this function as distinct arguments).

```
sockobj.listen(5)
```
Starts listening for incoming client connections and allows for a backlog of up to five pending requests. The value passed sets the number of incoming client requests queued by the operating system before new requests are denied (which only happens if a server isn't fast enough to process requests before the queues fill up). A value of 5 is usually enough for most socket-based programs; the value must be at least 1.

At this point, the server is ready to accept connection requests from client programs running on remote machines (or the same machine), and falls into an infinite loop waiting for them to arrive:

```
connection, address = sockobj.accept()
```
Waits for the next client connection request to occur; when it does, the `accept` call returns a brand new socket object over which data can be transferred from and to the connected client. Connections are accepted on `sockobj`, but communication with a client happens on `connection`, the new socket. This call actually returns a two-item tuple—`address` is the connecting client's Internet address. We can call `accept` more than one time, to service multiple client connections; that's why each call returns a new, distinct socket for talking to a particular client.

Once we have a client connection, we fall into another loop to receive data from the client in blocks of 1024 bytes at a time, and echo each block back to the client:

```
data = connection.recv(1024)
```
Reads at most 1024 more bytes of the next message sent from a client (i.e., coming across the network), and returns it to the script as a string. We get back an empty string when the client has finished—end-of-file is triggered when the client closes its end of the socket.

```
connection.send('Echo=>' + data)
```
> Sends the latest data block back to the client program, prepending the string `'Echo=>'` to it first. The client program can then **recv** what we **send** here— the next reply line.

```
connection.close()
```
> Shuts down the connection with this particular client.

After talking with a given client, the server goes back to its infinite loop, and waits for the next client connection request.

Client socket calls

On the other hand, client programs like the one shown in Example 10-2 follow simpler call sequences. The main thing to keep in mind is that the client and server must specify the same port number when opening their sockets, and the client must identify the machine on which the server is running (in our scripts, server and client agree to use port number 50007 for their conversation, outside the standard protocol range):

```
sockobj = socket(AF_INET, SOCK_STREAM)
```
> Creates a Python socket object in the client program, just like the server.

```
sockobj.connect((serverHost, serverPort))
```
> Opens a connection to the machine and port on which the server program is listening for client connections. This is where the client specifies the name of the service to be contacted. In the client, we can either specify the name of the remote machine as a domain name (e.g., *starship.python.net*) or numeric IP address. We can also give the server name as *localhost* to specify that the server program is running on the same machine as the client; that comes in handy for debugging servers without having to connect to the Net. And again, the client's port number must match the server's exactly. Note the nested parentheses again—just as in server **bind** calls, we really pass the server's host/port address to **connect** in a tuple object.

Once the client establishes a connection to the server, it falls into a loop sending a message one line at a time and printing whatever the server sends back after each line is sent:

```
sockobj.send(line)
```
> Transfers the next message line to the server over the socket.

```
data = sockobj.recv(1024)
```
> Reads the next reply line sent by the server program. Technically, this reads up to 1024 bytes of the next reply message and returns it as a string.

```
sockobj.close()
```
> Closes the connection with the server, sending it the end-of-file signal.

And that's it. The server exchanges one or more lines of text with each client that connects. The operating system takes care of locating remote machines, routing bytes sent between programs across the Internet, and (with TCP) making sure that our messages arrive intact. That involves a lot of processing, too—our strings may ultimately travel around the world, crossing phone wires, satellite links, and more along the way. But we can be happily ignorant of what goes on beneath the socket call layer when programming in Python.

In older Python code, you may see the `AF_INET` server address passed to the server-side `bind` and client-side `connect` socket methods as two distinct arguments, instead of a two-item tuple:

```
soc.bind(host,port)      vs  soc.bind((host,port))
soc.connect(host,port)   vs  soc.connect((host,port))
```

This two-argument form is now deprecated, and only worked at all due to a shortcoming in earlier Python releases (unfortunately, the Python library manual's socket example used the two-argument form too!). The tuple server address form is preferred, and, in a rare Python break with full backward-compatibility, will likely be the only one that will work in future Python releases.

Running socket programs locally

Okay, let's put this client and server to work. There are two ways to run these scripts—either on the same machine or on two different machines. To run the client and the server on the same machine, bring up two command-line consoles on your computer, start the server program in one, and run the client repeatedly in the other. The server keeps running and responds to requests made each time you run the client script in the other window.

For instance, here is the text that shows up in the MS-DOS console window where I've started the server script:

```
C:\...\PP2E\Internet\Sockets>python echo-server.py
Server connected by ('127.0.0.1', 1025)
Server connected by ('127.0.0.1', 1026)
Server connected by ('127.0.0.1', 1027)
```

The output here gives the address (machine IP name and port number) of each connecting client. Like most servers, this one runs perpetually, listening for client connection requests. This one receives three, but I have to show you the client window's text for you to understand what this means:

```
C:\...\PP2E\Internet\Sockets>python echo-client.py
Client received: 'Echo=>Hello network world'

C:\...\PP2E\Internet\Sockets>python echo-client.py localhost spam Spam SPAM
Client received: 'Echo=>spam'
```

```
Client received: 'Echo=>Spam'
Client received: 'Echo=>SPAM'

C:\...\PP2E\Internet\Sockets>python echo-client.py localhost Shrubbery
Client received: 'Echo=>Shrubbery'
```

Here, I ran the client script three times, while the server script kept running in the other window. Each client connected to the server, sent it a message of one or more lines of text, and read back the server's reply—an echo of each line of text sent from the client. And each time a client is run, a new connection message shows up in the server's window (that's why we got three).

It's important to notice that clients and server are running on the *same machine* here (a Windows PC). The server and client agree on port number, but use machine names "" and "localhost" respectively, to refer to the computer that they are running on. In fact, there is no Internet connection to speak of. Sockets also work well as cross-program communications tools on a single machine.

Running socket programs remotely

To make these scripts talk over the Internet instead of on a single machine, we have to do some extra work to run the server on a different computer. First, upload the server's source file to a remote machine where you have an account and a Python. Here's how I do it with FTP; your server name and upload interface details may vary, and there are other ways to copy files to a computer (e.g., email, web-page post forms, etc.):*

```
C:\...\PP2E\Internet\Sockets>ftp starship.python.net
Connected to starship.python.net.
User (starship.python.net:(none)): lutz
331 Password required for lutz.
Password:
230 User lutz logged in.
ftp> put echo-server.py
200 PORT command successful.
150 Opening ASCII mode data connection for echo-server.py.
226 Transfer complete.
ftp: 1322 bytes sent in 0.06Seconds 22.03Kbytes/sec.
ftp> quit
```

Once you have the server program loaded on the other computer, you need to run it there. Connect to that computer and start the server program. I usually tel-net into my server machine and start the server program as a perpetually running

---

* The FTP command is standard on Windows machines and most others. On Windows, simply type it in a DOS console box to connect to an FTP server (or start your favorite FTP program); on Linux, type the FTP command in an xterm window. You'll need to supply your account name and password to connect to a non-anonymous FTP site. For anonymous FTP, use "anonymous" for the username and your email address for the password (anonymous FTP sites are generally limited).

process from the command line.* The & syntax in Unix/Linux shells can be used to run the server script in the background; we could also make the server directly executable with a #! line and a *chmod* command (see Chapter 2, *System Tools*, for details). Here is the text that shows up in a Window on my PC that is running a Telnet session connected to the Linux server where I have an account (less a few deleted informational lines):

```
C:\...\PP2E\Internet\Sockets>telnet starship.python.net
Red Hat Linux release 6.2 (Zoot)
Kernel 2.2.14-5.0smp on a 2-processor i686
login: lutz
Password:
[lutz@starship lutz]$ python echo-server.py &
[1] 4098
```

Now that the server is listening for connections on the Net, run the client on your local computer multiple times again. This time, the client runs on a different machine than the server, so we pass in the server's domain or IP name as a client command-line argument. The server still uses a machine name of "" because it always listens on whatever machine it runs upon. Here is what shows up in the server's Telnet window:

```
[lutz@starship lutz]$ Server connected by ('166.93.68.61', 1037)
Server connected by ('166.93.68.61', 1040)
Server connected by ('166.93.68.61', 1043)
Server connected by ('166.93.68.61', 1050)
```

And here is what appears in the MS-DOS console box where I run the client. A "connected by" message appears in the server Telnet window each time the client script is run in the client window:

```
C:\...\PP2E\Internet\Sockets>python echo-client.py starship.python.net
Client received: 'Echo=>Hello network world'

C:\...\PP2E\Internet\Sockets>python echo-client.py starship.python.net ni Ni NI
Client received: 'Echo=>ni'
Client received: 'Echo=>Ni'
Client received: 'Echo=>NI'

C:\...\PP2E\Internet\Sockets>python echo-client.py starship.python.net Shrubbery
Client received: 'Echo=>Shrubbery'

C:\...\PP2E\Internet\Sockets>ping starship.python.net
Pinging starship.python.net [208.185.174.112] with 32 bytes of data:
Reply from 208.185.174.112: bytes=32 time=311ms TTL=246
ctrl-C
C:\...\PP2E\Internet\Sockets>python echo-client.py 208.185.174.112 Does she?
Client received: 'Echo=>Does'
Client received: 'Echo=>she?'
```

---

* Telnet is a standard command on Windows and Linux machines, too. On Windows, type it at a DOS console prompt or in the Start/Run dialog box (it can also be started via a clickable icon). Telnet usually runs in a window of its own.

The "ping" command can be used to get an IP address for a machine's domain name; either machine name form can be used to connect in the client. This output is perhaps a bit understated—a lot is happening under the hood. The client, running on my Windows laptop, connects with and talks to the server program running on a Linux machine perhaps thousands of miles away. It all happens about as fast as when client and server both run on the laptop, and it uses the same library calls; only the server name passed to clients differs.

Socket pragmatics

Before we move on, there are three practical usage details you should know. First of all, you can run the client and server like this on any two Internet-aware machines where Python is installed. Of course, to run clients and server on different computers, you need both a live Internet connection and access to another machine on which to run the server. You don't need a big, expensive Internet link, though—a simple modem and dialup Internet account will do for clients. When sockets are opened, Python is happy to use whatever connectivity you have, be it a dedicated T1 line, or a dialup modem account.

On my laptop PC, for instance, Windows automatically dials out to my ISP when clients are started or when Telnet server sessions are opened. In this book's examples, server-side programs that run remotely are executed on a machine called *starship.python.net*. If you don't have an account of your own on such a server, simply run client and server examples on the same machine, as shown earlier; all you need then is a computer that allows sockets, and most do.

Secondly, the socket module generally raises exceptions if you ask for something invalid. For instance, trying to connect to a nonexistent server (or unreachable servers, if you have no Internet link) fails:

```
C:\...\PP2E\Internet\Sockets>python echo-client.py www.nonesuch.com hello
Traceback (innermost last):
  File "echo-client.py", line 24, in ?
    sockobj.connect((serverHost, serverPort))   # connect to server machine...
  File "<string>", line 1, in connect
socket.error: (10061, 'winsock error')
```

Finally, also be sure to kill the server process before restarting it again, or else the port number will be still in use, and you'll get another exception:

```
[lutz@starship uploads]$ ps -x
  PID TTY     STAT   TIME COMMAND
 5570 pts/0   S      0:00 -bash
 5570 pts/0   S      0:00 -bash
 5633 pts/0   S      0:00 python echo-server.py
 5634 pts/0   R      0:00 ps -x
```

```
[lutz@starship uploads]$ python echo-server.py
Traceback (most recent call last):
  File "echo-server.py", line 14, in ?
    sockobj.bind((myHost, myPort))                    # bind it to server port number
socket.error: (98, 'Address already in use')
```

Under Python 1.5.2, a series of Ctrl-C's will kill the server on Linux (be sure to type *fg* to bring it to the foreground first if started with an &):

```
[lutz@starship uploads]$ python echo-server.py
ctrl-c
Traceback (most recent call last):
  File "echo-server.py", line 18, in ?
    connection, address = sockobj.accept()   # wait for next client connect
KeyboardInterrupt
```

A Ctrl-C kill key combination *won't* kill the server on my Windows machine, however. To kill the perpetually running server process running locally on Windows, you may need to type a Ctrl-Alt-Delete key combination, and then end the Python task by selecting it in the process listbox that appears. You can usually also kill a server on Linux with a `kill -9 pid` shell command if it is running in another window or in the background, but Ctrl-C is less typing.

Spawning clients in parallel

To see how the server handles the load, let's fire up eight copies of the client script in parallel using the script in Example 10-3 (see the end of Chapter 3, *Parallel System Tools*, for details on the `launchmodes` module used here to spawn clients).

Example 10-3. PP2E\Internet\Sockets\testecho.py

```
import sys, string
from PP2E.launchmodes import QuietPortableLauncher

numclients = 8
def start(cmdline): QuietPortableLauncher(cmdline, cmdline)()

# start('echo-server.py')              # spawn server locally if not yet started

args = string.join(sys.argv[1:], ' ')  # pass server name if running remotely
for i in range(numclients):
    start('echo-client.py %s' % args)  # spawn 8? clients to test the server
```

To run this script, pass no arguments to talk to a server listening on port 50007 on the local machine; pass a real machine name to talk to a server running remotely. On Windows, the clients' output is discarded when spawned from this script:

```
C:\...\PP2E\Internet\Sockets>python testecho.py

C:\...\PP2E\Internet\Sockets>python testecho.py starship.python.net
```

If the spawned clients connect to a server run *locally*, connection messages show up in the server's window on the local machine:

```
C:\...\PP2E\Internet\Sockets>python echo-server.py
Server connected by ('127.0.0.1', 1283)
Server connected by ('127.0.0.1', 1284)
Server connected by ('127.0.0.1', 1285)
Server connected by ('127.0.0.1', 1286)
Server connected by ('127.0.0.1', 1287)
Server connected by ('127.0.0.1', 1288)
Server connected by ('127.0.0.1', 1289)
Server connected by ('127.0.0.1', 1290)
```

If the server is running *remotely*, the client connection messages instead appear in the window displaying the Telnet connection to the remote computer:

```
[lutz@starship lutz]$ python echo-server.py
Server connected by ('166.93.68.61', 1301)
Server connected by ('166.93.68.61', 1302)
Server connected by ('166.93.68.61', 1308)
Server connected by ('166.93.68.61', 1309)
Server connected by ('166.93.68.61', 1313)
Server connected by ('166.93.68.61', 1314)
Server connected by ('166.93.68.61', 1307)
Server connected by ('166.93.68.61', 1312)
```

Keep in mind, however, that this works for our simple scripts only because the server doesn't take a long time to respond to each client's requests—it can get back to the top of the server script's outer `while` loop in time to process the next incoming client. If it could not, we would probably need to change the server to handle each client in *parallel*, or some might be denied a connection. Technically, client connections would fail after five clients are already waiting for the server's attention, as specified in the server's `listen` call. We'll see how servers can handle multiple clients robustly in the next section.

Talking to reserved ports

It's also important to know that this client and server engage in a proprietary sort of discussion, and so use a port number 50007 outside the range reserved for standard protocols (0–1023). There's nothing preventing a client from opening a socket on one of these special ports, however. For instance, the following client-side code connects to programs listening on the standard email, FTP, and HTTP web server ports on three different server machines:

```
C:\...\PP2E\Internet\Sockets>python
>>> from socket import *
>>> sock = socket(AF_INET, SOCK_STREAM)
>>> sock.connect(('mail.rmi.net', 110))          # talk to RMI POP mail server
>>> print sock.recv(40)
+OK Cubic Circle's v1.31 1998/05/13 POP3
>>> sock.close()
```

```
>>> sock = socket(AF_INET, SOCK_STREAM)
>>> sock.connect(('www.python.org', 21))          # talk to Python FTP server
>>> print sock.recv(40)
220 python.org FTP server (Version wu-2.
>>> sock.close()

>>> sock = socket(AF_INET, SOCK_STREAM)
>>> sock.connect(('starship.python.net', 80))     # starship HTTP web server
>>> sock.send('GET /\r\n')                         # fetch root web page
7
>>> sock.recv(60)
'<!DOCTYPE HTML PUBLIC "-//W3C//DTD HTML 3.2 Final//EN">\012<HTM'
>>> sock.recv(60)
'L>\012 <HEAD>\012  <TITLE>Starship Slowly Recovering</TITLE>\012 </HE'
```

If we know how to interpret the output returned by these ports' servers, we could use raw sockets like this to fetch email, transfer files, and grab web pages and invoke server-side scripts. Fortunately, though, we don't have to worry about all the underlying details—Python's `poplib`, `ftplib`, `httplib`, and `urllib` modules provide higher-level interfaces for talking to servers on these ports. Other Python protocol modules do the same for other standard ports (e.g., NNTP, Telnet, and so on). We'll meet some of these client-side protocol modules in the next chapter.[*]

By the way, it's okay to open client-side connections on reserved ports like this, but you can't install your own *server-side* scripts for these ports unless you have special permission:

```
[lutz@starship uploads]$ python
>>> from socket import *
>>> sock = socket(AF_INET, SOCK_STREAM)
>>> sock.bind(('', 80))
Traceback (most recent call last):
  File "<stdin>", line 1, in ?
socket.error: (13, 'Permission denied')
```

Even if run by a user with the required permission, you'll get the different exception we saw earlier if the port is already being used by a real web server. On computers being used as general servers, these ports really are reserved.

Handling Multiple Clients

The `echo` client and server programs shown previously serve to illustrate socket fundamentals. But the server model suffers from a fairly major flaw: if multiple clients try to connect to the server, and it takes a long time to process a given clients'

---

[*] You might be interested to know that the last part of this example, talking to port 80, is exactly what your web browser does as you surf the Net: followed links direct it to download web pages over this port. In fact, this lowly port is the primary basis of the Web. In Chapter 12, we will meet an entire application environment based upon sending data over port 80—CGI server-side scripting.

request, the server will fail. More accurately, if the cost of handling a given request prevents the server from returning to the code that checks for new clients in a timely manner, it won't be able to keep up with all the requests, and some clients will eventually be denied connections.

In real-world client/server programs, it's far more typical to code a server so as to avoid blocking new requests while handling a current client's request. Perhaps the easiest way to do so is to service each client's request in *parallel*—in a new process, in a new thread, or by manually switching (multiplexing) between clients in an event loop. This isn't a socket issue per se, and we've already learned how to start processes and threads in Chapter 3. But since these schemes are so typical of socket server programming, let's explore all three ways to handle client requests in parallel here.

Forking Servers

The script in Example 10-4 works like the original `echo` server, but instead forks a new process to handle each new client connection. Because the `handleClient` function runs in a new process, the `dispatcher` function can immediately resume its main loop, to detect and service a new incoming request.

Example 10-4. PP2E\Internet\Sockets\fork-server.py

```
#############################################################
# Server side: open a socket on a port, listen for
# a message from a client, and send an echo reply;
# forks a process to handle each client connection;
# child processes share parent's socket descriptors;
# fork is less portable than threads--not yet on Windows;
#############################################################

import os, time, sys
from socket import *                     # get socket constructor and constants
myHost = ''                              # server machine, '' means local host
myPort = 50007                           # listen on a non-reserved port number

sockobj = socket(AF_INET, SOCK_STREAM)      # make a TCP socket object
sockobj.bind((myHost, myPort))              # bind it to server port number
sockobj.listen(5)                           # allow 5 pending connects

def now():                                  # current time on server
    return time.ctime(time.time())

activeChildren = []
def reapChildren():                         # reap any dead child processes
    while activeChildren:                   # else may fill up system table
        pid,stat = os.waitpid(0, os.WNOHANG)  # don't hang if no child exited
        if not pid: break
        activeChildren.remove(pid)
```

Example 10-4. PP2E\Internet\Sockets\fork-server.py (continued)

```
def handleClient(connection):              # child process: reply, exit
    time.sleep(5)                          # simulate a blocking activity
    while 1:                               # read, write a client socket
        data = connection.recv(1024)       # till eof when socket closed
        if not data: break
        connection.send('Echo=>%s at %s' % (data, now()))
    connection.close()
    os._exit(0)

def dispatcher():                          # listen until process killed
    while 1:                               # wait for next connection,
        connection, address = sockobj.accept()   # pass to process for service
        print 'Server connected by', address,
        print 'at', now()
        reapChildren()                     # clean up exited children now
        childPid = os.fork()               # copy this process
        if childPid == 0:                  # if in child process: handle
            handleClient(connection)
        else:                              # else: go accept next connect
            activeChildren.append(childPid)   # add to active child pid list

dispatcher()
```

Running the forking server

Parts of this script are a bit tricky, and most of its library calls work only on Unix-like platforms (not Windows). But before we get into too many details, let's start up our server and handle a few client requests. First off, notice that to simulate a long-running operation (e.g., database updates, other network traffic), this server adds a five-second `time.sleep` delay in its client handler function, `handleClient`. After the delay, the original echo reply action is performed. That means that when we run a server and clients this time, clients won't receive the echo reply until five seconds after they've sent their requests to the server.

To help keep track of requests and replies, the server prints *its* system time each time a client connect request is received, and adds *its* system time to the reply. Clients print the reply time sent back from the server, not their own—clocks on the server and client may differ radically, so to compare apples to apples, all times are server times. Because of the simulated delays, we also usually must start each client in its own console window on Windows (on some platforms, clients will hang in a blocked state while waiting for their reply).

But the grander story here is that this script runs one main parent process on the server machine, which does nothing but watch for connections (in `dispatcher`), plus one child process per active client connection, running in parallel with both the main parent process and the other client processes (in `handleClient`). In principle, the server can handle any number of clients without bogging down. To test, let's start the server remotely in a Telnet window, and start three clients locally in three distinct console windows:

```
[server telnet window]
[lutz@starship uploads]$ uname -a
Linux starship …
[lutz@starship uploads]$ python fork-server.py
Server connected by ('38.28.162.194', 1063) at Sun Jun 18 19:37:49 2000
Server connected by ('38.28.162.194', 1064) at Sun Jun 18 19:37:49 2000
Server connected by ('38.28.162.194', 1067) at Sun Jun 18 19:37:50 2000

[client window 1]
C:\...\PP2E\Internet\Sockets>python echo-client.py starship.python.net
Client received: 'Echo=>Hello network world at Sun Jun 18 19:37:54 2000'

[client window 2]
C:\...\PP2E\Internet\Sockets>python echo-client.py starship.python.net Bruce
Client received: 'Echo=>Bruce at Sun Jun 18 19:37:54 2000'

[client window 3]
C:\...\PP2E\Internet\Sockets>python echo-client.py starship.python.net The
Meaning of Life
Client received: 'Echo=>The at Sun Jun 18 19:37:55 2000'
Client received: 'Echo=>Meaning at Sun Jun 18 19:37:56 2000'
Client received: 'Echo=>of at Sun Jun 18 19:37:56 2000'
Client received: 'Echo=>Life at Sun Jun 18 19:37:56 2000'
```

Again, all times here are on the server machine. This may be a little confusing because there are four windows involved. In English, the test proceeds as follows:

1. The server starts running remotely.

2. All three clients are started and connect to the server at roughly the same time.

3. On the server, the client requests trigger three forked child processes, which all immediately go to sleep for five seconds (to simulate being busy doing something useful).

4. Each client waits until the server replies, which eventually happens five seconds after their initial requests.

In other words, all three clients are serviced at the same time, by forked processes, while the main parent process continues listening for new client requests. If clients were *not* handled in parallel like this, no client could connect until the currently connected client's five-second delay expired.

In a more realistic application, that delay could be fatal if many clients were trying to connect at once—the server would be stuck in the action we're simulating with `time.sleep`, and not get back to the main loop to `accept` new client requests. With process forks per request, all clients can be serviced in parallel.

Notice that we're using the same client script here (*echo-client.py*), just a different server; clients simply send and receive data to a machine and port, and don't care how their requests are handled on the server. Also note that the server is running remotely on a Linux machine. (As we learned in Chapter 3, the `fork` call is not supported on Windows in Python at the time this book was written.) We can also run this test on a Linux server entirely, with two Telnet windows. It works about the same as when clients are started locally, in a DOS console window, but here "local" means a remote machine you're telneting to locally:

```
[one telnet window]
[lutz@starship uploads]$ python fork-server.py &
[1] 3379
Server connected by ('127.0.0.1', 2928) at Sun Jun 18 22:44:50 2000
Server connected by ('127.0.0.1', 2929) at Sun Jun 18 22:45:08 2000
Server connected by ('208.185.174.112', 2930) at Sun Jun 18 22:45:50 2000

[another telnet window, same machine]
[lutz@starship uploads]$ python echo-client.py
Client received: 'Echo=>Hello network world at Sun Jun 18 22:44:55 2000'

[lutz@starship uploads]$ python echo-client.py localhost niNiNI
Client received: 'Echo=>niNiNI at Sun Jun 18 22:45:13 2000'

[lutz@starship uploads]$ python echo-client.py starship.python.net Say no More!
Client received: 'Echo=>Say at Sun Jun 18 22:45:55 2000'
Client received: 'Echo=>no at Sun Jun 18 22:45:55 2000'
Client received: 'Echo=>More! at Sun Jun 18 22:45:55 2000'
```

Now let's move on to the tricky bits. This server script is fairly straightforward as forking code goes, but a few comments about some of the library tools it employs are in order.

Forking processes

We met `os.fork` in Chapter 3, but recall that forked processes are essentially a copy of the process that forks them, and so they inherit file and socket descriptors from their parent process. Because of that, the new child process that runs the `handleClient` function has access to the connection socket created in the parent process. Programs know they are in a forked child process if the fork call returns 0; otherwise, the original parent process gets back the new child's ID.

Exiting from children

In earlier fork examples, child processes usually call one of the **exec** variants to start a new program in the child process. Here, instead, the child process simply calls a function in the same program and exits with `os._exit`. It's imperative to call `os._exit` here—if we did not, each child would live on after `handleClient` returns, and compete for accepting new client requests.

In fact, without the exit call, we'd wind up with as many perpetual server processes as requests served—remove the exit call and do a *ps* shell command after running a few clients, and you'll see what I mean. With the call, only the single parent process listens for new requests. `os._exit` is like `sys.exit`, but it exits the calling process immediately without cleanup actions. It's normally only used in child processes, and `sys.exit` is used everywhere else.

Killing the zombies

Note, however, that it's not quite enough to make sure that child processes exit and die. On systems like Linux, parents must also be sure to issue a `wait` system call to remove the entries for dead child processes from the system's process table. If we don't, the child processes will no longer run, but they will consume an entry in the system process table. For long-running servers, these bogus entries may become problematic.

It's common to call such dead-but-listed child processes "zombies": they continue to use system resources even though they've already passed over to the great operating system beyond. To clean up after child processes are gone, this server keeps a list, `activeChildren`, of the process IDs of all child processes it spawns. Whenever a new incoming client request is received, the server runs its `reapChildren` to issue a `wait` for any dead children by issuing the standard Python `os.waitpid(0,os.WNOHANG)` call.

The `os.waitpid` call attempts to wait for a child process to exit and returns its process ID and exit status. With a 0 for its first argument, it waits for any child process. With the `WNOHANG` parameter for its second, it does nothing if no child process has exited (i.e., it does not block or pause the caller). The net effect is that this call simply asks the operating system for the process ID of any child that has exited. If any have, the process ID returned is removed both from the system process table and from this script's `activeChildren` list.

To see why all this complexity is needed, comment out the `reapChildren` call in this script, run it on a server, and then run a few clients. On my Linux server, a `ps -f` full process listing command shows that all the dead child processes stay in the system process table (show as `<defunct>`):

```
[lutz@starship uploads]$ ps -f
UID        PID  PPID  C STIME TTY          TIME CMD
lutz      3270  3264  0 22:33 pts/1    00:00:00 -bash
lutz      3311  3270  0 22:37 pts/1    00:00:00 python fork-server.py
lutz      3312  3311  0 22:37 pts/1    00:00:00 [python <defunct>]
lutz      3313  3311  0 22:37 pts/1    00:00:00 [python <defunct>]
lutz      3314  3311  0 22:37 pts/1    00:00:00 [python <defunct>]
lutz      3316  3311  0 22:37 pts/1    00:00:00 [python <defunct>]
lutz      3317  3311  0 22:37 pts/1    00:00:00 [python <defunct>]
lutz      3318  3311  0 22:37 pts/1    00:00:00 [python <defunct>]
lutz      3322  3270  0 22:38 pts/1    00:00:00 ps -f
```

When the `reapChildren` command is reactivated, dead child zombie entries are cleaned up each time the server gets a new client connection request, by calling the Python `os.waitpid` function. A few zombies may accumulate if the server is heavily loaded, but will remain only until the next client connection is received:

```
[lutz@starship uploads]$ ps -f
UID        PID  PPID  C STIME TTY        TIME CMD
lutz       3270 3264  0 22:33 pts/1   00:00:00 -bash
lutz       3340 3270  0 22:41 pts/1   00:00:00 python fork-server.py
lutz       3341 3340  0 22:41 pts/1   00:00:00 [python <defunct>]
lutz       3342 3340  0 22:41 pts/1   00:00:00 [python <defunct>]
lutz       3343 3340  0 22:41 pts/1   00:00:00 [python <defunct>]
lutz       3344 3270  6 22:41 pts/1   00:00:00 ps -f
[lutz@starship uploads]$
Server connected by ('38.28.131.174', 1170) at Sun Jun 18 22:41:43 2000

[lutz@starship uploads]$ ps -f
UID        PID  PPID  C STIME TTY        TIME CMD
lutz       3270 3264  0 22:33 pts/1   00:00:00 -bash
lutz       3340 3270  0 22:41 pts/1   00:00:00 python fork-server.py
lutz       3345 3340  0 22:41 pts/1   00:00:00 [python <defunct>]
lutz       3346 3270  0 22:41 pts/1   00:00:00 ps -f
```

If you type fast enough, you can actually see a child process morph from a real running program into a zombie. Here, for example, a child spawned to handle a new request (process ID 11785) changes to `<defunct>` on exit. Its process entry will be removed completely when the next request is received:

```
[lutz@starship uploads]$
Server connected by ('38.28.57.160', 1106) at Mon Jun 19 22:34:39 2000
[lutz@starship uploads]$ ps -f
UID         PID  PPID  C STIME TTY        TIME CMD
lutz       11089 11088  0 21:13 pts/2   00:00:00 -bash
lutz       11780 11089  0 22:34 pts/2   00:00:00 python fork-server.py
lutz       11785 11780  0 22:34 pts/2   00:00:00 python fork-server.py
lutz       11786 11089  0 22:34 pts/2   00:00:00 ps -f

[lutz@starship uploads]$ ps -f
UID         PID  PPID  C STIME TTY        TIME CMD
lutz       11089 11088  0 21:13 pts/2   00:00:00 -bash
lutz       11780 11089  0 22:34 pts/2   00:00:00 python fork-server.py
lutz       11785 11780  0 22:34 pts/2   00:00:00 [python <defunct>]
lutz       11787 11089  0 22:34 pts/2   00:00:00 ps -f
```

Preventing zombies with signal handlers

On some systems, it's also possible to clean up zombie child processes by resetting the signal handler for the `SIGCHLD` signal raised by the operating system when a child process exits. If a Python script assigns the `SIG_IGN` (ignore) action as the `SIGCHLD` signal handler, zombies will be removed automatically and immediately as child processes exit; the parent need not issue wait calls to clean up

after them. Because of that, this scheme is a simpler alternative to manually reap-
ing zombies (on platforms where it is supported).

If you've already read Chapter 3, you know that Python's standard **signal** module
lets scripts install handlers for *signals*—software-generated events. If you haven't
read that chapter, here is a brief bit of background to show how this pans out for
zombies. The program in Example 10-5 installs a Python-coded signal handler function to respond to whatever signal number you type on the command line.

Example 10-5. PP2E\Internet\Sockets\signal-demo.py

```
#########################################################
# Demo Python's signal module; pass signal number as a
# command-line arg, use a "kill -N pid" shell command
# to send this process a signal; e.g., on my linux
# machine, SIGUSR1=10, SIGUSR2=12, SIGCHLD=17, and
# SIGCHLD handler stays in effect even if not restored:
# all other handlers restored by Python after caught,
# but SIGCHLD is left to the platform's implementation;
# signal works on Windows but defines only a few signal
# types; signals are not very portable in general;
#########################################################

import sys, signal, time

def now():
    return time.ctime(time.time())

def onSignal(signum, stackframe):            # python signal handler
    print 'Got signal', signum, 'at', now()  # most handlers stay in effect
    if signum == signal.SIGCHLD:             # but sigchld handler is not
        print 'sigchld caught'
        #signal.signal(signal.SIGCHLD, onSignal)

signum = int(sys.argv[1])
signal.signal(signum, onSignal)              # install signal handler
while 1: signal.pause()                      # sleep waiting for signals
```

To run this script, simply put it in the background and send it signals by typing the
kill -signal-number process-id shell command line. Process IDs are listed in
the PID column of *ps* command results. Here is this script in action catching signal
numbers 10 (reserved for general use) and 9 (the unavoidable terminate signal):

```
[lutz@starship uploads]$ python signal-demo.py 10 &
[1] 11297
[lutz@starship uploads]$ ps -f
UID        PID  PPID  C STIME TTY        TIME CMD
lutz     11089 11088  0 21:13 pts/2   00:00:00 -bash
lutz     11297 11089  0 21:49 pts/2   00:00:00 python signal-demo.py 10
lutz     11298 11089  0 21:49 pts/2   00:00:00 ps -f

[lutz@starship uploads]$ kill -10 11297
```

```
Got signal 10 at Mon Jun 19 21:49:27 2000

[lutz@starship uploads]$ kill -10 11297
Got signal 10 at Mon Jun 19 21:49:29 2000

[lutz@starship uploads]$ kill -10 11297
Got signal 10 at Mon Jun 19 21:49:32 2000

[lutz@starship uploads]$ kill -9 11297
[1]+  Killed                    python signal-demo.py 10
```

And here the script catches signal 17, which happens to be SIGCHLD on my Linux server. Signal numbers vary from machine to machine, so you should normally use their names, not their numbers. SIGCHLD behavior may vary per platform as well (see the signal module's library manual entry for more details):

```
[lutz@starship uploads]$ python signal-demo.py 17 &
[1] 11320
[lutz@starship uploads]$ ps -f
UID         PID  PPID  C STIME TTY          TIME CMD
lutz      11089 11088  0 21:13 pts/2    00:00:00 -bash
lutz      11320 11089  0 21:52 pts/2    00:00:00 python signal-demo.py 17
lutz      11321 11089  0 21:52 pts/2    00:00:00 ps -f

[lutz@starship uploads]$ kill -17 11320
Got signal 17 at Mon Jun 19 21:52:24 2000
[lutz@starship uploads] sigchld caught

[lutz@starship uploads]$ kill -17 11320
Got signal 17 at Mon Jun 19 21:52:27 2000
[lutz@starship uploads]$ sigchld caught
```

Now, to apply all this to kill zombies, simply set the SIGCHLD signal handler to the SIG_IGN ignore handler action; on systems where this assignment is supported, child processes will be cleaned up when they exit. The forking server variant shown in Example 10-6 uses this trick to manage its children.

Example 10-6. PP2E\Internet\Sockets\fork-server-signal.py

```
#######################################################
# Same as fork-server.py, but use the Python signal
# module to avoid keeping child zombie processes after
# they terminate, not an explicit loop before each new
# connection; SIG_IGN means ignore, and may not work with
# SIG_CHLD child exit signal on all platforms; on Linux,
# socket.accept cannot be interrupted with a signal;
#######################################################

import os, time, sys, signal, signal
from socket import *                      # get socket constructor and constants
myHost = ''                               # server machine, '' means local host
myPort = 50007                            # listen on a non-reserved port number
```

Example 10-6. PP2E\Internet\Sockets\fork-server-signal.py (continued)

```
sockobj = socket(AF_INET, SOCK_STREAM)          # make a TCP socket object
sockobj.bind((myHost, myPort))                  # bind it to server port number
sockobj.listen(5)                               # up to 5 pending connects
signal.signal(signal.SIGCHLD, signal.SIG_IGN)   # avoid child zombie processes

def now():                                      # time on server machine
    return time.ctime(time.time())

def handleClient(connection):                   # child process replies, exits
    time.sleep(5)                               # simulate a blocking activity
    while 1:                                     # read, write a client socket
        data = connection.recv(1024)
        if not data: break
        connection.send('Echo=>%s at %s' % (data, now()))
    connection.close()
    os._exit(0)

def dispatcher():                               # listen until process killed
    while 1:                                     # wait for next connection,
        connection, address = sockobj.accept()  # pass to process for service
        print 'Server connected by', address,
        print 'at', now()
        childPid = os.fork()                    # copy this process
        if childPid == 0:                       # if in child process: handle
            handleClient(connection)            # else: go accept next connect

dispatcher()
```

Where applicable, this technique is:

- Much simpler—we don't need to manually track or reap child processes.

- More accurate—it leaves no zombies temporarily between client requests.

In fact, there is really only one line dedicated to handling zombies here: the `signal.signal` call near the top, to set the handler. Unfortunately, this version is also even *less* portable than using `os.fork` in the first place, because signals may work slightly different from platform to platform. For instance, some platforms may not allow `SIG_IGN` to be used as the `SIGCHLD` action at all. On Linux systems, though, this simpler forking server variant works like a charm:

```
[lutz@starship uploads]$
Server connected by ('38.28.57.160', 1166) at Mon Jun 19 22:38:29 2000

[lutz@starship uploads]$ ps -f
UID        PID  PPID  C STIME TTY          TIME CMD
lutz     11089 11088  0 21:13 pts/2    00:00:00 -bash
lutz     11827 11089  0 22:37 pts/2    00:00:00 python fork-server-signal.py
lutz     11835 11827  0 22:38 pts/2    00:00:00 python fork-server-signal.py
lutz     11836 11089  0 22:38 pts/2    00:00:00 ps -f

[lutz@starship uploads]$ ps -f
```

```
UID         PID  PPID  C STIME TTY          TIME CMD
lutz      11089 11088  0 21:13 pts/2    00:00:00 -bash
lutz      11827 11089  0 22:37 pts/2    00:00:00 python fork-server-signal.py
lutz      11837 11089  0 22:38 pts/2    00:00:00 ps -f
```

Notice that in this version, the child process's entry goes away as soon as it exits, even before a new client request is received; no "defunct" zombie ever appears. More dramatically, if we now start up the script we wrote earlier that spawns eight clients in parallel (*testecho.py*) to talk to this server, all appear on the server while running, but are removed immediately as they exit:

```
[lutz@starship uploads]$ ps -f
UID         PID  PPID  C STIME TTY          TIME CMD
lutz      11089 11088  0 21:13 pts/2    00:00:00 -bash
lutz      11827 11089  0 22:37 pts/2    00:00:00 python fork-server-signal.py
lutz      11839 11827  0 22:39 pts/2    00:00:00 python fork-server-signal.py
lutz      11840 11827  0 22:39 pts/2    00:00:00 python fork-server-signal.py
lutz      11841 11827  0 22:39 pts/2    00:00:00 python fork-server-signal.py
lutz      11842 11827  0 22:39 pts/2    00:00:00 python fork-server-signal.py
lutz      11843 11827  0 22:39 pts/2    00:00:00 python fork-server-signal.py
lutz      11844 11827  0 22:39 pts/2    00:00:00 python fork-server-signal.py
lutz      11845 11827  0 22:39 pts/2    00:00:00 python fork-server-signal.py
lutz      11846 11827  0 22:39 pts/2    00:00:00 python fork-server-signal.py
lutz      11848 11089  0 22:39 pts/2    00:00:00 ps -f

[lutz@starship uploads]$ ps -f
UID         PID  PPID  C STIME TTY          TIME CMD
lutz      11089 11088  0 21:13 pts/2    00:00:00 -bash
lutz      11827 11089  0 22:37 pts/2    00:00:00 python fork-server-signal.py
lutz      11849 11089  0 22:39 pts/2    00:00:00 ps -f
```

Threading Servers

But don't do that. The forking model just described works well on some platforms in general, but suffers from some potentially big limitations:

Performance

> On some machines, starting a new process can be fairly expensive in terms of time and space resources.

Portability

> Forking processes is a Unix device; as we just noted, the fork call currently doesn't work on non-Unix platforms such as Windows.

Complexity

> If you think that forking servers can be complicated, you're right. As we just saw, forking also brings with it all the shenanigans of managing zombies— cleaning up after child processes that live shorter lives than their parents.

If you read Chapter 3, you know that the solution to all of these dilemmas is usually to use threads instead of processes. Threads run in parallel and share global (i.e., module and interpreter) memory, but they are usually less expensive to start, and work both on Unix-like machines and Microsoft Windows today. Furthermore, threads are simpler to program—child threads die silently on exit, without leaving behind zombies to haunt the server.

Example 10-7 is another mutation of the echo server that handles client request in parallel by running them in threads, rather than processes.

Example 10-7. PP2E\Internet\Sockets\thread-server.py

```
#########################################################
# Server side: open a socket on a port, listen for
# a message from a client, and send an echo reply;
# echos lines until eof when client closes socket;
# spawns a thread to handle each client connection;
# threads share global memory space with main thread;
# this is more portable than fork--not yet on Windows;
#########################################################

import thread, time
from socket import *                    # get socket constructor and constants
myHost = ''                             # server machine, '' means local host
myPort = 50007                          # listen on a non-reserved port number

sockobj = socket(AF_INET, SOCK_STREAM)     # make a TCP socket object
sockobj.bind((myHost, myPort))             # bind it to server port number
sockobj.listen(5)                          # allow up to 5 pending connects

def now():
    return time.ctime(time.time())         # current time on the server

def handleClient(connection):              # in spawned thread: reply
    time.sleep(5)                          # simulate a blocking activity
    while 1:                               # read, write a client socket
        data = connection.recv(1024)
        if not data: break
        connection.send('Echo=>%s at %s' % (data, now()))
    connection.close()

def dispatcher():                          # listen until process killd
    while 1:                               # wait for next connection,
        connection, address = sockobj.accept()  # pass to thread for service
        print 'Server connected by', address,
        print 'at', now()
        thread.start_new(handleClient, (connection,))

dispatcher()
```

This **dispatcher** delegates each incoming client connection request to a newly spawned thread running the **handleClient** function. Because of that, this server can process multiple clients at once, and the main dispatcher loop can get quickly back to the top to check for newly arrived requests. The net effect is that new clients won't be denied service due to a busy server.

Functionally, this version is similar to the `fork` solution (clients are handled in parallel), but it will work on any machine that supports threads, including Windows and Linux. Let's test it on both. First, start the server on a Linux machine and run clients on both Linux and Windows:

```
[window 1: thread-based server process, server keeps accepting
client connections while threads are servicing prior requests]
[lutz@starship uploads]$ /usr/bin/python thread-server.py
Server connected by ('127.0.0.1', 2934) at Sun Jun 18 22:52:52 2000
Server connected by ('38.28.131.174', 1179) at Sun Jun 18 22:53:31 2000
Server connected by ('38.28.131.174', 1182) at Sun Jun 18 22:53:35 2000
Server connected by ('38.28.131.174', 1185) at Sun Jun 18 22:53:37 2000

[window 2: client, but on same server machine]
[lutz@starship uploads]$ python echo-client.py
Client received: 'Echo=>Hello network world at Sun Jun 18 22:52:57 2000'

[window 3: remote client, PC]
C:\...\PP2E\Internet\Sockets>python echo-client.py starship.python.net
Client received: 'Echo=>Hello network world at Sun Jun 18 22:53:36 2000'

[window 4: client PC]
C:\...\PP2E\Internet\Sockets>python echo-client.py starship.python.net Bruce
Client received: 'Echo=>Bruce at Sun Jun 18 22:53:40 2000'

[window 5: client PC]
C:\...\PP2E\Internet\Sockets>python echo-client.py starship.python.net The
Meaning of Life
Client received: 'Echo=>The at Sun Jun 18 22:53:42 2000'
Client received: 'Echo=>Meaning at Sun Jun 18 22:53:42 2000'
Client received: 'Echo=>of at Sun Jun 18 22:53:42 2000'
Client received: 'Echo=>Life at Sun Jun 18 22:53:42 2000'
```

Because this server uses threads instead of forked processes, we can run it portably on both Linux and a Windows PC. Here it is at work again, running on the same local Windows PC as its clients; again, the main point to notice is that new clients are accepted while prior clients are being processed in parallel with other clients and the main thread (in the five-second sleep delay):

```
[window 1: server, on local PC]
C:\...\PP2E\Internet\Sockets>python thread-server.py
Server connected by ('127.0.0.1', 1186) at Sun Jun 18 23:46:31 2000
Server connected by ('127.0.0.1', 1187) at Sun Jun 18 23:46:33 2000
Server connected by ('127.0.0.1', 1188) at Sun Jun 18 23:46:34 2000

[window 2: client, on local PC]
C:\...\PP2E\Internet\Sockets>python echo-client.py
Client received: 'Echo=>Hello network world at Sun Jun 18 23:46:36 2000'
```

[window 3: client]
```
C:\...\PP2E\Internet\Sockets>python echo-client.py localhost Brian
Client received: 'Echo=>Brian at Sun Jun 18 23:46:38 2000'
```

[window 4: client]
```
C:\...\PP2E\Internet\Sockets>python echo-client.py localhost Bright side of Life
Client received: 'Echo=>Bright at Sun Jun 18 23:46:39 2000'
Client received: 'Echo=>side at Sun Jun 18 23:46:39 2000'
Client received: 'Echo=>of at Sun Jun 18 23:46:39 2000'
Client received: 'Echo=>Life at Sun Jun 18 23:46:39 2000'
```

Recall that a thread silently exits when the function it is running returns; unlike the process `fork` version, we don't call anything like `os._exit` in the client handler function (and we shouldn't—it may kill all threads in the process!). Because of this, the thread version is not only more portable, but is also simpler.

Doing It with Classes: Server Frameworks

Now that I've shown you how to write forking and threading servers to process clients without blocking incoming requests, I should also tell you that there are standard tools in the Python library to make this process easier. In particular, the `SocketServer` module defines classes that implement all flavors of forking and threading servers that you are likely to be interested in. Simply create the desired kind of imported server object, passing in a handler object with a callback method of your own, as shown in Example 10-8.

Example 10-8. PP2E\Internet\Sockets\class-server.py

```
#######################################################
# Server side: open a socket on a port, listen for
# a message from a client, and send an echo reply;
# this version uses the standard library module
# SocketServer to do its work; SocketServer allows
# us to make a simple TCPServer, a ThreadingTCPServer,
# a ForkingTCPServer, and more, and routes each client
# connect request to a new instance of a passed-in
# request handler object's handle method; also supports
# UDP and Unix domain sockets; see the library manual.
#######################################################

import SocketServer, time            # get socket server, handler objects
myHost = ''                          # server machine, '' means local host
myPort = 50007                       # listen on a non-reserved port number
def now():
    return time.ctime(time.time())

class MyClientHandler(SocketServer.BaseRequestHandler):
    def handle(self):                          # on each client connect
        print self.client_address, now()       # show this client's address
        time.sleep(5)                          # simulate a blocking activity
        while 1:                               # self.request is client socket
```

Example 10-8. PP2E\Internet\Sockets\class-server.py (continued)

```
        data = self.request.recv(1024)      # read, write a client socket
        if not data: break
        self.request.send('Echo=>%s at %s' % (data, now()))
    self.request.close()

# make a threaded server, listen/handle clients forever
myaddr = (myHost, myPort)
server = SocketServer.ThreadingTCPServer(myaddr, MyClientHandler)
server.serve_forever()
```

This server works the same as the threading server we wrote by hand in the previous section, but instead focuses on service implementation (the customized `handle` method), not on threading details. It's run the same way, too—here it is processing three clients started by hand, plus eight spawned by the `testecho` script shown in Example 10-3:

```
[window1: server, serverHost='localhost' in echo-client.py]
C:\...\PP2E\Internet\Sockets>python class-server.py
('127.0.0.1', 1189) Sun Jun 18 23:49:18 2000
('127.0.0.1', 1190) Sun Jun 18 23:49:20 2000
('127.0.0.1', 1191) Sun Jun 18 23:49:22 2000
('127.0.0.1', 1192) Sun Jun 18 23:49:50 2000
('127.0.0.1', 1193) Sun Jun 18 23:49:50 2000
('127.0.0.1', 1194) Sun Jun 18 23:49:50 2000
('127.0.0.1', 1195) Sun Jun 18 23:49:50 2000
('127.0.0.1', 1196) Sun Jun 18 23:49:50 2000
('127.0.0.1', 1197) Sun Jun 18 23:49:50 2000
('127.0.0.1', 1198) Sun Jun 18 23:49:50 2000
('127.0.0.1', 1199) Sun Jun 18 23:49:50 2000

[window2: client]
C:\...\PP2E\Internet\Sockets>python echo-client.py
Client received: 'Echo=>Hello network world at Sun Jun 18 23:49:23 2000'

[window3: client]
C:\...\PP2E\Internet\Sockets>python echo-client.py localhost Robin
Client received: 'Echo=>Robin at Sun Jun 18 23:49:25 2000'

[window4: client]
C:\...\PP2E\Internet\Sockets>python echo-client.py localhost Brave Sir Robin
Client received: 'Echo=>Brave at Sun Jun 18 23:49:27 2000'
Client received: 'Echo=>Sir at Sun Jun 18 23:49:27 2000'
Client received: 'Echo=>Robin at Sun Jun 18 23:49:27 2000'

C:\...\PP2E\Internet\Sockets>python testecho.py

[window4: contact remote server instead—times skewed]
C:\...\PP2E\Internet\Sockets>python echo-client.py starship.python.net Brave
Sir Robin
Client received: 'Echo=>Brave at Sun Jun 18 23:03:28 2000'
Client received: 'Echo=>Sir at Sun Jun 18 23:03:28 2000'
Client received: 'Echo=>Robin at Sun Jun 18 23:03:29 2000'
```

To build a forking server instead, just use class name `ForkingTCPServer` when creating the server object. The `SocketServer` module is more powerful than shown by this example; it also supports synchronous (nonparallel) servers, UDP and Unix sockets, and so on. See Python's library manual for more details. Also see the end of Chapter 15 for more on Python server implementation tools.[*]

Multiplexing Servers with select

So far we've seen how to handle multiple clients at once with both forked processes and spawned threads, and we've looked at a library class that encapsulates both schemes. Under both approaches, all client handlers seem to run in parallel with each other and with the main dispatch loop that continues watching for new incoming requests. Because all these tasks run in parallel (i.e., at the same time), the server doesn't get blocked when accepting new requests or when processing a long-running client handler.

Technically, though, threads and processes don't really run in parallel, unless you're lucky enough to have a machine with arbitrarily many CPUs. Instead, your operating system performs a juggling act—it divides the computer's processing power among all active tasks. It runs part of one, then part of another, and so on. All the tasks appear to run in parallel, but only because the operating system switches focus between tasks so fast that you don't usually notice. This process of switching between tasks is sometimes called time-slicing when done by an operating system; it is more generally known as *multiplexing*.

When we spawn threads and processes, we rely on the operating system to juggle the active tasks, but there's no reason that a Python script can't do so as well. For instance, a script might divide tasks into multiple steps—do a step of one task, then one of another, and so on, until all are completed. The script need only know how to divide its attention among the multiple active tasks to multiplex on its own.

Servers can apply this technique to yield yet another way to handle multiple clients at once, a way that requires neither threads nor forks. By multiplexing client connections and the main dispatcher with the `select` system call, a *single event loop* can process clients and accept new ones in parallel (or at least close enough to avoid stalling). Such servers are sometimes call *asynchronous*, because they service clients in spurts, as each becomes ready to communicate. In asynchronous servers, a single main loop run in a single process and thread decides which clients should get a bit of attention each time through. Client requests and the main dispatcher are each given a small slice of the server's attention if they are ready to converse.

---

[*] Incidentally, Python also comes with library tools that allow you to implement a full-blown HTTP (web) server that knows how to run server-side CGI scripts, in a few lines of Python code. We'll explore those tools in Chapter 15.

Most of the magic behind this server structure is the operating system **select** call, available in Python's standard **select** module. Roughly, **select** is asked to monitor a list of input sources, output sources, and exceptional condition sources, and tells us which sources are ready for processing. It can be made to simply poll all the sources to see which are ready, wait for a maximum time period for sources to become ready, or wait indefinitely until one or more sources are ready for processing.

However used, **select** lets us direct attention to sockets ready to communicate, so as to avoid blocking on calls to ones that are not. That is, when the sources passed to **select** are sockets, we can be sure that socket calls like **accept**, **recv**, and **send** will not block (pause) the server when applied to objects returned by **select**. Because of that, a single-loop server that uses **select** need not get stuck communicating with one client or waiting for new ones, while other clients are starved for the server's attention.

A select-based echo server

Let's see how all this translates into code. The script in Example 10-9 implements another echo server, one that can handle multiple clients without ever starting new processes or threads.

Example 10-9. PP2E\Internet\Sockets\select-server.py

```
##############################################################
# Server: handle multiple clients in parallel with select.
# use the select module to multiplex among a set of sockets:
# main sockets which accept new client connections, and
# input sockets connected to accepted clients; select can
# take an optional 4th arg--0 to poll, n.m to wait n.m secs,
# ommitted to wait till any socket is ready for processing.
##############################################################

import sys, time
from select import select
from socket import socket, AF_INET, SOCK_STREAM
def now(): return time.ctime(time.time())

myHost = ''                              # server machine, '' means local host
myPort = 50007                           # listen on a non-reserved port number
if len(sys.argv) == 3:                   # allow host/port as cmdline args too
    myHost, myPort = sys.argv[1:]
numPortSocks = 2                         # number of ports for client connects

# make main sockets for accepting new client requests
mainsocks, readsocks, writesocks = [], [], []
for i in range(numPortSocks):
    portsock = socket(AF_INET, SOCK_STREAM)   # make a TCP/IP spocket object
    portsock.bind((myHost, myPort))           # bind it to server port number
    portsock.listen(5)                        # listen, allow 5 pending connects
```

Example 10-9. PP2E\Internet\Sockets\select-server.py (continued)

```
    mainsocks.append(portsock)              # add to main list to identify
    readsocks.append(portsock)              # add to select inputs list
    myPort = myPort + 1                      # bind on consecutive ports

# event loop: listen and multiplex until server process killed
print 'select-server loop starting'
while 1:
    #print readsocks
    readables, writeables, exceptions = select(readsocks, writesocks, [])
    for sockobj in readables:
        if sockobj in mainsocks:            # for ready input sockets
            # port socket: accept new client
            newsock, address = sockobj.accept()    # accept should not block
            print 'Connect:', address, id(newsock) # newsock is a new socket
            readsocks.append(newsock)       # add to select list, wait
        else:
            # client socket: read next line
            data = sockobj.recv(1024)       # recv should not block
            print '\tgot', data, 'on', id(sockobj)
            if not data:                     # if closed by the clients
                sockobj.close()             # close here and remv from
                readsocks.remove(sockobj)   # del list else reselected
            else:
                # this may block: should really select for writes too
                sockobj.send('Echo=>%s at %s' % (data, now()))
```

The bulk of this script is the big **while** event loop at the end that calls **select** to find out which sockets are ready for processing (these include main port sockets on which clients can connect, and open client connections). It then loops over all such ready sockets, accepting connections on main port sockets, and reading and echoing input on any client sockets ready for input. Both the **accept** and **recv** calls in this code are guaranteed to not block the server process after **select** returns; because of that, this server can get quickly back to the top of the loop to process newly arrived client requests and already-connected clients' inputs. The net effect is that all new requests and clients are serviced in pseudo-parallel fashion.

To make this process work, the server appends the connected socket for each client to the **readables** list passed to **select**, and simply waits for the socket to show up in the selected inputs list. For illustration purposes, this server also listens for new clients on more than one port—on ports 50007 and 50008 in our examples. Because these main port sockets are also interrogated with **select**, connection requests on either port can be accepted without blocking either already-connected clients or new connection requests appearing on the other port. The **select** call returns whatever sockets in list **readables** are ready for processing—both main port sockets and sockets connected to clients currently being processed.

Running the select server

Let's run this script locally to see how it does its stuff (the client and server can also be run on different machines, as in prior socket examples). First of all, we'll assume we've already started this server script in one window, and run a few clients to talk to it. The following code is the interaction in two such client windows running on Windows (MS-DOS consoles). The first client simply runs the echo-client script twice to contact the server, and the second also kicks off the testecho script to spawn eight echo-client programs running in parallel. As before, the server simply echoes back whatever text that clients send. Notice that the second client window really runs a script called echo-client-50008 so as to connect to the second port socket in the server; it's the same as echo-client, with a different port number (alas, the original script wasn't designed to input a port):

```
[client window 1]
C:\...\PP2E\Internet\Sockets>python echo-client.py
Client received: 'Echo=>Hello network world at Sun Aug 13 22:52:01 2000'

C:\...\PP2E\Internet\Sockets>python echo-client.py
Client received: 'Echo=>Hello network world at Sun Aug 13 22:52:03 2000'

[client window 2]
C:\...\PP2E\Internet\Sockets>python echo-client-50008.py localhost Sir Lancelot
Client received: 'Echo=>Sir at Sun Aug 13 22:52:57 2000'
Client received: 'Echo=>Lancelot at Sun Aug 13 22:52:57 2000'

C:\...\PP2E\Internet\Sockets>python testecho.py
```

Now, in the next code section is the sort of interaction and output that shows up in the window where the server has been started. The first three connections come from echo-client runs; the rest is the result of the eight programs spawned by testecho in the second client window. Notice that for testecho, new client connections and client inputs are all multiplexed together. If you study the output closely, you'll see that they overlap in time, because all activity is dispatched by the single event loop in the server.[*] Also note that the sever gets an empty string when the client has closed its socket. We take care to close and delete these sockets at the server right away, or else they would be needlessly reselected again and again, each time through the main loop:

```
[server window]
C:\...\PP2E\Internet\Sockets>python select-server.py
select-server loop starting
Connect: ('127.0.0.1', 1175) 7965520
        got Hello network world on 7965520
        got    on 7965520
Connect: ('127.0.0.1', 1176) 7964288
        got Hello network world on 7964288
```

---

[*] And the trace output on the server will probably look a bit different every time it runs. Clients and new connections are interleaved almost at random due to timing differences on the host machines.

```
         got   on 7964288
Connect: ('127.0.0.1', 1177) 7963920
         got Sir on 7963920
         got Lancelot on 7963920
         got   on 7963920
```

[testecho results]

```
Connect: ('127.0.0.1', 1178) 7965216
         got Hello network world on 7965216
         got   on 7965216
Connect: ('127.0.0.1', 1179) 7963968
Connect: ('127.0.0.1', 1180) 7965424
         got Hello network world on 7963968
Connect: ('127.0.0.1', 1181) 7962976
         got Hello network world on 7965424
         got   on 7963968
         got Hello network world on 7962976
         got   on 7965424
         got   on 7962976
Connect: ('127.0.0.1', 1182) 7963648
         got Hello network world on 7963648
         got   on 7963648
Connect: ('127.0.0.1', 1183) 7966640
         got Hello network world on 7966640
         got   on 7966640
Connect: ('127.0.0.1', 1184) 7966496
         got Hello network world on 7966496
         got   on 7966496
Connect: ('127.0.0.1', 1185) 7965888
         got Hello network world on 7965888
         got   on 7965888
```

A subtle but crucial point: a `time.sleep` call to simulate a long-running task doesn't make sense in the server here—because all clients are handled by the same single loop, sleeping would pause everything (and defeat the whole point of a multiplexing server). Here are a few additional notes before we move on:

Select call details

> Formally, `select` is called with three lists of selectable objects (input sources, output sources, and exceptional condition sources), plus an optional timeout. The timeout argument may be a real *wait* expiration value in seconds (use floating-point numbers to express fractions of a second), a zero value to mean simply poll and return immediately, or be omitted to mean wait until at least one object is ready (as done in our server script earlier). The call returns a triple of ready objects—subsets of the first three arguments—any or all of which may be empty if the timeout expired before sources became ready.

Select portability

> The `select` call works only for sockets on Windows, but also works for things like files and pipes on Unix and Macintosh. For servers running over the Internet, of course, sockets are the primary devices we are interested in.

Nonblocking sockets

select lets us be sure that socket calls like accept and recv won't block (pause) the caller, but it's also possible to make Python sockets nonblocking in general. Call the setblocking method of socket objects to set the socket to blocking or nonblocking mode. For example, given a call like sock. setblocking(flag), the socket sock is set to nonblocking mode if the flag is zero, and set to blocking mode otherwise. All sockets start out in blocking mode initially, so socket calls may always make the caller wait.

But when in nonblocking mode, a socket.error exception is raised if a recv socket call doesn't find any data, or if a send call can't immediately transfer data. A script can catch this exception to determine if the socket is ready for processing. In blocking mode, these calls always block until they can proceed. Of course, there may be much more to processing client requests than data transfers (requests may also require long-running computations), so nonblocking sockets don't guarantee that servers won't stall in general. They are simply another way to code multiplexing servers. Like select, they are better suited when client requests can be serviced quickly.

The asyncore module framework

If you're interested in using select, you will probably also be interested in checking out the *asyncore.py* module in the standard Python library. It implements a class-based callback model, where input and output callbacks are dispatched to class methods by a precoded select event loop. As such, it allows servers to be constructed without threads or forks. We'll learn more about this tool at the end of Chapter 15.

Choosing a Server Scheme

So when should you use select to build a server instead of threads or forks? Needs vary per application, of course, but servers based on the select call are generally considered to perform very well when client transactions are relatively short. If they are not short, threads or forks may be a better way to split processing among multiple clients. Threads and forks are especially useful if clients require long-running processing above and beyond socket calls.

It's important to remember that schemes based on select (and nonblocking sockets) are not completely immune to blocking. In the example earlier, for instance, the send call that echoes text back to a client might block, too, and hence stall the entire server. We could work around that blocking potential by using select to make sure that the output operation is ready before we attempt it (e.g., use the writesocks list and add another loop to send replies to ready output sockets), albeit at a noticeable cost in program clarity.

In general, though, if we cannot split up the processing of a client's request in such a way that it can be multiplexed with other requests and not block the server's loop, `select` may not be the best way to construct the server. Moreover, `select` also seems more complex than spawning either processes or threads, because we need to manually transfer control among all tasks (for instance, compare the threaded and `select` versions of this server, even without write selects). As usual, though, the degree of that complexity may vary per application.

A Simple Python File Server

Time for something more realistic. Let's conclude this chapter by putting some of these socket ideas to work in something a bit more useful than echoing text back and forth. Example 10-10 implements both the server-side and client-side logic needed to ship a requested file from server to client machines over a raw socket.

In effect, this script implements a simple file download system. One instance of the script is run on the machine where downloadable files live (the server), and another on the machines you wish to copy files to (the clients). Command-line arguments tell the script which flavor to run and optionally name the server machine and port number over which conversations are to occur. A server instance can respond to any number of client file requests at the port on which it listens, because it serves each in a thread.

Example 10-10. PP2E\Internet\Sockets\getfile.py

```
#########################################################
# implement client and server side logic to transfer an
# arbitrary file from server to client over a socket;
# uses a simple control-info protocol rather than
# separate sockets for control and data (as in ftp),
# dispatches each client request to a handler thread,
# and loops to transfer the entire file by blocks; see
# ftplib examples for a higher-level transport scheme;
#########################################################

import sys, os, thread, time
from socket import *
def now(): return time.ctime(time.time())

blksz = 1024
defaultHost = 'localhost'
defaultPort = 50001

helptext = """
Usage...
server=> getfile.py  -mode server          [-port nnn] [-host hhh|localhost]
client=> getfile.py [-mode client] -file fff [-port nnn] [-host hhh|localhost]
"""

def parsecommandline():
    dict = {}                          # put in dictionary for easy lookup
    args = sys.argv[1:]                # skip program name at front of args
    while len(args) >= 2:              # example: dict['-mode'] = 'server'
        dict[args[0]] = args[1]
```

Example 10-10. PP2E\Internet\Sockets\getfile.py (continued)

```python
        args = args[2:]
    return dict

def client(host, port, filename):
    sock = socket(AF_INET, SOCK_STREAM)
    sock.connect((host, port))
    sock.send(filename + '\n')                  # send remote name with dir
    dropdir = os.path.split(filename)[1]        # file name at end of dir path
    file = open(dropdir, 'wb')                  # create local file in cwd
    while 1:
        data = sock.recv(blksz)                 # get up to 1K at a time
        if not data: break                      # till closed on server side
        file.write(data)                        # store data in local file
    sock.close()
    file.close()
    print 'Client got', filename, 'at', now()


def serverthread(clientsock):
    sockfile = clientsock.makefile('r')         # wrap socket in dup file obj
    filename = sockfile.readline()[:-1]         # get filename up to end-line
    try:
        file = open(filename, 'rb')
        while 1:
            bytes = file.read(blksz)            # read/send 1K at a time
            if not bytes: break                 # until file totally sent
            sent = clientsock.send(bytes)
            assert sent == len(bytes)
    except:
        print 'Error downloading file on server:', filename
    clientsock.close()


def server(host, port):
    serversock = socket(AF_INET, SOCK_STREAM)   # listen on tcp/ip socket
    serversock.bind((host, port))               # serve clients in threads
    serversock.listen(5)
    while 1:
        clientsock, clientaddr = serversock.accept()
        print 'Server connected by', clientaddr, 'at', now()
        thread.start_new_thread(serverthread, (clientsock,))


def main(args):
    host = args.get('-host', defaultHost)       # use args or defaults
    port = int(args.get('-port', defaultPort))  # is a string in argv
    if args.get('-mode') == 'server':           # None if no -mode: client
        if host == 'localhost': host = ''       # else fails remotely
        server(host, port)
    elif args.get('-file'):                     # client mode needs -file
        client(host, port, args['-file'])
    else:
        print helptext


if __name__ == '__main__':
    args = parsecommandline()
    main(args)
```

This script doesn't do much different than the examples we saw earlier. Depending on the command-line arguments passed, it invokes one of two functions:

- The **server** function farms out each incoming client request to a thread that transfers the requested file's bytes.

- The **client** function sends the server a file's name and stores all the bytes it gets back in a local file of the same name.

The most novel feature here is the protocol between client and server: the client starts the conversation by shipping a filename string up to the server, terminated with an end-of-line character, and including the file's directory path in the server. At the server, a spawned thread extracts the requested file's name by reading the client socket, and opens and transfers the requested file back to the client, one chunk of bytes at a time.

Running the File Server and Clients

Since the server uses threads to process clients, we can test both client and server on the same Windows machine. First, let's start a server instance, and execute two client instances on the same machine while the server runs:

```
[server window, localhost]
C:\...\PP2E\Internet\Sockets>python getfile.py -mode server
Server connected by ('127.0.0.1', 1089) at Thu Mar 16 11:54:21 2000
Server connected by ('127.0.0.1', 1090) at Thu Mar 16 11:54:37 2000

[client window, localhost]
C:\...\Internet\Sockets>ls
class-server.py    echo.out.txt     testdir            thread-server.py
echo-client.py     fork-server.py   testecho.py
echo-server.py     getfile.py       testechowait.py

C:\...\Internet\Sockets>python getfile.py -file testdir\python15.lib -port 50001
Client got testdir\python15.lib at Thu Mar 16 11:54:21 2000

C:\...\Internet\Sockets>python getfile.py -file testdir\textfile
Client got testdir\textfile at Thu Mar 16 11:54:37 2000
```

Clients run in the directory where you want the downloaded file to appear—the client instance code strips the server directory path when making the local file's name. Here the "download" simply copied the requested files up to the local parent directory (the DOS *fc* command compares file contents):

```
C:\...\Internet\Sockets>ls
class-server.py    echo.out.txt     python15.lib       testechowait.py
echo-client.py     fork-server.py   testdir            textfile
echo-server.py     getfile.py       testecho.py        thread-server.py

C:\...\Internet\Sockets>fc /B python1.lib testdir\python15.lib
Comparing files python15.lib and testdir\python15.lib
FC: no differences encountered
```

```
C:\...\Internet\Sockets>fc /B textfile testdir\textfile
Comparing files textfile and testdir\textfile
FC: no differences encountered
```

As usual, we can run server and clients on different machines as well. Here the script is being used to run a remote server on a Linux machine and a few clients on a local Windows PC (I added line breaks to some of the command lines to make them fit). Notice that client and server machine times are different now—they are fetched from different machine's clocks and so may be arbitrarily skewed:

[server telnet window: first message is the python15.lib request in client window1]

```
[lutz@starship lutz]$ python getfile.py -mode server
Server connected by ('166.93.216.248', 1185) at Thu Mar 16 16:02:07 2000
Server connected by ('166.93.216.248', 1187) at Thu Mar 16 16:03:24 2000
Server connected by ('166.93.216.248', 1189) at Thu Mar 16 16:03:52 2000
Server connected by ('166.93.216.248', 1191) at Thu Mar 16 16:04:09 2000
Server connected by ('166.93.216.248', 1193) at Thu Mar 16 16:04:38 2000
```

[client window 1: started first, runs in thread while other client requests are made in client window 2, and processed by other threads]

```
C:\...\Internet\Sockets>python getfile.py -mode client
                        -host starship.python.net
                        -port 50001 -file python15.lib
Client got python15.lib at Thu Mar 16 14:07:37 2000

C:\...\Internet\Sockets>fc /B python15.lib testdir\python15.lib
Comparing files python15.lib and testdir\python15.lib
FC: no differences encountered
```

[client window 2: requests made while client window 1 request downloading]

```
C:\...\Internet\Sockets>python getfile.py
                        -host starship.python.net -file textfile
Client got textfile at Thu Mar 16 14:02:29 2000

C:\...\Internet\Sockets>python getfile.py
                        -host starship.python.net -file textfile
Client got textfile at Thu Mar 16 14:04:11 2000

C:\...\Internet\Sockets>python getfile.py
                        -host starship.python.net -file textfile
Client got textfile at Thu Mar 16 14:04:21 2000

C:\...\Internet\Sockets>python getfile.py
                        -host starship.python.net -file index.html
Client got index.html at Thu Mar 16 14:06:22 2000

C:\...\Internet\Sockets>fc textfile testdir\textfile
Comparing files textfile and testdir\textfile
FC: no differences encountered
```

One subtle security point here: the server instance code is happy to send any server-side file whose pathname is sent from a client, as long as the server is run with a username that has read access to the requested file. If you care about keeping some of your server-side files private, you should add logic to suppress downloads of restricted files. I'll leave this as a suggested exercise here, but will implement such filename checks in the `getfile` download tool in Chapter 12.[*]

Making Sockets Look Like Files

For illustration purposes, `getfile` uses the socket object `makefile` method to wrap the socket in a file-like object. Once so wrapped, the socket can be read and written using normal file methods; `getfile` uses the file `readline` call to read the filename line sent by the client.

This isn't strictly required in this example—we could have read this line with the socket `recv` call, too. In general, though, the `makefile` method comes in handy any time you need to pass a socket to an interface that expects a file.

For example, the `pickle` module's `load` and `dump` methods expect an object with a file-like interface (e.g., `read` and `write` methods), but don't require a physical file. Passing a TCP/IP socket wrapped with the `makefile` call to the pickler allows us to ship serialized Python objects over the Internet. See Chapter 16, *Databases and Persistence*, for more details on object serialization interfaces.

More generally, any component that expects a file-like method protocol will gladly accept a socket wrapped with a socket object `makefile` call. Such interfaces will also accept strings wrapped with the built-in `StringIO` module, and any other sort of object that supports the same kinds of method calls as built-in file objects. As always in Python, we code to *protocols*—object interfaces—not to specific datatypes.

Adding a User-Interface Frontend

You might have noticed that we have been living in the realm of the command line for all of this chapter—our socket clients and servers have been started from simple DOS or Linux shells. There is nothing stopping us from adding a nice

---

[*] We'll see three more `getfile` programs before we leave Internet scripting. The next chapter's *getfile.py* fetches a file with the higher-level FTP interface rather than using raw socket calls, and its *http-getfile* scripts fetch files over the HTTP protocol. Chapter 12 presents a *getfile.cgi* script that transfers file contents over the HTTP port in response to a request made in a web browser client (files are sent as the output of a CGI script). All four of the download schemes presented in this text ultimately use sockets, but only the version here makes that use explicit.

point-and-click user interface to some of these scripts, though; GUI and network scripting are not mutually exclusive techniques. In fact, they can be arguably sexy when used together well.

For instance, it would be easy to implement a simple Tkinter GUI frontend to the client-side portion of the `getfile` script we just met. Such a tool, run on the client machine, may simply pop up a window with `Entry` widgets for typing the desired filename, server, and so on. Once download parameters have been input, the user interface could either import and call the `getfile.client` function with appropriate option arguments, or build and run the implied *getfile.py* command line using tools such as `os.system`, `os.fork`, `thread`, etc.

Using Frames and command lines

To help make this all more concrete, let's very quickly explore a few simple scripts that add a Tkinter frontend to the `getfile` client-side program. The first, in Example 10-11, creates a dialog for inputting server, port, and filename information, and simply constructs the corresponding `getfile` command line and runs it with `os.system`.

Example 10-11. PP2E\Internet\Sockets\getfilegui-1.py

```
##########################################################
# launch getfile script client from simple Tkinter GUI;
# could also or os.fork+exec, os.spawnv (see Launcher);
# windows: replace 'python' with 'start' if not on path;
##########################################################

import sys, os
from Tkinter import *
from tkMessageBox import showinfo

def onReturnKey():
    cmdline = ('python getfile.py -mode client -file %s -port %s -host %s' %
                    (content['File'].get(),
                     content['Port'].get(),
                     content['Server'].get()))
    os.system(cmdline)
    showinfo('getfilegui-1', 'Download complete')

box = Frame(Tk())
box.pack(expand=YES, fill=X)
lcol, rcol = Frame(box), Frame(box)
lcol.pack(side=LEFT)
rcol.pack(side=RIGHT, expand=Y, fill=X)

labels = ['Server', 'Port', 'File']
content = {}
for label in labels:
    Label(lcol, text=label).pack(side=TOP)
```

Example 10-11. PP2E\Internet\Sockets\getfilegui-1.py (continued)

```
    entry = Entry(rcol)
    entry.pack(side=TOP, expand=YES, fill=X)
    content[label] = entry

box.master.title('getfilegui-1')
box.master.bind('<Return>', (lambda event: onReturnKey()))
mainloop()
```

When run, this script creates the input form shown in Figure 10-1. Pressing the Enter key (<Return>) runs a client-side instance of the `getfile` program; when the generated `getfile` command line is finished, we get the verification pop-up displayed in Figure 10-2.

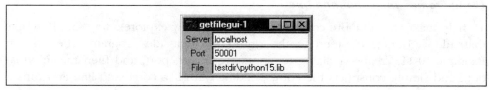

Figure 10-1. getfilegui-1 in action

Figure 10-2. getfilegui-1 verification pop-up

Using grids and function calls

The first user-interface script (Example 10-11) uses the **pack** geometry manager and `Frames` to layout the input form, and runs the `getfile` client as a stand-alone program. It's just as easy to use the `grid` manager for layout, and import and call the client-side logic function instead of running a program. The script in Example 10-12 shows how.

Example 10-12. PP2E\Internet\Sockets\getfilegui-2.py

```
###########################################################
# same, but with grids and import+call, not packs and cmdline;
# direct function calls are usually faster than running files;
###########################################################


import getfile
from Tkinter import *
from tkMessageBox import showinfo
```

Example 10-12. PP2E\Internet\Sockets\getfilegui-2.py (continued)

```
def onSubmit():
    getfile.client(content['Server'].get(),
                   int(content['Port'].get()),
                   content['File'].get())
    showinfo('getfilegui-2', 'Download complete')

box    = Tk()
labels = ['Server', 'Port', 'File']
rownum = 0
content = {}
for label in labels:
    Label(box, text=label).grid(col=0, row=rownum)
    entry = Entry(box)
    entry.grid(col=1, row=rownum, sticky=E+W)
    content[label] = entry
    rownum = rownum + 1

box.columnconfigure(0, weight=0)    # make expandable
box.columnconfigure(1, weight=1)
Button(text='Submit', command=onSubmit).grid(row=rownum, col=0, columnspan=2)

box.title('getfilegui-2')
box.bind('<Return>', (lambda event: onSubmit()))
mainloop()
```

This version makes a similar window (Figure 10-3), but adds a button at the bottom that does the same thing as an Enter key press—it runs the `getfile` client procedure. Generally speaking, importing and calling functions (as done here) is faster than running command lines, especially if done more than once. The `getfile` script is set up to work either way—as program or function library.

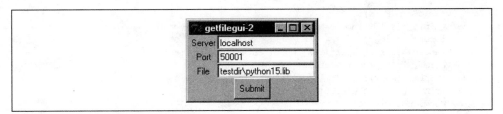

Figure 10-3. getfilegui-2 in action

Using a reusable form-layout class

If you're like me, though, writing all the GUI form layout code in those two scripts can seem a bit tedious, whether you use packing or grids. In fact, it became so tedious to me that I decided to write a general-purpose form-layout class, shown in Example 10-13, that handles most of the GUI layout grunt work.

Example 10-13. PP2E\Internet\Sockets\form.py

```
# a reusable form class, used by getfilegui (and others)

from Tkinter import *
entrysize = 40

class Form:                                         # add non-modal form box
    def __init__(self, labels, parent=None):        # pass field labels list
        box = Frame(parent)
        box.pack(expand=YES, fill=X)
        rows = Frame(box, bd=2, relief=GROOVE)       # box has rows, button
        lcol = Frame(rows)                           # rows has lcol, rcol
        rcol = Frame(rows)                           # button or return key,
        rows.pack(side=TOP, expand=Y, fill=X)        # runs onSubmit method
        lcol.pack(side=LEFT)
        rcol.pack(side=RIGHT, expand=Y, fill=X)
        self.content = {}
        for label in labels:
            Label(lcol, text=label).pack(side=TOP)
            entry = Entry(rcol, width=entrysize)
            entry.pack(side=TOP, expand=YES, fill=X)
            self.content[label] = entry
        Button(box, text='Cancel', command=self.onCancel).pack(side=RIGHT)
        Button(box, text='Submit', command=self.onSubmit).pack(side=RIGHT)
        box.master.bind('<Return>', (lambda event, self=self: self.onSubmit()))

    def onSubmit(self):                              # override this
        for key in self.content.keys():             # user inputs in
            print key, '\t=>\t', self.content[key].get()   # self.content[k]

    def onCancel(self):                              # override if need
        Tk().quit()                                  # default is exit

class DynamicForm(Form):
    def __init__(self, labels=None):
        import string
        labels = string.split(raw_input('Enter field names: '))
        Form.__init__(self, labels)
    def onSubmit(self):
        print 'Field values...'
        Form.onSubmit(self)
        self.onCancel()

if __name__ == '__main__':
    import sys
    if len(sys.argv) == 1:
        Form(['Name', 'Age', 'Job'])       # precoded fields, stay after submit
    else:
        DynamicForm()                       # input fields, go away after submit
    mainloop()
```

Running this module standalone triggers its self-test code at the bottom. Without arguments (and when double-clicked in a Windows file explorer), the self-test generates a form with canned input fields captured in Figure 10-4, and displays the fields' values on Enter key presses or Submit button clicks:

```
C:\...\PP2E\Internet\Sockets>python form.py
Job      =>      Educator, Entertainer
Age      =>      38
Name     =>      Bob
```

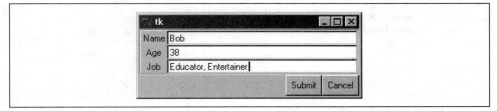

Figure 10-4. Form test, canned fields

With a command-line argument, the form class module's self-test code prompts for an arbitrary set of field names for the form; fields can be constructed as dynamically as we like. Figure 10-5 shows the input form constructed in response to the following console interaction. Field names could be accepted on the command line, too, but `raw_input` works just as well for simple tests like this. In this mode, the GUI goes away after the first submit, because `DynamicForm.onSubmit` says so:

```
C:\...\PP2E\Internet\Sockets>python form.py -
Enter field names: Name Email Web Locale
Field values...
Email    =>      lutz@rmi.net
Locale   =>      Colorado
Web      =>      http://rmi.net/~lutz
Name     =>      mel
```

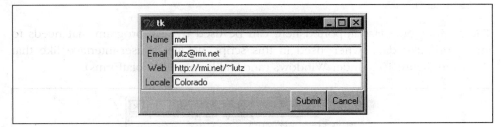

Figure 10-5. Form test, dynamic fields

And last but not least, Example 10-14 shows the `getfile` user interface again, this time constructed with the reusable form layout class. We need to fill in only the form labels list, and provide an `onSubmit` callback method of our own. All of the work needed to construct the form comes "for free," from the imported and widely reusable `Form` superclass.

Example 10-14. PP2E\Internet\Sockets\getfilegui.py

```
###############################################################
# launch getfile client with a reusable gui form class;
# os.chdir to target local dir if input (getfile stores in cwd);
# to do: use threads, show download status and getfile prints;
###############################################################

from form import Form
from Tkinter import Tk, mainloop
from tkMessageBox import showinfo
import getfile, os

class GetfileForm(Form):
    def __init__(self, oneshot=0):
        root = Tk()
        root.title('getfilegui')
        labels = ['Server Name', 'Port Number', 'File Name', 'Local Dir?']
        Form.__init__(self, labels, root)
        self.oneshot = oneshot
    def onSubmit(self):
        Form.onSubmit(self)
        localdir   = self.content['Local Dir?'].get()
        portnumber = self.content['Port Number'].get()
        servername = self.content['Server Name'].get()
        filename   = self.content['File Name'].get()
        if localdir:
            os.chdir(localdir)
        portnumber = int(portnumber)
        getfile.client(servername, portnumber, filename)
        showinfo('getfilegui', 'Download complete')
        if self.oneshot: Tk().quit()  # else stay in last localdir

if __name__ == '__main__':
    GetfileForm()
    mainloop()
```

The form layout class imported here can be used by any program that needs to
input form-like data; when used in this script, we get a user-interface like that
shown in Figure 10-6 under Windows (and similar on other platforms).

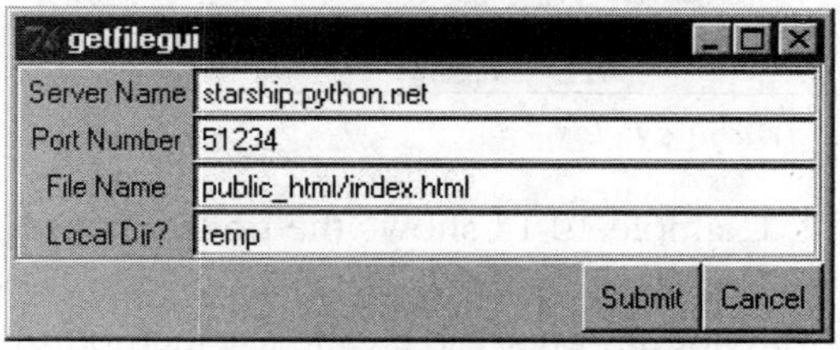

Figure 10-6. getfilegui in action

Pressing this form's Submit button or the Enter key makes the `getfilegui` script call the imported `getfile.client` client-side function as before. This time, though, we also first change to the local directory typed into the form, so that the fetched file is stored there (`getfile` stores in the current working directory, whatever that may be when it is called). As usual, we can use this interface to connect to servers running locally on the same machine, or remotely. Here is some of the interaction we get for both modes:

```
[talking to a local server]
C:\...\PP2E\Internet\Sockets>python getfilegui.py
Port Number      =>     50001
Local Dir?       =>     temp
Server Name      =>     localhost
File Name        =>     testdir\python15.lib
Client got testdir\python15.lib at Tue Aug 15 22:32:34 2000

[talking to a remote server]
[lutz@starship lutz]$ /usr/bin/python getfile.py -mode server -port 51234
Server connected by ('38.28.130.229', 1111) at Tue Aug 15 21:48:13 2000

C:\...\PP2E\Internet\Sockets>python getfilegui.py
Port Number      =>     51234
Local Dir?       =>     temp
Server Name      =>     starship.python.net
File Name        =>     public_html/index.html
Client got public_html/index.html at Tue Aug 15 22:42:06 2000
```

One caveat worth pointing out here: the GUI is essentially dead while the download is in progress (even screen redraws aren't handled—try covering and uncovering the window and you'll see what I mean). We could make this better by running the download in a thread, but since we'll see how in the next chapter, you should consider this problem a preview.

In closing, a few final notes. First of all, I should point out that the scripts in this chapter use Tkinter tricks we've seen before and won't go into here in the interest of space; be sure to see the GUI chapters in this book for implementation hints.

Keep in mind, too, that these interfaces all just *add* a GUI on top of the existing script to reuse its code; any command-line tool can be easily GUI-ified in this way to make them more appealing and user-friendly. In the next chapter, for example, we'll meet a more useful client-side Tkinter user interface for reading and sending email over sockets (PyMailGui), which largely just adds a GUI to mail-processing tools. Generally speaking, GUIs can often be added as almost an afterthought to a program. Although the degree of user-interface and core logic separation can vary per program, keeping the two distinct makes it easier to focus on each.

And finally, now that I've shown you how to build user interfaces on top of this chapter's `getfile`, I should also say that they aren't really as useful as they might seem. In particular, `getfile` clients can talk only to machines that are running a `getfile` server. In the next chapter, we'll discover another way to download files—FTP—which also runs on sockets, but provides a higher-level interface, and is available as a standard service on many machines on the Net. We don't generally need to start up a custom server to transfer files over FTP, the way we do with `getfile`. In fact, the user-interface scripts in this chapter could be easily changed to fetch the desired file with Python's FTP tools, instead of the `getfile` module. But rather than spilling all the beans here, I'll just say "read on."

Using Serial Ports on Windows

Sockets, the main subject of this chapter, are the programmer's interface to network connections in Python scripts. As we've seen, they let us write scripts that converse with computers arbitrarily located on a network, and they form the backbone of the Internet and the Web.

If you're looking for a more low-level way to communicate with devices in general, though, you may also be interested in the topic of Python's serial port interfaces. This isn't quite related to Internet scripting and applies only on Windows machines, but it's similar enough in spirit and is discussed often enough on the Net to merit a quick look here.

Serial ports are known as "COM" ports on Windows (not to be confused with the COM object model), and are identified as "COM1", "COM2", and so on. By using interfaces to these ports, scripts may engage in low-level communication with things like mice, modems, and a wide variety of serial devices. Serial port interfaces are also used to communicate with devices connected over infrared ports (e.g., hand-held computers and remote modems). There are often other higher-level ways to access such devices (e.g., the PyRite package for ceasing Palm Pilot databases, or RAS for using modems), but serial port interfaces let scripts tap into raw data streams and implement device protocols of their own.

There are at least three ways to send and receive data over serial ports in Python scripts—a public domain C extension package known as Serial, the proprietary MSComm COM server object interface published by Microsoft, and the low-level CreateFile file API call exported by the Python Windows extensions package, available via links at *http://www.python.org*.

Unfortunately, there's no time to cover any of these in detail in this text. For more information, the O'Reilly book *Python Programming on Win32* includes an entire section dedicated to serial port communication topics. Also be sure to use the search tools at Python's web site for up-to-date details on this front.

11

Client-Side Scripting

"Socket to Me!"

The previous chapter introduced Internet fundamentals and explored *sockets*—the underlying communications mechanism over which bytes flow on the Net. In this chapter, we climb the encapsulation hierarchy one level, and shift our focus to Python tools that support the client-side interfaces of common Internet protocols.

We talked about the Internet's higher-level *protocols* in the abstract at the start of the last chapter, and you should probably review that material if you skipped over it the first time around. In short, protocols define the structure of the conversations that take place to accomplish most of the Internet tasks we're all familiar with—reading email, transferring files by FTP, fetching web pages, and so on.

At the most basic level, all these protocol dialogs happen over sockets using fixed and standard message structures and ports, so in some sense this chapter builds upon the last. But as we'll see, Python's protocol modules hide most of the underlying details—scripts generally need deal only with simple objects and methods, and Python automates the socket and messaging logic required by the protocol.

In this chapter, we'll concentrate on the FTP and email protocol modules in Python, and peek at a few others along the way (NNTP news, HTTP web pages, and so on). All of the tools employed in examples here are in the standard Python library and come with the Python system. All of the examples here are also designed to run on the *client* side of a network connection—these scripts connect to an already-running server to request interaction and can be run from a simple PC. In the next chapter, we'll move on to explore scripts designed to be run on the server side instead. For now, let's focus on the client.

Transferring Files over the Net

As we saw in the previous chapter, sockets see plenty of action on the Net. For instance, the `getfile` example at the end of that chapter allowed us to transfer entire files between machines. In practice, though, higher-level protocols are behind much of what happens on the Net. Protocols run on top of sockets, but hide much of the complexity of the network scripting examples we've just seen.

FTP—the File Transfer Protocol—is one of the more commonly used Internet protocols. It defines a higher-level conversation model that is based on exchanging command strings and file contents over sockets. By using FTP, we can accomplish the same task as the prior chapter's `getfile` script, but the interface is simpler, and standard—FTP lets us ask for files from any server machine that supports FTP, without requiring that it run our custom `getfile` script. FTP also supports more advanced operations such as uploading files to the server, getting remote directory listings, and more.

Really, FTP runs on top of *two* sockets: one for passing control commands between client and server (port 21), and another for transferring bytes. By using a two-socket model, FTP avoids the possibility of deadlocks (i.e., transfers on the data socket do not block dialogs on the control socket). Ultimately, though, Python's `ftplib` support module allows us to upload and download files at a remote server machine by FTP, without dealing in raw socket calls or FTP protocol details.

FTP: Fetching Python with Python

Because the Python FTP interface is so easy to use, let's jump right into a realistic example. The script in Example 11-1 automatically fetches and builds Python with Python. No, this isn't a recursive chicken-and-egg thought exercise—you must already have installed Python to run this program. More specifically, this Python script does the following:

1. Downloads the Python source distribution by FTP

2. Unpacks and compiles the distribution into a Python executable

The download portion will run on any machine with Python and sockets; the unpacking and compiling code assumes a Unix-like build environment as coded here, but could be tweaked to work with other platforms.

Example 11-1. PP2E\Internet\Ftp\getpython.py

```
#!/usr/local/bin/python
##############################################################
# A Python script to download and build Python's source code.
# Uses ftplib, the ftp protocol handler which uses sockets.
# Ftp runs on 2 sockets (one for data, one for control--on
# ports 20 and 21) and imposes message text formats, but the
```

Example 11-1. PP2E\Internet\Ftp\getpython.py (continued)

```python
# Python ftplib module hides most of this protocol's details.
##############################################################

import os
from ftplib import FTP                     # socket-based ftp tools
Version = '1.5'                            # version to download
tarname = 'python%s.tar.gz' % Version      # remote/local file name

print 'Connecting...'
localfile  = open(tarname, 'wb')           # where to store download
connection = FTP('ftp.python.org')         # connect to ftp site
connection.login()                         # default is anonymous login
connection.cwd('pub/python/src')           # xfer 1k at a time to localfile

print 'Downloading...'
connection.retrbinary('RETR ' + tarname, localfile.write, 1024)
connection.quit()
localfile.close()

print 'Unpacking...'
os.system('gzip -d ' + tarname)            # decompress
os.system('tar -xvf ' + tarname[:-3])      # strip .gz

print 'Building...'
os.chdir('Python-' + Version)              # build Python itself
os.system('./configure')                   # assumes unix-style make
os.system('make')
os.system('make test')
print 'Done: see Python-%s/python.' % Version
```

Most of the FTP protocol details are encapsulated by the Python `ftplib` module imported here. This script uses some of the simplest interfaces in `ftplib` (we'll see others in a moment), but they are representative of the module in general:

```python
connection = FTP('ftp.python.org')         # connect to ftp site
```

To open a connection to a remote (or local) FTP server, create an instance of the `ftplib.FTP` object, passing in the name (domain or IP-style) of the machine you wish to connect to. Assuming this call doesn't throw an exception, the resulting FTP object exports methods that correspond to the usual FTP operations. In fact, Python scripts act much like typical FTP client programs—just replace commands you would normally type or select with method calls:

```python
connection.login()                         # default is anonymous login
connection.cwd('pub/python/src')           # xfer 1k at a time to localfile
```

Once connected, we log in, and go to the remote directory we want to fetch a file from. The `login` method allows us to pass in additional optional arguments to specify a username and password; by default it performs anonymous FTP:

```python
connection.retrbinary('RETR ' + tarname, localfile.write, 1024)
connection.quit()
```

Once we're in the target directory, we simply call the `retrbinary` method to download the target server file in binary mode. The `retrbinary` call will take awhile to complete, since it must download a big file. It gets three arguments:

- An FTP command string—here, a string `RETR` *filename*, which is the standard format for FTP retrievals.

- A function or method to which Python passes each chunk of the downloaded file's bytes—here, the `write` method of a newly created and opened local file.

- A size for those chunks of bytes—here, 1024 bytes are downloaded at a time, but the default is reasonable if this argument is omitted.

Because this script creates a local file named `localfile`, of the same name as the remote file being fetched, and passes its `write` method to the FTP retrieval method, the remote file's contents will automatically appear in a local, client-side file after the download is finished. By the way, notice that this file is opened in "wb" binary output mode; if this script is run on Windows, we want to avoid automatically expanding and \n bytes into \r\n byte sequences (that happens automatically on Windows when writing files opened in "w" text mode).

Finally, we call the FTP `quit` method to break the connection with the server and manually `close` the local file to force it to be complete before it is further processed by the shell commands spawned by `os.system` (it's not impossible that parts of the file are still held in buffers before the `close` call):

```
connection.quit()
localfile.close()
```

And that's all there is to it; all the FTP, socket, and networking details are hidden behind the `ftplib` interface module. Here is this script in action on a Linux machine, with a couple thousand output lines cut in the interest of brevity:

```
[lutz@starship test]$ python getpython.py
Connecting...
Downloading...
Unpacking...
Python-1.5/
Python-1.5/Doc/
Python-1.5/Doc/ref/
Python-1.5/Doc/ref/.cvsignore
Python-1.5/Doc/ref/fixps.py
...
...lots of tar lines deleted...
...
Python-1.5/Tools/webchecker/webchecker.py
Python-1.5/Tools/webchecker/websucker.py
Building...
creating cache ./config.cache
checking MACHDEP... linux2
checking CCC...
checking for --without-gcc... no
```

```
checking for gcc... gcc
...
...lots of build lines deleted...
...
Done: see Python-1.5/python.

[lutz@starship test]$ cd Python-1.5/
[lutz@starship Python-1.5]$ ./python
Python 1.5 (#1, Jul 12 2000, 12:35:52)   [GCC egcs-2.91.66 19990314/Li on linux2
Copyright 1991-1995 Stichting Mathematisch Centrum, Amsterdam
>>> print 'The Larch!'
The Larch!
```

Such a script could be automatically executed at regular intervals (e.g., by a Unix *cron* job) to update a local Python install with a fresh build. But the thing to notice here is that this otherwise typical Python script fetches information from an arbitrarily remote FTP site and machine. Given an Internet link, *any* information published by an FTP server on the Net can be fetched by and incorporated into Python scripts using interfaces such as these.

Using urllib to FTP files

In fact, FTP is just one way to transfer information across the Net, and there are more general tools in the Python library to accomplish the prior script's download. Perhaps the most straightforward is the Python `urllib` module: given an Internet address string—a URL, or Universal Resource Locator—this module opens a connection to the specified server and returns a file-like object ready to be read with normal file object method calls (e.g., `read`, `readlines`).

We can use such a higher-level interface to download anything with an address on the Web—files published by FTP sites (using URLs that start with "ftp://"), web pages and outputs of scripts that live on remote servers (using "http://" URLs), local files (using "file://" URLs), Gopher server data, and more. For instance, the script in Example 11-2 does the same as the one in Example 11-1, but it uses the general `urllib` module to fetch the source distribution file, instead of the protocol-specific `ftplib`.

Example 11-2. PP2E\Internet\Ftp\getpython-urllib.py

```
#!/usr/local/bin/python
##################################################################
# A Python script to download and build Python's source code
# use higher-level urllib instead of ftplib to fetch file
# urllib supports ftp, http, and gopher protocols, and local files
# urllib also allows downloads of html pages, images, text, etc.;
# see also Python html/xml parsers for web pages fetched by urllib;
##################################################################

import os
import urllib                          # socket-based web tools
Version = '1.5'                        # version to download
```

Example 11-2. PP2E\Internet\Ftp\getpython-urllib.py (continued)

```
tarname = 'python%s.tar.gz' % Version    # remote/local file name

remoteaddr = 'ftp://ftp.python.org/pub/python/src/' + tarname
print 'Downloading', remoteaddr

# this works too:
# urllib.urlretrieve(remoteaddr, tarname)

remotefile = urllib.urlopen(remoteaddr)      # returns input file-like object
localfile  = open(tarname, 'wb')             # where to store data locally
localfile.write(remotefile.read())
localfile.close()
remotefile.close()

# the rest is the same
execfile('buildPython.py')
```

Don't sweat the details of the URL string used here; we'll talk much more about URLs in the next chapter. We'll also use `urllib` again in this and later chapters to fetch web pages, format generated URL strings, and get the output of remote scripts on the Web.* Technically speaking, `urllib` supports a variety of Internet protocols (HTTP, FTP, Gopher, and local files), is only used for reading remote objects (not writing or uploading them), and retrievals must generally be run in threads if blocking is a concern. But the basic interface shown in this script is straightforward. The call:

```
    remotefile = urllib.urlopen(remoteaddr)       # returns input file-like object
```

contacts the server named in the `remoteaddr` URL string and returns a file-like object connected to its download stream (an FTP-based socket). Calling this file's `read` method pulls down the file's contents, which are written to a local client-side file. An even simpler interface:

```
    urllib.urlretrieve(remoteaddr, tarname)
```

also does the work of opening a local file and writing the downloaded bytes into it—things we do manually in the script as coded. This comes in handy if we mean to download a file, but is less useful if we want to process its data immediately.

Either way, the end result is the same: the desired server file shows up on the client machine. The remainder of the script—unpacking and building—is identical to the original version, so it's been moved to a reusable Python file run with the `execfile` built-in (recall that `execfile` runs a file as though its code were pasted into the place where the `execfile` appears). The script is shown in Example 11-3.

---

* For more `urllib` download examples, see the section on HTTP in this chapter. In bigger terms, tools like `urllib.urlopen` allow scripts to both download remote files and invoke programs that are located on a remote server machine. In Chapter 12, *Server-Side Scripting*, we'll also see that `urllib` includes tools for formatting (escaping) URL strings for safe transmission.

Example 11-3. PP2E\Internet\Ftp\buildPython.py

```
#!/usr/local/bin/python
############################################################
# A Python script to build Python from its source code.
# Run me in directory where Python source distribution lives.
############################################################

import os
Version = '1.5'                       # version to build
tarname = 'python%s.tar.gz' % Version  # remote/local file name

print 'Unpacking...'
os.system('gzip -d '  + tarname)       # decompress file
os.system('tar -xvf ' + tarname[:-3])  # untar without '.gz'

print 'Building...'
os.chdir('Python-' + Version)          # build Python itself
os.system('./configure')               # assumes unix-style make
os.system('make')
os.system('make test')
print 'Done: see Python-%s/python.' % Version
```

The output this time is almost identical to the output of Example 11-1, so I'll show
only a few portions (the `gzip` message appears if you don't delete a tar file left by
a run in the past):

```
[lutz@starship test]$ python getpython-urllib.py
Downloading ftp://ftp.python.org/pub/python/src/python1.5.tar.gz
Unpacking...
gzip: python1.5.tar already exists; do you wish to overwrite (y or n)? y
...tar lines...
Building...
...build lines...
Done: see Python-1.5/python.

[lutz@starship test]$ python buildPython.py
Unpacking...
...tar and build lines...
```

In fact, although the original script is all top-level code that runs immediately and
accomplishes only one task, there really are two potentially reusable activities
within it: fetching a file and building Python from source. By splitting each part off
into a module of its own, we can reuse its program logic in other contexts, which
naturally leads us to the topic in the next section.

FTP get and put Utilities

Almost invariably, when I present the `ftplib` interfaces in Python classes, students ask why programmers need to supply the RETR string in the retrieval
method. It's a good question—the RETR string is the name of the download command in the FTP protocol, but `ftplib` is supposed to *encapsulate* that protocol.

As we'll see in a moment, we have to supply an arguably odd STOR string for uploads as well. It's boilerplate code that you accept on faith once you see it, but that begs the question. You could always email Guido a proposed `ftplib` patch, but that's not really a good answer for beginning Python students.[*]

A better answer is that there is no law against extending the standard library modules with higher-level interfaces of our own—with just a few lines of reusable code, we can make the FTP interface look any way we want in Python. For instance, we could, once and for all, write utility modules that wrap the `ftplib` interfaces to hide the RETR string. If we place these utility modules in a directory on PYTHONPATH, they become just as accessible as `ftplib` itself, automatically reusable in any Python script we write in the future. Besides removing the RETR string requirement, a wrapper module could also make assumptions that simplify FTP operations into single function calls.

For instance, given a module that encapsulates and simplifies `ftplib`, our Python fetch-and-build script could be further reduced to the script shown in Example 11-4—essentially just a function call and file execution.

Example 11-4. PP2E\Internet\Ftp\getpython-modular.py

```
#!/usr/local/bin/python
################################################################
# A Python script to download and build Python's source code.
# Uses getfile.py, a utility module which encapsulates ftp step.
################################################################

import getfile
Version = '1.5'                          # version to download
tarname = 'python%s.tar.gz' % Version    # remote/local file name

# fetch with utility
getfile.getfile(tarname, 'ftp.python.org', 'pub/python/src')

# rest is the same
execfile('buildPython.py')
```

Besides having a line count that is much more impressive to marketeers, the meat of this script has been split off into files for reuse elsewhere. If you ever need to download a file again, simply import an existing function rather than copying code with cut-and-paste editing. Changes in download operations would need to be made in only one file, not everywhere we've copied boilerplate code; `getfile.getfile`

---

[*] This is one point in the class where I also usually threaten to write Guido's home phone number on the whiteboard. But that's generally an empty promise made just for comic effect. If you do want to discuss Python language issues, Guido's email address, as well as contact points for other Python core developers, are readily available on the Net. As someone who's gotten anonymous Python-related calls at home, I never do give out phone numbers (and dialing 1-800-Hi-Guido is only funny the first time).

could even be changed to use `urllib` instead of `ftplib` without effecting any of
its clients. It's good engineering.

Download utility

So just how would we go about writing such an FTP interface wrapper (he asks,
knowingly)? Given the `ftplib` library module, wrapping downloads of a particular file in a particular directory is straightforward. Connected FTP objects support
two download methods:

- The `retrbinary` method downloads the requested file in *binary* mode, sending its bytes in chunks to a supplied function, without line-feed mapping. Typically, the supplied function is a write method of an open local file object,
  such that the bytes are placed in the local file on the client.

- The `retrlines` method downloads the requested file in ASCII *text* mode,
  sending each line of text to a supplied function with all end-of-line characters
  stripped. Typically, the supplied function adds a `\n` newline (mapped appropriately for the client machine), and writes the line to a local file.

We will meet the `retrlines` method in a later example; the `getfile` utility module in Example 11-5 transfers in *binary* mode always with `retrbinary`. That is,
files are downloaded exactly as they were on the server, byte for byte, with the
server's line-feed conventions in text files. You may need to convert line-feeds
after downloads if they look odd in your text editor—see the converter tools in
Chapter 5, *Larger System Examples II*, for pointers.

Example 11-5. PP2E\Internet\Ftp\getfile.py

```
#!/usr/local/bin/python
################################################
# Fetch an arbitrary file by ftp.  Anonymous
# ftp unless you pass a user=(name, pswd) tuple.
# Gets the Monty Python theme song by default.
################################################

from ftplib  import FTP            # socket-based ftp tools
from os.path import exists         # file existence test

file = 'sousa.au'                  # default file coordinates
site = 'ftp.python.org'            # monty python theme song
dir  = 'pub/python/misc'

def getfile(file=file, site=site, dir=dir, user=(), verbose=1, force=0):
    """
    fetch a file by ftp from a site/directory
    anonymous or real login, binary transfer
    """
    if exists(file) and not force:
        if verbose: print file, 'already fetched'
```

Example 11-5. PP2E\Internet\Ftp\getfile.py (continued)

```
    else:
        if verbose: print 'Downloading', file
        local = open(file, 'wb')                    # local file of same name
        try:
            remote = FTP(site)                      # connect to ftp site
            apply(remote.login, user)               # anonymous=() or (name, pswd)
            remote.cwd(dir)
            remote.retrbinary('RETR ' + file, local.write, 1024)
            remote.quit()
        finally:
            local.close()                           # close file no matter what
            if verbose: print 'Download done.'      # caller handles exceptions

if __name__ == '__main__': getfile()                # anonymous python.org login
```

This module is mostly just a repackaging of the FTP code we used to fetch the
Python source distribution earlier, to make it simpler and reusable. Because it is a
callable function, the exported `getfile.getfile` here tries to be as robust and
generally useful as possible, but even a function this small implies some design
decisions. Here are a few usage notes:

FTP mode

> The `getfile` function in this script runs in anonymous FTP mode by default,
> but a two-item tuple containing a username and password string may be
> passed to the `user` argument to log in to the remote server in non-anonymous
> mode. To use anonymous FTP, either don't pass the user argument or pass it
> an empty tuple, `()`. The FTP object `login` method allows two optional argu-
> ments to denote a username and password, and the `apply` call in
> Example 11-5 sends it whatever argument tuple you pass to `user`.

Processing modes

> If passed, the last two arguments (`verbose`, `force`) allow us to turn off status
> messages printed to the `stdout` stream (perhaps undesirable in a GUI con-
> text) and force downloads to happen even if the file already exists locally (the
> download overwrites the existing local file).

Exception protocol

> The caller is expected to handle exceptions; this function wraps downloads in
> a `try`/`finally` statement to guarantee that the local output file is closed, but
> lets exceptions propagate. If used in a GUI or run from a thread, for instance,
> exceptions may require special handling unknown in this file.

Self-test

> If run standalone, this file downloads a *sousa.au* audio file from *http://www.
> python.org* as a self-test, but the function will normally be passed FTP file-
> names, site names, and directory names as well.

File mode

> This script is careful to open the local output file in "wb" binary mode to suppress end-line mapping, in case it is run on Windows. As we learned in Chapter 2, *System Tools*, it's not impossible that true binary data files may have bytes whose value is equal to a \n line-feed character; opening in "w" text mode instead would make these bytes be automatically expanded to a \r\n two-byte sequence when written locally on Windows. This is only an issue for portability to Windows (mode "w" works elsewhere). Again, see Chapter 5 for line-feed converter tools.

Directory model

> This function currently uses the same filename to identify both the remote file and the local file where the download should be stored. As such, it should be run in the directory where you want the file to show up; use `os.chdir` to move to directories if needed. (We could instead assume *filename* is the local file's name, and strip the local directory with `os.path.split` to get the remote name, or accept two distinct filename arguments—local and remote.)

Notice also that, despite its name, this module is very different than the *getfile.py* script we studied at the end of the sockets material in the previous chapter. The socket-based `getfile` implemented client and server-side logic to download a server file to a client machine over raw sockets.

This new `getfile` here is a *client-side* tool only. Instead of raw sockets, it uses the simpler FTP protocol to request a file from a server; all socket-level details are hidden in the `ftplib` module's implementation of the FTP client protocol. Furthermore, the server here is a perpetually running program on the server machine, which listens for and responds to FTP requests on a socket, on the dedicated FTP port (number 21). The net functional effect is that this script requires an FTP server to be running on the machine where the desired file lives, but such a server is much more likely to be available.

Upload utility

While we're at it, let's write a script to upload a single file by FTP to a remote machine. The upload interfaces in the FTP module are symmetric with the download interfaces. Given a connected FTP object:

- Its `storbinary` method can be used to upload bytes from an open local file object.

- Its `storlines` method can be used to upload text in ASCII mode from an open local file object.

Unlike the download interfaces, both of these methods are passed a file *object* as a whole, not a file object method (or other function). We will meet the `storlines` method in a later example. The utility module in Example 11-6 uses `storbinary` such that the file whose name is passed in is always uploaded verbatim—in binary mode, without line-feed translations for the target machine's conventions. If this script uploads a text file, it will arrive exactly as stored on the machine it came from, client line-feed markers and all.

Example 11-6. PP2E\Internet\Ftp\putfile.py

```python
#!/usr/local/bin/python
################################################
# Store an arbitrary file by ftp.  Anonymous
# ftp unless you pass a user=(name, pswd) tuple.
################################################

import ftplib                      # socket-based ftp tools

file = 'sousa.au'                  # default file coordinates
site = 'starship.python.net'       # monty python theme song
dir  = 'upload'

def putfile(file=file, site=site, dir=dir, user=(), verbose=1):
    """
    store a file by ftp to a site/directory
    anonymous or real login, binary transfer
    """
    if verbose: print 'Uploading', file
    local  = open(file, 'rb')                # local file of same name
    remote = ftplib.FTP(site)                # connect to ftp site
    apply(remote.login, user)                # anonymous or real login
    remote.cwd(dir)
    remote.storbinary('STOR ' + file, local, 1024)
    remote.quit()
    local.close()
    if verbose: print 'Upload done.'

if __name__ == '__main__':
    import sys, getpass
    pswd = getpass.getpass(site + ' pswd?')          # filename on cmdline
    putfile(file=sys.argv[1], user=('lutz', pswd))   # non-anonymous login
```

Notice that for portability, the local file is opened in "rb" binary mode this time to suppress automatic line-feed character conversions in case this is run on Windows; if this is binary information, we don't want any bytes that happen to have the value of the `\r` carriage-return character to mysteriously go away during the transfer.

Also observe that the standard Python `getpass.getpass` is used to ask for an FTP password in standalone mode. Like the `raw_input` built-in function, this call prompts for and reads a line of text from the console user; unlike `raw_input`, `getpass` does not *echo* typed characters on the screen at all (in fact, on Windows it uses the low-level direct keyboard interface we met in the stream redirection section of Chapter 2). This comes in handy for protecting things like passwords from potentially prying eyes.

Like the download utility, this script uploads a local copy of an audio file by default as a self-test, but you will normally pass in real remote filename, site name, and directory name strings. Also like the download utility, you may pass a (username, password) tuple to the user argument to trigger non-anonymous FTP mode (anonymous FTP is the default).

Playing the Monty Python theme song

Wake up—it's time for a bit of fun. Let's make use of these scripts to transfer and play the Monty Python theme song audio file maintained at Python's web site. First off, let's write a module that downloads and plays the sample file, as shown in Example 11-7.

Example 11-7. PP2E\Internet\Ftp\sousa.py

```
#!/usr/local/bin/python
##################################################
# Usage: % sousa.py
# Fetch and play the Monty Python theme song.
# This may not work on your system as is: it
# requires a machine with ftp access, and uses
# audio filters on Unix and your .au player on
# Windows.  Configure playfile.py as needed.
##################################################

import os, sys
from PP2E.Internet.Ftp.getfile  import getfile
from PP2E.Internet.Ftp.playfile import playfile
sample = 'sousa.au'

getfile(sample)     # fetch audio file by ftp
playfile(sample)    # send it to audio player
```

This script will run on any machine with Python, an Internet link, and a recognizable audio player; it works on my Windows laptop with a dialup Internet connection (if I could insert an audio file hyperlink here to show what it sounds like, I would):

```
C:\...\PP2E\Internet\Ftp>python sousa.py
Downloading sousa.au
Download done.

C:\...\PP2E\Internet\Ftp>python sousa.py
sousa.au already fetched
```

The getfile and putfile modules can be used to move the sample file around, too. Both can either be imported by clients that wish to use their functions, or run as top-level programs to trigger self-tests. Let's run these scripts from a command line and the interactive prompt to see how they work. When run standalone, parameters are passed in the command line, and the default file settings are used:

```
C:\...\PP2E\Internet\Ftp>python putfile.py sousa.au
starship.python.net pswd?
Uploading sousa.au
Upload done.
```

When imported, parameters are passed explicitly to functions:

```
C:\...\PP2E\Internet\Ftp>python
>>> from getfile import getfile
>>> getfile(file='sousa.au', site='starship.python.net', dir='upload',
...                          user=('lutz', '****'))
Downloading sousa.au
Download done.
>>> from playfile import playfile
>>> playfile('sousa.au')
```

I've left one piece out of the puzzle: all that's left is to write a module that attempts to play an audio file portably (see Example 11-8). Alas, this is the least straightforward task because audio players vary per platform. On Windows, the following module uses the DOS *start* command to launch whatever you have registered to play audio files (exactly as if you had double-clicked on the file's icon in a file explorer); on the Windows 98 side of my Sony notebook machine, this DOS command line:

```
C:\...\PP2E\Internet\Ftp>python playfile.py sousa.au
```

pops up a media bar playing the sample. On Unix, it attempts to pass the audio file to a command-line player program, if one has been added to the `unixfilter` table—tweak this for your system (*cat*'ing audio files to */dev/audio* works on some Unix systems, too). On other platforms, you'll need to do a bit more; there has been some work towards portable audio interfaces in Python, but it's notoriously platform-specific. Web browsers generally know how to play audio files, so passing the filename in a URL to a browser located via the *LaunchBrowser.py* script we met in Chapter 4, *Larger System Examples I*, is perhaps a portable solution here as well (see that chapter for interface details).

Example 11-8. PP2E\Internet\Ftp\playfile.py

```
#!/usr/local/bin/python
################################################
# Try to play an arbitrary audio file.
# This may not work on your system as is; it
# uses audio filters on Unix, and filename
# associations on Windows via the start command
# line (i.e., whatever you have on your machine
# to run *.au files--an audio player, or perhaps
# a web browser); configure me as needed. We
```

Example 11-8. PP2E\Internet\Ftp\playfile.py (continued)

```
# could instead launch a web browser here, with
# LaunchBrowser.py.  See also: Lib/audiodev.py.
#################################################

import os, sys
sample = 'sousa.au'  # default audio file

unixhelpmsg = """
Sorry: can't find an audio filter for your system!
Add an entry for your system to the "unixfilter"
dictionary in playfile.py, or play the file manually.
"""

unixfilter = {'sunos5':  '/usr/bin/audioplay',
              'linux2':  '<unknown>',
              'sunos4':  '/usr/demo/SOUND/play'}

def playfile(sample=sample):
    """
    play an audio file: use name associations
    on windows, filter command-lines elsewhere
    """
    if sys.platform[:3] == 'win':
        os.system('start ' + sample)   # runs your audio player
    else:
        if not (unixfilter.has_key(sys.platform) and
                os.path.exists(unixfilter[sys.platform])):
            print unixhelpmsg
        else:
            theme = open(sample, 'r')
            audio = os.popen(unixfilter[sys.platform], 'w')  # spawn shell tool
            audio.write(theme.read())                        # send to its stdin

if __name__ == '__main__': playfile()
```

Adding user interfaces

If you read the last chapter, you'll recall that it concluded with a quick look at scripts that added a user interface to a socket-based `getfile` script—one that transferred files over a proprietary *socket* dialog, instead of FTP. At the end of that presentation, I mentioned that FTP is a much more generally useful way to move files around, because FTP servers are so widely available on the Net. For illustration purposes, Example 11-9 shows a simple mutation of the last chapter's user interface, implemented as a new subclass of the last chapter's general form builder.

Example 11-9. P2E\Internet\Ftp\getfilegui.py

```
#############################################################
# launch ftp getfile function with a reusable form gui class;
# uses os.chdir to goto target local dir (getfile currently
# assumes that filename has no local directory path prefix);
```

Example 11-9. P2E\Internet\Ftp\getfilegui.py (continued)

```
# runs getfile.getfile in thread to allow more than one to be
# running at once and avoid blocking gui during downloads;
# this differs from socket-based getfilegui, but reuses Form;
# supports both user and anonymous ftp as currently coded;
# caveats: the password field is not displayed as stars here,
# errors are printed to the console instead of shown in the
# gui (threads can't touch the gui on Windows), this isn't
# 100% thread safe (there is a slight delay between os.chdir
# here and opening the local output file in getfile) and we
# could display both a save-as popup for picking the local dir,
# and a remote directory listings for picking the file to get;
##############################################################

from Tkinter import Tk, mainloop
from tkMessageBox import showinfo
import getfile, os, sys, thread               # ftp getfile here, not socket
from PP2E.Internet.Sockets.form import Form    # reuse form tool in socket dir

class FtpForm(Form):
    def __init__(self):
        root = Tk()
        root.title(self.title)
        labels = ['Server Name', 'Remote Dir', 'File Name',
                    'Local Dir',   'User Name?', 'Password?']
        Form.__init__(self, labels, root)
        self.mutex = thread.allocate_lock()
        self.threads = 0
    def transfer(self, filename, servername, remotedir, userinfo):
        try:
            self.do_transfer(filename, servername, remotedir, userinfo)
            print '%s of "%s" successful'  % (self.mode, filename)
        except:
            print '%s of "%s" has failed:' % (self.mode, filename),
            print sys.exc_info()[0], sys.exc_info()[1]
        self.mutex.acquire()
        self.threads = self.threads - 1
        self.mutex.release()
    def onSubmit(self):
        Form.onSubmit(self)
        localdir   = self.content['Local Dir'].get()
        remotedir  = self.content['Remote Dir'].get()
        servername = self.content['Server Name'].get()
        filename   = self.content['File Name'].get()
        username   = self.content['User Name?'].get()
        password   = self.content['Password?'].get()
        userinfo   = ()
        if username and password:
            userinfo = (username, password)
        if localdir:
            os.chdir(localdir)
        self.mutex.acquire()
        self.threads = self.threads + 1
        self.mutex.release()
```

Example 11-9. P2E\Internet\Ftp\getfilegui.py (continued)

```
        ftpargs = (filename, servername, remotedir, userinfo)
        thread.start_new_thread(self.transfer, ftpargs)
        showinfo(self.title, '%s of "%s" started' % (self.mode, filename))
    def onCancel(self):
        if self.threads == 0:
            Tk().quit()
        else:
            showinfo(self.title,
                     'Cannot exit: %d threads running' % self.threads)

class FtpGetfileForm(FtpForm):
    title = 'FtpGetfileGui'
    mode  = 'Download'
    def do_transfer(self, filename, servername, remotedir, userinfo):
        getfile.getfile(filename, servername, remotedir, userinfo, 0, 1)


if __name__ == '__main__':
    FtpGetfileForm()
    mainloop()
```

If you flip back to the end of the previous chapter, you'll find that this version is similar in structure to its counterpart there; in fact, it has the same name (and is distinct only because it lives in a different directory). The class here, though, knows how to use the FTP-based `getfile` module from earlier in this chapter, instead of the socket-based `getfile` module we met a chapter ago. When run, this version also implements more input fields, as we see in Figure 11-1.

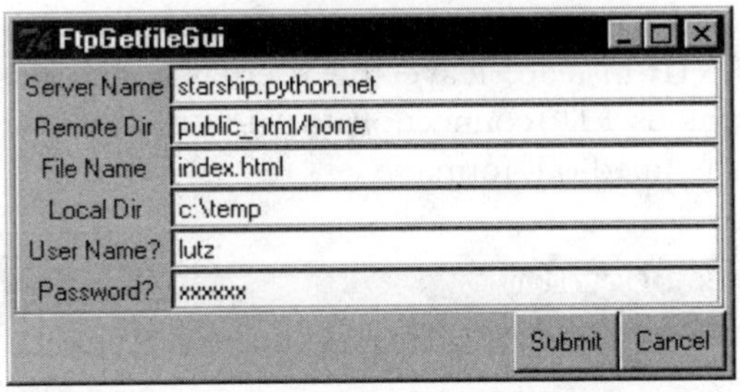

Figure 11-1. FTP getfile input form

Notice that a full file path is entered for the local directory here. Otherwise, the script assumes the current working directory, which changes after each download and can vary depending on where the GUI is launched (e.g., the current directory differs when this script is run by the PyDemos program at the top of the examples tree). When we click this GUI's Submit button (or press the Enter key), this script simply passes the form's input field values as arguments to the `getfile.getfile` FTP utility function shown earlier in this section. It also posts a pop-up to tell us the download has begun (Figure 11-2).

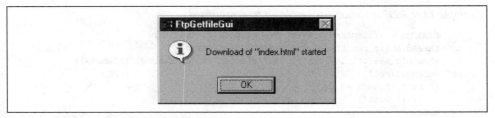

Figure 11-2. FTP getfile info pop-up

As currently coded, further download status messages from this point on show up in the console window; here are the messages for a successful download, as well as one that failed when I mistyped my password (no, it's not really "xxxxxx"):

```
User Name?      =>      lutz
Server Name     =>      starship.python.net
Local Dir       =>      c:\temp
Password?       =>      xxxxxx
File Name       =>      index.html
Remote Dir      =>      public_html/home
Download of "index.html" successful

User Name?      =>      lutz
Server Name     =>      starship.python.net
Local Dir       =>      c:\temp
Password?       =>      xxxxxx
File Name       =>      index.html
Remote Dir      =>      public_html/home
Download of "index.html" has failed: ftplib.error_perm 530 Login incorrect.
```

Given a username and password, the downloader logs into the specified account. To do anonymous FTP instead, leave the username and password fields blank. Let's start an anonymous FTP connection to fetch the Python source distribution; Figure 11-3 shows the filled-out form.

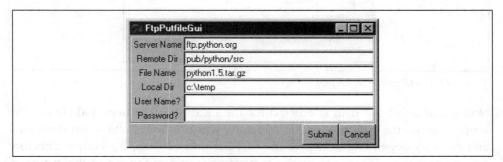

Figure 11-3. FTP getfile input form, anonymous FTP

Pressing Submit on this form starts a download running in the background as before; we get the pop-up shown in Figure 11-4 to verify the startup.

Figure 11-4. FTP getfile info pop-up

Now, to illustrate the *threading* capabilities of this GUI, let's start another download while this one is in progress. The GUI stays active while downloads are under way, so we simply change the input fields and press Submit again, as done in Figure 11-5.

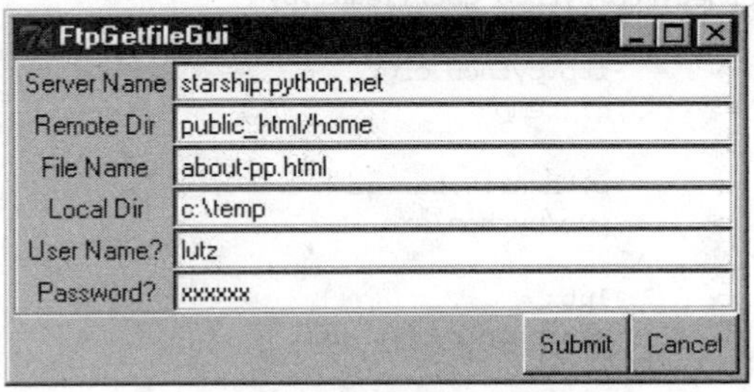

Figure 11-5. FTP getfile input form, second thread

This second download starts in parallel with the one attached to *ftp.python.org*, because each download is run in a thread, and more than one Internet connection can be active at once. In fact, the GUI itself stays active during downloads only because downloads are run in threads; if they were not, even screen redraws wouldn't happen until a download finished.

We discussed threads in Chapter 3, *Parallel System Tools*, but this script illustrates some practical thread concerns:

- This program takes care to not do anything GUI-related in a download thread. At least in the current release on Windows, only the thread that makes GUIs can process them (a Windows-only rule that has nothing to do with Python or Tkinter).

- To avoid killing spawned download threads on some platforms, the GUI must also be careful to not exit while any downloads are in progress. It keeps track of the number of in-progress threads, and just displays the pop-up in Figure 11-6 if we try to kill the GUI while both of these downloads are in progress by pressing the Cancel button.

Figure 11-6. FTP getfile busy pop-up

We'll see ways to work around the no-GUI rule for threads when we explore the **PyMailGui** example near the end of this chapter. To be portable, though, we can't really close the GUI until the active-thread count falls to zero. Here is the sort of output that appears in the console window for these two downloads:

```
C:\...\PP2E\Internet\Ftp>python getfilegui.py
User Name?        =>
Server Name       =>       ftp.python.org
Local Dir         =>       c:\temp
Password?         =>
File Name         =>       python1.5.tar.gz
Remote Dir        =>       pub/python/src

User Name?        =>       lutz
Server Name       =>       starship.python.net
Local Dir         =>       c:\temp
Password?         =>       xxxxxx
File Name         =>       about-pp.html
Remote Dir        =>       public_html/home
Download of "about-pp.html" successful
Download of "python1.5.tar.gz" successful
```

This all isn't much more useful than a command-line-based tool, of course, but it can be easily modified by changing its Python code, and it provides enough of a GUI to qualify as a simple, first-cut FTP user interface. Moreover, because this GUI runs downloads in Python threads, more than one can be run at the same time from this GUI without having to start or restart a different FTP client tool.

While we're in a GUI mood, let's add a simple interface to the **putfile** utility, too. The script in Example 11-10 creates a dialog that starts uploads in threads. It's almost the same as the **getfile** GUI we just wrote, so there's nothing new to say. In fact, because get and put operations are so similar from an interface perspective, most of the get form's logic was deliberately factored out into a single generic class (**FtpForm**) such that changes need only be made in a single place. That is, the put GUI here is mostly just a reuse of the get GUI, with distinct output labels and transfer method. It's in a file by itself to make it easy to launch as a stand-alone program.

Example 11-10. PP2E\Internet\Ftp\putfilegui.py

```
#############################################################
# launch ftp putfile function with a reusable form gui class;
# see getfilegui for notes: most of the same caveats apply;
# the get and put forms have been factored into a single
# class such that changes need only be made in one place;
#############################################################

from Tkinter import mainloop
import putfile, getfilegui

class FtpPutfileForm(getfilegui.FtpForm):
    title = 'FtpPutfileGui'
    mode  = 'Upload'
    def do_transfer(self, filename, servername, remotedir, userinfo):
        putfile.putfile(filename, servername, remotedir, userinfo, 0)

if __name__ == '__main__':
    FtpPutfileForm()
    mainloop()
```

Running this script looks much like running the download GUI, because it's almost entirely the same code at work. Let's upload a couple of files from the client machine to the *starship* server; Figure 11-7 shows the state of the GUI while starting one.

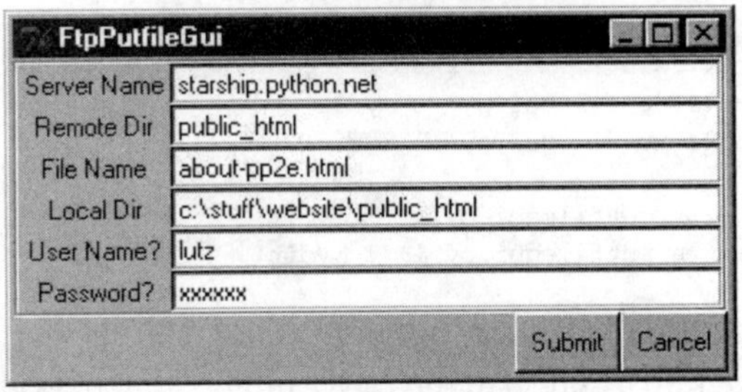

Figure 11-7. FTP putfile input form

And here is the console window output we get when uploading two files in parallel; here again, uploads run in threads, so if we start a new upload before one in progress is finished, they overlap in time:

```
User Name?     =>     lutz
Server Name    =>     starship.python.net
Local Dir      =>     c:\stuff\website\public_html
Password?      =>     xxxxxx
File Name      =>     about-pp2e.html
Remote Dir     =>     public_html
```

```
User Name?        =>      lutz
Server Name       =>      starship.python.net
Local Dir         =>      c:\stuff\website\public_html
Password?         =>      xxxxxx
File Name         =>      about-ppr2e.html
Remote Dir        =>      public_html
Upload of "about-pp2e.html" successful
Upload of "about-ppr2e.html" successful
```

Finally, we can bundle up both GUIs in a single *launcher script* that knows how to start the get and put interfaces, regardless of which directory we are in when the script is started, and independent of the platform on which it runs. Example 11-11 shows this process.

Example 11-11. PP2E\Internet\Ftp\PyFtpGui.pyw

```
###############################################################
# spawn ftp get and put guis no matter what dir I'm run from;
# os.getcwd is not necessarily the place this script lives;
# could also hard-code a path from $PP2EHOME, or guessLocation;
# could also do this but need the DOS popup for status messages:
# from PP2E.launchmodes import PortableLauncher
# PortableLauncher('getfilegui', '%s/getfilegui.py' % mydir)()
###############################################################

import os, sys
from PP2E.Launcher import findFirst
mydir = os.path.split(findFirst(os.curdir, 'PyFtpGui.pyw'))[0]

if sys.platform[:3] == 'win':
    os.system('start %s/getfilegui.py' % mydir)
    os.system('start %s/putfilegui.py' % mydir)
else:
    os.system('python %s/getfilegui.py &' % mydir)
    os.system('python %s/putfilegui.py &' % mydir)
```

When this script is started, both the get and put GUIs appear as distinct, independently running programs; alternatively, we might attach both forms to a single interface. We could get much fancier than these two interfaces, of course. For instance, we could pop up local file selection dialogs, and we could display widgets that give status of downloads and uploads in progress. We could even list files available at the remote site in a selectable list box by requesting remote directory listings over the FTP connection. To learn how to add features like that, though, we need to move on to the next section.

Downloading Web Sites (Mirrors)

Once upon a time, Telnet was all I needed. My web site lived at an Internet Service Provider (ISP) that provided general and free Telnet access for all its customers. It was a simple time. All of my site's files lived only in *one* place—at my account directory on my ISP's server machine. To make changes to web pages, I simply started a Telnet session connected to my ISP's machine and edited my web pages there online. Moreover, because Telnet sessions can be run from almost any machine with an Internet link, I was able to tweak my web pages *everywhere*— from my PC, from machines I had access to on the training road, from archaic machines I played with when I was bored at my day job, and so on. Life was good.

But times have changed. Due to a security breach, my ISP made a blanket decision to revoke Telnet access from all of their customers (except, of course, those who elected to pay a substantial premium to retain it). Seemingly, we weren't even supposed to have known about Telnet in the first place. As a replacement, the ISP mandated that all Telnet-inclined users should begin maintaining web page files locally on their own machines, and upload them by FTP after every change.

That's nowhere near as nice as editing files kept in a single place from almost any computer on the planet, of course, and this triggered plenty of complaints and cancellations among the technically savvy. Unfortunately, the technically savvy is a financially insignificant subset; more to the point, my web page's address had by this time been published in multiple books sold around the world, so changing ISPs would have been no less painful than changing update procedures.

After the shouting, it dawned on me that Python could help here: by writing Python scripts to automate the upload and download tasks associated with maintaining my web site on my PC, I could at least get back some of the mobility and ease of use that I'd lost. Because Python FTP scripts will work on any machine with sockets, I could run them both on my PC and on nearly any other computer where Python was installed. Furthermore, the same scripts used to transfer page files to and from my PC could be used to copy ("mirror") my site to another web server as a backup copy, should my ISP experience an outage (trust me—it happens).

The following two scripts were born of all of the above frustrations. The first, *mirrorflat.py*, automatically downloads (i.e., copies) by FTP all the files in a directory at a remote site, to a directory on the local machine. I keep the main copy of my web site files on my PC these days, but really use this script in two ways:

- To download my web site to client machines where I want to make edits, I fetch the contents of my *public_html* web directory of my account on my ISP's machine.

- To mirror my site to my account on the *starship.python.net* server, I run this script periodically from a Telnet session on the *starship* machine (as I wrote this, *starship* still clung to the radical notion that users are intelligent enough to run Telnet).

More generally, this script (shown in Example 11-12) will download a directory full of files to any machine with Python and sockets, from any machine running an FTP server.

Example 11-12. PP2E\Internet\Ftp\mirrorflat.py

```
#!/bin/env python
#########################################################
# use ftp to copy (download) all files from a remote site
# and directory to a directory on the local machine; e.g.,
# run me periodically to mirror a flat ftp site;
#########################################################

import os, sys, ftplib
from getpass import getpass

remotesite = 'home.rmi.net'
remotedir  = 'public_html'
remoteuser = 'lutz'
remotepass = getpass('Please enter password for %s: ' % remotesite)
localdir   = (len(sys.argv) > 1 and sys.argv[1]) or '.'
if sys.platform[:3] == 'win': raw_input()  # clear stream
cleanall   = raw_input('Clean local directory first? ')[:1] in ['y', 'Y']

print 'connecting...'
connection = ftplib.FTP(remotesite)             # connect to ftp site
connection.login(remoteuser, remotepass)        # login as user/password
connection.cwd(remotedir)                        # cd to directory to copy

if cleanall:
    for localname in os.listdir(localdir):      # try to delete all locals
        try:                                     # first to remove old files
            print 'deleting local', localname
            os.remove(os.path.join(localdir, localname))
        except:
            print 'cannot delete local', localname

count = 0                                         # download all remote files
remotefiles = connection.nlst()                  # nlst() gives files list
                                                 # dir()  gives full details
for remotename in remotefiles:
    localname = os.path.join(localdir, remotename)
    print 'copying', remotename, 'to', localname
    if remotename[-4:] == 'html' or remotename[-3:] == 'txt':
        # use ascii mode xfer
        localfile = open(localname, 'w')
        callback  = lambda line, file=localfile: file.write(line + '\n')
        connection.retrlines('RETR ' + remotename, callback)
    else:
        # use binary mode xfer
        localfile = open(localname, 'wb')
        connection.retrbinary('RETR ' + remotename, localfile.write)
    localfile.close()
    count = count+1

connection.quit()
print 'Done:', count, 'files downloaded.'
```

There is not a whole lot new to speak of in this script, compared to other FTP examples we've seen thus far. We open a connection with the remote FTP server, log in with a username and password for the desired account (this script never uses anonymous FTP), and go to the desired remote directory. New here, though, are loops to iterate over all the files in local and remote directories, text-based retrievals, and file deletions:

Deleting all local files

This script has a `cleanall` option, enabled by interactive prompt. If selected, the script first deletes all the files in the local directory before downloading, to make sure there are no extra files there that aren't also on the server (there may be junk here from a prior download). To delete local files, the script calls `os.listdir` to get a list of filenames in the directory, and `os.remove` to delete each; see Chapter 2 earlier in this book (or the Python library manual) for more details if you've forgotten what these calls do.

Notice the use of `os.path.join` to concatenate a directory path and filename according to the host platform's conventions; `os.listdir` returns filenames without their directory paths, and this script is not necessarily run in the local directory where downloads will be placed. The local directory defaults to the current directory ("."), but can be set differently with a command-line argument to the script.

Fetching all remote files

To grab all the files in a remote directory, we first need a list of their names. The FTP object's `nlst` method is the remote equivalent of `os.listdir`: `nlist` returns a list of the string names of all files in the current remote directory. Once we have this list, we simply step through it in a loop, running FTP retrieval commands for each filename in turn (more on this in a minute).

The `nlst` method is, more or less, like requesting a directory listing with an `ls` command in typical interactive FTP programs, but Python automatically splits up the listing's text into a list of filenames. We can pass it a remote directory to be listed; by default it lists the current server directory. A related FTP method, `dir`, returns the list of line strings produced by an FTP *LIST* command; its result is like typing a *dir* command in an FTP session, and its lines contain complete file information, unlike `nlst`. If you need to know more about all the remote files, parse the result of a `dir` method call.

Text-based retrievals

To keep line-feeds in sync with the machines that my web files live on, this script distinguishes between binary and text files. It uses a simple heuristic to do so: filenames ending in *.html* or *.txt* are assumed to be ASCII text data (HTML web pages and simple text files), and all others are assumed to be

binary files (e.g., GIF and JPEG images, audio files, tar archives). This simple
rule won't work for every web site, but it does the trick at mine.

Binary files are pulled down with the `retrbinary` method we met earlier and
a local open mode of "wb" to suppress line-feed byte mapping (this script
may be run on Windows or Unix-like platforms). We don't use a chunk size
third argument here, though—it defaults to a reasonable 8K if omitted.

For ASCII text files, the script instead uses the `retrlines` method, passing in
a function to be called for each line in the text file downloaded. The text line
handler function mostly just writes the line to a local file. But notice that the
handler function created by the `lambda` here also adds an `\n` newline character to the end of the line it is passed. Python's `retrlines` method strips all
line-feed characters from lines to side-step platform differences. By adding an
`\n`, the script is sure to add the proper line-feed marker character sequence
for the local platform on which this script runs (`\n` or `\r\n`). For this
automapping of the `\n` in the script to work, of course, we must also open
text output files in "w" text mode, not "wb"—the mapping from `\n` to `\r\n` on
Windows happens when data is written to the file.

All of this is simpler in action than in words. Here is the command I use to download my entire web site from my ISP server account to my Windows 98 laptop PC,
in a single step:

```
C:\Stuff\Website\public_html>python %X%\internet\ftp\mirrorflat.py
Please enter password for home.rmi.net:
Clean local directory first?
connecting...
copying UPDATES to .\UPDATES
copying PythonPowered.gif to .\PythonPowered.gif
copying Pywin.gif to .\Pywin.gif
copying PythonPoweredAnim.gif to .\PythonPoweredAnim.gif
copying PythonPoweredSmall.gif to .\PythonPoweredSmall.gif
copying about-hopl.html to .\about-hopl.html
copying about-lp.html to .\about-lp.html
...
...lines deleted...
...
copying training.html to .\training.html
copying trainingCD.GIF to .\trainingCD.GIF
copying uk-1.jpg to .\uk-1.jpg
copying uk-2.jpg to .\uk-2.jpg
copying uk-3.jpg to .\uk-3.jpg
copying whatsnew.html to .\whatsnew.html
copying whatsold.html to .\whatsold.html
copying xlate-lp.html to .\xlate-lp.html
copying uploadflat.py to .\uploadflat.py
copying ora-lp-france.gif to .\ora-lp-france.gif
Done: 130 files downloaded.
```

This can take awhile to complete (it's bound by network speed constraints), but it is much more accurate and easy than downloading files by hand. The script simply iterates over all the remote files returned by the `nlst` method, and downloads each with the FTP protocol (i.e., over sockets) in turn. It uses text transfer mode for names that imply obviously text data, and binary mode for others.

With the script running this way, I make sure the initial assignments in it reflect the machines involved, and then run the script from the local directory where I want the site copy to be stored. Because the download directory is usually not where the script lives, I need to give Python the full path to the script file (`%X%` evaluates a shell variable containing the top-level path to book examples on my machine). When run on the *starship* server in a Telnet session window, the execution and script directory paths are different, but the script works the same way.

If you elect to delete local files in the download directory, you may also see a batch of "deleting local…" messages scroll by on the screen before any "copying…" lines appear:

```
...
deleting local uploadflat.py
deleting local whatsnew.html
deleting local whatsold.html
deleting local xlate-lp.html
deleting local old-book.html
deleting local about-pp2e.html
deleting local about-ppr2e.html
deleting local old-book2.html
deleting local mirrorflat.py
...
copying about-pp-japan.html to ./about-pp-japan.html
copying about-pp.html to ./about-pp.html
copying about-ppr-germany.html to ./about-ppr-germany.html
copying about-ppr-japan.html to ./about-ppr-japan.html
copying about-ppr-toc.html to ./about-ppr-toc.html
...
```

By the way, if you botch the input of the remote site password, a Python exception is raised; I sometimes need to run again (and type slower):

```
C:\Stuff\Website\public_html>python %X%\internet\ftp\mirrorflat.py
Please enter password for home.rmi.net:
Clean local directory first?
connecting...
Traceback (innermost last):
  File "C:\PP2ndEd\examples\PP2E\internet\ftp\mirrorflat.py", line 20, in ?
    connection.login(remoteuser, remotepass)         # login as user/pass..
  File "C:\Program Files\Python\Lib\ftplib.py", line 316, in login
    if resp[0] == '3': resp = self.sendcmd('PASS ' + passwd)
  File "C:\Program Files\Python\Lib\ftplib.py", line 228, in sendcmd
    return self.getresp()
  File "C:\Program Files\Python\Lib\ftplib.py", line 201, in getresp
    raise error_perm, resp
ftplib.error_perm: 530 Login incorrect.
```

It's worth noting that this script is at least partially configured by assignments near the top of the file. In addition, the password and deletion options are given by interactive inputs, and one command-line argument is allowed—the local directory name to store the downloaded files (it defaults to ".", the directory where the script is run). Command-line arguments could be employed to universally configure all the other download parameters and options, too; but because of Python's simplicity and lack of compile/link steps, changing settings in the text of Python scripts is usually just as easy as typing words on a command line.

Windows input note: If you study the previous code closely, you'll notice that an extra `raw_input` call is made on Windows only, after the `getpass` password input call and before the `cleanall` option setting is input. This is a workaround for what seems like a bug in Python 1.5.2 for Windows.

Oddly, the Windows port sometimes doesn't synchronize command-line input and output streams as expected. Here, this seems to be due to a `getpass` bug or constraint—because `getpass` uses the low-level `msvcrt` keyboard interface module we met in Chapter 2, it appears to not mix well with the `stdin` stream buffering used by `raw_input`, and botches the input stream in the process. The extra `raw_input` clears the input stream (`sys.stdin.flush` doesn't help).

In fact, without the superfluous `raw_input` for Windows, this script prompts for `cleanall` option input, but never stops to let you type a reply! This effectively disables `cleanall` altogether. To force distinct input and output lines and correct `raw_input` behavior, some scripts in this book run extra `print` statements or `raw_input` calls to sync up streams before further user interaction. There may be other fixes, and this may be improved in future releases; try this script without the extra `raw_input` to see if this has been repaired in your Python.

Uploading Web Sites

Uploading a full directory is symmetric to downloading: it's mostly a matter of swapping the local and remote machines and operations in the program we just met. The script in Example 11-13 uses FTP to copy all files in a directory on the local machine on which it runs, up to a directory on a remote machine.

I really use this script, too, most often to upload all of the files maintained on my laptop PC to my ISP account in one fell swoop. I also sometimes use it to copy my site from my PC to its *starship* mirror machine, or from the mirror machine back to my ISP. Because this script runs on *any* computer with Python and sockets, it happily transfers a directory from any machine on the Net to any machine running an

FTP server. Simply change the initial setting in this module as appropriate for the transfer you have in mind.

Example 11-13. PP2E\Internet\Ftp\uploadflat.py

```
#!/bin/env python
#########################################################################
# use ftp to upload all files from a local dir to a remote site/directory;
# e.g., run me to copy a web/ftp site's files from your PC to your ISP;
# assumes a flat directory upload: uploadall.py does nested directories.
# to go to my ISP, I change setting to 'home.rmi.net', and 'public_html'.
#########################################################################

import os, sys, ftplib, getpass

remotesite = 'starship.python.net'              # upload to starship site
remotedir  = 'public_html/home'                 # from win laptop or other
remoteuser = 'lutz'
remotepass = getpass.getpass('Please enter password for %s: ' % remotesite)
localdir   = (len(sys.argv) > 1 and sys.argv[1]) or '.'
if sys.platform[:3] == 'win': raw_input()       # clear stream
cleanall   = raw_input('Clean remote directory first? ')[:1] in ['y', 'Y']

print 'connecting...'
connection = ftplib.FTP(remotesite)             # connect to ftp site
connection.login(remoteuser, remotepass)        # login as user/password
connection.cwd(remotedir)                        # cd to directory to copy

if cleanall:
    for remotename in connection.nlst():         # try to delete all remotes
        try:                                     # first to remove old files
            print 'deleting remote', remotename
            connection.delete(remotename)
        except:
            print 'cannot delete remote', remotename

count = 0
localfiles = os.listdir(localdir)                # upload all local files
                                                 # listdir() strips dir path
for localname in localfiles:
    localpath = os.path.join(localdir, localname)
    print 'uploading', localpath, 'to', localname
    if localname[-4:] == 'html' or localname[-3:] == 'txt':
        # use ascii mode xfer
        localfile = open(localpath, 'r')
        connection.storlines('STOR ' + localname, localfile)
    else:
        # use binary mode xfer
        localfile = open(localpath, 'rb')
        connection.storbinary('STOR ' + localname, localfile, 1024)
    localfile.close()
    count = count+1

connection.quit()
print 'Done:', count, 'files uploaded.'
```

Like the mirror download script, the program here illustrates a handful of new FTP interfaces and a set of FTP scripting techniques:

Deleting all remote files

Just like the mirror script, the upload begins by asking if we want to delete all the files in the remote target directory before copying any files there. This `cleanall` option is useful if we've deleted files in the local copy of the directory in the client—the deleted files would remain on the server-side copy unless we delete all files there first. To implement the remote cleanup, this script simply gets a listing of all the files in the remote directory with the FTP `nlst` method, and deletes each in turn with the FTP `delete` method. Assuming we have delete permission, the directory will be emptied (file permissions depend on the account we logged into when connecting to the server). We've already moved to the target remote directory when deletions occur, so no directory paths must be prepended to filenames here.

Storing all local files

To apply the upload operation to each file in the local directory, we get a list of local filenames with the standard `os.listdir` call, and take care to prepend the local source directory path to each filename with the `os.path.join` call. Recall that `os.listdir` returns filenames without directory paths, and the source directory may not be the same as the script's execution directory if passed on the command line.

Text-based uploads

This script may be run on both Windows and Unix-like clients, so we need to handle text files specially. Like the mirror download, this script picks text or binary transfer modes by inspecting each filename's extension—HTML and text files are moved in FTP text mode. We've already met the `storbinary` FTP object method used to upload files in binary mode—an exact, byte-for-byte copy appears at the remote site.

Text mode transfers work almost identically: the `storlines` method accepts an FTP command string and a local file (or file-like) object opened in text mode, and simply copies each line in the local file to a same-named file on the remote machine. As usual, if we run this script on Windows, opening the input file in "r" text mode means that DOS-style \r\n end-of-line sequences are mapped to the \n character as lines are read. When the script is run on Unix and Linux, lines end in a single \n already, so no such mapping occurs. The net effect is that data is read portably, with \n characters to represent end-of-line. For binary files, we open in "rb" mode to suppress such automatic mapping everywhere (we don't want bytes that happen to have the same value as \r to magically disappear when read on Windows).*

As for the mirror download script, this program simply iterates over all files to be transferred (files in the local directory listing this time), and transfers each in turn—in either text or binary mode, depending on the files' names. Here is the command I use to upload my entire web site from my laptop Windows 98 PC to the remote Unix server at my ISP, in a single step:

```
C:\Stuff\Website\public_html>python %X%\Internet\Ftp\uploadflat.py
Please enter password for starship.python.net:
Clean remote directory first?
connecting...
uploading .\LJsuppcover.jpg to LJsuppcover.jpg
uploading .\PythonPowered.gif to PythonPowered.gif
uploading .\PythonPoweredAnim.gif to PythonPoweredAnim.gif
uploading .\PythonPoweredSmall.gif to PythonPoweredSmall.gif
uploading .\Pywin.gif to Pywin.gif
uploading .\UPDATES to UPDATES
uploading .\about-hopl.html to about-hopl.html
uploading .\about-lp.html to about-lp.html
uploading .\about-pp-japan.html to about-pp-japan.html
...
...lines deleted...
...
uploading .\trainingCD.GIF to trainingCD.GIF
uploading .\uk-1.jpg to uk-1.jpg
uploading .\uk-2.jpg to uk-2.jpg
uploading .\uk-3.jpg to uk-3.jpg
uploading .\uploadflat.py to uploadflat.py
uploading .\whatsnew.html to whatsnew.html
uploading .\whatsold.html to whatsold.html
uploading .\xlate-lp.html to xlate-lp.html
Done: 131 files uploaded.
```

Like the mirror example, I usually run this command from the local directory where my web files are kept, and I pass Python the full path to the script. When I run this on the *starship* Linux server, it works the same, but the paths to the script and my web files directory differ. If you elect to clean the remote directory before uploading, you'll get a bunch of "deleting remote..." messages before the "uploading..." lines here, too:

```
...
deleting remote uk-3.jpg
deleting remote whatsnew.html
```

---

* Technically, Python's `storlines` method automatically sends all lines to the server with \r\n line-feed sequences, no matter what it receives from the local file's `readline` method (\n or \r\n). Because of that, the most important distinctions for uploads are to use the "rb" for binary mode and the `storlines` method for text. Consult module *ftplib.py* in the Python source library directory for more details.

```
deleting remote whatsold.html
deleting remote xlate-lp.html
deleting remote uploadflat.py
deleting remote ora-lp-france.gif
deleting remote LJsuppcover.jpg
deleting remote sonyz505js.gif
deleting remote pic14.html
...
```

Uploads with Subdirectories

Perhaps the biggest limitation of the web site download and upload scripts we just met are that they assume the site directory is flat (hence their names)—i.e., both transfer simple files only, and neither handles nested subdirectories within the web directory to be transferred.

For my purposes, that's a reasonable constraint. I avoid nested subdirectories to keep things simple, and I store my home web site as a simple directory of files. For other sites (including one I keep at the *starship* machine), site transfer scripts are easier to use if they also automatically transfer subdirectories along the way.

It turns out that supporting directories is fairly simple—we need to add only a bit of recursion and remote directory creation calls. The upload script in Example 11-14 extends the one we just saw, to handle uploading all subdirectories nested within the transferred directory. Furthermore, it recursively transfers subdirectories within subdirectories—the entire directory tree contained within the top-level transfer directory is uploaded to the target directory at the remote server.

Example 11-14. PP2E\Internet\Ftp\uploadall.py

```
#!/bin/env python
#########################################################################
# use ftp to upload all files from a local dir to a remote site/directory;
# this version supports uploading nested subdirectories too, but not the
# cleanall option (that requires parsing ftp listings to detect remote
# dirs, etc.);  to upload subdirectories, uses os.path.isdir(path) to see
# if a local file is really a directory, FTP().mkd(path) to make the dir
# on the remote machine (wrapped in a try in case it already exists there),
# and recursion to upload all files/dirs inside the nested subdirectory.
# see also: uploadall-2.py, which doesn't assume the topremotedir exists.
#########################################################################

import os, sys, ftplib
from getpass import getpass

remotesite   = 'home.rmi.net'           # upload from pc or starship to rmi.net
topremotedir = 'public_html'
remoteuser   = 'lutz'
remotepass   = getpass('Please enter password for %s: ' % remotesite)
toplocaldir  = (len(sys.argv) > 1 and sys.argv[1]) or '.'
```

Example 11-14. PP2E\Internet\Ftp\uploadall.py (continued)

```
print 'connecting...'
connection = ftplib.FTP(remotesite)          # connect to ftp site
connection.login(remoteuser, remotepass)     # login as user/password
connection.cwd(topremotedir)                 # cd to directory to copy to
                                             # assumes topremotedir exists

def uploadDir(localdir):
    global fcount, dcount
    localfiles = os.listdir(localdir)
    for localname in localfiles:
        localpath = os.path.join(localdir, localname)
        print 'uploading', localpath, 'to', localname
        if os.path.isdir(localpath):
            # recur into subdirs
            try:
                connection.mkd(localname)
                print localname, 'directory created'
            except:
                print localname, 'directory not created'
            connection.cwd(localname)
            uploadDir(localpath)
            connection.cwd('..')
            dcount = dcount+1
        else:
            if localname[-4:] == 'html' or localname[-3:] == 'txt':
                # use ascii mode xfer
                localfile = open(localpath, 'r')
                connection.storlines('STOR ' + localname, localfile)
            else:
                # use binary mode xfer
                localfile = open(localpath, 'rb')
                connection.storbinary('STOR ' + localname, localfile, 1024)
            localfile.close()
            fcount = fcount+1

fcount = dcount = 0
uploadDir(toplocaldir)
connection.quit()
print 'Done:', fcount, 'files and', dcount, 'directories uploaded.'
```

Like the flat upload script, this one can be run on any machine with Python and sockets and upload to any machine running an FTP server; I run it both on my laptop PC and on *starship* by Telnet to upload sites to my ISP.

In the interest of space, I'll leave studying this variant in more depth as a suggested exercise. Two quick pointers, though:

- The crux of the matter here is the os.path.isdir test near the top; if this test detects a directory in the current local directory, we create a same-named directory on the remote machine with connection.mkd and descend into it with connection.cwd, and recur into the subdirectory on the local machine. Like all FTP object methods, mkd and cwd methods issue FTP commands to the remote server. When we exit a local subdirectory, we run a remote `cwd('..')` to climb to the remote parent directory and continue. The rest of the script is roughly the same as the original.

- Note that this script handles only directory tree *uploads*; recursive uploads are generally more useful than recursive downloads, if you maintain your web sites on your local PC and upload to a server periodically, as I do. If you also want to download (mirror) a web site that has subdirectories, see the mirror scripts in the Python source distribution's Tools directory (currently, at file location *Tools/scripts/ftpmirror.py*). It's not much extra work, but requires parsing the output of a remote listing command to detect remote directories, and that is just complicated enough for me to omit here. For the same reason, the recursive upload script shown here doesn't support the remote directory cleanup option of the original—such a feature would require parsing remote listings as well.

For more context, also see the *uploadall-2.py* version of this script in the examples distribution; it's similar, but coded so as not to assume that the top-level remote directory already exists.

Processing Internet Email

Some of the other most common higher-level Internet protocols have to do with reading and sending email messages: POP and IMAP for fetching email from servers,[*] SMTP for sending new messages, and other formalisms such as `rfc822` for specifying email message contents and format. You don't normally need to know about such acronyms when using common email tools; but internally, programs like Microsoft Outlook talk to POP and SMTP servers to do your bidding.

Like FTP, email ultimately consists of formatted commands and byte streams shipped over sockets and ports (port 110 for POP; 25 for SMTP). But also like FTP, Python has standard modules to simplify all aspects of email processing. In this section, we explore the POP and SMTP interfaces for fetching and sending email at servers, and the `rfc822` interfaces for parsing information out of email header lines; other email interfaces in Python are analogous and are documented in the Python library reference manual.

POP: Reading Email

I used to be an old-fashioned guy. I admit it: up until recently, I preferred to check my email by telneting to my ISP and using a simple command-line email interface.

---

[*] IMAP, or Internet Message Access Protocol, was designed as an alternative to POP, but is not as widely used today, and so is not presented in this text. See the Python library manual for IMAP support details.

Of course, that's not ideal for mail with attachments, pictures, and the like, but its portability is staggering—because Telnet runs on almost any machine with a network link, I was able to check my mail quickly and easily from anywhere on the planet. Given that I make my living traveling around the world teaching Python classes, this wild accessibility was a big win.

If you've already read the web site mirror scripts sections earlier in this chapter, you've already heard my tale of ISP woe, so I won't repeat it here. Suffice it to say that times have changed on this front too: when my ISP took away Telnet access, they also took away my email access.* Luckily, Python came to the rescue here, too—by writing email access scripts in Python, I can still read and send email from any machine in the world that has Python and an Internet connection. Python can be as portable a solution as Telnet.

Moreover, I can still use these scripts as an alternative to tools suggested by the ISP, such as Microsoft Outlook. Besides not being a big fan of delegating control to commercial products of large companies, tools like Outlook generally download mail to your PC and delete it from the mail server as soon as you access it. This keeps your email box small (and your ISP happy), but isn't exactly friendly to traveling Python salespeople—once accessed, you cannot re-access a prior email from any machine except the one where it was initially downloaded to. If you need to see an old email and don't have your PC handy, you're out of luck.

The next two scripts represent one solution to these portability and single-machine constraints (we'll see others in this and later chapters). The first, *popmail.py*, is a simple mail reader tool, which downloads and prints the contents of each email in an email account. This script is admittedly primitive, but it lets you read your email on any machine with Python and sockets; moreover, it leaves your email intact on the server. The second, *smtpmail.py*, is a one-shot script for writing and sending a new email message.

Mail configuration module

Before we get to either of the two scripts, though, let's first take a look a common module they both import and use. The module in Example 11-15 is used to configure email parameters appropriately for a particular user. It's simply a collection of assignments used by all the mail programs that appear in this book; isolating these configuration settings in this single module makes it easy to configure the book's email programs for a particular user.

---

* In the process of losing Telnet, my email account and web site were taken down for weeks on end, and I lost forever a backlog of thousands of messages saved over the course of a year. Such outages can be especially bad if your income is largely driven by email and web contacts, but that's a story for another night, boys and girls.

If you want to use any of this book's email programs to do mail processing of your own, be sure to change its assignments to reflect your servers, account user-names, and so on (as shown, they refer to my email accounts). Not all of this module's settings are used by the next two scripts; we'll come back to this module at later examples to explain some of the settings here.

Example 11-15. PP2E\Internet\Email\mailconfig.py

```
###############################################################
# email scripts get their server names and other email config
# options from this module: change me to reflect your machine
# names, sig, etc.; could get some from the command line too;
###############################################################

#-------------------------------------------
# SMTP email server machine name (send)
#-------------------------------------------

smtpservername = 'smtp.rmi.net'          # or starship.python.net, 'localhost'


#-------------------------------------------
# POP3 email server machine, user (retrieve)
#-------------------------------------------

popservername  = 'pop.rmi.net'           # or starship.python.net, 'localhost'
popusername    = 'lutz'                   # password fetched of asked wehen run


#-------------------------------------------
# local file where pymail saves pop mail
# PyMailGui insead asks with a popup dialog
#-------------------------------------------

savemailfile  = r'c:\stuff\etc\savemail.txt'      # use dialog in PyMailGui


#----------------------------------------------------------------
# PyMailGui: optional name of local one-line text file with your
# pop password; if empty or file cannot be read, pswd requested
# when run; pswd is not encrypted so leave this empty on shared
# machines; PyMailCgi and pymail always ask for pswd when run.
#----------------------------------------------------------------

poppasswdfile = r'c:\stuff\etc\pymailgui.txt'      # set to '' to be asked


#----------------------------------------------------------------
# personal information used by PyMailGui to fill in forms;
# sig  -- can be a triple-quoted block, ignored if empty string;
# addr -- used for initial value of "From" field if not empty,
# else tries to guess From for replies, with varying success;
#----------------------------------------------------------------

myaddress   = 'lutz@rmi.net'
mysignature = '--Mark Lutz  (http://rmi.net/~lutz)  [PyMailGui 1.0]'
```

POP mail reader module

On to reading email in Python: the script in Example 11-16 employs Python's standard `poplib` module, an implementation of the client-side interface to POP—the Post Office Protocol. POP is just a well-defined way to fetch email from servers over sockets. This script connects to a POP server to implement a simple yet portable email download and display tool.

Example 11-16. PP2E\Internet\Email\popmail.py

```
#!/usr/local/bin/python
#####################################################
# use the Python POP3 mail interface module to view
# your pop email account messages; this is just a
# simple listing--see pymail.py for a client with
# more user interaction features, and smtpmail.py
# for a script which sends mail; pop is used to
# retrieve mail, and runs on a socket using port
# number 110 on the server machine, but Python's
# poplib hides all protocol details; to send mail,
# use the smtplib module (or os.popen('mail...').
# see also: unix mailfile reader in App framework.
#####################################################

import poplib, getpass, sys, mailconfig

mailserver = mailconfig.popservername    # ex: 'pop.rmi.net'
mailuser   = mailconfig.popusername      # ex: 'lutz'
mailpasswd = getpass.getpass('Password for %s?' % mailserver)

print 'Connecting...'
server = poplib.POP3(mailserver)
server.user(mailuser)                    # connect, login to mail server
server.pass_(mailpasswd)                 # pass is a reserved word

try:
    print server.getwelcome()            # print returned greeting message
    msgCount, msgBytes = server.stat()
    print 'There are', msgCount, 'mail messages in', msgBytes, 'bytes'
    print server.list()
    print '-'*80
    if sys.platform[:3] == 'win': raw_input()   # windows getpass is odd
    raw_input('[Press Enter key]')

    for i in range(msgCount):
        hdr, message, octets = server.retr(i+1)  # octets is byte count
        for line in message: print line          # retrieve, print all mail
        print '-'*80                             # mail box locked till quit
        if i < msgCount - 1:
            raw_input('[Press Enter key]')
finally:                                 # make sure we unlock mbox
    server.quit()                        # else locked till timeout
print 'Bye.'
```

Though primitive, this script illustrates the basics of reading email in Python. To establish a connection to an email server, we start by making an instance of the `poplib.POP3` object, passing in the email server machine's name:

```
server = poplib.POP3(mailserver)
```

If this call doesn't raise an exception, we're connected (by socket) to the POP server listening for requests on POP port number 110 at the machine where our email account lives. The next thing we need to do before fetching messages is tell the server our username and password; notice that the password method is called `pass_`—without the trailing underscore, `pass` would name a reserved word and trigger a syntax error:

```
server.user(mailuser)              # connect, login to mail server
server.pass_(mailpasswd)           # pass is a reserved word
```

To keep things simple and relatively secure, this script always asks for the account password interactively; the `getpass` module we met in the FTP section of this chapter is used to input but not display a password string typed by the user.

Once we've told the server our username and password, we're free to fetch mailbox information with the `stat` method (number messages, total bytes among all messages), and fetch a particular message with the `retr` method (pass the message number; they start at 1):

```
msgCount, msgBytes = server.stat()
hdr, message, octets = server.retr(i+1)    # octets is byte count
```

When we're done, we close the email server connection by calling the POP object's `quit` method:

```
server.quit()                      # else locked till timeout
```

Notice that this call appears inside the `finally` clause of a `try` statement that wraps the bulk of the script. To minimize complications associated with changes, POP servers lock your email box between the time you first connect and the time you close your connection (or until an arbitrarily long system-defined time-out expires). Because the POP `quit` method also unlocks the mailbox, it's crucial that we do this before exiting, whether an exception is raised during email processing or not. By wrapping the action in a `try/finally` statement, we guarantee that the script calls `quit` on exit to unlock the mailbox to make it accessible to other processes (e.g., delivery of incoming email).

Here is the popmail script in action, displaying two messages in my account's mailbox on machine *pop.rmi.net*—the domain name of the mail server machine at *rmi.net*, configured in module `mailconfig`:

```
C:\...\PP2E\Internet\Email>python popmail.py
Password for pop.rmi.net?
Connecting...
+OK Cubic Circle's v1.31 1998/05/13 POP3 ready <4860000073ed6c39@chevalier>
```

```
There are 2 mail messages in 1386 bytes
('+OK 2 messages (1386 octets)', ['1 744', '2 642'], 14)
--------------------------------------------------------------------------------


[Press Enter key]
Received: by chevalier (mbox lutz)
  (with Cubic Circle's cucipop (v1.31 1998/05/13) Wed Jul 12 16:13:33 2000)
X-From_: lumber.jack@TheLarch.com  Wed Jul 12 16:10:28 2000
Return-Path: <lumber.jack@TheLarch.com>
Received: from VAIO (dial-218.101.denco.rmi.net [166.93.218.101])
        by chevalier.rmi.net (8.9.3/8.9.3) with ESMTP id QAA21434
        for <lutz@rmi.net>; Wed, 12 Jul 2000 16:10:27 -0600 (MDT)
From: lumber.jack@TheLarch.com
Message-Id: <200007122210.QAA21434@chevalier.rmi.net>
To: lutz@rmi.net
Date: Wed Jul 12 16:03:59 2000
Subject: I'm a Lumberjack, and I'm okay
X-Mailer: PyMailGui Version 1.0 (Python)

I cut down trees, I skip and jump,
I like to press wild flowers...


--------------------------------------------------------------------------------


[Press Enter key]
Received: by chevalier (mbox lutz)
  (with Cubic Circle's cucipop (v1.31 1998/05/13) Wed Jul 12 16:13:54 2000)
X-From_: lutz@rmi.net  Wed Jul 12 16:12:42 2000
Return-Path: <lutz@chevalier.rmi.net>
Received: from VAIO (dial-218.101.denco.rmi.net [166.93.218.101])
        by chevalier.rmi.net (8.9.3/8.9.3) with ESMTP id QAA24093
        for <lutz@rmi.net>; Wed, 12 Jul 2000 16:12:37 -0600 (MDT)
Message-Id: <200007122212.QAA24093@chevalier.rmi.net>
From: lutz@rmi.net
To: lutz@rmi.net
Date: Wed Jul 12 16:06:12 2000
Subject: testing
X-Mailer: PyMailGui Version 1.0 (Python)

Testing Python mail tools.

--------------------------------------------------------------------------------


Bye.
```

This interface is about as simple as it could be—after connecting to the server, it prints the complete raw text of one message at a time, pausing between each until you type the enter key. The `raw_input` built-in is called to wait for the key press between message displays.[*] The pause keeps messages from scrolling off the

---

[*] An extra `raw_input` is inserted on Windows only, in order to clear the stream damage of the **getpass** call; see the note about this issue in the FTP section of this chapter.

screen too fast; to make them visually distinct, emails are also separated by lines of dashes. We could make the display more fancy (e.g., we'll pick out parts of messages in later examples with the `rfc822` module), but here we simply display the whole message that was sent.

If you look closely at these mails' text, you may notice that they were actually sent by another program called PyMailGui (a program we'll meet near the end of this chapter). The "X-Mailer" header line, if present, typically identifies the sending program. In fact, there are a variety of extra header lines that can be sent in a message's text. The "Received:" headers, for example, trace the machines that a message passed though on its way to the target mailbox. Because `popmail` prints the entire raw text of a message, you see all headers here, but you may see only a few by default in end-user-oriented mail GUIs such as Outlook.

Before we move on, I should also point out that this script never deletes mail from the server. Mail is simply retrieved and printed and will be shown again the next time you run the script (barring deletion in another tool). To really remove mail permanently, we need to call other methods (e.g., `server.dele(msgnum)`) but such a capability is best deferred until we develop more interactive mail tools.

SMTP: Sending Email

There is a proverb in hackerdom that states that every useful computer program eventually grows complex enough to send email. Whether such somewhat ancient wisdom rings true or not in practice, the ability to automatically initiate email from within a program is a powerful tool.

For instance, test systems can automatically email failure reports, user interface programs can ship purchase orders to suppliers by email, and so on. Moreover, a portable Python mail script could be used to send messages from any computer in the world with Python and an Internet connection. Freedom from dependence on mail programs like Outlook is an attractive feature if you happen to make your living traveling around teaching Python on all sorts of computers.

Luckily, sending email from within a Python script is just as easy as reading it. In fact, there are at least four ways to do so:

Calling os.popen to launch a command-line mail program

On some systems, you can send email from a script with a call of the form:

```
os.popen('mail -s "xxx" a@b.c', 'w').write(text)
```

As we've seen earlier in the book, the `popen` tool runs the command-line string passed to its first argument, and returns a file-like object connected to it. If we use an open mode of "w", we are connected to the command's standard input stream—here, we write the text of the new mail message to the standard Unix `mail` command-line program. The net effect is as if we had run `mail` interactively, but it happens inside a running Python script.

Running the sendmail program

The open source `sendmail` program offers another way to initiate mail from a program. Assuming it is installed and configured on your system, you can launch it using Python tools like the `os.popen` call of the previous paragraph.

Using the standard smtplib Python module

Python's standard library comes with support for the client-side interface to SMTP—the Simple Mail Transfer Protocol—a higher-level Internet standard for sending mail over sockets. Like the `poplib` module we met in the previous section, `smtplib` hides all the socket and protocol details, and can be used to send mail on any machine with Python and a socket-based Internet link.

Fetching and using third party packages and tools

Other tools in the open source library provide higher-level mail handling packages for Python (accessible from *http://www.python.org*). Most build upon one of the prior three techniques.

Of these four options, `smtplib` is by far the most portable and powerful. Using `popen` to spawn a mail program usually works on Unix-like platforms only, not on Windows (it assumes a command-line mail program). And although the `sendmail` program is powerful, it is also somewhat Unix-biased, complex, and may not be installed even on all Unix-like machines.

By contrast, the `smtplib` module works on any machine that has Python and an Internet link, including Unix, Linux, and Windows. Moreover, SMTP affords us much control over the formatting and routing of email. Since it is arguably the best option for sending mail from a Python script, let's explore a simple mailing program that illustrates its interfaces. The Python script shown in Example 11-17 is intended to be used from an interactive command line; it reads a new mail message from the user and sends the new mail by SMTP using Python's `smtplib` module.

Example 11-17. PP2E\Internet\Email\smtpmail.py

```
#!/usr/local/bin/python
####################################################
# use the Python SMTP mail interface module to send
# email messages; this is just a simple one-shot
# send script--see pymail, PyMailGui, and PyMailCgi
# for clients with more user interaction features,
# and popmail.py for a script which retrieves mail;
####################################################

import smtplib, string, sys, time, mailconfig
mailserver = mailconfig.smtpservername       # ex: starship.python.net
```

Example 11-17. PP2E\Internet\Email\smtpmail.py (continued)

```
From = string.strip(raw_input('From? '))        # ex: lutz@rmi.net
To   = string.strip(raw_input('To?   '))        # ex: python-list@python.org
To   = string.split(To, ';')                    # allow a list of recipients
Subj = string.strip(raw_input('Subj? '))

# prepend standard headers
date = time.ctime(time.time())
text = ('From: %s\nTo: %s\nDate: %s\nSubject: %s\n\n'
                    % (From, string.join(To, ';'), date, Subj))

print 'Type message text, end with line=(ctrl + D or Z)'
while 1:
    line = sys.stdin.readline()
    if not line:
        break                          # exit on ctrl-d/z
  # if line[:4] == 'From':
  #     line = '>' + line              # servers escape for us
    text = text + line

if sys.platform[:3] == 'win': print
print 'Connecting...'
server = smtplib.SMTP(mailserver)                # connect, no login step
failed = server.sendmail(From, To, text)
server.quit()
if failed:                                       # smtplib may raise exceptions
    print 'Failed recipients:', failed           # too, but let them pass here
else:
    print 'No errors.'
print 'Bye.'
```

Most of this script is *user interface*—it inputs the sender's address ("From"), one or more recipient addresses ("To", separated by ";" if more than one), and a subject line. The sending date is picked up from Python's standard `time` module, standard header lines are formatted, and the `while` loop reads message lines until the user types the end-of-file character (Ctrl-Z on Windows, Ctrl-D on Linux).

The rest of the script is where all the SMTP magic occurs: to send a mail by SMTP, simply run these two sorts of calls:

`server = smtplib.SMTP(mailserver)`

Make an instance of the SMTP object, passing in the name of the SMTP server that will dispatch the message first. If this doesn't throw an exception, you're connected to the SMTP server via a socket when the call returns.

`failed = server.sendmail(From, To, text)`

Call the SMTP object's `sendmail` method, passing in the sender address, one or more recipient addresses, and the text of the message itself with as many standard mail header lines as you care to provide. To be robust, add a blank line between the header lines and the body in the message's text.

When you're done, call the object's **quit** method to disconnect from the server. Notice that, on failure, the **sendmail** method may either raise an exception or return a list of the recipient addresses that failed; the script handles the latter case but lets exceptions kill the script with a Python error message.

Sending messages

Okay—let's ship a few messages across the world. The **smtpmail** script is a one-shot tool: each run allows you to send a single new mail message. Like most of the client-side tools in this chapter, it can be run from any computer with Python and an Internet link. Here it is running on Windows 98:

```
C:\...\PP2E\Internet\Email>python smtpmail.py
From? Eric.the.Half.a.Bee@semibee.com
To?   lutz@rmi.net
Subj? A B C D E F G
Type message text, end with line=(ctrl + D or Z)
Fiddle de dum, Fiddle de dee,
Eric the half a bee.

Connecting...
No errors.
Bye.
```

This mail is sent to my address (*lutz@rmi.net*), so it ultimately shows up in my mailbox at my ISP, but only after being routed through an arbitrary number of machines on the Net, and across arbitrarily distant network links. It's complex at the bottom, but usually, the Internet "just works."

Notice the "From" address, though—it's completely fictitious (as far as I know, at least). It turns out that we can usually provide any "From" address we like because SMTP doesn't check its validity (only its general format is checked). Furthermore, unlike POP, there is no notion of a username or password in SMTP, so the sender is more difficult to determine. We need only pass email to any machine with a server listening on the SMTP port, and don't need an account on that machine. Here, *Eric.the.Half.a.Bee@semibee.com* works fine as the sender; *Marketing.Geek. From.Hell@spam.com* would work just as well.

I'm going to tell you something now for instructional purposes only: it turns out that this behavior is the basis of all those annoying junk emails that show up in your mailbox without a real sender's address.* Salesmen infected with e-millionaire mania will email advertising to all addresses on a list without providing a real "From" address, to cover their tracks.

---

* Such junk mail is usually referred to as *spam,* a reference to a Monty Python skit where people trying to order breakfast at a restaurant were repeatedly drowned out by a group of Vikings singing an increasingly loud chorus of "spam, spam, spam,..." (no, really). While spam can be used in many ways, this usage differs both from its appearance in this book's examples, and its much-lauded role as a food product.

Normally, of course, you should use the same "To" address in the message and the SMTP call, and provide your real email address as the "From" value (that's the only way people will be able to reply to your message). Moreover, apart from teasing your significant other, sending phony addresses is just plain bad Internet citizenship. Let's run the script again to ship off another mail with more politically correct coordinates:

```
C:\...\PP2E\Internet\Email>python smtpmail.py
From? lutz@rmi.net
To?  lutz@rmi.net
Subj? testing smtpmail
Type message text, end with line=(ctrl + D or Z)
Lovely Spam! Wonderful Spam!
Connecting...
No errors.
Bye.
```

At this point, we could run whatever email tool we normally use to access our mailbox to verify the results of these two send operations; the two new emails should show up in our mailbox regardless of which mail client is used to view them. Since we've already written a Python script for reading mail, though, let's put it to use as a verification tool—running the `popmail` script from the last section reveals our two new messages at the end of the mail list:

```
C:\...\PP2E\Internet\Email>python popmail.py
Password for pop.rmi.net?
Connecting...
+OK Cubic Circle's v1.31 1998/05/13 POP3 ready <c4050000b6ee6c39@chevalier>
There are 6 mail messages in 10941 bytes
('+OK 6 messages (10941 octets)', ['1 744', '2 642', '3 4456', '4 697', '5 3791'
, '6 611'], 44)
--------------------------------------------------------------------------------
...
...lines omitted...
...
[Press Enter key]
Received: by chevalier (mbox lutz)
  (with Cubic Circle's cucipop (v1.31 1998/05/13) Wed Jul 12 16:19:20 2000)
X-From_: Eric.the.Half.a.Bee@semibee.com  Wed Jul 12 16:16:31 2000
Return-Path: <Eric.the.Half.a.Bee@semibee.com>
Received: from VAIO (dial-218.101.denco.rmi.net [166.93.218.101])
        by chevalier.rmi.net (8.9.3/8.9.3) with ESMTP id QAA28647
        for <lutz@rmi.net>; Wed, 12 Jul 2000 16:16:30 -0600 (MDT)
From: Eric.the.Half.a.Bee@semibee.com
Message-Id: <200007122216.QAA28647@chevalier.rmi.net>
To: lutz@rmi.net
Date: Wed Jul 12 16:09:21 2000
Subject: A B C D E F G

Fiddle de dum, Fiddle de dee,
Eric the half a bee.
```

```
---------------------------------------------------------------------------
[Press Enter key]
Received: by chevalier (mbox lutz)
  (with Cubic Circle's cucipop (v1.31 1998/05/13) Wed Jul 12 16:19:51 2000)
X-From_: lutz@rmi.net  Wed Jul 12 16:17:58 2000
Return-Path: <lutz@chevalier.rmi.net>
Received: from VAIO (dial-218.101.denco.rmi.net [166.93.218.101])
        by chevalier.rmi.net (8.9.3/8.9.3) with ESMTP id QAA00415
        for <lutz@rmi.net>; Wed, 12 Jul 2000 16:17:57 -0600 (MDT)
Message-Id: <200007122217.QAA00415@chevalier.rmi.net>
From: lutz@rmi.net
To: lutz@rmi.net
Date: Wed Jul 12 16:10:55 2000
Subject: testing smtpmail

Lovely Spam! Wonderful Spam!

---------------------------------------------------------------------------

Bye.
```

More ways to abuse the Net

The first mail here was the one we sent with a fictitious address; the second was the more legitimate message. Like "From" addresses, header lines are a bit arbitrary under SMTP, too. smtpmail automatically adds "From:" and "To:" header lines in the message's text with the same addresses as passed to the SMTP interface, but only as a polite convention. Sometimes, though, you can't tell who a mail was sent *to* either—to obscure the target audience, spammers also may play games with "Bcc" blind copies or the contents of headers in the message's text.

For example, if we change smtpmail to not automatically generate a "To:" header line with the same address(es) sent to the SMTP interface call, we can manually type a "To:" header that differs from the address we're really sending to:

```
C:\...\PP2E\Internet\Email>python smtpmail-noTo.py
From? Eric.the.Half.a.Bee@semibee.com
To?    lutz@starship.python.net
Subj? a b c d e f g
Type message text, end with line=(ctrl + D or Z)
To: nobody.in.particular@marketing.com
Fiddle de dum, Fiddle de dee,
Eric the half a bee.
Connecting...
No errors.
Bye.
```

In some ways, the "From" and "To" addresses in send method calls and message header lines are similar to addresses on envelopes and letters in envelopes. The former is used for routing, but the latter is what the reader sees. Here, I gave the

"To" address as my mailbox on the *starship.python.net* server, but gave a fictitious name in the manually typed "To:" header line; the first address is where it really goes. A command-line mail tool running on *starship* by Telnet reveals two bogus mails sent—one with a bad "From:", and the one with an additionally bad "To:" that we just sent:

```
[lutz@starship lutz]$ mail
Mail version 8.1 6/6/93.  Type ? for help.
"/home/crew/lutz/Mailbox": 22 messages 12 new 22 unread
...more...
>N 21 Eric.the.Half.a.Bee@  Thu Jul 13 20:22   20/789   "A B C D E F G"
 N 22 Eric.the.Half.a.Bee@  Thu Jul 13 20:26   19/766   "a b c d e f g"

& 21
Message 21:
From Eric.the.Half.a.Bee@semibee.com Thu Jul 13 20:21:18 2000
Delivered-To: lutz@starship.python.net
From: Eric.the.Half.a.Bee@semibee.com
To: lutz@starship.python.net
Date: Thu Jul 13 14:15:55 2000
Subject: A B C D E F G

Fiddle de dum, Fiddle de dee,
Eric the half a bee.

& 22
Message 22:
From Eric.the.Half.a.Bee@semibee.com Thu Jul 13 20:26:34 2000
Delivered-To: lutz@starship.python.net
From: Eric.the.Half.a.Bee@semibee.com
Date: Thu Jul 13 14:20:22 2000
Subject: a b c d e f g
To: nobody.in.particular@marketing.com

Fiddle de dum, Fiddle de dee,
Eric the half a bee.
```

If your mail tool picks out the "To:" line, such mails look odd when viewed. For instance, here's another sent to my *rmi.net* mailbox:

```
C:\...\PP2E\Internet\Email>python smtpmail-noTo.py
From? Arthur@knights.com
To?  lutz@rmi.net
Subj? Killer bunnies
Type message text, end with line=(ctrl + D or Z)
To: you@home.com
Run away!  Run away! ...
Connecting...
No errors.
Bye.
```

When it shows up in my mailbox on *rmi.net*, it's difficult to tell much about its origin or destination in either Outlook or a Python-coded mail tool we'll meet near the end of this chapter (see Figures 11-8 and 11-9). And its raw text will only show the machines it has been routed through.

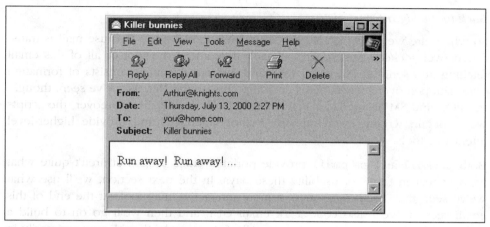

Figure 11-8. Bogus mail in Outlook

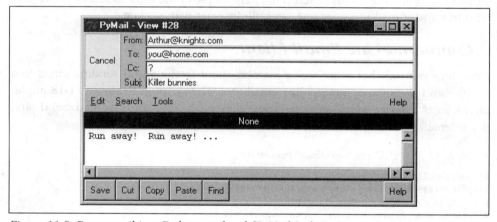

Figure 11-9. Bogus mail in a Python mail tool (PyMailGui)

Once again, though—don't do this unless you have good reason. I'm showing it for header-line illustration purposes (e.g., in a later section, we'll add an "X-mailer:" header line to identify the sending program). Furthermore, to stop a criminal, you sometimes need to think like one—you can't do much about spam mail unless you understand how it is generated. To write an automatic spam filter that deletes incoming junk mail, for instance, you need to know the telltale signs to look for in a message's text. And "To" address juggling may be useful in the context of legitimate mailing lists.

But really, sending email with bogus "From:" and "To:" lines is equivalent to making anonymous phone calls. Most mailers won't even let you change the "From" line, and don't distinguish between the "To" address and header line, but SMTP is wide open in this regard. Be good out there; okay?

Back to the big Internet picture

So where are we at in the Internet abstraction model now? Because mail is transferred over sockets (remember sockets?), they are at the root of all of this email fetching and sending. All email read and written ultimately consists of formatted bytes shipped over sockets between computers on the Net. As we've seen, though, the POP and SMTP interfaces in Python hide all the details. Moreover, the scripts we've begun writing even hide the Python interfaces and provide higher-level interactive tools.

Both `popmail` and `smtpmail` provide portable email tools, but aren't quite what we'd expect in terms of usability these days. In the next section, we'll use what we've seen thus far to implement a more interactive mail tool. At the end of this email section, we'll also code a Tk email GUI, and then we'll go on to build a web-based interface in a later chapter. All of these tools, though, vary primarily in terms of user interface only; each ultimately employs the mail modules we've met here to transfer mail message text over the Internet with sockets.

A Command-Line Email Client

Now, let's put together what we've learned about fetching and sending email in a simple but functional command-line email tool. The script in Example 11-18 implements an interactive email session—users may type commands to read, send, and delete email messages.

Example 11-18. PP2E\Internet\Emal\pymail.py

```
#!/usr/local/bin/python
#####################################################
# A simple command-line email interface client in
# Python; uses Python POP3 mail interface module to
# view pop email account messages; uses rfc822 and
# StringIO modules to extract mail message headers;
#####################################################

import poplib, rfc822, string, StringIO

def connect(servername, user, passwd):
    print 'Connecting...'
    server = poplib.POP3(servername)
    server.user(user)                      # connect, login to mail server
    server.pass_(passwd)                   # pass is a reserved word
    print server.getwelcome()              # print returned greeting message
    return server

def loadmessages(servername, user, passwd, loadfrom=1):
    server = connect(servername, user, passwd)
```

Example 11-18. PP2E\Internet\Emal\pymail.py (continued)

```
    try:
        print server.list()
        (msgCount, msgBytes) = server.stat()
        print 'There are', msgCount, 'mail messages in', msgBytes, 'bytes'
        print 'Retrieving:',
        msgList = []
        for i in range(loadfrom, msgCount+1):      # empty if low >= high
            print i,                                # fetch mail now
            (hdr, message, octets) = server.retr(i) # save text on list
            msgList.append(string.join(message, '\n')) # leave mail on server
        print
    finally:
        server.quit()                               # unlock the mail box
    assert len(msgList) == (msgCount - loadfrom) + 1  # msg nums start at 1
    return msgList

def deletemessages(servername, user, passwd, toDelete, verify=1):
    print 'To be deleted:', toDelete
    if verify and raw_input('Delete?')[:1] not in ['y', 'Y']:
        print 'Delete cancelled.'
    else:
        server = connect(servername, user, passwd)
        try:
            print 'Deleting messages from server.'
            for msgnum in toDelete:                  # reconnect to delete mail
                server.dele(msgnum)                  # mbox locked until quit()
        finally:
            server.quit()

def showindex(msgList):
    count = 0
    for msg in msgList:                             # strip,show some mail headers
        strfile = StringIO.StringIO(msg)            # make string look like a file
        msghdrs = rfc822.Message(strfile)           # parse mail headers into a dict
        count   = count + 1
        print '%d:\t%d bytes' % (count, len(msg))
        for hdr in ('From', 'Date', 'Subject'):
            try:
                print '\t%s=>%s' % (hdr, msghdrs[hdr])
            except KeyError:
                print '\t%s=>(unknown)' % hdr
            #print '\n\t%s=>%s' % (hdr, msghdrs.get(hdr, '(unknown)'))
        if count % 5 == 0:
            raw_input('[Press Enter key]')  # pause after each 5

def showmessage(i, msgList):
    if 1 <= i <= len(msgList):
        print '-'*80
        print msgList[i-1]                          # this prints entire mail--hdrs+text
        print '-'*80                                # to get text only, call file.read()
    else:                                           # after rfc822.Message reads hdr lines
        print 'Bad message number'
```

Example 11-18. PP2E\Internet\Emal\pymail.py (continued)

```
def savemessage(i, mailfile, msgList):
    if 1 <= i <= len(msgList):
        open(mailfile, 'a').write('\n' + msgList[i-1] + '-'*80 + '\n')
    else:
        print 'Bad message number'

def msgnum(command):
    try:
        return string.atoi(string.split(command)[1])
    except:
        return -1   # assume this is bad

helptext = """
Available commands:
i      - index display
l n?   - list all messages (or just message n)
d n?   - mark all messages for deletion (or just message n)
s n?   - save all messages to a file (or just message n)
m      - compose and send a new mail message
q      - quit pymail
?      - display this help text
"""

def interact(msgList, mailfile):
    showindex(msgList)
    toDelete = []
    while 1:
        try:
            command = raw_input('[Pymail] Action? (i, l, d, s, m, q, ?) ')
        except EOFError:
            command = 'q'

        # quit
        if not command or command == 'q':
            break

        # index
        elif command[0] == 'i':
            showindex(msgList)

        # list
        elif command[0] == 'l':
            if len(command) == 1:
                for i in range(1, len(msgList)+1):
                    showmessage(i, msgList)
            else:
                showmessage(msgnum(command), msgList)

        # save
        elif command[0] == 's':
            if len(command) == 1:
                for i in range(1, len(msgList)+1):
                    savemessage(i, mailfile, msgList)
```

Example 11-18. PP2E\Internet\Emal\pymail.py (continued)

```
            else:
                savemessage(msgnum(command), mailfile, msgList)

        # delete
        elif command[0] == 'd':
            if len(command) == 1:
                toDelete = range(1, len(msgList)+1)     # delete all later
            else:
                delnum = msgnum(command)
                if (1 <= delnum <= len(msgList)) and (delnum not in toDelete):
                    toDelete.append(delnum)
                else:
                    print 'Bad message number'

        # mail
        elif command[0] == 'm':                 # send a new mail via smtp
            try:                                # reuse existing script
                execfile('smtpmail.py', {})     # run file in own namespace
            except:
                print 'Error - mail not sent'   # don't die if script dies

        elif command[0] == '?':
            print helptext
        else:
            print 'What? -- type "?" for commands help'
    return toDelete

if __name__ == '__main__':
    import sys, getpass, mailconfig
    mailserver = mailconfig.popservername        # ex: 'starship.python.net'
    mailuser   = mailconfig.popusername          # ex: 'lutz'
    mailfile   = mailconfig.savemailfile         # ex: r'c:\stuff\savemail'
    mailpswd   = getpass.getpass('Password for %s?' % mailserver)

    if sys.platform[:3] == 'win': raw_input()    # clear stream
    print '[Pymail email client]'
    msgList    = loadmessages(mailserver, mailuser, mailpswd)     # load all
    toDelete   = interact(msgList, mailfile)
    if toDelete: deletemessages(mailserver, mailuser, mailpswd, toDelete)
    print 'Bye.'
```

There isn't much new here—just a combination of user-interface logic and tools we've already met, plus a handful of new tricks:

Loads

This client loads all email from the server into an in-memory Python list only once, on startup; you must exit and restart to reload newly arrived email.

Saves

On demand, `pymail` saves the raw text of a selected message into a local file, whose name you place in the `mailconfig` module.

Deletions

> We finally support on-request deletion of mail from the server here: in
> `pymail`, mails are selected for deletion by number, but are still only physi-
> cally removed from your server on exit, and then only if you verify the opera-
> tion. By deleting only on exit, we avoid changing mail message numbers
> during a session—under POP, deleting a mail not at the end of the list decre-
> ments the number assigned to all mails following the one deleted. Since mail
> is cached in memory by `pymail`, future operations on the numbered mes-
> sages in memory may be applied to the wrong mail if deletions were done
> immediately.*

Parsing messages

> Pymail still displays the entire raw text of a message on listing commands, but
> the mail index listing only displays selected headers parsed out of each mes-
> sage. Python's `rfc822` module is used to extract headers from a message: the
> call `rfc822.Message(strfile)` returns an object with dictionary interfaces
> for fetching the value of a message header by name string (e.g., index the
> object on string "From" to get the value of the "From" header line).

> Although unused here, anything not consumed from `strfile` after a `Message`
> call is the *body* of the message, and can be had by calling `strfile.read`.
> `Message` reads the message headers portion only. Notice that `strfile` is really
> an instance of the standard `StringIO.StringIO` object. This object wraps the
> message's raw text (a simple string) in a file-like interface; `rfc822.Message`
> expects a file interface, but doesn't care if the object is a true file or not. Once
> again, *interfaces* are what we code to in Python, not specific *types*. Module
> `StringIO` is useful anytime you need to make a string look like a file.

By now, I expect that you know enough Python to read this script for a deeper
look, so rather than saying more about its design here, let's jump into an interactive `pymail` session to see how it works.

Running the pymail command-line client

Let's start up `pymail` to read and delete email at our mail server and send new
messages. Pymail runs on any machine with Python and sockets, fetches mail
from any email server with a POP interface on which you have an account, and
sends mail via the SMTP server you've named in the `mailconfig` module.

Here it is in action running on my Windows 98 laptop machine; its operation is
identical on other machines. First, we start the script, supply a POP password

---

* More on POP message numbers when we study PyMailGui later in this chapter. Interestingly, the list of
  message numbers to be deleted need not be sorted; they remain valid for the duration of the connection.

Does Anybody Really Know What Time It Is?

Minor caveat: the simple date format used in the `smtpmail` program (and others in this book) doesn't quite follow the SMTP date formatting standard. Most servers don't care, and will let any sort of date text appear in date header lines. In fact, I've never seen a mail fail due to date formats.

If you want to be more in line with the standard, though, you could format the date header with code like this (adopted from standard module `urllib`, and parseable with standard tools such as the `rfc822` module and the `time.strptime` call):

```
import time
gmt = time.gmtime(time.time())
fmt = '%a, %d %b %Y %H:%M:%S GMT'
str = time.strftime(fmt, gmt)
hdr = 'Date: ' + str
print hdr
```

The `hdr` variable looks like this when this code is run:

```
Date: Fri, 02 Jun 2000 16:40:41 GMT
```

instead of the date format currently used by the `smtpmail` program:

```
>>> import time
>>> time.ctime(time.time())
'Fri Jun 02 10:23:51 2000'
```

The `time.strftime` call allows arbitrary date and time formatting (`time.ctime` is just one standard format), but we will leave rooting out the workings of all these calls as a suggested exercise for the reader; consult the `time` module's library manual entry. We'll also leave placing such code in a reusable file to the more modular among you. Time and date formatting rules are necessary, but aren't pretty.

(remember, SMTP servers require no password), and wait for the `pymail` email list index to appear:

```
C:\...\PP2E\Internet\Email>python pymail.py
Password for pop.rmi.net?

[Pymail email client]
Connecting...
+OK Cubic Circle's v1.31 1998/05/13 POP3 ready <870f000002f56c39@chevalier>
('+OK 5 messages (7150 octets)', ['1 744', '2 642', '3 4456', '4 697', '5 611'],
 36)
There are 5 mail messages in 7150 bytes
Retrieving: 1 2 3 4 5
1:      676 bytes
```

```
           From=>lumber.jack@TheLarch.com
           Date=>Wed Jul 12 16:03:59 2000
           Subject=>I'm a Lumberjack, and I'm okay
2:         587 bytes
           From=>lutz@rmi.net
           Date=>Wed Jul 12 16:06:12 2000
           Subject=>testing
3:         4307 bytes
           From=>"Mark Hammond" <MarkH@ActiveState.com>
           Date=>Wed, 12 Jul 2000 18:11:58 -0400
           Subject=>[Python-Dev] Python .NET (was Preventing 1.5 extensions...
4:         623 bytes
           From=>Eric.the.Half.a.Bee@semibee.com
           Date=>Wed Jul 12 16:09:21 2000
           Subject=>A B C D E F G
5:         557 bytes
           From=>lutz@rmi.net
           Date=>Wed Jul 12 16:10:55 2000
           Subject=>testing smtpmail
[Press Enter key]
[Pymail] Action? (i, l, d, s, m, q, ?) 1 5
-----------------------------------------------------------------------------

Received: by chevalier (mbox lutz)
  (with Cubic Circle's cucipop (v1.31 1998/05/13) Wed Jul 12 16:45:38 2000)
X-From_: lutz@rmi.net  Wed Jul 12 16:17:58 2000
Return-Path: <lutz@chevalier.rmi.net>
Received: from VAIO (dial-218.101.denco.rmi.net [166.93.218.101])
        by chevalier.rmi.net (8.9.3/8.9.3) with ESMTP id QAA00415
        for <lutz@rmi.net>; Wed, 12 Jul 2000 16:17:57 -0600 (MDT)
Message-Id: <200007122217.QAA00415@chevalier.rmi.net>
From: lutz@rmi.net
To: lutz@rmi.net
Date: Wed Jul 12 16:10:55 2000
Subject: testing smtpmail

Lovely Spam! Wonderful Spam!


-----------------------------------------------------------------------------

[Pymail] Action? (i, l, d, s, m, q, ?) 1 4
-----------------------------------------------------------------------------

Received: by chevalier (mbox lutz)
  (with Cubic Circle's cucipop (v1.31 1998/05/13) Wed Jul 12 16:45:38 2000)
X-From_: Eric.the.Half.a.Bee@semibee.com  Wed Jul 12 16:16:31 2000
Return-Path: <Eric.the.Half.a.Bee@semibee.com>
Received: from VAIO (dial-218.101.denco.rmi.net [166.93.218.101])
        by chevalier.rmi.net (8.9.3/8.9.3) with ESMTP id QAA28647
        for <lutz@rmi.net>; Wed, 12 Jul 2000 16:16:30 -0600 (MDT)
From: Eric.the.Half.a.Bee@semibee.com
Message-Id: <200007122216.QAA28647@chevalier.rmi.net>
To: lutz@rmi.net
Date: Wed Jul 12 16:09:21 2000
Subject: A B C D E F G
```

```
Fiddle de dum, Fiddle de dee,
Eric the half a bee.
```

Once `pymail` downloads your email to a Python list on the local client machine, you type command letters to process it. The "l" command lists (prints) the contents of a given mail number; here, we used it to list the two emails we wrote with the `smtpmail` script in the last section.

Pymail also lets us get command help, delete messages (deletions actually occur at the server on exit from the program), and save messages away in a local text file whose name is listed in the `mailconfig` module we saw earlier:

```
[Pymail] Action? (i, l, d, s, m, q, ?) ?

Available commands:
i      - index display
l n?   - list all messages (or just message n)
d n?   - mark all messages for deletion (or just message n)
s n?   - save all messages to a file (or just message n)
m      - compose and send a new mail message
q      - quit pymail
?      - display this help text

[Pymail] Action? (i, l, d, s, m, q, ?) d 1
[Pymail] Action? (i, l, d, s, m, q, ?) s 4
```

Now, let's pick the "m" mail *compose* option—`pymail` simply executes the `smptmail` script we wrote in the prior section and resumes its command loop (why reinvent the wheel?). Because that script sends by SMTP, you can use arbitrary "From" addresses here; but again, you generally shouldn't do that (unless, of course, you're trying to come up with interesting examples for a book).

The `smtpmail` script is run with the built-in `execfile` function; if you look at `pymail`'s code closely, you'll notice that it passes an empty dictionary to serve as the script's namespace to prevent its names from clashing with names in `pymail` code. `execfile` is a handy way to reuse existing code written as a top-level script, and thus is not really importable. Technically speaking, code in the file *smtplib.py* would run when imported, but only on the first import (later imports would simply return the loaded module object). Other scripts that check the __name__ attribute for __main__ won't generally run when imported at all:

```
[Pymail] Action? (i, l, d, s, m, q, ?) m
From? Cardinal@nice.red.suits.com
To?   lutz@rmi.net
Subj? Among our weapons are these:
Type message text, end with line=(ctrl + D or Z)
Nobody Expects the Spanish Inquisition!
Connecting...
No errors.
Bye.
```

```
[Pymail] Action? (i, l, d, s, m, q, ?) q
To be deleted: [1]
Delete?y
Connecting...
+OK Cubic Circle's v1.31 1998/05/13 POP3 ready <8e2e0000aff66c39@chevalier>
Deleting messages from server.
Bye.
```

As mentioned, deletions really happen only on exit; when we quit `pymail` with
the "q" command, it tells us which messages are queued for deletion, and verifies
the request. If verified, `pymail` finally contacts the mail server again and issues
POP calls to delete the selected mail messages.

Because `pymail` downloads mail from your server into a local Python list only
once at startup, though, we need to start `pymail` again to re-fetch mail from the
server if we want to see the result of the mail we sent and the deletion we made.
Here, our new mail shows up as number 5, and the original mail assigned number 1 is gone:

```
C:\...\PP2E\Internet\Email>python pymail.py
Password for pop.rmi.net?

[Pymail email client]
Connecting...
+OK Cubic Circle's v1.31 1998/05/13 POP3 ready <40310000d5f66c39@chevalier>
...
There are 5 mail messages in 7090 bytes
Retrieving: 1 2 3 4 5
1:      587 bytes
        From=>lutz@rmi.net
        Date=>Wed Jul 12 16:06:12 2000
        Subject=>testing
2:      4307 bytes
        From=>"Mark Hammond" <MarkH@ActiveState.com>
        Date=>Wed, 12 Jul 2000 18:11:58 -0400
        Subject=>[Python-Dev] Python .NET (was Preventing 1.5 extensions...
3:      623 bytes
        From=>Eric.the.Half.a.Bee@semibee.com
        Date=>Wed Jul 12 16:09:21 2000
        Subject=>A B C D E F G
4:      557 bytes
        From=>lutz@rmi.net
        Date=>Wed Jul 12 16:10:55 2000
        Subject=>testing smtpmail
5:      615 bytes
        From=>Cardinal@nice.red.suits.com
        Date=>Wed Jul 12 16:44:58 2000
        Subject=>Among our weapons are these:
[Press Enter key]
[Pymail] Action? (i, l, d, s, m, q, ?) 1 5
--------------------------------------------------------------------------

Received: by chevalier (mbox lutz)
  (with Cubic Circle's cucipop (v1.31 1998/05/13) Wed Jul 12 16:53:24 2000)
```

```
X-From_: Cardinal@nice.red.suits.com  Wed Jul 12 16:51:53 2000
Return-Path: <Cardinal@nice.red.suits.com>
Received: from VAIO (dial-218.101.denco.rmi.net [166.93.218.101])
        by chevalier.rmi.net (8.9.3/8.9.3) with ESMTP id QAA11127
        for <lutz@rmi.net>; Wed, 12 Jul 2000 16:51:52 -0600 (MDT)
From: Cardinal@nice.red.suits.com
Message-Id: <200007122251.QAA11127@chevalier.rmi.net>
To: lutz@rmi.net
Date: Wed Jul 12 16:44:58 2000
Subject: Among our weapons are these:

Nobody Expects the Spanish Inquisition!

-------------------------------------------------------------------------------

[Pymail] Action? (i, l, d, s, m, q, ?) q
Bye.
```

Finally, here is the mail save file, containing the one message we asked to be
saved in the prior session; it's simply the raw text of saved emails, with separator
lines. This is both human- and machine-readable—in principle, another script
could load saved mail from this file into a Python list, by calling the **string.
split** function on the file's text with the separator line as a delimiter:

```
C:\...\PP2E\Internet\Email>type c:\stuff\etc\savemail.txt

Received: by chevalier (mbox lutz)
  (with Cubic Circle's cucipop (v1.31 1998/05/13) Wed Jul 12 16:45:38 2000)
X-From_: Eric.the.Half.a.Bee@semibee.com  Wed Jul 12 16:16:31 2000
Return-Path: <Eric.the.Half.a.Bee@semibee.com>
Received: from VAIO (dial-218.101.denco.rmi.net [166.93.218.101])
        by chevalier.rmi.net (8.9.3/8.9.3) with ESMTP id QAA28647
        for <lutz@rmi.net>; Wed, 12 Jul 2000 16:16:30 -0600 (MDT)
From: Eric.the.Half.a.Bee@semibee.com
Message-Id: <200007122216.QAA28647@chevalier.rmi.net>
To: lutz@rmi.net
Date: Wed Jul 12 16:09:21 2000
Subject: A B C D E F G

Fiddle de dum, Fiddle de dee,
Eric the half a bee.
-------------------------------------------------------------------------------
```

Decoding Mail Message Attachments

In the last section, we learned how to parse out email message headers and bodies with the `rfc822` and `StringIO` modules. This isn't quite enough for some
messages, though. In this section, I will introduce tools that go further, to handle
complex information in the bodies of email messages.

One of the drawbacks of stubbornly clinging to a Telnet command-line email interface is that people sometimes send email with all sorts of attached information—
pictures, MS Word files, uuencoded tar files, base64-encoded documents, HTML

pages, and even executable scripts that can trash your computer if opened.* Not all attachments are crucial, of course, but email isn't always just ASCII text these days.

Before I overcame my Telnet habits, I needed a way to extract and process all those attachments from a command line (I tried the alternative of simply ignoring all attachments completely, but that works only for a while). Luckily, Python's library tools make handling attachments and common encodings easy and portable. For simplicity, all of the following scripts work on the raw text of a saved email message (or parts of such), but they could just as easily be incorporated into the email programs in this book to extract email components automatically.

Decoding base64 data

Let's start with something simple. Mail messages and attachments are frequently sent in an encoding format such as uu or base64; binary data files in particular must be encoded in a textual format for transit using one of these encoding schemes. On the receiving end, such encoded data must first be decoded before it can be viewed, opened, or otherwise used. The Python program in Example 11-19 knows how to perform base64 decoding on data stored in a file.

Example 11-19. PP2E\Internet\Email\decode64.py

```
#!/usr/bin/env python
##############################################
# Decode mail attachments sent in base64 form.
# This version assumes that the base64 encoded
# data has been extracted into a separate file.
# It doesn't understand mime headers or parts.
# uudecoding is similar (uu.decode(iname)),
# as is binhex decoding (binhex.hexbin(iname)).
# You can also do this with module mimetools:
# mimetools.decode(input, output, 'base64').
##############################################

import sys, base64

iname = 'part.txt'
oname = 'part.doc'

if len(sys.argv) > 1:
```

---

* I should explain this one: I'm referring to email viruses that appeared in 2000. The short story behind most of them is that Microsoft Outlook sported a "feature" that allowed email attachments to embed and contain executable scripts, and allowed these scripts to gain access to critical computer components when open and run. Furthermore, Outlook had another feature that automatically ran such attached scripts when an email was inspected, whether the attachment was manually opened or not. I'll leave the full weight of such a security hole for you to ponder, but I want to add that if you use Python's attachment tools in any of the mail programs in this book, please do not execute attached programs under any circumstance, unless you also run them with Python's restricted execution mode presented in Chapter 15, *Advanced Internet Topics.*

Example 11-19. PP2E\Internet\Email\decode64.py (continued)

```
    iname, oname = sys.argv[1:]          # % python prog [iname oname]?

input  = open(iname, 'r')
output = open(oname, 'wb')               # need wb on windows for docs
base64.decode(input, output)             # this does most of the work
print 'done'
```

There's not much to look at here, because all the low-level translation work happens in the Python `base64` module; we simply call its `decode` method with open input and output files. Other transmission encoding schemes are supported by different Python modules—uu for uuencoding, `binhex` for binhex format, and so on. All of these export interfaces that are analogous to `base64`, and are as easy to use; uu and `binhex` use the output filename in the data (see the library manual for details).

At a slightly higher level of generality, the `mimetools` module exports a `decode` method, which supports all encoding schemes. The desired decoding is given by a passed-in argument, but the net result is the same, as shown in Example 11-20.

Example 11-20. PP2E\Internet\Email\decode64_b.py

```
#!/usr/bin/env python
################################################
# Decode mail attachments sent in base64 form.
# This version tests the mimetools module.
################################################

import sys, mimetools

iname = 'part.txt'
oname = 'part.doc'

if len(sys.argv) > 1:
    iname, oname = sys.argv[1:]          # % python prog [iname oname]?

input  = open(iname, 'r')
output = open(oname, 'wb')
mimetools.decode(input, output, 'base64')      # or 'uuencode', etc.
print 'done'
```

To use either of these scripts, you must first extract the base64-encoded data into a text file. Save a mail message in a text file using your favorite email tool, then edit the file to save only the base64-encoded portion with your favorite text editor. Finally, pass the data file to the script, along with a name for the output file where the decoded data will be saved. Here are the base64 decoders at work on a saved data file; the generated output file turns out to be the same as the one saved for an attachment in MS Outlook earlier:

```
C:\Stuff\Mark\etc\jobs\test>python ..\decode64.py t4.64 t4.doc
done
```

```
C:\Stuff\Mark\etc\jobs\test>fc /B cand.agr10.22.doc t4.doc
Comparing files cand.agr10.22.doc and t4.doc
FC: no differences encountered


C:\Stuff\Mark\etc\jobs\test>python ..\decode64_b.py t4.64 t4.doc
done

C:\Stuff\Mark\etc\jobs\test>fc /B cand.agr10.22.doc t4.doc
Comparing files cand.agr10.22.doc and t4.doc
FC: no differences encountered
```

Extracting and decoding all parts of a message

The decoding procedure in the previous section is very manual and error-prone;
moreover, it handles only one type of encoding (base64), and decodes only a single component of an email message. With a little extra logic, we can improve on
this dramatically with the Python mhlib module's multipart message-decoding
tools. For instance, the script in Example 11-21 knows how to extract, decode, and
save every component in an email message in one step.

Example 11-21. PP2E\Internet\Email\decodeAll.py

```
#!/usr/bin/env python
####################################################
# Decode all mail attachments sent in encoded form:
# base64, uu, etc. To use, copy entire mail message
# to mailfile and run:
#     % python ..\decodeAll.py mailfile
# which makes one or more mailfile.part* outputs.
####################################################

import sys, mhlib
from types import *
iname = 'mailmessage.txt'

if len(sys.argv) == 3:
    iname, oname = sys.argv[1:]          # % python prog [iname [oname]?]?
elif len(sys.argv) == 2:
    iname = sys.argv[1]
    oname = iname + '.part'

def writeparts(part, oname):
    global partnum
    content = part.getbody()                 # decoded content or list
    if type(content) == ListType:            # multiparts: recur for each
        for subpart in content:
            writeparts(subpart, oname)
    else:                                    # else single decoded part
        assert type(content) == StringType   # use filename if in headers
        print; print part.getparamnames()    # else make one with counter
        fmode = 'wb'
        fname = part.getparam('name')
        if not fname:
```

Example 11-21. PP2E\Internet\Email\decodeAll.py (continued)

```
            fmode = 'w'
            fname = oname + str(partnum)
            if part.gettype() == 'text/plain':
                fname = fname + '.txt'
            elif part.gettype() == 'text/html':
                fname = fname + '.html'
        output = open(fname, fmode)               # mode must be 'wb' on windows
        print 'writing:', output.name             # for word doc files, not 'w'
        output.write(content)
        partnum = partnum + 1

partnum = 0
input   = open(iname, 'r')                        # open mail file
message = mhlib.Message('.', 0, input)            # folder, number args ignored
writeparts(message, oname)
print 'done: wrote %s parts' % partnum
```

Because `mhlib` recognizes message components, this script processes an entire mail message; there is no need to edit the message to extract components manually. Moreover, the components of an `mhlib.Message` object represent the already-decoded parts of the mail message—any necessary uu, base64, and other decoding steps have already been automatically applied to the mail components by the time we fetch them from the object. `mhlib` is smart enough to determine and perform decoding automatically; it supports all common encoding schemes at once, not just a particular format such as base64.

To use this script, save the raw text of an email message in a local file (using whatever mail tool you like), and pass the file's name on the script's command line. Here the script is extracting and decoding the components of two saved mail message files, *t4.eml* and *t5.eml*:

```
C:\Stuff\Mark\etc\jobs\test>python ..\decodeall.py t4.eml

['charset']
writing: t4.eml.part0.txt

['charset']
writing: t4.eml.part1.html

['name']
writing: cand.agr10.22.doc
done: wrote 3 parts


C:\Stuff\Mark\etc\jobs\test>python ..\decodeall.py t5.eml

['charset']
writing: t5.eml.part0.txt

['name']
writing: US West Letter.doc
done: wrote 2 parts
```

The end result of decoding a message is a set of one or more local files containing the decoded contents of each part of the message. Because the resulting local files are the crux of this script's purpose, it must assign meaningful names to files it creates. The following naming rules are applied by the script:

1. If a component has an associated "name" parameter in the message, the script stores the component's bytes in a local file of that name. This generally reuses the file's original name on the machine where the mail originated.

2. Otherwise, the script generates a unique filename for the component by adding a "partN" suffix to the original mail file's name, and trying to guess a file extension based on the component's file type given in the message.

For instance, the message saved away as *t4.eml* consists of the message body, an alternative HTML encoding of the message body, and an attached Word doc file. When decoding *t4.eml*:

- The first two message components have no "name" parameter, so the script generates names based on the filename and component types—*t4.eml.part0.txt* and *t4.eml.part1.html*—plain text and HTML code, respectively. On most machines, clicking on the HTML output file should open it in a web browser for formatted viewing.

- The last attachment was given an explicit name when attached—*cand.agr10. 22.doc*—so it is used as the output file's name directly. Notice that this was an attached MS Word doc file when sent; assuming all went well in transit, double-clicking on the third output file generated by this script should open it in Word.

There are additional tools in the Python library for decoding data fetched over the Net, but we'll defer to the library manual for further details. Again, using this decoding script still involves some manual intervention—users must save the mail file and type a command to split off its parts into distinct files—but it's sufficient for handling multipart mail, and it works portably on any machine with Python. Moreover, the decoding interfaces it demonstrates can be adopted in a more automatic fashion by interactive mail clients.

For instance, the decoded text of a message component could be automatically passed to handler programs (e.g., browsers, text editors, Word) when selected, rather than written to local files. It could also be saved in and automatically opened from local temporary files (on Windows, running a simple DOS *start* command with `os.system` would open the temporary file). In fact, popular email tools like Outlook use such schemes to support opening attachments. Python-coded email user interfaces could do so, too—which is a hint about where this chapter is headed next.

The PyMailGui Email Client

As a finale for this chapter's email tools coverage, this section presents *PyMailGui*—a Python/Tkinter program that implements a client-side email processing user interface. It is presented both as an instance of Python Internet scripting and as an example that ties together other tools we've already seen, such as threads and Tkinter GUIs.

Like the `pymail` program we wrote earlier, PyMailGui runs entirely on your local computer. Your email is fetched from and sent to remote mail servers over sockets, but the program and its user interface run locally. Because of that, PyMailGui is called an email *client*: it employs Python's client-side tools to talk to mail servers from the local machine. In fact, in some ways, PyMailGui builds on top of `pymail` to add a GUI. Unlike `pymail`, though, PyMailGui is a fairly full-featured user interface: email operations are performed with point-and-click operations.

Why PyMailGui?

Like many examples presented in this text, PyMailGui is also a practical, useful program. In fact, I run it on all kinds of machines to check my email while traveling around the world teaching Python classes (it's another workaround for Telnet-challenged ISPs). Although PyMailGui won't put Microsoft Outlook out of business anytime soon, I like it for two reasons:

It's portable

PyMailGui runs on any machine with sockets and a Python with Tkinter installed. Because email is transferred with the Python libraries, any Internet connection will do. Moreover, because the user interface is coded with the Tkinter extension, PyMailGui should work, unchanged, on Windows, the X Windows system (Unix, Linux), and the Macintosh.

Microsoft Outlook is a more feature-rich package, but it has to be run on Windows, and more specifically, on a single Windows machine. Because it generally deletes email from a server as it is downloaded and stores it on the client, you cannot run Outlook on multiple machines without spreading your email across all those machines. By contrast, PyMailGui saves and deletes email only on request, and so it is a bit more friendly to people who check their email in an ad-hoc fashion on arbitrary computers.

It's scriptable

PyMailGui can become anything you want it to be, because it is fully programmable. In fact, this is the real killer feature of PyMailGui and of open source software like Python in general—because you have full access to PyMailGui's source code, you are in complete control of where it evolves from here. You have nowhere near as much control over commercial, closed products like

Outlook; you generally get whatever a large company decided you need, along with whatever bugs that company might have introduced.

As a Python script, PyMailGui is a much more flexible tool. For instance, I can change its layout, disable features, and add completely new functionality quickly, by changing its Python source code. Don't like the mail list display? Change a few lines of code to customize it. Want to save and delete your mail automatically as it is loaded? Add some more code and buttons. Tired of seeing junk mail? Add a few lines of text-processing code to the load function to filter spam. These are just a few examples. The point is that because PyMailGui is written in a high-level, easy-to-maintain scripting language, such customizations are relatively simple, and might even be a lot of fun.*

It's also worth mentioning that PyMailGui achieves this portability and scriptability, and implements a full-featured email interface along the way, in roughly 500 lines of program code. It doesn't have as many bells and whistles as commercial products, but the fact that it gets as close as it does in so few lines of code is a testament to the power of both the Python language and its libraries.

Running PyMailGui

Of course, to script PyMailGui on your own, you'll need to be able to run it. PyMailGui only requires a computer with some sort of Internet connectivity (a PC with a dialup account and modem will do) and an installed Python with the Tkinter extension enabled. The Windows port of Python has this capability, so Windows PC users should be able to run this program immediately by clicking its icon (the Windows port self-installer is on this book's CD and also at *http://www.python.org*). You'll also want to change the file *mailconfig.py* in the email examples directory to reflect your account's parameters; more on this as we interact with the system.

Presentation Strategy

PyMailGui is easily one of the longest programs in this book (its main script is some 500 lines long, counting blank lines and comments), but it doesn't introduce many library interfaces that we haven't already seen in this book. For instance:

*   The PyMailGui interface is built with Python's Tkinter, using the familiar listboxes, buttons, and text widgets we met earlier.

*   Python's `rfc822` email header parser module is applied to pull out headers and text of messages.

---

* Example: I added code to pull the POP password from a local file instead of a pop-up in about 10 minutes, and less than 10 lines of code. Of course, I'm familiar with the code, but the wait time for new features in Outlook would be noticeably longer.

- Python's POP and SMTP library modules are used to fetch, send, and delete mail over sockets.

- Python threads, if installed in your Python interpreter, are put to work to avoid blocking during long-running mail operations (loads, sends, deletions).

We're also going to reuse the `TextEditor` object we wrote in Chapter 9, *Larger GUI Examples*, to view and compose messages, the simple `pymail` module's tools we wrote earlier in this chapter to load and delete mail from the server, and the `mailconfig` module of this chapter to fetch email parameters. PyMailGui is largely an exercise in combining existing tools.

On the other hand, because this program is so long, we won't exhaustively document all of its code. Instead, we'll begin by describing how PyMailGui works from an end-user's perspective. After that, we'll list the system's new source code modules without any additional comments, for further study.

Like most longer case studies in this book, this section assumes that you already know enough Python to make sense of the code on your own. If you've been reading this book linearly, you should also know enough about Tkinter, threads, and mail interfaces to understand the library tools applied here. If you get stuck, you may wish to brush-up on the presentation of these topics earlier in the book.

Interacting with PyMailGui

To make this case study easier to understand, let's begin by seeing what PyMailGui actually does—its user interaction and email processing functionality—before jumping into the Python code that implements that behavior. As you read this part, feel free to jump ahead to the code listings that appear after the screen shots, but be sure to read this section, too; this is where I will explain all the subtleties of PyMailGui's design. After this section, you are invited to study the system's Python source code listings on your own for a better and more complete explanation than can be crafted in English.

Getting started

PyMailGui is a Python/Tkinter program, run by executing its top-level script file, *PyMailGui.py*. Like other Python programs, PyMailGui can be started from the system command line, by clicking on its filename icon in a file explorer interface, or by pressing its button in the PyDemos or PyGadgets launcher bars. However it is started, the first window PyMailGui presents is shown in Figure 11-10.

This is the PyMailGui main window—every operation starts here. It consists of:

- A help button (the light blue bar at the top)

- A clickable email list area for fetched emails (the middle white section)

- A button bar at the bottom for processing messages selected in the list area

Open Source Software and Camaros

An analogy might help underscore the importance of PyMailGui's scriptability. There are still a few of us who remember a time when it was completely normal for car owners to work on and repair their own automobiles. I still fondly remember huddling with friends under the hood of a 1970 Camaro in my youth, tweaking and customizing its engine. With a little work, we could make it as fast, flashy, and loud as we liked. Moreover, a breakdown in one of those older cars wasn't necessarily the end of the world. There was at least some chance that I could get the car going again on my own.

That's not quite true today. With the introduction of electronic controls and diabolically cramped engine compartments, car owners are usually better off taking their cars back to the dealer or other repair professional for all but the simplest kinds of changes. By and large, cars are no longer user-maintainable products. And if I have a breakdown in my shiny new Jeep, I'm probably going to be completely stuck until an authorized repairperson can get around to towing and fixing my ride.

I like to think of the closed and open software models in the same terms. When I use Microsoft Outlook, I'm stuck both with the feature set that a large company dictates, as well as any bugs that it may harbor. But with a programmable tool like PyMailGui, I can still get under the hood. I can add features, customize the system, and work my way out of any lurking bugs. And I can do so long before the next Outlook patch or release.

At the end of the day, open source software is about freedom. Users, not an arbitrarily far-removed company, have the final say. Not everyone wants to work on his or her own car, of course. On the other hand, software tends to fail much more often than cars, and Python scripting is considerably less greasy than auto mechanics.

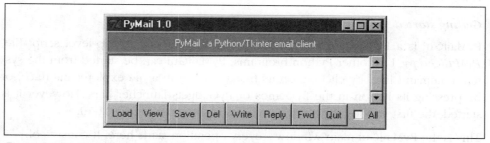

Figure 11-10. PyMailGui main window start

In normal operation, users load their email, select an email from the list area by clicking on it, and press a button at the bottom to process it. No mail messages are shown initially; we need to first load them, as we'll see in a moment. Before we do, though, let's press the blue help bar at the top to see what sort of help is available; Figure 11-11 shows the help window pop-up that appears.

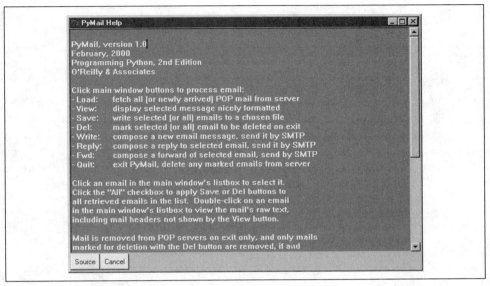

Figure 11-11. PyMailGui help pop-up

The main part of this window is simply a block of text in a scrolled-text widget, along with two buttons at the bottom. The entire help text is coded as a single triple-quoted string in the Python program. We could get more fancy and spawn a web browser to view HTML-formatted help, but simple text does the job here.* The Cancel button makes this nonmodal (i.e., nonblocking) window go away; more interestingly, the Source button pops up a viewer window with the source code of PyMailGui's main script, as shown in Figure 11-12.

Not every program shows you its source code, but PyMailGui follows Python's open source motif. Politics aside, the main point of interest here is that this source viewer window is the same as PyMailGui's email viewer window. All the information here comes from PyMailGui internally; but this same window is used to display and edit mail shipped across the Net, so let's look at its format here:

- The top portion consists of a Cancel button to remove this nonmodal window, along with a section for displaying email header lines—"From:", "To:", and so on.

---

* Actually, the help display started life even less fancy: it originally displayed help text in a standard information box pop-up, generated by the Tkinter `showinfo` call used earlier in the book. This worked fine on Windows (at least with a small amount of help text), but failed on Linux because of a default line-length limit in information pop-up boxes—lines were broken so badly as to be illegible. The moral: if you're going to use `showinfo` and care about Linux, be sure to make your lines short and your text strings small.

Figure 11-12. PyMailGui source code viewer window

- The bulk of this window is just another reuse of the `TextEditor` class object we wrote earlier in the book for the PyEdit program—PyMailGui simply attaches an instance of `TextEditor` to every view and compose window, to get a full-featured text editor component for free. In fact, everything but the Cancel button and header lines on this window are implemented by `TextEditor`, not PyMailGui.

For instance, if we pick the Tools menu of the text portion of this window, and select its Info entry, we get the standard PyEdit `TextEditor` object's file text statistics box—the exact same pop-up we'd get in the standalone PyEdit text editor, and the PyView image view programs we wrote in Chapter 9 (see Figure 11-13).

In fact, this is the *third* reuse of `TextEditor` in this book: PyEdit, PyView, and now PyMaiGui all present the same text editing interface to users, simply because they all use the same `TextEditor` object. For purposes of showing source code, we could also simply spawn the PyEdit program with the source file's name as a command-line argument (see PyEdit earlier in the text for more details). PyMailGui attaches an instance instead.

To display email, PyMailGui inserts its text into an attached `TextEditor` object; to compose mail, PyMailGui presents a `TextEditor` and later fetches all its text out

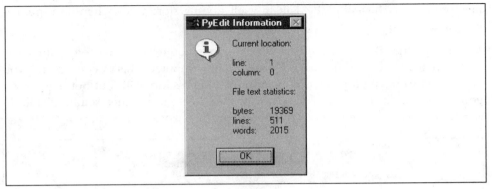

Figure 11-13. PyMailGui attached TextEditor info box

to ship over the Net. Besides the obvious simplification here, this code reuse also makes it easy to pick up improvements and fixes—any changes in the **TextEditor** object are automatically inherited by PyMailGui, PyView, and PyEdit.

Loading mail

Now, let's go back to the PyMailGui main window, and click the Load button to retrieve incoming email over the POP protocol. Like `pymail`, PyMailGui's load function gets account parameters from the `mailconfig` module listed in Example 11-15, so be sure to change this file to reflect your email account parameters (i.e., server names and usernames) if you wish to use PyMailGui to read your own email.

The account *password* parameter merits a few extra words. In PyMailGui, it may come from one of two places:

Local file
If you put the name of a local file containing the password in the `mailconfig` module, PyMailGui loads the password from that file as needed.

Pop-up dialog
If you don't put a password filename in `mailconfig` (or PyMailGui can't load it from the file for whatever reason), PyMailGui will instead ask you for your password any time it is needed.

Figure 11-14 shows the password input prompt you get if you haven't stored your password in a local file. Note that the password you type is not shown—a `show='*'` option for the `Entry` field used in this pop-up tells Tkinter to echo typed characters as stars (this option is similar in spirit to both the `getpass` console input module we met earlier in this chapter, and an HTML `type=password` option we'll meet in a later chapter). Once entered, the password lives only in memory on your machine; PyMailGui itself doesn't store it anywhere in a permanent way.

Also notice that the local file password option requires you to store your password unencrypted in a file on the local client computer. This is convenient (you don't need to retype a password every time you check email), but not generally a good idea on a machine you share with others; leave this setting blank in `mailconfig` if you prefer to always enter your password in a pop-up.

Figure 11-14. PyMailGui password input dialog

Once PyMailGui fetches your mail parameters and somehow obtains your password, it will next attempt to pull down all your incoming email from your POP server. PyMailGui reuses the load-mail tools in the `pymail` module listed in Example 11-18, which in turn uses Python's standard `poplib` module to retrieve your email.

Threading long-running email transfers

Ultimately, though, the load function must download your email over a socket. If you get as much email as I do, this can take awhile. Rather than blocking the GUI while the load is in progress, PyMailGui spawns a thread to do the mail download operation in parallel with the rest of the program. The main program continues responding to window events (e.g., redrawing the display after another window has been moved over it) while your email is being downloaded. To let you know that a download is in progress in the background, PyMailGui pops up the wait dialog box shown in Figure 11-15.

Figure 11-15. PyMailGui load mail wait box (thread running)

This dialog grabs focus and thus effectively disables the rest of the GUI's buttons while a download is in progress. It stays up for the duration of the download, and goes away automatically when the download is complete. Similar wait pop-ups appear during other long-running socket operations (email *send* and *delete* operations), but the GUI itself stays alive because the operations run in a thread.

On systems without threads, PyMailGui instead goes into a blocked state during such long-running operations (it stubs out the thread spawn operation to perform a simple function call). Because the GUI is essentially dead without threads, covering and uncovering the GUI during a mail load on such platforms will erase or otherwise distort its contents.* Threads are enabled by default on most platforms that Python runs on (including Windows), so you probably won't see such oddness on your machine.

One note here: as mentioned when we met the FTP GUIs earlier in this chapter, on MS Windows, only the thread that creates windows can process them. Because of that, PyMailGui takes care to not do anything related to the user interface within threads that load, send, or delete email. Instead, the main program continues responding to user interface events and updates, and watches for a global "I'm finished" flag to be set by the email transfer threads. Recall that threads share global (i.e., module) memory; since there is at most only two threads active in PyMailGui at once—the main program and an email transfer thread—a single global flag is all the cross-thread communication mechanism we need.

Load server interface

Because the load operation is really a socket operation, PyMailGui will automatically connect to your email server using whatever connectivity exists on the machine on which it is run. For instance, if you connect to the Net over a modem, and you're not already connected, Windows automatically pops up the standard connection dialog; Figure 11-16 shows the one I get on my laptop. If PyMailGui runs on a machine with a dedicated Internet link, it uses that instead.

After PyMailGui finishes loading your email, it populates the main window's list box with all of the messages on your email server, and scrolls to the most recently received. Figure 11-17 shows what the main windows looks like on my machine.

Technically, the Load button fetches all your mail the first time it is pressed, but fetches only newly arrived email on later presses. PyMailGui keeps track of the last email loaded, and requests only higher email numbers on later loads. Already-loaded mail is kept in memory, in a Python list, to avoid the cost of downloading it again. Like the simple `pymail` command-line interface shown earlier, PyMailGui

---

* If you want to see how this works, change PyMailGui's code such that the `fakeThread` class near the top of file *PyMailGui.py* is always defined (by default, it is created only if the import of the `thread` module fails), and try covering and uncovering the main window during a load, send, or delete operation. The window won't be redrawn because a single-threaded PyMailGui is busy talking over a socket.

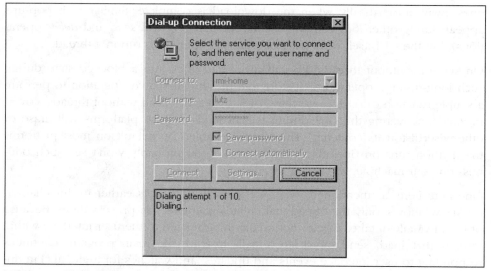

Figure 11-16. PyMailGui connection dialog (Windows)

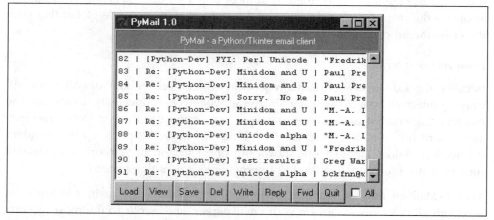

Figure 11-17. PyMailGui main window after load

does not delete email from your server when it is loaded; if you really want to not see an email on a later load, you must explicitly delete it (more on this later).

Like most GUIs in this book, the main window can be resized; Figure 11-18 shows what it looks like when stretched to reveal more email details. Entries in the main list show just enough to give the user an idea of what the message contains—each entry gives the concatenation of portions of the message's "Subject:", "From:", and "Date:" header lines, separated by | characters, and prefixed with the message's POP number (e.g., there are 91 emails in this list). The columns don't always line up neatly (some headers are shorter than others), but it's enough to hint at the message's contents.

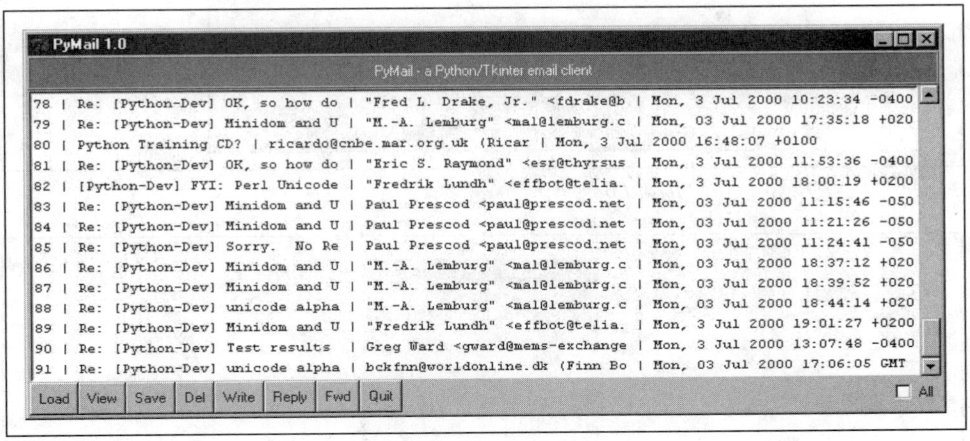

Figure 11-18. PyMailGui main window resized

As we've seen, much magic happens when downloading email—the client (the machine on which PyMailGui runs) must connect to the server (your email account machine) over a socket, and transfer bytes over arbitrary Internet links. If things go wrong, PyMailGui pops up standard error dialog boxes to let you know what happened. For example, if PyMailGui cannot establish a connection at all, you'll get a window like that shown in Figure 11-19.

Figure 11-19. PyMailGui connection error box

The details displayed here are just the Python exception type and exception data. If you typed an incorrect username or password for your account (in the `mailconfig` module or in the password pop-up), you'll see the message in Figure 11-20.

This box shows the exception raised by the Python `poplib` module. If PyMailGui cannot contact your server (e.g., it's down, or you listed its name wrong in `mailconfig`), you'll get the pop-up shown in Figure 11-21.

Figure 11-20. PyMailGui invalid password error box

Figure 11-21. PyMailGui invalid or down server error box

Sending email

Once we've loaded email, we can process our messages with buttons on the main window. We can, however, send new emails at any time, even before a load. Pressing the Write button on the main window generates a mail composition window; one has been captured in Figure 11-22.

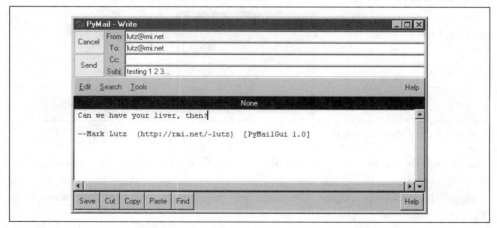

Figure 11-22. PyMailGui write mail compose window

This window is just like the help source code viewer we saw a moment ago—it has fields for entering header line details, and an attached TextEditor object for writing the body of the new email. For write operations, PyMailGui automatically fills the "From" line and inserts a signature text line ("—Mark..."), from your `mailconfig` module settings. You can change these to any text you like, but the defaults are filled in automatically from your `mailconfig`.*

There is also a new "Send" button here: when pressed, the text you typed into the the body of this window is mailed to the addresses you typed into the "To" and "Cc" lines, using Python's `smtplib` module. PyMailGui adds the header fields you type as mail header lines in the sent message. To send to more than one address, separate them with a ";" in the "To" and "Cc" lines (we'll see an example of this in a moment). In this mail, I fill in the "To" header with my own email address, to send the message to myself for illustration purposes.

As we've seen, `smtplib` ultimately sends bytes to a server over a socket. Since this can be a long-running operation, PyMailGui delegates this operation to a spawned thread, too. While the send thread runs, the wait window in Figure 11-23 appears, and the entire GUI stays alive; redraw and move events are handled in the main program thread, while the send thread talks to the SMTP server.

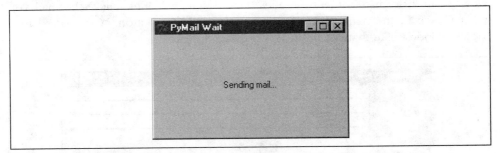

Figure 11-23. PyMailGui send mail wait box (thread running)

You'll get an error pop-up if Python cannot send a message to any of the target recipients, for any reason. If you don't get an error pop-up, everything worked correctly, and your mail will show up in the recipients' mailboxes on their email servers. Since I sent the message above to myself, it shows up in mine the next time I press the main window's Load button, as we see in Figure 11-24.

If you look back to the last main window shot, you'll notice that there are only two new emails now—numbers 92 (from Python-Help) and 93 (the one I just wrote); PyMailGui is smart enough to download only the two new massages, and tack them onto the end of the loaded email list.

---

* Like earlier examples in this chapter, PyMailGui sends mail by SMTP, so you can usually use any address you like in the "From" line; most servers don't check to see if it's valid or not, as long as it's in a valid format for email addresses in general. But once again, you really shouldn't—please put your *own* email address in your copy of *mailconfig.py*, or type it in the "From" field of composition windows.

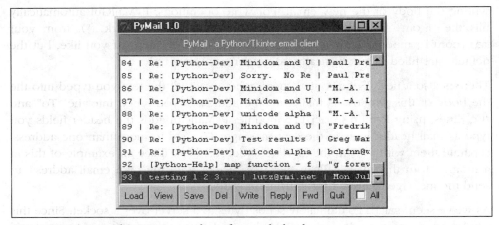

Figure 11-24. PyMailGui main window after sends, load

Viewing email

Now, let's view the mail message that was sent and received. PyMailGui lets us view email in formatted or raw modes. First, highlight (single-click) the mail you want to see in the main window, and press the View button. A formatted mail viewer window like that shown in Figure 11-25 appears.

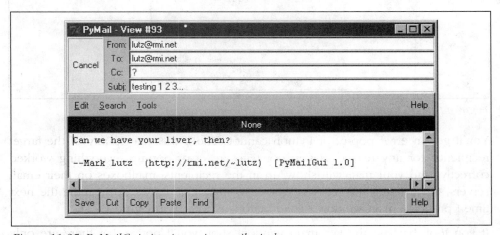

Figure 11-25. PyMailGui view incoming mail window

This is the exact same window we saw displaying source code earlier, only now all the information is filled in by extracting bits of the selected email message. Python's `rfc822` module is used to parse out header lines from the raw text of the email message; their text is placed into the fields in the top right of the window. After headers are parsed, the message's body text is left behind (in a `StringIO` file-like string wrapper), and is read and stuffed into a new `TextEditor` object for display (the white part in the middle of the window).

Besides the nicely formatted view window, PyMailGui also lets us see the raw text of a mail message. Double-click on a message's entry in the main window's list to bring up a simple unformatted display of the mail's text. The raw version of the mail I sent to myself is shown in Figure 11-26.

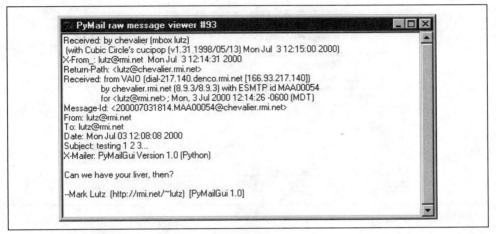

Figure 11-26. PyMailGui raw mail text view window

This raw text display can be useful to see special mail headers not shown in the formatted view. For instance, the optional "X-Mailer:" header in the raw text display identifies the program that transmitted a message; PyMailGui adds it automatically, along with standard headers like "From:" and "To:". Other headers are added as the mail is transmitted: the "Received:" headers name machines that the message was routed through on its way to our email server.

And really, the raw text form is all there is to an email message—it's what is transferred from machine to machine when mail is sent. The nicely formatted display simply parses out pieces of the mail's raw text with standard Python tools and places them in associated fields of the display of Figure 11-25.

Email replies and forwards

Besides allowing reading and writing email, PyMailGui also lets users forward and reply to incoming email sent from others. To reply to an email, select its entry in the main window's list and click the Reply button. If I reply to the mail I just sent to myself (arguably narcissistic, but demonstrative), the mail composition window shown in Figure 11-27 appears.

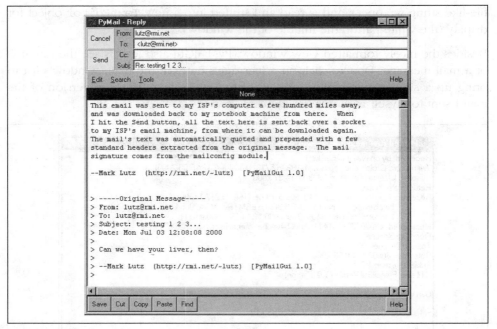

Figure 11-27. PyMailGui reply compose window

This window is identical in format to the one we saw for the "Write" operation, except that PyMailGui fills in some parts automatically:

- The "From" line is set to your email address in your `mailconfig` module.

- The "To" line is initialized to the original message's "From" address (we're replying to the original sender, after all). See the sidebar "More on Reply Addresses" for additional details on the target address.

- The "Subject" line is set to the original message's subject line prepended with a "Re:", the standard follow-up subject line form.

- The body of the reply is initialized with the signature line in `mailconfig`, along with the original mail message's text. The original message text is quoted with > characters and prepended with a few header lines extracted from the original message to give some context.

Luckily, all of this is much easier than it may sound. Python's standard `rfc822` module is used to extract all the original message's header lines, and a single `string.replace` call does the work of adding the > quotes to the original message body. I simply type what I wish to say in reply (the initial paragraph in the mail's text area), and press the Send button to route the reply message to the mailbox on my mail server again. Physically sending the reply works the same as sending a brand new message—the mail is routed to your SMTP server in a spawned send mail thread, and the send mail wait pop-up appears.

Forwarding a message is similar to replying: select the message in the main window, press the "Fwd" button, and fill in the fields and text area of the popped-up composition window. Figure 11-28 shows the window created to forward the mail we originally wrote and received.

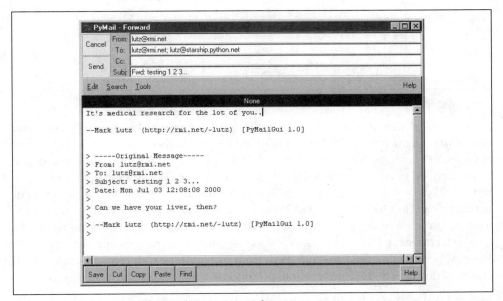

Figure 11-28. PyMailGui forward compose window

Much like replies, "From" is filled from `mailconfig`, the original text is automatically quoted in the message body again, and the subject line is preset to the original message's subject prepended with the string "Fwd:". I have to fill in the "To" line manually, though, because this is not a direct reply (it doesn't necessarily go back to the original sender). Notice that I'm forwarding this message to two different addresses; multiple recipient addresses are separated with a ";" character in "To" and "Cc" header fields. The Send button in this window fires the forward message off to all addresses listed in "To" and "Cc".

Okay, I've now written a new message, and replied to and forwarded it. The reply and forward were sent to my email address, too; if we press the main window's Load button again, the reply and forward messages should show up in the main window's list. In Figure 11-29, they appear as messages 94 and 95.

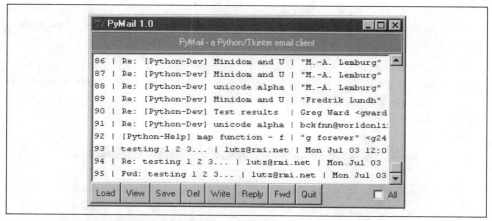

Figure 11-29. PyMailGui mail list after sends and load

Keep in mind that PyMailGui runs on the local computer, but the messages you see in the main window's list actually live in a mailbox on your email server machine. Every time we press Load, PyMailGui downloads but does not delete newly arrived email from the server to your computer. The three messages we just wrote (93–95) will also appear in any other email program you use on your account (e.g., in Outlook). PyMailGui does not delete messages as they are downloaded, but simply stores them in your computer's memory for processing. If we now select message 95 and press View, we see the forward message we sent, as in Figure 11-30. Really, this message went from my machine to a remote email server, and was downloaded from there into a Python list from which it is displayed.

Figure 11-31 shows what the forward message's raw text looks like; again, double-click on a main window's entry to display this form. The formatted display in Figure 11-30 simply extracts bits and pieces out of the text shown in the raw display form.

Saving and deleting email

So far, we've covered everything except two of the main window's processing buttons and the All checkbox. PyMailGui lets us save mail messages in local text files, and delete messages from the server permanently, such that we won't see them the next time we access our account. Moreover, we can save and delete a single mail at a time, or all mails displayed in the main windows list:

- To save one email, select it in the main window's list and press the Save button.

- To save all the emails in the list in one step, click the All checkbox at the bottom right corner of the main window and then press Save.

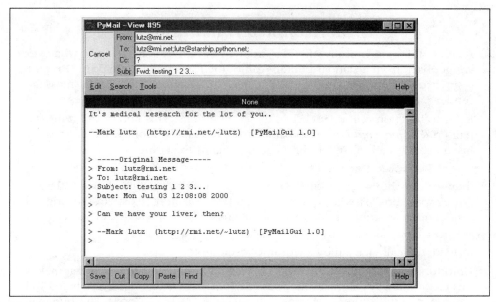

Figure 11-30. PyMailGui view forwarded mail

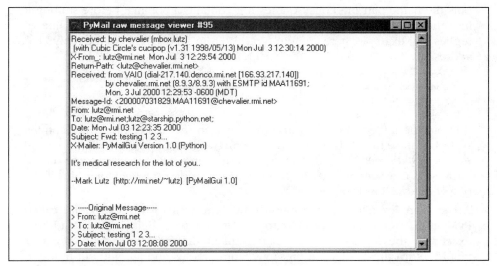

Figure 11-31. PyMailGui view forwarded mail, raw

Delete operations are kicked off the same way, but press the Del button instead. In typical operation, I eventually delete email I'm not interested in, and save and delete emails that are important. Save operations write the raw text of one or more emails to a local text file you pick in the pop-up dialog shown in Figure 11-32.

More on Reply Addresses

A subtle thing: technically, the "To" address in replies is made from whatever we get back from a standard library call of the form `hdrs.getaddr('From')` —an `rfc822` module interface that parses and formats the original message sender's address automatically—plus quotes added in a few rare cases.

Refer to function `onReplyMail` in the code listings. This library call returns a pair (*full name, email address*) parsed from the mail's "From:" header line. For instance, if a mail's first "From:" header contains the string:

```
'joe@spam.net (Joe Blow)'
```

then a call `hdrs.getaddr('From')` will yield the pair (`'Joe Blow'`, `'joe@spam.net'`), with an empty name string if none exists in the original sender address string. If the header contains:

```
'Joe Blow <joe@spam.net>'
```

instead, the call yields the exact same result tuple.

Unfortunately, though, the Python 1.5.2 `rfc822` module had a bug that makes this call not always correct: the `getaddr` function yields bogus results if a full name part of the address contains a comma (e.g., `"Blow, Joe"`). This bug may be fixed in Python 2.0, but to work around it for earlier releases, PyMailGui puts the name part in explicit quotes if it contains a comma, before stuffing it into the target *full-name <email-address>* address used in the "To:" line of replies. For example, here are four typical "From" addresses and the reply "To" address PyMailGui generates for each (after the =>):

```
joe@spam.net  =>  <joe@spam.net>
Joe Blow <joe@spam.net>      => Joe Blow <joe@spam.net>
joe@spam.net (Joe Blow)      => Joe Blow <joe@spam.net>
"Blow, Joe" <joe@spam.net> => "Blow, Joe" <joe@spam.net>
```

Without the added quotes around the name in the last of these, the comma would confuse my SMTP server into seeing two recipients—*Blow@rmi.net* and *Joe <joe@spam.net>* (the first incorrectly gets my ISP's domain name added because it is assumed to be a local user). The added quotes won't hurt if the bug is removed in later releases.

A less complex alternative solution (and one we'll use in a program called PyMailCgi later in this book) is to simply use the original "From" address exactly as the reply's "To". A library call of the form `hdrs.get('From')` would return the sender's address verbatim, quotes and all, without trying to parse out its components at all.

As coded, the PyMailGui reply address scheme works on every message I've ever replied to, but may need to be tweaked for some unique address formats or future Python releases. I've tested and used this program a lot, but much can happen on the Net, despite mail address standards. Officially speaking, any remaining bugs you find in it are really suggested exercises in disguise (at least I didn't say they were "features").

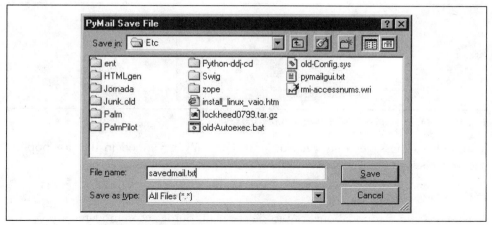

Figure 11-32. PyMailGui save mail dialog

Technically, saves always append raw message text to the chosen file; the file is opened in `'a'` mode, which creates the file if needed, and writes at its end. The save operation is also smart enough to remember the last directory you selected; the file dialog begins navigation there the next time you press Save.

Delete operations can also be applied to one or all messages. Unlike other operations, though, delete requests are simply queued up for later action. Messages are actually deleted from your mail server only as PyMailGui is exiting. For instance, if we've selected some messages for deletion and press the main window's Quit button, a standard verification dialog appears (Figure 11-33).

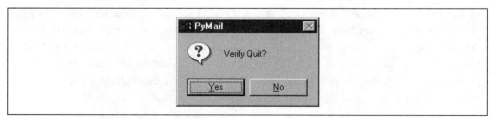

Figure 11-33. PyMailGui quit verification

If we then verify the quit request, a second dialog appears (Figure 11-34), asking us to verify deletion of the queued up messages. If we press No here, no deletes happen, and PyMailGui silently exits. If we select Yes, PyMailGui spawns one last thread to send deletion requests to the email server for all the emails selected for deletion during the session. Another wait-state pop-up appears while the delete thread is running; when that thread is finished, PyMailGui exits as well.

By default and design, no mail is ever removed: you will see the same messages the next time PyMailGui runs. It deletes mail from your server only when you ask

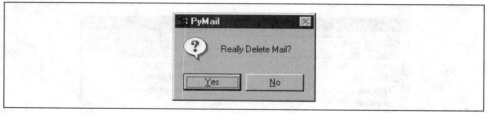

Figure 11-34. PyMailGui delete verification on quit

it to, deletes messages only on exit, and then only if verified in the last pop-up shown (this is your last chance to prevent permanent mail removal).

POP message numbers

This may seem a roundabout way to delete mail, but it accommodates a property of the POP interface. POP assigns each message a sequential number, starting from 1, and these numbers are passed to the server to fetch and delete messages. It's okay if new mail arrives while we're displaying the result of a prior download—the new mail is assigned higher numbers, beyond what is displayed on the client. But if we delete a message in the middle of a mailbox, the numbers of all messages after the one deleted change (they are decremented by one). That means that some message numbers may be no longer valid if deletions are made while viewing previously loaded email (deleting by some number N may really delete message N+1!).

PyMailGui could adjust all the displayed numbers to work around this. To keep things simple, though, it postpones deletions instead. Notice that if you run multiple instances of PyMailGui at once, you shouldn't delete in one and then another because message numbers may become confused. You also may not be happy with the results of running something like Outlook at the same time as a PyMailGui session, but the net effect of such a combination depends on how another mail client handles deletions. In principle, PyMailGui could be extended to prevent other instances from running at the same time, but we leave that as an exercise.

Windows and status messages

Before we close this section, I want to point out that PyMailGui is really meant to be a *multiple-window* interface—something not made obvious by the earlier screen shots. For example, Figure 11-35 shows PyMailGui with a main list box, help, and three mail view windows. All these windows are nonmodal; that is, they are all active and independent, and do not block other windows from being selected. This interface all looks slightly different on Linux, but has the same functionality.

In general, you can have any number of mail view or compose windows up at once, and cut and paste between them. This matters, because PyMailGui must take care to make sure that each window has a *distinct* text editor object. If the text

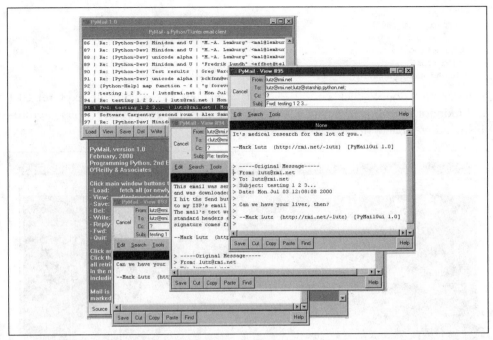

Figure 11-35. PyMailGui multiple windows and text editors

editor object was a global, or used globals internally, you'd likely see the same text in each window (and the send operations might wind up sending text from another window). To avoid this, PyMailGui creates and attaches a new **TextEditor** instance to each view and compose window it creates, and associates the new editor with the Send button's callback handler to make sure we get the right text.

Finally, PyMailGui prints a variety of status messages as it runs, but you see them only if you launch the program from the system command line (e.g., a DOS box on Windows or an xterm on Linux), or by double-clicking on its filename icon (its main script is a *.py*, not a *.pyw*). On Windows, you won't see these message when it is started from another program, such as the PyDemos or PyGadgets launcher bar GUIs. These status messages print server information, show mail loading status, and trace the load, store, and delete threads that are spawned along the way. If you want PyMailGui to be more verbose, launch it from a command line and watch:

```
C:\...\PP2E\Internet\Email>python PyMailGui.py
load start
Connecting...
+OK Cubic Circle's v1.31 1998/05/13 POP3 ready <594100005a655e39@chevalier>
('+OK 5 messages (8470 octets)', ['1 709', '2 1136', '3 998', '4 2679',
'5 2948'], 38)
There are 5 mail messages in 8470 bytes
Retrieving: 1 2 3 4 5
```

```
load exit
thread exit caught
send start
Connecting to mail... ['<lutz@rmi.net>']
send exit
thread exit caught
```

You can also double-click on the *PyMailGui.py* filename in your file explorer GUI and monitor the popped-up DOS console box on Windows; Figure 11-36 captures this window in action.

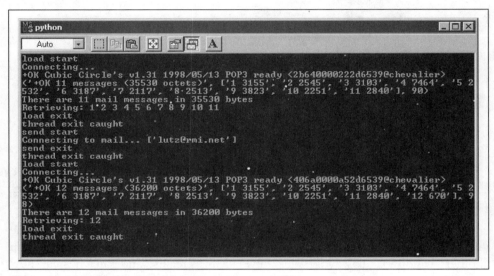

Figure 11-36. PyMailGui console status message window

PyMailGui status messages display the mail currently being downloaded (i.e., the "Retrieving:" lines are appended with a new mail number as each message is downloaded), and so give a more informative download status indicator than the wait pop-up window.

Implementing PyMailGui

Last but not least, we get to the code. There are really only two new modules here: one where the help text is stored and another that implements the system.

In fact, PyMailGui gets a lot of mileage out of reusing modules we wrote earlier and won't repeat here: `pymail` for mail load and delete operations, `mailconfig` for mail parameters, the GUI section's `TextEditor` for displaying and editing mail message text, and so on. In addition, standard Python modules used here such as `poplib`, `smtplib`, and `rfc822` hide most of the details of pushing bytes around the Net and extracting message components. `Tkinter` implements GUI components in a portable fashion.

Help text module

The net effect of all this reuse is that PyMailGui implements a fairly feature-rich email program in roughly 500 lines of code, plus one support module. Example 11-22 shows the support module—used only to define the help text string, to avoid cluttering the main script file.

Example 11-22. PP2E\Internet\Email\PyMailGuiHelp.py

```
#####################################################################
# PyMailGui help text string, in this seperate module only to avoid
# distracting from executable code.  As coded, we throw up this text
# in a simple scrollable text box; in the future, we might instead
# use an HTML file opened under a web browser (e.g., run a "netscape
# help.html" or DOS "start help.html" command using os.system call
#####################################################################

# must be narrow for Linux info box popups;
# now uses scrolledtext with buttons instead;

helptext = """
PyMail, version 1.0
February, 2000
Programming Python, 2nd Edition
O'Reilly & Associates

Click main window buttons to process email:
- Load:\t fetch all (or newly arrived) POP mail from server
- View:\t display selected message nicely formatted
- Save:\t write selected (or all) emails to a chosen file
- Del:\t mark selected (or all) email to be deleted on exit
- Write:\t compose a new email message, send it by SMTP
- Reply:\t compose a reply to selected email, send it by SMTP
- Fwd:\t compose a forward of selected email, send by SMTP
- Quit:\t exit PyMail, delete any marked emails from server

Click an email in the main window's listbox to select it.
Click the "All" checkbox to apply Save or Del buttons to
all retrieved emails in the list.  Double-click on an email
in the main window's listbox to view the mail's raw text,
including mail headers not shown by the View button.

Mail is removed from POP servers on exit only, and only mails
marked for deletion with the Del button are removed, if and
only if you verify the deletion in a confirmation popup.

Change the mailconfig.py module file on your own machine to
reflect your email server names, user name, email address,
and optional mail signature line added to all composed mails.
Miscellaneous hints:

- Passwords are requested if needed, and not stored by PyMail.
- You may put your password in a file named in mailconfig.py.
```

Example 11-22. PP2E\Internet\Email\PyMailGuiHelp.py (continued)

```
- Use ';' between multiple addresses in "To" and "Cc" headers.
- Reply and Fwd automatically quote the original mail text.
- Save pops up a dialog for selecting a file to hold saved mails.
- Load only fetches newly-arrived email after the first load.

This client-side program currently requires Python and Tkinter.
It uses Python threads, if installed, to avoid blocking the GUI.
Sending and loading email requires an Internet connection.
"""

if __name__ == '__main__':
    print helptext                      # to stdout if run alone
    raw_input('Press Enter key')        # pause in DOS console popups
```

Main module

And finally, here is the main PyMailGui script—the file run to start the system (see Example 11-23). I've already told what it does and why, so studying this listing's code and its comments for a deeper look is left as a suggested exercise. Python is so close to pseudocode already, that additional narrative here would probably be redundant.

Although I use this example on a daily basis as is, it is also prime for extension. For instance:

- Deleted messages could be marked as such graphically.

- Email attachments could be displayed, parsed out, decoded, and opened automatically when clicked using the Python multipart email extraction tools we met earlier in this chapter.

- Download status could be made more informative during mail load operations by updating a progress bar after each fetch (e.g., by periodically reconfiguring the size of a rectangle drawn on a popped-up canvas).

- Hyperlink URLs within messages could be highlighted visually and made to spawn a web browser automatically when clicked, by using the launcher tools we met in the GUI and system tools parts of this book.

- Because Internet newsgroup posts are similar in structure to emails (header lines plus body text: see the nntplib example in the next section), this script could in principle be extended to display both email messages and news articles. Classifying such a possible mutation as clever generalization or diabolical hack is left as an exercise in itself.

- This script still uses the nonstandard but usually harmless sending date format discussed in an earlier sidebar in this chapter; it would be trivial to import a conforming date format function from the pymail module.

- PyMailGui displays a wait dialog box during mail transfers that effectively disables the rest of the GUI. This is by design, to minimize timing complexity. In principle, though, the system could allow mail operation threads to overlap in time (e.g., allow the user to send new messages while a download is in progress). Since each transfer runs on a socket of its own, PyMailGui need not block other operations during transfers. This might be implemented with periodic Tkinter `after` events that check the status of transfers in progress. See the PyFtpGui scripts earlier in this chapter for an example of overlapping transfer threads.

And so on; because this software is open source, it is also necessarily open-ended. Suggested exercises in this category are delegated to your imagination.

Example 11-23. PP2E\Internet\Email\PyMailGui.py

```
#####################################################
# PyMailGui 1.0 - A Python/Tkinter email client.
# Adds a Tkinter-based GUI interface to the pymail
# script's functionality.  Works for POP/SMTP based
# email accounts using sockets on the machine on
# which this script is run.  Uses threads if
# installed to run loads, sends, and deletes with
# no blocking; threads are standard on Windows.
# GUI updates done in main thread only (Windows).
# Reuses and attaches TextEditor class object.
# Run from command-line to see status messages.
# See use notes in help text in PyMailGuiHelp.py.
# To do: support attachments, shade deletions.
#####################################################

# get services
import pymail, mailconfig
import rfc822, StringIO, string, sys
from Tkinter        import *
from tkFileDialog   import asksaveasfilename, SaveAs
from tkMessageBox   import showinfo, showerror, askyesno
from PP2E.Gui.TextEditor.textEditor import TextEditorComponentMinimal

# run if no threads
try:                                    # raise ImportError to
    import thread                       # run with gui blocking
except ImportError:                     # no wait popups appear
    class fakeThread:
        def start_new_thread(self, func, args):
            apply(func, args)
    thread = fakeThread()

# init global/module vars
msgList     = []                        # list of retrieved emails text
toDelete    = []                        # msgnums to be deleted on exit
listBox     = None                      # main window's scrolled msg list
rootWin     = None                      # the main window of this program
```

Example 11-23. PP2E\Internet\Email\PyMailGui.py (continued)

```
allModeVar    = None              # for All mode checkbox value
threadExitVar = 0                 # used to signal child thread exit
debugme       = 0                 # enable extra status messages

mailserver = mailconfig.popservername   # where to read pop email from
mailuser   = mailconfig.popusername     # smtp server in mailconfig too
mailpswd   = None                       # pop passwd via file or popup here
#mailfile  = mailconfig.savemailfile    # from a file select dialog here


def fillIndex(msgList):
    # fill all of main listbox
    listBox.delete(0, END)
    count = 1
    for msg in msgList:
        hdrs = rfc822.Message(StringIO.StringIO(msg))
        msginfo = '%02d' % count
        for key in ('Subject', 'From', 'Date'):
            if hdrs.has_key(key): msginfo = msginfo + ' | ' + hdrs[key][:30]
        listBox.insert(END, msginfo)
        count = count+1
    listBox.see(END)           # show most recent mail=last line


def selectedMsg():
    # get msg selected in main listbox
    # print listBox.curselection()
    if listBox.curselection() == ():
        return 0                                     # empty tuple:no selection
    else:                                            # else zero-based index
        return eval(listBox.curselection()[0]) + 1   # in a 1-item tuple of str


def waitForThreadExit(win):
    import time
    global threadExitVar         # in main thread, watch shared global var
    delay = 0.0                  # 0.0=no sleep needed on Win98 (but hogs cpu)
    while not threadExitVar:
        win.update()             # dispatch any new GUI events during wait
        time.sleep(delay)        # if needed, sleep so other thread can run
    threadExitVar = 0            # at most one child thread active at once


def busyInfoBoxWait(message):
    # popup wait message box, wait for a thread exit
    # main gui event thread stays alive during wait
    # as coded returns only after thread has finished
    # popup.wait_variable(threadExitVar) may work too

    popup = Toplevel()
    popup.title('PyMail Wait')
    popup.protocol('WM_DELETE_WINDOW', lambda:0)      # ignore deletes
    label = Label(popup, text=message+'...')
```

Example 11-23. PP2E\Internet\Email\PyMailGui.py (continued)

```
        label.config(height=10, width=40, cursor='watch')  # busy cursor
        label.pack()
        popup.focus_set()                          # grab application
        popup.grab_set()                           # wait for thread exit
        waitForThreadExit(popup)                   # gui alive during wait
        print 'thread exit caught'
        popup.destroy()



def loadMailThread():
    # load mail while main thread handles gui events
    global msgList, errInfo, threadExitVar
    print 'load start'
    errInfo = ''
    try:
        nextnum = len(msgList) + 1
        newmail = pymail.loadmessages(mailserver, mailuser, mailpswd, nextnum)
        msgList = msgList + newmail
    except:
        exc_type, exc_value = sys.exc_info()[:2]                # thread exc
        errInfo = '\n' + str(exc_type) + '\n' + str(exc_value)
    print 'load exit'
    threadExitVar = 1   # signal main thread



def onLoadMail():
    # load all (or new) pop email
    getpassword()
    thread.start_new_thread(loadMailThread, ())
    busyInfoBoxWait('Retrieving mail')
    if errInfo:
        global mailpswd            # zap pswd so can reinput
        mailpswd = None
        showerror('PyMail', 'Error loading mail\n' + errInfo)
    fillIndex(msgList)



def onViewRawMail():
    # view selected message - raw mail text with header lines
    msgnum = selectedMsg()
    if not (1 <= msgnum <= len(msgList)):
        showerror('PyMail', 'No message selected')
    else:
        text = msgList[msgnum-1]                    # put in ScrolledText
        from ScrolledText import ScrolledText
        window  = Toplevel()
        window.title('PyMail raw message viewer #' + str(msgnum))
        browser = ScrolledText(window)
        browser.insert('0.0', text)
        browser.pack(expand=YES, fill=BOTH)



def onViewFormatMail():
    # view selected message - popup formatted display
```

Example 11-23. PP2E\Internet\Email\PyMailGui.py (continued)

```
    msgnum = selectedMsg()
    if not (1 <= msgnum <= len(msgList)):
        showerror('PyMail', 'No message selected')
    else:
        mailtext = msgList[msgnum-1]            # put in a TextEditor form
        textfile = StringIO.StringIO(mailtext)
        headers  = rfc822.Message(textfile)     # strips header lines
        bodytext = textfile.read()              # rest is message body
        editmail('View #%d' % msgnum,
                   headers.get('From', '?'),
                   headers.get('To', '?'),
                   headers.get('Subject', '?'),
                   bodytext,
                   headers.get('Cc', '?'))


# use objects that retain prior directory for the next
# select, instead of simple asksaveasfilename() dialog

saveOneDialog = saveAllDialog = None

def myasksaveasfilename_one():
    global saveOneDialog
    if not saveOneDialog:
        saveOneDialog = SaveAs(title='PyMail Save File')
    return saveOneDialog.show()


def myasksaveasfilename_all():
    global saveAllDialog
    if not saveAllDialog:
        saveAllDialog = SaveAs(title='PyMail Save All File')
    return saveAllDialog.show()


def onSaveMail():
    # save selected message in file
    if allModeVar.get():
        mailfile = myasksaveasfilename_all()
        if mailfile:
            try:
                # maybe this should be a thread
                for i in range(1, len(msgList)+1):
                    pymail.savemessage(i, mailfile, msgList)
            except:
                showerror('PyMail', 'Error during save')
    else:
        msgnum = selectedMsg()
        if not (1 <= msgnum <= len(msgList)):
            showerror('PyMail', 'No message selected')
        else:
            mailfile = myasksaveasfilename_one()
            if mailfile:
                try:
```

Example 11-23. PP2E\Internet\Email\PyMailGui.py (continued)

```
                    pymail.savemessage(msgnum, mailfile, msgList)
            except:
                showerror('PyMail', 'Error during save')


def onDeleteMail():
    # mark selected message for deletion on exit
    global toDelete
    if allModeVar.get():
        toDelete = range(1, len(msgList)+1)
    else:
        msgnum = selectedMsg()
        if not (1 <= msgnum <= len(msgList)):
            showerror('PyMail', 'No message selected')
        elif msgnum not in toDelete:
            toDelete.append(msgnum)      # fails if in list twice


def sendMailThread(From, To, Cc, Subj, text):
    # send mail while main thread handles gui events
    global errInfo, threadExitVar
    import smtplib, time
    from mailconfig import smtpservername
    print 'send start'

    date  = time.ctime(time.time())
    Cchdr = (Cc and 'Cc: %s\n' % Cc) or ''
    hdrs  = ('From: %s\nTo: %s\n%sDate: %s\nSubject: %s\n'
                    % (From, To, Cchdr, date, Subj))
    hdrs  = hdrs + 'X-Mailer: PyMailGui Version 1.0 (Python)\n\n'

    Ccs = (Cc and string.split(Cc, ';')) or []     # some servers reject ['']
    Tos = string.split(To, ';') + Ccs              # cc: hdr line, and To list
    Tos = map(string.strip, Tos)                   # some addrs can have ','s
    print 'Connecting to mail...', Tos             # strip spaces around addrs

    errInfo = ''
    failed  = {}                                   # smtplib may raise except
    try:                                           # or return failed Tos dict
        server = smtplib.SMTP(smtpservername)
        failed = server.sendmail(From, Tos, hdrs + text)
        server.quit()
    except:
        exc_type, exc_value = sys.exc_info()[:2]   # thread exc
        excinfo = '\n' + str(exc_type) + '\n' + str(exc_value)
        errInfo = 'Error sending mail\n' + excinfo
    else:
        if failed: errInfo = 'Failed recipients:\n' + str(failed)

    print 'send exit'
    threadExitVar = 1                              # signal main thread
```

Example 11-23. PP2E\Internet\Email\PyMailGui.py (continued)

```python
def sendMail(From, To, Cc, Subj, text):
    # send completed email
    thread.start_new_thread(sendMailThread, (From, To, Cc, Subj, text))
    busyInfoBoxWait('Sending mail')
    if errInfo:
        showerror('PyMail', errInfo)


def onWriteReplyFwdSend(window, editor, hdrs):
    # mail edit window send button press
    From, To, Cc, Subj = hdrs
    sendtext = editor.getAllText()
    sendMail(From.get(), To.get(), Cc.get(), Subj.get(), sendtext)
    if not errInfo:
        window.destroy()     # else keep to retry or save


def editmail(mode, From, To='', Subj='', origtext='', Cc=''):
    # create a new mail edit/view window
    win = Toplevel()
    win.title('PyMail - '+ mode)
    win.iconname('PyMail')
    viewOnly = (mode[:4] == 'View')

    # header entry fields
    frm =  Frame(win); frm.pack( side=TOP,    fill=X)
    lfrm = Frame(frm); lfrm.pack(side=LEFT,   expand=NO,  fill=BOTH)
    mfrm = Frame(frm); mfrm.pack(side=LEFT,   expand=NO,  fill=NONE)
    rfrm = Frame(frm); rfrm.pack(side=RIGHT,  expand=YES, fill=BOTH)
    hdrs = []
    for (label, start) in [('From:', From),
                           ('To:',   To),              # order matters on send
                           ('Cc:',   Cc),
                           ('Subj:', Subj)]:
        lab = Label(mfrm, text=label, justify=LEFT)
        ent = Entry(rfrm)
        lab.pack(side=TOP, expand=YES, fill=X)
        ent.pack(side=TOP, expand=YES, fill=X)
        ent.insert('0', start)
        hdrs.append(ent)

    # send, cancel buttons (need new editor)
    editor = TextEditorComponentMinimal(win)
    sendit = (lambda w=win, e=editor, h=hdrs: onWriteReplyFwdSend(w, e, h))

    for (label, callback) in [('Cancel', win.destroy), ('Send', sendit)]:
        if not (viewOnly and label == 'Send'):
            b = Button(lfrm, text=label, command=callback)
            b.config(bg='beige', relief=RIDGE, bd=2)
            b.pack(side=TOP, expand=YES, fill=BOTH)

    # body text editor: pack last=clip first
    editor.pack(side=BOTTOM)                             # may be multiple editors
```

Example 11-23. PP2E\Internet\Email\PyMailGui.py (continued)

```
    if (not viewOnly) and mailconfig.mysignature:     # add auto signature text?
        origtext = ('\n%s\n' % mailconfig.mysignature) + origtext
    editor.setAllText(origtext)


def onWriteMail():
    # compose new email
    editmail('Write', From=mailconfig.myaddress)


def quoteorigtext(msgnum):
    origtext = msgList[msgnum-1]
    textfile = StringIO.StringIO(origtext)
    headers  = rfc822.Message(textfile)              # strips header lines
    bodytext = textfile.read()                       # rest is message body
    quoted   = '\n-----Original Message-----\n'
    for hdr in ('From', 'To', 'Subject', 'Date'):
        quoted = quoted + ( '%s: %s\n' % (hdr, headers.get(hdr, '?')) )
    quoted   = quoted + '\n' + bodytext
    quoted   = '\n' + string.replace(quoted, '\n', '\n> ')
    return quoted


def onReplyMail():
    # reply to selected email
    msgnum = selectedMsg()
    if not (1 <= msgnum <= len(msgList)):
        showerror('PyMail', 'No message selected')
    else:
        text = quoteorigtext(msgnum)
        hdrs = rfc822.Message(StringIO.StringIO(msgList[msgnum-1]))
        toname, toaddr = hdrs.getaddr('From')
        if toname and ',' in toname: toname = '"%s"' % toname
        To   = '%s <%s>' % (toname, toaddr)
        From = mailconfig.myaddress or ('%s <%s>' % hdrs.getaddr('To'))
        Subj = 'Re: ' + hdrs.get('Subject', '(no subject)')
        editmail('Reply', From, To, Subj, text)


def onFwdMail():
    # forward selected email
    msgnum = selectedMsg()
    if not (1 <= msgnum <= len(msgList)):
        showerror('PyMail', 'No message selected')
    else:
        text = quoteorigtext(msgnum)
        hdrs = rfc822.Message(StringIO.StringIO(msgList[msgnum-1]))
        From = mailconfig.myaddress or ('%s <%s>' % hdrs.getaddr('To'))
        Subj = 'Fwd: ' + hdrs.get('Subject', '(no subject)')
        editmail('Forward', From, '', Subj, text)


def deleteMailThread(toDelete):
    # delete mail while main thread handles gui events
```

Example 11-23. PP2E\Internet\Email\PyMailGui.py (continued)

```python
    global errInfo, threadExitVar
    print 'delete start'
    try:
        pymail.deletemessages(mailserver, mailuser, mailpswd, toDelete, 0)
    except:
        exc_type, exc_value = sys.exc_info()[:2]
        errInfo = '\n' + str(exc_type) + '\n' + str(exc_value)
    else:
        errInfo = ''
    print 'delete exit'
    threadExitVar = 1    # signal main thread


def onQuitMail():
    # exit mail tool, delete now
    if askyesno('PyMail', 'Verify Quit?'):
        if toDelete and askyesno('PyMail', 'Really Delete Mail?'):
            getpassword()
            thread.start_new_thread(deleteMailThread, (toDelete,))
            busyInfoBoxWait('Deleting mail')
            if errInfo:
                showerror('PyMail', 'Error while deleting:\n' + errInfo)
            else:
                showinfo('PyMail', 'Mail deleted from server')
        rootWin.quit()


def askpassword(prompt, app='PyMail'):    # getpass.getpass uses stdin, not GUI
    win = Toplevel()                      # tkSimpleDialog.askstring echos input
    win.title(app + ' Prompt')
    Label(win, text=prompt).pack(side=LEFT)
    entvar = StringVar()
    ent = Entry(win, textvariable=entvar, show='*')
    ent.pack(side=RIGHT, expand=YES, fill=X)
    ent.bind('<Return>', lambda event, savewin=win: savewin.destroy())
    ent.focus_set(); win.grab_set(); win.wait_window()
    win.update()
    return entvar.get()     # ent widget is now gone


def getpassword():
    # unless known, set global pop password
    # from client-side file or popup dialog
    global mailpswd
    if mailpswd:
        return
    else:
        try:
            localfile = open(mailconfig.poppasswdfile)
            mailpswd = localfile.readline()[:-1]
            if debugme: print 'local file password', repr(mailpswd)
        except:
            prompt    = 'Password for %s on %s?' % (mailuser, mailserver)
```

Example 11-23. PP2E\Internet\Email\PyMailGui.py (continued)

```
            mailpswd = askpassword(prompt)
            if debugme: print 'user input password', repr(mailpswd)


def decorate(rootWin):
    # window manager stuff for main window
    rootWin.title('PyMail 1.0')
    rootWin.iconname('PyMail')
    rootWin.protocol('WM_DELETE_WINDOW', onQuitMail)


def makemainwindow(parent=None):
    # make the main window
    global rootWin, listBox, allModeVar
    if parent:
        rootWin = Frame(parent)                  # attach to a parent
        rootWin.pack(expand=YES, fill=BOTH)
    else:
        rootWin = Tk()                           # assume I'm standalone
        decorate(rootWin)

    # add main buttons at bottom
    frame1 = Frame(rootWin)
    frame1.pack(side=BOTTOM, fill=X)
    allModeVar = IntVar()
    Checkbutton(frame1, text="All", variable=allModeVar).pack(side=RIGHT)
    actions = [ ('Load',  onLoadMail),  ('View',  onViewFormatMail),
                ('Save',  onSaveMail),  ('Del',   onDeleteMail),
                ('Write', onWriteMail), ('Reply', onReplyMail),
                ('Fwd',   onFwdMail),   ('Quit',  onQuitMail) ]
    for (title, callback) in actions:
        Button(frame1, text=title, command=callback).pack(side=LEFT, fill=X)

    # add main listbox and scrollbar
    frame2  = Frame(rootWin)
    vscroll = Scrollbar(frame2)
    fontsz  = (sys.platform[:3] == 'win' and 8) or 10
    listBox = Listbox(frame2, bg='white', font=('courier', fontsz))

    # crosslink listbox and scrollbar
    vscroll.config(command=listBox.yview, relief=SUNKEN)
    listBox.config(yscrollcommand=vscroll.set, relief=SUNKEN, selectmode=SINGLE)
    listBox.bind('<Double-1>', lambda event: onViewRawMail())
    frame2.pack(side=TOP, expand=YES, fill=BOTH)
    vscroll.pack(side=RIGHT, fill=BOTH)
    listBox.pack(side=LEFT, expand=YES, fill=BOTH)
    return rootWin


# load text block string
from PyMailGuiHelp import helptext

def showhelp(helptext=helptext, appname='PyMail'):   # show helptext in
    from ScrolledText import ScrolledText             # a non-modal dialog
```

Example 11-23. PP2E\Internet\Email\PyMailGui.py (continued)

```
    new   = Toplevel()                              # make new popup window
    bar   = Frame(new)                              # pack first=clip last
    bar.pack(side=BOTTOM, fill=X)
    code = Button(bar, bg='beige', text="Source", command=showsource)
    quit = Button(bar, bg='beige', text="Cancel", command=new.destroy)
    code.pack(pady=1, side=LEFT)
    quit.pack(pady=1, side=LEFT)
    text = ScrolledText(new)                         # add Text + scrollbar
    text.config(font='system',  width=70)            # too big for showinfo
    text.config(bg='steelblue', fg='white')          # erase on btn or return
    text.insert('0.0', helptext)
    text.pack(expand=YES, fill=BOTH)
    new.title(appname + " Help")
    new.bind("<Return>", (lambda event, new=new: new.destroy()))


def showsource():
    # tricky, but open
    try:                                             # like web getfile.cgi
        source = open('PyMailGui.py').read()         # in cwd or below it?
    except:
        try:                                         # or use find.find(f)[0],
            import os                                 # $PP2EHOME, guessLocation
            from PP2E.Launcher import findFirst       # or spawn pyedit with arg
            here   = os.curdir
            source = open(findFirst(here, 'PyMailGui.py')).read()
        except:
            source = 'Sorry - cannot find my source file'
    subject = 'Main script [see also: PyMailGuiHelp, pymail, mailconfig]'
    editmail('View Source Code', 'PyMailGui', 'User', subject, source)


def container():
    # use attachment to add help button
    # this is a bit easier with classes
    root  = Tk()
    title = Button(root, text='PyMail - a Python/Tkinter email client')
    title.config(bg='steelblue', fg='white', relief=RIDGE)
    title.config(command=showhelp)
    title.pack(fill=X)
    decorate(root)
    return root


if __name__ == '__main__':
    # run stand-alone or attach
    rootWin = makemainwindow(container())      # or makemainwindow()
    rootWin.mainloop()
```

Other Client-Side Tools

So far in this chapter, we have focused on Python's FTP and email processing tools and have met a handful of client-side scripting modules along the way: `ftplib`, `poplib`, `smtplib`, `mhlib`, `mimetools`, `urllib`, `rfc822`, and so on. This set is representative of Python's library tools for transferring and processing information over the Internet, but it's not at all complete. A more or less comprehensive list of Python's Internet-related modules appears at the start of the previous chapter. Among other things, Python also includes client-side support libraries for Internet news, Telnet, HTTP, and other standard protocols.

NNTP: Accessing Newsgroups

Python's `nntplib` module supports the client-side interface to *NNTP*—the Network News Transfer Protocol—which is used for reading and posting articles to Usenet newsgroups in the Internet. Like other protocols, NNTP runs on top of sockets and merely defines a standard message protocol; like other modules, `nntplib` hides most of the protocol details and presents an object-based interface to Python scripts.

We won't get into protocol details here, but in brief, NNTP servers store a range of articles on the server machine, usually in a flat-file database. If you have the domain or IP name of a server machine that runs an NNTP server program listening on the NNTP port, you can write scripts that fetch or post articles from any machine that has Python and an Internet connection. For instance, the script in Example 11-24 by default fetches and displays the last 10 articles from Python's Internet news group, *comp.lang.python*, from the *news.rmi.net* NNTP server at my ISP.

Example 11-24. PP2E\Internet\Other\readnews.py

```
################################################
# fetch and print usenet newsgroup postings
# from comp.lang.python via the nntplib module
# which really runs on top of sockets; nntplib
# also supports posting new messages, etc.;
# note: posts not deleted after they are read;
################################################

listonly = 0
showhdrs = ['From', 'Subject', 'Date', 'Newsgroups', 'Lines']
try:
    import sys
    servername, groupname, showcount = sys.argv[1:]
    showcount  = int(showcount)
except:
    servername = 'news.rmi.net'
    groupname  = 'comp.lang.python'      # cmd line args or defaults
    showcount  = 10                      # show last showcount posts
```

Example 11-24. PP2E\Internet\Other\readnews.py (continued)

```
# connect to nntp server
print 'Connecting to', servername, 'for', groupname
from nntplib import NNTP
connection = NNTP(servername)
(reply, count, first, last, name) = connection.group(groupname)
print '%s has %s articles: %s-%s' % (name, count, first, last)

# get request headers only
fetchfrom = str(int(last) - (showcount-1))
(reply, subjects) = connection.xhdr('subject', (fetchfrom + '-' + last))

# show headers, get message hdr+body
for (id, subj) in subjects:                    # [-showcount:] if fetch all hdrs
    print 'Article %s [%s]' % (id, subj)
    if not listonly and raw_input('=> Display?') in ['y', 'Y']:
        reply, num, tid, list = connection.head(id)
        for line in list:
            for prefix in showhdrs:
                if line[:len(prefix)] == prefix:
                    print line[:80]; break
        if raw_input('=> Show body?') in ['y', 'Y']:
            reply, num, tid, list = connection.body(id)
            for line in list:
                print line[:80]
    print
print connection.quit()
```

As for FTP and email tools, the script creates an NNTP object and calls its methods to fetch newsgroup information and articles' header and body text. The **xhdr** method, for example, loads selected headers from a range of messages. When run, this program connects to the server and displays each article's subject line, pausing to ask whether it should fetch and show the article's header information lines (headers listed in variable **showhdrs** only) and body text:

```
C:\...\PP2E\Internet\Other>python readnews.py
Connecting to news.rmi.net for comp.lang.python
comp.lang.python has 3376 articles: 30054-33447
Article 33438 [Embedding? file_input and eval_input]
=> Display?

Article 33439 [Embedding? file_input and eval_input]
=> Display?y
From: James Spears <jimsp@ichips.intel.com>
Newsgroups: comp.lang.python
Subject: Embedding? file_input and eval_input
Date: Fri, 11 Aug 2000 10:55:39 -0700
Lines: 34
=> Show body?

Article 33440 [Embedding? file_input and eval_input]
=> Display?
```

```
   Article 33441 [Embedding? file_input and eval_input]
   => Display?

   Article 33442 [Embedding? file_input and eval_input]
   => Display?

   Article 33443 [Re: PYHTONPATH]
   => Display?y
   Subject: Re: PYHTONPATH
   Lines: 13
   From: sp00fd <sp00fdNOspSPAM@yahoo.com.invalid>
   Newsgroups: comp.lang.python
   Date: Fri, 11 Aug 2000 11:06:23 -0700
   => Show body?y
   Is this not what you were looking for?

   Add to cgi script:
   import sys
   sys.path.insert(0, "/path/to/dir")
   import yourmodule

   ----------------------------------------------------------
   Got questions?  Get answers over the phone at Keen.com.
   Up to 100 minutes free!
   http://www.keen.com

   Article 33444 [Loading new code...]
   => Display?

   Article 33445 [Re: PYHTONPATH]
   => Display?

   Article 33446 [Re: Compile snags on AIX & IRIX]
   => Display?

   Article 33447 [RE: string.replace() can't replace newline characters???]
   => Display?

   205 GoodBye
```

We can also pass this script an explicit server name, newsgroup, and display count on the command line to apply it in different ways. Here is this Python script checking the last few messages in Perl and Linux newsgroups:

```
C:\...\PP2E\Internet\Other>python readnews.py news.rmi.net comp.lang.perl.misc 5
Connecting to news.rmi.net for comp.lang.perl.misc
comp.lang.perl.misc has 5839 articles: 75543-81512
Article 81508 [Re: Simple Argument Passing Question]
=> Display?

Article 81509 [Re: How to Access a hash value?]
=> Display?

Article 81510 [Re: London =?iso-8859-1?Q?=A330-35K?= Perl Programmers Required]
=> Display?
```

```
Article 81511 [Re: ODBC question]
=> Display?

Article 81512 [Re: ODBC question]
=> Display?

205 GoodBye


C:\...\PP2E\Internet\Other>python readnews.py news.rmi.net comp.os.linux 4
Connecting to news.rmi.net for comp.os.linux
comp.os.linux has 526 articles: 9015-9606
Article 9603 [Re: Simple question about CD-Writing for Linux]
=> Display?

Article 9604 [Re: How to start the ftp?]
=> Display?

Article 9605 [Re: large file support]
=> Display?

Article 9606 [Re: large file support]
=> Display?y
From: andy@physast.uga.edu (Andreas Schweitzer)
Newsgroups: comp.os.linux.questions,comp.os.linux.admin,comp.os.linux
Subject: Re: large file support
Date: 11 Aug 2000 18:32:12 GMT
Lines: 19
=> Show body?n

205 GoodBye
```

With a little more work, we could turn this script into a full-blown news interface. For instance, new articles could be posted from within a Python script with code of this form (assuming the local file already contains proper NNTP header lines):

```
# to post, say this (but only if you really want to post!)
connection = NNTP(servername)
localfile = open('filename')        # file has proper headers
connection.post(localfile)          # send text to newsgroup
connection.quit()
```

We might also add a Tkinter-based GUI frontend to this script to make it more usable, but we'll leave such an extension on the suggested exercise heap (see also the PyMailGui interface's suggested extensions in the previous section).

HTTP: Accessing Web Sites

Python's standard library (that is, modules that are installed with the interpreter) also includes client-side support for HTTP—the Hypertext Transfer Protocol—a message structure and port standard used to transfer information on the World

Wide Web. In short, this is the protocol that your web browser (e.g., Internet Explorer, Netscape) uses to fetch web pages and run applications on remote servers as you surf the Net. At the bottom, it's just bytes sent over port 80.

To really understand HTTP-style transfers, you need to know some of the server-side scripting topics covered in the next three chapters (e.g., script invocations and Internet address schemes), so this section may be less useful to readers with no such background. Luckily, though, the basic HTTP interfaces in Python are simple enough for a cursory understanding even at this point in the book, so let's take a brief look here.

Python's standard `httplib` module automates much of the protocol defined by HTTP and allows scripts to fetch web pages much like web browsers. For instance, the script in Example 11-25 can be used to grab any file from any server machine running an HTTP web server program. As usual, the file (and descriptive header lines) is ultimately transferred over a standard socket port, but most of the complexity is hidden by the `httplib` module.

Example 11-25. PP2E\Internet\Other\http-getfile.py

```
#######################################################################
# fetch a file from an http (web) server over sockets via httplib;
# the filename param may have a full directory path, and may name a cgi
# script with query parameters on the end to invoke a remote program;
# fetched file data or remote program output could be saved to a local
# file to mimic ftp, or parsed with string.find or the htmllib module;
#######################################################################

import sys, httplib
showlines = 6
try:
    servername, filename = sys.argv[1:]                # cmdline args?
except:
    servername, filename = 'starship.python.net', '/index.html'

print servername, filename
server = httplib.HTTP(servername)                      # connect to http site/server
server.putrequest('GET', filename)                     # send request and headers
server.putheader('Accept', 'text/html')                # POST requests work here too
server.endheaders()                                    # as do cgi script file names

errcode, errmsh, replyheader = server.getreply()       # read reply info headers
if errcode != 200:                                     # 200 means success
    print 'Error sending request', errcode
else:
    file = server.getfile()                            # file obj for data received
    data = file.readlines()
    file.close()                                       # show lines with eoln at end
    for line in data[:showlines]: print line,          # to save, write data to file
```

Desired server names and filenames can be passed on the command line to override hardcoded defaults in the script. You need to also know something of the HTTP protocol to make the most sense of this code, but it's fairly straightforward to decipher. When run on the client, this script makes a HTTP object to connect to the server, sends it a GET request along with acceptable reply types, and then reads the server's reply. Much like raw email message text, the HTTP server's reply usually begins with a set of descriptive header lines, followed by the contents of the requested file. The HTTP object's `getfile` method gives us a file object from which we can read the downloaded data.

Let's fetch a few files with this script. Like all Python client-side scripts, this one works on any machine with Python and an Internet connection (here it runs on a Windows client). Assuming that all goes well, the first few lines of the downloaded file are printed; in a more realistic application, the text we fetch would probably be saved to a local file, parsed with Python's `htmllib` module, and so on. Without arguments, the script simply fetches the HTML index page at *http:// starship.python.org*:

```
C:\...\PP2E\Internet\Other>python http-getfile.py
starship.python.net /index.html
<HTML>
<HEAD>
  <META NAME="GENERATOR" CONTENT="HTMLgen">
  <TITLE>Starship Python</TITLE>
  <SCRIPT language="JavaScript">
<!-- // mask from the infidel
```

But we can also list a server and file to be fetched on the command line, if we want to be more specific. In the following code, we use the script to fetch files from two different web sites by listing their names on the command lines (I've added line breaks to make these lines fit in this book). Notice that the filename argument can include an arbitrary remote directory path to the desired file, as in the last fetch here:

```
C:\...\PP2E\Internet\Other>python http-getfile.py www.python.org /index.html
www.python.org /index.html
<HTML>
<!-- THIS PAGE IS AUTOMATICALLY GENERATED.  DO NOT EDIT. -->
<!-- Wed Aug 23 17:29:24 2000 -->
<!-- USING HT2HTML 1.1 -->
<!-- SEE http://www.python.org/~bwarsaw/software/pyware.html -->
<!-- User-specified headers:

C:\...\PP2E\Internet\Other>python http-getfile.py www.python.org /index
www.python.org /index
Error sending request 404

C:\...\PP2E\Internet\Other>python http-getfile.py starship.python.net
                                     /~lutz/index.html
```

```
starship.python.net /~lutz/index.html
<HTML>
<HEAD><TITLE>Mark Lutz's Starship page</TITLE></HEAD>
<BODY>

<H1>Greetings</H1>
```

Also notice the second attempt in this code: if the request fails, the script receives and displays an HTTP error code from the server (we forgot the *.html* on the filename). With the raw HTTP interfaces, we need to be precise about what we want.

Technically, the string we call `filename` in the script can refer to either a simple static web page file, or a server-side program that generates HTML as its output. Those server-side programs are usually called CGI scripts—the topic of the next three chapters. For now, keep in mind that when `filename` refers to a script, this program can be used to invoke another program that resides on a remote server machine. In that case, we can also specify parameters (called a query string) to be passed to the remote program after a ?. Here, for instance, we pass a `language=Python` parameter to a CGI script we will meet in the next chapter:

```
C:\...\PP2E\Internet\Other>python http-getfile.py starship.python.net
                          /~lutz/Basics/languages.cgi?language=Python
starship.python.net /~lutz/Basics/languages.cgi?language=Python
<TITLE>Languages</TITLE>
<H1>Syntax</H1><HR>
<H3>Python</H3><P><PRE>
 print 'Hello World'
</PRE></P><BR>
<HR>
```

This book has much more to say about HTML, CGI scripts, and the meaning of an HTTP GET request (one way to format information sent to a HTTP server) later, so we'll skip additional details here. Suffice it to say, though, that we could use the HTTP interfaces to write our own web browsers and build scripts that use web sites as though they were subroutines. By sending parameters to remote programs and parsing their results, web sites can take on the role of simple in-process functions (albeit, much more slowly and indirectly).

urllib revisited

The `httplib` module we just met provides low-level control for HTTP clients. When dealing with items available on the Web, though, it's often easier to code downloads with Python's standard `urllib` module introduced in the FTP section of this chapter. Since this module is another way to talk HTTP, let's expand on its interfaces here.

Recall that given a URL, `urllib` either downloads the requested object over the Net to a local file, or gives us a file-like object from which we can read the requested object's contents. Because of that, the script in Example 11-26 does the same work as the `httplib` script we just wrote, but requires noticeably less typing.

Example 11-26. PP2E\Internet\Other\http-getfile-urllib1.py

```
###################################################################
# fetch a file from an http (web) server over sockets via urllib;
# urllib supports http, ftp, files, etc. via url address strings;
# for hhtp, the url can name a file or trigger a remote cgi script;
# see also the urllib example in the ftp section, and the cgi
# script invocation in a later chapter; files can be fetched over
# the net with Python in many ways that vary in complexity and
# server requirements: sockets, ftp, http, urllib, cgi outputs;
# caveat: should run urllib.quote on filename--see later chapters;
###################################################################

import sys, urllib
showlines = 6
try:
    servername, filename = sys.argv[1:]                # cmdline args?
except:
    servername, filename = 'starship.python.net', '/index.html'

remoteaddr = 'http://%s%s' % (servername, filename)   # can name a cgi script too
print remoteaddr
remotefile = urllib.urlopen(remoteaddr)               # returns input file object
remotedata = remotefile.readlines()                   # read data directly here
remotefile.close()
for line in remotedata[:showlines]: print line,
```

Almost all HTTP transfer details are hidden behind the `urllib` interface here. This version works about the same as the `httplib` version we wrote first, but builds and submits an Internet URL address to get its work done (the constructed URL is printed as the script's first output line). As we saw in the FTP section of this chapter, the `urllib urlopen` function returns a file-like object from which we can read the remote data. But because the constructed URLs begin with "http://" here, the `urllib` module automatically employs the lower-level HTTP interfaces to download the requested file, not FTP:

```
C:\...\PP2E\Internet\Other>python http-getfile-urllib1.py
http://starship.python.net/index.html
<HTML>
<HEAD>
  <META NAME="GENERATOR" CONTENT="HTMLgen">
  <TITLE>Starship Python</TITLE>
  <SCRIPT language="JavaScript">
<!-- // mask from the infidel

C:\...\PP2E\Internet\Other>python http-getfile-urllib1.py www.python.org /index
http://www.python.org/index
<HTML>
<!-- THIS PAGE IS AUTOMATICALLY GENERATED.  DO NOT EDIT. -->
<!-- Fri Mar  3 10:28:30 2000 -->
```

```
<!-- USING HT2HTML 1.1 -->
<!-- SEE http://www.python.org/~bwarsaw/software/pyware.html -->
<!-- User-specified headers:

C:\...\PP2E\Internet\Other>python http-getfile-urllib1.py starship.python.net
                                               /~lutz/index.html
http://starship.python.net/~lutz/index.html
<HTML>
<HEAD><TITLE>Mark Lutz's Starship page</TITLE></HEAD>
<BODY>

<H1>Greetings</H1>

C:\...\PP2E\Internet\Other>python http-getfile-urllib1.py starship.python.net
                                /~lutz/Basics/languages.cgi?language=Java
http://starship.python.net/~lutz/Basics/languages.cgi?language=Java
<TITLE>Languages</TITLE>
<H1>Syntax</H1><HR>
<H3>Java</H3><P><PRE>
  System.out.println("Hello World");
</PRE></P><BR>
<HR>
```

As before, the filename argument can name a simple file or a program invocation
with optional parameters at the end. If you read this output carefully, you'll notice
that this script still works if you leave the *.html* off the end of a filename (in the
second command line); unlike the raw HTTP version, the URL-based interface is
smart enough to do the right thing.

Other urllib interfaces

One last mutation: the following `urllib` downloader script uses the slightly
higher-level `urlretrieve` interface in that module to automatically save the
downloaded file or script output to a local file on the client machine. This interface is handy if we really mean to store the fetched data (e.g., to mimic the FTP
protocol). If we plan on processing the downloaded data immediately, though,
this form may be less convenient than the version we just met: we need to open
and read the saved file. Moreover, we need to provide extra protocol for specifying or extracting a local filename, as in Example 11-27.

Example 11-27. PP2E\Internet\Other\http-getfile-urllib2.py

```
###################################################################
# fetch a file from an http (web) server over sockets via urlllib;
# this version uses an interface that saves the fetched data to a
# local file; the local file name is either passed in as a cmdline
# arg or stripped from the url with urlparse: the filename argument
# may have a directory path at the front and query parmams at end,
# so os.path.split is not enough (only splits off directory path);
# caveat: should run urllib.quote on filename--see later chapters;
###################################################################
```

Example 11-27. PP2E\Internet\Other\http-getfile-urllib2.py (continued)

```
import sys, os, urllib, urlparse
showlines = 6
try:
    servername, filename = sys.argv[1:3]            # first 2 cmdline args?
except:
    servername, filename = 'starship.python.net', '/index.html'

remoteaddr = 'http://%s%s' % (servername, filename)   # any address on the net
if len(sys.argv) == 4:                                # get result file name
    localname = sys.argv[3]
else:
    (scheme, server, path, parms, query, frag) = urlparse.urlparse(remoteaddr)
    localname = os.path.split(path)[1]

print remoteaddr, localname
urllib.urlretrieve(remoteaddr, localname)             # can be file or script
remotedata = open(localname).readlines()             # saved to local file
for line in remotedata[:showlines]: print line,
```

Let's run this last variant from a command line. Its basic operation is the same as the last two versions: like the prior one, it builds a URL, and like both of the last two, we can list an explicit target server and file path on the command line:

```
C:\...\PP2E\Internet\Other>python http-getfile-urllib2.py
http://starship.python.net/index.html index.html
<HTML>
<HEAD>
  <META NAME="GENERATOR" CONTENT="HTMLgen">
  <TITLE>Starship Python</TITLE>
  <SCRIPT language="JavaScript">
<!-- // mask from the infidel

C:\...\PP2E\Internet\Other>python http-getfile-urllib2.py
                                      www.python.org /index.html
http://www.python.org/index.html index.html
<HTML>
<!-- THIS PAGE IS AUTOMATICALLY GENERATED.  DO NOT EDIT. -->
<!-- Wed Aug 23 17:29:24 2000 -->
<!-- USING HT2HTML 1.1 -->
<!-- SEE http://www.python.org/~bwarsaw/software/pyware.html -->
<!-- User-specified headers:
```

Because this version uses an `urllib` interface that automatically saves the downloaded data in a local file, it's more directly like FTP downloads in spirit. But this script must also somehow come up with a local filename for storing the data. You can either let the script strip and use the base filename from the constructed URL, or explicitly pass a local filename as a last command-line argument. In the prior run, for instance, the downloaded web page is stored in local file *index.html*—the base filename stripped from the URL (the script prints the URL and local filename as its first output line). In the next run, the local filename is passed explicitly as *python-org-index.html*:

```
C:\...\PP2E\Internet\Other>python http-getfile-urllib2.py www.python.org
                                      /index.html python-org-index.html
http://www.python.org/index.html python-org-index.html
<HTML>
<!-- THIS PAGE IS AUTOMATICALLY GENERATED.  DO NOT EDIT. -->
<!-- Wed Aug 23 17:29:24 2000 -->
<!-- USING HT2HTML 1.1 -->
<!-- SEE http://www.python.org/~bwarsaw/software/pyware.html -->
<!-- User-specified headers:

C:\...\PP2E\Internet\Other>python http-getfile-urllib2.py starship.python.net
                                      /~lutz/home/index.html
http://starship.python.net/~lutz/home/index.html index.html
<HTML>

<HEAD>
<TITLE>Mark Lutz's Home Page</TITLE>
</HEAD>

C:\...\PP2E\Internet\Other>python http-getfile-urllib2.py starship.python.net
                                      /~lutz/home/about-pp.html
http://starship.python.net/~lutz/home/about-pp.html about-pp.html
<HTML>

<HEAD>
<TITLE>About "Programming Python"</TITLE>
</HEAD>
```

Below is a listing showing this third version being used to trigger a remote program. As before, if you don't give the local filename explicitly, the script strips the base filename out of the filename argument. That's not always easy or appropriate for program invocations—the filename can contain both a remote directory path at the front, and query parameters at the end for a remote program invocation.

Given a script invocation URL and no explicit output filename, the script extracts the base filename in the middle by using first the standard `urlparse` module to pull out the file path, and then `os.path.split` to strip off the directory path. However, the resulting filename is a remote script's name, and may or may not be an appropriate place to store the data locally. In the first run below, for example, the script's output goes in a local file called *languages.cgi*, the script name in the middle of the URL; in the second, we name the output *CxxSyntax.html* explicitly instead to suppress filename extraction:

```
C:\...\PP2E\Internet\Other>python http-getfile-urllib2.py starship.python.net
                               /~lutz/Basics/languages.cgi?language=Perl
http://starship.python.net/~lutz/Basics/languages.cgi?language=Perl
                                          languages.cgi

<TITLE>Languages</TITLE>
```

```
<H1>Syntax</H1><HR>
<H3>Perl</H3><P><PRE>
 print "Hello World\n";
</PRE></P><BR>
<HR>

C:\...\PP2E\Internet\Other>python http-getfile-urllib2.py starship.python.net
                     /~lutz/Basics/languages.cgi?language=C++ CxxSyntax.html
http://starship.python.net/~lutz/Basics/languages.cgi?language=C++
                                              CxxSyntax.html

<TITLE>Languages</TITLE>
<H1>Syntax</H1><HR>
<H3>C   </H3><P><PRE>
Sorry--I don't know that language
</PRE></P><BR>
<HR>
```

The remote script returns a not-found message when passed "C++" in the last
command here. It turns out that "+" is a special character in URL strings (meaning
a space), and to be robust, both of the `urllib` scripts we've just written should
really run the `filename` string though something called `urllib.quote`, a tool
that escapes special characters for transmission. We will talk about this in depth in
the next chapter, so consider this all a preview for now. But to make this invocation work, we need to use special sequences in the constructed URL; here's how
to do it by hand:

```
C:\...\PP2E\Internet\Other>python http-getfile-urllib2.py  starship.python.net
                     /~lutz/Basics/languages.cgi?language=C%2b%2b CxxSyntax.html
http://starship.python.net/~lutz/Basics/languages.cgi?language=C%2b%2b
                                              CxxSyntax.html

<TITLE>Languages</TITLE>
<H1>Syntax</H1><HR>
<H3>C++</H3><P><PRE>
 cout &lt;&lt; "Hello World" &lt;&lt; endl;
</PRE></P><BR>
<HR>
```

The odd "%2b" strings in this command line are not entirely magical: the escaping
required for URLs can be seen by running standard Python tools manually (this is
what these scripts should do automatically to handle all possible cases well):

```
C:\...\PP2E\Internet\Other>python
Python 1.5.2 (#0, Apr 13 1999, 10:51:12) [MSC 32 bit (Intel)] on win32
Copyright 1991-1995 Stichting Mathematisch Centrum, Amsterdam
>>> import urllib
>>> urllib.quote('C++')
'C%2b%2b'
```

Again, don't work too hard at understanding these last few commands; we will
revisit URLs and URL escapes in the next chapter, while exploring server-side
scripting in Python. I will also explain there why the C++ result came back with
other oddities like <<—HTML escapes for <<.

Other Client-Side Scripting Options

In this chapter, we've focused on client-side interfaces to standard protocols that run over sockets, but client-side programming can take other forms, too. For instance, in Chapter 15 we'll also see that Python code can be embedded inside the HTML code that defines a web page, with the Windows Active Scripting extension. When Internet Explorer downloads such a web page file from a web server, the embedded Python scripts are actually executed on the client machine, with an object API that gives access to the browser's context. Code in HTML is downloaded over a socket initially, but its execution is not bound up with a socket-based protocol.

In Chapter 15, we'll also meet client-side options such as the *JPython* (a.k.a. "Jython") system, a compiler that supports Python-coded Java *applets*—general-purpose programs downloaded from a server and run locally on the client when accessed or referenced by a URL. We'll also peek at Python tools for processing *XML*—structured text that may become a common language of client/server dialogs in the future.

In deference to time and space, though, we won't go into further details on these and other client-side tools here. If you are interested in using Python to script clients, you should take a few minutes to become familiar with the list of Internet tools documented in the Python library reference manual. All work on similar principles, but have slightly distinct interfaces.

In the next chapter, we'll hop the fence to the other side of the Internet world and explore scripts that run on server machines. Such programs give rise to the grander notion of applications that live entirely on the Web and are launched by web browsers. As we take this leap in structure, keep in mind that the tools we met in this and the previous chapter are often sufficient to implement all the distributed processing that many applications require, and they can work in harmony with scripts that run on a server. To completely understand the web world view, though, we need to explore the server realm, too.

12

Server-Side Scripting

"Oh What a Tangled Web We Weave"

This chapter is the third part of our look at Python Internet programming. In the last two chapters, we explored sockets and basic client-side programming interfaces such as FTP and email. In this chapter, our main focus will be on writing *server-side scripts* in Python—a type of program usually referred to as *CGI scripts*. Server-side scripting and its derivatives are at the heart of much of what happens on the Web these days.

As we'll see, Python makes an ideal language for writing scripts to implement and customize web sites, due to both its ease of use and its library support. In the following two chapters, we will use the basics we learn in this chapter to implement full-blown web sites. After that, we will wrap up with a chapter that looks at other Internet-related topics and technologies. Here, our goal is to understand the fundamentals of server-side scripting, before exploring systems that build upon that basic model.

What's a Server-Side CGI Script?

Simply put, CGI scripts implement much of the interaction you typically experience on the Web. They are a standard and widely used mechanism for programming web site interaction. There are other ways to add interactive behavior to web sites with Python, including client-side solutions (e.g., JPython applets and Active Scripting), as well as server-side technologies, which build upon the basic CGI model (e.g., Active Server Pages and Zope), and we will discuss these briefly at the end of Chapter 15, *Advanced Internet Topics*, too. But by and large, CGI server-side scripts are used to program much of the activity on the Web.

A House upon the Sand

As you read the next three chapters of this book, please keep in mind that they are intended only as an introduction to server-side scripting with Python. The webmaster domain is large and complex, changes continuously, and often prescribes many ways to accomplish a given goal—some of which can vary from browser to browser and server to server. For instance, the password encryption scheme of the next chapter may be unnecessary under certain scenarios, and special HTML tags may sometimes obviate some work we'll do here.

Given such a large and shifting knowledge base, this part of the book does not even pretend to be a complete look at the server-side scripting domain. To become truly proficient in this area, you should study other texts for additional webmaster-y details and tricks (e.g., O'Reilly's *HTML & XHTML: The Definitive Guide*). Here, you will meet Python's CGI toolset and learn enough to start writing substantial web sites of your own in Python. But you should not take this text as the final word on the subject.

The Script Behind the Curtain

Formally speaking, CGI scripts are programs that run on a server machine and adhere to the Common Gateway Interface—a model for browser/server communications, from which CGI scripts take their name. Perhaps a more useful way to understand CGI, though, is in terms of the interaction it implies.

Most people take this interaction for granted when browsing the Web and pressing buttons in web pages, but there is a lot going on behind the scenes of every transaction on the Web. From the perspective of a user, it's a fairly familiar and simple process:

1. *Submission.* When you visit a web site to purchase a product or submit information online, you generally fill in a form in your web browser, press a button to submit your information, and begin waiting for a reply.

2. *Response.* Assuming all is well with both your Internet connection and the computer you are contacting, you eventually get a reply in the form of a new web page. It may be a simple acknowledgement (e.g, "Thanks for your order") or a new form that must be filled out and submitted again.

And, believe it or not, that simple model is what makes most of the Web hum. But internally, it's a bit more complex. In fact, there is a subtle client/server socket-based architecture at work—your web browser running on your computer is the *client*, and the computer you contact over the Web is the *server*. Let's examine the interaction scenario again, with all the gory details that users usually never see.

Submission

When you fill out a form page in a web browser and press a submission button, behind the scenes your web browser sends your information across the Internet to the server machine specified as its receiver. The server machine is usually a remote computer that lives somewhere else in both cyberspace and reality. It is named in the URL you access (the Internet address string that appears at the top of your browser). The target server and file can be named in a URL you type explicitly, but more typically they are specified in the HTML that defines the submission page itself—either in a hyperlink, or in the "action" tag of a form's HTML. However the server is specified, the browser running on your computer ultimately sends your information to the server as bytes over a socket, using techniques we saw in the last two chapters. On the server machine, a program called an HTTP server runs perpetually, listening on a socket for incoming data from browsers, usually on port number 80.

Processing

When your information shows up at the server machine, the HTTP server program notices it first and decides how to handle the request. If the requested URL names a simple *web page* (e.g., a URL ending in *.html*), the HTTP server opens the named HTML file on the server machine and sends its text back to the browser over a socket. On the client, the browser reads the HTML and uses it to construct the next page you see. But if the URL requested by the browser names an *executable program* instead (e.g., a URL ending in *.cgi*), the HTTP server starts the named program on the server machine to process the request and redirects the incoming browser data to the spawned program's `stdin` input stream and environment variables. That program is usually a CGI script— a program run on the remote server machine somewhere in cyberspace, not on your computer. The CGI script is responsible for handling the request from this point on; it may store your information in a database, charge your credit card, and so on.

Response

Ultimately, the CGI script prints HTML to generate a new response page in your browser. When a CGI script is started, the HTTP server takes care to connect the script's `stdout` standard output stream to a socket that the browser is listening to. Because of this, HTML code printed by the CGI script is sent over the Internet, back to your browser, to produce a new page. The HTML printed back by the CGI script works just as if it had been stored and read in from an HTML file; it can define a simple response page or a brand new form coded to collect additional information.

In other words, CGI scripts are something like *callback handlers* for requests generated by web browsers that require a program to be run dynamically; they are automatically run on the server machine in response to actions in a browser.

Although CGI scripts ultimately receive and send standard structured messages over sockets, CGI is more like a higher-level procedural convention for sending and receiving information between a browser and a server.

Writing CGI Scripts in Python

If all of the above sounds complicated, relax—Python, as well as the resident HTTP server, automates most of the tricky bits. CGI scripts are written as fairly autonomous programs, and they assume that startup tasks have already been accomplished. The HTTP web server program, not the CGI script, implements the server-side of the HTTP protocol itself. Moreover, Python's library modules automatically dissect information sent up from the browser and give it to the CGI script in an easily digested form. The upshot is that CGI scripts may focus on application details like processing input data and producing a result page.

As mentioned earlier, in the context of CGI scripts, the `stdin` and `stdout` streams are automatically tied to sockets connected to the browser. In addition, the HTTP server passes some browser information to the CGI script in the form of shell environment variables. To CGI programmers, that means:

- *Input* data sent from the browser to the server shows up as a stream of bytes in the `stdin` input stream, along with shell environment variables.

- *Output* is sent back from the server to the client by simply printing properly formatted HTML to the `stdout` output stream.

The most complex parts of this scheme include parsing all the input information sent up from the browser and formatting information in the reply sent back. Happily, Python's standard library largely automates both tasks:

Input

> With the Python `cgi` module, inputs typed into a web browser form or appended to a URL string show up as values in a dictionary-like object in Python CGI scripts. Python parses the data itself and gives us an object with one `key:value` pair per input sent by the browser that is fully independent of transmission style (form or URL).

Output

> The `cgi` module also has tools for automatically escaping strings so that they are legal to use in HTML (e.g., replacing embedded <, >, and & characters with HTML escape codes). Module `urllib` provides other tools for formatting text inserted into generated URL strings (e.g., adding `%XX` and + escapes).

We'll study both of these interfaces in detail later in this chapter. For now, keep in mind that although any language can be used to write CGI scripts, Python's standard modules and language attributes make it a snap.

Less happily, CGI scripts are also intimately tied to the syntax of HTML, since they must generate it to create a reply page. In fact, it can be said that Python CGI scripts embed HTML, which is an entirely distinct language in its own right. As we'll also see, the fact that CGI scripts create a user interface by printing HTML syntax means that we have to take special care with the text we insert into a web page's code (e.g., escaping HTML operators). Worse, CGI scripts require at least a cursory knowledge of HTML forms, since that is where the inputs and target script's address are typically specified. This book won't teach HTML in-depth; if you find yourself puzzled by some of the arcane syntax of the HTML generated by scripts here, you should glance at an HTML introduction, such as O'Reilly's *HTML and XHTML: The Definitive Guide.*

Running Server-Side Examples

Like GUIs, web-based systems are highly interactive, and the best way to get a feel for some of these examples is to test-drive them live. Before we get into some code, it's worth noting that all you need to *run* the examples in the next few chapters is a web browser. That is, all the Web examples we will see here can be run from any web browser on any machine, whether you've installed Python on that machine or not. Simply type this URL at the top:[*]

```
http://starship.python.net/~lutz/PyInternetDemos.html
```

That address loads a launcher page with links to all the example files installed on a server machine whose domain name is *starship.python.net* (a machine dedicated to Python developers). The launcher page itself appears as shown in Figure 12-1, running under Internet Explorer. It looks similar in other browsers. Each major example has a link on this page, which runs when clicked.

The launcher page, and all the HTML files in this chapter, can also be loaded locally, from the book's example distribution directory on your machine. They can even be opened directly off the book's CD and may be opened by buttons on the top-level book demo launchers. However, the CGI scripts ultimately invoked by some of the example links must be run on a server, and thus require a live Internet connection. If you browse root pages locally on your machine, your browser will either display the scripts' source code or tell you when you need to connect to the Web to run a CGI script. On Windows, a connection dialog will likely pop up automatically, if needed.

---

[*] Given that this edition may not be updated for many years, it's not impossible that the server name in this address *starship.python.net* might change over time. If this address fails, check the book updates at *http://rmi.net/~lutz/about-pp.html* to see if a new examples site address has been posted. The rest of the main page's URL will likely be unchanged. Note, though, that some examples hardcode the *starship* host server name in URLs; these will be fixed on the new server if moved, but not on your book CD. Run script *fixsitename.py* later in this chapter to change site names automatically.

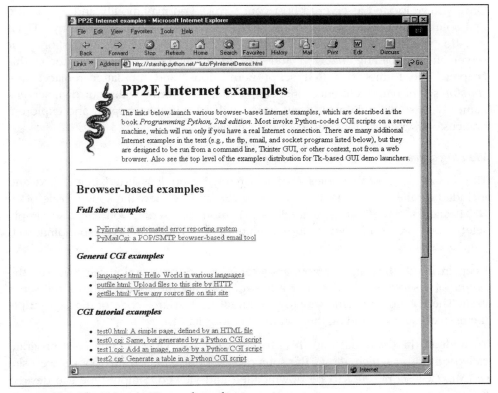

Figure 12-1. The PyInternetDemos launcher page

Changing server-side examples

Of course, running scripts in your browser isn't quite the same as writing scripts on your own. If you do decide to change these CGI programs or write new ones from scratch, you must be able to access web server machines:

- To change server-side scripts, you need an account on a web server machine with an installed version of Python. A basic account on such a server is often enough. Then edit scripts on your machine and upload to the server by FTP.

- To type explicit command lines on a server machine or edit scripts on the server directly, you will need to also have shell access on the web server. Such access lets you telnet to that machine to get a command-line prompt.

Unlike the last chapter's examples, Python server-side scripts require both Python and a server. That is, you'll need access to a web server machine that supports CGI scripts in general and that either already has an installed Python interpreter or lets you install one of your own. Some Internet Service Providers (ISPs) are more supportive than others on this front, but there are many options here, both commercial and free (more on this later).

Once you've located a server to host your scripts, you may modify and upload the CGI source code file from this book's CD to your own server and site by FTP. If you do, you may also want to run two Python command-line scripts on your server after uploading: *fixcgi.py* and *fixsitename.py*, both presented later in this chapter. The former sets CGI script permissions, and the latter replaces any *starship* server name references in example links and forms with your own server's name. We'll study additional installation details later in this chapter, and explore a few custom server options at the end of Chapter 15.

Viewing server-side examples and output

The source code of examples in this part of the book is listed in the text and included on the book's CD. In all cases, if you wish to view the source code of an HTML file, or the HTML generated by a Python CGI script, you can also simply select your browser's View Source menu option while the corresponding web page is displayed.

Keep in mind, though, that your browser's View Source option lets you see the *output* of a server-side script after it has run, but not the source code of the script itself. There is no automatic way to view the Python source code of the CGI scripts themselves, short of finding them in this book or its CD.

To address this issue, later in this chapter we'll also write a CGI-based program called `getfile`, which allows the source code of any file on this book's web site (HTML, CGI script, etc.) to be downloaded and viewed. Simply type the desired file's name into a web page form referenced by the *getfile.html* link on the Internet demos launcher page, or add it to the end of an explicitly typed URL as a parameter like this:

```
http://.../getfile.cgi?filename=somefile.cgi
```

In response, the server will ship back the text of the named file to your browser. This process requires explicit interface steps, though, and much more knowledge than we've gained thus far, so see ahead for details.

Climbing the CGI Learning Curve

Okay, it's time to get into concrete programming details. This section introduces CGI coding one step at a time—from simple, noninteractive scripts to larger programs that utilize all the common web page user input devices (what we called "widgets" in the Tkinter GUI chapters of Part II, *GUI Programming*). We'll move slowly at first, to learn all the basics; the next two chapters will use the ideas presented here to build up larger and more realistic web site examples. For now, let's work though a simple CGI tutorial, with just enough HTML thrown in to write basic server-side scripts.

A First Web Page

As mentioned, CGI scripts are intimately bound up with HTML, so let's start with a simple HTML page. The file *test0.html*, shown in Example 12-1, defines a bona fide, fully functional web page—a text file containing HTML code, which specifies the structure and contents of a simple web page.

Example 12-1. PP2E\Internet\Cgi-Web\Basics\test0.html

```
<HTML><BODY>
<TITLE>HTML 101</TITLE>
<H1>A First HTML page</H1>
<P>Hello, HTML World!</P>
</BODY></HTML>
```

If you point your favorite web browser to the Internet address of this file (or to its local path on your own machine), you should see a page like that shown in Figure 12-2. This figure shows the Internet Explorer browser at work; other browsers render the page similarly.

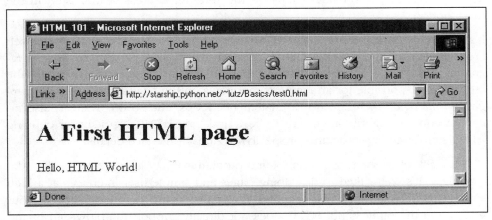

Figure 12-2. A simple web page from an HTML file

To truly understand how this little file does its work, you need to know something about permission rules, HTML syntax, and Internet addresses. Let's take a quick first look at each of these topics before we move on to larger examples.

HTML file permission constraints

First of all, if you want to install this code on a different machine, it's usually necessary to grant web page files and their directories world-readable permission. That's because they are loaded by arbitrary people over the Web (actually, by someone named "nobody", who we'll introduce in a moment). An appropriate *chmod* command can be used to change permissions on Unix-like machines. For instance, a `chmod 755 `*filename* shell command usually suffices; it makes `filename` readable and executable by everyone, and writable by you only.[*] These directory and file permission details are typical, but they can vary from server to server. Be sure to find out about the local server's conventions if you upload this file to your site.

HTML basics

I promised that I wouldn't teach much HTML in this book, but you need to know enough to make sense of examples. In short, HTML is a descriptive markup language, based on *tags*—items enclosed in <> pairs. Some tags stand alone (e.g., <HR> specifies a horizontal rule). Others appear in begin/end pairs where the end tag includes an extra slash.

For instance, to specify the text of a level-1 header line, we write HTML code of the form <H1>*text*</H1>; the text between the tags shows up on the web page. Some tags also allow us to specify options. For example, a tag pair like <A href="*address*">*text*</A> specifies a *hyperlink*: pressing the link's text in the page directs the browser to access the Internet address (URL) listed in the `href` option.

It's important to keep in mind that HTML is used only to describe pages: your web browser reads it and translates its description to a web page with headers, paragraphs, links, and the like. Notably absent is both *layout information*—the browser is responsible for arranging components on the page—and syntax for *programming logic*—there are no "if" statements, loops, and so on. There is also no Python code in this file anywhere to be found; raw HTML is strictly for defining pages, not for coding programs or specifying all user-interface details.

HTML's lack of user interface control and programmability is both a strength and a weakness. It's well-suited to describing pages and simple user interfaces at a high level. The browser, not you, handles physically laying out the page on your screen. On the other hand, HTML does not directly support full-blown GUIs and requires us to introduce CGI scripts (and other technologies) to web sites, in order to add dynamic programmability to otherwise static HTML.

Internet addresses (URLs)

Once you write an HTML file, you need to put it some place where the outside world can find it. Like all HTML files, *test0.html* must be stored in a directory on the server machine, from which the resident web server program allows browsers

---

[*] These are not necessarily magic numbers. On Unix machines, mode 755 is a bit mask. The first 7 simply means that you (the file's owner) can read, write, and execute the file (7 in binary is 111—each bit enables an access mode). The two 5s (binary 101) say that everyone else (your group and others) can read and execute (but not write) the file. See your system's manpage on the *chmod* command for more details.

to fetch pages. On the server where this example lives, the page's file must be stored in or below the *public_html* directory of my personal home directory—that is, somewhere in the directory tree rooted at */home/lutz/public_html*. For this section, examples live in a *Basics* subdirectory, so the complete Unix pathname of this file on the server is:

```
/home/lutz/public_html/Basics/test0.html
```

This path is different than its *PP2E\Internet\Cgi-Web\Basics* location on the book's CD, as given in the example file listing's title. When you reference this file on the client, though, you must specify its Internet address, sometimes called a *URL*, instead. To load the remote page, type the following text in your browser's address field (or click the example root page's *test0.html* hyperlink, which refers to same address):

```
http://starship.python.net/~lutz/Basics/test0.html
```

This string is a URL composed of multiple parts:

Protocol name: http
> The protocol part of this URL tells the browser to communicate with the HTTP server program on the server machine, using the HTTP message protocol. URLs used in browsers can also name different protocols—for example, *ftp://* to reference a file managed by the FTP protocol and server, *telnet* to start a Telnet client session, and so on.

Server machine name: starship.python.net
> A URL also names the target server machine following the protocol type. Here, we list the domain name of the server machine were the examples are installed; the machine name listed is used to open a socket to talk to the server. For HTTP, the socket is usually connected to port number 80.

File path: ~lutz/Basics/test0.html
> Finally, the URL gives the path to the desired file on the remote machine. The HTTP web server automatically translates the URL's file path to the file's true Unix pathname: on my server, *~lutz* is automatically translated to the *public_html* directory in my home directory. URLs typically map to such files, but can reference other sorts of items as well.

Parameters (used in later examples)
> URLs may also be followed by additional input parameters for CGI programs. When used, they are introduced by a ? and separated by & characters; for instance, a string of the form ?name=bob&job=hacker at the end of a URL passes parameters named name and job to the CGI script named earlier in the URL. These values are sometimes called URL *query string parameters* and are treated the same as form inputs. More on both forms and parameters in a moment.

For completeness, you should also know that URLs can contain additional information (e.g., the server name part can specify a port number following a `:`), but we'll ignore these extra formatting rules here. If you're interested in more details, you might start by reading the `urlparse` module's entry in Python's library manual, as well as its source code in the Python standard library. You might also notice that a URL you type to access a page looks a bit different after the page is fetched (spaces become + characters, `%`s are added, etc.). This is simply because browsers must also generally follow URL escaping (i.e., translation) conventions, which we'll explore later in this chapter.

Using minimal URLs

Because browsers remember the prior page's Internet address, URLs embedded in HTML files can often omit the protocol and server names, as well as the file's directory path. If missing, the browser simply uses these components' values from the last page's address. This minimal syntax works both for URLs embedded in hyperlinks and form actions (we'll meet forms later in this chapter). For example, within a page that was fetched from directory *dirpath* on server *www.server.com*, minimal hyperlinks and form actions such as:

```
<A HREF="more.html">
<FORM ACTION="next.cgi"  ...>
```

are treated exactly as if we had specified a complete URL with explicit server and path components, like the following:

```
<A HREF="http://www.server.com/dirpath/more.html">
<FORM ACTION="http://www.server.com/dirpath/next.cgi"  ...>
```

The first minimal URL refers to file *more.html* on the same server and in the same directory that the page containing this hyperlink was fetched from; it is expanded to a complete URL within the browser. URLs can also employ Unix-style relative path syntax in the file path component. For instance, a hyperlink tag like `<A HREF="../spam.gif">` names a GIF file on the server machine and parent directory of the file that contains this link's URL.

Why all the fuss about shorter URLs? Besides extending the life of your keyboard and eyesight, the main advantage of such minimal URLs is that they don't need to be changed if you ever move your pages to a new directory or server—the server and path are inferred when the page is used, not hardcoded into its HTML. The flipside of this can be fairly painful: examples that do include explicit site and pathnames in URLs embedded within HTML code cannot be copied to other servers without source code changes. Scripts can help here, but editing source code can be error-prone.[*]

---

[*] To make this process easier, the *fixsitename.py* script presented in the next section largely automates the necessary changes by performing global search-and-replace operations and directory walks. A few book examples do use complete URLs, so be sure to run this script after copying examples to a new site.

The downside of minimal URLs is that they don't trigger automatic Internet connection when followed. This becomes apparent only when you load pages from local files on your computer. For example, we can generally open HTML pages without connecting to the Internet at all, by pointing a web browser to a page's file that lives on the local machine (e.g., by clicking on its file icon). When browsing a page locally like this, following a fully specified URL makes the browser automatically connect to the Internet to fetch the referenced page or script. Minimal URLs, though, are opened on the local machine again; usually, the browser simply displays the referenced page or script's source code.

The net effect is that minimal URLs are more portable, but tend to work better when running all pages live on the Internet. To make it easier to work with the examples in this book, they will often omit the server and path components in URLs they contain. In this book, to derive a page or script's true URL from a minimal URL, imagine that the string:

```
http://starship.python.net/~lutz/subdir
```

appears before the filename given by the URL. Your browser will, even if you don't.

A First CGI Script

The HTML file we just saw is just that—an HTML file, not a CGI script. When referenced by a browser, the remote web server simply sends back the file's text to produce a new page in the browser. To illustrate the nature of CGI scripts, let's recode the example as a Python CGI program, as shown in Example 12-2.

Example 12-2. PP2E\Internet\Cgi-Web\Basics\test0.cgi

```
#!/usr/bin/python
#####################################################
# runs on the server, prints html to create a new page;
# executable permissions, stored in ~lutz/public_html,
# url=http://starship.python.net/~lutz/Basics/test0.cgi
#####################################################

print "Content-type: text/html\n"
print "<TITLE>CGI 101</TITLE>"
print "<H1>A First CGI script</H1>"
print "<P>Hello, CGI World!</P>"
```

This file, *test0.cgi*, makes the same sort of page if you point your browser at it (simply replace *.html* with *.cgi* in the URL). But it's a very different kind of animal—it's an *executable program* that is run on the server in response to your access request. It's also a completely legal Python program, in which the page's HTML is printed dynamically, rather than being precoded in a static file. In fact, there is little that is

CGI-specific about this Python program at all; if run from the system command line, it simply prints HTML rather than generating a browser page:

```
C:\...\PP2E\Internet\Cgi-Web\Basics>python test0.cgi
Content-type: text/html

<TITLE>CGI 101</TITLE>
<H1>A First CGI script</H1>
<P>Hello, CGI World!</P>
```

When run by the HTTP server program on a web server machine, however, the standard output stream is tied to a socket read by the browser on the client machine. In this context, all the output is sent across the Internet to your browser. As such, it must be formatted per the browser's expectations. In particular, when the script's output reaches your browser, the first printed line is interpreted as a header, describing the text that follows. There can be more than one header line in the printed response, but there must always be a blank line between the headers and the start of the HTML code (or other data).

In this script, the first header line tells the browser that the rest of the transmission is HTML text (*text/html*), and the newline character (\n) at the end of the first **print** statement generates one more line-feed than the **print** statement itself. The rest of this program's output is standard HTML and is used by the browser to generate a web page on a client, exactly as if the HTML lived in a static HTML file on the server.[*]

CGI scripts are accessed just like HTML files: you either type the full URL of this script into your browser's address field, or click on the *test0.cgi* link line in the examples root page (which follows a minimal hyperlink that resolves to the script's full URL). Figure 12-3 shows the result page generated if you point your browser at this script to make it go.

Installing CGI scripts

Like HTML files, CGI scripts are simple text files that you can either create on your local machine and upload to the server by FTP, or write with a text editor running directly on the server machine (perhaps using a telnet client). However, because CGI scripts are run as programs, they have some unique installation requirements that differ from simple HTML files. In particular, they usually must be stored and named specially, and they must be configured as programs that are executable by arbitrary users. Depending on your needs, CGI scripts may also need help finding

---

[*] Notice that the script does not generate the enclosing <HEAD> and <BODY> tags in the static HTML file of the prior section. Strictly speaking, it should—HTML without such tags is invalid. But all commonly used browsers simply ignore the omission.

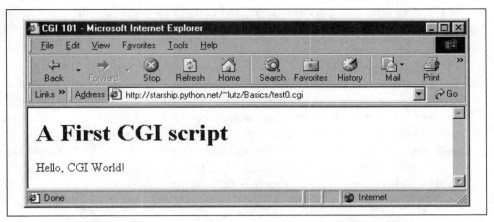

Figure 12-3. A simple web page from a CGI script

imported modules and may need to be converted to the server platform's text file format after being uploaded. Let's look at each install constraint in more depth:

Directory and filename conventions

First of all, CGI scripts need to be placed in a directory that your web server recognizes as a program directory, and they need to be given a name that your server recognizes as a CGI script. On the server where these examples reside, CGI scripts can be stored in each user's *public_html* directory just like HTML files, but must have a filename ending in a *.cgi* suffix, not *.py*. Some servers allow *.py* filename suffixes too, and may recognize other program directories (*cgi-bin* is common), but this varies widely, too, and can sometimes be configured per server or user.

Execution conventions

Because they must be executed by the web server on behalf of arbitrary users on the Web, CGI script files also need to be given executable file permissions to mark them as programs, and they must be made executable by others. Again, a shell command `chmod 0755 `*filename* does the trick on most servers. CGI scripts also generally need the special `#!` line at the top, to identify the Python interpreter that runs the file's code. The text after the `#!` in the first line simply gives the directory path to the Python executable on your server machine. See Chapter 2, *System Tools*, for more details on this special first line, and be sure to check your server's conventions for more details on non-Unix platforms.

One subtlety worth noting. As we saw earlier in the book, the special first line in executable text files can normally contain either a hardcoded path to the Python interpreter (e.g., *#!/usr/bin/python*) or an invocation of the **env** program (e.g., *#!/usr/bin/env python*), which deduces where Python lives from environment variable settings (i.e., your $PATH). The **env** trick is less useful in

CGI scripts, though, because their environment settings are those of user "nobody" (not your own), as explained in the next paragraph.

Module search path configuration (optional)

HTTP servers generally run CGI scripts with username "nobody" for security reasons (this limits the user's access to the server machine). That's why files you publish on the Web must have special permission settings that make them accessible to other users. It also means that CGI scripts can't rely on the Python module search path to be configured in any particular way. As we've seen, the module path is normally initialized from the user's PYTHONPATH setting plus defaults. But because CGI scripts are run by user "nobody", PYTHONPATH may be arbitrary when a CGI script runs.

Before you puzzle over this too hard, you should know that this is often not a concern in practice. Because Python usually searches the current directory for imported modules by default, this is not an issue if all of your scripts and any modules and packages they use are stored in your web directory (which is the installation structure on the book's site). But if the module lives elsewhere, you may need to tweak the `sys.path` list in your scripts to adjust the search path manually before imports (e.g., with `sys.path.append(dirname)` calls, index assignments, and so on).

End-of-line conventions (optional)

Finally, on some Unix (and Linux) servers, you might also have to make sure that your script text files follow the Unix end-of-line convention (\n), not DOS (\r\n). This isn't an issue if you edit and debug right on the server (or on another Unix machine) or FTP files one by one in text mode. But if you edit and upload your scripts from a PC to a Unix server in a tar file (or in FTP binary mode), you may need to convert end-of-lines after the upload. For instance, the server that was used to develop this text returns a default error page for scripts whose end-of-lines are in DOS format (see later in this chapter for a converter script).

This installation process may sound a bit complex at first glance, but it's not bad once you've worked through it on your own: it's only a concern at install time and can usually be automated to some extent with Python scripts run on the server. To summarize, most Python CGI scripts are text files of Python code, which:

- Are named according to your web server's conventions (e.g., *file.cgi*)

- Are stored in a directory recognized by your web server (e.g., *cgi-bin/*)

- Are given executable file permissions (e.g., `chmod 755 file.cgi`)

- Usually have the special `#!pythonpath` line at the top (but not **env**)

- Configure `sys.path` only if needed to see modules in other directories

- Use Unix end-of-line conventions, only if your server rejects DOS format

- Print headers and HTML to generate a response page in the browser, if any

- Use the `cgi` module to parse incoming form data, if any (more about forms later in this chapter)

Even if you must use a server machine configured by someone else, most of the machine's conventions should be easy to root out. For instance, on some servers you can rename this example to *test0.py* and it will continue to be run when accessed. On others, you might instead see the file's source code in a popped-up text editor when you access it. Try a *.cgi* suffix if the text is displayed rather than executed. CGI directory conventions can vary, too, but try the directory where you normally store HTML files first. As usual, you should consult the conventions for any machine that you plan to copy these example files to.

Automating installation steps

But wait—why do things the hard way? Before you start installing scripts by hand, remember that Python programs can usually do much of your work for you. It's easy to write Python scripts that automate some of the CGI installation steps using the operating systems tools that we met earlier in the book.

For instance, while developing the examples in this chapter, I did all editing on my PC (it's generally more dependable than a telnet client). To install, I put all the examples in a `tar` file, which is uploaded to the Linux server by FTP in a single step. Unfortunately, my server expects CGI scripts to have Unix (not DOS) end-of-line markers; unpacking the `tar` file did not convert end-of-lines or retain executable permission settings. But rather than tracking down all the web CGI scripts and fixing them by hand, I simply run the Python script in Example 12-3 from within a Unix *find* command after each upload.

Example 12-3. PP2E\Internet\Cgi-Web\fixcgi.py

```
#######################################################################
# run fom a unix find command to automate some cgi script install steps;
# example:  find . -name "*.cgi" -print -exec python fixcgi.py \{} \;
# which converts all cgi scripts to unix line-feed format (needed on
# starship) and gives all cgi files executable mode, else won't be run;
# do also: chmod 777 PyErrata/DbaseFiles/*, vi Extern/Email/mailconfig*;
# related: fixsitename.py, PyTools/fixeoln*.py, System/Filetools
#######################################################################

# after: ungzip, untar, cp -r Cgi-Web/* ~/public_html

import sys, string, os
fname = sys.argv[1]
old   = open(fname, 'rb').read()
new   = string.replace(old, '\r\n', '\n')
open(fname, 'wb').write(new)
if fname[-3:] == 'cgi': os.chmod(fname, 0755)        # note octal int: rwx,sgo
```

This script is kicked off at the top of the *Cgi-Web* directory, using a Unix `csh` shell command to apply it to every CGI file in a directory tree, like this:

```
% find . -name "*.cgi" -print -exec python fixcgi.py \{} \;
./Basics/languages-src.cgi
./Basics/getfile.cgi
./Basics/languages.cgi
./Basics/languages2.cgi
./Basics/languages2reply.cgi
./Basics/putfile.cgi
...more...
```

Recall from Chapter 2 that there are various ways to walk directory trees and find matching files in pure Python code, including the `find` module, `os.path.walk`, and one we'll use in the next section's script. For instance, a pure Python and more portable alternative could be kicked off like this:

```
C:\...\PP2E\Internet\Cgi-Web>python
>>> import os
>>> from PP2E.PyTools.find import find
>>> for filename in find('*.cgi', '.'):
...     print filename
...     stat = os.system('python fixcgi.py ' + filename)
...
.\Basics\getfile.cgi
.\Basics\languages-src.cgi
.\Basics\languages.cgi
.\Basics\languages2.cgi
...more...
```

The Unix *find* command simply does the same, but outside the scope of Python: the command line after –exec is run for each matching file found. For more details about the `find` command, see its manpage. Within the Python script, `string.replace` translates to Unix end-of-line markers, and `os.chmod` works just like a shell *chmod* command. There are other ways to translate end-of-lines, too; see Chapter 5, *Larger System Examples II*.

Automating site move edits

Speaking of installation tasks, a common pitfall of web programming is that hard-coded site names embedded in HTML code stop working the minute you relocate the site to a new server. Minimal URLs (just the filename) are more portable, but for various reasons are not always used. Somewhere along the way, I also grew tired of updating URLs in hyperlinks and form actions, and wrote a Python script to do it all for me (see Example 12-4).

Example 12-4. PP2E\Internet\Cgi-Web\fixsitename.py

```
#!/usr/bin/env python
#############################################################
# run this script in Cgi-Web dir after copying book web
# examples to a new server--automatically changes all starship
```

Example 12-4. PP2E\Internet\Cgi-Web\fixsitename.py (continued)

```
# server references in hyperlinks and form action tags to the
# new server/site; warns about references that weren't changed
# (may need manual editing); note that starship references are
# not usually needed or used--since browsers have memory, server
# and path can usually be omitted from a URL in the prior page
# if it lives at the same place (e.g., "file.cgi" is assumed to
# be in the same server/path as a page that contains this name,
# with a real url like "http://lastserver/lastpath/file.cgi"),
# but a handful of URLs are fully specified in book examples;
# reuses the Visitor class developed in the system chapters,
# to visit and convert all files at and below current dir;
#############################################################

import os, string
from PP2E.PyTools.visitor import FileVisitor        # os.path.walk wrapper

listonly = 0
oldsite  = 'starship.python.net/~lutz'              # server/rootdir in book
newsite  = 'XXXXXX/YYYYYY'                           # change to your site
warnof   = ['starship.python', 'lutz']              # warn if left after fix
fixext   = ['.py', '.html', '.cgi']                 # file types to check

class FixStarship(FileVisitor):
    def __init__(self, listonly=0):                 # replace oldsite refs
        FileVisitor.__init__(self, listonly=listonly)  # in all web text files
        self.changed, self.warning = [], []         # need diff lists here
    def visitfile(self, fname):                     # or use find.find list
        FileVisitor.visitfile(self, fname)
        if self.listonly:
            return
        if os.path.splitext(fname)[1] in fixext:
            text = open(fname, 'r').read()
            if string.find(text, oldsite) != -1:
                text = string.replace(text, oldsite, newsite)
                open(fname, 'w').write(text)
                self.changed.append(fname)
            for word in warnof:
                if string.find(text, word) != -1:
                    self.warning.append(fname); break

if __name__ == '__main__':
    # don't run auto if clicked
    go = raw_input('This script changes site in all web files; continue?')
    if go != 'y':
        raw_input('Canceled - hit enter key')
    else:
        walker = FixStarship(listonly)
        walker.run()
        print 'Visited %d files and %d dirs' % (walker.fcount, walker.dcount)

        def showhistory(label, flist):
            print '\n%s in %d files:' % (label, len(flist))
```

Example 12-4. PP2E\Internet\Cgi-Web\fixsitename.py (continued)

```
        for fname in flist:
            print '=>', fname
    showhistory('Made changes', walker.changed)
    showhistory('Saw warnings', walker.warning)

    def edithistory(flist):
        for fname in flist:                        # your editor here
            os.system('vi ' + fname)
    if raw_input('Edit changes?') == 'y':  edithistory(walker.changed)
    if raw_input('Edit warnings?') == 'y': edithistory(walker.warning)
```

This is a more complex script that reuses the *visitor.py* module we wrote in
Chapter 5 to wrap the `os.path.walk` call. If you read that chapter, this script will
make sense. If not, we won't go into many more details here again. Suffice it to
say that this program visits all source code files at and below the directory where
it is run, globally changing all *starship.python.net/~lutz* appearances to whatever
you've assigned to variable `newsite` within the script. On request, it will also
launch your editor to view files changed, as well as files that contain potentially
suspicious strings. As coded, it launches the Unix vi text editor at the end, but you
can change this to start whatever editor you like (this is Python, after all):

```
C:\...\PP2E\Internet\Cgi-Web>python fixsitename.py
This script changes site in all web files; continue?y
. ...
1 => .\PyInternetDemos.html
2 => .\README.txt
3 => .\fixcgi.py
4 => .\fixsitename.py
5 => .\index.html
6 => .\python_snake_ora.gif
.\Basics ...
7 => .\Basics\mlutz.jpg
8 => .\Basics\languages.html
9 => .\Basics\languages-src.cgi
...more...
146 => .\PyMailCgi\temp\secret.doc.txt
Visited 146 files and 16 dirs

Made changes in 8 files:
=> .\fixsitename.py
=> .\Basics\languages.cgi
=> .\Basics\test3.html
=> .\Basics\test0.py
=> .\Basics\test0.cgi
=> .\Basics\test5c.html
=> .\PyMailCgi\commonhtml.py
=> .\PyMailCgi\sendurl.py

Saw warnings in 14 files:
=> .\PyInternetDemos.html
=> .\fixsitename.py
```

```
=> .\index.html
=> .\Basics\languages.cgi
...more...
=> .\PyMailCgi\pymailcgi.html
=> .\PyMailCgi\commonhtml.py
=> .\PyMailCgi\sendurl.py
Edit changes?n
Edit warnings?y
```

The net effect is that this script automates part of the site relocation task: running it will update all pages' URLs for the new site name automatically, which is considerably less aggravating than manually hunting down and editing each such reference by hand.

There aren't many hardcoded *starship* site references in web examples in this book (the script found and fixed eight above), but be sure to run this script in the *Cgi-Web* directory from a command line, after copying the book examples to your own site. To use this script for other site moves, simply set both `oldsite` and `newsite` as appropriate. The truly ambitious scriptmaster might even run such a script from within another that first copies a site's contents by FTP (see `ftplib` in the previous chapter).*

Finding Python on the server

One last install pointer: even though Python doesn't have to be installed on any *clients* in the context of a server-side web application, it does have to exist on the *server* machine where your CGI scripts are expected to run. If you are using a web server that you did not configure yourself, you must be sure that Python lives on that machine. Moreover, you need to find where it is on that machine so that you can specify its path in the `#!` line at the top of your script.

By now, Python is a pervasive tool, so this generally isn't as big a concern as it once was. As time goes by, it will become even more common to find Python as a standard component of server machines. But if you're not sure if or where Python lives on yours, here are some tips:

* Especially on Unix systems, you should first assume that Python lives in a standard place (e.g., */usr/local/bin/python*), and see if it works. Chances are that Python already lives on such machines. If you have Telnet access on your server, a Unix *find* command starting at */usr* may help.

---

* As I mentioned at the start of this chapter, there are often multiple ways to accomplish any given webmaster-y task. For instance, the HTML `<BASE>` tag may provide an alternative way to map absolute URLs, and FTPing your web site files to your server individually and in text mode might obviate line-end issues. There are undoubtedly other ways to handle such tasks, too. On the other hand, such alternatives wouldn't be all that useful in a book that illustrates Python coding techniques.

- If your server runs Linux, you're probably set to go. Python ships as a standard part of Linux distributions these days, and many web sites and Internet Service Providers (ISPs) run the Linux operating system; at such sites, Python probably already lives at */usr/bin/python*.

- In other environments where you cannot control the server machine yourself, it may be harder to obtain access to an already-installed Python. If so, you can relocate your site to a server that does have Python installed, talk your ISP into installing Python on the machine you're trying to use, or install Python on the server machine yourself.

If your ISP is unsympathetic to your need for Python and you are willing to relocate your site to one that is, you can find lists of Python-friendly ISPs by searching *http://www.python.org*. And if you choose to install Python on your server machine yourself, be sure to check out the *freeze* tool shipped with the Python source distribution (in the *Tools* directory). With *freeze*, you can create a single executable program file that contains the entire Python interpreter, as well as all the standard library modules. Such a frozen interpreter can be uploaded to your web account by FTP in a single step, and it won't require a full-blown Python installation on the server.

Adding Pictures and Generating Tables

Now let's get back to writing server-side code. As anyone who's ever surfed the Web knows, web pages usually consist of more than simple text. Example 12-5 is a Python CGI script that prints an <IMG> HTML tag in its output to produce a graphic image in the client browser. There's not much Python-specific about this example, but note that just as for simple HTML files, the image file (*ppsmall.gif*) lives on and is downloaded from the server machine when the browser interprets the output of this script.

Example 12-5. PP2E\Internet\Cgi-Web\Basics\test1.cgi

```
#!/usr/bin/python

text = """Content-type: text/html

<TITLE>CGI 101</TITLE>
<H1>A Second CGI script</H1>
<HR>
<P>Hello, CGI World!</P>
<IMG src="ppsmall.gif" BORDER=1 ALT=[image]>
<HR>
"""

print text
```

Notice the use of the triple-quoted string block here; the entire HTML string is sent to the browser in one fell swoop, with the print statement at the end. If client and server are both functional, a page that looks like Figure 12-4 will be generated when this script is referenced and run.

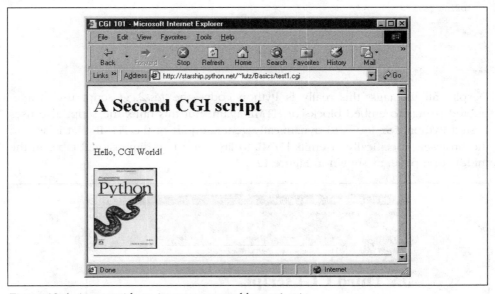

Figure 12-4. A page with an image generated by test1.cgi

So far, our CGI scripts have been putting out canned HTML that could have just as easily been stored in an HTML file. But because CGI scripts are executable programs, they can also be used to generate HTML on the fly, dynamically—even, possibly, in response to a particular set of user inputs sent to the script. That's the whole purpose of CGI scripts, after all. Let's start using this to better advantage now, and write a Python script that builds up response HTML programmatically (see Example 12-6).

Example 12-6. PP2E\Internet\Cgi-Web\Basics\test2.cgi

```
#!/usr/bin/python

print """Content-type: text/html

<TITLE>CGI 101</TITLE>
<H1>A Third CGI script</H1>
<HR>
<P>Hello, CGI World!</P>

<table border=1>
"""
```

Example 12-6. PP2E\Internet\Cgi-Web\Basics\test2.cgi (continued)

```
for i in range(5):
    print "<tr>"
    for j in range(4):
        print "<td>%d.%d</td>" % (i, j)
    print "</tr>"

print """
</table>
<HR>
"""
```

Despite all the tags, this really is Python code—the *test2.cgi* script uses triple-quoted strings to embed blocks of HTML again. But this time, the script also uses nested Python `for` loops to dynamically generate part of the HTML that is sent to the browser. Specifically, it emits HTML to lay out a two-dimensional table in the middle of a page, as shown in Figure 12-5.

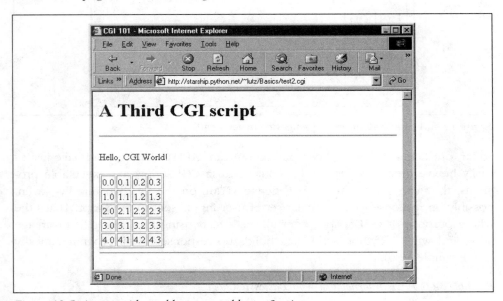

Figure 12-5. A page with a table generated by test2.cgi

Each row in the table displays a "row.column" pair, as generated by the executing Python script. If you're curious how the generated HTML looks, select your browser's View Source option after you've accessed this page. It's a single HTML page composed of the HTML generated by the first `print` in the script, then the `for` loops, and finally the last `print`. In other words, the concatenation of this script's output is an HTML document with headers.

Table tags

This script generates HTML table tags. Again, we're not out to learn HTML here, but we'll take a quick look just so you can make sense of the example. Tables are declared by the text between `<table>` and `</table>` tags in HTML. Typically, a table's text in turn declares the contents of each table row between `<tr>` and `</tr>` tags and each column within a row between `<td>` and `</td>` tags. The loops in our script build up HTML to declare five rows of four columns each, by printing the appropriate tags, with the current row and column number as column values. For instance, here is part of the script's output, defining the first two rows:

```
<table border=1>
<tr>
<td>0.0</td>
<td>0.1</td>
<td>0.2</td>
<td>0.3</td>
</tr>
<tr>
<td>1.0</td>
<td>1.1</td>
<td>1.2</td>
<td>1.3</td>
</tr>
. . .
</table>
```

Other table tags and options let us specify a row title (`<th>`), layout borders, and so on. We'll see more table syntax put to use to lay out forms in a later section.

Adding User Interaction

CGI scripts are great at generating HTML on the fly like this, but they are also commonly used to implement interaction with a user typing at a web browser. As described earlier in this chapter, web interactions usually involve a two-step process and two distinct web pages: you fill out a form page and press submit, and a reply page eventually comes back. In between, a CGI script processes the form input.

Submission

That description sounds simple enough, but the process of collecting user inputs requires an understanding of a special HTML tag, `<form>`. Let's look at the implementation of a simple web interaction to see forms at work. First off, we need to define a form page for the user to fill out, as shown in Example 12-7.

Example 12-7. PP2E\Internet\Cgi-Web\Basics\test3.html

```
<html><body>
<title>CGI 101</title>
<H1>A first user interaction: forms</H1>
<hr>
<form method=POST action="http://starship.python.net/~lutz/Basics/test3.cgi">
    <P><B>Enter your name:</B>
    <P><input type=text name=user>
    <P><input type=submit>
</form>
</BODY></HTML>
```

test3.html is a simple HTML file, not a CGI script (though its contents could be printed from a script as well). When this file is accessed, all the text between its <form> and </form> tags generate the input fields and Submit button shown in Figure 12-6.

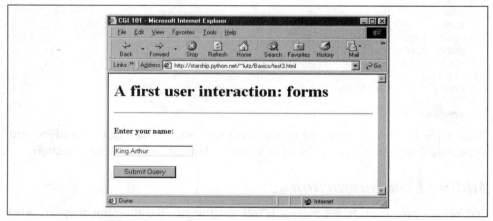

Figure 12-6. A simple form page generated by test3.html

More on form tags

We won't go into all the details behind coding HTML forms, but a few highlights are worth underscoring. Within a form's HTML code:

- The form's action option gives the URL of a CGI script that will be invoked to process submitted form data. This is the link from a form to its handler program—in this case, a program called *test3.cgi* in my web home directory, on a server machine called *starship.python.net*. The action option is the moral equivalent to command options in Tkinter buttons—it's where a callback handler (here, a remote handler) is registered to the browser.

- Input controls are specified with nested <input> tags. In this example, input tags have two key options. The type option accepts values such as text for text fields and submit for a Submit button (which sends data to the server and is labeled "Submit Query" by default). The *name* option is the hook used to identify the entered value by key, once all the form data reaches the server. For instance, the server-side CGI script we'll see in a moment uses the string user as a key to get the data typed into this form's text field. As we'll see in later examples, other input tag options can specify initial values (value=X), display-only mode (readonly), and so on. Other input *type* option values may transmit hidden data (type=hidden), reinitialize fields (type=reset), or make multiple-choice buttons (type=checkbox).

- Forms also include a method option to specify the encoding style to be used to send data over a socket to the target server machine. Here, we use the post style, which contacts the server and then ships it a stream of user input data in a separate transmission. An alternative get style ships input information to the server in a single transmission step, by adding user inputs to the end of the URL used to invoke the script, usually after a ? character (more on this soon). With get, inputs typically show up on the server in environment variables or as arguments in the command line used to start the script. With post, they must be read from standard input and decoded. Luckily, Python's cgi module transparently handles either encoding style, so our CGI scripts don't need to know or care which is used.

Notice that the action URL in this example's form spells out the full address for illustration. Because the browser remembers where the enclosing HTML page came from, it works the same with just the script's filename, as shown in Example 12-8.

Example 12-8. PP2E\Internet\Cgi-Web\Basics\test3-minimal.html

```
<html><body>
<title>CGI 101</title>
<H1>A first user interaction: forms</H1>
<hr>
<form method=POST action="test3.cgi">
    <P><B>Enter your name:</B>
    <P><input type=text name=user>
    <P><input type=submit>
</form>
</BODY></HTML>
```

It may help to remember that URLs embedded in form action tags and hyperlinks are directions to the browser first, not the script. The *test3.cgi* script itself doesn't care which URL form is used to trigger it—minimal or complete. In fact, all parts of a URL through the script filename (and up to URL query parameters) is used in the conversation between browser and HTTP server, before a CGI script is ever spawned. As long as the browser knows which server to contact, the URL will work, but URLs outside of a page (e.g., typed into a browser's address field or sent to Python's urllib module) usually must be completely specified, because there is no notion of a prior page.

Response

So far, we've created only a static page with an input field. But the Submit button on this page is loaded to work magic. When pressed, it triggers the remote program whose URL is listed in the form's **action** option, and passes this program the input data typed by the user, according to the form's **method** encoding style option. On the server, a Python script is started to handle the form's input data while the user waits for a reply on the client, as shown in Example 12-9.

Example 12-9. PP2E\Internet\Cgi-Web\Basics\test3.cgi

```
#!/usr/bin/python
###################################################
# runs on the server, reads form input, prints html;
# url=http://server-name/root-dir/Basics/test3.cgi
###################################################

import cgi
form = cgi.FieldStorage()               # parse form data
print "Content-type: text/html"         # plus blank line

html = """
<TITLE>test3.cgi</TITLE>
<H1>Greetings</H1>
<HR>
<P>%s</P>
<HR>"""

if not form.has_key('user'):
    print html % "Who are you?"
else:
    print html % ("Hello, %s." % form['user'].value)
```

As before, this Python CGI script prints HTML to generate a response page in the client's browser. But this script does a bit more: it also uses the standard **cgi** module to parse the input data entered by the user on the prior web page (see Figure 12-6). Luckily, this is all automatic in Python: a call to the **cgi** module's **FieldStorage** class automatically does all the work of extracting form data from the input stream and environment variables, regardless of how that data was passed—in a **post** style stream or in **get** style parameters appended to the URL. Inputs sent in both styles look the same to Python scripts.

Scripts should call **cgi.FieldStoreage** only once and before accessing any field values. When called, we get back an object that looks like a dictionary—user input fields from the form (or URL) show up as values of keys in this object. For example, in the script, **form['user']** is an object whose **value** attribute is a string containing the text typed into the form's text field. If you flip back to the form page's HTML, you'll notice that the input field's **name** option was **user**—the name in the form's HTML has become a key we use to fetch the input's value from a dictionary. The object returned by **FieldStorage** supports other dictionary operations, too—for instance, the `has_key` method may be used to check if a field is present in the input data.

Before exiting, this script prints HTML to produce a result page that echoes back what the user typed into the form. Two string-formatting expressions (`%`) are used to insert the input text into a reply string, and the reply string into the triple-quoted HTML string block. The body of the script's output looks like this:

```
<TITLE>test3.cgi</TITLE>
<H1>Greetings</H1>
<HR>
<P>Hello, King Arthur.</P>
<HR>
```

In a browser, the output is rendered into a page like the one in Figure 12-7.

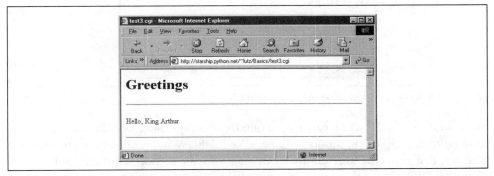

Figure 12-7. test3.cgi result for parameters in a form

Passing parameters in URLs

Notice that the URL address of the script that generated this page shows up at the top of the browser. We didn't type this URL itself—it came from the `action` tag of the prior page's `form` HTML. However, there is nothing stopping us from typing the script's URL explicitly in our browser's address field to invoke the script, just as we did for our earlier CGI script and HTML file examples.

But there's a catch here: where does the input field's value come from if there is no form page? That is, if we type the CGI script's URL ourselves, how does the input field get filled in? Earlier, when we talked about URL formats, I mentioned that the `get` encoding scheme tacks input parameters onto the end of URLs. When we type script addresses explicitly, we can also append input values on the end of URLs, where they serve the same purpose as `<input>` fields in forms. Moreover, the Python `cgi` module makes URL and form inputs look identical to scripts.

For instance, we can skip filling out the input form page completely, and directly invoke our *test3.cgi* script by visiting a URL of the form:

```
http://starship.python.net/~lutz/Basics/test3.cgi?user=Brian
```

In this URL, a value for the input named **user** is specified explicitly, as if the user had filled out the input page. When called this way, the only constraint is that the parameter name **user** must match the name expected by the script (and hard-coded in the form's HTML). We use just one parameter here, but in general, URL parameters are typically introduced with a **?** and followed by one or more **name=value** assignments, separated by **&** characters if there is more than one. Figure 12-8 shows the response page we get after typing a URL with explicit inputs.

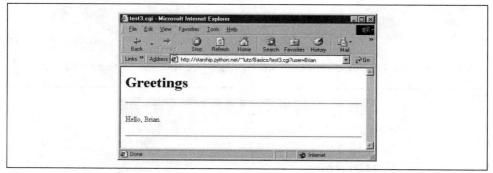

Figure 12-8. test3.cgi result for parameters in a URL

In general, any CGI script can be invoked either by filling out and submitting a form page or by passing inputs at the end of a URL. When CGI scripts are invoked with explicit input parameters this way, it's difficult to not see their similarity to *functions*, albeit ones that live remotely on the Net. Passing data to scripts in URLs is similar to keyword arguments in Python functions, both operationally and syntactically. In fact, in Chapter 15, we will meet a system called Zope that makes the relationship between URLs and Python function calls even more literal (URLs become more direct function calls).

Incidentally, if you clear out the name input field in the form input page (i.e., make it empty) and press submit, the **user** name field becomes empty. More accurately, the browser may not send this field along with the form data at all, even though it is listed in the form layout HTML. The CGI script detects such a missing field with the dictionary **has_key** method and produces the page captured in Figure 12-9 in response.

In general, CGI scripts must check to see if any inputs are missing, partly because they might not be typed by a user in the form, but also because there may be no form at all—input fields might not be tacked on to the end of an explicitly typed URL. For instance, if we type the script's URL without any parameters at all (i.e., omit the text **?** and beyond), we get this same error response page. Since we can invoke any CGI through a form or URL, scripts must anticipate both scenarios.

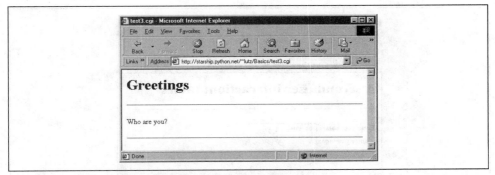

Figure 12-9. An empty name field produces an error page

Using Tables to Lay Out Forms

Now let's move on to something a bit more realistic. In most CGI applications, input pages are composed of multiple fields. When there is more than one, input labels and fields are typically laid out in a table, to give the form a well-structured appearance. The HTML file in Example 12-10 defines a form with two input fields.

Example 12-10. PP2E\Internet\Cgi-Web\Basics\test4.html

```
<html><body>
<title>CGI 101</title>
<H1>A second user interaction: tables</H1>
<hr>
<form method=POST action="test4.cgi">
  <table>
    <TR>
      <TH align=right>Enter your name:
      <TD><input type=text name=user>
    <TR>
      <TH align=right>Enter your age:
      <TD><input type=text name=age>
    <TR>
      <TD colspan=2 align=center>
      <input type=submit value="Send">
  </table>
</form>
</body></html>
```

The <TH> tag defines a column like <TD>, but also tags it as a header column, which generally means it is rendered in a bold font. By placing the input fields and labels in a table like this, we get an input page like that shown in Figure 12-10. Labels and inputs are automatically lined up vertically in columns much as they were by the Tkinter GUI geometry managers we met earlier in this book.

When this form's Submit button (labeled "Send" by the page's HTML) is pressed, it causes the script in Example 12-11 to be executed on the server machine, with the inputs typed by the user.

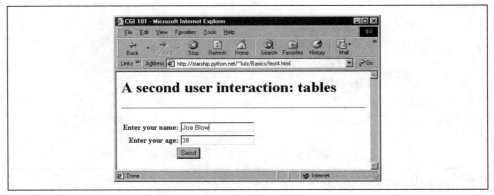

Figure 12-10. A form laid out with table tags

Example 12-11. PP2E\Internet\Cgi-Web\Basics\test4.cgi

```
#!/usr/bin/python
#####################################################
# runs on the server, reads form input, prints html;
# url http://server-name/root-dir/Basics/test4.cgi
#####################################################

import cgi, sys
sys.stderr = sys.stdout              # errors to browser
form = cgi.FieldStorage()            # parse form data
print "Content-type: text/html\n"    # plus blank line

# class dummy:
#     def __init__(self, s): self.value = s
# form = {'user': dummy('bob'), 'age':dummy('10')}

html = """
<TITLE>test4.cgi</TITLE>
<H1>Greetings</H1>
<HR>
<H4>%s</H4>
<H4>%s</H4>
<H4>%s</H4>
<HR>"""

if not form.has_key('user'):
    line1 = "Who are you?"
else:
    line1 = "Hello, %s." % form['user'].value

line2 = "You're talking to a %s server." % sys.platform

line3 = ""
if form.has_key('age'):
    try:
        line3 = "Your age squared is %d!" % (int(form['age'].value) ** 2)
    except:
```

Example 12-11. PP2E\Internet\Cgi-Web\Basics\test4.cgi (continued)

```
        line3 = "Sorry, I can't compute %s ** 2." % form['age'].value
print html % (line1, line2, line3)
```

The table layout comes from the HTML file, not this Python CGI script. In fact, this script doesn't do much new—it uses string formatting to plug input values into the response page's HTML triple-quoted template string as before, this time with one line per input field. There are, however, a few new tricks here worth noting, especially regarding CGI script debugging and security. We'll talk about them in the next two sections.

Converting strings in CGI scripts

Just for fun, the script echoes back the name of the server platform by fetching `sys.platform` along with the square of the `age` input field. Notice that the `age` input's value must be converted to an integer with the built-in `int` function; in the CGI world, all inputs arrive as strings. We could also convert to an integer with the built-in `string.atoi` or `eval` function. Conversion (and other) errors are trapped gracefully in a `try` statement to yield an error line, rather than letting our script die.

You should never use `eval` to convert strings that were sent over the Internet like the `age` field in this example, unless you can be absolutely sure that the string is not even potentially malicious code. For instance, if this example were available on the general Internet, it's not impossible that someone could type a value into the `age` field (or append an `age` parameter to the URL) with a value like: `os.system('rm *')`. When passed to `eval`, such a string might delete all the files in your server script directory!

We talk about ways to minimize this risk with Python's restricted execution mode (module `rexec`) in Chapter 15. But by default, strings read off the Net can be very bad things to say in CGI scripting. You should never pass them to dynamic coding tools like `eval` and `exec`, or to tools that run arbitrary shell commands such as `os. popen` and `os.system`, unless you can be sure that they are safe, or unless you enable Python's restricted execution mode in your scripts.

Debugging CGI scripts

Errors happen, even in the brave new world of the Internet. Generally speaking, debugging CGI scripts can be much more difficult than debugging programs that run on your local machine. Not only do errors occur on a remote machine, but scripts generally won't run without the context implied by the CGI model. The script in Example 12-11 demonstrates the following two common debugging tricks.

Error message trapping

This script assigns `sys.stderr` to `sys.stdout` so that Python error messages wind up being displayed in the response page in the browser. Normally, Python error messages are written to `stderr`. To route them to the browser, we must make `stderr` reference the same file object as `stdout` (which is connected to the browser in CGI scripts). If we don't do this assignment, Python errors, including program errors in our script, never show up in the browser.

Test case mock-up

The `dummy` class definition, commented out in this final version, was used to debug the script before it was installed on the Net. Besides not seeing `stderr` messages by default, CGI scripts also assume an enclosing context that does not exist if they are tested outside the CGI environment. For instance, if run from the system command line, this script has no form input data. Uncomment this code to test from the system command line. The `dummy` class masquerades as a parsed form field object, and `form` is assigned a dictionary containing two form field objects. The net effect is that `form` will be plug-and-play compatible with the result of a `cgi.FieldStorage` call. As usual in Python, object interfaces (not datatypes) are all we must adhere to.

Here are a few general tips for debugging your server-side CGI scripts:

Run the script from the command line.

It probably won't generate HTML as is, but running it standalone will detect any syntax errors in your code. Recall that a Python command line can run source code files regardless of their extension: e.g., `python somescript.cgi` works fine.

Assign sys.stderr to sys.stdout as early as possible in your script.

This will make the text of Python error messages and stack dumps appear in your client browser when accessing the script. In fact, short of wading through server logs, this may be the only way to see the text of error messages after your script aborts.

Mock up inputs to simulate the enclosing CGI context.

For instance, define classes that mimic the CGI inputs interface (as done with the `dummy` class in this script), so that you can view the script's output for various test cases by running it from the system command line.[*] Setting environment variables to mimic form or URL inputs sometimes helps, too (we'll see how later in this chapter).

---

[*] This technique isn't unique to CGI scripts, by the way. In Chapter 15, we'll meet systems that embed Python code inside HTML. There is no good way to test such code outside the context of the enclosing system, without extracting the embedded Python code (perhaps by using the `htmllib` HTML parser that comes with Python) and running it with a passed-in mock-up of the API that it will eventually use.

Call utilities to display CGI context in the browser.

The CGI module includes utility functions that send a formatted dump of CGI environment variables and input values to the browser (e.g., `cgi.test`, `cgi.print_form`). Sometimes, this is enough to resolve connection problems. We'll use some of these in the mailer case study in the next chapter.

Show exceptions you catch.

If you catch an exception that Python raises, the Python error message won't be printed to `stderr` (that is simply the default behavior). In such cases, it's up to your script to display the exception's name and value in the response page; exception details are available in the built-in `sys` module. We'll use this in a later example, too.

Run it live.

Of course, once your script is at least half working, your best bet is likely to start running it live on the server, with real inputs coming from a browser.

When this script is run by submitting the input form page, its output produces the new reply page shown in Figure 12-11.

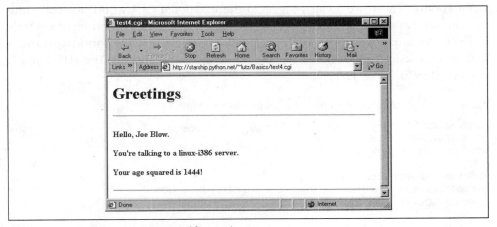

Figure 12-11. Reply page generated by test4.cgi

As usual, we can pass parameters to this CGI script at the end of a URL, too. Figure 12-12 shows the page we get when passing a **user** and **age** explicitly in the URL. Notice that we have two parameters after the **?** this time; we separate them with **&**. Also note that we've specified a blank space in the **user** value with **+**. This is a common URL encoding convention. On the server side, the **+** is automatically replaced with a space again. It's also part of the standard escape rule for URL strings, which we'll revisit later.

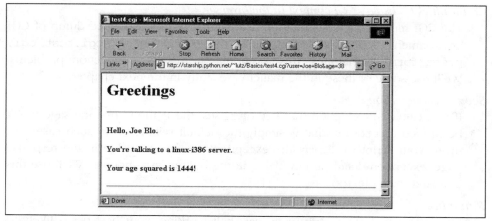

Figure 12-12. Reply page generated by test4.cgi for parameters in URL

Adding Common Input Devices

So far, we've been typing inputs into text fields. HTML forms support a handful of input controls (what we'd call widgets in the traditional GUI world) for collecting user inputs. Let's look at a CGI program that shows all the common input controls at once. As usual, we define both an HTML file to lay out the form page and a Python CGI script to process its inputs and generate a response. The HTML file is presented in Example 12-12.

Example 12-12. PP2E\Internet\Cgi-Web\Basics\test5a.html

```
<HTML><BODY>
<TITLE>CGI 101</TITLE>
<H1>Common input devices</H1>
<HR>
<FORM method=POST action="test5.cgi">
  <H3>Please complete the following form and click Send</H3>
  <P><TABLE>
    <TR>
      <TH align=right>Name:
      <TD><input type=text name=name>
    <TR>
      <TH align=right>Shoe size:
      <TD><table>
      <td><input type=radio name=shoesize value=small>Small
      <td><input type=radio name=shoesize value=medium>Medium
      <td><input type=radio name=shoesize value=large>Large
      </table>
    <TR>
      <TH align=right>Occupation:
      <TD><select name=job>
        <option>Developer
        <option>Manager
```

Example 12-12. PP2E\Internet\Cgi-Web\Basics\test5a.html (continued)

```
        <option>Student
        <option>Evangelist
        <option>Other
      </select>
    <TR>
      <TH align=right>Political affiliations:
      <TD><table>
      <td><input type=checkbox name=language value=Python>Pythonista
      <td><input type=checkbox name=language value=Perl>Perlmonger
      <td><input type=checkbox name=language value=Tcl>Tcler
      </table>
    <TR>
      <TH align=right>Comments:
      <TD><textarea name=comment cols=30 rows=2>Enter text here</textarea>
    <TR>
      <TD colspan=2 align=center>
      <input type=submit value="Send">
  </TABLE>
</FORM>
<HR>
</BODY></HTML>
```

When rendered by a browser, the page in Figure 12-13 appears.

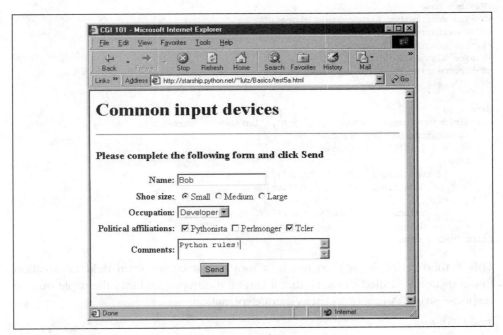

Figure 12-13. Form page generated by test5a.html

This page contains a simple text field as before, but it also has radiobuttons, a pull-down selection list, a set of multiple-choice checkbuttons, and a multiple-line text input area. All have a **name** option in the HTML file, which identifies their selected value in the data sent from client to server. When we fill out this form and click the Send submit button, the script in Example 12-13 runs on the server to process all the input data typed or selected in the form.

Example 12-13. PP2E\Internet\Cgi-Web\Basics\test5.cgi

```python
#!/usr/bin/python
#####################################################
# runs on the server, reads form input, prints html;
# url=http://server-name/root-dir/Basics/test5.cgi
#####################################################

import cgi, sys, string
form = cgi.FieldStorage()              # parse form data
print "Content-type: text/html"        # plus blank line

html = """
<TITLE>test5.cgi</TITLE>
<H1>Greetings</H1>
<HR>
<H4>Your name is %(name)s</H4>
<H4>You wear rather %(shoesize)s shoes</H4>
<H4>Your current job: %(job)s</H4>
<H4>You program in %(language)s</H4>
<H4>You also said:</H4>
<P>%(comment)s</P>
<HR>"""

data = {}
for field in ['name', 'shoesize', 'job', 'language', 'comment']:
    if not form.has_key(field):
        data[field] = '(unknown)'
    else:
        if type(form[field]) != type([]):
            data[field] = form[field].value
        else:
            values = map(lambda x: x.value, form[field])
            data[field] = string.join(values, ' and ')
print html % data
```

This Python script doesn't do much; it mostly just copies form field information into a dictionary called **data**, so that it can be easily plugged into the triple-quoted response string. A few of its tricks merit explanation:

Field validation

> As usual, we need to check all expected fields to see if they really are present in the input data, using the dictionary **has_key** method. Any or all of the input fields may be missing if they weren't entered on the form or appended to an explicit URL.

String formatting

We're using dictionary key references in the format string this time—recall that %(name)s means pull out the value for key name in the data dictionary and perform a to-string conversion on its value.

Multiple-choice fields

We're also testing the type of all the expected fields' values to see if they arrive as a list instead of the usual string. Values of multiple-choice input controls, like the language choice field in this input page, are returned from cgi.FieldStorage as a list of objects with value attributes, rather than a simple single object with a value. This script copies simple field values to the dictionary verbatim, but uses map to collect the value fields of multiple-choice selections, and string.join to construct a single string with an and inserted between each selection value (e.g., Python and Tcl).*

When the form page is filled out and submitted, the script creates the response shown in Figure 12-14—essentially just a formatted echo of what was sent.

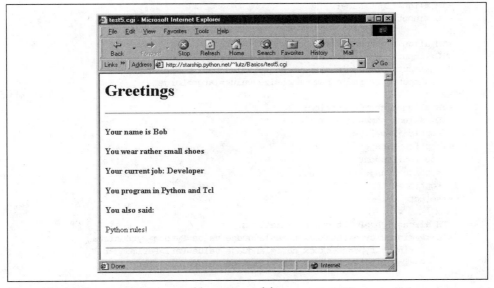

Figure 12-14. Response page created by test5.cgi (1)

Changing input layouts

Suppose that you've written a system like this, and your users, clients, and significant other start complaining that the input form is difficult to read. Don't worry.

---

* Two forward references are worth noting here. Besides simple strings and lists, later we'll see a third type of form input object, returned for fields that specify file uploads. The script in this example should really also escape the echoed text inserted into the HTML reply to be robust, lest it contain HTML operators. We will discuss escapes in detail later.

Because the CGI model naturally separates the *user interface* (the HTML page definition) from the *processing logic* (the CGI script), it's completely painless to change
the form's layout. Simply modify the HTML file; there's no need to change the CGI
code at all. For instance, Example 12-14 contains a new definition of the input that
uses tables a bit differently to provide a nicer layout with borders.

Example 12-14. PP2E\Internet\Cgi-Web\Basics\test5b.html

```
<HTML><BODY>
<TITLE>CGI 101</TITLE>
<H1>Common input devices: alternative layout</H1>
<P>Use the same test5.cgi server side script, but change the
layout of the form itself.  Notice the separation of user interface
and processing logic here; the CGI script is independent of the
HTML used to interact with the user/client.</P><HR>

<FORM method=POST action="test5.cgi">
  <H3>Please complete the following form and click Submit</H3>
  <P><TABLE border cellpadding=3>
    <TR>
      <TH align=right>Name:
      <TD><input type=text name=name>
    <TR>
      <TH align=right>Shoe size:
      <TD><input type=radio name=shoesize value=small>Small
          <input type=radio name=shoesize value=medium>Medium
          <input type=radio name=shoesize value=large>Large
    <TR>
      <TH align=right>Occupation:
      <TD><select name=job>
        <option>Developer
        <option>Manager
        <option>Student
        <option>Evangelist
        <option>Other
      </select>
    <TR>
      <TH align=right>Political affiliations:
      <TD><P><input type=checkbox name=language value=Python>Pythonista
          <P><input type=checkbox name=language value=Perl>Perlmonger
          <P><input type=checkbox name=language value=Tcl>Tcler
    <TR>
      <TH align=right>Comments:
      <TD><textarea name=comment cols=30 rows=2>Enter spam here</textarea>
    <TR>
      <TD colspan=2 align=center>
      <input type=submit value="Submit">
      <input type=reset  value="Reset">
  </TABLE>
</FORM>
</BODY></HTML>
```

When we visit this alternative page with a browser, we get the interface shown in Figure 12-15.

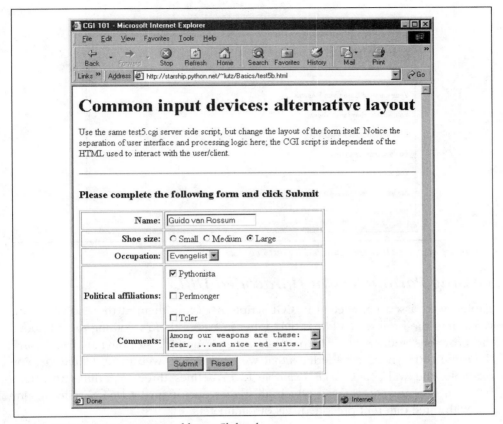

Figure 12-15. Form page created by test5b.html

Now, before you go blind trying to detect the differences in this and the prior HTML file, I should note that the HTML differences that produce this page are much less important than the fact that the action fields in these two pages' forms reference identical URLs. Pressing this version's Submit button triggers the exact same and totally unchanged Python CGI script again, *test5.cgi* (Example 12-13).

That is, scripts are completely independent of the layout of the user-interface used to send them information. Changes in the response page require changing the script, of course; but we can change the input page's HTML as much as we like, without impacting the server-side Python code. Figure 12-16 shows the response page produced by the script this time around.

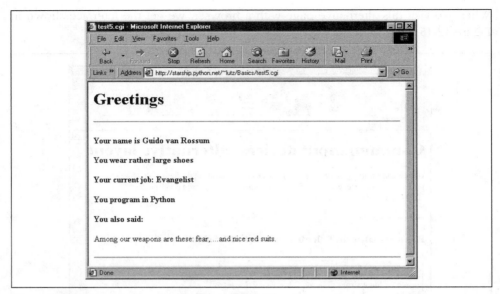

Figure 12-16. Response page created by test5.cgi (2)

Passing Parameters in Hardcoded URLs

Earlier, we passed parameters to CGI scripts by listing them at the end of a URL typed into the browser's address field (after a ?). But there's nothing sacred about the browser's address field. In particular, there's nothing stopping us from using the same URL syntax in hyperlinks that we hardcode in web page definitions. For example, the web page from Example 12-15 defines three hyperlinks (the text between <A> and </A> tags), which all trigger our original *test5.cgi* script again, but with three different precoded sets of parameters.

Example 12-15. PP2E\Internet\Cgi-Web\Basics\test5c.html

```
<HTML><BODY>
<TITLE>CGI 101</TITLE>
<H1>Common input devices: URL parameters</H1>

<P>This demo invokes the test5.cgi server-side script again,
but hardcodes input data to the end of the script's URL,
within a simple hyperlink (instead of packaging up a form's
inputs).  Click your browser's "show page source" button
to view the links associated with each list item below.

<P>This is really more about CGI than Python, but notice that
Python's cgi module handles both this form of input (which is
also produced by GET form actions), as well as POST-ed forms;
they look the same to the Python CGI script.  In other words,
cgi module users are independent of the method used to submit
data.
```

Example 12-15. PP2E\Internet\Cgi-Web\Basics\test5c.html (continued)

```
<P>Also notice that URLs with appended input values like this
can be generated as part of the page output by another CGI script,
to direct a next user click to the right place and context; together
with type 'hidden' input fields, they provide one way to
save state between clicks.
</P><HR>

<UL>
<LI><A href="test5.cgi?name=Bob&shoesize=small">Send Bob, small</A>
<LI><A href="test5.cgi?name=Tom&language=Python">Send Tom, Python</A>
<LI><A href=
"http://starship.python.net/~lutz/Basics/test5.cgi?job=Evangelist&comment=spam">
Send Evangelist, spam</A>
</UL>

<HR></BODY></HTML>
```

This static HTML file defines three hyperlinks—the first two are minimal and the third is fully specified, but all work similarly (again, the target script doesn't care). When we visit this file's URL, we see the page shown in Figure 12-17. It's mostly just a page for launching canned calls to the CGI script.

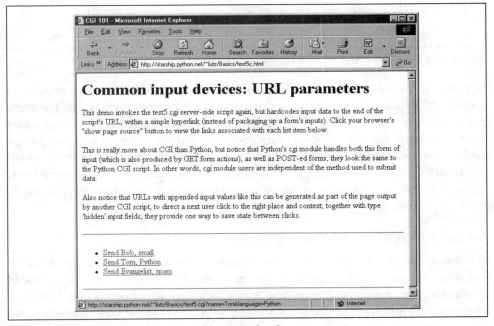

Figure 12-17. Hyperlinks page created by test5c.html

Clicking on this page's second link creates the response page in Figure 12-18. This link invokes the CGI script, with the name parameter set to "Tom" and the `language` parameter set to "Python," simply because those parameters and values are hardcoded in the URL listed in the HTML for the second hyperlink. It's exactly as if we had manually typed the line shown at the top of the browser in Figure 12-18.

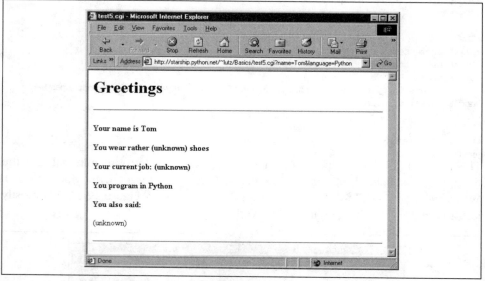

Figure 12-18. Response page created by test5.cgi (3)

Notice that lots of fields are missing here; the *test5.cgi* script is smart enough to detect and handle missing fields and generate an unknown message in the reply page. It's also worth pointing out that we're reusing the Python CGI script again here. The script itself is completely independent of both the user-interface format of the submission page, as well as the technique used to invoke it (from a submitted form or a hardcoded URL). By separating user interface from processing logic, CGI scripts become reusable software components, at least within the context of the CGI environment.

Saving CGI script state information

But the real reason for showing this technique is that we're going to use it extensively in the larger case studies in the next two chapters to implement lists of dynamically generated selections that "know" what to do when clicked. Precoded parameters in URLs are a way to retain state information between pages—they can be used to direct the action of the next script to be run. As such, hyperlinks with such parameters are sometimes known as "smart links."

Normally, CGI scripts run autonomously, with no knowledge of any other scripts that may have run before. That hasn't mattered in our examples so far, but larger systems are usually composed of multiple user interaction steps and many scripts, and we need a way to keep track of information gathered along the way. Generating hardcoded URLs with parameters is one way for a CGI script to pass data to the next script in the application. When clicked, such URL parameters send pre-programmed selection information back to another server-side handler script.

For example, a site that lets you read your email may present you with a list of viewable email messages, implemented in HTML as a list of hyperlinks generated by another script. Each hyperlink might include the name of the message viewer script, along with parameters identifying the selected message number, email server name, and so on—as much data as is needed to fetch the message associated with a particular link. A retail site may instead serve up a generated list of product links, each of which triggers a hardcoded hyperlink containing the product number, its price, and so on.

In general, there are a variety of ways to pass or retain state information between CGI script executions:

- *Hardcoded URL parameters* in dynamically generated hyperlinks and embedded in web pages (as discussed here)
- *Hidden form input fields* that are attached to form data and embedded in web pages, but not displayed on web pages
- *HTTP "cookies"* that are stored on the client machine and transferred between client and server in HTTP message headers
- *General server-side data stores* that include databases, persistent object shelves, flat files, and so on

We'll meet most of these mediums in later examples in this chapter and in the two chapters that follow.

The Hello World Selector

It's now time for something a bit more useful (well, more entertaining, at least). This section presents a program that displays the basic syntax required by various programming languages to print the string "Hello World", the classic language benchmark. To keep this simple, it assumes the string shows up in the standard output stream, not a GUI or web page. It also gives just the output command itself, not the complete programs. The Python version happens to be a complete program, but we won't hold that against its competitors here.

Structurally, the first cut of this example consists of a main page HTML file, along with a Python-coded CGI script that is invoked by a form in the main HTML page. Because no state or database data is stored between user clicks, this is still a fairly simple example. In fact, the main HTML page implemented by Example 12-16 is really just one big pull-down selection list within a form.

Example 12-16. PP2E\Internet\Cgi-Web\Basics\languages.html

```
<html><body>
<title>Languages</title>
<h1>Hello World selector</h1>

<P>This demo shows how to display a "hello world" message in various
programming languages' syntax.  To keep this simple, only the output command
is shown (it takes more code to make a complete program in some of these
languages), and only text-based solutions are given (no GUI or HTML
construction logic is included). This page is a simple HTML file; the one
you see after pressing the button below is generated by a Python CGI script
which runs on the server. Pointers:

<UL>
<LI>To see this page's HTML, use the 'View Source' command in your browser.
<LI>To view the Python CGI script on the server,
    <A HREF="languages-src.cgi">click here</A> or
    <A HREF="getfile.cgi?filename=languages.cgi">here</A>.
<LI>To see an alternative version that generates this page dynamically,
    <A HREF="languages2.cgi">click here</A>.
<LI>For more syntax comparisons, visit
    <A HREF="http://www.ionet.net/~timtroyr/funhouse/beer.html">this site</A>.
</UL></P>

<hr>
<form method=POST action="languages.cgi">
    <P><B>Select a programming language:</B>
    <P><select name=language>
        <option>All
        <option>Python
        <option>Perl
        <option>Tcl
        <option>Scheme
        <option>SmallTalk
        <option>Java
        <option>C
        <option>C++
        <option>Basic
        <option>Fortran
        <option>Pascal
        <option>Other
    </select>
    <P><input type=Submit>
</form>

</body></html>
```

For the moment, let's ignore some of the hyperlinks near the middle of this file; they introduce bigger concepts like file transfers and maintainability that we will explore in the next two sections. When visited with a browser, this HTML file is downloaded to the client and rendered into the new browser page shown in Figure 12-19.

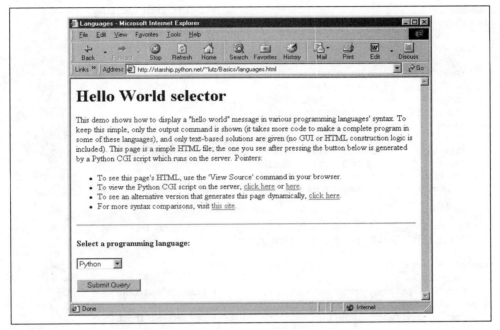

Figure 12-19. The "Hello World" main page

That widget above the Submit button is a pull-down selection list that lets you choose one of the <option> tag values in the HTML file. As usual, selecting one of these language names and pressing the Submit button at the bottom (or pressing your Enter key) sends the selected language name to an instance of the server-side CGI script program named in the form's **action** option. Example 12-17 contains the Python script that runs on the server upon submission.

Example 12-17. PP2E\Internet\Cgi-Web\Basics\languages.cgi

```
#!/usr/bin/python
#######################################################
# show hello world syntax for input language name;
# note that it uses r'...' raw strings so that '\n'
# in the table are left intact, and cgi.escape() on
# the string so that things like '<<' don't confuse
# browsers--they are translated to valid html code;
# any language name can arrive at this script: e.g.,
# can type "http://starship.python.net/~lutz/Basics
# /languages.cgi?language=Cobol" in any web browser.
# caveats: the languages list appears in both the cgi
# and html files--could import from a single file if
```

Example 12-17. PP2E\Internet\Cgi-Web\Basics\languages.cgi (continued)

```
# selection list generated by another cgi script too;
########################################################

debugme  = 0                                    # 1=test from cmd line
inputkey = 'language'                           # input parameter name

hellos = {
    'Python':    r" print 'Hello World'                ",
    'Perl':      r' print "Hello World\n";             ',
    'Tcl':       r' puts "Hello World"                 ',
    'Scheme':    r' (display "Hello World") (newline)  ',
    'SmallTalk': r" 'Hello World' print.               ",
    'Java':      r' System.out.println("Hello World"); ',
    'C':         r' printf("Hello World\n");           ',
    'C++':       r' cout << "Hello World" << endl;     ',
    'Basic':     r' 10 PRINT "Hello World"             ',
    'Fortran':   r" print *, 'Hello World'             ",
    'Pascal':    r" WriteLn('Hello World');            "
}

class dummy:                                     # mocked-up input obj
    def __init__(self, str): self.value = str

import cgi, sys
if debugme:
    form = {inputkey: dummy(sys.argv[1])}        # name on cmd line
else:
    form = cgi.FieldStorage()                    # parse real inputs

print "Content-type: text/html\n"                # adds blank line
print "<TITLE>Languages</TITLE>"
print "<H1>Syntax</H1><HR>"

def showHello(form):                             # html for one language
    choice = form[inputkey].value
    print "<H3>%s</H3><P><PRE>" % choice
    try:
        print cgi.escape(hellos[choice])
    except KeyError:
        print "Sorry--I don't know that language"
    print "</PRE></P><BR>"

if not form.has_key(inputkey) or form[inputkey].value == 'All':
    for lang in hellos.keys():
        mock = {inputkey: dummy(lang)}
        showHello(mock)
else:
    showHello(form)
print '<HR>'
```

And as usual, this script prints HTML code to the standard output stream to produce a response page in the client's browser. There's not much new to speak of in this script, but it employs a few techniques that merit special focus:

Raw strings

Notice the use of *raw strings* (string constants preceded by an "r" character) in the language syntax dictionary. Recall that raw strings retain \ backslash characters in the string literally, rather than interpreting them as string escape-code introductions. Without them, the \n newline character sequences in some of the language's code snippets would be interpreted by Python as line-feeds, rather than being printed in the HTML reply as \n.

Escaping text embedded in HTML and URLs

This script takes care to format the text of each language's code snippet with the `cgi.escape` utility function. This standard Python utility automatically translates characters that are special in HTML into HTML escape code sequences, such that they are not treated as HTML operators by browsers. Formally, `cgi.escape` translates characters to escape code sequences, according to the standard HTML convention: <, >, and & become <, >, and &. If you pass a second true argument, the double-quote character (") is also translated to ".

For example, the << left-shift operator in the C++ entry is translated to <<—a pair of HTML escape codes. Because printing each code snippet effectively embeds it in the HTML response stream, we must escape any special HTML characters it contains. HTML parsers (including Python's standard `htmllib` module) translate escape codes back to the original characters when a page is rendered.

More generally, because CGI is based upon the notion of passing formatted strings across the Net, escaping special characters is a ubiquitous operation. CGI scripts almost always need to escape text generated as part of the reply to be safe. For instance, if we send back arbitrary text input from a user or read from a data source on the server, we usually can't be sure if it will contain HTML characters or not, so we must escape it just in case.

In later examples, we'll also find that characters inserted into URL address strings generated by our scripts may need to be escaped as well. A literal & in a URL is special, for example, and must be escaped if it appears embedded in text we insert into a URL. However, URL syntax reserves different special characters than HTML code, and so different escaping conventions and tools must be used. As we'll see later in this chapter, `cgi.escape` implements escape translations in HTML code, but `urllib.quote` (and its relatives) escapes characters in URL strings.

Mocking up form inputs

Here again, form inputs are "mocked up" (simulated), both for debugging and for responding to a request for all languages in the table. If the script's global `debugme` variable is set to a true value, for instance, the script creates a dictionary that is plug-and-play compatible with the result of a `cgi.FieldStorage` call—its "languages" key references an instance of the `dummy` mock-up class. This class in turn creates an object that has the same interface as the contents of a `cgi.FieldStorage` result—it makes an object with a `value` attribute set to a passed-in string.

The net effect is that we can test this script by running it from the system command line: the generated dictionary fools the script into thinking it was invoked by a browser over the Net. Similarly, if the requested language name is "All," the script iterates over all entries in the languages table, making a mocked-up form dictionary for each (as though the user had requested each language in turn). This lets us reuse the existing `showHello` logic to display each language's code in a single page. As always in Python, object interfaces and protocols are what we usually code for, not specific datatypes. The `showHello` function will happily process any object that responds to the syntax `form['language'].value`.*

Now let's get back to interacting with this program. If we select a particular language, our CGI script generates an HTML reply of the following sort (along with the required content-type header and blank line):

```
<TITLE>Languages</TITLE>
<H1>Syntax</H1><HR>
<H3>Scheme</H3><P><PRE>
  (display "Hello World") (newline)
</PRE></P><BR>
<HR>
```

Program code is marked with a `<PRE>` tag to specify preformatted text (the browser won't reformat it like a normal text paragraph). This reply code shows what we get when we pick "Scheme." Figure 12-20 shows the page served up by the script after selecting "Python" in the pull-down selection list.

Our script also accepts a language name of "All," and interprets it as a request to display the syntax for every language it knows about. For example, here is the HTML that is generated if we set global variable `debugme` to 1 and run from the

---

* If you are reading closely, you might notice that this is the second time we've used mock-ups in this chapter (see the earlier *test4.cgi* example). If you find this technique generally useful, it would probably make sense to put the `dummy` class, along with a function for populating a form dictionary on demand, into a module so it can be reused. In fact, we will do that in the next section. Even for two-line classes like this, typing the same code the third time around will do much to convince you of the power of code reuse.

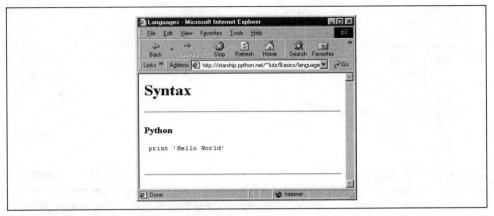

Figure 12-20. Response page created by languages.cgi

command line with a single argument, "All." This output is the same as what's printed to the client's browser in response to an "All" request:[*]

```
C:\...\PP2E\Internet\Cgi-Web\Basics>python languages.cgi All
Content-type: text/html

<TITLE>Languages</TITLE>
<H1>Syntax</H1><HR>
<H3>Perl</H3><P><PRE>
 print "Hello World\n";
</PRE></P><BR>
<H3>SmallTalk</H3><P><PRE>
 'Hello World' print.
</PRE></P><BR>
<H3>Basic</H3><P><PRE>
 10 PRINT "Hello World"
</PRE></P><BR>
<H3>Scheme</H3><P><PRE>
 (display "Hello World") (newline)
</PRE></P><BR>
<H3>Python</H3><P><PRE>
 print 'Hello World'
</PRE></P><BR>
<H3>C++</H3><P><PRE>
 cout &lt;&lt; "Hello World" &lt;&lt; endl;
</PRE></P><BR>
<H3>Pascal</H3><P><PRE>
 WriteLn('Hello World');
</PRE></P><BR>
<H3>Java</H3><P><PRE>
```

---

[*] Interestingly, we also get the "All" reply if debugme is set to 0 when we run the script from the command line. The cgi.FieldStorage call returns an empty dictionary if called outside the CGI environment rather than throwing an exception, so the test for a missing key kicks in. It's likely safer to not rely on this behavior, however.

```
   System.out.println("Hello World");
  </PRE></P><BR>
 <H3>C</H3><P><PRE>
  printf("Hello World\n");
  </PRE></P><BR>
 <H3>Tcl</H3><P><PRE>
  puts "Hello World"
  </PRE></P><BR>
 <H3>Fortran</H3><P><PRE>
  print *, 'Hello World'
  </PRE></P><BR>
 <HR>
```

Each language is represented here with the same code pattern—the showHello
function is called for each table entry, along with a mocked-up form object. Notice
the way that C++ code is escaped for embedding inside the HTML stream; this is
the **cgi.escape** call's handiwork. When viewed with a browser, the "All"
response page is rendered as shown in Figure 12-21.

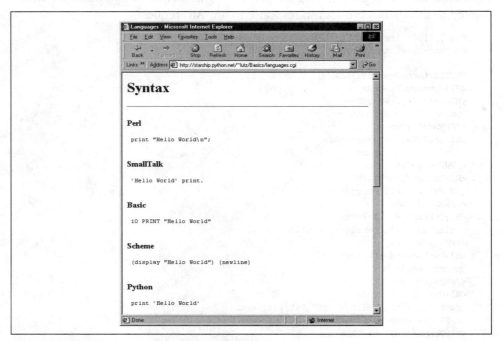

Figure 12-21. Response page for "all languages" choice

Checking for Missing and Invalid Inputs

So far, we've been triggering the CGI script by selecting a language name from the
pull-down list in the main HTML page. In this context, we can be fairly sure that
the script will receive valid inputs. Notice, though, that there is nothing to prevent

a user from passing the requested language name at the end of the CGI script's URL as an explicit parameter, instead of using the HTML page form. For instance, a URL of the form:

```
http://starship.python.net/~lutz/Basics/languages.cgi?language=Python
```

yields the same "Python" response page shown in Figure 12-20.[*] However, because it's always possible for a user to bypass the HTML file and use an explicit URL, it's also possible that a user could invoke our script with an unknown language name that is not in the HTML file's pull-down list (and so not in our script's table). In fact, the script might be triggered with no language input at all, if someone explicitly types its URL with no parameter at the end.

To be robust, the script checks for both cases explicitly, as all CGI scripts generally should. For instance, here is the HTML generated in response to a request for the fictitious language "GuiDO":

```
<TITLE>Languages</TITLE>
<H1>Syntax</H1><HR>
<H3>GuiDO</H3><P><PRE>
Sorry--I don't know that language
</PRE></P><BR>
<HR>
```

If the script doesn't receive any language name input, it simply defaults to the "All" case. If we didn't detect these cases, chances are that our script would silently die on a Python exception and leave the user with a mostly useless half-complete page or with a default error page (we didn't assign `stderr` to `stdout` here, so no Python error message would be displayed). In pictures, Figure 12-22 shows the page generated if the script is invoked with an explicit URL like this:

```
http://starship.python.net/~lutz/Basics/languages.cgi?language=COBOL
```

To test this error case, the pull-down list includes an "Unknown" name, which produces a similar error page reply. Adding code to the script's table for the COBOL "Hello World" program is left as an exercise for the reader.

Coding for Maintainability

Let's step back from coding details for just a moment to gain some design perspective. As we've seen, Python code, by and large, automatically lends itself to systems that are easy to read and maintain; it has a simple syntax that cuts much of

---

[*] See the `urllib` module examples in the prior and following chapters for a way to send this URL from a Python script. `urllib` lets programs fetch web pages and invoke remote CGI scripts by building and submitting URL strings like this one, with any required parameters filled in at the end of the string. You could use this module, for instance, to automatically send information to order Python books at an online bookstore from within a Python script, without ever starting a web browser.

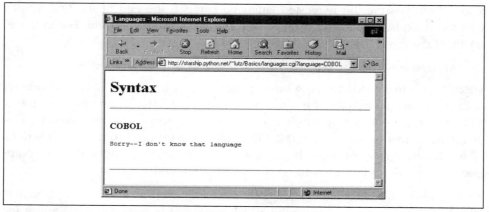

Figure 12-22. Response page for unknown language

the clutter of other tools. On the other hand, coding styles and program design can often impact maintainability as much as syntax. For example, the "Hello World" selector pages earlier in this chapter work as advertised, and were very easy and fast to throw together. But as currently coded, the languages selector suffers from substantial maintainability flaws.

Imagine, for instance, that you actually take me up on that challenge posed at the end of the last section, and you attempt to add another entry for COBOL. If you add COBOL to the CGI script's table, you're only half done: the list of supported languages lives redundantly in two places—in the HTML for the main page as well as the script's syntax dictionary. Changing one does not change the other. More generally, there are a handful of ways that this program might fail the scrutiny of a rigorous code review:

Selection list
> As just mentioned, the list of languages supported by this program lives in two places: the HTML file and the CGI script's table.

Field name
> The field name of the input parameter, "language," is hardcoded into both files, as well. You might remember to change it in the other if you change it in one, but you might not.

Form mock ups
> We've redundantly coded classes to mock-up form field inputs twice in this chapter already; the "dummy" class here is clearly a mechanism worth reusing.

HTML Code
> HTML embedded in and generated by the script is sprinkled throughout the program in `print` statements, making it difficult to implement broad web page layout changes.

This is a short example, of course, but issues of redundancy and reuse become more acute as your scripts grow larger. As a rule of thumb, if you find yourself changing multiple source files to modify a single behavior, or if you notice that you've taken to writing programs by cut-and-paste copying of existing code, then it's probably time to think more about rational program structures. To illustrate coding styles and practices that are more friendly to maintainers, let's rewrite this example to fix all of these weaknesses in a single mutation.

Step 1: Sharing Objects Between Pages

We can remove the first two maintenance problems listed above with a simple transformation; the trick is to generate the main page dynamically, from an executable script, rather than from a precoded HTML file. Within a script, we can import the input field name and selection list values from a common Python module file, shared by the main and reply page generation scripts. Changing the selection list or field name in the common module changes both clients automatically. First, we move shared objects to a common module file, as shown in Example 12-18.

Example 12-18. PP2E\Internet\Cgi-Web\Basics\languages2common.py

```
#######################################################
# common objects shared by main and reply page scripts;
# need change only this file to add a new language.
#######################################################

inputkey = 'language'                       # input parameter name

hellos = {
    'Python':    r" print 'Hello World'                ",
    'Perl':      r' print "Hello World\n";             ',
    'Tcl':       r' puts "Hello World"                 ',
    'Scheme':    r' (display "Hello World") (newline)  ',
    'SmallTalk': r" 'Hello World' print.               ",
    'Java':      r' System.out.println("Hello World"); ',
    'C':         r' printf("Hello World\n");           ',
    'C++':       r' cout << "Hello World" << endl;     ',
    'Basic':     r' 10 PRINT "Hello World"             ',
    'Fortran':   r" print *, 'Hello World'             ",
    'Pascal':    r" WriteLn('Hello World');            "
}
```

Module `languages2common` contains all the data that needs to agree between pages: the field name, as well as the syntax dictionary. The `hellos` syntax dictionary isn't quite HTML code, but its keys list can be used to generate HTML for the selection list on the main page dynamically. Next, in Example 12-19, we recode the main page as an executable script, and populate the response HTML with values imported from the common module file in the previous example.

Example 12-19. PP2E\Internet\Cgi-Web\Basics\languages2.cgi

```
#!/usr/bin/python
###################################################################
# generate html for main page dynamically from an executable
# Python script, not a pre-coded HTML file; this lets us
# import the expected input field name and the selection table
# values from a common Python module file; changes in either
# now only have to be made in one place, the Python module file;
###################################################################

REPLY = """Content-type: text/html

<html><body>
<title>Languages2</title>
<h1>Hello World selector</h1>
<P>Similar to file <a href="languages.html">languages.html</a>, but
this page is dynamically generated by a Python CGI script, using
selection list and input field names imported from a common Python
module on the server. Only the common module must be maintained as
new languages are added, because it is shared with the reply script.

To see the code that generates this page and the reply, click
<a href="getfile.cgi?filename=languages2.cgi">here</a>,
<a href="getfile.cgi?filename=languages2reply.cgi">here</a>,
<a href="getfile.cgi?filename=languages2common.py">here</a>, and
<a href="getfile.cgi?filename=formMockup.py">here</a>.</P>
<hr>
<form method=POST action="languages2reply.cgi">
    <P><B>Select a programming language:</B>
    <P><select name=%s>
        <option>All
        %s
        <option>Other
    </select>
    <P><input type=Submit>
</form>
</body></html>
"""

import string
from languages2common import hellos, inputkey

options = []
for lang in hellos.keys():
    options.append('<option>' + lang)      # wrap table keys in html code
options = string.join(options, '\n\t')
print REPLY % (inputkey, options)          # field name and values from module
```

Here again, ignore the `getfile` hyperlinks in this file for now; we'll learn what
they mean in the next section. You should notice, though, that the HTML page
definition becomes a printed Python string here (named REPLY), with `%s` format

targets where we plug in values imported from the common module.* It's otherwise similar to the original HTML file's code; when we visit this script's URL, we get a similar page, shown in Figure 12-23. But this time, the page is generated by running a script on the server that populates the pull-down selection list from the keys list of the common syntax table.

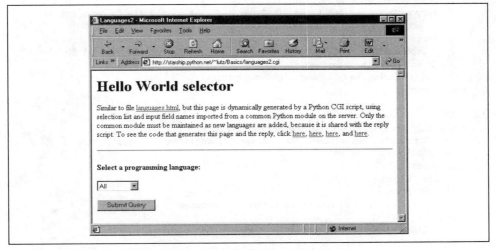

Figure 12-23. Alternative main page made by languages2.cgi

Step 2: A Reusable Form Mock-up Utility

Moving the languages table and input field name to a module file solves the first two maintenance problems we noted. But if we want to avoid writing a dummy field mock-up class in every CGI script we write, we need to do something more. Again, it's merely a matter of exploiting the Python module's affinity for code reuse: let's move the dummy class to a utility module, as in Example 12-20.

Example 12-20. PP2E\Internet\Cgi-Web\Basics\formMockup.py

```
##############################################################
# Tools for simulating the result of a cgi.FieldStorage()
# call; useful for testing CGI scripts outside the web
##############################################################

import types

class FieldMockup:                                  # mocked-up input object
```

---

* The HTML code template could be loaded from an external text file, too, but external text files are no more easily changed than Python scripts. In fact, Python scripts *are* text files, and this is a major feature of the language: it's usually easy to change the Python scripts of an installed system onsite, without re-compile or re-link steps.

Example 12-20. PP2E\Internet\Cgi-Web\Basics\formMockup.py (continued)

```
        def __init__(self, str):
            self.value = str

def formMockup(**kwargs):                            # pass field=value args
    mockup = {}                                      # multi-choice: [value,...]
    for (key, value) in kwargs.items():
        if type(value) is not types.ListType:        # simple fields have .value
            mockup[key] = FieldMockup(str(value))
        else:                                        # multi-choice have list
            mockup[key] = []                         # to do: file upload fields
            for pick in value:
                mockup[key].append(FieldMockup(pick))
    return mockup

def selftest():
    # use this form if fields can be hard-coded
    form = formMockup(name='Bob', job='hacker', food=['Spam', 'eggs', 'ham'])
    print form['name'].value
    print form['job'].value
    for item in form['food']:
        print item.value,
    # use real dict if keys are in variables or computed
    print
    form = {'name':FieldMockup('Brian'), 'age':FieldMockup(38)}
    for key in form.keys():
        print form[key].value

if __name__ == '__main__': selftest()
```

By placing our mock-up class in this module, *formMockup.py*, it automatically becomes a reusable tool, and may be imported by any script we care to write.[*] For readability, the dummy field simulation class has been renamed FieldMockup here. For convenience, we've also added a formMockup utility function that builds up an entire form dictionary from passed-in keyword arguments. Assuming you can hardcode the names of the form to be faked, the mock-up can be created in a single call. This module includes a self-test function invoked when the file is run from the command line, which demonstrates how its exports are used. Here is its test output, generated by making and querying two form mock-up objects:

```
C:\...\PP2E\Internet\Cgi-Web\Basics>python formMockup.py
Bob
hacker
```

---

[*] This assumes, of course, that this module can be found on the Python module search path when those scripts are run. See the search path discussion earlier in this chapter. Since Python searches the current directory for imported modules by default, this always works without sys.path changes if all of our files are in our main web directory.

```
Spam eggs ham
38
Brian
```

Since the mock-up now lives in a module, we can reuse it any time we want to test a CGI script offline. To illustrate, the script in Example 12-21 is a rewrite of the *test5.cgi* example we saw earlier, using the form mock-up utility to simulate field inputs. If we had planned ahead, we could have tested this script like this without even needing to connect to the Net.

Example 12-21. PP2E\Internet\Cgi-Web\Basics\test5_mockup.cgi

```
#!/usr/bin/python
###################################################################
# run test5 logic with formMockup instead of cgi.FieldStorage()
# to test: python test5_mockup.cgi > temp.html, and open temp.html
###################################################################

from formMockup import formMockup
form = formMockup(name='Bob',
                  shoesize='Small',
                  language=['Python', 'C++', 'HTML'],
                  comment='ni, Ni, NI')

# rest same as original, less form assignment
```

Running this script from a simple command line shows us what the HTML response stream will look like:

```
C:\...\PP2E\Internet\Cgi-Web\Basics>python test5_mockup.cgi
Content-type: text/html

<TITLE>test5.cgi</TITLE>
<H1>Greetings</H1>
<HR>
<H4>Your name is Bob</H4>
<H4>You wear rather Small shoes</H4>
<H4>Your current job: (unknown)</H4>
<H4>You program in Python and C++ and HTML</H4>
<H4>You also said:</H4>
<P>ni, Ni, NI</P>
<HR>
```

Running it live yields the page in Figure 12-24. Field inputs here are hardcoded, similar in spirit to the *test5* extension that embedded input parameters at the end of hyperlink URLs. Here, they come from form mock-up objects created in the reply script that cannot be changed without editing the script. Because Python code runs immediately, though, modifying a Python script during the debug cycle goes as quickly as you can type.

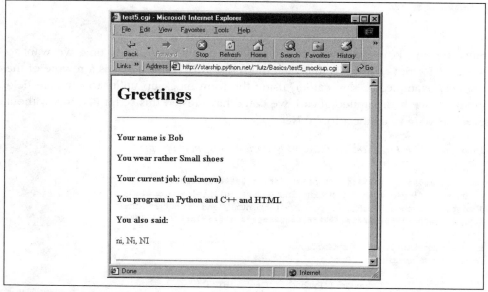

Figure 12-24. A response page with simulated inputs

Step 3: Putting It All Together—A New Reply Script

There's one last step on our path to software maintenance nirvana: we still must recode the reply page script itself, to import data that was factored out to the common module and import the reusable form mock-up module's tools. While we're at it, we move code into functions (in case we ever put things in this file that we'd like to import in another script), and all HTML code to triple-quoted string blocks (see Example 12-22). Changing HTML is generally easier when it has been isolated in single strings like this, rather than being sprinkled throughout a program.

Example 12-22. PP2E\Internet\Cgi-Web\Basics\languages2reply.cgi

```
#!/usr/bin/python
#####################################################
# for easier maintenance, use html template strings, get
# the language table and input key from common mdule file,
# and get reusable form field mockup utilities module.
#####################################################

import cgi, sys
from formMockup import FieldMockup              # input field simulator
from languages2common import hellos, inputkey   # get common table, name
debugme = 0

hdrhtml = """Content-type: text/html\n
<TITLE>Languages</TITLE>
<H1>Syntax</H1><HR>"""
```

Example 12-22. PP2E\Internet\Cgi-Web\Basics\languages2reply.cgi (continued)

```
langhtml = """
<H3>%s</H3><P><PRE>
%s
</PRE></P><BR>"""

def showHello(form):                                   # html for one language
    choice = form[inputkey].value                      # escape lang name too
    try:
        print langhtml % (cgi.escape(choice),
                          cgi.escape(hellos[choice]))
    except KeyError:
        print langhtml % (cgi.escape(choice),
                          "Sorry--I don't know that language")

def main():
    if debugme:
        form = {inputkey: FieldMockup(sys.argv[1])}    # name on cmd line
    else:
        form = cgi.FieldStorage()                      # parse real inputs

    print hdrhtml
    if not form.has_key(inputkey) or form[inputkey].value == 'All':
        for lang in hellos.keys():
            mock = {inputkey: FieldMockup(lang)}
            showHello(mock)
    else:
        showHello(form)
    print '<HR>'

if __name__ == '__main__': main()
```

When global **debugme** is set to 1, the script can be tested offline from a simple command line as before:

```
C:\...\PP2E\Internet\Cgi-Web\Basics>python languages2reply.cgi Python
Content-type: text/html

<TITLE>Languages</TITLE>
<H1>Syntax</H1><HR>

<H3>Python</H3><P><PRE>
 print 'Hello World'
</PRE></P><BR>
<HR>
```

When run online, we get the same reply pages we saw for the original version of this example (we won't repeat them here again). This transformation changed the program's architecture, not its user interface.

Most of the code changes in this version of the reply script are straightforward. If you test-drive these pages, the only differences you'll find are the URLs at the top of your browser (they're different files, after all), extra blank lines in the generated

HTML (ignored by the browser), and a potentially different ordering of language names in the main page's pull-down selection list.

This selection list ordering difference arises because this version relies on the order of the Python dictionary's keys list, not on a hardcoded list in an HTML file. Dictionaries, you'll recall, arbitrarily order entries for fast fetches; if you want the selection list to be more predictable, simply sort the keys list before iterating over it using the list `sort` method.

Faking Inputs with Shell Variables

If you know what you're doing, you can sometimes also test CGI scripts from the command line by setting the same environment variables that HTTP servers set, and then launching your script. For example, we can pretend to be a web server by storing input parameters in the QUERY_STRING environment variable, using the same syntax we employ at the end of a URL string after the ?:

```
$ setenv QUERY_STRING "name=Mel&job=trainer,+writer"
$ python test5.cgi
Content-type: text/html

<TITLE>test5.cgi<?TITLE>
<H1>Greetings</H1>
<HR>
<H4>Your name is Mel</H4>
<H4>You wear rather (unknown) shoes</H4>
<H4>Your current job: trainer, writer</H4>
<H4>You program in (unknown)</H4>
<H4>You also said:</H4>
<P>(unknown)</P>
<HR>
```

Here, we mimic the effects of a GET style form submission or explicit URL. HTTP servers place the query string (parameters) in the shell variable QUERY_STRING. Python's `cgi` module finds them there as though they were sent by a browser. POST-style inputs can be simulated with shell variables, too, but it's more complex—so much so that you're likely best off not learning how. In fact, it may be more robust in general to mock-up inputs with Python objects (e.g., as in *formMockup.py*). But some CGI scripts may have additional environment or testing constraints that merit unique treatment.

More on HTML and URL Escapes

Perhaps the most subtle change in the last section's rewrite is that, for robustness, this version also calls `cgi.escape` for the language *name*, not just for the language's code snippet. It's unlikely but not impossible that someone could pass the script a language name with an embedded HTML character. For example, a URL like:

```
http://starship.python.net/~lutz/Basics/languages2reply.cgi?language=a<b
```

embeds a < in the language name parameter (the name is a<b). When submitted, this version uses `cgi.escape` to properly translate the < for use in the reply HTML, according to the standard HTML escape conventions discussed earlier:

```
<TITLE>Languages</TITLE>
<H1>Syntax</H1><HR>

<H3>a&lt;b</H3><P><PRE>
Sorry--I don't know that language
</PRE></P><BR>
<HR>
```

The original version doesn't escape the language name, such that the embedded <b is interpreted as an HTML tag (which may make the rest of the page render in bold font!). As you can probably tell by now, text escapes are pervasive in CGI scripting—even text that you may think is safe must generally be escaped before being inserted into the HTML code in the reply stream.

URL Escape Code Conventions

Notice, though, that while it's wrong to embed an unescaped < in the HTML code reply, it's perfectly okay to include it literally in the earlier URL string used to trigger the reply. In fact, HTML and URLs define completely different characters as special. For instance, although & must be escaped as &amp inside HTML code, we have to use other escaping schemes to code a literal & within a URL string (where it normally separates parameters). To pass a language name like a&b to our script, we have to type the following URL:

```
http://starship.python.net/~lutz/Basics/languages2reply.cgi?language=a%26b
```

Here, %26 represents &—the & is replaced with a % followed by the hexadecimal value (0x26) of its ASCII code value (38). By URL standard, most nonalphanumeric characters are supposed to be translated to such escape sequences, and spaces are replaced by + signs. Technically, this convention is known as the *application/x-www-form-urlencoded* query string format, and it's part of the magic behind those bizarre URLs you often see at the top of your browser as you surf the Web.

Python HTML and URL Escape Tools

If you're like me, you probably don't have the hexadecimal value of the ASCII code for & committed to memory. Luckily, Python provides tools that automatically implement URL escapes, just as `cgi.escape` does for HTML escapes. The main thing to keep in mind is that HTML code and URL strings are written with entirely different syntax, and so they employ distinct escaping conventions. Web users don't generally care, unless they need to type complex URLs explicitly (browsers handle most escape code details internally). But if you write scripts that must generate HTML or URLs, you need to be careful to escape characters that are reserved in either syntax.

Because HTML and URLs have different syntaxes, Python provides two distinct sets of tools for escaping their text. In the standard Python library:

- `cgi.escape` escapes text to be embedded in HTML.

- `urllib.quote` and `quote_plus` escape text to be embedded in URLs.

The `urllib` module also has tools for undoing URL escapes (`unquote`, `unquote_plus`), but HTML escapes are undone during HTML parsing at large (`htmllib`). To illustrate the two escape conventions and tools, let's apply each toolset to a few simple examples.

Escaping HTML Code

As we saw earlier, `cgi.escape` translates code for inclusion within HTML. We normally call this utility from a CGI script, but it's just as easy to explore its behavior interactively:

```
>>> import cgi
>>> cgi.escape('a < b > c & d "spam"', 1)
'a &lt; b &gt; c &amp; d &quot;spam&quot;'

>>> s = cgi.escape("1<2 <b>hello</b>")
>>> s
'1&lt;2 &lt;b&gt;hello&lt;/b&gt;'
```

Python's `cgi` module automatically converts characters that are special in HTML syntax according to the HTML convention. It translates <, >, &, and with an extra true argument, ", into escape sequences of the form `&X;`, where the X is a mnemonic that denotes the original character. For instance, `&lt;` stands for the "less than" operator (<) and `&amp;` denotes a literal ampersand (&).

There is no *un*-escaping tool in the CGI module, because HTML escape code sequences are recognized within the context of an HTML parser, like the one used by your web browser when a page is downloaded. Python comes with a full HTML parser, too, in the form of standard module `htmllib`, which imports and specializes tools in module `sgmllib` (HTML is a kind of SGML syntax). We won't go into details on the HTML parsing tools here (see the library manual for details), but to illustrate how escape codes are eventually undone, here is the SGML module at work reading back the last output above:

```
>>> from sgmllib import TestSGMLParser
>>> p = TestSGMLParser(1)
>>> s
```

```
'1&lt;2 &lt;b&gt;hello&lt;/b&gt;'
>>> for c in s:
...     p.feed(c)
...
>>> p.close()
data: '1<2 <b>hello</b>'
```

Escaping URLs

By contrast, URLs reserve other characters as special and must adhere to different escape conventions. Because of that, we use different Python library tools to escape URLs for transmission. Python's `urllib` module provides two tools that do the translation work for us: `quote`, which implements the standard `%XX` hexadecimal URL escape code sequences for most nonalphanumeric characters, and `quote_plus`, which additionally translates spaces to + plus signs. The `urllib` module also provides functions for unescaping quoted characters in a URL string: `unquote` undoes `%XX` escapes, and `unquote_plus` also changes plus signs back to spaces. Here is the module at work, at the interactive prompt:

```
>>> import urllib
>>> urllib.quote("a & b #! c")
'a%20%26%20b%20%23%21%20c'

>>> urllib.quote_plus("C:\stuff\spam.txt")
'C%3a%5cstuff%5cspam.txt'

>>> x = urllib.quote_plus("a & b #! c")
>>> x
'a+%26+b+%23%21+c'

>>> urllib.unquote_plus(x)
'a & b #! c'
```

URL escape sequences embed the hexadecimal values of non-safe characters following a `%` sign (usually, their ASCII codes). In `urllib`, non-safe characters are usually taken to include everything except letters, digits, a handful of safe special characters (any of `_,.-`), and / by default). You can also specify a string of safe characters as an extra argument to the quote calls to customize the translations; the argument defaults to /, but passing an empty string forces / to be escaped:

```
>>> urllib.quote_plus("uploads/index.txt")
'uploads/index.txt'

>>> urllib.quote_plus("uploads/index.txt", '')
'uploads%2findex.txt'
```

Note that Python's `cgi` module also translates URL escape sequences back to their original characters and changes + signs to spaces during the process of extracting input information. Internally, `cgi.FieldStorage` automatically calls `urllib.unquote` if needed to parse and unescape parameters passed at the end of URLs (most of the translation happens in `cgi.parse_qs`). The upshot is that CGI scripts get back the original, unescaped URL strings, and don't need to unquote values on their own. As we've seen, CGI scripts don't even need to know that inputs came from a URL at all.

Escaping URLs Embedded in HTML Code

But what do we do for URLs inside HTML? That is, how do we escape when we generate and embed text inside a URL, which is itself embedded inside generated HTML code? Some of our earlier examples used hardcoded URLs with appended input parameters inside `<A HREF>` hyperlink tags; file *languages2.cgi*, for instance, prints HTML that includes a URL:

```
<a href="getfile.cgi?filename=languages2.cgi">
```

Because the URL here is embedded in HTML, it must minimally be escaped according to HTML conventions (e.g., any < characters must become <), and any spaces should be translated to + signs. A `cgi.escape(url)` call, followed by a `string.replace(url, " ", "+")` would take us this far, and would probably suffice for most cases.

That approach is not quite enough in general, though, because HTML escaping conventions are not the same as URL conventions. To robustly escape URLs embedded in HTML code, you should instead call `urllib.quote_plus` on the URL string before adding it to the HTML text. The escaped result also satisfies HTML escape conventions, because `urllib` translates more characters than `cgi.escape`, and the `%` in URL escapes is not special to HTML.

But there is one more wrinkle here: you also have to be careful with & characters in URL strings that are embedded in HTML code (e.g., within `<A>` hyperlink tags). Even if parts of the URL string are URL-escaped, when more than one parameter is separated by a &, the & separator might also have to be escaped as `&amp;` according to HTML conventions. To see why, consider the following HTML hyperlink tag:

```
<A HREF="file.cgi?name=a&job=b&amp=c&sect=d&lt=e">hello</a>
```

When rendered in most browsers I've tested, this URL link winds up looking incorrectly like this (the "S" character is really a non-ASCII section marker):

```
file.cgi?name=a&job=b&=c&S=d<=e
```

The first two parameters are retained as expected (`name=a`, `job=b`), because `name` is not preceded with an &, and `&job` is not recognized as a valid HTML character escape code. However, the `&amp`, `&sect`, and `&lt` parts are interpreted as special characters, because they do name valid HTML escape codes. To make this work as expected, the & separators should be escaped:

```
<A HREF="file.cgi?name=a&amp;job=b&amp;amp=c&amp;sect=d&amp;lt=e">hello</a>
```

Browsers render this fully escaped link as expected:

```
file.cgi?name=a&job=b&amp=c&sect=d&lt=e
```

The moral of this story is that unless you can be sure that the names of all but the leftmost URL query parameters embedded in HTML are not the same as the name of any HTML character escape code like amp, you should generally run the entire URL through `cgi.escape` after escaping its parameter names and values with `urllib.quote_plus`:

```
>>> import cgi
>>> cgi.escape('file.cgi?name=a&job=b&amp=c&sect=d&lt=e')
'file.cgi?name=a&amp;job=b&amp;amp=c&amp;sect=d&amp;lt=e'
```

Having said that, I should add that some examples in this book do not escape & URL separators embedded within HTML simply because their URL parameter names are known to not conflict with HTML escapes. This is not, however, the most general solution; when in doubt, escape much and often.

"Always Look on the Bright Side of Life"

Lest these formatting rules sound too clumsy (and send you screaming into the night!), note that the HTML and URL escaping conventions are imposed by the Internet itself, not by Python. (As we've seen, Python has a different mechanism for escaping special characters in string constants with backslashes.) These rules stem from the fact that the Web is based upon the notion of shipping formatted strings around the planet, and they were surely influenced by the tendency of different interest groups to develop very different notations.

You can take heart, though, in the fact that you often don't need to think in such cryptic terms; when you do, Python automates the translation process with library tools. Just keep in mind that any script that generates HTML or URLs dynamically probably needs to call Python's escaping tools to be robust. We'll see both the HTML and URL escape tool sets employed frequently in later examples in this chapter and the next two. In Chapter 15, we'll also meet systems such as Zope that aim to get rid of some of the low-level complexities that CGI scripters face. And as usual in programming, there is no substitute for brains; amazing technologies like the Internet come at a cost in complexity.

Sending Files to Clients and Servers

It's time to explain a bit of HTML code we've been keeping in the shadows. Did you notice those hyperlinks on the language selector example's main page for showing the CGI script's source code? Normally, we can't see such script source code, because accessing a CGI script makes it execute (we can see only its HTML output, generated to make the new page). The script in Example 12-23, referenced by a hyperlink in the main `language.html` page, works around that by opening the source file and sending its text as part of the HTML response. The text is marked with `<PRE>` as pre-formatted text, and escaped for transmission inside HTML with `cgi.escape`.

Example 12-23. PP2E\Internet\Cgi-Web\Basics\languages-src.cgi

```
#!/usr/bin/python
###############################################################
# Display languages.cgi script code without running it.
###############################################################

import cgi
filename = 'languages.cgi'

print "Content-type: text/html\n"        # wrap up in html
print "<TITLE>Languages</TITLE>"
print "<H1>Source code: '%s'</H1>" % filename
print '<HR><PRE>'
print cgi.escape(open(filename).read())
print '</PRE><HR>'
```

When we visit this script on the Web via the hyperlink or a manually typed URL, the script delivers a response to the client that includes the text of the CGI script source file. It appears as in Figure 12-25.

Note that here, too, it's crucial to format the text of the file with `cgi.escape`, because it is embedded in the HTML code of the reply. If we don't, any characters in the text that mean something in HTML code are interpreted as HTML tags. For example, the C++ `<` operator character within this file's text may yield bizarre results if not properly escaped. The `cgi.escape` utility converts it to the standard sequence `&lt;` for safe embedding.

Displaying Arbitrary Server Files on the Client

Almost immediately after writing the languages source code viewer script in the previous example, it occurred to me that it wouldn't be much more work, and would be much more useful, to write a generic version—one that could use a passed-in filename to display *any* file on the site. It's a straightforward mutation on the server side; we merely need to allow a filename to be passed in as an input. The *getfile.cgi* Python script in Example 12-24 implements this generalization. It assumes the filename is either typed into a web page form or appended to the end of the URL as a parameter. Remember that Python's `cgi` module handles both cases transparently, so there is no code in this script that notices any difference.

Figure 12-25. Source code viewer page

Example 12-24. PP2E\Internet\Cgi-Web\Basics\getfile.cgi

```
#!/usr/bin/python
###################################################################
# Display any cgi (or other) server-side file without running it.
# The filename can be passed in a URL param or form field; e.g.,
# http://server/~lutz/Basics/getfile.cgi?filename=somefile.cgi.
# Users can cut-and-paste or "View source" to save file locally.
# On IE, running the text/plain version (formatted=0) sometimes
# pops up Notepad, but end-of-lines are not always in DOS format;
# Netscape shows the text correctly in the browser page instead.
# Sending the file in text/html mode works on both browsers--text
# is displayed in the browser response page correctly. We also
# check the filename here to try to avoid showing private files;
# this may or may not prevent access to such files in general.
###################################################################

import cgi, os, sys
formatted = 1                            # 1=wrap text in html
privates  = ['../PyMailCgi/secret.py']   # don't show these

html = """
<html><title>Getfile response</title>
```

Example 12-24. PP2E\Internet\Cgi-Web\Basics\getfile.cgi (continued)

```
<h1>Source code for: '%s'</h1>
<hr>
<pre>%s</pre>
<hr></html>"""

def restricted(filename):
    for path in privates:
        if os.path.samefile(path, filename):    # unify all paths by os.stat
            return 1                             # else returns None=false

try:
    form = cgi.FieldStorage()
    filename = form['filename'].value            # url param or form field
except:
    filename = 'getfile.cgi'                     # else default filename

try:
    assert not restricted(filename)              # load unless private
    filetext = open(filename).read()
except AssertionError:
    filetext = '(File access denied)'
except:
    filetext = '(Error opening file: %s)' % sys.exc_value

if not formatted:
    print "Content-type: text/plain\n"           # send plain text
    print filetext                                # works on NS, not IE
else:
    print "Content-type: text/html\n"             # wrap up in html
    print html % (filename, cgi.escape(filetext))
```

This Python server-side script simply extracts the filename from the parsed CGI inputs object, and reads and prints the text of the file to send it to the client browser. Depending on the **formatted** global variable setting, it either sends the file in plain text mode (using **text/plain** in the response header) or wrapped up in an HTML page definition (**text/html**).

Either mode (and others) works in general under most browsers, but Internet Explorer doesn't handle the plain text mode as gracefully as Netscape—during testing, it popped up the Notepad text editor to view the downloaded text, but end-of-line characters in Unix format made the file appear as one long line. (Netscape instead displays the text correctly in the body of the response web page itself.) HTML display mode works more portably with current browsers. More on this script's restricted file logic in a moment.

Let's launch this script by typing its URL at the top of a browser, along with a desired filename appended after the script's name. Figure 12-26 shows the page we get by visiting this URL:

```
http://starship.python.net/~lutz/Basics/getfile.cgi?filename=languages-src.cgi
```

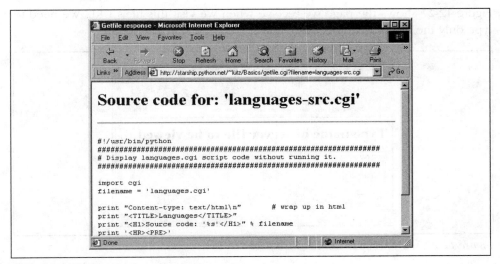

Figure 12-26. Generic source code viewer page

The body of this page shows the text of the server-side file whose name we passed at the end of the URL; once it arrives, we can view its text, cut-and-paste to save it in a file on the client, and so on. In fact, now that we have this generalized source code viewer, we could replace the hyperlink to script *languages-src.cgi* in *language.html,* with a URL of this form:

```
http://starship.python.net/~lutz/Basics/getfile.cgi?filename=languages.cgi
```

For illustration purposes, the main HTML page in Example 12-16 has links both to the original source code display script, as well as to the previous URL (less the server and directory paths, since the HTML file and `getfile` script live in the same place). Really, URLs like these are direct calls (albeit, across the Web) to our Python script, with filename parameters passed explicitly. As we've seen, parameters passed in URLs are treated the same as field inputs in forms; for convenience, let's also write a simple web page that allows the desired file to be typed directly into a form, as shown in Example 12-25.

Example 12-25. PP2E\Internet\Cgi-Web\Basics\getfile.html

```
<html><title>Getfile: download page</title>
<body>
<form method=get action="getfile.cgi">
  <h1>Type name of server file to be viewed</h1>
  <p><input type=text size=50 name=filename>
  <p><input type=submit value=Download>
</form>
<hr><a href="getfile.cgi?filename=getfile.cgi">View script code</a>
</body></html>
```

Figure 12-27 shows the page we receive when we visit this file's URL. We need to type only the filename in this page, not the full CGI script address.

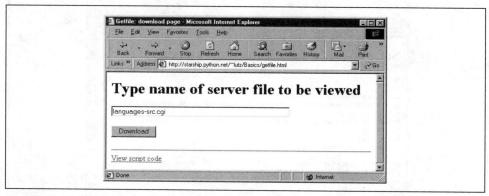

Figure 12-27. source code viewer selection page

When we press this page's Download button to submit the form, the filename is transmitted to the server, and we get back the same page as before, when the file-name was appended to the URL (see Figure 12-26). In fact, the filename *will* be appended to the URL here, too; the `get` method in the form's HTML instructs the browser to append the filename to the URL, exactly as if we had done so manually. It shows up at the end of the URL in the response page's address field, even though we really typed it into a form.*

Handling private files and errors

As long as CGI scripts have permission to open the desired server-side file, this script can be used to view and locally save *any* file on the server. For instance, Figure 12-28 shows the page we're served after asking for file path *../PyMailCgi/ index.html*—an HTML text file in another application's subdirectory, nested within the parent directory of this script.† Users can specify both relative and absolute paths to reach a file—any path syntax the server understands will do.

More generally, this script will display any file path for which the user "nobody" (the username under which CGI scripts usually run) has read access. Just about

---

* You may notice one difference in the response pages produced by the form and an explicitly typed URL: for the form, the value of the "filename" parameter at the end of the URL in the response may contain URL escape codes for some characters in the file path you typed. Browsers automatically trans-late some non-ASCII characters into URL escapes (just like `urllib.quote`). URL escapes are discussed earlier in this chapter; we'll see an example of this automatic browser escaping at work in a moment.

† PyMailCgi is described in the next chapter. If you're looking for source files for PyErrata (also in the next chapter), use a path like *../PyErrata/xxx*. In general, the top level of the book's web site corre-sponds to the top level of the *Internet/Cgi-Web* directory in the examples on the book's CD-ROM; `getfile` runs in subdirectory *Basics*.

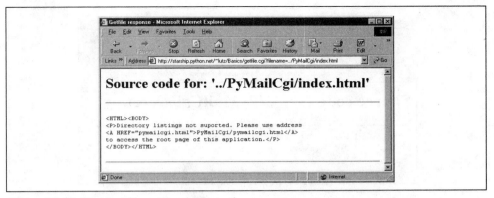

Figure 12-28. Viewing files with relative paths

every server-side file used in web applications will, or else they wouldn't be accessible from browsers in the first place. That makes for a flexible tool, but it's also potentially dangerous. What if we don't want users to be able to view some files on the server? For example, in the next chapter, we will implement an encryption module for email account passwords. Allowing users to view that module's source code would make encrypted passwords shipped over the Net much more vulnerable to cracking.

To minimize this potential, the `getfile` script keeps a list, `privates`, of restricted filenames, and uses the `os.path.samefile` built-in to check if a requested filename path points to one of the names on `privates`. The `samefile` call checks to see if the `os.stat` built-in returns the same identifying information for both file paths; because of that, pathnames that look different syntactically but reference the same file are treated as identical. For example, on my server, the following paths to the encryptor module are different strings, but yield a true result from `os.path.samefile`:[*]

```
../PyMailCgi/secret.py
/home/crew/lutz/public_html/PyMailCgi/secret.py
```

Accessing either path form generates an error page like that in Figure 12-29.

Notice that bona fide file errors are handled differently. Permission problems and accesses to nonexistent files, for example, are trapped by a different exception handler clause, and display the exception's message to give additional context. Figure 12-30 shows one such error page.

---

[*] The `os.path.samefile` call works on POSIX machines (e.g., Unix and Linux), but may not be supported on every machine on which you can run a web server (e.g., it isn't available on Windows 98 under Python 1.5.2). If it is absent, you can fall back on other ways to detect file path sameness, such as calling `os.stat` manually or checking for substring matches. For instance, any server path string that ends in *PyMailCgi/secret.py* after backslash conversions will likely lead to this private file.

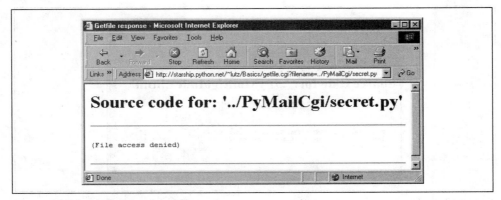

Figure 12-29. Accessing private files

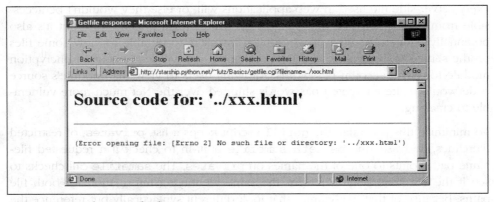

Figure 12-30. File errors display

As a general rule of thumb, file-processing exceptions should always be reported in detail, especially during script debugging. If we catch such exceptions in our scripts, it's up to us to display the details (assigning `sys.stderr` to `sys.stdout` won't help if Python doesn't print an error message). The current exception's type, data, and traceback objects are always available in the `sys` module for manual display.

The private files list check does prevent the encryption module from being viewed directly with this script, but it still may or may not be vulnerable to attack by malicious users. This book isn't about security, so I won't go into further details here, except to say that on the Internet, a little paranoia goes a long way. Especially for systems installed on the general Internet (instead of closed intranets), you should assume that the worst-case scenario will eventually happen.

Uploading Client Files to the Server

The `getfile` script lets us view server files on the client, but in some sense, it is a general-purpose file download tool. Although not as direct as fetching a file by FTP or over raw sockets, it serves similar purposes. Users of the script can either cut-and-paste the displayed code right off the web page or use their browser's View Source option to view and cut.

But what about going the other way—uploading a file from the client machine to the server? As we saw in the last chapter, that is easy enough to accomplish with a client-side script that uses Python's FTP support module. Yet such a solution doesn't really apply in the context of a web browser; we can't usually ask all of our program's clients to start up a Python FTP script in another window to accomplish an upload. Moreover, there is no simple way for the server-side script to request the upload explicitly, unless there happens to be an FTP server running on the client machine (not at all the usual case).

So is there no way to write a web-based program that lets its users upload files to a common server? In fact, there is, though it has more to do with HTML than with Python itself. HTML `<input>` tags also support a `type=file` option, which produces an input field, along with a button that pops up a file-selection dialog. The name of the client-side file to be uploaded can either be typed into the control, or selected with the pop-up dialog. The HTML page file in Example 12-26 defines a page that allows any client-side file to be selected and uploaded to the server-side script named in the form's `action` option.

Example 12-26. PP2E\Internet\Cgi-Web\Basics\putfile.html

```
<html><title>Putfile: upload page</title>
<body>
<form enctype="multipart/form-data"
      method=post
      action="putfile.cgi">
  <h1>Select client file to be uploaded</h1>
  <p><input type=file size=50 name=clientfile>
  <p><input type=submit value=Upload>
</form>
<hr><a href="getfile.cgi?filename=putfile.cgi">View script code</a>
</body></html>
```

One constraint worth noting: forms that use `file` type inputs must also specify a `multipart/form-data` encoding type and the `post` submission method, as shown in this file; `get` style URLs don't work for uploading files. When we visit this page, the page shown in Figure 12-31 is delivered. Pressing its Browse button opens a file-selection dialog, while Upload sends the file.

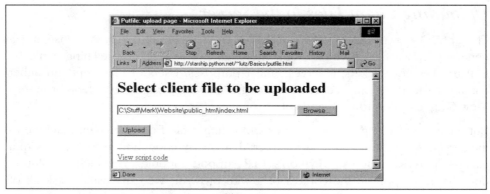

Figure 12-31. File upload selection page

On the client side, when we press this page's Upload button, the browser opens and reads the selected file, and packages its contents with the rest of the form's input fields (if any). When this information reaches the server, the Python script named in the form `action` tag is run as always, as seen in Example 12-27.

Example 12-27. PP2E\Internet\Cgi-Web\Basics\putfile.cgi

```
#!/usr/bin/python
#####################################################
# extract file uploaded by http from web browser;
# users visit putfile.html to get the upload form
# page, which then triggers this script on server;
# note: this is very powerful, and very dangerous:
# you will usually want to check the filename, etc.
# this will only work if file or dir is writeable;
# a unix 'chmod 777 uploads' command may suffice;
# file path names arrive in client's path format;
#####################################################

import cgi, string, os, sys
import posixpath, dospath, macpath      # for client paths
debugmode   = 0                         # 1=print form info
loadtextauto = 0                        # 1=read file at once
uploaddir   = './uploads'               # dir to store files

sys.stderr = sys.stdout                 # show error msgs
form = cgi.FieldStorage()               # parse form data
print "Content-type: text/html\n"       # with blank line
if debugmode: cgi.print_form(form)      # print form fields

# html templates

html = """
<html><title>Putfile response page</title>
<body>
<h1>Putfile response page</h1>
```

Example 12-27. PP2E\Internet\Cgi-Web\Basics\putfile.cgi (continued)

```
%s
</html>"""

goodhtml = html % """
<p>Your file, '%s', has been saved on the server as '%s'.
<p>An echo of the file's contents received and saved appears below.
</p><hr>
<p><pre>%s</pre>
</p><hr>
"""


# process form data

def splitpath(origpath):                                # get file at end
    for pathmodule in [posixpath, dospath, macpath]:    # try all clients
        basename = pathmodule.split(origpath)[1]        # may be any server
        if basename != origpath:
            return basename                             # lets spaces pass
    return origpath                                     # failed or no dirs

def saveonserver(fileinfo):                             # use file input form data
    basename = splitpath(fileinfo.filename)             # name without dir path
    srvrname = os.path.join(uploaddir, basename)        # store in a dir if set
    if loadtextauto:
        filetext = fileinfo.value                       # reads text into string
        open(srvrname, 'w').write(filetext)             # save in server file
    else:
        srvrfile = open(srvrname, 'w')                  # else read line by line
        numlines, filetext = 0, ''                      # e.g., for huge files
        while 1:
            line = fileinfo.file.readline()
            if not line: break
            srvrfile.write(line)
            filetext = filetext + line
            numlines = numlines + 1
        filetext = ('[Lines=%d]\n' % numlines) + filetext
    os.chmod(srvrname, 0666)    # make writeable: owned by 'nobody'
    return filetext, srvrname

def main():
    if not form.has_key('clientfile'):
        print html % "Error: no file was received"
    elif not form['clientfile'].filename:
        print html % "Error: filename is missing"
    else:
        fileinfo = form['clientfile']
        try:
            filetext, srvrname = saveonserver(fileinfo)
        except:
            errmsg = '<h2>Error</h2><p>%s<p>%s' % (sys.exc_type, sys.exc_value)
            print html % errmsg
        else:
```

Example 12-27. PP2E\Internet\Cgi-Web\Basics\putfile.cgi (continued)

```
        print goodhtml % (cgi.escape(fileinfo.filename),
                          cgi.escape(srvrname),
                          cgi.escape(filetext))
main()
```

Within this script, the Python-specific interfaces for handling uploaded files are employed. They aren't much different, really; the file comes into the script as an entry in the parsed form object returned by `cgi.FieldStorage` as usual; its key is `clientfile`, the input control's `name` in the HTML page's code.

This time, though, the entry has additional attributes for the file's name on the client. Moreover, accessing the `value` attribute of an uploaded file input object will automatically read the file's contents all at once into a string on the server. For very large files, we can instead read line by line (or in chunks of bytes). For illustration purposes, the script implements either scheme: based on the setting of the `loadtextauto` global variable, it either asks for the file contents as a string, or reads it line by line.* In general, the CGI module gives us back objects with the following attributes for file upload controls:

`filename`
: The name of the file as specified on the client

`file`
: A file object from which the uploaded file's contents can be read

`value`
: The contents of the uploaded file (read from file on demand)

There are additional attributes not used by our script. Files represent a third input field object; as we've also seen, the `value` attribute is a *string* for simple input fields, and we may receive a *list* of objects for multiple-selection controls.

For uploads to be saved on the server, CGI scripts (run by user "nobody") must have write access to the enclosing directory if the file doesn't yet exist, or to the file itself if it does. To help isolate uploads, the script stores all uploads in whatever server directory is named in the `uploaddir` global. On my site's Linux server, I had to give this directory a mode of 777 (universal read/write/execute permissions) with `chmod` to make uploads work in general. Your mileage may vary, but be sure to check permissions if this script fails.

---

* Note that reading line means that this CGI script is biased towards uploading text files, not binary data files. The fact that it also uses a "w" open mode makes it ill suited for binary uploads if run on a Windows server—`\r` characters might be added to the data when written. See Chapter 2 for details if you've forgotten why.

The script also calls `os.chmod` to set the permission on the server file such that it can be read and written by everyone. If created anew by an upload, the file's owner will be "nobody," which means anyone out in cyberspace can view and upload the file. On my server, though, the file will also be only writable by user "nobody" by default, which might be inconvenient when it comes time to change that file outside the Web (the degree of pain can vary per operation).

> Isolating client-side file uploads by placing them in a single directory on the server helps minimize security risks: existing files can't be overwritten arbitrarily. But it may require you to copy files on the server after they are uploaded, and it still doesn't prevent all security risks—mischievous clients can still upload huge files, which we would need to trap with additional logic not present in this script as is. Such traps may only be needed in scripts open to the Internet at large.

If both client and server do their parts, the CGI script presents us with the response page shown in Figure 12-32, after it has stored the contents of the client file in a new or existing file on the server. For verification, the response gives the client and server file paths, as well as an echo of the uploaded file with a line count (in line-by-line reader mode).

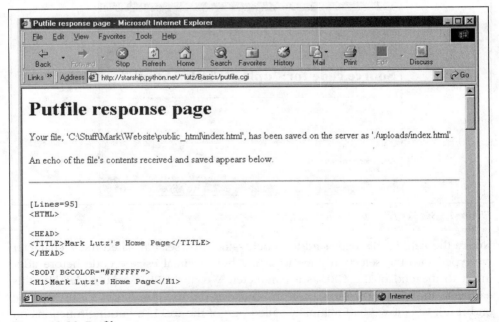

Figure 12-32. Putfile response page

Incidentally, we can also verify the upload with the `getfile` program we wrote in
the prior section. Simply access the selection page to type the pathname of the file
on the server, as shown in Figure 12-33.

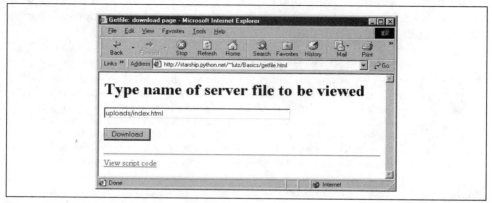

Figure 12-33. Verifying putfile with getfile — selection

Assuming uploading the file was successful, Figure 12-34 shows the resulting
viewer page we will obtain. Since user "nobody" (CGI scripts) was able to write
the file, "nobody" should be able to view it as well.

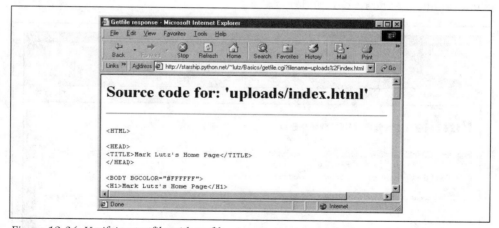

Figure 12-34. Verifying putfile with getfile — response

Notice the URL in this page's address field—the browser translated the / character
we typed into the selection page to a `%2F` hexadecimal escape code before adding it to the end of the URL as a parameter. We met URL escape codes like this
earlier in this chapter. In this case, the browser did the translation for us, but the
end result is as if we had manually called one of the `urllib` quoting functions on
the file path string.

Technically, the %2F escape code here represents the standard URL translation for non-ASCII characters, under the default encoding scheme browsers employ. Spaces are usually translated to + characters as well. We can often get away without manually translating most non-ASCII characters when sending paths explicitly (in typed URLs). But as we saw earlier, we sometimes need to be careful to escape characters (e.g., &) that have special meaning within URL strings with urllib tools.

Handling client path formats

In the end, the *putfile.cgi* script stores the uploaded file on the server, within a hardcoded uploaddir directory, under the filename at the end of the file's path on the client (i.e., less its client-side directory path). Notice, though, that the splitpath function in this script needs to do extra work to extract the base name of the file on the right. Browsers send up the filename in the directory path format used on the *client* machine; this path format may not be the same as that used on the server where the CGI script runs.

The standard way to split up paths, os.path.split, knows how to extract the base name, but only recognizes path separator characters used on the platform it is running on. That is, if we run this CGI script on a Unix machine, os.path.split chops up paths around a / separator. If a user uploads from a DOS or Windows machine, however, the separator in the passed filename is \, not /. Browsers running on a Macintosh may send a path that is more different still.

To handle client paths generically, this script imports platform-specific, path-processing modules from the Python library for each client it wishes to support, and tries to split the path with each until a filename on the right is found. For instance, posixpath handles paths sent from Unix-style platforms, and dospath recognizes DOS and Windows client paths. We usually don't import these modules directly since os.path.split is automatically loaded with the correct one for the underlying platform; but in this case, we need to be specific since the path comes from another machine. Note that we could have instead coded the path splitter logic like this to avoid some split calls:

```
def splitpath(origpath):                                # get name at end
    basename = os.path.split(origpath)[1]               # try server paths
    if basename == origpath:                            # didn't change it?
        if '\\' in origpath:
            basename = string.split(origpath, '\\')[-1]   # try dos clients
        elif '/' in origpath:
            basename = string.split(origpath, '/')[-1]    # try unix clients
    return basename
```

But this alternative version may fail for some path formats (e.g., DOS paths with a drive but no backslashes). As is, both options waste time if the filename is already a base name (i.e., has no directory paths on the left), but we need to allow for the more complex cases generically.

This upload script works as planned, but a few caveats are worth pointing out before we close the book on this example:

- First, `putfile` doesn't do anything about cross-platform incompatibilities in filenames themselves. For instance, spaces in a filename shipped from a DOS client are not translated to nonspace characters; they will wind up as spaces in the server-side file's name, which may be legal but which are difficult to process in some scenarios.

- Second, the script is also biased towards uploading text files; it opens the output file in text mode (which will convert end-of-line marker codes in the file to the end-of-line convention on the web server machine), and reads input line-by-line (which may fail for binary data).

If you run into any of these limitations, you will have crossed over into the domain of suggested exercises.

More Than One Way to Push Bits Over the Net

Finally, let's discuss some context. We've seen three `getfile` scripts at this point in the book. The one in this chapter is different than the other two we wrote in earlier chapters, but it accomplishes a similar goal:

- This chapter's `getfile` is a server-side CGI script that displays files over the HTTP protocol (on port 80).

- In Chapter 10, *Network Scripting*, we built a client and server-side `getfile` to transfer with raw sockets (on port 50001) and Chapter 11 implemented a client-side `getfile` to ship over FTP (on port 21)

The CGI- and HTTP-based `putfile` script here is also different from the FTP-based `putfile` in the last chapter, but it can be considered an alternative to both socket and FTP uploads. To help underscore the distinctions, Figures 12-35 and 12-36 show the new `putfile` uploading the original socket-based `getfile`.[*]

Really, the `getfile` CGI script in this chapter simply displays files only, but can be considered a download tool when augmented with cut-and-paste operations in a web browser. Figures 12-37 and 12-38 show the CGI `getfile` displaying the uploaded socket-based `getfile`.

---

[*] Shown here being loaded from a now defunct *Part2* directory—replace *Part2* with *PP2E* to find its true location, and don't be surprised if a few difference show up in transferred files contents if you run such examples yourself. Like I said, engineers love to change things.

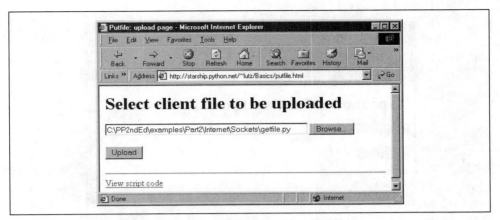

Figure 12-35. A new putfile with the socket-based getfile uploaded

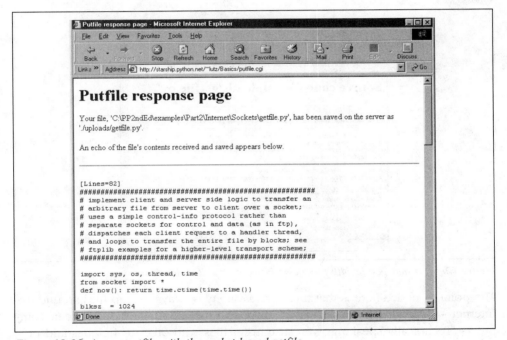

Figure 12-36. A new putfile with the socket-based getfile

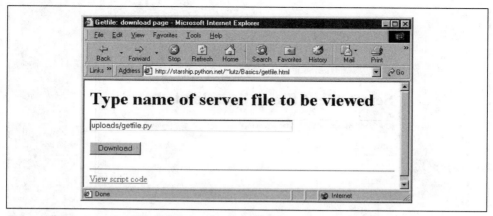

Figure 12-37. A new getfile with the socket-based getfile

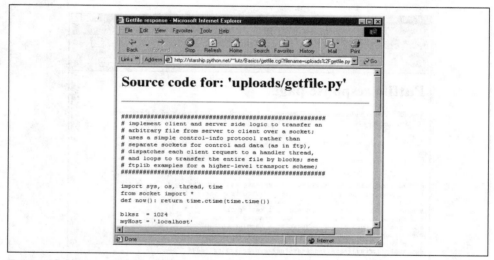

Figure 12-38. A new getfile with the socket-based getfile downloaded

The point to notice here is that there are a variety of ways to ship files around the Internet—sockets, FTP, and HTTP (web pages) can all move files between computers. Technically speaking, we can transfer files with other techniques and protocols, too—POP email, NNTP news, and so on.

Each technique has unique properties but does similar work in the end: moving bits over the Net. All ultimately run over sockets on a particular port, but protocols like FTP add additional structure to the socket layer, and application models like CGI add both structure and programmability.

13

Larger Web Site Examples I

"Things to Do When Visiting Chicago"

This chapter is the fourth part of our look at Python Internet programming, and continues the last chapter's discussion. In the prior chapter, we explored the fundamentals of server-side CGI scripting in Python. Armed with that knowledge, in this and the following chapter we move on to two larger case studies that underscore advanced CGI topics:

PyMailCgi

> This chapter presents *PyMailCgi*, a web site for reading and sending email that illustrates security concepts, hidden form fields, URL generation, and more. Because this system is similar in spirit to the PyMailGui program shown in Chapter 11, *Client-Side Scripting*, this example also serves as a comparison of web and non-web applications.

PyErrata

> Chapter 14, *Larger Web Site Examples II*, presents *PyErrata,* a web site for posting book comments and bugs that introduces database concepts in the CGI domain. This system demonstrates common ways to store data persistently on the server between web transactions, and addresses concurrent update problems inherent in the CGI model.

Both of these case studies are based on CGI scripting, but implement full-blown web sites that do something more useful than the last chapter's examples.

As usual, these chapters split their focus between application-level details and Python programming concepts. Because both of the case studies presented are fairly large, they illustrate system design concepts that are important in actual projects. They also say more about CGI scripts in general. PyMailCgi, for example, introduces the notions of state retention in hidden fields and URLs, as well as security concerns and encryption. PyErrata provides a vehicle for exploring persistent database concepts in the context of web sites.

Neither system here is particularly flashy or feature-rich as web sites go (in fact, the initial cut of PyMailCgi was thrown together during a layover at a Chicago airport). Alas, you will find neither dancing bears nor blinking lights at either of these sites. On the other hand, they were written to serve real purposes, speak more to us about CGI scripting, and hint at just how far Python server-side programs can take us. In Chapter 15, *Advanced Internet Topics*, we will explore higher-level systems and tools that build upon ideas we will apply here. For now, let's have some fun with Python on the Web.

The PyMailCgi Web Site

Near the end of Chapter 11, we built a program called PyMailGui that implemented a complete Python+Tk email client GUI (if you didn't read that section, you may want to take a quick look at it now). Here, we're going to do something of the same, but on the Web: the system presented in this section, PyMailCgi, is a collection of CGI scripts that implement a simple web-based interface for sending and reading email in any browser.

Our goal in studying this system is partly to learn a few more CGI tricks, partly to learn a bit about designing larger Python systems in general, and partly to underscore the trade-offs between systems implemented for the Web (PyMailCgi) and systems written to run locally (PyMailGui). This chapter hints at some of these trade-offs along the way, and returns to explore them in more depth after the presentation of this system.

Implementation Overview

At the top level, PyMailCgi allows users to view incoming email with the POP interface and to send new mail by SMTP. Users also have the option of replying to, forwarding, or deleting an incoming email while viewing it. As implemented, anyone can send email from the PyMailCgi site, but to view your email, you generally have to install PyMailCgi at your own site with your own mail server information (due to security concerns described later).

Viewing and sending email sounds simple enough, but the interaction involved involves a number of distinct web pages, each requiring a CGI script or HTML file of its own. In fact, PyMailCgi is a fairly linear system—in the most complex user interaction scenario, there are six states (and hence six web pages) from start to finish. Because each page is usually generated by a distinct file in the CGI world, that also implies six source files.

To help keep track of how all of PyMailCgi's files fit into the overall system, I wrote the file in Example 13-1 before starting any real programming. It informally sketches the user's flow through the system and the files invoked along the way. You can certainly use more formal notations to describe the flow of control and information through states such as web pages (e.g., dataflow diagrams), but for this simple example this file gets the job done.

Example 13-1. PP2E\Internet\Cgi-Web\PyMailCgi\pageflow.txt

```
file or script                     creates
--------------                     -------

[pymailcgi.html]                   Root window
 => [onRootViewLink.cgi]           Pop password window
    => [onViewPswdSubmit.cgi]      List window (loads all pop mail)
       => [onViewListLink.cgi]     View Window + pick=del|reply|fwd (fetch)
          => [onViewSubmit.cgi]    Edit window, or delete+confirm (del)
             => [onSendSubmit.cgi] Confirmation (sends smtp mail)
                => back to root


 => [onRootSendLink.cgi]           Edit Window
    => [onSendSubmit.cgi]          Confirmation (sends smtp mail)
       => back to root
```

This file simply lists all the source files in the system, using => and indentation to denote the scripts they trigger.

For instance, links on the *pymailcgi.html* root page invoke *onRootViewLink.cgi* and *onRootSendLink.cgi*, both executable scripts. The script *onRootViewLink.cgi* generates a password page, whose Submit button in turn triggers *onViewPswdSubmit.cgi*, and so on. Notice that both the view and send actions can wind up triggering *onSendSubmit.cgi* to send a new mail; view operations get there after the user chooses to reply to or forward an incoming mail.

In a system like this, CGI scripts make little sense in isolation, so it's a good idea to keep the overall page flow in mind; refer to this file if you get lost. For additional context, Figure 13-1 shows the overall contents of this site, viewed on Windows with the PyEdit "Open" function.

The *temp* directory was used only during development. To install this site, all the files you see here are uploaded to a *PyMailCgi* subdirectory of my *public_html* web directory. Besides the page-flow HTML and CGI script files invoked by user interaction, PyMailCgi uses a handful of utility modules as well:

- *commonhtml.py* is a library of HTML tools.
- *externs.py* isolates access to modules imported from other systems.
- *loadmail.py* encapsulates mailbox fetches.
- *secret.py* implements configurable password encryption.

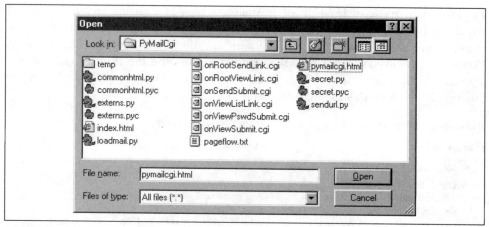

Figure 13-1. PyMailCgi contents

PyMailCgi also reuses parts of the *pymail.py* and *mailconfig.py* modules we wrote in Chapter 11; on my web server, these are installed in a special directory that is not necessarily the same as their location in the examples distribution (they show up in another server directory, not shown in Figure 13-1). As usual, PyMailCgi also uses a variety of standard Python library modules: `smtplib`, `poplib`, `rfc822`, `cgi`, `urllib`, `time`, `rotor`, and the like.

Carry-on Software

PyMailCgi works as planned and illustrates more CGI and email concepts, but I want to point out a few caveats up front. The application was initially written during a two-hour layover in Chicago's O'Hare airport (though debugging took a few hours more). I wrote it to meet a specific need—to be able to read and send email from any web browser while traveling around the world teaching Python classes. I didn't design it to be aesthetically pleasing to others and didn't spend much time focusing on its efficiency.

I also kept this example intentionally simple for this book. For example, PyMailCgi doesn't provide all the features of the PyMailGui program in Chapter 11, and reloads email more than it probably should. In other words, you should consider this system a work in progress; it's not yet software worth selling. On the other hand, it does what it was intended to do, and can be customized by tweaking its Python source code—something that can't be said of all software sold.

Presentation Overview

PyMailCgi is a challenge to present in a book like this, because most of the "action" is encapsulated in shared utility modules (especially one called *commonhtml.py*); the CGI scripts that implement user interaction don't do much by themselves. This architecture was chosen deliberately, to make scripts simple and implement a common look-and-feel. But it means you must jump between files to understand how the system works.

To make this example easier to digest, we're going to explore its code in two chunks: page scripts first, and then the utility modules. First, we'll study screen shots of the major web pages served up by the system and the HTML files and top-level Python CGI scripts used to generate them. We begin by following a send mail interaction, and then trace how existing email is processed. Most implementation details will be presented in these sections, but be sure to flip ahead to the utility modules listed later to understand what the scripts are really doing.

I should also point out that this is a fairly complex system, and I won't describe it in exhaustive detail; be sure to read the source code along the way for details not made explicit in the narrative. All of the system's source code appears in this section (and on the book's CD), and we will study the key concepts in this system here. But as usual with case studies in this book, I assume that you can read Python code by now and will consult the example's source code for more details. Because Python's syntax is so close to executable pseudocode, systems are sometimes better described in Python than in English.

The Root Page

Let's start off by implementing a main page for this example. The file shown in Example 13-2 is primarily used to publish links to the Send and View functions' pages. It is coded as a static HTML file, because there is nothing to generate on the fly here.

Example 13-2. PP2E\Internet\Cgi-Web\PyMailCgi\pymailcgi.html

```
<HTML><BODY>
<TITLE>PyMailCgi Main Page</TITLE>
<H1 align=center>PyMailCgi</H1>
<H2 align=center>A POP/SMTP Email Interface</H2>
<P align=center><I>Version 1.0, April 2000</I></P>

<table><tr><td><hr>
<P>
<A href="http://rmi.net/~lutz/about-pp.html">
<IMG src="../PyErrata/ppsmall.gif" align=left
alt="[Book Cover]" border=1 hspace=10></A>
```

Example 13-2. PP2E\Internet\Cgi-Web\PyMailCgi\pymailcgi.html (continued)

This site implements a simple web-browser interface to POP/SMTP email
accounts. Anyone can send email with this interface, but for security
reasons, you cannot view email unless you install the scripts with your
own email account information, in your own server account directory.
PyMailCgi is implemented as a number of Python-coded CGI scripts that run on
a server machine (not your local computer), and generate HTML to interact
with the client/browser. See the book <I>Programming Python, 2nd Edition</I>
for more details.</P>

```
<tr><td><hr>
<h2>Actions</h2>
<P><UL>
<LI><a href="onRootViewLink.cgi">View, Reply, Forward, Delete POP mail</a>
<LI><a href="onRootSendLink.cgi">Send a new email message by SMTP</a>
</UL></P>
```

```
<tr><td><hr>
<P>Caveats: PyMailCgi 1.0 was initially written during a 2-hour layover at
Chicago's O'Hare airport.  This release is not nearly as fast or complete
as PyMailGui (e.g., each click requires an Internet transaction, there
is no save operation, and email is reloaded often).  On the other hand,
PyMailCgi runs on any web broswer, whether you have Python (and Tk)
installed on your machine or not.
```

```
<P>Also note that if you use these scripts to read your own email, PyMailCgi
does not guarantee security for your account password, so be careful out there.
See the notes in the View action page as well as the book for more information
on security policies.  Also see:
```

```
<UL>
<li>The <I>PyMailGui</I> program in the Email directory, which
        implements a client-side Python+Tk email GUI
<li>The <I>pymail.py</I> program in the Email directory, which
        provides a simple command-line email interface
<li>The Python imaplib module which supports the IMAP email protocol
        instead of POP
<li>The upcoming openSSL support for secure transactions in the new
        Python 1.6 socket module
</UL></P>
</table><hr>
```

```
<A href="http://www.python.org">
<IMG SRC="../PyErrata/PythonPoweredSmall.gif" ALIGN=left
ALT="[Python Logo]" border=0 hspace=15></A>
<A href="../PyInternetDemos.html">More examples</A>
</BODY></HTML>
```

The file *pymailcgi.html* is the system's root page and lives in a *PyMailCgi* subdirectory of my web directory that is dedicated to this application (and helps keep its files separate from other examples). To access this system, point your browser to:

> *http://starship.python.net/~lutz/PyMailCgi/pymailcgi.html*

If you do, the server will ship back a page like that shown in Figure 13-2.

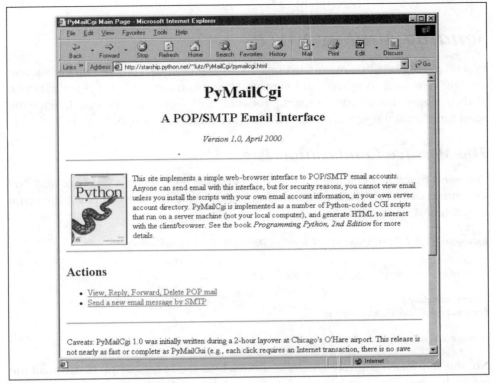

Figure 13-2. PyMailCgi main page

Now, before you click on the View link here expecting to read your own email, I should point out that by default, PyMailCgi allows anybody to send email from this page with the Send link (as we learned earlier, there are no passwords in SMTP). It does not, however, allow arbitrary users on the Web to read their email accounts without typing an explicit and unsafe URL or doing a bit of installation and configuration. This is on purpose, and has to do with security constraints; as we'll see later, I wrote the system such that it never associates your email user-name and password together without encryption.

By default, then, this page is set up to read my (the author's) email account, and requires my POP password to do so. Since you probably can't guess my password (and wouldn't find my email helpful if you could), PyMailCgi is not incredibly useful as installed at this site. To use it to read your email instead, you should install the system's source code on your own server and tweak a mail configuration file that we'll see in a moment. For now, let's proceed by using the system as it is installed on my server, with my POP email account; it works the same way, regardless of which account it accesses.

Sending Mail by SMTP

PyMailCgi supports two main functions (as links on the root page): composing and sending new mail to others, and viewing your incoming mail. The View function leads to pages that let users reply to, forward, and delete existing email. Since the Send function is the simplest, let's start with its pages and scripts first.

The Message Composition Page

The Send function steps users through two pages: one to edit a message and one to confirm delivery. When you click on the Send link on the main page, the script in Example 13-3 runs on the server.

Example 13-3. PP2E\Internet\Cgi-Web\PyMailCgi\onRootSendLink.cgi

```
#!/usr/bin/python
# On 'send' click in main root window

import commonhtml
from externs import mailconfig

commonhtml.editpage(kind='Write', headers={'From': mailconfig.myaddress})
```

No, this file wasn't truncated; there's not much to see in this script, because all the action has been encapsulated in the `commonhtml` and `externs` modules. All that we can tell here is that the script calls something named `editpage` to generate a reply, passing in something called `myaddress` for its "From" header. That's by design—by hiding details in utility modules, we make top-level scripts like this much easier to read and write. There are no inputs to this script either; when run, it produces a page for composing a new message, as shown in Figure 13-3.

Send Mail Script

Much like the Tkinter-based PyMailGui client program we met in Chapter 11, this page provides fields for entering common header values as well as the text of the message itself. The "From" field is prefilled with a string imported from a module called `mailconfig`. As we'll discuss in a moment, that module lives in another directory on the server in this system, but its contents are the same as in the PyMailGui example. When we click the Send button of the edit page, Example 13-4 runs on the server.

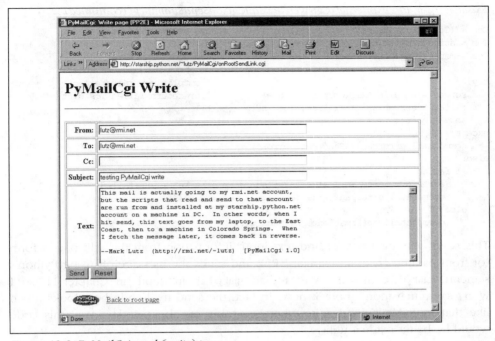

Figure 13-3. PyMailCgi send (write) page

Example 13-4. PP2E\Internet\Cgi-Web\PyMailCgi\onSendSubmit.cgi

```python
#!/usr/bin/python
# On submit in edit window--finish a write, reply, or forward

import cgi, smtplib, time, string, commonhtml
#commonhtml.dumpstatepage(0)
form = cgi.FieldStorage()                      # parse form input data

# server name from module or get-style url
smtpservername = commonhtml.getstandardsmtpfields(form)

# parms assumed to be in form or url here
from commonhtml import getfield              # fetch value attributes
From = getfield(form, 'From')                # empty fields may not be sent
To   = getfield(form, 'To')
Cc   = getfield(form, 'Cc')
Subj = getfield(form, 'Subject')
text = getfield(form, 'text')

# caveat: logic borrowed from PyMailGui
date = time.ctime(time.time())
Cchdr = (Cc and 'Cc: %s\n' % Cc) or ''
hdrs = ('From: %s\nTo: %s\n%sDate: %s\nSubject: %s\n'
                % (From, To, Cchdr, date, Subj))
hdrs = hdrs + 'X-Mailer: PyMailCgi Version 1.0 (Python)\n\n'
```

Example 13-4. PP2E\Internet\Cgi-Web\PyMailCgi\onSendSubmit.cgi (continued)

```
Ccs = (Cc and string.split(Cc, ';')) or []    # some servers reject ['']
Tos = string.split(To, ';') + Ccs             # cc: hdr line, and To list
Tos = map(string.strip, Tos)                  # some addrs can have ','s

try:                                           # smtplib may raise except
    server = smtplib.SMTP(smtpservername)      # or return failed Tos dict
    failed = server.sendmail(From, Tos, hdrs + text)
    server.quit()
except:
    commonhtml.errorpage('Send mail error')
else:
    if failed:
        errInfo = 'Send mail error\nFailed recipients:\n' + str(failed)
        commonhtml.errorpage(errInfo)
    else:
        commonhtml.confirmationpage('Send mail')
```

This script gets mail header and text input information from the edit page's form (or from parameters in an explicit URL), and sends the message off using Python's standard `smtplib` module. We studied `smtplib` in depth in Chapter 11, so I won't say much more about it now. In fact, the send mail code here looks much like that in PyMailGui (despite what I've told you about code reuse; this code would be better made a utility).

A utility in `commonhtml` ultimately fetches the name of the SMTP server to receive the message from either the `mailconfig` module or the script's inputs (in a form field or URL parameter). If all goes well, we're presented with a generated confirmation page, as in Figure 13-4.

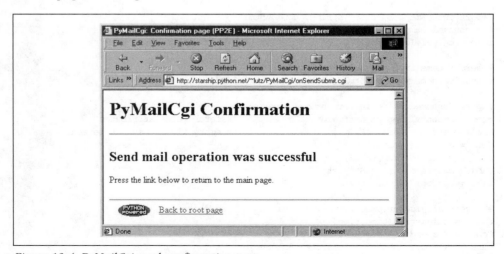

Figure 13-4. PyMailCgi send confirmation page

Notice that there are no usernames or passwords to be found here; as we saw in Chapter 11, SMTP requires only a server that listens on the SMTP port, not a user account or password. As we also saw in that chapter, SMTP send operations that fail either raise a Python exception (e.g., if the server host can't be reached) or return a dictionary of failed recipients.

If there is a problem during mail delivery, we get an error page like the one shown in Figure 13-5. This page reflects a failed recipient—the `else` clause of the `try` statement we used to wrap the send operation. On an actual exception, the Python error message and extra details would be displayed.

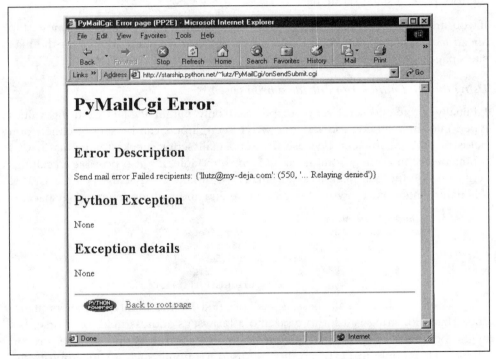

Figure 13-5. PyMailCgi send error page

Before we move on, you should know that this send mail script is also used to deliver *reply* and *forward* messages for incoming POP mail. The user interface for those operations is slightly different than for composing new email from scratch, but as in PyMailGui, the submission handler logic is the same code—they are really just mail send operations.

It's also worth pointing out that the `commonhtml` module encapsulates the generation of both the confirmation and error pages, so that all such pages look the same in PyMailCgi no matter where and when they are produced. Logic that generates the mail edit page in commonhtml is reused by the reply and forward actions too (but with different mail headers).

In fact, commonhtml makes all pages look similar—it also provides common page *header* (top) and *footer* (bottom) generation functions, which are used everywhere in the system. You may have already noticed that all the pages so far follow the same pattern: they start with a title and horizontal rule, have something unique in the middle, and end with another rule, followed by a Python icon and link at the bottom. This *common look-and-feel* is the product of commonhtml; it generates everything but the middle section for every page in the system (except the root page, a static HTML file).

If you are interested in seeing how this encapsulated logic works right now, flip ahead to Example 13-14. We'll explore its code after we study the rest of the mail site's pages.

Using the send mail script outside a browser

I initially wrote the send script to be used only within PyMailCgi, using values typed into the mail edit form. But as we've seen, inputs can be sent in either form fields or URL parameters; because the send mail script checks for inputs in CGI inputs before importing from the mailconfig module, it's also possible to call this script outside the edit page to send email. For instance, explicitly typing a URL of this nature into your browser (but all on one line and with no intervening spaces):

```
http://starship.python.net/~lutz/
    PyMailCgi/onSendSubmit.cgi?site=smtp.rmi.net&
                            From=lutz@rmi.net&
                            To=lutz@rmi.net&
                            Subject=test+url&
                            text=Hello+Mark;this+is+Mark
```

will indeed send an email message as specified by the input parameters at the end. That URL string is a lot to type into a browser's address field, of course, but might be useful if generated automatically by another script. As we saw in Chapter 11, module urllib can then be used to submit such a URL string to the server from within a Python program. Example 13-5 shows one way to do it.

Example 13-5. PP2E\Internet\Cgi-Web\PyMailCgi\sendurl.py

```
#####################################################################
# Send email by building a URL like this from inputs:
# http://starship.python.net/~lutz/
#       PyMailCgi/onSendSubmit.cgi?site=smtp.rmi.net&
#                               From=lutz@rmi.net&
#                               To=lutz@rmi.net&
#                               Subject=test+url&
#                               text=Hello+Mark;this+is+Mark
#####################################################################
```

Example 13-5. PP2E\Internet\Cgi-Web\PyMailCgi\sendurl.py (continued)

```
from urllib import quote_plus, urlopen

url = 'http://starship.python.net/~lutz/PyMailCgi/onSendSubmit.cgi'
url = url + '?site=%s'    % quote_plus(raw_input('Site>'))
url = url + '&From=%s'    % quote_plus(raw_input('From>'))
url = url + '&To=%s'      % quote_plus(raw_input('To  >'))
url = url + '&Subject=%s' % quote_plus(raw_input('Subj>'))
url = url + '&text=%s'    % quote_plus(raw_input('text>'))    # or input loop

print 'Reply html:'
print urlopen(url).read()      # confirmation or error page html
```

Running this script from the system command line is yet another way to send an email message—this time, by contacting our CGI script on a remote server machine to do all the work. Script *sendurl.py* runs on any machine with Python and sockets, lets us input mail parameters interactively, and invokes another Python script that lives on a remote machine. It prints HTML returned by our CGI script:

```
C:\...\PP2E\Internet\Cgi-Web\PyMailCgi>python sendurl.py
Site>smtp.rmi.net
From>lutz@rmi.net
To  >lutz@rmi.net
Subj>test sendurl.py
text>But sir, it's only wafer-thin...
Reply html:
<html><head><title>PyMailCgi: Confirmation page (PP2E)</title></head>
<body bgcolor="#FFFFFF"><h1>PyMailCgi Confirmation</h1><hr>
<h2>Send mail operation was successful</h2>
<p>Press the link below to return to the main page.</p>
</p><hr><a href="http://www.python.org">
<img src="../PyErrata/PythonPoweredSmall.gif"
align=left alt="[Python Logo]" border=0 hspace=15></a>
<a href="pymailcgi.html">Back to root page</a>
</body></html>
```

The HTML reply printed by this script would normally be rendered into a new web page if caught by a browser. Such cryptic output might be less than ideal, but you could easily search the reply string for its components to determine the result (e.g., using `string.find` to look for "successful"), parse out its components with Python's standard `htmllib` module, and so on. The resulting mail message—viewed, for variety, with Chapter 11's PyMailGui program—shows up in my account as seen in Figure 13-6.

Of course, there are other, less remote ways to send email from a client machine. For instance, the Python `smtplib` module itself depends only upon the client and POP server connections being operational, whereas this script also depends on the CGI server machine (requests go from client to CGI server to POP server and back). Because our CGI script supports general URLs, though, it can do more than

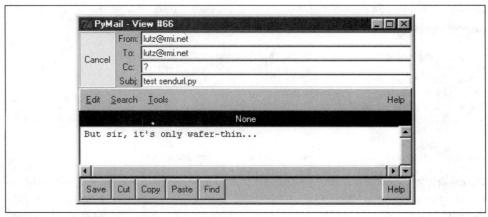

Figure 13-6. sendurl.py result

a "mailto:" HTML tag, and can be invoked with `urllib` outside the context of a running web browser. For instance, scripts like *sendurl.py* can be used to invoke and *test* server-side programs.

Reading POP Email

So far, we've stepped through the path the system follows to *send* new mail. Let's now see what happens when we try to *view* incoming POP mail.

The POP Password Page

If you flip back to the main page in Figure 13-2, you'll see a View link; pressing it triggers the script in Example 13-6 to run on the server:

Example 13-6. PP2E\Internet\Cgi-Web\PyMailCgi\onRootViewLink.cgi

```
#!/usr/bin/python
############################################################
# on view link click on main/root html page
# this could almost be a html file because there are likely
# no input params yet, but I wanted to use standard header/
# footer functions and display the site/user names which must
# be fetched;  On submission, doesn't send the user along with
# password here, and only ever sends both as URL params or
# hidden fields after the password has been encrypted by a
# user-uploadable encryption module; put html in commonhtml?
############################################################

# page template

pswdhtml = """
```

Example 13-6. PP2E\Internet\Cgi-Web\PyMailCgi\onRootViewLink.cgi (continued)

```
<form method=post action=%s/onViewPswdSubmit.cgi>
<p>
Please enter POP account password below, for user "%s" and site "%s".
<p><input name=pswd type=password>
<input type=submit value="Submit"></form></p>

<hr><p><i>Security note</i>: The password you enter above will be transmitted
over the Internet to the server machine, but is not displayed, is never
transmitted in combination with a username unless it is encrypted, and is
never stored anywhere: not on the server (it is only passed along as hidden
fields in subsequent pages), and not on the client (no cookies are generated).
This is still not totally safe; use your browser's back button to back out of
PyMailCgi at any time.</p>
"""

# generate the password input page

import commonhtml                                           # usual parms case:
user, pswd, site = commonhtml.getstandardpopfields({})      # from module here,
commonhtml.pageheader(kind='POP password input')            # from html|url later
print pswdhtml % (commonhtml.urlroot, user, site)
commonhtml.pagefooter()
```

This script is almost all embedded HTML: the triple-quoted `pswdhtml` string is printed, with string formatting, in a single step. But because we need to fetch the user and server names to display on the generated page, this is coded as an executable script, not a static HTML file. Module `commonhtml` either loads user and server names from script inputs (e.g., appended to the script's URL), or imports them from the `mailconfig` file; either way, we don't want to hardcode them into this script or its HTML, so an HTML file won't do.

Since this is a script, we can also make use of the `commonhtml` page header and footer routines to render the generated reply page with the common look-and-feel; this is shown in Figure 13-7.

At this page, the user is expected to enter the password for the POP email account of the user and server displayed. Notice that the actual password isn't displayed; the input field's HTML specifies `type=password`, which works just like a normal text field, but shows typed input as stars. (See also Example 11-6 for doing this at a console, and Example 11-23 for doing this in a GUI.)

The Mail Selection List Page

After filling out the last page's password field and pressing its Submit button, the password is shipped off to the script shown in Example 13-7.

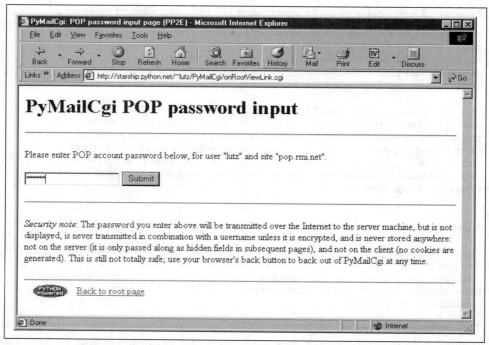

Figure 13-7. PyMailCgi view password login page

Example 13-7. PP2E\Internet\Cgi-Web\PyMailCgi\onViewPswdSubmit.cgi

```
#!/usr/bin/python
# On submit in pop password input window--make view list

import cgi, StringIO, rfc822, string
import loadmail, commonhtml
from    secret import encode        # user-defined encoder module
MaxHdr = 35                         # max length of email hdrs in list

# only pswd comes from page here, rest usually in module
formdata = cgi.FieldStorage()
mailuser, mailpswd, mailsite = commonhtml.getstandardpopfields(formdata)

try:
    newmail  = loadmail.loadnewmail(mailsite, mailuser, mailpswd)
    mailnum  = 1
    maillist = []
    for mail in newmail:
        msginfo = []
        hdrs = rfc822.Message(StringIO.StringIO(mail))
        for key in ('Subject', 'From', 'Date'):
            msginfo.append(hdrs.get(key, '?')[:MaxHdr])
        msginfo = string.join(msginfo, ' | ')
        maillist.append((msginfo, commonhtml.urlroot + '/onViewListLink.cgi',
                                   {'mnum': mailnum,
                                    'user': mailuser,              # data params
```

Example 13-7. PP2E\Internet\Cgi-Web\PyMailCgi\onViewPswdSubmit.cgi (continued)

```
                                  'pswd': encode(mailpswd),   # pass in url
                                  'site': mailsite}))         # not inputs
        mailnum = mailnum+1
    commonhtml.listpage(maillist, 'mail selection list')
except:
    commonhtml.errorpage('Error loading mail index')
```

This script's main purpose is to generate a selection list page for the user's email account, using the password typed into the prior page (or passed in a URL). As usual with encapsulation, most of the details are hidden in other files:

- `loadmail.loadnewmail` reuses the mail module from Example 11-8 to fetch email with the POP protocol; we need a message count and mail headers here to display an index list.

- `commonhtml.listpage` generates HTML to display a passed-in list of (`text`, `URL`, `parameter-dictionary`) tuples as a list of hyperlinks in the reply page; parameter values show up at the end of URLs in the response.

The `maillist` list built here is used to create the body of the next page—a clickable email message selection list. Each generated hyperlink in the list page references a constructed URL that contains enough information for the next script to fetch and display a particular email message.

If all goes well, the mail selection list page HTML generated by this script is rendered as in Figure 13-8. If you get as much email as I do, you'll probably need to scroll down to see the end of this page. It looks like Figure 13-9, and follows the common look-and-feel for all PyMailCgi pages, thanks to `commonhtml`.[*]

If the script can't access your email account (e.g., because you typed the wrong password), then its `try` statement handler instead produces a commonly formatted error page. Figure 13-10 shows one that gives the Python exception and details as part of the reply after a genuine exception is caught.

Passing state information in URL link parameters

The central mechanism at work in Example 13-7 is the generation of URLs that embed message numbers and mail account information. Clicking on any of the View links in the selection list triggers another script, which uses information in the link's URL parameters to fetch and display the selected email. As mentioned in

---

[*] The keen-eyed reader may notice that the hyperlink shown at the bottom of this screen shot shows the POP password in a different format than shown elsewhere. This is just an alternative encoding scheme in utility module *secret.py*, which yields a string of ASCII digits separated by dashes, instead of using the default URL encoding scheme. Some readers might also notice that the password on this page has fewer characters than in other screen shots; because I'm publishing my password decryptor code in this book, all passwords here are changed often. Did you really think it would be that easy? :-)

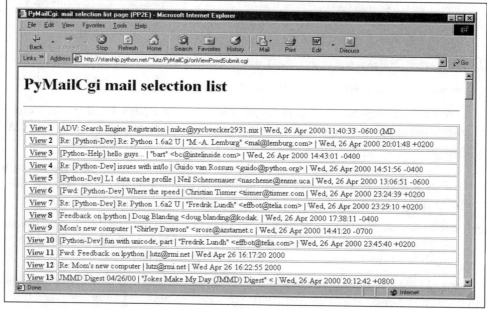

Figure 13-8. PyMailCgi view selection list page, top

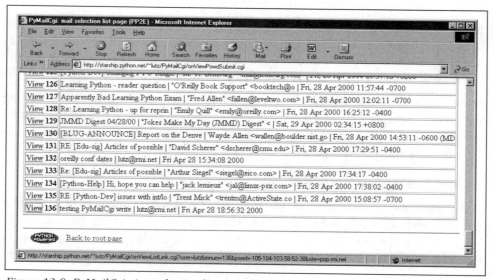

Figure 13-9. PyMailCgi view selection list page, bottom

the prior chapter, because the list's links are effectively programmed to "know" how to load a particular message, it's not too far-fetched to refer to them as *smart links*—URLs that remember what to do next. Figure 13-11 shows part of the HTML generated by this script.

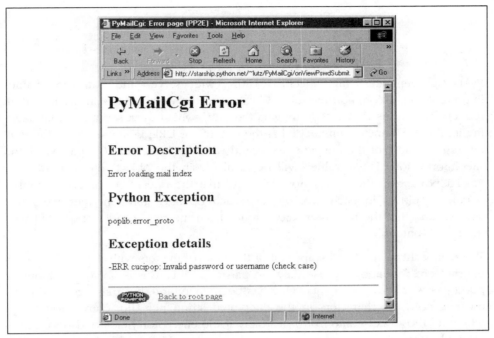

Figure 13-10. PyMailCgi login error page

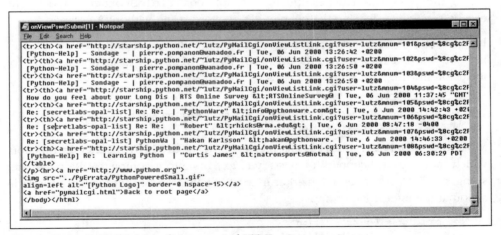

Figure 13-11. PyMailCgi view list, generated HTML

Did you get all that? You may not be able to read generated HTML like this, but your browser can. For the sake of readers afflicted with human parsing limitations, here is what one of those link lines looks like, reformatted with line breaks and spaces to make it easier to understand:

```
<tr><th><ahref="http://starship.python.net/~lutz/
                PyMailCgi/onViewListLink.cgi
```

```
                                    ?user=lutz&
                                    mnum=66&
                                    pswd=%8cg%c2P%1e%f3%5b%c5J%1c%f0&
                                    site=pop.rmi.net">View</a> 66
        <td>test sendurl.py | lutz@rmi.net | Mon Jun  5 17:51:11 2000
```

PyMailCgi generates fully specified URLs (with server and pathname values imported from a common module). Clicking on the word "View" in the hyperlink rendered from this HTML code triggers the onViewListLink script as usual, passing it all the parameters embedded at the end of the URL: POP username, the POP message number of the message associated with this link, and POP password and site information. These values will be available in the object returned by cgi. FieldStorage in the next script run. Note that the mnum POP message number parameter differs in each link because each opens a different message when clicked, and that the text after <td> comes from message headers extracted with the rfc822 module.

The commonhtml module escapes all of the link parameters with the urllib module, not cgi.escape, because they are part of a URL. This is obvious only in the pswd password parameter—its value has been encrypted, but urllib additionally escapes non-safe characters in the encrypted string per URL convention (that's where all those %xx come from). It's okay if the encryptor yields odd—even non-printable—characters, because URL encoding makes them legible for transmission. When the password reaches the next script, cgi.FieldStorage undoes URL escape sequences, leaving the encrypted password string without % escapes.

It's instructive to see how commonhtml builds up the smart link parameters. Earlier, we learned how to use the urllib.quote_plus call to escape a string for inclusion in URLs:

```
>>> import urllib
>>> urllib.quote_plus("There's bugger all down here on Earth")
'There%27s+bugger+all+down+here+on+Earth'
```

Module commonhtml, though, calls the higher-level urllib.urlencode function, which translates a dictionary of *name:value* pairs into a complete URL parameter string, ready to add after a ? marker in a URL. For instance, here is urlencode in action at the interactive prompt:

```
>>> parmdict = {'user': 'Brian',
...             'pswd': '#!/spam',
...             'text': 'Say no more, squire!'}

>>> urllib.urlencode(parmdict)
'pswd=%23%21/spam&user=Brian&text=Say+no+more,+squire%21'

>>> "%s?%s" % ("http://scriptname.cgi", urllib.urlencode(parmdict))
'http://scriptname.cgi?pswd=%23%21/spam&user=Brian&text=Say+no+more,+squire%21'
```

Internally, `urlencode` passes each name and value in the dictionary to the built-in `str` function (to make sure they are strings) and then runs each one through `urllib.quote_plus` as they are added to the result. The CGI script builds up a list of similar dictionaries and passes it to `commonhtml` to be formatted into a selection list page.*

In broader terms, generating URLs with parameters like this is one way to pass state information to the next script (along with databases and hidden form input fields, discussed later). Without such state information, the user would have to re-enter the username, password, and site name on every page they visit along the way. We'll use this technique again in the next case study, to generate links that "know" how to fetch a particular database record.

Incidentally, the list generated by this script is not radically different in functionality from what we built in the PyMailGui program of Chapter 11. Figure 13-12 shows this strictly client-side GUI's view on the same email list displayed in Figures 13-8 and 13-9.

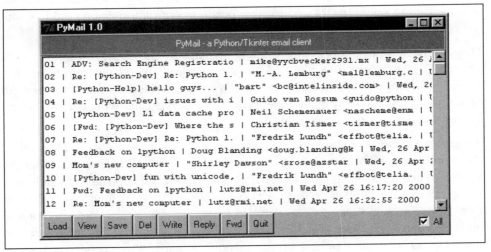

Figure 13-12. PyMailGui displaying the same view list

However, PyMailGui uses the Tkinter GUI library to build up a user interface instead of sending HTML to a browser. It also runs entirely on the client and downloads mail from the POP server to the client machine over sockets on demand. In contrast, PyMailCgi runs on the server machine and simply displays

---

* Technically, again, you should generally escape & separators in generated URL links like by running the URL through `cgi.escape`, if any parameter's name could be the same as that of an HTML character escape code (e.g., `"&amp=high"`). See the prior chapter for more details; they aren't escaped here because there are no clashes.

mail text on the client's browser—mail is downloaded from the POP server machine to the *starship* server, where CGI scripts are run. These architecture differences have some important ramifications, which we'll discuss in a few moments.

Security protocols

In onViewPswdSubmit's source code (Example 13-7), notice that password inputs are passed to an encode function as they are added to the parameters dictionary, and hence show up encrypted in hyperlink URLs. They are also URL-encoded for transmission (with % escapes) and are later decoded and decrypted within other scripts as needed to access the POP account. The password encryption step, encode, is at the heart of PyMailCgi's security policy.

Beginning in Python 1.6, the standard socket module will include optional support for *OpenSSL,* an open source implementation of secure sockets that prevents transmitted data from being intercepted by eavesdroppers on the Net. Unfortunately, this example was developed under Python 1.5.2, so an alternative scheme was devised to minimize the chance that email account information could be stolen off the Net in transit.

Here's how it works. When this script is invoked by the password input page's form, it gets only one input parameter: the password typed into the form. The username is imported from a mailconfig module installed on the server instead of transmitted together with the unencrypted password (that would be much too easy for malicious users to intercept).

To pass the POP username and password to the next page as state information, this script adds them to the end of the mail selection list URLs, but only after the password has been encrypted by secret.encode—a function in a module that lives on the server and may vary in every location that PyMailCgi is installed. In fact, PyMailCgi was written to not have to know about the password encryptor at all; because the encoder is a separate module, you can provide any flavor you like. Unless you also publish your encoder module, the encoded password shipped with the username won't be of much help to snoopers.

That upshot is that normally, PyMailGui never sends or receives both user and password values together in a single transaction unless the password is encrypted with an encryptor of your choice. This limits its utility somewhat (since only a single account username can be installed on the server), but the alternative of popping up two pages—one for password entry and one for user—is even more unfriendly. In general, if you want to read your mail with the system as coded, you have to install its files on your server, tweak its *mailconfig.py* to reflect your account details, and change its *secret.py* encryptor as desired.

One exception: since any CGI script can be invoked with parameters in an explicit URL instead of form field values, and since `commonhtml` tries to fetch inputs from the form object before importing them from `mailconfig`, it is possible for any person to use this script to check his or her mail without installing and configuring a copy of PyMailCgi. For example, a URL like the following (but without the linebreak used to make it fit here):

```
http://starship.python.net/~lutz/PyMailCgi/
onViewPswdSubmit.cgi?user=lutz&pswd=asif&site=pop.rmi.net
```

will actually load email into a selection list using whatever user, password, and mail site names are appended. From the selection list, you may then view, reply, forward, and delete email. Notice that at this point in the interaction, the password you send in a URL of this form is *not* encrypted. Later scripts expect that the password inputs will be sent encrypted, though, which makes it more difficult to use them with explicit URLs (you would need to match the encrypted form produced by the `secret` module on the server). Passwords are encrypted as they are added to links in the reply page's selection list, and remain encrypted in URLs and hidden form fields thereafter.

But please don't use a URL like this, unless you don't care about exposing your email password. Really. Sending both your unencrypted mail user ID and password strings across the Net in a URL like this is extremely unsafe and wide open to snoopers. In fact, it's like giving them a loaded gun—anyone who intercepts this URL will have complete access to your email account. It is made even more treacherous by the fact that this URL format appears in a book that will be widely distributed all around the world.

If you care about security and want to use PyMailCgi, install it on your own server and configure `mailconfig` and `secret`. That should at least guarantee that your user and password information will never both be transmitted unencrypted in a single transaction. This scheme still is not foolproof, so be careful out there, folks. Without secure sockets, the Internet is a "use at your own risk" medium.

The Message View Page

Back to our page flow. At this point, we are still viewing the message selection list in Figure 13-8. When we click on one of its generated hyperlinks, the smart URL invokes the script in Example 13-8 on the server, sending the selected message number and mail account information (user, password, and site) as parameters on the end of the script's URL.

Example 13-8. PP2E\Internet\Cgi-Web\PyMailCgi\onViewListLink.cgi

```
#!/usr/bin/python
###########################################################
# On user click of message link in main selection list;
# cgi.FieldStorage undoes any urllib escapes in the link's
# input parameters (%xx and '+' for spaces already undone);
###########################################################

import cgi, rfc822, StringIO
import commonhtml, loadmail
from secret import decode
#commonhtml.dumpstatepage(0)

form = cgi.FieldStorage()
user, pswd, site = commonhtml.getstandardpopfields(form)
try:
    msgnum   = form['mnum'].value                          # from url link
    newmail  = loadmail.loadnewmail(site, user, decode(pswd))
    textfile = StringIO.StringIO(newmail[int(msgnum) - 1])    # don't eval!
    headers  = rfc822.Message(textfile)
    bodytext = textfile.read()
    commonhtml.viewpage(msgnum, headers, bodytext, form)     # encoded pswd
except:
    commonhtml.errorpage('Error loading message')
```

Again, most of the work here happens in the `loadmail` and `commonhtml` modules, which are listed later in this section (Examples 13-12 and 13-14). This script adds logic to decode the input password (using the configurable `secret` encryption module) and extract the selected mail's headers and text using the `rfc822` and `StringIO` modules, just as we did in Chapter 11.[*]

If the message can be loaded and parsed successfully, the result page (shown in Figure 13-13) allows us to view, but not edit, the mail's text. The function `commonhtml.viewpage` generates a "read-only" HTML option for all the text widgets in this page.

View pages like this have a pull-down action selection list near the bottom; if you want to do more, use this list to pick an action (Reply, Forward, or Delete), and click on the Next button to proceed to the next screen. If you're just in a browsing frame of mind, click the "Back to root page" link at the bottom to return to the main page, or use your browser's Back button to return to the selection list page.

---

[*] Notice that the message number arrives as a string and must be converted to an integer in order to be used to fetch the message. But we're careful not convert with **eval** here, since this is a string passed over the Net and could have arrived embedded at the end of an arbitrary URL (remember that earlier warning?).

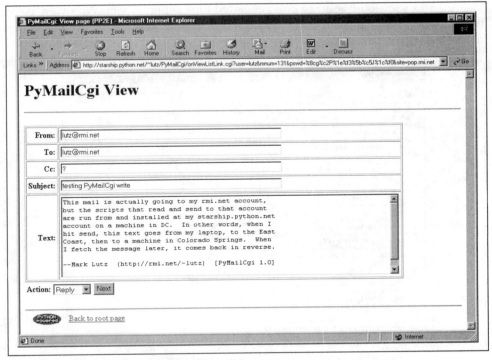

Figure 13-13. PyMailCgi view page

Passing state information in HTML hidden input fields

What you don't see on the view page in Figure 13-13 is just as important as what you do. We need to refer to Example 13-14 for details, but there's something new going on here. The original message number, as well as the POP user and (still encrypted) password information sent to this script as part of the smart link's URL, wind up being copied into the HTML used to create this view page, as the values of "hidden" input fields in the form. The hidden field generation code in `commonhtml` looks like this:

```
print '<form method=post action="%s/onViewSubmit.cgi">' % urlroot
print '<input type=hidden name=mnum value="%s">' % msgnum
print '<input type=hidden name=user value="%s">' % user    # from page|url
print '<input type=hidden name=site value="%s">' % site    # for deletes
print '<input type=hidden name=pswd value="%s">' % pswd    # pswd encoded
```

Much like parameters in generated hyperlink URLs, hidden fields in a page's HTML allow us to embed state information inside this web page itself. Unless you view that page's source, you can't see this state information, because hidden fields are never displayed. But when this form's Submit button is clicked, hidden field values are automatically transmitted to the next script along with the visible fields on the form.

Figure 13-14 shows the source code generated for a different message's view page; the hidden input fields used to pass selected mail state information are embedded near the top.

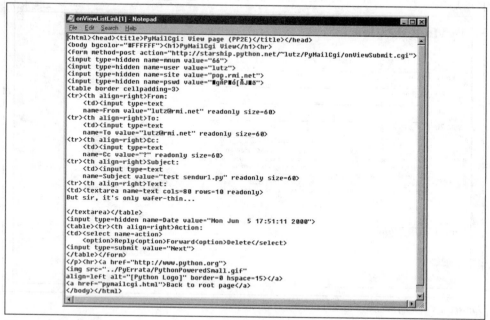

Figure 13-14. PyMailCgi view page, generated HTML

The net effect is that hidden input fields in HTML, just like parameters at the end of generated URLs, act like temporary storage areas and retain state between pages and user interaction steps. Both are the Web's equivalent to programming language variables. They come in handy any time your application needs to remember something between pages.

Hidden fields are especially useful if you cannot invoke the next script from a generated URL hyperlink with parameters. For instance, the next action in our script is a form submit button (Next), not a hyperlink, so hidden fields are used to pass state. As before, without these hidden fields, users would need to re-enter POP account details somewhere on the view page if they were needed by the next script (in our example, they are required if the next action is Delete).

Escaping mail text and passwords in HTML

Notice that everything you see on the message view page in Figure 13-13 is escaped with `cgi.escape`. Header fields and the text of the mail itself might contain characters that are special to HTML and must be translated as usual. For instance, because some mailers allow you to send messages in HTML format, it's possible that an email's text could contain a `</textarea>` tag, which would throw the reply page hopelessly out of sync if not escaped.

One subtlety here: HTML escapes are important only when text is sent to the browser initially (by the CGI script). If that text is later sent out again to another script (e.g., by sending a reply), the text will be back in its original, non-escaped format when received again on the server. The browser parses out escape codes and does not put them back again when uploading form data, so we don't need to undo escapes later. For example, here is part of the escaped text area sent to a browser during a Reply transaction (use your browser's View Source option to see this live):

```
<tr><th align=right>Text:
<td><textarea name=text cols=80 rows=10 readonly>
more stuff

--Mark Lutz   (http://rmi.net/~lutz)   [PyMailCgi 1.0]


&gt; -----Original Message-----
&gt; From: lutz@rmi.net
&gt; To: lutz@rmi.net
&gt; Date: Tue May  2 18:28:41 2000
&gt;
&gt; &lt;table&gt;&lt;textarea&gt;
&gt; &lt;/textarea&gt;&lt;/table&gt;
&gt; --Mark Lutz   (http://rmi.net/~lutz)   [PyMailCgi 1.0]
&gt;
&gt;
&gt; &gt; -----Original Message-----
```

After this reply is delivered, its text looks as it did before escapes (and exactly as it appeared to the user in the message edit web page):

```
more stuff

--Mark Lutz   (http://rmi.net/~lutz)   [PyMailCgi 1.0]


> -----Original Message-----
> From: lutz@rmi.net
> To: lutz@rmi.net
> Date: Tue May  2 18:28:41 2000
>
> <table><textarea>
> </textarea></table>
> --Mark Lutz   (http://rmi.net/~lutz)   [PyMailCgi 1.0]
>
>
> > -----Original Message-----
```

Did you notice the odd characters in the hidden password field of the generated HTML screen shot (Figure 13-14)? It turns out that the POP password is still encrypted when placed in hidden fields of the HTML. For security, they have to be: values of a page's hidden fields can be seen with a browser's View Source option, and it's not impossible that the text of this page could be intercepted off the Net.

The password is no longer URL-encoded when put in the hidden field, though, even though it was when it appeared at the end of the smart link URL. Depending on your encryption module, the password might now contain non-printable characters when generated as a hidden field value here; the browser doesn't care, as long as the field is run through `cgi.escape` like everything else added to the HTML reply stream. The `commonhtml` module is careful to route all text and headers through `cgi.escape` as the view page is constructed.

As a comparison, Figure 13-15 shows what the mail message captured in Figure 13-13 looks like when viewed in PyMailGui, the client-side Tkinter-based email tool from Chapter 11. PyMailGui doesn't need to care about things like passing state in URLs or hidden fields (it saves state in Python variables) or escaping HTML and URL strings (there are no browsers, and no network transmission steps once mail is downloaded). It does require Python to be installed on the client, but we'll get into that in a few pages.

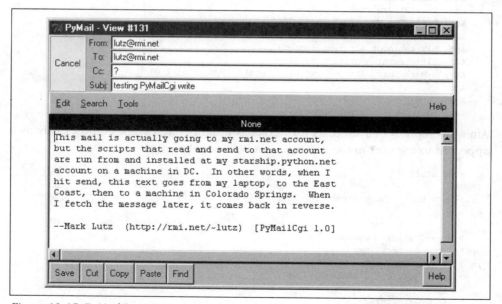

Figure 13-15. PyMailGui viewer, same message

The Message Action Pages

At this point in our hypothetical PyMailCgi web interaction, we are viewing an email message (Figure 13-13) that was chosen from the selection list page. On the message view page, selecting an action from the pull-down list and clicking the

Next button invokes the script in Example 13-9 on the server to perform a reply,
forward, or delete operation for the selected message.

Example 13-9. PP2E\Internet\Cgi-WebPyMaiCgi\onViewSubmit.cgi

```
#!/usr/bin/python
# On submit in mail view window, action selected=(fwd, reply, delete)

import cgi, string
import commonhtml, secret
from    externs import pymail, mailconfig
from    commonhtml import getfield

def quotetext(form):
    """
    note that headers come from the prior page's form here,
    not from parsing the mail message again; that means that
    commonhtml.viewpage must pass along date as a hidden field
    """
    quoted = '\n-----Original Message-----\n'
    for hdr in ('From', 'To', 'Date'):
        quoted = quoted + '%s: %s\n' % (hdr, getfield(form, hdr))
    quoted = quoted + '\n' +  getfield(form, 'text')
    quoted = '\n' + string.replace(quoted, '\n', '\n> ')
    return quoted

form = cgi.FieldStorage()   # parse form or url data
user, pswd, site = commonhtml.getstandardpopfields(form)

try:
    if form['action'].value    == 'Reply':
        headers = {'From':    mailconfig.myaddress,
                   'To':      getfield(form, 'From'),
                   'Cc':      mailconfig.myaddress,
                   'Subject': 'Re: ' + getfield(form, 'Subject')}
        commonhtml.editpage('Reply', headers, quotetext(form))

    elif form['action'].value == 'Forward':
        headers = {'From':    mailconfig.myaddress,
                   'To':      '',
                   'Cc':      mailconfig.myaddress,
                   'Subject': 'Fwd: ' + getfield(form, 'Subject')}
        commonhtml.editpage('Forward', headers, quotetext(form))

    elif form['action'].value == 'Delete':
        msgnum = int(form['mnum'].value)         # or string.atoi, but not eval()
        commonhtml.runsilent(                    # mnum field is required here
            pymail.deletemessages,
                (site, user, secret.decode(pswd), [msgnum], 0) )
        commonhtml.confirmationpage('Delete')

    else:
        assert 0, 'Invalid view action requested'
except:
    commonhtml.errorpage('Cannot process view action')
```

This script receives all information about the selected message as form input field data (some hidden, some not) along with the selected action's name. The next step in the interaction depends upon the action selected:

- Reply and Forward actions generate a message edit page with the original message's lines automatically quoted with a leading >.

- Delete actions trigger immediate deletion of the email being viewed, using a tool imported from the **pymail** module from Chapter 11.

All these actions use data passed in from the prior page's form, but only the Delete action cares about the POP username and password and must decode the password received (it arrives here from hidden form input fields generated in the prior page's HTML).

Reply and forward

If you select Reply as the next action, the message edit page in Figure 13-16 is generated by the script. Text on this page is editable, and pressing this page's Send button again triggers the send mail script we saw in Example 13-4. If all goes well, we'll receive the same confirmation page we got earlier when writing new mail from scratch (Figure 13-4).

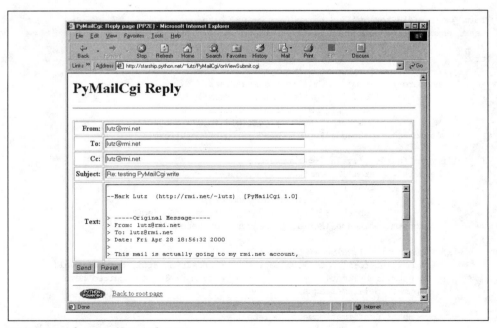

Figure 13-16. PyMailCgi reply page

Forward operations are virtually the same, except for a few email header differences. All of this busy-ness comes "for free," because Reply and Forward pages are generated by calling `commonhtml.editpage`, the same utility used to create a new mail composition page. Here, we simply pass the utility preformatted header line strings (e.g., replies add "Re:" to the subject text). We applied the same sort of reuse trick in PyMailGui, but in a different context. In PyMailCgi, one script handles three pages; in PyMailGui, one callback function handles three buttons, but the architecture is similar.

Delete

Selecting the Delete action on a message view page and pressing Next will cause the `onViewSubmit` script to immediately delete the message being viewed. Deletions are performed by calling a reusable delete utility function coded in Example 11-18; the call to the utility is wrapped in a `commonhtml.runsilent` call that prevents `print` statements in the utility from showing up in the HTML reply stream (they are just status messages, not HTML code). Figure 13-17 shows a delete operation in action.

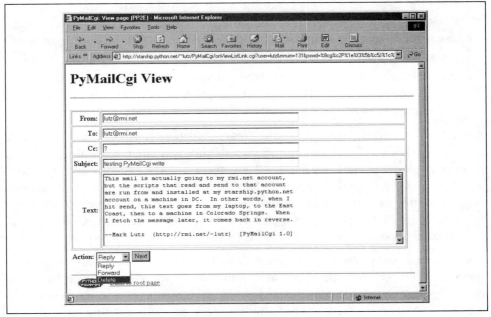

Figure 13-17. PyMailCgi view page, delete selected

As mentioned, Delete is the only action that uses the POP account information (user, password, and site) that was passed in from hidden fields on the prior (message view) page. By contrast, the Reply and Forward actions format an edit page, which ultimately sends a message to the SMTP server; no POP information is needed or passed. But at this point in the interaction, the POP password has racked up more than a few frequent flyer miles. In fact, it may have crossed phone lines, satellite links, and continents on its journey from machine to machine. This process is illustrated here:

1. Input (Client): The password starts life by being typed into the login page on the client (or being embedded in an explicit URL), unencrypted. If typed into the input form in a web browser, each character is displayed as a star (*).

2. Load index (Client to CGI server to POP server): It is next passed from the client to the CGI server, which sends it on to your POP server in order to load a mail index. The client sends only the password, unencrypted.

3. List page URLs (CGI server to client): To direct the next script's behavior, the password is embedded in the mail selection list web page itself as hyperlink URL parameters, encrypted and URL-encoded.

4. Load message (Client to CGI server to POP server): When an email is selected from the list, the password is sent to the next script within the script's URL; the CGI script decrypts it and passes it on to the POP server to fetch the selected message.

5. View page fields (CGI server to client): To direct the next script's behavior, the password is embedded in the view page itself as HTML hidden input fields, encrypted and HTML-escaped.

6. Delete (Client to CGI server to POP server): Finally, the password is again passed from client to CGI server, this time as hidden form field values; the CGI script decrypts it and passes it to the POP server to delete.

Along the way, scripts have passed the password between pages as both a URL parameter and an HTML hidden input field; either way, they have always passed its encrypted string, and never passed an unencrypted password and username together in any transaction. Upon a Delete request, the password must be decoded here using the `secret` module before passing it to the POP server. If the script can access the POP server again and delete the selected message, another confirmation page appears, as shown in Figure 13-18.

Note that you really *should* click "Back to root page" after a successful deletion— don't use your browser's Back button to return to the message selection list at this point, because the delete has changed the relative numbers of some messages in the list. PyMilGui worked around this problem by only deleting on exit, but PyMailCgi deletes mail immediately since there is no notion of "on exit." Clicking on a view link in an old selection list page may not bring up the message you think it should, if it comes after a message that was deleted.

This is a property of POP email in general: incoming mail simply adds to the mail list with higher message numbers, but deletions remove mail from arbitrary locations in the list and hence change message numbers for all mail following the ones

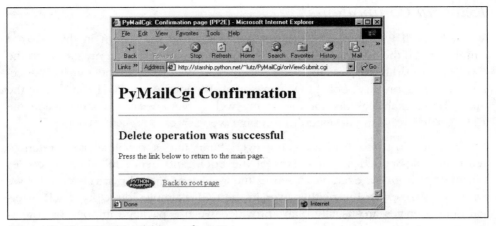

Figure 13-18. PyMailCgi delete confirmation

deleted. Even PyMailGui may get some message numbers wrong if mail is deleted by another program while the GUI is open (e.g., in a second PyMailGui instance). Alternatively, both mailers could delete all email off the server as soon as it is downloaded, such that deletions wouldn't impact POP identifiers (Microsoft Outlook uses this scheme, for instance), but this requires additional mechanisms for storing deleted email persistently for later access.

One subtlety: for replies and forwards, the `onViewSubmit` mail action script builds up a >-quoted representation of the original message, with original "From:", "To:", and "Date:" header lines prepended to the mail's original text. Notice, though, that the original message's headers are fetched from the CGI form input, not by reparsing the original mail (the mail is not readily available at this point). In other words, the script gets mail header values from the form input fields of the view page. Because there is no "Date" field on the view page, the original message's date is also passed along to the action script as a hidden input field to avoid reloading the message. Try tracing through the code in this chapter's listings to see if you can follow dates from page to page.

Utility Modules

This section presents the source code of the utility modules imported and used by the page scripts shown above. There aren't any new screen shots to see here, because these are utilities, not CGI scripts (notice their *.py* extensions). Moreover, these modules aren't all that useful to study in isolation, and are included here primarily to be referenced as you go through the CGI scripts' code. See earlier in this chapter for additional details not repeated here.

External Components

When I install PyMailCgi and other server-side programs shown in this book, I simply upload the contents of the *Cgi-Web* examples directory on my laptop to the top-level web directory on my server account (*public_html*). The *Cgi-Web* directory also lives on this book's CD, a mirror of the one on my PC. I don't copy the entire book examples distribution to my web server, because code outside the *Cgi-Web* directory isn't designed to run on a web server.

When I first installed PyMailCgi, however, I ran into a problem: it's written to reuse modules coded in other parts of the book, and hence in other directories outside *Cgi-Web*. For example, it reuses the `mailconfig` and `pymail` modules we wrote in Chapter 11, but neither lives in the CGI examples directory. Such external dependencies are usually okay, provided we use package imports or configure `sys.path` appropriately on startup. In the context of CGI scripts, though, what lives on my development machine may not be what is available on the web server machine where the scripts are installed.

To work around this (and avoid uploading the full book examples distribution to my web server), I define a directory at the top-level of *Cgi-Web* called *Extern*, to which any required external modules are copied as needed. For this system, *Extern* includes a subdirectory called *Email*, where the `mailconfig` and `pymail` modules are copied for upload to the server.

Redundant copies of files are less than ideal, but this can all be automated with install scripts that automatically copy to *Extern* and then upload *Cgi-Web* contents via FTP using Python's `ftplib` module (discussed in Chapter 11). Just in case I change this structure, though, I've encapsulated all external name accesses in the utility module in Example 13-10.

Example 13-10. PP2E\Internet\Cgi-Web\PyMailCgi\externs.py

```
###############################################################
# Isolate all imports of modules that live outside of the
# PyMailCgi PyMailCgi directory.  Normally, these would come
# from PP2E.Internet.Email, but when I install PyMailCgi,
# I copy just the Cgi-Web directory's contents to public_html
# on the server, so there is no PP2E directory on the server.
# Instead, I either copy the imports referenced in this file to
# the PyMailCgi parent directory, or tweak the dir appended to
# the sys.path module search path here.  Because all other
# modules get the externals from here, there is only one place
# to change when they are relocated.  This may be arguably
# gross, but I only put Internet code on the server machine.
###############################################################

import sys
sys.path.append('..')                  # see dir where Email installed on server
```

Example 13-10. PP2E\Internet\Cgi-Web\PyMailCgi\externs.py (continued)

```
from   Extern import Email              # assumes a ../Extern dir with Email dir
from   Extern.Email import pymail       # can use names Email.pymail or pymail
from   Extern.Email import mailconfig
```

This module appends the parent directory of PyMailCgi to `sys.path` to make the *Extern* directory visible (remember, PYTHONPATH might be anything when CGI scripts are run as user "nobody") and preimports all external names needed by PyMailCgi into its own namespace. It also supports future changes; because all external references in PyMailCgi are made through this module, I have to change only this one file if externals are later installed differently.

As a reference, Example 13-11 lists part of the external `mailconfig` module again. For PyMailCgi, it's copied to *Extern*, and may be tweaked as desired on the server (for example, the signature string differs slightly in this context). See the *pymail.py* file in Chapter 11, and consider writing an automatic copy-and-upload script for the *Cgi-Web\Extern* directory a suggested exercise; it's not proved painful enough to compel me to write one of my own.

Example 13-11. PP2E\Internet\Cgi-Web\Extern\Email\mailconfig.py

```
#############################################
# email scripts get server names from here:
# change to reflect your machine/user names;
# could get these in command line instead
#############################################

# SMTP email server machine (send)
smtpservername = 'smtp.rmi.net'          # or starship.python.net, 'localhost'

# POP3 email server machine, user (retrieve)
popservername  = 'pop.rmi.net'           # or starship.python.net, 'localhost'
popusername    = 'lutz'                   # password is requested when run

...rest omitted

# personal info used by PyMailGui to fill in forms;
# sig-- can be a triple-quoted block, ignored if empty string;
# addr--used for initial value of "From" field if not empty,

myaddress   = 'lutz@rmi.net'
mysignature = '--Mark Lutz  (http://rmi.net/~lutz)  [PyMailCgi 1.0]'
```

POP Mail Interface

The `loadmail` utility module in Example 13-12 depends on external files and encapsulates access to mail on the remote POP server machine. It currently exports one function, `loadnewmail`, which returns a list of all mail in the specified POP account; callers are unaware of whether this mail is fetched over the Net, lives in memory, or is loaded from a persistent storage medium on the CGI server machine. That is by design—loadmail changes won't impact its clients.

Example 13-12. PP2E\Internet\Cgi-Web\PyMailCgi\loadmail.py

```
###################################################################
# mail list loader; future--change me to save mail list between
# cgi script runs, to avoid reloading all mail each time; this
# won't impact clients that use the interfaces here if done well;
# for now, to keep this simple, reloads all mail on each operation
###################################################################

from commonhtml import runsilent          # suppress print's (no verbose flag)
from externs     import Email

# load all mail from number 1 up
# this may trigger an exception

def loadnewmail(mailserver, mailuser, mailpswd):
    return runsilent(Email.pymail.loadmessages,
                            (mailserver, mailuser, mailpswd))
```

It's not much to look at—just an interface and calls to other modules. The Email. pymail.loadmessages function (reused here from Chapter 11) uses the Python poplib module to fetch mail over sockets. All this activity is wrapped in a commonhtml.runsilent function call to prevent pymail print statements from going to the HTML reply stream (although any pymail exceptions are allowed to propagate normally).

As it is, though, loadmail loads all incoming email to generate the selection list page, and reloads all email again every time you fetch a message from the list. This scheme can be horribly inefficient if you have lots of email sitting on your server; I've noticed delays on the order of a dozen seconds when my mailbox is full. On the other hand, servers can be slow in general, so the extra time taken to reload mail isn't always significant; I've witnessed similar delays on the server for empty mailboxes and simple HTML pages too.

More importantly, loadmail is intended only as a first-cut mail interface—something of a usable prototype. If I work on this system further, it would be straightforward to cache loaded mail in a file, shelve, or database on the server, for example. Because the interface exported by loadmail would not need to change to introduce a caching mechanism, clients of this module would still work. We'll explore server storage options in the next chapter.

POP Password Encryption

Time to call the cops. We discussed the approach to password security adopted by PyMailCgi earlier. In brief, it works hard to avoid ever passing the POP account username and password across the Net together in a single transaction, unless the password is encrypted according to module *secret.py* on the server. This module can be different everywhere PyMailCgi is installed and can be uploaded anew at any time—encrypted passwords aren't persistent and live only for the duration of one mail-processing interaction session.[*] Example 13-13 is the encryptor module I installed on my server while developing this book.

Example 13-13. PP2E\Internet\Cgi-Web\PyMailCgi\secret.py

```
###########################################################################
# PyMailCgi encodes the pop password whenever it is sent to/from client over
# the net with a user name as hidden text fields or explicit url params; uses
# encode/decode functions in this module to encrypt the pswd--upload your own
# version of this module to use a different encryption mechanism; pymail also
# doesn't save the password on the server, and doesn't echo pswd as typed, but
# this isn't 100% safe--this module file itself might be vulnerable to some
# malicious users; Note: in Python 1.6, the socket module will include standard
# (but optional) support for openSSL sockets on the server, for programming
# secure Internet transactions in Python; see 1.6 socket module docs;
###########################################################################

forceReadablePassword = 0
forceRotorEncryption  = 1

import time, string
dayofweek = time.localtime(time.time())[6]


###########################################################################
# string encoding schemes
###########################################################################

if not forceReadablePassword:
    # don't do anything by default: the urllib.quote or
    # cgi.escape calls in commonhtml.py will escape the
    # password as needed to embed in in URL or HTML; the
    # cgi module undoes escapes automatically for us;

    def stringify(old):   return old
    def unstringify(old): return old

else:
    # convert encoded string to/from a string of digit chars,
    # to avoid problems with some special/nonprintable chars,
    # but still leave the result semi-readable (but encrypted);
    # some browser had problems with escaped ampersands, etc.;

    separator = '-'
```

---

[*] Note that there are other ways to handle password security, beyond the custom encryption schemes described in this section. For instance, Python's socket module now supports the server-side portion of the OpenSSL secure sockets protocol. With it, scripts may delegate the security task to web browsers and servers. On the other hand, such schemes do not afford as good an excuse to introduce Python's standard encryption tools in this book.

Example 13-13. PP2E\Internet\Cgi-Web\PyMailCgi\secret.py (continued)

```
    def stringify(old):
        new = ''
        for char in old:
            ascii = str(ord(char))
            new   = new + separator + ascii        # '-ascii-ascii-ascii'
        return new

    def unstringify(old):
        new = ''
        for ascii in string.split(old, separator)[1:]:
            new = new + chr(int(ascii))
        return new


###########################################################################
# encryption schemes
###########################################################################

if (not forceRotorEncryption) and (dayofweek % 2 == 0):
    # use our own scheme on evenly-numbered days (0=monday)
    # caveat: may fail if encode/decode over midnite boundary

    def do_encode(pswd):
        res = ''
        for char in pswd:
            res = res + chr(ord(char) + 1)         # add 1 to each ascii code
        return str(res)

    def do_decode(pswd):
        res = ''
        for char in pswd:
            res = res + chr(ord(char) - 1)
        return res

else:
    # use the standard lib's rotor module to encode pswd
    # this does a better job of encryption than code above

    import rotor
    mykey = 'pymailcgi'

    def do_encode(pswd):
        robj = rotor.newrotor(mykey)               # use enigma encryption
        return robj.encrypt(pswd)

    def do_decode(pswd):
        robj = rotor.newrotor(mykey)
        return robj.decrypt(pswd)


###########################################################################
# top-level entry points
###########################################################################
```

Example 13-13. PP2E\Internet\Cgi-Web\PyMailCgi\secret.py (continued)

```
def encode(pswd):
    return stringify(do_encode(pswd))          # encrypt plus string encode

def decode(pswd):
    return do_decode(unstringify(pswd))
```

This encryptor module implements two alternative encryption schemes: a simple ASCII character code mapping, and Enigma-style encryption using the standard `rotor` module. The `rotor` module implements a sophisticated encryption strategy, based on the "Enigma" encryption machine used by the Nazis to encode messages during World War II. Don't panic, though; Python's `rotor` module is much less prone to cracking than the Nazis'!

In addition to encryption, this module also implements an *encoding* method for already-encrypted strings. By default, the encoding functions do nothing, and the system relies on straight URL encoding. An optional encoding scheme translates the encrypted string to a string of ASCII code digits separated by dashes. Either encoding method makes non-printable characters in the encrypted string printable.

Default encryption scheme: rotor

To illustrate, let's test this module's tools interactively. First off, we'll experiment with Python's standard `rotor` module, since it's at the heart of the default encoding scheme. We import the module, make a new rotor object with a key (and optionally, a rotor count), and call methods to encrypt and decrypt:

```
C:\...\PP2E\Internet\Cgi-Web\PyMailCgi>python
>>> import rotor
>>> r = rotor.newrotor('pymailcgi')        # (key, [,numrotors])
>>> r.encrypt('abc123')                    # may return non-printable chars
' \323an\021\224'

>>> x = r.encrypt('spam123')               # result is same len as input
>>> x
'* _\344\011pY'
>>> len(x)
7
>>> r.decrypt(x)
'spam123'
```

Notice that the same rotor object can encrypt multiple strings, that the result may contain non-printable characters (printed as `\ascii` escape codes when displayed, possibly in octal form), and that the result is always the same length as the original string. Most importantly, a string encrypted with `rotor` can be decrypted in a different process (e.g., in a later CGI script) if we recreate the rotor object:

```
C:\...\PP2E\Internet\Cgi-Web\PyMailCgi>python
>>> import rotor
```

```
>>> r = rotor.newrotor('pymailcgi')        # can be decrypted in new process
>>> r.decrypt('* _\344\011pY')             # use "\ascii" escapes for two chars
'spam123'
```

Our secret module by default simply uses rotor to encrypt, and does no additional encoding of its own. It relies on URL encoding when the password is embedded in a URL parameter, and HTML escaping when the password is embedded in hidden form fields. For URLs, the following sorts of calls occur:

```
>>> from secret import encode, decode
>>> x = encode('abc$#<>&+')                # CGI scripts do this (rotor)
>>> x
' \323a\016\317\326\023\0163'

>>> import urllib                          # urllib.urlencode does this
>>> y = urllib.quote_plus(x)
>>> y
'+%d3a%0e%cf%d6%13%0e3'

>>> a = urllib.unquote_plus(y)             # cgi.FieldStorage does this
>>> a
' \323a\016\317\326\023\0163'

>>> decode(a)                              # CGI scripts do this (rotor)
'abc$#<>&+'
```

Alternative encryption schemes

To show how to write alternative encryptors and encoders, secret also includes a digits-string encoder and a character-code shuffling encryptor; both are enabled with global flag variables at the top of the module:

forceReadablePassword
> If set to *true*, the encrypted password is encoded into a string of ASCII code digits separated by dashes. Defaults to *false* to fall back on URL and HTML escape encoding.

forceRotorEncryption
> If set to *false* and the encryptor is used on an even-numbered day of the week, the simple character-code encryptor is used instead of rotor. Defaults to *true* to force rotor encryption.

To show how these alternatives work, let's set forceReadablePassword to 1 and forceRotorEncryption to 0, and reimport. Note that these are global variables that must be set *before* the module is imported (or reloaded), because they control the selection of alternative def statements. Only one version of each kind of function is ever made by the module:

```
C:\...\PP2E\Internet\Cgi-Web\PyMailCgi>python
>>> from secret import *
>>> x = encode('abc$#<>&+')
>>> x
```

```
'-98-99-100-37-36-61-63-39-44'

>>> y = decode(x)
>>> y
'abc$#<>&+'
```

This really happens in two steps, though—encryption and then encoding (the top-level encode and decode functions orchestrate the two steps). Here's what the steps look like when run separately:

```
>>> t = do_encode('abc$#<>&+')          # just our encryption
>>> t
"bcd%$=?',"
>>> stringify(t)                        # add our own encoding
'-98-99-100-37-36-61-63-39-44'

>>> unstringify(x)                      # undo encoding
"bcd%$=?',"
>>> do_decode(unstringify(x))           # undo both steps
'abc$#<>&+'
```

This alternative encryption scheme merely adds 1 to the each character's ASCII code value, and the encoder inserts the ASCII code integers of the result. It's also possible to combine rotor encryption and our custom encoding (set both forceReadablePassword and forceRotorEncryption to 1), but URL encoding provided by urllib works just as well. Here are a variety of schemes in action; *secret.py* is edited and saved before each reload:

```
>>> import secret
>>> secret.encode('spam123')            # default: rotor, no extra encoding
'* _\344\011pY'

>>> reload(secret)                      # forcereadable=1, forcerotor=0
<module 'secret' from 'secret.py'>
>>> secret.encode('spam123')
'-116-113-98-110-50-51-52'

>>> reload(secret)                      # forcereadable=1, forcerotor=1
<module 'secret' from 'secret.py'>
>>> secret.encode('spam123')
'-42-32-95-228-9-112-89'
>>> ord('Y')                            # the last one is really a 'Y'
89

>>> reload(secret)                      # back to default rotor, no stringify
<module 'secret' from 'secret.pyc'>
>>> import urllib
>>> urllib.quote_plus(secret.encode('spam123'))
'%2a+_%e4%09pY'
>>> 0x2a                                # the first is really 42, '*'
42
>>> chr(42)
'*'
```

You can provide any kind of encryption and encoding logic you like in a custom *secret.py*, as long as it adheres to the expected protocol—encoders and decoders must receive and return a string. You can also alternate schemes by days of the week as done here (but note that this can fail if your system is being used when the clock turns over at midnight!), and so on. A few final pointers:

Other Python encryption tools

There are additional encryption tools that come with Python or are available for Python on the Web; see *http://www.python.org* and the library manual for details. Some encryption schemes are considered serious business and may be protected by law from export, but these rules change over time.

Secure sockets support

As mentioned, Python 1.6 (not yet out as I wrote this) will have standard support for OpenSSL secure sockets in the Python `socket` module. OpenSSL is an open source implementation of the secure sockets protocol (you must fetch and install it separately from Python—see *http://www.openssl.org*). Where it can be used, this will provide a better and less limiting solution for securing information like passwords than the manual scheme we've adopted here.

For instance, secure sockets allow usernames and passwords to be entered into and submitted from a single web page, thereby supporting arbitrary mail readers. The best we can do without secure sockets is to either avoid mixing unencrypted user and password values and assume that some account data and encryptors live on the server (as done here), or to have two distinct input pages or URLs (one for each value). Neither scheme is as user-friendly as a secure sockets approach. Most browsers already support SSL; to add it to Python on your server, see the Python 1.6 (and beyond) library manual.

Internet security is a much bigger topic than can be addressed fully here, and we've really only scratched its surface. For additional information on security issues, consult books geared exclusively towards web programming techniques.

On my server, the *secret.py* file will be changed over time, in case snoopers watch the book's web site. Moreover, its source code cannot be viewed with the `getfile` CGI script coded in Chapter 12, *Server-Side Scripting*. That means that if you run this system live, passwords in URLs and hidden form fields may look very different than seen in this book. My password will have changed by the time you read these words too, or else it would be possible to know my password from this book alone!

Common Utilities Module

The file *commonhtml.py*, shown in Example 13-14, is the Grand Central Station of this application—its code is used and reused by just about every other file in the system. Most of it is self-explanatory, and I've already said most of what I wanted to say about it earlier, in conjunction with the CGI scripts that use it.

I haven't talked about its *debugging* support, though. Notice that this module assigns `sys.stderr` to `sys.stdout`, in an attempt to force the text of Python error messages to show up in the client's browser (remember, uncaught exceptions print details to `sys.stderr`). That works sometimes in PyMailCgi, but not always—the error text shows up in a web page only if a `page_header` call has already printed a response preamble. If you want to see all error messages, make sure you call `page_header` (or print `Content-type:` lines manually) before any other processing. This module also defines functions that dump lots of raw CGI environment information to the browser (`dumpstatepage`), and that wrap calls to functions that print status messages so their output isn't added to the HTML stream (`runsilent`).

I'll leave the discovery of any remaining magic in this code up to you, the reader. You are hereby admonished to go forth and read, refer, and reuse.

Example 13-14. PP2E\Internet\Cgi-Web\PyMailCgi\commonhtml.py

```
#!/usr/bin/python
###########################################################
# generate standard page header, list, and footer HTML;
# isolates html generation-related details in this file;
# text printed here goes over a socket to the client,
# to create parts of a new web page in the web browser;
# uses one print per line, instead of string blocks;
# uses urllib to escape parms in url links auto from a
# dict, but cgi.escape to put them in html hidden fields;
# some of the tools here are useful outside pymailcgi;
# could also return html generated here instead of
# printing it, so it could be included in other pages;
# could also structure as a single cgi script that gets
# and tests a next action name as a hidden form field;
# caveat: this system works, but was largely written
# during a 2-hour layover at the Chicago O'Hare airport:
# some components could probably use a bit of polishing;
# to run standalone on starship via a commandline, type
# "python commonhtml.py"; to run standalone via a remote
# web brower, rename file with .cgi and run fixcgi.py.
###########################################################

import cgi, urllib, string, sys
sys.stderr = sys.stdout             # show error messages in browser
from externs import mailconfig      # from a package somewhere on server
```

Example 13-14. PP2E\Internet\Cgi-Web\PyMailCgi\commonhtml.py (continued)

```
# my address root
urlroot = 'http://starship.python.net/~lutz/PyMailCgi'


def pageheader(app='PyMailCgi', color='#FFFFFF', kind='main', info=''):
    print 'Content-type: text/html\n'
    print '<html><head><title>%s: %s page (PP2E)</title></head>' % (app, kind)
    print '<body bgcolor="%s"><h1>%s %s</h1><hr>' % (color, app, (info or kind))


def pagefooter(root='pymailcgi.html'):
    print '</p><hr><a href="http://www.python.org">'
    print '<img src="../PyErrata/PythonPoweredSmall.gif" '
    print 'align=left alt="[Python Logo]" border=0 hspace=15></a>'
    print '<a href="%s">Back to root page</a>' % root
    print '</body></html>'


def formatlink(cgiurl, parmdict):
    """
    make "%url?key=val&key=val" query link from a dictionary;
    escapes str() of all key and val with %xx, changes ' ' to +
    note that url escapes are different from html (cgi.escape)
    """
    parmtext = urllib.urlencode(parmdict)              # calls urllib.quote_plus
    return '%s?%s' % (cgiurl, parmtext)                # urllib does all the work


def pagelistsimple(linklist):                          # show simple ordered list
    print '<ol>'
    for (text, cgiurl, parmdict) in linklist:
        link = formatlink(cgiurl, parmdict)
        text = cgi.escape(text)
        print '<li><a href="%s">\n    %s</a>' % (link, text)
    print '</ol>'


def pagelisttable(linklist):                           # show list in a table
    print '<p><table border>'                          # escape text to be safe
    count = 1
    for (text, cgiurl, parmdict) in linklist:
        link = formatlink(cgiurl, parmdict)
        text = cgi.escape(text)
        print '<tr><th><a href="%s">View</a> %d<td>\n %s' % (link, count, text)
        count = count+1
    print '</table>'


def listpage(linkslist, kind='selection list'):
    pageheader(kind=kind)
    pagelisttable(linkslist)            # [('text', 'cgiurl', {'parm':'value'})]
    pagefooter()


def messagearea(headers, text, extra=''):
    print '<table border cellpadding=3>'
    for hdr in ('From', 'To', 'Cc', 'Subject'):
        val = headers.get(hdr, '?')
        val = cgi.escape(val, quote=1)
        print '<tr><th align=right>%s:' % hdr
```

Example 13-14. PP2E\Internet\Cgi-Web\PyMailCgi\commonhtml.py (continued)

```
        print '     <td><input type=text '
        print '     name=%s value="%s" %s size=60>' % (hdr, val, extra)
    print '<tr><th align=right>Text:'
    print '<td><textarea name=text cols=80 rows=10 %s>' % extra
    print '%s\n</textarea></table>' % (cgi.escape(text) or '?')    # if has </>s

def viewpage(msgnum, headers, text, form):
    """
    on View + select (generated link click)
    very subtle thing: at this point, pswd was url encoded in the
    link, and then unencoded by cgi input parser; it's being embedded
    in html here, so we use cgi.escape; this usually sends nonprintable
    chars in the hidden field's html, but works on ie and ns anyhow:
    in url:   ?user=lutz&mnum=3&pswd=%8cg%c2P%1e%f0%5b%c5J%1c%f3&...
    in html: <input type=hidden name=pswd value="...nonprintables..">
    could urllib.quote the html field here too, but must urllib.unquote
    in next script (which precludes passing the inputs in a URL instead
    of the form); can also fall back on numeric string fmt in secret.py
    """
    pageheader(kind='View')
    user, pswd, site = map(cgi.escape, getstandardpopfields(form))
    print '<form method=post action="%s/onViewSubmit.cgi">' % urlroot
    print '<input type=hidden name=mnum value="%s">' % msgnum
    print '<input type=hidden name=user value="%s">' % user         # from page|url
    print '<input type=hidden name=site value="%s">' % site         # for deletes
    print '<input type=hidden name=pswd value="%s">' % pswd         # pswd encoded
    messagearea(headers, text, 'readonly')

    # onViewSubmit.quotetext needs date passed in page
    print '<input type=hidden name=Date value="%s">' % headers.get('Date','?')
    print '<table><tr><th align=right>Action:'
    print '<td><select name=action>'
    print '     <option>Reply<option>Forward<option>Delete</select>'
    print '<input type=submit value="Next">'
    print '</table></form>'                        # no 'reset' needed here
    pagefooter()

def editpage(kind, headers={}, text=''):
    # on Send, View+select+Reply, View+select+Fwd
    pageheader(kind=kind)
    print '<form method=post action="%s/onSendSubmit.cgi">' % urlroot
    if mailconfig.mysignature:
        text = '\n%s\n%s' % (mailconfig.mysignature, text)
    messagearea(headers, text)
    print '<input type=submit value="Send">'
    print '<input type=reset  value="Reset">'
    print '</form>'
    pagefooter()

def errorpage(message):
    pageheader(kind='Error')                       # or sys.exc_type/exc_value
    exc_type, exc_value = sys.exc_info()[:2]        # but safer,thread-specific
    print '<h2>Error Description</h2><p>', message
```

Example 13-14. PP2E\Internet\Cgi-Web\PyMailCgi\commonhtml.py (continued)

```
      print '<h2>Python Exception</h2><p>',  cgi.escape(str(exc_type))
      print '<h2>Exception details</h2><p>', cgi.escape(str(exc_value))
      pagefooter()

def confirmationpage(kind):
      pageheader(kind='Confirmation')
      print '<h2>%s operation was successful</h2>' % kind
      print '<p>Press the link below to return to the main page.</p>'
      pagefooter()

def getfield(form, field, default=''):
      # emulate dictionary get method
      return (form.has_key(field) and form[field].value) or default

def getstandardpopfields(form):
      """
      fields can arrive missing or '' or with a real value
      hard-coded in a url; default to mailconfig settings
      """
      return (getfield(form, 'user', mailconfig.popusername),
              getfield(form, 'pswd', '?'),
              getfield(form, 'site', mailconfig.popservername))

def getstandardsmtpfields(form):
      return  getfield(form, 'site', mailconfig.smtpservername)

def runsilent(func, args):
      """
      run a function without writing stdout
      ex: suppress print's in imported tools
      else they go to the client/browser
      """
      class Silent:
          def write(self, line): pass
      save_stdout = sys.stdout
      sys.stdout  = Silent()                    # send print to dummy object
      try:                                      # which has a write method
          result = apply(func, args)            # try to return func result
      finally:                                  # but always restore stdout
          sys.stdout = save_stdout
      return result

def dumpstatepage(exhaustive=0):
      """
      for debugging: call me at top of a cgi to
      generate a new page with cgi state details
      """
      if exhaustive:
          cgi.test()                            # show page with form, environ, etc.
      else:
          pageheader(kind='state dump')
          form = cgi.FieldStorage()             # show just form fields names/values
          cgi.print_form(form)
```

Example 13-14. PP2E\Internet\Cgi-Web\PyMailCgi\commonhtml.py (continued)

```
        pagefooter()
    sys.exit()

def selftest(showastable=0):                     # make phony web page
    links = [                                    # [(text, url, {parms})]
        ('text1', urlroot + '/page1.cgi', {'a':1}),
        ('text2', urlroot + '/page1.cgi', {'a':2, 'b':'3'}),
        ('text3', urlroot + '/page2.cgi', {'x':'a b', 'y':'a<b&c', 'z':'?'}),
        ('te<>4', urlroot + '/page2.cgi', {'<x>':'', 'y':'<a>', 'z':None})]
    pageheader(kind='View')
    if showastable:
        pagelisttable(links)
    else:
        pagelistsimple(links)
    pagefooter()

if __name__ == '__main__':                       # when run, not imported
    selftest(len(sys.argv) > 1)                  # html goes to stdout
```

CGI Script Trade-offs

As shown in this chapter, PyMailCgi is still something of a system in the making, but it does work as advertised: by pointing a browser at the main page's URL, I can check and send email from anywhere I happen to be, as long as I can find a machine with a web browser. In fact, any machine and browser will do: Python doesn't even have to be installed.* That's not the case with the PyMailGui client-side program we wrote in Chapter 11.

But before we all jump on the collective Internet bandwagon and utterly abandon traditional APIs like Tkinter, a few words of larger context are in order. Besides illustrating larger CGI applications in general, this example was chosen to under-score some of the trade-offs you run into when building applications to run on the Web. PyMailGui and PyMailCgi do roughly the same things, but are radically different in implementation:

- PyMailGui is a traditional user-interface program: it runs entirely on the local machine, calls out to an in-process GUI API library to implement interfaces, and talks to the Internet through sockets only when it has to (e.g., to load or send email on demand). User requests are routed immediately to callback handler functions or methods running locally, with shared variables that automatically retain state between requests. For instance, PyMailGui only loads email once, keeps it in memory, and only fetches newly arrived messages on future loads because its memory is retained between events.

---

* This property can be especially useful when visiting government institutions, which seem to generally provide web browser accessibility, but restrict administrative functions and broader network connectivity to officially cleared system administrators (and international spies).

- PyMailCgi, like all CGI systems, consists of scripts that reside and run on a server machine, and generate HTML to interact with a user at a web browser on the client machine. It runs only in the context of a web browser, and handles user requests by running CGI scripts remotely on the server. Unless we add a real database system, each request handler runs autonomously, with no state information except that which is explicitly passed along by prior states as hidden form fields or URL parameters. As coded, PyMailCgi must reload all email whenever it needs to process incoming email in any way.

On a basic level, both systems use the Python POP and SMTP modules to fetch and send email through sockets. But the implementation alternatives they represent have some critical ramifications that you should know about when considering delivering systems on the Web:

Performance costs

Networks are slower than CPUs. As implemented, PyMailCgi isn't nearly as fast or as complete as PyMailGui. In PyMailCgi, every time the user clicks a submit button, the request goes across the network. More specifically, every user request incurs a network transfer overhead, every callback handler (usually) takes the form of a newly spawned process on the server, parameters come in as text strings that must be parsed out, and the lack of state information on the server between pages means that mail needs to be reloaded often. In contrast, user clicks in PyMailGui trigger in-process function calls instead of network traffic and process forks, and state is easily saved as Python in-process variables (e.g., the loaded-mail list is retained between clicks). Even with an ultra-fast Internet connection, a server-side CGI system is slower than a client-side program.[*]

Some of these bottlenecks may be designed away at the cost of extra program complexity. For instance, some web servers use threads and process pools to minimize process creation for CGI scripts. Moreover, some state information can be manually passed along from page to page in hidden form fields and generated URL parameters, and state can be saved between pages in a concurrently accessible database to minimize mail reloads (see the PyErrata case study in Chapter 14 for an example). But there's no getting past the fact that routing events over a network to scripts is much slower than calling a Python function directly.

Complexity costs

HTML isn't pretty. Because PyMailCgi must generate HTML to interact with the user in a web browser, it is also more complex (or at least, less readable) than

---

[*] To be fair, some Tkinter operations are sent to the underlying Tcl library as strings too, which must be parsed. This may change in time; but the contrast here is with CGI scripts versus GUI libraries in general, not with a particular library's implementation.

PyMailGui. In some sense, CGI scripts embed HTML code in Python. Because the end result of this is a mixture of two very different languages, creating an interface with HTML in a CGI script can be much less straightforward than making calls to a GUI API such as Tkinter.

Witness, for example, all the care we've taken to escape HTML and URLs in this chapter's examples; such constraints are grounded in the nature of HTML. Furthermore, changing the system to retain loaded-mail list state in a database between pages would introduce further complexities to the CGI-based solution. Secure sockets (e.g., OpenSSL, to be supported in Python 1.6) would eliminate manual encryption costs, but introduce other overheads.

Functionality costs

HTML can only say so much. HTML is a portable way to specify simple pages and forms, but is poor to useless when it comes to describing more complex user interfaces. Because CGI scripts create user interfaces by writing HTML back to a browser, they are highly limited in terms of user-interface constructs.

For example, consider implementing an image-processing and animation program as CGI scripts: HTML doesn't apply once we leave the domain of fill-out forms and simple interactions. This is precisely the limitation that Java applets were designed to address—programs that are stored on a server but pulled down to run on a client on demand, and given access to a full-featured GUI API for creating richer user interfaces. Nevertheless, strictly server-side programs are inherently limited by the constraints of HTML. The animation scripts we wrote at the end of Chapter 8, *A Tkinter Tour, Part 2*, for example, are well beyond the scope of server-side scripts.

Portability benefits

All you need is a browser. On the client side, at least. Because PyMailCgi runs over the Web, it can be run on any machine with a web browser, whether that machine has Python and Tkinter installed or not. That is, Python needs to be installed on only one computer: the web server machine where the scripts actually live and run. As long as you know that the users of your system have an Internet browser, installation is simple.

Python and Tkinter, you will recall, are very portable too—they run on all major window systems (X, Windows, Mac)—but to run a client-side Python/Tk program such as PyMailGui, you need Python and Tkinter on the client machine itself. Not so with an application built as CGI scripts: they will work on Macintosh, Linux, Windows, and any other machine that can somehow render HTML web pages. In this sense, HTML becomes a sort of portable GUI API language in CGI scripts, interpreted by your web browser. You don't even need the source code or bytecode for the CGI scripts themselves—they run on a remote server that exists somewhere else on the Net, not on the machine running the browser.

Execution requirements

But you do need a browser. That is, the very nature of web-enabled systems can render them useless in some environments. Despite the pervasiveness of the Internet, there are still plenty of applications that run in settings that don't have web browsers or Internet access. Consider, for instance, embedded systems, real-time systems, and secure government applications. While an Intranet (a local network without external connections) can sometimes make web applications feasible in some such environments, I have recently worked at more than one company whose client sites had no web browsers to speak of. On the other hand, such clients may be more open to installing systems like Python on local machines, as opposed to supporting an internal or external network.

Administration requirements

You really need a server too. You can't write CGI-based systems at all without access to a web sever. Further, keeping programs on a centralized server creates some fairly critical administrative overheads. Simply put, in a pure client/server architecture, clients are simpler, but the server becomes a critical path resource and a potential performance bottleneck. If the centralized server goes down, you, your employees, and your customers may be knocked out of commission. Moreover, if enough clients use a shared server at the same time, the speed costs of web-based systems become even more pronounced. In fact, one could make the argument that moving towards a web server architecture is akin to stepping backwards in time—to the time of centralized mainframes and dumb terminals. Whichever way we step, offloading and distributing processing to client machines at least partially avoids this processing bottleneck.

So what's the best way to build applications for the Internet—as client-side programs that talk to the Net, or as server-side programs that live and breathe on the Net? Naturally, there is no one answer to that question, since it depends upon each application's unique constraints. Moreover, there are more possible answers to it than we have proposed here; most common CGI problems already have common proposed solutions. For example:

Client-side solutions

Client- and server-side programs can be mixed in many ways. For instance, *applet* programs live on a server, but are downloaded to and run as client-side programs with access to rich GUI libraries (more on applets when we discuss JPython in Chapter 15). Other technologies, such as embedding JavaScript or Python directly in HTML code, also support client-side execution and richer GUI possibilities; such scripts live in HTML on the server, but run on the client when downloaded and access browser components through an exposed object model (see the discussion "Windows Web Scripting Extensions" near the end of Chapter 15). The emerging Dynamic HTML (DHTML) extensions provide yet another client-side scripting option for changing web pages after they have been constructed. All of these client-side technologies add extra complexities all their own, but ease some of the limitations imposed by straight HTML.

State retention solutions

Some web application servers (e.g., Zope, described in Chapter 15) naturally support state retention between pages by providing concurrently accessible object databases. Some of these systems have a real underlying database component (e.g., Oracle and mySql); others may make use of files or Python persistent object shelves with appropriate locking (as we'll explore in the next chapter). Scripts can also pass state information around in hidden form fields and generated URL parameters, as done in PyMailCgi, or store it on the client machine itself using the standard cookie protocol.

Cookies are bits of information stored on the client upon request from the server. A cookie is created by sending special headers from the server to the client within the response HTML (`Set-Cookie: name=value`). It is then accessed in CGI scripts as the value of a special environment variable containing cookie data uploaded from the client (`HTTP_COOKIE`). Search *http://www. python.org* for more details on using cookies in Python scripts, including the freely available *cookie.py* module, which automates the cookie translation process.[*] Cookies are more complex than program variables and are somewhat controversial (some see them as intrusive), but they can offload some simple state retention tasks.

HTML generation solutions

Add-ons can also take some of the complexity out of embedding HTML in Python CGI scripts, albeit at some cost to execution speed. For instance, the HTMLgen system described in Chapter 15 lets programs build pages as trees of Python objects that "know" how to produce HTML. When a system like this is employed, Python scripts deal only with objects, not the syntax of HTML itself. Other systems such as PHP and Active Server Pages (described in the same chapter) allow scripting language code to be embedded in HTML and executed on the server, to dynamically generate or determine part of the HTML that is sent back to a client in response to requests.

Clearly, Internet technology does imply some design trade-offs, and is still evolving rapidly. It is nevertheless an appropriate delivery context for many (though not all) applications. As with every design choice, you must be the judge. While delivering systems on the Web may have some costs in terms of performance, functionality, and complexity, it is likely that the significance of those overheads will diminish with time.

---

[*] Also see the new standard `cookie` module in Python release 2.0.

14

Larger Web Site Examples II

"Typos Happen"

This chapter presents the second of two server-side Python web programming case studies. It covers the design and implementation of *PyErrata*, a CGI-based web site implemented entirely in Python that allows users to post book comments and error reports, and demonstrates the concepts underlying persistent database storage in the CGI world. As we'll see, this case study teaches both server-side scripting and Python development techniques.

The PyErrata Web Site

The last chapter concluded with a discussion of the downsides of deploying applications on the Web. But now that I've told you all the reasons you might *not* want to design systems for the Web, I'm going to completely contradict myself and present a system that cries out for a web-based implementation. This chapter presents the PyErrata web site, a Python program that lets arbitrary people on arbitrary machines submit book comments and bug reports (usually called *errata*) over the Web, using just a web browser.

PyErrata is in some ways simpler than the PyMailCgi case study presented in the previous chapter. From a user's perspective, PyErrata is more hierarchical than linear: user interactions are shorter and spawn fewer pages. There is also little state retention in web pages themselves in PyErrata; URL parameters pass state in only one isolated case, and no hidden form fields are generated.

On the other hand, PyErrata introduces an entirely new dimension: *persistent data storage*. State (error and comment reports) is stored permanently by this system on the server, either in flat pickle files or a shelve-based database. Both raise the specter of concurrent updates, since any number of users out in cyberspace may be accessing the site at the same time.

System Goals

Before you ponder too long over the seeming paradox of a book that comes with its own bug-reporting system, I should provide a little background. Over the last five years, I've been fortunate enough to have had the opportunity to write four books, a large chapter in a reference book, and various magazine articles and training materials. Changes in the Python world have also provided opportunities to rewrite books from the ground up. It's been both wildly rewarding and lucrative work (well, rewarding, at least).

But one of the first big lessons one learns upon initiation in the publishing business is that typos are a fact of life. Really. No matter how much of a perfectionist you are, books will have bugs. Furthermore, big books tend to have more bugs than little books, and in the technical publishing domain, readers are often sufficiently savvy and motivated to send authors email when they find those bugs.

That's a terrific thing, and helps authors weed out typos in reprints. I always encourage and appreciate email from readers. But I get lots of email—at times, so much so that given my schedule, I find it difficult to even reply to every message, let alone investigate and act on every typo report. I get lots of other email too, and can miss a reader's typo report if I'm not careful.

About a year ago, I realized that I just couldn't keep up with all the traffic and started thinking about alternatives. One obvious way to cut down on the overhead of managing reports is to delegate responsibility—to offload at least some report-processing tasks to the people who generate the reports. That is, I needed to somehow provide a widely available system, separate from my email account, that automates report posting and logs reports to be reviewed as time allows.

Of course, that's exactly the sort of need that the Internet is geared to. By implementing an error-reporting system as a web site, any reader can visit and log reports from any machine with a browser, whether they have Python installed or not. Moreover, those reports can be logged in a database at the web site for later inspection by both author and readers, instead of requiring manual extraction from incoming email.

The implementation of these ideas is the PyErrata system—a web site implemented with server-side Python programs. PyErrata allows readers to post bug reports and comments about this edition of *Programming Python*, as well as view the collection of all prior posts by various sort keys. Its goal is to replace the traditional errata list pages I've had to maintain manually for other books in the past.

More than any other web-based example in this book, PyErrata demonstrates just how much work can be saved with a little Internet scripting. To support the first edition of this book, I hand-edited an HTML file that listed all known bugs. With PyErrata, server-side programs generate such pages dynamically from a user-populated database. Because list pages are produced on demand, PyErrata not only publishes and automates list creation, it also provides multiple ways to view report data. I wouldn't even try to reorder the first edition's static HTML file list.

PyErrata is something of an experiment in open systems, and as such is vulnerable to abuse. I still have to manually investigate reports, as time allows. But it at least has the potential to ease one of the chores that generally goes unmentioned in typical publishing contracts.

Implementation Overview

Like other web-based systems in this part of the book, PyErrata consists of a collection of HTML files, Python utility modules, and Python-coded CGI scripts that run on a shared server instead of on a client. Unlike those other web systems, PyErrata also implements a persistent database and defines additional directory structures to support it. Figure 14-1 shows the top-level contents of the site, seen on Windows from a PyEdit Open dialog.

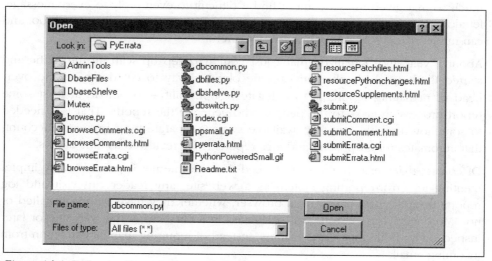

Figure 14-1. PyErrata site contents

You will find a similar structure on this book's CD-ROM. To install this site on the Net, all the files and directories you see here are uploaded to the server machine and stored in a *PyErrata* subdirectory within the root of the directory that is exposed to the Web (my *public_html* directory). The top-level files of this site implement browse and submit operations as well as database interfaces. A few resource page files and images show up in this listing too, but are ignored in this book. Besides files, this site has subdirectories of its own:

- *Mutex* is a Python package that contains a mutual-exclusion utility module used for shelves, as well as test scripts for this utility model.

- *AdminTools* includes system utility scripts that are run standalone from the command line.

- *DbaseFiles* holds the file-based database, with separate subdirectories for errata and comment pickle files.

- *DbaseShelve* contains the shelve-based database, with separate shelve files for errata and comments.

We'll meet the contents of the database subdirectories later in this chapter, when exploring the database implementation.

Presentation Strategy

PyErrata takes logic factoring, code reuse, and encapsulation to extremes. Top-level scripts, for example, are often just a few lines long and ultimately invoke generic logic in common utility modules. With such an architecture, mixing short code segments with lots of screen shots makes it tough to trace the flow of control through the program.

To make this system easier to study, we're going to take a slightly different approach here. PyErrata's implementation will be presented in three main sections corresponding to major functional areas of the system: report browsing, report submission, and database interfaces. The site root page will be shown before these three sections, but mostly just for context; it's simple, static HTML.

Within the browsing and submission sections, all user interaction models (and screen shots) are shown first, followed by all the source code used to implement that interaction. Like the PyForm example in Chapter 16, *Databases and Persistence*, PyErrata is at heart a database-access program, and its database interfaces are ultimately the core of the system. Because these interfaces encapsulate most low-level storage details, though, we'll save their presentation for last.

Although you still may have to jump around some to locate modules across functional boundaries, this organization of all the code for major chunks of the system in their own sections should help minimize page-flipping.

Use the Source, Luke

I want to insert the standard case-study caveat here: although this chapter does explain major concepts along the way, understanding the whole story is left partly up to you. As always, please consult the source code listings in this chapter (and on the CD) for details not spelled out explicitly. I've taken this minimal approach deliberately, mostly because I assume you already know a lot about CGI scripting and the Python language by this point in the book, but also because real-world development time is spent as much on reading other people's code as on writing your own. Python makes both tasks relatively easy, but now is your chance to see how for yourself.

I also wish to confess right off that this chapter has a hidden agenda. PyErrata not only shows more server-side scripting techniques, but also illustrates common Python development concepts at large. Along the way, we focus on this system's current software architecture and point out a variety of design alternatives. Be sure to pay special attention to the way that logic has been layered into multiple abstraction levels. For example, by separating database and user-interface (page generation) code, we minimize code redundancy and cross-module dependencies and maximize code reuse. Such techniques are useful in all Python systems, web-based or not.

The Root Page

Let's start at the top. In this chapter we will study the complete implementation of PyErrata, but readers are also encouraged to visit the web site where it lives to sample the flavor of its interaction first-hand. Unlike PyMailCgi, there are no password constraints in PyErrata, so you can access all of its pages without any configuration steps.

PyErrata installs as a set of HTML files and Python CGI scripts, along with a few image files. As usual, you can simply point your web browser to the system's root page to run the system live while you study this chapter. Its root page currently lives here:[*]

>   *http://starship.python.net/~lutz/PyErrata/pyerrata.html*

If you go to this address, your browser will be served the page shown in Figure 14-2. PyErrata supports both submission and browsing of comments and

---

[*] But be sure to see this book's web site, *http://rmi.net/~lutz/about-pp.html*, for an updated link if the one listed here no longer works by the time you read this book. Web sites seem to change addresses faster than developers change jobs.

error reports; the four main links on this page essentially provide write and read access to its databases over the Web.

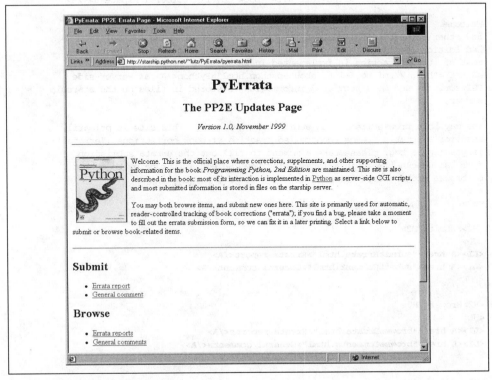

Figure 14-2. PyErrata main page

The static HTML code file downloaded to produce this page is listed in Example 14-1. The only parts we're interested in are shown in bold: links to the submission and browsing pages for comments and errata. There is more to this page, but we're only dealing with the parts shown in the screen shot. For instance, the site will eventually also include resource page HTML files (e.g., Python resources and changes), but we'll ignore those components in this book.

Example 14-1. PP2E\Internet\Cgi-Web\PyErrata\pyerrata.html

```
<HTML><BODY>
<TITLE>PyErrata: PP2E Errata Page</TITLE>
<H1 align=center>PyErrata</H1>
<H2 align=center>The PP2E Updates Page</H2>
<P  align=center><I>Version 1.0, November 1999</I></P>

<HR><P>
```

Example 14-1. PP2E\Internet\Cgi-Web\PyErrata\pyerrata.html (continued)

```
<A href="http://rmi.net/~lutz/about-pp.html">
<IMG src="ppsmall.gif" align=left alt="[Book Cover]" border=1 hspace=8></A>

Welcome.  This is the official place where corrections, supplements,
and other supporting information for the book <I>Programming Python,
2nd Edition</I> are maintained.  This site is also described in the book:
most of its interaction is implemented in
<A HREF="http://rmi.net/~lutz/about-python.html">Python</A> as server-side
CGI scripts, and most submitted information is stored in files on the starship
server.
<P>
You may both browse items, and submit new ones here.  This site is primarily
used for automatic, reader-controlled tracking of book corrections ("errata");
if you find a bug, please take a moment to fill out the errata submission
form, so we can fix it in a later printing.  Select a link below to submit
or browse book-related items.
</P>
<HR>

<H2>Submit</H2>
<UL>
<LI><A href="submitErrata.html">Errata report</A>
<LI><A href="submitComment.html">General comment</A>
</UL>

<H2>Browse</H2>
<UL>
<LI><A href="browseErrata.html">Errata reports</A>
<LI><A href="browseComments.html">General comments</A>
</UL>

<H2>Library</H2>
<UL>
<LI><A href="resourceSupplements.html">Supplements</A>
<LI><A href="resourcePythonchanges.html">Python changes</A>
<LI><A href="resourcePatchfiles.html">Program patch files</A>
</UL>

<HR>
<A href="http://www.python.org">
<IMG SRC="PythonPoweredSmall.gif"
 ALIGN=left ALT="[Python Logo]" border=0 hspace=10></A>
<A href="../PyInternetDemos.html">More examples</A>
</BODY></HTML>
```

Browsing PyErrata Reports

On to the first major system function: browsing report records. Before we study
the code used to program browse operations, let's get a handle on the sort of user

interaction it is designed to produce. If you're the sort that prefers to jump into code right away, it's okay to skip the next two sections for now, but be sure to come back here to refer to the screen shots as you study code listed later.

User Interface: Browsing Comment Reports

As shown in Figure 14-2, PyErrata lets us browse and submit two kinds of reports: general comments and errata (bug) reports. Clicking the "General comments" link in the Browse section of the root page brings up the page shown in Figure 14-3.

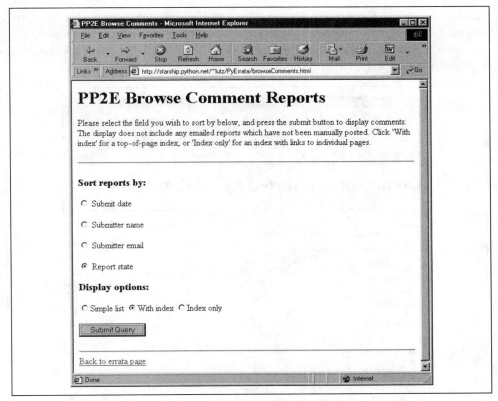

Figure 14-3. Browse comments, selection page

Now, the first thing you should know about PyErrata's browse feature is that it allows users to query and view the report database in multiple ways. Reports may be ordered by any report field and displayed in three different formats. The top-level browse pages essentially serve to configure a query against the report database and the presentation of its result.

To specify an ordering, first select a sort criterion: a report field name by which report listings are ordered. Fields take the form of radio buttons on this page. To specify a report display format, select one of three option buttons:

- *Simple list* yields a simple sorted list page.
- *With index* generates a sorted list page, with hyperlinks at the top that jump to the starting point of each sort key value in the page when clicked.
- *Index only* produces a page containing only hyperlinks for each sort key value, which fetch and display matching records when clicked.

Figure 14-4 shows the simple case produced by clicking the "Submit date" sort key button, selecting the "Simple list" display option, and pressing the Submit Query button to contact a Python script on the server. It's a scrollable list of all comment reports in the database ordered by submission date.

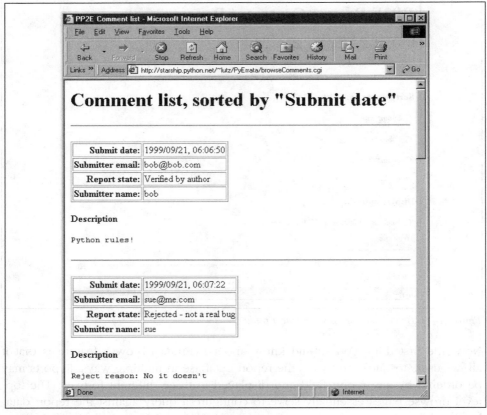

Figure 14-4. Browse comments, "Simple list" option

In all query results, each record is displayed as a table of attribute field values (as many as are present in the record) followed by the text of the record's description field. The description is typically multiple lines long, so it's shown separately and without any HTML reformatting (i.e., as originally typed). If there are multiple records in a list, they are separated by horizontal lines.

Simple lists like this work well for small databases, but the other two display options are better suited to larger report sets. For instance, if we instead pick the "With index" option, we are served up a page that begins with a list of links to other locations in the page, followed by a list of records ordered and grouped by a sort key's value. Figure 14-5 shows the "With index" option being used with the "Report state" sort key.

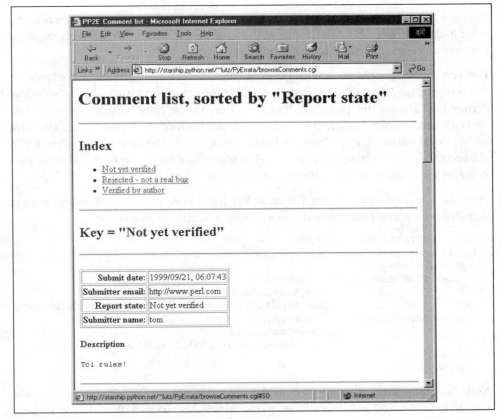

Figure 14-5. Browse comments, "With index" option

To view reports, the user can either scroll through the list or click on one of the links at the top; they follow in-page hyperlinks to sections of the report list where a

given key value's records begin. Internally, these hyperlinks use *file.*
html#section section-link syntax that is supported by most browsers, and in-page
tags. The important parts of the generated HTML code look like this:

```
<title>PP2E Comment list</title>
<h1>Comment list, sorted by "Report state"</h1><hr>
<h2>Index</h2><ul>
<li><a href="#S0">Not yet verified</a>
<li><a href="#S1">Rejected - not a real bug</a>
<li><a href="#S2">Verified by author</a>
</ul><hr>
<h2><a name="#S0">Key = "Not yet verified"</a></h2><hr>
<p><table border>
<tr><th align=right>Submit date:<td>1999/09/21, 06:07:43
...more...
```

Figure 14-6 shows the result of clicking one such link in a page sorted instead by
submit date. Notice the #S4 at the end of the result's URL. We'll see how these
tags are automatically generated in a moment.

For very large databases, it may be impractical to list every record's contents on
the same page; the third PyErrata display format option provides a solution.
Figure 14-7 shows the page produced by the "Index only" display option, with
"Submit date" chosen for report order. There are no records on this page, just a list
of hyperlinks that "know" how to fetch records with the listed key value when
clicked. They are another example of what we've termed *smart links*—they embed
key and value information in the hyperlink's URL.

PyErrata generates these links dynamically; they look like the following, except
that I've added line-feeds to make them more readable in this book:

```
<title>PP2E Comment list</title>
<h1>Comment list, sorted by "Submit date"</h1><hr>
<h2>Index</h2><ul>
<li><a href="index.cgi?kind=Comment&
                   sortkey=Submit+date&
                   value=1999/09/21,+06%3a06%3a50">1999/09/21, 06:06:50</a>
<li><a href="index.cgi?kind=Comment&
                   sortkey=Submit+date&
                   value=1999/09/21,+06%3a07%3a22">1999/09/21, 06:07:22</a>
...more...
</ul><hr>
```

Note the URL-encoded parameters in the links this time; as you'll see in the code,
this is Python's `urllib` module at work again. Also notice that unlike the last
chapter's PyMailCgi example, PyErrata generates minimal URLs in lists (without
server and path names—they are inferred and added by the browser from the

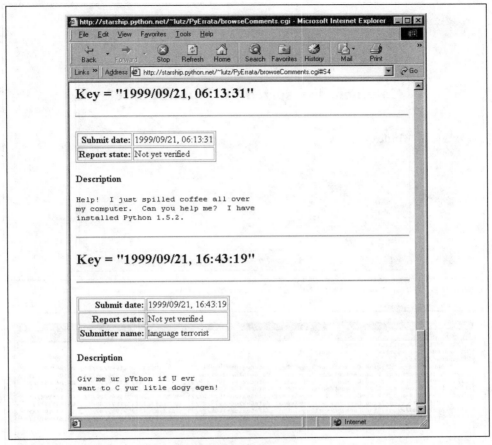

Figure 14-6. Browse comments, "With index" listing

prior page's address). If you view the generated page's source code, the underlying smart links are more obvious; Figure 14-8 shows one such index page's code.[*]

Clicking on a link in the "Index only" page fetches and displays all records in the database with the displayed value in the displayed key field. For instance, pressing the second to last link in the index page (Figure 14-7) yields the page shown in Figure 14-9. As usual, generated links appear in the address field of the result.

If we ask for an index based on field "Submitter name," we generate similar results but with different key values in the list and URLs; Figure 14-10 shows the result of

---

[*] Like PyMailCgi, the & character in the generated URLs is not escaped by PyErrata, since its parameter name doesn't clash with HTML character escape names. If yours might, be sure to use `cgi.escape` on URLs to be inserted into web pages.

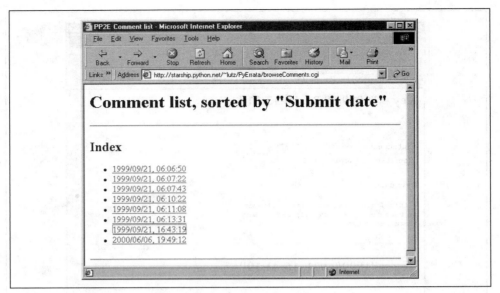

Figure 14-7. Browse comments, "Index only" selection list

```
browseComments[1] - Notepad
File  Edit  Search  Help
<title>PP2E Comment list</title>
<h1>Comment list, sorted by "Submit date"</h1><hr>
<h2>Index</h2><ul>
<li><a href="index.cgi?kind=Comment&sortkey=Submit+date&value=1999/09/21,+06%3a06%3a50">1999/09/21, 06:06:50</a>
<li><a href="index.cgi?kind=Comment&sortkey=Submit+date&value=1999/09/21,+06%3a07%3a22">1999/09/21, 06:07:22</a>
<li><a href="index.cgi?kind=Comment&sortkey=Submit+date&value=1999/09/21,+06%3a07%3a43">1999/09/21, 06:07:43</a>
<li><a href="index.cgi?kind=Comment&sortkey=Submit+date&value=1999/09/21,+06%3a10%3a22">1999/09/21, 06:10:22</a>
<li><a href="index.cgi?kind=Comment&sortkey=Submit+date&value=1999/09/21,+06%3a11%3a08">1999/09/21, 06:11:08</a>
<li><a href="index.cgi?kind=Comment&sortkey=Submit+date&value=1999/09/21,+06%3a13%3a31">1999/09/21, 06:13:31</a>
<li><a href="index.cgi?kind=Comment&sortkey=Submit+date&value=1999/09/21,+16%3a43%3a19">1999/09/21, 16:43:19</a>
<li><a href="index.cgi?kind=Comment&sortkey=Submit+date&value=2000/06/11,+23%3a08%3a28">2000/06/11, 23:08:28</a>
</ul><hr>
```

Figure 14-8. PyErrata generated links code

clicking such an index page link. This is the same record as Figure 14-9, but was accessed via name key, not submit date. By treating records generically, PyErrata provides multiple ways to view and access stored data.

User Interface: Browsing Errata Reports

PyErrata maintains two distinct databases—one for general comments and one for genuine error reports. To PyErrata, records are just objects with fields; it treats both comments and errata the same, and is happy to use whatever database it is passed. Because of that, the interface for browsing errata records is almost identical to that for comments, and as we'll see in the implementation section, it largely uses the same code.

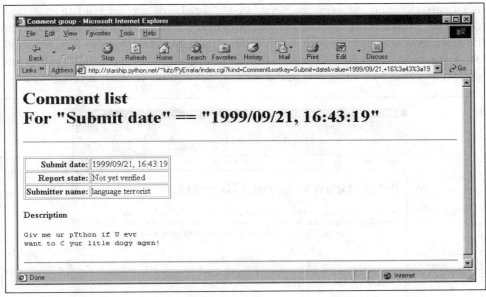

Figure 14-9. Browse comments, "Index only" link clicked

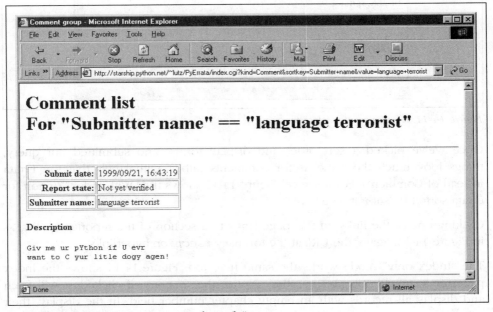

Figure 14-10. Browse comments, "Index only" page

Errata reports differ, though, in the fields they contain. Because there are many more fields that can be filled out here, the root page of the errata browse function is slightly different. As seen in Figure 14-11, sort fields are selected from a pull-down *selection list* rather than radiobuttons. Every attribute of an errata report can be used as a sort key, even if some reports have no value for the field selected. Most fields are optional; as we'll see later, reports with empty field values are shown as value ? in index lists and grouped under value (none) in report lists.

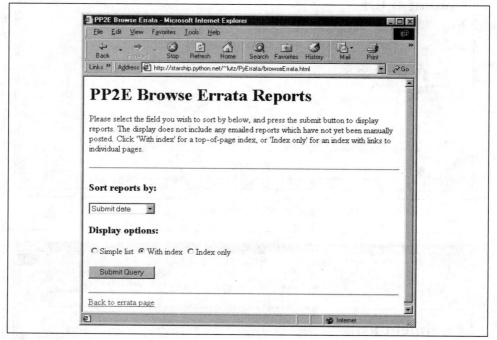

Figure 14-11. Browse errata, selection page

Once we've picked a sort order and display format and submitted our query, things look much the same as for comments (albeit with labels that say Errata instead of Comment). For instance, Figure 14-12 shows the "With index" option for errata sorted by submit date.

Clicking one of the links on this page leads to a section of the report page list, as in Figure 14-13; again, the URL at the top uses #*section* hyperlinks.

The "Index only" mode works the same here too: Figure 14-14 shows the index page for sort field "Chapter number". Notice the "?" entry; if clicked, it will fetch and display all records with an empty chapter number field. In the display, their empty key values print as (none). In the database, it's really an empty string.

Clicking on the "16" entry brings up all errata tagged with that chapter number in the database; Figure 14-15 shows that only one was found this time.

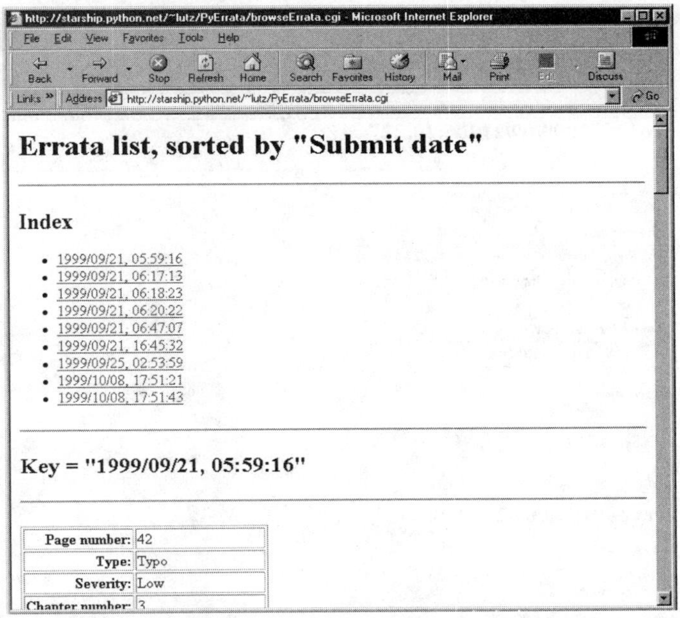

Figure 14-12. Browse errata, "With index" display

Using Explicit URLs with PyErrata

Because Python's `cgi` module treats form inputs and URL parameters the same way, you can also use explicit URLs to generate most of the pages shown so far. In fact, PyErrata does too; the URL shown at the top of Figure 14-15:

```
http://starship.python.net/~lutz/
      PyErrata/index.cgi?kind=Errata&sortkey=Chapter+number&value=16
```

was generated by PyErrata internally to represent a query to be sent to the next script (mostly—the browser actually adds the first part, through *PyErrata/*). But there's nothing preventing a user (or another script) from submitting that fully specified URL explicitly to trigger a query and reply. Other pages can be fetched with direct URLs too; this one loads the index page itself:

```
http://starship.python.net/~lutz/
      PyErrata/browseErrata.cgi?key=Chapter+number&display=indexonly
```

Likewise, if you want to query the system for all comments submitted under a given name, you can either navigate through the system's query pages, or type a URL like this:

```
http://starship.python.net/~lutz/
      PyErrata/index.cgi?kind=Comment&sortkey=Submitter+name&value=Bob
```

Figure 14-13. Browse errata, report list

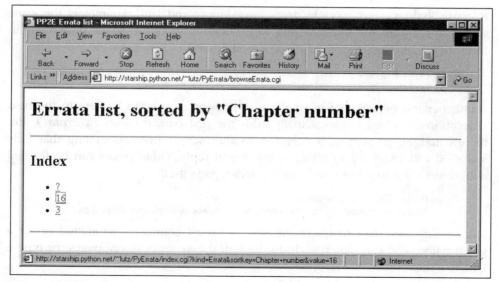

Figure 14-14. Browse errata, "Index only" link page

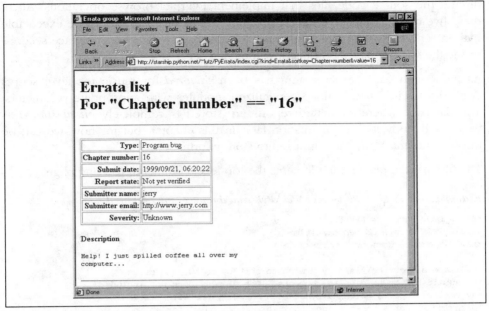

Figure 14-15. Browse errata, "Index only" link clicked

You'll get a page with Python exception information if there are no matches for the key and value in the specified database. If you instead just want to fetch a comment list sorted by submit dates (e.g., to parse in another script), type this:

```
http://starship.python.net/~lutz/
         PyErrata/browseComments.cgi?key=Submit+date&display=list
```

If you access this system outside the scope of its form pages like this, be sure to specify a complete URL and URL-encoded parameter values. There is no notion of a prior page, and because most key values originate from values in user-provided reports, they may contain arbitrary characters.

It's also possible to use explicit URLs to submit new reports—each field may be passed as a URL's parameter to the submit script:

```
http://starship.python.net/~lutz/
         PyErrata/submitComment.cgi?Description=spam&Submitter+name=Bob
```

but we won't truly understand what this does until we reach the section "Submitting PyErrata Reports" later in this chapter.

Implementation: Browsing Comment Reports

Okay, now that we've seen the external behavior of the browse function, let's roll up our sleeves and dig into its implementation. The following sections list and discuss the source code files that implement PyErrata browse operations. All of these live on the web server; some are static HTML files and others are executable Python scripts. As you read, remember to refer back to the user interface sections to see the sorts of pages produced by the code.

As mentioned earlier, this system has been *factored* for reuse: top-level scripts don't do much but call out to generalized modules with appropriate parameters. The database where submitted reports are stored is completely *encapsulated* as well; we'll study its implementation later in this chapter, but for now we can be mostly ignorant of the medium used to store information.

The file in Example 14-2 implements the top-level comment browsing page.

Example 14-2. PP2E\Internet\Cgi-Web\PyErrata\browseComments.html

```
<html><body bgcolor="#FFFFFF">
<title>PP2E Browse Comments</title>
<h1>PP2E Browse Comment Reports</h1>

<p>Please select the field  you wish to sort by below, and press
the submit button to display comments.  The display does not include
any emailed reports which have not been manually posted.  Click
'With index' for a top-of-page index, or 'Index only' for an index
with links to individual pages.
</p>

<hr>
<form method=POST action="browseComments.cgi">
      <h3>Sort reports by:</h3>

      <p><input type=radio name=key value="Submit date" checked> Submit date
      <p><input type=radio name=key value="Submitter name"> Submitter name
      <p><input type=radio name=key value="Submitter email"> Submitter email
      <p><input type=radio name=key value="Report state"> Report state

      <h3>Display options:</h3>
       <p><input type=radio name=display value="list">Simple list
          <input type=radio name=display value="indexed" checked>With index
          <input type=radio name=display value="indexonly">Index only
      <p><input type=submit>
</form>

<hr>
<a href="pyerrata.html">Back to errata page</A>
</body></html>
```

This is straight and static HTML code, as opposed to a script (there's nothing to construct dynamically here). As with all forms, clicking its submit button triggers a CGI script (Example 14-3) on the server, passing all the input fields' values.

Example 14-3. PP2E\Internet\Cgi-Web\PyErrata\browseComments.cgi

```
#!/usr/bin/python

from dbswitch import DbaseComment      # dbfiles or dbshelve
from browse   import generatePage      # reuse html formatter
generatePage(DbaseComment, 'Comment')  # load data, send page
```

There's not much going on here, because all the machinery used to perform a query has been split off to the **browse** module (shown in Example 14-6) so that it can be reused to browse errata reports too. Internally, browsing both kinds of records is handled the same way; here, we pass in only items that vary between comment and errata browsing operations. Specifically, we pass in the comment database object and a "Comment" label for use in generated pages. Module **browse** is happy to query and display records from any database we pass to it.

The **dbswitch** module used here (and listed in Example 14-13) simply selects between flat-file and shelve database mechanisms. By making the mechanism choice in a single module, we need to update only one file to change to a new medium; this CGI script is completely independent of the underlying database mechanism. Technically, the object **dbswitch.DbaseComment** is a *class* object, used later to construct a database interface object in the **browse** module.

Implementation: Browsing Errata Reports

The file in Example 14-4 implements the top-level errata browse page, used to select a report sort order and display format. Fields are in a pull-down selection list this time, but otherwise this page is similar to that for comments.

Example 14-4. PP2E\Internet\Cgi-Web\PyErrata\browseErrata.html

```
<html><body bgcolor="#FFFFFF">
<title>PP2E Browse Errata</title>
<h1>PP2E Browse Errata Reports</h1>

<p>Please select the field  you wish to sort by below, and press
the submit button to display reports.  The display does not include
any emailed reports which have not yet been manually posted.  Click
'With index' for a top-of-page index, or 'Index only' for an index
with links to individual pages.
</p>


<hr>
<form method=POST action="browseErrata.cgi">
    <h3>Sort reports by:</h3>
    <select name=key>
        <option>Page number
        <option>Type
        <option>Submit date
        <option>Severity
```

Example 14-4. PP2E\Internet\Cgi-Web\PyErrata\browseErrata.html (continued)

```
        <option>Chapter number
        <option>Part number
        <option>Printing date
        <option>Submitter name
        <option>Submitter email
        <option>Report state
    </select>
    <h3>Display options:</h3>
     <p><input type=radio name=display value="list">Simple list
        <input type=radio name=display value="indexed" checked>With index
        <input type=radio name=display value="indexonly">Index only
     <p><input type=submit>
</form>

<hr>
<a href="pyerrata.html">Back to errata page</A>
</body></html>
```

When submitted, the form in this HTML file invokes the script in Example 14-5 on the server.

Example 14-5. PP2E\Internet\Cgi-Web\PyErrata\browseErrata.cgi

```
#!/usr/bin/python

from dbswitch import DbaseErrata          # dbfiles or dbshelve
from browse    import generatePage        # reuse html formatter
generatePage(DbaseErrata)                 # load data, send page
```

Again, there's not much to speak of here. In fact, it's nearly identical to the comment browse script, because both use the logic split off into the **browse** module. Here, we just pass a different database for the browse logic to process.

Common Browse Utility Modules

To fully understand how browse operations work, we need to explore the module in Example 14-6, which is used by both comment and errata browse operations.

Example 14-6. PP2E\Internet\Cgi-Web\PyErrata\browse.py

```
###########################################################
# on browse requests: fetch and display data in new page;
# report data is stored in dictionaries on the database;
# caveat: the '#Si' section links generated for top of page
# indexes work on a recent Internet Explorer, but have been
# seen to fail on an older Netscape; if they fail, try
# using 'index only' mode, which uses url links to encode
# information for creating a new page; url links must be
# encoded with urllib, not cgi.escape (for text embedded in
# the html reply stream; IE auto changes space to %20 when
# url is clicked so '+' replacement isn't always needed,
```

Example 14-6. PP2E\Internet\Cgi-Web\PyErrata\browse.py (continued)

```python
# but urllib.quote_plus is more robust; web browser adds
# http://server-name/root-dir/PyErrata/ to indexurl;
############################################################

import cgi, urllib, sys, string
sys.stderr = sys.stdout                # show errors in browser
indexurl = 'index.cgi'                 # minimal urls in links

def generateRecord(record):
    print '<p><table border>'
    rowhtml = '<tr><th align=right>%s:<td>%s\n'
    for field in record.keys():
        if record[field] != '' and field != 'Description':
            print rowhtml % (field, cgi.escape(str(record[field])))

    print '</table></p>'
    field = 'Description'
    text  = string.strip(record[field])
    print '<p><b>%s</b><br><pre>%s</pre><hr>' % (field, cgi.escape(text))

def generateSimpleList(dbase, sortkey):
    records = dbase().loadSortedTable(sortkey)        # make list
    for record in records:
        generateRecord(record)

def generateIndexOnly(dbase, sortkey, kind):
    keys, index = dbase().loadIndexedTable(sortkey)   # make index links
    print '<h2>Index</h2><ul>'                         # for load on click
    for key in keys:
        html = '<li><a href="%s?kind=%s&sortkey=%s&value=%s">%s</a>'
        htmlkey    = cgi.escape(str(key))
        urlkey     = urllib.quote_plus(str(key))       # html or url escapes
        urlsortkey = urllib.quote_plus(sortkey)        # change spaces to '+'
        print html % (indexurl,
                    kind, urlsortkey, (urlkey or '(none)'), (htmlkey or '?'))
    print '</ul><hr>'

def generateIndexed(dbase, sortkey):
    keys, index = dbase().loadIndexedTable(sortkey)
    print '<h2>Index</h2><ul>'
    section = 0                                         # make index
    for key in keys:
        html = '<li><a href="#S%d">%s</a>'
        print html % (section, cgi.escape(str(key)) or '?')
        section = section + 1
    print '</ul><hr>'
    section = 0                                         # make details
    for key in keys:
        html = '<h2><a name="#S%d">Key = "%s"</a></h2><hr>'
        print html % (section, cgi.escape(str(key)))
        for record in index[key]:
            generateRecord(record)
```

Example 14-6. PP2E\Internet\Cgi-Web\PyErrata\browse.py (continued)

```
        section = section + 1

def generatePage(dbase, kind='Errata'):
    form = cgi.FieldStorage()
    try:
        sortkey = form['key'].value
    except KeyError:
        sortkey = None

    print 'Content-type: text/html\n'
    print '<title>PP2E %s list</title>' % kind
    print '<h1>%s list, sorted by "%s"</h1><hr>' % (kind, str(sortkey))

    if not form.has_key('display'):
        generateSimpleList(dbase, sortkey)

    elif form['display'].value == 'list':          # dispatch on display type
        generateSimpleList(dbase, sortkey)          # dict would work here too

    elif form['display'].value == 'indexonly':
        generateIndexOnly(dbase, sortkey, kind)

    elif form['display'].value == 'indexed':
        generateIndexed(dbase, sortkey)
```

This module in turn heavily depends on the top-level database interfaces we'll meet in a few moments. For now, all we need to know at this high level of abstraction is that the database exports *interfaces* for loading report records and sorting and grouping them by key values, and that report records are stored away as *dictionaries* in the database with one key per field in the report. Two top-level interfaces are available for accessing stored reports:

- `dbase().loadSortedTable(sortkey)` loads records from the generated database interface object into a simple list, sorted by the key whose name is passed in. It returns a list of record dictionaries sorted by a record field.

- `dbase().loadIndexedTable(sortkey)` loads records from the generated database interface object into a dictionary of lists, grouped by values of the passed-in key (one dictionary entry per sort key value). It returns both a dictionary of record-dictionary lists to represent the grouping by key, as well as a sorted-keys list to give ordered access into the groups dictionary (remember, dictionaries are unordered).

The simple list display option uses the first call, and both index display options use the second to construct key-value lists and sets of matching records. We will see the implementation of these calls and record store calls later. Here, we only care that they work as advertised.

Technically speaking, any mapping for storing a report record's fields in the database will do, but dictionaries are the storage unit in the system as currently coded. This representation was chosen for good reasons:

- It blends well with the CGI form field inputs object returned by `cgi.FieldStorage`. Submit scripts simply merge form field input dictionaries into expected field dictionaries to configure a record.

- It's more direct than other representations. For instance, it's easy to generically process all fields by stepping through the record dictionary's keys list, while using classes and attribute names for fields is less direct and might require frequent `getattr` calls.

- It's more flexible than other representations. For instance, dictionary keys can have values that attribute names cannot (e.g., embedded spaces), and so map well to arbitrary form field names.

More on the database later. For the "Index only" display mode, the `browse` module generates links that trigger the script in Example 14-7 when clicked. There isn't a lot to see in this file either, because most page generation is again delegated to the `generateRecord` function in the `browse` module in Example 14-6. The passed-in "kind" field is used to select the appropriate database object class to query here; the passed-in sort field name and key values are then used to extract matching records returned by the database interface.

Example 14-7. PP2E\Internet\Cgi-Web\PyErrata\index.cgi

```python
#!/usr/bin/python
#####################################################
# run when user clicks on a hyperlink generated for
# index-only mode by browse.py; input parameters are
# hard-coded into the link url, but there's nothing
# stopping someone from creating a similar link on
# their own--don't eval() inputs (security concern);
# note that this script assumes that no data files
# have been deleted since the index page was created;
# cgi.FieldStorage undoes any urllib escapes in the
# input parameters (%xx and '+' for spaces undone);
#####################################################

import cgi, sys, dbswitch
from browse import generateRecord
sys.stderr = sys.stdout
form = cgi.FieldStorage()                               # undoes url encoding

inputs = {'kind':'?', 'sortkey':'?', 'value':'?'}
for field in inputs.keys():
    if form.has_key(field):
        inputs[field] = cgi.escape(form[field].value)   # adds html encoding
```

Example 14-7. PP2E\Internet\Cgi-Web\PyErrata\index.cgi (continued)

```
if inputs['kind'] == 'Errata':
    dbase = dbswitch.DbaseErrata
else:
    dbase = dbswitch.DbaseComment

print 'Content-type: text/html\n'
print '<title>%s group</title>' % inputs['kind']
print '<h1>%(kind)s list<br>For "%(sortkey)s" == "%(value)s"</h1><hr>' % inputs

keys, index = dbase().loadIndexedTable(inputs['sortkey'])
key = inputs['value']
if key == '(none)': key = ''
for record in index[key]:
    generateRecord(record)
```

In a sense, this **index** script is a continuation of **browse**, with a page in between. We could combine these source files with a bit more work and complexity, but their logic really must be run in distinct *processes*. In interactive client-side programs, a pause for user input might simply take the form of a function call (e.g., to **raw_input**); in the CGI world, though, such a pause generally requires spawning a distinct process to handle the input.

There are two additional points worth underscoring before we move on. First of all, the "With index" option has its limitations. Notice how the **browse** module generates in-page *#section* hyperlinks, and then tags each key's section in the records list with a header line that embeds an **<A name=#section>** tag, using a counter to generate unique section labels. This all relies on the fact that the database interface knows how to return records grouped by key values (one list per key). Unfortunately, in-page links like this may not work on all browsers (they've failed on older Netscapes); if they don't work in yours, use the "Index only" option to access records by key groups.

The second point is that since all report fields are optional, the system must handle empty or missing fields gracefully. Because submit scripts (described in the next section) define a fixed set of fields for each record type, the database never really has "missing" fields in records; empty fields are simply stored as empty strings and omitted in record displays. When empty values are used in index lists, they are displayed as ?; within key labels and URLs, they are denoted as string **(none)**, which is internally mapped to the empty string in the **index** and **browse** modules just listed (empty strings don't work well as URL parameters). This is subtle, so see these modules for more details.

A word on redundancy: notice that the list of possible sort fields displayed in the browse input pages is hardcoded into their HTML files. Because the submit scripts we'll explore next ensure that all records in a database have the same set of fields, the HTML files' lists will be redundant with records stored away in the databases.

We could in principle build up the HTML sort field lists by inspecting the keys of any record in the comment and errata databases (much as we did in the language selector example in Chapter 12, *Server-Side Scripting*), but that may require an extra database operation. These lists also partially overlap with the fields list in both submit page HTML and submit scripts, but seem different enough to warrant some redundancy.

Submitting PyErrata Reports

The next major functional area in PyErrata serves to implement user-controlled submission of new comment and errata reports. As before, let's begin by getting a handle on this component's user-interface model before inspecting its code.

User Interface: Submitting Comment Reports

As we've seen, PyErrata supports two user functions: browsing the reports database and adding new reports to it. If you click the "General comment" link in the Submit section of the root page shown in Figure 14-2, you'll be presented with the comment submission page shown in Figure 14-16.

This page initially comes up empty; the data we type into its form fields is submitted to a server-side script when we press the submit button at the bottom. If the system was able to store the data as a new database record, a confirmation like the one in Figure 14-17 is reflected back to the client.

All fields in submit forms are optional except one; if we leave the "Description" field empty and send the form, we get the error page shown in Figure 14-18 (generated during an errata submission). Comments and error reports without descriptions aren't incredibly useful, so we kick such requests out. All other report fields are stored empty if we send them empty (or missing altogether) to the submit scripts.

Once we've submitted a comment, we can go back to the browse pages to view it in the database; Figure 14-19 shows the one we just added, accessed by key "Submitter name" and in "With index" display format mode.

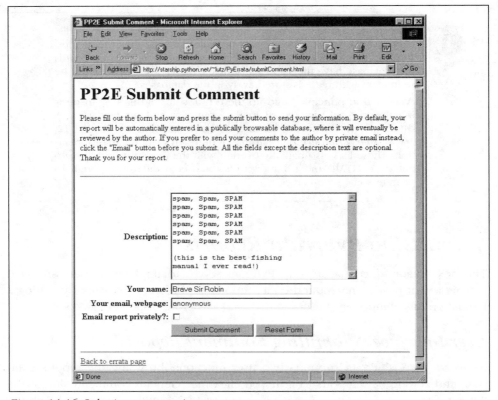

Figure 14-16. Submit comments, input page

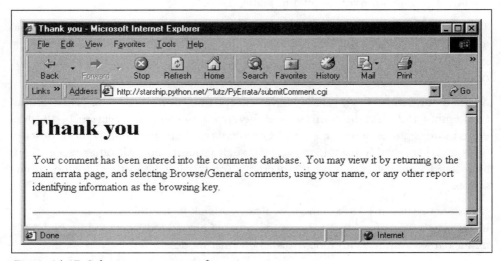

Figure 14-17. Submit comments, confirmation page

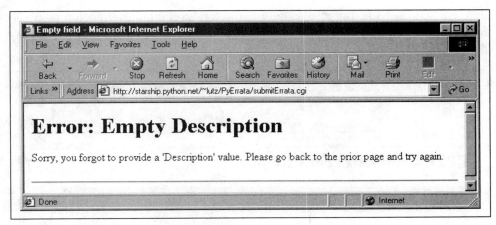

Figure 14-18. Submit, missing field error page

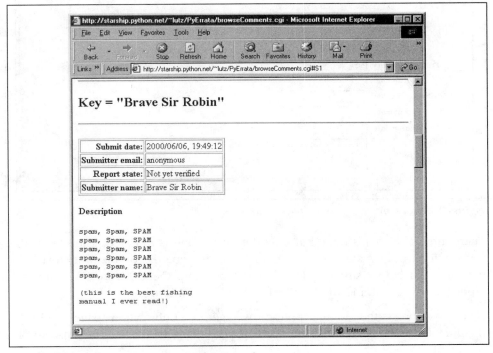

Figure 14-19. Submit comments, verifying result

User Interface: Submitting Errata Reports

Here again, the pages generated to submit errata reports are virtually identical to the ones we just saw for submitting comments, as comments and errata are treated the same within the system. Both are instances of generic database records with different sets of fields. But also as before, the top-level errata submission page differs, because there are many more fields that can be filled in; Figure 14-20 shows the top of this input page.

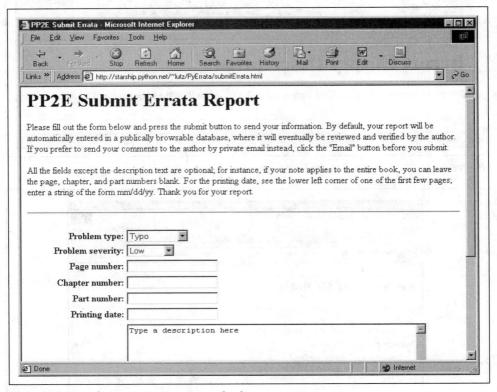

Figure 14-20. Submit errata, input page (top)

There are lots of fields here, but only the description is required. The idea is that users will fill in as many fields as they like to describe the problem; all text fields default to an empty string if no value is typed into them. Figure 14-21 shows a report in action with most fields filled with relevant information.

When we press the submit button, we get a confirmation page as before (Figure 14-22), this time with text customized to thank us for an errata instead of a comment.

As before, we can verify a submission with the browse pages immediately after it has been confirmed. Let's bring up an index list page for submission dates and click on the new entry at the bottom (Figure 14-23). Our report is fetched from the errata database and displayed in a new page (Figure 14-24). Note that the display doesn't include a "Page number" field: we left it blank on the submit form. PyErrata displays only nonempty record fields when formatting web pages. Because it treats

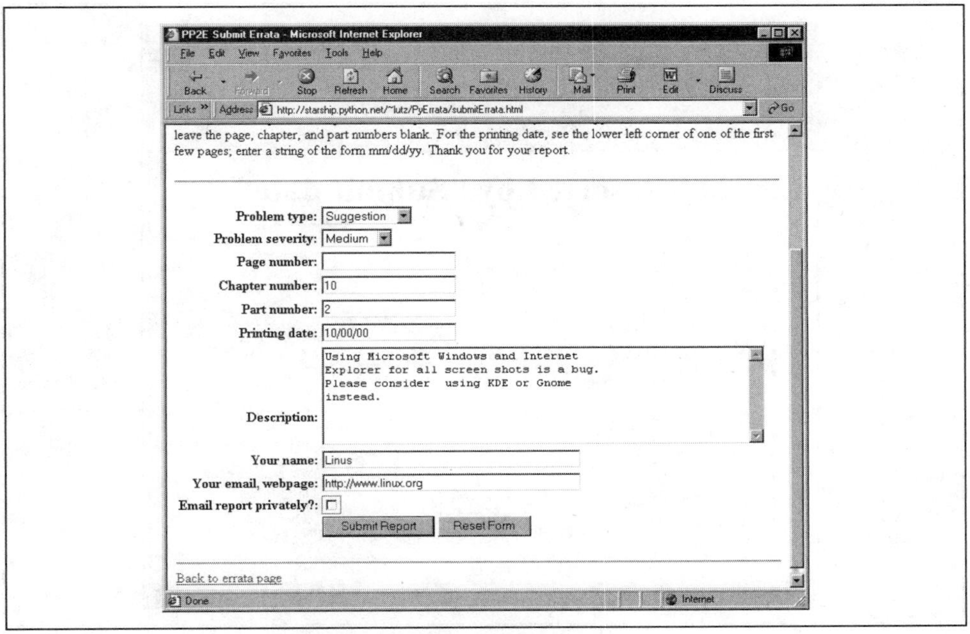

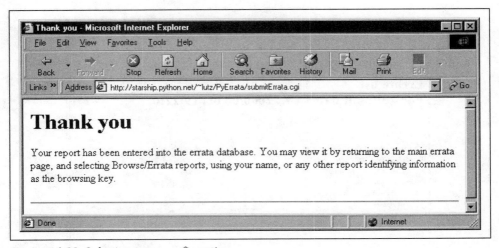

Figure 14-21. Submit errata, input page (filled)

Figure 14-22. Submit errata, confirmation

all records generically, the same is true for comment reports; at its core, PyErrata is a very generic system that doesn't care about the meaning of data stored in records.

Because not everyone wants to post to a database viewable by everyone in the world with a browser, PyErrata also allows both comments and errata to be sent by email instead of being automatically added to the database. If we click the "Email report privately" checkbox near the bottom of the submit pages before submission,

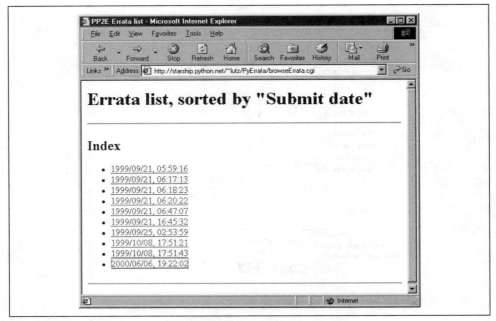

Figure 14-23. Submit errata, verify result (index)

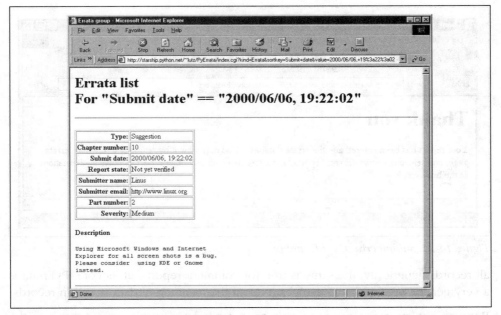

Figure 14-24. Submit errata, verify result (record)

the report's details are emailed to me (their fields show up as a message in my mailbox), and we get the reply in Figure 14-25.

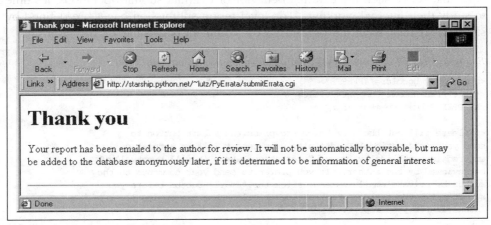

Figure 14-25. Submit errata, email mode confirmation

Finally, if the directory or shelve file that represents the database does not grant write access to everyone (remember, CGI scripts run as user "nobody"), our scripts won't be able to store the new record. Python generates an exception, which is displayed in the client's browser because PyErrata is careful to route exception text to `sys.stdout`. Figure 14-26 shows an exception page I received before making the database directory in question writable with the shell command `chmod 777 DbaseFiles/errataDB`.

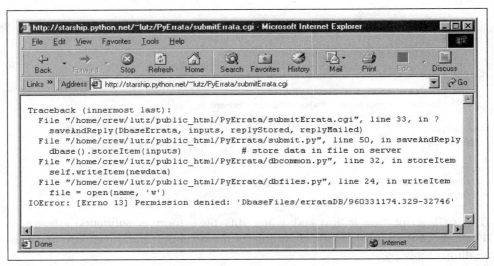

Figure 14-26. Submit errata, exception (need chmod 777 dir)

Implementation: Submitting Comment Reports

Now that we've seen the external behavior of PyErrata submit operations, it's time to study their internal workings. Top-level report submission pages are defined by static HTML files. Example 14-8 shows the comment page's file.

Example 14-8. PP2E\Internet\Cgi-Web\PyErrata\submitComment.html

```
<html><body bgcolor="#FFFFFF">
<title>PP2E Submit Comment</title>
<h1>PP2E Submit Comment</h1>

<p>Please fill out the form below and press the submit button to
send your information.  By default, your report will be automatically
entered in a publically browsable database, where it will eventually
be reviewed by the author.  If you prefer to send your comments to the
author by private email instead, click the "Email" button before you
submit.  All the fields except the description text are optional.
Thank you for your report.
</p>

<hr>
<form method=POST action="submitComment.cgi">
  <table>
    <tr>
      <th align=right>Description:
      <td><textarea name="Description" cols=40 rows=10>Type your comment here
        </textarea>
    <tr>
      <th align=right>Your name:
      <td><input type=text size=35 name="Submitter name">
    <tr>
      <th align=right>Your email, webpage:
      <td><input type=text size=35 name="Submitter email">
    <tr>
      <th align=right>Email report privately?:
      <td><input type=checkbox name="Submit mode" value="email">
    <tr>
      <th></th>
      <td><input type=submit value="Submit Comment">
          <input type=reset  value="Reset Form">
  </table>
</form>

<hr>
<A href="pyerrata.html">Back to errata page</A>
</body></html>
```

The CGI script that is invoked when this file's form is submitted, shown in Example 14-9, does the work of storing the form's input in the database and generating a reply page.

Example 14-9. PP2E\Internet\Cgi-Web\PyErrata\submitComment.cgi

```
#!/usr/bin/python

DEBUG=0
if DEBUG:
    import sys
    sys.stderr = sys.stdout
    print "Content-type: text/html"; print

import traceback
try:
    from dbswitch import DbaseComment        # dbfiles or dbshelve
    from submit    import saveAndReply        # reuse save logic

    replyStored = """
    Your comment has been entered into the comments database.
    You may view it by returning to the main errata page, and
    selecting Browse/General comments, using your name, or any
    other report identifying information as the browsing key."""

    replyMailed = """
    Your comment has been emailed to the author for review.
    It will not be automatically browsable, but may be added to
    the database anonymously later, if it is determined to be
    information of general use."""

    inputs = {'Description':'',       'Submit mode':'',
              'Submitter name':'',   'Submitter email':''}

    saveAndReply(DbaseComment, inputs, replyStored, replyMailed)

except:
    print "\n\n<PRE>"
    traceback.print_exc()
```

Don't look too hard for database or HTML-generation code here; it's all been factored out to the submit module, listed in a moment, so it can be reused for errata submissions too. Here, we simply pass it things that vary between comment and errata submits: database, expected input fields, and reply text.

As before, the database interface object is fetched from the switch module to select the currently supported storage medium. Customized text for confirmation pages (replyStored, replyMailed) winds up in web pages and is allowed to vary per database.

The inputs dictionary in this script provides default values for missing fields and defines the format of comment records in the database. In fact, this dictionary *is* stored in the database: within the submit module, input fields from the form or an explicit URL are merged in to the inputs dictionary created here, and the result is written to the database as a record.

More specifically, the submit module steps through all keys in inputs and picks up values of those keys from the parsed form input object, if present. The result is that this script guarantees that records in the comments database will have all the fields listed in inputs, but no others. Because all submit requests invoke this script, this is true even if superfluous fields are passed in an explicit URL; only fields in inputs are stored in the database.

Notice that almost all of this script is wrapped in a try statement with an empty except clause. This guarantees that every (uncaught) exception that can possibly happen while our script runs will return to this try and run its exception handler; here, it runs the standard traceback.print_exc call to print exception details to the web browser in unformatted (<PRE>) mode.

Implementation: Submitting Errata Reports

The top-level errata submission page in Figures 14-20 and 14-21 is also rendered from a static HTML file on the server, listed in Example 14-10. There are more input fields here, but it's similar to comments.

Example 14-10. PP2E\Internet\Cgi-Web\PyErrata\submitErrata.html

```
<html><body bgcolor="#FFFFFF">
<title>PP2E Submit Errata</title>
<h1>PP2E Submit Errata Report</h1>

<p>Please fill out the form below and press the submit button to
send your information.  By default, your report will be automatically
entered in a publically browsable database, where it will eventually
be reviewed and verified by the author.  If you prefer to send your
comments to the author by private email instead, click the "Email"
button before you submit.

<p>All the fields except the description text are optional;
for instance, if your note applies to the entire book, you can leave
the page, chapter, and part numbers blank.  For the printing date, see
the lower left corner of one of the first few pages; enter a string of
the form mm/dd/yy.  Thank you for your report.
</p>

<hr>
<form method=POST action="submitErrata.cgi">
  <table>
    <tr>
      <th align=right>Problem type:
      <td><select name="Type">
        <option>Typo
        <option>Grammar
        <option>Program bug
        <option>Suggestion
        <option>Other
```

```
      </select>
    <tr>
      <th align=right>Problem severity:
      <td><select name="Severity">
          <option>Low
          <option>Medium
          <option>High
          <option>Unknown
      </select>
    <tr>
      <th align=right>Page number:
      <td><input type=text name="Page number">
    <tr>
      <th align=right>Chapter number:
      <td><input type=text name="Chapter number">
    <tr>
      <th align=right>Part number:
      <td><input type=text name="Part number">
    <tr>
      <th align=right>Printing date:
      <td><input type=text name="Printing date">
    <tr>
      <th align=right>Description:
      <td><textarea name="Description" cols=60 rows=10>Type a description here
          </textarea>
    <tr>
      <th align=right>Your name:
      <td><input type=text size=40 name="Submitter name">
    <tr>
      <th align=right>Your email, webpage:
      <td><input type=text size=40 name="Submitter email">
    <tr>
      <th align=right>Email report privately?:
      <td><input type=checkbox name="Submit mode" value="email">
    <tr>
      <th></th>
      <td><input type=submit value="Submit Report">
          <input type=reset  value="Reset Form">
  </table>
</form>

<hr>
<A href="pyerrata.html">Back to errata page</A>
</body></html>
```

The script triggered by the form on this page, shown in Example 14-11, also looks remarkably similar to the submitComment script shown in Example 14-9. Because both scripts simply use factored-out logic in the submit module, all we need do here is pass in appropriately tailored confirmation pages text and expected input fields. As before, real CGI inputs are merged into the script's inputs dictionary to yield a database record; the stored record will contain exactly the fields listed here.

Example 14-11. PP2E\Internet\Cgi-Web\PyErrata\submitErrata.cgi

```python
#!/usr/bin/python

DEBUG=0
if DEBUG:
    import sys
    sys.stderr = sys.stdout
    print "Content-type: text/html"; print

import traceback
try:
    from dbswitch import DbaseErrata         # dbfiles or dbshelve
    from submit    import saveAndReply       # reuse save logic

    replyStored = """
Your report has been entered into the errata database.
You may view it by returning to the main errata page, and
selecting Browse/Errata reports, using your name, or any
other report identifying information as the browsing key."""

    replyMailed = """
Your report has been emailed to the author for review.
It will not be automatically browsable, but may be added to
the database anonymously later, if it is determined to be
information of general interest."""

    # 'Report state' and 'Submit date' are added when written

    inputs = {'Type':'',               'Severity':'',
                'Page number':'',        'Chapter number':'',    'Part number':'',
                'Printing Date':'',      'Description':'',        'Submit mode':'',
                'Submitter name':'',     'Submitter email':''}

    saveAndReply(DbaseErrata, inputs, replyStored, replyMailed)

except:
    print "\n\n<pre>"
    traceback.print_exc()
```

Common Submit Utility Module

Both comment and errata reports ultimately invoke functions in the module in Example 14-12 to store to the database and generate a reply page. Its primary goal is to merge real CGI inputs into the expected inputs dictionary and post the result to the database or email. We've already described the basic ideas behind this module's code, so we don't have much new to say here.

Notice, though, that email-mode submissions (invoked when the submit page's email checkbox is checked) use an `os.popen` shell command call to send the report by email; messages arrive in my mailbox with one line per nonempty report field. This works on my Linux web server, but other mail schemes such as the smptlib module (discussed in Chapter 11, *Client-Side Scripting*) are more portable.

Example 14-12. PP2E\Internet\Cgi-Web\PyErrata\submit.py

```
############################################################
# on submit request: store or mail data, send reply page;
# report data is stored in dictionaries on the database;
# we require a description field (and return a page with
# an error message if it's empty), even though the dbase
# mechanism could handle empty description fields--it
# makes no sense to submit a bug without a description;
############################################################

import cgi, os, sys, string
mailto = 'lutz@rmi.net'                 # or lutz@starship.python.net
sys.stderr = sys.stdout                 # print errors to browser
print "Content-type: text/html\n"

thankyouHtml = """
<TITLE>Thank you</TITLE>
<H1>Thank you</H1>
<P>%s</P>
<HR>"""

errorHtml = """
<TITLE>Empty field</TITLE>
<H1>Error: Empty %s</H1>
<P>Sorry, you forgot to provide a '%s' value.
Please go back to the prior page and try again.</P>
<HR>"""

def sendMail(inputs):                        # email data to author
    text = ''                                # or 'mailto:' form action
    for key, val in inputs.items():          # or smtplib.py or sendmail
        if val != '':
            text = text + ('%s = %s\n' % (key, val))
    mailcmd = 'mail -s "PP2E Errata" %s' % mailto
    os.popen(mailcmd, 'w').write(text)

def saveAndReply(dbase, inputs, replyStored, replyMailed):
    form = cgi.FieldStorage()
    for key in form.keys():
        if key in inputs.keys():
            inputs[key] = form[key].value        # pick out entered fields

    required = ['Description']
    for field in required:
        if string.strip(inputs[field]) == '':
            print errorHtml % (field, field)     # send error page to browser
            break
        else:
            if inputs['Submit mode'] == 'email':
                sendMail(inputs)                  # email data direct to author
```

Example 14-12. PP2E\Internet\Cgi-Web\PyErrata\submit.py (continued)

```
        print thankyouHtml % replyMailed
    else:
        dbase().storeItem(inputs)              # store data in file on server
        print thankyouHtml % replyStored
```

This module makes use of one additional database interface to store record dictionaries: `dbase().storeItem(inputs)`. However, we need to move on to the next section to fully understand the processing that this call implies.

 Another redundancy caveat: the list of expected fields in the `inputs` dictionaries in submit scripts is the same as the input fields list in submit HTML files. In principle again, we could instead generate the HTML file's fields list using data in a common module to remove this redundancy. However, that technique may not be as directly useful here, since each field requires description text in the HTML file only.

PyErrata Database Interfaces

Now that we've seen the user interfaces and top-level implementations of browse and submit operations, this section proceeds down one level of abstraction to the third and last major functional area in the PyErrata system.

Compared to other systems in this part of the book, one of the most unique technical features of PyErrata is that it must manage *persistent data*. Information posted by readers needs to be logged in a database for later review. PyErrata stores reports as dictionaries, and includes logic to support two database storage mediums—flat pickle files and shelves—as well as tools for synchronizing data access.

The Specter of Concurrent Updates

There is a variety of ways for Python scripts to store data persistently: files, object pickling, object shelves, real databases, and so on. In fact, Chapter 16 is devoted exclusively to this topic and provides more in-depth coverage than we require here.* Those storage mediums all work in the context of server-side CGI scripts too, but the CGI environment almost automatically introduces a new challenge: *concurrent updates*. Because the CGI model is inherently parallel, scripts must

---

* But see Chapter 16 if you could use a bit of background information on this topic. The current chapter introduces and uses only the simplest interfaces of the object `pickle` and `shelve` modules, and most module interface details are postponed until that later chapter.

take care to ensure that database writes and reads are properly synchronized to avoid data corruption and incomplete records.

Here's why. With PyErrata, a given reader may visit the site and post a report or view prior posts. But in the context of a web application, there is no way to know how many readers may be posting or viewing at once: any number of people may press a form's submit button at the same time. As we've seen, form submissions generally cause the HTTP server to spawn a new process to handle the request. Because these handler processes all run in parallel, if one hundred users all press submit at the same time, there will be one hundred CGI script processes running in parallel on the server, all of which may try to update (or read) the reports database at the same time.

Due to all this potential parallel traffic, server-side programs that maintain a database must somehow guarantee that database updates happen one at a time, or the database could be corrupted. The likelihood of two particular scenarios increases with the number of site users:

- *Concurrent writers*: If two processes try to update the same file at once, we may wind up with part of one process's new data intermixed with another's, lose part of one process's data, or otherwise corrupt stored data.

- *Concurrent reader and writer*: Similarly, if a process attempts to read a record that is being written by another, it may fetch an incomplete report. In effect, the database must be managed as a shared resource among all possible CGI handler processes, whether they update or not.

Constraints vary per database medium, and while it's generally okay for multiple processes to *read* a database at the same time, *writers* (and updates in general) almost always need to have exclusive access to a shared database. There is a variety of ways to make database access safe in a potentially concurrent environment such as CGI-based web sites:

Database systems
> If you are willing to accept the extra complexity of using a full-blown database system in your application (e.g, Sybase, Oracle, mySql), most provide support for concurrent access in one form or another.

Central database servers
> It's also possible to coordinate access to shared data stores by routing all data requests to a perpetually running manager program that you implement yourself. That is, each time a CGI script needs to hit the database, it must ask a data server program for access via a communications protocol such as socket calls.

File naming conventions

   If it is feasible to store each database record in a separate flat file, we can
   sometimes avoid or minimize the concurrent access problems altogether by
   giving each flat file a distinct name. For instance, if each record's filename
   includes both the file's creation time and the ID of the process that created it,
   it will be unique for all practical purposes, since a given process updates only
   one particular file. In this scheme, we rely on the operating system's filesystem to make records distinct, by storing them in unique files.

File locking protocols

   If the entire database is physically stored as a single file, we can use operating-system tools to lock the file during update operations. On Unix and Linux
   servers, exclusively locking a file will block other processes that need it until
   the lock is released; when used consistently by all processes, such a mechanism automatically synchronizes database accesses. Python shelves support
   concurrent readers but not concurrent updates, so we must add locks of our
   own to use them as dynamic data stores in CGI scripting.

In this section, we implement both of the last two schemes for PyErrata to illustrate concurrent data-access fundamentals.

Database Storage Structure

First of all, let's get a handle on what the system really stores. If you flip back to
Figure 14-1, you'll notice that there are two top-level database directories:
DbaseShelve (for the shelve mechanism) and *DbaseFiles* (for file-based storage).
Each of these directories has unique contents.

Shelve database

For shelve-based databases, the *DbaseShelve* directory's contents are shown in
Figure 14-27. The commentDB and errataDB files are the shelves used to store
reports, and the *.lck* and *.log* files are lock and log files generated by the system.
To start a new installation from scratch, only the two *.lck* files are needed initially (and can be simply empty files); the system creates the shelve and log files
as records are stored.

We'll explore the Python shelve module in more detail in the next part of this
book, but the parts of it used in this chapter are straightforward. Here are the basic
shelve interfaces we'll use in this example:

```
import shelve                          # load the standard shelve module
dbase = shelve.open('filename')        # open shelve (create if doesn't yet exist)
dbase['key'] = object                  # store almost any object in shelve file
object = dbase['key']                  # fetch object from shelve in future run
dbase.keys()                           # list of keys stored in the shelve
dbase.close()                          # close shelve's file
```

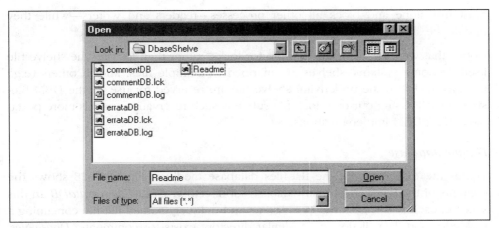

Figure 14-27. PyErrata shelve-based directory contents

In other words, shelves are like dictionaries of Python objects that are mapped to an external file, and so persist between program runs. Objects in a shelve are stored away and later fetched with a key. In fact, it's not inaccurate to think of shelves as dictionaries that live on after a program exits, and must be explicitly opened.

Like dictionaries, each distinct value stored in a shelve must have a *unique key.* Because there is no field in a comment or errata report that is reliably unique among all reports, we need to generate one of our own. Record submit time is close to being unique, but there is no guarantee that two users (and hence two processes) won't submit a report in the same second.

To assign each record a unique slot in the shelve, the system generates a unique key string for each, containing the submission time (seconds since the Unix "epoch" as a floating-point value) and the process ID of the storing CGI script. Since the dictionary values stored in the shelve contain all the report information we're interested in, shelve keys need only be unique, not meaningful. Records are loaded by blindly iterating over the shelve's keys list.

In addition to generating unique keys for records, shelves must accommodate *concurrent updates.* Because shelves are mapped to single files in the filesystem (here, `errataDB` and `commentDB`), we must synchronize all access to them in a potentially parallel process environment such as CGI scripting.

In its current form, the Python `shelve` module supports concurrent readers but not concurrent updates, so we need to add such functionality ourselves. The PyErrata implementation of the shelve database-storage scheme uses locks on the *.lck* files to make sure that writers (submit processes) gain exclusive access to the shelve before performing updates. Any number of readers may run in parallel, but writers must run alone and block all other processes—readers and writers—while they update the shelve.

Notice that we use a separate *.lck* file for locks, rather than locking the shelve file itself. In some systems, shelves are mapped to multiple files, and in others (e.g., GDBM), locks on the underlying shelve file are reserved for use by the DBM file-system itself. Using our own lock file subverts such reservations and is more portable among DBM implementations.

Flat-file database

Things are different with the flat-files database medium; Figure 14-28 shows the contents of the file-based errata database subdirectory, *DbaseFiles/errataDB*. In this scheme, each report is stored in a distinct and uniquely named flat file containing a pickled report-data dictionary. A similar directory exists for comments, *DbaseFiles/commentDB*. To start from scratch here, only the two subdirectories must exist; files are added as reports are submitted.

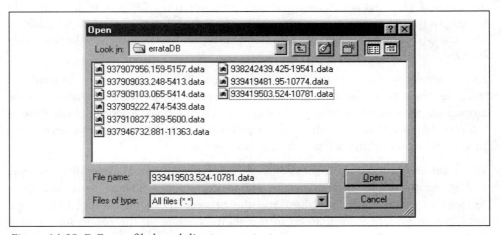

Figure 14-28. PyErrata file-based directory contents

Python's object pickler converts ("serializes") in-memory objects to and from specially coded strings in a single step, and therefore comes in handy for storing complex objects like the dictionaries PyErrata uses to represent report records.* We'll

---

* PyErrata could also simply write report record dictionaries to files with one field key and value per text line, and split lines later to rebuild the record. It could also just convert the record dictionary to its string representation with the str built-in function, write that string to the file manually, and convert the string back to a dictionary later with the built-in eval function (which may or may not be slower, due to the general parsing overhead of eval). As we'll see in the next part of this book, though, object pickling is a much more powerful and general approach to object storage—it also handles things like class instance objects and shared and cyclic object references well. See table wrapper classes in the PyForm example in Chapter 16 for similar topics.

also study the `pickle` module in depth in Part IV, *Assorted Topics*, but its interfaces employed by PyErrata are simple as well:

```
pickle.dump(object, outputfile)          # store object in a file
object = pickle.load(inputfile)          # load object back from file
```

For flat files, the system-generated *key* assigned to a record follows the same format as for shelves, but here it is used to name the report's file. Because of that,
record keys are more apparent (we see them when listing the directory), but still
don't need to convey any real information. They need only be unique for each
stored record to yield a unique file. In this storage scheme, records are processed
by iterating over directory listings returned by the standard `glob.glob` call on
name pattern `*.data` (see Chapter 2, *System Tools*, for a refresher on the `glob`
module).

In a sense, this flat-file approach uses the filesystem as a shelve and relies on the
operating system to segregate records as files. It also doesn't need to care much
about *concurrent access* issues; because generated filenames make sure that each
report is stored in its own separate file, it's impossible for two submit processes to
be writing the same file at once. Moreover, it's okay to read one report while
another is being created; they are truly distinct files.

We still need to be careful, though, to avoid making a file visible to reader directory listings until it is complete, or else we may read a half-finished file. This case
is unlikely in practice—it can happen only if the writer still hasn't finished by the
time the reader gets around to that file in its directory listing. But to avoid problems, submit scripts first write data to a temporary file, and move the temporary
file to the real `*.data` name only after it is complete.

Database Switch

On to code listings. The first database module, shown in Example 14-13, simply
selects between a file-based mechanism and shelve-based mechanism; we make
the choice here alone to avoid impacting other files when we change storage
schemes.

Example 14-13. PP2E\Internet\Cgi-Web\PyErrata\dbswitch.py

```
#############################################################
# for testing alternative underlying database mediums;
# since the browse, submit, and index cgi scripts import
# dbase names from here only, they'll get whatever this
# module loads; in other words, to switch mediums, simply
# change the import here; eventually we could remove this
# interface module altogether, and load the best medium's
# module directly, but the best may vary by use patterns;
#############################################################
```

Example 14-13. PP2E\Internet\Cgi-Web\PyErrata\dbswitch.py (continued)

```
#
# one directory per dbase, one flat pickle file per submit
#

from dbfiles import DbaseErrata, DbaseComment


#
# one shelve per dbase, one key per submit, with mutex update locks
#

# from dbshelve import DbaseErrata, DbaseComment
```

Storage-Specific Classes for Files and Shelves

The next two modules implement file- and shelve-based database-access objects;
the classes they define are the objects passed and used in the browse and submit
scripts. Both are really just subclasses of the more generic class in dbcommon; in
Example 14-14, we fill in methods that define storage scheme–specific behavior,
but the superclass does most of the work.

Example 14-14. PP2E\Internet\Cgi-Web\PyErrata\dbfiles.py

```
##############################################################
# store each item in a distinct flat file, pickled;
# dbcommon assumes records are dictionaries, but we don't here;
# chmod to 666 to allow admin access (else 'nobody' owns);
# subtlety: unique filenames prevent multiple writers for any
# given file, but it's still possible that a reader (browser)
# may try to read a file while it's being written, if the
# glob.glob call returns the name of a created but still
# incomplete file;  this is unlikely to happen (the file
# would have to still be incomplete after the time from glob
# to unpickle has expired), but to avoid this risk, files are
# created with a temp name, and only moved to the real name
# when they have been completely written and closed;
# cgi scripts with persistent data are prone to parallel
# updates, since multiple cgi scripts may be running at once;
##############################################################

import dbcommon, pickle, glob, os

class Dbase(dbcommon.Dbase):
    def writeItem(self, newdata):
        name = self.dirname + self.makeKey()
        file = open(name, 'w')
        pickle.dump(newdata, file)             # store in new file
        file.close()
        os.rename(name, name+'.data')          # visible to globs
        os.chmod(name+'.data', 0666)           # owned by 'nobody'
```

Example 14-14. PP2E\Internet\Cgi-Web\PyErrata\dbfiles.py (continued)

```python
    def readTable(self):
        reports = []
        for filename in glob.glob(self.dirname + '*.data'):
            reports.append(pickle.load(open(filename, 'r')))
        return reports

class DbaseErrata(Dbase):
    dirname = 'DbaseFiles/errataDB/'

class DbaseComment(Dbase):
    dirname = 'DbaseFiles/commentDB/'
```

The shelve interface module listed in Example 14-15 provides the same methods interface, but implements them to talk to shelves. Its class also mixes in the mutual-exclusion class to get file locking; we'll study that class's code in a few pages.

Notice that this module extends `sys.path` so that a platform-specific FCNTL module (described later in this chapter) becomes visible to the file-locking tools. This is necessary in the CGI script context only, because the module search path given to CGI user "nobody" doesn't include the platform-specific extension modules directory. Both the file and shelve classes set newly created file permissions to octal 0666, so that users besides "nobody" can read and write. If you've forgotten whom "nobody" is, see earlier discussions of permission and ownership issues in this and the previous two chapters.

Example 14-15. PP2E\Internet\Cgi-Web\PyErrata\dbshelve.py

```python
#########################################################
# store items in a shelve, with file locks on writes;
# dbcommon assumes items are dictionaries (not here);
# chmod call assumes single file per shelve (e.g., gdbm);
# shelve allows simultaneous reads, but if any program
# is writing, no other reads or writes are allowed,
# so we obtain the lock before all load/store ops
# need to chown to 0666, else only 'nobody' can write;
# this file doesn't know about fcntl, but mutex doesn't
# know about cgi scripts--one of the 2 needs to add the
# path to FCNTL module for cgi script use only (here);
# we circumvent whatever locking mech the underlying
# dbm system may have, since we acquire alock on our own
# non-dbm file before attempting any dbm operation;
# allows multiple simultaneous readers, but writers
# get exclusive access to the shelve; lock calls in
# MutexCntl block and later resume callers if needed;
#########################################################

# cgi runs as 'nobody' without
# the following default paths
import sys
sys.path.append('/usr/local/lib/python1.5/plat-linux2')
```

Example 14-15. PP2E\Internet\Cgi-Web\PyErrata\dbshelve.py (continued)

```python
import dbcommon, shelve, os
from Mutex.mutexcntl import MutexCntl

class Dbase(MutexCntl, dbcommon.Dbase):              # mix mutex, dbcommon, mine
    def safe_writeItem(self, newdata):
        dbase = shelve.open(self.filename)           # got excl access: update
        dbase[self.makeKey()] = newdata              # save in shelve, safely
        dbase.close()
        os.chmod(self.filename, 0666)                # else others can't change

    def safe_readTable(self):
        reports = []                                 # got shared access: load
        dbase = shelve.open(self.filename)           # no writers will be run
        for key in dbase.keys():
            reports.append(dbase[key])               # fetch data, safely
        dbase.close()
        return reports

    def writeItem(self, newdata):
        self.exclusiveAction(self.safe_writeItem, newdata)

    def readTable(self):
        return self.sharedAction(self.safe_readTable)

class DbaseErrata(Dbase):
    filename = 'DbaseShelve/errataDB'

class DbaseComment(Dbase):
    filename = 'DbaseShelve/commentDB'
```

Top-Level Database Interface Class

Here, we reach the top-level database interfaces that our CGI scripts actually call. The class in Example 14-16 is "abstract" in the sense that it cannot do anything by itself. We must provide and create instances of subclasses that define storage-specific methods, rather than making instances of this class directly.

In fact, this class deliberately leaves the underlying storage scheme undefined and raises assertion errors if a subclass doesn't fill in the required details. Any storage-specific class that provides writeItem and readTable methods can be plugged into this top-level class's interface model. This includes classes that interface with flat files, shelves, and other specializations we might add in the future (e.g., schemes that talk to full-blown SQL or object databases, or that cache data in persistent servers).

In a sense, subclasses take the role of embedded component objects here; they simply need to provide expected interfaces. Because the top-level interface has been factored out to this single class, we can change the underlying storage scheme simply by selecting a different storage-specific subclass (as in dbswitch);

the top-level database calls remain unchanged. Moreover, changes and optimizations to top-level interfaces will likely impact this file alone.

Since this is a superclass common to storage-specific classes, we also here define record key generation methods and insert common generated attributes (submit date, initial report state) into new records before they are written.

Example 14-16. PP2E\Internet\Cgi-Web\PyErrata\dbcommon.py

```
#############################################################
# an abstract superclass with shared dbase access logic;
# stored records are assumed to be dictionaries (or other
# mapping), one key per field; dbase medium is undefined;
# subclasses: define writeItem and readTable as appropriate
# for the underlying file medium--flat files, shelves, etc.
# subtlety: the 'Submit date' field added here could be kept
# as a tuple, and all sort/select logic will work; but since
# these values may be embedded in a url string, we don't want
# to convert from string to tuple using eval in index.cgi;
# for consistency and safety, we convert to strings here;
# if not for the url issue, tuples work fine as dict keys;
# must use fixed-width columns in time string to sort;
# this interface may be optimized in future releases;
#############################################################

import time, os

class Dbase:

    # store

    def makeKey(self):
        return "%s-%s" % (time.time(), os.getpid())

    def writeItem(self, newdata):
        assert 0, 'writeItem must be customized'

    def storeItem(self, newdata):
        secsSinceEpoch          = time.time()
        timeTuple               = time.localtime(secsSinceEpoch)
        y_m_d_h_m_s             = timeTuple[:6]
        newdata['Submit date']  = '%s/%02d/%02d, %02d:%02d:%02d' % y_m_d_h_m_s
        newdata['Report state'] = 'Not yet verified'
        self.writeItem(newdata)

    # load

    def readTable(self):
        assert 0, 'readTable must be customized'

    def loadSortedTable(self, field=None):          # returns a simple list
        reports = self.readTable()                  # ordered by field sort
        if field:
```

Example 14-16. PP2E\Internet\Cgi-Web\PyErrata\dbcommon.py (continued)

```
            reports.sort(lambda x, y, f=field: cmp(x[f], y[f]))
        return reports

    def loadIndexedTable(self, field):
        reports = self.readTable()
        index = {}
        for report in reports:
            try:
                index[report[field]].append(report)    # group by field values
            except KeyError:
                index[report[field]] = [report]         # add first for this key
        keys = index.keys()
        keys.sort()                                     # sorted keys, groups dict
        return keys, index
```

Mutual Exclusion for Shelves

We've at last reached the bottom of the PyErrata code hierarchy: code that encapsulates file locks for synchronizing shelve access. The class listed in Example 14-17 provides tools to synchronize operations, using a lock on a file whose name is provided by systems that use the class.

It includes methods for locking and unlocking the file, but also exports higher-level methods for running function calls in exclusive or shared mode. Method sharedAction is used to run read operations, and exclusiveAction handles writes. Any number of *shared* actions can occur in parallel, but *exclusive* actions occur all by themselves and block all other action requests in parallel processes. Both kinds of actions are run in try-finally statements to guarantee that file locks are unlocked on action exit, normal or otherwise.

Example 14-17. PP2E\Internet\Cgi-Web\PyErrata\Mutex\mutexcntl.py

```
#######################################################
# generally useful mixin, so a separate module;
# requires self.filename attribute to be set, and
# assumes self.filename+'.lck' file already exists;
# set mutexcntl.debugMutexCntl to toggle logging;
# writes lock log messages to self.filename+'.log';
#######################################################

import fcntl, os, time
from FCNTL import LOCK_SH, LOCK_EX, LOCK_UN

debugMutexCntl = 1
processType = {LOCK_SH: 'reader', LOCK_EX: 'writer'}

class MutexCntl:
    def lockFile(self, mode):
        self.logPrelock(mode)
        self.lock = open(self.filename + '.lck')     # lock file in this process
```

Example 14-17. PP2E\Internet\Cgi-Web\PyErrata\Mutex\mutexcntl.py (continued)

```
        fcntl.flock(self.lock.fileno(), mode)        # waits for lock if needed
        self.logPostlock()

    def lockFileRead(self):                          # allow > 1 reader: shared
        self.lockFile(LOCK_SH)                       # wait if any write lock

    def lockFileWrite(self):                         # writers get exclusive lock
        self.lockFile(LOCK_EX)                       # wait if any lock: r or w

    def unlockFile(self):
        self.logUnlock()
        fcntl.flock(self.lock.fileno(), LOCK_UN)     # unlock for other processes

    def sharedAction(self, action, *args):           # higher level interface
        self.lockFileRead()                          # block if a write lock
        try:
            result = apply(action, args)             # any number shared at once
        finally:                                     # but no exclusive actions
            self.unlockFile()                        # allow new writers to run
        return result

    def exclusiveAction(self, action, *args):
        self.lockFileWrite()                         # block if any other locks
        try:
            result = apply(action, args)             # no other actions overlap
        finally:
            self.unlockFile()                        # allow new readers/writers
        return result

    def logmsg(self, text):
        if not debugMutexCntl: return
        log = open(self.filename + '.log', 'a')      # append to the end
        log.write('%s\t%s\n' % (time.time(), text))  # output won't overwrite
        log.close()                                  # but it may intermingle

    def logPrelock(self, mode):
        self.logmsg('Requested: %s, %s' % (os.getpid(), processType[mode]))
    def logPostlock(self):
        self.logmsg('Aquired: %s' % os.getpid())
    def logUnlock(self):
        self.logmsg('Released: %s' % os.getpid())
```

This file lock management class is coded in its own module by design, because it is potentially worth reusing. In PyErrata, shelve database classes mix it in with *multiple inheritance* to implement mutual exclusion for database writers.

This class assumes that a lockable file exists as name `self.filename` (defined in client classes) with a *.lck* extension; like all instance attributes, this name can vary per client of the class. If a global variable is true, the class also optionally logs all lock operations in a file of the same name as the lock, but with a *.log* extension.

Notice that the log file is opened in a append mode; on Unix systems, this mode guarantees that the log file text written by each process appears on a line of its own, not intermixed (multiple copies of this class may write to the log from parallel CGI script processes). To really understand how this class works, though, we need to say more about Python's file-locking interface.

Using fcntl.flock to lock files

When we studied threads in Chapter 3, *Parallel System Tools*, we saw that the Python thread module includes a mutual-exclusion lock mechanism that can be used to synchronize threads' access to shared global memory resources. This won't usually help us much in the CGI environment, however, because each database request generally comes from a distinct process spawned by the HTTP server to handle an incoming request. That is, thread locks work only within the same process, because all threads run within a *single* process.

For CGI scripts, we usually need a locking mechanism that spans multiple processes instead. On Unix systems, the Python standard library exports a tool based on locking files, and therefore may be used across process boundaries. All of this magic happens in these two lines in the PyErrata mutex class:

```
fcntl.flock(self.lock.fileno(), mode)       # waits for lock if needed
fcntl.flock(self.lock.fileno(), LOCK_UN)    # unlock for other processes
```

The `fcntl.flock` call in the standard Python library attempts to acquire a lock associated with a file, and by default blocks the calling process if needed until the lock can be acquired. The call accepts a *file descriptor* integer code (the `stdio` file object's `fileno` method returns one for us) and a *mode flag* defined in standard module FCNTL, which takes one of three values in our system:

- LOCK_EX requests an exclusive lock, typically used for writers. This lock is granted only if no other locks are held (exclusive or shared) and blocks all other lock requests (exclusive or shared) until the lock is released. This guarantees that exclusive lock holders run alone.

- LOCK_SH requests a shared lock, typically used for readers. Any number of processes can hold shared locks at the same time, but one is granted only if no exclusive lock is held, and new exclusive lock requests are blocked until all shared locks are released.

- LOCK_UN unlocks a lock previously acquired by the calling process so that other processes can acquire locks and resume execution.

In database terms, the net effect is that readers wait only if a write lock is held by another process, and writers wait if any lock is held—read or write. Though used to synchronize processes, this scheme is more complex and powerful than the simple acquire/release model for locks in the Python **thread** module, and is different from the class tools available in the higher-level **threading** module. However, it could be emulated by both these thread modules.

fcntl.flock internally calls out to whatever file-locking mechanism is available in the underlying operating system,[*] and therefore you can consult the corresponding Unix or Linux manpage for more details. It's also possible to avoid blocking if a lock can't be acquired, and there are other synchronization tools in the Python library (e.g., "fifos"), but we will ignore such options here.

Mutex test scripts

To help us understand the PyErrata synchronization model, let's get a better feel for the underlying file-locking primitives by running a few simple experiments. Examples 14-18 and 14-19 implement simple reader and writer processes using the **flock** call directly instead of our class. They request shared and exclusive locks, respectively.

Example 14-18. PP2E\Internet\Cgi-Web\PyErrata\Mutex\testread.py

```
#!/usr/bin/python

import os, fcntl, time
from FCNTL import LOCK_SH, LOCK_UN
print os.getpid(), 'start reader', time.time()

file = open('test.lck', 'r')                      # open the lock file for fd
fcntl.flock(file.fileno(), LOCK_SH)               # block if a writer has lock
print os.getpid(), 'got read lock', time.time()   # any number of readers can run

time.sleep(3)
print 'lines so far:', os.popen('wc -l Shared.txt').read(),

print os.getpid(), 'unlocking\n'
fcntl.flock(file.fileno(), LOCK_UN)               # resume blocked writers now
```

In this simple test, locks on text file *test.lck* are used to synchronize read and write access to a text file appended by writers. The appended text file plays the role of PyErrata shelve databases, and the reader and writer scripts in Examples 14-18 and 14-19 stand in for its browse and submit script processes.

Example 14-19. PP2E\Internet\Cgi-Web\PyErrata\Mutex\testwrite.py

```
#!/usr/bin/python

import os, fcntl, time
from FCNTL import LOCK_EX, LOCK_UN
```

---

[*] Locking mechanisms vary per platform and may not exist at all. For instance, the **flock** call is not currently supported on Windows as of Python 1.5.2, so you may need to replace this call with a platform-specific alternative on some server machines.

Example 14-19. PP2E\Internet\Cgi-Web\PyErrata\Mutex\testwrite.py (continued)

```
print os.getpid(), 'start writer', time.time()

file = open('test.lck', 'r')                        # open the lock file
fcntl.flock(file.fileno(), LOCK_EX)                 # block if any read or write
print os.getpid(), 'got write lock', time.time()   # only 1 writer at a time

log = open('Shared.txt', 'a')
time.sleep(3)
log.write('%d Hello\n' % os.getpid())

print os.getpid(), 'unlocking\n'
fcntl.flock(file.fileno(), LOCK_UN)                 # resume blocked read or write
```

To start a set of readers and writers running in parallel, Example 14-20 uses the Unix **fork**/**execl** call combination to launch program processes (both calls are described in Chapter 3).

Example 14-20. PP2E\Internet\Cgi-Web\PyErrata\Mutex\launch-test.py

```
#!/usr/bin/python
###################################################
# launch test program processes
# run with ./launch-test.py > launch-test.out
# try spawning reader before writer, then writer
# before reader--second process blocks till first
# unlocks in both cases; if launches 2 readers
# initially, both get lock and block writer; if
# launch 2 writers first then 2 readers, 2nd writer
# waits for first, both readers wait for both
# writers, and both readers get lock at same time;
# in test below, the first writer runs, then all
# readers run before any writer;  if readers are
# first, all run before any writer; (all on linux)
###################################################

import os

for i in range(1):
    if os.fork() == 0:
        os.execl("./testwrite.py")

for i in range(2):                          # copy this process
    if os.fork() == 0:                      # if in new child process
        os.execl("./testread.py")           # overlay with test program

for i in range(2):
    if os.fork() == 0:
        os.execl("./testwrite.py")          # same, but start writers

for i in range(2):
    if os.fork() == 0:
        os.execl("./testread.py")
```

Example 14-20. PP2E\Internet\Cgi-Web\PyErrata\Mutex\launch-test.py (continued)

```
for i in range(1):
    if os.fork() == 0:
        os.execl("./testwrite.py")
```

Comments in this script give the results for running its logic various ways on Linux. Pragmatic note: after copying these files over from Windows in an FTP'd `tar` file, I first had to give them executable permissions and convert them from DOS to Unix line-feed format before Linux would treat them as executable programs:[*]

```
[mark@toy .../PyErrata/Mutex]$ chmod +x *.py
[mark@toy .../PyErrata/Mutex]$ python $X/PyTools/fixeoln_all.py tounix "*.py"
__init__.py
launch-mutex-simple.py
launch-mutex.py
launch-test.py
mutexcntl.py
testread-mutex.py
testread.py
testwrite-mutex.py
testwrite.py
```

Once they've been so configured as executables, we can run all three of these scripts from the Linux command line. The reader and writer scripts access a *Shared.txt* file, which is meant to simulate a shared resource in a real parallel application (e.g., a database in the CGI realm):

```
[mark@toy ...PyErrata/Mutex]$ ./testwrite.py
1010 start writer 960919842.773
1010 got write lock 960919842.78
1010 unlocking

[mark@toy ...PyErrata/Mutex]$ ./testread.py
1013 start reader 960919900.146
1013 got read lock 960919900.153
lines so far:      132 Shared.txt
1013 unlocking
```

The `launch-test` script simply starts a batch of the reader and writer scripts that run as parallel processes to simulate a concurrent environment (e.g., web browsers contacting a CGI script all at once):

```
[mark@toy ...PyErrata/Mutex]$ python launch-test.py
1016 start writer 960919933.206
1016 got write lock 960919933.213
1017 start reader 960919933.416
1018 start reader 960919933.455
```

---

[*] The +x syntax in the *chmod* shell command here means "set the executable bit" in the file's permission bit-string for "self", the current user. At least on my machine, *chmod* accepts both the integer bit-strings used earlier and symbolic forms like this. Note that we run these tests on Linux because the Python `os.fork` call doesn't work on Windows, at least as of Python 1.5.2. It may eventually, but for now Windows scripts use `os.spawnv` instead (see Chapter 3 for details).

```
1022 start reader 960919933.474
1021 start reader 960919933.486
1020 start writer 960919933.497
1019 start writer 960919933.508
1023 start writer 960919933.52
1016 unlocking

1017 got read lock 960919936.228
1018 got read lock 960919936.234
1021 got read lock 960919936.24
1022 got read lock 960919936.246
lines so far:       133 Shared.txt
1022 unlocking

lines so far:       133 Shared.txt
1018 unlocking

lines so far:       133 Shared.txt
1017 unlocking

lines so far:       133 Shared.txt
1021 unlocking

1019 got write lock 960919939.375
1019 unlocking

1020 got write lock 960919942.379
1020 unlocking

1023 got write lock 960919945.388
1023 unlocking
```

This output is a bit cryptic; most lines list process ID, text, and system time, and each process inserts a three-second delay (via `time.sleep`) to simulate real activities. If you look carefully, you'll notice that all processes start at roughly the same time, but access to the shared file is synchronized into this sequence:

1. One writer grabs the file first.

2. Next, all readers get it at the same time, three seconds later.

3. Finally, all other writers get the file one after another, three seconds apart.

The net result is that writer processes always access the file alone while all others are blocked. Such a sequence will avoid concurrent update problems.

Mutex class test scripts

To test our mutex class outside the scope of PyErrata, we simply rewrite these scripts to hook into the class's interface. The output of Examples 14-21 and 14-22 is similar to the raw `fcntl` versions shown previously, but an additional log file is produced to help trace lock operations.

Example 14-21. PP2E\Internet\Cgi-Web\PyErrata\Mutex\testread-mutex.py

```
#!/usr/bin/python
import os, time
from mutexcntl import MutexCntl

class app(MutexCntl):
    def go(self):
        self.filename = 'test'
        print os.getpid(), 'start mutex reader'
        self.sharedAction(self.report)          # can report with others
                                                 # but not during update
    def report(self):
        print os.getpid(), 'got read lock'
        time.sleep(3)
        print 'lines so far:', os.popen('wc -l Shared.txt').read(),
        print os.getpid(), 'unlocking\n'

if __name__ == '__main__': app().go()
```

Unlike PyErrata, we don't need to change `sys.path` to allow `FCNTL` imports in the `mutexcntl` module in Examples 14-21 and 14-22, because we'll run these scripts as ourself, not the CGI user "nobody" (my path includes the directory where `FCNTL` lives).

Example 14-22. PP2E\Internet\Cgi-Web\PyErrata\Mutex\testwrite-mutex.py

```
#!/usr/bin/python
import os, time
from mutexcntl import MutexCntl

class app(MutexCntl):
    def go(self):
        self.filename = 'test'
        print os.getpid(), 'start mutex writer'
        self.exclusiveAction(self.update)       # must do this alone;
                                                 # no update or report
    def update(self):                            # can run at same time
        print os.getpid(), 'got write lock'
        log = open('Shared.txt', 'a')
        time.sleep(3)
        log.write('%d Hello\n' % os.getpid())
        print os.getpid(), 'unlocking\n'

if __name__ == '__main__': app().go()
```

The launcher is the same as Example 14-20, but Example 14-23 starts multiple copies of the class-based readers and writers. Run Example 14-23 on your server with various process counts to follow the locking mechanism.

Example 14-23. PP2E\Internet\Cgi-Web\PyErrata\launch-mutex.py

```
#!/usr/bin/python
# launch test program processes
# same, but start mutexcntl clients

import os

for i in range(1):
    if os.fork() == 0:
        os.execl("./testwrite-mutex.py")

for i in range(2):
    if os.fork() == 0:
        os.execl("./testread-mutex.py")

for i in range(2):
    if os.fork() == 0:
        os.execl("./testwrite-mutex.py")

for i in range(2):
    if os.fork() == 0:
        os.execl("./testread-mutex.py")

for i in range(1):
    if os.fork() == 0:
        os.execl("./testwrite-mutex.py")
```

The output of the class-based test is more or less the same. Processes start up in a different order, but the synchronization behavior is identical—one writer writes, all readers read, then remaining writers write one at a time:

```
[mark@toy .../PyErrata/Mutex]$ python launch-mutex.py
1035 start mutex writer
1035 got write lock
1037 start mutex reader
1040 start mutex reader
1038 start mutex writer
1041 start mutex reader
1039 start mutex writer
1036 start mutex reader
1042 start mutex writer
1035 unlocking

1037 got read lock
1041 got read lock
1040 got read lock
1036 got read lock
lines so far:     137 Shared.txt
1036 unlocking

lines so far:     137 Shared.txt
1041 unlocking
```

```
        lines so far:     137 Shared.txt
        1040 unlocking

        lines so far:     137 Shared.txt
        1037 unlocking

        1038 got write lock
        1038 unlocking

        1039 got write lock
        1039 unlocking

        1042 got write lock
        1042 unlocking
```

All times have been removed from launcher output this time, because our mutex class automatically logs lock operations in a separate file, with times and process IDs; the three-second sleep per process is more obvious in this format:

```
[mark@toy .../PyErrata/Mutex]$ cat test.log
960920109.518   Requested: 1035, writer
960920109.518   Aquired: 1035
960920109.626   Requested: 1040, reader
960920109.646   Requested: 1038, writer
960920109.647   Requested: 1037, reader
960920109.661   Requested: 1041, reader
960920109.674   Requested: 1039, writer
960920109.69    Requested: 1036, reader
960920109.701   Requested: 1042, writer
960920112.535   Released: 1035
960920112.542   Aquired: 1037
960920112.55    Aquired: 1041
960920112.557   Aquired: 1040
960920112.564   Aquired: 1036
960920115.601   Released: 1036
960920115.63    Released: 1041
960920115.657   Released: 1040
960920115.681   Released: 1037
960920115.681   Aquired: 1038
960920118.689   Released: 1038
960920118.696   Aquired: 1039
960920121.709   Released: 1039
960920121.716   Aquired: 1042
960920124.728   Released: 1042
```

Finally, this is what the shared text file looks like after all these processes have exited stage left. Each writer simply added a line with its process ID; it's not the most amazing of parallel process results, but if you pretend that this is our PyErrata shelve-based *database*, these tests seem much more meaningful:

```
[mark@toy .../PyErrata/Mutex]$ cat Shared.txt
1010 Hello
1016 Hello
1019 Hello
```

```
1020 Hello
1023 Hello
1035 Hello
1038 Hello
1039 Hello
1042 Hello
```

Administrative Tools

Now that we have finished implementing a Python-powered, web-enabled, concurrently accessible report database, and published web pages and scripts that make that database accessible to the cyberworld at large, we can sit back and wait for reports to come in. Or almost; there still is no way for the site owner to view or delete records offline. Moreover, all records are tagged as "not yet verified" on submission, and must somehow be verified or rejected.

This section lists a handful of tersely documented PyErrata scripts that accomplish such tasks. All are Python programs shipped in the top-level *AdminTools* directory and are assumed to be run from a shell command line on the server (or other machine, after database downloads). They implement simple database content dumps, database backups, and database state-changes and deletions for use by the errata site administrator.

These tasks are infrequent, so not much work has gone into these tools. Frankly, some fall into the domain of "quick and dirty" hackerage and aren't as robust as they could be. For instance, because these scripts bypass the database interface classes and speak directly to the underlying file structures, changes in the underlying file mechanisms will likely break these tools. Also in a more polished future release, these tools might instead sprout GUI- or web-based user interfaces to support over-the-net administration. For now, such extensions are left as exercises for the ambitious reader.

Backup Tools

System backup tools simply spawn the standard Unix `tar` and `gzip` command-line programs to copy databases into single compressed files. You could write a shell script for this task too, but Python works just as well, as shown in Examples 14-24 and 14-25.

Example 14-24. PP2E\Internet\Cgi-Web\PyErrata\AdminTools\backupFiles.py

```
#!/usr/bin/python
import os
os.system('tar -cvf DbaseFiles.tar ../DbaseFiles')
os.system('gzip DbaseFiles.tar')
```

Example 14-25. PP2E\Internet\Cgi-Web\PyErrata\AdminTools\backupShelve.py

```
#!/usr/bin/python
import os
os.system('tar -cvf DbaseShelve.tar ../DbaseShelve')
os.system('gzip DbaseShelve.tar')
```

Display Tools

The scripts in Examples 14-26 and 14-27 produce raw dumps of each database structure's contents. Because the databases use pure Python storage mechanisms (pickles, shelves), these scripts can work one level below the published database interface classes; whether they should depends on how much code you're prepared to change when your database model evolves. Apart from printing generated record filenames and shelve keys, there is no reason that these scripts couldn't be made less brittle by instead calling the database classes' `loadSortedTable` methods. Suggested exercise: do better.

Example 14-26. PP2E\Internet\Cgi-Web\PyErrata\AdminTools\dumpFiles.py

```
#!/usr/bin/python
import glob, pickle

def dump(kind):
    print '\n', kind, '='*60, '\n'
    for file in glob.glob("../DbaseFiles/%s/*.data" % kind):
        print '\n', '-'*60
        print file
        print pickle.load(open(file, 'r'))

dump('errataDB')
dump('commentDB')
```

Example 14-27. PP2E\Internet\Cgi-Web\PyErrata\AdminTools\dumpShelve.py

```
#!/usr/bin/python
import shelve
e = shelve.open('../DbaseShelve/errataDB')
c = shelve.open('../DbaseShelve/commentDB')

print '\n', 'Errata', '='*60, '\n'
print e.keys()
for k in e.keys(): print '\n', k, '-'*60, '\n', e[k]

print '\n', 'Comments', '='*60, '\n'
print c.keys()
for k in c.keys(): print '\n', k, '-'*60, '\n', c[k]
```

Running these scripts produces the following sorts of results (truncated at 80 characters to fit in this book). It's not nearly as pretty as the web pages generated for the user in PyErrata, but could be piped to other command-line scripts for further

offline analysis and processing. For instance, the dump scripts' output could be
sent to a report-generation script that knows nothing of the Web:

```
[mark@toy .../Internet/Cgi-Web/PyErrata/AdminTools]$ python dumpFiles.py

errataDB ========================================================


------------------------------------------------------------
../DbaseFiles/errataDB/937907956.159-5157.data
{'Page number': '42', 'Type': 'Typo', 'Severity': 'Low', 'Chapter number': '3'...

------------------------------------------------------------
...more...

commentDB =========================================================


------------------------------------------------------------
../DbaseFiles/commentDB/937908410.203-5352.data
{'Submit date': '1999/09/21, 06:06:50', 'Submitter email': 'bob@bob.com',...

------------------------------------------------------------
...more...

[mark@toy .../Internet/Cgi-Web/PyErrata/AdminTools]$ python dumpShelve.py

Errata ===========================================================

['938245136.363-20046', '938244808.434-19964']

938245136.363-20046 ------------------------------------------------------------
{'Page number': '256', 'Type': 'Program bug', 'Severity': 'High', 'Chapter nu...

938244808.434-19964 ------------------------------------------------------------
{'Page number': 'various', 'Type': 'Suggestion', 'Printing Date': '', 'Chapte...

Comments =========================================================

['938245187.696-20054']

938245187.696-20054 ------------------------------------------------------------
{'Submit date': '1999/09/25, 03:39:47', 'Submitter email': 'bob@bob.com', 'Re...
```

Report State-Change Tools

Our last batch of command-line tools allows the site owner to mark reports as verified or rejected and to delete reports altogether. The idea is that someone will
occasionally run these scripts offline, as time allows, to change states after investi-
gating reports. And this is the end to our quest for errata automation: the investiga-
tion process itself is assumed to require both time and brains.

There are no interfaces in the database's classes for changing existing reports, so these scripts can at least make a case for going below the classes to the physical storage mediums. On the other hand, the classes could be extended to support such update operations too, with interfaces that could also be used by future state-change tools (e.g., web interfaces).

To minimize some redundancy, let's first define state-change functions in a common module listed in Example 14-28, so they may be shared by both the file and shelve scripts.

Example 14-28. PP2E\Internet\Cgi-Web\PyErrata\AdminTools\verifycommon.py

```
################################################################
# put common verify code in a shared module for consistency and
# reuse; could also generalize dbase update scan, but this helps
################################################################

def markAsVerify(report):
    report['Report state'] = 'Verified by author'

def markAsReject(report):
    reason = ''                             # input reject reason text
    while 1:                                # prepend to original desc
        try:
            line = raw_input('reason>')
        except EOFError:
            break
        reason = reason + line + '\n'
    report['Report state'] = 'Rejected - not a real bug'
    report['Description']  = ('Reject reason: ' + reason +
                '\n[Original description=>]\n' + report['Description'])
```

To process state changes on the *file*-based database, we simply iterate over all the pickle files in the database directories, as shown in Example 14-29.

Example 14-29. PP2E\Internet\Cgi-Web\PyErrata\AdminTools\verifyFiles.py

```
#!/usr/bin/python
######################################################
# report state change and deletion operations;
# also need a tool for anonymously publishing reports
# sent by email that are of general interest--for now,
# they can be entered with the submit forms manually;
# this is text-based: the idea is that records can be
# browsed in the errata page first (sort by state to
# see unverified ones), but an edit gui or web-based
# verification interface might be very useful to add;
######################################################

import glob, pickle, os
from verifycommon import markAsVerify, markAsReject
```

Example 14-29. PP2E\Internet\Cgi-Web\PyErrata\AdminTools\verifyFiles.py (continued)

```
def analyse(kind):
    for file in glob.glob("../DbaseFiles/%s/*.data" % kind):
        data = pickle.load(open(file, 'r'))
        if data['Report state'] == 'Not yet verified':
            print data
            if raw_input('Verify?') == 'y':
                markAsVerify(data)
                pickle.dump(data, open(file, 'w'))
            elif raw_input('Reject?') == 'y':
                markAsReject(data)
                pickle.dump(data, open(file, 'w'))
            elif raw_input('Delete?') == 'y':
                os.remove(file)   # same as os.unlink

print 'Errata...';   analyse('errataDB')
print 'Comments...'; analyse('commentDB')
```

When run from the command line, the script displays one report's contents at a time and pauses after each to ask if it should be verified, rejected, or deleted. Here is the beginning of one file database verify session, shown with line wrapping so you can see what I see (it's choppy but compact):

```
[mark@toy .../Internet/Cgi-Web/PyErrata/AdminTools]$ python verifyFiles.py
Errata...
{'Page number': '12', 'Type': 'Program bug', 'Printing Date': '', 'Chapter numbe
r': '', 'Submit date': '1999/09/21, 06:17:13', 'Report state': 'Not yet verified
', 'Submitter name': 'Lisa Lutz', 'Submitter email': '', 'Description': '1 + 1 =
 2, not 3...\015\012', 'Submit mode': '', 'Part number': '', 'Severity
': 'High'}
Verify?n
Reject?n
Delete?n
{'Page number': '', 'Type': 'Program bug', 'Printing Date': '', 'Chapter number'
: '16', 'Submit date': '1999/09/21, 06:20:22', 'Report state': 'Not yet verified
', 'Submitter name': 'jerry', 'Submitter email': 'http://www.jerry.com', 'Descri
ption': 'Help! I just spilled coffee all over my\015\012computer...\015\012
     ', 'Submit mode': '', 'Part number': '', 'Severity': 'Unknown'}
Verify?n
Reject?y
reason>It's not Python's fault
reason>(ctrl-d)
...more...
```

Verifications and rejections change records, but deletions actually remove them from the system. In `verifycommon`, a report rejection prompts for an explanation and concatenates it to the original description. Deletions delete the associated file with `os.remove`; this feature may come in handy if the system is ever abused by a frivolous user (including me, while writing examples for this book). The *shelve*-based version of the verify script looks and feels similar, but deals in shelves instead of flat files, as shown in Example 14-30.

Example 14-30. PP2E\Internet\Cgi-Web\PyErrata\AdminTools\verifyShelve.py

```
#!/usr/bin/python
######################################################
# like verifyFiles.py, but do it to shelves;
# caveats: we should really obtain a lock before shelve
# updates here, and there is some scan logic redundancy
######################################################

import shelve
from verifycommon import markAsVerify, markAsReject

def analyse(dbase):
    for k in dbase.keys():
        data = dbase[k]
        if data['Report state'] == 'Not yet verified':
            print data
            if raw_input('Verify?') == 'y':
                markAsVerify(data)
                dbase[k] = data
            elif raw_input('Reject?') == 'y':
                markAsReject(data)
                dbase[k] = data
            elif raw_input('Delete?') == 'y':
                del dbase[k]

print 'Errata...';    analyse(shelve.open('../DbaseShelve/errataDB'))
print 'Comments...';  analyse(shelve.open('../DbaseShelve/commentDB'))
```

Note that the verifycommon module helps ensure that records are marked consistently and avoids some redundancy. However, the file and shelve verify scripts still look very similar; it might be better to further generalize the notion of database update scans by moving this logic into the storage-specific database interface classes shown earlier.

Short of doing so, there is not much we can do about the scan-logic redundancy or storage-structure dependencies of the file and shelve verify scripts. The existing load-list database class methods won't help, because they don't provide the generated filename and shelve key details we need to rewrite records here. To make the administrative tools more robust, some database class redesign would probably be in order—which seems as good a segue to the next section as any.

Designing for Reuse and Growth

I admit it: PyErrata may be thrifty, but it's also a bit self-centered. The database interfaces presented in the prior sections work as planned and serve to separate all database processing from CGI scripting details. But as shown in this book, these interfaces aren't as generally reusable as they could be; moreover, they are not yet designed to scale up to larger database applications.

Let's wrap up this chapter by donning our software code review hats for just a few moments and exploring some design alternatives for PyErrata. In this section, I highlight the PyErrata database interface's obstacles to general applicability, not as self-deprecation, but to show how programming decisions can impact reusability.

Something else is going on in this section too. There is more concept than code here, and the code that is here is more like an experimental design than a final product. On the other hand, because that design is coded in Python, it can be run to test the feasibility of design alternatives; as we've seen, Python can be used as a form of *executable pseudocode*.

Reusability

As we saw, code reuse is pervasive within PyErrata: top-level calls filter down to common browse and submit modules, which in turn call database classes that reuse a common module. But what about sharing PyErrata code with other systems? Although not designed with generality in mind, PyErrata's database interface modules could *almost* be reused to implement other kinds of file- and shelve-based databases outside the context of PyErrata itself. However, we need a few more tweaks to turn these interfaces into widely useful tools.

As is, shelve and file-directory names are hardcoded into the storage-specific subclass modules, but another system could import and reuse their Dbase classes and provide different directory names. Less generally, though, the dbcommon module adds two attributes to all new records (submit-time and report-state) that may or may not be relevant outside PyErrata. It also assumes that stored values are mappings (dictionaries), but that is less PyErrata-specific.

If we were to rewrite these classes for more general use, it would make sense to first repackage the four DbaseErrata and DbaseComment classes in modules of their own (they are very specific instances of file and shelve databases). We would probably also want to somehow relocate dbcommon's insertion of submit-time and report-state attributes from the dbcommon module to these four classes themselves (these attributes are specific to PyErrata databases). For instance, we might define a new DbasePyErrata class that sets these attributes and is a mixed-in superclass to the four PyErrata storage-specific database classes:

```
# in new module
class DbasePyErrata:
    def storeItem(self, newdata):
        secsSinceEpoch          = time.time()
        timeTuple               = time.localtime(secsSinceEpoch)
        y_m_d_h_m_s             = timeTuple[:6]
        newdata['Submit date']  = '%s/%02d/%02d, %02d:%02d:%02d' % y_m_d_h_m_s
        newdata['Report state'] = 'Not yet verified'
        self.writeItem(newdata)
```

```
# in dbshelve
class Dbase(MutexCntl, dbcommon.Dbase):
    # as is

# in dbfiles
class Dbase(dbcommon.Dbase):
    # as is

# in new file module
class DbaseErrata(DbasePyErrata,  dbfiles.Dbase):
    dirname = 'DbaseFiles/errataDB/'
class DbaseComment(DbasePyErrata, dbfiles.Dbase):
    dirname = 'DbaseFiles/commentDB/'

# in new shelve module
class DbaseErrata(DbasePyErrata,  dbshelve.Dbase):
    filename = 'DbaseShelve/errataDB'
class DbaseComment(DbasePyErrata, dbshelve.Dbase):
    filename = 'DbaseShelve/commentDB'
```

There are more ways to structure this than we have space to cover here. The point is that by factoring out application-specific code, dbshelve and dbfiles modules not only serve to keep PyErrata interface and database code distinct, but also become generally useful data-storage tools.

Scalability

PyErrata's database interfaces were designed for this specific application's storage requirements alone and don't directly support very large databases. If you study the database code carefully, you'll notice that submit operations update a single item, but browse requests load entire report databases all at once into memory. This scheme works fine for the database sizes expected in PyErrata, but performs badly for larger data sets. We could extend the database classes to handle larger data sets too, but they would likely require new top-level interfaces altogether.

Before I stopped updating it, the static HTML file used to list errata from the first edition of this book held just some 60 reports, and I expect a similarly small data set for other books and editions. With such small databases, it's reasonable to load an entire database into memory (i.e., into Python lists and dictionaries) all at once, and frequently. Indeed, the time needed to transfer a web page containing 60 records across the Internet likely outweighs the time it takes to load 60 report files or shelve keys on the server.

On the other hand, the database may become too slow if many more reports than expected are posted. There isn't much we could do to optimize the "Simple list" and "With index" display options, since they really do display all records. But for the "Index only" option, we might be able to change our classes to load only records having a selected value in the designated report field.

For instance, we could work around database load bottlenecks by changing our classes to implement *delayed loading* of records: rather than returning the real database, load requests could return objects that look the same but fetch actual records only when needed. Such an approach might require no changes in the rest of the system's code, but may be complex to implement.

Multiple shelve field indexing

Perhaps a better approach would be to define an entirely new top-level interface for the "Index only" option—one that really does load only records matching a field value query. For instance, rather than storing all records in a single shelve, we could implement the database as a *set of index shelves*, one per record field, to associate records by field values. Index shelve *keys* would be values of the associated field; shelve *values* would be lists of records having that field value. The shelve entry lists might contain either redundant copies of records, or unique names of flat files holding the pickled record dictionaries, external to the index shelves (as in the current flat-file model).

For example, the PyErrata comment database could be structured as a *directory of flat files* to hold pickled report dictionaries, together with five shelves to index the values in all record fields (submitter-name, submitter-email, submit-mode, submit-date, report-state). In the report-state shelve, there would be one entry for each possible report state (verified, rejected, etc.); each entry would contain a list of records with just that report-state value. Field value queries would be fast, but store and load operations would become more complex:

- To store a record in such a scheme, we would first pickle it to a uniquely named flat file, then insert that file's name into lists in all five shelves, using each field's value as shelve key.

- To load just the records matching a field/value combination, we would first index that field's shelve on the value to fetch a filename list, and step through that list to load matching records only, from flat pickle files.

Let's take the leap from hypothetical to concrete, and prototype these ideas in Python. If you're following closely, you'll notice that what we're really talking about here is an *extension* to the flat-file database structure, one that merely adds index shelves. Hence, one possible way to implement the model is as a subclass of the current flat-file classes. Example 14-31 does just that, as proof of the design concept.

Example 14-31. PP2E\Internet\PyErrata\AdminTools\dbaseindexed.py

```
###########################################################################
# add field index shelves to flat-file database mechanism;
# to optimize "index only" displays, use classes at end of this file;
# change browse, index, submit to use new loaders for "Index only" mode;
```

Example 14-31. PP2E\Internet\PyErrata\AdminTools\dbaseindexed.py (continued)

```
# minor nit: uses single lock file for all index shelve read/write ops;
# storing record copies instead of filenames in index shelves would be
# slightly faster (avoids opening flat files), but would take more space;
# falls back on original brute-force load logic for fields not indexed;
# shelve.open creates empty file if doesn't yet exist, so never fails;
# to start, create DbaseFilesIndex/{commentDB,errataDB}/indexes.lck;
##########################################################################

import sys; sys.path.insert(0, '..')      # check admin parent dir first
from Mutex import mutexcntl                # fcntl path okay: not 'nobody'
import dbfiles, shelve, pickle, string, sys

class Dbase(mutexcntl.MutexCntl, dbfiles.Dbase):
    def makeKey(self):
        return self.cachedKey
    def cacheKey(self):                                   # save filename
        self.cachedKey = dbfiles.Dbase.makeKey(self)      # need it here too
        return self.cachedKey

    def indexName(self, fieldname):
        return self.dirname + string.replace(fieldname, ' ', '-')

    def safeWriteIndex(self, fieldname, newdata, recfilename):
        index = shelve.open(self.indexName(fieldname))
        try:
            keyval  = newdata[fieldname]                  # recs have all fields
            reclist = index[keyval]                       # fetch, mod, rewrite
            reclist.append(recfilename)                   # add to current list
            index[keyval] = reclist
        except KeyError:
            index[keyval] = [recfilename]                 # add to new list

    def safeLoadKeysList(self, fieldname):
        if fieldname in self.indexfields:
            keys = shelve.open(self.indexName(fieldname)).keys()
            keys.sort()
        else:
            keys, index = self.loadIndexedTable(fieldname)
        return keys

    def safeLoadByKey(self, fieldname, fieldvalue):
        if fieldname in self.indexfields:
            dbase = shelve.open(self.indexName(fieldname))
            try:
                index = dbase[fieldvalue]
                reports = []
                for filename in index:
                    pathname = self.dirname + filename + '.data'
                    reports.append(pickle.load(open(pathname, 'r')))
                return reports
            except KeyError:
                return []
        else:
```

Example 14-31. PP2E\Internet\PyErrata\AdminTools\dbaseindexed.py (continued)

```
            key, index = self.loadIndexedTable(fieldname)
            try:
                return index[fieldvalue]
            except KeyError:
                return []

    # top-level interfaces (plus dbcommon and dbfiles)

    def writeItem(self, newdata):
        # extend to update indexes
        filename = self.cacheKey()
        dbfiles.Dbase.writeItem(self, newdata)
        for fieldname in self.indexfields:
            self.exclusiveAction(self.safeWriteIndex,
                                 fieldname, newdata, filename)

    def loadKeysList(self, fieldname):
        # load field's keys list only
        return self.sharedAction(self.safeLoadKeysList, fieldname)

    def loadByKey(self, fieldname, fieldvalue):
        # load matching recs lisy only
        return self.sharedAction(self.safeLoadByKey, fieldname, fieldvalue)

class DbaseErrata(Dbase):
    dirname     = 'DbaseFilesIndexed/errataDB/'
    filename    = dirname + 'indexes'
    indexfields = ['Submitter name', 'Submit date', 'Report state']

class DbaseComment(Dbase):
    dirname     = 'DbaseFilesIndexed/commentDB/'
    filename    = dirname + 'indexes'
    indexfields = ['Submitter name', 'Report state']     # index just these

#
# self-test
#

if __name__ == '__main__':
    import os
    dbase = DbaseComment()
    os.system('rm %s*'         % dbase.dirname)           # empty dbase dir
    os.system('echo > %s.lck' % dbase.filename)           # init lock file

    # 3 recs; normally have submitter-email and description, not page
    # submit-date and report-state are added auto by rec store method
    records = [{'Submitter name': 'Bob',   'Page': 38, 'Submit mode': ''},
               {'Submitter name': 'Brian', 'Page': 40, 'Submit mode': ''},
               {'Submitter name': 'Bob',   'Page': 42, 'Submit mode': 'email'}]
    for rec in records: dbase.storeItem(rec)

    dashes = '-'*80
    def one(item):
```

Example 14-31. PP2E\Internet\PyErrata\AdminTools\dbaseindexed.py (continued)

```
        print dashes; print item
    def all(list):
        print dashes
        for x in list: print x

    one('old stuff')
    all(dbase.loadSortedTable('Submitter name'))              # load flat list
    all(dbase.loadIndexedTable('Submitter name'))             # load, grouped
#one(dbase.loadIndexedTable('Submitter name')[0])
#all(dbase.loadIndexedTable('Submitter name')[1]['Bob'])
#all(dbase.loadIndexedTable('Submitter name')[1]['Brian'])

    one('new stuff')
    one(dbase.loadKeysList('Submitter name'))                 # bob, brian
    all(dbase.loadByKey('Submitter name', 'Bob'))             # two recs match
    all(dbase.loadByKey('Submitter name', 'Brian'))           # one rec mathces
    one(dbase.loadKeysList('Report state'))                   # all match
    all(dbase.loadByKey('Report state',   'Not yet verified'))

    one('boundary cases')
    all(dbase.loadByKey('Submit mode',    ''))                # not indexed: load
    one(dbase.loadByKey('Report state',    'Nonesuch'))       # unknown value: []
    try:           dbase.loadByKey('Nonesuch',  'Nonesuch')   # bad fields: exc
    except: print 'Nonesuch failed'
```

This module's code is something of an executable prototype, but that's much of the point here. The fact that we can actually run experiments coded in Python helps pinpoint problems in a model early on.

For instance, I had to redefine the makeKey method here to cache filenames locally (they are needed for index shelves too). That's not quite right, and if I were to adopt this database interface, I would probably change the file class to return generated filenames, not discard them. Such misfits can often be uncovered only by writing real code—a task that Python optimizes by design.

If this module is run as a top-level script, its self-test code at the bottom of the file executes with the following output. I don't have space to explain it in detail, but try to match it up with the module's self-test code to trace how queries are satisfied with and without field indexes:

```
[mark@toy .../Internet/Cgi-Web/PyErrata/AdminTools]$ python dbaseindexed.py
--------------------------------------------------------------------------
old stuff
--------------------------------------------------------------------------
{'Submit date': '2000/06/13, 11:45:01', 'Page': 38, 'Submit mode': '', 'Report s
tate': 'Not yet verified', 'Submitter name': 'Bob'}
{'Submit date': '2000/06/13, 11:45:01', 'Page': 42, 'Submit mode': 'email', 'Rep
ort state': 'Not yet verified', 'Submitter name': 'Bob'}
{'Submit date': '2000/06/13, 11:45:01', 'Page': 40, 'Submit mode': '', 'Report s
tate': 'Not yet verified', 'Submitter name': 'Brian'}
--------------------------------------------------------------------------
```

```
['Bob', 'Brian']
{'Bob': [{'Submit date': '2000/06/13, 11:45:01', 'Page': 38, 'Submit mode': '',
'Report state': 'Not yet verified', 'Submitter name': 'Bob'}, {'Submit date': '2
000/06/13, 11:45:01', 'Page': 42, 'Submit mode': 'email', 'Report state': 'Not y
et verified', 'Submitter name': 'Bob'}], 'Brian': [{'Submit date': '2000/06/13,
11:45:01', 'Page': 40, 'Submit mode': '', 'Report state': 'Not yet verified', 'S
ubmitter name': 'Brian'}]}
-------------------------------------------------------------------------------
new stuff
-------------------------------------------------------------------------------
['Bob', 'Brian']
-------------------------------------------------------------------------------
{'Submit date': '2000/06/13, 11:45:01', 'Page': 38, 'Submit mode': '', 'Report s
tate': 'Not yet verified', 'Submitter name': 'Bob'}
{'Submit date': '2000/06/13, 11:45:01', 'Page': 42, 'Submit mode': 'email', 'Rep
ort state': 'Not yet verified', 'Submitter name': 'Bob'}
-------------------------------------------------------------------------------
{'Submit date': '2000/06/13, 11:45:01', 'Page': 40, 'Submit mode': '', 'Report s
tate': 'Not yet verified', 'Submitter name': 'Brian'}
-------------------------------------------------------------------------------
['Not yet verified']
-------------------------------------------------------------------------------
{'Submit date': '2000/06/13, 11:45:01', 'Page': 38, 'Submit mode': '', 'Report s
tate': 'Not yet verified', 'Submitter name': 'Bob'}
{'Submit date': '2000/06/13, 11:45:01', 'Page': 40, 'Submit mode': '', 'Report s
tate': 'Not yet verified', 'Submitter name': 'Brian'}
{'Submit date': '2000/06/13, 11:45:01', 'Page': 42, 'Submit mode': 'email', 'Rep
ort state': 'Not yet verified', 'Submitter name': 'Bob'}
-------------------------------------------------------------------------------
boundary cases
-------------------------------------------------------------------------------
{'Submit date': '2000/06/13, 11:45:01', 'Page': 38, 'Submit mode': '', 'Report s
tate': 'Not yet verified', 'Submitter name': 'Bob'}
{'Submit date': '2000/06/13, 11:45:01', 'Page': 40, 'Submit mode': '', 'Report s
tate': 'Not yet verified', 'Submitter name': 'Brian'}
-------------------------------------------------------------------------------
[]
Nonesuch failed

[mark@toy .../PyErrata/AdminTools]$ ls DbaseFilesIndexed/commentDB/
960918301.263-895.data  960918301.506-895.data  Submitter-name  indexes.log
960918301.42-895.data    Report-state            indexes.lck

[mark@toy .../PyErrata/AdminTools]$ more DbaseFilesIndexed/commentDB/indexes.log
960918301.266   Requested: 895, writer
960918301.266   Aquired: 895
960918301.36    Released: 895
960918301.36    Requested: 895, writer
960918301.361   Aquired: 895
960918301.419   Released: 895
960918301.422   Requested: 895, writer
960918301.422   Aquired: 895
960918301.46    Released: 895
...more...
```

One drawback to this interface is that it works only on a machine that supports the `fcntl.flock` call (notice that I ran the previous test on Linux). If you want to use these classes to support indexed file/shelve databases on other machines, you could delete or stub out this call in the **mutex** module to do nothing and return. You won't get safe updates if you do, but many applications don't need to care:

```
try:
    import fcntl
    from FCNTL import *
except ImportError:
    class fakeFcntl:
        def flock(self, fileno, flag): return
    fcntl = fakeFcntl()
    LOCK_SH = LOCK_EX = LOCK_UN = 0
```

You might instead instrument `MutexCntl.lockFile` to do nothing in the presence of a command-line argument flag, mix in a different `MutexCntl` class at the bottom that does nothing on lock calls, or hunt for platform-specific locking mechanisms (e.g., the Windows extensions package exports a Windows-only file locking call; see its documentation for details).

Regardless of whether you use locking or not, the **dbaseindexed** flat-files plus multiple-shelve indexing scheme can speed access by keys for large databases. However, it would also require changes to the top-level CGI script logic that implements "Index only" displays, and so is not without seams. It may also perform poorly for very large databases, as record information would span multiple files. If pressed, we could finally extend the database classes to talk to a real database system such as Oracle, MySQL, PostGres, or Gadfly (described in Chapter 16).

All of these options are not without trade-offs, but we have now come dangerously close to stepping beyond the scope of this chapter. Because the PyErrata database modules were designed with neither general applicability nor broad scalability in mind, additional mutations are left as suggested exercises.

15

Advanced Internet Topics

"Surfing on the Shoulders of Giants"

This chapter concludes our look at Python Internet programming by exploring a handful of Internet-related topics and packages. We've covered many Internet topics in the previous five chapters—socket basics, client and server-side scripting tools, and programming full-blown web sites with Python. Yet we still haven't seen many of Python's standard built-in Internet modules in action. Moreover, there is a rich collection of third-party extensions for scripting the Web with Python that we have not touched on at all.

In this chapter, we explore a grab-bag of additional Internet-related tools and third-party extensions of interest to Python Internet developers. Along the way, we meet larger Internet packages, such as HTMLgen, JPython, Zope, PSP, Active Scripting, and Grail. We'll also study standard Python tools useful to Internet programmers, including Python's restricted execution mode, XML support, COM interfaces, and techniques for implementing proprietary servers. In addition to their practical uses, these systems demonstrate just how much can be achieved by wedding a powerful object-oriented scripting language such as Python to the Web.

Before we start, a disclaimer: none of these topics is presented in much detail here, and undoubtedly some interesting Internet systems will not be covered at all. Moreover, the Internet evolves at lightning speed, and new tools and techniques are certain to emerge after this edition is published; indeed, most of the systems in this chapter appeared in the five years *after* the first edition of this book was written, and the next five years promise to be just as prolific. As always, the standard moving-target caveat applies: read the Python library manual's Internet section for details we've skipped, and stay in touch with the Python community at *http://www.python.org* for information about extensions not covered due to a lack of space or a lack of clairvoyance.

Zope: A Web Publishing Framework

Zope is an open source web-application server and toolkit, written in and customizable with Python. It is a server-side technology that allows web designers to implement sites and applications by publishing Python object hierarchies on the Web. With Zope, programmers can focus on writing objects, and let Zope handle most of the underlying HTTP and CGI details. If you are interested in implementing more complex web sites than the form-based interactions we've seen in the last three chapters, you should investigate Zope: it can obviate many of the tasks that web scripters wrestle with on a daily basis.

Sometimes compared to commercial web toolkits such as ColdFusion, Zope is made freely available over the Internet by a company called Digital Creations and enjoys a large and very active development community. Indeed, many attendees at a recent Python conference were attracted by Zope, which had its own conference track. The use of Zope has spread so quickly that many Pythonistas now look to it as Python's "killer application"—a system so good that it naturally pushes Python into the development spotlight. At the least, Zope offers a new, higher-level way of developing sites for the Web, above and beyond raw CGI scripting.*

Zope Components

Zope began life as a set of tools (part of which was named "Bobo") placed in the public domain by Digital Creations. Since then, it has grown into a large system with many components, a growing body of add-ons (called "products" in Zope parlance), and a fairly steep learning curve. We can't do it any sort of justice in this book, but since Zope is one of the most popular Python-based applications at this writing, I'd be remiss if I didn't provide a few details here.

In terms of its core components, Zope includes the following parts:

Zope Object Request Broker (ORB)
> At the heart of Zope, the ORB dispatches incoming HTTP requests to Python objects and returns results to the requestor, working as a perpetually running middleman between the HTTP CGI world and your Python objects. The Zope ORB is described further in the next section.

---

* Over the years, observers have also pointed to other systems as possible Python "killer applications," including Grail, Python's COM support on Windows, and JPython. I hope they're all right, and fully expect new killers to arise after this edition is published. But at the time that I write this, Zope is attracting an astonishing level of interest among both developers and investors.

HTML document templates

Zope provides a simple way to define web pages as templates, with values automatically inserted from Python objects. Templates allow an object's HTML representation to be defined independently of the object's implementation. For instance, values of attributes in a class instance object may be automatically plugged into a template's text by name. Template coders need not be Python coders, and vice versa.

Object database

To record data persistently, Zope comes with a full object-oriented database system for storing Python objects. The Zope object database is based on the Python `pickle` serialization module we'll meet in the next part of this book, but adds support for transactions, lazy object fetches (sometimes called delayed evaluation), concurrent access, and more. Objects are stored and retrieved by key, much as they are with Python's standard `shelve` module, but classes must subclass an imported `Persistent` superclass, and object stores are instances of an imported `PickleDictionary` object. Zope starts and commits transactions at the start and end of HTTP requests.

Zope also includes a management framework for administrating sites, as well as a product API used to package components. Zope ships with these and other components integrated into a whole system, but each part can be used on its own as well. For instance, the Zope object database can be used in arbitrary Python applications by itself.

What's Object Publishing?

If you're like me, the concept of publishing objects on the Web may be a bit vague at first glance, but it's fairly simple in Zope: the Zope ORB automatically maps URLs requested by HTTP into calls on Python objects. Consider the Python module and function in Example 15-1.

Example 15-1. PP2E\Internet\Other\messages.py

```
"A Python module published on the Web by Zope"

def greeting(size='brief', topic='zope'):
    "a published Python function"
    return 'A %s %s introduction' % (size, topic)
```

This is normal Python code, of course, and says nothing about Zope, CGI, or the Internet at large. We may call the function it defines from the interactive prompt as usual:

```
C:\...\PP2E\Internet\Other>python
>>> import messages
>>> messages.greeting()
```

```
'A brief zope introduction'

>>> messages.greeting(size='short')
'A short zope introduction'

>>> messages.greeting(size='tiny', topic='ORB')
'A tiny ORB introduction'
```

But if we place this module file, along with Zope support files, in the appropriate directory on a server machine running Zope, it automatically becomes visible on the Web. That is, the function becomes a *published object*—it can be invoked through a URL, and its return value becomes a response page. For instance, if placed in a `cgi-bin` directory on a server called `myserver.net`, the following URLs are equivalent to the three calls above:

```
http://www.myserver.net/cgi-bin/messages/greeting
http://www.myserver.net/cgi-bin/messages/greeting?size=short
http://www.myserver.net/cgi-bin/messages/greeting?size=tiny&topic=ORB
```

When our function is accessed as a URL over the Web this way, the Zope ORB performs two feats of magic:

- The URL is automatically translated into a call to the Python function. The first part of the URL after the directory path (`messages`) names the Python module, the second (`greeting`) names a function or other callable object within that module, and any parameters after the `?` become keyword arguments passed to the named function.

- After the function runs, its return value automatically appears in a new page in your web browser. Zope does all the work of formatting the result as a valid HTTP response.

In other words, URLs in Zope become *remote function calls*, not just script invocations. The functions (and methods) called by accessing URLs are coded in Python, and may live at arbitrary places on the Net. It's as if the Internet itself becomes a Python namespace, with one module directory per server.

Zope is a server-side technology based on *objects*, not text streams; the main advantage of this scheme is that the details of CGI input and output are handled by Zope, while programmers focus on writing domain objects, not on text generation. When our function is accessed with a URL, Zope automatically finds the referenced object, translates incoming parameters to function call arguments, runs the function, and uses its return value to generate an HTTP response. In general, a URL like:

```
http://servername/dirpath/module/object1/object2/method?arg1=val1&arg2=val2
```

is mapped by the Zope ORB running on `servername` into a call to a Python object in a Python module file installed in `dirpath`, taking the form:

```
module.object1.object2.method(arg1=val1, arg2=val2)
```

The return value is formatted into an HTML response page sent back to the client requestor (typically a browser). By using longer paths, programs can publish complete hierarchies of objects; Zope simply uses Python's generic object-access protocols to fetch objects along the path.

As usual, a URL like those listed here can appear as the text of a hyperlink, typed manually into a web browser, or used in an HTTP request generated by a program (e.g., using Python's `urllib` module in a client-side script). Parameters are listed at the end of these URLs directly, but if you post information to this URL with a form instead, it works the same way:

```
<form action="http://www.myserver.net/cgi-bin/messages/greeting" method=POST>
    Size:  <input type=text name=size>
    Topic: <input type=text name=topic value=zope>
    <input type=submit>
</form>
```

Here, the `action` tag references our function's URL again; when the user fills out this form and presses its submit button, inputs from the form sent by the browser magically show up as arguments to the function again. These inputs are typed by the user, not hardcoded at the end of a URL, but our published function doesn't need to care. In fact, Zope recognizes a variety of parameter sources and translates them all into Python function or method arguments: form inputs, parameters at the end of URLs, HTTP headers and cookies, CGI environment variables, and more.

This just scratches the surface of what published objects can do, though. For instance, published functions and methods can use the Zope object database to save state permanently, and Zope provides many more advanced tools such as debugging support, precoded HTTP servers for use with the ORB, and finer-grained control over responses to URL requestors.

For all things Zope, visit *http://www.zope.org*. There, you'll find up-to-date releases, as well as documentation ranging from tutorials to references to full-blown Zope example sites. Also see this book's CD for a copy of the Zope distribution, current as of the time we went to press.

Python creator Guido van Rossum and his Pythonlabs team of core Python developers have moved from BeOpen to Digital Creations, home of the Zope framework introduced here. Although Python itself remains an open source system, Guido's presence at Digital Creations is seen as a strategic move that will foster future growth of both Zope and Python.

HTMLgen: Web Pages from Objects

One of the things that makes CGI scripts complex is their inherent dependence on HTML: they must embed and generate legal HTML code to build user interfaces. These tasks might be easier if the syntax of HTML were somehow removed from CGI scripts and handled by an external tool.

HTMLgen is a third-party Python tool designed to fill this need. With it, programs build web pages by constructing trees of Python objects that represent the desired page and "know" how to format themselves as HTML. Once constructed, the program asks the top of the Python object tree to generate HTML for itself, and out comes a complete, legally formatted HTML web page.

Programs that use HTMLgen to generate pages need never deal with the syntax of HTML; instead, they can use the higher-level object model provided by HTMLgen and trust it to do the formatting step. HTMLgen may be used in any context where you need to generate HTML. It is especially suited for HTML generated periodically from static data, but can also be used for HTML creation in CGI scripts (though its use in the CGI context incurs some extra speed costs). For instance, HTMLgen would be ideal if you run a nightly job to generate web pages from database contents. HTMLgen can also be used to generate documents that don't live on the Web at all; the HTML code it produces works just as well when viewed offline.

A Brief HTMLgen Tutorial

We can't investigate HTMLgen in depth here, but let's look at a few simple examples to sample the flavor of the system. HTMLgen is shipped as a collection of Python modules that must be installed on your machine; once it's installed, you simply import objects from the `HTMLgen` module corresponding to the tag you wish to generate, and make instances:

```
C:\Stuff\HTMLgen\HTMLgen>python
>>> from HTMLgen import *
>>> p = Paragraph("Making pages from objects is easy\n")
>>> p
<HTMLgen.Paragraph instance at 7dbb00>
>>> print p
<P>Making pages from objects is easy
</P>
```

Here, we make a `HTMLgen.Paragraph` object (a class instance), passing in the text to be formatted. All HTMLgen objects implement `__str__` methods and can emit legal HTML code for themselves. When we print the `Paragraph` object, it emits an HTML paragraph construct. HTMLgen objects also define `append` methods, which do the right thing for the object type; Paragraphs simply add appended text to the end of the text block:

```
>>> p.append("Special < characters > are & escaped")
>>> print p
<P>Making pages from objects is easy
Special &lt; characters &gt; are &amp; escaped</P>
```

Notice that HTMLgen escaped the special characters (e.g., < means <) so that they are legal HTML; you don't need to worry about writing either HTML or escape codes yourself. HTMLgen has one class for each HTML tag; here is the List object at work, creating an ordered list:

```
>>> choices = ['python', 'tcl', 'perl']
>>> print List(choices)
<UL>
<LI>python
<LI>tcl
<LI>perl
</UL>
```

In general, HTMLgen is smart about interpreting data structures you pass to it. For instance, embedded sequences are automatically mapped to the HTML code for displaying nested lists:

```
>>> choices = ['tools', ['python', 'c++'], 'food', ['spam', 'eggs']]
>>> l = List(choices)
>>> print l
<UL>
<LI>tools
    <UL>
    <LI>python
    <LI>c++
    </UL>
<LI>food
    <UL>
    <LI>spam
    <LI>eggs
    </UL>
</UL>
```

Hyperlinks are just as easy: simply make and print an Href object with the link target and text. (The text argument can be replaced by an image, as we'll see later in Example 15-3.)

```
>>> h = Href('http://www.python.org', 'python')
>>> print h
<A HREF="http://www.python.org">python</A>
```

To generate HTML for complete pages, we create one of the HTML document objects, append its component objects, and print the document object. HTMLgen emits a complete page's code, ready to be viewed in a browser:

```
>>> d = SimpleDocument(title='My doc')
>>> p = Paragraph('Web pages made easy')
```

```
>>> d.append(p)
>>> d.append(h)
>>> print d
<!DOCTYPE HTML PUBLIC "-//W3C//DTD HTML 3.2//EN">
<HTML>

<!-- This file generated using Python HTMLgen module. -->
<HEAD>
   <META NAME="GENERATOR" CONTENT="HTMLgen 2.2.2">
      <TITLE>My doc</TITLE>
</HEAD>
<BODY>
<P>Web pages made easy</P>

<A HREF="http://www.python.org">python</A>

</BODY> </HTML>
```

There are other kinds of document classes, including a `SeriesDocument` that implements a standard layout for pages in a series. `SimpleDocument` is simple indeed: it's essentially a container for other components, and generates the appropriate wrapper HTML code. HTMLgen also provides classes such as `Table`, `Form`, and so on, one for each kind of HTML construct.

Naturally, you ordinarily use HTMLgen from within a script, so you can capture the generated HTML in a file or send it over an Internet connection in the context of a CGI application (remember, printed text goes to the browser in the CGI script environment). The script in Example 15-2 does roughly what we just did interactively, but saves the printed text in a file.

Example 15-2. PP2E\Internet\Other\htmlgen101.py

```
import sys
from HTMLgen import *

p = Paragraph('Making pages from objects is easy.\n')
p.append('Special < characters > are & escaped')

choices = ['tools', ['python', 'c++'], 'food', ['spam', 'eggs']]
l = List(choices)

s = SimpleDocument(title="HTMLgen 101")
s.append(Heading(1, 'Basic tags'))
s.append(p)
s.append(l)
s.append(HR())
s.append(Href('http://www.python.org', 'Python home page'))

if len(sys.argv) == 1:
    print s                      # send html to sys.stdout or real file
else:
    open(sys.argv[1], 'w').write(str(s))
```

This script also uses the HR object to format a horizontal line, and Heading to insert a header line. It either prints HTML to the standard output stream (if no arguments are listed) or writes HTML to an explicitly named file; the str built-in function invokes object __str__ methods just as print does. Run this script from the system command line to make a file, using one of the following:

```
C:\...\PP2E\Internet\Other>python htmlgen101.py > htmlgen101.html
C:\...\PP2E\Internet\Other>python htmlgen101.py htmlgen101.html
```

Either way, the script's output is a legal HTML page file, which you can view in your favorite browser by typing the output filename in the address field or clicking on the file in your file explorer. Either way, it will look a lot like Figure 15-1.

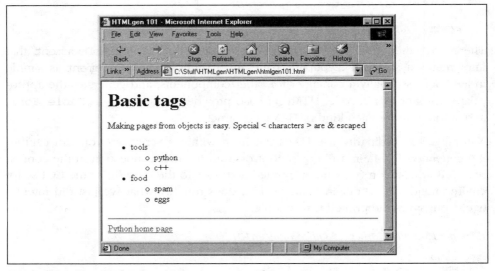

Figure 15-1. Viewing htmlgen101.py output in a browser

See file *htmlgen101.html* in the examples distribution if you wish to inspect the HTML generated to describe this page directly (it looks much like the prior document's output). Example 15-3 shows another script that does something less hard-coded: it constructs a web page to display its own source code.

Example 15-3. PP2E\Internet\Other\htmlgen101-b.py

```
import sys
from HTMLgen import *
d = SimpleDocument(title="HTMLgen 101 B")

# show this script
text = open('htmlgen101-b.py', 'r').read()
d.append(Heading(1, 'Source code'))
```

Example 15-3. PP2E\Internet\Other\htmlgen101-b.py (continued)

```
d.append(Paragraph( PRE(text) ))

# add gif and links
site  = 'http://www.python.org'
gif   = 'PythonPoweredSmall.gif'
image = Image(gif, alt='picture', align='left', hspace=10, border=0)

d.append(HR())
d.append(Href(site, image))
d.append(Href(site, 'Python home page'))

if len(sys.argv) == 1:
    print d
else:
    open(sys.argv[1], 'w').write(str(d))
```

We use the `PRE` object here to specify preformatted text, and the `Image` object to generate code to display a GIF file on the generated page. Notice that HTML tag options such as `alt` and `align` are specified as keyword arguments when making HTMLgen objects. Running this script and pointing a browser at its output yields the page shown in Figure 15-2; the image at the bottom is also a hyperlink, because it was embedded inside an `Href` object.

And that (along with a few nice advanced features) is all there is to using HTMLgen. Once you become familiar with it, you can construct web pages by writing Python code, without ever needing to manually type HTML tags again. Of course, you still must write code with HTMLgen instead of using a drag-and-drop page layout tool, but that code is incredibly simple and supports the addition of more complex programming logic where needed to construct pages dynamically.

In fact, now that you're familiar with HTMLgen, you'll see that many of the HTML files shown earlier in this book could have been simplified by recoding them to use HTMLgen instead of direct HTML code. The earlier CGI scripts could have used HTMLgen as well, albeit with additional speed overheads—printing text directly is faster than generating it from object trees, though perhaps not significantly so (CGI scripts are generally bound to network speeds, not CPU speed).

HTMLgen is open source software, but it is not a standard part of Python and must therefore be installed separately. You can find a copy of HTMLgen on this book's CD, but the Python web site should have its current location and version. Once installed, simply add the HTMLgen path to your PYTHONPATH variable setting to gain access to its modules. For more documentation about HTMLgen, see the package itself: its *html* subdirectory includes the HTMLgen manual in HTML format.

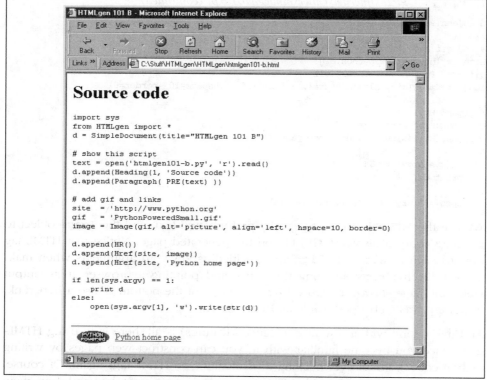

Figure 15-2. Viewing htmlgen101-b.py output in a browser

JPython (Jython): Python for Java

JPython (recently renamed "Jython") is an entirely distinct implementation of the
Python programming language that allows programmers to use Python as a scripting component in Java-based applications. In short, JPython makes Python code
look like Java, and consequently offers a variety of technology options inherited
from the Java world. With JPython, Python code may be run as client-side applets
in web browsers, as server-side scripts, and in a variety of other roles. JPython is
distinct from other systems mentioned in this section in terms of its scope: while it
is based on the core Python language we've seen in this book, it actually replaces
the underlying implementation of that language rather than augmenting it.*

---

* At this writing, JPython is the second implementation of the Python language. By contrast, the standard,
original implementation of Python is sometimes now referred to as "CPython," because it is implemented in ANSI C. Among other things, the JPython implementation is driving a clearer definition of the
Python language itself, independent of a particular implementation's effects. A new Python implementation for Microsoft's C#/.NET environment is also on the way (see later in this chapter) and may further
drive a definition of what it means to be Python.

This section briefly explores JPython and highlights some of the reasons you may or may not want to use it instead of the standard Python implementation. Although JPython is primarily of interest to programmers writing Java-based applications, it underscores integration possibilities and language definition issues that merit the attention of all Python users. Because JPython is Java-centric, you need to know something about Java development to make the most sense of JPython, and this book doesn't pretend to teach that in the next few pages. For more details, interested readers should consult other materials, including JPython documentation at *http://www.jpython.org.*

 The JPython port is now called "Jython." Although you are likely to still see it called by its original JPython name on the Net (and in this book) for some time, the new Jython title will become more common as time goes by.

A Quick Introduction to JPython

Functionally speaking, JPython is a collection of Java classes that run Python code. It consists of a Python compiler, written in Java, that translates Python scripts to Java bytecodes so they can be executed by a *Java virtual machine*—the runtime component that executes Java programs and is used by major web browsers. Moreover, JPython automatically exposes all Java class libraries for use in Python scripts. In a nutshell, here's what comes with the JPython system:

Python-to-Java-bytecode compiler
> JPython always compiles Python source code into Java bytecode and passes it to a Java virtual machine (JVM) runtime engine to be executed. A command-line compiler program, jpythonc, is also able to translate Python source code files into Java *.class* and *.jar* files, which can then be used as Java applets, beans, servlets, and so on. To the JVM, Python code run through JPython looks the same as Java code. Besides making Python code work on a JVM, JPython code also inherits all aspects of the Java runtime system, including Java's garbage collection and security models. jpythonc also imposes Java source file class rules.

Access to Java class libraries (extending)
> JPython uses Java's *reflection API* (runtime type information) to expose all available Java class libraries to Python scripts. That is, Python programs written for the JPython system can call out to any resident Java class automatically simply by importing it. The Python-to-Java interface is completely automatic and remarkably seamless—Java class libraries appear as though they are

coded in Python. Import statements in JPython scripts may refer to either JPython modules or Java class libraries. For instance, when a JPython script imports `java.awt`, it gains access to all the tools available in the `awt` library. JPython internally creates a "dummy" Python module object to serve as an interface to `awt` at import time. This dummy module consists of hooks for dispatching calls from JPython code to Java class methods and automatically converting datatypes between Java and Python representations as needed. To JPython scripts, Java class libraries look and feel exactly like normal Python modules (albeit with interfaces defined by the Java world).

Unified object model

JPython objects are actually Java objects internally. In fact, JPython implements Python types as instances of a Java `PyObject` class. By contrast, C Python classes and types are still distinct in the current release. For instance, in JPython, the number 123 is an instance of the `PyInteger` Java class, and you can specify things like `[].__class__` since all objects are class instances. That makes data mapping between languages simple: Java can process Python objects automatically, because they are Java objects. JPython automatically converts types between languages according to a standard type map as needed to call out to Java libraries, and selects among overloaded Java method signatures.

API for running Python from Java (embedding)

JPython also provides interfaces that allow Java programs to execute JPython code. As for embedding in C and C++, this allows Java applications to be customized by bits of dynamically written JPython code. For instance, JPython ships with a Java `PythonInterpreter` class, which allows Java programs to create objects that function as Python namespaces for running Python code. Each `PythonInterpreter` object is roughly a Python module, with methods such as `exec` (a string of Python code), `execfile` (a Python filename), and `get` and `set` methods for assigning Python global variables. Because Python objects are really instances of a Java `PyObject` class, an enclosing Java layer can access and process data created by Python code naturally.

Interactive Python command line

Like the standard Python implementation, JPython comes with an interactive command line that runs code immediately after it is typed. JPython's `jpython` program is equivalent to the `python` executable we've been using in this book; without arguments, it starts an interactive session. Among other things, this allows JPython programmers to import and test class components actually written in Java. This ability alone is compelling enough to interest many Java programmers.

Interface automations

Java libraries are somewhat easier to use in JPython code than in Java. That's because JPython automates some of the coding steps Java implies. For instance, *callback handlers* for Java GUI libraries may be simple Python functions, even though Java coders need to provide methods in fully specified classes (Java does not have first-class function objects). JPython also makes Java class *data members* accessible as both Python attribute names (`object.name`) and object constructor keyword arguments (`name=value`); such Python syntax is translated into calls to `getName` and `setName` accessor methods in Java classes. We'll see these automation tricks in action in the following examples. You don't have to use any of these (and they may confuse Java programmers at first glance), but they further simplify coding in JPython, and give Java class libraries a more Python-like flavor.

The net effect of all this is that JPython allows us to write Python programs that can run on any Java-aware machine—in particular, in the context of most web browsers. More importantly, because Python programs are translated into Java bytecodes, JPython provides an incredibly seamless and natural integration between the two languages. Both walk and talk in terms of the Java model, so calls across language boundaries are trivial. With JPython's approach, it's even possible to subclass a Java class in Python and vice versa.

So why go to all this trouble to mix Python into Java environments? The most obvious answer is that JPython makes Java components easier to use: JPython scripts are typically a fraction of the size of their Java equivalents, and much less complex. More generally, the answer is really the same as it is for C and C++ environments: Python, as an easy-to-use, object-oriented scripting language, naturally complements the Java programming language.

By now, it is clear to most people that Java is too complex to serve as a scripting or rapid-development tool. But this is exactly where Python excels; by adding Python to the mix with JPython, we add a scripting component to Java systems, exactly as we do when integrating Python with C or C++. For instance, we can use JPython to quickly prototype Java systems, test Java classes interactively, and open up Java systems for end-user customization. In general, adding Python to Java development can significantly boost programmer productivity, just as it does for C and C++ systems.

A Simple JPython Example

Once a Python program is compiled with JPython, it is all Java: the program is translated to Java bytecodes, it uses Java classes to do its work, and there is no Python left except for the original source code. Because the compiler tool itself is also written in Java, JPython is sometimes called "100% pure Java." That label may

JPython Versus the Python C API

Functionally, JPython is primarily an integration system: it allows us to mix Python with Java components. We also study ways to integrate Python with C and C++ components in the next part of this book. It's worth noting that we need different techniques to integrate Python with Java (such as the JPython compiler), because Java is a somewhat closed system: it prefers an all-Java mix. The C and C++ integration tools are generally less restrictive in terms of language assumptions, and any C-compatible language components will do. Java's strictness is partly due to its security goals, but the net effect is to foster integration techniques that are specific to Java alone.

On the other hand, because Java exposes runtime type information through its reflection API, JPython can largely automate the conversions and dispatching needed to access Java components from Python scripts; Python code simply imports and calls Java components. When mixing Python with C or C++, we must provide a "glue" code layer that integrates the two languages explicitly. Some of this can be automated (with the SWIG system we'll meet later in this text). No glue code is required in JPython, however, because JPython's (and Java's) developers have done all the linkage work already, in a generic fashion. It is also possible to mix in C/C++ components with Java via its native call interface (JNI), but this can be cumbersome and may cancel out Java's reported portability and security benefits.

be more profound to marketeers than programmers, though, because JPython scripts are still written using standard Python syntax. For instance, Example 15-4 is a legal JPython program, derived from an example originally written by Guido van Rossum.

Example 15-4. PP2E\Internet\Other\jpython.py

```
############################################
# implement a simple calculator in JPython;
# evaluation runs a full expression all at
# once using the Python eval() built-in--
# JPython's compiler is present at run-time
############################################

from java import awt                # get access to Java class libraries
from pawt import swing               # they look like Python modules here

labels = ['0', '1', '2', '+',        # labels for calculator buttons
          '3', '4', '5', '-',        # will be used for a 4x4 grid
          '6', '7', '8', '*',
          '9', '.', '=', '/' ]

keys = swing.JPanel(awt.GridLayout(4, 4))    # do Java class library magic
```

Example 15-4. PP2E\Internet\Other\jpython.py (continued)

```
display = swing.JTextField()              # Python data auto-mapped to Java

def push(event):                          # callback for regular keys
    display.replaceSelection(event.actionCommand)

def enter(event):                         # callback for the '=' key
    display.text = str(eval(display.text))  # use Python eval() to run expr
    display.selectAll()

for label in labels:                      # build up button widget grid
    key = swing.JButton(label)            # on press, invoke Python funcs
    if label == '=':
        key.actionPerformed = enter
    else:
        key.actionPerformed = push
    keys.add(key)

panel = swing.JPanel(awt.BorderLayout())  # make a swing panel
panel.add("North", display)               # text plus key grid in middle
panel.add("Center", keys)
swing.test(panel)                         # start in a GUI viewer
```

The first thing you should notice is that this is genuine Python code—JPython scripts use the same core language that we've been using all along in this book. That's good news, both because Python is such an easy language to use and because you don't need to learn a new, proprietary scripting language to use JPython. It also means that all of Python's high-level language syntax and tools are available. For example, in this script, the Python `eval` built-in function is used to parse and evaluate constructed expressions all at once, saving us from having to write an expression evaluator from scratch.

Interface Automation Tricks

The previous calculator example also illustrates two interface automations performed by JPython: function callback and attribute mappings. Java programmers may have already noticed that this example doesn't use classes. Like standard Python and unlike Java, JPython supports but does not impose OOP. Simple Python functions work fine as *callback handlers*. In Example 15-4, assigning `key.actionPerformed` to a Python function object has the same effect as registering an instance of a class that defines a callback handler method:

```
def push(event):
    ...
key = swing.JButton(label)
key.actionPerformed = push
```

This is noticeably simpler than the more Java-like:

```
class handler(awt.event.ActionListener):
    def actionPerformed(self, event):
```

```
       ...
key = swing.JButton(label)
key.addActionListener(handler())
```

JPython automatically maps Python functions to the Java class method callback model. Java programmers may now be wondering why we can assign to something named `key.actionPerformed` in the first place. JPython's second magic feat is to make Java data members look like simple *object attributes* in Python code. In abstract terms, JPython code of the form:

```
X = Object(argument)
X.property = value + X.property
```

is equivalent to the more traditional and complex Java style:

```
X = Object(argument)
X.setProperty(value + X.getProperty())
```

That is, JPython automatically maps attribute assignments and references to Java accessor method calls by inspecting Java class signatures (and possibly Java Bean-Info files if used). Moreover, properties can be assigned with *keyword arguments* in object constructor calls, such that:

```
X = Object(argument, property=value)
```

is equivalent to both this more traditional form:

```
X = Object(argument)
X.setProperty(value)
```

as well as the following, which relies on attribute name mapping:

```
X = Object(argument)
X.property = value
```

We can combine both callback and property automation for an even simpler version of the callback code snippet:

```
def push(event):
    ...
key = swing.JButton(label, actionPerformed=push)
```

You don't need to use these automation tricks, but again, they make JPython scripts simpler, and that's most of the point behind mixing Python with Java.

Writing Java Applets in JPython

I would be remiss if I didn't include a brief example of JPython code that more directly masquerades as a Java *applet*: code that lives on a server machine but is downloaded to and run on the client machine when its Internet address is referenced. Most of the magic behind this is subclassing the appropriate Java class in a JPython script, demonstrated in Example 15-5.

Example 15-5. PP2E\Internet\Other\jpython-applet.py

```
#######################################
# a simple java applet coded in Python
#######################################

from java.applet import Applet                          # get java superclass

class Hello(Applet):
    def paint(self, gc):                                # on paint callback
        gc.drawString("Hello applet world", 20, 30)     # draw text message

if __name__ == '__main__':                              # if run standalone
    import pawt                                          # get java awt lib
    pawt.test(Hello())                                  # run under awt loop
```

The Python class in this code inherits all the necessary applet protocol from the standard Java **Applet** superclass, so there is not much new to see here. Under JPython, Python classes can always subclass Java classes, because Python objects really are Java objects when compiled and run. The Python-coded **paint** method in this script will be automatically run from the Java AWT event loop as needed; it simply uses the passed-in **gc** user-interface handle object to draw a text message.

If we use JPython's **jpythonc** command-line tool to compile this into a Java *.class* file and properly store that file on a web server, it can then be used exactly like applets written in Java. Because most web browsers include a JVM, this means that such Python scripts may be used as client-side programs that create sophisticated user-interface devices within the browser, and so on.

JPython Trade-offs

Depending on your background, though, the somewhat less good news about JPython is that even though the calculator and applet scripts discussed here are straight Python code, the libraries they use are different than what we've seen so far. In fact, the library calls employed are radically different. The calculator, for example, relies primarily on imported Java class libraries, not standard Python libraries. You really need to understand Java's **awt** and **swing** libraries to make sense of its code, and this *library skew* between language implementations becomes more acute as programs grow larger. The applet example is even more Java-bound: it depends both on Java user-interface libraries and Java applet protocols.

If you are already familiar with Java libraries, this isn't an issue at all, of course. But because most of the work performed by realistic programs is done by using libraries, the fact that most JPython code relies on very different libraries makes compatibility with standard Python less potent than it may seem at first glance. To put that more strongly, apart from very trivial core language examples, many JPython programs won't run on the standard Python interpreter, and many standard Python programs won't work under JPython.

Generally, JPython presents a number of trade-offs, partly due to its relative immaturity as of this writing. I want to point out up front that JPython is indeed an excellent Java scripting tool—arguably the best one available, and most of its trade-offs are probably of little or no concern to Java developers. For instance, if you are coming to JPython from the Java world, the fact that Java libraries are at the heart of JPython scripts may be more asset than downside. But if you are presented with a choice between the standard and Java-based Python language implementations, some of JPython's implications are worth knowing about:

JPython is not yet fully compatible with the standard Python language

At this writing, JPython is not yet totally compatible with the standard Python language, as defined by the original C implementation. In subtle ways, the core Python language itself works differently in JPython. For example, until very recently, assigning file-like objects to the standard input `sys.stdin` failed, and exceptions were still strings, not class objects. The list of incompatibilities (viewable at *http://www.jpython.org*) will likely shrink over time, but will probably never go away completely. Moreover, new language features are likely to show up later in JPython than in the standard C-based implementation.

JPython requires programmers to learn Java development too

Language syntax is only one aspect of programming. The library skew mentioned previously is just one example of JPython's dependence on the Java system. Not only do you need to learn Java libraries to get real work done in JPython, but you also must come to grips with the Java programming environment in general. Many standard Python libraries have been ported to JPython, and others are being adopted regularly. But major Python tools such as Tkinter GUIs may show up late or never in JPython (and instead are replaced with Java tools).* In addition, many core Python library features cannot be supported in JPython, because they would violate Java's security constraints. For example, the `os.system` call for running shell commands may never become available in JPython.

JPython applies only where a JVM is installed or shipped

You need the Java runtime to run JPython code. This may sound like a non-issue given the pervasiveness of the Internet, but I have very recently worked in more than one company for which delivering applications to be run on JVMs was not an option. Simply put, there was no JVM to be found at the customer's site. In such scenarios, JPython is either not an option, or will require

---

* But see the note at the end of the later section on Grail; an early port of Tkinter for JPython is already available on the Net.

you to ship a JVM with your application just to run your compiled JPython code. Shipping the standard Python system with your products is completely free; shipping a JVM may require licensing and fees. This may become less of a concern as robust open source JVMs appear. But if you wish to use JPython today and can't be sure that your clients will be able to run your systems in Java-aware browsers (or other JVM components), you should consider the potential costs of shipping a Java runtime system with your products.*

JPython doesn't support Python extension modules written in C or C++

At present, no C or C++ extension modules written to work with the C Python implementation will work with JPython. This is a major impediment to deploying JPython outside the scope of applications run in a browser. To date, the half-million-strong Python user community has developed thousands of extensions written for C Python, and these constitute much of the substance of the Python development world. JPython's current alternative is to instead expose Java class libraries and ask programmers to write new extensions in Java. But this dismisses a vast library of prior and future Python art. In principle, C extensions could be supported by Java's native call interface, but it's complex, has not been done, and can negate Java portability and security.

JPython is noticeably slower than C Python

Today, Python code generally runs slower under the JPython implementation. How much slower depends on what you test, which JVM you use to run your test, whether a just-in-time (JIT) compiler is available, and which tester you cite. Posted benchmarks have run the gamut from 1.7 times slower than C Python, to 10 times slower, and up to 100 times slower. Regardless of the exact number, the extra layer of logic JPython requires to map Python to the Java execution model adds speed overheads to an already slow JVM and makes it unlikely that JPython will ever be as fast as the C Python implementation. Given that C Python is already slower than compiled languages like C, the additional slowness of JPython makes it less useful outside the realm of Java scripting. Furthermore, the `Swing` GUI library used by JPython scripts is powerful, but generally considered to be the slowest and largest of all Python GUI options. Given that Python's Tkinter library is a portable and standard GUI solution, Java's proprietary user-interface tools by themselves are probably not reason enough to use the JPython implementation.

---

* Be sure you can get a JVM to develop those products too! Installing JPython on Windows 98 while writing this book proved painful, not because of JPython, but because I also had to come to grips with Java commands to run during installation, and track down and install a JVM other than the one provided by Microsoft. Depending on your platform, you may be faced with JPython's Java-dependence even before you type your first line of code.

JPython is less robust than C Python

At this writing, JPython is substantially more buggy than the standard C implementation of the language. This is certainly due to its younger age and smaller user base and varies from JVM to JVM, but you are more likely to hit snags in JPython. In contrast, C Python has been amazingly bug-free since its introduction in 1990.

JPython may be less portable than C Python

It's also worth noting that as of this writing, the core Python language is far more portable than Java (despite marketing statements to the contrary). Because of that, deploying standard Python code with the Java-based JPython implementation may actually *lessen* its portability. Naturally, this depends on the set of extensions you use, but standard Python runs today on everything from handheld PDAs and PCs to Cray supercomputers and IBM mainframes.

Some incompatibilities between JPython and standard Python can be very subtle. For instance, JPython inherits all of the Java runtime engine's behavior, including Java security constraints and garbage collection. Java garbage collection is not based on standard Python's reference count scheme, and therefore can automatically collect cyclic objects.* It also means that some common Python programming idioms won't work. For example, it's typical in Python to code file-processing loops in this form:

```
for filename in bigfilenamelist:
    text = open(filename).read()
    dostuffwith(text)
```

That works because files are automatically closed when garbage-collected in standard Python, and we can be sure that the file object returned by the open call will be immediately garbage collected (it's a temporary, so there are no more references as soon as we call read). It won't work in JPython, though, because we can't be sure when the temporary file object will be reclaimed. To avoid running out of file descriptors, we usually need to code this differently for JPython:

```
for filename in bigfilenamelist:
    file = open(filename)
    text = file.read()
    dostuffwith(text)
    file.close()
```

You may face a similar implementation mismatch if you assume that output files are immediately closed: open(name, 'w').write(bytes) collects and closes the temporary file object and hence flushes the bytes out to the file under the standard C implementation of Python only, while JPython instead collects the file

---

* But Python 2.0's garbage collector can now collect cyclic objects too. See the 2.0 release notes and Appendix A, *Recent Python Changes*.

object at some arbitrary time in the future. In addition to such file-closing concerns, Python __del__ class destructors are never called in JPython, due to complications associated with object termination.

Picking Your Python

Because of concerns such as those just mentioned, the JPython implementation of the Python language is probably best used only in contexts where Java integration or web browser interoperability are crucial design concerns. You should always be the judge, of course, but the standard C implementation seems better suited to most other Python applications. Still, that leaves a very substantial domain to JPython—almost all Java systems and programmers can benefit from adding JPython to their tool sets.

JPython allows programmers to write programs that use Java class libraries in a fraction of the code and complexity required by Java-coded equivalents. Hence, JPython excels as an extension language for Java-based systems, especially those that will run in the context of web browsers. Because Java is a standard component of most web browsers, JPython scripts will often run automatically without extra install steps on client machines. Furthermore, even Java-coded applications that have nothing to do with the Web can benefit from JPython's ease of use; its seamless integration with Java class libraries makes JPython simply the best Java scripting and testing tool available today.

For most other applications, though, the standard Python implementation, possibly integrated with C and C++ components, is probably a better design choice. The resulting system will likely run faster, cost less to ship, have access to all Python extension modules, be more robust and portable, and be more easily maintained by people familiar with standard Python.

On the other hand, I want to point out again that the trade-offs listed here are mostly written from the Python perspective; if you are a Java developer looking for a scripting tool for Java-based systems, many of these detriments may be of minor concern. And to be fair, some of JPython's problems may be addressed in future releases; for instance, its speed will probably improve over time. Yet even as it exists today, JPython clearly makes an ideal extension-language solution for Java-based applications, and offers a much more complete Java scripting solution than those currently available for other scripting languages.[*]

---

[*] Other scripting languages have addressed Java integration by reimplementing a Java virtual machine in the underlying scripting language or by integrating their original C implementations with Java using the Java native call interface. Neither approach is anywhere near as seamless and powerful as generating real Java bytecode.

For more details, see the JPython package included on this book's CD, and consult the JPython home page, currently maintained at *http://www.jpython.org*. At least one rumor has leaked concerning an upcoming JPython book as well, so check *http://www.python.org* for developments on this front. See also the sidebar later in this chapter about the new Python implementation for the C#/.NET environment on Windows. It seems likely that there will be three Pythons to choose from very soon (not just two), and perhaps more in the future. All will likely implement the same core Python language we've used in this text, but may emphasize alternative integration schemes, application domains, development environments, and so on.

Grail: A Python-Based Web Browser

I briefly mentioned the Grail browser near the start of Chapter 10. Many of Python's Internet tools date back to and reuse the work that went into Grail, a full-blown Internet web browser that:

- Is written entirely in Python
- Uses the Tkinter GUI API to implement its user interface and render pages
- Downloads and runs Python/Tkinter scripts as client-side applets

As mentioned earlier, Grail was something of a proof-of-concept for using Python to code large-scale Internet applications. It implements all the usual Internet protocols and works much like common browsers such as Netscape and Internet Explorer. Grail pages are implemented with the Tk text widgets that we met in the GUI part of this book.

More interestingly, the Grail browser allows applets to be written in Python. Grail applets are simply bits of Python code that live on a server but are run on a client. If an HTML document references a Python class and file that live on a server machine, Grail automatically downloads the Python code over a socket and runs it on the client machine, passing it information about the browser's user interface. The downloaded Python code may use the passed-in browser context information to customize the user interface, add new kinds of widgets to it, and perform arbitrary client-side processing on the local machine. Roughly speaking, Python applets in Grail serve the same purposes as Java applets in common Internet browsers: they perform client-side tasks that are too complex or slow to implement with other technologies such as server-side CGI scripts and generated HTML.

A Simple Grail Applet Example

Writing Grail applets is remarkably straightforward. In fact, applets are really just Python/Tkinter programs; with a few exceptions, they don't need to "know" about Grail at all. Let's look at a short example; the code in Example 15-6 simply adds a button to the browser, which changes its appearance each time it's pressed (its bitmap is reconfigured in the button callback handler).

There are two components to this page definition: an HTML file and the Python applet code it references. As usual, the *grail.html* HTML file that follows describes how to format the web page when the HTML's URL address is selected in a browser. But here, the APP tag also specifies a Python applet (class) to be run by the browser. By default, the Python module is assumed to have the same name as the class and must be stored in the same location (URL directory) as the HTML file that references it. Additional APP tag options can override the applet's default location.

Example 15-6. PP2E\Internet\Other\grail.html

```
<HEAD>
<TITLE>Grail Applet Test Page</TITLE>
</HEAD>
<BODY>
<H1>Test an Applet Here!</H1>
Click this button!
<APP CLASS=Question>
</BODY>
```

The applet file referenced by the HTML is a Python script that adds widgets to the Tkinter-based Grail browser. Applets are simply classes in Python modules. When the APP tag is encountered in the HTML, the Grail browser downloads the *Question.py* source code module (Example 15-7) and makes an instance of its Question class, passing in the browser widget as the master (parent). The master is the hook that lets applets attach new widgets to the browser itself; applets extend the GUI constructed by the HTML in this way.

Example 15-7. PP2E\Internet\Other\Question.py

```
# Python applet file: Question.py
# in the same location (URL) as the html file
# that references it; adds widgets to browser;

from Tkinter import *

class Question:                          # run by grail?
    def __init__(self, parent):          # parent=browser
        self.button = Button(parent,
                             bitmap='question',
                             command=self.action)
        self.button.pack()

    def action(self):
        if self.button['bitmap'] == 'question':
            self.button.config(bitmap='questhead')
        else:
            self.button.config(bitmap='question')
```

Example 15-7. PP2E\Internet\Other\Question.py (continued)

```
if __name__ == '__main__':
    root = Tk()                       # run standalone?
    button = Question(root)           # parent=Tk: top-level
    root.mainloop()
```

Notice that nothing in this class is Grail- or Internet-specific; in fact, it can be run (and tested) standalone as a Python/Tkinter program. Figure 15-3 is what it looks like if run standalone on Windows (with a Tk application root object as the master); when run by Grail (with the browser/page object as the master), the button appears as part of the web page instead. Either way, its bitmap changes on each press.

Figure 15-3. Running a Grail applet standalone

In effect, Grail applets are simply Python modules that are linked into HTML pages by using the APP tag. The Grail browser downloads the source code identified by an APP tag and runs it locally on the client during the process of creating the new page. New widgets added to the page (like the button here) may run Python callbacks on the client later, when activated by the user.

Applets interact with the user by creating one or more arbitrary Tk widgets. Of course, the previous example is artificial; but notice that the button's callback handler could do anything we can program in Python: updating persistent information, popping up new user interaction dialogs, calling C extensions, etc. However, by working in concert with Python's restricted execution mode (discussed later) applets can be prevented from performing potentially unsafe operations, like opening local files and talking over sockets.

Figure 15-4 shows a screen shot of Grail in action, hinting at what's possible with Python code downloaded to and run on a client. It shows the animated "game of life" demo; everything you see here is implemented using Python and the Tkinter GUI interface. To run the demo, you need to install Python with the Tk extension and download the Grail browser to run locally on your machine or copy it off the CD. Then point your browser to a URL where any Grail demo lives.

Having said all that, I should add that Grail is no longer formally maintained, and is now used primarily for research purposes (Guido never intended for Grail to put Netscape or Microsoft out of business). You can still get it for free (find it at *http://www.python.org*) and use it for surfing the Web or experimenting with alternative web browser concepts, but it is not the active project it was a few years ago.

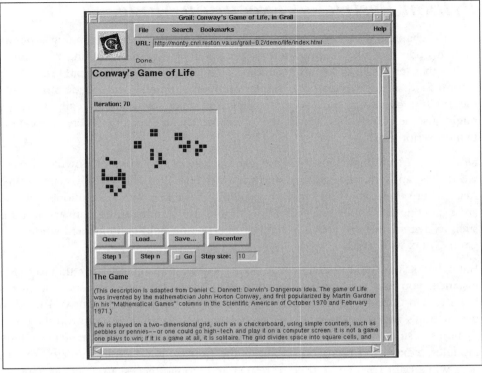

Figure 15-4. A Grail applet demo

If you want to code web browser applets in Python, the more common approach today is to use the JPython system described previously to compile your scripts into Java applet bytecode files, and use Java libraries for your scripts' user-interface portions. Embedding Python code in HTML with the Active Scripting extension described later in this chapter is yet another way to integrate client-side code.

Alas, this advice may change over time too. For instance, if Tkinter is ever ported to JPython, you will be able to build GUIs in applet files with Tkinter, rather than with Java class libraries. In fact, as I wrote this, an early release of a complete Java JNI implementation of the Python built-in _tkinter module (which allows JPython scripts to import and use the Tkinter module in the standard Python library) was available on the Net at *http://jtkinter.sourceforge.net.* Whether this makes Tkinter a viable GUI option under JPython or not, all current approaches are subject to change. Grail, for instance, was a much more prominent tool when the first edition of this book was written. As ever, be sure to keep in touch with developments in the Python community at *http://www.python.org;* clairvoyance isn't all it's cracked up to be.

Python Restricted Execution Mode

In prior chapters, I've been careful to point out the dangers of running arbitrary Python code that was shipped across the Internet. There is nothing stopping a malicious user, for instance, from sending a string such as `os.system('rm *')` in a form field where we expect a simple number; running such a code string with the built-in `eval` function or `exec` statement may, by default, really work—it might just delete all the files in the server or client directory where the calling Python script runs!

Moreover, a truly malicious user can use such hooks to view or download password files, and otherwise access, corrupt, or overload resources on your machine. Alas, where there is a hole, there is probably a hacker. As I've cautioned, if you are expecting a number in a form, you should use simpler string conversion tools such as `int` or `string.atoi` instead of interpreting field contents as Python program syntax with `eval`.

But what if you really want to run Python code transmitted over the Net? For instance, you may wish to put together a web-based training system that allows users to run code from a browser. It is possible to do this safely, but you need to use Python's *restricted execution mode* tools when you ask Python to run the code. Python's restricted execution mode support is provided in two standard library modules, `rexec` and `bastion`. `rexec` is the primary interface to restricted execution, while `bastion` can be used to restrict and monitor access to object attributes.

On Unix systems, you can also use the standard `resource` module to limit things like CPU time and memory consumption while the code is running. Python's library manual goes into detail on these modules, but let's take a brief look at `rexec` here.

Using rexec

The restricted execution mode implemented by `rexec` is optional—by default, all Python code runs with full access to everything available in the Python language and library. But when we enable restricted mode, code executes in what is commonly called a "sandbox" model—access to components on the local machine is limited. Operations that are potentially unsafe are either disallowed or must be approved by code you can customize by subclassing. For example, the script in Example 15-8 runs a string of program code in a restricted environment and customizes the default `rexec` class to restrict file access to a single, specific directory.

Example 15-8. PP2E\Internet\Other\restricted.py

```
#!/usr/bin/python
import rexec, sys
Test = 1
if sys.platform[:3] == 'win':
```

Example 15-8. PP2E\Internet\Other\restricted.py (continued)

```
    SafeDir = r'C:\temp'
else:
    SafeDir = '/tmp/'

def commandLine(prompt='Input (ctrl+z=end) => '):
    input = ''
    while 1:
        try:
            input = input + raw_input(prompt) + '\n'
        except EOFError:
            break
    print                                # clear for Windows
    return input

if not Test:
    import cgi                          # run on the web? - code from form
    form = cgi.FieldStorage()           # else input interactively to test
    input = form['input'].value
else:
    input = commandLine()

# subclass to customize default rules: default=write modes disallowed
class Guard(rexec.RExec):
    def r_open(self, name, mode='r', bufsz=-1):
        if name[:len(SafeDir)] != SafeDir:
            raise SystemError, 'files outside %s prohibited' % SafeDir
        else:
            return open(name, mode, bufsz)

# limit system resources (not available on Windows)
if sys.platform[:3] != 'win':
    import resource                     # at most 5 cpu seconds
    resource.setrlimit(resource.RLIMIT_CPU, (5, 5))

# run code string safely
guard = Guard()
guard.r_exec(input)          # ask guard to check and do opens
```

When we run Python code strings with this script on Windows, safe code works as usual, and we can read and write files that live in the *C:\temp* directory, because our custom `Guard` class's `r_open` method allows files with names beginning with "C:\temp" to proceed. The default `r_open` in `rexec.RExec` allows all files to be read, but all write requests fail. Here, we type code interactively for testing, but it's exactly as if we received this string over the Internet in a CGI script's form field:

```
C:\...\PP2E\Internet\Other>python restricted.py
Input (ctrl+z=end) => x = 5
Input (ctrl+z=end) => for i in range(x): print 'hello%d' % i,
Input (ctrl+z=end) => hello0 hello1 hello2 hello3 hello4

C:\...\PP2E\Internet\Other>python restricted.py
Input (ctrl+z=end) => open(r'C:\temp\rexec.txt', 'w').write('Hello rexec\n')
```

```
Input (ctrl+z=end) =>

C:\...\PP2E\Internet\Other>python restricted.py
Input (ctrl+z=end) => print open(r'C:\temp\rexec.txt', 'r').read()
Input (ctrl+z=end) => Hello rexec
```

On the other hand, attempting to access files outside the allowed directory will fail in our custom class, as will inherently unsafe things such as opening sockets, which rexec always makes out of bounds by default:

```
C:\...\PP2E\Internet\Other>python restricted.py
Input (ctrl+z=end) => open(r'C:\stuff\mark\hack.txt', 'w').write('BadStuff\n')
Input (ctrl+z=end) => Traceback (innermost last):
  File "restricted.py", line 41, in ?
    guard.r_exec(input)         # ask guard to check and do opens
  File "C:\Program Files\Python\Lib\rexec.py", line 253, in r_exec
    exec code in m.__dict__
  File "<string>", line 1, in ?
  File "restricted.py", line 30, in r_open
    raise SystemError, 'files outside %s prohibited' % SafeDir
SystemError: files outside C:\temp prohibited

C:\...\PP2E\Internet\Other>python restricted.py
Input (ctrl+z=end) => open(r'C:\stuff\mark\secret.py', 'r').read()
Input (ctrl+z=end) => Traceback (innermost last):
  File "restricted.py", line 41, in ?
    guard.r_exec(input)         # ask guard to check and do opens
  File "C:\Program Files\Python\Lib\rexec.py", line 253, in r_exec
    exec code in m.__dict__
  File "<string>", line 1, in ?
  File "restricted.py", line 30, in r_open
    raise SystemError, 'files outside %s prohibited' % SafeDir
SystemError: files outside C:\temp prohibited

C:\...\PP2E\Internet\Other>python restricted.py
Input (ctrl+z=end) => from socket import *
Input (ctrl+z=end) => s = socket(AF_INET, SOCK_STREAM)
Input (ctrl+z=end) => Traceback (innermost last):
  File "restricted.py", line 41, in ?
    guard.r_exec(input)         # ask guard to check and do opens
  ...part ommitted...
  File "C:\Program Files\Python\Lib\ihooks.py", line 324, in load_module
    exec code in m.__dict__
  File "C:\Program Files\Python\Lib\plat-win\socket.py", line 17, in ?
    _realsocketcall = socket
NameError: socket
```

And what of that nasty rm * problem? It's possible in normal Python mode like everything else, but not when running in restricted mode. Python makes some potentially dangerous attributes of the os module, such as system (for running shell commands), disallowed in restricted mode:

```
C:\temp>python
>>> import os
>>> os.system('ls -l rexec.txt')
```

```
-rwxrwxrwa   1 0      0              13 May  4 15:45 rexec.txt
0
>>>
C:\temp>python %X%\Part2\internet\other\restricted.py
Input (ctrl+z=end) => import os
Input (ctrl+z=end) => os.system('rm *.*')
Input (ctrl+z=end) => Traceback (innermost last):
  File "C:\PP2ndEd\examples\Part2\internet\other\restricted.py", line 41, in ?
    guard.r_exec(input)      # ask guard to check and do opens
  File "C:\Program Files\Python\Lib\rexec.py", line 253, in r_exec
    exec code in m.__dict__
  File "<string>", line 2, in ?
AttributeError: system
```

Internally, restricted mode works by taking away access to certain APIs (imports are controlled, for example) and changing the __builtins__ dictionary in the module where the restricted code runs to reference a custom and safe version of the standard __builtin__ built-in names scope. For instance, the custom version of name __builtins__.open references a restricted version of the standard file open function. rexec also keeps customizable lists of safe built-in modules, safe os and sys module attributes, and more. For the rest of this story, see the Python library manual.

 Restricted execution mode is not necessarily tied to Internet scripting. It can be useful any time you need to run Python code of possibly dubious origin. For instance, we will use Python's eval and exec built-ins to evaluate arithmetic expressions and input commands in a calculator program later in the book. Because user input is evaluated as executable code in this context, there is nothing preventing a user from knowingly or unknowingly entering code that can do damage when run (e.g., they might accidentally type Python code that deletes files). However, the risk of running raw code strings becomes more prevalent in applications that run on the Web, since they are inherently open to both use and abuse. Although JPython inherits the underlying Java security model, pure Python systems such as Zope, Grail, and custom CGI scripts can all benefit from restricted execution of strings sent over the Net.

XML Processing Tools

Python ships with XML parsing support in its standard library and plays host to a vigorous XML special-interest group. *XML* (eXtended Markup Language) is a tag-based markup language for describing many kinds of structured data. Among other things, it has been adopted in roles such as a standard database and Internet content representation by many companies. As an object-oriented scripting language,

Python mixes remarkably well with XML's core notion of structured document interchange, and promises to be a major player in the XML arena.

XML is based upon a tag syntax familiar to web page writers. Python's `xmllib` library module includes tools for parsing XML. In short, this XML parser is used by defining a subclass of an `XMLParser` Python class, with methods that serve as callbacks to be invoked as various XML structures are detected. Text analysis is largely automated by the library module. This module's source code, file *xmllib.py* in the Python library, includes self-test code near the bottom that gives additional usage details. Python also ships with a standard HTML parser, `htmllib`, that works on similar principles and is based upon the `sgmllib` SGML parser module.

Unfortunately, Python's XML support is still evolving, and describing it is well beyond the scope of this book. Rather than going into further details here, I will instead point you to sources for more information:

Standard library

First off, be sure to consult the Python library manual for more on the standard library's XML support tools. At the moment, this includes only the `xmllib` parser module, but may expand over time.

PyXML SIG package

At this writing, the best place to find Python XML tools and documentation is at the XML SIG (Special Interest Group) web page at *http://www.python.org* (click on the "SIGs" link near the top). This SIG is dedicated to wedding XML technologies with Python, and publishes a free XML tools package distribution called *PyXML*. That package contains tools not yet part of the standard Python distribution, including XML parsers implemented in both C and Python, a Python implementation of SAX and DOM (the XML Document Object Model), a Python interface to the `Expat` parser, sample code, documentation, and a test suite.

Third-party tools

You can also find free, third-party Python support tools for XML on the Web by following links at the XML SIGs web page. These include a DOM implementation for CORBA environments (4DOM) that currently supports two ORBs (ILU and Fnorb) and much more.

Documentation

As I wrote these words, a book dedicated to XML processing with Python was on the eve of its publication; check the books list at *http://www.python.org* or your favorite book outlet for details.

Given the rapid evolution of XML technology, I wouldn't wager on any of these resources being up to date a few years after this edition's release, so be sure to check Python's web site for more recent developments on this front.

In fact, the XML story changed substantially between the time I wrote this section and when I finally submitted it to O'Reilly. In Python 2.0, some of the tools described here as the PyXML SIG package have made their way into a standard `xml` module package in the Python library. In other words, they ship and install with Python itself; see the Python 2.0 library manual for more details. O'Reilly has a book in the works on this topic called *Python and XML*.

Windows Web Scripting Extensions

Although this book doesn't cover the Windows-specific extensions available for Python in detail, a quick look at Internet scripting tools available to Windows programmers is in order here. On Windows, Python can be used as a scripting language for both the Active Scripting and Active Server Pages systems, which provide client- and server-side control of HTML-based applications. More generally, Python programs can also take the role of COM and DCOM clients and servers on Windows.

You should note that at this point in time, everything in this section works only on Microsoft tools, and HTML embedding runs only under Internet Explorer (on the client) and Internet Information Server (on the server). If you are interested in portability, other systems in this chapter may address your needs better (see JPython's client-side applets, PSP's server-side scripting support, and Zope's server-side object publishing model). On the other hand, if portability isn't a concern, the following techniques provide powerful ways to script both sides of a web conversation.

Active Scripting: Client-Side Embedding

Active Scripting is a technology that allows scripting languages to communicate with hosting applications. The hosting application provides an application-specific *object model API*, which exposes objects and functions for use in the scripting language programs.

In one if its more common roles, Active Scripting provides support that allows scripting language code embedded in HTML pages to communicate with the local web browser through an automatically exposed object model API. Internet Explorer, for instance, utilizes Active Scripting to export things such as global functions and user-interface objects for use in scripts embedded in HTML. With Active Scripting, Python code may be embedded in a web page's HTML between special tags; such code is executed on the client machine and serves the same roles as embedded JavaScript and VBScript.

Active Scripting basics

Unfortunately, embedding Python in client-side HTML works only on machines where Python is installed and Internet Explorer is configured to know about the Python language (by installing the `win32all` extension package discussed in a moment). Because of that, this technology doesn't apply to most of the browsers in cyberspace today. On the other hand, if you can configure the machines on which a system is to be delivered, this is a nonissue.

Before we get into a Python example, let's look at the way standard browser installations handle other languages embedded in HTML. By default, IE (Internet Explorer) knows about JavaScript (really, Microsoft's Jscript implementation of it) and VBScript (a Visual Basic derivative), so you can embed both of those languages in any delivery scenario. For instance, the HTML file in Example 15-9 embeds JavaScript code, the default IE scripting language on my PC.

Example 15-9. PP2E\Internet\Other\activescript-js.html

```
<HTML>
<BODY>
<H1>Embedded code demo: JavaScript</H1>
<SCRIPT>

// popup 3 alert boxes while this page is
// being constructed on client side by IE;
// JavaScript is the default script language,
// and alert is an automatically exposed name

function message(i) {
    if (i == 2) {
        alert("Finished!");
    }
    else {
        alert("A JavaScript-generated alert => " + i);
    }
}

for (count = 0; count < 3; count += 1) {
    message(count);
}

</SCRIPT>
</BODY></HTML>
```

All the text between the `<SCRIPT>` and `</SCRIPT>` tags in this file is JavaScript code. Don't worry about its syntax—this book isn't about JavaScript, and we'll see a simpler Python equivalent in a moment. The important thing to know is how this code is used by the browser.

When a browser detects a block of code like this while building up a new page, it locates the appropriate interpreter, tells the interpreter about global object names, and passes the code to the interpreter for execution. The global names become variables in the embedded code and provide links to browser context. For instance, the name `alert` in the code block refers to a global function that creates a message box. Other global names refer to objects that give access to the browser's user interface: window objects, document objects, and so on.

This HTML file can be run on the local machine by clicking on its name in a file explorer. It can also be stored on a remote server and accessed via its URL in a browser. Whichever way you start it, three pop-up alert boxes created by the embedded code appear during page construction. Figure 15-5 shows one under IE.

Figure 15-5. IE running embedded JavaScript code

The VBScript (Visual Basic) version of this example appears in Example 15-10, so you can compare and contrast.* It creates three similar pop-ups when run, but the windows say "VBScript" everywhere. Notice the Language option in the `<SCRIPT>` tag here; it must be used to declare the language to IE (in this case, VBScript) unless your embedded scripts speak in its default tongue. In the JavaScript version in Example 15-9, Language wasn't needed, because JavaScript was

---

* Again, feel free to ignore most of this example's syntax. I'm not going to teach either JavaScript or VBScript syntax in this book, nor will I tell you which of the three versions of this example is clearer (though you can probably guess my preference). The first two versions are included partly for comparison by readers with a web development background.

the default language. Other than this declaration, IE doesn't care what language you insert between `<SCRIPT>` and `</SCRIPT>`; in principle, Active Scripting is a language-neutral scripting engine.

Example 15-10. PP2E\Internet\Other\activescript-vb.html

```
<HTML>
<BODY>
<H1>Embedded code demo: VBScript</H1>
<SCRIPT Language=VBScript>

' do the same but with embedded VBScript;
' the Language option in the SCRIPT tag
' tells IE which interpreter to use

sub message(i)
    if i = 2 then
        alert("Finished!")
    else
        alert("A VBScript-generated alert => " & i)
    end if
end sub

for count = 0 to 2 step 1
    message(count)
next

</SCRIPT>
</BODY></HTML>
```

So how about putting Python code in that page, then? Alas, we need to do a bit more first. Although IE is language-neutral in principle, it does support some languages better than others, at least today. Moreover, other browsers may be more rigid and not support the Active Scripting concept at all.

For example, on my machine and with my installed browser versions (IE 5, Netscape 4), the previous JavaScript example works on both IE and Netscape, but the Visual Basic version works only on IE. That is, IE directly supports VBScript and JavaScript, while Netscape handles only JavaScript. Neither browser as installed can run embedded Python code, even though Python itself is already installed on my machine. There's more to do before we can replace the JavaScript and VBScript code in our HTML pages with Python.

Teaching IE about Python

To make the Python version work, you must do more than simply installing Python on your PC. You must also register Python with IE. Luckily, this is mostly an automatic process, thanks to the work of the Python Windows extension developers; you merely need to install a package of Windows extensions.

Here's how this works. The tool to perform the registration is part of the Python Win32 extensions, which are not included in the standard Python system. To make Python known to IE, you must:

1. First install the standard Python distribution your PC (you should have done this already by now—simply double-click the Python self-installer).

2. Then download and install the `win32all` package separately from *http:// www.python.org* (you can also find it on this book's CD).[*]

The `win32all` package includes the `win32COM` extensions for Python, plus the *PythonWin* IDE (a simple interface for editing and running Python programs, written with the MFC interfaces in `win32all`) and lots of other Windows-specific tools not covered in this book. The relevant point here is that installing `win32all` automatically registers Python for use in IE. If needed, you can also perform this registration manually by running the following Python script file located in the win32 extensions package: *python\win32comext\axscript\client\pyscript.py.*

Once you've registered Python with IE this way, Python code embedded in HTML works just like our JavaScript and VBScript examples—IE presets Python global names to expose its object model and passes the embedded code to your Python interpreter for execution. Example 15-11 shows our alerts example again, programmed with embedded Python code.

Example 15-11. PP2E\Internet\Other\activescript-py.html

```
<HTML>
<BODY>
<H1>Embedded code demo: Python</H1>
<SCRIPT Language=Python>

# do the same but with python, if configured;
# embedded python code shows three alert boxes
# as page is loaded; any Python code works here,
# and uses auto-imported global funcs and objects

def message(i):
    if i == 2:
        alert("Finished!")
    else:
        alert("A Python-generated alert => %d" % i)

for count in range(3): message(count)

</SCRIPT>
</BODY></HTML>
```

---

[*] However, you may not need to download the `win32all` package. The ActivePython Python distribution available from ActiveState (*http://www.activestate.com*), for example, comes with the Windows extensions package.

Figure 15-6 shows one of the three pop-ups you should see when you open this file in IE after installing the win32all package (you can simply click on the file's icon in Windows' file explorer to open it). Note that the first time you access this page, IE may need to load Python, which could induce an apparent delay on slower machines; later accesses generally start up much faster because Python has already been loaded.

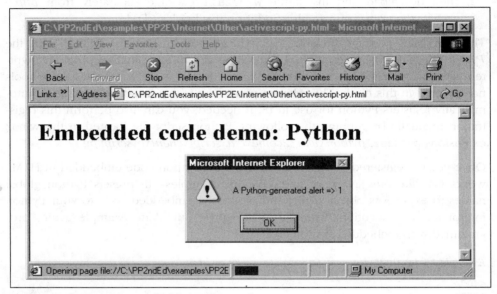

Figure 15-6. IE running embedded Python code

Regrettably, this example still works only on IE Version 4 and higher, and not on the Netscape browser on my machine (and reportedly fails on Netscape 6 and Mozilla as well). In other words (at least today and barring new browser releases), not only is Active Scripting a Windows-only technology, but using it as a client-side web browser tool for Python works only on machines where Python is installed and registered to IE, and even then only under IE.

It's also worth knowing that even when you do get Python to work under IE, your Python code runs in *restricted mode*, with limited access to machine resources (e.g., your code can't open sockets—see the rexec module description earlier in this chapter for details). That's probably what you want when running code down-loaded over the Net, and can be changed locally (the implementation is coded in Python), but it limits the utility and scope of your Python scripts embedded in HTML.

The good news is that this does work—with a simple configuration step, Python code can be embedded in HTML and be made to run under IE, just like JavaScript and VBScript. For many applications, the Windows and IE-only constraint is completely acceptable. Active Scripting is a straightforward way to add client-side Python scripting for web browsers, especially when you can control the target delivery environment. For instance, machines running on an Intranet within a company may have well-known configurations. In such scenarios, Active Scripting lets developers apply all the power of Python in their client-side scripts.

Active Server Pages: Server-Side Embedding

Active Server Pages (ASPs) use a similar model: Python code is embedded in the HTML that defines a web page. But ASP is a *server-side* technology; embedded Python code runs on the server machine and uses an object-based API to dynamically generate portions of the HTML that is ultimately sent back to the client-side browser. As we saw in the last three chapters, Python server-side CGI scripts embed and generate HTML, and deal with raw inputs and output streams. By contrast, server-side ASP scripts are embedded in HTML and use a higher-level object model to get their work done.

Just like client-side Active Scripting, ASP requires you to install Python and the Python Windows `win32all` extensions package. But because ASP runs embedded code on the server, you need to configure Python only on one machine. Like CGI scripts in general, this generally makes Python ASP scripting much more widely applicable, as you don't need Python support on every client. Unlike CGI scripts, however, ASP requires you to run Microsoft's IIS (Internet Information Server) today.

A short ASP example

We can't discuss ASP in any real detail here, but here's an example of what an ASP file looks like when Python code is embedded:

```
<HTML><BODY>
<SCRIPT RunAt=Server Language=Python>
#
# code here is run at the server
#
</SCRIPT>
</BODY></HTML>
```

As before, code may be embedded inside `SCRIPT` tag pairs. This time, we tell ASP to run the code at the server with the `RunAt` option; if omitted, the code and its tags are passed through to the client and run by IE (if configured properly). ASP also recognizes code enclosed in `<%` and `%>` delimiters and allows a language to be specified for the entire page. This form is more handy if there are multiple chunks of code in a page, as shown in Example 15-12.

Example 15-12. PP2E\Internet\Other\asp-py.asp

```
<HTML><BODY>
<%@ Language=Python %>

<%
#
# Python code here, using global names Request (input), Response (output), etc.
#
Response.Write("Hello ASP World from URL %s" %
                      Request.ServerVariables("PATH_INFO"))
%>
</BODY></HTML>
```

However the code is marked, ASP executes it on the server after passing in a handful of named objects that the code may use to access input, output and server context. For instance, the automatically imported **Request** and **Response** objects give access to input and output context. The code here calls a **Response.Write** method to send text back to the browser on the client (much like a print statement in a simple Python CGI script), as well as **Request.ServerVariables** to access environment variable information. To make this script run live, you'll need to place it in the proper directory on a server machine running IIS with ASP support.

The COM Connection

At their core, both IE and IIS are based on the COM (Component Object Model) integration system—they implement their object APIs with standard COM interfaces and look to the rest of the world like any other COM object. From a broader perspective, Python can be used as both a scripting and implementation language for any COM object. Although the COM mechanism used to run Python code embedded within HTML is automated and hidden, it can also be employed explicitly to make Python programs take the role of both COM clients and servers. COM is a general integration technology and is not strictly tied to Internet scripting, but a brief introduction here might help demystify some of the Active Scripting magic behind HTML embedding.

A brief introduction to COM

COM is a Microsoft technology for language-neutral component integration. It is sometimes marketed as ActiveX, partially derived from a system called OLE, and is the technological heart of the Active Scripting system we met earlier.* COM also sports a distributed extension known as DCOM that allows communicating objects

---

* Roughly, OLE (Object Linking and Embedding) was a precursor to COM, and Active Scripting is just a technology that defines COM interfaces for activities such as passing objects to arbitrary programming language interpreters by name. Active Scripting is not much more than COM itself with a few extensions, but acronym- and buzzword-overload seem to run rampant in the Windows development world.

to be run on remote machines. Implementing DCOM often simply involves running through Windows registry configuration steps to associate servers with machines on which they run.

Operationally, COM defines a standard way for objects implemented in arbitrary languages to talk to each other, using a published object model. For example, COM components can be written in and used by programs written in Visual Basic, Visual C++, Delphi, PowerBuilder, and Python. Because the COM indirection layer hides the differences between all the languages involved, it's possible for Visual Basic to use an object implemented in Python and vice versa.

Moreover, many software packages register COM interfaces to support end-user scripting. For instance, Microsoft Excel publishes an object model that allows any COM-aware scripting language to start Excel and programmatically access spreadsheet data. Similarly, Microsoft Word can be scripted through COM to automatically manipulate documents. COM's language-neutrality means that programs written in any programming language with a COM interface, including Visual Basic and Python, can be used to automate Excel and Word processing.

Of most relevance to this chapter, Active Scripting also provides COM objects that allow scripts embedded in HTML to communicate with Microsoft's Internet Explorer (on the client) and Internet Information Server (on the server). Both systems register their object models with Windows such that they can be invoked from any COM-aware language. For example, when Internet Explorer extracts and executes Python code embedded in HTML, some Python variable names are automatically preset to COM object components that give access to IE context and tools (`alert` in Example 15-11). Calls to such components from Python code are automatically routed through COM back to IE.

Python COM clients

With the `win32all` Python extension package installed, though, we can also write Python programs that serve as registered COM servers and clients, even if they have nothing to do with the Internet at all. For example, the Python program in Example 15-13 acts as a client to the Microsoft Word COM object.

Example 15-13. PP2E\Internet\Other\Com\comclient.py

```
####################################################################
# a COM client coded in Python: talk to MS-Word via its COM object
# model; uses either dynamic dispatch (run-time lookup/binding),
# or the static and faster type-library dispatch if makepy.py has
# been run; install the windows win32all extensions package to use
# this interface; Word runs hidden unless Visible is set to 1 (and
# Visible lets you watch, but impacts interactive Word sessions);
####################################################################
```

Example 15-13. PP2E\Internet\Other\Com\comclient.py (continued)

```
from sys import argv
docdir = 'C:\\temp\\'
if len(argv) == 2: docdir = argv[1]              # ex: comclient.py a:\

from win32com.client import Dispatch             # early or late binding
word  = Dispatch('Word.Application')             # connect/start word
word.Visible = 1                                 # else word runs hidden

# create and save new doc file
newdoc = word.Documents.Add()                    # call word methods
spot   = newdoc.Range(0,0)
spot.InsertBefore('Hello COM client world!')     # insert some text
newdoc.SaveAs(docdir + 'pycom.doc')              # save in doc file
newdoc.SaveAs(docdir + 'copy.doc')
newdoc.Close()

# open and change a doc file
olddoc = word.Documents.Open(docdir + 'copy.doc')
finder = word.Selection.Find
finder.text = 'COM'
finder.Execute()
word.Selection.TypeText('Automation')
olddoc.Close()

# and so on: see Word's COM interface specs
```

This particular script starts Microsoft Word—known as **Word.Application** to scripting clients—if needed, and converses with it through COM. That is, calls in this script are automatically routed from Python to Microsoft Word and back. This code relies heavily on calls exported by Word, which are not described in this book. Armed with documentation for Word's object API, though, we could use such calls to write Python scripts that automate document updates, insert and replace text, create and print documents, and so on.

For instance, Figure 15-7 shows the two Word *.doc* files generated when the previous script is run on Windows: both are new files, and one is a copy of the other with a text replacement applied. The interaction that occurs while the script runs is more interesting: because Word's **Visible** attribute is set to 1, you can actually *watch* Word inserting and replacing text, saving files, etc., in response to calls in the script. (Alas, I couldn't quite figure out how to paste a movie clip in this book.)

In general, Python COM client calls may be dispatched either dynamically by runtime look-ups in the Windows registry, or statically using type libraries created by running a Python utility script at development time (*makepy.py*). These dispatch modes are sometimes called *late* and *early* dispatch binding, respectively. Dynamic

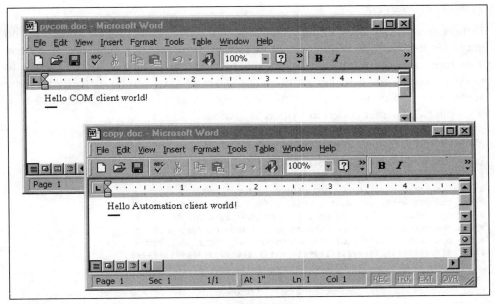

Figure 15-7. Word files generated by Python COM client

(late) dispatch skips a development step but is slower when clients are running, due to all the required look-ups.*

Luckily, we don't need to know which scheme will be used when we write client scripts. The `Dispatch` call used in Example 15-13 to connect to Word is smart enough to use static binding if server type libraries exist, or dynamic binding if they do not. To force dynamic binding and ignore any generated type libraries, replace the first line with this:

```
from win32com.client.dynamic import Dispatch      # always late binding
```

However calls are dispatched, the Python COM interface performs all the work of locating the named server, looking up and calling the desired methods or attributes, and converting Python datatypes according to a standard type map as needed. In the context of Active Scripting, the underlying COM model works the same way, but the server is something like IE or IIS (not Word), the set of available calls differs, and some Python variables are preassigned to COM server objects. The notions of "client" and "server" can become somewhat blurred in these scenarios, but the net result is similar.

---

* Actually, `makepy` can also be executed at runtime now, so you may no longer need to manually run it during development. See the `makepy` documentation available in the latest Windows extensions package for breaking details.

Python COM servers

Python scripts can also be deployed as COM *servers*, and provide methods and attributes that are accessible to any COM-aware programming language or system. This topic is too complex to cover well here, but exporting a Python object to COM is mostly just a matter of providing a set of class attributes to identify the server and utilizing the proper `win32com` registration utility calls. Example 15-14 is a simple COM server coded in Python as a class.

Example 15-14. PP2E\Internet\Other\Com\comserver.py

```
###############################################################
# a COM server coded in Python; the _reg_ class attributes
# give registry parameters, and others list methods and attrs;
# for this to work, you must install Python and the win32all
# package, this module file must live on your Python path,
# and the server must be registered to COM (see code at end);
# run pythoncom.CreateGuid() to make your own _reg_clsid_ key;
###############################################################

import sys
from   win32com.server.exception import COMException      # what to raise
import win32com.server.util                               # server tools
globhellos = 0

class MyServer:

    # com info settings
    _reg_clsid_      = '{1BA63CC0-7CF8-11D4-98D8-BB74DD3DDE3C}'
    _reg_desc_       = 'Example Python Server'
    _reg_progid_     = 'PythonServers.MyServer'            # external name
    _reg_class_spec_ = 'comserver.MyServer'               # internal name
    _public_methods_ = ['Hello', 'Square']
    _public_attrs_   = ['version']

    # python methods
    def __init__(self):
        self.version = 1.0
        self.hellos  = 0
    def Square(self, arg):                                 # exported methods
        return arg ** 2
    def Hello(self):                                       # global variables
        global globhellos                                 # retain state, but
        globhellos  = globhellos  + 1                     # self vars don't
        self.hellos = self.hellos + 1
        return 'Hello COM server world [%d, %d]' % (globhellos, self.hellos)

# registration functions
def Register(pyclass=MyServer):
    from win32com.server.register import UseCommandLine
    UseCommandLine(pyclass)
```

Example 15-14. PP2E\Internet\Other\Com\comserver.py (continued)

```
def Unregister(classid=MyServer._reg_clsid_):
    from win32com.server.register import UnregisterServer
    UnregisterServer(classid)

if __name__ == '__main__':          # register server if file run or clicked
    Register()                      # unregisters if --unregister cmd-line arg
```

As usual, this Python file must be placed in a directory in Python's module search path. Besides the server class itself, the file includes code at the bottom to automatically register and unregister the server to COM when the file is run:

- To *register* a server, simply call the UseCommandLine function in the win32com.server.register package and pass in the Python server class. This function uses all the special class attribute settings to make the server known to COM. The file is set to automatically call the registration tools if it is run by itself (e.g., when clicked in a file explorer).

- To *unregister* a server, simply pass an --unregister argument on the command line when running this file. When run this way, the script automatically calls UseCommandLine again to unregister the server; as its name implies, this function inspects command-line arguments and knows to do the right thing when --unregister is passed. You can also unregister servers explicitly with the UnregisterServer call demonstrated near the end of this script, though this is less commonly used.

Perhaps the more interesting part of this code, though, is the special *class attribute* assignments at the start of the Python class. These class annotations can provide server registry settings (the _reg_ attributes), accessibility constraints (the _public_ names), and more. Such attributes are specific to the Python COM framework, and their purpose is to configure the server.

For example, the _reg_class_spec_ is simply the Python module and class names separated by a period. If set, the resident Python interpreter uses this attribute to import the module and create an instance of the Python class it defines, when accessed by a client.[*]

Other attributes may be used to identify the server in the Windows registry. The _reg_clsid_ attribute, for instance, gives a *globally unique identifier* (GUID) for the server and should vary in every COM server you write. In other words, don't

---

[*] But note that the _reg_class_spec_ attribute is no longer strictly needed, and not specifying it avoids a number of PYTHONPATH issues. Because such settings are prone to change, you should always consult the latest Windows extensions package reference manuals for details on this and other class annotation attributes.

use the value in this script. Instead, do what I did to make this ID, and paste the result returned on your machine into your script:[*]

```
A:\>python
>>> import pythoncom
>>> pythoncom.CreateGuid()
<iid:{1BA63CC0-7CF8-11D4-98D8-BB74DD3DDE3C}>
```

GUIDs are generated by running a tool shipped with the Windows extensions package; simply import and call the `pythoncom.CreateGuid()` function and insert the returned text in the script. Windows uses the ID stamped into your network card to come up with a complex ID that is likely to be unique across servers and machines. The more symbolic Program ID string, `_reg_progid_`, can be used by clients to name servers too, but is not as likely to be unique.

The rest of the server class is simply pure-Python methods, which implement the exported behavior of the server; that is, things to be called from clients. Once this Python server is annotated, coded, and registered, it can be used in any COM-aware language. For instance, programs written in Visual Basic, C++, Delphi, and Python may access its public methods and attributes through COM; of course, other Python programs can also simply import this module, but the point of COM is to open up components for even wider reuse.[†]

Using the Python server from a Python client. Let's put this Python COM server to work. The Python script in Example 15-15 tests the server two ways: first by simply importing and calling it directly, and then by employing Python's client-side COM interfaces shown earlier to invoke it less directly. When going through COM, the `PythonServers.MyServer` symbolic program ID we gave the server (by setting class attribute `_reg_progid_`) can be used to connect to this server from any language (including Python).

Example 15-15. PP2E\Internet\Other\Com\comserver-test.py

```
###########################################################
# test the Python-coded COM server from Python two ways
###########################################################

def testViaPython():                                    # test without com
```

---

[*] The `A:/>` prompt shows up here only because I copied the COM scripts to a floppy so I could run them on a machine with the `win32all` extension installed. You should be able to run from the directory where these scripts live in the examples tree.

[†] But you should be aware of a few type rules. In Python 1.5.2, Python-coded COM servers must be careful to use a fixed number of function arguments, and convert passed-in strings with the `str` built-in function. The latter of these constraints arises because COM passes strings as Unicode strings. Because Python 1.6 and 2.0 now support both Unicode and normal strings, though, this constraint should disappear soon. When using COM as a client (i.e., code that calls COM), you may pass a string or Unicode object, and the conversion is done automatically; when coding a COM server (i.e., code called by COM), strings are always passed in as Unicode objects.

Example 15-15. PP2E\Internet\Other\Com\comserver-test.py (continued)

```
    from comserver import MyServer        # use Python class name
    object = MyServer()                   # works as for any class
    print object.Hello()
    print object.Square(8)
    print object.version

def testViaCom():
    from win32com.client import Dispatch  # test via client-side com
    server = Dispatch('PythonServers.MyServer')  # use Windows registry name
    print server.Hello()                  # call public methods
    print server.Square(12)
    print server.version                  # access attributes

if __name__ == '__main__':
    testViaPython()
    testViaCom()                          # test module, server
    testViaCom()                          # com object retains state
```

If we've properly configured and registered the Python COM server, we can talk to it by running this Python test script. In the following, we run the server and client files from an MS-DOS console box (though they can usually be run by mouse clicks as well). The first command runs the server file by itself to register the server to COM; the second executes the test script to exercise the server both as an imported module (`testViaPython`) and as a server accessed through COM (`testViaCom`):

```
A:\>python comserver.py
Registered: PythonServers.MyServer

A:\>python comserver-test.py
Hello COM server world [1, 1]
64
1.0
Hello COM server world [2, 1]
144
1.0
Hello COM server world [3, 1]
144
1.0

A:\>python comserver.py --unregister
Unregistered: PythonServers.MyServer
```

Notice the two numbers at the end of the `Hello` output lines: they reflect current values of a global variable and a server instance attribute. Global variables in the server's module retain state as long as the server module is loaded; by contrast, each COM `Dispatch` (and Python class) call makes a new instance of the server class, and hence new instance attributes. The third command unregisters the server in COM, as a cleanup step. Interestingly, once the server has been unregistered, it's no longer usable, at least not through COM:

```
A:\>python comserver-test.py
Hello COM server world [1, 1]
64
1.0
Traceback (innermost last):
  File "comserver-test.py", line 21, in ?
    testViaCom()                                    # com object retains
  File "comserver-test.py", line 14, in testViaCom
    server = Dispatch('PythonServers.MyServer')     # use Windows register
  ...more deleted...
pywintypes.com_error: (-2147221005, 'Invalid class string', None, None)
```

Using the Python server from a VB client. The *comserver-test.py* script just listed demonstrates how to use a Python COM server from a Python COM client. Once we've created and registered a Python COM server, though, it's available to any language that sports a COM interface. For instance, Example 15-16 shows the sort of code we write to access the Python server from Visual Basic. Clients coded in other languages (e.g., Delphi or Visual C++) are analogous, but syntax and instantiation calls may vary.

Example 15-16. PP2E\Internet\Other\Com\comserver-test.bas

```
Sub runpyserver()
    ' use python server from vb client
    ' alt-f8 in word to start macro editor
    Set server = CreateObject("PythonServers.MyServer")
    hello1 = server.hello()
    square = server.square(32)
    pyattr = server.Version
    hello2 = server.hello()
    sep = Chr(10)
    Result = hello1 & sep & square & sep & pyattr & sep & hello2
    MsgBox Result
End Sub
```

The real trick (at least for someone as naive about VB as this author) is how to make this code go. Because VB is embedded in Microsoft Office products such as Word, one approach is to test this code in the context of those systems. Try this: start Word, press Alt and F8 together, and you'll wind up in the Word macro dialog. There, enter a new macro name, press Create, and you'll find yourself in a development interface where you can paste and run the VB code just shown.

I don't teach VB tools in this book, so you'll need to consult other documents if this fails on your end. But it's fairly simple once you get the knack—running the VB code in this context produces the Word pop-up box in Figure 15-8, showing the results of VB calls to our Python COM server. Global variable and instance attribute values at the end of both `Hello` reply messages are the same this time, because we make only one instance of the Python server class: in VB, by calling `CreateObject`, with the program ID of the desired server.

Figure 15-8. VB client running Python COM server

But because we've now learned how to embed VBScript in HTML pages, another way to kick off the VB client code is to put it in a web page and rely on IE to launch it for us. The bulk of the HTML file in Example 15-17 is the same as the Basic file shown previously, but tags have been added around the code to make it a bona fide web page.

Example 15-17. PP2E\Internet\Other\Com\comserver-test-vbs.html

```
<HTML><BODY>
<P>Run Python COM server from VBScript embedded in HTML via IE</P>
<SCRIPT Language=VBScript>

Sub runpyserver()
    ' use python server from vb client
    ' alt-f8 in word to start macro editor
    Set server = CreateObject("PythonServers.MyServer")
    hello1 = server.hello()
    square = server.square(9)
    pyattr = server.Version
    hello2 = server.hello()
    sep = Chr(10)
    Result = hello1 & sep & square & sep & pyattr & sep & hello2
    MsgBox Result
End Sub

runpyserver()

</SCRIPT>
</BODY></HTML>
```

There is an incredible amount of routing going on here, but the net result is similar to running the VB code by itself. Clicking on this file starts Internet Explorer (assuming it is registered to handle HTML files), which strips out and runs the embedded VBScript code, which in turn calls out to the Python COM server. That is, IE runs VBScript code that runs Python code—a control flow spanning three systems, an HTML file, a Python file, and the IE implementation. With COM, it just works. Figure 15-9 shows IE in action running the HTML file above; the pop-up box is generated by the embedded VB code as before.

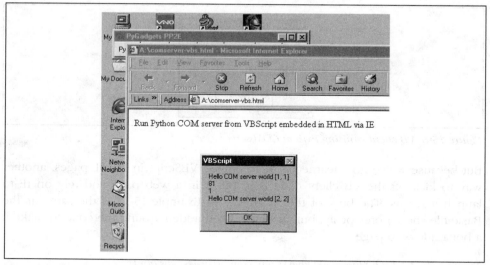

Figure 15-9. IE running a VBScript client running a Python COM server

If your client code runs but generates a COM error, make sure that the `win32all` package has been installed, that the server module file is in a directory on Python's path, and that the server file has been run by itself to register the server with COM. If none of that helps, you're probably already beyond the scope of this text. (Please see additional Windows programming resources for more details.)

The bigger COM picture

So what does writing Python COM servers have to do with the Internet motif of this chapter? After all, Python code embedded in HTML simply plays the role of COM client to IE or IIS systems that usually run locally. Besides showing how such systems work their magic, I've presented this topic here because COM, at least in its grander world view, is also about communicating over networks.

Although we can't get into details in this text, COM's *distributed* extensions make it possible to implement Python-coded COM servers to run on machines that are arbitrarily remote from clients. Although largely transparent to clients, COM object calls like those in the preceding client scripts may imply network transfers of arguments and results. In such a configuration, COM may be used as a general client/server implementation model and a replacement for technologies such as RPC (Remote Procedure Calls).

For some applications, this distributed object approach may even be a viable alternative to Python's other client and server-side scripting tools we've studied in this part of the book. Moreover, even when not distributed, COM is an alternative to the lower-level Python/C integration techniques we'll meet later in this book.

Once its learning curve is scaled, COM is a straightforward way to integrate arbitrary components and provides a standardized way to script and reuse systems. However, COM also implies a level of dispatch indirection overhead and is a Windows-only solution at this writing. Because of that, it is generally not as fast or portable as some of the other client/server and C integration schemes discussed in this book. The relevance of such trade-offs varies per application.

As you can probably surmise, there is much more to the Windows scripting story than we cover here. If you are interested in more details, O'Reilly's *Python Programming on Win32* provides an excellent presentation of these and other Windows development topics. Much of the effort that goes into writing scripts embedded in HTML involves using the exposed object model APIs, which are deliberately skipped in this book; see Windows documentation sources for more details.

The New C# Python Compiler

Late-breaking news: a company called ActiveState (*http://www.activestate.com*) announced a new compiler for Python after this chapter was completed. This system (tentatively titled Python.NET) is a new, independent Python language implementation like the JPython system described earlier in this chapter, but compiles Python scripts for use in the Microsoft C# language environment and .NET framework (a software component system based on XML that fosters cross-language interoperability). As such, it opens the door to other Python web scripting roles and modes in the Windows world.

If successful, this new compiler system promises to be the third Python implementation (with JPython and the standard C implementation) and an exciting development for Python in general. Among other things, the C#-based port allows Python scripts to be compiled to binary *.exe* files and developed within the Visual Studio IDE. As in the JPython Java-based implementation, scripts are coded using the standard Python core language presented in this text, and translated to be executed by the underlying C# system. Moreover, .NET interfaces are automatically integrated for use in Python scripts: Python classes may subclass, act as, and use .NET components.

Also like JPython, this new alternative implementation of Python has a specific target audience and will likely prove to be of most interest to developers concerned with C# and .NET framework integration. ActiveState also plans to roll out a whole suite of Python development products besides this new compiler; be sure to watch the Python and ActiveState web sites for more details.

Python Server Pages

Though still somewhat new at this writing, Python Server Pages (PSP) is a server-side technology that embeds JPython code inside HTML. PSP is a Python-based answer to other server-side embedded scripting approaches.

The PSP scripting engine works much like Microsoft's Active Server Pages (ASP, described earlier) and Sun's Java Server Pages (JSP) specification. At the risk of pushing the acronym tolerance envelope, PSP has also been compared to PHP, a server-side scripting language embedded in HTML. All of these systems, including PSP, embed scripts in HTML and run them on the server to generate the response stream sent back to the browser on the client; scripts interact with an exposed object model API to get their work done. PSP is written in pure Java, however, and so is portable to a wide variety of platforms (ASP applications can be run only on Microsoft platforms).

PSP uses JPython as its scripting language, reportedly a vastly more appropriate choice for scripting web sites than the Java language used in Java Server Pages. Since JPython code is embedded under PSP, scripts have access to the large number of Python and JPython tools and add-ons from within PSPs. In addition, scripts may access all Java libraries, thanks to JPython's Java integration support.

We can't cover PSP in detail here; but for a quick look, Example 15-18, adapted from an example in the PSP documentation, illustrates the structure of PSPs.

Example 15-18. PP2E\Internet\Other\hello.psp

```
$[
# Generate a simple message page with the client's IP address
]$
<HTML><HEAD>
<TITLE>Hello PSP World</TITLE>
</HEAD>
<BODY>
$[include banner.psp]$
<H1>Hello PSP World</H1>
<BR>
$[
Response.write("Hello from PSP, %s." % (Request.server["REMOTE_ADDR"]) )
]$
<BR>
</BODY></HTML>
```

A page like this would be installed on a PSP-aware server machine and referenced by URL from a browser. PSP uses $[and]$ delimiters to enclose JPython code embedded in HTML; anything outside these pairs is simply sent to the client browser, while code within these markers is executed. The first code block here is a JPython comment (note the # character); the second is an **include** statement that simply inserts another PSP file's contents.

The third piece of embedded code is more useful. As in Active Scripting technologies, Python code embedded in HTML uses an exposed object API to interact with the execution context—in this case, the `Response` object is used to write output to the client's browser (much like a `print` in a CGI script), and `Request` is used to access HTTP headers for the request. The `Request` object also has a `params` dictionary containing `GET` and `POST` input parameters, as well as a `cookies` dictionary holding cookie information stored on the client by a PSP application.

Notice that the previous example could have just as easily been implemented with a Python CGI script using a Python `print` statement, but PSP's full benefit becomes clearer in large pages that embed and execute much more complex JPython code to produce a response.

PSP runs as a Java servlet and requires the hosting web site to support the Java Servlet API, all of which is beyond the scope of this text. For more details about PSP, visit its web site, currently located at *http://www.ciobriefings.com/psp*, but search *http://www.python.org* for other links if this one changes over time.

Rolling Your Own Servers in Python

Most of the Internet modules we looked at in the last few chapters deal with client-side interfaces such as FTP and POP, or special server-side protocols such as CGI that hide the underlying server itself. If you want to build servers in Python by hand, you can do so either manually or by using higher-level tools.

Coding Solutions

We saw the sort of code needed to build servers manually in Chapter 10, *Network Scripting*. Python programs typically implement servers either by using raw socket calls with threads, forks, or selects to handle clients in parallel, or by using the `SocketServer` module.

In either case, to serve requests made in terms of higher-level protocols such as FTP, NNTP, and HTTP, you must listen on the protocol's port and add appropriate code to handle the protocol's message conventions. If you go this route, the client-side protocol modules in Python's standard library can help you understand the message conventions used. You may also be able to uncover protocol server examples in the Demos and Tools directories of the Python source distribution and on the Net at large (search *http://www.python.org*). See prior chapters for more details on writing socket-based servers.

As a higher-level interface, Python also comes with precoded HTTP web protocol server implementations, in the form of three standard modules. `BaseHTTPServer` implements the server itself; this class is derived from the standard `SocketServer.TCPServer` class. `SimpleHTTPServer` and `CGIHTTPServer` implement standard handlers for incoming HTTP requests; the former handles simple web page file requests, while the latter also runs referenced CGI scripts on the server machine by forking processes.

For example, to start a CGI-capable HTTP server, simply run Python code like that shown in Example 15-19 on the server machine.

Example 15-19. PP2E\Internet\Other\webserver.py

```
#!/usr/bin/python
###########################################
# implement a HTTP server in Python which
# knows how to run server-side CGI scripts;
# change root dir for your server machine
###########################################

import os
from BaseHTTPServer import HTTPServer
from CGIHTTPServer   import CGIHTTPRequestHandler
os.chdir("/home/httpd/html")                        # run in html root dir
srvraddr = ("", 80)                                 # my hostname, portnumber
srvrobj  = HTTPServer(srvraddr, CGIHTTPRequestHandler)
srvrobj.serve_forever()                             # run as perpetual demon
```

This assumes that you have appropriate permissions to run such a script, of course; see the Python library manual for more details on precoded HTTP server and request handler modules. Once you have your server running, you can access it in any web browser or by using either the Python `httplib` module, which implements the client side of the HTTP protocol, or the Python `urllib` module, which provides a file-like interface to data fetched from a named URL address (see the `urllib` examples in Chapter 11, *Client-Side Scripting*, and Chapter 13, *Larger Web Site Examples I*, and use a URL of the form "http://..." to access HTTP documents).

Packaged Solutions

Finally, you can deploy full-blown, open source, and Python-friendly web servers and tools that are freely available on the Net. These may change over time too, but here are a few current options:

Medusa, asyncore

> The Medusa system (*http://www.nightmare.com/medusa*) is an architecture for building long-running, high-performance network servers in Python, and is used in several mission-critical systems. Beginning in Python 1.5.2, the core of Medusa is now standard in Python, in the form of the `asyncore` and `asynchat` library modules. These standard modules may be used by themselves to build high-performance network servers, based on an asynchronous, multiplexing, single-process model. They use an event loop built using the `select` system call presented in Chapter 10 of this book to provide concurrency without spawning threads or processes, and are well-suited to handling

short-lived transactions. See the Python library for details. The complete Medusa system (not shipped with Python) also provides precoded HTTP and FTP servers; it is free for noncommercial use, but requires a license otherwise.

Zope

If you are doing any server-side work at all, be sure to consider the Zope open source web application server, described earlier in this chapter and at *http://www.zope.org*. Zope provides a full-featured web framework that implements an object model that is well beyond standard server-side CGI scripting. The Zope world has also developed full-blown servers (e.g., Zserver).

Mailman

If you are looking for email list support, be sure to explore the GNU mailing list manager, otherwise known as Mailman. Written in Python, Mailman provides a robust, quick, and feature-rich email discussion list tool. Mailman allows users to subscribe over the Web, supports web-based administration, and provides mail-to-news gateways and integrated spam prevention (spam of the junk mail variety, that is). At this time, *http://www.list.org* is the place to find more Mailman details.

Apache

If you are adventurous, you may be interested in the highly configurable Apache open source web server. Apache is one of the dominant servers used on the Web today, despite its free nature. Among many other things, it supports running Python server-side scripts in a variety of modes; see the site *http://www.apache.org* for details on Apache itself.

PyApache

If you use Apache, also search the Python web site for information on the *PyApache* Apache server module (sometimes called `mod_pyapache`), which embeds a Python interpreter inside Apache to speed up the process of launching Python server-side scripts. CGI scripts are passed to the embedded interpreter directly, avoiding interpreter startup costs. PyApache also opens up the possibility of scripting Apache's internal components.

mod_python

As I wrote this chapter, another package for embedding Python within the Apache web server appeared on the open source landscape: `mod_python`, available at *http://www.modpython.org*. According to its release notes, `mod_python` also allows Python to be embedded in Apache, with a substantial boost in performance and added flexibility. The beta release announcement for this system appeared on *comp.lang.python* the very week that this section was written, so check the Web for its current status.

Be sure to watch *http://www.python.org* for new developments on the server front, as well as late-breaking advances in Python web scripting techniques in general.

IV

Assorted Topics

This part of the book is a collection of additional Python application topics. Most of the tools presented along the way can be used in a wide variety of application domains. You'll find the following chapters here:

- Chapter 16, *Databases and Persistence*. This chapter covers commonly used and advanced Python techniques for storing information between program executions—DBM files, object pickling (serialization), object shelves, and Python's SQL database interfaces.

- Chapter 17, *Data Structures*. This chapter explores techniques for implementing more advanced data structures in Python—stacks, sets, binary search trees, graphs, and the like. In Python, these take the form of object implementations.

- Chapter 18, *Text and Language*. This chapter addresses Python tools and techniques for parsing text-based information—string splits and joins, regular expression matching, recursive descent parsing, and advanced language-based topics.

This is the last pure Python part of the book and makes heavy use of tools presented earlier in the text, especially the Tkinter GUI library. For instance, a tree browser is used to illustrate various object structures, a form browser helps make database concepts more concrete, and a calculator GUI serves to demonstrate language processing and code reuse concepts.

16

Databases and Persistence

"Give Me an Order of Persistence, but Hold the Pickles"

So far in this book, we've used Python in the system programming, GUI development, and Internet scripting domains—three of Python's most common applications. In the next three chapters, we're going to take a quick look at other major Python programming topics: persistent data, data structure techniques, and text and language processing tools. None of these are covered exhaustively (each could easily fill a book alone), but we'll sample Python in action in these domains and highlight their core concepts. If any of these chapters spark your interest, additional resources are readily available in the Python world.

Persistence Options in Python

In this chapter, our focus is on *persistent* data—the kind that outlives a program that creates it. That's not true by default for objects a script constructs; things like lists, dictionaries, and even class instance objects live in your computer's memory and are lost as soon as the script ends. To make data longer-lived, we need to do something special. In Python programming, there are at least five traditional ways to save information between program executions:

- Flat files: storing text and bytes
- DBM keyed files: keyed access to strings
- Pickled objects: serializing objects to byte streams
- Shelve files: storing pickled objects in DBM keyed files
- Database systems: full-blown SQL and object database systems

We studied Python's simple (or "flat") file interfaces in earnest in Chapter 2, *System Tools*, and have been using them ever since. Python provides standard access to both the `stdio` filesystem (through the built-in `open` function), as well as lower-level descriptor-based files (with the built-in `os` module). For simple data storage tasks, these are all that many scripts need. To save for use in a future program run, simply write data out to a newly opened file on your computer and read it back from that file later. As we've seen, for more advanced tasks, Python also supports other file-like interfaces such as pipes, fifos, and sockets.

Since we've already explored flat files, I won't say more about them here. The rest of this chapter introduces the remaining topics on the list earlier in this section. At the end, we'll also meet a GUI program for browsing the contents of things like shelves and DBM files. Before that, though, we need to learn what manner of beast these are.

DBM Files

Flat files are handy for simple persistence tasks, but are generally geared towards a sequential processing mode. Although it is possible to jump around to arbitrary locations with `seek` calls, flat files don't provide much structure to data beyond the notion of bytes and text lines.

DBM files, a standard tool in the Python library for database management, improve on that by providing key-based access to stored text strings. They implement a random-access, single-key view on stored data. For instance, information related to objects can be stored in a DBM file using a unique key per object and later can be fetched back directly with the same key. DBM files are implemented by a variety of underlying modules (including one coded in Python), but if you have Python, you have a DBM.

Using DBM Files

Although DBM filesystems have to do a bit of work to map chunks of stored data to keys for fast retrieval (technically, they generally use a technique called hashing to store data in files), your scripts don't need to care about the action going on behind the scenes. In fact, DBM is one of the easiest ways to save information in Python—DBM files behave so much like in-memory dictionaries that you may forget you're actually dealing with a file. For instance, given a DBM file object:

- Indexing by key fetches data from the file.

- Assigning to an index stores data in the file.

DBM file objects also support common dictionary methods such as keys-list fetches and tests, and key deletions. The DBM library itself is hidden behind this simple model. Since it is so simple, let's jump right into an interactive example that creates a DBM file and shows how the interface works:

```
% python
>>> import anydbm                          # get interface: dbm, gdbm, ndbm,..
>>> file = anydbm.open('movie', 'c')       # make a dbm file called 'movie'
>>> file['Batman'] = 'Pow!'                # store a string under key 'Batman'
>>> file.keys()                            # get the file's key directory
['Batman']
>>> file['Batman']                         # fetch value for key 'Batman'
'Pow!'

>>> who  = ['Robin', 'Cat-woman', 'Joker']
>>> what = ['Bang!', 'Splat!', 'Wham!']
>>> for i in range(len(who)):
...     file[who[i]] = what[i]             # add 3 more "records"
...
>>> file.keys()
['Joker', 'Robin', 'Cat-woman', 'Batman']
>>> len(file), file.has_key('Robin'), file['Joker']
(4, 1, 'Wham!')
>>> file.close()                           # close sometimes required
```

Internally, importing anydbm automatically loads whatever DBM interface is available in your Python interpreter, and opening the new DBM file creates one or more external files with names that start with the string "movie" (more on the details in a moment). But after the import and open, a DBM file is virtually indistinguishable from a dictionary. In effect, the object called `file` here can be thought of as a dictionary mapped to an external file called `movie`.

Unlike normal dictionaries, though, the contents of `file` are retained between Python program runs. If we come back later and restart Python, our dictionary is still available. DBM files are like dictionaries that must be opened:

```
% python
>>> import anydbm
>>> file = anydbm.open('movie', 'c')       # open existing dbm file
>>> file['Batman']
'Pow!'

>>> file.keys()                            # keys gives an index list
['Joker', 'Robin', 'Cat-woman', 'Batman']
>>> for key in file.keys(): print key, file[key]
...
Joker Wham!
Robin Bang!
Cat-woman Splat!
Batman Pow!

>>> file['Batman'] = 'Ka-Boom!'            # change Batman slot
>>> del file['Robin']                      # delete the Robin entry
>>> file.close()                           # close it after changes
```

Apart from having to import the interface and open and close the DBM file, Python programs don't have to know anything about DBM itself. DBM modules achieve this integration by overloading the indexing operations and routing them to more primitive library tools. But you'd never know that from looking at this Python code—DBM files look like normal Python dictionaries, stored on external files. Changes made to them are retained indefinitely:

```
% python
>>> import anydbm                          # open dbm file again
>>> file = anydbm.open('movie', 'c')
>>> for key in file.keys(): print key, file[key]
...
Joker Wham!
Cat-woman Splat!
Batman Ka-Boom!
```

As you can see, this is about as simple as it can be. Table 16-1 lists the most commonly used DBM file operations. Once such a file is opened, it is processed just as though it were an in-memory Python dictionary. Items are fetched by indexing the file object by key and stored by assigning to a key.

Table 16-1. DBM File Operations

Python Code	Action	Description
`import anydbm`	Import	Get dbm, gdbm,... whatever is installed
`file = anydbm.open('filename', 'c')`	Open[a]	Create or open an existing DBM file
`file['key'] = 'value'`	Store	Create or change the entry for key
`value = file['key']`	Fetch	Load the value for entry key
`count = len(file)`	Size	Return the number of entries stored
`index = file.keys()`	Index	Fetch the stored keys list
`found = file. has_key('key')`	Query	See if there's an entry for key
`del file['key']`	Delete	Remove the entry for key
`file.close()`	Close	Manual close, not always needed

[a] In Python versions 1.5.2 and later, be sure to pass a string c as a second argument when calling anydbm. open, to force Python to create the file if it does not yet exist, and simply open it otherwise. This used to be the default behavior but is no longer. You do not need the c argument when opening shelves discussed ahead—they still use an "open or create" mode by default if passed no open mode argument. Other open mode strings can be passed to anydbm (e.g., n to always create the file, and r for read only—the new default); see the library reference manuals for more details.

Despite the dictionary-like interface, DBM files really do map to one or more external files. For instance, the underlying gdbm interface writes two files, *movie.dir* and *movie.pag*, when a GDBM file called movie is made. If your Python was built with a different underlying keyed-file interface, different external files might show up on your computer.

Technically, module `anydbm` is really an interface to whatever DBM-like filesystem you have available in your Python. When creating a new file, `anydbm` today tries to load the `dbhash`, `gdbm`, and `dbm` keyed-file interface modules; Pythons without any of these automatically fall back on an all-Python implementation called `dumbdbm`. When opening an already-existing DBM file, `anydbm` tries to determine the system that created it with the `whichdb` module instead. You normally don't need to care about any of this, though (unless you delete the files your DBM creates).

Note that DBM files may or may not need to be explicitly closed, per the last entry in Table 16-1. Some DBM files don't require a close call, but some depend on it to flush changes out to disk. On such systems, your file may be corrupted if you omit the close call. Unfortunately, the default DBM on the 1.5.2 Windows Python port, `dbhash` (a.k.a., `bsddb`), is one of the DBM systems that requires a close call to avoid data loss. As a rule of thumb, always close your DBM files explicitly after making changes and before your program exits, to avoid potential problems. This rule extends by proxy to shelves, a topic we'll meet later in this chapter.

Pickled Objects

Probably the biggest limitation of DBM keyed files is in what they can store: data stored under a key must be a simple text string. If you want to store Python objects in a DBM file, you can sometimes manually convert them to and from strings on writes and reads (e.g., with `str` and `eval` calls), but this only takes you so far. For arbitrarily complex Python objects like class instances, you need something more. Class instance objects, for example, cannot be later recreated from their standard string representations.

The Python `pickle` module, a standard part of the Python system, provides the conversion step needed. It converts Python in-memory objects to and from a single linear string format, suitable for storing in flat files, shipping across network sockets, and so on. This conversion from object to string is often called *serialization*—arbitrary data structures in memory are mapped to a serial string form. The string representation used for objects is also sometimes referred to as a byte-stream, due to its linear format.

Using Object Pickling

Pickling may sound complicated the first time you encounter it, but the good news is that Python hides all the complexity of object-to-string conversion. In fact, the pickle module's interfaces are incredibly simple to use. The following list describes a few details of this interface.

`P = pickle.Pickler(`*file*`)`
> Make a new pickler for pickling to an open output file object `file`.

`P.dump(`*object*`)`
> Write an object onto the pickler's file/stream.

`pickle.dump(`*object, file*`)`
> Same as the last two calls combined: pickle an object onto an open file.

`U = pickle.Unpickler(`*file*`)`
> Make an unpickler for unpickling from an open input file object `file`.

`object = U.load()`
> Read an object from the unpickler's file/stream.

`object = pickle.load(`*file*`)`
> Same as the last two calls combined: unpickle an object from an open file.

`string = pickle.dumps(`*object*`)`
> Return the pickled representation of `object` as a character string.

`object = pickle.loads(`*string*`)`
> Read an object from a character string instead of a file.

`Pickler` and `Unpickler` are exported classes. In all of these, `file` is either an open file object or any object that implements the same attributes as file objects:

- `Pickler` calls the file's `write` method with a string argument.

- `Unpickler` calls the file's `read` method with a byte count, and `readline` without arguments.

Any object that provides these attributes can be passed in to the "file" parameters. In particular, `file` can be an instance of a Python class that provides the read/write methods. This lets you map pickled streams to in-memory objects, for arbitrary use. It also lets you ship Python objects across a network, by providing sockets wrapped to look like files in pickle calls at the sender and unpickle calls at the receiver (see the sidebar "Making Sockets Look Like Files" in Chapter 10, *Network Scripting*, for more details).

In more typical use, to pickle an object to a flat file, we just open the file in write-mode, and call the `dump` function; to unpickle, reopen and call `load`:

```
% python
>>> import pickle
>>> table = {'a': [1, 2, 3], 'b': ['spam', 'eggs'], 'c':{'name':'bob'}}
>>> mydb  = open('dbase', 'w')
>>> pickle.dump(table, mydb)

% python
>>> import pickle
>>> mydb  = open('dbase', 'r')
```

```
>>> table = pickle.load(mydb)
>>> table
```

```
{'b': ['spam', 'eggs'], 'a': [1, 2, 3], 'c': {'name': 'bob'}}
```

To make this process simpler still, the module in Example 16-1 wraps pickling and unpickling calls in functions that also open the files where the serialized form of the object is stored.

Example 16-1. PP2E\Dbase\filepickle.py

```
import pickle

def saveDbase(filename, object):
    file = open(filename, 'w')
    pickle.dump(object, file)      # pickle to file
    file.close()                   # any file-like object will do

def loadDbase(filename):
    file = open(filename, 'r')
    object = pickle.load(file)     # unpickle from file
    file.close()                   # recreates object in memory
    return object
```

To store and fetch now, simply call these module functions:

```
C:\...\PP2E\Dbase>python
>>> from filepickle import *
>>> L = [0]
>>> D = {'x':0, 'y':L}
>>> table = {'A':L, 'B':D}      # L appears twice
>>> saveDbase('myfile', table)   # serialize to file

C:\...\PP2E\Dbase>python
>>> from filepickle import *
>>> table = loadDbase('myfile')  # reload/unpickle
>>> table
{'B': {'x': 0, 'y': [0]}, 'A': [0]}
>>> table['A'][0] = 1
>>> saveDbase('myfile', table)

C:\...\PP2E\Dbase>python
>>> from filepickle import *
>>> print loadDbase('myfile')    # both L's updated as expected
{'B': {'x': 0, 'y': [1]}, 'A': [1]}
```

Python can pickle just about anything, except compiled code objects, instances of classes that do not follow importability rules we'll meet later, and instances of some built-in and user-defined types that are coded in C or depend upon transient operating system states (e.g., open file objects cannot be pickled). A `PicklingError` is raised if an object cannot be pickled.

Refer to Python's library manual for more information on the pickler. And while you are flipping (or clicking) through that manual, be sure to also see the entries for the `cPickle` module—a reimplementation of `pickle` coded in C for faster performance. Also check out `marshal`, a module that serializes an object, too, but can only handle simple object types. If available in your Python, the `shelve` module automatically chooses the `cPickle` module for faster serialization, not `pickle`. I haven't explained `shelve` yet, but I will now.

Shelve Files

Pickling allows you to store arbitrary objects on files and file-like objects, but it's still a fairly unstructured medium; it doesn't directly support easy access to members of collections of pickled objects. Higher-level structures can be added, but they are not inherent:

- You can sometimes craft your own higher-level pickle file organizations with the underlying filesystem (e.g., you can store each pickled object in a file whose name uniquely identifies the object), but such an organization is not part of pickling itself and must be manually managed.

- You can also store arbitrarily large dictionaries in a pickled file and index them by key after they are loaded back into memory; but this will load the entire dictionary all at once when unpickled, not just the entry you are interested in.

Shelves provide some structure to collections of pickled objects. They are a type of file that stores arbitrary Python objects by key for later retrieval, and they are a standard part of the Python system. Really, they are not much of a new topic—shelves are simply a combination of DBM files and object pickling:

- To store an in-memory object by key, the `shelve` module first serializes the object to a string with the `pickle` module, and then it stores that string in a DBM file by key with the `anydbm` module.

- To fetch an object back by key, the `shelve` module first loads the object's serialized string by key from a DBM file with the `anydbm` module, and then converts it back to the original in-memory object with the `pickle` module.

Because `shelve` uses `pickle` internally, it can store any object that `pickle` can: strings, numbers, lists, dictionaries, cyclic objects, class instances, and more.

Using Shelves

In other words, `shelve` is just a go-between; it serializes and deserializes objects so that they can be placed in DBM files. The net effect is that shelves let you store nearly arbitrary Python objects on a file by key, and fetch them back later with the same key. Your scripts never see all this interfacing, though. Like DBM files, shelves provide an interface that looks like a dictionary that must be opened. To gain access to a shelve, import the module and open your file:

```
import shelve
dbase = shelve.open("mydbase")
```

Internally, Python opens a DBM file with name *mydbase*, or creates it if it does not yet exist. Assigning to a shelve key stores an object:

```
dbase['key'] = object
```

Internally, this assignment converts the object to a serialized byte-stream and stores it by key on a DBM file. Indexing a shelve fetches a stored object:

```
value = dbase['key']
```

Internally, this index operation loads a string by key from a DBM file and unpickles it into an in-memory object that is the same as the object originally stored. Most dictionary operations are supported here, too:

```
len(dbase)        # number of items stored
dbase.keys()      # stored item key index
```

And except for a few fine points, that's really all there is to using a shelve. Shelves are processed with normal Python dictionary syntax, so there is no new database API to learn. Moreover, objects stored and fetched from shelves are normal Python objects; they do not need to be instances of special classes or types to be stored away. That is, Python's persistence system is external to the persistent objects themselves. Table 16-2 summarizes these and other commonly used shelve operations.

Table 16-2. Shelve File Operations

Python Code	Action	Description
`import shelve`	Import	Get dbm, gdbm,... whatever is installed
`file = shelve.open('filename')`	Open	Create or open an existing DBM file
`file['key'] = anyvalue`	Store	Create or change the entry for key
`value = file['key']`	Fetch	Load the value for entry key
`count = len(file)`	Size	Return the number of entries stored
`index = file.keys()`	Index	Fetch the stored keys list
`found = file. has_key('key')`	Query	See if there's an entry for key
`del file['key']`	Delete	Remove the entry for key
`file.close()`	Close	Manual close, not always needed

Because shelves export a dictionary-like interface, too, this table is almost identical to the DBM operation table. Here, though, the module name **anydbm** is replaced by **shelve**, **open** calls do not require a second c argument, and stored

values can be nearly arbitrary kinds of objects, not just strings. You still should
close shelves explicitly after making changes to be safe, though; shelves use
anydbm internally and some underlying DBMs require closes to avoid data loss or
damage.

Storing Built-in Object Types

Let's run an interactive session to experiment with shelve interfaces:

```
% python
>>> import shelve
>>> dbase = shelve.open("mydbase")
>>> object1 = ['The', 'bright', ('side', 'of'), ['life']]
>>> object2 = {'name': 'Brian', 'age': 33, 'motto': object1}
>>> dbase['brian']  = object2
>>> dbase['knight'] = {'name': 'Knight', 'motto': 'Ni!'}
>>> dbase.close()
```

Here, we open a shelve and store two fairly complex dictionary and list data structures away permanently by simply assigning them to shelve keys. Because shelve
uses pickle internally, almost anything goes here—the trees of nested objects are
automatically serialized into strings for storage. To fetch them back, just reopen
the shelve and index:

```
% python
>>> import shelve
>>> dbase = shelve.open("mydbase")
>>> len(dbase)                        # entries
2

>>> dbase.keys()                      # index
['knight', 'brian']

>>> dbase['knight']                   # fetch
{'motto': 'Ni!', 'name': 'Knight'}

>>> for row in dbase.keys():
...     print row, '=>'
...     for field in dbase[row].keys():
...         print '  ', field, '=', dbase[row][field]
...
knight =>
   motto = Ni!
   name = Knight
brian =>
   motto = ['The', 'bright', ('side', 'of'), ['life']]
   age = 33
   name = Brian
```

The nested loops at the end of this session step through nested dictionaries—the
outer scans the shelve, and the inner scans the objects stored in the shelve. The

crucial point to notice is that we're using normal Python syntax both to store and to fetch these persistent objects as well as to process them after loading.

Storing Class Instances

One of the more useful kinds of objects to store in a shelve is a class instance. Because its attributes record state and its inherited methods define behavior, persistent class objects effectively serve the roles of both database records and database-processing programs. For instance, consider the simple class shown in Example 16-2, which is used to model people.

Example 16-2. PP2E\Dbase\person.py (version 1)

```
# a person object: fields + behavior

class Person:
    def __init__(self, name, job, pay=0):
        self.name = name
        self.job  = job
        self.pay  = pay          # real instance data
    def tax(self):
        return self.pay * 0.25   # computed on call
    def info(self):
        return self.name, self.job, self.pay, self.tax()
```

We can make some persistent objects from this class by simply creating instances as usual, and storing them by key on an opened shelve:

```
C:\...\PP2E\Dbase>python
>>> from person import Person
>>> bob   = Person('bob', 'psychologist', 70000)
>>> emily = Person('emily', 'teacher', 40000)
>>>
>>> import shelve
>>> dbase = shelve.open('cast')      # make new shelve
>>> for obj in (bob, emily):         # store objects
...     dbase[obj.name] = obj        # use name for key
>>> dbase.close()                    # need for bsddb
```

When we come back and fetch these objects in a later Python session or script, they are recreated in memory as they were when they were stored:

```
C:\...\PP2E\Dbase>python
>>> import shelve
>>> dbase = shelve.open('cast')      # reopen shelve
>>>
>>> dbase.keys()                     # both objects are here
['emily', 'bob']
>>> print dbase['emily']
<person.Person instance at 799940>
>>>
>>> print dbase['bob'].tax()         # call: bob's tax
17500.0
```

Notice that calling Bob's `tax` method works even though we didn't import the
`Person` class here. Python is smart enough to link this object back to its original
class when unpickled, such that all the original methods are available through
fetched objects.

Changing Classes of Stored Objects

Technically, Python reimports a class to recreate its stored instances as they are
fetched and unpickled. Here's how this works:

Store

> When Python pickles a class instance to store it in a shelve, it saves the
> instance's attributes plus a reference to the instance's class. Really, Python seri-
> alizes and stores the instance's `__dict__` attribute dictionary along with
> source file information for the class's module.

Fetch

> When Python unpickles a class instance fetched from a shelve, it recreates the
> instance object in memory by reimporting the class and assigning the saved
> attribute dictionary to a new empty instance of the class.

The key point in this is that the class itself is not stored with its instances, but is
instead reimported later when instances are fetched. The upshot is that by modifying external classes in module files, we can change the way stored objects' data is
interpreted and used without actually having to change those stored objects. It's as
if the class is a program that processes stored records.

To illustrate, suppose the `Person` class from the previous section was changed to
the source code in Example 16-3.

Example 16-3. PP2E\Dbase\person.py (version 2)

```
# a person object: fields + behavior
# change: the tax method is now a computed attribute

class Person:
    def __init__(self, name, job, pay=0):
        self.name = name
        self.job  = job
        self.pay  = pay                # real instance data
    def __getattr__(self, attr):       # on person.attr
        if attr == 'tax':
            return self.pay * 0.30     # computed on access
        else:
            raise AttributeError       # other unknown names
    def info(self):
        return self.name, self.job, self.pay, self.tax
```

This revision has a new tax rate (30%), introduces a __getattr__ qualification overload method, and deletes the original `tax` method. Tax attribute references are intercepted and computed when accessed:

```
C:\...\PP2E\Dbase>python
>>> import shelve
>>> dbase = shelve.open('cast')      # reopen shelve
>>>
>>> print dbase.keys()               # both objects are here
['emily', 'bob']
>>> print dbase['emily']
<person.Person instance at 79aea0>
>>>
>>> print dbase['bob'].tax           # no need to call tax()
21000.0
```

Because the class has changed, `tax` is now simply qualified, not called. In addition, because the tax rate was changed in the class, Bob pays more this time around. Of course, this example is artificial, but when used well, this separation of classes and persistent instances can eliminate many traditional database update programs—in most cases, you can simply change the class, not each stored instance, for new behavior.

Shelve Constraints

Although shelves are generally straightforward to use, there are a few rough edges worth knowing about.

Keys must be strings

First of all, although they can store arbitrary objects, keys must still be strings. The following fails, unless you convert the integer 42 to string "42" manually first:

```
dbase[42] = value       # fails, but str(42) will work
```

This is different from in-memory dictionaries, which allow any immutable object to be used as a key, and derives from the shelve's use of DBM files internally.

Objects are only unique within a key

Although the `shelve` module is smart enough to detect multiple occurrences of a nested object and recreate only one copy when fetched, this only holds true within a given slot:

```
dbase[key] = [object, object]     # okay: only one copy stored and fetched

dbase[key1] = object
dbase[key2] = object              # bad?: two copies of object in the shelve
```

When `key1` and `key2` are fetched, they reference independent copies of the original shared object; if that object is mutable, changes from one won't be reflected in the other. This really stems from the fact the each key assignment runs an independent pickle operation—the pickler detects repeated objects but only within each pickle call. This may or may not be a concern in your practice and can be avoided with extra support logic, but an object can be duplicated if it spans keys.

Updates must treat shelves as fetch-modify-store mappings

Because objects fetched from a shelve don't know that they came from a shelve, operations that change components of a fetched object only change the in-memory copy, not the data on a shelve:

```
dbase[key].attr = value    # shelve unchanged
```

To really change an object stored on a shelve, fetch it into memory, change its parts, and then write it back to the shelve as a whole by key assignment:

```
object = dbase[key]        # fetch it
object.attr = value        # modify it
dbase[key] = object        # store back-shelve changed
```

Concurrent updates not allowed

As we learned near the end of Chapter 14, *Larger Web Site Examples II*, the `shelve` module does not currently support simultaneous updates. Simultaneous readers are okay, but writers must be given exclusive access to the shelve. You can trash a shelve if multiple processes write to it at the same time, and this is a common potential in things like CGI server-side scripts. If your shelves may be hit by multiple processes, be sure to wrap updates in calls to the `fcntl.flock` built-in we explored in Chapter 14.

Pickler class constraints

In addition to these shelve constraints, storing class instances in a shelve adds a set of additional rules you need to be aware of. Really, these are imposed by the `pickle` module, not `shelve`, so be sure to follow these if you store class objects with `pickle` directly, too.

Classes must be importable

The Python pickler stores instance attributes only when pickling an instance object, and reimports the class later to recreate the instance. Because of that, the classes of stored objects must be importable when objects are unpickled—they must be coded unnested at the top level of a module file visible on PYTHONPATH. Further, they must be associated with a real module when instances are pickled, not a top-level script (with module name `__main__`), and you need to be careful about moving class modules after instances are stored. When an instance is unpickled, Python must find its class's module on

PYTHONPATH using the original module name (including any package path prefixes), and fetch the class from that module using the original class name. If the module or class has been moved or renamed, it might not be found.

Class changes must be backwards-compatible

Although Python lets you change a class while instances of it are stored on a shelve, those changes must be backwards-compatible with the objects already stored. For instance, you cannot change the class to expect an attribute not associated with already-stored persistent instances unless you first manually update those stored instances or provide extra conversion protocols on the class.

In a prior Python release, persistent object classes also had to either use constructors with no arguments, or they had to provide defaults for all constructor arguments (much like the notion of a C++ copy constructor). This constraint was dropped as of Python 1.5.2—classes with non-defaulted constructor arguments now work fine in the pickling system.[*]

Other persistence limitations

In addition to the above constraints, keep in mind that files created by an underlying DBM system are not necessarily compatible with all possible DBM implementations. For instance, a file generated by `gdbm` may not be readable by a Python with another DBM module installed, unless you explicitly import `gdbm` instead of `anydbm` (assuming it's installed at all). If DBM file portability is a concern, make sure that all the Pythons that will read your data use compatible DBM modules.

Finally, although shelves store objects persistently, they are not really object-oriented database systems (OODBs). Such systems also implement features like object decomposition and delayed ("lazy") component fetches, based on generated object IDs: parts of larger objects are loaded into memory only as they are accessed. It's possible to extend shelves to support such features, but you don't need to—the Zope system described in Chapter 15, *Advanced Internet Topics*, includes an implementation of a more complete OODB system. It is constructed on top of Python's built-in persistence support, but offers additional features for advanced data stores. See the previous chapter for information and links.

---

[*] Subtle thing: internally, Python now avoids calling the class to recreate a pickled instance and instead simply makes a class object generically, inserts instance attributes, and sets the instance's `__class__` pointer to the original class directly. This avoids the need for defaults, but it also means that the class `__init__` constructors are no longer called as objects are unpickled, unless you provide extra methods to force the call. See the library manual for more details, and see the `pickle` module's source code (*pickle.py* in the source library) if you're curious about how this works. Better yet, see the `formtable` module listed ahead in this chapter—it does something very similar with `__class__` links to build an instance object from a class and dictionary of attributes, without calling the class's `__init__` constructor. This makes constructor argument defaults unnecessary in classes used for records browsed by PyForm, but it's the same idea.

SQL Database Interfaces

Shelves are a powerful tool; they allow scripts to throw Python objects on a keyed-access file and load them back later in a single step. They aren't quite a full-blown database system, though; objects (records) are accessed with a single key, and there is no notion of SQL queries. It's as if shelves were a database with a single index and no other query-processing support.

Although it's possible to build a multiple-index interface to store data with multiple shelves, it's not a trivial task and requires manually coded extensions (see the dbaseindexed module in the PyErrata system near the end of Chapter 14 for a prototype of this concept).

For industrial-strength persistence needs, Python also supports relational database systems. Today, there are freely available interfaces that let Python scripts utilize all common database systems, both free and commercial: Oracle, Sybase, Informix, mSql, MySql, Interbase, Postgres, ODBC, and more. In addition, the Python community has defined a database API specification that works portably with a variety of underlying database packages. Scripts written for this API can be migrated to different database vendor packages with minimal or no source code changes.

Interface Overview

Unlike all the persistence topics presented in this chapter and book so far, though, SQL databases are optional extensions that are not part of Python itself, and you need to know SQL to make the most sense of their interfaces. Because I don't have space to teach SQL in this text, this section instead gives a brief overview of the API; please consult other SQL references and the database API resources mentioned in the next section for more details.

The good news is that you can access SQL databases from Python, through a straightforward and portable model. The Python database API specification defines an interface for communicating with underlying database systems from Python scripts. Vendor-specific database interfaces for Python may or may not conform to this API completely, but all database extensions for Python seem minor variations on a theme. SQL databases in Python are grounded on a few concepts:

*   *Connection objects* represent a connection to a database, are the interface to rollback and commit operations, and generate cursor objects.

*   *Cursor objects* represent a single SQL statement submitted as a string, and can be used to step through SQL statement results.

- *Query results* of SQL `select` statements are returned to scripts as Python lists of Python tuples, representing database tables of rows. Within these row tuples, field values are normal Python objects such as strings, integers, and floats, or special types (e.g., `[('bob',38), ('emily',37)]`).

Beyond this, the API defines a standard set of database exception types, special database type object constructors (e.g., nulls and dates), and informational calls.

For instance, to establish a database connection under the Python API-compliant Oracle interface available from Digital Creations, install the extension and then run a line of this form:

```
connobj = Connect("user/password@system")
```

The string argument's contents may vary per database and vendor, but they generally contain what you provide to log in to your database system. Once you have a connection object, there a variety of things you can do with it, including:

`connobj.close()`	*close connection now (not at object __del__ time)*
`connobj.commit()`	*commit any pending transactions to the database*
`connobj.rollback()`	*roll database back to start of pending transactions*
`connobj.getSource(proc)`	*fetch stored procedure's code*

But one of the most useful things to do with a connection object is to generate a cursor object:

```
cursobj = connobj.cursor()       return a new cursor object for running SQL
```

Cursor objects have a set of methods, too (e.g., `close` to close the cursor before its destructor runs), but the most important may be this one:

```
cursobj.execute(sqlstring [, parm, parm,...])    run SQL query or command string
```

The `execute` method can be used to run a variety of SQL statement strings:

- *DDL* definition statements (e.g., CREATE TABLE)

- *DML* modification statements (e.g., UPDATE or INSERT)

- *DQL* query statements (e.g., SELECT)

For DML statements, `execute` returns the number of rows effected. For DQL query statements, a `None` is returned and you must call one of the `fetch` methods to complete the operation:

```
tuple       = cursobj.fetchone()      fetch next row of a query result
listoftuple = cursobj.fetchmany([size])  fetch next set of rows of query result
listoftuple = cursobj.fetchall()      fetch all remaining rows of the result
```

And once you've received fetch method results, table information is processed using normal Python list and tuple object operations (e.g., you can step through the tuples in a `fetchall` result list with a simple `for` loop). Most Python database interfaces also allow you to provide values to be passed to SQL statement strings, by providing targets and a tuple of parameters. For instance:

```
query = 'SELECT name, shoesize FROM spam WHERE job = ? AND age = ?'
cursobj.execute(query, (value1, value2))
results = cursobj.fetchall()
for row in results: ...
```

In this event, the database interface utilizes prepared statements (an optimization and convenience) and correctly passes the parameters to the database regardless of their Python types. The notation used to code targets in the query string may vary in some database interfaces (e.g., ":p1" and ":p2", rather than "?" and "?"); in any event, this is not the same as Python's "%" string formatting operator.

Finally, if your database supports stored procedures, you can generally call them with the `callproc` method, or by passing an SQL CALL or EXEC statement string to the `execute` method; use a `fetch` variant to retrieve its results.

Resources

There is more to database interfaces than the basics just mentioned, but additional API documentation is readily available on the Web. Perhaps the best resource for information about database extensions today is the home page of the Python database special interest group (SIG). Go to *http://www.python.org*, click on the SIGs link near the top, and navigate to the database group's page (or go straight to *http://www.python.org/sigs/db-sig*, the page's current address at the time of writing). There, you'll find API documentation, links to database vendor-specific extension modules, and more.

While you're at *python.org*, be sure to also explore the Gadfly database package—a Python-specific SQL-based database extension, which sports wide portability, socket connections for client/server modes, and more. Gadfly loads data into memory, so it is currently somewhat limited in scope. On the other hand, it is ideal for prototyping database applications—you can postpone cutting a check to a vendor until it's time to scale up for deployment. Moreover, Gadfly is suitable by itself for a variety of applications—not every system needs large data stores, but many can benefit from the power of SQL.

PyForm: A Persistent Object Viewer

Rather than going into additional database interface details that are freely available at *python.org*, I'm going to close out this chapter by showing you one way to combine the GUI technology we met earlier in the text with the persistence techniques introduced in this chapter. This section presents *PyForm*, a Tkinter GUI designed to let you browse and edit tables of records:

- *Tables* browsed are shelves, DBM files, in-memory dictionaries, or any other object that looks and feels like a dictionary.

- *Records* within tables browsed can be class instances, simple dictionaries, strings, or any other object that can be translated to and from a dictionary.

Although this example is about GUIs and persistence, it also illustrates Python design techniques. To keep its implementation both simple and type-independent, the PyForm GUI is coded to expect tables to look like *dictionaries of dictionaries*. To support a variety of table and record types, PyForm relies on separate wrapper classes to translate tables and records to the expected protocol:

- At the top table level, the translation is easy—shelves, DBM files, and in-memory dictionaries all have the same key-based interface.

- At the nested record level, the GUI is coded to assume that stored items have a dictionary-like interface, too, but classes intercept dictionary operations to make records compatible with the PyForm protocol. Records stored as strings are converted to and from the dictionary objects on fetches and stores; records stored as class instances are translated to and from attribute dictionaries. More specialized translations can be added in new table wrapper classes.

The net effect is that PyForm can be used to browse and edit a wide variety of table types, despite its dictionary interface expectations. When PyForm browses shelves and DBM files, table changes made within the GUI are persistent—they are saved in the underlying files. When used to browse a shelve of class instances, PyForm essentially becomes a GUI frontend to a simple object database, one built using standard Python persistence tools.

Doing It the Hard Way

Before we get to the GUI, though, let's see why you'd want one in the first place. To experiment with shelves in general, I first coded a canned test data file. The script in Example 16-4 hardcodes a dictionary used to populate databases (`cast`), as well as a class used to populate shelves of class instances (`Actor`).

Example 16-4. PP2E\Dbase\testdata.py

```
# definitions for testing shelves, dbm, and formgui

cast = {
    'rob':   {'name': ('Rob', 'P'),   'job': 'writer', 'spouse': 'Laura'},
    'buddy': {'name': ('Buddy', 'S'), 'job': 'writer', 'spouse': 'Pickles'},
    'sally': {'name': ('Sally', 'R'), 'job': 'writer'},
    'laura': {'name': ('Laura', 'P'), 'spouse': 'Rob',   'kids':1},
    'milly': {'name': ('Milly', '?'), 'spouse': 'Jerry', 'kids':2},
    'mel':   {'name': ('Mel', 'C'),   'job': 'producer'},
    'alan':  {'name': ('Alan', 'B'),  'job': 'comedian'}
```

Example 16-4. PP2E\Dbase\testdata.py (continued)

```
}

class Actor:                                       # unnested file-level class
    def __init__(self, name=(), job=''):           # no need for arg defaults,
        self.name = name                           # for new pickler or formgui
        self.job  = job
    def __setattr__(self, attr, value):            # on setattr(): validate
        if attr == 'kids' and value > 10:          # but set it regardless
            print 'validation error: kids =', value
        if attr == 'name' and type(value) != type(()):
            print 'validation error: name type =', type(value)
        self.__dict__[attr] = value                # don't trigger __setattr__
```

The cast object here is intended to represent a table of records (it's really a dictionary of dictionaries when written out in Python syntax like this). Now, given this test data, it's easy to populate a shelve with cast dictionaries. Simply open a shelve and copy over cast, key for key, as shown in Example 16-5.

Example 16-5. PP2E\Dbase\castinit.py

```
import shelve
from testdata import cast
db = shelve.open('data/castfile')          # create a new shelve
for key in cast.keys():
    db[key] = cast[key]                    # store dictionaries in shelve
```

Once you've done that, it's almost as easy to verify your work with a script that prints the contents of the shelve, as shown in Example 16-6.

Example 16-6. PP2E\Dbase\castdump.py

```
import shelve
db = shelve.open('data/castfile')          # reopen shelve
for key in db.keys():                      # show each key,value
    print key, db[key]
```

Here are these two scripts in action, populating and displaying a shelve of dictionaries:

```
C:\...\PP2E\Dbase>python castinit.py
C:\...\PP2E\Dbase>python castdump.py
alan {'job': 'comedian', 'name': ('Alan', 'B')}
mel {'job': 'producer', 'name': ('Mel', 'C')}
buddy {'spouse': 'Pickles', 'job': 'writer', 'name': ('Buddy', 'S')}
sally {'job': 'writer', 'name': ('Sally', 'R')}
rob {'spouse': 'Laura', 'job': 'writer', 'name': ('Rob', 'P')}
milly {'spouse': 'Jerry', 'name': ('Milly', '?'), 'kids': 2}
laura {'spouse': 'Rob', 'name': ('Laura', 'P'), 'kids': 1}
```

So far, so good. But here is where you reach the limitations of manual shelve processing: to modify a shelve, you need much more general tools. You could write little Python scripts that each perform very specific updates. Or you might even get by for awhile typing such update commands by hand in the interactive interpreter:

```
>>> import shelve
>>> db  = shelve.open('data/castfile')
>>> rec = db['rob']
>>> rec['job'] = 'hacker'
>>> db['rob'] = rec
```

For all but the most trivial databases, though, this will get tedious in a hurry—especially for a system's end users. What you'd really like is a GUI that lets you view and edit shelves arbitrarily, and can be started up easily from other programs and scripts, as shown in Example 16-7.

Example 16-7. PP2E\Dbase\castview.py

```
import shelve
from TableBrowser.formgui import FormGui    # after initcast
db = shelve.open('data/castfile')           # reopen shelve file
FormGui(db).mainloop()                       # browse existing shelve-of-dicts
```

To make this particular script work, we need to move on to the next section.

Doing It the Graphical Way

The path traced in the last section really is what led me to write PyForm, a GUI tool for editing arbitrary tables of records. When those tables are shelves and DBM files, the data PyForm displays is persistent; it lives beyond the GUI's lifetime. Because of that, PyForm can be seen as a simple database browser.

PyForm GUI code

We've already met all the GUI interfaces PyForm uses earlier in this book, so I won't go into all of its implementation details here (see the chapters in Part II, *GUI Programming*, for background details). Before we see the code at all, though, let's see what it does. Figure 16-1 shows PyForm in action on Windows, browsing a shelve of persistent instance objects, created from the `testdata` module's `Actor` class. It looks slightly different but works the same on Linux and Macs.

PyForm uses a three-window interface to the table being browsed; all windows are packed for proper window expansion and clipping, as set by the rules we studied earlier in this book. The window in the upper left of Figure 16-1 is the main window, created when PyForm starts; it has buttons for navigating through a table, finding items by key, and updating, creating, and deleting records (more useful when browsing tables that persist between runs). The table (dictionary) key of the record currently displayed shows up in the input field in the middle of this window.

The "index" button pops up the listbox window in the upper right, and selecting a record in either window at the top creates the form window at the bottom. The

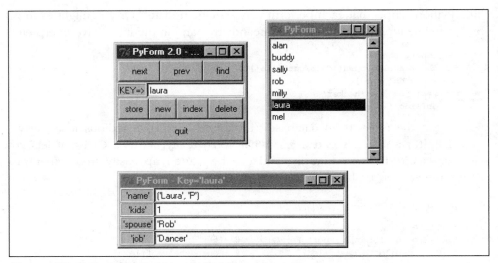

Figure 16-1. PyForm displaying a shelf of Actor objects

form window is used both to display a record and to edit it—if you change field values and press "store," the record is updated. Pressing "new" clears the form for input of new values (fill in the "Key=>" field and press "store" to save the new record).

Field values are typed with Python syntax, so strings are quoted (more on this later). When browsing a table with records that contain different sets of field names, PyForm erases and redraws the form window for new field sets as new records are selected; to avoid seeing the window recreated, use the same format for all records within a given table.

On to the code. The first thing I did when writing PyForm was to code utility functions to hide some of the details of widget creation. By making a few simplifying assumptions (e.g., packing protocol), the module in Example 16-8 helps keep some GUI coding details out of the rest of the PyForm implementation.

Example 16-8. PP2E\Dbase\guitools.py

```
# added extras for entry width, calcgui font/color

from Tkinter import *

def frame(root, side, **extras):
    widget = Frame(root)
    widget.pack(side=side, expand=YES, fill=BOTH)
    if extras: apply(widget.config, (), extras)
    return widget

def label(root, side, text, **extras):
    widget = Label(root, text=text, relief=RIDGE)
```

Example 16-8. PP2E\Dbase\guitools.py (continued)

```
        widget.pack(side=side, expand=YES, fill=BOTH)
        if extras: apply(widget.config, (), extras)
        return widget

def button(root, side, text, command, **extras):
    widget = Button(root, text=text, command=command)
    widget.pack(side=side, expand=YES, fill=BOTH)
    if extras: apply(widget.config, (), extras)
    return widget

def entry(root, side, linkvar, **extras):
    widget = Entry(root, relief=SUNKEN, textvariable=linkvar)
    widget.pack(side=side, expand=YES, fill=BOTH)
    if extras: apply(widget.config, (), extras)
    return widget
```

Armed with this utility module, the file in Example 16-9 implements the rest of the
PyForm GUI. It uses the `GuiMixin` module we wrote in Chapter 9, *Larger GUI
Examples*, for simple access to standard popup dialogs. It's also coded as a class
that can be specialized in subclasses, or attached to a larger GUI. I run PyForm as
a standalone program. Attaching its `FormGui` class really attaches its main window only, but it can be used to provide a pre-coded table browser widget for
other GUIs.

This file's `FormGui` class creates the GUI shown in Figure 16-1, and responds to
user interaction in all three of the interface's windows. Because we've already covered all the GUI tools that PyForm uses, you should study this module's source
code listing for additional implementation details. Notice, though, that this file
knows almost nothing about the table being browsed, other than that it looks and
feels like a dictionary of dictionaries. To understand how PyForm supports browsing things like shelves of class instances, you will need to look elsewhere (or at
least wait for the next module).

Example 16-9. PP2E\Dbase\TableBrowser\formgui.py

```
#!/usr/local/bin/python
############################################################################
# PyForm: a persistent table viewer GUI. Uses guimixin for std dialogs.
# Assumes the browsed table has a dictionary-of-dictionary interface, and
# relies on table wrapper classes to convert other structures as needed.
# Store an initial record with dbinit script to start a dbase from scratch.
# Caveat: doesn't do object method calls, shows complex field values poorly.
############################################################################

from Tkinter   import *                      # Tk widgets
from guitools import frame, label, button, entry    # widget builders
from PP2E.Gui.Tools.guimixin import GuiMixin         # common methods

class FormGui(GuiMixin, Frame):
```

Example 16-9. PP2E\Dbase\TableBrowser\formgui.py (continued)

```
    def __init__(self, mapping):                    # an extended frame
        Frame.__init__(self)                        # on default top-level
        self.pack(expand=YES, fill=BOTH)            # all parts expandable
        self.master.title('PyForm 2.0 - Table browser')
        self.master.iconname("PyForm")
        self.makeMainBox()
        self.table     = mapping                    # a dict, dbm, shelve, Table,..
        self.index     = mapping.keys()             # list of table keys
        self.cursor    = -1                         # current index position
        self.currslots = []                         # current form's (key,text)s
        self.currform  = None                       # current form window
        self.listbox   = None                       # index listbox window

    def makeMainBox(self):
        frm = frame(self, TOP)
        frm.config(bd=2)
        button(frm, LEFT, 'next', self.onNext)      # next in list
        button(frm, LEFT, 'prev', self.onPrev)      # backup in list
        button(frm, LEFT, 'find', self.onFind)      # find from key
        frm = frame(self, TOP)
        self.keytext = StringVar()                  # current record's key
        label(frm, LEFT, 'KEY=>')                   # change before 'find'
        entry(frm, LEFT, self.keytext)
        frm = frame(self, TOP)
        frm.config(bd=2)
        button(frm, LEFT, 'store', self.onStore)    # updated entry data
        button(frm, LEFT, 'new', self.onNew)        # clear fields
        button(frm, LEFT, 'index', self.onMakeList) # show key list
        button(frm, LEFT, 'delete', self.onDelete)  # show key list
        button(self, BOTTOM,'quit', self.quit)      # from guimixin

    def onPrev(self):
        if self.cursor <= 0:
            self.infobox('Backup', "Front of table")
        else:
            self.cursor = self.cursor - 1
            self.display()

    def onNext(self):
        if self.cursor >= len(self.index)-1:
            self.infobox('Advance', "End of table")
        else:
            self.cursor = self.cursor + 1
            self.display()

    def sameKeys(self, record):                     # can we reuse the same form?
        keys1 = record.keys()
        keys2 = map(lambda x:x[0], self.currslots)
        keys1.sort(); keys2.sort()                  # keys list order differs
        return keys1 == keys2                        # if insertion-order differs

    def display(self):
```

Example 16-9. PP2E\Dbase\TableBrowser\formgui.py (continued)

```
        key = self.index[self.cursor]             # show record at index cursor
        self.keytext.set(key)                     # change key in main box
        record = self.table[key]                  # in dict, dbm, shelf, class
        if self.sameKeys(record):
            self.currform.title('PyForm - Key=' + `key`)
            for (field, text) in self.currslots:
                text.set(`record[field]`)         # same fields? reuse form
        else:                                     # expr `x` works like repr(x)
            if self.currform:
                self.currform.destroy()           # different fields?
            new = Toplevel()                      # replace current box
            new.title('PyForm - Key=' + `key`)    # new resizable window
            new.iconname("pform")
            left  = frame(new, LEFT)
            right = frame(new, RIGHT)
            self.currslots = []                   # list of (field, entry)
            for field in record.keys():
                label(left, TOP, `field`)         # key,value to strings
                text = StringVar()                # we could sort keys here
                text.set( `record[field]` )
                entry(right, TOP, text, width=40)
                self.currslots.append((field, text))
            self.currform = new
            new.protocol('WM_DELETE_WINDOW', lambda:0)   # ignore destroy's
        self.selectlist()                         # update listbox

    def onStore(self):
        if not self.currform: return
        key = self.keytext.get()
        if key in self.index:                     # change existing record
            record = self.table[key]              # not: self.table[key][field]=
        else:
            record = {}                           # create a new record
            self.index.append(key)                # add to index and listbox
            if self.listbox:
                self.listbox.insert(END, key)     # or at len(self.index)-1
        for (field, text) in self.currslots:
            try:                                  # fill out dictionary rec
                record[field] = eval(text.get())  # convert back from string
            except:
                self.errorbox('Bad data: "%s" = "%s"' % (field, text.get()))
                record[field] = None
        self.table[key] = record                  # add to dict, dbm, shelf,...
        self.onFind(key)                          # readback: set cursor,listbox

    def onNew(self):
        if not self.currform: return              # clear input form and key
        self.keytext.set('?%d' % len(self.index)) # default key unless typed
        for (field, text) in self.currslots:      # clear key/fields for entry
            text.set('')
        self.currform.title('Key: ?')
```

Example 16-9. PP2E\Dbase\TableBrowser\formgui.py (continued)

```
    def onFind(self, key=None):
        target = key or self.keytext.get()         # passed in, or entered
        try:
            self.cursor = self.index.index(target)  # find label in keys list
            self.display()
        except:
            self.infobox('Not found', "Key doesn't exist", 'info')

    def onDelete(self):
        if not self.currform or not self.index: return
        currkey = self.index[self.cursor]
        del self.table[currkey]                     # table, index, listbox
        del self.index[self.cursor:self.cursor+1]   # like "list[i:i+1] = []"
        if self.listbox:
            self.listbox.delete(self.cursor)        # delete from listbox
        if self.cursor < len(self.index):
            self.display()                          # show next record if any
        elif self.cursor > 0:
            self.cursor = self.cursor-1             # show prior if delete end
            self.display()
        else:                                       # leave box if delete last
            self.onNew()

    def onList(self,evnt):
        if not self.index: return                   # on listbox double-click
        index = self.listbox.curselection()         # fetch selected key text
        label = self.listbox.get(index)             # or use listbox.get(ACTIVE)
        self.onFind(label)                          # and call method here

    def onMakeList(self):
        if self.listbox: return                     # already up?
        new = Toplevel()                            # new resizable window
        new.title("PyForm - Key Index")             # select keys from a listbox
        new.iconname("pindex")
        frm    = frame(new, TOP)
        scroll = Scrollbar(frm)
        list   = Listbox(frm, bg='white')
        scroll.config(command=list.yview, relief=SUNKEN)
        list.config(yscrollcommand=scroll.set, relief=SUNKEN)
        scroll.pack(side=RIGHT, fill=BOTH)
        list.pack(side=LEFT, expand=YES, fill=BOTH) # pack last, clip first
        for key in self.index:                      # add to list-box
            list.insert(END, key)                   # or: sort list first
        list.config(selectmode=SINGLE, setgrid=1)   # select,resize modes
        list.bind('<Double-1>', self.onList)        # on double-clicks
        self.listbox = list
        if self.index and self.cursor >= 0:         # highlight position
            self.selectlist()
        new.protocol('WM_DELETE_WINDOW', lambda:0)  # ignore destroy's

    def selectlist(self):                           # listbox tracks cursor
        if self.listbox:
```

Example 16-9. PP2E\Dbase\TableBrowser\formgui.py (continued)

```
        self.listbox.select_clear(0, self.listbox.size())
        self.listbox.select_set(self.cursor)

if __name__ == '__main__':
    from PP2E.Dbase.testdata import cast      # self-test code
    for k in cast.keys(): print k, cast[k]    # view in-memory dict-of-dicts
    FormGui(cast).mainloop()
    for k in cast.keys(): print k, cast[k]    # show modified table on exit
```

The file's self-test code starts up the PyForm GUI to browse the in-memory dictionary of dictionaries called `cast` in the `testdata` module listed earlier. To start PyForm, you simply make and run the `FormGui` class object this file defines, passing in the table to be browsed. Here are the messages that show up in `stdout` after running this file and editing a few entries displayed in the GUI; the dictionary is displayed on GUI startup and exit:

```
C:\...\PP2E\Dbase\TableBrowser>python formgui.py
alan {'job': 'comedian', 'name': ('Alan', 'B')}
sally {'job': 'writer', 'name': ('Sally', 'R')}
rob {'spouse': 'Laura', 'job': 'writer', 'name': ('Rob', 'P')}
mel {'job': 'producer', 'name': ('Mel', 'C')}
milly {'spouse': 'Jerry', 'name': ('Milly', '?'), 'kids': 2}
buddy {'spouse': 'Pickles', 'job': 'writer', 'name': ('Buddy', 'S')}
laura {'spouse': 'Rob', 'name': ('Laura', 'P'), 'kids': 1}

alan {'job': 'comedian', 'name': ('Alan', 'B')}
jerry {'spouse': 'Milly', 'name': 'Jerry', 'kids': 0}
sally {'job': 'writer', 'name': ('Sally', 'R')}
rob {'spouse': 'Laura', 'job': 'writer', 'name': ('Rob', 'P')}
mel {'job': 'producer', 'name': ('Mel', 'C')}
milly {'spouse': 'Jerry', 'name': ('Milly', '?'), 'kids': 2}
buddy {'spouse': 'Pickles', 'job': 'writer', 'name': ('Buddy', 'S')}
laura {'name': ('Laura', 'P'), 'kids': 3, 'spouse': 'bob'}
```

The last line (in bold) represents a change made in the GUI. Since this is an in-memory table, changes made in the GUI are not retained (dictionaries are not persistent by themselves). To see how to use the PyForm GUI on persistent stores like DBM files and shelves, we need to move on to the next topic.

PyForm table wrappers

The following file defines generic classes that "wrap" (interface with) various kinds of tables for use in PyForm. It's what makes PyForm useful for a variety of table types.

The prior module was coded to handle GUI chores, and assumes that tables expose a dictionary-of-dictionaries interface. Conversely, this next module knows nothing about the GUI, but provides the translations necessary to browse non-dictionary objects in PyForm. In fact, this module doesn't even import Tkinter at all—it strictly deals in object protocol conversions and nothing else. Because PyForm's implementation is divided into functionally distinct modules like this, it's easier to focus on each module's task in isolation.

Here is the hook between the two modules: for special kinds of tables, PyForm's `FormGui` is passed an instance of the `Table` class coded here. The `Table` class intercepts table index fetch and assignment operations, and uses an embedded record wrapper class to convert records to and from dictionary format as needed.

For example, because DBM files can store only strings, `Table` converts real dictionaries to and from their printable string representation on table stores and fetches. For class instances, `Table` extracts the object's `__dict__` attribute dictionary on fetches, and copies a dictionary's fields to attributes of a newly generated class instance on stores.* The end result is that the GUI thinks the table is all dictionaries, even if it is really something very different here.

While you study this module's listing, shown in Example 16-10, notice that there is nothing here about the record formats of any particular database. In fact, there was none in the GUI-related `formgui` module either. Because neither module cares about the structure of fields used for database records, both can be used to browse arbitrary records.

Example 16-10. PP2E\Dbase\formtable.py

```
#############################################################################
# PyForm table wrapper classes and tests
# Because PyForm assumes a dictionary-of-dictionary interface, this module
# converts strings and class instance records to and from dicts.  PyForm
# contains the table mapping--Table is not a PyForm subclass.  Note that
# some of the wrapper classes may be useful outside PyForm--DbmOfString can
# wrap a dbm containing arbitrary datatypes.  Run the dbinit scripts to
# start a new database from scratch, and run the dbview script to browse
# a database other than the one tested here.  No longer requires classes to
# have defaults in constructor args, and auto picks up record class from the
# first one fetched if not passed in to class-record wrapper.  Caveat: still
# assumes that all instances in a table are instances of the same class.
#############################################################################


#############################################################################
# records within tables
#############################################################################

class DictionaryRecord:
    def todict(self, value):
```

---

* Subtle thing revisited: like the new `pickle` module, PyForm tries to generate a new class instance on store operations by simply setting a generic instance object's `__class__` pointer to the original class; only if this fails does PyForm fall back on calling the class with no arguments (in which case the class must have defaults for any constructor arguments other than "self"). Assignment to `__class__` can fail in restricted execution mode. See class `InstanceRecord` in the source listing for further details.

Example 16-10. PP2E\Dbase\formtable.py (continued)

```
        return value              # to dictionary: no need to convert
    def fromdict(self, value):
        return value              # from dictionary: no need to convert

class StringRecord:
    def todict(self, value):
        return eval(value)        # convert string to dictionary (or any)
    def fromdict(self, value):
        return str(value)         # convert dictionary (or any) to string

class InstanceRecord:
    def __init__(self, Class=None):   # need class object to make instances
        self.Class = Class
    def todict(self, value):          # convert instance to attr dictionary
        if not self.Class:            # get class from obj if not yet known
            self.Class = value.__class__
        return value.__dict__
    def fromdict(self, value):        # convert attr dictionary to instance
        try:
            class Dummy: pass                 # try what new pickle does
            instance = Dummy()                # fails in restricted mode
            instance.__class__ = self.Class
        except:                               # else call class, no args
            instance = self.Class()           # init args need defaults
        for attr in value.keys():
            setattr(instance, attr, value[attr])   # set instance attributes
        return instance                       # may run Class.__setattr__

###########################################################################
# table containing records
###########################################################################

class Table:
    def __init__(self, mapping, converter):   # table object, record converter
        self.table  = mapping                 # wrap arbitrary table mapping
        self.record = converter               # wrap arbitrary record types

    def storeItems(self, items):              # initialize from dictionary
        for key in items.keys():              # do __setitem__ to xlate, store
            self[key] = items[key]

    def printItems(self):                     # print wrapped mapping
        for key in self.keys():               # do self.keys to get table keys
            print key, self[key]              # do __getitem__ to fetch, xlate

    def __getitem__(self, key):               # on tbl[key] index fetch
        rawval = self.table[key]              # fetch from table mapping
        return self.record.todict(rawval)     # translate to dictionary

    def __setitem__(self, key, value):        # on tbl[key]=val index assign
        rawval = self.record.fromdict(value)  # translate from dictionary
        self.table[key] = rawval              # store in table mapping
```

Example 16-10. PP2E\Dbase\formtable.py (continued)

```python
    def __delitem__(self, key):                  # delete from table mapping
        del self.table[key]

    def keys(self):                              # get table mapping keys index
        return self.table.keys()

    def close(self):
        if hasattr(self.table, 'close'):         # call table close if has one
            self.table.close()                   # may need for shelves, dbm


###########################################################################
# table/record combinations
###########################################################################

import shelve, anydbm

def ShelveOfInstance(filename, Class=None):
    return Table(shelve.open(filename), InstanceRecord(Class))
def ShelveOfDictionary(filename):
    return Table(shelve.open(filename), DictionaryRecord())
def ShelveOfString(filename):
    return Table(shelve.open(filename), StringRecord())

def DbmOfString(filename):
    return Table(anydbm.open(filename, 'c'), StringRecord())

def DictOfInstance(dict, Class=None):
    return Table(dict, InstanceRecord(Class))
def DictOfDictionary(dict):
    return Table(dict, DictionaryRecord())
def DictOfString(filename):
    return Table(dict, StringRecord())

ObjectOfInstance   = DictOfInstance          # other mapping objects
ObjectOfDictionary = DictOfDictionary        # classes that look like dicts
ObjectOfString     = DictOfString


###########################################################################
# test common applications
###########################################################################

if __name__ == '__main__':
    from sys import argv
    from formgui import FormGui                 # get dict-based gui
    from PP2E.Dbase.testdata import Actor, cast # get class, dict-of-dicts

    TestType   = 'shelve'                        # shelve, dbm, dict
    TestInit   = 0                               # init file on startup?
    TestFile   = '../data/shelve1'               # external filename
    if len(argv) > 1: TestType = argv[1]
    if len(argv) > 2: TestInit = int(argv[2])
    if len(argv) > 3: TestFile = argv[3]
```

Example 16-10. PP2E\Dbase\formtable.py (continued)

```
    if TestType == 'shelve':                               # python formtbl.py shelve?
        print 'shelve-of-instance test'
        table = ShelveOfInstance(TestFile, Actor)         # wrap shelf in Table object
        if TestInit:
            table.storeItems(cast)                         # python formtbl.py shelve 1
        FormGui(table).mainloop()
        table.close()
        ShelveOfInstance(TestFile).printItems()           # class picked up on fetch

    elif TestType == 'dbm':                                # python formtbl.py dbm
        print 'dbm-of-dictstring test'
        table = DbmOfString(TestFile)                      # wrap dbm in Table object
        if TestInit:
            table.storeItems(cast)                         # python formtbl.py dbm 1
        FormGui(table).mainloop()
        table.close()
        DbmOfString(TestFile).printItems()                # dump new table contents
```

Besides the `Table` and record-wrapper classes, the module defines generator functions (e.g., `ShelveOfInstance`) that create a `Table` for all reasonable table and record combinations. Not all combinations are valid; DBM files, for example, can only contain dictionaries coded as strings, because class instances don't easily map to the string value format expected by DBM. However, these classes are flexible enough to allow additional `Table` configurations to be introduced.

The only thing that is GUI-related about this file at all is its self-test code at the end. When run as a script, this module starts a PyForm GUI to browse and edit either a shelve of persistent `Actor` class instances or a DBM file of dictionaries, by passing in the right kind of `Table` object. The GUI looks like the one we saw in Figure 16-1 earlier; when run without arguments, the self-test code lets you browse a shelve of class instances:

```
C:\...\PP2E\Dbase\TableBrowser>python formtable.py
shelve-of-instance test
...display of contents on exit...
```

Because PyForm displays a shelve this time, any changes you make are retained after the GUI exits. To reinitialize the shelve from the cast dictionary in `testdata`, pass a second argument of "1" ("0" means don't reinitialize the shelve). To override the script's default shelve filename, pass a different name as a third argument:

```
C:\...\PP2E\Dbase\TableBrowser>python formtable.py shelve 1
C:\...\PP2E\Dbase\TableBrowser>python formtable.py shelve 0 ../data/shelve1
```

To instead test PyForm on a DBM file of dictionaries mapped to strings, pass a `dbm` in the first command-line argument; the next two arguments work the same:

```
C:\...\PP2E\Dbase\TableBrowser>python formtable.py dbm 1 ..\data\dbm1
dbm-of-dictstring test
...display of contents on exit...
```

Finally, because these self-tests ultimately process concrete shelve and DBM files, you can manually open and inspect their contents using normal library calls. Here is what they look like when opened in an interactive session:

```
C:\...\PP2E\Dbase\data>ls
dbm1          myfile          shelve1

C:\...\PP2E\Dbase\data>python
>>> import shelve
>>> db = shelve.open('shelve1')
>>> db.keys()
['alan', 'buddy', 'sally', 'rob', 'milly', 'laura', 'mel']
>>> db['laura']
<PP2E.Dbase.testdata.Actor instance at 799850>

>>> import anydbm
>>> db = anydbm.open('dbm1')
>>> db.keys()
['alan', 'mel', 'buddy', 'sally', 'rob', 'milly', 'laura']
>>> db['laura']
"{'name': ('Laura', 'P'), 'kids': 2, 'spouse': 'Rob'}"
```

The shelve file contains real `Actor` class instance objects, and the DBM file holds dictionaries converted to strings. Both formats are retained in these files between GUI runs and are converted back to dictionaries for later redisplay.[*]

PyForm creation and view utility scripts

The `formtable` module's self-test code proves that it works, but it is limited to canned test case files and classes. What about using PyForm for other kinds of databases that store more useful kinds of data?

Luckily, both the `formgui` and `formtable` modules are written to be generic—they are independent of a particular database's record format. Because of that, it's easy to point PyForm to databases of your own; simply import and run the `FormGui` object with the (possibly wrapped) table you wish to browse.

The required startup calls are not too complex, and you could type them at the interactive prompt every time you want to browse a database; but it's usually easier to store them in scripts so they can be reused. The script in Example 16-11, for example, can be run to open PyForm on *any* shelve containing records stored in class instance or dictionary format.

---

[*] Note that DBM files of dictionaries use `str` and `eval` to convert to and from strings, but could also simply store the pickled representations of record dictionaries in DBM files instead using `pickle`. But since this is exactly what a `shelve` of dictionaries does, the `str`/`eval` scheme was chosen for illustration purposes here instead. Suggested exercise: add a new `PickleRecord` record class based upon the `pickle` module's `loads` and `dumps` functions described earlier in this chapter, and compare its performance to `StringRecord`. See also the `pickle` file database structure in Chapter 14; its directory scheme with one flat-file per record could be used to implement a "table" here, too, with appropriate `Table` subclassing.

Example 16-11. PP2E\Dbase\dbview.py

```
#################################################################
# view any existing shelve directly; this is more general than a
# "formtable.py shelve 1 filename" cmdline--only works for Actor;
# pass in a filename (and mode) to use this to browse any shelve:
# formtable auto picks up class from the first instance fetched;
# run dbinit1 to (re)initialize dbase shelve with a template.
#################################################################

from sys import argv
from formtable import *
from formgui import FormGui

mode = 'class'
file = '../data/mydbase-' + mode
if len(argv) > 1: file = argv[1]                    # dbview.py file? mode??
if len(argv) > 2: mode = argv[2]

if mode == 'dict':
    table = ShelveOfDictionary(file)                # view dictionaries
else:
    table = ShelveOfInstance(file)                  # view class objects

FormGui(table).mainloop()
table.close()                                       # close needed for some dbm
```

The only catch here is that PyForm doesn't handle completely *empty* tables very well; there is no way to add new records within the GUI unless a record is already present. That is, PyForm has no record layout design tool; its "new" button simply clears an existing input form.

Because of that, to start a new database from scratch, you need to add an initial record that gives PyForm the field layout. Again, this requires only a few lines of code that could be typed interactively, but why not instead put it in generalized scripts for reuse? The file in Example 16-12, shows one way to go about initializing a PyForm database with a first empty record.

Example 16-12. PP2E\Dbase\dbinit1.py

```
####################################################################
# store a first record in a new shelve to give initial fields list;
# PyForm GUI requires an existing record before you can more records;
# delete the '?' key template record after real records are added;
# change mode, file, template to use this for other kinds of data;
# if you populate shelves from other data files you don't need this;
# see dbinit2 for object-based version, and dbview to browse shelves.
####################################################################

import os
from sys import argv
mode = 'class'
```

Example 16-12. PP2E\Dbase\dbinit1.py (continued)

```
file = '../data/mydbase-' + mode
if len(argv) > 1: file = argv[1]                        # dbinit1.py file? mode??
if len(argv) > 2: mode = argv[2]
try:
    os.remove(file)                                     # delete if present
except: pass

if mode == 'dict':
    template = {'name': None, 'age': None, 'job': None}  # start dict shelve
else:
    from PP2E.Dbase.person import Person                 # one arg defaulted
    template = Person(None, None)                        # start object shelve

import shelve
dbase = shelve.open(file)                                # create it now
dbase['?empty?'] = template
dbase.close()
```

Now, simply change some of this script's settings or pass in command-line arguments to generate a new shelve-based database for use in PyForm. You can substitute any fields list or class name in this script to maintain a simple object database with PyForm that keeps track of real-world information (we'll see two such databases in action in a moment). The empty record shows up with key "?empty?" when you first browse the database with **dbview**; replace it with a first real record using the PyForm "store" key, and you are in business. As long as you don't change the database's shelve outside of the GUI, all its records will have the same fields format, as defined in the initialization script.

But notice that the **dbinit1** script goes straight to the shelve file to store the first record; that's fine today, but might break if PyForm is ever changed to do something more custom with its stored data representation. Perhaps a better way to populate tables outside the GUI is to use the **Table** wrapper classes it employs. The following alternative script, for instance, initializes a PyForm database with generated **Table** objects, not direct shelve operations (see Example 16-13).

Example 16-13. PP2E\Dbase\dbinit2.py

```
###############################################################
# this works too--based on Table objects not manual shelve ops;
# store a first record in shelve, as required by PyForm GUI.
###############################################################

from formtable import *
import sys, os

mode = 'dict'
file = '../data/mydbase-' + mode
if len(sys.argv) > 1: file = sys.argv[1]
if len(sys.argv) > 2: mode = sys.argv[2]
```

Example 16-13. PP2E\Dbase\dbinit2.py (continued)

```
try:
    os.remove(file)
except: pass

if mode == 'dict':
    table    = ShelveOfDictionary(file)
    template = {'name': None, 'shoesize': None, 'language': 'Python'}
else:
    from PP2E.Dbase.person import Person
    table    = ShelveOfInstance(file, Person)
    template = Person(None, None).__dict__

table.storeItems({'?empty?': template})
table.close()
```

Let's put these scripts to work to initialize and edit a couple of custom databases. Figure 16-2 shows one being browsed after initializing the database with a script, and adding a handful of real records within the GUI.

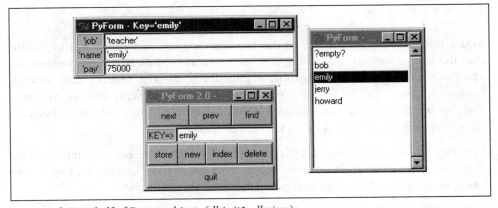

Figure 16-2. A shelf of Person objects (dbinit1, dbview)

The listbox here shows the record I added to the shelve within the GUI. I ran the following commands to initialize the database with a starter record and open it in PyForm to add records (that is, Person class instances):

```
C:\...\PP2E\Dbase\TableBrowser>python dbinit1.py
```

```
C:\...\PP2E\Dbase\TableBrowser>python dbview.py
```

You can tweak the class name or fields dictionary in the dbinit scripts to initialize records for any sort of database you care to maintain with PyForm; use dictionaries if you don't want to represent persistent objects with classes (but classes let you add other sorts of behavior as methods not visible under PyForm). Be sure to use a distinct filename for each database; the initial "?empty?" record can be deleted as soon as you add a real entry (later, simply select an entry from the list-box and press "new" to clear the form for input of a new record's values).

The data displayed in the GUI represents a true shelve of persistent `Person` class instance objects—changes and additions made in the GUI will be retained for the next time you view this shelve with PyForm. If you like to type, though, you can still open the shelve directly to check PyForm's work:

```
C:\...\PP2E\Dbase\data>ls
mydbase-class  myfile        shelve1

C:\...\PP2E\Dbase\data>python
>>> import shelve
>>> db = shelve.open('mydbase-class')
>>> db.keys()
['emily', 'jerry', '?empty?', 'bob', 'howard']
>>> db['bob']
<PP2E.Dbase.person.Person instance at 798d70>
>>> db['emily'].job
'teacher'
>>> db['bob'].tax
30000.0
```

Notice that "bob" is an instance of the `Person` class we met earlier in this chapter (see the shelve section). Assuming that the `person` module is still the version that introduced a `__getattr__` method, asking for a shelved object's `tax` attribute computes a value on the fly, because this really invokes a class *method*. Also note that this works even though `Person` was never imported here—Python loads the class internally when recreating its shelved instances.

You can just as easily base a PyForm-compatible database on an internal dictionary structure, instead of classes. Figure 16-3 shows one being browsed, after being initialized with a script and populated with the GUI.

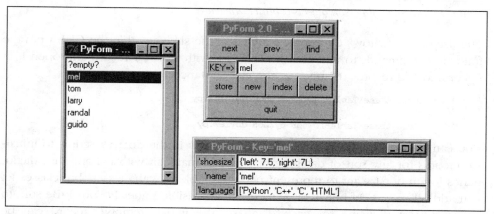

Figure 16-3. A shelf of dictionaries (dbinit2, dbview)

Besides its different internal format, this database has a different record structure (its record's field names differ from the last example), and it is stored in a shelve file of its own. Here are the commands I used to initialize and edit this database:

```
C:\...\PP2E\Dbase\TableBrowser>python dbinit2.py ../data/mydbase-dict dict

C:\...\PP2E\Dbase\TableBrowser>python dbview.py ../data/mydbase-dict dict
```

After adding a few records (that is, *dictionaries*) to the shelve, you can either view them again in PyForm or open the shelve manually to verify PyForm's work:

```
C:\...\PP2E\Dbase\data>ls
mydbase-class  mydbase-dict  myfile          shelve1

C:\...\PP2E\Dbase\data>python
>>> db = shelve.open('mydbase-dict')
>>> db.keys()
['tom', 'guido', '?empty?', 'larry', 'randal', 'mel']
>>> db['guido']
{'shoesize': 42, 'name': 'benevolent dictator', 'language': 'Python'}
>>> db['mel']['shoesize']
{'left': 7.5, 'right': 7L}
```

This time, shelve entries are really dictionaries, not instances of a class or converted strings. PyForm doesn't care, though—because all tables are wrapped to conform to PyForm's interface, both formats look the same when browsed in the GUI.

Notice that the "shoe size" and "language" fields in this screen shot really are a dictionary and list. You can type any Python expression syntax into this GUI's form fields to give values (that's why strings are quoted there). PyForm uses the Python backquotes expression to convert value objects for display (`` `x` `` is like `repr(x)`, which is like `str(x)`, but quotes are added around strings). To convert from a string back to value objects, PyForm uses the Python `eval` function to parse and evaluate the code typed in fields. The key entry/display field in the main window does not add or accept quotes around the key string, because keys must still be strings in things like shelves (even though fields can be arbitrary types).

As we've seen at various points in this book, `eval` (and its statement cousin, `exec`) is powerful but dangerous—you never know when a user might type something that removes files, hangs the system, emails your boss, and so on. If you can't be sure that field values won't contain harmful code (whether malicious or otherwise), use the `rexec` restricted execution mode tools we met in Chapter 15 to evaluate strings. Alternatively, you can simply limit the kinds of expressions allowed and evaluate them with simpler tools (e.g., `int`, `str`, `string.atoi`).

Although PyForm expects to find a dictionary-of-dictionary interface (protocol) in the tables it browses, a surprising number of objects fit this mold because dictionaries are so pervasive in Python object internals. In fact, PyForm can be used to browse things that have nothing to do with the notion of database tables of records at all, as long as they can be made to conform to the protocol.

For instance, the Python `sys.modules` table we met in Chapter 2 is a built-in dictionary of loaded module objects. With an appropriate wrapper class to make modules look like dictionaries, there's no reason we can't browse the in-memory `sys.modules` with PyForm too, as shown in Example 16-14.

Example 16-14. PP2E\Dbase\TableBrowser\viewsysmod.py

```
# view the sys.modules table in FormGui

class modrec:
    def todict(self, value):
        return value.__dict__      # not dir(value): need dict
    def fromdict(self, value):
        assert 0, 'Module updates not supported'

import sys
from formgui import FormGui
from formtable import Table
FormGui(Table(sys.modules, modrec())).mainloop()
```

This script defines a class to pull out a module's `__dict__` attribute dictionary (`formtable`'s `InstanceRecord` won't do, because it also looks for a `__class__`). The rest of it simply passes `sys.modules` to PyForm (`FormGui`) wrapped in a `Table` object; the result appears in Figure 16-4.

With similar record and table wrappers, all sorts of objects could be viewed in PyForm. As usual in Python, all that matters is that they provide a compatible interface.

PyForm limitations

Although the `sys.modules` viewer script works, it also highlights a few limitations of PyForm's current design:

Two levels only

PyForm is set up to handle a two-dimensional table/record mapping structure only. You can't descend further into fields shown in the form, large data structures in fields print as long strings, and complex objects like nested modules, classes, and functions that contain attributes of their own simply show their default print representation. We could add object viewers to inspect nested objects interactively, but they might be complex to code.

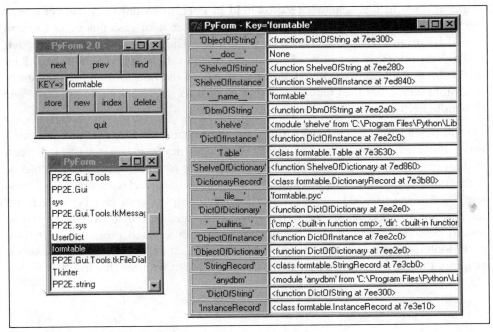

Figure 16-4. FormGui browsing sys.modules (viewsysmod)

No big (giant) forms

PyForm is not equipped to handle a large number of record fields—if you select the `os` module's entry in the index listbox in Figure 16-4, you'll get a huge form that is likely too big to even fit on your screen (the `os` module has lots and lots of attributes; it goes off my screen after about 40). We could fix this with a scrollbar, but it's unlikely that records in the databases that PyForm was designed to view will have many dozens of fields.

Data attributes only

PyForm displays record attribute values, but does not support calling method functions of objects being browsed, and cannot display dynamically computed attributes (e.g., the `tax` attribute in `Person` objects).

One class per table

PyForm currently assumes all instances in a table are of the same class, even though that's not a requirement for shelves in general.

In other words, there is room for improvement if you care to experiment. There are other coding styles you might wish to explore, as well. For instance, PyForm current overloads *table* index fetch and assignment, and the GUI uses dictionaries to represent records internally. It would be almost as easy to overload *record* field index fetch and assignment instead, and add a `Table` method for creating a new empty record. In this scheme, records held in PyForm would be whatever object the table stores (not dictionaries), and each field fetch or assignment in PyForm would be routed back to record wrapper classes. The downside of this approach is that PyForm could not browse any object unless it is wrapped in a `Table`. Raw dictionaries would not work, because they have no method for making new empties. Moreover, DBM files that map whole records to strings might need extra logic to handle field-at-a-time requests.

On the other hand, extensions in this domain are somewhat open-ended, so we'll leave them as suggested exercises. PyForm was never meant to be a general Python object viewer. But as a simple GUI interface to tables of persistent objects, it meets its design goals as planned. Python's shelves and classes make such systems both easy to code and powerful to use. Complex data can be stored and fetched in a single step, and augmented with methods that provide dynamic record behavior. As an added bonus, by programming such programs in Python and Tkinter, they are automatically portable among all major GUI platforms. When you mix Python persistence and GUIs, you get a lot of features "for free."

17

Data Structures

"Roses Are Red, Violets Are Blue; Lists Are Mutable, and So Is Class Foo"

Data structures are a central theme in most programs, whether you know it or not. It may not always be obvious, because Python provides a set of built-in types that make it easy to deal with structured data: lists, strings, tuples, dictionaries, and the like. For simple systems, these types are usually enough. Technically, dictionaries make many of the classical searching algorithms unnecessary in Python, and lists replace much of the work you'd do to support collections in lower-level languages. Both are so easy to use, though, that you generally never give them a second thought.

But for advanced applications, we may need to add more sophisticated types of our own to handle extra requirements. In this chapter, we'll explore a handful of advanced data structure implementations in Python: sets, stacks, graphs, and so on. As we'll see, data structures take the form of new object types in Python, integrated into the language's type model. That is, objects we code in Python become full-fledged datatypes—they can look and feel just like built-in lists, numbers, and dictionaries, to the scripts that use them.

Although the examples in this chapter illustrate advanced programming techniques, they also underscore Python's support for writing reusable software. By coding object implementations with classes, modules, and other Python tools, they naturally become generally useful components, which may be used in any program that imports them. In effect, we will be building libraries of data structure classes, whether we plan for it or not.

In addition, although the examples in this chapter are pure Python code, we will also be building a path towards the next part of the book here. From the most general perspective, new Python objects can be implemented in either Python or an integrated language such as C. In particular, pay attention to the stack objects implemented in the first section of this chapter; they will later be reimplemented in C to gauge both the benefits and complexity of C migration.

Implementing Stacks

Stacks are a common and straightforward data structure, used in a variety of applications: language processing, graph searches, etc. In short, stacks are a last-in-first-out collection of objects: the last item added to the collection is always the next one to be removed. Clients use stacks by:

- Pushing items onto the top
- Popping items off the top

Depending on client requirements, there may also be tools for such tasks as testing if the stack is empty, fetching the top item without popping it, iterating over a stack's items, testing for item membership, etc.

In Python, a simple list is often adequate for implementing a stack: because we can change lists in place, we can either add and delete items from the front (left) or end (right). Table 17-1 summarizes various built-in operations available for implementing stack-like behavior with Python lists, depending on whether the stack "top" is the first or last node in the list. In this table, string `'c'` is the top item on the stack.

Table 17-1. Stacks as Lists

Operation	Top is end-of-list	Top is front-of-list	Top is front-of-list
New	`stack=['a','b','c']`	`stack=['c','b','a']`	`stack=['c','b','a']`
Push	`stack.append('d')`	`stack.insert(0,'d')`	`stack[0:0] = ['d']`
Pop[a]	`X = stack[-1];` `del stack[-1]`	`x = stack[0];` `del stack[:1]`	`x = stack[0];` `stack[:1] = []`

[a] In fact, Python 1.5 introduced a list **pop** method designed to be used in conjunction with **append** to implement stacks: to *push*, say `list.append(value)`, to *pop*, say `x=list.pop()`. The **pop** method is equivalent to fetching and then deleting the last item at offset –1 (and equal to the last row in column 2 of Table 17-1). Because lists are a type (not a class), though, you still may need to use the stack class techniques in this chapter to do something custom.

This list arrangement works and will be relatively fast. But it also binds stack-based programs to the stack representation chosen: stack operations will all be hardcoded. If we later want to change how a stack is represented, or extend its basic operations, we're stuck: every stack-based program will have to be updated.

For instance, to add logic that monitors the number of stack operations a program performs, we'd have to add code around each hardcoded stack operation. In a large system, this operation may be nontrivial. As we'll see in the next chapter, we may also decide to move stacks to a C-based implementation, if they prove to be a performance bottleneck. As a general rule, hardcoded operations on built-in data structures don't support future migrations as well as we'd sometimes like.

A Stack Module

Perhaps a better approach is to encapsulate stack implementations using Python's code reuse tools. Let's begin by implementing a stack as a module containing a Python list, plus functions to operate on it (see Example 17-1).

Example 17-1. PP2E\Dstruct\Basic\stack1.py

```
stack = []                                  # on first import
error = 'stack1.error'                      # local exceptions

def push(obj):
    global stack                            # use 'global' to change
    stack = [obj] + stack                   # add item to the front

def pop():
    global stack
    if not stack:
        raise error, 'stack underflow'      # raise local error
    top, stack = stack[0], stack[1:]        # remove item at front
    return top

def top():
    if not stack:
        raise error, 'stack underflow'      # raise local error
    return stack[0]                         # or let IndexError occur

def empty():       return not stack         # is the stack []?
def member(obj):   return obj in stack      # item in stack?
def item(offset):  return stack[offset]     # index the stack
def length():      return len(stack)        # number entries
def dump():        print '<Stack:%s>' % stack
```

This module creates a list object (**stack**) and exports functions to manage access to it. The stack is declared global in functions that change it, but not in those that just reference it. The module also defines an error object (**error**) that can be used to catch exceptions raised locally in this module. Some stack errors are built-in exceptions: method **item** triggers **IndexError** for out-of-bounds indexes.

Most of the stack's functions just delegate the operation to the embedded list used to represent the stack. In fact, the module is really just a wrapper around a Python list. But this extra layer of interface logic makes clients independent of the actual implementation of the stack. So, we're able to change the stack later without impacting its clients.

As usual, one of the best ways to understand such code is to see it in action. Here's an interactive session that illustrates the module's interfaces:

```
C:\...\PP2E\Dstruct\Basic>python
>>> import stack1
>>> stack1.push('spam')
>>> stack1.push(123)
>>> stack1.top()
123
>>> stack1.stack
[123, 'spam']
>>> stack1.pop()
123
>>> stack1.dump()
<Stack:['spam']>
>>> stack1.pop()
'spam'
>>> stack1.empty()
1
>>> for c in 'spam': stack1.push(c)
...
>>> while not stack1.empty():
...        print stack1.pop(),
...
m a p s
```

Other operations are analogous, but the main thing to notice here is that all stack operations are module *functions*. For instance, it's possible to iterate over the stack, but we need to use counter-loops and indexing function calls (item). There's nothing preventing clients from accessing (and changing) stack1.stack directly, but doing so defeats the purpose of interfaces like this one.

A Stack Class

Perhaps the biggest drawback of the module-based stack is that it supports only a single stack object. All clients of the stack module effectively share the same stack. Sometimes we want this feature: a stack can serve as a shared-memory object for multiple modules. But to implement a true stack datatype, we need to use classes.

To illustrate, let's define a full-featured stack *class*. The Stack class shown in Example 17-2 defines a new datatype, with a variety of behavior. Like the module, the class uses a Python list to hold stacked objects. But this time, each instance gets its own list. The class defines both "real" methods, and specially named methods that implement common type operations. Comments in the code describe special methods.

Example 17-2. PP2E\Dstruct\Basic\stack2.py

```
error = 'stack2.error'                          # when imported: local exception

class Stack:
    def __init__(self, start=[]):               # self is the instance object
        self.stack = []                         # start is any sequence: stack..
        for x in start: self.push(x)
        self.reverse()                          # undo push's order reversal
    def push(self, obj):                        # methods: like module + self
        self.stack = [obj] + self.stack         # top is front of list
    def pop(self):
        if not self.stack: raise error, 'underflow'
        top, self.stack = self.stack[0], self.stack[1:]
        return top
    def top(self):
        if not self.stack: raise error, 'underflow'
        return self.stack[0]
    def empty(self):
        return not self.stack                                # instance.empty()

    # overloads
    def __repr__(self):
        return '[Stack:%s]' % self.stack                     # print, backquotes,..
    def __cmp__(self, other):
        return cmp(self.stack, other.stack)                  # '==', '>', '<=', '!=',..
    def __len__(self):
        return len(self.stack)                               # len(instance), not instance
    def __add__(self, other):
        return Stack(self.stack + other.stack)               # instance1 + instance2
    def __mul__(self, reps):
        return Stack(self.stack * reps)                      # instance * reps
    def __getitem__(self, offset):
        return self.stack[offset]                            # intance[offset], in, for
    def __getslice__(self, low, high):
        return Stack(self.stack[low : high])                 # instance[low:high]
    def __getattr__(self, name):
        return getattr(self.stack, name)                     # instance.sort()/reverse()/..
```

Now distinct instances are created by calling the `Stack` class like a function. In most respects, the `Stack` class implements operations exactly like the **stack** module in Example 17-1. But here, access to the stack is qualified by `self`, the subject instance object. Each instance has its own **stack** attribute, which refers to the instance's own list. Furthermore, instance stacks are created and initialized in the **__init__** constructor method, not when the module is imported. Let's make a couple of stacks to see how this all works in practice:

```
>>> from stack2 import Stack
>>> x = Stack()                     # make a stack object, push items
>>> x.push('spam')
>>> x.push(123)
>>> x                               # __repr__ prints a stack
[Stack:[123, 'spam']]
```

```
>>> y = Stack()                    # two distinct stacks objects
>>> y.push(3.1415)                 # they do not share content
>>> y.push(x.pop())
>>> x, y
([Stack:['spam']], [Stack:[123, 3.1415]])


>>> z = Stack()                    # third distinct stack object
>>> for c in 'spam': z.push(c)
...
>>> while z: print z.pop(),        # __len__ tests stack truth
...
m a p s

>>> z = x + y                      # __add__ handles stack +
>>> z                              # holds three different types
[Stack:['spam', 123, 3.1415]]
>>> for item in z: print item,     # __getitem__ does for
...
spam 123 3.1415
```

Like lists and dictionaries, Stack defines both methods and operators for manipulating instances by attribute qualification and expressions. Additionally, it defines the __getattr__ metaclass method to intercept references to attributes not defined in the class and to route them to the wrapped list object (to support list methods: sort, append, reverse, etc.). Many of the module's operations become operators in the class. Table 17-2 shows the equivalence of module and class operations (columns 1 and 2) and gives the class method that comes into play for each (column 3).

Table 17-2. Module/Class Operation Comparison

Module Operations	Class Operations	Class Method
module.empty()	not instance	__len__
module.member(x)	x in instance	__getitem__
module.item(i)	instance[i]	__getitem__
module.length()	len(instance)	__len__
module.dump()	print instance	__repr__
range() *counter loops*	for x in instance	__getitem__
manual loop logic	instance + instance	__add__
module.stack.reverse()	instance.reverse()	__getattr__
module.push/pop/top	instance.push/pop/top	push/pop/top

In effect, classes let us extend Python's set of built-in types with reusable types implemented in Python modules. Class-based types may be used just like built-in types: depending on which operation methods they define, classes can implement numbers, mappings, and sequences, and may be mutable or not. Class-based types may also fall somewhere in between these categories.

Customization: Performance Monitors

So far we've seen how classes support multiple instances and integrate better with Python's object model by defining operator methods. One of the other main reasons for using classes is to allow for future extensions and customizations. By implementing stacks with a class, we can later add subclasses that specialize the implementation for new demands.

For instance, suppose we've started using the `Stack` class in Example 17-2, but we start running into performance problems. One way to isolate bottlenecks is to instrument data structures with logic that keeps track of usage statistics, which we can analyze after running client applications. Because `Stack` is a class, we can add such logic in a new subclass, without affecting the original stack module (or its clients). The subclass in Example 17-3 extends `Stack` to keep track of overall push/pop usage frequencies and to record the maximum size of each instance.

Example 17-3. PP2E\Dstruct\Basic\stacklog.py

```
from stack2 import Stack                         # extends imported Stack

class StackLog(Stack):
    pushes = pops = 0                            # count pushes/pops, max-size
    def __init__(self, start=[]):                # shared/static class members
        self.maxlen = 0                          # could also be module vars
        Stack.__init__(self, start)
    def push(self, object):
        Stack.push(self, object)                 # do real push
        StackLog.pushes = StackLog.pushes + 1    # overall stats
        self.maxlen = max(self.maxlen, len(self)) # per-instance stats
    def pop(self):
        StackLog.pops = StackLog.pops + 1        # overall counts
        return Stack.pop(self)                   # not 'self.pops': instance
    def stats(self):
        return self.maxlen, self.pushes, self.pops # get counts from instance
```

This subclass works the same as the original `Stack`; it just adds monitoring logic. The new `stats` method is used to get a statistics tuple through an instance:

```
>>> from stacklog import StackLog
>>> x = StackLog()
>>> y = StackLog()                               # make two stack objects
>>> for i in range(3): x.push(i)                 # and push object on them
...
>>> for c in 'spam':   y.push(c)
...
>>> x, y                                          # run inherited __repr__
([Stack:[2, 1, 0]], [Stack:['m', 'a', 'p', 's']])
>>> x.stats(), y.stats()
((3, 7, 0), (4, 7, 0))
>>>
>>> y.pop(), x.pop()
('m', 2)
```

```
>>> x.stats(), y.stats()                      # my maxlen, all pushes, all pops
((3, 7, 2), (4, 7, 2))
```

Notice the use of *class* attributes to record overall pushes and pops, and *instance* attributes for per-instance maximum length. By hanging attributes on different objects, we can expand or narrow their scopes.

Optimization: Tuple Tree Stacks

One of the nice things about wrapping objects up in classes is that you are free to change the underlying implementation without breaking the rest of your program. Optimizations can be added in the future, for instance, with minimal impact; the interface is unchanged, even if the internals are. There are a variety of ways to implement stacks, some more efficient than others. So far, our stacks have used slicing and concatenation to implement pushing and popping. This method is relatively inefficient: both operations make copies of the wrapped list object. For large stacks, this practice can add a significant time penalty.

One way to speed up such code is to change the underlying data structure completely. For example, we can store the stacked objects in a binary tree of tuples: each item may be recorded as a pair: (object, tree), where object is the stacked item, and tree is either another tuple pair giving the rest of the stack or None to designate an empty stack. A stack of items [1,2,3,4] would be internally stored as a tuple tree (1,(2,(3,(4,None)))).

This tuple-based representation is similar to the notion of "cons-cells" in Lisp-family languages: the object on the left is the car, and the rest of the tree on the right is the cdr. Because we add or remove only a top tuple to push and pop items, this structure avoids copying the entire stack. For large stacks, the benefit might be significant. The next class, shown in Example 17-4, implements these ideas.

Example 17-4. PP2E\Dstruct\Basic\stack3.py

```
class Stack:
    def __init__(self, start=[]):          # init from any sequence
        self.stack = None                  # even other (fast)stacks
        for i in range(-len(start), 0):
            self.push(start[-i - 1])       # push in reverse order
    def push(self, node):                  # grow tree 'up/left'
        self.stack = node, self.stack      # new root tuple: (node, tree)
    def pop(self):
        node, self.stack = self.stack      # remove root tuple
        return node                        # TypeError if empty
    def empty(self):
        return not self.stack              # is it 'None'?
    def __len__(self):                     # on: len, not
        len, tree = 0, self.stack
        while tree:
            len, tree = len+1, tree[1]     # visit right subtrees
        return len
```

Example 17-4. PP2E\Dstruct\Basic\stack3.py (continued)

```
    def __getitem__(self, index):            # on: x[i], in, for
        len, tree = 0, self.stack
        while len < index and tree:          # visit/count nodes
            len, tree = len+1, tree[1]
        if tree:
            return tree[0]                    # IndexError if out-of-bounds
        else: raise IndexError                # so 'in' and 'for' stop
    def __repr__(self): return '[FastStack:' + `self.stack` + ']'
```

This class's __getitem__ method handles indexing, in tests, and for loop iteration as before, but this version has to traverse a tree to find a node by index. Notice that this isn't a subclass of the original Stack class. Since nearly every operation is implemented differently here, inheritance won't really help. But clients that restrict themselves to the operations that are common to both classes can still use them interchangeably—they just need to import a stack class from a different module to switch implementations. Here's a session with this stack version; as long as we stick to pushing, popping, indexing, and iterating, this version is essentially indistinguishable from the original:

```
>>> from stack3 import Stack
>>> x = Stack()
>>> y = Stack()
>>> for c in 'spam': x.push(c)
...
>>> for i in range(3): y.push(i)
...
>>> x
[FastStack:('m', ('a', ('p', ('s', None))))]
>>> y
[FastStack:(2, (1, (0, None)))]

>>> len(x), x[2], x[-1]
(4, 'p', 'm')
>>> x.pop()
'm'
>>> x
[FastStack:('a', ('p', ('s', None)))]
>>>
>>> while y: print y.pop(),
...
2 1 0
```

Optimization: In-place List Modifications

Perhaps a better way to speed up the stack object, though, is to fall back on the mutability of Python's list object. Because lists can be changed in place, they can be modified more quickly than any of the prior examples. In-place change operations like append are prone to complications when a list is referenced from more than one place. But because the list inside the stack object isn't meant to be used directly, we're probably safe here. The module in Example 17-5 shows one way to implement a stack with in-place changes; some operator overloading methods have been dropped to keep this simple. The new Python `pop` method it uses is equivalent to indexing and deleting the item at offset −1 (top is end-of-list here).

Example 17-5. PP2E\Dstruct\Basic\stack4.py

```
error = 'stack4.error'                       # when imported: local exception

class Stack:
    def __init__(self, start=[]):            # self is the instance object
        self.stack = []                      # start is any sequence: stack..
        for x in start: self.push(x)
    def push(self, obj):                     # methods: like module + self
        self.stack.append(obj)               # top is end of list
    def pop(self):
        if not self.stack: raise error, 'underflow'
        return self.stack.pop()              # like fetch and delete stack[-1]
    def top(self):
        if not self.stack: raise error, 'underflow'
        return self.stack[-1]
    def empty(self):
        return not self.stack                # instance.empty()
    def __len__(self):
        return len(self.stack)               # len(instance), not intance
    def __getitem__(self, offset):
        return self.stack[offset]            # instance[offset], in, for
    def __repr__(self): return '[Stack:%s]' % self.stack
```

This version works like the original in module `stack2`, too—just replace `stack2` with `stack4` in the previous interaction to get a feel for its operation. The only obvious difference is that stack items are in reverse when printed (i.e., the top is the end):

```
>>> from stack4 import Stack
>>> x = Stack()
>>> x.push('spam')
>>> x.push(123)
>>> x
[Stack:['spam', 123]]
>>>
>>> y = Stack()
>>> y.push(3.1415)
>>> y.push(x.pop())
>>> x, y
([Stack:['spam']], [Stack:[3.1415, 123]])
>>> y.top()
123
```

Timing the Improvements

The in-place changes stack object probably runs faster than both the original and the tuple-tree version, but the only way to really be sure how much faster is to time the alternative implementations. Since this could be something we'll want to do more than once, let's first define a general module for timing functions in Python. In Example 17-6, the built-in `time` module provides a `clock` function that we can use to get the current CPU time in floating-point seconds, and the function `timer.test` simply calls a function `reps` times and returns the number of elapsed seconds by subtracting stop from start CPU times.

Example 17-6. PP2E\Dstruct\Basic\timer.py

```
def test(reps, func, *args):
    import time
    start = time.clock()                # current CPU tim in float seconds
    for i in xrange(reps):              # call function reps times
        apply(func, args)               # discard any return value
    return time.clock() - start         # stop time - start time
```

Next, we define a test driver script (see Example 17-7). It expects three command-line arguments: the number of pushes, pops, and indexing operations to perform (we'll vary these arguments to test different scenarios). When run at the top level, the script creates 200 instances of the original and optimized stack classes, and performs the specified number of operations on each stack.* Pushes and pops change the stack; indexing just accesses it.

Example 17-7. PP2E\Dstruct\Basic\stacktime.py

```
import stack2         # list-based stacks: [x]+y
import stack3         # tuple-tree stacks: (x,y)
import stack4         # in-place stacks:  y.append(x)
import timer          # general function timer function

rept = 200
from sys import argv
pushes, pops, items = eval(argv[1]), eval(argv[2]), eval(argv[3])

def stackops(stackClass):
    #print stackClass.__module__
    x = stackClass('spam')              # make a stack object
    for i in range(pushes): x.push(i)   # exercise its methods
    for i in range(items): t = x[i]
    for i in range(pops):   x.pop()

print 'stack2:', timer.test(rept, stackops, stack2.Stack)   # pass class to test
print 'stack3:', timer.test(rept, stackops, stack3.Stack)   # rept*(push+pop+ix)
print 'stack4:', timer.test(rept, stackops, stack4.Stack)
```

Here are some of the timings reported by the test driver script. The three outputs represent the measured run times in seconds for the original, tuple, and in-place stacks. For each stack type, the first test creates 200 stack objects and performs

---

* If you have a copy of the first edition of this book lying around, you might notice that I had to scale all test factors way up to get even close to the run times I noticed before. Both Python and chips have gotten a lot faster in five years.

roughly 120,000 stack operations (200 rept × (200 pushes + 200 indexes + 200 pops)), in the test duration times listed. These results were obtained on a 650 MHz Pentium III Windows machine, and a Python 1.5.2 install:

```
C:\...\PP2E\Dstruct\Basic>python stacktime.py 200 200 200
stack2: 1.67890008213
stack3: 7.70020952413
stack4: 0.694291724635

C:\...\PP2E\Dstruct\Basic>python stacktime.py 200 50 200
stack2: 1.06876246669
stack3: 7.48964866994
stack4: 0.477584270605

C:\...\PP2E\Dstruct\Basic>python stacktime.py 200 200 50
stack2: 1.34536448817
stack3: 0.795615917129
stack4: 0.57297976835

C:\...\PP2E\Dstruct\Basic>python stacktime.py 200 200 0
stack2: 1.33500477715
stack3: 0.300776077373
stack4: 0.533050336077
```

If you look closely enough, you'll notice that the results show that the tuple-based stack (stack3) performs better when we do more pushing and popping, but worse if we do much indexing. Indexing lists is extremely fast for built-in lists, but very slow for tuple trees—the Python class must traverse the tree manually. The in-place change stacks (stack4) are almost always fastest, unless no indexing is done at all—tuples won by a hair in the last test case. Since pushes and pops are most of what clients would do to a stack, tuples are a contender, despite their poor indexing performance. Of course, we're talking about fractions of a second after many tens of thousands of operations; in many applications, your users probably won't care either way.

Implementing Sets

Another commonly used data structure is the *set,* a collection of objects that support operations such as:

Intersection
    Make a new set with all items in common.

Union
    Make a new set with all items in either operand.

Membership
    Test if an item exists in a set.

And there are others, depending on the intended use. Sets come in handy for dealing with more abstract group combinations. For instance, given a set of engineers and a set of writers, you can pick out individuals who do both activities by intersecting the two sets. A union of such sets would contain either type of individual, but only include any given individual once.

Python lists, tuples, and strings come close to the notion of a set: the `in` operator tests membership, `for` iterates, etc. Here, we add operations not directly supported by Python sequences. The idea is that we're *extending* built-in types for unique requirements.

Set Functions

As before, let's first start out with a function-based set manager. But this time, instead of managing a shared set object in a module, let's define functions to implement set operations on passed-in Python sequences (see Example 17-8).

Example 17-8. PP2E\Dstruct\Basic\inter.py

```python
def intersect(seq1, seq2):
    res = []                       # start with an empty list
    for x in seq1:                 # scan the first sequence
        if x in seq2:
            res.append(x)          # add common items to the end
    return res

def union(seq1, seq2):
    res = list(seq1)               # make a copy of seq1
    for x in seq2:                 # add new items in seq2
        if not x in res:
            res.append(x)
    return res
```

These functions work on any type of sequence—lists strings, tuples, and other objects that conform to the sequence protocols expected by these functions (`for` loops, `in` membership tests). In fact, we can even use them on mixed object types: the last two commands in the following code compute the intersection and union of a list and a tuple. As usual in Python, the object *interface* is what matters, not the specific types:

```
C:\...\PP2E\Dstruct\Basic>python
>>> from inter import *
>>> s1 = "SPAM"
>>> s2 = "SCAM"
>>> intersect(s1, s2), union(s1, s2)
(['S', 'A', 'M'], ['S', 'P', 'A', 'M', 'C'])
>>> intersect([1,2,3], (1,4))
[1]
>>> union([1,2,3], (1,4))
[1, 2, 3, 4]
```

Notice that the result is always a list here, regardless of the type of sequences passed in. We could work around this by converting types or by using a class to sidestep this issue (and we will in a moment). But type conversions aren't clear-cut if the operands are mixed-type sequences. Which type do we convert to?

Supporting multiple operands

If we're going to use the intersect and union functions as general tools, one useful extension is support for multiple arguments (i.e., more than two). The functions in Example 17-9 use Python's variable-length argument lists feature to compute the intersection and union of arbitrarily many operands.

Example 17-9. PP2E\Dstruct\Basic\inter2.py

```
def intersect(*args):
    res = []
    for x in args[0]:            # scan the first list
        for other in args[1:]:   # for all other arguments
            if x not in other: break   # this item in each one?
        else:
            res.append(x)        # add common items to the end
    return res

def union(*args):
    res = []
    for seq in args:             # for all sequence-arguments
        for x in seq:            # for all nodes in argument
            if not x in res:
                res.append(x)    # add new items to result
    return res
```

The multi-operand functions work on sequences in the same way as the original functions, but they support three or more operands. Notice that the last two examples in the following session work on lists with embedded compound objects: the in tests used by the intersect and union functions apply equality testing to sequence nodes recursively, as deep as necessary to determine collection comparison results:

```
C:\...\PP2E\Dstruct\Basic>python
>>> from inter2 import *
>>> s1, s2, s3 = 'SPAM', 'SLAM', 'SCAM'
>>> intersect(s1, s2)
['S', 'A', 'M']
>>> intersect(s1, s2, s3)
['S', 'A', 'M']
>>> intersect(s1, s2, s3, 'HAM')
['A', 'M']

>>> union(s1, s2), union(s1, s2, s3)
(['S', 'P', 'A', 'M', 'L'], ['S', 'P', 'A', 'M', 'L', 'C'])
>>> intersect([1,2,3], (1,4), range(5))
[1]
```

```
>>> s1 = (9, (3.14, 1), "bye", [1,2], "mello")
>>> s2 = [[1,2], "hello", (3.14, 0), 9]
>>> intersect(s1, s2)
[9, [1, 2]]
>>> union(s1, s2)
[9, (3.14, 1), 'bye', [1, 2], 'mello', 'hello', (3.14, 0)]
```

Set Classes

The set functions can operate on a variety of sequences, but they aren't as friendly as true objects. Among other things, your scripts need to keep track of the sequences passed into these functions manually. Classes can do better: the class in Example 17-10 implements a set object that can hold any type of object. Like the stack classes, it's essentially a wrapper around a Python list with extra set operations.

Example 17-10. PP2E\Dstruct\Basic\set.py

```
class Set:
    def __init__(self, value = []):        # on object creation
        self.data = []                     # manages a local list
        self.concat(value)
    def intersect(self, other):            # other is any sequence type
        res = []                           # self is the instance subject
        for x in self.data:
            if x in other:
                res.append(x)
        return Set(res)                    # return a new Set
    def union(self, other):
        res = self.data[:]                 # make a copy of my list
        for x in other:
            if not x in res:
                res.append(x)
        return Set(res)
    def concat(self, value):               # value: a list, string, Set...
        for x in value:                    # filters out duplicates
            if not x in self.data:
                self.data.append(x)

    def __len__(self):        return len(self.data)
    def __getitem__(self, key): return self.data[key]
    def __and__(self, other): return self.intersect(other)
    def __or__(self, other):  return self.union(other)
    def __repr__(self):       return '<Set:' + `self.data` + '>'
```

The Set class is used like the Stack class we saw earlier in this chapter: we make instances and apply sequence operators plus unique set operations to them. Intersection and union can be called as methods, or by using the & and | operators normally used for built-in integer objects. Because we can string operators in expressions now (e.g., x & y & z), there is no obvious need to support multiple operands in intersect/union methods here. As with all objects, we can either use the `Set` class within a program, or test it interactively as follows:

```
>>> from set import Set
>>> users1 = Set(['Bob', 'Emily', 'Howard', 'Peeper'])
>>> users2 = Set(['Jerry', 'Howard', 'Carol'])
>>> users3 = Set(['Emily', 'Carol'])
>>> users1 & users2
<Set:['Howard']>
>>> users1 | users2
<Set:['Bob', 'Emily', 'Howard', 'Peeper', 'Jerry', 'Carol']>
>>> users1 | users2 & users3
<Set:['Bob', 'Emily', 'Howard', 'Peeper', 'Carol']>
>>> (users1 | users2) & users3
<Set:['Emily', 'Carol']>
>>> users1.data
['Bob', 'Emily', 'Howard', 'Peeper']
```

Optimization: Moving Sets to Dictionaries

Once you start using the `Set` class, the first problem you might encounter is its performance: its nested `for` loops and `in` scans become exponentially slow. That slowness may or may not be significant in your applications, but library classes should generally be coded as efficiently as possible.

One way to optimize set performance is by changing the implementation to use dictionaries instead of lists, for storing sets internally—items may be stored as the keys of a dictionary whose values are all `None`. Because lookup time is constant and short for dictionaries, the `in` list scans of the original set may be replaced with direct dictionary fetches in this scheme. In traditional terms, moving sets to dictionaries replaces slow linear searches with fast hash tables.

The module in Example 17-11 implements this idea. Its class is a subclass of the original set, and redefines the methods that deal with the internal representation but inherits others. The inherited `&` and `|` methods trigger the new intersect and union methods here, and the inherited `len` method works on dictionaries as is. As long as `Set` clients are not dependent on the order of items in a set, they can switch to this version directly by just changing the name of the module where `Set` is imported from; the class name is the same.

Example 17-11. PP2E\Dstruct\Basic\fastset.py

```
import set
                                        # fastset.Set extends set.Set
class Set(set.Set):
    def __init__(self, value = []):
        self.data = {}                  # manages a local dictionary
        self.concat(value)              # hashing: linear search times
    def intersect(self, other):
```

Example 17-11. PP2E\Dstruct\Basic\fastset.py (continued)

```
        res = {}
        for x in other:                        # other: a sequence or Set
            if self.data.has_key(x):           # use hash-table lookup
                res[x] = None
        return Set(res.keys())                 # a new dictionary-based Set
    def union(self, other):
        res = {}                               # other: a sequence or Set
        for x in other:                        # scan each set just once
            res[x] = None
        for x in self.data.keys():             # '&' and '|' come back here
            res[x] = None                      # so they make new fastset's
        return Set(res.keys())
    def concat(self, value):
        for x in value: self.data[x] = None

    # inherit and, or, len
    def __getitem__(self, key):  return self.data.keys()[key]
    def __repr__(self):          return '<Set:' + `self.data.keys()` + '>'
```

This works about the same as the previous version:

```
>>> from fastset import Set
>>> users1 = Set(['Bob', 'Emily', 'Howard', 'Peeper'])
>>> users2 = Set(['Jerry', 'Howard', 'Carol'])
>>> users3 = Set(['Emily', 'Carol'])
>>> users1 & users2
<Set:['Howard']>
>>> users1 | users2
<Set:['Emily', 'Howard', 'Jerry', 'Carol', 'Peeper', 'Bob']>
>>> users1 | users2 & users3
<Set:['Emily', 'Howard', 'Carol', 'Peeper', 'Bob']>
>>> (users1 | users2) & users3
<Set:['Emily', 'Carol']>
>>> users1.data
{'Emily': None, 'Bob': None, 'Peeper': None, 'Howard': None}
```

The main functional difference in this version is the *order* of items in the set: because dictionaries are randomly ordered, this set's order will differ from the original. For instance, you can store compound objects in sets, but the order of items varies in this version:

```
>>> import set, fastset
>>> a = set.Set([(1,2), (3,4), (5,6)])
>>> b = set.Set([(3,4), (7,8)])
>>> a & b
<Set:[(3, 4)]>
>>> a | b
<Set:[(1, 2), (3, 4), (5, 6), (7, 8)]>

>>> a = fastset.Set([(1,2), (3,4), (5,6)])
>>> b = fastset.Set([(3,4), (7,8)])
>>> a & b
```

```
<Set:[(3, 4)]>
>>> a | b
<Set:[(3, 4), (1, 2), (7, 8), (5, 6)]>
>>> b | a
<Set:[(3, 4), (5, 6), (1, 2), (7, 8)]>
```

Sets aren't supposed to be ordered anyhow, so this isn't a showstopper. A deviation that might matter, though, is that this version cannot be used to store unhashable objects. This stems from the fact that dictionary keys must be immutable. Because values are stored in keys, dictionary sets can contain only things like tuples, strings, numbers, and class objects with immutable signatures. Mutable objects like lists and dictionaries won't work directly. For example, the call:

```
fastset.Set([[1,2],[3,4]])
```

raises an exception with this dictionary-based set, but works with the original set class. Tuples work here because they are immutable; Python computes hash values and tests key equality as expected.

Timing the results

So how did we do on the optimization front? Example 17-12 contains a script to compare set class performance. It reuses the **timer** module used earlier to test stacks.

Example 17-12. PP2E\Dstruct\Basic\settime.py

```
import timer, sys
import set, fastset

def setops(Class):
    a = Class(range(50))                # a 50-integer set
    b = Class(range(20))                # a 20-integer set
    c = Class(range(10))
    d = Class(range(5))
    for i in range(5):
        t = a & b & c & d               # 3 intersections
        t = a | b | c | d               # 3 unions

if __name__ == '__main__':
    rept = int(sys.argv[1])
    print 'set =>   ', timer.test(rept, setops, set.Set)
    print 'fastset =>', timer.test(rept, setops, fastset.Set)
```

The **setops** function makes four sets and combines them with intersection and union operators five times. A command-line argument controls the number of times this whole process is repeated. More accurately, each call to **setops** makes 34 Set instances (4 + [5 × (3 + 3)]), and runs the **intersect** and **union** methods

15 times each (5 × 3) in the `for` loop's body. On the same test machine, the performance improvement is equally dramatic this time around:

```
C:\...\PP2E\Dstruct\Basic>python settime.py 50
set =>     1.5440352671
fastset => 0.446057593993

C:\...\PP2E\Dstruct\Basic>python settime.py 100
set =>     2.77783486146
fastset => 0.888354648921

C:\...\PP2E\Dstruct\Basic>python settime.py 200
set =>     5.7762634305
fastset => 1.77677885985
```

At least for this test case, the simple set implementation is over three times slower than dictionary-based sets. In fact, this threefold speedup is probably sufficient. Python dictionaries are already optimized hash tables that you might be hard-pressed to improve on. Unless there is evidence that dictionary-based sets are still too slow, our work here is probably done.

Using the Python Profiler

The Python profiler provides another way to gather performance data besides timing sections of code as done in this chapter. Because the profiler tracks all function calls, it provides much more information in a single blow. As such, it's a more powerful way to isolate bottlenecks in slow programs—after profiling, you should have a good idea where to focus your optimization efforts.

The profiler ships with Python as the standard library module called `profile`, and provides a variety of interfaces for measuring code performance. It is structured and used much like the `pdb` command-line debugger: import the `profile` module and call its functions with a code string to measure performance. The simplest profiling interface is its `profile.run(statementstring)` function. When invoked, the profiler runs the code string, collects statistics during the run, and issues a report on the screen when the statement completes.

The report's format is straightforward and well-documented in the Python library manual. By default, it lists the number of calls and times spent in each function invoked during the run. When the profiler is enabled, each interpreter event is routed to a Python handler. This gives an accurate picture of performance, but tends to make the program being profiled run much slower than normal.

Optimizing fastset by Coding Techniques (or Not)

As coded, there seems to be a bottleneck in the `fastset` class: each time we call a dictionary's `keys` method, Python makes a new list to hold the result, and this can happen repeatedly during intersections and unions. If you are interested in trying to optimize this further, see the following files in the book CD:

- *PP2E\Dstruct\Basic\fastset2.py*
- *PP2E\Dstruct\Basic\fastset3.py*

I wrote these to try to speed up sets further, but failed miserably. It turns out that adding extra code to try to shave operations usually negates the speedup you obtain. There may be faster codings, but the biggest win here was likely in changing the underlying data structure to dictionaries, not in minor code tweaks.

As a rule of thumb, your intuition about performance is almost always wrong in a dynamic language like Python: the algorithm is usually the real culprit behind performance problems, not the coding style or even the implementation language. By removing the combinatorial list scanning algorithm of the original set class, the Python implementation became dramatically faster.

In fact, moving the original set class to C without fixing the algorithm would not have addressed the real performance problem. Coding tricks don't usually help as much either, and they make your programs difficult to understand. In Python, it's almost always best to code for readability first and optimize later if needed. Despite its simplicity, `fastset` is fast indeed.

Adding Relational Algebra to Sets (CD)

If you are interested in studying additional set-like operations coded in Python, see the following files on this book's CD:

- *PP2E\Dstruct\Basic\rset.py*: `RSet` implementation
- *PP2E\Dstruct\Basic\reltest.py*: Test script for `RSet`

The `RSet` subclass defined in *rset.py* adds basic relational algebra operations for sets of dictionaries. It assumes the items in sets are mappings (rows), with one entry per column (field). `RSet` inherits all the original `Set` operations (iteration, intersection, union, & and | operators, uniqueness filtering, etc.), and adds new operations as methods:

Select
> Return a set of nodes that have a field equal to a given value.

Bagof
> Collect set nodes that satisfy an expression string.

Find

Select tuples according to a comparison, field, and value.

Match

Find nodes in two sets with the same values for common fields.

Product

Compute a Cartesian product: concatenate tuples from two sets.

Join

Combine tuples from two sets that have the same value for a field.

Project

Extract named fields from the tuples in a table.

Difference

Remove one set's tuples from another.

Alternative implementations of set *difference* operations can also be found in the *diff.py* file in the same CD directory.

Binary Search Trees

Binary trees are a data structure that impose an order on inserted nodes: items less than a node are stored in its left subtree, and items greater than a node are inserted in the right. At the bottom, the subtrees are empty. Because of this structure, binary trees naturally support quick, recursive traversals—at least ideally, every time you follow a link to a subtree, you divide the search space in half.[*]

Binary trees are named for the implied branch-like structure of their subtree links. Typically, their nodes are implemented as a triple of values: (`LeftSubtree`, `NodeValue`, `RightSubtree`). Beyond that, there is fairly wide latitude in the tree implementation. Here we'll use a class-based approach:

- *BinaryTree* is a header object, which initializes and manages the actual tree.
- *EmptyNode* is the empty object, shared at all empty subtrees (at the bottom).
- *BinaryNode* objects are nonempty tree nodes with a value and two subtrees.

Rather than coding distinct search functions, binary trees are constructed with "smart" objects (class instances) that know how to handle insert/lookup and printing requests and pass them to subtree objects. In fact, this is another example of the OOP composition relationship in action: tree nodes embed other tree nodes and pass search requests off to the embedded subtrees. A single empty class

---

[*] If you're looking for a more graphical image of binary trees, skip ahead to the PyTree examples at the end of this chapter, or simply run it on your own machine.

instance is shared by all empty subtrees in a binary tree, and inserts replace an
EmptyNode with a BinaryNode at the bottom (see Example 17-13).

Example 17-13. PP2E\Dstruct\Classics\btree.py

```
class BinaryTree:
    def __init__(self):        self.tree = EmptyNode()
    def __repr__(self):        return `self.tree`
    def lookup(self, value):   return self.tree.lookup(value)
    def insert(self, value):   self.tree = self.tree.insert(value)

class EmptyNode:
    def __repr__(self):
        return '*'
    def lookup(self, value):                            # fail at the bottom
        return 0
    def insert(self, value):
        return BinaryNode(self, value, self)       # add new node at bottom

class BinaryNode:
    def __init__(self, left, value, right):
        self.data, self.left, self.right  =  value, left, right
    def lookup(self, value):
        if self.data == value:
            return 1
        elif self.data > value:
            return self.left.lookup(value)              # look in left
        else:
            return self.right.lookup(value)             # look in right
    def insert(self, value):
        if self.data > value:
            self.left = self.left.insert(value)         # grow in left
        elif self.data < value:
            self.right = self.right.insert(value)       # grow in right
        return self
    def __repr__(self):
        return '( %s, %s, %s )' % (`self.left`, `self.data`, `self.right`)
```

As usual, BinaryTree can contain objects of any type that support the expected
interface protocol—here, > and < comparisons. This includes class instances with
the __cmp__ method. Let's experiment with this module's interfaces. The following code stuffs five integers into a new tree, and then searches for values 0...9:

```
C:\...\PP2E\Dstruct\Classics>python
>>> from btree import BinaryTree
>>> x = BinaryTree()
>>> for i in [3,1,9,2,7]:  x.insert(i)
...
>>> for i in range(10):  print (i, x.lookup(i)),
...
(0, 0) (1, 1) (2, 1) (3, 1) (4, 0) (5, 0) (6, 0) (7, 1) (8, 0) (9, 1)
```

To watch this tree grow, add a print statement after each insert. Tree nodes print themselves as triples, and empty nodes print as *. The result reflects tree nesting:

```
>>> y = BinaryTree()
>>> y
*
>>> for i in [3,1,9,2,7]:
...     y.insert(i); print y
...
( *, 3, * )
( ( *, 1, * ), 3, * )
( ( *, 1, * ), 3, ( *, 9, * ) )
( ( *, 1, ( *, 2, * ) ), 3, ( *, 9, * ) )
( ( *, 1, ( *, 2, * ) ), 3, ( ( *, 7, * ), 9, * ) )
```

At the end of this chapter, we'll see another way to visualize trees in a GUI (which means you're invited to flip ahead now). Node values in this tree object can be any comparable Python object; for instances, here is a tree of strings:

```
>>> z = BinaryTree()
>>> for c in 'badce':  z.insert(c)
...
>>> z
( ( *, 'a', * ), 'b', ( ( *, 'c', * ), 'd', ( *, 'e', * ) ) )
>>> z = BinaryTree()
>>> for c in 'abcde':  z.insert(c)
...
>>> z
( *, 'a', ( *, 'b', ( *, 'c', ( *, 'd', ( *, 'e', * ) ) ) ) )
```

Notice the last result here: if items inserted into a binary tree are already ordered, then you wind up with a *linear* structure, and you lose the search-space partitioning magic of binary trees (the tree grows in right branches only). This is a worst-case scenario, and binary trees generally do a good job of dividing up values in practice. But if you are interested in pursuing this topic further, see a data structures text for tree-balancing techniques that automatically keep the tree as dense as possible.

Also note that to keep the code simple, these trees store a value only, and look-ups return a 1 or 0 (true or false). In practice, you sometimes may want to store both a key and an associated value (or even more) at each tree node. Example 17-14 shows what such a tree object looks like, for any prospective lumberjacks in the audience.

Example 17-14. PP2E\Dstruct\Classics\btree-keys.py

```
class KeyedBinaryTree:
    def __init__(self):           self.tree = EmptyNode()
    def __repr__(self):           return `self.tree`
    def lookup(self, key):        return self.tree.lookup(key)
    def insert(self, key, val):   self.tree = self.tree.insert(key, val)
```

Example 17-14. PP2E\Dstruct\Classics\btree-keys.py (continued)

```
class EmptyNode:
    def __repr__(self):
        return '*'
    def lookup(self, key):                              # fail at the bottom
        return None
    def insert(self, key, val):
        return BinaryNode(self, key, val, self)         # add node at bottom

class BinaryNode:
    def __init__(self, left, key, val, right):
        self.key,  self.val   = key, val
        self.left, self.right = left, right
    def lookup(self, key):
        if self.key == key:
            return self.val
        elif self.key > key:
            return self.left.lookup(key)                # look in left
        else:
            return self.right.lookup(key)               # look in right
    def insert(self, key, val):
        if self.key == key:
            self.val = val
        elif self.key > key:
            self.left = self.left.insert(key, val)      # grow in left
        elif self.key < key:
            self.right = self.right.insert(key, val)    # grow in right
        return self
    def __repr__(self):
        return ('( %s, %s=%s, %s )' %
                (`self.left`, `self.key`, `self.val`, `self.right`))

if __name__ == '__main__':
    t = KeyedBinaryTree()
    for (key, val) in [('bbb', 1), ('aaa', 2), ('ccc', 3)]:
        t.insert(key, val)
    print t
    print t.lookup('aaa'), t.lookup('ccc')
    t.insert('ddd', 4)
    t.insert('aaa', 5)                        # changes key's value
    print t
```

And here is this script's self-test code at work; nodes simply have more content this time around:

```
C:\...\PP2E\Dstruct\Classics>python btree-keys.py
( ( *, 'aaa'=2, * ), 'bbb'=1, ( *, 'ccc'=3, * ) )
2 3
( ( *, 'aaa'=5, * ), 'bbb'=1, ( *, 'ccc'=3, ( *, 'ddd'=4, * ) ) )
```

Graph Searching

Many problems can be represented as a graph, which is a set of states with transitions ("arcs") that lead from one state to another. For example, planning a route for a trip is really a graph search problem in disguise—the states are places you'd like to visit, and the arcs are the transportation links between them.

This section presents simple Python programs that search through a directed, cyclic graph to find the paths between a start state and a goal. Graphs can be more general than trees, because links may point at arbitrary nodes—even ones already searched (hence the word "cyclic").

The graph used to test searchers in this section is sketched in Figure 17-1. Arrows at the end of arcs indicate valid paths (e.g., *A* leads to *B*, *E*, and *G*). The search algorithms will traverse this graph in a depth-first fashion, and trap cycles in order to avoid looping. If you pretend that this is a map, where nodes represent cities, and arcs represent roads, this example will probably seem a bit more meaningful.

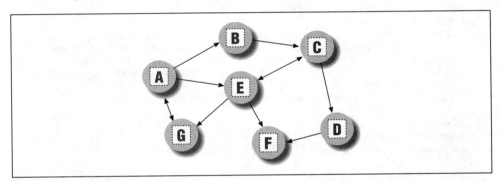

Figure 17-1. A directed graph

The first thing we need to do is choose a way to represent this graph in a Python script. One approach is to use built-in datatypes and searcher functions. The file in Example 17-15 builds the test graph as a simple dictionary: each state is a dictionary key, with a list of keys of nodes it leads to (i.e., its arcs). This file also defines a function that we'll use to run a few searches in the graph.

Example 17-15. PP2E\Dstruct\Classics\gtestfunc.py

```
Graph = {'A': ['B', 'E', 'G'],
         'B': ['C'],                    # a directed, cyclic graph
         'C': ['D', 'E'],               # stored as a dictionary
         'D': ['F'],                    # 'key' leads-to [nodes]
         'E': ['C', 'F', 'G'],
         'F': [ ],
         'G': ['A']  }
```

Example 17-15. PP2E\Dstruct\Classics\gtestfunc.py (continued)

```
def tests(searcher):                        # test searcher function
    print searcher('E', 'D', Graph)         # find all paths from 'E' to 'D'
    for x in ['AG', 'GF', 'BA', 'DA']:
        print x, searcher(x[0], x[1], Graph)
```

Now let's code two modules that implement the actual search algorithms. They are
both independent of the graph to be searched (it is passed in as an argument).
The first searcher, in Example 17-16, uses *recursion* to walk through the graph.

Example 17-16. PP2E\Dstruct\Classics\gsearch1.py

```
# find all paths from start to goal in graph

def search(start, goal, graph):
    solns = []
    generate([start], goal, solns, graph)        # collect paths
    solns.sort( lambda x, y: cmp(len(x), len(y)) )   # sort by path length
    return solns

def generate(path, goal, solns, graph):
    state = path[-1]
    if state == goal:                            # found goal here
        solns.append(path)                       # change solns in-place
    else:                                        # check all arcs here
        for arc in graph[state]:                 # skip cycles on path
            if arc not in path:
                generate(path + [arc], goal, solns, graph)

if __name__ == '__main__':
    import gtestfunc
    gtestfunc.tests(search)
```

The second searcher, in Example 17-17, uses an explicit *stack* of paths to be
expanded using the tuple-tree stack representation we explored earlier in this
chapter.

Example 17-17. PP2E\Dstruct\Classics\gsearch2.py

```
# use paths stack instead of recursion

def search(start, goal, graph):
    solns = generate( ([start], []), goal, graph)
    solns.sort( lambda x, y: cmp(len(x), len(y)) )
    return solns

def generate(paths, goal, graph):               # returns solns list
    solns = []                                  # use a tuple-stack
    while paths:
        front, paths = paths                    # pop the top path
        state = front[-1]
        if state == goal:
```

Example 17-17. PP2E\Dstruct\Classics\gsearch2.py (continued)

```
            solns.append(front)                    # goal on this path
        else:
            for arc in graph[state]:               # add all extensions
                if arc not in front:
                    paths = (front + [arc]), paths
    return solns

if __name__ == '__main__':
    import gtestfunc
    gtestfunc.tests(search)
```

Both searchers keep track of nodes visited along a path, to avoid cycles. If an extension is already on the current path, it is a loop. The resulting solutions list is sorted by increasing lengths using the list **sort** method and the built-in **cmp** comparison function. To test the searcher modules, simply run them; their self-test code calls the canned search test in the **gtestfunc** module:

```
C:\...\PP2E\Dstruct\Classics>python gsearch1.py
[['E', 'C', 'D'], ['E', 'G', 'A', 'B', 'C', 'D']]
AG [['A', 'G'], ['A', 'E', 'G'], ['A', 'B', 'C', 'E', 'G']]
GF [['G', 'A', 'E', 'F'], ['G', 'A', 'B', 'C', 'D', 'F'],
    ['G', 'A', 'B', 'C', 'E', 'F'], ['G', 'A', 'E', 'C', 'D', 'F']]
BA [['B', 'C', 'E', 'G', 'A']]
DA []

C:\...\PP2E\Dstruct\Classics>python gsearch2.py
[['E', 'C', 'D'], ['E', 'G', 'A', 'B', 'C', 'D']]
AG [['A', 'G'], ['A', 'E', 'G'], ['A', 'B', 'C', 'E', 'G']]
GF [['G', 'A', 'E', 'F'], ['G', 'A', 'E', 'C', 'D', 'F'],
    ['G', 'A', 'B', 'C', 'E', 'F'], ['G', 'A', 'B', 'C', 'D', 'F']]
BA [['B', 'C', 'E', 'G', 'A']]
DA []
```

This output shows lists of possible paths through the test graph; I added two line breaks to make it more readable. Notice that both searchers find the same paths in all tests, but the order in which they find those solutions may differ. The **gsearch2** order depends on how and when extensions are added to its path's stack.

Moving Graphs to Classes

Using dictionaries to represent graphs is efficient: connected nodes are located by a fast hashing operation. But depending on the application, other representations might make more sense. For instance, classes can be used to model nodes in a network, too, much like the binary tree example earlier. As classes, nodes may contain content useful for more sophisticated searches. To illustrate, Example 17-18 shows an alternative coding for our graph searcher; its algorithm is closest to **gsearch1**.

Example 17-18. PP2E\Dstruct\Classics\graph.py

```
# build graph with objects that know how to search

class Graph:
    def __init__(self, label, extra=None):
        self.name = label                           # nodes=inst objects
        self.data = extra                           # graph=linked objs
        self.arcs = []
    def __repr__(self):
        return self.name
    def search(self, goal):
        Graph.solns = []
        self.generate([self], goal)
        Graph.solns.sort(lambda x,y: cmp(len(x), len(y)))
        return Graph.solns
    def generate(self, path, goal):
        if self == goal:                            # class == tests addr
            Graph.solns.append(path)                # or self.solns: same
        else:
            for arc in self.arcs:
                if arc not in path:
                    arc.generate(path + [arc], goal)

if __name__ == '__main__':
    import gtestobj1
    gtestobj1.tests(Graph)
```

In this version, graphs are represented as a network of embedded class instance objects. Each node in the graph contains a list of the node objects it leads to (arcs), which it knows how to search. The generate method walks through the objects in the graph. But this time, links are directly available on each node's arcs list; there is no need to index (or pass) a dictionary to find linked objects.

To test, the module in Example 17-19 builds the test graph again, this time using linked instances of the Graph class. Notice the use of exec in the self-test code: it executes dynamically constructed strings to do the work of seven assignment statements (A=Graph('A'), B=Graph('B'), etc.).

Example 17-19. PP2E\Dstruct\Classics\gtestobj1.py

```
def tests(Graph):
    for name in "ABCDEFG":                          # make objects first
        exec "%s = Graph('%s')" % (name, name)      # label=variable-name

    A.arcs = [B, E, G]
    B.arcs = [C]                                    # now configure their links:
    C.arcs = [D, E]                                 # embedded class-instance list
    D.arcs = [F]
    E.arcs = [C, F, G]
    G.arcs = [A]
```

Example 17-19. PP2E\Dstruct\Classics\gtestobj1.py (continued)

```
A.search(G)
for (start, stop) in [(E,D), (A,G), (G,F), (B,A), (D,A)]:
    print start.search(stop)
```

You run this test by running the **graph** module to pass in a graph class, like this:

```
C:\...\PP2E\Dstruct\Classics>python graph.py
[[E, C, D], [E, G, A, B, C, D]]
[[A, G], [A, E, G], [A, B, C, E, G]]
[[G, A, E, F], [G, A, B, C, D, F], [G, A, B, C, E, F], [G, A, E, C, D, F]]
[[B, C, E, G, A]]
[]
```

The results are the same as for the functions, but node name labels are not quoted: nodes on path lists here are **Graph** instances, and this class's **__repr__** scheme suppresses quotes. Example 17-20 is one last graph test before we move on; sketch the nodes and arcs on paper if you have more trouble following the paths than Python.

Example 17-20. PP2E\Dstruct\Classics\gtestobj2.py

```
from graph import Graph

S = Graph('s')
P = Graph('p')          # a graph of spam
A = Graph('a')          # make node objects
M = Graph('m')

S.arcs = [P, M]         # S leads to P and M
P.arcs = [S, M, A]      # arcs: embedded objects
A.arcs = [M]
print S.search(M)       # find all paths from S to M
```

This test finds three paths in its graph between nodes S and M. If you'd like to see more Python graph code, check out the files in directory **MoreGraphs** on the CD. These are roughly the same as the ones listed here, but add user interaction as each solution is found. In addition, we've really only scratched the surface of this domain here; see other books for additional topics (e.g., breadth- and best-first search):

```
C:\...\PP2E\Dstruct\Classics>python gtestobj2.py
[[s, m], [s, p, m], [s, p, a, m]]
```

Reversing Sequences

Reversal of collections is another typical operation. We can code it either recursively or iteratively in Python, and as functions or class methods. Example 17-21 is a first attempt at two simple reversal functions.

Example 17-21. PP2E\Dstruct\Classics\rev1.py

```
def reverse(list):                    # recursive
    if list == []:
        return []
    else:
        return reverse(list[1:]) + list[:1]

def ireverse(list):                   # iterative
    res = []
    for x in list: res = [x] + res
    return res
```

Both reversal functions work correctly on lists. But if we try reversing nonlist sequences (strings, tuples, etc.) we're in trouble: the `ireverse` function always returns a list for the result regardless of the type of sequence passed:

```
>>> ireverse("spam")
['m', 'a', 'p', 's']
```

Much worse, the recursive **reverse** version won't work at all for nonlists—it gets stuck in an infinite loop. The reason is subtle: when **reverse** reaches the empty string (`""`), it's not equal to the empty list (`[]`), so the `else` clause is selected. But slicing an empty sequence returns another empty sequence (indexes are scaled): the `else` clause recurs again with an empty sequence, and without raising an exception. The net effect is that this function gets stuck in a loop, calling itself over and over again until Python runs out of memory.

The versions in Example 17-22 fix both problems by using generic sequence handling techniques:

- **reverse** uses the `not` operator to detect the end of the sequence and returns the empty sequence itself, rather than an empty list constant. Since the empty sequence is the type of the original argument, the `+` operation always builds the correct type sequence as the recursion unfolds.

- **ireverse** makes use of the fact that slicing a sequence returns a sequence of the same type. It first initializes the result to the slice `[:0]`, a new, empty slice of the argument's type. Later, it uses slicing to extract one-node sequences to add to the result's front, instead of a list constant.

Example 17-22. PP2E\Dstruct\Classics\rev2.py

```
def reverse(list):
    if not list:                          # empty? (not always [])
        return list                       # the same sequence type
    else:
        return reverse(list[1:]) + list[:1]   # add front item on the end

def ireverse(list):
    res = list[:0]                        # empty, of same type
```

Example 17-22. PP2E\Dstruct\Classics\rev2.py (continued)

```
    for i in range(len(list)):
        res = list[i:i+1] + res          # add each item to front
    return res
```

These functions work on any sequence, and return a new sequence of the same type as the sequence passed in. If we pass in a string, we get a new string as the result. In fact, they reverse any sequence object that responds to slicing, concatenation, and `len`—even instances of Python classes and C types. In other words, they can reverse any object that has sequence interface protocols. Here they are working on lists, strings, and tuples:

```
% python
>>> from rev2 import *
>>> reverse([1,2,3]), ireverse([1,2,3])
([3, 2, 1], [3, 2, 1])
>>> reverse("spam"), ireverse("spam")
('maps', 'maps')
>>> reverse((1.2, 2.3, 3.4)), ireverse((1.2, 2.3, 3.4))
((3.4, 2.3, 1.2), (3.4, 2.3, 1.2))
```

Permuting Sequences

The functions defined in Example 17-23 shuffle sequences in a number of ways:

- `permute` constructs a list with all valid permutations of any sequence.

- `subset` constructs a list with all valid permutations of a specific length.

- `combo` works like `subset`, but order doesn't matter: permutations of the same items are filtered out.

These results are useful in a variety of algorithms: searches, statistical analysis, and more. For instance, one way to find an optimal ordering for items is to put them in a list, generate all possible permutations, and simply test each one in turn. All three of the functions make use of the generic sequence slicing tricks of the reversal functions in the prior section, so that the result list contains sequences of the same type as the one passed in (e.g., when we permute a string, we get back a list of strings).

Example 17-23. PP2E\Dstruct\Classics\permcomb.py

```
def permute(list):                              # shuffle any sequence
    if not list:                                # empty sequence
        return [list]
    else:
        res = []
        for i in range(len(list)):
            rest = list[:i] + list[i+1:]        # delete current node
            for x in permute(rest):             # permute the others
```

Example 17-23. PP2E\Dstruct\Classics\permcomb.py (continued)

```
            res.append(list[i:i+1] + x)              # add node at front
        return res

def subset(list, size):
    if size == 0 or not list:                        # order matters here
        return [list[:0]]                            # an empty sequence
    else:
        result = []
        for i in range(len(list)):
            pick = list[i:i+1]                       # sequence slice
            rest = list[:i] + list[i+1:]             # keep [:i] part
            for x in subset(rest, size-1):
                result.append(pick + x)
        return result

def combo(list, size):
    if size == 0 or not list:                        # order doesn't matter
        return [list[:0]]                            # xyz == yzx
    else:
        result = []
        for i in range(0, (len(list) - size) + 1):   # iff enough left
            pick = list[i:i+1]
            rest = list[i+1:]                        # drop [:i] part
            for x in combo(rest, size - 1):
                result.append(pick + x)
        return result
```

As in the reversal functions, all three of these work on any sequence object that supports len, slicing, and concatenation operations. For instance, we can use **permute** on instances of some of the stack classes defined at the start of this chapter; we'll get back a list of stack instance objects with shuffled nodes.

Here are our sequence shufflers in action. Permuting a list enables us to find all the ways the items can be arranged. For instance, for a four-item list, there are 24 possible permutations ($4 \times 3 \times 2 \times 1$). After picking one of the four for the first position, there are only three left to choose from for the second, and so on. Order matters: [1,2,3] is not the same as [1,3,2], so both appear in the result:

```
C:\...\PP2E\Dstruct\Classics>python
>>> from permcomb import *
>>> permute([1,2,3])
[[1, 2, 3], [1, 3, 2], [2, 1, 3], [2, 3, 1], [3, 1, 2], [3, 2, 1]]
>>> permute('abc')
['abc', 'acb', 'bac', 'bca', 'cab', 'cba']
>>> permute('help')
['help', 'hepl', 'hlep', 'hlpe', 'hpel', 'hple', 'ehlp', 'ehpl', 'elhp', 'elph',
 'ephl', 'eplh', 'lhep', 'lhpe', 'lehp', 'leph', 'lphe', 'lpeh', 'phel', 'phle',
 'pehl', 'pelh', 'plhe', 'pleh']
```

combo results are related to permutations, but a fixed-length constraint is put on the result, and order doesn't matter: abc is the same as acb, so only one is added to the result set:

```
>>> combo([1,2,3], 3)
[[1, 2, 3]]
>>> combo('abc', 3)
['abc']
>>> combo('abc', 2)
['ab', 'ac', 'bc']
>>> combo('abc', 4)
[]
>>> combo((1, 2, 3, 4), 3)
[(1, 2, 3), (1, 2, 4), (1, 3, 4), (2, 3, 4)]
>>> for i in range(0, 6): print i, combo("help", i)
...
0 ['']
1 ['h', 'e', 'l', 'p']
2 ['he', 'hl', 'hp', 'el', 'ep', 'lp']
3 ['hel', 'hep', 'hlp', 'elp']
4 ['help']
5 []
```

Finally, subset is just fixed-length permutations; order matters, so the result is larger than for combo. In fact, calling subset with the length of the sequence is identical to permute:

```
>>> subset([1,2,3], 3)
[[1, 2, 3], [1, 3, 2], [2, 1, 3], [2, 3, 1], [3, 1, 2], [3, 2, 1]]
>>> subset('abc', 3)
['abc', 'acb', 'bac', 'bca', 'cab', 'cba']
>>> for i in range(0, 6): print i, subset("help", i)
...
0 ['']
1 ['h', 'e', 'l', 'p']
2 ['he', 'hl', 'hp', 'eh', 'el', 'ep', 'lh', 'le', 'lp', 'ph', 'pe', 'pl']
3 ['hel', 'hep', 'hle', 'hlp', 'hpe', 'hpl', 'ehl', 'ehp', 'elh', 'elp', 'eph',
   'epl', 'lhe', 'lhp', 'leh', 'lep', 'lph', 'lpe', 'phe', 'phl', 'peh', 'pel',
   'plh', 'ple']
4 ['help', 'hepl', 'hlep', 'hlpe', 'hpel', 'hple', 'ehlp', 'ehpl', 'elhp',
   'elph', 'ephl', 'eplh', 'lhep', 'lhpe', 'lehp', 'leph', 'lphe', 'lpeh',
   'phel', 'phle', 'pehl', 'pelh', 'plhe', 'pleh']
5 ['help', 'hepl', 'hlep', 'hlpe', 'hpel', 'hple', 'ehlp', 'ehpl', 'elhp',
   'elph', 'ephl', 'eplh', 'lhep', 'lhpe', 'lehp', 'leph', 'lphe', 'lpeh',
   'phel', 'phle', 'pehl', 'pelh', 'plhe', 'pleh']
```

Sorting Sequences

Another staple of many systems is sorting: ordering items in a collection according to some constraint. The script in Example 17-24 defines a simple sort routine in Python, which orders a list of objects on a field. Because Python indexing is generic, the field can be an index or key—this function can sort lists of either sequences or mappings.

Example 17-24. PP2E\Dstruct\Classics\sort1.py

```
def sort(list, field):
    res = []                                    # always returns a list
    for x in list:
        i = 0
        for y in res:
            if x[field] <= y[field]: break      # list node goes here?
            i = i+1
        res[i:i] = [x]                          # insert in result slot
    return res

if __name__ == '__main__':
    table = [ {'name':'john', 'age':25}, {'name':'doe', 'age':32} ]
    print sort(table, 'name')
    print sort(table, 'age')
    table = [ ('john', 25), ('doe', 32) ]
    print sort(table, 0)
    print sort(table, 1)
```

Here is this module's self-test code in action:

```
C:\...\PP2E\Dstruct\Classics>python sort1.py
[{'age': 32, 'name': 'doe'}, {'age': 25, 'name': 'john'}]
[{'age': 25, 'name': 'john'}, {'age': 32, 'name': 'doe'}]
[('doe', 32), ('john', 25)]
[('john', 25), ('doe', 32)]
```

Adding Comparison Functions

Since functions can be passed in like any other object, we can easily allow for an optional comparison function. In the next version (Example 17-25), the second argument takes a function that should return *true* if its first argument should be placed before its second. A `lambda` is used to provide an ascending-order test by default. This sorter also returns a new sequence that is the same type as the sequence passed in, by applying the slicing techniques used in earlier sections: if you sort a tuple of nodes, you get back a tuple.

Example 17-25. PP2E\Dstruct\Classics\sort2.py

```
def sort(seq, func=(lambda x,y: x <= y)):       # default: ascending
    res = seq[:0]                               # return seq's type
    for j in range(len(seq)):
        i = 0
        for y in res:
            if func(seq[j], y): break
            i = i+1
        res = res[:i] + seq[j:j+1] + res[i:]    # seq can be immutable
```

Example 17-25. PP2E\Dstruct\Classics\sort2.py (continued)

```
    return res

if __name__ == '__main__':
    table = ({'name':'doe'}, {'name':'john'})
    print sort(list(table),  (lambda x, y: x['name'] > y['name']))
    print sort(tuple(table), (lambda x, y: x['name'] <= y['name']))
    print sort('axbyzc')
```

This time, the table entries are ordered per a field comparison function passed in:

```
C:\...\PP2E\Dstruct\Classics>python sort2.py
[{'name': 'john'}, {'name': 'doe'}]
({'name': 'doe'}, {'name': 'john'})
abcxyz
```

This version also dispenses with the notion of a field altogether and lets the passed-in function handle indexing if needed. That makes this version much more general; for instance, it's also useful for sorting strings.

Data Structures Versus Python Built-ins

Now that I've shown you all these complicated algorithms, I need to also tell you that at least in some cases, they may not be an optimal approach. Built-in types like lists and dictionaries are often a simpler and more efficient way to represent data. For instance:

Binary trees

These may be useful in many applications, but Python dictionaries already provide a highly optimized, C-coded, search table tool. Indexing a dictionary by key is likely to be faster than searching a Python-coded tree structure:

```
>>> x = {}
>>> for i in [3,1,9,2,7]: x[i] = None              # insert
>>> for i in range(10): print (i, x.has_key(i)),   # lookup
(0, 0) (1, 1) (2, 1) (3, 1) (4, 0) (5, 0) (6, 0) (7, 1) (8, 0) (9, 1)
```

Because dictionaries are built in to the language, they are always available, and will usually be faster than Python-based data structure implementations.

Graph algorithms

These serve many purposes, but a purely Python-coded implementation of a very large graph might be less efficient than you want in some applications. Graph programs tend to require peak performance; using dictionaries instead of class instances to represent graphs may boost performance some, but using linked-in compiled extensions may as well.

Sorting algorithms

These are an important part of many programs too, but Python's built-in list **sort** method is so fast that you would be hard pressed to beat it in Python in most scenarios. In fact, it's generally better to convert sequences to lists first just so you can use the built-in:

```
temp = list(sequence)
temp.sort()
...use items in temp...
```

For custom sorts, simply pass in a comparison function of your own:

```
>>> L = [{'n':3}, {'n':20}, {'n':0}, {'n':9}]
>>> L.sort( lambda x, y: cmp(x['n'], y['n']) )
>>> L
[{'n': 0}, {'n': 3}, {'n': 9}, {'n': 20}]
```

Reversal algorithms

These are generally superfluous by the same token—because Python lists provide a fast **reverse** method, you may be better off converting a non-list to a list first, just so that you can run the built-in list method.

Don't misunderstand: sometimes you really do need objects that add functionality to built-in types, or do something more custom. The set classes we met, for instance, add tools not directly supported by Python today, and the tuple-tree stack implementation was actually faster than one based upon built-in lists for common usage patterns. Permutations are something you need to add on your own too.

Moreover, class encapsulations make it possible to change and extend object internals without impacting the rest of your system. They also support reuse much better than built-in types—types are not classes today, and cannot be specialized directly without wrapper class logic.

Yet because Python comes with a set of built-in, flexible, and optimized datatypes, data structure implementations are often not as important in Python as they are in lesser-equipped languages such as C or C++. Before you code that new datatype, be sure to ask yourself if a built-in type or call might be more in line with the Python way of thinking.

PyTree: A Generic Tree Object Viewer

Up to now, this chapter has been command-line-oriented. To wrap up, I want to show you a program that merges the GUI technology we studied earlier in the book with some of the data structure ideas we've met in this chapter.

This program is called *PyTree,* a generic tree data structure viewer written in Python with the Tkinter GUI library. PyTree sketches out the nodes of a tree on screen as boxes connected by arrows. It also knows how to route mouseclicks on drawn tree nodes back to the tree, to trigger tree-specific actions. Because PyTree lets you visualize the structure of the tree generated by a set of parameters, it's a fun way to explore tree-based algorithms.

PyTree supports arbitrary tree types by "wrapping" real trees in interface objects. The interface objects implement a standard protocol by communicating with the underlying tree object. For the purposes of this chapter, PyTree is instrumented to display *binary search trees*; for the next chapter, it's also set up to render *expression parse trees*. New trees can be viewed by coding wrapper classes to interface to new tree types.

The GUI interfaces PyTree utilizes were covered in depth earlier in this book, so I won't go over this code in much detail here. See Part II, *GUI Programming*, for background details, and be sure to run this program on your own computer to get a better feel for its operation. Because it is written with Python and Tkinter, it should be portable to Windows, Unix, and Macs.

Running PyTree

Before we get to the code, let's see what PyTree looks like. You can launch PyTree from the PyDemos launcher bar (see the top-level of the examples distribution source tree on this book's CD), or by directly running the *treeview.py* file listed in Example 17-27. Figure 17-2 shows PyTree in action displaying the binary tree created by the "test1" button. Trees are sketched as labels embedded in a canvas, and connected by lines with arrows. The lines reflect parent-to-child relationships in the actual tree; PyTree attempts to layout the tree to produce a more or less uniform display like this one.

PyTree's window consists of a canvas with vertical and horizontal scrolls, and a set of controls at the bottom—radiobuttons for picking the type of tree you wish to display, a set of buttons that trigger canned tree drawing tests, and an input field for typing text to specify and generate a new tree. The set of test buttons changes if you pick the Parser radiobutton (you get one less test button); PyTree use widget `pack_forget` and `pack` methods to hide and show tree-specific buttons on the fly.

When you pick one of the canned test buttons, it displays in the input field the string you would type to generate the tree drawn. For binary trees, type a list of values separated by spaces and press the "input" button or the Enter key to generate a new tree; the new tree is the result of inserting the typed values from left to right. For parse trees, you input an expression string in the input field instead (more on this later). Figure 17-3 shows the result of typing a set of values into the input field and submitting; the resulting binary tree shows up in the canvas.

Notice the pop-up in this screen shot; left-clicking on a displayed tree node with your mouse runs whatever action a tree wrapper class defines, and displays its

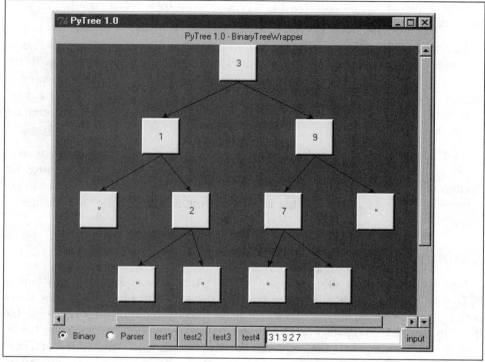

Figure 17-2. PyTree viewing a binary search tree (test1)

result in the pop-up. Binary trees have no action to run, so we get a default message in the pop-up, but parse tress use the mouseclick to evaluate the subtree rooted at the clicked node (again, more on parse trees later).

Just for fun, maximize this window and press the "test4" button—it inserts 100 numbers from 0 through 99 into a new binary tree at random, and displays the result. Figure 17-4 captures one portion of this tree; it's much too large to fit on one screen (or on one book page), but you can move around the tree with the canvas scrollbars.

PyTree uses an algorithm to connect all parents to their children in this tree without crossing their connecting lines. It does some up-front analysis to try and arrange descendents at each level to be as close to their parents as possible. This analysis step also yields the overall size of a new tree—PyTree uses it to reset the scrollable area size of the canvas for each tree drawn.

Pytree Source Code

Let's move on to the code. Similar to PyForm in the prior chapter, PyTree is coded as two modules; here, one module handles the task of sketching trees in the GUI,

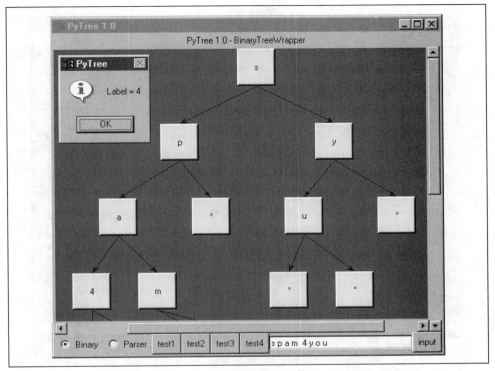

Figure 17-3. A binary tree typed manually with on-click pop-up

and another implements wrappers to interface to various tree types and extends the GUI with extra widgets.

Tree-independent GUI implementation

The module in Example 17-26 does the work of drawing trees in a canvas. It's coded to be independent of any particular tree structure—its `TreeViewer` class delegates to its `TreeWrapper` class when it needs tree-specific information for the drawing (e.g., node label text, node child links). `TreeWrapper` in turn expects to be subclassed for a specific kind of tree; in fact it raises assertion errors if you try to use it without subclassing. In design terms, `TreeViewer` embeds a `TreeWrapper`; it's almost as easy to code `TreeViewer` subclasses per tree type, but that limits a viewer GUI to one particular kind of tree (see *treeview_subclasses.py* in the CD for a subclassing-based alternative).

Trees are drawn in two steps—a planning traversal the builds a layout data structure that links parents and children, and a drawing step that uses the generated plan to draw and link node labels on the canvas. The two-step approach simplifies some of the logic required to layout trees uniformly. Study this listing for more details.

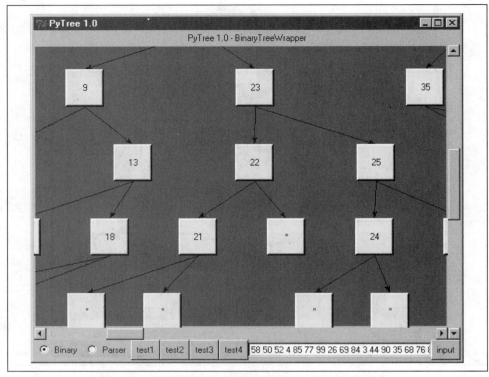

Figure 17-4. PyTree viewing a large binary search tree (test4)

Example 17-26. PP2E\Dstruct\TreeView\treeview_wrappers.py

```
#########################################################################
# PyTree: sketch arbitrary tree data structures in a scrolled canvas;
# this version uses tree wrapper classes embedded in the viewer gui
# to support arbitrary trees (i.e.. composition, not viewer subclassing);
# also adds tree node label click callbacks--run tree specific actions;
# see treeview_subclasses.py for subclass-based alternative structure;
# subclassing limits one tree viewer to one tree type, wrappers do not;
# see treeview_left.py for an alternative way to draw the tree object;
# see and run treeview.py for binary and parse tree wrapper test cases;
#########################################################################

from Tkinter import *
from tkMessageBox import showinfo

Width, Height = 350, 350                    # start canvas size (reset per tree)
Rowsz = 100                                 # pixels per tree row
Colsz = 100                                 # pixels per tree col


##################################
# interface to tree object's nodes
##################################
```

Example 17-26. PP2E\Dstruct\TreeView\treeview_wrappers.py (continued)

```
class TreeWrapper:                             # subclass for a tree type
    def children(self, treenode):
        assert 0, 'children method must be specialized for tree type'
    def label(self, treenode):
        assert 0, 'label method must be specialized for tree type'
    def value(self, treenode):
        return ''
    def onClick(self, treenode):               # node label click callback
        return ''
    def onInputLine(self, line, viewer):       # input line sent callback
        pass


###########$######################
# tree view gui, tree independent
#################################

class TreeViewer(Frame):
    def __init__(self, wrapper, parent=None, tree=None, bg='brown', fg='beige'):
        Frame.__init__(self, parent)
        self.pack(expand=YES, fill=BOTH)
        self.makeWidgets(bg)                       # build gui: scrolled canvas
        self.master.title('PyTree 1.0')            # assume I'm run standalone
        self.wrapper = wrapper                     # embed a TreeWrapper object
        self.fg = fg                               # setTreeType changes wrapper
        if tree:
            self.drawTree(tree)

    def makeWidgets(self, bg):
        self.title = Label(self, text='PyTree 1.0')
        self.canvas = Canvas(self, bg=bg, borderwidth=0)
        vbar = Scrollbar(self)
        hbar = Scrollbar(self, orient='horizontal')

        self.title.pack(side=TOP, fill=X)
        vbar.pack(side=RIGHT,  fill=Y)                   # pack canvas after bars
        hbar.pack(side=BOTTOM, fill=X)
        self.canvas.pack(side=TOP, fill=BOTH, expand=YES)

        vbar.config(command=self.canvas.yview)           # call on scroll move
        hbar.config(command=self.canvas.xview)
        self.canvas.config(yscrollcommand=vbar.set)      # call on canvas move
        self.canvas.config(xscrollcommand=hbar.set)
        self.canvas.config(height=Height, width=Width)   # viewable area size

    def clearTree(self):
        mylabel = 'PyTree 1.0 - ' + self.wrapper.__class__.__name__
        self.title.config(text=mylabel)
        self.unbind_all('<Button-1>')
        self.canvas.delete('all')                        # clear events, drawing

    def drawTree(self, tree):
        self.clearTree()
```

Example 17-26. PP2E\Dstruct\TreeView\treeview_wrappers.py (continued)

```
        wrapper = self.wrapper
        levels, maxrow = self.planLevels(tree, wrapper)
        self.canvas.config(scrollregion=(                  # scrollable area
            0, 0, (Colsz * maxrow), (Rowsz * len(levels)) ))   # upleft, lowright
        self.drawLevels(levels, maxrow, wrapper)

    def planLevels(self, root, wrap):
        levels = []
        maxrow = 0                                         # traverse tree to
        currlevel = [(root, None)]                         # layout rows, cols
        while currlevel:
            levels.append(currlevel)
            size = len(currlevel)
            if size > maxrow: maxrow = size
            nextlevel = []
            for (node, parent) in currlevel:
                if node != None:
                    children = wrap.children(node)         # list of nodes
                    if not children:
                        nextlevel.append((None, None))     # leave a hole
                    else:
                        for child in children:
                            nextlevel.append((child, node))  # parent link
            currlevel = nextlevel
        return levels, maxrow

    def drawLevels(self, levels, maxrow, wrap):
        rowpos = 0                                         # draw tree per plan
        for level in levels:                               # set click handlers
            colinc = (maxrow * Colsz) / (len(level) + 1)   # levels is treenodes
            colpos = 0
            for (node, parent) in level:
                colpos = colpos + colinc
                if node != None:
                    text = wrap.label(node)
                    more = wrap.value(node)
                    if more: text = text + '=' + more
                    win = Label(self.canvas, text=text,
                                    bg=self.fg, bd=3, relief=RAISED)
                    win.pack()
                    win.bind('<Button-1>',
                        lambda e, n=node, handler=self.onClick: handler(e, n))
                    self.canvas.create_window(colpos, rowpos, anchor=NW,
                            window=win, width=Colsz*.5, height=Rowsz*.5)
                    if parent != None:
                        self.canvas.create_line(
                            parent.__colpos + Colsz*.25,    # from x-y, to x-y
                            parent.__rowpos + Rowsz*.5,
                            colpos + Colsz*.25, rowpos, arrow='last', width=1)
                    node.__rowpos = rowpos
                    node.__colpos = colpos                 # mark node, private attrs
            rowpos = rowpos + Rowsz
```

Example 17-26. PP2E\Dstruct\TreeView\treeview_wrappers.py (continued)

```
def onClick(self, event, node):
    label = event.widget
    wrap  = self.wrapper
    text  = 'Label = ' + wrap.label(node)      # on label click
    value = wrap.value(node)
    if value:
        text = text + '\nValue = ' + value      # add tree text if any
    result = wrap.onClick(node)                  # run tree action if any
    if result:
        text = text + '\n' + result              # add action result
    showinfo('PyTree', text)                     # popup std dialog

def onInputLine(self, line):                     # feed text to tree wrapper
    self.wrapper.onInputLine(line, self)         # ex: parse and redraw tree

def setTreeType(self, newTreeWrapper):           # change tree type drawn
    if self.wrapper != newTreeWrapper:           # effective on next draw
        self.wrapper = newTreeWrapper
        self.clearTree()                         # else old node, new wrapper
```

Tree wrappers and test widgets

The other half of PyTree consists of a module that defines **TreeWrapper** sub-classes that interface to binary and parser trees, implements canned test case buttons, and adds the control widgets to the bottom of the PyTree window.[*] These control widgets were split off into this separate module (in Example 17-27) on purpose, because the PyTree canvas might be useful as a viewer component in other GUI applications.

Example 17-27. PP2E\Dstruct\TreeView\treeview.py

```
# PyTree launcher script
# wrappers for viewing tree types in the book, plus test cases/gui

import string
from Tkinter import *
from treeview_wrappers import TreeWrapper, TreeViewer
from PP2E.Dstruct.Classics import btree
from PP2E.Lang.Parser import parser2


#################################################################
# binary tree wrapper
#################################################################

class BinaryTreeWrapper(TreeWrapper):           # embed binary tree in viewer
    def children(self, node):                   # adds viewer protocols
        try:                                    # to interface with tree
```

---

[*] If you're looking for a coding exercise, try adding another wrapper class and radiobutton to view the **KeyedBinaryTree** we wrote earlier in this chapter. You'll probably want to display the key in the GUI, and pop up the associated value on clicks.

Example 17-27. PP2E\Dstruct\TreeView\treeview.py (continued)

```
            return [node.left, node.right]
        except:
            return None
    def label(self, node):
        try:
            return str(node.data)
        except:
            return str(node)
    def onInputLine(self, line, viewer):          # on test entry at bottom
        items = string.split(line)                # make tree from text input
        t = btree.BinaryTree()                    # draw resulting btree
        for x in items: t.insert(x)               # no onClick handler here
        viewer.drawTree(t.tree)


###################################################################
# binary tree extension
###################################################################

class BinaryTree(btree.BinaryTree):
    def __init__(self, viewer):                   # embed viewer in tree
        btree.BinaryTree.__init__(self)           # but viewer has a wrapper
        self.viewer  = viewer
    def view(self):
        self.viewer.drawTree(self.tree)


###################################################################
# parse tree wrapper
###################################################################

class ParseTreeWrapper(TreeWrapper):
    def __init__(self):                           # embed parse tree in viewer
        self.dict = {}                            # adds viewer protocols
    def children(self, node):
        try:
            return [node.left, node.right]
        except:
            try:
                return [node.var, node.val]
            except:
                return None
    def label(self, node):
        for attr in ['label', 'num', 'name']:
            if hasattr(node, attr):
                return str(getattr(node, attr))
        return 'set'
    def onClick(self, node):                       # on tree label click
        try:                                       # tree-specific action
            result = node.apply(self.dict)         # evaluate subtree
            return 'Value = ' + str(result)        # show result in popup
        except:
            return 'Value = <error>'
    def onInputLine(self, line, viewer):           # on input line
```

Example 17-27. PP2E\Dstruct\TreeView\treeview.py (continued)

```
        p = parser2.Parser()                    # parse expr text
        p.lex.newtext(line)                     # draw resulting tree
        t = p.analyse()
        if t: viewer.drawTree(t)


###################################################################
# canned test cases (or type new nodelists/exprs in input field)
###################################################################

def shownodes(sequence):
    sequence = map(str, sequence)               # convert nodes to strings
    entry.delete(0, END)                        # show nodes in text field
    entry.insert(0, string.join(sequence, ' '))

def test1_binary():                             # tree type is binary wrapper
    nodes = [3, 1, 9, 2, 7]                      # make a binary tree
    tree  = BinaryTree(viewer)                   # embed viewer in tree
    for i in nodes: tree.insert(i)
    shownodes(nodes)                            # show nodes in input field
    tree.view()                                 # sketch tree via embedded viewer

def test2_binary():
    nodes = 'badce'
    tree  = btree.BinaryTree()                   # embed wrapper in viewer
    for c in nodes: tree.insert(c)               # make a binary tree
    shownodes(nodes)
    viewer.drawTree(tree.tree)                   # ask viewer to draw it

def test3_binary():
    nodes = 'abcde'
    tree  = BinaryTree(viewer)
    for c in nodes: tree.insert(c)
    shownodes(nodes)
    tree.view()

def test4_binary():
    tree = BinaryTree(viewer)
    import random                                # make a big binary tree
    nodes = range(100)                           # insert 100 nodes at random
    order = []                                   # and sketch in viewer
    while nodes:
        item = random.choice(nodes)
        nodes.remove(item)
        tree.insert(item)
        order.append(item)
    shownodes(order)
    tree.view()

def test_parser(expr):
    parser = parser2.Parser()                    # tree type is parser wrapper
    parser.lex.newtext(expr)                     # subtrees evaluate when clicked
```

Example 17-27. PP2E\Dstruct\TreeView\treeview.py (continued)

```
        tree    = parser.analyse()          # input line parses new expr
        entry.delete(0, END)                # vars set in wrapper dictionary
        entry.insert(0, expr)               # see lang/text chapter for parser
        if tree: viewer.drawTree(tree)


def test1_parser(): test_parser("1 + 3 * (2 * 3 + 4)")
def test2_parser(): test_parser("set temp 1 + 3 * 2 * 3 + 4")
def test3_parser(): test_parser("set result temp + ((1 + 3) * 2) * (3 + 4)")


###################################################################
# build viewer with extra widgets to test tree types
###################################################################

if __name__ == '__main__':
    root = Tk()                             # build a single viewer gui
    bwrapper = BinaryTreeWrapper()          # add extras: input line, test btns
    pwrapper = ParseTreeWrapper()           # make wrapper objects
    viewer   = TreeViewer(bwrapper, root)   # start out in binary mode

    def onRadio():
        if var.get() == 'btree':
            viewer.setTreeType(bwrapper)             # change viewer's wrapper
            for btn in p_btns: btn.pack_forget()     # erase parser test buttons
            for btn in b_btns: btn.pack(side=LEFT)   # unhide binary buttons
        elif var.get() == 'ptree':
            viewer.setTreeType(pwrapper)
            for btn in b_btns: btn.pack_forget()
            for btn in p_btns: btn.pack(side=LEFT)

    var = StringVar()
    var.set('btree')
    Radiobutton(root, text='Binary', command=onRadio,
                      variable=var, value='btree').pack(side=LEFT)
    Radiobutton(root, text='Parser', command=onRadio,
                      variable=var, value='ptree').pack(side=LEFT)
    b_btns = []
    b_btns.append(Button(root, text='test1', command=test1_binary))
    b_btns.append(Button(root, text='test2', command=test2_binary))
    b_btns.append(Button(root, text='test3', command=test3_binary))
    b_btns.append(Button(root, text='test4', command=test4_binary))
    p_btns = []
    p_btns.append(Button(root, text='test1', command=test1_parser))
    p_btns.append(Button(root, text='test2', command=test2_parser))
    p_btns.append(Button(root, text='test3', command=test3_parser))
    onRadio()

    def onInputLine():
        line = entry.get()                  # use per current tree wrapper type
        viewer.onInputLine(line)            # type a node list or expression

    Button(root, text='input', command=onInputLine).pack(side=RIGHT)
    entry = Entry(root)
```

Example 17-27. PP2E\Dstruct\TreeView\treeview.py (continued)

```
    entry.pack(side=RIGHT, expand=YES, fill=X)
    entry.bind('<Return>', lambda event: onInputLine())   # button or enter key
    root.mainloop()                                        # start up the gui
```

Pytree Does Parse Trees, Too

Finally, I want to show you what happens when you click the Parser radiobutton in the PyTree window. The GUI changes over to an expression parse tree viewer, by simply using a different tree wrapper class: the label at the top changes, the test buttons change, and input is now entered as an arithmetic expression to be parsed and sketched. Figure 17-5 shows a tree generated for the expression string displayed in the input field.

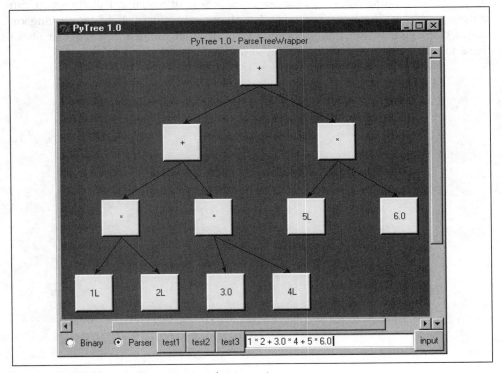

Figure 17-5. PyTree viewing an expression parse tree

PyTree is designed to be generic—it displays both binary and parse trees, but is easy to extend for new tree types with new wrapper classes. On the GUI, you can switch between binary and parser tree types at any time by clicking the radiobuttons. Input typed into the input field is always evaluated according to the current tree type. When the viewer is in parse tree mode, clicking on a node in the tree evaluates the part of the expression represented by the parse tree rooted at the node you clicked. Figure 17-6 shows the pop-up you get when you click the root node of the tree displayed.

Figure 17-6. PyTree pop-up after clicking a parse tree node

When viewing parse trees, PyTree becomes a sort of visual calculator—you can generate arbitrary expression trees and evaluate any part of them by clicking on nodes displayed. But at this point, there is not much more I can tell you about these kinds of trees until you move on to the next chapter.

18

Text and Language

"See Jack Hack. Hack, Jack, Hack"

In one form or another, processing text-based information is one of the more common tasks that applications need to perform. This can include anything from scanning a text file by columns to analyzing statements in a language defined by a formal grammar. Such processing usually is called *parsing*—analyzing the structure of a text string. In this chapter, we'll explore ways to handle language and text-based information and summarize some Python development concepts in sidebars along the way.

Some of this material is advanced, but the examples are small. For instance, recursive descent parsing is illustrated with a simple example to show how it can be implemented in Python. We'll also see that it's often unnecessary to write custom parsers for each language processing task in Python. They can usually be replaced by exporting APIs for use in Python programs, and sometimes by a single built-in function call. Finally, this chapter closes by presenting *PyCalc*—a calculator GUI written in Python, and the last major Python coding example in this text. As we'll see, writing calculators isn't much more difficult than juggling stacks while scanning text.

Strategies for Parsing Text in Python

In the grand scheme of things, there are a variety of ways to handle text processing in Python:

- Built-in string objects
- String module (and method) utilities
- Regular expression matching

- Parser-generator integrations
- Hand-coded parsers
- Running Python code with `eval` and `exec` built-ins

For simpler tasks, Python's built-in string object is often all we really need. Python strings can be indexed, concatenated, sliced, and processed both with built-in functions and with the `string` module. Our emphasis in this chapter, though, is on higher-level tools and techniques for analyzing textual information. Let's briefly explore each of the other approaches above with representative examples.

String Module Utilities

Python's `string` module includes a variety of text-processing utilities that go above and beyond string expression operators. For instance:

- `string.find` performs substring searches.
- `string.atoi` converts strings to integers.
- `string.strip` removes leading and trailing whitespace.
- `string.upper` converts to uppercase.
- `string.replace` performs substring substitutions.

The Python library manual includes an exhaustive list of available tools. Moreover, as of Python 2.0, Unicode (wide) strings are fully supported by Python string tools, and most of the `string` module's functions are also now available as string object *methods*. For instance, in Python 2.0, the following two expressions are equivalent:

```
string.find(str, substr)     # traditional
str.find(substr)             # new in 2.0
```

except that the second form does not require callers to import the `string` module first. As usual, you should consult the library manuals and Appendix A, *Recent Python Changes*, for late-breaking news on the string tools front.

In terms of this chapter's main focus, though, Python's built-in tools for splitting and joining strings around tokens turn out to be especially useful when it comes to parsing text:

`string.split`

   Splits a string into substrings, using either whitespace (tabs, spaces, newlines) or an explicitly passed string as a delimiter.

`string.join`

   Concatenates a list or tuple of substrings, adding a space or an explicitly passed separator string between each.

As we saw earlier in this book, `split` chops a string into a list of substrings, and `join` puts them back together:[*]

```
>>> import string
>>> string.split('A B C D')
['A', 'B', 'C', 'D']
>>> string.split('A+B+C+D', '+')
['A', 'B', 'C', 'D']
>>> string.join(['a', 'b', 'c'], '--')
'a--b--c'
```

Despite their simplicity, they can handle surprisingly complex text-parsing tasks. Moreover, the `string` module is very fast because it has been migrated to C. For instance, to quickly replace all tabs in a file with four periods, pipe the file into a script that looks like this:

```
from sys import *
from string import *
stdout.write( join( split(stdin.read(), '\t'), '.'*4) )
```

The `split` call here divides input around tabs, and the `join` puts it back together with periods where tabs had been. The combination of the two calls is equivalent to using the global replacement call in the `string` module as follows:

```
stdout.write( replace(stdin.read(), '\t', '.'*4) )
```

Summing Columns in a File

Let's look at a couple of practical applications of string splits and joins. In many domains, scanning files by columns is a fairly common task. For instance, suppose you have a file containing columns of numbers output by another system, and you need to sum each column's numbers. In Python, string splitting does the job (see Example 18-1). As an added bonus, it's easy to make the solution a reusable tool in Python.

Example 18-1. PP2E\Lang\summer.py

```
#!/usr/local/bin/python
import string

def summer(numCols, fileName):
    sums = [0] * numCols                          # make list of zeros
    for line in open(fileName, 'r').readlines():  # scan file's lines
        cols = string.split(line)                 # split up columns
        for i in range(numCols):                  # around blanks/tabs
            sums[i] = sums[i] + eval(cols[i])      # add numbers to sums
    return sums
```

---

[*] Earlier Python releases had similar tools called `spitfields` and `joinfields`; the more modern (and less verbose) `split` and `join` are the preferred way to spell these today.

Example 18-1. PP2E\Lang\summer.py (continued)

```
if __name__ == '__main__':
    import sys
    print summer(eval(sys.argv[1]), sys.argv[2])      # '% summer.py cols file'
```

As usual, you can both *import* this module and call its function, and *run* it as a shell tool from the command line. The summer calls `split` to make a list of strings representing the line's columns, and `eval` to convert column strings to numbers. Here's an input file that uses both blanks and tabs to separate columns:

```
C:\...\PP2E\Lang>type table1.txt
1       5       10      2   1.0
2       10      20      4   2.0
3       15      30      8   3
4       20      40      16  4.0
C:\...\PP2E\Lang>python summer.py 5 table1.txt
[10, 50, 100, 30, 10.0]
```

Notice that because the summer script uses `eval` to convert file text to numbers, you could really store arbitrary Python expressions in the file. Here, for example, it's run on a file of Python code snippets:

```
C:\...\PP2E\Lang>type table2.txt
2       1+1             1<<1        eval("2")
16      2*2*2*2         pow(2,4)    16.0
3       len('abc')      [1,2,3][2]  {'spam':3}['spam']

C:\...\PP2E\Lang>python summer.py 4 table2.txt
[21, 21, 21, 21.0]
```

We'll revisit `eval` later in this chapter when we explore expression evaluators.[*]

Parsing and Unparsing Rule Strings

Example 18-2 demonstrates one way that splitting and joining strings can be used to parse sentences in a simple language. It is taken from a rule-based expert system shell (holmes) that is written in Python and included on this book's CD (see the top-level *Ai* examples directory). Rule strings in holmes take the form:

```
"rule <id> if <test1>, <test2>... then <conclusion1>, <conclusion2>..."
```

Tests and conclusions are conjunctions of terms ("," means "and"). Each term is a list of words or variables separated by spaces; variables start with `?`. To use a rule, it is translated to an internal form—a dictionary with nested lists. To display a rule, it is translated back to the string form. For instance, given a call:

```
rules.internal_rule('rule x if a ?x, b then c, d ?x')
```

---

[*] Also see the grid examples in Chapter 8, *A Tkinter Tour, Part 2*, for another example of `eval` table magic at work. The summer script here is a much simpler version of that chapter's column sum logic.

the conversion in function `internal_rule` proceeds as follows:

```
string = 'rule x if a ?x, b then c, d ?x'
i = ['rule x', 'a ?x, b then c, d ?x']
t = ['a ?x, b', 'c, d ?x']
r = ['', 'x']
result = {'rule':'x', 'if':[['a','?x'], ['b']], 'then':[['c'], ['d','?x']]}
```

It first splits around the `if`, then around the `then`, and finally around `rule`. The result is the three substrings that were separated by the keywords. Test and conclusion substrings are split around "," and spaces last. `join` is used to convert back (unparse) to the original string for display. Example 18-2 is the concrete implementation of this scheme.

Example 18-2. PP2E\Lang\rules.py

```
from string import split, join, strip

def internal_rule(string):
    i = split(string, ' if ')
    t = split(i[1],    ' then ')
    r = split(i[0],    'rule ')
    return {'rule':strip(r[1]), 'if':internal(t[0]), 'then':internal(t[1])}

def external_rule(rule):
    return ('rule '      + rule['rule']                +
            ' if '       + external(rule['if'])        +
            ' then '     + external(rule['then']) + '.')

def internal(conjunct):
    res = []                                # 'a b, c d'
    for clause in split(conjunct, ','):     # -> ['a b', ' c d']
        res.append(split(clause))           # -> [['a','b'], ['c','d']]
    return res

def external(conjunct):
    strs = []                               # [['a','b'], ['c','d']]
    for clause in conjunct:                 # -> ['a b', 'c d']
        strs.append(join(clause))           # -> 'a b, c d'
    return join(strs, ', ')
```

As usual, we can test components of this module interactively:

```
>>> import rules
>>> rules.internal('a ?x, b')
[['a', '?x'], ['b']]

>>> rules.internal_rule('rule x if a ?x, b then c, d ?x')
{'if': [['a', '?x'], ['b']], 'rule': 'x', 'then': [['c'], ['d', '?x']]}

>>> r = rules.internal_rule('rule x if a ?x, b then c, d ?x')
>>> rules.external_rule(r)
'rule x if a ?x, b then c, d ?x.'
```

Parsing by splitting strings around tokens like this only takes you so far: there is no direct support for recursive nesting of components, and syntax errors are not handled very gracefully. But for simple language tasks like this, string splitting might be enough, at least for prototyping systems. You can always add a more robust rule parser later or reimplement rules as embedded Python code or classes.

Lesson 1: Prototype and Migrate

As a rule of thumb, use the `string` module's functions instead of things like regular expressions whenever you can. They tend to be much faster, because they've been moved to a C language implementation. When you import `string`, it internally replaces most of its content with functions imported from the `strop` C extension module; `strop` methods are reportedly 100–1000 times faster than their Python-coded equivalents.[a]

The `string` module was originally written in Python but demands for string efficiency prompted recoding it in C. The result was dramatically faster performance for `string` client programs without impacting the interface. That is, string module clients became instantly faster without having to be modified for the new C-based module. A similar migration was applied to the `pickle` module we met in Chapter 16, *Databases and Persistence*—the newer `cPickle` recoding is compatible but much faster.

Which is a great lesson about Python development: modules can be coded quickly in Python at first, and translated to C later for efficiency if required. Because the interface to Python and C extension modules is identical (both are imported), C translations of modules are backward compatible with their Python prototypes. The only impact of the translation of such modules on clients is an improvement in performance.

There is usually no need to move every module to C for delivery of an application: you can pick and choose performance-critical modules (like `string` and `pickle`) for translation, and leave others coded in Python. Use the timing and profiling techniques of the prior chapter to isolate which modules will give the most improvement when translated to C. C-based extension modules are introduced in the next part of this book.

---

a. Actually, in Python 2.0, the `string` module has changed its implementation again: it is now a frontend to new string *methods*, which are able to also handle Unicode strings. As mentioned, most `string` functions are also available as object methods in 2.0. For instance, `string.split(X)` is now simply a synonym for `X.split()`; both forms are supported, but the latter may become prevalent over time. Either way, clients of the original `string` module are not affected by this change—yet another lesson!

More on the holmes expert system shell

So how are these rules actually used? As mentioned, the rule parser we just met is part of the Python-coded holmes expert system shell. This book does not cover holmes in detail due to lack of space; see the *PP2E\AI\ExpertSystem* directory on the book CD for its code and documentation. But by way of introduction, holmes is an inference engine that performs forward and backward chaining deduction on rules that you supply. For example, a rule:

```
rule pylike if ?X likes coding, ?X likes spam then ?X likes Python
```

can be used both to prove whether someone likes Python (backward, from "then" to "if"), and to deduce that someone likes Python from a set of known facts (forward, from "if" to "then"). Deductions may span multiple rules, and rules that name the same conclusion represent alternatives. Holmes also performs simple pattern-matching along the way to assign the variables that appear in rules (e.g., ?X), and is able to explain its work.

To make this all more concrete, let's step through a simple holmes session. The += interactive command adds a new rule to the rule base by running the rule parser, and @@ prints the current rule base:

```
C:`..\PP2E\Ai\ExpertSystem\holmes\holmes>python holmes.py
-Holmes inference engine-
holmes> += rule pylike if ?X likes coding, ?X likes spam then ?X likes Python
holmes> @@
rule pylike if ?X likes coding, ?X likes spam then ?X likes Python.
```

Now, to kick off a backward-chaining proof of a goal, use the ?- command. A proof explanation is shown here; holmes can also tell you why it is asking a question. Holmes pattern variables can show up in both rules and queries; in rules, variables provide generalization; in a query, they provide an answer:

```
holmes> ?- mel likes Python
is this true: "mel likes coding" ? y
is this true: "mel likes spam" ? y
yes: (no variables)

show proof ? yes
   "mel likes Python" by rule pylike
       "mel likes coding" by your answer
       "mel likes spam" by your answer
more solutions? n

holmes> ?- linda likes ?X
is this true: "linda likes coding" ? y
is this true: "linda likes spam" ? y
yes: linda likes Python
```

Forward-chaining from a set of facts to conclusions is started with a +- command. Here, the same rule is being applied but in a different way:

```
holmes> +- chris likes spam, chris likes coding
I deduced these facts...
    chris likes Python
I started with these facts...
    chris likes spam
    chris likes coding
time: 0.0
```

More interestingly, deductions chain through multiple rules when part of a rule's "if" is mentioned in another rule's "then":

```
holmes> += rule 1 if thinks ?x then human ?x
holmes> += rule 2 if human ?x then mortal ?x
holmes> ?- mortal bob
is this true: "thinks bob" ? y
yes: (no variables)

holmes> +- thinks bob
I deduced these facts...
    human bob
    mortal bob
I started with these facts...
    thinks bob
time: 0.0
```

Finally, the @= command is used to load files of rules that implement more sophisticated knowledgebases; the rule parser is run on each rule in the file. Here is a file that encodes animal classification rules; other example files are available on the CD if you'd like to experiment:

```
holmes> @= ..\bases\zoo.kb
holmes> ?- it is a penguin
is this true: "has feathers" ? why
to prove "it is a penguin" by rule 17
this was part of your original query.
is this true: "has feathers" ? y
is this true: "able to fly" ? n
is this true: "black color" ? y
yes: (no variables)
```

Type "stop" to end a session and "help" for a full commands list, and see the text files in the holmes directories for more details. Holmes is an old system written before Python 1.0 (and around 1993), but still works unchanged on all platforms under Python 1.5.2.

Regular Expression Matching

Splitting and joining strings is a simple way to process text, as long as it follows the format you expect. For more general text analysis tasks, Python provides regular expression matching utilities. Regular expressions (REs) are simply strings that define *patterns* to be matched against other strings. You supply a pattern and a string, and ask if the string matches your pattern. After a match, parts of the string matched by parts of the pattern are made available to your script. That is, matches not only give a yes/no answer, but they can pick out substrings as well.

Regular expression pattern strings can be complicated (let's be honest—they can be downright gross to look at). But once you get the hang of them, they can replace larger hand-coded string search routines. In Python, regular expressions are not part of the syntax of the Python language itself, but are supported by extension modules that you must import to use. The modules define functions for compiling pattern strings into pattern objects, matching these objects against strings, and fetching matched substrings after a match.

Beyond those generalities, Python's regular expression story is complicated a little by history:

The regex module (old)
> In earlier Python releases, a module called **regex** was the standard (and only) RE module. It was fast and supported patterns coded in *awg*, *grep*, and *emacs* style, but it is now somewhat deprecated (though it will likely still be available for some time to come).

The re module (new)
> Today, you should use **re**, a new RE module for Python, that was introduced sometime around Python release 1.5. This module provides a much richer RE pattern syntax that tries to be close to that used to code patterns in the Perl language (yes, REs are a feature of Perl worth emulating). For instance, **re** supports the notions of named groups, character classes, and *non-greedy* matches—RE pattern operators that match as few characters as possible (other RE pattern operators always match the longest possible substring).

Up until very recently, **re** was generally slower than **regex**, so you had to choose between speed and Perl-like RE syntax. Today, though, **re** has been optimized with the **sre** implementation, to the extent that **regex** no longer offers any clear advantages. Moreover, **re** in Python 2.0 now supports matching Unicode strings (strings with 16-bit wide characters for representing large character sets).

Because of this migration, I've recoded RE examples in this text to use the new **re** module instead of **regex**. The old **regex**-based versions are still available on the book's CD, in directory *PP2E\lang\old-regex*. If you find yourself having to migrate old **regex** code, you can also find a document describing the translation steps needed at *http://www.python.org*. Both modules' interfaces are similar, but **re** introduces a match object and changes pattern syntax in minor ways.

Having said that, I also want to warn you that REs are a complex topic that cannot be covered in depth here. If this area sparks your interest, the text *Mastering Regular Expressions* from O'Reilly is a good next step to take.

Using the re Module

The Python **re** module comes with functions that can search for patterns right away or make compiled *pattern objects* for running matches later. Pattern objects (and module search calls) in turn generate *match objects*, which contain information about successful matches and matched substrings. The next few sections describe the module's interfaces and some of the operators you can use to code patterns.

Module functions

The top level of the module provides functions for matching, substitution, precompiling, and so on:

compile(pattern [, flags])
> Compile a RE **pattern** string into a regular expression object, for later matching. See the reference manual for the flags argument's meaning.

match(pattern, string [, flags])
> If zero or more characters at start of **string** match the **pattern** string, return a corresponding MatchObject instance, or None if no match is found.

search(pattern, string [, flags])
> Scan through **string** for a location matching **pattern**, and return a corresponding MatchObject instance, or None if no match is found.

split(pattern, string [, maxsplit])
> Split **string** by occurrences of **pattern**. If capturing ( ) are used in the pattern, then occurrences of patterns or subpatterns are also returned.

sub(pattern, repl, string [, count])
> Return the string obtained by replacing the (first **count**) leftmost non-overlapping occurrences of **pattern** (a string or a RE object) in **string** by **repl**.

subn(pattern, repl, string [, count])
> Same as **sub**, but returns a tuple: (new-string, number-of-changes-made).

Compiled pattern objects

At the next level, pattern objects provide similar attributes, but the pattern string is implied. The re.compile function in the previous section is useful to optimize patterns that may be matched more than once (compiled patterns match faster). Pattern objects returned by re.compile have these sorts of attributes:

```
match(string [, pos] [, endpos])
search(string [, pos] [, endpos])
split(string [, maxsplit])
sub(repl, string [, count])
subn(repl, string [, count])
```

> Same as the re functions, but the pattern is implied, and pos and endpos give start/end string indexes for the match.

Match objects

Finally, when a match or search function or method is successful, you get back a match object (None comes back on failed matches). Match objects export a set of attributes of their own, including:

group([g1, g2, ...])
> Returns the substring that matched a parenthesized groups in the pattern.

groups()
> Returns a tuple of all groups' substrings of the match.

start([group]), end([group])
> Indices of the start and end of the substring matched by group (or the entire matched string, if no group).

span([group])
> Returns the two-item tuple: (start(group),end(group)).

Regular expression patterns

Regular expression strings are built up by concatenating single-character regular expression forms, shown in Table 18-1. The longest-matching string is usually matched by each form, except for the non-greedy operators. In the table, R means any regular expression form, C is a character, and N denotes a digit.

Table 18-1. re Pattern Syntax

.	Matches any character (including newline if DOTALL flag specified)
^	Matches start of the string (of every line in MULTILINE mode)
$	Matches end of the string (of every line in MULTILINE mode)
C	Any non-special character matches itself
R*	Zero or more of preceding regular expression R (as many as possible)

Table 18-1. re Pattern Syntax (continued)

R+	One or more of preceding regular expression R (as many as possible)
R?	Zero or one occurrence of preceding regular expression R
R{m,n}	Matches from m to n repetitions of preceding regular expression R
R*?, R+?, R??, R{m,n}?	Same as *, +, and ? but matches as few characters/times as possible; these are known as *non-greedy* match operators (unlike others, they match and consume as few characters as possible)
[ ]	Defines character set: e.g. [a-zA-Z] to match all letters
[^]	Defines complemented character set: matches if char is not in set
\	Escapes special chars (e.g., *?+|()) and introduces special sequences
\\	Matches a literal \ (write as \\\\ in pattern, or r\\)
R|R	Alternative: matches left or right R
RR	Concatenation: match both Rs
(R)	Matches any RE inside (), and forms a group (retains matched substring)
(?: R)	Same but doesn't delimit a group
(?= R)	Matches if R matches next, but doesn't consume any of the string (e.g., X (?=Y) matches X only if followed by Y)
(?! R)	Matches if R doesn't match next. Negative of (?=R)
(?P<name>R)	Matches any RE inside (), and delimits a named group
(?P=name)	Matches whatever text was matched by the earlier group named name
(?#...)	A comment; ignored
(?letter)	Set mode flag; letter is one of i, L, m, s, x (see library manual)

Within patterns, ranges and selections can be combined. For instance, [a-zA-Z0-9_]+ matches the longest possible string of one or more letters, digits, or underscores. Special characters can be escaped as usual in Python strings: [\t]* matches zero or more tabs and spaces (i.e., it skips whitespace).

The parenthesized grouping construct, (R), lets you extract matched substrings after a successful match. The portion of the string matched by the expression in parentheses is retained in a numbered register. It's available through the group method of a match object after a successful match.

In addition to the entries in this table, special sequences in Table 18-2 can be used in patterns, too. Due to Python string rules, you sometimes must double up on backslashes (\\) or use Python raw strings (r'...') to retain backslashes in the pattern.

Table 18-2. re Special Sequences

\num	Match text of group num (numbered from 1)
\A	Matches only at the start of the string
\b	Empty string at word boundaries

Table 18-2. re Special Sequences (continued)

\B	Empty string not at word boundary
\d	Any decimal digit (like [0-9])
\D	Any nondecimal digit character (like [^0-9])
\s	Any whitespace character (like [\t\n\r\f\v])
\S	Any nonwhitespace character (like [^ \t\n\r\f\v])
\w	Any alphanumeric character (uses LOCALE flag)
\W	Any nonalphanumeric character (uses LOCALE flag)
\Z	Matches only at the end of the string

The Python library manual gives additional details. But to demonstrate how the **re** interfaces are typically used, we'll turn to some short examples.

Basic Patterns

To illustrate how to combine RE operators, let's start with a few short test files that match simple pattern forms. Comments in Example 18-3 describe the operations exercised; check Table 18-1 to see which operators are used in these patterns.

Example 18-3. PP2E\lang\re-basics.py

```
# literals, sets, ranges    (all print 2 = offset where pattern found)

import re                                  # the one to use today

pattern, string = "A.C.", "xxABCDxx"       # nonspecial chars match themself
matchobj = re.search(pattern, string)      # '.' means any one char
if matchobj:                               # search returns match object or None
    print matchobj.start()                 # start is index where matched

pattobj  = re.compile("A.*C.*")            # 'R*' means zero or more Rs
matchobj = pattobj.search("xxABCDxx")      # compile returns pattern obj
if matchobj:                               # patt.search returns match obj
    print matchobj.start()

# selection sets
print re.search(" *A.C[DE][D-F][^G-ZE]G\t+ ?", "..ABCDEFG\t..").start()

# alternatives
print re.search("A|XB|YC|ZD", "..AYCD..").start()    # R1|R2 means R1 or R2

# word boundaries
print re.search(r"\bABCD", "..ABCD ").start()        # \b means word boundary
print re.search(r"ABCD\b", "..ABCD ").start()        # use r'...' to escape '\'
```

Notice that there are a variety of ways to kick off a match with **re**—by calling module search functions and by making compiled pattern objects. In either event, you can hang on to the resulting match object or not. All the print statements in this script show a result of 2—the offset where the pattern was found in the string.

In the first test, for example, "A.C." matches the "ABCD" at offset 2 in the search string (i.e., after the first "xx"):

```
C:\...\PP2E\Lang>python re-basic.py
2
2
2
2
2
2
```

In Example 18-4, parts of the pattern strings enclosed in parentheses delimit *groups*; the parts of the string they matched are available after the match.

Example 18-4. PP2E\lang\re-groups.py

```
# groups (extract substrings matched by REs in '()' parts)

import re

patt = re.compile("A(.)B(.)C(.)")
mobj = patt.match("A0B1C2")                        # saves 3 substrings
print mobj.group(1), mobj.group(2), mobj.group(3)  # each '()' is a group, 1..n
                                                   # group() gives substring

patt = re.compile("A(.*)B(.*)C(.*)")               # saves 3 substrings
mobj = patt.match("A000B111C222")                  # groups() gives all groups
print mobj.groups()

print re.search("(A|X)(B|Y)(C|Z)D", "..AYCD..").groups()

patt = re.compile(r"[\t ]*#\s*define\s*([a-z0-9_]*)\s*(.*)")
mobj = patt.search(" # define    spam  1 + 2 + 3") # parts of C #define
print mobj.groups()                                # \s is whitespace
```

In the first test here, for instance, the three (.) groups each match a single character, but retain the character matched; calling **group** pulls out the bits matched. The second test's (.*) groups match and retain any number of characters. The last test here matches C **#define** lines; more on this later.

```
C:\...\PP2E\Lang>python re-groups.py
0 1 2
('000', '111', '222')
('A', 'Y', 'C')
('spam', '1 + 2 + 3')
```

Finally, besides matches and substring extraction, **re** also includes tools for string replacement or substitution (see Example 18-5).

Example 18-5. PP2E\lang\re-subst.py

```
# substitutions (replace occurrences of patt with repl in string)

import re
print re.sub('[ABC]', '*', 'XAXAXBXBXCXC')
print re.sub('[ABC]_', '*', 'XA-XA_XB-XB_XC-XC_')
```

In the first test, all characters in the set are replaced; in the second, they must be followed by an underscore:

```
C:\...\PP2E\Lang>python re-subst.py
X*X*X*X*X*X*
XA-X*XB-X*XC-X*
```

Scanning C Header Files for Patterns

The script in Example 18-6 puts these pattern operators to more practical use. It uses regular expressions to find #define and #include lines in C header files and extract their components. The generality of the patterns makes them detect a variety of line formats; pattern groups (the parts in parentheses) are used to extract matched substrings from a line after a match.

Example 18-6. PP2E\Lang\cheader.py

```
#! /usr/local/bin/python
import sys, re
from string import strip

pattDefine = re.compile(                            # compile to pattobj
    '^#[\t ]*define[\t ]+([a-zA-Z0-9_]+)[\t ]*(.*)')   # "# define xxx yyy..."

pattInclude = re.compile(
    '^#[\t ]*include[\t ]+[<"]([a-zA-Z0-9_/\.]+)')     # "# include <xxx>..."

def scan(file):
    count = 0
    while 1:                                        # scan line-by-line
        line = file.readline()
        if not line: break
        count = count + 1
        matchobj = pattDefine.match(line)           # None if match fails
        if matchobj:
            name = matchobj.group(1)                # substrings for (...) parts
            body = matchobj.group(2)
            print count, 'defined', name, '=', strip(body)
            continue
        matchobj = pattInclude.match(line)
        if matchobj:
            start, stop = matchobj.span(1)          # start/stop indexes of (...)
            filename = line[start:stop]             # slice out of line
            print count, 'include', filename        # same as matchobj.group(1)

if len(sys.argv) == 1:
    scan(sys.stdin)                     # no args: read stdin
else:
    scan(open(sys.argv[1], 'r'))        # arg: input file name
```

To test, let's run this script on the text file in Example 18-7.

Example 18-7. PP2E\Lang\test.h

```
#ifndef TEST_H
#define TEST_H

#include <stdio.h>
#include <lib/spam.h>
#  include   "Python.h"

#define DEBUG
#define HELLO 'hello regex world'
#  define SPAM    1234

#define EGGS sunny + side + up
#define  ADDER(arg) 123 + arg
#endif
```

Notice the spaces after # in some of these lines; regular expressions are flexible enough to account for such departures from the norm. Here is the script at work, picking out #include and #define lines and their parts; for each matched line, it prints the line number, the line type, and any matched substrings:

```
C:\...\PP2E\Lang>python cheader.py test.h
2 defined TEST_H =
4 include stdio.h
5 include lib/spam.h
6 include Python.h
8 defined DEBUG =
9 defined HELLO = 'hello regex world'
10 defined SPAM = 1234
12 defined EGGS = sunny + side + up
13 defined ADDER = (arg) 123 + arg
```

A File Pattern Search Utility

The next script searches for patterns in a set of files, much like the **grep** command-line program. We wrote file and directory searchers earlier, in Chapter 5, *Larger System Examples II*. Here, the file searches look for patterns instead of simple strings (see Example 18-8). The patterns are typed interactively separated by a space, and the files to be searched are specified by an input pattern for Python's **glob.glob** filename expansion tool we studied earlier, too.

Example 18-8. PP2E\Lang\pygrep1.py

```
#!/usr/local/bin/python
import sys, re, glob
from string import split

help_string = """
Usage options.
interactive:  % pygrep1.py
"""
```

Example 18-8. PP2E\Lang\pygrep1.py (continued)

```
def getargs():
    if len(sys.argv) == 1:
        return split(raw_input("patterns? >")), raw_input("files? >")
    else:
        try:
            return sys.argv[1], sys.argv[2]
        except:
            print help_string
            sys.exit(1)

def compile_patterns(patterns):
    res = []
    for pattstr in patterns:
        try:
            res.append(re.compile(pattstr))          # make re patt object
        except:                                       # or use re.match
            print 'pattern ignored:', pattstr
    return res

def searcher(pattfile, srchfiles):
    patts = compile_patterns(pattfile)                # compile for speed
    for file in glob.glob(srchfiles):                 # all matching files
        lineno = 1                                    # glob uses re too
        print '\n[%s]' % file
        for line in open(file, 'r').readlines():      # all lines in file
            for patt in patts:
                if patt.search(line):                 # try all patterns
                    print '%04d)' % lineno, line,     # match if not None
                    break
            lineno = lineno+1

if __name__ == '__main__':
    apply(searcher, getargs())
```

Here's what a typical run of this script looks like; it searches all Python files in the current directory for two different patterns, compiled for speed. Notice that files are named by a pattern, too—Python's `glob` module also uses `re` internally:

```
C:\...\PP2E\Lang>python pygrep1.py
patterns? >import.*string spam
files? >*.py

[cheader.py]

[finder2.py]
0002) import string, glob, os, sys

[patterns.py]
0048) mobj = patt.search(" # define  spam  1 + 2 + 3")

[pygrep1.py]
```

```
[rules.py]

[summer.py]
0002) import string

[__init__.py]
```

Parser Generators

If you have any background in parsing theory, you may know that neither regular expressions nor string splitting is powerful enough to handle more complex language grammars (roughly, they don't have the "memory" required by true grammars). For more sophisticated language analysis tasks, we sometimes need a full-blown parser. Since Python is built for integrating C tools, we can write integrations to traditional parser generator systems such as *yacc* and *bison*. Better yet, we could use an integration that already exists.

There are also Python-specific parsing systems accessible from Python's web site. Among them, the *kwParsing* system, developed by Aaron Watters, is a parser generator written in Python, and the *SPARK* toolkit, developed by John Aycock, is a lightweight system that employs the Earley algorithm to work around technical problems with LALR parser generation (if you don't know what that means, you probably don't need to care). Since these are all complex tools, though, we'll skip their details in this text. Consult *http://www.python.org* for information on parser generator tools available for use in Python programs.

Lesson 2: Don't Reinvent the Wheel

Speaking of parser generators: to use some of these tools in Python programs, you'll need an extension module that integrates them. The first step in such scenarios should always be to see if the extension already exists in the public domain. Especially for common tools like these, chances are that someone else has already written an integration that you can use off-the-shelf instead of writing one from scratch.

Of course, not everyone can donate all their extension modules to the public domain, but there's a growing library of available components that you can pick up for free and a community of experts to query. Visit *http://www.python.org* for links to Python software resources. With some half a million Python users out there as I write this book, there is much that can be found in the prior-art department.

Of special interest to this chapter, also see YAPPS—Yet Another Python Parser System. YAPPS is a parser generator written in Python. It uses supplied rules to generate human-readable Python code that implements a recursive descent parser. The parsers generated by YAPPS look much like (and are inspired by) the hand-coded expression parsers shown in the next section. YAPPS creates LL(1) parsers, which are not as powerful as LALR parsers, but sufficient for many language tasks. For more on YAPPS, see *http://theory.standford.edu/~amitp/Yapps*.

Hand-Coded Parsers

Since Python is a general purpose programming language, it's also reasonable to consider writing a hand-coded parser. For instance, *recursive descent parsing* is a fairly well-known technique for analyzing language-based information. Since Python is a very high-level language, writing the parser itself is usually easier than it would be in a traditional language like C or C++.

To illustrate, this section develops a custom parser for a simple grammar: it parses and evaluates arithmetic expression strings. This example also demonstrates the utility of Python as a general-purpose programming language. Although Python is often used as a frontend or rapid development language, it's also useful for the kinds of things we'd normally write in a systems development language like C or C++.

The Expression Grammar

The grammar our parser will recognize can be described as follows:

```
goal -> <expr> END                              [number, variable, ( ]
goal -> <assign> END                            [set]

assign -> 'set' <variable> <expr>               [set]

expr -> <factor> <expr-tail>                    [number, variable, ( ]

expr-tail -> ^                                  [END, ) ]
expr-tail -> '+' <factor> <expr-tail>           [+]
expr-tail -> '-' <factor> <expr-tail>           [-]

factor -> <term> <factor-tail>                  [number, variable, ( ]

factor-tail -> ^                                [+, -, END, ) ]
factor-tail -> '*' <term> <factor-tail>         [*]
factor-tail -> '/' <term> <factor-tail>         [/]

term -> <number>                                [number]
term -> <variable>                              [variable]
term -> '(' <expr> ')'                          [(]

tokens: (, ), num, var, -, +, /, *, set, end
```

This is a fairly typical grammar for a simple expression language, and it allows for arbitrary expression nesting (some example expressions appear at the end of the `testparser` module listing in Example 18-11). Strings to be parsed are either an expression or an assignment to a variable name (`set`). Expressions involve numbers, variables, and the operators +, -, *, and /. Because `factor` is nested in `expr` in the grammar, * and / have higher precedence (i.e., bind tighter) than + and -. Expressions can be enclosed in parentheses to override precedence, and all operators are left associative—that is, group on the left (e.g., 1-2-3 is treated the same as (1-2)-3).

Tokens are just the most primitive components of the expression language. Each grammar rule earlier is followed in square brackets by a list of tokens used to select it. In recursive descent parsing, we determine the set of tokens that can possibly start a rule's substring, and use that information to predict which rule will work ahead of time. For rules that iterate (the -`tail` rules), we use the set of possibly following tokens to know when to stop. Typically, tokens are recognized by a string processor (a "scanner"), and a higher-level processor (a "parser") uses the token stream to predict and step through grammar rules and substrings.

The Parser's Code

The system is structured as two modules, holding two classes:

- The *scanner* handles low-level character-by-character analysis.
- The *parser* embeds a scanner and handles higher-level grammar analysis.

The parser is also responsible for computing the expression's value and testing the system. In this version, the parser evaluates the expression while it is being parsed. To use the system, we create a parser with an input string and call its `parse` method. We can also call `parse` again later with a new expression string.

There's a deliberate division of labor here. The scanner extracts tokens from the string, but knows nothing about the grammar. The parser handles the grammar, but is naive about the string itself. This modular structure keeps the code relatively simple. And it's another example of the OOP composition relationship at work: parsers embed and delegate to scanners.

The module in Example 18-9 implements the lexical analysis task—detecting the expression's basic tokens by scanning the text string left to right on demand. Notice that this is all straightforward logic here; such analysis can sometimes be performed with regular expressions instead (described earlier), but the pattern needed to detect and extract tokens in this example would be too complex and fragile for my tastes. If your tastes vary, try recoding this module with `re`.

Example 18-9. PP2E\Lang\Parser\scanner.py

```python
##################################################
# the scanner (lexical analyser)
##################################################

import string
SyntaxError    = 'SyntaxError'          # local errors
LexicalError   = 'LexicalError'

class Scanner:
    def __init__(self, text):
        self.next = 0
        self.text = text + '\0'

    def newtext(self, text):
        Scanner.__init__(self, text)

    def showerror(self):
        print '=> ', self.text
        print '=> ', (' ' * self.start) + '^'

    def match(self, token):
        if self.token != token:
            raise SyntaxError, [token]
        else:
            value = self.value
            if self.token != '\0':
                self.scan()                 # next token/value
            return value                    # return prior value

    def scan(self):
        self.value = None
        ix = self.next
        while self.text[ix] in string.whitespace:
            ix = ix+1
        self.start = ix

        if self.text[ix] in ['(', ')', '-', '+', '/', '*', '\0']:
            self.token = self.text[ix]
            ix = ix+1

        elif self.text[ix] in string.digits:
            str = ''
            while self.text[ix] in string.digits:
                str = str + self.text[ix]
                ix = ix+1
            if self.text[ix] == '.':
                str = str + '.'
                ix = ix+1
                while self.text[ix] in string.digits:
                    str = str + self.text[ix]
                    ix = ix+1
                self.token = 'num'
                self.value = string.atof(str)
```

Example 18-9. PP2E\Lang\Parser\scanner.py (continued)

```
        else:
            self.token = 'num'
            self.value = string.atol(str)

    elif self.text[ix] in string.letters:
        str = ''
        while self.text[ix] in (string.digits + string.letters):
            str = str + self.text[ix]
            ix = ix+1
        if string.lower(str) == 'set':
            self.token = 'set'
        else:
            self.token = 'var'
            self.value = str

    else:
        raise LexicalError
    self.next = ix
```

The parser module's class creates and embeds a scanner for its lexical chores, and handles interpretation of the expression grammar's rules and evaluation of the expression's result, as shown in Example 18-10.

Example 18-10. PP2E\Lang\Parser\parser1.py

```
#########################################################
# the parser (syntax analyser, evaluates during parse)
#########################################################

UndefinedError = 'UndefinedError'
from scanner import Scanner, LexicalError, SyntaxError

class Parser:
    def __init__(self, text=''):
        self.lex  = Scanner(text)               # embed a scanner
        self.vars = {'pi':3.14159}              # add a variable

    def parse(self, *text):
        if text:                                # main entry-point
            self.lex.newtext(text[0])           # reuse this parser?
        try:
            self.lex.scan()                     # get first token
            self.Goal()                         # parse a sentence
        except SyntaxError:
            print 'Syntax Error at column:', self.lex.start
            self.lex.showerror()
        except LexicalError:
            print 'Lexical Error at column:', self.lex.start
            self.lex.showerror()
        except UndefinedError, name:
            print "'%s' is undefined at column:" % name, self.lex.start
            self.lex.showerror()
```

Example 18-10. PP2E\Lang\Parser\parser1.py (continued)

```python
    def Goal(self):
        if self.lex.token in ['num', 'var', '(']:
            val = self.Expr()
            self.lex.match('\0')                    # expression?
            print val
        elif self.lex.token == 'set':               # set command?
            self.Assign()
            self.lex.match('\0')
        else:
            raise SyntaxError

    def Assign(self):
        self.lex.match('set')
        var = self.lex.match('var')
        val = self.Expr()
        self.vars[var] = val            # assign name in dict

    def Expr(self):
        left = self.Factor()
        while 1:
            if self.lex.token in ['\0', ')']:
                return left
            elif self.lex.token == '+':
                self.lex.scan()
                left = left + self.Factor()
            elif self.lex.token == '-':
                self.lex.scan()
                left = left - self.Factor()
            else:
                raise SyntaxError

    def Factor(self):
        left = self.Term()
        while 1:
            if self.lex.token in ['+', '-', '\0', ')']:
                return left
            elif self.lex.token == '*':
                self.lex.scan()
                left = left * self.Term()
            elif self.lex.token == '/':
                self.lex.scan()
                left = left / self.Term()
            else:
                raise SyntaxError

    def Term(self):
        if self.lex.token == 'num':
            val = self.lex.match('num')             # numbers
            return val
        elif self.lex.token == 'var':
            if self.vars.has_key(self.lex.value):
                val = self.vars[self.lex.value]     # lookup name's value
                self.lex.scan()
```

Example 18-10. PP2E\Lang\Parser\parser1.py (continued)

```
                return val
        else:
                raise UndefinedError, self.lex.value
        elif self.lex.token == '(':
            self.lex.scan()
            val = self.Expr()                                # sub-expression
            self.lex.match(')')
            return val
        else:
            raise SyntaxError

if __name__ == '__main__':
    import testparser                                # self-test code
    testparser.test(Parser, 'parser1')              # test local Parser
```

If you study this code closely, you'll notice that the parser keeps a dictionary (`self.vars`) to manage variable names: they're stored in the dictionary on a *set* command and fetched from it when they appear in an expression. Tokens are represented as strings, with an optional associated value (a numeric value for numbers and a string for variable names).

The parser uses iteration (`while` loops) instead of recursion, for the `expr-tail` and `factor-tail` rules. Other than this optimization, the rules of the grammar map directly onto parser methods: tokens become calls to the scanner, and nested rule references become calls to other methods.

When file *parser1.py* is run as a top-level program, its self-test code is executed, which in turn simply runs a canned test in the module shown in Example 18-11. Note that all integer math uses Python long integers (unlimited precision integers), because the scanner converts numbers to strings with `string.atol`. Also notice that mixed integer/floating-point operations cast up to floating point since Python operators are used to do the actual calculations.

Example 18-11. PP2E\Lang\Parser\testparser.py

```
####################################################
# parser test code
####################################################

def test(ParserClass, msg):
    print msg, ParserClass
    x = ParserClass('4 / 2 + 3')                     # allow different Parser's
    x.parse()

    x.parse('3 + 4 / 2')                             # like eval('3 + 4 / 2')...
    x.parse('(3 + 4) / 2')
    x.parse('4 / (2 + 3)')
    x.parse('4.0 / (2 + 3)')
    x.parse('4 / (2.0 + 3)')
    x.parse('4.0 / 2 * 3')
```

Example 18-11. PP2E\Lang\Parser\testparser.py (continued)

```
    x.parse('(4.0 / 2) * 3')
    x.parse('4.0 / (2 * 3)')
    x.parse('(((3))) + 1')

    y = ParserClass()
    y.parse('set a 4 / 2 + 1')
    y.parse('a * 3')
    y.parse('set b 12 / a')
    y.parse('b')

    z = ParserClass()
    z.parse('set a 99')
    z.parse('set a a + 1')
    z.parse('a')

    z = ParserClass()
    z.parse('pi')
    z.parse('2 * pi')
    z.parse('1.234 + 2.1')

def interact(ParserClass):                        # command-line entry
    print ParserClass
    x = ParserClass()
    while 1:
        cmd = raw_input('Enter=> ')
        if cmd == 'stop':
            break
        x.parse(cmd)
```

Correlate the following results to print statements in the self-test module:

```
C:\...\PP2E\Lang\Parser>python parser1.py
parser1 __main__.Parser
5L
5L
3L
0L
0.8
0.8
6.0
6.0
0.666666666667
4L
9L
4L
100L
3.14159
6.28318
3.334
```

As usual, we can also test and use the system interactively:

```
% python
>>> import parser1
```

```
>>> x = parser1.Parser()
>>> x.parse('1 + 2')
3L
```

Error cases are trapped and reported:

```
>>> x.parse('1 + a')
'a' is undefined at column: 4
=>  1 + a
=>        ^
>>> x.parse('1+a+2')
'a' is undefined at column: 2
=>  1+a+2
=>     ^
>>> x.parse('1 * 2 $')
Lexical Error at column: 6
=>  1 * 2 $
=>          ^
>>> x.parse('1 * - 1')
Syntax Error at column: 4
=>  1 * - 1
=>        ^
>>> x.parse('1 * (9')
Syntax Error at column: 6
=>  1 * (9
=>          ^
```

Pathologically big numbers are handled well, because Python's built-in objects and operators are used along the way:

```
>>> x.parse('8888888888888888888888888888888888888888888888.9999999')
8.88888888889e+44
>>> x.parse('9999999999999999999999999999999999999999 + 2')
10000000000000000000000000000000000000001L
>>> x.parse('999999999999999999999999999999.88888888888 + 1.1')
1e+30
```

In addition, there is an interactive loop interface in the `testparser` module, if you want to use the parser as a simple command-line calculator (or if you get tired of typing parser method calls). Pass the `Parser` class, so `testparser` can make one of its own:

```
>>> import testparser
>>> testparser.interact(parser1.Parser)
Enter=> 4 * 3 + 5
17L
Enter=> 5 + 4 * 3
17L
Enter=> (5 + 4) * 3
27L
Enter=> set a 99
Enter=> set b 66
Enter=> a + b
165L
Enter=> # + 1
```

```
Lexical Error at column: 0
=>  # + 1
=>  ^
Enter=> a * b + c
'c' is undefined at column: 8
=>  a * b + c
=>          ^
Enter=> a * b * + c
Syntax Error at column: 8
=>  a * b * + c
=>          ^
Enter=> a
99L
Enter=> a * a * a
970299L
Enter=> stop
>>>
```

Lesson 3: Divide and Conquer

As the parser system demonstrates, modular program design is almost always a major win. By using Python's program structuring tools (functions, modules, classes, etc.), big tasks can be broken down into small, manageable parts that can be coded and tested independently.

For instance, the scanner can be tested without the parser by making an instance with an input string and calling its **scan** or **match** methods repeatedly. We can even test it like this interactively, from Python's command line. By separating programs into logical components, they become easier to understand and modify. Imagine what the parser would look like if the scanner's logic was embedded rather than called.

Adding a Parse Tree Interpreter

One weakness in the `parser1` program is that it embeds expression evaluation logic in the parsing logic: the result is computed while the string is being parsed. This makes evaluation quick, but it can also make it difficult to modify the code, especially in larger systems. To simplify, we could restructure the program to keep expression parsing and evaluation separate. Instead of evaluating the string, the parser can build up an intermediate representation of it that can be evaluated later. As an added incentive, building the representation separately makes it available to other analysis tools (e.g., optimizers, viewers, and so on).

Example 18-12 shows a variant of `parser1` that implements this idea. The parser analyzes the string and builds up a *parse tree*—that is, a tree of class instances that represents the expression and that may be evaluated in a separate step. The parse tree is built from classes that "know" how to evaluate themselves: to compute the expression, we just ask the tree to evaluate itself. Root nodes in the tree ask their children to evaluate themselves and then combine the results by applying a single operator. In effect, evaluation in this version is simply a recursive traversal of a tree of embedded class instances constructed by the parser.

Example 18-12. PP2E\Lang\Parser\parser2.py

```
TraceDefault    = 0
UndefinedError = "UndefinedError"
from scanner import Scanner, SyntaxError, LexicalError


####################################################
# the interpreter (a smart objects tree)
####################################################

class TreeNode:
    def validate(self, dict):          # default error check
        pass
    def apply(self, dict):             # default evaluator
        pass
    def trace(self, level):            # default unparser
        print '.'*level + '<empty>'

# ROOTS

class BinaryNode(TreeNode):
    def __init__(self, left, right):           # inherited methods
        self.left, self.right = left, right    # left/right branches
    def validate(self, dict):
        self.left.validate(dict)               # recurse down branches
        self.right.validate(dict)
    def trace(self, level):
        print '.'*level + '[' + self.label + ']'
        self.left.trace(level+3)
        self.right.trace(level+3)

class TimesNode(BinaryNode):
    label = '*'
    def apply(self, dict):
        return self.left.apply(dict) * self.right.apply(dict)

class DivideNode(BinaryNode):
    label = '/'
    def apply(self, dict):
        return self.left.apply(dict) / self.right.apply(dict)

class PlusNode(BinaryNode):
    label = '+'
    def apply(self, dict):
        return self.left.apply(dict) + self.right.apply(dict)

class MinusNode(BinaryNode):
```

Example 18-12. PP2E\Lang\Parser\parser2.py (continued)

```
        label = '-'
        def apply(self, dict):
            return self.left.apply(dict) - self.right.apply(dict)


# LEAVES

class NumNode(TreeNode):
    def __init__(self, num):
        self.num = num                      # already numeric
    def apply(self, dict):                  # use default validate
        return self.num
    def trace(self, level):
        print '.'*level + `self.num`


class VarNode(TreeNode):
    def __init__(self, text, start):
        self.name   = text                  # variable name
        self.column = start                 # column for errors
    def validate(self, dict):
        if not dict.has_key(self.name):
            raise UndefinedError, (self.name, self.column)
    def apply(self, dict):
        return dict[self.name]              # validate before apply
    def assign(self, value, dict):
        dict[self.name] = value             # local extension
    def trace(self, level):
        print '.'*level + self.name


# COMPOSITES

class AssignNode(TreeNode):
    def __init__(self, var, val):
        self.var, self.val = var, val
    def validate(self, dict):
        self.val.validate(dict)             # don't validate var
    def apply(self, dict):
        self.var.assign( self.val.apply(dict), dict )
    def trace(self, level):
        print '.'*level + 'set '
        self.var.trace(level + 3)
        self.val.trace(level + 3)



##################################################
# the parser (syntax analyser, tree builder)
##################################################

class Parser:
    def __init__(self, text=''):
        self.lex     = Scanner(text)        # make a scanner
        self.vars    = {'pi':3.14159}       # add constants
        self.traceme = TraceDefault

    def parse(self, *text):                 # external interface
```

Example 18-12. PP2E\Lang\Parser\parser2.py (continued)

```
        if text:
            self.lex.newtext(text[0])        # reuse with new text
        tree = self.analyse()                # parse string
        if tree:
            if self.traceme:                 # dump parse-tree?
                print; tree.trace(0)
            if self.errorCheck(tree):        # check names
                self.interpret(tree)         # evaluate tree

    def analyse(self):
        try:
            self.lex.scan()                  # get first token
            return self.Goal()               # build a parse-tree
        except SyntaxError:
            print 'Syntax Error at column:', self.lex.start
            self.lex.showerror()
        except LexicalError:
            print 'Lexical Error at column:', self.lex.start
            self.lex.showerror()

    def errorCheck(self, tree):
        try:
            tree.validate(self.vars)         # error checker
            return 'ok'
        except UndefinedError, varinfo:
            print "'%s' is undefined at column: %d" % varinfo
            self.lex.start = varinfo[1]
            self.lex.showerror()             # returns None

    def interpret(self, tree):
        result = tree.apply(self.vars)       # tree evals itself
        if result != None:                   # ignore 'set' result
            print result

    def Goal(self):
        if self.lex.token in ['num', 'var', '(']:
            tree = self.Expr()
            self.lex.match('\0')
            return tree
        elif self.lex.token == 'set':
            tree = self.Assign()
            self.lex.match('\0')
            return tree
        else:
            raise SyntaxError

    def Assign(self):
        self.lex.match('set')
        vartree = VarNode(self.lex.value, self.lex.start)
        self.lex.match('var')
        valtree = self.Expr()
        return AssignNode(vartree, valtree)              # two subtrees
```

Example 18-12. PP2E\Lang\Parser\parser2.py (continued)

```python
    def Expr(self):
        left = self.Factor()                          # left subtree
        while 1:
            if self.lex.token in ['\0', ')']:
                return left
            elif self.lex.token == '+':
                self.lex.scan()
                left = PlusNode(left, self.Factor())  # add root-node
            elif self.lex.token == '-':
                self.lex.scan()
                left = MinusNode(left, self.Factor()) # grows up/right
            else:
                raise SyntaxError

    def Factor(self):
        left = self.Term()
        while 1:
            if self.lex.token in ['+', '-', '\0', ')']:
                return left
            elif self.lex.token == '*':
                self.lex.scan()
                left = TimesNode(left, self.Term())
            elif self.lex.token == '/':
                self.lex.scan()
                left = DivideNode(left, self.Term())
            else:
                raise SyntaxError

    def Term(self):
        if self.lex.token == 'num':
            leaf = NumNode(self.lex.match('num'))
            return leaf
        elif self.lex.token == 'var':
            leaf = VarNode(self.lex.value, self.lex.start)
            self.lex.scan()
            return leaf
        elif self.lex.token == '(':
            self.lex.scan()
            tree = self.Expr()
            self.lex.match(')')
            return tree
        else:
            raise SyntaxError


###################################################
# self-test code: use my parser, parser1's tester
###################################################

if __name__ == '__main__':
    import testparser
    testparser.test(Parser, 'parser2')    # run with Parser class here
```

When `parser2` is run as a top-level program, we get the same test code output as for `parser1`. In fact, it reuses the same test code: both parsers pass in their parser class object to `testparser.test`. And since classes are objects, we can also pass this version of the parser to `testparser`'s interactive loop: `testparser.inter-act(parser2.Parser)`. The new parser's external behavior is identical to that of the original.

Notice that the new parser reuses the same scanner module, too. To catch errors raised by scanner, it also imports the specific strings that identify the scanner's exceptions. The scanner and parser can both raise exceptions on errors (lexical errors, syntax errors, and undefined name errors). They're caught at the top level of the parser, and end the current parse. There's no need to set and check status flags to terminate the recursion. Since math is done using long integers, floating-point numbers, and Python's operators, there's usually no need to trap numeric overflow or underflow errors. But as is, the parser doesn't handle errors like division by zero: they make the parser system exit with a Python stack dump. Uncovering the cause and fix for this is left as an exercise.

Parse Tree Structure

The intermediate representation of an expression is a tree of class instances, whose shape reflects the order of operator evaluation. This parser also has logic to print an indented listing of the constructed parse tree if the `traceme` attribute is set. Indentation gives the nesting of subtrees, and binary operators list left subtrees first. For example:

```
% python
>>> import parser2
>>> p = parser2.Parser()
>>> p.traceme = 1
>>> p.parse('5 + 4 * 2')

[+]
...5L
...[*]
......4L
......2L
13L
```

When this tree is evaluated, the `apply` method recursively evaluates subtrees and applies root operators to their results. Here, `*` is evaluated before `+`, since it's lower in the tree. The `Factor` method consumes the `*` substring before returning a right subtree to `Expr`:

```
>>> p.parse('5 * 4 - 2')

[-]
```

```
...[*]
......5L
......4L
...2L
18L
```

In this example, * is evaluated before −. The `Factor` method loops though a substring of * and / expressions before returning the resulting left subtree to `Expr`:

```
>>> p.parse('1 + 3 * (2 * 3 + 4)')

[+]
...1L
...[*]
......3L
......[+]
.........[*]
............2L
............3L
.........4L
31L
```

Trees are made of nested class instances. From an OOP perspective, it's another way to use composition. Since tree nodes are just class instances, this tree could be created and evaluated manually, too:

```
PlusNode( NumNode(1),
         TimesNode( NumNode(3),
                   PlusNode( TimesNode(NumNode(2), NumNode(3)),
                            NumNode(4) ))).apply({})
```

But we might as well let the parser build it for us (Python is not that much like Lisp, despite what you may have heard).

Exploring Parse Trees with Pytree

But wait—there is a better way to explore parse tree structures. Figure 18-1 shows the parse tree generated for string "1 + 3 * (2 * 3 + 4)", displayed in PyTree, the tree visualization GUI presented at the end of the previous chapter. This only works because the `parser2` module builds the parse tree explicitly (`parser1` evaluates during a parse instead), and because PyTree's code is generic and reusable.

If you read the last chapter, you'll recall that PyTree can draw most any tree data structure, but it is preconfigured to handle binary search trees and the parse trees we're studying in this chapter. You might also remember that clicking on nodes in a displayed parse tree evaluates the subtree rooted there. Figure 18-2 shows the pop-up generated after clicking the tree's root node (you get different results if you click other parts of tree, because smaller subtrees are evaluated).

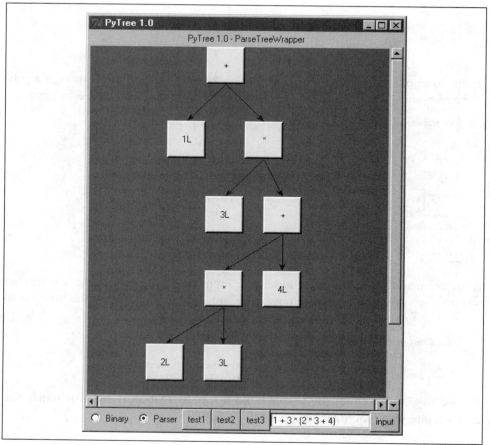

Figure 18-1. Parse tree built for 1 + 3 * (2 * 3 + 4)

Figure 18-2. Clicking the root node to evaluate a tree

PyTree makes it easy to learn about and experiment with the parser. To determine the tree shape produced for a given expression, start PyTree, click on its Parser radiobutton, type the expression in the input field at the bottom, and press "input" (or your Enter key). The parser class is run to generate a tree from your input, and the GUI displays the result. For instance, Figure 18-3 sketches the parse tree generated if we remove the parentheses from the first expression in the input field. The root node evaluates to 23 this time, due to the different shape's evaluation order.

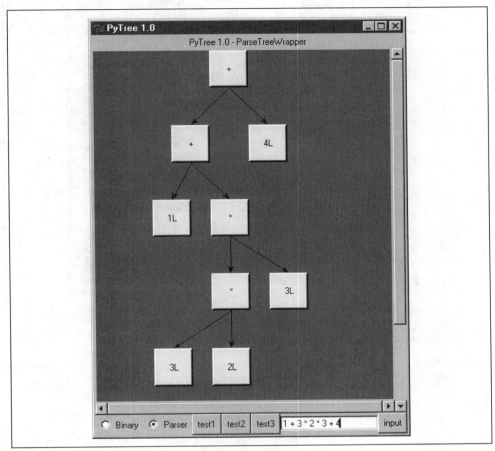

Figure 18-3. Parse tree for 1 + 3 * 2 * 3 + 4, result=23

To generate an even more different shape, try introducing more parentheses to the expression and hitting the Enter key again. Figure 18-4 shows a much flatter tree structure produced by adding a few parentheses to override operator precedence. Because these parentheses change the tree shape, they also change the expression's overall result again. Figure 18-5 shows the result pop-up after clicking the root node in this display.

Depending upon the operators used within an expression, some very differently shaped trees yield the same result when evaluated. For instance, Figure 18-6

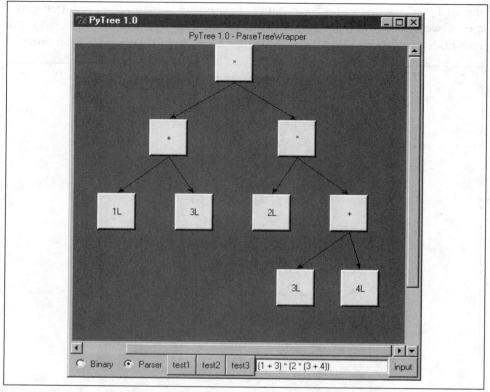

*Figure 18-4. Parse tree built for "(1 + 3) * (2 * (3 + 4))"*

Figure 18-5. Clicking and evaluating the root node

shows a more left-heavy tree generated from a different expression string that evaluates to 56 nevertheless.

Finally, Figure 18-7 shows a parsed assignment statement; clicking the "set" root assigns variable **spam**, and clicking node **spam** then evaluates to −4. If you find the parser puzzling, try running PyTree like this on your computer to get a better feel for the parsing process. (I'd like to show more example trees, but I ran out of page real estate at this point in the book.)

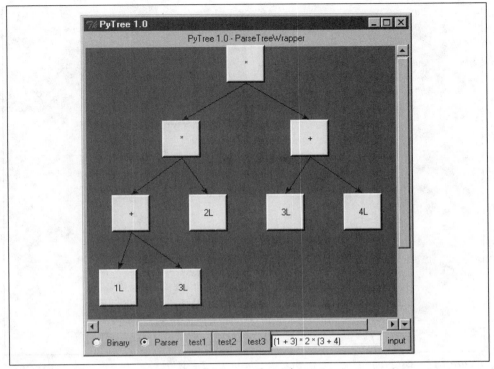

Figure 18-6. Parse tree for "(1 + 3) * 2 * (3 + 4)", result=56

Parsers Versus Python

The hand-coded parser programs shown earlier illustrate some interesting concepts and underscore the power of Python for general-purpose programming. Depending on your job description, they may also be typical of the sort of thing you'd write regularly in a traditional language like C. Parsers are an important component in a wide variety of applications, but in some cases, they're not as necessary as you might think. Let me explain why.

So far, we started with an expression parser and added a parse tree interpreter to make the code easier to modify. As is, the parser works, but it may be slow compared to a C implementation. If the parser is used frequently, we could speed it up by moving parts to C extension modules. For instance, the scanner might be moved to C initially, since it's often called from the parser. Ultimately, we might add components to the grammar that allow expressions to access application-specific variables and functions.

All of the these steps constitute good engineering. But depending on your application, this approach may not be the best one in Python. The easiest way to evaluate

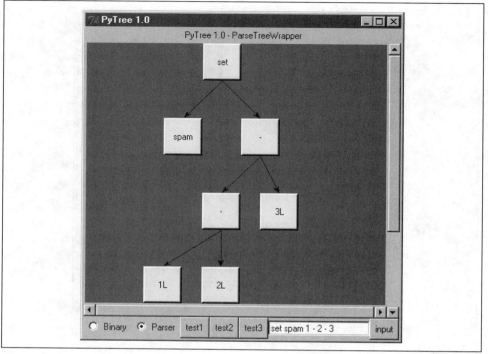

Figure 18-7. Assignment, left-grouping: "set spam 1 – 2 – 3"

input expressions in Python is often to let Python do it, by calling the `eval` built-in function. In fact, we can usually replace the entire expression evaluation program with one function call. The next example will demonstrate how this is done.

More importantly, the next section underscores a core idea behind the language: if you already have an extensible, embeddable, high-level language system, why invent another? Python itself can often satisfy language-based component needs.

PyCalc: A Calculator Program/Object

To wrap up this chapter, I'm going to show you a practical application for some of the parsing technology introduced in the previous section. This section presents *PyCalc*—a Python calculator program with a graphical interface similar to the calculator programs available on most window systems. But like most of the GUI examples in this book, PyCalc offers a few advantages over existing calculators. Because PyCalc is written in Python, it is both easily customized and widely portable across window platforms. And because it is implemented with classes, it is both a standalone program and a reusable object library.

A Simple Calculator GUI

Before I show you how to write a full-blown calculator, though, the module shown in Example 18-13 starts this discussion in simpler terms. It implements a limited calculator GUI, whose buttons just add text to the input field at the top, to compose a Python expression string. Fetching and running the string all at once produces results. Figure 18-8 shows the window this module makes when run as a top-level script.

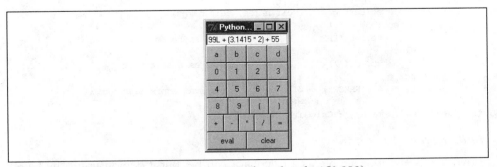

Figure 18-8. The calc0 script in action on Windows (result=160.283)

Example 18-13. PP2E\Lang\Calculator\calc0.py

```
#!/usr/local/bin/python
# a simple calculator GUI: expressions run all at once with eval/exec

from Tkinter  import *
from PP2E.Dbase.TableBrowser.guitools import frame, button, entry

class CalcGui(Frame):
    def __init__(self, parent=None):            # an extended frame
        Frame.__init__(self, parent)            # on default top-level
        self.pack(expand=YES, fill=BOTH)        # all parts expandable
        self.master.title('Python Calculator 0.1')   # 6 frames plus entry
        self.master.iconname("pcalc1")

        self.names = {}                         # namespace for variables
        text = StringVar()
        entry(self, TOP, text)

        rows = ["abcd", "0123", "4567", "89()"]
        for row in rows:
            frm = frame(self, TOP)
            for char in row: button(frm, LEFT, char,
                            lambda x=text, y=char: x.set(x.get() + y))

        frm = frame(self, TOP)
        for char in "+-*/=": button(frm, LEFT, char,
                        lambda x=text, y=char: x.set(x.get()+' '+y+' '))
```

Example 18-13. PP2E\Lang\Calculator\calc0.py (continued)

```
        frm = frame(self, BOTTOM)
        button(frm, LEFT, 'eval',  lambda x=self, y=text: x.eval(y) )
        button(frm, LEFT, 'clear', lambda x=text: x.set('') )

    def eval(self, text):
        try:
            text.set(`eval(text.get(), self.names, self.names)`)
        except SyntaxError:
            try:
                exec(text.get(), self.names, self.names)
            except:
                text.set("ERROR")          # bad as statement too?
            else:
                text.set('')               # worked as a statement
        except:
            text.set("ERROR")              # other eval expression errors

if __name__ == '__main__': CalcGui().mainloop()
```

Building the GUI

Now, this is about as simple as a calculator can be, but it demonstrates the basics. This window comes up with buttons for entry of numbers, variable names, and operators. It is built by attaching buttons to frames: each row of buttons is a nested `Frame`, and the GUI itself is a `Frame` subclass, with an attached `Entry` and six embedded row frames (grids would work here, too). The calculator's frame, entry field, and buttons are made expandable in the imported `guitools` utility module.

This calculator builds up a string to pass to the Python interpreter all at once on "eval" button presses. Because you can type any Python expression or statement in the entry field, the buttons are really just a convenience. In fact, the entry field isn't much more than a command line. Try typing `import sys` and then `dir(sys)` to display `sys` module attributes in the input field at the top—it's not what you normally do with a calculator, but demonstrative nevertheless.[*]

In `CalcGui`'s constructor, buttons are coded as lists of strings; each string represents a row and each character in the string represents a button. Lambdas with default argument values are used to set callback data for each button. The callback functions save the button's character and the linked text entry variable, so that the character can be added to the end of the entry widget's current string on a press.

---

[*] And once again, I need to warn you about running strings like this if you can't be sure they won't cause damage. See the `rexec` restricted execution mode module in Chapter 15, *Advanced Internet Topics*, for more details.

Lesson 4: Embedding Beats Parsers

The calculator uses `eval` and `exec` to call Python's parser/interpreter at run-time instead of analyzing and evaluating expressions manually. In effect, the calculator runs embedded Python code from a Python program. This works because Python's development environment (the parser and byte-code compiler) is always a part of systems that use Python. Because there is no difference between the development and delivery environments, Python's parser can be used by Python programs.

The net effect here is that the entire expression evaluator has been replaced with a single call to `eval`. In broader terms, this is a powerful technique to remember: the Python language itself can replace many small custom languages. Besides saving development time, clients have to learn just one language, one that's potentially simple enough for end-user coding.

Furthermore, Python can take on the flavor of any application. If a language interface requires application-specific extensions, just add Python classes, or export an API for use in embedded Python code as a C extension. By evaluating Python code that uses application-specific extensions, custom parsers become almost completely unnecessary.

There's also a critical added benefit to this approach: embedded Python code has access to all the tools and features of a powerful, full-blown programming language. It can use lists, functions, classes, external modules, and even larger Python tools like Tkinter, shelves, threads, and sockets. You'd probably spend years trying to provide similar functionality in a custom language parser. Just ask Guido.

Running code strings

This module implements a GUI calculator in 45 lines of code (counting comments and blank lines). But to be honest, it cheats: expression evaluation is delegated to Python. In fact, the built-in `eval` and `exec` tools do most of the work here:

- `eval` parses, evaluates, and returns the result of a Python expression represented as a string.

- `exec` runs an arbitrary Python statement represented as a string; there's no return value because the code is a string.

Both accept optional dictionaries to be used as global and local namespaces for assigning and evaluating names used in the code strings. In the calculator, `self.names` becomes a symbol table for running calculator expressions. A related Python function, `compile`, can be used to precompile code strings before passing them to `eval` and `exec` (use it if you need to run the same string many times).

By default a code string's namespace defaults to the caller's namespaces. If we didn't pass in dictionaries here, the strings would run in the `eval` method's namespace. Since the method's local namespace goes away after the method call returns, there would be no way to retain names assigned in the string. Notice the use of nested exception handlers in the `eval` method:

- It first assumes the string is an expression and tries the built-in `eval` function.

- If that fails due to a syntax error, it tries evaluating the string as a statement using `exec`.

- Finally, if both attempts fail, it reports an error in the string (a syntax error, undefined name, etc.).

Statements and invalid expressions might be parsed twice, but the overhead doesn't matter here, and you can't tell if a string is an expression or a statement without parsing it manually. Note that the "eval" button evaluates expressions, but = sets Python variables by running an assignment statement. Variable names are combinations of letter keys abcd (or any name typed directly). They are assigned and evaluated in a dictionary used to represent the calculator's namespace.

Extending and attaching

Clients that reuse this calculator are as simple as the calculator itself. Like most class-based Tkinter GUIs, this one can be extended in subclasses—Example 18-14 customizes the simple calculator's constructor to add extra widgets.

Example 18-14. PP2E\Lang\Calculator\calc0ext.py

```
from Tkinter import *
from calc0 import CalcGui

class Inner(CalcGui):                                    # extend gui
    def __init__(self):
        CalcGui.__init__(self)
        Label(self,  text='Calc Subclass').pack()        # add after
        Button(self, text='Quit', command=self.quit).pack()    # top implied

Inner().mainloop()
```

It can also be embedded in a container class—Example 18-15 attaches the simple calculator's widget package, and extras, to a common parent.

Example 18-15. PP2E\Lang\Calculator\calc0emb.py

```
from Tkinter  import *
from calc0 import CalcGui                      # add parent, no master calls
```

Example 18-15. PP2E\Lang\Calculator\calc0emb.py (continued)

```
class Outer:
    def __init__(self, parent):              # embed gui
        Label(parent, text='Calc Attachment').pack()   # side=top
        CalcGui(parent)                      # add calc frame
        Button(parent, text='Quit', command=parent.quit).pack()

root = Tk()
Outer(root)
root.mainloop()
```

Figure 18-9 shows the result of running both of these scripts from different command lines. Both have a distinct input field at the top. This works; but to see a more practical application of such reuse techniques, we need to make the underlying calculator more practical, too.

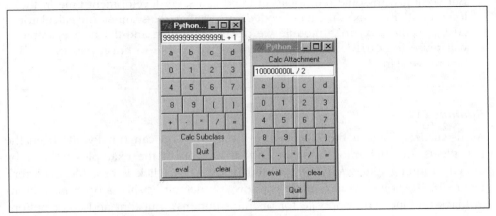

Figure 18-9. The calc0 script's object attached and extended

Pycalc—A Real Calculator GUI

Of course, real calculators don't usually work by building up expression strings and evaluating them all at once; that approach is really little more than a glorified Python command line. Traditionally, expressions are evaluated in piecemeal fashion as they are entered, and temporary results are displayed as soon as they are computed. Implementing this behavior is a bit more work: expressions must be evaluated manually instead of calling the `eval` function only once. But the end result is much more useful and intuitive.

This section presents the implementation of PyCalc—a Python/Tkinter program that implements such a traditional calculator GUI. Although its evaluation logic is more complex than the simpler calculator above, it demonstrates advanced programming techniques and serves as an interesting finale for this chapter.

Lesson 5: Reusability Is Power

Though simple, attaching and subclassing the calculator graphically, as shown in Figure 18-9, illustrates the power of Python as a tool for writing reusable software. By coding programs with modules and classes, components written in isolation almost automatically become general-purpose tools. Python's program organization features promote reusable code.

In fact, code reuse is one of Python's major strengths and has been one of the main themes of this book thus far. Good object-oriented design takes some practice and forethought, and the benefits of code reuse aren't apparent immediately. And sometimes we're more interested in a quick fix rather than a future use for the code.

But coding with some reusability in mind can save development time in the long run. For instance, the hand-coded parsers shared a scanner, the calculator GUI uses the `guitools` module we discussed earlier, and the next example will reuse the `GuiMixin` class. Sometimes we're able to finish part of a job before we start.

Running PyCalc

As usual, let's look at the GUI before the code. You can run PyCalc from the PyGadgets and PyDemos launcher bars at the top of the examples tree, or by directly running file *calculator.py* listed below (e.g., click it in a file explorer). Figure 18-10 shows PyCalc's main window. By default, it shows operand buttons in black-on-blue (and opposite for operator buttons), but font and color options can be passed in to the GUI class's constructor method. Of course, that means gray-on-gray in this book, so you'll have to run PyCalc yourself to see what I mean.

If you do run this, you'll notice that PyCalc implements a normal calculator model—expressions are evaluated as entered, not all at once at the end. That is, parts of an expression are computed and displayed as soon as operator precedence and manually typed parentheses allow. I'll explain how this evaluation works in a moment.

PyCalc's `CalcGui` class builds the GUI interface as frames of buttons much like the simple calculator of the previous section, but PyCalc adds a host of new features. Among them are another row of action buttons, inherited methods from `GuiMixin` (presented in Chapter 9, *Larger GUI Examples*), a new "cmd" button that pops up nonmodal dialogs for entry of arbitrary Python code, and a recent calculations history pop-up. Figure 18-11 captures some of PyCalc's pop-up windows.

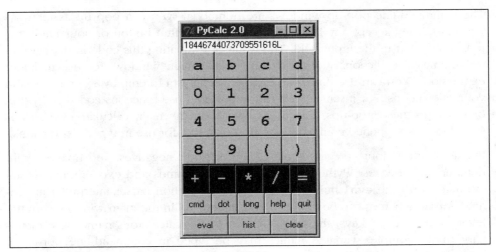

Figure 18-10. PyCalc calculator at work on Windows

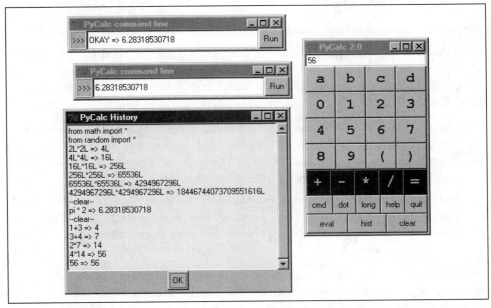

Figure 18-11. PyCalc calculator with some of its pop-ups

You may enter expressions in PyCalc by clicking buttons in the GUI, typing full expressions in command-line pop-ups, or typing keys on your keyboard. PyCalc intercepts key press events and interprets them the same as corresponding button presses; typing + is like pressing button +, the space bar key is "clear", Enter is "eval", backspace erases a character, and ? is like pressing "help".

The command-line pop-up windows are nonmodal (you can pop up as many as you like). They accept any Python code—press the Run button or your Enter key to evaluate text in the input field. The result of evaluating this code in the calculator's namespace dictionary is thrown up in the main window, for use in larger expressions. You can use this as an escape mechanism to employ external tools in your calculations. For instance, you can import and use functions coded in Python or C within these pop-ups. The current value in the main calculator window is stored in newly opened command-line pop-ups, too, for use in typed expressions.

PyCalc supports long integers (unlimited precision), negatives, and floating-point numbers, just because Python does: individual operands and expressions are still evaluated with the `eval` built-in, which calls the Python parser/interpreter at runtime. Variable names can be assigned and referenced in the main window with the letter, =, and "eval" keys; they are assigned in the calculator's namespace dictionary (more complex variable names may be typed in command-line pop-ups). Note the use of `pi` in the history window: PyCalc preimports names in the `math` and `random` modules into the namespace where expressions are evaluated.

Evaluating expressions with stacks

Now that you have the general idea of what PyCalc does, I need to say a little bit about how it does what it does. Most of the changes in this version involve managing the expression display and evaluating expressions. PyCalc is structured as two classes:

- The `CalcGui` class manages the GUI itself. It controls input events and is in charge of the main window's display field at the top. It doesn't evaluate expressions, though; for that, it sends operators and operands entered in the GUI to an embedded instance of the `Evaluator` class.

- The `Evaluator` class manages two stacks. One stack records pending *operators* (e.g., +), and one records pending *operands* (e.g, 3.141). Temporary results are computed as new operators are sent from `CalcGui` and pushed onto the operands stack.

As you can see from this, the magic of expression evaluation boils down to juggling the operator and operand stacks. While scanning expression strings from left to right as they are entered, operands are pushed along the way, but operators delimit operands and may trigger temporary results before they are pushed. Here's the general scenario:

- When a new operator is seen (i.e., when an operator button or key is pressed), the prior operand in the entry field is pushed onto the operands stack.

- The operator is then added to the operators stack, but only after all pending operators of higher precedence have been popped and applied to pending operands (e.g., pressing + makes any pending * operators on the stack fire).

- When "eval" is pressed, all remaining operators are popped and applied to all remaining operands, and the result is the last remaining value on the operands stack.

In the end, the last value on the operands stack is displayed in the calculator's entry field, ready for use in another operation. This evaluation algorithm is probably best described by working through examples. Let's step through the entry of a few expressions and watch the evaluation stacks grow.

PyCalc stack tracing is enabled with the debugme flag in the module; if true, the operator and operand stacks are displayed on stdout each time the Evaluator class is about to apply an operator and reduce (pop) the stacks. A tuple holding the stack lists (*operators*, *operands*) is printed on each stack reduction; tops of stack are at the ends of the lists. For instance, here is the console output after typing and evaluating a simple string:

```
1) Entered keys: "5 * 3 + 4 <eval>" [result = 19]

(['*'], ['5', '3'])     [on '+' press: displays "15"]
(['+'], ['15', '4'])    [on 'eval' press: displays "19"]
```

Note that the pending (stacked) * subexpression is evaluated when the + is pressed: * operators bind tighter than +, so the code is evaluated immediately before the + operator is pushed. When the + button is pressed, the entry field contains 3. In general, the entry field always holds the prior operand when an operator button is pressed. Since the text entry's value is pushed onto the operands stack before the operator is applied, we have to pop results before displaying them after "eval" or) is pressed (otherwise the results are pushed onto the stack twice):

```
2) "5 + 3 * 4 <eval>" [result = 17]

(['+', '*'], ['5', '3', '4'])    [on 'eval' press]
(['+'], ['5', '12'])             [displays "17"]
```

Here, the pending + isn't evaluated when the * button is pressed: since * binds tighter, we need to postpone the + until the * can be evaluated. The * operator isn't popped until its right operand has been seen. On the "eval" press there are two operators to pop and apply to operand stack entries:

```
3) "5 + 3 + 4 <eval>" [result = 12]

(['+'], ['5', '3'])     [on the second '+']
(['+'], ['8', '4'])     [on 'eval']
```

For strings of same-precedence operators like this one, we pop and evaluate immediately as we scan left to right, instead of postponing evaluation. This results in a left-associative evaluation, in the absence of parentheses: 5+3+4 is evaluated as ((5+3)+4). Order doesn't matter for + and * operations:

```
4) "1 + 3 * ( 1 + 3 * 4 ) <eval>" [result = 40]

(['+', '*', '(', '+', '*'], ['1', '3', '1', '3', '4'])      [on ')']
(['+', '*', '(', '+'], ['1', '3', '1', '12'])               [displays "13"]
(['+', '*'], ['1', '3', '13'])                              [on 'eval']
(['+'], ['1', '39'])
```

In this case, all the operators and operands are stacked (postponed) until we press the) button at the end. When the) button is pressed, the parenthesized subexpression is popped and evaluated, and 13 is displayed in the entry field. On pressing "eval", the rest is evaluated, and the final result (40) is shown. The result is the left operand of another operator. In fact, any temporary result can be used again: if we keep pressing an operator button without typing new operands, it's reapplied to the result of the prior press. Figure 18-12 shows how the two stacks look at their highest level while scanning the expression in the preceding example trace. The top operator is applied to the top two operands and the result is pushed back for the operator below:

```
5) "1 + 3 * ( 1 + 3 * 4 <eval>" [result = *ERROR*]

(['+', '*', '(', '+', '*'], ['1', '3', '1', '3', '4'])      [on eval]
(['+', '*', '(', '+'], ['1', '3', '1', '12'])
(['+', '*', '('], ['1', '3', '13'])
(['+', '*'], ['1', '*ERROR*'])
(['+'], ['*ERROR*'])
(['+'], ['*ERROR*', '*ERROR*'])
```

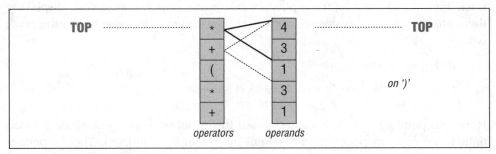

*Figure 18-12. Evaluation stacks: 1 + 3 * (1 + 3 * 4)*

This string triggers an error. PyCalc is casual about error handling. Many errors are made impossible by the algorithm itself, but things like unmatched parentheses still trip up the evaluator. But instead of trying to detect all possible error cases explicitly, a general `try` statement in the `reduce` method is used to catch them all: expression errors, undefined name errors, syntax errors, etc.

Operands and temporary results are always stacked as strings, and each operator is applied by calling `eval`. When an error occurs inside an expression, a result operand of *ERROR* is pushed, which makes all remaining operators fail in `eval`, too. *ERROR* percolates to the top of the expression. At the end, it's the last operand and is displayed in the text entry field to alert you of the mistake.

PyCalc source code

Example 18-16 contains the PyCalc source module that puts these ideas to work in the context of a GUI. It's a single-file implementation (not counting utilities imported and reused). Study the source for more details; and as usual, there's no substitute for interacting with the program on your own to get a better feel for its functionality.

Example 18-16. PP2E\Lang\Calculator\calculator.py

```python
#!/usr/local/bin/python
##########################################################################
# PyCalc 2.0: a Python/Tkinter calculator program and GUI component.
# evaluates expressions as they are entered, catches keyboard keys
# for expression entry; adds integrated command-line popups, recent
# calculations history display popup, fonts and colors configuration,
# help and about popups, preimported math/random constants, and more;
##########################################################################

from Tkinter import *                             # widgets, consts
from PP2E.Gui.Tools.guimixin import GuiMixin      # quit method
from PP2E.Dbase.TableBrowser.guitools import *    # widget builders
Fg, Bg, Font = 'black', 'skyblue', ('courier', 16, 'bold')   # default config

debugme = 1
def trace(*args):
    if debugme: print args


#########################################
# the main class - handles user interface;
# an extended Frame, on new Toplevel, or
# embedded in another container widget
#########################################

class CalcGui(GuiMixin, Frame):
    Operators = "+-*/="                           # button lists
    Operands  = ["abcd", "0123", "4567", "89()"]  # customizable

    def __init__(self, parent=None, fg=Fg, bg=Bg, font=Font):
        Frame.__init__(self, parent)
        self.pack(expand=YES, fill=BOTH)          # all parts expandable
        self.eval = Evaluator()                   # embed a stack handler
```

Example 18-16. PP2E\Lang\Calculator\calculator.py (continued)

```
        self.text = StringVar()                     # make a linked variable
        self.text.set("0")
        self.erase = 1                              # clear "0" text next
        self.makeWidgets(fg, bg, font)              # build the gui itself
        if not parent or not isinstance(parent, Frame):
            self.master.title('PyCalc 2.0')         # title iff owns window
            self.master.iconname("PyCalc")          # ditto for key bindings
            self.master.bind('<KeyPress>', self.onKeyboard)
            self.entry.config(state='disabled')
        else:
            self.entry.config(state='normal')
            self.entry.focus()

    def makeWidgets(self, fg, bg, font):            # 7 frames plus text-entry
        self.entry = entry(self, TOP, self.text)    # font, color configurable
        for row in self.Operands:
            frm = frame(self, TOP)
            for char in row:
                button(frm, LEFT, char,
                            lambda x=self, y=char: x.onOperand(y),
                        fg=fg, bg=bg, font=font)

        frm = frame(self, TOP)
        for char in self.Operators:
            button(frm, LEFT, char,
                        lambda x=self, y=char: x.onOperator(y),
                    fg=bg, bg=fg, font=font)

        frm = frame(self, TOP)
        button(frm, LEFT, 'cmd ', self.onMakeCmdline)
        button(frm, LEFT, 'dot ', lambda x=self: x.onOperand('.'))
        button(frm, LEFT, 'long', lambda x=self: x.text.set(x.text.get()+'L'))
        button(frm, LEFT, 'help', self.help)
        button(frm, LEFT, 'quit', self.quit)        # from guimixin

        frm = frame(self, BOTTOM)
        button(frm, LEFT, 'eval ', self.onEval)
        button(frm, LEFT, 'hist ', self.onHist)
        button(frm, LEFT, 'clear', self.onClear)

    def onClear(self):
        self.eval.clear()
        self.text.set('0')
        self.erase = 1

    def onEval(self):
        self.eval.shiftOpnd(self.text.get())        # last or only opnd
        self.eval.closeall()                        # apply all optrs left
        self.text.set(self.eval.popOpnd())          # need to pop: optr next?
        self.erase = 1

    def onOperand(self, char):
        if char == '(':
```

Example 18-16. PP2E\Lang\Calculator\calculator.py (continued)

```
            self.eval.open()
            self.text.set('(')                          # clear text next
            self.erase = 1
        elif char == ')':
            self.eval.shiftOpnd(self.text.get())        # last or only nested opnd
            self.eval.close()                           # pop here too: optr next?
            self.text.set(self.eval.popOpnd())
            self.erase = 1
        else:
            if self.erase:
                self.text.set(char)                     # clears last value
            else:
                self.text.set(self.text.get() + char)   # else append to opnd
            self.erase = 0

    def onOperator(self, char):
        self.eval.shiftOpnd(self.text.get())            # push opnd on left
        self.eval.shiftOptr(char)                       # eval exprs to left?
        self.text.set(self.eval.topOpnd())              # push optr, show opnd|result
        self.erase = 1                                  # erased on next opnd|'('

    def onMakeCmdline(self):
        new = Toplevel()                                # new top-level window
        new.title('PyCalc command line')                # arbitrary python code
        frm = frame(new, TOP)                           # only the Entry expands
        label(frm, LEFT, '>>>').pack(expand=NO)
        var = StringVar()
        ent = entry(frm, LEFT, var, width=40)
        onButton = (lambda s=self, v=var, e=ent: s.onCmdline(v,e))
        onReturn = (lambda event, s=self, v=var, e=ent: s.onCmdline(v,e))
        button(frm, RIGHT, 'Run', onButton).pack(expand=NO)
        ent.bind('<Return>', onReturn)
        var.set(self.text.get())

    def onCmdline(self, var, ent):                      # eval cmdline popup input
        try:
            value = self.eval.runstring(var.get())
            var.set('OKAY')                             # run in eval namespace dict
            if value != None:                           # expression or statement
                self.text.set(value)
                self.erase = 1
                var.set('OKAY => '+ value)
        except:                                         # result in calc field
            var.set('ERROR')                            # status in popup field
        ent.icursor(END)                                # insert point after text
        ent.select_range(0, END)                        # select msg so next key deletes

    def onKeyboard(self, event):
        pressed = event.char                            # on keyboard press event
        if pressed != '':                               # pretend button was pressed
            if pressed in self.Operators:
                self.onOperator(pressed)
```

Example 18-16. PP2E\Lang\Calculator\calculator.py (continued)

```
            else:
                for row in self.Operands:
                    if pressed in row:
                        self.onOperand(pressed)
                        break
                else:
                    if pressed == '.':
                        self.onOperand(pressed)            # can start opnd
                    if pressed in 'Ll':
                        self.text.set(self.text.get()+'L')  # can't: no erase
                    elif pressed == '\r':
                        self.onEval()                       # enter key = eval
                    elif pressed == ' ':
                        self.onClear()                      # spacebar = clear
                    elif pressed == '\b':
                        self.text.set(self.text.get()[:-1]) # backspace
                    elif pressed == '?':
                        self.help()

    def onHist(self):
        # show recent calcs log popup
        # self.infobox('PyCalc History', self.eval.getHist())
        from ScrolledText import ScrolledText
        new = Toplevel()                                    # make new window
        ok = Button(new, text="OK", command=new.destroy)
        ok.pack(pady=1, side=BOTTOM)                         # pack first=clip last
        text = ScrolledText(new, bg='beige')                # add Text + scrollbar
        text.insert('0.0', self.eval.getHist())             # get Evaluator text
        text.pack(expand=YES, fill=BOTH)

        # new window goes away on ok press or enter key
        new.title("PyCalc History")
        new.bind("<Return>", (lambda event, new=new: new.destroy()))
        ok.focus_set()                                      # make new window modal:
        new.grab_set()                                      # get keyboard focus, grab app
        new.wait_window()                                   # don't return till new.destroy

    def help(self):
        self.infobox('PyCalc', 'PyCalc 2.0\n'
                               'A Python/Tk calculator\n'
                               'August, 1999\n'
                               'Programming Python 2E\n\n'
                               'Use mouse or keyboard to\n'
                               'input numbers and operators,\n'
                               'or type code in cmd popup')


####################################
# the expression evaluator class
# embedded in and used by a CalcGui
# instance, to perform calculations
####################################
```

Example 18-16. PP2E\Lang\Calculator\calculator.py (continued)

```
class Evaluator:
    def __init__(self):
        self.names = {}                         # a names-space for my vars
        self.opnd, self.optr = [], []           # two empty stacks
        self.hist = []                          # my prev calcs history log
        self.runstring("from math import *")    # preimport math modules
        self.runstring("from random import *")  # into calc's namespace

    def clear(self):
        self.opnd, self.optr = [], []           # leave names intact
        if len(self.hist) > 64:                 # don't let hist get too big
            self.hist = ['clear']
        else:
            self.hist.append('--clear--')

    def popOpnd(self):
        value = self.opnd[-1]                    # pop/return top|last opnd
        self.opnd[-1:] = []                      # to display and shift next
        return value

    def topOpnd(self):
        return self.opnd[-1]                     # top operand (end of list)

    def open(self):
        self.optr.append('(')                    # treat '(' like an operator

    def close(self):                             # on ')' pop downto higest '('
        self.shiftOptr(')')                      # ok if empty: stays empty
        self.optr[-2:] = []                      # pop, or added again by optr

    def closeall(self):
        while self.optr:                         # force rest on 'eval'
            self.reduce()                        # last may be a var name
        try:
            self.opnd[0] = self.runstring(self.opnd[0])
        except:
            self.opnd[0] = '*ERROR*'             # pop else added again next:

    afterMe = {'*': ['+', '-', '(', '='],        # class member
               '/': ['+', '-', '(', '='],        # optrs to not pop for key
               '+': ['(', '='],                  # if prior optr is this: push
               '-': ['(', '='],                  # else: pop/eval prior optr
               ')': ['(', '='],                  # all left-associative as is
               '=': ['('] }

    def shiftOpnd(self, newopnd):                # push opnd at optr, ')', eval
        self.opnd.append(newopnd)

    def shiftOptr(self, newoptr):                # apply ops with <= priority
        while (self.optr and
               self.optr[-1] not in self.afterMe[newoptr]):
            self.reduce()
```

Example 18-16. PP2E\Lang\Calculator\calculator.py (continued)

```
            self.optr.append(newoptr)              # push this op above result
                                                   # optrs assume next opnd erases

    def reduce(self):
        trace(self.optr, self.opnd)
        try:                                       # collapse the top expr
            operator      = self.optr[-1]          # pop top optr (at end)
            [left, right] = self.opnd[-2:]         # pop top 2 opnds (at end)
            self.optr[-1:] = []                    # delete slice in-place
            self.opnd[-2:] = []
            result = self.runstring(left + operator + right)
            if result == None:
                result = left                      # assignment? key var name
            self.opnd.append(result)               # push result string back
        except:
            self.opnd.append('*ERROR*')            # stack/number/name error

    def runstring(self, code):
        try:
            result = `eval(code, self.names, self.names)`  # try expr: string
            self.hist.append(code + ' => ' + result)       # add to hist log
        except:
            exec code in self.names, self.names    # try stmt: None
            self.hist.append(code)
            result = None
        return result

    def getHist(self):
        import string
        return string.join(self.hist, '\n')

def getCalcArgs():
    from sys import argv
    config = {}                                    # get cmdline args in a dict
    for arg in argv[1:]:                           # ex: -bg black -fg red
        if arg in ['-bg', '-fg']:                  # font not yet supported
            try:
                config[arg[1:]] = argv[argv.index(arg) + 1]
            except:
                pass
    return config

if __name__ == '__main__':
    apply(CalcGui, (), getCalcArgs()).mainloop()   # on default toplevel window
```

Using PyCalc as a component

PyCalc serves a standalone program on my desktop, but it's also useful in the context of other GUIs. Like most of the GUI classes in this book, PyCalc can be customized with subclass extensions, or embedded in a larger GUI with attachment. The module in Example 18-17 demonstrates one way to reuse PyCalc's `CalcGui` class by extending and embedding, much as done for the simple calculator earlier.

Example 18-17. PP2E\Lang\Calculator\calculator_test.py

```
######################################################################
# test calculator use as an extended and embedded gui component;
######################################################################

from Tkinter import *
from calculator import CalcGui
from PP2E.Dbase.TableBrowser.guitools import *

def calcContainer(parent=None):
    frm = Frame(parent)
    frm.pack(expand=YES, fill=BOTH)
    Label(frm, text='Calc Container').pack(side=TOP)
    CalcGui(frm)
    Label(frm, text='Calc Container').pack(side=BOTTOM)
    return frm

class calcSubclass(CalcGui):
    def makeWidgets(self, fg, bg, font):
        Label(self, text='Calc Subclass').pack(side=TOP)
        Label(self, text='Calc Subclass').pack(side=BOTTOM)
        CalcGui.makeWidgets(self, fg, bg, font)
        #Label(self, text='Calc Subclass').pack(side=BOTTOM)

if __name__ == '__main__':
    import sys
    if len(sys.argv) == 1:              # % calculator_test.py
        root = Tk()                     # run 3 calcs in same process
        CalcGui(Toplevel())             # each in a new toplevel window
        calcContainer(Toplevel())
        calcSubclass(Toplevel())
        Button(root, text='quit', command=root.quit).pack()
        root.mainloop()
    if len(sys.argv) == 2:              # % calculator_test1.py -
        CalcGui().mainloop()            # as a standalone window (default root)
    elif len(sys.argv) == 3:            # % calculator_test.py - -
        calcContainer().mainloop()      # as an embedded component
    elif len(sys.argv) == 4:            # % calculator_test.py - - -
        calcSubclass().mainloop()       # as a customized superclass
```

Figure 18-13 shows the result of running this script with no command-line arguments. We get instances of the original calculator class, plus the container and subclass classes defined in this script, all attached to new top-level windows.

These two windows on the right reuse the core PyCalc code running in the window on the left. All these windows all run in the same process (e.g., quitting one quits them all), but they all function as independent windows. Note that when running three calculators in the same process like this, each has its own distinct expression evaluation namespace because it's a class instance attribute, not a global module-level variable. Because of that, variables set in one calculator are set in that calculator only, and don't overwrite settings made in other windows. Similarly,

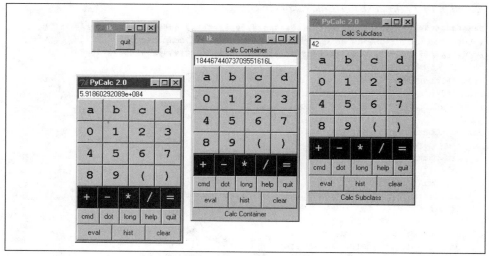

Figure 18-13. The calculator_test script: attaching and extending

each calculator has its own evaluation stack manager object, such that calculations in one window don't appear in or impact other windows at all.

The two extensions in this script are artificial, of course—they simply add labels at the top and bottom of the window—but the concept is widely applicable. You could reuse the calculator's class by attaching it to any GUI that needs a calculator, and customize it with subclasses arbitrarily. It's a reusable widget.

Adding new buttons in new components

One obvious way to reuse the calculator is to add additional expression feature buttons—square roots, inverses, cubes, and the like. You can type such operations in the command-line pop-ups, but buttons are a bit more convenient. Such features could also be added to the main calculator implementation itself; but since the set of features that will be useful may vary per user and application, a better approach may be to add them in separate extensions. For instance, the class in Example 18-18 adds a few extra buttons to PyCalc by embedding (i.e., attaching) it in a container.

Example 18-18. PP2E\Lang\Calculator\calculator_plus_emb.py

```
#####################################################################
# a container with an extra row of buttons for common operations;
# a more useful customization: adds buttons for more operations (sqrt,
# 1/x, etc.) by embedding/composition, not subclassing; new buttons are
# added after entire CalGui frame because of the packing order/options;
#####################################################################

from Tkinter import *
```

Example 18-18. PP2E\Lang\Calculator\calculator_plus_emb.py (continued)

```
from calculator import CalcGui, getCalcArgs
from PP2E.Dbase.TableBrowser.guitools import frame, button, label

class CalcGuiPlus(Toplevel):
    def __init__(self, **args):
        Toplevel.__init__(self)
        label(self, TOP, 'PyCalc Plus - Container')
        self.calc = apply(CalcGui, (self,), args)
        frm = frame(self, BOTTOM)
        extras = [('sqrt', 'sqrt(%s)'),
                  ('x^2 ', '(%s)**2'),
                  ('x^3 ', '(%s)**3'),
                  ('1/x ', '1.0/(%s)')]
        for (lab, expr) in extras:
            button(frm, LEFT, lab, (lambda m=self.onExtra, e=expr: m(e)) )
        button(frm, LEFT, ' pi ', self.onPi)
    def onExtra(self, expr):
        text = self.calc.text
        eval = self.calc.eval
        try:
            text.set(eval.runstring(expr % text.get()))
        except:
            text.set('ERROR')
    def onPi(self):
        self.calc.text.set(self.calc.eval.runstring('pi'))

if __name__ == '__main__':
    root = Tk()
    button(root, TOP, 'Quit', root.quit)
    apply(CalcGuiPlus, (), getCalcArgs()).mainloop()      # -bg,-fg to calcgui
```

Because PyCalc is coded as a Python class, you can always achieve a similar effect by extending PyCalc in a new subclass instead of embedding it, as shown in Example 18-19.

Example 18-19. PP2E\Lang\Calculator\calculator_plus_ext.py

```
#############################################################################
# a customization with an extra row of buttons for common operations;
# a more useful customization: adds buttons for more operations (sqrt,
# 1/x, etc.) by subclassing to extend the original class, not embedding;
# new buttons show up before frame attached to bottom be calcgui class;
#############################################################################

from Tkinter import *
from calculator import CalcGui, getCalcArgs
from PP2E.Dbase.TableBrowser.guitools import *

class CalcGuiPlus(CalcGui):
    def makeWidgets(self, *args):
        label(self, TOP, 'PyCalc Plus - Subclass')
        apply(CalcGui.makeWidgets, (self,) + args)
```

Example 18-19. PP2E\Lang\Calculator\calculator_plus_ext.py (continued)

```
        frm = frame(self, BOTTOM)
        extras = [('sqrt', 'sqrt(%s)'),
                  ('x^2 ', '(%s)**2'),
                  ('x^3 ', '(%s)**3'),
                  ('1/x ', '1.0/(%s)')]
        for (lab, expr) in extras:
            button(frm, LEFT, lab, (lambda m=self.onExtra, e=expr: m(e)) )
        button(frm, LEFT, ' pi ', self.onPi)
    def onExtra(self, expr):
        try:
            self.text.set(self.eval.runstring(expr % self.text.get()))
        except:
            self.text.set('ERROR')
    def onPi(self):
        self.text.set(self.eval.runstring('pi'))

if __name__ == '__main__':
    apply(CalcGuiPlus, (), getCalcArgs()).mainloop()      # passes -bg, -fg on
```

Notice that these buttons' callbacks use `1.0/x` to force float-point division to be used for inverses (integer division truncates remainders), and wrap entry field values in parentheses (to sidestep precedence issues). They could instead convert the entry's text to a number and do real math, but Python does all the work automatically when expression strings are run raw.

Also note that the buttons added by these scripts simply operate on the current value in the entry field, immediately. That's not quite the same as expression operators applied with the stacks evaluator (additional customizations are needed to make them true operators). Still, these buttons prove the point these scripts are out to make—they use PyCalc as a component, both from the outside and below.

Finally, to test both of the extended calculator classes, as well as PyCalc configuration options, the script in Example 18-20 puts up four distinct calculator windows (this is the script run by PyDemos).

Example 18-20. PP2E\Lang\Calculator\calculator_plusplus.py

```
#!/usr/local/bin/python
from Tkinter import Tk, Button, Toplevel
import calculator, calculator_plus_ext, calculator_plus_emb

# demo all 3 calculator flavors at once
# each is a distinct calculator object and window

root=Tk()
calculator.CalcGui(Toplevel())
calculator.CalcGui(Toplevel(), fg='white', bg='purple')
calculator_plus_ext.CalcGuiPlus(Toplevel(), fg='gold', bg='black')
calculator_plus_emb.CalcGuiPlus(fg='black', bg='red')
```

Example 18-20. PP2E\Lang\Calculator\calculator_plusplus.py (continued)

```
Button(root, text='Quit Calcs', command=root.quit).pack()
root.mainloop()
```

Figure 18-14 shows the result—four independent calculators in top-level windows within the same process. The windows on the left and right represent specialized reuses of PyCalc as a component. Although it may not be obvious in this book, all four use different color schemes; calculator classes accept color and font configuration options and pass them down the call chain as needed.

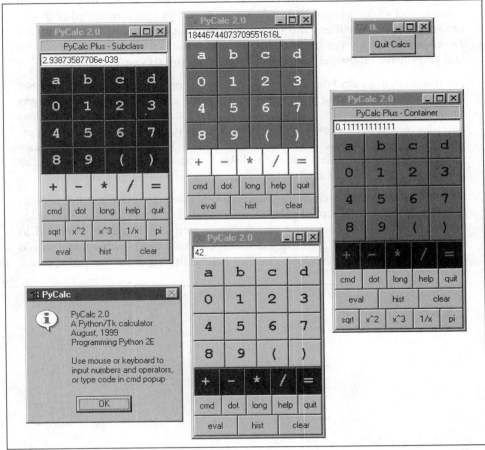

Figure 18-14. The calculator_plusplus script: extend, embed, and configure

As we learned earlier, these calculators could also be run as independent processes by spawning command lines with the `launchmodes` module we met in Chapter 3, *Parallel System Tools*. In fact, that's how the PyGadgets and PyDemos launcher bars run calculators, so see their code for more details.

Lesson 6: Have Fun

In closing, here's a less tangible but important aspect of Python programming. A common remark among new users is that it's easy to "say what you mean" in Python without getting bogged down in complex syntax or obscure rules. It's a programmer-friendly language. In fact, it's not too uncommon for Python programs to run on the first attempt.

As we've seen in this book, there are a number of factors behind this distinction—lack of declarations, no compile steps, simple syntax, useful built-in objects, and so on. Python is specifically designed to optimize speed of development (an idea we'll expand on in Chapter 21, *Conclusion: Python and the Development Cycle*). For many users, the end result is a remarkably expressive and responsive language, which can actually be fun to use.

For instance, the calculator programs shown earlier were first thrown together in one afternoon, starting from vague, incomplete goals. There was no analysis phase, no formal design, and no official coding stage. I typed up some ideas and they worked. Moreover, Python's interactive nature allowed me to experiment with new ideas and get immediate feedback. Since its initial development, the calculator has been polished and expanded, but · the core implementation remains unchanged.

Naturally, such a laid-back programming mode doesn't work for every project. Sometimes more up-front design is warranted. For more demanding tasks, Python has modular constructs and fosters systems that can be extended in either Python or C. And, a simple calculator GUI may not be what some would call "serious" software development. But maybe that's part of the point, too.

V

Integration

This part of the book explores Python's interfaces for communicating with software components written in other programming languages. Its emphasis is on mixing Python with programs written in C and C++, but other integration techniques are also introduced along the way. This part contains two chapters that address the two primary modes of Python/C integration:

- Chapter 19, *Extending Python*. This chapter presents tools that allow Python scripts to call out to C components. C components take the form of new modules or object types. This chapter also covers SWIG—a system that automatically generates the glue code needed to export C and C++ libraries to Python scripts and hides much of the complexity underlying extensions.

- Chapter 20, *Embedding Python*. This chapter presents tools that allow C programs to execute Python scripts. These tools live in the Python runtime API—a collection of functions exposed by the Python interpreter and linked in to your C/C++ program. This chapter concludes with a look at other integration topics and systems—JPython, COM, CORBA, and so on.

This part of the book assumes that you know how to read C programs, and is useful mostly to developers responsible for implementing application integration layers that route control to and from Python scripts. Yet because C components are at the heart of many Python systems, a basic understanding of integration concepts can be useful even to scripters who code strictly in Python.

19

Extending Python

"I Am Lost at C"

So far in this book, we've been using Python as it comes out of the box. We have used interfaces to services outside Python, and coded extensions as Python modules. But we haven't added any external services beyond the built-in set. For many users, this makes perfect sense: such standalone programming is one of the main ways people apply Python. As we've seen, Python comes with batteries included —interfaces to system tools, Internet protocols, GUIs, filesystems, and much more.

But for many systems, Python's ability to integrate with C-compatible components is a crucial feature of the language. In fact, Python's role as an extension and interface language in larger systems is one of the reasons for its popularity and why it is often called a "scripting" language. Its design supports *hybrid* systems that mix components written in a variety of programming languages. Because different languages have different strengths, being able to pick and choose on a component-by-component basis is a powerful concept. You can add Python to the mix anywhere you need an easy-to-use and flexible language tool.

For instance, compiled languages such as C and C++ are optimized for speed of *execution*, but are complex to program—for developers, but especially for end users. Because Python is optimized for speed of *development*, using Python scripts to control or customize software components written in C or C++ can yield more flexible systems and dramatically faster development modes. Systems designed to delegate customizations to Python scripts don't need to be shipped with full source code and don't require end users to learn complex or proprietary languages. Moreover, moving selected components of a pure Python program to C can optimize program performance.

Integration Topics

The last two technical chapters of this book introduce Python's tools for interfacing to the outside world, and discuss both its ability to be used as an embedded language tool in other systems and its interfaces for extending Python scripts with new modules and types implemented in C-compatible languages. I'll also summarize other integration techniques that are less C-specific, such as COM and JPython.

When you mix Python with C components, either Python or C can be "on top." Because of that, there are two distinct integration APIs:

- The *extending* interface for running C extensions from Python programs
- The *embedding* interface for running Python code from C programs

This chapter covers extending, and the next explores embedding. Some systems use only one scheme, but many use both. For instance, embedded Python code run from C can also use linked-in C extensions to interface with the enclosing application. And in callback-based systems, C code accessed through extending interfaces may later use embedding techniques to run Python callback handlers. Python has an open and reentrant architecture that lets you mix languages arbitrarily.

Before we get into details, I should mention that Python/C integration is a big topic—in principle, the entire set of *extern* C functions in the Python system makes up its runtime interface. The next two chapters concentrate only on the tools commonly used to implement integration with external modules. For additional examples beyond this book and its CD, see the Python source code itself; its `Modules` and `Objects` directories are a wealth of code resources. Most of the Python built-ins we have used in this book—from simple things such as integers and strings to more advanced tools such as files, system calls, Tkinter, and DBM—utilize integration APIs and can be studied in Python's source code distribution.

These chapters assume that you know basic C programming concepts. If you don't, you won't miss much by skipping or skimming these chapters. Typically, C developers code the extending and embedding interfaces of a system, and others do the bulk of the system's programming with Python alone. But if you know enough about C programming to recognize a need for an extension language, you probably already have the required background knowledge for this chapter. The good news in both chapters is that much of the complexity inherent in integrating Python with a static compiled language like C can be automated with tools such as SWIG in the extension domain, and higher-level APIs in the embedding world.

C Extensions Overview

Because Python itself is coded in C today, compiled Python extensions can be coded in any language that is C-compatible in terms of call stacks and linking. That includes C, but also C++ with appropriate "extern C" declarations (which are automatically provided in Python header files). Python extensions coded in a C-compatible language can take two forms:

- *C modules*, which look and feel to their clients like Python module files

- *C types*, which behave like standard built-in types (numbers, lists, etc.)

Generally, C modules are used to implement flat function libraries, and C types are used to code objects that generate multiple instances. Because built-in types are really just precoded C extension types, your C extension types can do anything that built-in types can: method calls, addition, indexing, slicing, and so on.[*] In the current Python release, though, types are not quite classes—you cannot customize types by coding a Python subclass unless you add "wrapper" classes as frontend interfaces to the type. More on this later.

Both C modules and types register their operations with the Python interpreter as C function pointers. In all cases, the C layer is responsible for converting arguments passed from Python to C form, and converting results from C to Python form. Python scripts simply import C extensions and use them as though they were really coded in Python; C code does all the translation work.

C modules and types are also responsible for communicating errors back to Python, detecting errors raised by Python API calls, and managing garbage-collector reference counters on objects retained by the C layer indefinitely—Python objects held by your C code won't be garbage-collected as long as you make sure their reference counts don't fall to zero. C modules and types may either be linked to Python statically (at build time) or dynamically (when first imported).

A Simple C Extension Module

At least that's the short story; we need to turn to some code to make this more concrete. C types generally export a C module with a constructor function.

---

[*] Yes, every time you make an integer or string in Python, you generate a new C type instance object (whether you know it or not). This isn't as inefficient as you may think, though; as we'll see, type operations are dispatched through fast C pointers, and Python internally caches some integers and strings to avoid object creation when possible.

Because of that (and because they are simpler), let's start off by studying the basics of C *module* coding with a quick example.

When you add new or existing C components to Python, you need to code an interface (or "glue") logic layer in C that handles cross-language dispatching and data translation. The C source file in Example 19-1 shows how to code one by hand. It implements a simple C extension module named `hello` for use in Python scripts, with a function named `message` that simply returns its input string argument with extra text prepended.

Example 19-1. PP2E\Integrate\Extend\Hello\hello.c

```
/**********************************************************************
 * A simple C extension module for Python, called "hello"; compile
 * this into a ".so" on python path, import and call hello.message;
 **********************************************************************/

#include <Python.h>
#include <string.h>

/* module functions */
static PyObject *                             /* returns object */
message(PyObject *self, PyObject *args)        /* self unused in modules */
{                                              /* args from python call */
    char *fromPython, result[64];
    if (! PyArg_Parse(args, "(s)", &fromPython))  /* convert Python -> C */
        return NULL;                           /* null=raise exception */
    else {
        strcpy(result, "Hello, ");             /* build up C string */
        strcat(result, fromPython);            /* add passed Python string */
        return Py_BuildValue("s", result);     /* convert C -> Python */
    }
}

/* registration table  */
static struct PyMethodDef hello_methods[] = {
    {"message", message, 1},         /* method name, C func ptr, always-tuple */
    {NULL, NULL}                     /* end of table marker */
};

/* module initializer */
void inithello()                         /* called on first import */
{                                        /* name matters if loaded dynamically */
    (void) Py_InitModule("hello", hello_methods);   /* mod name, table ptr */
}
```

Ultimately, Python code will call this C file's `message` function with a string object and get a new string object back. First, though, it has to be somehow linked into the Python interpreter. To use this C file in a Python script, compile it into a dynamically loadable object file (e.g., *hello.so* on Linux) with a makefile like the one listed in Example 19-2, and drop the resulting object file into a directory listed on your PYTHONPATH module search path setting exactly as though it were a *.py* or *.pyc* file.*

Example 19-2. PP2E\Integrate\Extend\Hello\makefile.hello

```
#############################################################
# Compile hello.c into a shareable object file on Linux,
# to be loaded dynamically when first imported by Python.
# MYPY is the directory where your Python header files live.
#############################################################

PY = $(MYPY)

hello.so: hello.c
    gcc hello.c -g -I$(PY)/Include -I$(PY) -fpic -shared -o hello.so

clean:
    rm -f hello.so core
```

This is a Linux makefile (other platforms will vary); to use it to build the extension module, simply type `make -f makefile.hello` at your shell. Be sure to include the path to Python's install directory with `-I` flags to access Python include (a.k.a. "header") files. When compiled this way, Python automatically loads and links the C module when it is first imported by a Python script.

Finally, to call the C function from a Python program, simply import module `hello` and call its `hello.message` function with a string:

```
[mark@toy ~/.../PP2E/Integrate/Extend/Hello]$ make -f makefile.hello

[mark@toy ~/.../PP2E/Integrate/Extend/Hello]$ python
>>> import hello                              # import a C module
>>> hello.message('world')                    # call a C function
'Hello, world'
>>> hello.message('extending')
'Hello, extending'
```

And that's it—you've just called an integrated C module's function from Python. The most important thing to notice here is that the C function looks exactly as if it were coded in Python. Python callers send and receive normal string objects from the call; the Python interpreter handles routing calls to the C function, and the C function itself handles Python/C data conversion chores.

---

* Because Python always searches the current working directory on imports, this chapter's examples will run from the directory you compile them in (".") without any file copies or moves. Being on PYTHON-PATH matters more in larger programs and installs.

In fact, there is little to distinguish `hello` as a C extension module at all, apart from its filename. Python code imports the module and fetches its attributes as if it had been written in Python. C extension modules even respond to `dir` calls as usual, and have the standard module and filename attributes (though the filename doesn't end in a *.py* or *.pyc* this time around):

```
>>> dir(hello)                              # C module attributes
['__doc__', '__file__', '__name__', 'message']

>>> hello.__name__, hello.__file__
('hello', './hello.so')

>>> hello.message                           # a C function object
<built-in function message>
>>> hello                                   # a C module object
<module 'hello' from './hello.so'>
```

Like any module in Python, you can also access the C extension from a script file. The Python file in Example 19-3, for instance, imports and uses the C extension module.

Example 19-3. PP2E\Integrate\Extend\Hello\hellouse.py

```
import hello

print hello.message('C')
print hello.message('module ' + hello.__file__)

for i in range(3):
    print hello.message(str(i))
```

Run this script as any other—when the script first imports module `hello`, Python automatically finds the C module's *.so* object file in a directory on PYTHONPATH and links it into the process dynamically. All of this script's output represents strings returned from the C function in file *hello.c*:

```
[mark@toy ~/.../PP2E/Integrate/Extend/Hello]$ python hellouse.py
Hello, C
Hello, module ./hello.so
Hello, 0
Hello, 1
Hello, 2
```

Compilation and Linking

Now that I've shown you the somewhat longer story, let's fill in the rest of the details. You always must compile and somehow link C extension files like the *hello.c* example with the Python interpreter to make them accessible to Python scripts, but there is some flexibility on how you go about doing so. For example, the following rule could be used to compile this C file on Linux too:

```
hello.so: hello.c
        gcc hello.c -c -g -fpic -I$(PY)/Include -I$(PY) -o hello.o
        gcc -shared hello.o -o hello.so
        rm -f hello.o
```

To compile the C file into a shareable object file on Solaris, you might instead say something like this:

```
hello.so: hello.c
        cc hello.c -c -KPIC -o hello.o
        ld -G hello.o -o hello.so
        rm hello.o
```

On other platforms, it's more different still. Because compiler options vary widely, you'll have to consult your C or C++ compiler's documentation or Python's extension manuals for platform- and compiler-specific details. The point is to determine how to compile a C source file into your platform's notion of a shareable or dynamically loaded object file. Once you have, the rest is easy; Python supports dynamic loading of C extensions on all major platforms today.

Dynamic binding

Technically, what I've been showing you so far is called "dynamic binding," and represents one of two ways to link compiled C extensions with the Python interpreter. Since the alternative, "static binding," is more complex, dynamic binding is almost always the way to go. To bind dynamically, simply:

1. Compile *hello.c* into a shareable object file

2. Put the object file in a directory on Python's module search path

That is, once you've compiled the source code file into a shareable object file, simply copy or move the object file to a directory listed in PYTHONPATH. It will be automatically loaded and linked by the Python interpreter at runtime when the module is first imported anywhere in the Python process (e.g., from the interactive prompt, a standalone or embedded Python program, or a C API call).

Notice that the only non-static name in the *hello.c* example C file is the initialization function. Python calls this function by name after loading the object file, so its name must be a C global and should generally be of the form "initX", where "X" is both the name of the module in Python import statements and the name passed to Py_InitModule. All other names in C extension files are arbitrary, because they are accessed by C pointer, not by name (more on this later). The name of the C source file is arbitrary too—at import time, Python cares only about the compiled object file.

Static binding

Under static binding, extensions are added to the Python interpreter permanently. This is more complex, though, because you must rebuild Python itself, and hence need access to the Python source distribution (an interpreter executable won't do). To link this example statically, add a line like:

```
hello ~/PP2E/Integrate/Extend/Hello/hello.c
```

to the `Modules/Setup` configuration file in the Python source code tree. Alternatively, you can copy your C file to the `Modules` directory (or add a link to it there with an *ln* command) and add a line to `Setup` like `hello hello.c`.

Then, rebuild Python itself by running a *make* command at the top level of the Python source tree. Python reconstructs its own makefiles to include the module you added to `Setup`, such that your code becomes part of the interpreter and its libraries. In fact, there's really no distinction between C extensions written by Python users and services that are a standard part of the language; Python is built with this same interface. The full format of module declaration lines looks like this (but see the `Modules/Setup` configuration file for more details):

```
<module> ... [<sourceOrObjectFile> ...] [<cpparg> ...] [<library> ...]
```

Under this scheme, the name of the module's initialization function must match the name used in the `Setup` file, or you'll get linking errors when you rebuild Python. The name of the source or object file doesn't have to match the module name; the leftmost name is the resulting Python module's name.

Static versus dynamic binding

Static binding works on any platform and requires no extra makefile to compile extensions. It can be useful if you don't want to ship extensions as separate files, or if you're on a platform without dynamic linking support. Its downsides are that you need to update the Python `Setup` configuration file and rebuild the Python interpreter itself, so you must therefore have the full source distribution of Python to use static linking at all. Moreover, all statically linked extensions are always added to your interpreter, whether or not they are used by a particular program. This can needlessly increase the memory needed to run all Python programs.

With dynamic binding, you still need Python include files, but can add C extensions even if all you have is a binary Python interpreter executable. Because extensions are separate object files, there is no need to rebuild Python itself or to access the full source distribution. And because object files are only loaded on demand in this mode, it generally makes for smaller executables too—Python loads into memory only the extensions actually imported by each program run. In other words, if you can use dynamic linking on your platform, you probably should.

Anatomy of a C Extension Module

Though simple, the *hello.c* example illustrates the structure common to all C modules. This structure can vary somewhat, but this file consists of fairly typical boilerplate code:

Python header files
> The C file first includes the standard *Python.h* header file (from the installed Python Include directory). This file defines almost every name exported by the Python API to C, and serves as a starting point for exploring the API itself.

Method functions
> The file then defines a function to be called from the Python interpreter in response to calls in Python programs. C functions receive two Python objects as input, and send either a Python object back to the interpreter as the result, or a NULL to trigger an exception in the script (more on this later). In C, a PyObject* represents a generic Python object pointer; you can use more specific type names, but don't always have to. C module functions can all be declared C "static" (local to the file), because Python calls them by pointer, not name.

Registration table
> Near the end, the file provides an initialized table (array) that maps function *names* to function *pointers* (addresses). Names in this table become module attribute names that Python code uses to call the C functions. Pointers in this table are used by the interpreter to dispatch C function calls. In effect, the table "registers" attributes of the module. A NULL entry terminates the table.

Initialization function
> Finally, the C file provides an initialization function, which Python calls the first time this module is imported into a Python program. This function calls the API function Py_InitModule to build up the new module's attribute dictionary from the entries in the registration table and create an entry for the C module on the sys.modules table (described in Chapter 2, *System Tools*). Once so initialized, calls from Python are routed directly to the C function through the registration table's function pointers.

Data conversions

C module functions are responsible for converting Python objects to and from C datatypes. In Example 19-1, message gets two Python input objects passed from the Python interpreter: args is a Python tuple holding the arguments passed from the Python caller (the values listed in parentheses in a Python program), and self is ignored; it is useful only for extension *types* (discussed later in this chapter).

After finishing its business, the C function can return any of the following to the Python interpreter: a Python object (known in C as `PyObject*`), for an actual result; a Python `None`, (known in C as `Py_None`), if the function returns no real result; or a C `NULL` pointer, to flag an error and raise a Python exception.

There are distinct API tools for handling input conversions (Python to C) and output conversions (C to Python). It's up to C functions to implement their call signatures (argument lists and types) by using these tools properly.

Python to C: Using Python argument lists

When the C function is run, the arguments passed from a Python script are available in the `args` Python tuple object. The API function `PyArg_Parse` (and `PyArg_ParseTuple`, its cousin that assumes it is converting a tuple object) is probably the easiest way to extract and convert passed arguments to C form.

`PyArg_Parse` takes a Python object, a format string, and a variable-length list of C target addresses. It converts the items in the tuple to C datatype values according to the format string, and stores the results in the C variables whose addresses are passed in. The effect is much like C's `scanf` string function. For example, the `hello` module converts a passed-in Python string argument to a C `char*` using the `s` convert code:

```
PyArg_Parse(args, "(s)", &fromPython)        # or PyArg_ParseTuple(args, "s",...
```

To handle multiple arguments, simply string format codes together and include corresponding C targets for each code in the string. For instance, to convert an argument list holding a string, an integer, and another string to C, say this:

```
PyArg_Parse(args, "(sis)", &s1, &i, &s2)     # or PyArg_ParseTuple(args, "sis",...
```

To verify that no arguments were passed, use an empty format string like this: `PyArg_Parse(args, "()")`. This API call checks that the number and types of the arguments passed from Python matches the format string in the call. If there is a mismatch, it sets an exception and returns zero to C (more on errors below).

Python to C: Using Python return values

As we'll see in Chapter 20, *Embedding Python*, API functions may also return Python objects to C as results when Python is being run as an embedded language. Converting Python return values in this mode is almost the same as converting Python arguments passed to C extension functions, except that Python return values are not always tuples. To convert returned Python objects to C form, simply use `PyArg_Parse`. Unlike `PyArg_ParseTuple`, this call takes the same kinds of arguments but doesn't expect the Python object to be a tuple.

C to Python: Returning values to Python

There are two ways to convert C data to Python objects: by using type-specific API functions, or the general object-builder function `Py_BuildValue`. The latter is more general, and is essentially the inverse of `PyArg_Parse`, in that `Py_BuildValue` converts C data to Python objects according to a format string. For instance, to make a Python string object from a C `char*`, the `hello` module uses an `s` convert code:

```
    return Py_BuildValue("s", result)          # "result" is a C char []/*
```

More specific object constructors can be used instead:

```
    return PyString_FromString(result)         # same effect
```

Both calls make a Python string object from a C character array pointer. See the now-standard Python extension and runtime API manuals for an exhaustive list of such calls available. Besides being easier to remember, though, `Py_BuildValue` has syntax that allows you to build lists in a single step, described next.

Common conversion codes

With a few exceptions, `PyArg_Parse(Tuple)` and `Py_BuildValue` use the same conversion codes in format strings. A list of all supported conversion codes appears in Python's extension manuals. The most commonly used are shown in Table 19-1; the tuple, list, and dictionary formats can be nested.

Table 19-1. Common Python/C Data Conversion Codes

Format-String Code	C Datatype	Python Object Type
s	char*	String
s#	char*, int	String, length
i	int	Integer
l	long int	Integer
c	char	String
f	float	Floating-point
d	double	Floating-point
O	PyObject*	Raw (unconverted) object
O&	&converter, void*	Converted object (calls converter)
(*items*)	Targets or values	Nested tuple
[*items*]	Series of arguments/values	List
{*items*}	Series of key,value arguments	Dictionary

These codes are mostly what you'd expect (e.g., `i` maps between a C `int` and a Python integer object), but here are a few usage notes on this table's entries:

- Pass in the address of a `char*` for `s` codes when converting *to* C, not the address of a `char` array: Python copies out the address of an existing C string (and you must copy it to save it indefinitely on the C side: use `strdup`).

- The `O` code is useful to pass raw Python objects between languages; once you have a raw object pointer, you can use lower-level API tools to access object attributes by name, index and slice sequences, and so on.

- The `O&` code lets you pass in C converter functions for custom conversions. This comes in handy for special processing to map an object to a C datatype not directly supported by conversion codes (for instance, when mapping to or from an entire C struct or C++ class-instance). See the extensions manual for more details.

- The last two entries, `[...]` and `{...}`, are currently supported only by `Py_BuildValue`: you can construct lists and dictionaries with format strings, but can't unpack them. Instead, the API includes type-specific routines for accessing sequence and mapping components given a raw object pointer.

`PyArg_Parse` supports some extra codes, which must not be nested in tuple formats (`(...)`):

| The remaining arguments are all optional (*varargs*). The C targets are unchanged if arguments are missing in the Python tuple. For instance, `si|sd` requires two arguments but allows up to four.

: The function name follows, for use in error messages set by the call (argument mismatches). Normally Python sets the error message to a generic string.

; A full error message follows, running to the end of the format string.

This format code list isn't exhaustive, and the set of convert codes may expand over time; refer to Python's extension manual for further details.

Error Handling

When you write C extensions, you need to be aware that errors can occur on either side of the languages fence. The following sections address both possibilities.

Raising Python exceptions in C

C extension module functions return a C `NULL` value for the result object to flag an error. When control returns to Python, the `NULL` result triggers a normal Python exception in the Python code that called the C function. To name an exception, C code can also set the type and extra data of the exceptions it triggers. For instance, the `PyErr_SetString` API function sets the exception object to a Python object and sets the exception's extra data to a character string:

```
PyErr_SetString(ErrorObject, message)
```

We will use this in the next example to be more specific about exceptions raised when C detects an error. C modules may also set a built-in Python exception; for instance, returning `NULL` after saying this:

```
PyErr_SetString(PyExc_IndexError, "index out-of-bounds")
```

raises a standard Python `IndexError` exception with the message string data. When an error is raised inside a Python API function, both the exception object and its associated "extra data" are automatically set by Python; there is no need to set it again in the calling C function. For instance, when an argument-passing error is detected in the `PyArg_Parse` function, the `hello` stack module just returns `NULL` to propagate the exception to the enclosing Python layer, instead of setting its own message.

Detecting errors that occur in Python

Python API functions may be called from C extension functions, or from an enclosing C layer when Python is embedded. In either case, C callers simply check the return value to detect errors raised in Python API functions. For pointer result functions, Python returns `NULL` pointers on errors. For integer result functions, Python generally returns a status code of –1 to flag an error and a 0 or positive value on success. (`PyArg_Parse` is an exception to this rule: it returns 0 when it detects an error.) To make your programs robust, you should check return codes for error indicators after most Python API calls; some calls can fail for reasons you may not have expected (e.g., memory overflow).

Reference Counts

The Python interpreter uses a reference-count scheme to implement garbage collection. Each Python object carries a count of the number of places it is referenced; when that count reaches zero, Python reclaims the object's memory space automatically. Normally, Python manages the reference counts for objects behind the scenes; Python programs simply make and use objects without concern for managing storage space.

When extending or embedding Python, though, integrated C code is responsible for managing the reference counts of the Python objects it uses. How important this becomes depends on how many raw Python objects a C module processes and which Python API functions it calls. In simple programs, reference counts are of minor, if any, concern; the `hello` module, for instance, makes no reference-count management calls at all.

When the API is used extensively, however, this task can become significant. In later examples, we'll see calls of these forms show up:

- `Py_INCREF(obj)` increments an object's reference count.

- `Py_DECREF(obj)` decrements an object's reference count (reclaim if zero).

- `Py_XINCREF(obj)` is similar to `Py_INCREF(obj)`, but ignores a `NULL` object pointer.

- `Py_XDECREF(obj)` is similar to `py_DECREF(obj)`, but ignores a `NULL` object pointer.

C module functions are expected to return either an object with an incremented reference count, or `NULL` to signal an error. As a general rule, API functions that create new objects increment their reference counts before returning them to C; unless a new object is to be passed back to Python, the C program that creates it should eventually decrement the object's counts. In the extending scenario, things are relatively simple; argument object reference counts need not be decremented, and new result objects are passed back to Python with their reference counts intact.

The upside of reference counts is that Python will never reclaim a Python object held by C as long as C increments the object's reference count (or doesn't decrement the count on an object it owns). Although it requires counter management calls, Python's garbage collector scheme is fairly well-suited to C integration.

The SWIG Integration Code Generator

But don't do that. I'm introducing C extension basics so you understand the underlying structure, but today, C extensions are usually better and more easily implemented with the SWIG integration code generator.

SWIG—the Simplified Wrapper and Interface Generator—is an open source system created by Dave Beazley. It uses C and C++ type declarations to generate complete C extension modules that integrate existing libraries for use in Python scripts. The generated C extension modules are complete: they automatically handle data conversion, error protocols, reference-count management, and more.

That is, SWIG automatically generates all the "glue" code needed to plug C and C++ components into Python programs; simply compile its output and your extension work is done. You still have to manage compilation and linking details, but the rest of the C extension task is done by SWIG.

A Simple SWIG Example

For instance, instead of writing all that C code in the prior section, write the C function you want to use from Python without any Python integration logic at all, as though it is to be used from C alone. This is illustrated in Example 19-4.

Example 19-4. PP2E\Integrate\Extend\HelloLib\hellolib.c

```
/**********************************************************************
 * A simple C library file, with a single function, "message",
 * which is to be made available for use in Python programs.
 * There is nothing about Python here--this C function can be
 * called from a C program, as well as Python (with glue code).
 **********************************************************************/

#include <string.h>
#include <hellolib.h>

static char result[64];                    /* this isn't exported */

char *
message(char *label)                       /* this is exported */
{
    strcpy(result, "Hello, ");             /* build up C string */
    strcat(result, label);                 /* add passed-in label */
    return result;                         /* return a temporary */
}
```

While you're at it, define the usual C header file to declare the function externally; as shown in Example 19-5. This is probably overkill, but will prove a point.

Example 19-5. PP2E\Integrate\Extend\HelloLib\hellolib.h

```
/**********************************************************************
 * Define hellolib.c exports to the C namespace, not to Python
 * programs--the latter is defined by a method registration
 * table in a Python extension module's code, not by this .h;
 **********************************************************************/

extern char *message(char *label);
```

Now, instead of all the Python extension glue code shown in the prior section, simply write a SWIG type declarations input file, as in Example 19-6.

Example 19-6. PP2E\Integrate\Extend\Swig\hellolib.i

```
/*****************************************************
 * Swig module description file, for a C lib file.
 * Generate by saying "swig -python hellolib.i".
 *****************************************************/

%module hellowrap
```

Example 19-6. PP2E\Integrate\Extend\Swig\hellolib.i (continued)

```
%{
#include <hellolib.h>
%}

extern char *message(char*);     /* or: %include "../HelloLib/hellolib.h"   */
                                 /* or: %include hellolib.h, and use -I arg */
```

This file spells out the C function's type signature. In general, SWIG scans files containing ANSI C and C++ declarations. Its input file can take the form of an interface description file (usually with an *.i* suffix), or a C/C++ header or source file. Interface files like this one are the most common input form; they can contain *comments* in C or C++ format, type *declarations* just like standard header files, and SWIG *directives* that all start with %. For example:

- **%module** sets the module's name as known to Python importers.

- **%{...%}** encloses code added to generated wrapper file verbatim.

- **extern** statements declare exports in normal ANSI C/C++ syntax.

- **%include** makes SWIG scan another file (–I flags give search paths).

In this example, SWIG could also be made to read the *hellolib.h* header file directly. But one of the advantages of writing special SWIG input files like *hellolib.i* is that you can pick and choose which functions are wrapped and exported to Python; scanning a library's entire header file wraps everything it defines.

SWIG is really a utility that you run from your build scripts, not a programming language, so there is not much more to show here. Simply add a step to your makefile that runs SWIG, and compile its output to be linked with Python. Example 19-7 shows one way to do it on Linux.

Example 19-7. PP2E\Integrate\Extend\Swig\makefile.hellolib-swig

```
###############################################################
# Use SWIG to integrate hellolib.c for use in Python programs.
###############################################################

# unless you've run make install
SWIG = ./myswig

PY   = $(MYPY)
LIB  = ../HelloLib

# the library plus its wrapper
hellowrap.so: hellolib_wrap.o $(LIB)/hellolib.o
	ld -shared hellolib_wrap.o $(LIB)/hellolib.o -o hellowrap.so

# generated wrapper module code
hellolib_wrap.o: hellolib_wrap.c $(LIB)/hellolib.h
	gcc hellolib_wrap.c -c -g -I$(LIB) -I$(PY)/Include -I$(PY)
```

Example 19-7. PP2E\Integrate\Extend\Swig\makefile.hellolib-swig (continued)

```
hellolib_wrap.c: hellolib.i
    $(SWIG) -python -I$(LIB) hellolib.i

# C library code (in another directory)
$(LIB)/hellolib.o: $(LIB)/hellolib.c $(LIB)/hellolib.h
    gcc $(LIB)/hellolib.c -c -g -I$(LIB) -o $(LIB)/hellolib.o

clean:
    rm -f *.o *.so core
force:
    rm -f *.o *.so core hellolib_wrap.c hellolib_wrap.doc
```

When run on the *hellolob.i* input file by this makefile, SWIG generates two files:

- *hellolib_wrap.doc* is a text summary of the functions in the module.

- *hellolib_wrap.c* is the generated C extension module glue code file.*

This makefile simply runs SWIG, compiles the generated C glue code file into an *.o* object file, and then combines it with *hellolib.c*'s compiled object file to produce *hellowrap.so*. The latter is the dynamically loaded C extension module file, and the one to place in a directory on your Python module search path (or "." if you're working in the directory where you compile).

Assuming you've got SWIG set to go, run the makefile to generate and compile wrappers for the C function. Here is the build process running on Linux:

```
[mark@toy ~/.../PP2E/Integrate/Extend/Swig]$ make -f makefile.hellolib-swig
./myswig -python -I../HelloLib hellolib.i
Generating wrappers for Python
gcc hellolib_wrap.c -c -g -I../HelloLib ...more text deleted here...
ld -shared hellolib_wrap.o ../HelloLib/hellolib.o -o hellowrap.so
```

And once you've run this makefile, you are finished. The generated C module is used exactly like the manually coded version shown before, except that SWIG has taken care of the complicated parts automatically:

```
[mark@toy ~/.../PP2E/Integrate/Extend/Swig]$ python
>>> import hellowrap                          # import the glue+library file
>>> hellowrap.__file__                        # cwd always searched on imports
'./hellowrap.so'
>>> hellowrap.message('swig world')
'Hello, swig world'
```

In other words, once you learn how to use SWIG, you can largely forget all the integration coding details introduced in this chapter. In fact, SWIG is so adept at generating Python glue code that it's usually much easier and less error-prone to

---

* You can wade through this generated file on the book's CD if you are so inclined. Also see file *PP2E\Integrate\Extend\HelloLib\hellolib_wrapper.c* on the CD for a hand-coded equivalent; it's shorter because SWIG also generates extra support code.

code C extensions for Python as purely C or C++-based libraries first, and later add them to Python by running their header files through SWIG, as demonstrated here.

SWIG Details

Of course, you must have SWIG before you can run SWIG; it's not part of Python itself. Unless it is already on your system, fetch SWIG off the Web (or find it on this book's CD) and build it from its source code. You'll need a C++ compiler (e.g., g++), but the install is very simple; see SWIG's README file for more details. SWIG is a command-line program, and generally can be run just by saying this:

```
swig -python hellolib.i
```

In my build environment, things are a bit more complex because I have a custom SWIG build. I run SWIG from this **csh** script called **myswig**:

```
#!/bin/csh
# run custom swig install

source $PP2EHOME/Integrate/Extend/Swig/setup-swig.csh
swig $*
```

This file in turn sets up pointers to the SWIG install directory by loading the following **csh** file, called *setup-swig.csh*:

```
# source me in csh to run SWIG with an unofficial install

setenv SWIG_LIB /home/mark/PP2ndEd/dev/examples/SWIG/SWIG1.1p5/swig_lib
alias swig "/home/mark/PP2ndEd/dev/examples/SWIG/SWIG1.1p5/swig"
```

But you won't need either of these files if you run a **make install** command in the SWIG source directory to copy it to standard places.

Along the way in this chapter, I'll show you a few more SWIG-based alternatives to the remaining examples. You should consult the SWIG Python user manual for the full scoop, but here is a quick look at a few more SWIG highlights:

C++ "shadow" classes

Later in the chapter, I'll also show you how to use SWIG to integrate C++ classes for use in your Python scripts. When given C++ class declarations, SWIG generates glue code that makes C++ classes look just like Python classes in Python scripts. In fact, C++ classes *are* Python classes under SWIG; you get what SWIG calls a C++ "shadow" class that interfaces with a C++ coded extension module, which in turn talks to C++ classes. Because the integration's outer layer is Python classes, those classes may be subclassed in Python and their instances processed with normal Python object syntax.

Variables

Besides functions and C++ classes, SWIG can also wrap C global variables and constants for use in Python: they become attributes of an object named `cvar` inserted in generated modules (e.g., `module.cvar.name` fetches the value of C's variable `name` from a SWIG-generated wrapper module).

Pointers

SWIG passes pointers between languages as strings (not as special Python types) for uniformity, and to allow type safety tests. For instance, a pointer to a `Vector` type may look like `_100f8e2_Vector_p`. You normally won't care, because pointer values are not much to look at in C either. SWIG can also be made to handle output parameters and C++ references.

Structs

C `structs` are converted into a set of `get` and `set` *accessor* functions that are called to fetch and assign fields with a `struct` object pointer (e.g., `module.Vector_fieldx_get(v)` fetches C's `Vector.fieldx` from a `Vector` pointer v, like C's `v->fieldx`). Similar accessor functions are generated for data members and methods of C++ classes (the C++ `class` is roughly a `struct` with extra syntax), but the SWIG shadow class feature allows you to treat wrapped classes just like Python classes, instead of calling the lower-level accessor functions.

Although the SWIG examples in this book are simple, you should know that SWIG handles industrial-strength libraries just as easily. For instance, Python developers have successfully used SWIG to integrated libraries as complex as Windows extensions and commonly used graphics APIs.

SWIG can also generate integration code for other scripting languages such as Tcl and Perl. In fact, one of its underlying goals is to make components independent of scripting language choices—C/C++ libraries can be plugged in to whatever scripting language you prefer to use (I prefer to use Python, but I might be biased). SWIG's support for things like classes seems strongest for Python, though, probably because Python is considered to be strong in the classes department. As a language-neutral integration tool, SWIG addresses some of the same goals as systems like COM and CORBA (described in Chapter 20), but provides a code-generation-based alternative instead of an object model.

You can find SWIG on this book's CD or at its home page on the Web, *http://www.swig.org*. Along with full source code, SWIG comes with outstanding documentation (including a manual specifically for Python), so I won't cover all of its features in this book. The documentation also describes how to build SWIG extensions on Windows. A SWIG book is reportedly in the works as I write this, so be sure to check the books list at *http://www.python.org* for additional resources.

Wrapping C Environment Calls

Let's move on to a more useful application of C extension modules. The hand-coded C file in Example 19-8 integrates the standard C library's **getenv** and **putenv** shell environment variable calls for use in Python scripts.

Example 19-8. PP2E\Integrate\Extend\CEnviron\cenviron.c

```c
/*********************************************************************
 * A C extension module for Python, called "cenviron".  Wraps the
 * C library's getenv/putenv routines for use in Python programs.
 *********************************************************************/

#include <Python.h>
#include <stdlib.h>
#include <string.h>

/***********************/
/* 1) module functions */
/***********************/

static PyObject *                                   /* returns object */
wrap_getenv(PyObject *self, PyObject *args)          /* self not used */
{                                                    /* args from python */
    char *varName, *varValue;
    PyObject *returnObj = NULL;                          /* null=exception */

    if (PyArg_Parse(args, "s", &varName)) {             /* Python -> C */
        varValue = getenv(varName);                     /* call C getenv */
        if (varValue != NULL)
            returnObj = Py_BuildValue("s", varValue);   /* C -> Python */
        else
            PyErr_SetString(PyExc_SystemError, "Error calling getenv");
    }
    return returnObj;
}

static PyObject *
wrap_putenv(PyObject *self, PyObject *args)
{
    char *varName, *varValue, *varAssign;
    PyObject *returnObj = NULL;

    if (PyArg_Parse(args, "(ss)", &varName, &varValue))
    {
        varAssign = malloc(strlen(varName) + strlen(varValue) + 2);
        sprintf(varAssign, "%s=%s", varName, varValue);
        if (putenv(varAssign) == 0) {
            Py_INCREF(Py_None);                         /* C call success */
            returnObj = Py_None;                        /* reference None */
        }
```

Example 19-8. PP2E\Integrate\Extend\CEnviron\cenviron.c (continued)

```
        else
            PyErr_SetString(PyExc_SystemError, "Error calling putenv");
    }
    return returnObj;
}

/*************************/
/* 2) registration table  */
/*************************/

static struct PyMethodDef cenviron_methods[] = {
    {"getenv", wrap_getenv},
    {"putenv", wrap_putenv},           /* method name, address */
    {NULL, NULL}
};

/************************/
/* 3) module initializer */
/************************/

void initcenviron()                    /* called on first import */
{
    (void) Py_InitModule("cenviron", cenviron_methods);    /* mod name, table */
}
```

This example is less useful now than it was in the first edition of this book—as we learned in Part I, *System Interfaces*, not only can you fetch shell environment variables by indexing the os.environ table, but assigning to a key in this table automatically calls C's putenv to export the new setting to the C code layer in the process. That is, os.environ['key'] fetches the value of shell variable 'key', and os.environ['key']=value assigns a variable both in Python and C.

The second action—pushing assignments out to C—was added to Python releases after the first edition of this book was published. Besides demonstrating additional extension coding techniques, though, this example still serves a practical purpose: even today, changes made to shell variables by the C code linked in to a Python process are not picked up when you index os.environ in Python code. That is, once your program starts, os.environ reflects only subsequent changes made by Python code.

If you want your Python code to be truly integrated with shell settings made by your C extension modules' code, you still must rely on calls to the C library's environment tools: putenv is available as os.putenv, but getenv is not present in the Python library. This will probably rarely, if ever, be an issue; but this C extension module is not completely without purpose (at least until Guido tightens this up again).[*]

This *cenviron.c* C file creates a Python module called `cenviron` that does a bit more than the last example—it exports two functions, sets some exception descriptions explicitly, and makes a reference count call for the Python **None** object (it's not created anew, so we need to add a reference before passing it to Python). As before, to add this code to Python, compile and link into an object file; the Linux makefile in Example 19-9 builds the C source code for dynamic binding.

Example 19-9. PP2E\Integrate\Extend\Cenviron\makefile.cenviron

```
###############################################################
# Compile cenviron.c into cenviron.so--a shareable object file
# on Linux, which is loaded dynamically when first imported.
###############################################################

PY = $(MYPY)

cenviron.so: cenviron.c
    gcc cenviron.c -g -I$(PY)/Include -I$(PY) -fpic -shared -o cenviron.so

clean:
    rm -f *.pyc cenviron.so
```

To build, type `make -f makefile.cenviron` at your shell. To run, make sure the *.so* file is in a directory on Python's module path ("." works too):

```
[mark@toy ~/.../PP2E/Integrate/Extend/Cenviron]$ python
>>> import cenviron
>>> cenviron.getenv('USER')                 # like os.environ[key] but refetched
'mark'
>>> cenviron.putenv('USER', 'gilligan')     # like os.environ[key]=value
>>> cenviron.getenv('USER')                 # C sees the changes too
'gilligan'
```

As before, `cenviron` is a bona fide Python module object after it is imported, with all the usual attached information:

```
>>> dir(cenviron)
['__doc__', '__file__', '__name__', 'getenv', 'putenv']
>>> cenviron.__file__
'./cenviron.so'
>>> cenviron.__name__
'cenviron'
>>> cenviron.getenv
```

---

[*] This code is also open to customization (e.g., it can limit the set of shell variables read and written by checking names), but you could do the same by wrapping `os.environ`. In fact, because `os.environ` is simply a Python `UserDict` subclass that preloads shell variables on startup, you could *almost* add the required `getenv` call to load C layer changes by simply wrapping `os.environ` accesses in a Python class whose `__getitem__` calls `gentenv` before passing the access off to `os.environ`. But you still need C's `getenv` call in the first place, and it's not available in `os` today.

```
<built-in function getenv>
>>> cenviron
<module 'cenviron' from './cenviron.so'>
>>> print cenviron.getenv('HOST'), cenviron.getenv('DISPLAY')
toy :0.0
```

Here is an example of the problem this module addresses (but you have to pretend that the getenv calls are made by linked-in C code, not Python):

```
>>> import os
>>> os.environ['USER']                     # initialized from the shell
'skipper'
>>> from cenviron import getenv, putenv    # direct C library call access
>>> getenv('USER')
'skipper'
>>> putenv('USER', 'gilligan')             # changes for C but not Python
>>> getenv('USER')
'gilligan'
>>> os.environ['USER']                     # oops—does not fetch values again
'skipper'
```

As is, the C extension module exports a function-based interface, but you can wrap its functions in Python code that makes the interface look any way you like. For instance, Example 19-10 makes the functions accessible by dictionary indexing, and integrates with the os.environ object.

Example 19-10. PP2E\Integrate\Extend\Cenviron\envmap.py

```
import os
from cenviron import getenv, putenv     # get C module's methods

class EnvMapping:                        # wrap in a Python class
    def __setitem__(self, key, value):
        os.environ[key] = value          # on writes: Env[key]=value
        putenv(key, value)               # put in os.environ too

    def __getitem__(self, key):
        value = getenv(key)              # on reads: Env[key]
        os.environ[key] = value          # integrity check
        return value

Env = EnvMapping()                       # make one instance
```

And Example 19-11 exports the functions as qualified attribute names instead of calls. The point here is that you can graft many different sorts of interface models on top of extension functions by providing Python wrappers (an idea we'll revisit when we meet type wrappers and SWIG shadow classes later in this chapter).

Example 19-11. PP2E\Integrate\Extend\Cenviron\envattr.py

```
import os
from cenviron import getenv, putenv     # get C module's methods
```

Example 19-11. PP2E\Integrate\Extend\Cenviron\envattr.py (continued)

```
class EnvWrapper:                           # wrap in a Python class
    def __setattr__(self, name, value):
        os.environ[name] = value            # on writes: Env.name=value
        putenv(name, value)                 # put in os.environ too

    def __getattr__(self, name):
        value = getenv(name)                # on reads: Env.name
        os.environ[name] = value            # integrity check
        return value

Env = EnvWrapper()                          # make one instance
```

But Don't Do That Either—SWIG

You can manually code extension modules like we just did, but you don't necessarily have to. Because this example really just wraps functions that already exist in standard C libraries, the entire *cenviron.c* C code file of Example 19-8 can be replaced with a simple SWIG input file that looks like Example 19-12.

Example 19-12. PP2E\Integrate\Extend\Swig\Environ\environ.i

```
/***************************************************************
 * Swig module description file, to generate all Python wrapper
 * code for C lib getenv/putenv calls: "swig -python environ.i".
 ***************************************************************/

%module environ

%{
#include <stdlib.h>
%}

extern char * getenv(const char *varname);
extern int    putenv(const char *assignment);
```

And you're done. Well, almost; you still need to run this file through SWIG and compile its output. As before, simply add a SWIG step to your makefile, compile its output file into a shareable object, and you're in business. Example 19-13 is a Linux makefile that does the job.

Example 19-13. PP2E\Integrate\Extend\Swig\Environ\makefile.environ-swig

```
# build environ.so extension from SWIG generated code

# unless you've run make install
SWIG = ../myswig
PY   = $(MYPY)

environ.so: environ_wrap.c
    gcc environ_wrap.c -g -I$(PY)/Include -I$(PY) -shared -o environ.so
```

Example 19-13. PP2E\Integrate\Extend\Swig\Environ\makefile.environ-swig (continued)

```
environ_wrap.c: environ.i
    $(SWIG) -python environ.i

clean:
    rm -f *.o *.so core
force:
    rm -f *.o *.so core environ_wrap.c environ_wrap.doc
```

When run on *environ.i*, SWIG generates two files—*environ_wrap.doc* (a list of wrapper function descriptions) and *environ_wrap.c* (the glue code module file). Because the functions being wrapped here live in standard linked-in C libraries, there is nothing to combine with the generated code; this makefile simply runs SWIG and compiles the wrapper file into a C extension module, ready to be imported:

```
[mark@toy ~/....../Integrate/Extend/Swig/Environ]$ make -f makefile.environ-swig
../myswig -python environ.i
Generating wrappers for Python
gcc environ_wrap.c -g -I/...more... -shared -o environ.so
```

And now you're really done. The resulting C extension module is linked when imported, and used as before (except that SWIG handled all the gory bits):

```
[mark@toy ~/....../Integrate/Extend/Swig/Environ]$ python
>>> import environ
>>> environ.getenv('USER')
'mark'
>>> environ.putenv('USER=gilligan')            # use C lib call pattern now
0
>>> environ.getenv('USER')
'gilligan'

>>> dir(environ)
['__doc__', '__file__', '__name__', 'getenv', 'putenv']
>>> environ.__name__, environ.__file__, environ
('environ', './environ.so', <module 'environ' from './environ.so'>)
```

You could also run SWIG over the C header file where `getenv` and `putenv` are defined, but that would result in wrappers for every function in the header file. With the input file coded here, you'll wrap only two library functions.

A C Extension Module String Stack

Let's kick it up another notch—the following C extension module implements a stack of strings for use in Python scripts. Example 19-14 demonstrates additional API calls, but also serves as a basis of comparison. It is roughly equivalent to the Python stack module we met earlier in Chapter 17, *Data Structures*, but it stacks only strings (not arbitrary objects), has limited string storage and stack lengths, and is written in C.

Alas, the last point makes for a complicated program listing—C code is never quite as nice to look at as equivalent Python code. C must declare variables, manage memory, implement data structures, and include lots of extra syntax. Unless you're a big fan of C, you should focus on the Python interface code in this file, not the internals of its functions.

Example 19-14. PP2E\Integrate\Extend\Stacks\stackmod.c

```c
/***************************************************
 * stackmod.c: a shared stack of character-strings;
 * a C extension module for use in Python programs;
 * linked into python libraries or loaded on import;
 ***************************************************/

#include "Python.h"            /* Python header files */
#include <stdio.h>             /* C header files */
#include <string.h>

static PyObject *ErrorObject;   /* locally-raised exception */

#define onError(message) \
        { PyErr_SetString(ErrorObject, message); return NULL; }

/****************************************************************************
 * LOCAL LOGIC/DATA (THE STACK)
 ****************************************************************************/

#define MAXCHARS 2048
#define MAXSTACK MAXCHARS

static int  top = 0;                   /* index into 'stack' */
static int  len = 0;                   /* size of 'strings' */
static char *stack[MAXSTACK];          /* pointers into 'strings' */
static char strings[MAXCHARS];         /* string-storage area */

/****************************************************************************
 * EXPORTED MODULE METHODS/FUNCTIONS
 ****************************************************************************/

static PyObject *
stack_push(PyObject *self, PyObject *args)       /* args: (string) */
{
    char *pstr;
    if (!PyArg_ParseTuple(args, "s", &pstr))     /* convert args: Python->C */
        return NULL;                             /* NULL triggers exception */
    if (top == MAXSTACK)                         /* python sets arg-error msg */
        onError("stack overflow")                /* iff maxstack < maxchars */
    if (len + strlen(pstr) + 1 >= MAXCHARS)
        onError("string-space overflow")
    else {
        strcpy(strings + len, pstr);             /* store in string-space */
        stack[top++] = &(strings[len]);          /* push start address */
        len += (strlen(pstr) + 1);               /* new string-space size */
```

Example 19-14. PP2E\Integrate\Extend\Stacks\stackmod.c (continued)

```c
        Py_INCREF(Py_None);                          /* a 'procedure' call */
        return Py_None;                              /* None: no errors */
    }
}

static PyObject *
stack_pop(PyObject *self, PyObject *args)
{                                                    /* no arguments for pop */
    PyObject *pstr;
    if (!PyArg_ParseTuple(args, ""))                 /* verify no args passed */
        return NULL;
    if (top == 0)
        onError("stack underflow")                   /* return NULL = raise */
    else {
        pstr = Py_BuildValue("s", stack[--top]);     /* convert result: C->Py */
        len -= (strlen(stack[top]) + 1);
        return pstr;                                 /* return new python string */
    }                                                /* pstr ref-count++ already */
}

static PyObject *
stack_top(PyObject *self, PyObject *args)            /* almost same as item(-1) */
{                                                    /* but different errors */
    PyObject *result = stack_pop(self, args);        /* get top string */
    if (result != NULL)
        len += (strlen(stack[top++]) + 1);           /* undo pop */
    return result;                                   /* NULL or string object */
}

static PyObject *
stack_empty(PyObject *self, PyObject *args)          /* no args: '()' */
{
    if (!PyArg_ParseTuple(args, ""))                 /* or PyArg_NoArgs */
        return NULL;
    return Py_BuildValue("i", top == 0);             /* boolean: a python int */
}

static PyObject *
stack_member(PyObject *self, PyObject *args)
{
    int i;
    char *pstr;
    if (!PyArg_ParseTuple(args, "s", &pstr))
        return NULL;
    for (i = 0; i < top; i++)                        /* find arg in stack */
        if (strcmp(pstr, stack[i]) == 0)
            return PyInt_FromLong(1);                /* send back a python int */
    return PyInt_FromLong(0);                        /* same as Py_BuildValue("i" */
}

static PyObject *
stack_item(PyObject *self, PyObject *args)           /* return Python string or NULL */
```

Example 19-14. PP2E\Integrate\Extend\Stacks\stackmod.c (continued)

```c
{                                              /* inputs = (index): Python int */
    int index;
    if (!PyArg_ParseTuple(args, "i", &index))  /* convert args to C */
        return NULL;                           /* bad type or arg count? */
    if (index < 0)
        index = top + index;                   /* negative: offset from end */
    if (index < 0 || index >= top)
        onError("index out-of-bounds")         /* return NULL = 'raise' */
    else
        return Py_BuildValue("s", stack[index]); /* convert result to Python */
}                                              /* no need to INCREF new obj */

static PyObject *
stack_len(PyObject *self, PyObject *args)      /* return a Python int or NULL */
{                                              /* no inputs */
    if (!PyArg_ParseTuple(args, ""))
        return NULL;
    return PyInt_FromLong(top);                /* wrap in python object */
}

static PyObject *
stack_dump(PyObject *self, PyObject *args)     /* not "print": reserved word */
{
    int i;
    if (!PyArg_ParseTuple(args, ""))
        return NULL;
    printf("[Stack:\n");
    for (i=top-1; i >= 0; i--)                 /* formatted output */
        printf("%d: '%s'\n", i, stack[i]);
    printf("]\n");
    Py_INCREF(Py_None);
    return Py_None;
}

/**************************************************************************
 * METHOD REGISTRATION TABLE: NAME-STRING -> FUNCTION-POINTER
 **************************************************************************/

static struct PyMethodDef stack_methods[] = {
    {"push",       stack_push,      1},        /* name, address */
    {"pop",        stack_pop,       1},        /* '1'=always tuple args */
    {"top",        stack_top,       1},
    {"empty",      stack_empty,     1},
    {"member",     stack_member,    1},
    {"item",       stack_item,      1},
    {"len",        stack_len,       1},
    {"dump",       stack_dump,      1},
    {NULL,         NULL}                        /* end, for initmodule */
};

/**************************************************************************
 * INITIALIZATION FUNCTION (IMPORT-TIME)
 **************************************************************************/
```

Example 19-14. PP2E\Integrate\Extend\Stacks\stackmod.c (continued)

```
void
initstackmod()
{
    PyObject *m, *d;

    /* create the module and add the functions */
    m = Py_InitModule("stackmod", stack_methods);        /* registration hook */

    /* add symbolic constants to the module */
    d = PyModule_GetDict(m);
    ErrorObject = Py_BuildValue("s", "stackmod.error");  /* export exception */
    PyDict_SetItemString(d, "error", ErrorObject);       /* add more if need */

    /* check for errors */
    if (PyErr_Occurred())
        Py_FatalError("can't initialize module stackmod");
}
```

This C extension file is compiled and statically or dynamically linked with the interpreter just like in previous examples. File *makefile.stack* on the CD handles the build with a rule like this:

```
stackmod.so: stackmod.c
    gcc stackmod.c -g -I$(PY)/Include -I$(PY) -fpic -shared -o stackmod.so
```

The whole point of implementing such a stack in a C extension module (apart from demonstrating API calls in a Python book) is *optimization*: in theory, this code should present a similar interface to the Python stack module we wrote earlier, but run considerably faster due to its C coding. The interface is roughly the same, though we've sacrificed some Python flexibility by moving to C—there are limits on size and stackable object types:

```
[mark@toy ~/.../PP2E/Integrate/Extend/Stacks]$ python
>>> import stackmod                          # load C module
>>> stackmod.push('new')                     # call C functions
>>> stackmod.dump()                          # dump format differs
[Stack:
0: 'new'
]
>>> for c in "SPAM": stackmod.push(c)
...
>>> stackmod.dump()
[Stack:
4: 'M'
3: 'A'
2: 'P'
1: 'S'
0: 'new'
]
>>> stackmod.len(), stackmod.top()
(5, 'M')
```

```
>>> x = stackmod.pop()
>>> x
'M'
>>> stackmod.dump()
[Stack:
3: 'A'
2: 'P'
1: 'S'
0: 'new'
]
>>> stackmod.push(99)
Traceback (innermost last):
  File "<stdin>", line 1, in ?
TypeError: argument 1: expected string, int found
```

Some of the C stack's type and size limitations could be removed by alternate C coding (which might eventually create something that looks and performs almost exactly like a Python built-in list). Before we check on this stack's speed, though, we'll see what can be done about also optimizing our stack *classes* with a C *type*.

But Don't Do That Either—SWIG

You can manually code extension modules like this, but you don't necessarily have to. As we saw earlier, if you instead code the stack module's functions without any notion of Python integration, they can be integrated into Python automatically by running their type signatures through SWIG. I haven't coded these functions that way here, because I also need to teach the underlying Python C extension API. But if I were asked to write a C string stack for Python in any other context, I'd do it with SWIG instead.

A C Extension Type String Stack

To implement multiple-instance objects in C, you need to code a C extension *type*, not a module. Like Python classes, C types generate multiple-instance objects and can overload (i.e., intercept and implement) Python expression operators and type operations. Unlike classes, though, types do not support attribute inheritance by themselves—attributes are fetched from a flat names table, not a namespace objects tree. That makes sense if you realize that Python's built-in types are simply precoded C extension types; when you ask for the list **append** method, for instance, inheritance never enters the picture. We can add inheritance for types by coding "wrapper" classes, but it is a manual process (more on this later).

One of the biggest drawbacks of types, though, is their size—to implement a realistically equipped C type, you need to code lots of not-very-pretty C code, and fill out type descriptor tables with pointers to link up operation handlers. In fact, C extension types are so complex that I'm going to cut some details here. To give you a feel for the overall structure, Example 19-15 presents a C string stack type implementation, but with the bodies of all its functions stripped out. For the complete implementation, see this file on the book's CD.

This C type roughly implements the same interface as the stack classes we met earlier in Chapter 17, but imposes a few limits on the stack itself and does not support specialization by subclassing (it's a type, not a class). The stripped parts use the same algorithms as the C module in Example 19-14, but operate on the passed-in `self` object, which now refers to the particular type instance object being processed, just as the first argument does in class methods. In types, `self` is a pointer to an allocated C `struct` that represents a type instance object.

Example 19-15. PP2E\Integrate\Extend\Stacks\stacktyp.c

```
/****************************************************
 * stacktyp.c: a character-string stack data-type;
 * a C extension type, for use in Python programs;
 * stacktype module clients can make multiple stacks;
 * similar to stackmod, but 'self' is the instance,
 * and we can overload sequence operators here;
 ***************************************************/

#include "Python.h"

static PyObject *ErrorObject;       /* local exception */
#define onError(message) \
        { PyErr_SetString(ErrorObject, message); return NULL; }


/***********************************************************************
 * STACK-TYPE INFORMATION
 **********************************************************************/

#define MAXCHARS 2048
#define MAXSTACK MAXCHARS

typedef struct {                    /* stack instance object format */
    PyObject_HEAD                   /* python header: ref-count + &typeobject */
    int top, len;
    char *stack[MAXSTACK];          /* per-instance state info */
    char strings[MAXCHARS];         /* same as stackmod, but multiple copies */
} stackobject;


/***********************************************************************
 * INSTANCE METHODS
 **********************************************************************/

static PyObject *                   /* on "instance.push(arg)" */
stack_push(self, args)              /* 'self' is the stack instance object */
    stackobject *self;              /* 'args' are args passed to self.push method */
    PyObject    *args;
{   ...
}
```

Example 19-15. PP2E\Integrate\Extend\Stacks\stacktyp.c (continued)

```c
static PyObject *
stack_pop(self, args)
    stackobject *self;
    PyObject    *args;          /* on "instance.pop()" */
{   ...
}
static PyObject *
stack_top(self, args)
    stackobject *self;
    PyObject    *args;
{   ...
}
static PyObject *
stack_empty(self, args)
    stackobject *self;
    PyObject    *args;
{   ...
}
static struct PyMethodDef stack_methods[] = {      /* instance methods */
  {"push",        stack_push,     1},              /* name/address table */
  {"pop",         stack_pop,      1},              /* like list append,sort */
  {"top",         stack_top,      1},
  {"empty",       stack_empty,    1},              /* extra ops besides optrs */
  {NULL,          NULL}                            /* end, for getattr here */
};


/************************************************************************
 * BASIC TYPE-OPERATIONS
 ************************************************************************/

static stackobject *                /* on "x = stacktype.Stack()" */
newstackobject()                    /* instance constructor function */
{   ...                               /* these don't get an 'args' input */
}
static void                         /* instance destructor function */
stack_dealloc(self)                 /* when reference-count reaches zero */
    stackobject *self;
{   ...                               /* do cleanup activity */
}
static int
stack_print(self, fp, flags)
    stackobject *self;
    FILE *fp;
    int flags;                      /* print self to file */
{   ...
}
static PyObject *
stack_getattr(self, name)           /* on "instance.attr" reference */
    stackobject *self;              /* make a bound-method or member */
    char *name;
{   ...
}
static int
```

Example 19-15. PP2E\Integrate\Extend\Stacks\stacktyp.c (continued)

```c
stack_compare(v, w)                     /* on all comparisons */
    stackobject *v, *w;
{   ...
}


/****************************************************************************
 * SEQUENCE TYPE-OPERATIONS
 ****************************************************************************/


static int
stack_length(self)
    stackobject *self;                  /* called on "len(instance)" */
{   ...
}
static PyObject *
stack_concat(self, other)
    stackobject *self;                  /* on "instance + other" */
    PyObject    *other;                 /* 'self' is the instance */
{   ...
}
static PyObject *
stack_repeat(self, n)                   /* on "instance * N" */
    stackobject *self;                  /* new stack = repeat self n times */
    int n;
{   ...
}
static PyObject *
stack_item(self, index)                 /* on "instance[offset]", "in/for" */
    stackobject *self;                  /* return the i-th item of self */
    int index;                          /* negative index pre-adjusted */
{   ...
}
static PyObject *
stack_slice(self, ilow, ihigh)
    stackobject *self;                  /* on "instance[ilow:ihigh]" */
    int ilow, ihigh;                    /* negative-adjusted, not scaled */
{   ...
}


/****************************************************************************
 * TYPE DESCRIPTORS
 ****************************************************************************/


static PySequenceMethods stack_as_sequence = {  /* sequence supplement    */
        (inquiry)        stack_length,      /* sq_length    "len(x)"   */
        (binaryfunc)     stack_concat,      /* sq_concat    "x + y"    */
        (intargfunc)     stack_repeat,      /* sq_repeat    "x * n"    */
        (intargfunc)     stack_item,        /* sq_item      "x[i], in" */
        (intintargfunc)  stack_slice,       /* sq_slice     "x[i:j]"   */
        (intobjargproc)  0,                 /* sq_ass_item  "x[i] = v" */
        (intintobjargproc) 0,               /* sq_ass_slice "x[i:j]=v" */
};
```

Example 19-15. PP2E\Integrate\Extend\Stacks\stacktyp.c (continued)

```c
static PyTypeObject Stacktype = {       /* main python type-descriptor */
  /* type header */                     /* shared by all instances */
     PyObject_HEAD_INIT(&PyType_Type)
     0,                                 /* ob_size */
     "stack",                           /* tp_name */
     sizeof(stackobject),               /* tp_basicsize */
     0,                                 /* tp_itemsize */

  /* standard methods */
     (destructor)  stack_dealloc,       /* tp_dealloc  ref-count==0   */
     (printfunc)   stack_print,         /* tp_print    "print x"      */
     (getattrfunc) stack_getattr,       /* tp_getattr  "x.attr"       */
     (setattrfunc) 0,                   /* tp_setattr  "x.attr=v"     */
     (cmpfunc)     stack_compare,       /* tp_compare  "x > y"        */
     (reprfunc)    0,                   /* tp_repr     `x`, print x   */

  /* type categories */
     0,                                 /* tp_as_number   +,-,*,/,%,&,>>,...*/
     &stack_as_sequence,                /* tp_as_sequence +,[i],[i:j],len, ...*/
     0,                                 /* tp_as_mapping  [key], len, ...*/

  /* more methods */
     (hashfunc)    0,                   /* tp_hash     "dict[x]" */
     (ternaryfunc) 0,                   /* tp_call     "x()"     */
     (reprfunc)    0,                   /* tp_str      "str(x)"  */

};  /* plus others: see Include/object.h */

/****************************************************************************
 * MODULE LOGIC
 ****************************************************************************/

static PyObject *
stacktype_new(self, args)               /* on "x = stacktype.Stack()" */
    PyObject *self;                     /* self not used */
    PyObject *args;                     /* constructor args */
{
    if (!PyArg_ParseTuple(args, ""))    /* Module-method function */
        return NULL;
    return (PyObject *)newstackobject(); /* make a new type-instance object */
}                                       /* the hook from module to type... */

static struct PyMethodDef stacktype_methods[] = {
    {"Stack",  stacktype_new, 1},               /* one function: make a stack */
    {NULL,     NULL}                            /* end marker, for initmodule */
};

void
initstacktype()                 /* on first "import stacktype" */
{
    PyObject *m, *d;
    m = Py_InitModule("stacktype", stacktype_methods);   /* make the module, */
```

Example 19-15. PP2E\Integrate\Extend\Stacks\stacktyp.c (continued)

```
    d = PyModule_GetDict(m);                        /* with 'Stack' func */
    ErrorObject = Py_BuildValue("s", "stacktype.error");
    PyDict_SetItemString(d, "error", ErrorObject);   /* export exception */
    if (PyErr_Occurred())
        Py_FatalError("can't initialize module stacktype");
}
```

Anatomy of a C Extension Type

Although most of file *stacktyp.c* is missing, there is enough here to illustrate the global structure common to C type implementations:

Instance struct

The file starts off by defining a C struct called `stackobject` that will be used to hold per-instance state information—each generated instance object gets a newly `malloc`'d copy of the struct. It serves the same function as class instance attribute dictionaries, and contains data that was saved in global variables by the C stack module.

Instance methods

As in the module, a set of instance methods follows next; they implement method calls such as `push` and `pop`. But here, method functions process the implied instance object, passed in to the `self` argument. This is similar in spirit to class methods. Type instance methods are looked up in the registration table of the code listing (Example 19-15) when accessed.

Basic type operations

Next, the file defines functions to handle basic operations common to all types: creation, printing, qualification, and so on. These functions have more specific type signatures than instance method handlers. The object creation handler allocates a new stack `struct`, and initializes its header fields: the reference count is set to 1, and its type object pointer is set to the `Stacktype` type descriptor that appears later in the file.

Sequence operations

Functions for handling sequence type operations come next. Stacks respond to most sequence operators: `len`, `+`, `*`, and `[i]`. Much like the `__getitem__` class method, the `stack_item` indexing handler performs indexing, but also in membership tests and `for` iterator loops. These latter two work by indexing an object until an `IndexError` exception is caught by Python.

Type descriptors

The type descriptor tables (really, `structs`) that appear near the end of the file are the crux of the matter for types—Python uses these tables to dispatch an operation performed on an instance object to the corresponding C handler function in this file. In fact, everything is routed through these tables; even method attribute lookups start by running a C `stack_getattr` function listed in the table (which in turn looks up the attribute name in a name/function-pointer table). The main `Stacktype` table includes a link to the supplemental `stack_as_sequence` table where sequence operation handlers are registered; types can provide such tables to register handlers for mapping, number, and sequence operation sets. See Python's integer and dictionary objects' source code for number and mapping examples; they are analogous to the sequence type here, but their operation tables vary.*

Constructor module

Besides defining a C type, this file also creates a simple C *module* at the end that exports a `stacktype.Stack` constructor function, which Python scripts call to generate new stack instance objects. The initialization function for this module is the only C name in this file that is not `static` (local to the file); everything else is reached by following pointers—from instance, to type descriptor, to C handler function.

Again, see the book CD for the full C stack type implementation. But to give you the general flavor of C type methods, here is what the C type's `pop` function looks like; compare this with the C module's `pop` function to see how the `self` argument is used to access per-instance information in types:

```
static PyObject *
stack_pop(self, args)
    stackobject *self;
    PyObject *args;                          /* on "instance.pop()" */
{
    PyObject *pstr;
    if (!PyArg_ParseTuple(args, ""))         /* verify no args passed */
        return NULL;
    if (self->top == 0)
        onError("stack underflow")           /* return NULL = raise */
    else {
        pstr = Py_BuildValue("s", self->stack[--self->top]);
        self->len -= (strlen(self->stack[self->top]) + 1);
        return pstr;
    }
}
```

---

* Note that type descriptor layouts, like most C API tools, are prone to change over time, and you should always consult *Include/object.h* in the Python distribution for an up-to-date list of fields. Some new Python releases may also require that types written to work with earlier releases be recompiled to pick up descriptor changes. As always, see Python's extension manuals and its full source code distribution for more information and examples.

Compiling and Running

This C extension file is compiled and dynamically or statically linked like previous examples; file *makefile.stack* on the CD handles the build like this:

```
stacktype.so: stacktyp.c
        gcc stacktyp.c -g -I$(PY)/Include -I$(PY) -fpic -shared -o stacktype.so
```

Once compiled, you can import the C module and make and use instances of the C type it defines much as if it were a Python class (but without inheritance). You would normally do this from a Python script, but the interactive prompt is a convenient place to test the basics:

```
[mark@toy ~/.../PP2E/Integrate/Extend/Stacks]$ python
>>> import stacktype              # import C constructor module
>>> x = stacktype.Stack()         # make C type instance object
>>> x.push('new')                 # call C type methods
>>> x                             # call C type print handler
[Stack:
0: 'new'
]

>>> x[0]                          # call C type index handler
'new'
>>> y = stacktype.Stack()         # make another type instance
>>> for c in 'SPAM': y.push(c)    # a distinct stack object
...
>>> y
[Stack:
3: 'M'
2: 'A'
1: 'P'
0: 'S'
]

>>> z = x + y                     # call C type concat handler
>>> z
[Stack:
4: 'M'
3: 'A'
2: 'P'
1: 'S'
0: 'new'
]

>>> y.pop()
'M'
>>> len(z), z[0], z[-1]           # for loops work too (indexing)
(5, 'new', 'M')
```

Timing the C Implementations

So how did we do on the optimization front this time? Let's resurrect that timer module we wrote back in Example 17-6 to compare the C stack module and type to the Python stack module and classes we coded in Chapter 17. Example 19-16 calculates the system time in seconds that it takes to run tests on all of this book's stack implementations.

Example 19-16. PP2E\Integrate\Extend\Stacks\exttime.py

```
#!/usr/local/bin/python
# time the C stack module and type extensions
# versus the object chapter's Python stack implementations

from PP2E.Dstruct.Basic.timer  import test       # second count function
from PP2E.Dstruct.Basic import stack1            # python stack module
from PP2E.Dstruct.Basic import stack2            # python stack class: +/slice
from PP2E.Dstruct.Basic import stack3            # python stack class: tuples
from PP2E.Dstruct.Basic import stack4            # python stack class: append/pop
import stackmod, stacktype                       # c extension type, module

from sys import argv
rept, pushes, pops, items = 200, 200, 200, 200   # default: 200 * (600 ops)
try:
    [rept, pushes, pops, items] = map(int, argv[1:])
except: pass
print 'reps=%d * [push=%d+pop=%d+fetch=%d]' % (rept, pushes, pops, items)

def moduleops(mod):
    for i in range(pushes): mod.push('hello')    # strings only for C
    for i in range(items):  t = mod.item(i)
    for i in range(pops):   mod.pop()

def objectops(Maker):                            # type has no init args
    x = Maker()                                  # type or class instance
    for i in range(pushes): x.push('hello')      # strings only for C
    for i in range(items):  t = x[i]
    for i in range(pops):   x.pop()

# test modules: python/c
print "Python module:", test(rept, moduleops, stack1)
print "C ext module: ", test(rept, moduleops, stackmod), '\n'

# test objects: class/type
print "Python simple Stack:", test(rept, objectops, stack2.Stack)
print "Python tuple  Stack:", test(rept, objectops, stack3.Stack)
print "Python append Stack:", test(rept, objectops, stack4.Stack)
print "C ext type Stack:   ", test(rept, objectops, stacktype.Stack)
```

Running this script on Linux produces the following results. As we saw before, the Python tuple stack is slightly better than the Python in-place **append** stack in typical use (when the stack is only pushed and popped), but it is slower when indexed. The first test here runs 200 repetitions of 200 stack pushes and pops, or 80,000 stack operations (200 × 400); times listed are test duration seconds:

```
[mark@toy ~/.../PP2E/Integrate/Extend/Stacks]$ python exttim.py 200 200 200 0
reps=200 * [push=200+pop=200+fetch=0]
Python module: 2.09
C ext module:  0.68

Python simple Stack: 2.15
Python tuple  Stack: 0.68
Python append Stack: 1.16
C ext type Stack:    0.5

[mark@toy ~/.../PP2E/Integrate/Extend/Stacks]$ python exttim.py 100 300 300 0
reps=100 * [push=300+pop=300+fetch=0]
Python module: 1.86
C ext module:  0.52

Python simple Stack: 1.91
Python tuple  Stack: 0.51
Python append Stack: 0.87
C ext type Stack:    0.38
```

At least when there are no indexing operations on the stack as in these two tests (just pushes and pops), the C type is only slightly faster than the best Python stack (tuples). In fact, it's almost a draw—in these first two tests, the C type reports only a tenth of a second speedup after 200 stacks and 80,000 stack operations. It's not exactly the kind of performance difference that would generate a bug report.*

The C module comes in at roughly three times faster than the Python module, but these results are flawed. The `stack1` Python module tested here uses the same slow stack implementation as the Python "simple" stack (`stack2`). If it was recoded to use the *tuple* stack representation used in Chapter 17, its speed would be similar to the "tuple" figures listed here, and almost identical to the speed of the C module in the first two tests:

```
[mark@toy ~/.../PP2E/Integrate/Extend/Stacks]$ python exttim.py 200 200 200 50
reps=200 * [push=200+pop=200+fetch=50]
Python module: 2.17
C ext module:  0.79

Python simple Stack: 2.24
Python tuple  Stack: 1.94
Python append Stack: 1.25
C ext type Stack:    0.52
```

---

* Interestingly, Python has gotten much faster since this book's first edition, relative to C. Back then, the C type was still almost three times faster than the best Python stack (tuples) when no indexing was performed. Today, it's almost a draw. One might infer from this that C migrations have become a third as important as they once were.

```
[mark@toy ~/.../PP2E/Integrate/Extend/Stacks]$ python exttim.py
reps=200 * [push=200+pop=200+fetch=200]
Python module: 2.42
C ext module:  1.1

Python simple Stack: 2.54
Python tuple  Stack: 19.09
Python append Stack: 1.54
C ext type Stack:    0.63
```

But under the different usage patterns simulated in these two tests, the C type wins the race. It is about twice as fast as the best Python stack (`append`) when indexing is added to the test mix, as illustrated by two of the preceding test runs that ran with a nonzero fetch count. Similarly, the C module would be twice as fast as the best Python module coding in this case as well.

In other words, the fastest Python stacks are as good as the C stacks if you stick to pushes and pops, but the C stacks are roughly twice as fast if any indexing is performed. Moreover, since you have to pick one representation, if indexing is possible at all you would likely pick the Python `append` stack; assuming they represent the best case, C stacks would always be twice as fast.

Of course, the measured time differences are so small that in many applications you won't care. Further, the C stacks are much more difficult to program, and achieve their speed by imposing substantial functional limits; in many ways, this is not quite an apples-to-apples comparison. But as a rule of thumb, C extensions can not only integrate existing components for use in Python scripts, they can also optimize time-critical components of pure Python programs. In other scenarios, migration to C might yield an even larger speedup.

On the other hand, C extensions should generally be used only as a last resort. As we learned earlier, algorithms and data structures are often bigger influences on program performance than implementation language. The fact that Python-coded tuple stacks are just as fast as the C stacks under common usage patterns speaks volumes about the importance of data structure representation.

Wrapping C Types in Classes

In the current Python implementation, to add inheritance to C types you must have a class somewhere. The most common way to support type customization is to introduce a *wrapper* class—a Python class that does little but keep a reference to a type object and pass all operations off to the type. Because such a wrapper adds a class interface on top of the type, though, it allows the underlying type to be subclassed and extended as though the type was a class. This is illustrated in Example 19-17.

Example 19-17. PP2E\Integrate\Extend\Stacks\oopstack.py

```
import stacktype                        # get the C type/module
class Stack:
    def __init__(self, start=None):     # make/wrap a C type-instance
        self._base = start or stacktype.Stack()  # deleted when class-instance is
    def __getattr__(self, name):
        return getattr(self._base, name)          # methods/members: type-instance
    def __cmp__(self, other):
        return cmp(self._base, other)
    def __repr__(self):                 # 'print' is not really repr
        print self._base,; return ''
    def __add__(self, other):           # operators: special methods
        return Stack(self._base + other._base)    # operators are not attributes
    def __mul__(self, n):
        return Stack(self._base * n)    # wrap result in a new Stack
    def __getitem__(self, i):
        return self._base[i]            # 'item': index, in, for
    def __len__(self):
        return len(self._base)
```

This wrapper class can be used the same as the C type, because it delegates all operations to the type instance stored away in the class instance's `self._base`:

```
[mark@toy ~/.../PP2E/Integrate/Extend/Stacks]$ python
>>> import oopstack
>>> x = oopstack.Stack()
>>> y = oopstack.Stack()
>>> x.push('class')
>>> for c in "SPAM": y.push(c)
...
>>> x
[Stack:
0: 'class'
]

>>> y[2]
'A'
>>> z = x + y
>>> for s in z: print s,
...
class S P A M

>>> z.__methods__, z.__members__, z.pop()
(['empty', 'pop', 'push', 'top'], ['len'], 'M')
>>> type(z), type(z._base)
(<type 'instance'>, <type 'stack'>)
```

The point of coding such a wrapper is to better support extensions in Python. Subclasses really subclass the wrapper class, but because the wrapper is just a thin interface to the type, it's like subclassing the type itself, as in Example 19-18.

Example 19-18. PP2E\Integrate\Extend\Stacks\substack.py

```
from oopstack import Stack              # get the 'stub' class (C-type wrapper)

class Substack(Stack):
    def __init__(self, start=[]):       # extend the 'new' operation
        Stack.__init__(self)            # initialize stack from any sequence
        for str in start:               # start can be another stack too
            self.push(str)
    def morestuff(self):                # add a new method
        print 'more stack stuff'
    def __getitem__(self, i):           # extend 'item' to trace accesses
        print 'accessing cell', i
        return Stack.__getitem__(self, i)
```

This subclass extends the type (wrapper) to support an initial value at construction time, prints trace messages when indexed, and introduces a brand new morestuff method. This subclass is limited (e.g., the result of a + is a Stack, not a Substack), but proves the point—wrappers let you apply inheritance and composition techniques we've met in this book to new types coded in C:

```
>>> import substack
>>> a = substack.Substack(x + y)
>>> a
[Stack:
4: 'M'
3: 'A'
2: 'P'
1: 'S'
0: 'class'
]

>>> a[3]
accessing cell 3
'A'
>>> a.morestuff()
more stack stuff
>>> b = substack.Substack("C" + "++")
>>> b.pop(), b.pop()
('+', '+')
>>> c = b + substack.Substack(['-', '-'])
>>> for s in c: print s,
...
C - -
```

But Don't Do That Either—SWIG

You can code C types manually like this, but you don't necessarily have to. Because SWIG knows how to generate glue code for C++ classes, you can instead *automatically* generate all the C extension and wrapper class code required to integrate such a stack object, simply by running SWIG over an appropriate class declaration. The next section shows how.

Wrapping C++ Classes with SWIG

One of the neater tricks SWIG can perform is class wrapper generation—given a C++ class declaration and special command-line settings, SWIG generates:

- A C++ coded Python extension module with accessor functions that interface with the C++ class's methods and members

- A Python coded wrapper class (called a "shadow" class in SWIG-speak) that interfaces with the C++ class accessor functions module

As before, simply run SWIG in your makefile to scan the C++ class declaration and compile its outputs. The end result is that by importing the shadow class in your Python scripts, you can utilize C++ classes as though they were really coded in Python. Not only can Python programs make and use instances of the C++ class, they can also customize it by subclassing the generated shadow class.

A Little C++ Class (But Not Too Much)

To see how this all works, we need a C++ class. To illustrate, let's code a simple one to be used in Python scripts.* The following C++ files define a **Number** class with three methods (**add, sub, display**), a data member (**data**), and a constructor and destructor. Example 19-19 shows the header file.

Example 19-19. PP2E\Integrate\Extend\Swig\Shadow\number.h

```
class Number
{
public:
    Number(int start);
    ~Number();
    void add(int value);
    void sub(int value);
    void display();
    int data;
};
```

And Example 19-20 is the C++ class's implementation file; each method prints a message when called to trace class operations.

---

* For a more direct comparison, you could translate the stack type in Example 19-15 to a C++ class too, but that yields much more C++ code than I care to show in this Python book. Moreover, such a translation would sacrifice the type's operator overloading features (SWIG does not currently map C++ operator overloads).

Example 19-20. PP2E\Integrate\Extend\Swig\Shadow\number.cxx

```cpp
#include "number.h"
#include "iostream.h"
// #include "stdio.h"

Number::Number(int start) {
   data = start;
   cout << "Number: " << data << endl;      // cout and printf both work
   // printf("Number: %d\n", data);          // python print goes to stdout
}

Number::~Number() {
   cout << "~Number: " << data << endl;
}

void Number::add(int value) {
   data += value;
   cout << "add " << value << endl;
}

void Number::sub(int value) {
   data -= value;
   cout << "sub " << value << endl;
}

void Number::display() {
   cout << "Number = " << data << endl;
}
```

Just so that you can compare languages, here is how this class is used in a C++ program; Example 19-21 makes a **Number** object, call its methods, and fetches and sets its data attribute directly (C++ distinguishes between "members" and "methods," while they're usually both called "attributes" in Python).

Example 19-21. PP2E\Integrate\Extend\Swig\Shadow\main.cxx

```cpp
#include "iostream.h"
#include "number.h"

main()
{
    Number *num;
    num = new Number(1);            // make a C++ class instance
    num->add(4);                    // call its methods
    num->display();
    num->sub(2);
    num->display();

    num->data = 99;                 // set C++ data member
    cout << num->data << endl;      // fetch C++ data member
    num->display();
    delete num;
}
```

You can use the g++ command-line C++ compiler program to compile and run this code on Linux. If you don't run Linux, you'll have to extrapolate (there are far too many C++ compiler differences to list here).

```
[mark@toy ~/.../PP2E/Integrate/Extend/Swig/Shadow]$ g++ main.cxx number.cxx
[mark@toy ~/.../PP2E/Integrate/Extend/Swig/Shadow]$ a.out
Number: 1
add 4
Number = 5
sub 2
Number = 3
99
Number = 99
~Number: 99
```

Wrapping the C++ Class with SWIG

Lets get back to Python. To use the C++ Number class in Python scripts, you need to code or generate a glue logic layer between the two languages, as in prior examples. To generate that layer automatically, just write a SWIG input file like the one shown in Example 19-22.

Example 19-22. PP2E\Integrate\Extend\Swig\Shadow\number.i

```
/********************************************************
 * Swig module description file for wrapping a C++ class.
 * Generate by saying "swig -python -shadow number.i".
 * The C module is generated in file number_wrap.c; here,
 * module 'number' refers to the number.py shadow class.
 ********************************************************/

%module number

%{
#include "number.h"
%}

%include number.h
```

This interface file simply directs SWIG to read the C++ class's type signature information from the included *number.h* header file. This time, SWIG uses the class declaration to generate three files, and two different Python modules:

- *number_wrap.doc*, a simple wrapper function description file
- *number_wrap.c*, a C++ extension module with class accessor functions
- *number.py*, a Python shadow class module that wraps accessor functions

The Linux makefile shown in Example 19-23 combines the generated C++ wrapper code module with the C++ class implementation file to create a *numberc.so*,

the dynamically loaded extension module that must be in a directory on your
Python module search path when imported from a Python script.

Example 19-23. PP2E\Integrate\Extend\Swig\Shadow\makefile.number-swig

```
###########################################################################
# Use SWIG to integrate the number.h C++ class for use in Python programs.
# Note: name "numberc.so" matters, because shadow class imports numberc.
###########################################################################

# unless you've run make install
SWIG = ../myswig
PY   = $(MYPY)


all: numberc.so number.py

# wrapper + real class
numberc.so: number_wrap.o number.o
    g++ -shared number_wrap.o number.o -o numberc.so

# generated class wrapper module
number_wrap.o: number_wrap.c number.h
    g++ number_wrap.c -c -g -I$(PY)/Include -I$(PY)

number_wrap.c: number.i
    $(SWIG) -c++ -python -shadow number.i

number.py: number.i
    $(SWIG) -c++ -python -shadow number.i

# wrapped C++ class code
number.o: number.cxx number.h
    g++ -c -g number.cxx

cxxtest:
    g++ main.cxx number.cxx

clean:
    rm -f *.pyc *.o *.so core a.out
force:
    rm -f *.pyc *.o *.so core a.out number.py number_wrap.c number_wrap.doc
```

As usual, run this makefile to generate and compile the necessary glue code into
an extension module that can be imported by Python programs:

```
[mark@toy ~/....../Integrate/Extend/Swig/Shadow]$ make -f makefile.number-swig
Generating wrappers for Python
g++ number_wrap.c -c -g -I/...
g++ -c -g number.cxx
g++ -shared number_wrap.o number.o -o numberc.so
```

To help demystify SWIG's magic somewhat, here is a portion of the generated C++
number_wrap.c accessor functions module. You can find the full source file on

the book's CD (or simply generate it yourself). Notice that this file defines a simple C extension module of functions that generally expect a C++ object pointer to be passed in (i.e., a "this" pointer in C++ lingo). This is a slightly different structure than Example 19-17, which wrapped a C *type* with a Python class instead, but the net effect is similar:

```
..._wrap function implementations that run C++ operation syntax...

#define new_Number(_swigarg0) (new Number(_swigarg0))
static PyObject *_wrap_new_Number(PyObject *self, PyObject *args) {
    ...body deleted...
}

#define Number_add(_swigobj,_swigarg0)  (_swigobj->add(_swigarg0))
static PyObject *_wrap_Number_add(PyObject *self, PyObject *args) {
    ...body deleted...
}

#define Number_data_get(_swigobj) ((int ) _swigobj->data)
static PyObject *_wrap_Number_data_get(PyObject *self, PyObject *args) {
    ...body deleted...
}

static PyMethodDef numbercMethods[] = {
     { "Number_data_get", _wrap_Number_data_get, 1 },
     { "Number_data_set", _wrap_Number_data_set, 1 },
     { "Number_display", _wrap_Number_display, 1 },
     { "Number_sub", _wrap_Number_sub, 1 },
     { "Number_add", _wrap_Number_add, 1 },
     { "delete_Number", _wrap_delete_Number, 1 },
     { "new_Number", _wrap_new_Number, 1 },
     { NULL, NULL }
};

SWIGEXPORT(void,initnumberc)() {
     PyObject *m, *d;
     SWIG_globals = SWIG_newvarlink();
     m = Py_InitModule("numberc", numbercMethods);
     d = PyModule_GetDict(m);
```

On top of the accessor functions module, SWIG generates *number.py*, the following shadow class that Python scripts import as the actual interface to the class. This code is a bit more complicated than the wrapper class we saw in the prior section, because it manages object ownership and therefore handles new and existing objects differently. The important thing to notice is that it is a straight Python class that saves the C++ "this" pointer of the associated C++ object, and passes control to accessor functions in the generated C++ extension module:

```
import numberc
class NumberPtr :
    def __init__(self,this):
```

```
              self.this = this
              self.thisown = 0
         def __del__(self):
              if self.thisown == 1 :
                   numberc.delete_Number(self.this)
         def add(self,arg0):
              val = numberc.Number_add(self.this,arg0)
              return val
         def sub(self,arg0):
              val = numberc.Number_sub(self.this,arg0)
              return val
         def display(self):
              val = numberc.Number_display(self.this)
              return val
         def __setattr__(self,name,value):
              if name == "data" :
                   numberc.Number_data_set(self.this,value)
                   return
              self.__dict__[name] = value
         def __getattr__(self,name):
              if name == "data" :
                   return numberc.Number_data_get(self.this)
              raise AttributeError,name
         def __repr__(self):
              return "<C Number instance>"
    class Number(NumberPtr):
         def __init__(self,arg0) :
              self.this = numberc.new_Number(arg0)
              self.thisown = 1
```

A subtle thing: the generated C++ module file is named *number_wrap.c,* but the
Python module name it gives in its initialization function is numberc, which is the
name also imported by the shadow class. The import works because the combination of the glue code module and the C++ library file is linked into a file *numberc.
so* such that the imported module file and initialization function names match.
When using shadow classes and dynamic binding, the compiled object file's name
must generally be the module name given in the *.i* file with an appended "c". In
general, given an input file named *interface.i*:

```
%module interface
...declarations...
```

SWIG generates glue code file *interface_wrap.c,* which you should somehow compile into an *interfacec.so* file to be dynamically loaded on import:

```
swig -python -shadow interface.i
g++ -c interface.c interface_wrap.c ...more...
g++ -shared interface.o interface_wrap.o -o interfacec.so
```

The module name interface is reserved for the generated shadow class module,
interface.py. Keep in mind that this implementation structure is subject to change

at the whims of SWIG's creator, but the interface it yields should remain the
same—a Python class that shadows the C++ class, attribute for attribute.*

Using the C++ Class in Python

Once the glue code is generated and compiled, Python scripts can access the C++
class as though it were coded in Python. Example 19-24 repeats the *main.cxx* file's
class tests; here, though, the C++ class is being utilized from the Python programming language.

Example 19-24. PP2E\Integrate\Extend\Swig\Shadow\main.py

```
from number import Number      # use C++ class in Python (shadow class)
                              # runs same tests as main.cxx C++ file
num = Number(1)               # make a C++ class object in Python
num.add(4)                    # call its methods from Python
num.display()                 # num saves the C++ 'this' pointer
num.sub(2)
num.display()


num.data = 99                 # set C++ data member, generated __setattr__
print num.data                # get C++ data member, generated __getattr__
num.display()
del num                       # runs C++ destructor automatically
```

Because the C++ class and its wrappers are automatically loaded when imported
by the **number** shadow class, you run this script like any other:

```
[mark@toy ~/....../Integrate/Extend/Swig/Shadow]$ python main.py
Number: 1
add 4
Number = 5
sub 2
Number = 3
99
Number = 99
~Number: 99
```

This output is mostly coming from the C++ class's methods, and is the same as the
main.cxx results shown in Example 19-21. If you really want to use the generated
accessor functions module, you can, as shown in Example 19-25.

---

* While I wrote this, Guido suggested a few times that a future Python release may merge the ideas of
  Python classes and C types more closely, and may even be rewritten in C++ to ease C++ integration in
  general. If and when that happens, it's possible that SWIG may use C types to wrap C++ classes, instead
  of the current accessor functions + Python class approach. Or not. Watch *http://www.swig.org* for more
  recent developments beyond the details presented in this book.

Example 19-25. PP2E\Integrate\Extend\Swig\Shadow\main_low.py

```
from numberc import *              # same test as main.cxx
                                   # use low-level C accessor function interface
num = new_Number(1)
Number_add(num, 4)                 # pass C++ 'this' pointer explicitly
Number_display(num)                # use accessor functions in the C module
Number_sub(num, 2)
Number_display(num)

Number_data_set(num, 99)
print Number_data_get(num)
Number_display(num)
delete_Number(num)
```

This script generates the same output as *main.py*, but there is no obvious advantage to moving from the shadow class to functions here. By using the shadow class, you get both an object-based interface to C++ and a customizable Python object. For instance, the Python module shown in Example 19-26 extends the C++ class, adding an extra print statement to the C++ **add** method, and defining a brand new **mul** method. Because the shadow class is pure Python, this works naturally.

Example 19-26. PP2E\Integrate\Extend\Swig\Shadow\main_subclass.py

```
from number import Number         # sublass C++ class in Python (shadow class)

class MyNumber(Number):
    def add(self, other):
        print 'in Python add...'
        Number.add(self, other)
    def mul(self, other):
        print 'in Python mul...'
        self.data = self.data * other

num = MyNumber(1)                 # same test as main.cxx
num.add(4)                        # using Python subclass of shadow class
num.display()                     # add() is specialized in Python
num.sub(2)
num.display()

num.data = 99
print num.data
num.display()

num.mul(2)                        # mul() is implemented in Python
num.display()
del num
```

Now we get extra messages out of **add** calls, and **mul** changes the C++ class's data member automatically when it assigns **self.data**:

```
[mark@toy ~/....../Integrate/Extend/Swig/Shadow]$ python main_subclass.py
Number: 1
```

```
in Python add...
add 4
Number = 5
sub 2
Number = 3
99
Number = 99
in Python mul...
Number = 198
~Number: 198
```

In other words, SWIG makes it easy to use C++ class libraries as base classes in your Python scripts. As usual, you can import the C++ class interactively to experiment with it some more:

```
[mark@toy ~/....../Integrate/Extend/Swig/Shadow]$ python
>>> import numberc
>>> numberc.__file__              # the C++ class plus generated glue module
'./numberc.so'
>>> import number                 # the generated Python shadow class module
>>> number.__file__
'number.pyc'

>>> x = number.Number(2)          # make a C++ class instance in Python
Number: 2
>>> y = number.Number(4)          # make another C++ object
Number: 4
>>> x, y
(<C Number instance>, <C Number instance>)

>>> x.display()                   # call C++ method (like C++ x->display())
Number = 2
>>> x.add(y.data)                 # fetch C++ data member, call C++ method
add 4
>>> x.display()
Number = 6

>>> y.data = x.data + y.data + 32      # set C++ data member
>>> y.display()                        # y records the C++ this pointer
Number = 42
```

So what's the catch? Nothing much, really, but if you start using SWIG in earnest, the biggest downside is that SWIG cannot handle every feature of C++ today. If your classes use advanced C++ tools such as operator overloading and templates, you may need to hand-code simplified class type declarations for SWIG, instead of running SWIG over the original class header files.

Also, SWIG's current string-based pointer representation sidesteps conversion and type-safety issues and works well in most cases, but it has sometimes been accused of creating performance or interface complications when wrapping existing libraries. SWIG development is ongoing, so you should consult the SWIG manuals and web site for more details on these and other topics.

In return for any such trade-offs, though, SWIG can completely obviate the need to code glue layers to access C and C++ libraries from Python scripts. If you have ever coded such layers by hand in the past, you already know that this is a *very* big win.

If you do go the manual route, though, consult Python's standard extension manuals for more details on both API calls used in this and the next chapter, as well as additional extension tools we don't have space to cover in this text. C extensions can run the gamut from short SWIG input files to code that is staunchly wedded to the internals of the Python interpreter; as a rule of thumb, the former survives the ravages of time much better than the latter.

Mixing Python and C++

Python's standard implementation is currently coded in C, so all the normal rules about mixing C programs with C++ programs apply to the Python interpreter. In fact, there is nothing special about Python in this context, but here are a few pointers.

When embedding Python in a C++ program, there are no special rules to follow. Simply link in the Python library and call its functions from C++. Python's header files automatically wrap themselves in **extern "C" {...}** declarations to suppress C++ name-mangling. Hence, the Python library looks like any other C component to C++; there is no need to recompile Python itself with a C++ compiler.

When extending Python with C++ components, Python header files are still C++-friendly, so Python API calls in C++ extensions work like any other C++ to C call. But be sure to wrap the parts of your extension code made visible to Python with **extern "C"** declarations so that they may be called by Python's C code. For example, to wrap a C++ class, SWIG generates a C++ extension module that declares its initialization function this way, though the rest of the module is pure C++.

The only other potential complication involves C++ static or global object constructor methods when extending. If Python (a C program) is at the top level of a system, such C++ constructors may not be run when the system starts up. This behavior may vary per compiler, but if your C++ objects are not initialized on startup, make sure that your main program is linked by your C++ compiler, not C.

If you are interested in Python/C++ integration in general, be sure to consult the C++ special interest group (SIG) pages at *http://www.python.org* for information about work in this domain. The CXX system, for instance, makes it easier to extend Python with C++.

20

Embedding Python

"Add Python. Mix Well. Repeat."

In the last chapter, we explored half of the Python/C integration picture—calling C services from Python. This mode lets programmers speed up operations by moving them to C, and utilize external libraries by wrapping them in C extension modules and types. But the inverse can be just as useful—calling Python from C. By delegating selected components of an application to embedded Python code, we can open them up to onsite changes without having to ship a system's code.

This chapter tells this other half of the Python/C integration tale. It introduces the Python C interfaces that make it possible for programs written in C-compatible languages to run Python program code. In this mode, Python acts as an embedded control language (what some call a "macro" language). Although embedding is mostly presented in isolation here, keep in mind that Python's integration support is best viewed as a whole. A system's structure usually determines an appropriate integration approach: C extensions, embedded code calls, or both. To wrap up, this chapter concludes by discussing a handful of larger integration platforms, such as COM and JPython, that present broader component integration possibilities.

C Embedding API Overview

The first thing you should know about Python's embedded-call API is that it is less structured than the extension interfaces. Embedding Python in C may require a bit more creativity on your part than extending; you must pick tools from a general collection of calls to implement the Python integration, rather than coding to a boilerplate structure. The upside of this loose structure is that programs can combine embedding calls and strategies to build up arbitrary integration architectures.

The lack of a more rigid model for embedding is largely the result of a less clear-cut goal. When *extending* Python, there is a distinct separation for Python and C responsibilities and a clear structure for the integration. C modules and types are required to fit the Python module/type model by conforming to standard extension structures. This makes the integration seamless for Python clients: C extensions look like Python objects and handle most of the work.

But when Python is *embedded*, the structure isn't as obvious; because C is the enclosing level, there is no clear way to know what model the embedded Python code should fit. C may want to run objects fetched from modules, strings fetched from files or parsed out of documents, and so on. Instead of deciding what C can and cannot do, Python provides a collection of general embedding interface tools, which you use and structure according to your embedding goals.

Most of these tools correspond to tools available to Python programs. Table 20-1 lists some of the more common API calls used for embedding, and their Python equivalents. In general, if you can figure out how to accomplish your embedding goals in pure Python code, you can probably find C API tools that achieve the same results.

Table 20-1. Common API Functions

C API Call	Python Equivalent
PyImport_ImportModule	import module, __import__
PyImport_ReloadModule	reload(module)
PyImport_GetModuleDict	sys.modules
PyModule_GetDict	module.__dict__
PyDict_GetItemString	dict[key]
PyDict_SetItemString	dict[key]=val
PyDict_New	dict = {}
PyObject_GetAttrString	getattr(obj, attr)
PyObject_SetAttrString	setattr(obj, attr, val)
PyEval_CallObject	apply(funcobj, argstuple)
PyRun_String	eval(exprstr), exec stmtstr
PyRun_File	execfile(filename)

Because embedding relies on API call selection, though, becoming familiar with the Python C API is fundamental to the embedding task. This chapter presents a handful of representative embedding examples and discusses common API calls, but does not provide a comprehensive list of all tools in the API. Once you've mastered the examples here, you'll probably need to consult Python's integration manuals for more details on available calls in this domain. The most recent Python release comes with two standard manuals for C/C++ integration programmers: *Extending and Embedding*, an integration tutorial; and *Python/C API*, the Python runtime library reference.

You can find these manuals on the book's CD, or fetch their most recent releases at *http://www.python.org*. Beyond this chapter, these manuals are likely to be your best resource for up-to-date and complete Python API tool information.

What Is Embedded Code?

Before we jump into details, let's get a handle on some of the core ideas in the embedding domain. When this book speaks of "embedded" Python code, it simply means any Python program structure that can be executed from C. Generally speaking, embedded Python code can take a variety of forms:

Code strings
> C programs can represent Python programs as character strings, and run them as either expressions or statements (like `eval` and `exec`).

Callable objects
> C programs can load or reference Python callable objects such as functions, methods, and classes, and call them with argument lists (like `apply`).

Code files
> C programs can execute entire Python program files by importing modules and running script files though the API or general system calls (e.g., `popen`).

The Python binary library is usually what is physically embedded in the C program; the actual Python code run from C can come from a wide variety of sources:

- *Code strings* might be loaded from files, fetched from persistent databases and shelves, parsed out of HTML or XML files, read over sockets, built or hard-coded in a C program, passed to C extension functions from Python registration code, and so on.

- *Callable objects* might be fetched from Python modules, returned from other Python API calls, passed to C extension functions from Python registration code, and so on.

- *Code files* simply exist as files, modules, and executable scripts.

Registration is a technique commonly used in callback scenarios that we will explore in more detail later in this chapter. But especially for strings of code, there are as many possible sources as there are for C character strings. For example, C programs can construct arbitrary Python code dynamically by building and running strings.

Finally, once you have some Python code to run, you need a way to communicate with it: the Python code may need to use inputs passed in from the C layer, and may want to generate outputs to communicate results back to C. In fact, embedding generally becomes interesting only when the embedded code has access to the enclosing C layer. Usually, the form of the embedded code suggests its communication mediums:

- *Code strings* that are Python expressions return an *expression result* as their output. Both inputs and outputs can take the form of *global variables* in the namespace in which a code string is run—C may set variables to serve as input, run Python code, and fetch variables as the code's result. Inputs and outputs can also be passed with exported C *extension calls*—Python code may use C modules or types to get or set variables in the enclosing C layer. Communications schemes are often combined; for instance, C may preassign global names to objects that export state and interface calls to the embedded Python code.[*]

- *Callable objects* may accept inputs as function *arguments* and produce results as function *return values*. Passed-in mutable arguments (e.g., lists, dictionaries, class instances) can be used as both input and output for the embedded code—changes made in Python are retained in objects held by C. Objects can also make use of the global variable and C extension interface techniques described for strings to communicate with C.

- *Code files* can communicate with most of the same techniques as code strings; when run as separate programs, files can also employ IPC techniques.

Naturally, all embedded code forms can also communicate with C using general system-level tools: files, sockets, pipes, and so on. These techniques are generally less direct and slower, though.

Basic Embedding Techniques

As you can probably tell from the preceding overview, there is much flexibility in the embedding domain. To illustrate common embedding techniques in action, this section presents a handful of short C programs that run Python code in one form or another. Most of these examples make use of the simple Python module file shown in Example 20-1.

---

[*] If you want an example, flip back to the discussion of Active Scripting in Chapter 15, *Advanced Internet Topics*. This system fetches Python code embedded in an HTML web page file, assigns global variables in a namespace to objects that give access to the web browser's environment, and runs the Python code in the namespace where the objects were assigned. I recently worked on a project where we did something similar, but Python code was embedded in XML documents, and objects preassigned to globals in the code's namespace represented widgets in a GUI.

Example 20-1. PP2E\Integrate\Embed\Basics\usermod.py

```
#########################################################
# C runs Python code in this module in embedded mode.
# Such a file can be changed without changing the C layer.
# There is just standard Python code (C does conversions).
# You can also run code in standard modules like string.
#########################################################

import string

message = 'The meaning of life...'

def transform(input):
    input = string.replace(input, 'life', 'Python')
    return string.upper(input)
```

If you know any Python at all, you know that this file defines a string and a function; the function returns whatever it is passed with string substitution and uppercase conversions applied. It's easy to use from Python:

```
[mark@toy ~/.../PP2E/Integrate/Embed/Basics]$ python
>>> import usermod                        # import a module
>>> usermod.message                       # fetch a string
'The meaning of life...'
>>> usermod.transform(usermod.message)    # call a function
'THE MEANING OF PYTHON...'
```

With proper API use, it's not much more difficult to use this module the same way in C.

Running Simple Code Strings

Perhaps the simplest way to run Python code from C is by calling the `PyRun_SimpleString` API function. With it, C programs can execute Python programs represented as C character string arrays. This call is also very limited: all code runs in the same namespace (module `__main__`), the code strings must be Python statements (not expressions), and there is no easy way to communicate inputs or outputs with the Python code run. Still, it's a simple place to start; the C program in Example 20-2 runs Python code to accomplish the same results as the interactive session listed in the prior section.

Example 20-2. PP2E\Integrate\Embed\Basics\embed-simple.c

```
/*****************************************************
 * simple code strings: C acts like the interactive
 * prompt, code runs in __main__, no output sent to C;
 *****************************************************/

#include <Python.h>      /* standard API def */
```

Example 20-2. PP2E\Integrate\Embed\Basics\embed-simple.c (continued)

```
main() {
    printf("embed-simple\n");
    Py_Initialize();
    PyRun_SimpleString("import usermod");              /* load .py file */
    PyRun_SimpleString("print usermod.message");       /* on python path */
    PyRun_SimpleString("x = usermod.message");         /* compile and run */
    PyRun_SimpleString("print usermod.transform(x)");
}
```

The first thing you should notice here is that when Python is embedded, C programs always call `Py_Initialize` to initialize linked-in Python libraries before using any other API functions. The rest of this code is straightforward—C submits hardcoded strings to Python that are roughly what we typed interactively. Internally, `PyRun_SimpleString` invokes the Python compiler and interpreter to run the strings sent from C; as usual, the Python compiler is always available in systems that contain Python.

Compiling and running

To build a standalone executable from this C source file, you need to link its compiled form with the Python library file. In this chapter, "library" usually means the binary library file (e.g., an *.a* file on Unix) that is generated when Python is compiled, not the Python source code library.

Today, everything about Python you need in C is compiled into a single *.a* library file when the interpreter is built. The program's **main** function comes from your C code, and depending on the extensions installed in your Python, you may also need to link any external libraries referenced by the Python library.

Assuming no extra extension libraries are needed, Example 20-3 is a minimal Linux makefile for building the C program in Example 20-2. Again, makefile details vary per platform, but see Python manuals for hints. This makefile uses the Python include-files path to find *Python.h* in the compile step, and adds the Python library file to the final link step to make API calls available to the C program.

Example 20-3. PP2E\Integrate\Embed\Basics\makefile.1

```
# a linux makefile that builds a C executable that embeds
# Python, assuming no external module libs must be linked in;
# uses Python header files, links in the Python lib file;
# both may be in other dirs (e.g., /usr) in your install;
# set MYPY to your Python install tree, change lib version;

PY    = $(MYPY)
PYLIB = $(PY)/libpython1.5.a
PYINC = -I$(PY)/Include -I$(PY)

embed-simple: embed-simple.o
```

Example 20-3. PP2E\Integrate\Embed\Basics\makefile.1 (continued)

```
    gcc embed-simple.o $(PYLIB) -g -export-dynamic -lm -ldl -o embed-simple

embed-simple.o: embed-simple.c
    gcc embed-simple.c -c -g $(PYINC)
```

Things may not be quite this simple in practice, though, at least not without some coaxing. The makefile in Example 20-4 is the one I actually used to build all of this section's C programs on Linux.

Example 20-4. PP2E\Integrate\Embed\Basics\makefile.basics

```
# build all 5 basic embedding examples
# with external module libs linked in;
# source setup-pp-embed.csh if needed

PY    = $(MYPY)
PYLIB = $(PY)/libpython1.5.a
PYINC = -I$(PY)/Include -I$(PY)

LIBS = -L/usr/lib \
       -L/usr/X11R6/lib \
       -lgdbm -ltk8.0 -ltcl8.0 -lX11 -lm -ldl

BASICS = embed-simple embed-string embed-object embed-dict embed-bytecode

all: $(BASICS)

embed%: embed%.o
    gcc embed$*.o $(PYLIB) $(LIBS) -g -export-dynamic -o embed$*

embed%.o: embed%.c
    gcc embed$*.c -c -g $(PYINC)

clean:
    rm -f *.o *.pyc $(BASICS) core
```

This version links in Tkinter libraries because the Python library file it uses was built with Tkinter enabled. You may have to link in arbitrarily many more externals for your Python library, and frankly, chasing down all the linker dependencies can be tedious. Required libraries may vary per platform and Python install, so there isn't a lot of advice I can offer to make this process simple (this is C, after all).

But if you're going to do much embedding work, you might want to build Python on your machine from its source with all unnecessary extensions *disabled* in the `Modules/Setup` file. This produces a Python library with minimal external dependencies, which links much more easily. For example, if your embedded code won't be building GUIs, Tkinter can simply be removed from the library; see the `Setup` file for details. You can also find a list of external libraries referenced from your Python in the generated makefiles located in the Python source tree. In any event, the good news is that you only need to resolve linker dependencies once.

Once you've gotten the makefile to work, run it to build the C program with python libraries linked in. Run the resulting C program as usual:[*]

```
[mark@toy ~/.../PP2E/Integrate/Embed/Basics]$ embed-simple
embed-simple
The meaning of life...
THE MEANING OF PYTHON...
```

Most of this output is produced by Python `print` statements sent from C to the linked-in Python library. It's as if C has become an interactive Python programmer.

However, strings of Python code run by C probably would not be hardcoded in a C program file like this. They might instead be loaded from a text file, extracted from HTML or XML files, fetched from a persistent database or socket, and so on. With such external sources, the Python code strings that are run from C could be changed arbitrarily without having to recompile the C program that runs them. They may even be changed onsite, and by end users of a system. To make the most of code strings, though, we need to move on to more flexible API tools.

Running Code Strings with Results and Namespaces

Example 20-5 uses the following API calls to run code strings that return expression results back to C:

- `Py_Initialize` initializes linked-in Python libraries as before
- `PyImport_ImportModule` imports a Python module, returns pointer to it
- `PyModule_GetDict` fetches a module's attribute dictionary object
- `PyRun_String` runs a string of code in explicit namespaces
- `PyObject_SetAttrString` assigns an object attribute by name string
- `PyArg_Parse` converts a Python return value object to C form

The import calls are used to fetch the namespace of the `usermod` module listed in Example 20-1 earlier, so that code strings can be run there directly (and will have

---

[*] My build environment is a little custom (really, odd), so I first need to `source $PP2E/Config/setup-pp-embed.csh` to set up PYTHONPATH to point to the source library directory of a custom Python build on my machine. In Python 1.5.2., at least, Python may have trouble locating standard library directories when it is embedded, especially if there are multiple Python installs on the same machine (e.g., the interpreter and library versions may not match). This probably won't be an issue in your build environment, but see the sourced file's contents for more details if you get startup errors when you try to run a C program that embeds Python. You may need to customize your login scripts or source such a setup configuration file before running the embedding examples, but only if your Python lives in dark places.

access to names defined in that module without qualifications). `Py_Import_ImportModule` is like a Python `import` statement, but the imported module object is returned to C, not assigned to a Python variable name. Because of that, it's probably more similar to the Python `__import__` built-in function we used in Example 7-32.

The `PyRun_String` call is the one that actually runs code here, though. It takes a code string, a parser mode flag, and dictionary object pointers to serve as the global and local namespaces for running the code string. The mode flag can be `Py_eval_input` to run an expression, or `Py_file_input` to run a statement; when running an expression, the result of evaluating the expression is returned from this call (it comes back as a `PyObject*` object pointer). The two namespace dictionary pointer arguments allow you to distinguish global and local scopes, but they are typically passed the same dictionary such that code runs in a single namespace.*

Example 20-5. PP2E\Integrate\Embed\Basics\embed-string.c

```
/* code-strings with results and namespaces */

#include <Python.h>

main() {
    char *cstr;
    PyObject *pstr, *pmod, *pdict;
    printf("embed-string\n");
    Py_Initialize();

    /* get usermod.message */
    pmod  = PyImport_ImportModule("usermod");
    pdict = PyModule_GetDict(pmod);
    pstr  = PyRun_String("message", Py_eval_input, pdict, pdict);

    /* convert to C */
    PyArg_Parse(pstr, "s", &cstr);
    printf("%s\n", cstr);

    /* assign usermod.X */
    PyObject_SetAttrString(pmod, "X", pstr);

    /* print usermod.transform(X) */
    (void) PyRun_String("print transform(X)", Py_file_input, pdict, pdict);
    Py_DECREF(pmod);
    Py_DECREF(pstr);
}
```

---

* A related function lets you run *files* of code but is not demonstrated in this chapter: `PyObject* PyRun_File(FILE *fp, char *filename, mode, globals, locals)`. Because you can always load a file's text and run it as a single code string with `PyRun_String`, the `PyRun_File` call is not always necessary. In such multiline code strings, the `\n` character terminates lines and indentation groups blocks as usual.

When compiled and run, this file produces the same result as its predecessor:

```
[mark@toy ~/.../PP2E/Integrate/Embed/Basics]$ embed-string
embed-string
The meaning of life...
THE MEANING OF PYTHON...
```

But very different work goes into producing this output. This time, C fetches, converts, and prints the value of the Python module's `message` attribute directly by running a string expression, and assigns a global variable (`X`) within the module's namespace to serve as input for a Python `print` statement string.

Because the string execution call in this version lets you specify namespaces, you can better partition the embedded code your system runs—each grouping can have a distinct namespace to avoid overwriting other groups' variables. And because this call returns a result, you can better communicate with the embedded code—expression results are outputs, and assignments to globals in the namespace in which code runs can serve as inputs.

Before we move on, I need to explain two coding issues here. First of all, this program also decrements the *reference count* on objects passed to it from Python, using the `Py_DECREF` call introduced in Chapter 19, *Extending Python*. These calls are not strictly needed here (the objects' space is reclaimed when the programs exits anyhow), but demonstrate how embedding interfaces must manage reference counts when Python passes their ownership to C. If this was a function called from a larger system, for instance, you would generally want to decrement the count to allow Python to reclaim the objects.

Secondly, in a realistic program, you should generally test the return values of *all* the API calls in this program immediately to detect errors (e.g., import failure). Error tests are omitted in this section's example to keep the code simple, but will appear in later code listings and should be included in your programs to make them more robust.

Calling Python Objects

The last two sections dealt with running strings of code, but it's easy for C programs to deal in terms of Python objects too. Example 20-6 accomplishes the same task as Examples 20-2 and 20-5, but uses other API tools to interact with objects in the Python module directly:

- `PyImport_ImportModule` imports the module from C as before
- `PyObject_GetAttrString` fetches an object's attribute value by name
- `PyEval_CallObject` calls a Python function (or class, or method)
- `PyArg_Parse` converts Python objects to C values
- `Py_BuildValue` converts C values to Python objects

We met both the data conversion functions in the last chapter. The `PyEval_CallObject` call in this version is the key call here: it runs the imported function with a tuple of arguments, much like the Python `apply` built-in function. The Python function's return value comes back to C as a `PyObject*`, a generic Python object pointer.

Example 20-6. PP2E\Integrate\Embed\Basics\embed-object.c

```
/* fetch and call objects in modules */

#include <Python.h>

main() {
    char *cstr;
    PyObject *pstr, *pmod, *pfunc, *pargs;
    printf("embed-object\n");
    Py_Initialize();

    /* get usermod.message */
    pmod = PyImport_ImportModule("usermod");
    pstr = PyObject_GetAttrString(pmod, "message");

    /* convert string to C */
    PyArg_Parse(pstr, "s", &cstr);
    printf("%s\n", cstr);
    Py_DECREF(pstr);

    /* call usermod.transform(usermod.message) */
    pfunc = PyObject_GetAttrString(pmod, "transform");
    pargs = Py_BuildValue("(s)", cstr);
    pstr  = PyEval_CallObject(pfunc, pargs);
    PyArg_Parse(pstr, "s", &cstr);
    printf("%s\n", cstr);

    /* free owned objects */
    Py_DECREF(pmod);
    Py_DECREF(pstr);
    Py_DECREF(pfunc);         /* not really needed in main() */
    Py_DECREF(pargs);         /* since all memory goes away  */
}
```

When compiled and run, the result is the same again:

```
[mark@toy ~/.../PP2E/Integrate/Embed/Basics]$ embed-object
embed-object
The meaning of life...
THE MEANING OF PYTHON...
```

But this output is all generated by C this time—first by fetching the Python module's `message` attribute value, and then by fetching and calling the module's `transform` function object directly and printing its return value that is sent back to C. Input to the `transform` function is a function argument here, not a preset global variable. Notice that `message` is fetched as a module attribute this time, instead of by running its name as a code string; there is often more than one way to accomplish the same goals with different API calls.

Running functions in modules like this is a simple way to structure embedding; code in the module file can be changed arbitrarily without having to recompile the C program that runs it. It also provides a direct communication model: inputs and outputs to Python code can take the form of function arguments and return values.

Running Strings in Dictionaries

When we used `PyRun_String` earlier to run expressions with results, code was executed in the namespace of an existing Python module. However, sometimes it's more convenient to create a brand new namespace for running code strings that is independent of any existing module files. The C file in Example 20-7 shows how; the new namespace is created as a new Python dictionary object, and a handful of new API calls are employed in the process:

- `PyDict_New` makes a new empty dictionary object

- `PyDict_SetItemString` assigns to a dictionary's key

- `PyDict_GetItemString` fetches (indexes) a dictionary value by key

- `PyRun_String` runs a code string in namespaces, as before

- `PyEval_GetBuiltins` gets the built-in scope's module

The main trick here is the new dictionary. Inputs and outputs for the embedded code strings are mapped to this dictionary by passing it as the code's namespace dictionaries in the `PyRun_String` call. The net effect is that the C program in Example 20-7 works exactly like this Python code:

```
>>> d = {}
>>> d['Y'] = 2
>>> exec 'X = 99' in d, d
>>> exec 'X = X + Y' in d, d
>>> print d['X']
101
```

But here, each Python operation is replaced by a C API call.

Example 20-7. PP2E\Integrate\Embed\Basics\embed-dict.c

```
/**************************************************
 * make a new dictionary for code string namespace;
 **************************************************/

#include <Python.h>

main() {
    int cval;
    PyObject *pdict, *pval;
```

Example 20-7. PP2E\Integrate\Embed\Basics\embed-dict.c (continued)

```
    printf("embed-dict\n");
    Py_Initialize();

    /* make a new namespace */
    pdict = PyDict_New();
    PyDict_SetItemString(pdict, "__builtins__", PyEval_GetBuiltins());

    PyDict_SetItemString(pdict, "Y", PyInt_FromLong(2));    /* dict['Y'] = 2    */
    PyRun_String("X = 99",  Py_file_input, pdict, pdict);   /* run statements   */
    PyRun_String("X = X+Y", Py_file_input, pdict, pdict);   /* same X and Y     */
    pval = PyDict_GetItemString(pdict, "X");               /* fetch dict['X']  */

    PyArg_Parse(pval, "i", &cval);                          /* convert to C     */
    printf("%d\n", cval);                                   /* result=101       */
    Py_DECREF(pdict);
}
```

When compiled and run, this C program creates this sort of output:

```
[mark@toy ~/.../PP2E/Integrate/Embed/Basics]$ embed-dict
embed-dict
101
```

The output is different this time: it reflects the value of Python variable **X** assigned by the embedded Python code strings and fetched by C. In general, C can fetch module attributes either by calling **PyObject_GetAttrString** with the module, or by using **PyDict_GetItemString** to index the module's attribute dictionary (expression strings work too, but are less direct). Here, there is no module at all, so dictionary indexing is used to access the code's namespace in C.

Besides allowing you to partition code string namespaces independent of any Python module files on the underlying system, this scheme provides a natural communication mechanism. Values stored in the new dictionary before code is run serve as inputs, and names assigned by the embedded code can later be fetched out of the dictionary to serve as code outputs. For instance, the variable **Y** in the second string run refers to a name set to 2 by C; **X** is assigned by the Python code and fetched later by C code as the printed result.

There is one trick in this code that I need to explain. Each module namespace in Python has a link to the built-in scope's namespace, where names like **open** and **len** live. In fact, this is the link Python follows during the last step of its local/global/built-in three-scope name lookup procedure.[*] Today, embedding code is responsible for setting the **__builtins__** scope link in dictionaries that serve as namespaces. Python sets this link automatically in all other namespaces that host

---

[*] This link also plays a part in Python's restricted-execution mode, described in Chapter 15. By changing the built-in scope link to a module with limited attribute sets and customized versions of built-in calls like **open**, the **rexec** module can control machine access from code run through its interface.

code execution, and this embedding requirement may be lifted in the future (it seems a bit too magical to be required for long). For now, simply do what this example does to initialize the built-ins link, in dictionaries you create for running code in C.

Precompiling Strings to Bytecode

When you call Python function objects from C, you are actually running the already-compiled bytecode associated with the object (e.g., a function body). When running strings, Python must compile the string before running it. Because compilation is a slow process, this can be a substantial overhead if you run a code string more than once. Instead, precompile the string to a bytecode object to be run later, using the API calls illustrated in Example 20-8:[*]

- `Py_CompileString` compiles a string of code, returns a bytecode object

- `PyEval_EvalCode` runs a compiled bytecode object

The first of these takes the mode flag normally passed to `PyRun_String`, and a second string argument that is only used in error messages. The second takes two namespace dictionaries. These two API calls are used in Example 20-8 to compile and execute three strings of Python code.

Example 20-8. PP2E\Integrate\Embed\Basics\embed-bytecode.c

```
/* precompile code strings to bytecode objects */

#include <Python.h>
#include <compile.h>
#include <eval.h>

main() {
    int i;
    char *cval;
    PyObject *pcode1, *pcode2, *pcode3, *presult, *pdict;
    char *codestr1, *codestr2, *codestr3;
    printf("embed-bytecode\n");

    Py_Initialize();
    codestr1 = "import usermod\nprint usermod.message";      /* statements */
    codestr2 = "usermod.transform(usermod.message)";          /* expression */
    codestr3 = "print '%d:%d' % (X, X ** 2),";                /* use input X */
```

---

[*] Just in case you flipped ahead to this chapter early: *bytecode* is simply an intermediate representation for already compiled program code in the current standard Python implementation. It's a low-level binary format that can be quickly interpreted by the Python runtime system. Bytecode is usually generated automatically when you import a module, but there may be no notion of an import when running raw strings from C.

Example 20-8. PP2E\Integrate\Embed\Basics\embed-bytecode.c (continued)

```c
    /* make new namespace dictionary */
    pdict = PyDict_New();
    if (pdict == NULL) return -1;
    PyDict_SetItemString(pdict, "__builtins__", PyEval_GetBuiltins());

    /* precompile strings of code to bytecode objects */
    pcode1 = Py_CompileString(codestr1, "<embed>", Py_file_input);
    pcode2 = Py_CompileString(codestr2, "<embed>", Py_eval_input);
    pcode3 = Py_CompileString(codestr3, "<embed>", Py_file_input);

    /* run compiled bytecode in namespace dict */
    if (pcode1 && pcode2 && pcode3) {
        (void)    PyEval_EvalCode((PyCodeObject *)pcode1, pdict, pdict);
        presult = PyEval_EvalCode((PyCodeObject *)pcode2, pdict, pdict);
        PyArg_Parse(presult, "s", &cval);
        printf("%s\n", cval);
        Py_DECREF(presult);

        /* rerun code object repeatedly */
        for (i = 0; i <= 10; i++) {
            PyDict_SetItemString(pdict, "X", PyInt_FromLong(i));
            (void) PyEval_EvalCode((PyCodeObject *)pcode3, pdict, pdict);
        }
        printf("\n");
    }

    /* free referenced objects */
    Py_XDECREF(pdict);
    Py_XDECREF(pcode1);
    Py_XDECREF(pcode2);
    Py_XDECREF(pcode3);
}
```

This program combines a variety of technique we've already seen. The namespace in which the compiled code strings run, for instance, is a newly created dictionary (not an existing module object), and inputs for code strings are passed as preset variables in the namespace. When built and executed, the first part of the output is similar to previous examples in this section, but the last line represents running the same precompiled code string 11 times:

```
[mark@toy ~/.../PP2E/Integrate/Embed/Basics]$ embed-bytecode
embed-bytecode
The meaning of life...
THE MEANING OF PYTHON...
0:0 1:1 2:4 3:9 4:16 5:25 6:36 7:49 8:64 9:81 10:100
```

If your system executes strings multiple times, it is a major speedup to precompile to bytecode in this fashion.

Registering Callback Handler Objects

In examples thus far, C has been running and calling Python code from a standard main program flow of control. That's not always the way programs work, though; in some cases, programs are modeled on an *event-driven* architecture where code is executed only in response to some sort of event. The event might be an end user clicking a button in a GUI, the operating system delivering a signal, or simply software running an action associated with an entry in a table.

In any event (pun accidental), program code in such an architecture is typically structured as *callback handlers*—chunks of code dispatched by event-processing logic. It's easy to use embedded Python code to implement callback handlers in such a system; in fact, the event-processing layer can simply use the embedded-call API tools we saw earlier in this chapter to run Python handlers.

The only new trick in this model is how to make the C layer know what code should be run for each event. Handlers must somehow be registered to C to associate them with future events. In general, there is a wide variety of ways to achieve this code/event association; for instance, C programs can:

- Fetch and call *functions* by event name from one or more *module* files
- Fetch and run code *strings* associated with event names in a *database*
- Extract and run code associated with event *tags* in HTML or XML*
- Run Python code that calls back to C to tell it what should be run

And so on. Really, any place you can associate objects or strings with identifiers is a potential callback registration mechanism. Some of these techniques have advantages all their own. For instance, callbacks fetched from module files support dynamic reloading (as we learned in Chapter 9, *Larger GUI Examples*, `reload` works on modules and does not update objects held directly). And none of the first three schemes requires users to code special Python programs that do nothing but register handlers to be run later.

It is perhaps more common, though, to register callback handlers with the last approach: letting Python code register handlers with C by calling back to C through extensions interfaces. Although this scheme is not without trade-offs, it can provide a natural and direct model in scenarios where callbacks are associated with a large number of objects.

---

* And if C chooses to do so, it might even run embedded Python code that uses Python's standard HTML and XML processing tools to parse out the embedded code associated with an event tag. See the Python library manual for details on these parsers.

For instance, consider a GUI constructed by building a tree of widget objects in Python scripts. If each widget object in the tree can have an associated event handler, it may be easier to register handlers by simply calling methods of widgets in the tree. Associating handlers with widget objects in a separate structure such as a module file or HTML file requires extra cross-reference work to keep the handlers in sync with the tree.*

The following C and Python files demonstrate the basic coding techniques used to implement explicitly registered callback handlers. The C file in Example 20-9 implements interfaces for registering Python handlers, as well as code to run those handlers in response to events:

Event router
> The `Route_Event` function responds to an event by calling a Python function object previously passed from Python to C.

Callback registration
> The `Register_Handler` function saves a passed-in Python function object pointer in a C global variable. Python calls `Register_Handler` through a simple `cregister` C extension module created by this file.

Event trigger
> To simulate real-world events, the `Trigger_Event` function can be called from Python through the generated C module to trigger an event.

In other words, this example uses both the embedding and extending interfaces we've already met to register and invoke Python event handler code.

Example 20-9. PP2E\Integrate\Mixed\Regist\cregister.c

```c
#include <Python.h>
#include <stdlib.h>

/***********************************************/
/* 1) code to route events to Python object    */
/* note that we could run strings here instead */
/***********************************************/

static PyObject *Handler = NULL;      /* keep Python object in C */

void Route_Event(char *label, int count)
{
    char *cres;
```

---

* If you're looking for a more realistic example of Python callback handlers, see the Tkinter GUI system used extensively in this book. Tkinter uses both extending and embedding. Its *extending* interface (widget objects) is used to register Python callback handlers, which are later run with *embedding* interfaces in response to GUI events. You can study Tkinter's implementation in the Python source distribution for more details, though its Tk library interface logic makes it a somewhat challenging read.

Example 20-9. PP2E\Integrate\Mixed\Regist\cregister.c (continued)

```
    PyObject *args, *pres;

    /* call Python handler */
    args = Py_BuildValue("(si)", label, count);    /* make arg-list */
    pres = PyEval_CallObject(Handler, args);       /* apply: run a call */
    Py_DECREF(args);                               /* add error checks */

    if (pres != NULL) {
        /* use and decref handler result */
        PyArg_Parse(pres, "s", &cres);
        printf("%s\n", cres);
        Py_DECREF(pres);
    }
}


/****************************************************/
/* 2) python extension module to register handlers  */
/* python imports this module to set handler objects */
/****************************************************/

static PyObject *
Register_Handler(PyObject *self, PyObject *args)
{
    /* save Python callable object */
    Py_XDECREF(Handler);                /* called before? */
    PyArg_Parse(args, "O", &Handler);   /* one argument? */
    Py_XINCREF(Handler);                /* add a reference */
    Py_INCREF(Py_None);                 /* return 'None': success */
    return Py_None;
}

static PyObject *
Trigger_Event(PyObject *self, PyObject *args)
{
    /* let Python simulate event caught by C */
    static count = 0;
    Route_Event("spam", count++);
    Py_INCREF(Py_None);
    return Py_None;
}

static struct PyMethodDef cregister_methods[] = {
    {"setHandler",    Register_Handler},       /* name, address */
    {"triggerEvent",  Trigger_Event},
    {NULL, NULL}
};

void initcregister()                   /* this is called by Python */
{                                      /* on first "import cregister" */
    (void) Py_InitModule("cregister", cregister_methods);
}
```

Ultimately, this C file is an extension module for Python, not a standalone C program that embeds Python (though C could just as well be on top). To compile it into a dynamically loaded module file, run the makefile in Example 20-10 on Linux (and use something similar on other platforms). As we learned in the last chapter, the resulting *cregister.so* file will be loaded when first imported by a Python script if it is placed in a directory on Python's module search path (e.g., ".").

Example 20-10. PP2E\Integrate\Mixed\Regist\makefile.regist

```
#####################################################################
# Builds cregister.so, a dynamically-loaded C extension
# module (shareable), which is imported by register.py
#####################################################################

PY   = $(MYPY)
PYINC = -I$(PY)/Include -I$(PY)

CMODS = cregister.so

all: $(CMODS)

cregister.so: cregister.c
    gcc cregister.c -g $(PYINC) -fpic -shared -o cregister.so

clean:
    rm -f *.pyc $(CMODS)
```

Now that we have a C extension module set to register and dispatch Python handlers, all we need are some Python handlers. The Python module shown in Example 20-11 defines two callback handler functions and imports the C extension module to register handlers and trigger events.

Example 20-11. PP2E\Integrate\Mixed\Regist\register.py

```
#######################################################
# register for and handle event callbacks from C;
# compile C code, and run with 'python register.py'
#######################################################

#
# C calls these Python functions;
# handle an event, return a result
#

def callback1(label, count):
    return 'callback1 => %s number %i' % (label, count)

def callback2(label, count):
    return 'callback2 => ' +  label * count

#
# Python calls a C extension module
```

Example 20-11. PP2E\Integrate\Mixed\Regist\register.py (continued)

```
# to register handlers, trigger events
#

import cregister

print '\nTest1:'
cregister.setHandler(callback1)
for i in range(3):
    cregister.triggerEvent()          # simulate events caught by C layer

print '\nTest2:'
cregister.setHandler(callback2)
for i in range(3):
    cregister.triggerEvent()          # routes these events to callback2
```

That's it—the Python/C callback integration is set to go. To kick off the system, run the Python script; it registers one handler function, forces three events to be triggered, and then changes the event handler and does it again:

```
[mark@toy ~/.../PP2E/Integration/Mixed/Regist]$ python register.py

Test1:
callback1 => spam number 0
callback1 => spam number 1
callback1 => spam number 2

Test2:
callback2 => spamspamspam
callback2 => spamspamspamspam
callback2 => spamspamspamspamspam
```

This output is printed by the C event router function, but its content is the return values of the handler functions in the Python module. Actually, there is something pretty wild going on here under the hood. When Python forces an event to trigger, control flows between languages like this:

1. From Python to the C event router function

2. From the C event router function to the Python handler function

3. Back to the C event router function (where the output is printed)

4. And finally back to the Python script

That is, we jump from Python to C to Python and back again. Along the way, control passes through both extending and embedding interfaces. When the Python callback handler is running, there are two Python levels active, and one C level in the middle. Luckily, this works; Python's API is reentrant, so you don't need to be concerned about having multiple Python interpreter levels active at the same time. Each level runs different code and operates independently.

Using Python Classes in C

In the previous chapter, we saw how to use C++ classes in Python by wrapping them with SWIG. But what about going the other way—using Python classes from other languages? It turns out that this is really just a matter of applying interfaces already shown.

Recall that Python scripts generate class instance objects by *calling* class objects as though they were functions. To do it from C (or C++), you simply follow the same steps: import a class from a module (or elsewhere), build an arguments tuple, and call it to generate an instance using the same C API tools you use to call Python functions. Once you've got an instance, you can fetch attributes and methods with the same tools you use to fetch globals out of a module.

To illustrate how this works in practice, Example 20-12 defines a simple Python class in a module that we can utilize from C.

Example 20-12. PP2E\Integrate\Embed\ApiClients\module.py

```python
# call this class from C to make objects

class klass:
    def method(self, x, y):
        return "brave %s %s" % (x, y)    # run me from C
```

This is nearly as simple as it gets, but it's enough to illustrate the basics. As usual, make sure that this module is on your Python search path (e.g., in the current directory, or one listed on your PYTHONPATH setting), or else the import call to access it from C will fail, just as it would in a Python script. Now, here is how you might make use of this Python class from a Python program:

```
C:\...\PP2E\Integrate\Embed\ApiClients>python
>>> import module                          # import the file
>>> object = module.klass()                # make class instance
>>> result = object.method('sir', 'robin') # call class method
>>> print result
brave sir robin
```

This is fairly easy stuff in Python. You can do all these operations in C too, but it takes a bit more code. The C file in Example 20-13 implements these steps by arranging calls to the appropriate Python API tools.

Example 20-13. PP2E\Integrate\Embed\ApiClients\objects-low.c

```c
#include <Python.h>
#include <stdio.h>

main() {
  /* run objects with low-level calls */
  char *arg1="sir", *arg2="robin", *cstr;
```

Example 20-13. PP2E\Integrate\Embed\ApiClients\objects-low.c (continued)

```
    PyObject *pmod, *pclass, *pargs, *pinst, *pmeth, *pres;

    /* instance = module.klass() */
    Py_Initialize();
    pmod   = PyImport_ImportModule("module");              /* fetch module */
    pclass = PyObject_GetAttrString(pmod, "klass");        /* fetch module.class */
    Py_DECREF(pmod);

    pargs  = Py_BuildValue("()");
    pinst  = PyEval_CallObject(pclass, pargs);             /* call class() */
    Py_DECREF(pclass);
    Py_DECREF(pargs);

    /* result = instance.method(x,y) */
    pmeth  = PyObject_GetAttrString(pinst, "method");      /* fetch bound method */
    Py_DECREF(pinst);
    pargs  = Py_BuildValue("(ss)", arg1, arg2);            /* convert to Python */
    pres   = PyEval_CallObject(pmeth, pargs);              /* call method(x,y) */
    Py_DECREF(pmeth);
    Py_DECREF(pargs);

    PyArg_Parse(pres, "s", &cstr);                         /* convert to C */
    printf("%s\n", cstr);
    Py_DECREF(pres);
}
```

Step through this source file for more details; it's merely a matter of figuring out how you would accomplish the task in Python, and then calling equivalent C functions in the Python API. To build this source into a C executable program, run the makefile in the file's directory (it's analogous to makefiles we've already seen). After compiling, run it as you would any other C program:

```
[mark@toy ~/.../PP2E/Integrate/Embed/ApiClients]$ objects-low
brave sir robin
```

This output might seem anticlimactic, but it actually reflects the return values sent back to C by the class method in file *module.py*. C did a lot of work to get this little string: it imported the module, fetched the class, made an instance, and fetched and called the instance method, performing data conversions and reference count management every step of the way. In return for all the work, C gets to use the techniques shown in this file to reuse *any* Python class.

Of course, this example would be more complex in practice. As mentioned earlier, you generally need to check the return value of every Python API call to make sure it didn't fail. The module import call in this C code, for instance, can fail easily if the module isn't on the search path; if you don't trap the NULL pointer result, your program will almost certainly crash when it tries to use the pointer (at least eventually). Example 20-14 is a recoding of Example 20-13 with full error-checking; it's big, but it's robust.

Example 20-14. PP2E\Integrate\Embed\ApiClients\objects-err-low.c

```c
#include <Python.h>
#include <stdio.h>
#define error(msg) do { printf("%s\n", msg); exit(1); } while (1)

main() {
  /* run objects with low-level calls and full error checking */
  char *arg1="sir", *arg2="robin", *cstr;
  PyObject *pmod, *pclass, *pargs, *pinst, *pmeth, *pres;

  /* instance = module.klass() */
  Py_Initialize();
  pmod = PyImport_ImportModule("module");          /* fetch module */
  if (pmod == NULL)
      error("Can't load module");

  pclass = PyObject_GetAttrString(pmod, "klass");  /* fetch module.class */
  Py_DECREF(pmod);
  if (pclass == NULL)
      error("Can't get module.klass");

  pargs = Py_BuildValue("()");
  if (pargs == NULL) {
     Py_DECREF(pclass);
     error("Can't build arguments list");
  }
  pinst = PyEval_CallObject(pclass, pargs);         /* call class() */
  Py_DECREF(pclass);
  Py_DECREF(pargs);
  if (pinst == NULL)
      error("Error calling module.klass()");

  /* result = instance.method(x,y) */
  pmeth  = PyObject_GetAttrString(pinst, "method"); /* fetch bound method */
  Py_DECREF(pinst);
  if (pmeth == NULL)
      error("Can't fetch klass.method");

  pargs = Py_BuildValue("(ss)", arg1, arg2);       /* convert to Python */
  if (pargs == NULL) {
     Py_DECREF(pmeth);
     error("Can't build arguments list");
  }
  pres = PyEval_CallObject(pmeth, pargs);          /* call method(x,y) */
  Py_DECREF(pmeth);
  Py_DECREF(pargs);
  if (pres == NULL)
      error("Error calling klass.method");

  if (!PyArg_Parse(pres, "s", &cstr))              /* convert to C */
     error("Can't convert klass.method result");
  printf("%s\n", cstr);
  Py_DECREF(pres);
}
```

ppembed: A High-Level Embedding API

But don't do that. As you can probably tell from the last example, embedded-mode integration code can very quickly become as complicated as extending code for nontrivial use. Today, no automation solution solves the embedding problem as well as SWIG addresses extending. Because embedding does not impose the kind of structure that extension modules and types provide, it's much more of an open-ended problem; what automates one embedding strategy might be completely useless in another.

With a little up-front work, though, you can still automate common embedding tasks by wrapping up calls in a higher-level API. These APIs could handle things such as error detection, reference counts, data conversions, and so on. One such API, *ppembed*, is available on this book's CD. It merely combines existing tools in Python's standard C API to provide a set of easier-to-use calls for running Python programs from C.

Running Objects with ppembed

Example 20-15 demonstrates how to recode *objects-err-low.c* by linking ppembed's library files with your program.

Example 20-15. PP2E\Integrate\Embed\ApiClients\object-api.c

```
#include <stdio.h>
#include "ppembed.h"

main () {                                      /* with ppembed high-level api */
   int failflag;
   PyObject *pinst;
   char *arg1="sir", *arg2="robin", *cstr;

   failflag = PP_Run_Function("module", "klass", "O", &pinst, "()") ||
              PP_Run_Method(pinst, "method", "s", &cstr, "(ss)", arg1, arg2);

   printf("%s\n", (!failflag) ? cstr : "Can't call objects");
   Py_XDECREF(pinst); free(cstr);
}
```

This file uses two ppembed calls (the names that start with "PP") to make the class instance and call its method. Because ppembed handles error checks, reference counts, data conversions, and so on, there isn't much else to do here. When this program is run and linked with ppembed library code, it works like the original, but is much easier to read, write, and debug:

```
[mark@toy ~/.../PP2E/Integrate/Embed/ApiClients]$ objects-api
brave sir robin
```

Running Code Strings with ppembed

The ppembed API provides higher-level calls for most of the embedding techniques we've seen in this chapter. For example, the C program in Example 20-16 runs code strings to make the **string** module capitalize a simple text.

Example 20-16. PP2E\Integrate\Embed\ApiClients\codestring-low.c

```c
#include <Python.h>              /* standard API defs */
void error(char *msg) { printf("%s\n", msg); exit(1); }


main() {
    /* run strings with low-level calls */
    char *cstr;
    PyObject *pstr, *pmod, *pdict;              /* with error tests */
    Py_Initialize();

    /* result = string.upper('spam') + '!' */
    pmod = PyImport_ImportModule("string");     /* fetch module */
    if (pmod == NULL)                           /* for name-space */
        error("Can't import module");

    pdict = PyModule_GetDict(pmod);             /* string.__dict__ */
    Py_DECREF(pmod);
    if (pdict == NULL)
        error("Can't get module dict");

    pstr = PyRun_String("upper('spam') + '!'", Py_eval_input, pdict, pdict);
    if (pstr == NULL)
        error("Error while running string");

    /* convert result to C */
    if (!PyArg_Parse(pstr, "s", &cstr))
        error("Bad result type");
    printf("%s\n", cstr);
    Py_DECREF(pstr);            /* free exported objects, not pdict */
}
```

This C program file includes politically correct error tests after each API call. When run, it prints the result returned by running an uppercase conversion call in the namespace of the Python **string** module:

```
[mark@toy ~/.../PP2E/Integrate/Embed/ApiClients]$ codestring-low
SPAM!
```

You can implement such integrations by calling Python API functions directly, but you don't necessarily have to. With a higher-level embedding API like ppembed, the task can be noticeably simpler, as shown in Example 20-17.

Example 20-17. PP2E\Integrate\Embed\ApiClients\codestring-api.c

```c
#include "ppembed.h"
#include <stdio.h>
```

Example 20-17. PP2E\Integrate\Embed\ApiClients\codestring-api.c (continued)

```
                                            /* with ppembed high-level api */
main() {
    char *cstr;
    int err = PP_Run_Codestr(
                    PP_EXPRESSION,                          /* expr or stmt?  */
                    "upper('spam') + '!'", "string",        /* code, module   */
                    "s", &cstr);                            /* expr result    */
    printf("%s\n", (!err) ? cstr : "Can't run string");     /* and free(cstr) */
}
```

When linked with the ppembed library code, this version produces the same result as the former. Like most higher-level APIs, ppembed makes some usage mode assumptions that are not universally applicable; when they match the embedding task at hand, though, such wrapper calls can cut much clutter from programs that need to run embedded Python code.

Running Customizable Validations

Embedded Python code can do useful work as well. For instance, the C program in Example 20-18 calls ppembed functions to run a string of Python code fetched from a file that performs validation tests on inventory data. To save space, I'm not going list all the components used by this example (though you can find them on this book's CD). Still, this file shows the embedding portions relevant to this chapter: it sets variables in the Python code's namespace to serve as input, runs the Python code, and then fetches names out of the code's namespace as results.*

Example 20-18. PP2E\Integrate\Embed\Inventory\order-string.c

```
/* run embedded code-string validations */

#include <ppembed.h>
#include <stdio.h>
#include <string.h>
#include "ordersfile.h"

run_user_validation()
{                               /* python is initialized automatically */
    int i, status, nbytes;      /* caveat: should check status everywhere */
    char script[4096];          /* caveat: should malloc a big-enough block */
    char *errors, *warnings;
    FILE *file;

    file = fopen("validate1.py", "r");       /* customizable validations */
```

---

* This is more or less the kind of structure used when Python is embedded in HTML files in the Active Scripting extension, except that the globals set here (e.g., PRODUCT) become names preset to web browser objects, and the code is extracted from a web page, not fetched from a text file with a known name. See Chapter 15.

Example 20-18. PP2E\Integrate\Embed\Inventory\order-string.c (continued)

```
    nbytes = fread(script, 1, 4096, file);    /* load python file text */
    script[nbytes] = '\0';

    status = PP_Make_Dummy_Module("orders");  /* application's own namespace */
    for (i=0; i < numorders; i++) {           /* like making a new dictionary */
        printf("\n%d (%d, %d, '%s')\n",
            i, orders[i].product, orders[i].quantity, orders[i].buyer);

        PP_Set_Global("orders", "PRODUCT",  "i", orders[i].product);   /* int */
        PP_Set_Global("orders", "QUANTITY", "i", orders[i].quantity);  /* int */
        PP_Set_Global("orders", "BUYER",    "s", orders[i].buyer);     /* str */

        status = PP_Run_Codestr(PP_STATEMENT, script, "orders", "", NULL);
        if (status == -1) {
            printf("Python error during validation.\n");
            PyErr_Print();  /* show traceback */
            continue;
        }

        PP_Get_Global("orders", "ERRORS",   "s", &errors);    /* can split */
        PP_Get_Global("orders", "WARNINGS", "s", &warnings);  /* on blanks */

        printf("errors:   %s\n", strlen(errors)? errors : "none");
        printf("warnings: %s\n", strlen(warnings)? warnings : "none");
        free(errors); free(warnings);
        PP_Run_Function("inventory", "print_files", "", NULL, "()");
    }
}

main(int argc, char **argv)     /* C is on top, Python is embedded */
{                               /* but Python can use C extensions too */
    run_user_validation();      /* don't need sys.argv in embedded code */
}
```

There are a couple of things worth noticing here. First of all, in practice this program might fetch the Python code file's name or path from configurable shell variables; here, it is loaded from the current directory. Secondly, you could also code this program by using straight API calls instead of ppembed, but each of the "PP" calls here would then grow into a chunk of more complex code. As coded, you can compile and link this file with Python and ppembed library files to build a program. The Python code run by the resulting C program lives in Example 20-19; it uses preset globals and is assumed to set globals to send result strings back to C.

Example 20-19. PP2E\Integrate\Embed\Inventory\validate1.py

```
# embedded validation code, run from C
# input vars:  PRODUCT, QUANTITY, BUYER
# output vars: ERRORS, WARNINGS

import string           # all python tools are available to embedded code
import inventory        # plus C extensions, Python modules, classes,..
```

Example 20-19. PP2E\Integrate\Embed\Inventory\validate1.py (continued)

```
msgs, errs = [], []          # warning, error message lists

def validate_order():
    if PRODUCT not in inventory.skus():       # this function could be imported
        errs.append('bad-product')            # from a user-defined module too
    elif QUANTITY > inventory.stock(PRODUCT):
        errs.append('check-quantity')
    else:
        inventory.reduce(PRODUCT, QUANTITY)
        if inventory.stock(PRODUCT) / QUANTITY < 2:
            msgs.append('reorder-soon:' + `PRODUCT`)

first, last = BUYER[0], BUYER[1:]         # code is changeable on-site:
if first not in string.uppercase:         # this file is run as one long
    errs.append('buyer-name:' + first)    # code-string, with input and
if BUYER not in inventory.buyers():       # output vars used by the C app
    msgs.append('new-buyer-added')
    inventory.add_buyer(BUYER)
validate_order()

ERRORS   = string.join(errs)        # add a space between messages
WARNINGS = string.join(msgs)        # pass out as strings: "" == none
```

Don't sweat the details in this code; some components it uses are not listed here either (see the book's CD for the full implementation). The thing you should notice, though, is that this code file can contain any kind of Python code—it can define functions and classes, use sockets and threads, and so on. When you embed Python, you get a full-featured extension language for free. Perhaps even more importantly, because this file is Python code, it can be changed arbitrarily without having to recompile the C program. Such flexibility is especially useful after a system has been shipped and installed.

As discussed earlier, there is a variety of ways to structure embedded Python code. For instance, you can implement similar flexibility by delegating actions to Python *functions* fetched from *module* files, as illustrated in Example 20-20.

Example 20-20. PP2E\Integrate\Embed\Inventory\order-func.c

```
/* run embedded module-function validations */

#include <ppembed.h>
#include <stdio.h>
#include <string.h>
#include "ordersfile.h"

run_user_validation() {
    int i, status;                 /* should check status everywhere */
    char *errors, *warnings;       /* no file/string or namespace here */
    PyObject *results;
```

Example 20-20. PP2E\Integrate\Embed\Inventory\order-func.c (continued)

```
    for (i=0; i < numorders; i++) {
        printf("\n%d (%d, %d, '%s')\n",
            i, orders[i].product, orders[i].quantity, orders[i].buyer);

        status = PP_Run_Function(                  /* validate2.validate(p,q,b) */
                        "validate2", "validate",
                        "O",          &results,
                        "(iis)",      orders[i].product,
                                      orders[i].quantity, orders[i].buyer);
        if (status == -1) {
            printf("Python error during validation.\n");
            PyErr_Print();  /* show traceback */
            continue;
        }
        PyArg_Parse(results, "(ss)", &warnings, &errors);
        printf("errors:   %s\n", strlen(errors)? errors : "none");
        printf("warnings: %s\n", strlen(warnings)? warnings : "none");
        Py_DECREF(results);  /* ok to free strings */
        PP_Run_Function("inventory", "print_files", "", NULL, "()");
    }
}

main(int argc, char **argv) {
    run_user_validation();
}
```

The difference here is that the Python code file (shown in Example 20-21) is imported, and so must live on the Python module search path. It also is assumed to contain functions, not a simple list of statements. Strings can live anywhere—files, databases, web pages, and so on, and may be simpler for end users to code. But assuming that the extra requirements of module functions are not prohibitive, functions provide a natural communication model in the form of arguments and return values.

Example 20-21. PP2E\Integrate\Embed\Inventory\validate2.py

```
# embedded validation code, run from C
# input = args, output = return value tuple

import string
import inventory

def validate(product, quantity, buyer):      # function called by name
    msgs, errs = [], []                      # via mod/func name strings
    first, last = buyer[0], buyer[1:]
    if first not in string.uppercase:
        errs.append('buyer-name:' + first)
    if buyer not in inventory.buyers():
        msgs.append('new-buyer-added')
        inventory.add_buyer(buyer)
    validate_order(product, quantity, errs, msgs)      # mutable list args
```

Example 20-21. PP2E\Integrate\Embed\Inventory\validate2.py (continued)

```
    return string.join(msgs), string.join(errs)          # use "(ss)" format

def validate_order(product, quantity, errs, msgs):
    if product not in inventory.skus():
        errs.append('bad-product')
    elif quantity > inventory.stock(product):
        errs.append('check-quantity')
    else:
        inventory.reduce(product, quantity)
        if inventory.stock(product) / quantity < 2:
            msgs.append('reorder-soon:' + `product`)
```

ppembed Implementation

The ppembed API originally appeared as an example in the first edition of this book. Since then, it has been utilized in real systems and become too large to present here in its entirety. For instance, ppembed also supports debugging embedded code (by routing it to the pdb debugger module), dynamically reloading modules containing embedded code, and other features too complex to illustrate usefully here.

But if you are interested in studying another example of Python embedding calls in action, ppembed's full source code and makefile live in this directory on the enclosed CD:

   PP2E\Integration\Embed\HighLevelApi

As a sample of the kinds of tools you can build to simplify embedding, the ppembed API's header file is shown in Example 20-22. You are invited to study, use, copy, and improve its code as you like. Or simply write an API of your own; the main point to take from this section is that embedding programs need only be complicated if you stick with the Python runtime API as shipped. By adding convenience functions such as those in ppembed, embedding can be as simple as you make it. It also makes your C programs immune to changes in the Python C core; ideally, only the API must change if Python ever does.

Be sure to also see file *abstract.h* in the Python include directory if you are in the market for higher-level interfaces. That file provides generic type operation calls that make it easy to do things like creating, filling, indexing, slicing, and concatenating Python objects referenced by pointer from C. Also see the corresponding implementation file, *abstract.c*, as well as the Python built-in module and type implementations in the Python source distribution for more examples of lower-level object access. Once you have a Python object pointer in C, you can do all sorts of type-specific things to Python inputs and outputs.

Example 20-22. PP2E\Integrate\Embed\HighLevelApi\ppembed.h

```
/***********************************************************************
 * PPEMBED, VERSION 2.0
 * AN ENHANCED PYTHON EMBEDDED-CALL INTERFACE
 *
 * Wraps Python's run-time embedding API functions for easy use.
 * Most utilities assume the call is qualified by an enclosing module
 * (namespace). The module can be a file-name reference or a dummy module
 * created to provide a namespace for file-less strings. These routines
 * automate debugging, module (re)loading, input/output conversions, etc.
 *
 * Python is automatically initialized when the first API call occurs.
 * Input/output conversions use the standard Python conversion format
 * codes (described in the C API manual). Errors are flagged as either
 * a -1 int, or a NULL pointer result. Exported names use a PP_ prefix
 * to minimize clashes; names in the built-in Python API use Py prefixes
 * instead (alas, there is no "import" equivalent in C, just "from*").
 * Also note that the varargs code here may not be portable to certain
 * C compilers; to do it portably, see the text or file 'vararg.txt'
 * here, or search for string STDARG in Python's source code files.
 *
 * New in this version/edition: names now have a PP_ prefix, files
 * renamed, compiles to a single .a file, fixed pdb retval bug for
 * strings, and char* results returned by the "s" convert code now
 * point to new char arrays which the caller should free() when no
 * longer needed (this was a potential bug in prior version). Also
 * added new API interfaces for fetching exception info after errors,
 * precompiling code strings to byte code, and calling simple objects.
 *
 * Also fully supports Python 1.5 module package imports: module names
 * in this API can take the form "package.package.[...].module", where
 * Python maps the package names to a nested directories path in your
 * file system hierarchy;  package dirs all contain __init__.py files,
 * and the leftmost one is in a directory found on PYTHONPATH. This
 * API's dynamic reload feature also works for modules in packages;
 * Python stores the full path name in the sys.modules dictionary.
 *
 * Caveats: there is no support for advanced things like threading or
 * restricted execution mode here, but such things may be added with
 * extra Python API calls external to this API (see the Python/C API
 * manual for C-level threading calls; see modules rexec and bastion
 * in the library manual for restricted mode details).  For threading,
 * you may also be able to get by with C threads and distinct Python
 * namespaces per Python code segments, or Python language threads
 * started by Python code run from C (see the Python thread module).
 *
 * Note that Python can only reload Python modules, not C extensions,
 * but it's okay to leave the dynamic reload flag on even if you might
 * access dynamically-loaded C extension modules--in 1.5.2, Python
 * simply resets C extension modules to their initial attribute state
 * when reloaded, but doesn't actually reload the C extension file.
 ***********************************************************************/
```

Example 20-22. PP2E\Integrate\Embed\HighLevelApi\ppembed.h (continued)

```
#ifndef PPEMBED_H
#define PPEMBED_H

#ifdef __cplusplus
extern "C" {              /* a C library, but callable from C++ */
#endif

#include <stdio.h>
#include <Python.h>

extern int PP_RELOAD;     /* 1=reload py modules when attributes referenced */
extern int PP_DEBUG;      /* 1=start debugger when string/function/member run */

typedef enum {
    PP_EXPRESSION,        /* which kind of code-string */
    PP_STATEMENT          /* expressions and statements differ */
} PPStringModes;


/**************************************************/
/*  ppembed-modules.c: load,access module objects  */
/**************************************************/

extern char     *PP_Init(char *modname);
extern int       PP_Make_Dummy_Module(char *modname);
extern PyObject *PP_Load_Module(char *modname);
extern PyObject *PP_Load_Attribute(char *modname, char *attrname);
extern int       PP_Run_Command_Line(char *prompt);


/********************************************************/
/*  ppembed-globals.c: read,write module-level variables  */
/********************************************************/

extern int
    PP_Convert_Result(PyObject *presult, char *resFormat, void *resTarget);

extern int
    PP_Get_Global(char *modname, char *varname, char *resfmt, void *cresult);

extern int
    PP_Set_Global(char *modname, char *varname, char *valfmt, ... /*val*/);


/**************************************************/
/*  ppembed-strings.c: run strings of Python code  */
/**************************************************/

extern int                                 /* run C string of code */
    PP_Run_Codestr(PPStringModes mode,     /* code=expr or stmt?  */
                char *code,    char *modname,    /* codestr, modnamespace */
                char *resfmt, void *cresult);   /* result type, target */
```

Example 20-22. PP2E\Integrate\Embed\HighLevelApi\ppembed.h (continued)

```
extern PyObject*
    PP_Debug_Codestr(PPStringModes mode,              /* run string in pdb */
                     char *codestring, PyObject *moddict);

extern PyObject *
    PP_Compile_Codestr(PPStringModes mode,
                       char *codestr);                /* precompile to bytecode */

extern int
    PP_Run_Bytecode(PyObject *codeobj,                /* run a bytecode object */
                    char   *modname,
                    char   *resfmt, void *restarget);

extern PyObject *                                     /* run bytecode under pdb */
    PP_Debug_Bytecode(PyObject *codeobject, PyObject *moddict);


/****************************************************/
/*  ppembed-callables.c: call functions, classes, etc. */
/****************************************************/

extern int                                            /* mod.func(args) */
    PP_Run_Function(char *modname, char *funcname,     /* func|classname */
                    char *resfmt,  void *cresult,       /* result target */
                    char *argfmt, ... /* arg, arg... */ ); /* input arguments*/

extern PyObject*
    PP_Debug_Function(PyObject *func, PyObject *args);  /* call func in pdb */

extern int
    PP_Run_Known_Callable(PyObject *object,            /* func|class|method */
                          char *resfmt, void *restarget, /* skip module fetch */
                          char *argfmt, ... /* arg,.. */ );


/************************************************************/
/*  ppembed-attributes.c: run object methods, access members  */
/************************************************************/

extern int
    PP_Run_Method(PyObject *pobject, char *method,     /* uses Debug_Function */
                  char *resfmt,  void *cresult,         /* output */
                  char *argfmt, ... /* arg, arg... */ );  /* inputs */

extern int
    PP_Get_Member(PyObject *pobject, char *attrname,
                  char *resfmt,  void *cresult);         /* output */

extern int
    PP_Set_Member(PyObject *pobject, char *attrname,
                  char *valfmt, ... /* val, val... */ );  /* input */
```

Example 20-22. PP2E\Integrate\Embed\HighLevelApi\ppembed.h (continued)

```
/**********************************************************/
/*  ppembed-errors.c: get exception data after api error  */
/**********************************************************/

extern void PP_Fetch_Error_Text();     /* fetch (and clear) exception */

extern char PP_last_error_type[];      /* exception name text */
extern char PP_last_error_info[];      /* exception data text */
extern char PP_last_error_trace[];     /* exception traceback text */

extern PyObject *PP_last_traceback;    /* saved exception traceback object */


#ifdef __cplusplus
}
#endif

#endif (!PPEMBED_H)
```

Other Integration Examples on the CD

While writing this chapter, I ran out of space before I ran out of examples. Besides the ppembed API example described in the last section, you can find a handful of additional Python/C integration self-study examples on this book's CD:

PP2E\Integration\Embed\Inventory
> The full implementation of the validation examples listed earlier. This case study uses the ppembed API to run embedded Python order validations, both as embedded code strings and as functions fetched from modules. The inventory is implemented with and without shelves and pickle files for data persistence.

PP2E\Integration\Mixed\Exports
> A tool for exporting C variables for use in embedded Python programs.

PP2E\Integration\Embed\TestApi
> A simple ppembed test program, shown with and without package import paths to identify modules.

Some of these are large C examples that are probably better studied than listed.

Other Integration Topics

In this book, the term *integration* has largely meant mixing Python with components written in C or C++ (or other C-compatible languages) in extending and embedding modes. But from a broader perspective, integration also includes any other technology that lets us mix Python components into larger systems. This last section briefly looks at a handful of integration technologies beyond the C API tools we've seen in this part of the book.

JPython (a.k.a. Jython) Integration

We met JPython in Chapter 15, but it is worth another mention in the context of integration at large. As we saw earlier, JPython supports two kinds of integration:

- JPython uses Java's *reflection API* to allow Python programs to call out to Java class libraries automatically (extending). The Java reflection API provides Java type information at runtime, and serves the same purpose as the glue code we've generated to plug C libraries into Python in this part of the book. In JPython, however, this runtime type information allows largely automated resolution of Java calls in Python scripts—no glue code has to be written or generated.

- JPython also provides a Java `PythonInterpreter` class API that allows Java programs to run Python code in a namespace (embedding), much like the C API tools we've used to run Python code strings from C programs. In addition, because JPython implements all Python objects as instances of a Java `PyObject` class, it is straightforward for the Java layer that encloses embedded Python code to process Python objects.

In other words, JPython allows Python to be both extended and embedded in Java, much like the C integration strategies we've seen in this part of the book. With the addition of the JPython system, Python may be integrated with any C-compatible program by using C API tools, as well as any Java-compatible program by using JPython.

Although JPython provides a remarkably seamless integration model, Python code runs slower in the JPython implementation, and its reliance on Java class libraries and execution environments introduces Java dependencies that may be a concern in some development scenarios. See Chapter 15 for more JPython details; for the full story, read the documentation available online at *http://www.jpython.org* (also available in the JPython package on this book's CD).

COM Integration on Windows

We briefly discussed Python's support for the COM object model on Windows when we explored Active Scripting in Chapter 15, but it's really a general integration tool that is useful apart from the Internet too.

Recall that COM defines a standard and language-neutral object model with which components written in a variety of programming languages may integrate and communicate. Python's `win32all` Windows extension package tools allow Python programs to implement both server and client in the COM interface model.

As such, it provides a powerful way to integrate Python programs with programs written in other COM-aware languages such as Visual Basic, Delphi, Visual C++, PowerBuilder, and even other Python programs. Python scripts can also use COM calls to script popular Microsoft applications such as Word and Excel, since these systems register COM object interfaces of their own. Moreover, the newcomer Python implementation (tentatively called Python.NET) for Microsoft's C#/.NET technology mentioned in Chapter 15 provides another way to mix Python with other Windows components.

On the downside, COM implies a level of dispatch indirection and is a Windows-only solution at this writing. Because of that, it is not as fast or as portable as some of the lower-level integration schemes we've studied in this part of the book (linked-in, in-process, and direct calls between Python and C-compatible language components). For nontrivial use, COM is also considered to be a large system, and further details about it are well beyond the scope of this book.

For more information on COM support and other Windows extensions, refer to Chapter 15 in this book, and to O'Reilly's *Python Programming on Win32*. That book also describes how to use Windows compilers to do Python/C integration in much more detail than is possible here; for instance, it shows how to use Visual C++ tools to compile and link Python C/C++ integration layer code. The basic C code behind low-level extending and embedding on Windows is the same as shown in this book, but compiling and linking details vary.

CORBA Integration

There is also much support, some of it open source, for using Python in the context of a CORBA-based application. *CORBA* stands for the Common Object Request Broker; it's a language-neutral way to distribute systems among communicating components, which speak through an object model architecture. As such, it represents another way to integrate Python components into a larger system.

Python's CORBA support includes the public domain systems *ILU* (from Xerox) and *fnorb* (see *http://www.python.org*). At this writing, the *OMG* (Object Management Group, responsible for directing CORBA growth) is also playing host to an effort to elect Python as the standard scripting language for CORBA-based systems. Whether that ultimately transpires or not, Python is an ideal language for programming distributed objects, and is being used in such a role by many companies around the world.

Like COM, CORBA is a large system—too large for us to even scratch the surface in this text. For more details, search Python's web site for CORBA-related materials.

Integration Versus Optimization

Given so many integration options, choosing between them can be puzzling. When should you choose something like COM over writing C extension modules, for instance? As usual, it depends on why you're interested in mixing external components into your Python programs in the first place.

Basically, frameworks such as JPython, COM, and CORBA allow Python scripts to leverage existing libraries of software components, and do a great job of addressing goals like code reuse and integration. However, they say almost nothing about optimization: integrated components are not necessarily faster than the Python equivalents.

On the other hand, Python extension modules and types coded in a compiled language like C serve two roles: they too can be used to integrate existing components, but also tend to be a better approach when it comes to boosting system performance.

Framework roles

Let's consider the big picture here. Frameworks such as COM and CORBA can perhaps be understood as alternatives to the Python/C integration techniques we met in this part of the book. For example, packaging Python logic as a COM *server* makes it available for something akin to *embedding*—many languages (including C) can access it using the COM client-side interfaces we met in Chapter 15. And as we saw earlier, JPython allows Java to embed and run Python code and objects through a Java class interface.

Furthermore, frameworks allow Python scripts to use existing component libraries: standard Java class libraries in JPython, COM server libraries on Windows, and so on. In such a role, the external libraries exposed by such frameworks are more or less analogous to Python *extension* modules. For instance, Python scripts that use COM *client* interfaces to access an external object are acting much like importers of C extension modules (albeit through the COM indirection layer).

Extension module roles

Python's C API is designed to serve in many of the same roles. As we've seen, C extension modules can serve as code *reuse* and *integration* tools too—it's straightforward to plug existing C and C++ libraries into Python with SWIG. In most cases, we simply generate and import the glue code created with SWIG to make almost any existing compiled library available for use in Python scripts[*]. Moreover,

---

[*] In fact, it's *so* easy to plug in libraries with SWIG that extensions are usually best coded first as simple C/C++ libraries, and later wrapped for use in Python with SWIG. Adding a COM layer to an existing C library may or may not be as straightforward, but will clearly be less portable—COM is currently a Windows-only technology.

Python's embedding API allows other languages to run Python code, much like client-side interfaces in COM.

One of the primary reasons for writing C extension modules in the first place, though, is *optimization*: key parts of Python applications may be implemented or recoded as C or C++ extension modules to speed up the system at large (as in the last chapter's stack examples). Moving such components to compiled extension modules not only improves system performance, but is completely seamless— module interfaces in Python look the same no matter what programming language implements the module.

Picking an integration technology

By contrast, JPython, COM, and CORBA do not deal directly with optimization goals at all; they serve only to integrate. For instance, JPython allows Python scripts to automatically access Java libraries, but generally mandates that non-Python extensions be coded in Java, a language that is itself usually interpreted and no speed demon. COM and CORBA focus on the interfaces between components and leave the component implementation language ambiguous by design. Exporting a Python class as a COM server, for instance, can make its tools widely reusable on Windows, but has little to do with performance improvement.

Because of their different focus, frameworks are not quite replacements for the more direct Python/C extension modules and types we've studied in these last two chapters, and are less direct (and hence likely slower) than Python's C embedding API. It's possible to mix-and-match approaches, but the combinations are rarely any better than their parts. For example, although C libraries can be added to Java with its native call interface, it's neither a secure nor straightforward undertaking. And while C libraries can also be wrapped as COM servers to make them visible to Python scripts on Windows, the end result will probably be slower and no less complex than a more directly linked-in Python extension module.

As you can see, there are a lot of options in the integration domain. Perhaps the best parting advice I can give you is simply that different tools are meant for different tasks. C extension modules and types are ideal at optimizing systems and integrating libraries, but frameworks offer other ways to integrate components— JPython for mixing in Java tools, COM for reusing and publishing objects on Windows, and so on. As ever, your mileage may vary.

VI

The End

This last part of the book wraps up with:

- Chapter 21, *Conclusion: Python and the Development Cycle*. This chapter discusses Python roles and scope.

- Appendix A, *Recent Python Changes*. This appendix presents Python changes since the first edition.

- Appendix B, *Pragmatics*. This appendix gives common Python install and usage details.

- Appendix C, *Python Versus C++*. This appendix contrasts Python's class model with that of the C++ language, and is intended for C++ developers.

Note that there are no reference appendixes here. For additional reference resources, consult the Python standard manuals included on this book's CD-ROM, or commercially published reference books such as O'Reilly's *Python Pocket Reference*. For additional Python core language material, see O'Reilly's *Learning Python*. And for help on other Python-related topics, see the resources mentioned at the end of Appendix B and at Python's official web site, *http://www.python.org*.

21

*Conclusion: Python
and the Development
Cycle*

"That's the End of the Book, Now Here's the Meaning of Life"

Well, the meaning of Python, anyway. In the introduction to this book I promised that we'd return to the issue of Python's roles after seeing how it is used in practice. So in closing, here are some completely subjective comments on the broader implications of the language.

As I mentioned in the first chapter, Python's focus is on *productivity* and *integration*. I hope that this book has demonstrated some of the benefits of that focus in action. In this conclusion, let's now go back to the forest—to revisit Python's roles in more concrete terms. In particular, Python's role as a prototyping tool can profoundly affect the development cycle.

"Something's Wrong with the Way We Program Computers"

This has to be one of the most overused lines in the business. Still, given time to ponder the big picture, most of us would probably agree that we're not quite "there" yet. Over the last few decades, the computer software industry has made significant progress on streamlining the development task (anyone remember dropping punch cards?). But at the same time, the cost of developing potentially useful computer applications is often still high enough to make them impractical.

Moreover, systems built using modern tools and paradigms are often delivered far behind schedule. Software engineering remains largely defiant of the sort of

1187

quantitative measurements employed in other engineering fields. In the software world, it's not uncommon to take one's best time estimate for a new project and multiply by a factor of two or three to account for unforeseen overheads in the development task. This situation is clearly unsatisfactory for software managers, developers, and end users.

The "Gilligan Factor"

It has been suggested (tongue in cheek) that if there were a patron saint of software engineers, the honor would fall on none other than Gilligan, the character in the pervasively popular American television show of the 1960s, *Gilligan's Island*. Gilligan is the enigmatic, sneaker-clad first mate, widely held to be responsible for the shipwreck that stranded the now-residents of the island.

To be sure, Gilligan's situation seems oddly familiar. Stranded on a desert island with only the most meager of modern technological comforts, Gilligan and his cohorts must resort to scratching out a living using the resources naturally available. In episode after episode, we observe the Professor developing exquisitely intricate tools for doing the business of life on their remote island, only to be foiled in the implementation phase by the ever-bungling Gilligan.

But clearly it was never poor Gilligan's fault. How could one possibly be expected to implement designs for such sophisticated applications as home appliances and telecommunications devices, given the rudimentary technologies available in such an environment? He simply lacked the proper tools. For all we know, Gilligan may have had the capacity for engineering on the grandest level. But you can't get there with bananas and coconuts.

And pathologically, time after time, Gilligan wound up inadvertently sabotaging the best of the Professor's plans; misusing, abusing, and eventually destroying his inventions. If he could just pedal his makeshift stationary bicycle faster and faster (he was led to believe), all would be well. But in the end, inevitably, the coconuts were sent hurling into the air, the palm branches came crashing down around his head, and poor Gilligan was blamed once again for the failure of the technology.

Dramatic though this image may be, some observers would consider it a striking metaphor for the software industry. Like Gilligan, we software engineers are often asked to perform tasks with arguably inappropriate tools. Like Gilligan, our intentions are sound, but technology can hold us back. And like poor Gilligan, we inevitably must bear the brunt of management's wrath when our systems are delivered behind schedule. You can't get there with bananas and coconuts . . .

Doing the Right Thing

Of course, the Gilligan factor is a exaggeration, added for comic effect. But few would argue that the bottleneck between ideas and working systems has disappeared completely. Even today, the cost of developing software far exceeds the cost of computer hardware. Why must programming be so complex?

Let's consider the situation carefully. By and large, the root of the complexity in developing software isn't related to the role it's supposed to perform—usually this is a well-defined real-world process. Rather, it stems from the mapping of real-world tasks onto computer-executable models. And this mapping is performed in the context of programming languages and tools.

The path toward easing the software bottleneck must therefore lie, at least partially, in optimizing the act of programming itself by deploying the right tools. Given this realistic scope, there's much that can be done now—there are a number of purely artificial overheads inherent in our current tools.

The Static Language Build Cycle

Using traditional static languages, there is an unavoidable overhead in moving from coded programs to working systems: compile and link steps add a built-in delay to the development process. In some environments, it's common to spend many hours each week just waiting for a static language application's build cycle to finish. Given that modern development practice involves an iterative process of building, testing, and rebuilding, such delays can be expensive and demoralizing (if not physically painful).

Of course, this varies from shop to shop, and in some domains the demand for performance justifies build-cycle delays. But I've worked in C++ environments where programmers joked about having to go to lunch whenever they recompiled their systems. Except they weren't really joking.

Artificial Complexities

With many traditional programming tools, you can easily lose the forest for the trees: the act of programming becomes so complex that the real-world goal of the program is obscured. Traditional languages divert valuable attention to syntactic issues and development of bookkeeping code. Obviously, complexity isn't an end in itself; it must be clearly warranted. Yet some of our current tools are so complex that the language itself makes the task harder and lengthens the development process.

One Language Does Not Fit All

Many traditional languages implicitly encourage homogeneous, single-language systems. By making integration complex, they impede the use of multiple-language tools; therefore, instead of being able to select the right tool for the task at hand, developers are often compelled to use the same language for every component of an application. Since no language is good at everything, this constraint inevitably sacrifices both product functionality and programmer productivity.

Until our machines are as clever at taking directions as we are (arguably, not the most rational of goals), the task of programming won't go away. But for the time being, we can make substantial progress by making the mechanics of that task easier. And this topic is what I want to talk about now.

Enter Python

If this book has achieved its goals, you should by now have a good understanding of why Python has been called a "next-generation scripting language." Compared with similar tools, it has some critical distinctions that we're finally in a position to summarize:

Tcl

> Like Tcl, Python can be used as an embedded extension language. Unlike Tcl, Python is also a full-featured programming language. For many, Python's data structure tools and support for programming-in-the-large make it useful in more domains. Tcl demonstrated the utility of integrating interpreted languages with C modules. Python provides similar functionality plus a powerful, object-oriented language; it's not just a command string processor.

Perl

> Like Perl, Python can be used for writing shell tools, making it easy to use system services. Unlike Perl, Python has a simple, readable syntax and a remarkably coherent design. For some, this makes Python easier to use and a better choice for programs that must be reused or maintained by others. Without question, Perl is a powerful system administration tool. But once we move beyond processing text and files, Python's features become attractive.

Scheme/Lisp

> Like Scheme (and Lisp), Python supports dynamic typing, incremental development, and metaprogramming; it exposes the interpreter's state and supports runtime program construction. Unlike Lisp, Python has a procedural syntax that is familiar to users of mainstream languages such as C and Pascal. If extensions are to be coded by end users, this can be a major advantage.

Smalltalk

Like Smalltalk, Python supports object-oriented programming (OOP) in the context of a highly dynamic language. Unlike Smalltalk, Python doesn't extend the object system to include fundamental program control flow constructs. Users need not come to grips with the concept of *if* statements as message-receiving objects to use Python—Python is more conventional.

Icon

Like Icon, Python supports a variety of high-level datatypes and operations such as lists, dictionaries, and slicing. Unlike Icon, Python is fundamentally simple. Programmers (and end users) don't need to master esoteric concepts such as backtracking just to get started.

BASIC

Like modern structured BASIC dialects, Python has an interpretive/interactive nature. Unlike most BASICs, Python includes standard support for advanced programming features such as classes, modules, exceptions, high-level datatypes, and general C integration.

All of these languages (and others) have merit and unique strengths of their own—in fact, Python borrowed most of its features from languages such as these. It's not Python's goal to replace every other language; different tasks require different tools, and mixed-language development is one of Python's main ideas. But Python's blend of advanced programming constructs and integration tools make it a natural choice for the problem domains we've talked about in this book.

But What About That Bottleneck?

Back to our original question: how can the act of writing software be made easier? At some level, Python is really "just another computer language." It's certainly true that Python the language doesn't represent much that's radically new from a theoretical point of view. So why should we be excited about Python when so many languages have been tried already?

What makes Python of interest, and what may be its larger contribution to the development world, is not its syntax or semantics, but its world view: Python's combination of tools makes rapid development a realistic goal. In a nutshell, Python fosters rapid development by providing features like these:

- Fast build-cycle turnaround

- A very high-level, object-oriented language

- Integration facilities to enable mixed-language development

Specifically, Python attacks the software development bottleneck on four fronts, described in the following sections.

Python Provides Immediate Turnaround

Python's development cycle is dramatically shorter than that of traditional tools. In Python, there are no compile or link steps—Python programs simply import modules at runtime and use the objects they contain. Because of this, Python programs run immediately after changes are made. And in cases where dynamic module reloading can be used, it's even possible to change and reload parts of a running program without stopping it at all. Figure 21-1 shows Python's impact on the development cycle.

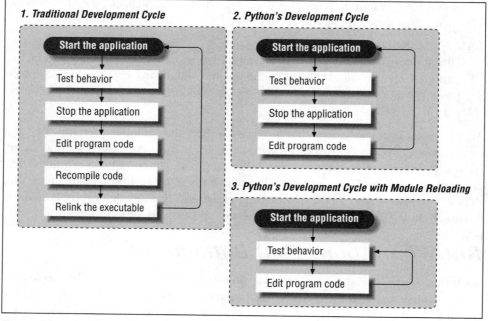

Figure 21-1. Development cycles

Because Python is interpreted, there's a rapid turnaround after program changes. And because Python's parser is embedded in Python-based systems, it's easy to modify programs at runtime. For example, we saw how GUI programs developed with Python allow developers to change the code that handles a button press while the GUI remains active; the effect of the code change may be observed immediately when the button is pressed again. There's no need to stop and rebuild.

More generally, the entire development process in Python is an exercise in rapid prototyping. Python lends itself to experimental, interactive program development, and encourages developing systems incrementally by testing components in isolation and putting them together later. In fact, we've seen that we can switch from testing components (unit tests) to testing whole systems (integration tests) arbitrarily, as illustrated in Figure 21-2.

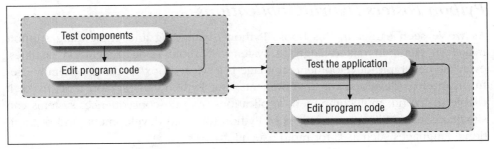

Figure 21-2. Incremental development

Python Is "Executable Pseudocode"

Python's very high-level nature means there's less for us to program and manage. Lack of compile and link steps isn't really enough to address the development-cycle bottleneck by itself. For instance, a C or C++ interpreter might provide fast turnaround but still be almost useless for rapid development: the language is too complex and low-level.

But because Python is also a simple language, coding is dramatically faster too. For example, its dynamic typing, built-in objects, and garbage collection eliminate much of the manual bookkeeping code required in lower-level languages such as C and C++. Since things like type declarations, memory management, and common data structure implementations are all conspicuously absent, Python programs are typically a fraction of the size of their C or C++ equivalents. There's less to write and read, and thus less opportunity for coding errors.

Because most bookkeeping code is missing, Python programs are easier to understand and more closely reflect the actual problem they're intended to address. And Python's high-level nature not only allows algorithms to be realized more quickly, but also makes it easier to learn the language.

Python Is OOP Done Right

For OOP to be useful, it must be easy to apply. Python makes OOP a flexible tool by delivering it in a dynamic language. More importantly, its class mechanism is a simplified subset of C++'s, and it's this simplification that makes OOP useful in the context of a rapid-development tool. For instance, when we looked at data structure classes in this book, we saw that Python's dynamic typing let us apply a single class to a variety of object types; we didn't need to write variants for each supported type.

In fact, Python's OOP is so easy to use that there's really no reason not to apply it in most parts of an application. Python's class model has features powerful enough for complex programs, yet because they're provided in simple ways, they don't interfere with the problem we're trying to solve.

Python Fosters Hybrid Applications

As we've seen earlier in this book, Python's extending and embedding support makes it useful in mixed-language systems. Without good integration facilities, even the best rapid-development language is a "closed box" and not generally useful in modern development environments. But Python's integration tools make it usable in hybrid, multicomponent applications. As one consequence, systems can simultaneously utilize the strengths of Python for rapid development, and of traditional languages such as C for rapid execution.

While it's possible to use Python as a standalone tool, it doesn't impose this mode. Instead, Python encourages an integrated approach to application development. By supporting arbitrary mixtures of Python and traditional languages, Python fosters a spectrum of development paradigms, ranging from pure prototyping to pure efficiency. Figure 21-3 shows the abstract case.

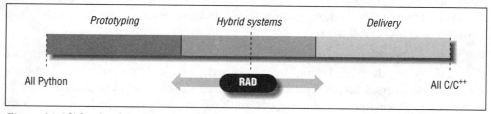

Figure 21-3. The development mode "slider"

As we move to the left extreme of the spectrum, we optimize speed of development. Moving to the right side optimizes speed of execution. And somewhere in between is an optimum mix for any given project. With Python, not only can we pick the proper mix for our project, but we can also later move the RAD slider in the picture arbitrarily as our needs change:

Going to the right

> Projects can be started on the left end of the scale in Python and gradually moved toward the right, module by module, as needed to optimize performance for delivery.

Going to the left

> Similarly, we can move strategic parts of existing C or C++ applications on the right end of the scale to Python, to support end-user programming and customization on the left end of the scale.

This flexibility of development modes is crucial in realistic environments. Python is optimized for speed of development, but that alone isn't enough. By themselves, neither C nor Python is adequate to address the development bottleneck; together, they can do much more. As shown in Figure 21-4, for instance, apart from standalone use, one of Python's most common roles splits systems into *frontend* components that can benefit from Python's ease-of use and *backend* modules that require the efficiency of static languages like C, C++, or FORTRAN.

Whether we add Python frontend interfaces to existing systems or design them in early on, such a division of labor can open up a system to its users without exposing its internals.

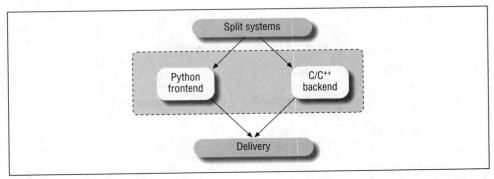

Figure 21-4. Hybrid designs

When developing new systems, we also have the option of writing entirely in Python at first and then optimizing as needed for delivery by moving performance-critical components to compiled languages. And because Python and C modules look the same to clients, migration to compiled extensions is transparent.

Prototyping doesn't make sense in every scenario. Sometimes splitting a system into a Python frontend and a C/C++ backend up front works best. And prototyping doesn't help much when enhancing existing systems. But where it can be applied, early prototyping can be a major asset. By prototyping in Python first, we can show results more quickly. Perhaps more critically, end users can be closely involved in the early stages of the process, as sketched in Figure 21-5. The result is systems that more closely reflect their original requirements.

On Sinking the Titanic

In short, Python is really more than a language; it implies a development philosophy. The concepts of prototyping, rapid development, and hybrid applications certainly aren't new. But while the benefits of such development modes are widely recognized, there has been a lack of tools that make them practical without sacrificing programming power. This is one of the main gaps that Python's design fills: *Python provides a simple but powerful rapid development language, along with the integration tools needed to apply it in realistic development environments.*

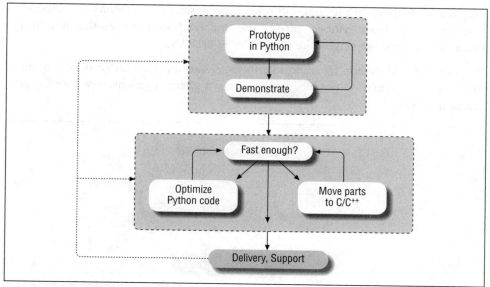

Figure 21-5. Prototyping with Python

This combination arguably makes Python unique among similar tools. For instance, Tcl is a good integration tool but not a full-blown language; Perl is a powerful system administration language but a weak integration tool. But Python's marriage of a powerful dynamic language and integration opens the door to fundamentally faster development modes. With Python, it's no longer necessary to choose between fast development and fast execution.

By now, it should be clear that a single programming language can't satisfy all our development goals. In fact, our needs are sometimes contradictory: the goals of efficiency and flexibility will probably always clash. Given the high cost of making software, the choice between development and execution speed is crucial. Although machine cycles are cheaper than programmers, we can't yet ignore efficiency completely.

But with a tool like Python, we don't need to decide between the two goals at all. Just as a carpenter wouldn't drive a nail with a chainsaw, software engineers are now empowered to use the right tool for the task at hand: Python when speed of development matters, compiled languages when efficiency dominates, and combinations of the two when our goals are not absolute.

Moreover, we don't have to sacrifice code reuse or rewrite exhaustively for delivery when applying rapid development with Python. We can have our rapid development cake and eat it too:

Reusability

Because Python is a high-level, object-oriented language, it encourages writing reusable software and well-designed systems.

Deliverability

Because Python is designed for use in mixed-language systems, we don't have to move to more efficient languages all at once.

In typical Python development, a system's frontend and infrastructure may be written in Python for ease of development and modification, but the kernel is still written in C or C++ for efficiency. Python has been called the tip of the iceberg in such systems—the part visible to end users of a package, as captured in Figure 21-6.

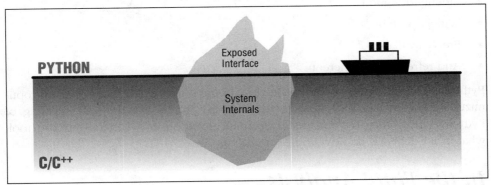

Figure 21-6. "Sinking the Titanic" with mixed-language systems

Such an architecture uses the best of both worlds: it can be extended by adding more Python code or by writing C extension modules, depending on performance requirements. But this is just one of many mixed-language development scenarios:

System interfaces

Packaging code as Python extension modules makes it more accessible.

End-user customization

Delegating logic to embedded Python code provides for onsite changes.

Pure prototyping

Python prototypes can be moved to C all at once or piecemeal.

Legacy code migration

Moving existing code from C to Python makes it simpler and more flexible.

Standalone use

Of course, using Python all by itself leverages its existing library of tools.

Python's design lets us apply it in whatever way makes sense for each project.

So What's Python: The Sequel

As we've seen in this book, Python is a multifaceted tool, useful in a wide variety of domains. What can we say about Python to sum up here? In terms of some of its best attributes, the Python language is:

- General-purpose
- Object-oriented
- Interpreted
- Very high-level
- Openly designed
- Widely portable
- Freely available
- And refreshingly coherent

Python is useful for both standalone development and extension work, and optimized to boost *developer productivity* on many fronts. But the real meaning of Python is really up to you, the reader. Since Python is a general-purpose tool, what it "is" depends on how you choose to use it.

In the Final Analysis...

I hope this book has taught you something about Python, both the language and its roles. Beyond this text, there is really no substitute for doing some original Python programming. Be sure to grab a reference source or two to help you along the way.

The task of programming computers will probably always be challenging. Perhaps happily, there will continue to be a need for intelligent software engineers, skilled at translating real-world tasks into computer-executable form, at least for the foreseeable future. (After all, if it were too easy, none of us would get paid. :-)

But current development practice and tools make our tasks unnecessarily difficult: many of the obstacles faced by software developers are purely artificial. We have come far in our quest to improve the speed of computers; the time has come to focus our attentions on improving the speed of development. In an era of constantly shrinking schedules, productivity must be paramount.

Python, as a mixed-paradigm tool, has the potential to foster development modes that simultaneously leverage the benefits of rapid development and of traditional languages. While Python won't solve all the problems of the software industry, it offers hope for making programming simpler, faster, and at least a little more enjoyable.

It may not get us off that island altogether, but it sure beats bananas and coconuts.

Postscript to the Second Edition

One of the luxuries of updating a book like this is that you get an opportunity to debate yourself, or at least your opinions, from years past. With the benefit of five years' retrospect, I'd like to add a few comments to the original conclusion.

Integration Isn't Everything

The conclusion for this book's first edition stressed the importance of Python's role as an integration tool. Although the themes underscored there are still valid, I should point out that not all Python applications rely explicitly on the ability to be mixed with components written in other languages. Many developers now use Python in standalone mode, either not having or not noticing integration layers.

For instance, developers who code CGI Internet scripts with Python often code in pure Python. Somewhere down the call chain, C libraries are called (to access sockets, databases, and so on), but Python coders often don't need to care. In fact, this has proven to be true in my own recent experience as well. While working on the new GUI, system, and Internet examples for this edition, I worked purely in Python for long periods of time. A few months later I also worked on a Python/C++ integration framework, but this integration project was entirely separate from the pure Python book examples programming effort. Many projects are implemented in Python alone.

That is not to say that Python's integration potential is not one of its most profound attributes—indeed, most Python systems *are* composed of combinations of Python and C. However, in many cases, the integration layer is implemented once by a handful of advanced developers, while others perform the bulk of the programming in Python alone. If you're fortunate enough to count yourself among the latter group, Python's overall ease of use may seem more crucial than its integration role.

The End of the Java Wars

In 1995, the Python community perceived a conflict between Java and Python in terms of competition for developer mind-share—hence the sidebar "Python versus Java: Round 1?" in the first edition. Since then, this has become virtually a nonissue; I've even deleted this sidebar completely.

This cooling of hostilities has come about partly because Java's role is now better understood: Java is recognized as a *systems development* language, not a scripting language. That is essentially what the sidebar proposed. Java's complexity is on the order of C++'s (from which it is derived), making it impractical for scripting work, where short development cycles are at a premium. This is by design—Java is meant for tasks where the extra complexity may make sense. Given the great disparity in their roles, the Python/Java conflict has fizzled.

The truce has also been called on account of the new *JPython* implementation of Python. JPython was described in Chapter 15, *Advanced Internet Topics*; in short, it integrates Python and Java programs such that applications can be developed as hybrids: parts can be coded in Python when scripting is warranted, and in Java for performance-intensive parts. This is exactly the argument made for C/C++ integration in the conclusion of the first edition; thanks to JPython, the same reasoning behind hybrid systems now applies to Java-based applications.

The claims made by the old Java sidebar are still true—Python is simpler, more open, and easier to learn and apply. But that is as it should be: as a scripting language, Python naturally complements systems languages like Java and C++, rather than competing with them. There are still some who would argue that Python is better suited for many applications now coded in Java. But just as for Python and C and C++, Python and Java seem to work best as a team.

It's also worth noting that as I write these words, Microsoft has just announced a new, proprietary language called C# that seems to be intended as a substitute for Java in Microsoft's systems language offerings. Moreover, a new Python port to the C#/.NET environment has been announced as well. See Chapter 15 for details—this port is roughly to C# what JPython is to Java. Time will tell if C# and Java will do battle for mindshare. But given that Python integrates with both, the outcome of these clashes between mega-companies is largely irrelevant; Pythonistas can watch calmly from the sidelines this time around.

We're Not Off That Island Yet

As I mentioned in the preface to this edition, Python has come far in the last five years. Companies around the world have adopted it, and Python now boasts a user base estimated at half a million strong. Yet for all the progress, there is still work to be done, both in improving and popularizing Python, and in simplifying software development in general.

As I travel around the world teaching Python classes at companies and organizations, I still meet many people who are utterly frustrated with the development tools they are required to use in their jobs. Some even change jobs (or careers) because of such frustrations. Even well after the onset of the Internet revolution, development is still harder than it needs to be.

On the other hand, I also meet people who find Python so much fun to use, they can't imagine going back to their old ways. They use Python both on and off the job for the pure pleasure of programming.

Five years from now, I hope to report that I meet many more people in the latter category than the former. After all, Guido may have appeared on the covers of *Linux Journal* and *Dr. Dobb's* since the first edition of this book, but we still have a bit more work to do before he makes the cover of *Rolling Stone*.

A Morality Tale of Perl Versus Python

(The following was posted recently to the *rec.humor.funny* Usenet newsgroup by Larry Hastings, and is reprinted here with the original author's permission. I don't necessarily condone language wars; okay?)

This has been percolating in the back of my mind for a while. It's a scene from *The Empire Strikes Back*, reinterpreted to serve a valuable moral lesson for aspiring programmers.

EXTERIOR: DAGOBAH--DAY

With Yoda strapped to his back, Luke climbs up one of the many thick vines that grow in the swamp until he reaches the Dagobah statistics lab. Panting heavily, he continues his exercises—grepping, installing new packages, logging in as root, and writing replacements for two-year-old shell scripts in Python.

YODA: Code! Yes. A programmer's strength flows from code maintainability. But beware of Perl. Terse syntax . . . more than one way to do it . . . default variables. The dark side of code maintainability are they. Easily they flow, quick to join you when code you write. If once you start down the dark path, forever will it dominate your destiny, consume you it will.

LUKE: Is Perl better than Python?

YODA: No . . . no . . . no. Quicker, easier, more seductive.

LUKE: But how will I know why Python is better than Perl?

YODA: You will know. When your code you try to read six months from now.

Recent Python Changes

This appendix summarizes prominent changes introduced in Python releases since the first edition of this book. It is divided into three sections, mostly because the sections on 1.6 and 2.0 changes were adapted from release note documents:

- Changes introduced in Python 2.0 (and 2.1)
- Changes introduced in Python 1.6
- Changes between the first edition and Python 1.5.2

Python 1.3 was the most recent release when the first edition was published (October 1996), and Python 1.6 and 2.0 were released just before this second edition was finished. 1.6 was the last release posted by CNRI, and 2.0 was released from BeOpen (Guido's two employers prior to his move to Digital Creations); 2.0 adds a handful of features to 1.6.

With a few notable exceptions, the changes over the last five years have introduced new features to Python, but have not changed it in incompatible ways. Many of the new features are widely useful (e.g., module packages), but some seem to address the whims of Python gurus (e.g., list comprehensions) and can be safely ignored by anyone else. In any event, although it is important to keep in touch with Python evolution, you should not take this appendix too seriously. Frankly, application library and tool usage is much more important in practice than obscure language additions.

For information on the Python changes that will surely occur after this edition's publication, consult either the resources I maintain at this book's web site (*http://rmi.net/~lutz/about-pp.html*), the resources available at Python's web site (*http://www.python.org*), or the release notes that accompany Python releases.

Major Changes in 2.0

This section lists changes introduced in Python release 2.0. Note that third-party extensions built for Python 1.5.x or 1.6 cannot be used with Python 2.0; these extensions must be rebuilt for 2.0. Python bytecode files (**.pyc* and **.pyo*) are not compatible between releases either.

Core Language Changes

The following sections describe changes made to the Python language itself.

Augmented assignment

After nearly a decade of complaints from C programmers, Guido broke down and added 11 new C-like assignment operators to the language:

```
+= -= *= /= %= **= <<= >>= &= ^= |=
```

The statement A += B is similar to A = A + B except that A is evaluated only once (useful if it is a complex expression). If A is a *mutable* object, it may be modified in place; for instance, if it is a list, A += B has the same effect as A.extend(B).

Classes and built-in object types can override the new operators in order to implement the in-place behavior; the non-in-place behavior is automatically used as a fallback when an object does not implement the in-place behavior. For classes, the method name is the method name for the corresponding non-in-place operator prepended with an "i" (e.g., __iadd__ implements in-place __add__).

List comprehensions

A new expression notation was added for lists whose elements are computed from another list (or lists):

```
[<expression> for <variable> in <sequence>]
```

For example, [i**2 for i in range(4)] yields the list [0,1,4,9]. This is more efficient than using map with a lambda, and at least in the context of scanning lists, avoids some scoping issues raised by lambdas (e.g., using defaults to pass in information from the enclosing scope). You can also add a condition:

```
[<expression> for <variable> in <sequence> if <condition>]
```

For example, [w for w in words if w == w.lower()] yields the list of words that contain no uppercase characters. This is more efficient than filter with a lambda. Nested for loops and more than one if is supported as well, though using this seems to yield code that is as complex as nested maps and lambdas (see Python manuals for more details).

Extended import statements

Import statements now allow an "as" clause (e.g., `import mod as name`), which saves an assignment of an imported module's name to another variable. This works with `from` statements and package paths too (e.g., `from mod import var as name`. The word "as" was not made a reserved word in the process. (To import odd filenames that don't map to Python variable names, see the `__import__` built-in function.)

Extended print statement

The print statement now has an option that makes the output go to a different file than the default `sys.stdout`. For instance, to write an error message to `sys.stderr`, you can now write:

```
print >> sys.stderr, "spam"
```

As a special case, if the expression used to indicate the file evaluates to `None`, the current value of `sys.stdout` is used (like not using `>>` at all). Note that you can always write to file objects such as `sys.stderr` by calling their `write` method; this optional extension simply adds the extra formatting performed by the print statement (e.g., string conversion, spaces between items).

Optional collection of cyclical garbage

Python is now equipped with a garbage collector that can hunt down cyclical references between Python objects. It does not replace reference counting (and in fact depends on the reference counts being correct), but can decide that a set of objects belongs to a cycle if all their reference counts are accounted for in their references to each other. A new module named `gc` lets you control parameters of the garbage collection; an option to the Python "configure" script lets you enable or disable the garbage collection. (See the 2.0 release notes or the library manual to check if this feature is enabled by default or not; because running this extra garbage collection step periodically adds performance overheads, the decision on whether to turn it on by default is pending.)

Selected Library Changes

This is a partial list of standard library changes introduced by Python release 2.0; see 2.0 release notes for a full description of the changes.

New zip function

A new function `zip` was added: `zip(seq1,seq2,...)` is equivalent to `map(None,seq1,seq2,...)` when the sequences have the same length. For instance, `zip([1, 2, 3], [10, 20, 30])` returns `[(1,10), (2,20), (3,30)]`. When the lists are not all the same length, the shortest list defines the result's length.

XML support

A new standard module named `pyexpat` provides an interface to the Expat XML parser. A new standard module package named `xml` provides assorted XML support code in (so far) three subpackages: `xml.dom`, `xml.sax`, and `xml.parsers`.

New web browser module

The new `webbrowser` module attempts to provide a platform-independent API to launch a web browser. (See also the `LaunchBrowser` script at the end of Chapter 4, *Larger System Examples I.*)

Python/C Integration API Changes

Portability was ensured to 64-bit platforms under both Linux and Win64, especially for the new Intel Itanium processor. Large file support was also added for Linux64 and Win64.

The garbage collection changes resulted in the creation of two new slots on an object, `tp_traverse` and `tp_clear`. The augmented assignment changes result in the creation of a new slot for each in-place operator. The GC API creates new requirements for container types implemented in C extension modules. See *Include/objimpl.h* in the Python source distribution.

Windows Changes

New `popen2`, `popen3`, and `popen4` calls were added in the `os` module.

The `os.popen` call is now much more usable on Windows 95 and 98. To fix this call for Windows 9x, Python internally uses the `w9xpopen.exe` program in the root of your Python installation (it is not a standalone program). See Microsoft Knowledge Base article Q150956 for more details.

Administrator privileges are no longer required to install Python on Windows NT or Windows 2000. The Windows installer also now installs by default in *\Python20* on the default volume (e.g., *C:\Python20*), instead of the older-style *\Program Files\Python-2.0*.

The Windows installer no longer runs a separate Tcl/Tk installer; instead, it installs the needed Tcl/Tk files directly in the Python directory. If you already have a Tcl/Tk installation, this wastes some disk space (about 4 MB) but avoids problems with conflicting Tcl/Tk installations and makes it much easier for Python to ensure that Tcl/Tk can find all its files.

Python 2.1 Alpha Features

Like the weather in Colorado, if you wait long enough, Python's feature set changes. Just before this edition went to the printer, the first alpha release of Python 2.1 was announced. Among its new weapons are these:

- Functions can now have arbitrary attributes attached to them; simply assign to function attribute names to associate extra information with the function (something coders had been doing with formatted documentation stings).

- A new rich comparison extension now allows classes to overload individual comparison operators with distinct methods (e.g., `__lt__` overloads < tests), instead of trying to handle all tests in the single `__cmp__` method.

- A warning framework provides an interface to messages issued for use of deprecated features (e.g., the `regex` module).

- The Python build system has been revamped to use the `Distutils` package.

- A new `sys.displayhook` attribute allows users to customize the way objects are printed at the interactive prompt.

- Line-by-line file input/output (the file `readline` method) was made much faster, and a new `xreadlines` file method reads just one line at a time in `for` loops.

- Also: the numeric coercion model used in C extensions was altered, modules may now set an `__all__` name to specify which names they export for `from *` imports, the `ftplib` module now defaults to "passive" mode to work better with firewalls, and so on.

- Other enhancements, such as statically nested scopes and weak references, were still on the drawing board in the alpha release.

As usual, of course, you should consult this book's web page (*http://www.rmi.net/~lutz/about-pp.html*) and Python 2.1 and later release notes for Python developments that will surely occur immediately after I ship this insert off to my publisher.

Major Changes in 1.6

This section lists changes introduced by Python release 1.6; by proxy, most are part of release 2.0 as well.

Incompatibilities

The `append` method for lists can no longer be invoked with more than one argument. This used to append a single tuple made out of all arguments, but was undocumented. To append a tuple, write `l.append((a, b, c))`.

The `connect`, `connect_ex`, and `bind` methods for sockets require exactly one argument. Previously, you could call `s.connect(host, port)`, but this was not by design; you must now write `s.connect((host, port))`.

The `str` and `repr` functions are now different more often. For long integers, `str` no longer appends an "L"; `str(1L)` is "1", which used to be "1L", and `repr(1L)` still returns "1L". For floats, `repr` now gives 17 digits of precision to ensure that no precision is lost (on all current hardware).

Some library functions and tools have been moved to the deprecated category, including some widely used tools such as `find`. The `string` module is now simply a frontend to the new string methods, but given that this module is used by almost every Python module written to date, it is very unlikely to go away.

Core Language Changes

The following sections describe changes made to the Python language itself.

Unicode strings

Python now supports Unicode (i.e., 16-bit wide character) strings. Release 1.6 added a new fundamental datatype (the Unicode string), a new built-in function `unicode`, and numerous C APIs to deal with Unicode and encodings. Unicode string constants are prefixed with the letter "u", much like raw strings (e.g., `u"..."`). See the file *Misc/unicode.txt* in your Python distribution for details, or visit web site *http://starship.python.net/crew/lemburg/unicode-proposal.txt*.

String methods

Many of the functions in the `string` module are now available as methods of string objects. For instance, you can now say `str.lower()` instead of importing the `string` module and saying `string.lower(str)`. The equivalent of `string.join(sequence,delimiter)` is `delimiter.join(sequence)`. (That is, you use `" ".join(sequence)` to mimic `string.join(sequence)`).

New (internal) regular expression engine

The new regular expression engine, SRE, is fully backward-compatible with the old engine, and is invoked using the same interface (the `re` module). That is, the `re` module's interface remains the way to write matches, and is unchanged; it is simply implemented to use SRE. You can explicitly invoke the old engine by importing `pre`, or the SRE engine by importing `sre`. SRE is faster than `pre`, and supports Unicode (which was the main reason to develop yet another underlying regular expression engine).

apply-like function calls syntax

Special function call syntax can be used instead of the `apply` function: `f(*args, **kwds)` is equivalent to `apply(f, args, kwds)`. You can also use variations like `f(a1, a2, *args, **kwds)`, and can leave one or the other out (e.g., `f(*args)`, `f(**kwds)`).

String to number conversion bases

The built-ins `int` and `long` take an optional second argument to indicate the conversion base, but only if the first argument is a string. This makes **`string.atoi`** and **`string.atol`** obsolete. (**`string.atof`** already was.)

Better errors for local name oddities

When a local variable is known to the compiler but undefined when used, a new exception `UnboundLocalError` is raised. This is a class derived from `NameError`, so code that catches `NameError` should still work. The purpose is to provide better diagnostics in the following example:

```
x = 1
def f():
    print x
    x = x+1
```

This used to raise a confusing `NameError` on the print statement.

Membership operator overloading

You can now override the `in` operator by defining a `__contains__` method. Note that it has its arguments backward: `x in a` runs `a.__contains__(x)` (that's why the name isn't `__in__`).

Selected Library Module Changes

This section lists some of the changes made to the Python standard library.

`distutils`
>   New; tools for distributing Python modules.

`zipfile`
>   New; read and write zip archives (module `gzip` does gzip files).

`unicodedata`
>   New; access to the Unicode 3.0 database.

`_winreg`
>   New; Windows registry access (one without the _ is in progress).

`socket`, `httplib`, `urllib`
>   Expanded to include optional OpenSSL secure socket support (on Unix only).

`_tkinter`
>   Support for Tk versions 8.0 through 8.3.

`string`
>   This module no longer uses the built-in C `strop` module, but takes advantage
>   of the new string methods to provide transparent support for both Unicode
>   and ordinary strings.

Selected Tools Changes

This section lists some of the changes made to Python tools.

IDLE
>   Completely overhauled. See the IDLE home page at *http://www.python.org* for
>   more information.

Tools/i18n/pygettext.py
>   Python equivalent of `xgettext` message text extraction tool used for interna-
>   tionalizing applications written in Python.

Major Changes Between 1.3 and 1.5.2

This section describes significant language, library, tool, and C API changes in
Python between the first edition of this book (Python 1.3) and Python release 1.5.2.

Core Language Changes

The following sections describe changes made to the Python language itself.

Pseudo-private class attributes

Python now provides a name-mangling protocol that hides attribute names used by
classes. Inside a class statement, a name of the form `__X` is automatically changed

by Python to _Class__X, where Class is the name of the class being defined by the statement. Because the enclosing class name is prepended, this feature limits the possibilities of name clashes when you extend or mix existing classes. Note that this is not a "private" mechanism at all, just a class name localization feature to minimize name clashes in hierarchies and the shared instance object's namespace at the bottom of the attribute inheritance links chain.

Class exceptions

Exceptions may now take the form of class (and class instance) objects. The intent is to support exception categories. Because an **except** clause will now match a raised exception if it names the raised class or any of its superclasses, specifying superclasses allows **try** statements to catch broad categories without listing all members explicitly (e.g., catching a numeric-error superclass exception will also catch specific kinds of numeric errors). Python's standard built-in exceptions are now classes (instead of strings) and have been organized into a shallow class hierarchy; see the library manual for details.

Package imports

Import statements may now reference directory paths on your computer by dotted-path syntax. For instance:

```
import directory1.directory2.module              # and use path
from   directory1.directory2.module import name  # and use "name"
```

Both load a module nested two levels deep in packages (directories). The left-most package name in an import path (**directory1**) must be a directory *within* a directory that is listed in the Python module search path (**sys.path** initialized from PYTHONPATH). Thereafter, the **import** statement's path denotes subdirectories to follow. Paths prevent module name conflicts when installing multiple Python systems on the same machine that expect to find their own version of the same module name (otherwise, only the first on PYTHONPATH wins).

Unlike the older **ni** module that this feature replaces, the new package support is always available (without running special imports) and requires each package directory along an import path to contain a (possibly empty) *__init__.py* module file to identify the directory as a package, and serve as its namespace if imported directly. Packages tend to work better with **from** than with **import**, since the full path must be repeated to use imported objects after an **import**.

New assert statement

Python 1.5 added a new statement:

```
assert test [, value]
```

which is the same as:

```
if __debug__:
    if not test:
        raise AssertionError, value
```

Assertions are mostly meant for debugging, but can also be used to specify program constraints (e.g., type tests on entry to functions).

Reserved word changes

The word "assert" was added to the list of Python reserved words; "access" was removed (it has now been deprecated in earnest).

New dictionary methods

A few convenience methods were added to the built-in dictionary object to avoid the need for manual loops: `D.clear()`, `D.copy()`, `D.update()`, and `D.get()`. The first two methods empty and copy dictionaries, respectively. `D1.update(D2)` is equivalent to the loop:

```
for k in D2.keys(): D1[k] = D2[k]
```

`D.get(k)` returns `D[k]` if it exists, or `None` (or its optional second argument) if the key does not exist.

New list methods

List objects have a new method, `pop`, to fetch and delete the last item of the list:

```
x = s.pop()     ...is the same as the two statements...    x = s[-1]; del s[-1]
```

and `extend`, to concatenate a list of items on the end, in place:

```
s.extend(x)     ...is the same as...                        s[len(s):len(s)] = x
```

The `pop` method can also be passed an index to delete (it defaults to –1). Unlike `append`, `extend` is passed an entire list and adds each of its items at the end.

"Raw" string constants

In support of regular expressions and Windows, Python allows string constants to be written in the form `r"...\..."`, which works like a normal string except that Python leaves any backslashes in the string alone. They remain as literal \ characters rather than being interpreted as special escape codes by Python.

Complex number type

Python now supports complex number constants (e.g., `1+3j`) and complex arithmetic operations (normal math operators, plus a `cmath` module with many of the `math` module's functions for complex numbers).

Printing cyclic objects doesn't core dump

Objects created with code like `L.append(L)` are now detected and printed specially by the interpreter. In the past, trying to print cyclic objects caused the interpreter to loop recursively (which eventually led to a core dump).

raise without arguments: re-raise

A `raise` statement without any exception or extra-data arguments now makes Python re-raise the most recently raised uncaught exception.

raise forms for class exceptions

Because exceptions can now either be string objects or classes and class instances, you can use any of the following `raise` statement forms:

```
raise string            # matches except with same string object
raise string, data      # same, with optional data

raise class, instance   # matches except with class or its superclass
raise instance          # same as: raise instance.__class__, instance

raise                   # reraise last exception
```

You can also use the following three forms, which are for backwards-compatibility with earlier releases where all built-in exceptions were strings:

```
raise class             # same as: raise class() (and: raise class, instance)
raise class, arg        # same as: raise class(arg)
raise class, (arg,...)  # same as: raise class(args...)
```

*Power operator X ** Y*

The new `**` binary operator computes the left operand raised to the power of the right operand. It works much like the built-in **pow** function.

Generalized sequence assignments

In an assignment (= statements and other assignment contexts), you can now assign any sort of sequence on the right to a list or tuple on the left (e.g., `(A,B) = seq`, `[A,B] = seq`). In the past, the sequence types had to match.

It's faster

Python 1.5 has been clocked at almost twice the speed of its predecessors on the *Lib/test/pystone.py* benchmark. (I've seen almost a threefold speedup in other tests.)

Library Changes

The following sections describe changes made to the Python standard library.

dir(X) now works on more objects

The built-in `dir` function now reports attributes for modules, classes, and class instances, as well as for built-in objects such as lists, dictionaries, and files. You don't need to use members like __methods__ (but you still can).

New conversions: int(X), float(X), list(S)

The `int` and `float` built-in functions now accept string arguments, and convert from strings to numbers exactly like `string.atoi/atof`. The new `list(S)` built-in function converts any sequence to a list, much like the older and obscure `map(None, S)` trick.

The new re regular expression module

A new regular expression module, `re`, offers full-blown Perl-style regular expression matching. See Chapter 18, *Text and Language*, for details. The older `regex` module described in the first edition is still available, but considered obsolete.

splitfields/joinfields became split/join

The `split` and `join` functions in the `string` module were generalized to do the same work as the original `splitfields` and `joinfields`.

Persistence: unpickler no longer calls __init__

Beginning in Python 1.5, the `pickle` module's unpickler (loader) no longer calls class __init__ methods to recreate pickled class instance objects. This means that classes no longer need defaults for all constructor arguments to be used for persistent objects. To force Python to call the __init__ method (as it did before), classes must provide a special __getinitargs__ method; see the library manual for details.

Object pickler coded in C: cPickle

An implementation of the `pickle` module in C is now a standard part of Python. It's called `cPickle` and is reportedly many times faster than the original pickle. If present, the `shelve` module loads it instead of `pickle` automatically.

anydbm.open now expects a "c" second argument for prior behavior

To open a DBM file in "create new or open existing for read+write" mode, pass a "c" in argument 2 to `anydbm.open`. This changed as of Python 1.5.2; passing a "c" now does what passing no second argument used to do (the second argument now defaults to "r"—read-only). This does not impact `shelve.open`.

rand module replaced by random module

The `rand` module is now deprecated; use `random` instead.

Assorted Tkinter changes

Tkinter became portable to and sprouted native look-and-feel for all major platforms (Windows, X, Macs). There has been a variety of changes in the Tkinter GUI interface:

StringVar objects can't be called
> The `__call__` method for `StringVar` class objects was dropped in Python 1.4; that means you need to explicitly call their `get()`/`set()` methods, instead of calling them with or without arguments.

ScrolledText changed
> The `ScrolledText` widget went through a minor interface change in Python 1.4, which was apparently backed out in release 1.5 due to code breakage (so never mind).

Gridded geometry manager
> Tkinter now supports Tk's new `grid` geometry manager. To use it, call the `grid` method of widget objects (much like `pack`, but passes row and column numbers, not constraints).

New Tkinter documentation site
> Fredrik Lundh now maintains a nice set of Tkinter documentation at *http://www.pythonware.com,* which provides references and tutorials.

CGI module interface change

The CGI interface changed. An older `FormContent` interface was deprecated in favor of the `FieldStorage` object's interface. See the library manual for details.

site.py, user.py, and PYTHONHOME

These scripts are automatically run by Python on startup, used to tailor initial paths configuration. See the library manuals for details.

Assignment to os.environ[key] calls putenv

Assigning to a key in the `os.environ` dictionary now updates the corresponding environment variable in the C environment. It triggers a call to the C library's `putenv` routine such that the changes are reflected in integrated C code layers as well as in the environment of any child processes spawned by the Python program. `putenv` is now exposed in the `os` module too (`os.putenv`).

New sys.exc_info() tuple

The new `exc_info()` function in the `sys` module returns a tuple of values corresponding to `sys.exc_type` and `sys.exc_value`. These older names access a single global exception; `exc_info` is specific to the calling thread..

The new operator module

There is a new standard module called `operator`, which provides functions that implement most of the built-in Python expression operators. For instance, `operator.add(X,Y)` does the same thing as `X+Y`, but because operator module exports are functions, they are sometimes handy to use in things like `map`, so you don't have to create a function or use a lambda form.

Tool Changes

The following sections describe major Python tool-related changes.

JPython (a.k.a. Jython): a Python-to-Java compiler

The new JPython system is an alternative Python implementation that compiles Python programs to Java Virtual Machine (JVM) bytecode and provides hooks for integrating Python and Java programs. See Chapter 15, *Advanced Internet Topics*.

MS-Windows ports: COM, Tkinter

The COM interfaces in the Python Windows ports have evolved substantially since the first edition's descriptions (it was "OLE" back then); see Chapter 15. Python also now ships as a self-installer for Windows, with built-in support for the Tkinter interface, DBM-style files, and more; it's a simple double-click to install today.

SWIG growth, C++ shadow classes

The SWIG system has become a primary extension writers' tool, with new "shadow classes" for wrapping C++ classes. See Chapter 19, *Extending Python*.

Zope (formerly Bobo): Python objects for the Web

This system for publishing Python objects on the Web has grown to become a popular tool for CGI programmers and web scripters in general. See the Zope section in Chapter 15.

HTMLgen: making HTML from Python classes

This tool for generating correct HTML files (web page layouts) from Python class object trees has grown to maturity. See Chapter 15.

PMW: Python mega-widgets for Tkinter

The PMW system provides powerful, higher-level widgets for Tkinter-based GUIs in Python. See Chapter 6, *Graphical User Interfaces*.

IDLE: an integrated development environment GUI

Python now ships with a point-and-click development interface named IDLE. Written in Python using the Tkinter GUI library, IDLE either comes in the source library's Tools directory or is automatically installed with Python itself (on Windows, see IDLE's entry in the Python menu within your Start button menus). IDLE offers a syntax-coloring text editor, a graphical debugger, an object browser, and more. If you have Python with Tk support enabled and are accustomed to more advanced development interfaces, IDLE provides a feature-rich alternative to the traditional Python command line. IDLE does not provide a GUI builder today.

Other tool growth: PIL, NumPy, Database API

The PIL image processing and NumPy numeric programming systems have matured considerably, and a portable database API for Python has been released. See Chapter 6 and Chapter 16, *Databases and Persistence*.

Python/C Integration API Changes

The following sections describe changes made to the Python C API.

A single Python.h header file

All useful Python symbols are now exported in the single *Python.h* header file; no other header files need be imported in most cases.

A single libpython*.a C library file

All Python interpreter code is now packaged in a single library file when you build Python. For instance, under Python 1.5, you need only link in *libpython1.5.a* when embedding Python (instead of the older scheme's four libraries plus .o's).

The "Great (Grand?) Renaming" is complete

All exposed Python symbols now start with a "Py" prefix.

Threading support, multiple interpreters

A handful of new API tools provide better support for threads when embedding Python. For instance, there are tools for finalizing Python (`Py_Finalize`) and for creating "multiple interpreters" (`Py_NewInterpreter`).

Note that spawning Python language threads may be a viable alternative to C-level threads, and multiple namespaces are often sufficient to isolate names used in independent system components; both schemes are easier to manage than multiple interpreters and threads. But in some threaded programs, it's also useful to have one copy of system modules and structures per thread, and this is where multiple interpreters come in handy (e.g., without one copy per thread, imports might find an already-loaded module in the `sys.modules` table if it was imported by a different thread). See the new C API documentation manuals for details.

New Python C API documentation

There is a new reference manual that ships with Python and documents major C API tools and behavior. It's not fully fleshed out yet, but it's a useful start.

B

Pragmatics

This appendix is a very brief introduction to some install-level details of Python use, and contains a list of Python Internet resources. More information on topics not covered fully here can be found at other resources:

- For additional install details, consult the various README text files in the examples distribution on this book's CD, as well as the README files and other documentation that accompany the Python distributions and other packages on the CD. In particular, the README files in the *Examples* and *Examples\PP2E* directories contain book example tree documentation and Python install details not repeated in this appendix.

- For more background information on running Python programs in general, see the Python manuals included on this book's CD, or the introductory-level O'Reilly text *Learning Python*.

- For more background information on the core Python language itself, refer to the Python standard manuals included on this book's CD, and the O'Reilly texts *Learning Python* and *Python Pocket Reference*.

- For more information about all things Python, see *http://www.python.org*. This site has online Python documentation, interpreter downloads, search engines, and links to just about every other relevant Python site on the Web. For links to information about this book, refer back to the Preface.

Installing Python

This section gives an overview of install-related details—instructions for putting the Python interpreter on your computer.

Windows

Python install details vary per platform and are described in the resources just listed. But as an overview, Windows users will find a Python self-installer executable on this book's CD (see the top-level Python 1.5.2 and 2.0 directories). Simply double-click the installer program and answer "yes," "next," or "default" to step through a default Windows install. Be sure to install Tcl/Tk too, if you are asked about it along the way.

After the install, you will find an entry for Python in your Start button's Programs menu; it includes options for running both the IDLE integrated GUI development interface and the command-line console session, viewing Python's standard manuals, and more. Python's manuals are installed with the interpreter in HTML form, and open locally in a web browser when selected.

Python also registers itself to open Python files on Windows, so you can simply click on Python scripts in a Windows file explorer window to launch them. You can also run Python scripts by typing `python file.py` command lines at any DOS command-line prompt, provided that the directory containing the `python.exe` Python interpreter program is added to your PATH DOS shell variable (see the configuration and running sections later).

Note that the standard Python package for Windows includes full Tkinter support. You do not need to install other packages or perform any extra install steps to run Tkinter GUIs on Windows; simply install Python. All necessary Tkinter components are installed by the Python self-installer, and Python automatically finds the necessary components without extra environment settings. The Windows install also includes the `bsddb` extension to support DBM-style files.

If you plan on doing any Windows-specific work such as COM development, you will probably want to install the extra `win32all` extensions package (available on the book's CD as well as at *http://www.python.org*). This package registers Python for Active Scripting, provides MFC wrappers and COM integration, and more (see Chapter 15, *Advanced Internet Topics*). Also note that Python distributions available from other sources (e.g., the ActivePython distribution from ActiveState, *http://www.activestate.com*) may include both Python and the Windows extensions package.

Unix and Linux

Python may already be available on these platforms (it's often installed as a standard part of Linux these days); check your */usr/bin* and */usr/local/bin* directories to see if a Python interpreter is lurking there. If not, Python is generally installed on these platforms from either an `rpm` package (which installs Python executables and libraries automatically) or the source code distribution package (which you unpack and compile locally on your computer). Compiling Python from its source on Linux is a trivial task—usually just a matter of typing two or three simple command lines. See the Python source distribution's top-level README files and Linux `rpm` documentation for more details.

Macintosh and Others

Please see the documentation associated with the Macintosh ports for install and usage details. For other platforms, you will likely need to find ports at *http://www.python.org* and consult the port's install notes or documentation.

Book Examples Distribution

This section briefly discusses the book's example source code distribution, and covers example usage details.

The Book Examples Package

The *Examples\PP2E* CD directory is a Python module package that contains source code files for all examples presented in this book (and more). The *PP2E* package in turn contains nested module packages that partition the example files into subdirectories by topic. You can either run files straight off the CD, or copy the *PP2E* directory onto your machine's hard drive (copying over allows you to change the files, and lets Python store their compiled bytecode for faster startups).

Either way, the directory that contains the *PP2E* root must generally be listed on the Python module search path (normally, the PYTHONPATH environment variable). This is the only entry that you must add to the Python path, though; import statements in book examples are always package import paths relative to the *PP2E* root directory unless the imported module lives in the same directory as the importer.

Also in the examples package, you'll find scripts for converting example files' linefeeds to and from Unix format (they are in DOS format on the CD), making files writable (useful after a drag-and-drop on Windows), and more. See the README files at the top of the *Examples* and *PP2E* directory trees for more details on package tree usage and utilities.

Running the Demo Launcher Scripts

The top level of the CD's *Examples\PP2E* package includes Python self-configuring scripts that can be run to launch major book examples, even if you do not configure your environment. That is, they should work even of you don't set your PATH or PYTHONPATH shell variables. These two scripts, PyDemos and PyGadgets, are presented in Chapter 8, *A Tkinter Tour, Part 2*, and described more fully in both this book's Preface and the CD's README files. In most cases, you should be able to run these scripts right off the book's CD by double-clicking on them in a file explorer GUI (assuming Python has been installed, of course).

Environment Configuration

This section introduces Python environment setup details and describes settings that impact Python programs.

Shell Variables

The following shell environment variables (among others) are usually important when using Python:

PYTHONPATH

> Python's module file search path. If set, it is used to locate modules at runtime when they're imported by a Python program—Python looks for an imported module file or package directory in each directory listed on PYTHONPATH, from left to right. Python generally searches the home directory of a script as well as the Python standard source code library directory automatically, so you don't need to add these. Hint: check `sys.path` interactively to see how the path is truly set up.

PYTHONSTARTUP

> An optional Python initialization file. If used, set this variable to the full pathname of a file of Python code (a module) that you want to be run each time the Python interactive command-line interpreter starts up. This is a convenient way to import modules you use frequently when working interactively.

PATH

> The operating system's executable search path variable. It is used to locate program files when you type their names at a command line without their full directory paths. Add the directory containing the `python` interpreter executable file (or else you must retype its directory path each time).

In addition, users on platforms other than Windows may need to set variables to use Tkinter if Tcl/Tk installations cannot be found normally. Set TK_LIBRARY and TCL_LIBRARY variables to point to the local *Tk* and *Tcl* library file directories.

Configuration Settings

The *Examples\PP2E\Config* directory on the CD contains example configuration files with comments for Python variable settings. On Windows NT, you can set these variables in the system settings GUI (more on this in a minute); on Windows 98, you can set them from DOS batch files, which can be run from your *C:\ autoexec.bat* file to make sure they are set every time you start your compute. For example, my *autoexec* file includes this line:

```
C:\PP2ndEd\examples\PP2E\Config\setup-pp.bat
```

which in turn invokes a file that contains these lines to add Python to the system PATH, and the book examples package root to PYTHONPATH:

```
REM PATH %PATH%;c:\Python20
PATH %PATH%;c:\"program files"\python

set PP2EHOME=C:\PP2ndEd\examples
set PYTHONPATH=%PP2EHOME%;%PYTHONPATH%
```

Pick (i.e., remove the REM from) one of the first two lines, depending upon your Python install—the first line assumes a Python 2.0 default install, and the second assumes Python 1.5.2. Also change the PP2EHOME setting here to the directory that contains the *PP2E* examples root on your machine (the one shown works on my computer). On Linux, my *~/.cshrc* startup file sources a *setup-pp.csh* file that looks similar:

```
setenv PATH $PATH:/usr/bin
setenv PP2EHOME /home/mark/PP2ndEd/examples
setenv PYTHONPATH $PP2EHOME:$PYTHONPATH
```

But the syntax used to set variables varies per shell (see the *PP2E\Config* CD directory for more details). Setting the PYTHONPATH shell variable to a list of directories like this works on most platforms, and is the typical way to configure your module search path. On some platforms, there are other ways to set the search path. Here are a few platform-specific hints:

Windows port

The Windows port allows the Windows registry to be used in addition to setting PYTHONPATH in DOS. On some versions of Windows, rather than changing *C:\autoexec.bat* and rebooting, you can also set your path by selecting the Control Panel, picking the System icon, clicking in the Environment Settings tab, and typing PYTHONPATH and the path you want (e.g., *C:\mydir*) in the resulting dialog box. Such settings are permanent, just like adding them to *autoexec.bat*.

JPython

Under JPython, the Java implementation of Python, the path may take the form of –Dpath command-line arguments on the Java command used to launch a program, or python.path assignments in Java registry files.

Configuring from a Program

In all cases, `sys.path` represents the search path to Python scripts and is initialized from path settings in your environment plus standard defaults. This is a normal Python list of strings that may be changed by Python programs to configure the search path dynamically. To extend your search path within Python, do this:

```
import sys
sys.path.append('mydirpath')
```

Because shell variable settings are available to Python programs in the built-in `os.environ` dictionary, a Python script may also say something like `sys.path.append(os.environ['MYDIR']))` to add the directory named by the MYDIR shell variable to the Python module search path at runtime. Because `os.pathsep` gives the character used to separate directory paths on your platform, and `string.split` knows how to split up strings around delimiters, this sequence:

```
import sys, os, string
path = os.environ['MYPYTHONPATH']
dirs = string.split(path, os.pathsep)
sys.path = sys.path + dirs
```

adds all names in the MYPYTHONPATH list setting to the module search path in the same way that Python usually does for PYTHONPATH. Such `sys.path` changes can be used to dynamically configure the module search path from within a script. They last only as long as the Python program or session that made them, though, so you are usually better off setting PYTHONPATH in most cases.

Running Python Programs

Python code can be typed at a `>>>` interactive prompt, run from a C program, or placed in text files and run. There is a variety of ways to run code in files:

Running from a command line

Python files can always be run by typing a command of the form `python file.py` in your system shell or console box, as long as the Python interpreter program is on your system's search path. On Windows, you can type this command in an MS-DOS console box; on Linux, use an xterm.

Running by clicking

Depending on your platform, you can usually start Python program files by double-clicking on their icons in a file explorer user interface. On Windows, for instance, *.py* Python files are automatically registered such that they can be run by being clicked (as are *.pyc* and *.pyw* files).

Running by importing and reloading

Files can also be run by importing them, either interactively or from within another module file. To rerun a module file's code again without exiting Python, be sure to run a call like `reload(module)`.

Running files in IDLE

For many, running a console window and one or more separate text editor windows constitutes an adequate Python development environment. For others, IDLE—the Python Integrated Development Environment (but really named for Monty Python's Eric Idle)—is a development environment GUI for Python. It can also be used to run existing program files or develop new systems from scratch. IDLE is written in Python/Tkinter, and thus is portable across Windows, X Windows (Unix), and Macintosh. It ships (for free) as a standard tool with the Python interpreter. On Windows, IDLE is installed automatically with Python; see the "Windows" section under "Installing Python" earlier in this appendix.

IDLE lets you edit, debug, and run Python programs. It does syntax coloring for edited Python code, sports an object browser the lets you step through your system's objects in parallel with its source code, and offers a point-and-click debugger interface for Python. See IDLE's help text and page at *http://www.python.org* for more details. Or simply play with it on your machine; most of its interfaces are intuitive and easy to learn. The only thing IDLE seems to lack today is a point-and-click GUI builder (but Tkinter's simplicity tends to make such builders less important in Python work).

Running files in Pythonwin

Pythonwin is another freely available, open source IDE for Python, but is targeted at Windows platforms only. It makes use of the MFC integration made available to Python programmers in the `win32all` Windows-specific Python extensions package described in Chapter 15. In fact, Pythonwin is something of an example application of these Windows tools. Pythonwin supports source code editing and launching much like IDLE does (and there has been some cross-pollination between these systems). It doesn't sport all the features or portability of IDLE, but offers tools all its own for Windows developers. Fetch and install the `win32all` Windows extensions package to experiment with Pythonwin. You can also find this package on this book's CD.

Running Python from other IDEs

If you are accustomed to more sophisticated development environments, see the Visual Python products from Active State (*http://www.activestate.com*), and the PythonWorks products from PythonWare (*http://www.pythonware.com*). Both are emerging as I write this, and promise to provide advanced integrated development tool suites for Python programmers. For instance, ActiveState's plans include support for developing Python programs under both Microsoft's Visual Studio and the Mozilla application environment, as well as a Python port to the C#/.NET environment. PythonWare's products support visual interface development and a suite of development tools.

Other platforms have additional ways to launch Python programs (e.g., dropping files on Mac icons). Here are a few more hints for Unix and Windows users:

Unix and Linux users

> You can also make Python module files directly executable by adding the special `#!/usr/bin/python` type line at the top of the file and giving the file executable permissions with a *chmod* command. If you do, you can run Python files simply by typing their names (e.g., *file.py*), as though they were compiled executables. See Chapter 2, *System Tools*, for more details.

Windows users

> If you see a flash when you click on a Python program in the file explorer, it's probably the console box that Python pops up to represent the program's standard input/output streams. If you want to keep the program's output up so that you can see it, add a call `raw_input()` to the bottom of your program; this call pauses until you press the Enter key. If you write your own GUI and don't want to see the console pop-up at all, name your source files with a *.pyw* extension instead of *.py*.

Windows NT and 2000

> You can also launch a Python script file from a command-line prompt simply by typing the name of the script's file (e.g., *file.py*). These platforms correctly run the script with the Python interpreter without requiring the special `#!` first line needed to run files directly in Unix. To run Python command lines on Windows 9x platforms, you'll need to add the word "python" before the filename and make sure the *python.exe* executable is on your PATH setting (as described earlier). On all Windows platforms, you may also click on Python filenames in a Windows explorer to start them.

Python Internet Resources

Finally, Table B-1 lists some of the most useful Internet sites for Python information and resources. Nearly all of these are accessible from Python's home page (*http://www.python.org*) and most are prone to change over time, so be sure to consult Python's home page for up-to-date details.

Table B-1. Python Internet Links

Resource	Address
Python's main web site	*http://www.python.org*
Python's FTP site	*ftp://ftp.python.org/pub/python*
Python's newsgroup	*comp.lang.python (python-list@cwi.nl)*
O'Reilly's main web site	*http://www.oreilly.com*
O'Reilly Python DevCenter	*http://www.oreillynet.com/python*
Book's web site	*http://www.rmi.net/~lutz/about-pp2e.html*
Author's web site	*http://www.rmi.net/~lutz*
Python support mail-list	*mailto:python-help@python.org*
Python online manuals	*http://www.python.org/doc*
Python online FAQ	*http://www.python.org/doc/FAQ.html*
Python special interest groups	*http://www.python.org/sigs*
Python resource searches	*http://www.python.org/search*
Starship (library)	*http://starship.python.net*
Vaults of Parnassus (library)	*http://www.vex.net/parnassus*
JPython's site	*http://www.jpython.org*
SWIG's site	*http://www.swig.org*
Tk's site	*http://www.scriptics.com*
Zope's site	*http://www.zope.org*
ActiveState (tools)	*http://www.activestate.com*
PythonWare (tools)	*http://www.pythonware.com*

C

Python Versus C++

This appendix briefly summarizes some of the differences between Python and C++ classes. Python's `class` system can be thought of as a subset of C++'s. Although the comparison to Modula 3 may be closer, C++ is the dominant OOP language today. But in Python, things are intentionally simpler—classes are simply *objects* with attached *attributes* that may have links to other class objects. They support generation of multiple instances, customization by attribute inheritance, and operator overloading, but the object model in Python is comparatively uncluttered. Here are some specific differences between Python and C++:

Attributes

There is no real distinction between data members and methods in Python; both simply designate named *attributes* of instances or classes, bound to functions or other kinds of objects. Attributes are names attached to objects, and accessed by qualification: `object.attribute`. Methods are merely class attributes assigned to functions normally created with nested `def` statements; members are just attribute names assigned to other kinds of objects.

Class object generation

Class statements create *class* objects and assign them to a name. Statements that assign names within a `class` statement generate class attributes, and classes inherit attributes from all other classes listed in their `class` statement header line (multiple inheritance is supported; this is discussed in a moment).

Instance object creation

Calling a class object as though it were a function generates a new class *instance* object. An instance begins with an empty namespace that inherits names in the class's namespace; assignments to instance attributes (e.g., to `self` attributes within class method functions) create attributes in the instance.

Object deletion

Both classes and instances (and any data they embed) are automatically reclaimed when no longer held. There is no **new** (classes are called instead) and Python's **del** statement removes just one reference, unlike C++'s *delete*.

Member creation

Class and instance attributes, like simple variables, spring into existence when assigned, are not declared ahead of time, and may reference any type of object (they may even reference different object datatypes at different times).

Inheritance

Python inheritance is generally kicked off to search for an attribute name's value: given an expression of the form **object.attribute**, Python searches the namespace object tree at **object** and above for the first appearance of name **attribute**. An inheritance search also occurs when expression operators and type operations are applied to objects. A new, independent inheritance search is performed for every **object.attribute** expression that is evaluated—even **self.attr** expressions within a method function search anew for **attr** at the instance object referenced by **self** and above.

Runtime type information

Python classes are *objects* in memory at runtime—they can be passed around a program to provide a sort of runtime type resource (e.g., a single function can generate instances of arbitrary classes passed in as an argument). Both class and instance objects carry interpreter information (e.g., a **__dict__** attribute dictionary), and Python's **type** function allows object type testing. Instance objects' **__class__** attributes reference the class they were created from, and class objects' **__bases__** attributes give class superclasses (base classes).

"this" pointer

Python's equivalent of the C++ **this** instance pointer is the first argument added to method function calls (and usually called **self** by convention). It is usually implicit in a call but is used explicitly in methods: there is no hidden instance scope for unqualified names. Python methods are just functions nested in a **class** statement that receive the implied instance objects in their leftmost parameters.

Virtual methods

In Python, all methods and data members are **virtual** in the C++ sense: there is no notion of a compile-time resolution of attributes based on an object's type. Every attribute qualification (**object.name**) is resolved at runtime, based on the qualified object's type.

Pure virtuals

Methods called by a superclass but not defined by it correspond to C++'s concept of "pure virtual" methods: methods that must be redefined in a subclass.

Since Python is not statically compiled, there is no need for C++'s special syntax to declare this case. Calls to undefined methods raise a name error exception at runtime, which may or may not be caught with `try` statements.

Static members

There is no `static` class data declaration; instead, assignments nested in a `class` statement generate attribute names associated with the class and shared by all its instances.

Private members

There is no notion of true access restrictions for attributes; every member and method is *public* in the C++ sense. Attribute hiding is a matter of convention rather than syntax: C++'s `public`, `private`, and `protected` constraints don't apply (but see also the new __X class name localization feature in Appendix A, *Recent Python Changes*).

Const interfaces

Objects may be immutable, but names are not—there is no equivalent of C++'s `const` modifier. Nothing prevents a name or object from being changed in a method, and methods can change mutable arguments (the `self` object, for example). Convention and common sense replaces extra syntax.

Reference parameters

There is no direct analogue for C++'s *reference* parameters. Python methods may return multiple values in a tuple and can change passed-in objects if they're mutable (for instance, by assigning to an object's attributes or changing lists and dictionaries in place). But there is no aliasing between names at the call and names in a function header: arguments are passed by assignment, which creates shared object references.

Operator overloading

Special method names overload operators: there is no `operator+`-like syntax but the effects are similar. For instance, a class attribute named __add__ overloads (intercepts and implements) application of the + operator to instances of the class; __getattr__ is roughly like C++ -> overloading. Arbitrary expressions require coding right-side methods (e.g., __radd__).

Templates

Python is dynamically typed—names are references to arbitrary objects, and there is no notion of type declarations. C++ templates are neither applicable nor necessary. Python classes and functions can generally be applied to any object type that implements the interface protocols (operations and operators) expected by the class's code. Subjects need not be of a certain datatype.

Friends

Everything is friendly in Python. Because there is no notion of privacy constraints, any class can access the internals of another.

Function overloading

Python polymorphism is based on virtual method calls: the type of a qualified object determines what its methods do. Since Python arguments' types are never declared (dynamically typed), there is nothing like C++'s function overloading for dispatching to different versions of a function based on the datatypes of its arguments. You can explicitly test types and argument list lengths in methods instead of writing separate functions for each type combination (see `type` built-in function and `*args` function argument form).

Multiple inheritance

Multiple inheritance is coded by listing more than one superclass in parentheses in a class statement header line. When multiple inheritance is used, Python simply uses the *first* appearance of an attribute found during a depth-first, left-to-right search through the superclass tree. Python resolves multiple inheritance conflicts this way instead of treating them as errors.

Virtual inheritance

C++'s notion of virtual base classes doesn't quite apply in Python. A Python class instance is a single namespace dictionary (with a class pointer for access to inherited attributes). Classes add attributes to the class instance dictionary by assignment. Because of this structure, each attribute exists in just one place—the instance dictionary. For inherited class attributes, the search of the superclass tree resolves references unambiguously.

Constructors

Python only runs the one `__init__` method found by the inheritance object tree search. It doesn't run all accessible classes' constructors automatically; if needed, we have to call other class constructors manually. But this is no harder than specifying superclass constructor arguments in C++. Python destructors (`__del__`) run when an instance is garbage-collected (i.e., deallocated), not in response to *delete* calls.

Scope operators

C++ scope operators of the form `Superclass::Method` are used to extend inherited methods and disambiguate inheritance conflicts. Python's closest equivalent is `Superclass.Method`, a class object qualification. It isn't required for inheritance conflict resolution, but can be used to override the default search rule and to call back to superclasses in method extensions.

Method pointers

Instead of special syntax, Python method references are *objects*; they may be passed, stored in data structures, and so on. Method objects come in two flavors: *bound* methods (when an instance is known) are instance/method pairs called later like simple functions, and *unbound* methods are simply references to a method function object and require an instance to be passed explicitly when called.

Naturally, Python has additional class features not found in C++, such as *meta-class protocols*: __setattr__ can be used to implement alternative interfaces, and an instance's __class__ pointer can be reset to change the class type of an object dynamically. Moreover, class attributes can be modified arbitrarily at runtime; classes are merely objects with attached attribute names.

In addition, Python differs from C++ in numerous ways besides its class model. For instance, there are neither type declarations nor compile and linking steps in Python; you cannot overload = in Python as you can in C++ (assignment isn't an operator in Python); and pointers, central to much C and C++ programming, are completely absent in Python (though object references can have some of the same effects). Instead of pointers, Python programs use first-class objects, which are automatically allocated and reclaimed.

Most of these differences stem from the fact that Python was designed for speed of development, not speed of execution; much of C++'s extra syntax would interfere with Python's purpose. See the O'Reilly text *Learning Python* for a complete introduction to Python classes and the remainder of the core Python language.

Index

We'd like to hear your suggestions for improving our indexes. Send email to *index@oreilly.com*.

About the Author

Mark Lutz is a Python trainer, writer, and software developer, and is one of the primary figures in the Python community. He is the author of the O'Reilly books *Programming Python* and *Python Pocket Reference*, and co-author of *Learning Python*. Mark has been involved with Python since 1992, and began teaching Python classes in 1997. In addition, he holds BS and MS degrees in computer science from the University of Wisconsin, and over the past two decades has worked on compilers, programming tools, scripting applications, and assorted client/server systems. Whenever Mark gets a break from spreading the Python word, he leads an ordinary, average life in Colorado. Mark can be reached by email at *lutz@rmi.net*, or on the Web at *http://rmi.net/~lutz*.

Colophon

Our look is the result of reader comments, our own experimentation, and feedback from distribution channels. Distinctive covers complement our distinctive approach to technical topics, breathing personality and life into potentially dry subjects.

The animal featured on the cover of *Programming Python, Second Edition* is an African rock python, one of approximately 18 species of python. Pythons are nonvenomous constrictor snakes that live in tropical regions of Africa, Asia, Australia, and some Pacific Islands. Pythons live mainly on the ground, but they are also excellent swimmers and climbers. Both male and female pythons retain vestiges of their ancestral hind legs. The male python uses these vestiges, or spurs, when courting a female. The python kills its prey by suffocation. While the snake's sharp teeth grip and hold the prey in place, the python's long body coils around its victim's chest, constricting tighter each time it breathes out. They feed primarily on mammals and birds. Python attacks on humans are extremely rare.

Emily Quill was the production editor for *Programming Python, Second Edition*. Clairemarie Fisher O'Leary, Nicole Arigo, and Emily Quill copyedited the book. Matt Hutchinson, Colleen Gorman, Rachel Wheeler, Mary Sheehan, and Jane Ellin performed quality control reviews. Gabe Weiss, Lucy Muellner, Deborah Smith, Molly Shangraw, Matt Hutchinson, and Mary Sheehan provided production assistance. Nancy Crumpton wrote the index.

Edie Freedman designed the cover of this book. The cover image is a 19th-century engraving from the Dover Pictorial Archive. Emma Colby produced the cover layout with QuarkXPress 4.1 using Adobe's ITC Garamond font.

David Futato and Melanie Wang designed the interior layout, based on a series design by Nancy Priest. Cliff Dyer converted the files from Microsoft Word to FrameMaker 5.5.6, using tools created by Mike Sierra. The text and heading fonts are ITC Garamond Light and Garamond Book; the code font is Constant Willison. The illustrations that appear in the book were produced by Robert Romano using Macromedia FreeHand 8 and Adobe Photoshop 5. This colophon was written by Nicole Arigo.

Whenever possible, our books use a durable and flexible lay-flat binding. If the page count exceeds this binding's limit, perfect binding is used.